Aircraft of the Soviet Union

AIRCRAFT of the

The encyclopaedia of Soviet aircraft

Bill Gunston

OSPREY

SOVIET UNION

since 1917

Published in 1983 by Osprey Publishing Limited
12–14 Long Acre, London WC2E 9LP
Member company of the George Philip Group

British Library Cataloguing in Publication Data

Gunston, Bill
Aircraft Of The Soviet Union
The Encyclopaedia Of Soviet Aircraft Since 1917
1. Aeronautics–Soviet Union–History–
Dictionaries
I. Title II. Baldry, Dennis
629.133'03'21 TL509

ISBN 0–85045–445–X

Editor Dennis Baldry

Filmset and printed and bound in Great Britain by Butler & Tanner Ltd, Frome and London

Cover artwork by Hussein Hussein

TITLE PAGES *Tu-144 prototype*

Contents

The Soviet Union keeps hardware in use much longer than most Western air forces. This Tu-16 Badger-H has probably flown 5000 hours in the past 25 years

Preface

This book is an attempt to describe all the aeroplanes, rotary-wing aircraft, transport gliders, and some more important sailplanes, produced in the Soviet Union. To have included aircraft of pre-revolutionary Russia would have added types either derived from foreign designs or of little technical interest. *Aircraft of the Soviet Union*, in contrast, form the biggest gap in contemporary aviation literature.

There are something like 850 types covered in this book. About 710 never graced the pages of *Jane's All the World's Aircraft*. This is no reflection on Jane's, because that unique annual can print only what it knows about in the current year. At least it never fell for the spate of 'secret Soviet military aircraft' that emerged in US magazines during the 1950s. These fictitious aircraft were invented by enthusiastic writers in Germany and other countries. No attempt was made to find out the facts.

I am sure there are no fictitious types in this book, and apologize for errors and omissions caused by lack of knowledge. It is obvious to the specialists that all I have done is put together information painstakingly assembled by others, notably V.B. Shavrov, A.N. Ponomaryev, N. Gordyukov, I. Rodionov, V. Klishin, Vaclav Něměcek, Jiři Horňat, Jean Alexander, and William Green. I must especially thank Pilot Press for assistance with three-view drawings, Mike Badrocke, Terry Hadler and Ray Hutchins for preparing many others, Wim Schoenmaker, Marina Evstigneeva (Tass), William Green (Pilot Press), John W.R. Taylor, Robert J. Ruffle, Robert Carlisle and Maj Lennart Berns (of Aeroproduction), for providing various photographs, Nigel Eastaway for unhesitatingly providing *Bulletins* of the Russian Aviation Research Group of Air Britain, and Sue Cozens and Bogda Smykala for assistance in elucidating the exact meaning of several tricky items in Russian and Polish. Finally, I would like to add a personal note of thanks to the Editor, Dennis Baldry, and Art Editor, Martin Richards for their limitless patience.

Bill Gunston
Haslemere, England
1983

Introduction

I was born on 1 March 1927. On the same day, some 1600 miles to the east, the German Junkers company formally closed its factory at Fili, near Moscow. It had ceased its unusual 'Russian Connection', in which the first communist state had relied heavily for technical assistance on an extremely capitalist private company. The parting of the ways was by mutual consent. It could hardly go on for ever, and Junkers had outlived its usefulness. Conversely, the German company was losing its fear of the Allied Control Commission, and felt it could flex its muscles in its own country in defiance of the Treaty of Versailles. The Soviet government, though still busy with massive internal repression, was no longer faced with a civil war. It had begun to plan for the future, with the first of its great Five-Year Plans. It was determined not only to be independent, but also to demonstrate the total superiority of the communist system, and nowhere more than in aviation. On 1 March 1927 the Fili plant acquired new red banners and ecstatic slogans. It immediately reopened as GAZ (State Aviation Factory) No 22. It was the day Soviet aircraft construction matured as a national industry.

For the next 15 years the rest of the world knew next to nothing about the aircraft of the Soviet Union. After the Spanish civil war the existence was known of two fighters called the Chato and Rata. Nobody seemed to appreciate that these were not real names but merely derogatory epithets applied by the enemy. In addition, one or two Soviet aircraft made courtesy visits to Prague, Milan and Paris and record-breaking flights as far as the USA via Siberia and the uncharted polar region. But when the Soviet Union became one of the Allies in the fight against Nazi Germany, Western editors scratched their heads as they concocted accounts of Soviet air power. As a young enthusiast I subscribed to that splendid weekly *The Aeroplane Spotter*. Its issue of 31 July 1941 presented the fullest account of the 'Red Air Fleet' it could compile. Of the 14 aircraft types illustrated, 13 were described as copies of well-known Western aircraft. The 14th, labelled the ANT-41 (TB-6B), was said to be 'most original' in a joking fashion with the implication it could hardly be taken seriously. (In fact it was not the TB-6 but the Bolkhovitinov DB-A and had nothing to do with any of the ANT family.)

Before the year was out the same magazine, in company with other publications, was busy telling its readers about the aircraft of another major power, Japan. Again we learned that they were all copies of Western designs, and probably inferior ones made mainly of bamboo and rice-paper—until the air combat reports began to come in. Perhaps we have now grown up, and if Haiti or the Central African Empire were to announce a homegrown aircraft industry, at least we would try to find out the facts. But, entirely because of the difficulty of finding out, even the aviation experts in the big world outside the Soviet Union have taken generations to piece together what is by far the biggest single jigsaw in the history of aircraft production. I have wanted to write this book since 1950, but for 30 years held-off in the conviction one could not do the subject justice. On many occasions I was slapped on the back by likeable Russians who explained why previous approaches had led nowhere. They told me exactly what I should do to get on the inside track with the *politburo*, the GUAP and everyone else from the president down. I am convinced most of them were sincere, and that the total lack of cooperation stemmed not from any dark plot aimed at keeping information from the West, but simply because in Soviet society it is safer to do nothing.

The Soviet Union—which, incidentally, is not the same thing as Russia, any more than the United States is the same thing as Texas, however much Texans may disagree—was born out of discord, with a heritage of distrust of its neighbours and embracing the totally new philosophies attributed to Marx and Lenin. These state in unyielding and invariant fashion that the capitalist world will always seek to destroy the Soviet state. The capitalist world hardly helped to refute this when, at that state's very birth, it sent in troops and aircraft to help the White Russians in the so-called War of Intervention, whose main result where aviation was concerned was to give the victorious Soviets a lot of modern aircraft. Naturally, in the bloody chaos of the ensuing civil war (which occupied almost the entire first half of the 1920s) technically trained engineers were busier doping fabric over bullet holes than with pencils and slide-rules. When around 1924 they began to form themselves into design teams it was as part of a socialist state.

This state was founded on what it called the *proletariat:* peasants, workers, soldiers and mechanics, united in the uniformity of their poverty. The state also included everyone else, and it was in their interest to try to get their hands dirty and merge into the background. It is not news to record that every individual became totally subservient to the state—most of them, not merely willingly but with enthusiasm. Despite its gigantic geographical area and the dissimilarity of its many ethnic populations, the state ruled henceforth by central decree and centralized planning. Political indoctrination became the central thread of life, from the crèche to the grave, and required the appointment of powerful figures called *commissars* to every school, every machine shop, every military unit and every design office, to offer political guidance and watch for the slightest sign of deviation.

On the face of it, there ought to be nothing wrong with either socialism or its ultimate form of communism. Millions of sincere people to this day passionately believe in it as morally better than capitalism. In practice the Soviet Union had to endure about a half-century in which distrust and intolerance blurred the original idealistic goals. To this day, Soviet society operates within a police state which persuades the people they are fortunate not to live in the brutally repressive societies of the capitalist West. One fervently hopes that, with the passing of years, mistrust will gradually give way to truer understanding on both sides.

Certainly, work in a Soviet OKB (aircraft design bureau) has changed dramatically. In Stalin's day the inevitable ulcers acquired by all designers grew extra ulcers on top through fear of the political system. It was part of the early Soviet system to combine ceaseless exhortation with punishment for failure. In our capitalist societies we used to fire employees for making mistakes. We can still fine an air force mechanic a week's pay for leaving a screwdriver where it can wreck compressor blades. But we never flung a designer in prison because a wing came off. Designers are pretty dedicated people, deeply aware of the tragic consequences of mistakes. We certainly never sent people to forced-labour camps because a jealous colleague 'informed' on them, not necessarily with a true charge. And we have yet to execute the leader of a design bureau for trumped-up charges of sabotage and crimes against the state. It may be that injustice was an inevitable part of the growing-up of a new form of society, though in the great purges of the late 1930s Stalin ordered the execution of countless engineers, military officers and many other sorts of people who would have made the nation much stronger in its hour of need from 22 June 1941.

One of the arguments for a socialist society is that not only are people more personally motivated, but the whole system is more efficient. So far the record shows the reverse is true. The greater the centralized control, the greater the chance of really big mistakes. Time and again in Stalin's day enormous errors were committed. Efficiency was often submerged under the sheer weight of bureaucracy, or the intrusion of personalities, or a natural unwillingness to take any decision. We can imagine Michaelson, Morshchikhin and their workforce clustered round the radical new MP prototype in Leningrad in 1938, and understand why the test-flight programme was never started: though potentially important to the nation, the MP might have crashed, and they would have seen Siberia. Again, we can imagine the out-of-favour Lavochkin at Novosibirsk in the 50-below temperatures of the first days of 1942, trying to get work done on the first LaGG-3 to be re-engined with the M-82 radial. The local factory director knew Stalin had lost interest with the designer, and had no wish to harm his career by having anything to do with him. The vital prototype, which was to lead to the La-5 that would sweep the fascist invaders from the sky, languished in the snow for weeks while Lavochkin tried to enlist some kind of official support to get it brought back inside the factory.

In fact, having regard to the political environment, it is surely remarkable that even in Stalin's day new design teams and radical new prototypes mushroomed up all over the Soviet Union. One of the facets of Soviet aircraft production that must surprise Western observers is its strength (or perhaps it should be its former strength, because the situation seems to have changed) in light aircraft built for fun. Thanks to all-union (ie, throughout the states of the Soviet Union) organizations set up for the purpose of applying state funds to desirable objectives, it has been possible for many individuals to launch quite substantial projects. In the case of aviation the chief funding organization is Osoaviakhim, a strange mixture of aviation and the chemical defence industries (explosives and war gases) which when the organization was set up were both likely to benefit from enthusiastic amateurs. Even now the Soviet Union continues to fund private light aircraft designs, though on a much-reduced scale, and it probably leads all other countries in the full-scale aircraft created in technical schools as diploma projects by senior students. Of more concern to the West, the Soviet output of qualified engineers has since 1945 far surpassed that of all other countries.

In the turbulent early days of the Soviet Union none of the former Russian aircraft design teams survived as a viable entity, and roughly half the lead designers died or emigrated. In the circumstances it was reasonable to rely heavily on the manufacture of foreign designs, and even complete imported aircraft. Nobody could quarrel with the two companies that provided the bulk of the early new-built machines: Junkers and Fokker. A handful of designers succeeded in satisfying the *commissars* of their political reliability, among them Tupolev, Grigorovich, Polikarpov and Kalinin. They were organized into teams called brigades within existing establishments such as TsAGI or new ones such as OSS and OMOS (respectively responsible for landplanes and seaplanes). A few designers of proven communist sympathy were imported from foreign countries, notably France and Italy. The worst gap was in engines. There had never been a national design capability in aero-engines, and though engine KBs (design bureaux) were set up by 1927, they based their work at first on proven foreign designs. Because of the challenging nature of engines they continued to do so for the next 20 years. To this day Soviet engine designers study foreign engines with even greater application than the aircraft designers study foreign aircraft.

In the mid-1920s it was a quite difficult enough objective for the Soviet Union to send homegrown aircraft, with slogans painted on their sides, on propaganda flights to foreign countries. The objective of self-sufficiency in military and commercial transport aircraft took much longer. Despite going against the grain, the GUAP (state aircraft-industry management) bought a license for the DC-3 as late as 1937, and the VVS (air force) decided in 1944 to adopt a local version of the Boeing B-29. There is no doubt one or two much later Western products, including one of the big-fan engines, have come close to being licensed for Soviet construction.

Between 1925 and 1935 the Junkers-taught TsAGI design brigades under Tupolev, led by Petlyakov, Sukhoi, Arkhangelskii and Myasishchyev, took the local technology of Kolchugaluminium—essentially the same alloy as the German Duralumin—to a high pitch of excellence, which in large cantilever monoplane wings outstripped all other countries. Supposed Soviet love of bigness certainly found full expression in their work, though the largest design of all, the TB-6, was abandoned before the prototype flew. Wisely it was regarded as inherently obsolescent and a bad investment; like Nazi Germany the VVS decided to fund smaller twin-engined bombers for tactical missions. So the mighty fleet of TB-3 heavy bombers—by far the greatest bombers of their day—had no real successor except a tiny handful of Pe-8s.

In extreme contrast, the Soviet designers learned that often greater success was to be gained by making aircraft simpler, cruder and slower. The U-2 light biplane trainer was built in staggering numbers and used for almost every possible purpose, including front-line duties against the might of the Nazi war machine. To build a reliable workhorse that anyone can fly, anyone can maintain and which needs no proper airfield is no mean achievement. We in the West are so imbued by a spirit of competition that we instinctively think in terms of stressed-skin construction, highly advanced engines and substantial paved runways; but as The Duke of Edinburgh said in his first big lecture on aviation, 'You don't have to be supersonic if your only competitor is a bullock-cart'. In 1947 a Western journal cited the Shchye-2 transport's maximum speed of 96 mph as evidence of Soviet backwardness. It failed to comprehend that this speed was about 93 mph faster than anything else available, and that the Shchye-2 was almost exactly right for the job.

If anything, the Soviet policymakers have been as much in error as their counterparts in the West in declaring things prematurely obsolete. In 1931 Grigorovich was told to lay off his old pusher flying boats. In Britain we wisely kept the Walrus in production until 1944 and then followed it with the Sea Otter. In 1938 the torpedo version of the R-5 was withdrawn from service in the Far East. Britain kept the even slower Swordfish in production almost to the end of the Second World War. In 1948 the Il-20 was curtly cancelled because it had a propeller; the United States (which thought the same way in 1948) found the Skyraider so invaluable during the Korean war it built 3180 non-stop to 1957, and then wished in Vietnam it had built even more. But on the whole these are the exceptions that prove the rule; the Soviet Union never cares much about appearance or unessential features, and is often quite happy with aircraft that others may think quaint. The outstanding example of recent years is the An-2 biplane. Little did I think when I saw its photograph in 1947 (and finally concluded the Russians really were backward) that it would be constructed in greater numbers than any other aircraft of the post-war era!

Though the main effort of Soviet aircraft production has always been military, it was in the field of small transports that the nation first achieved technical parity with other countries. The single-engined monoplanes of Kalinin and Moskalyev were technically excellent, and had they been continued (Moskalyev diversified and Kalinin was shot)—might have taken a lot of the world market away from de Havilland Canada. In larger civil transports the Soviet Union has made fantastic strides, but has cranked into its original calculations figures somewhat different from the rest of the world. Even today robust reliability in austere environments counts for more than the last decimal place off the fuel consumption; but the message has now got through that Western airliners actually last longer and are more reliable than the Soviet ones, at least when operated from smooth runways at well-equipped airports.

Surprisingly, since operating economy has never figured very large in the planning of Soviet transports, the 1930s saw a succession of Soviet transport prototypes designed for economy at the expense of almost everything else. Many had relatively large wings and were officially classed as *motor planer* (powered gliders). Almost always the engine was the ubiquitous M-11 of 100 hp, and Soviet constructors vied with each other to see who would make an M-11 carry most passengers (if they didn't get into double figures they weren't trying). Russian peasants must have been quite used to hearing the drone of the same M-11 for 15 minutes or more, and any kind of headwind must have been a major problem.

But it is in the field of military aircraft that Soviet designers have shown their most astonishing diversity. Their work in the inter-war period, almost unknown until recently, now fills copious volumes of fascinating reading. In terms of numbers of aircraft types the lead is held by the fighters, divided into single and two-seat, closely followed by the *Shturmoviks* or armoured attack aircraft, a class almost ignored by other countries. I would like to write reams here on the painstaking trials between manœuvrable biplane fighters and fast monoplanes, on the long and impressive history of heavy recoilless cannon (these stemmed from British guns of the First World War which had not been followed up in their country of origin) and how the Soviet Union at last made the rocket projectile a formidable weapon against aircraft, tanks, and ships. Certainly where aircraft armament is concerned the Soviet Union has been a world leader since the early 1930s both in the individual weapons and the diversity of their application.

It is a matter of historical importance that, having made numerous tough, fast and heavily armed prototypes throughout the 1930s, the Soviet Union should have been invaded on 22 June 1941 at the worst possible state of unpreparedness. True, the Pe-2 and Il-2 were already coming into production and were to play a central role in repelling the enemy; but in the vital matter of fighters the position could hardly have been worse. What was wanted were modern high-performance fighters combining good firepower with both combat agility and easy handling so that pilots used to slow biplanes could convert without fear. Instead there were a host of prototypes and early production fighters which combined poor firepower with dangerous handling, to the extent that pilot attrition became a serious problem.

Tu-144 first flight: from left, M. Kozlov, E. Elyan, A.A. Tupolev (later chief of Tu-144 programme), A.N. Tupolev, V.N. Benderov, and Yu. Seliverstov

A.S. Yakovlev in the foyer of his OKB, about 1970

This was especially remarkable in view of the fact that, unknown at the time to the rest of the world, the Soviet Union had done more work than any other country on variable-incidence, variable-profile and variable-area wings (and the only other variable-area effort worth mentioning was by an expatriate Russian, Ivan Makhonin, working in France). It is difficult to find a single interesting or promising technical development in aviation in the inter-war years that the Soviet designers did not investigate to their own satisfaction. This extended to man-powered flight and even flapping wings; in fact one is almost driven to conclude that a hare-brained aeronautical inventor stood a better chance of seeing his idea become hardware in the Soviet Union than in any other country. So much for the cosy Western belief at the time that all the Russian designers could do was copy others!

In the late 1930s the third five-year plan opened to a background of unprecedented purges of a high proportion of the nation's top people. There had also been serious shortfalls in industrial production, not least in steel (especially steel tube and all high-strength and stainless steels) and aluminium. This led to several prototype combat aircraft being designed mainly in wood, and unquestionably the Soviet Union led the world in the application of wood and wood-based materials, known by such names as *shpon* and *delta*, to high-performance aircraft. This was unknown to the designers at Hatfield in 1939 trying to get the Air Ministry in London to accept the idea of an unarmed bomber made of wood. Far from being obsolete, wood—especially in the advanced forms used in Soviet aircraft—had much to commend it. Its one big drawback was structural volume, which reduced the internal space available for fuel. It was for this reason that, as the Second World War drew to its close, Soviet designers replaced the wood-like materials by duralumin, despite the loss of some of the nation's chief aluminium smelting facilities in 1941–1942.

Whereas wood-based airframes would have caused terrible upheaval at most of the big US plants in the Second World War, it fitted in well with the widespread Soviet GAZ factories peopled by relatively unskilled personnel and with the absolute minimum of jigs, tooling and machine tools. From October 1941 more than 70% of the GAZ capacity had either already been wiped out by the invader or had to be evacuated thousands of kilometres to the east, beyond the Urals. Nothing remotely like this had ever been attempted before (and, of course, it had its counterpart in all the other defence industries). There are plenty of first-hand accounts of what it was like; the first, and still one of the best, is that by Yakovlev, who not only had to move his own OKB to Siberia but as a deputy minister in GUAP had to see that everyone else moved as well. In some cases the frantically working production factory found itself moved to a place weeks distant by train, or non-existent roads, to end up either in a disused brickworks or a field where a GAZ was to be built. Such places in Siberia in October are hardly encouraging, and the rapidity with which previous production levels were exceeded was astonishing. In many cases wood-based airframes undoubtedly speeded the process.

By 1945 the largely new dispersed GAZ network was building aircraft at the rate of over 40,000 per year, though none was four-engined and most were small single-engined machines. In the long-term the evacuation has exploited the vast region east of the Urals, and has accelerated further development. Aviation plays a central role in this process. It is extraordinary that until recently the Soviet Union had never built really capable transport aircraft on a scale similar to that of the stillborn TB-6, which really could have made a difference in opening up the undeveloped territories. Instead in 1944 the Ilyushin KB drew the Il-12 as the next major transport, to replace the Li-2 (Sovietized DC-3), and ended up with an aircraft that for various reasons was inferior to the DC-3. For 17 years Aeroflot restricted the number of passengers in Il-12s and Il-14s to a mere 18, though in power and general design the aircraft was closely similar to the contemporary Convair 240 which was much faster and seated 44! Operating economy was of no consequence, and well over 2000 of the Ilyushin transports were built. Yet the much bigger and faster Il-18 (the 1947 prototype, not the turboprop of ten years later) was never put into production, Aeroflot having no use for so capable a machine.

The same went for the Tu-70 transport of the same era, based on the captured B-29 bomber and in fact produced ahead of the Soviet copy of the bomber itself. The Tu-70 was an eminently successful aircraft, far better than anything used at the time by the GVF (civil air fleet) or VVS, yet it too languished as an unwanted prototype. The reason given by the officials was that such a machine simply did not fit the operating environment. Fields that were fine for the Po-2, and perhaps an An-2, were no place to land a 70-tonner with high-pressure tyres, large Fowler flaps and door cills four metres above the ground. One might have thought the answer would be to improve the airports. In 1957 a colleague asked a US airport administrator how he intended to extend a runway at what was then known as Idlewild Airport, New York, because the waters of Jamaica Bay stretched to the horizon. The instant answer was 'We'll fill in the lousy bay'. Cherishing this retort I found myself a few weeks later at Paris talking for the first time with the great Tupolev. He sidestepped the suggestion that maybe the airfields could have been improved by pointing out this was no concern of an aircraft designer who, he said, 'does what he is told'. Moral here surely?

Adoption of the B-29 at a stroke gave the Soviet Union a gigantic new spectrum of technology in structures, systems, armament and a host of detail engineering features throughout large and fast aircraft. A lot of B-29 style technology is flying today in Tu-16s and even a few bits have filtered through to the Tu-154, more than 40 years after the US bomber was on the Seattle drawing boards. Another amazing windfall was the 1945 election in Britain of a Labour government which, despite the severe shortages at home and absence of even a Royal Air Force requirement for an aeroplane powered by the powerful Nene turbojet, moved with impressive speed to ship crates of Nenes to Moscow. A copy of the Nene was created with great rapidity, built in vast numbers, and used to power a whole new generation of military aircraft including the notorious MiG-15 which was such a shock to the Allied pilots in Korea in 1950. New aerodynamic shapes were snapped up by the Soviet Union with all possible speed. The swept wing is a good example, and the gloved outboard-pivot swing wing is now used more widely than in the West.

We ought to know by now how the Soviet policymakers operate. They still take sweeping central decisions, they still investigate everything that shows even the smallest chance of success, and they still do everything they can to minimise risk in production programmes. Many observers have pointed out how, following millions of hours of research by TsAGI (and now by the larger OKBs, which have research facilities of their own) a new configuration may be officially adopted. Once accepted only a bold or rash designer dare propose anything else. Compare the aerodynamics of the MiG-15 with the Yak-30 and La-176, MiG-21 and Su-9, La-250 and M-52, and a whole generation of Tupolevs. Even the unlikely staggered-engine configuration was used with almost identical aerodynamics in the La-200, MiG I-320 and the first Su-15. TsAGI and other centralized bureaux settle the shapes; one was used for the MiG SM/MiG-19 and Sukhoi S (Su-7) series; another for Ye-6/MiG-21 and Sukhoi T family; another for Su-17 and Tu-22M; another for Ye-231/MiG-23 and Su-24.

When change has to be accepted, it is usually done in small doses and to a quick timescale; for example the Il-30, Il-46 and Il-54 were all taken from inception to first flight in 22 to 29 months, while Britain's V-bombers took 66 to 71 months, followed by up to another 59 months before they entered service. These long timescales in Britain were not due to laziness or lack of competition, but to vacillation by the officials representing the customer. Severe shortages of trained staff and crucial raw materials meant lead-times of up to four years for machine tools, large jigs, and flaw-free slabs of particular light alloys. They resulted from a 'relaxed' defence posture after 1945 which had no counterpart in other countries, and most certainly not in the Soviet Union.

Today prison is seldom in the minds of Soviet designers. The nation has matured, and those involved in the aircraft industry the world over would find working in the Soviet Union not disagreeable, and in many respects stimulating. Here is a land where there are no defence cutbacks, and where cancellation is unheard-of unless the aircraft simply refuses to perform as predicted, or unless it is the loser in a competitive evaluation. Competition is intense, and far from being regarded as a luxury (a word used by a number of MPs at Westminster in recent years) it is regarded as an essential, unless the technical risk is small and a rival design would have been of little value (eg, in the case of the Mi-26).

In some disciplines and industries central control and planning has, in the West at least, proved a route to decline if not disaster. In Soviet aircraft production a combination of professionalism and competition, without the threat of interference by powerful amateurs such as abound at Westminster, has led over the years to a procurement process that works at least as well as the best achieved in the West. Its only shortcomings have been that the inputs from the customer have been dictated 99% by the operational requirement and about 1% by such considerations as fuel burn, noise, maintenance man-hours, airframe life and even safety and cost. Times are changing, but detailed inspection of the latest civil transports confirms that at least into the 1970s Soviet designers worked to a set of ground rules different from, say, Airbus Industrie.

With every aircraft except sporting lightplanes the customer is the GVF (civil air fleet) or the military VVS or naval AV-MF. When one of these sees a future requirement for a new type, political and financial permission is sought for the entire planned programme at a single meeting attended by the MAP (including the Minister) and NTO VSNKh. In 1977 the author was assured that such permission never takes as long as a month, though of course often the answer is negative, or the requirement is combined with something else. Once a positive decision is reached, from two to six OKB heads or their nominees are summoned to Moscow for a preliminary meeting. The representative of the customer announces the requirement in general terms, and gives two or three basic numbers such as weapon load or payload, at least one speed and perhaps a turn rate or field length. Each OKB man (so far as is known ladies have not reached these meetings) is then asked to tell the meeting completely off-the-cuff what aircraft he would propose. Some may explain they are overloaded, or decline for some other true or contrived reason, but this is rare. A rep from TsIAM is present to answer questions on availability of future engines, and it is not unknown for a really important programme to be put back at this meeting while a new engine project is urgently launched. Usually at least two OKBs state that they can fulfil the requirement; they are bidden to attend a second meeting in three or four weeks, if necessary bringing several specialist engineers as well.

The second meeting has paper on the table, each OKB presenting its *Skitsovyi* (or *Eskiznyi*) *Proyekt* (preliminary design) with numerical data covering not only performance but also total programme quantities of materials, man-hours and timescale. Each submission is spelt out in the fullest detail, openly. Obviously the rivals may be surprised at one or two of the proposals or figures, and tempted either to alter their own submission or announce something that beats the competition. This is a big and important meeting, taking the whole of an arduous day, and with major programmes a second day. It is attended by the two OKB teams each led by the General Constructor, plus strong teams from the MAP, economics and finance ministries, customer, TsAGI, TsIAM, VIAM and possibly an all-union organization on electronics or weapons. Almost the whole meeting is quick-fire cross-examination, the 'customer/government' side not only

Ilyushin Il-18 at the closing stages of a major overhaul

trying to fault each proposal in front of the rival team, but also having an excellent opportunity to size up the General Constructor and his chosen team. There is no room for vagueness or waffle; an OKB that has not previously done its homework not only loses but may even be shut down, or find it has a new leader.

At the end of this tough SP conference there is invariably a winning design, but if there is a significant degree of technical risk in a major programme the final choice will be made after a fly-off. There is no such thing as proprietary information or a patented design feature. It is not uncommon for the selected design(s) to be an amalgam of two original submissions, and in some cases modern production aircraft have incorporated features originally proposed by three or even four OKBs. It also appears to be normal practice for this conference to be attended by the highest-ranking constructor (for many years A. S. Yakovlev) who as a father-figure may not be a competitor but plays the role of chief technical critic. The Soviet Union has a great belief in age and experience, as discussed in the box on the next page.

In 1958 Decca Navigator was asked to send engineers to Moscow to assist fitting their receivers and displays to the prototype Tu-114. Panel space had been provided for a Flight Log, but a small angle bracket got in the way. The Decca men began to work on the Simmonds-type nuts holding it at the back of the panel, but were told to stop. This was a job for the GVF senior instrument engineer. Eventually a lady of advanced years shuffled on the scene in carpet slippers, carrying a tool-bag. Morosely she listened to the instructions; then she attacked the bracket with a cold chisel and hammer. After a while the bracket was no longer part of the aircraft, and the lady silently departed, leaving a distorted panel holding unserviceable instruments. The Decca men asked who the lady was, to be told 'She is our senior instrument engineer ... you see, she has been in the department longest'.

Mark Lambert, then an assistant editor of *Flight International*, is so good a linguist he had little difficulty conversing with the pilot of Tu-104 No 42382 on an Aeroflot proving flight in 1959. He asked 'Do you not find the control forces with this aircraft excessive?' A powerful bass voice replied: 'In the Soviet Union there are many strong men'.

The Russian mind is attuned from birth to brain-washing. Russians do not understand Western criticism of the way the Soviet Union manages its news, even to the extent of omitting central facts that seem obvious. In his detailed description of the development of the Tu-4 V.B. Shavrov makes no mention of the Boeing B-29. In his account of the Kalinin VS-2 (K-12) he ends by stating the bomber was accepted for series production; he does not explain why no more were built, and makes no allusion to the execution of the designer. In a detailed account of the career of N.D. Kuznetsov in a 1981 magazine, the NK-12 turboprop is covered fully without reporting that the design team were originally captured Germans, led by an Austrian engineer. Kuznetsov's greatest engine, the NK-144 used in the Tu-144, is not mentioned even though the fact must be obvious to every Russian reader. The reader's thought-process is probably: the NK-144 is not mentioned; it is obviously in trouble; I must forget it is in trouble; I must forget it existed. So in a year or two, when a Western journalist says 'Tell me Ivan, what was wrong with the NK-144?' the reply comes back 'What NK-144?'

Though it is the SP meeting that eliminates most of the proposals, hardly ever ending up with more than two, there is a further round of critical assessment before go-ahead. The TP (*Tekhnichyeskii Proyekt*) conference follows the SP after anything from three to about 15 weeks, depending on the complexity of the aircraft. The difference at this meeting is that the OKBs bring a much more detailed engineering design and almost certainly preliminary tunnel data, a detailed weight breakdown, detailed schedules of airframe and systems components, refined timescale, and resource estimates. After the TP round only one design may be left, but in the past it has been common for two finalists to be built in numbers from two to five. It may be timed to receive the definitive engine, or the first may have to fly with an interim powerplant (MiG Ye-23). There is no rigid rule on production tooling, but good tooling is essential for large or supersonic airframes. Of course no OKB today can avoid major investment in tunnel models, systems rigs, fatigue and static-test airframes, mock-ups and all the other adjuncts to prototype construction. Timescales are invariably agreed only after great argument, the OKB being forced to accept timing that seems impossible. What certainly belongs to history is anything like the day and night hand-building of 15 MiG-9 jet fighters to take part in a previously scheduled flypast. Undertaken on Stalin's express order, this merely wasted effort and delayed production.

A typical timescale from TP meeting to first flight today is about 15 months. OKB testing is hurried through by the test pilots, after which there may be several prototypes ready for NII state testing and possibly for evaluation against the rival. It is not uncommon for this phase to overturn previously accepted decisions, because there is still an art in aircraft design and occasionally an experienced team comes badly unstuck. Even the accepted type may go through a protracted process of rectification, which in such extreme cases as the Il-62, Tu-144 and Yak-42 shows to the outside world. The loser is ruthlessly terminated, though if the OKB or anyone else can make a case for doing so the prototypes may be kept busy in useful programmes.

Long before the winner has been chosen GUAP has made plans for its production, and one or more GAZ has been assigned depending on the rate of output and production load throughout the GAZ system. For a fighter invariably a production batch is not fewer than 500 (it used to be 1000) and one batch may be assigned to each of two widely separated plants. A transport may be ordered in units of 100 or 300, hardly ever from more than one GAZ though today, as with Western wide-bodies, several factories may each make parts of the airframe. Mi-10 helicopters were used to carry Tu-144 parts from Kazan to Voronezh, and the Il-86 production plan involves the supply of major sections from Poland. At the start of production the design OKB assigns a team of 15 to 50 (usually about 35) specialist design engineers to each GAZ involved in manufacture. They live there throughout the programme, being replaced by the same number of GAZ production engineers who inject their viewpoint into the OKB during the same period. Thus the design team avoid an ivory-tower approach to production problems, while the GAZ management have experienced specialists available to speed production and get the new type quickly down the learning-curve.

Today even the Soviet Union has to acknowledge the universal pressure of inflation, and especially the rising price of fuel. It may have been a mistake to put wing-mounted engines on the Il-86, thereby making it difficult to fit high bypass-ratio turbofans when these eventually become available. Certainly long airframe life, system redundancy, engineering design for safety and digital electronics are areas where the Soviet designers are having to run at top speed to catch up with the West; but in the straightforward matter of providing airpower and airlift capability, especially with rotating wings, the boot is on the other foot. Moreover they get the fullest possible use from every airframe, and appear never to throw anything away if a use can be found for it. John W. R. Taylor is sure they have a squadron of *Ilya Mouromets* bombers from the First World War busy somewhere; but that aircraft is outside the scope of this book.

Soviet aircraft designations

Soviet aircraft designations

During the Civil War most aircraft were a motley collection of foreign types with no national designation system. The Soviet authorities laid down about 1923 a scheme for designating aircraft types according to function (R for reconnaissance, B for bombing, I for fighter and U for training, for example), while non-military machines were named or took the initials of the designer(s) or purchasing authority. By 1925 a scheme had been worked out designating all except light aircraft according to function; occasionally, by error, there was duplication eg, MDR-7. In 1940 this was replaced by a new scheme based on OKB General Constructor names, and these have been continued after the death of their founders. In addition types selected for series production receive VVS, GVF or other service designations, with odd numbers (originally) reserved strictly for fighters; thus MiG Ye-6 and Ye-66 became MiG-21, and Tu-95 became Tu-20. There are thus duplications as well as exceptions; Yak's bureau began with AIR (A.I. Rykov) numbers, switched to Ya and finally to Yak. Where identical designations are repeated asterisks are used here to avoid confusion, thus Yak-25* and Yak-25**, and Su-17*/Su-17**. Asterisks did not form part of original designation. There are many anomalies, eg Yak-104 was given VVS designation Yak-30 even though it failed to win series contract, and latest published service designations—Yak-36MP and Tu-22M—are in author's opinion a political cloak for their true identities.

A, Sukhoi Su-6
A-1 to A-15, Antonov, also TsAGI (autogyros)
A-5, Artseulov
A-7, Kamov, also Polikarpov
A-10, Mil Mi-24
A-40, Antonov KT
ACh-39, Tu-2 (reference to engines)
AIR-1 to AIR-18, Yakovlev
Aist (Stork), Antonov OKA-38
AK, Kamov/Mil
AK-1, Alexandrov/Kalinin
Alarm clock (Budilnik), Avietka
An series, Antonov
Anito, Avietka
ANT series, Tupolev
Antei (Antheus), Antonov An-22
AO, Polikarpov Po-2
AP, Polikarpov Po-2
Ar, Arkhangyelskii
Arab, Tikhonravov
ARK-3, Chyetverikov
ARK-5, Polikarpov R-5
ARK-Z, Zlokakov
ASh, Shavrov Sh-2
ASK, V. Ya. Krylov
AT, Antonov KT
AT-1, A. A. Krylov
Aviatourist, Putilov
Aviavnito-3, KhAI-3
AWF, Yakovlev (1924)
B, Sukhoi Su-8, also Arkhangyelskii Ar-2
B-1 to B-6, Chyetverikov MDR-6
B-5 to B-11, Bratukhin
BB-1, Sukhoi Su-2
BB-2, Grushin BB-MAI
BB-22, Yakovlev Yak-4
BB-MAI, Grushin
BDD, Bolkhovitinov DB-A
BDP, Polikarpov
Be series, Beriev
BI, Beresnyak-Isayev
BICh series (except BICh-17), Chyeranovskii
BICh-17, Kurchyevskii
Blokhi, (two types) Avietka, also KhAI-2
BOK series, BOK
Boldrev, Avietka
BOP, Avietka
BS, Antonov
BS-2, Kalinin K-12
BSB, Polikarpov SPB
BSh-1, Kochyerigin V-11
BSh-2, Ilyushin Il-2
Budilnik, Avietka
Buichok (Young Bull), Tupolev Tu-91
Burevestnik, Avietka
Ch-1, Avietka
Chaika (Seagull), Beriev Be-12, also Polikarpov I-15 and Avietka (Riga)
Chye-2, Chyetverikov MDR-6
Chkalov, Avietka (Ch-1)
Combine, see Kombine
D, Bolkhovitinov, also Borovkov/Florov, also Polikarpov SPB
D-2, Polikarpov
D-3, Polikarpov SPB
DAR, Bartini
DB-1, Tupolev ANT-36
DB-2, Tupolev ANT-37
DB-3, Ilyushin
DB-4, Ilyushin
DB-108, Myasishchyev
DB-240, Yermolayev Yer-2
DB-A, Bolkhovitinov
DB-LK, Belyayev
DBSh, Ilyushin Il-2
DDBSh, Sukhoi Su-8
DDI, Polikarpov VIT-2
DF-1, Fedorov
DG-52, Grigorovich IP-1
DG-53, Grigorovich IP-4
DG-54, Grigorovich IP-2
DG-55, Grigorovich E-2
DG-56, Grigorovich LK-3
DG-58, Grogorovich PB-1
DI, Yakovlev Yak-7
DI-1, Polikarpov 2I-N1
DI-2, Polikarpov D-2
DI-3, Grigorovich/Polikarpov
DI-4, Laville
DI-6, Kochyerigin
DI-8, Tupolev ANT-46
DIP, Tupolev ANT-29
DIS, MiG-5, also Myasishchyev
Diskoplan, KhAI-17
DIT, Polikarpov I-15bis
DKL, Kazan KAI
Dosaaf, Avietka
Dragonfly (Strekoza), Avietka (VEK)
Dubrovin, Avietka
DVB, Myasishchyev
Dzherjinski, Avietka
E, Polikarpov SPB
E 1, E 2, E 3, Avietka
E-2, Grigorovich, also Polikarpov SPB
E-23, Polikarpov Po-2
E-31, Yakovlev AIR-4
ED-1, Polikarpov R-5
EG, Yakovlev
EI, Belyayev, also Kozlov
EMZI, Avietka
Enthusiast, Avietka
Eska, Avietka
Evensen, see Ivensen, Avietka
Experiment, Avietka (RIIGA-14)
F, MiG I-300 (MiG-9**)
Fanera (Veneer) 1, NIAI-Bedunkovich LK-1
FT, Mikoyan/Guryevich MiG-9
G-1, Tupolev ANT-4
G-2, Tupolev ANT-6, also Bratukhin Omega II
G-2 to G-30, Gribovskii
G-3, Kamov/Mil AK
G-4, Bratukhin
G-5, Avietka
G-26 to G-61, Grokhovskii
GAZ-5, Groppius
Gibkolyet, KhAI-21

Gidro 1, Chyetverikov SPL
Gigant, Kozlov
GM-1, Mil Mi-1
GMK-1, Romeo-Gurko
Golub (Pigeon), Antonov
Gorbatch (Hunchback), Ilyushin Il-20
Gr-1, Grushin
GST, Amtorg
Gu-1, Gudkov
Gu-82, Lavochkin LaGG-3
Guep, Avietka
GUP, Avietka
HD.55, OMOS KR-1
Helicogyr, Isacco
I, Bolkhovitinov
I-1, Polikarpov, also Grigorovich
I-1/M-5, Polikarpov IL-400
I-2, Grigorovich
I-3, Polikarpov
I-4, Tupolev ANT-5, also Isacco
I-5, Tupolev ANT-12, then Polikarpov/Grigorovich VT-11
I-6, Polikarpov
I-7, Polikarpov (He 37c)
I-8, Tupolev ANT-13
I-9, Grigorovich
I-10, Grigorovich
I-11, Polikarpov
I-12, Tupolev ANT-23
I-13, Polikarpov
I-14, Tupolev ANT-31
I-15, Polikarpov
I-16, Polikarpov
I-17, Polikarpov
I-18, Polikarpov (not used except as I-180, 185, 187)
I-19, Polikarpov
I-21, Ilyushin, also Pashinin
I-22, Lavochkin LaGG-1
I-26, Yakovlev Yak-1
I-27, Yakovlev Yak-7
I-28, Yatsyenko, also Yakovlev Yak-9PD and Yak-1 Experimentals
I-29, Yakovlev Yak-4
I-30, Yakovlev Yak-1 Experimentals
I-61,MiG-1
I-75F, Mikoyan/Guryevich
I-105, Gorbunov
I-107, Sukhoi Su-5
I-110, Tomashyevich
I-120, Lavochkin La-7
I-130, Lavochkin La-9
I-138, Lavochkin La-9RD
I-140, Lavochkin La-11
I-142, Tupolev ANT-31
I-143, Tupolev ANT-31
I-152, Polikarpov I-15
I-153, Polikarpov I-15
I-180, Polikarpov
I-185, Polikarpov
I-187, Polikarpov I-185
I-190, Polikarpov I-153
I-195, Polikarpov I-153
I-200, Mikoyan/Guryevich MiG-3
I-207, Borovkov
I-210, Mikoyan/Guryevich MiG-3
I-211, Mikoyan/Guryevich Ye (MiG-9*), also Alekseyev
I-212, Alekseyev
I-215, Alekseyev
I-218, Alekseyev
I-220, Nikitin/Shyevchyenko, also MiG-11
I-221 to I-225, Mikoyan/Guryevich MiG-7
I-230, I-231, Mikoyan/Guryevich MiG-3
I-250, Mikoyan/Guryevich
I-270, Mikoyan/Guryevich
I-287, Yatsyenko I-28
I-300, Mikoyan/Guryevich MiG-9**
I-301, Lavochkin LaGG-3
I-301T, Mikoyan MiG-9UTI
I-302, Tikhonravov
I-305, Mikoyan MiG-9
I-310, Mikoyan MiG-15
I-320, Mikoyan MiG-17
I-330, Sukhoi Su-1
I-350, Mikoyan MiG-19
I-360, Sukhoi Su-3
IB, Ilyushin Il-2
IgA-2, Avietka
IL, Kurchyevskii
Il series, Ilyushin
IL-21, Pashinin
IL-400, Polikarpov
Inflatable, Grokhovskii
IP-1 to IP-4, Grigorovich
IP-21, Pashinin
IS, Silvanskii, also Nikitin/Shyevchyenko
Iskra (Spark), KhAI-4
IT-2, IT-4, IT-6 and IT-9, Avietka
ITP, Polikarpov
Ivanov, Polikarpov, Sukhoi, Tupolev (ANT-51) and KhAI (R-10), also Avietka
Ivensen, Avietka
IVS, Shchyerbakov
I-Z, Grigorovich
Jockey, Tupolev ANT-13
JRD, Yakovlev Yak-7
Ju, JuG, Junkers
K-1 to K-13, Kalinin
K-1, Kolpakov
K-17, BOK-7
K-30, Junkers
K-37, Gudkov
K-62, Polikarpov Po-2
Ka series, Kamov
KAI series, Kazan
Karas, Me 163 (see imported types list)
KaSkr-1, KaSkr-2, Kamov/Skrzhinskii
Katsur, Avietka (VO-4)
KB-2, designation of OKB
KD, Sukhoi Su-13
Keet (Whale), Antonov An-8
KhAI series, Kharkov
KhB, Putilov Stal-5
Komarov, Avietka
Kombine, Mozharovskii/Venyevidov
Kometa, Grigorovich E-2
Komsomolyets 1, Avietka (KSM-1)
Komta, Zhukovskii
Konjok Gorbunok, Khioni No 5
KOR-1, Beriev Be-2
KOR-2, Beriev Be-4
KPIR, Avietka
KR, Tupolev ANT-40
KR-1, OMOS
KR-6, Tupolev ANT-7
Kretchet, Gribovskii G-28
KSM, Avietka
KT, Antonov
KTs-20, Koleznikov
KuAI, Avietka (VIGR)
Kukuracha, Grokhovskii
Kukuruznik (Corn Cutter), Polikarpov Po-2
Kvant (Quantum), Avietka
L, Moskalyev Strela
L-760, Tupolev ANT-20bis
La series, Lavochkin
La-174, Lavochkin La-15
LaGG, Lavochkin/Gorbunov/Gudkov
LAKM, Avietka
LB-2LD, Kolpakov
LBSh, Kochyerigin R-9
LEM-2, Antonov
LEM-3, NIAI-Domrachyev
Leningradets, Avietka
Leningradskii Kombinat, NIAI LK-1
Leningradskii Komsomolyets, Bakshayev LK
Li-2, Lisunov
LIG-5, NIAI-Bedunkovich P-3
LIG-6, NIAI-Domrachyev LEM-3
LIG-7, Bakshayev RK
LIG-8, NIAI-Bakshayev
LIG-10, NIAI-Bedunkovich Skh-1
LiM-1, LiM-2, MiG-15 (Poland)
LK, NIAI-Bakshayev, also Sukhoi Su-11*
LK-1, NIAI-Bedunkovich
LK-2, Grokhovskii G-38
LK-3, Grigorovich
LK-4, NIAI-Bedunkovich
LL, Kurchyevskii IL
LL-1, LL-2, Tsybin
LL-143, Beriev Be-6
LM, Avietka
LM-2, Avietka LM
LNB, Polikarpov Po-2
LR, LR-2, Kochyerigin
LSh, Grigorovich LK-3, also Nikitin NV-5
M-1, M-2, Polikarpov ITP
M-4, Myasishchyev
M-5 to M-24, Grigorovich
M-10, Beriev Be-10
M-12, Beriev Be-12
M-50, Myasishchyev
MA, Polikarpov TIS
MA-1, V.Ya. Krylov/Rentel
Maksim Gorkii, Tupolev ANT-20
MAI-62, Avietka
Malyutka, Polikarpov
Marabou, Mil Mi-2
Mars, Avietka
MB, Avietka
MB-1, Avietka
MBR-2, Beriev
MBR-3, Samsonov
MBR-4, imported (S.M.62)
MBR-5, Samsonov
MBR-7, Beriev
MDR-1, Grigorovich ROM
MDR-2, Tupolev ANT-8
MDR-3, Chyetverikov
MDR-4, Tupolev ANT-27
MDR-5, Beriev
MDR-6, Chyetverikov
MDR-7, Samsonov, also Shavrov
MER, Tupolev ANT-8
MG, Tupolev ANT-20
Mi series, Mil
MI-3, Tupolev ANT-21
MiG series, Mikoyan/Guryevich
MIIT, Avietka
Mikrosamolyet, Avietka
MK-1, Tupolev ANT-22
MK-1, MK-21, Mikhelson
MM, Grigorovich
MMN, Arkhangyelskii
Molot (Hammer), Myasishchyev M-4
Moskit, Avietka
Moskva, Ilyushin Il-18**, also Ilyushin TsKB-30
Moskvich, Mil Mi-1
MP, Mikhelson/Morshchikhin, also Polikarpov BDP

TOM, Richard
TRD, Tu-2
Tri Druga, Avietka
Ts series, Tsybin
TS-1, Schchyerbakov Shchye-2
TsAGI-10, Polikarpov Po-2
TSh, MiG-6
TSh-1, Grigorovich
TSh-2, Grigorovich
TSh-3, Kochyerigin
TShB, Tupolev ANT-17
TSK, Avietka (Pissarenko)
TsKB-1, Kochyerigin LR
TsKB-3, Polikarpov I-15
TsKB-4, Kochyerigin TSh-3
TsKB-5, Grigorovich LSh-1
TsKB-6, Grigorovich TSh-1
TsKB-7, Grigorovich I-Z
TsKB-8, Grigorovich TB-5
TsKB-10, BICh-14
TsKB-11, Kochyerigin DI-6 (not MDR-3)
TsKB-12, Polikarpov I-16
TsKB-15, Polikarpov I-17 (1)
TsKB-18, Polikarpov I-16
TsKB-19, Polikarpov I-17 (2)
TsKB-21, Grigorovich TSh-2
TsKB-23, Grigorovich ShON
TsKB-24, Kochyerigin TSh-3
TsKB-25, Polikarpov I-17
TsKB-26, Ilyushin
TsKB-27, Kochyerigin SR
TsKB-29, Polikarpov I-16
TsKB-30, Ilyushin DB-3
TsKB-32, Ilyushin I-21
TsKB-33, Polikarpov I-17 (3)
TsKB-38, Kochyerigin DI-6Sh
TsKB-43, Polikarpov I-17
TsKB-44, Polikarpov VIT-1
TsKB-48, Polikarpov VIT-2
TsKB-55, Ilyushin Il-2
TsKB-56, Ilyushin DB-4
TsKB-57, Ilyushin Il-2
TsKB-65, MiG-6
Tu series, Tupolev
Turbolyet, Rafaelyants
U-1, Dudakov/Konstantinov
U-2, Polikarpov Po-2, also Rafaelyants
U-3, U-4, Mikhelson
U-5, Nikitin NV-5
Ukraina, Antonov An-10
ULK, Grokhovskii G-37
Upar, Antonov
UPB, KAI-3
UPO-22, Avietka
US, Antonov
USB, Tupolev ANT-40
UT-1, Yakovlev AIR-14
UT-2, Yakovlev Ya-20
UT-3, Yakovlev Ya-17
UT-15, Yakovlev AIR-15
UTB-2, Sukhoi but included in Tupolev Tu-2
UTI-1, Polikarpov/Grigorovich I-5
UTI-4, Polikarpov I-16UTI
UTI-5, Nikitin NV-2
UTI-6, Nikitin NV-6
UTI-26, Yakovlev Yak-1
Utka, Mikoyan/Guryevich
V-2, Mil Mi-2
V-8, Mil Mi-8
V-10, Mil Mi-10
V-11, Kochyerigin
V-12, Mil Mi-12
V-14, Mil Mi-14
VAT, Avietka (Chkalov)
VB-109, Myasishchyev
VEK, Avietka
Veneer-1, NIAI LK-1
VI-100, Petlyakov
VIGR (VIHR), Avietka
Vinogradov, Avietka
Vintokryl, Kamov Ka-22
VIT-1, VIT-2, Polikarpov
VNP, Bratukhin B-10
Vnuk Oktyabr, Avietka (VAT)
VO-4, Avietka
VP, VP(K), Polikarpov
VS-2, Kalinin K-12
VSI, Shchyerbakov
VT-2, Yakovlev Ya-20
VT-11, Polikarpov/Grigorovich I-5
VVA-1, Avietka
VVA-3, Yakovlev AIR-1
Ya series, Yakovlev
Yak series, Yakovlev
Yak No 104, Yakovlev Yak-30**
Yakov Alksnis, Grokhovskii G-31
Ye, Sukhoi Su-10
Ye, numbers up to at least 266, experimental MiGs
Yer, Yermolayev
Yer-4, Yermolayev Yer-2
Z, Grigorovich I-Z
Z-1 to Z-7, Vakhmistrov
ZAOR, Avietka
Zh, MiG I-270
Zhar Pteetsa (Firebird), Kalinin K-12
ZIG-1, Laville
Zlatoust, Avietka
Zvyeno, Vakhmistrov
1-EA, 2-EA etc, TsAGI
2A, 3A, Sukhoi Su-6
2I-N1, Polikarpov
2U-BZ, Moiseyenko
3B/M, Avietka
No 4, 5, Khioni
11, Chyetverikov MDR-3
28, Yak I-26
65, MiG
77, Tupolev Tu-12
81, Sukhoi Su-6
103, Tupolev ANT-58, ANT-59
104, Tupolev Tu-2 variant
105, Gorbunov
110, Tomashyevich
201-M, Myasishchyev
346, DFS 346, imports list (1945-1946)
4302, Florov
7211, Borovkov

Monino is at present closed to visitors, but it now contains this Mandrake derivative which is almost certainly the RV, with 21,5 m unswept wing and short body with glazed nose and large fin. RV probably meant 'record height' as explained on page 395. Tu-114 in background

Air weapons

The Soviet Union has for many years been a world leader in aircraft armament. No other nation has put into service so many types of aircraft gun, most of them of outstanding quality and performance. Rockets as air/ground weapons were pioneered in the Soviet Union. Guided missiles have tended to be large rather than advanced in design, but today the picture may have changed.

Guns

Until 1932 all aircraft guns were derived from the Maxim/Vickers machine guns, firing rimless ammunition in 7,62 mm (0·300 in) calibre. The designation DA stemmed from *Dyegtyaryev Aviatsionnyi* (Vasilii Dyegtyaryev was perhaps the greatest Soviet designer of small arms); this gun was normally used on pivoted hand-aimed mountings. The very similar PV-1 (*Pulyemet Vozdushnyi*, air machine-gun) was developed mainly by Nadashkyevich and used in fixed, synchronized and movable installations. In 1930 work began on large-calibre recoilless guns, discussed later. The first heavy cannon tested after 1920 was the Hispano *moteur canon*, but this never reached service units and instead B.G. Shpital'nyi created two superb new gas-operated guns, one almost a scale-up of the other. The rifle-calibre ShKAS (*Shpital'nyi/Komarnitskii Aviatsionnyi Skorostrel'nyi*) was the neatest, fastest-firing machine-gun of its day; a Hurricane with five would have had greater hitting-power and more strikes per second than with its eight Brownings. The 20 mm ShVAK (*Shpital'nyi/Vladimirov Aviatsionnyi Krupnokaliber*) was lighter and much smaller than the Hispano but fired with almost the same m.v. (muzzle velocity) at a much faster rate. Both guns were used in fixed, synchronized and movable installations. In 1940 they were joined by the first of the outstanding weapons designed by M.Ye. Beresin, the UB (*Universal'nyi Beresin*). With the same calibre as the famed 0·5 Browning, the Russian gun was much more compact, lighter, faster-firing and had a higher m.v.; it was used as the UBS (*Synkhronnom*), often abbreviated to BS, as the UBK (*Kryl'yenom*, in wing) and as the UBT (*Turel'nom*, turret). The VYa (*Volkov/Yartsyev*) had calibre only 3 mm greater than the ShVAK but was utterly different; with a projectile more than twice as heavy which at long air/ground ranges would 25 mm armour. Even this gun was dwarfed by the NS-37 (*Nudel'man/Suranov*), which had a bigger punch than US or German weapons of this calibre or the British RR or Vickers 40 mm, with almost guaranteed penetration of 40 mm armour at angles to 45°. The same gun was given a slightly shorter barrel of 45 mm calibre which was satisfactorily installed in Yak-9s (armour penetration, 58 mm) but the recoil of the immense 57 mm version proved to be too much. In 1945 Beresin brought in a lightweight 20 mm gun to replace the ShVAK; designated B-20 it was gas-operated from a point well down the barrel and was used in fighters and as the gun in the remotely directed four-turret PV-20 bomber defence system. The NS team replaced the VYa with their NS-23, the NS-23S variant being synchronized in fighters and two sub-types being used in bomber turrets. The later NR-23 (*Nudel'man/Rikhter*) used the same ammunition but had a higher cyclic rate and was used in fighters and also in bomber turrets (system PV-23) in place of the B-20. A. Suranov, V. Nyemenov, A. Rikhter

gun	year	calibre	mass		cyclic rate	m.v.
		mm	gun kg	projectile g	shots/min	m/s
PV, DA	1928	7,62	14,5	16	720/780	825
ShKAS	1932	7,62	10,0	16	1,800	825
UB	1940	12,7	21,5	48	1,000	860
ShVAK, MP	1936	20	45	96	800	800
VYa, MP-23	1940	23	66	200	600	900
NS-37	1942	37	150	735	250	900
NS-45	1944	45	152	1065	250	850
OKB-16-57	1944	57	290	2780	?	980
B-20	1945	20	25	96	800	800
NS-23	1945	23	37	200	550	690
N-37	1946	37	103	735	400	900
NR-23	1949	23	39	200	850	690
NR-30	1954	30	66	410	850, 1,000	780
AM-23	1954	23	43	200	1,300	690
GSh-23	1959	23	72	200	2,800	890
?	c1970	23	c150	200	c4,000	890

and P. Gribkov designed the N-37 used in early jet fighters, while from the NR-23 a series of original new features resulted in one of the most formidable single-barrel guns ever created, the NR-30, which, though much lighter than the rival Aden and DEFA of the same era, fired a far heavier projectile at the same m.v. For bombers the AM-23 offered a higher rate of fire, compared with the NR-23, and remains in use to this day. With considerably improved high-energy ammunition, 23 mm remains the chief calibre, both in single-barrel guns and in the twin-barrel GSh-23 which is commonly installed in the GP-9 pack with 200 or 320-round magazine. The latest gun of this calibre has six barrels.

Recoilless guns

As far as is known all Soviet guns of this type were derived from the British Davis of 1915 and, like most similar weapons, cancelled out recoil by firing two equal masses in opposite directions, the projectile down the barrel and gun gas and a balance weight to the rear. Development was headed by Leonid Vasil'yevich Kurchyevskii and led to a series of weapons known by APK designations, from *Avtomatichyeskaya pushka Kurchyevskogo* or as DRP, from *Dynamo-reaktivnoi pushkye*. The original basis had been laid earlier (1922–1926) by Prof Boris Sergeyevich Stechkin, who tested guns of from 1 in (25,4 mm) to 12 in (305 mm) calibre, and flew 6 in (152 mm) weapons under the wings of a Junkers F13 in 1923. Kurchyevskii appears to have picked up the work in 1930 with 3 in (76,2 mm) weapons, which in the APK-4 of June 1934 could fire repeatedly, though at a slow rate. At the same time the APK-100 of 4 in (101,6 mm) calibre was on test, intended for the I-12, and despite many problems such weapons continued to be developed for use against air and ground targets until the DI-8 (ANT-46). Kurchyevskii's KB was liquidated in February 1936.

Rockets

The roots of Soviet aircraft rocket projectiles lay in studies by artillery officers V.A. Artemyev and N.I. Tikhomirov during the Civil War of 1920-1922. Eventually this led to the GDL (gas dynamics lab) in the Peter and Paul Fortress, Leningrad, where basic designs were prepared under B.S. Petropavlovskii for finned, spinning missiles of 75, 82 and 132 mm calibre. Motor firings were in hand when in 1933 the programme was transferred to the newly formed RNII, where under Ivan T. Kleimenov the theory – completely elucidated by mathematician G. Ye. Langemak – was translated into practice. The 75 mm rocket, for use against aerial targets, went into pilot production as RS-75 (*Reaktivnyi Snaryad*, reaction missile) in summer 1937, and immediately underwent large-scale firing trials from I-16 and other aircraft, often against agile target gliders released by R-5s. About October 1937 Kleimenov and Langemak were arrested and never heard of again, but by 1939 all three missiles were in production, together with simple launch rails and electric ignition circuits for the aircraft. I-15 and I-16 fighters were progressively equipped to fire eight RS-75, and the first operational use came on 22 August

Air-to-air missiles (AAM)

Missile		Approx year	Guidance	Dimensions mm			Weight	Range
				Body diam	Length	Span	kg	km
AA-1	Alkali	1958	Radar beam rider	190	1880	578	91	8
AA-2	Atoll	1960	IR or SARH	120	2780	530	70	6,4
AA-3	Anab	1962	IR or SARH	280	3600	1300	275	32
AA-4	Awl	1961	?	305	5200	1800	400	60+
AA-5	Ash	1961	IR or SARH	305	5510	1300	390	64
AA-6	Acrid	c1972	IR or SARH	400	6300	2250	850	100
AA-7	Apex	c1975	IR or SAHR	260	4500	1400	320	48
AA-8	Aphid	1976	IR or SARH	130	2150	520	55	15

Air-to-surface missiles (ASM)

Missile		Approx year	Guidance	Dimensions mm			Weight	Range
				Body diam	Length	Span	kg	km
AS-1	Kennel	1957	A+ARH	1350	8230	4900	3000	120
AS-2	Kipper	1961	A+ARH	965	9400	4900	5000	212
AS-3	Kangaroo	1961	A+ARH	1400	14 960	9000	10 000	650
AS-4	Kitchen	1963	I	790	11 300	2400	7000	220
AS-5	Kelt	c1967	A+I+ARH	1350	9780	4750	4800	320
AS-6	Kingfish	1977	A+I+(ARH?)	790	10 700	2400	5000	650
AS-7	Kerry	c1980	RC	c400	c8500	?	1200	10
AS-8		1977	LS	c200	c2900	?	c180	10
AS-X-9		c1982	ARM	?	?	?	?	c90
AS-X-10		c1982	EO homing	?	?	?	c200	c10
ATASM		?	I+EO homing	?	?	?	c900	c40

Abbreviations: A, autopilot; ARH, active radar homing; ARM, anti-radiation missile; EO, electro-optical; I, inertial; IR, infra-red homing; LS, laser seeker; RC, radio command; SARH, semi-active radar homing.

1939 when 22-IAP (I-16 type 10) fired salvos against Japanese Ki-27s (Western accounts often give the rocket size as RS-82). The latter was made in far greater numbers (at least 2·5 million) than the other species, and was apparently a surprise to the Nazis and the Allies when fired against Panzers from Il-2s in June 1941. A simple projectile with ogive nose (with fuze windmill), drum central portion and four-fin conical tail, it was 864 mm long and weighed 6,82 kg. The RS-132 was 935 mm long and weighed 23,1 kg. After the war the Il-40 and Tu-91 were designed to carry the RS-182, TRS-190 and ARS-212. Modern rockets include the mass-produced S-5 series 57 mm, fired from UB8, 16, 19 and 32 pods; S-8, 80 mm; S-13, 130 mm; S-16, 160 mm; S-21 series, 210 mm; S-24, 240 mm; S-28, 280 mm; and S-32 series, 325 mm. Some of the S-21 and S-32 models have limited radio-command steering.

Missiles

At least in the early generations, Soviet air-launched guided missiles have appeared to be overlarge and clumsy. An exception is the AA-2 Atoll, a copy of the American Sidewinder. In this field the edge appears to have lain with the West, because of the latter's superior digital microelectronics, though in terms of the number of missile rounds the picture is quite the opposite. Lacking true designations (except for AA-2, believed to be K-13A or SB-06) NATO code designations and names are used in the table on page 22.

Free-fall stores

There are more than 1000 known species of Soviet bombs, mines, depth charges and torpedoes. Most have a prefix followed by a number giving the drop mass in kg. Typical prefixes include: FAB, GP HE bomb; OFAB, HE frag; ZAB, incendiary; ZAP, box of ZABs; BETAB, retarded/rocket-assisted anti-runway; PTAB, original hollow-charge bomblet; PTK, modern hollow-charge bomblet for cluster dispenser; RPK, frag bomblet for cluster; RRAB, incendiary for cluster; AK, mustard/Lewisite bomblet; KhAB or ChAB, large phosgene; VAP, tanks or spray dispensers for HCN or persistent Toxic-B; SOV-AB, new persistent Toxic-B dispense; NOV-AB, non-persist; PLAB, napalm; FAE, fuel/air explosive; N, TN, nuclear; DAP, DV-AB, smoke; FOTAB, photo-flash; PROSAB, parachute flare.

The MiG-23 and MiG-27 family of swing-wing fighter/bombers are probably being built at a greater rate than any other combat aircraft. This MiG-27 was photographed in March 1983, laden with 16 FAB-250s

Materials

Shorthand used in the text needs a brief explanation and some background on Soviet airframe construction.

Metals Russia had no aluminium smelting capability, but in 1920, at the height of the Civil War, the Soviet Union's infant VVF formed a committee to study light alloys under engineer (later professor) Ivan Ivanovich Sidorin. In August 1922 under his direction the first commercial quantities were made of a direct copy of the German alloy Duralumin, named Kolchugalumin from the town (north-east of Moscow) Kol'chugino where, at the Gospromtsvyetmet works, the ingots were produced. Standard fabricated bar, rolled sections, tube and sheet began to appear in October 1922, and small pieces flew in ANT-1 a year later. By 1939 the name had lapsed, and dural specifications were written for alloys D1 to D16 (sometimes written D-1 with hyphen). Aluminium is A or AMTs. Mild-steel specifications are prefaced M or MS. Stainless was first produced on a lab scale in October 1928, with the name *Enerzh*. By 1930 six grades existed, but none was in production; price rivalled silver. *Enerzh-6* was used at great cost to build early Stal aircraft. This was a basic 18/8 Ni/Cr steel, and by 1938 it had been improved to various grades of KhGSA (these are the chemical symbols in Russian). KhMA is a Cr/Mo steel, imported until late 1936. KhNZA or Chromansil is a Cr/Mn/Si alloy. Titanium sponge was produced from late 1953, and today Soviet output far exceeds that of Europe, to which it is an exporter. There are several T-series titanium alloys. Armour has received greater attention than in any other country, mainly because of work at VIAM of Sergei Kishkin and Nikolai Slkyarov from circa 1930 towards fabrication methods for AB-1 (*Aviatsionnaya Bronya*, aviation armour), based on Ni/Mo steel, which had to be formed to approximate shape before being hardened, and which after hardening was difficult to cut or to drill. Major problems continued to be distortion after initial shaping and drilling, so that the *Bronyekorpus* (armour body) did not match drawings, and an extreme scarcity of vital alloying elements.

Wood Soviet Union led world in application of wood to advanced airframes, without resorting to imported balsa widely used in British Mosquito. From two-dimensional plywood workers at several GAZ, assisted by VIAM, developed a 3-D technique called *shpon* in which layers (typically 1 mm) of birch or similar wood were glued one above another whilst formed over a male die giving single or double curvature. No heat or pressure was used, and adhesives were local casein or albumen glues. A major development, by L.I. Ryzhkov (director of a laminated propeller and ski factory), was *delta drevesina* (delta wood) in which each laminate was impregnated with an imported resin adhesive prior to bonding under pressure. Imported resin was finally, about December 1940, replaced by phenol-formaldehyde resin, later with trace additions of borax, often inserted in sheet form. After bonding at 150°C the result was called bakelite ply, widely used in the Second World War. Today wood-based laminates use epoxy resins.

When the Myasishchyev M-4 was designed 31 years ago it was impossible to achieve the stipulated range. But as an exercise in aircraft structures it was a remarkable achievement. This M-4 Bison-B was photographed near the UK in late 1982

Engines

From 1924 the NKAP assigned a simple M (*Motornyi*) number to each engine, all of which were then based on imported designs. The first indigenous engine to be qualified was Shvetsov's M-11. From 1941, as with aircraft types, General Constructors were permitted to use their own initials; in the following list engines designated by both schemes are described under the later 1941 scheme. Rocket and ramjet engines received different designations prior to 1941, and for turbojets other new schemes (eg, using the prefix RD, from *Reaktivnyi Dvigatyel*, reaction engine) were standardized. Today the designer's initials are used in older engine KBs but Lotaryev uses D (*Dvigatyel*), Tumanskii R (*Reaktivnyi*) and for FAI record submissions other (duplicative) systems are used. The following is strictly alphabetical purely for ease of reference.

A, A-117 Free-piston gas generator for long-range bombers, GAZ-117 (1949–1955), chief designer Mikhail Aleksandrovich Orlov, 10,000 hp class; complex, and low target s.f.c. never attained.

ACh-30, ACh-40 Important family of turbocharged two-stroke diesels developed from AN-1 by KB of Aleksei Dmitriyevich Charomskii, V-12, pressure-glycol-cooled, 180 × 200 cylinders (62,34 lit), typically 1200 kg. ACh-30, 1400 hp; 30B, BF, 1500 hp; 31, 32, 1550 hp; 39, 1800 hp; 39BF, 1900 hp; 40, 1500 hp.

ADG-4 Four-stroke flat-twin, 35 hp at 2400 rpm.

AI-4 Small aircooled flat-four four-stroke by Aleksandr G. Ivchyenko, qualified 1946 at 52 hp and produced in several forms (4B, 4G for helicopters) at 55 hp.

AI-10 Ivchyenko 5-cylinder radial, qualified 1946 at 80 hp.

AI-14 Ivchyenko 9-cylinder radial, built in many versions in large quantities for aeroplanes and helicopters, today in production only in Poland and China. Cylinders 105 × 130 (10,16 lit), qualified 1947 at 240 (later 260) hp, 14RF, 300 hp at 2400 rpm; 14VF, 285 hp; 14RA, 260 hp at 2350 rpm.

AI-20 Single-shaft turboprop, begun 1947 at Kuibyshyev as NK-4 under N. D. Kuznetsov with mainly German team as rival to VK-2; in 1952 found to have better s.f.c. and adopted, further development and preparation for production transferred to Zaporozhye under Ivchyenko and redesignated AI-20; qualified 1955 at 2800 kW, AI-20K, 2942 kW; AI-20M 3124 kW, uprated for An-32 to 3169 kW. Ten-stage compressor, p.r. 9·2, airflow 20,7 kg/s.

AI-24 Ivchyenko single-shaft turboprop scaled down from AI-20 to airflow 14,4 kg/s; qualified 1959 at 1875 kW; 24A, rating maintained hot/high by water; 24T, 2103 kW also maintained by water.

AI-25 Ivchyenko two-shaft turbofan, compressor 3 + 8, p.r. 1·695/4·68, b.p.r. 2; rating 1500 kg (14,68 kN); AI-25T, aircooled HP blades, 1750 kg (17,13 kN).

AI-26 Ivchyenko 7-cylinder radial, 155,5 × 155 (20,6 lit), qualified 1946 at 500 hp, subsequently many versions for normal or vertical installation including 26GR, 500 hp; GRF, 550; GRFL, 575; V, 575; later built in Poland, redesignated Lit-3 and developed into PZL-3.

AL-1 Small single-shaft turbojet by Arkhip Mikhailovich Lyul'ka, 1000 kg (9,8 kN).

AL-3 Lyul'ka turbojet of 1947, not flown.

AL-5 Lyul'ka single-shaft turbojet, 7-stage, prototype 1950 at 4500 kg (44,13 kN), qualified 1951 4600 kg (45,1 kN); AL-5F, 5000 kg (49,1 kN); 5G, 5500 kg (53,93 kN).

AL-7 Lyul'ka turbojet with supersonic LP stages in 9-stage compressor, qualified 1954 at 6500 kg (63,74 kN); 7F, afterburner, rated 7 t (68,64 kN) dry and 10 t (98,1 kN) max; 7PB, marine, 6500 kg (63,74 kN) dry only.

AL-9 Became AL-21?

AL-21 Lyul'ka turbojet derived from AL-7F; qualified about 1972, and series production of 21F-3 at 8165 kg (80,1 kN) dry and 11,1 t (109 kN) with afterburner.

AM-2 Single-shaft turbojet of Aleksandr Aleksandrovich Mikulin, tested about 1953 at 4600 kg (45,17 kN); incorrectly reported at thrusts in range 2720/2825 kg.

AM-3 Large single-shaft turbojet by Mikulin KB developed by team under P. F. Zubets as M-209 and with official designation RD-3; 8-stage compressor, p.r. 6·4; qualified 1952 at 6750 kg (66,2 kN); production 1954 of 3M at 8200 kg (80,4 kN), and numerous sub-types 1955–1959 including 3M-200 (8700 kg/85,34 kN) and 3M-500 (9500 kg/93,2 kN).

AM-5 Single-shaft turbojet in 2700-kg class (3040 with afterburner) redesignated RD-5 in 1956.

AM-13 Mikulin water-cooled V-12, qualified 1928 at 880 hp at 2,150 rpm.

AM-30 Baseline engine for important Mikulin series of V-12 water (later glycol) cooled, modified BMW VI cylinder blocks, 160 × 190 (46,7 lit), HS12 rear wheelcase, Allison supercharger and R-R Buzzard reduction gear, qualified 660 hp at 2000 rpm about 1931.

AM-34 Derived engine built in at least 14 versions from 1932 with compression ratio 6·25, 6·6 or 7·0 and powers 690 hp to 1285 hp; main variants M-34, 34N, V, NV, RNV, 830 hp; M-34 (c.r. 7·0) 874 hp; 34R, 34F, 830 hp; 34 FRN, 900 hp; 34R (6·6), 900 hp; 34R (7·0), 950 hp; 34RN, 970 hp; 34 FRNV, 1200 hp; 34 RNF, 1275 hp).

AM-35 Derived engine with improved cylinder head and supercharger and many minor changes, qualified 1939 at 1200 hp at 2050 rpm; 35A, 1350 hp.

AM-37 Derived engine, 1380 hp, 1940; 37F, 1400 hp.

AM-38 Major production engine, usual c.r. 6·8, numerous refinements; qualified 1941 at 1550 hp, later same year 1665 hp; 38F, 1700 hp, 1720 hp, 1760 hp.

AM-39 Further development, qualified 1942 at 1870 hp; FN-2, 1850 hp; A, 1900 hp; FB, 1800 hp.

AM-41 Prototype only, 1942.

AM-42 Qualified 1944 at 2000 hp; 42FB, 1900 hp with or without TK.

AM-43 Prototype 1944, four ratings 1950 hp (43B) to 2200 hp.

AM-47 Prototype 1946, ratings 2700 hp to 3100 hp (47F).

AN-1 First definitive two-stroke diesel by Charomskii, designation *Aviatsionnyi Nyeftyarnoi*, aviation/oil, tested 1933 at 850 hp, later 900 hp.

ASh-2 Lowest numerical designation of piston engine by Arkadiya Dmitriyevich Shvetsov, but last basic ASh type; basically two ASh-82 in tandem, 28-cylinder in line, 3300 hp in 1950–1951.

ASh-21 Shvetsov 7-cylinder radial with direct injection, ASh-82 cylinders 155,5 × 155 (20,6 lit); qualified 1947 at 700 hp, later 730 hp, then (1954) 760 hp; 21V, helicopter engine, 575 hp.

ASh-62 Originally M-62, long series of engines derived from Wright R-1820 Cyclone via M-25; qualified 1937 at 840 hp, later 900 hp and 920 hp; main wartime production 1000 hp on 100-octane; ASh-62IR standard An-2 at 1000 hp, with TK maintained to 9,5 km; 62M, 58 hp auxiliary drive-shaft for agricultural equipment. IR still produced in Poland (as ASz 62IR) and China.

ASh-63 Usually known as M-63, improved 1939 development of M-62, 1,100 hp.

ASh-71 Essentially two M-63 combined to form large 18-cylinder engine, qualified 1941 at 1700 hp, 1942 at 2000 hp; 71F, 2100 hp, later 2200 hp.

ASh-72 Improved M-71, rated 2000/2250 hp in 1943, qualified 1944 at 2300 hp.

ASh-73 Ultimate 18-cylinder Shvetsov, tested 1944 at 2300 hp, qualified 1945 at 2600 hp; 73TK, rated 2400 hp with TK maintained to 6,5 km; 73FN, 2400/2650 hp.

ASh-82 Important Shvetsov 14-cylinder radials originally (as M-82) using cylinder derived from M-62 but with stroke reduced to give engine capacity 41,2 lit instead of 42,7 lit (cylinders 155,5 × 155), resulting in compact engine around which KB and TsIAM achieved some of world's first really good radial installations; qualified 1940 at 1250 hp on 87-octane and subsequently made in 22 variants with different c.r. and fuel grades, inertia/electric/pneumatic starter and in direct-drive oblique helicopter variant; 82 qualified 1330 hp later 1400 hp in 1941; 82A, 1600 hp; 82FN, 1540 hp, 1630 hp, 1850 hp on 100-octane, direct injection; 82FNV, 1850 hp; NV, 1700 hp; T, civil, 1900 hp; V, helicopter, 1700 hp.

ASh-83 Derived engine, 1900 hp.

ASh-90 Derived engine with 18 cylinders; qualified 1941 at 1500 hp.

BD-500 Compound engine using same cylinder as M-501 supplying gas to turbine geared to prop; developed 1946–1953 at GAZ-500 under S.S. Balandin.

D-1 Series of liquid rocket engines developed at RNII by team led by L.S. Dushkin and V.A. Shtokolov, culminating in D-1A-1100, with HP pump feed of concentrated nitric acid (RFNA) and kerosene, SL thrust 1100 kg (10,8 kN), about 1300 kg at height.

D-15 Turbojet, generally assumed by Soloviev, rated from 1957 at 13 t (12,75 kN) dry and 15– 17,5 t (147/172 kN) with afterburner.

D-20 Two-shaft turbofan by P.A. Soloviev KB, known only in D-20P form; compressors 3 + 8, p.r. 13, b.p.r. 1·0; airflow 113 kg/s; rated 1962 at 5,4 t (52,96 kN).

D-25 Soloviev single-shaft free-turbine helicopter engine; 9-stage, p.r. 5·6, rated 1956 at 4101 kW as D-25V, also called TV-2BM; D-25VF rated about 1963 at 4850 kW (all ratings maintained to 3 km or 40° C).

D-30 Soloviev two-shaft turbofan; compressors 4 + 10, p.r. 17·4, b.p.r. 1, airflow 125 kg/s; rated circa 1964 at 6800 kg (66,68 kN).

D-30K Soloviev two-shaft turbofan not related to D-30; compressors 3 + 11, p.r. 20, b.p.r. 2·42, airflow 269 kg/s; rated 1966 at 11 t (108 kN) as D-30KU; D-30KP later rated 12 t (117,7 kN).

D-36 First engine developed by new team at Zaporozhye under Vladimir Lotarev (successor to Ivchyenko); three-shaft turbofan, p.r. 20, b.p.r. 5·6, rating 6,5 t (63,74 kN).

D-136 Turboshaft for large helicopters derived from D-36; compressors 6 + 6, p.r. 18·3; qualified 1980 at 8500 kW.

DM-1 Auxiliary ramjet, designation from *Dopolnityelnyi Motor* (supplementary motor), by Ivan A. Merkulov, 400-mm diameter, operating on same fuel as existing piston engine, tested 1939.

DM-2 Improved ramjet, 400-mm diameter, flown January 1940.

DM-4 Larger ramjet, 500-mm diameter, weight 30 kg, required special tank with ethyl alcohol added to existing piston fuel, flown October 1940.

ED-1 Soviet designation for series of two-stroke diesels based on Junkers Jumo 204 and 206, tested 1935–1940 at around 600 hp.

GAZ M-1 Modified 4-cylinder water-cooled car engine, Ye. V. Agitov at Gorkii works, 56 hp.

GDL Series of large space rockets, not used for aircraft.

GTD-3 Alternative designation (from *Gelikopter Turbo-Dvigatyel*) for TVD-10.

GTD-350 Small helicopter turboshaft developed by Sergei Pietrovich Isotov; compressor 7 + 1 centrifugal, p.r. 6·05, airflow 2,19 kg/s; rated circa 1964 at 295 kW, later uprated to 322 kW (350P, 331 kW); made only in Poland.

M-2 Soviet 120 hp Le Rhône 9.

M-5 Soviet 400 hp Liberty 12.

M-6 Soviet 300 hp Hispano-Suiza 8Fb.

M-8 Earliest known Soviet-designed engine, radial by A.D. Shvetsov circa 1925.

M-11 Classic engine derived from M-8 and over 100,000 built 1927–1959, probably about 125,000; 5-cylinder 125 × 140 (8,6 lit), qualified 1927 at 100 hp; 11G, 115 hp; D, 115 hp; K, 115 hp; Ye, 150 hp; F, 145/165 hp; FM, M, 145 hp; FR, 160 hp; FR-1, 165 hp; FN, 200 hp.

M-12 Developed M-11, 190 hp.

M-13 See M-18.

M-14 Modern refinement by Ivan M. Vedeneyev of AI-14; M-14V-26 helicopter engine rated 325 hp/242 kW; M-14P fixed-wing either same rating or 360 hp/269 kW.

M-15 Soviet (mainly Shvetsov) 9-cylinder radial, run 1928 at 450 hp, no production.

M-17 Soviet engines derived from BMW VI V-12 water-cooled; 17, 535/680 hp; 17F, 715 hp; 17B, 680 hp.

M-18 Following design of M-13 two-row radial circa 1926, NAMI team under A.A. Mikulin and N.R. Brilling built prototype M-18, two rows each based on Jupiter; passed 100-hour test at 750 hp and later gave 880 hp at 2100 rpm. No production.

M-20 Engine in Charomskii development series between AN-1 and M-30 (ACh-30).

M-21 Predecessor of Shvetsov MG-21.

M-22 Soviet engines originally licensed from GR9ASB (Bristol Jupiter VI) and later locally developed; in production 1930 at 480 hp.

M-23 Light 3-cylinder 4-stroke, also called NAMI-65, 65 hp, circa 1935.

M-25 Soviet engines originally licensed from Wright R-1820 Cyclone (SGR-1820-F3), cylinder 155,5 × 174,5 (29,8 lit); first series M-25 October 1934 at 700 hp; later rated 710 hp; 25A, 730 hp; 25V, 750 hp; 25Ye, 750 hp; led to M-62.

M-26 Soviet variant of Bristol/GR Titan using M-15 cylinders; run 300 hp early 1929 but unsuccessful.

M-27 Experimental derivative of M-17; improved cooling and larger radiator.

M-30 Experimental diesel in Charomskii series, later designated ACh-30.

M-31 Predecessor of MG-31.

M-32 Experimental radial run circa 1932 at 625 hp using improved M-22 cylinders.

M-34 See AM-34.

M-35 See AM-35.

M-36 Soviet radial in 550-hp class run circa 1931 as rival to Jupiter in I-5.

M-37 See AM-37.

M-40 Precursor of ACh-40, tested 1939.

M-41 Unknown engine (600/700 hp class) for I-10.

M-42 See AM-42.

M-48 Soviet (Shvetsov?) 7-cylinder radial tested 1934 at 200 hp.

M-61 Flat-twin motorcycle engine mid-1960s, 30·5 hp.

M-62 Derived by Shvetsov from M-25V by fitting two-speed supercharger and improving induction system and other parts. Later see ASh-62.

M-63 See ASh-63.

M-71 See ASh-71.

M-72 Motorcycle engine, 35 hp.

M-73 See ASh-73; same designation, 28-kW/37·5 hp motorcycle engine approved Dosaaf.

M-76 Licensed BMW flat-twin motorcycle engine, 45 hp.

M-81 Experimental 14-cylinder radial flown in I-185 at 1200 hp.

M-82 See ASh-82.

M-85 Baseline licensed version of Gnome-Rhône K14 Mistral Major 14-cylinder, 146 × 165 (38,65 lit), tested 1934 at 760 hp, assigned to Tumanskii within Mikulin KB and developed to 850 hp at 2400 rpm January 1936.

M-86 Tumanskii development to 870/960 hp in four sub-types 1936–1937.

M-87 Tumanskii development 1938–1939 to 930 hp; 87A, 930 hp; 87B, 950 hp.

M-88 Tumanskii development with direct injection and 100-octane fuel to 950/1000 hp October 1938; 88A, 1000 hp; 88B, 1100 hp; 88R, 1000 hp.

M-90 See ASh-90.

M-100 to **109** See VK-100.

M-120 Experimental Klimov engine with three M-103 cylinder blocks at 120° (one vertical above crankshaft), tested 1942 at 1500 hp, later 1820 hp; could have TK-3 maintaining power to high altitude.

M-300 Experimental engine with 16 cylinders in X arrangement, tested 1940 at 950 hp and flown in DI-6.

M-501 Experimental compound engine developed at GAZ-500 under V.M. Yakovlev (no relation) comprising gas turbine driven by 4-stroke diesel with 7 Al-monobloc banks each of 6 cylinders 160 × 170 (143,55 lit) with double-sided central compressor driven by exhaust turbine and separate two-speed geared supercharger; passed 200-hour test 1952 at 6000 hp at 2400 rpm with s.f.c. 0,22 kg/h/kW; transferred (in Stalin's last resolution, signed 28 February 1953) to marine use.

MB-100 Experimental engine developed under Aleksei Mikhailovich Dobrotvorskii using four M-103 cylinder blocks in X formation with superimposed crankshafts driving common gearbox; tested in neat 1,95-m diameter cowl at 3200 hp January 1945. Installed Yer-2, believed not flown.

MB-102 Unknown experimental engine, not necessarily by Dobrotvorskii, intended for DVB-102DM.

MG-11 Development of M-11 by M.A. Kossov, rated 1937 at 165 hp; 11F, 165 hp, later 180 hp.

MG-21 Basically 7-cylinder Kossov development MG-11, rated1938 at 200 hp.

MG-31 Basically 9-cylinder development by Kossov of M-11, rated 1938 at 300 hp; 31F, 330 hp.

MG-40 M-11 refined circa 1933–1934 by Kossov, 140 hp.

MM-1 Inverted 6-inline aircooled by A.A. Bessonev, tested 1937 at 220 hp.

MV-4 Soviet inverted 4-inline built 1936 under Renault license, 140 hp.

MV-6 Soviet inverted 6-inline built 1936–1939 under Renault license, 220 hp.

MV-12 Designation for 350/380 hp Renault inverted V-12, no Soviet production, imported only.

NII-1 Twin-chamber acid/kerosene rocket by V.P. Glushko, total 1200 kg at SL.

NK-2 First turboprop project at Kuibyshyev under Nikolai Dmitriyevich Kuznetsov (deputy to Klimov at Ufa plant in WW2), run 1951, qualified 3730 kW (later 3805 kW) 1954.

NK-4 Single-shaft Kuznetsov turboprop, became AI-20.

NK-6 First Kuznetsov turboprop to fly, in Tu-4 (circa January 1953); single-shaft axial, qualified 1954 at 3760 kW, later used in Tu-91 as TV-2F.

NK-8 Two-shaft Kuznetsov turbofan, compressors 2F/2LP + 6HP, p.r. 10·8, b.p.r. 1·02; qualified with reverser early 1966 and produced as NK-8-4, 10,1 t (99,1 kN); NK-8-2, 9,5 t (93,2 kN); NK-8-2U, 10,5 t (103 kN).

NK-12 Large single-shaft turboprop created by mainly German team at Kuibyshyev under Austrian Dipl-Ing Ferdinand Brandner, all virtual prisoners at Kuznetsov KB; 14-stage axial, p.r. varies 9 to 13; airflow 65 kg/s; constant 8300 rpm; run 1951 and qualified circa 1954 at about 8000 kW; in production 1955 as 12M at 8948 kW; 12MV, 11 033 kW; 12MA, 11 185 kW.

NK-86 NK-8 derived turbofan qualified circa 1980 at 13 t (127,5 kN).

NK-144 Family of afterburning turbofans derived from NK-8 first run 1963, qualified at 17,5 t (171,6 kN) 1970, later uprated to 20 t (196,1 kN).

OR-1 Original liquid rocket (OR, *Opytnyi Raketa*) by F.A. Tsander at TsIAM, later MosGIRD; tested on compressed air and various hydrocarbons 31, 5 kg thrust.

OR-2 First liquid engine to fly (BICh-11), run on bench by Tsander at GIRD on lox/petrol 18 March 1933, 50 kg.

ORM-65 Most important design in series of ORM (*Opytnyi reaktivnyi motor*) rocket engines designed and tested at GIRD and RNII under V.P. Glushko, S.P. Korolyev and G. Ye. Langemak; tested from 1936 on RFNA/kerosene at 175 kg and flown in RP-318 and No 212. Led to RD-1 series. Other members of family ORM-1 (N_2O_4/toluene), ORM-50 and large ORM-52 of 300 kg.

PVRD General abbreviation for ramjet.

R-11 Major series of single-shaft turbojets by KB of Sergei Konstantinovich Tumanskii, usually produced with afterburner; qualified 1956 at 5,1 t (50 kN) and series-produced in at least 12 variants with afterburning rating 53,5, 56,4, 58,4 and 60,8 kN; in FAI record submissions called R37 or R37F.

R-13 Development of R-11 with increased airflow but no change in size, major R-13-300 series having afterburning rating 6,6 t (64,72 kN).

R-25 Major current production Tumanskii afterburning turbojet, smaller than R-13 but normally rated at 7,5 t (73,58 kN).

R-27 New Tumanskii two-shaft turbofan, usually with large fully modulated afterburner; initial production circa 1971 at 10,2 t (100 kN).

R-29 Developed R-27, compressors 5 + 6, p.r. 12·4, airflow 105 kg/s; qualified circa 1975 at 11,5t (112,8 kN) with afterburner.

R-31 Tumanskii single-shaft afterburning turbojet for MiG-25; 5-stage compressor, p.r. 7, mainly steel/titanium, special T-6 fuel, water/methanol injection; qualified circa 1964 at 10 t (98,1 kN), subsequently series production at 11 t (107,9 kN) and 12,25 t (120 kN); in production as R-31F at 14 t (137,3 kN). Other designations TRD Mk 31, Ye-266, R-266 and RD-F.

R37 Soviet FAI reporting name for R-11; R37F with afterburner, R37V for record height submission.

RD-1 Used for two *Reaktivnyi Dvigatel*. (1) Liquid rocket developed from ORM-65 at RNII by Glushko's team, normal rating on RFNA/petrol 300 kg at SL (more at height); in RD-1/KhZ (chemical ignition) form, extensively tested on fighters/bombers from 1943. (2) First Lyul'ka axial turbojet with form of afterburner, abandoned after 22 June 1941.

RD-2 Next major step beyond RD-1 rocket, qualified at 600 kg late 1945; RD-2M with main chamber 1450-kg, cruise chamber 400.

RD-3 Turbopump-fed three-chamber engine, run at up to 1450 kg. Later engines by same KB were for missiles and space launcers.

RD-5 Redesignation of AM-5 after blacklisting of Mikulin, 1956.

RD-9 Important family of single-shaft turbojets developed in Mikulin's KB under Tumanskii 1951–1954, originally designated AM-9; qualified 1954 at 2,6 t (3,25 t with afterburner) and redesignated RD-9 on Mikulin's removal 1956.

RD-9BF qualified 1957 at 3,3 t and 9B-811 circa 1959 at 3,75 t (36,8 kN). All these produced without license in China with WP-6 designations.

RD-10 Soviet Junkers Jumo 004B, further developed at Kazan as RD-10, 900 or 910 kg; 10A, 1000 kg; 10F, 1100 kg.

RD-13 Refined derivative of As 014 (V-1) resonant pulsejet, flown on La-9RD.

RD-20 Soviet BMW 003A, further developed and series produced at GAZ-466; normal rating (20 and 20F) 800 kg.

RD-21 Derived from RD-20, 1000-kg rating.

RD-45 Soviet Rolls-Royce Nene, taking number from GAZ-45 production plant in Moscow despite GAZ-117 having swiftly done most of engineering effort and production of drawings (both plants headed by Maj-Gen V.Ya. Klimov); RD-45 in series production at 2270 kg late 1949.

RD-500 Soviet Rolls-Royce Derwent V, taking number from GAZ-500 under Vladimir Mikhailovich Yakovlev (see M-501 engine); in production January 1949 at 1590 kg.

RDA-1 Rocket engine developed by group under L.S. Dushkin and V.P. Glushko at Aviavnito from 1933, mainly on nitric acid and petrol and flown (RDA-1-150 No 1) February 1940 in RP-318 at 100 kg.

RU-9 Precursor prototype of RU-19, original engine of Yak-30.

RU-19 Tumanskii single-shaft turbojet initially rated for propulsion at 900 kg. Later used to power La-17 RPV/target and as aux booster/APU engine in transports at ratings from 2,16 kN (with heavy shaft loads) to 8,83 kN as turbojet.

S-18 Second Lyul'ka turbojet to run, 1250 kg August 1945, led to TR-1.

SPRD-110 Rocket a.t.o. unit, 3 t for 8 seconds.

TR-1 First Lyul'ka turbojet to fly, 8-stage axial derived from S-18, qualified December 1946 at 1,3 t; TR-1A qualified 1947–1948 at 1,5 t.

TR-3 Original designation of AL-5 before Lyul'ka became General Constructor.

TR-7 Prototype Lyul'ka supersonic compressor engine, led to AL-7.

TRD-29 Alternative designation of RU-19.

TS-20 Small Lyul'ka turbojet, 50 kg, also important APU.

TS-31 Small Lyul'ka turbojet, 55 kg; production form TS-31M.

TV-2 Service designation of NK-6 turboprop, not related to TV2-117.

TV2-117A Free-turbine turboshaft for helicopters developed at KB of Sergei Pietrovich Isotov: 10-stage, p.r. 6·6, qualified 1962 at 1267 kW.

TV3-117MT Derived free-turbine turboshaft, qualified circa 1978 at 1417 kW, 1640 kW contingency rating.

TVD-10 Free-turbine engine by Glushyenkov produced as turboshaft and turboprop with ratings in 700-kW range; designated GTD-3 (671-kW) in Ka-25; TVD-10B turboprop, 723 kW; series production in Poland as PZL-10, turboshaft 715 kW.

TVD-650 Isotov single-shaft turboprop, 600 kW.

TVD-850 Derivative of TVD-650, same rating.

U-1 First of series-produced a.t.o. rockets for military use, designation from *Uskoritel* (accelerator); U-5 and U-7 also in use.

VD-4 Extremely advanced and attractive piston engine family by KB of Vladimir Alekseyevich Dobrynin, four banks of six aircooled cylinders in X arrangement, diameter 1,4 m, length 2,5 m, nominal power in VD-4K form with TK turbosupercharger 3800 hp, 4300 hp for take-off; qualified spring 1951.

VD-7 Large high-compression turbojet by Koliesov (Dobrynin successor), produced in quantity as -7F with afterburner at 14t rating.

VD-251 Smaller related Dobrynin engine using two banks of same cylinders to give 2000 hp.

VK-1 Important centrifugal turbojet derived from RD-45 by GAZ-117 under Maj-Gen Vladimir Yakovlyevich Klimov (see VK-100); airflow increased 30% within same overall engine dimensions and advanced (for era) afterburner developed; qualified December 1948 at 2,7 t (26,5 kN); VK-1F with afterburner 2,6/3,38 t; VK-1A, 2,7/3,45 t, longer life, different accessory-gearbox system. Almost 40,000 delivered from GAZ-16, 19 and 45.

VK-2 Single-shaft axial turboprop developed at GAZ-117 under Klimov 1947 to termination 1952; 8-stage, 3357 kW at 9000 rpm.

VK-3 Klimov single-shaft by-pass jet, begun GAZ-117 mid-1952; first stage supersonic, first annular-chamber engine in Soviet Union; chief of design team Sergei Vasilyevich Lyunevich.

VK-5 Ultimate development of Nene at GAZ-117, in this case under project chief designer Anatolii Sergeyevich Mevius; enlarged dimensions and increased p.r. (5) with higher component efficiencies, 3,1 t (30,4 kN); ten built, two flown 1953 but could not compete against slim axials.

VK-7 Final turbojet design, derived from VK-3, to bear Klimov's initials; totally unrelated to RD-9.

VK-100 In search for powerful new fighter engine circa 1934 choice fell on Hispano-Suiza 12Y, imported and licensed by Aviatrust and assigned to new KB of V.Ya. Klimov as M-100 (all following engines redesignated with Klimov's initials December 1940 and VK used here). Baseline engine for most numerous family of Soviet engines, over 129,000 produced 1935/circa 1947. V-12, water-cooled, cylinders 148 × 170 (35,09 lit), single-speed supercharger, qualified 1935 at 750 hp; later 100A qualified 840 or 860hp, 2400 rpm.

VK-103 Development with two-speed supercharger, 860 hp January 1937, later 103U and 103A, 960 hp; qualified 1100 hp on 100-octane fuel.

VK-105 Chief WW2 liquid-cooled engine, normal compression ratio 7 on 94/95-octane fuel, qualified 1941 at 1050 hp at 2700 rpm; 105P, 1100 hp (in some maintained by TK to 4 km); PF, 1150/1260 hp; PF-2, 1180/1280 hp; R, RA, 1100 hp.

VK-106 Experimental derivative 1939–1940, 1200 hp; 106-I, 1350 hp.

VK-107 Revised valve gear (instead of two inlet, one exhaust, fitted with one inlet, two exhaust and one scav, three cams per cylinder), restressed for higher rpm, revised cylinder liners, equi-spaced exhaust outlets; January 1942, 1400 hp; 107A, 1943, 1650 hp.

VK-108 Experimental engine based on 107, 1800hp in 1945.

VK-109 Experimental engine, two series 1530 or 2073 hp, 1945.

VRD-2 First Lyul'ka turbojet to run, 700 kg, early 1943.

VRD-3 Original designation of S-18.

VRD-5 Original designation of TR-3.

VRD-430 Subsonic ramjet, believed 400-mm diameter, by M. Bondaryuk, flown September 1946.

ZhRD General abbreviation for a liquid rocket; also applied to series of two-chamber units run by L.S. Dushkin and A.M. Isayev at 1,1/1,14 t in 1945–1947 for Florov No 4302.

Soviet organisations

ADD Long-range aviation (bomber force) of VVS.
Aeroflot Civil air fleet.
AGOS Dept of aviation, hydro-aviation (seaplanes and hydroplanes) and experimental construction.
AMG *Maksim Gorkii* propaganda squadron.
Amtorg Organization for importing and licensing US products.
A-VDV Aviation of airborne forces of VVS.
Aviaarktika Independent Arctic directorate of Aeroflot.
Aviavnito Strictly AVIAvnito, aviation dept of Vnito, all-union scientific and technical research organization.
Aviatrust Original (Sept 23) central aviation management organization with direct authority over TsKB and external licensing.
AV-MF Naval aviation.
BAP Bomber regiment.
BNK Bureau of new construction.
BNT NKAP bureau of new technology.
BOK Bureau of special design.
DA Long-range (bomber) aviation, became ADD.
Deruluft Original (21) German/Russian airline company.
Dobrolyet Original (22) Soviet airline.
Dosaaf Voluntary society for assisting army, AF and navy.
Dosav Voluntary society for assisting AF.
GAZ State aviation factory.
GDL Gas dynamics lab.
Gird Group for studying reaction (in practice, rocket) engines.
GKAP State committee on aviation industry.
Glavkoavia Chief administration of aviation.
Glavsevmorput Chief administration of northern sea routes.
GosNII State scientific research institute of GVF.
Gros, Gross Civil experimental aeroplane construction.
Guap Chief administration of aviation industry.
GUGVF Chief administration of GVF.
GUSMP Chief administration of navy.
GUVVS Chief administration of air force.
GVF Civil air fleet (of which Aeroflot is operating branch).
IAP Fighter regiment.
IA-PVO Manned fighter branch of PVO
KAI Kazan aviation institute.
KB Constructor bureau ie, design office.
KhAI Kharkov aviation institute.
Komta Commission for heavy aviation.
Komsomol Young Communists.
Kosos Dept of experimental aeroplane construction.
LII Flight research institute.
LIIPS Leningrad institute for sail and communications engineers.
MA Naval aviation, became AV-MF.
MAI Moscow aviation institute.
MAP Ministry of aviation industry.
MAT Moscow aviation technical high school.
MGVF Ministry of civil aviation.
MosGird Moscow Gird.
MOS VAO All-union association for experimental marine aircraft.
MVTU Moscow higher technical school.
NAMI Scientific auto-motor institute.
NII Scientific test institute (more than 30, including many involved with aviation, eg, NII VVS, NII GVF).
NKAP State commissariat for aviation industry.
NKO State commissariat for defence.
NKTP State commissariat for heavy industry.
NKVD State commissariat for internal affairs, became KGB.
NTK Scientific and technical committee (of VVS).
NTU National technical administration.
OAVUK Society for aviation and gliding of Ukraine and Crimea.
ODVF Society of friends of the air fleet.
OGPU Predecessor of NKVD, leader Menzhinskii.
OKB Experimental construction (ie, design) bureau.
OKO Experimental design section (Kiev).
Omag Independent naval aviation group.
Omos Dept of marine experimental aircraft construction.
OOK Dept of special construction.
OOS Dept of experimental aircraft construction.
Osoaviakhim Society for assistance to aviation and chemical industry.
OSK Dept for special construction.
OSS Dept for experimental landplane construction.
Ostekhburo
OVI Dept for war invention of RKKA.
PVO Protective air defence (disbanded 1983, interceptor force being reorganized).
RKKA
RNII Reaction-engine scientific research institute.
SKB Student construction bureau; also *syerinom* KB, production bureau.
SNII Aeroplane scientific test institute of GVF.
Stavka Supreme command staff.
TsAGI Central aerodynamics and hydrodynamics institute.
TsIAM Central institute for aviation engines.
TsKB Central constructor (design) bureau.
TsKhA Trust for agricultural aviation.
TTT Tactical/technical requirements, ie military specification.
UK Training centre.
Ukrvosdukhput See UVP.
USR Special work control.
UVP Ukrvosdukhput, Ukrainian airline.
UVVS Administration of the VVS.
VIAM All-Union institute for aviation material.
VT Internal prison.
VVA Zhukovskii VVS academy.
VVF Military air fleet.
VVIA VVA engineering academy.
VVS Air force.
ZOK Factory for experimental construction, at GVF and at TsAGI.

Miscellaneous data

Russian language

The Soviet Union has a standardized Cyrillic alphabet:

capital	small	italic or handwritten	written or sounds like
А	а	*а*	as English
Б	б	*б*	B
В	в	*в*	V
Г	г	*г*	G as in give
Д	д	*д*	D
Е	е	*е*	Ye as in yen
Ё	ё	*ё*	Yo as in yo-yo
Ж	ж	*ж*	Zh as in measure
З	з	*з*	Z as in doze
И	и	*и*	I as in ink
К	к	*к*	as English
Л	л	*л*	L
М	м	*м*	as English
Н	н	*н*	N
О	о	*о*	O as in yo-yo
П	п	*п*	P
Р	р	*р*	R
С	с	*с*	S as in bus
Т	т	*т*	as English T
У	у	*у*	U as in rude
Ф	ф	*ф*	F
Х	х	*х*	Kh as in Scots loch
Ц	ц	*ц*	Ts as in Tsetse fly
Ч	ч	*ч*	Ch as in church
Ш	ш	*ш*	Sh as in push
Щ	щ	*щ*	Shch as in fish-chip
	ы	*ы*	y as in y'know
	ъ	*ъ*	hard sign
	ь	*ь*	soft sign
Э	э	*э*	E as in men
Ю	ю	*ю*	Yu as in few
Я	я	*я*	Ya as in Yarmouth

Though Russian is phonetic (pronounced exactly as written) English is not, and there are countless problems. Many of the accepted usages could be improved upon. Tupolev would be more faithfully written Toopolyev, but this would be hard to accept. I have written Alexander in the more accurate form Aleksandr, and Maxim Gorky is much better in the form Maksim Gorkii, but the OKB leader we call Tyrov actually begins with Ta and his Type 110 fighter is thus Ta-110 and not Ty-110. In any case Ty looks exactly like the Tupolev abbreviation written in Russian. I lacked the courage to interpret *Tsentral* as Central and thus write CAGI, because TsAGI is so universally accepted. The same goes for TsKB, Central Constructor Bureau. Names such as Mikoyan inevitably get pronounced with the middle syllable rhyming with boy; it should rhyme with go. In the same way the Russian word for a glider cannot be written in English in any better way than *planer*, and when seen by an English-speaking reader this is automatically rhymed with strainer; the sound is actually more like plunn-air.

In the reverse direction Russian documents often contain letters which look Cyrillic but are actually Western designations; an example is the Clark YHC wing section, which in a Soviet document is indistinguishable from Russian letters U (oo), N and S.

NATO names

To facilitate slick and unambiguous reporting of Soviet aircraft the NATO ASCC (Air Standards Co-ordinating Committee) assigns reporting names which sound different, even over a poor radio link, and give a clue to aircraft mission. Bombers and reconnaissance aircraft have names beginning with B, fighters with F, transports with C, helicopters with H, and miscellaneous types with M. Single-syllable names are assigned to propeller aircraft (with helicopters the number of syllables is arbitrary).

Backfin, Tu-98; Backfire, Tu-22M/Tu-26; Badger, Tu-16; Bank, US-supplied B-25; Barge, Tu-85; Bark, Il-2; Bat, Tu-2 and variants; Beagle, Il-28; Bear, Tu-20, -95, -142; Beast, Il-10; Beauty, changed to Blinder; Bison, M-4; Blackjack, Tu-? Ram-P; Blinder, Tu-22; Blowlamp, Il-54; Bob, Il-4; Boot, Tu-91; Bosun, Tu-14; Bounder, M-50, -52; Box, US-supplied A-20; Brassard, changed to Brewer; Brawny, Il-40; Brewer, Yak-28 except 28P; Buck, Pe-2; Bull, Tu-4; Butcher, changed to Beagle; Cab, Li-2 and DC-3 variants; Camber, Il-86; Camel, Tu-104; Camp, An-8; Candid, Il-76; Careless, Tu-154; Cart, Tu-70; Cash, An-28; Cat, An-10; Charger, Tu-144 and 144D; Clam, Il-18*; Clank, An-30; Classic, Il-62; Cleat, Tu-114; Cline, An-32; Clobber, Yak-42; Clod, An-14; Coach, Il-12; Coaler, An-72; Cock, An-22; Codling, Yak-40; Coke, An-24; Colt, An-2; Cooker, Tu-110; Cookpot, Tu-124; Coot, Il-18**; Cork, Yak-16; Crate, Il-14; Creek, Yak-12**; Crib, Yak-8; Crow, Yak-12*; Crusty, Tu-134; Cub, An-12; Cuff, Be-30; Curl, An-26; Faceplate, MiG Ye-2A; Fagot, MiG-15 except UTI; Faithless, MiG Ye-23 jet-lift; Fang, La-11; Fantail, La-15; Fargo, MiG-9; Farmer, MiG-19; Feather, Yak-17; Fencer, Su-24; Fiddler, Tu-28P; Fin, La-7; Firebar, changed to Brassard except retained for Yak-28P; Fishbed, MiG-21 except UTI; Fishpot, Su-9 and -11 except U; Fitter, Su-7, -17, -20 and -22 except U, UTI; Flagon, Su-15** incl trainer; Flanker, Su-27; Flashlight, Yak-25**; Flipper, MiG Ye-152M; Flogger, MiG-23; Flogger-D, MiG-27; Flora, Yak-23; Forger, Yak-36MP; Foxbat, MiG-25; Frank, Yak-9; Fred, US-supplied P-63; Freehand, Yak-36; Fresco, MiG-17; Fritz, La-9; Frogfoot, Su-25; Fulcrum, MiG-29; Halo, Mi-26; Hare, Mi-1; Harke, Mi-10 and 10K; Harp, Ka-25 prototype; Hat, Ka-10; Haze, Mi-14P; Helix, Ka-32; Hen, Ka-15; Hind, Mi-24; Hip, Mi-8 and -17, Hog, Ka-18; Homer, Mil V-12; Hoodlum, Ka-26; Hook, Mi-6; Hoop, Ka-22; Hoplite, Mi-2 and PZL successors; Hormone, Ka-25 production; Horse, Yak-24; Hound, Mi-4; Madge, Be-6; Maestro, Yak-28U; Magnet, Yak-17UTI; Magnum, Yak-30**; Maiden, Su-9U, -11U; Mail, Be-12; Mainstay, Il-76 'Awacs'; Mallow, Be-10; Mandrake, Yak-26 or -25RV; Mangrove, Yak-27R and variants; Mantis, Yak-32; Mare, Yak-14; Mark, Yak-7V; Mascot, Il-28U; Max, Yak-18 (and variants except -50, -52); May, Il-38; Midget, MiG-15UTI; Mink, UT-2; Mist, Ts-25; Mole, Be-8; Mongol, MiG-21U variants; Moose, Yak-11; Mop, GST and US-supplied PBY/PBN; Moss, Tu-126; Mote, MBR-2; Moujik, Su-7U; Mug, MDR-6; Mule, Po-2.

Some GAZ numbers

1 Khodinka (Moscow), the old Duks factory, in MiG-1 production October 1941 when evacuated Kuibyshyev.
2 Moscow, opened as Gnome-Rhône factory 1912.
3 *Krasnyi letchik* (Red airman) works, Leningrad.
4 Moscow plant of Motor Company, 1911.
5 Leningrad.
6 Kiev, basis of Antonov factory.
9 Zaporozhye (engines).
10 Kazan (RD-10 turbojet).
15 Simferopol (Anatra).
16 Ufa (engine production).
18 Voroshilov, Voronezh, Il production, evacuated Kuibyshyev, later participated Tu-144.
19 Kuibyshyev (engines).
21 Gorkii (Nizhni-Novgorod), Po OKB from 1935, then La OKB from October 1941.
22 Fili (Moscow), then Povolozhye (Kazan) on Pe-2 as 22A.
23 Fili (Moscow), series production of at least 12 types, Mya OKB 1950.
24 Moscow, AM-38 engine.
25 Moscow, OSS from 1925, from October 1941 Irtysh, near Omsk.
26 Rybinsk, M-100 and -103 engines.
29 Moscow, VT (TsKB-29) special prison.
30 Khodinka (Moscow), Aviatekhnikum and modern Il production (aircraft by road to Vnukovo).
31 Originally Moskalyev OKB, Voronezh, from 1941 evacuated Tbilisi on LaGG production, from 1946 Beriev OKB, Taganrog.
34 Il-14 production.
36 Moscow, Polikarpov OKB to 1935.
38 Ordzhonikidze works, Moscow Khodinka, Il-2 production.
39 Named for 10th anniversary of October revolution, Moscow, also housed V.P. Menzhinskii (chief of OGPU) factory where VT (internal prison) established December 1929, later TB-3 production and Il OKB.
43 Kiev, OKO.
45 Moscow, nation's largest engine plant.
51 Voronezh, Kalinin OKB from 1931, later Yer-2 production.
56 Moscow Central airfield, light aircraft including AIR-6.
64 Voronezh, former GAZ-18, later Tu-154 production.
81 Tushino (Moscow), Osoaviakhim and MKB (Gribovskii), Bartini Stal-7.
84 Khimki (Moscow), Li-2 KB and production.
89 Gorkii, GVF repair works, ZIG and Laville KBs.
115 Moscow, Leningradskii Prospekt, Yak OKB and production.
117 Leningrad, Klimov (now Isotov) engine KB.
124 Moscow, Yak production from 1942.
125 Kazan, Pe-8 followed by Pe-2 from GAZ-22.
153 Novosibirsk, first and largest Siberian series factory, LaGG then (42) Yak fighters, also location of Po, Su and initial An OKBs.
155 Moscow, MiG OKB.
156 Moscow, I-153 production, Tu detention 1936 at relocated TsKB-29 special prison, later evacuated to GAZ-166.
166 Omsk, believed Be OKB pre-46 and Tu-2 production.
243 Tashkent, Li-2 production, later Il-62.
266 Kulomzino, Irtysh.
286 Kamensk-Uralsk, Yak fighters.
292 Saratov, Yak fighters, then Yak-24 and Yak-40.
301 Moscow suburb, Dubrovin KB, BB-22 fuselage production, LaGG OKB 1938.
400 Vnukovo (Moscow), Tu-104, 114, and 154; also AI-20 engine (same location but different GAZ number).
401 Novosibirsk, Mil OKB and Mi-6 production.
402 Bykovo (Moscow) Il-18 production and D-30 engine.
412 Rostov-on-Don, An-12.
466 *Krasnyi Oktober*, Leningrad. RD-20 engines 1947.
500 Tushino (Moscow), turbine engines.
? Zhukovskii, near Moscow, Tu experimental base and Tu-144 assembly.
? Arsenyev, near Vladivostok, Progress Works, Yak light aircraft and An-14A and An-28 production.
? Jaroslavl, La fighters from 1943.
? Kharkov, Tu-104 and 134 production.
? Ulan-Ude, Ka OKB and An production.

Some Soviet 'firsts'

1913 Four-engined aeroplane, Sikorsky *Le Grand*.
1916 Controllable-incidence wing aircraft actually flown, K-1.
1923 Purpose-built agricultural aircraft, Khioni No 5.
1930 Modern four-engined monoplane bomber, ANT-6.
1931 Stainless-steel primary structure, Stal-2.
1932 Hi-lift wing, full-span flaps, rotary tip ailerons, Yak E-3.
1933 Manned aeroplane powered solely by liquid rocket engines (BICh-11).
1933 Modern monoplane fighter with retractable landing gear, I-16.
1933 Large aircraft boosted by a.t.o. rockets, TB-1.
1934 Magnesium-alloy primary structure, EMAI-1.
1934 Pneu inflatable aeroplane, Grokhovskii Naduvatsya.
1934 Steerable nosewheel, A-7 autogyro.
1935 V (butterfly) tail, R-5 and U-2.
1936 Flush cockpit and periscope, LL.
1936 Use of air-to-ground rockets, I-15 and I-16.
1936 So-called invisible aircraft, PS.
1938 Levered-suspension oleo main legs, Po Ivanov.
1938 Reverse-pitch braking/manœuvring props, SPB(P).
1938 Small fighter with four 20-mm cannon, I-16P.
1939 Prone-pilot research aircraft, U-2LPL.
1939 High-speed fully variable-incidence wing, EI.
1939 High-speed ducted-spinner engine installation, I-190 (just beat Fw 190).
1939 Regular service aircraft with drop tanks, I-153.
1940 Retractable-wing aircraft, IS-1.
1940 Air-cushion landing gear, UT-2-SYeN.
1941 Live test of ejection seat, TIS.
1944 Psy-war aircraft, Po-2GN.
1946 Braking parachute, Su-9*.
1946 Swivelling-pod VTOL jet fighter project, Shchye VSI.
1947 Fenced wing, La-160.
1947 Fighter with afterburner, La-150F.
1948 6%-thick wing, La-174TK.
1949 Escape-capsule nose fuselage, Su-17*.
1951 Supersonic fighter, La-190.
1954 All-swept turboprop aircraft, Tu-95.
1956 Swept-wing jetliner in service, Tu-104.
1956 Large twin-turbine helicopter (also first with auxiliary wing), Mi-6.
1962 Turbofan short-haul airliner, Tu-124.
1968 Supersonic transport, Tu-144.
1974 Large swing-wing intercontinental bomber, Tu-22M.

Foreign aircraft imported

This list excludes types captured in war or taken over in Latvia, Lithuania and Estonia 1940. Persistent reports of Fokker G.1 and Hall 'PTBH-2' appear unfounded. The Soviet Union makes important use of light general-aviation types made in Poland and Czechoslavakia, including the L29 and L39 jet trainers and L-410UVP turboprop transports.

1914–17 Very numerous; included licenses for Farmans, Moranes, Spad S.VII and Sopwith 1½-Strutter.
1919 Martinsyde F.4 (Hispano), Bristol F.2B (Hispano), Morane-Saulnier A-1.
1920 Left by retreating intervention forces, at least nine types notably de Havilland D.H.4 and 9a, Fairey III, Avro 504 and Avro Baby.
1921 Various Fokkers, including D.XI, D.XIII; Ansaldo Balilla and SVA.10.
1922 Vickers Vernon and Viking, Hanriot HD.14, Norman Thompson N.T.2B, Junkers F 13 (20, plus 5+ Dobrolyet-built), Handley Page Hanley, Airco/de Havilland D.H. 34.
1923 Various Junkers (see text); Savoia S.1bis.
1924 Junkers W 33 (10, plus 17 Soviet-built PS4), Farman Goliath.
1925 Savoia S.1ter, Dornier Wal (various 1925–1931), believed a Huff-Daland AT.
1926 Farman F 62 (Goliath series bombers), Savoia-Marchetti S.55, Heinkel He 5c.
1927 Dornier Komet and Merkur.
1930 Heinkel HD 55 (built by OMOS as KR-1).
1932 Heinkel He 34c (built as I-7), Savoia-Marchetti S.62 (MBR-4).
1935 Northrop 2-E, Seversky SEV-3M.
1936 Vultee V-1A, V-11A and V-11G, Martin W-136 (Cyclones) dissected at Leningrad LIIPS, Sikorsky S-43, Lockheed Electra, Dewoitine D.510 *moteur canon.*
1937 Douglas DC-3 (built as PS-84/Li-2), Douglas DF, Consolidated 28 (built as GST), Martin 156, Republic (then Seversky) 2PA-L.
1939 Bü 131, Bü 133, Fi 156.
1940 Nakajima Ki-27 (in addition to captures), He 100, Bf 109E, Bf 108, Bf 110C, Fw 58, Do 215B, Ju 88; also some 26 types from Finland, Latvia, Estonia, Lithuania, Poland and France.
1941–45 Numerous Lend-Lease and other Allied, including Hurricane, Spitfire, Hampden, Mosquito, Lancaster, A-20, B-17, B-25, P-51, P-39, P-40, P-47, P-63, UC-78, AT-7, C-47, UC-64, UC-61, L-4B.
1945 Fw 190D-9, B-29 (see text Tu-70 and Tu-4), Junkers EF.126, Ju 290 (Czech-built), Ju 352 (Czech-built, presented Stalin), Ar 396 (Czech-built), DFS 346, Me 163S, Ju 248, Aero C-3A (Si 204D).
1960 Sikorsky S-58, Vertol 44.

Exports

1935 ANT-40 (licensed as Avia 71).
1936 Republican Spain, various.
1937 ANT-40 to China.
1943 Various to Czechoslovakia, Poland, Free French, Jugoslavia.
1949 Various to China.
1950 Various to North Korea including Yak-9, La-11, MiG-15, Il-12, Il-10, Po-2, Yak-11, Yak-18, An-2, Li-2.
1959 Start of regular commercial export of military and later civil aircraft to countries outside Warsaw Pact.

Abbreviations (Russian)
Aircraft categories

AK Artillery correction (AOP).
ARK Arctic coastal reconnaissance.
ASK Amphibian for northern region.
BB Short-range bomber.
BSh Armoured attacker.
DB Long-range bomber.
DI Two-seat fighter.
F Frontal (tactical) or boosted (see next list).
G Helicopter.
GK Pressure cabin.
I Fighter.
IP Interceptor fighter.
IS Folding fighter.
L Limousine, cabin version, or radar-equipped.
LSh Light attack.
LL Flying laboratory.
MBR Sea short-range reconnaissance.
MDR Sea long-range reconnaissance.
MK Cruiser, armoured seaplane.
MP Sea passenger aircraft.
MR Sea reconnaissance.
MTB Sea heavy bomber.
MU Sea trainer.
P Passenger aircraft, or interceptor.
PS Passenger aircraft.
R Reconnaissance.
SB Fast bomber.
T Anti-tank.
TB Heavy bomber.
TSh Heavy attack.
U Trainer, or improved version.
UTI Fighter trainer.

Propulsion

AD Aviation engine.
APD Accessory gearbox.
F Boosted, increased power or afterburner.
PD Piston engine.
PVRD Ramjet.
RD Turbojet.
TK Turbo-supercharger
TRD Turbojet.
TRDD Two-spool (two-shaft) turbojet.
TV Turboshaft.
TVD Turboprop.
TvRDD Turbofan.
U ATO rocket motor.
VFSh Variable-pitch propeller.
VISh Constant-speed propeller.
VPSh Fixed-pitch propeller.
ZhRD Liquid-propellant rocket.

Abbreviations (English)

AC Alternating current.
AOA Angle of attack.

APU Auxiliary power unit.
ASW Anti-submarine warfare.
a.t.o. Assisted take-off.
b.p.r. Bypass ratio.
CG Centre of gravity.
c.p. Centre of pressure (where resultant wing lift acts).
c/s Constant speed.
c-s Constant section.
CSD Constant-speed drive.
DC Direct current.
FLIR Forward-looking infrared.
HP High pressure.
IAS Indicated airspeed.
ILS Instrument landing system.
ISA International standard atmosphere.
LE Leading edge.
LLTV Low-light television.
LP Low pressure.
MLW Maximum landing weight.
MTO Maximum take-off weight.
OWE Operating weight empty.
p.r. Pressure ratio.
SL Sea level.
SLAR Side-looking airborne radar.
SST supersonic transport.
TE Trailing edge.
UHF Ultra-high frequency.
VHF Very high frequency.
VOR VHF omni-range.
V-p Variable pitch.

A note on data

It is ridiculous to offer precise conversions from rough original figures (one Western publisher translated a ceiling of 9 km as 29,527 ft 6 in), so imperial conversions vary slightly according to the credibility of input. For speeds the best compromise was judged to be km/h and mph; apologies to modern aircrew who think in knots. All gallons are imperial (for US, multiply by 1·2). Commas are often used to denote what in imperial measures are decimal points; thus 42,3 t means 42·3 tonnes or 93,254 lb. Engine powers are (piston) max rating at best height, (jet) SL static.

A technical note

Camloc and Dzus fasteners are patented devices widely copied in the Soviet Union; Camloc is a lever-action latch, Dzus a rotary fastening turned by a screwdriver.

Fowler flaps fit under a fixed wing TE and run out on tracks initially to increase wing area, finally rotating down to increase drag.

Hucks dogs were a bayonet-type drive on the end of early propeller shafts, spun by an external power source (invariably a shaft of adjustable height and inclination on a converted motor vehicle) to start the engine. They were widely used throughout the Second World War after they had long been obsolete in other countries.

A *moteur canon* was a Hispano-Suiza patented arrangement of a gun (at first 20 mm, in the Soviet Union later much larger) lying between the cylinder blocks of a geared V-type engine to fire through the hub of the propeller.

A NACA cowl is a long-chord cowling over a radial engine to reduce drag and improve cooling.

Scheibe fins are vertical fins, with or without hinged rudders, attached at or near the tips of the wing. In some cases they have been canted inwards (seen from above, ie LEs closer together than TEs) but the purpose is to reduce tip-vortex formation and increase effective aspect ratio.

Schrenk flaps are split flaps, named for the originator, Dr Martin Schrenk, at the DVL, 1932.

A Townend ring was a simple short-chord cowl around a radial engine, much less efficacious than a NACA cowl.

Zap (or Zapp) flaps were invented by Zaparka in order to reduce the effort needed to lower the flaps against the airstream; they were split flaps pivoted to a series of arms well back from the flap LE so that the flap LE in effect slid backwards along the underside of the recess.

Aircraft of the Soviet Union
A-Z

Alexandrov -Kalinin

AK-1 Apart from *Komta* the first transport aircraft to be designed in Soviet Union. Its need was obvious, especially after failure of *Komta* in 1922. With full state backing, design was led at TsAGI by V. L. Alexandrov and V. V. Kalinin, assisted by A. M. Cheremukhin. Rather unusually for period, design job was done properly with at least one model tunnel-tested, others dropped from high towers and every part of primary structure stressed. Engine was from wartime imported Voisin LBS, and structure was mixed, with a 12%-thick wooden wing above steel-tube fuselage. Engine completely enclosed, with curved exhaust pipe ahead of open cockpit for pilot and mechanic, and a Lamblin radiator on each side. Up to three passenger seats could be installed in cabin, door being on right. Designated from initials of designers, in style not officially adopted until 1941, AK-1 was built at GAZ-5 (and was thus a rival to an aircraft designated for that factory and built there at same time) and first flown by A. I. Tomashevsky on 8 March 1924. Results were encouraging, and on 15 June AK-1 was taken on strength of Dobroyet and assigned to route Moscow-Novgorod-Kazan. Last heard of when it took part in flight to Pekin 10 June to 17 July 1925.
ENGINE One 160 hp Salmson (Canton-Unné) RB 9 nine-cylinder water-cooled radial.
DIMENSIONS Span 14,9 m (48 ft 10½ in); length 11,0 m (36 ft 1 in); wing area 37 m² (398 ft²).
WEIGHTS Empty 1145 kg (2524 lb); fuel/oil 197+24 kg (434+53 lb); maximum 1685 kg (3715 lb).
PERFORMANCE Max cruising speed 147 km/h (91 mph); time to 1000 m, 16 min; ceiling 2200 m (7200 ft).

AK-1

I-215

Alekseyev

Semyon Mikhailovich Alekseyev was lead designer in Lavochkin OKB from 1942 onwards, and was chiefly responsible for La-5 and La-7 detail design. After the Second World War he transferred from Lavochkin bureau and in 1946 was successful in establishing his own OKB to concentrate on high-performance combat aircraft. He is unrelated to Dr R.Y. Alekseyev, dean of Soviet hydrofoil designers.

I-211 Twin-jet fighter, similar in layout to British Meteor but with two of first locally produced axial engines and with twin-wheel landing gears. There was ample volume for fuel, and heavy armament of three NS-37 was fitted below floor of pressurized cockpit. Red-painted prototype flown by A. A. Efimov in 1947. While handling appears to have been good, engines were undeveloped and unreliable. It may have been same protype that formed the basis of I-215 that succeeded it on drawing board.
DIMENSIONS Span 12,25 m (40 ft 2¼ in); length 11,54 m (37 ft 10¼ in); wing area 25 m² (269·1 ft²).
ENGINES Two 1000 kg (2205 lb) Lyul'ka AL-1 turbojets replaced before first-flight by 1300 kg TR-1 turbojets.
WEIGHTS Empty not known; loaded 7450 kg (16,424 lb).
PERFORMANCE Maximum speed 935 km/h (581 mph) at sea level; time to 5000 m, 3 min.

I-212 Most challenging assignment awarded to Alekseyev OKB was this all-weather interceptor, essentially a scaled-up I-215 and in many ways remarkably similar to Canadian CF-100 (especially in appearance). Radar operator was to be seated behind pilot facing to rear; planned armament four of new B-20 guns each with 150 rounds. Radar never installed, and armament one NS-37 with 75 rounds and two NS-23 each with 100 rounds. Alekseyev also schemed a multi-camera reconnaissance nose, but this is not thought to have been constructed. Brief flight trials in 1948. According to one narrative it was Yakovlev's description of this aircraft as 'another copy of the Me 262' (a most inaccurate assessment) that brought about Alekseyev's downfall and closure of his OKB.
DIMENSIONS Span 16,2 m (53 ft 1¾ in); length 12,98 m (42 ft 7 in); wing area 33,0 m² (355 ft²).
ENGINES Two 2268 kg (5000 lb) R-R Nene 1, imported.
WEIGHTS Empty 5130 kg (11,310 lb); loaded 9250 kg (20,392 lb).
PERFORMANCE Maximum speed 1000 km/h (621 mph), probably at low level; 956 km/h (594 mph) at 8 km; time to 5000 m, 2·3 min; ceiling 14,800 m (48,556 ft); range 3100 km (1926 miles).

I-215 Despite Lyul'ka TR-1 engines, it was natural for Alekseyev to cast covetous eyes on imported Derwent turbojet because of its power and reliability. Later this went into production as RD-500, but two British-supplied engines were sent to Alekseyev and used as basis of the I-215, whose airframe was similar to (and may have been same as) I-211. Intention was to fit nose radar, but this almost certainly was absent from prototype. Pilot had an ejection seat, and the I-215 inherited a pressurized cockpit from the I-211. A downward-pointing searchlight is mentioned, although word for 'look down' also means jettisonable'—either way, puzzling. Speedbrakes were fitted to wings, with auto-

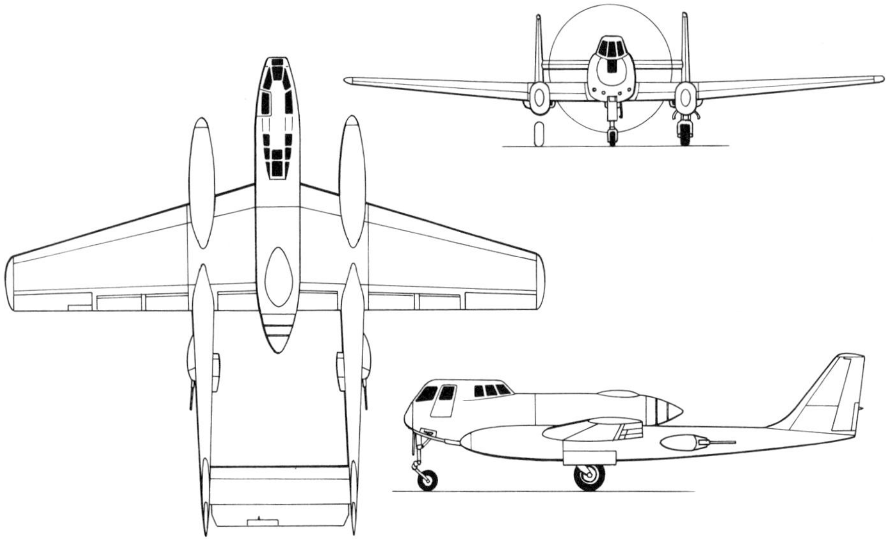

I-218

matic opening at critical speed, a common precaution in early Mach-limited jets. Armament schemes (probably not fitted) included three N-37 (30 rounds each), two NS-57 (35 rounds each) or two 113P-57 (35 rounds each), latter two schemes being for use against bombers. Flight trials began November 1947 in the hands of A. A. Efimov, S. N. Anokhin and M. L. Gallai.

DIMENSIONS Span 12,25 m (40 ft $2\frac{1}{4}$ in); length probably 11,54 m (37 ft $10\frac{1}{3}$ in) (Shavrov's 14,54 m is probably a misprint); wing area 25 m² (296·1 ft²).

ENGINES Two 1588 kg (3500 lb) R-R Derwent 5, imported.

WEIGHTS Empty not known; loaded 6890 kg (15,190 lb).

PERFORMANCE Maximum speed 970 km/h (603 mph) at sea level, 900 km/h (559 mph) at 6 km; time to 5000 m, 2·7 min; range 2300 km (1429 miles).

I-218 This was Alekseyev's last prototype, and was almost certainly a mistake in that it was outdated in concept (though history of American Skyraider may refute this.) It was a *Shturmovik*, a heavily armed and armoured attacker for close support and anti-armour use in a land war. At low-level jet engines suffer high fuel consumption, and Alekseyev chose Dobrynin's two-bank VD-251 piston engine, driving a pusher AV-28 contraprop with two three-blade units of 3·6 m (142 in) diameter. Pilot had an armoured cockpit with flat glass slabs giving good view, while backseater faced rear and aimed two defensive barbettes mounted in Me 410 style on tail booms, with arc of fire 25° above and below horizontal and out to 50° laterally. These were to be NR-23s with 120 rounds each, and there were various schemes for heavy forward-firing armament such as four NR-23 (150 rounds each), two N-37 (40 each) and two N-57 (30 each). Wing racks were to be provided for 16 rockets, and pylons under fuselage were to carry up to 1500 kg (3307 lb) of bombs, presumably aimed in dive attacks. Highly stressed or armoured parts were of a new nickel-steel, 30 KhGSNA. Prototype was flown 1948, but no further history known. OKB closed same year.

DIMENSIONS Span 16,43 m (53 ft $10\frac{3}{4}$ in); length 13,88 m (45 ft $6\frac{1}{2}$ in); wing area 45 m² (484·4 ft²).

ENGINE One 2000/2200 hp Dobrynin VD-251 V-12 piston engine.

WEIGHTS Empty not known; loaded 9000 kg (19,840 lb).

PERFORMANCE Maximum speed 520 km/h (323 mph) at sea level, 530 km/h (329 mph) at 2 km; time to 5000 m, 5·0 min; ceiling 6600 m (21,650 ft); range 1200 km (746 miles).

Amtorg

Throughout 1930s Soviet Union's vast coastal, river and water areas required good long-range flying boats, but except for small MBR-2 all Soviet marine aircraft were disappointing. Much was learned from importing Sikorsky S-43 and Douglas DF, but by 1936 it was clear the best foreign buy was a Consolidated 28 (PBY). This was released for export in 1938, and a manufacturing license was immediately concluded by Amtorg, Soviet state department responsible for licensing and importing US products. Three complete aircraft imported to approximately PBY-1 standard with 880 hp R-1830-64 engines but without radio or guns. Design of Isaac M. Laddon vastly impressed Russian engineers, but difficulty experienced in actually making boat, and numerous airframe details were altered to obviate need for tools or skills not then possessed by licensees. Russian designation **GST** (*Gidro Samolyet Transportnyi*, hydro aircraft transport), but primary purpose was military reconnaissance, bombing and many other tasks with MA (naval aviation). In 1939 production was still bogged down, but responsibility was transferred to MA headquarters, and to Aeroflot in respect of planned civil version, **MP-7**. Production is believed to have taken place at Taganrog (now Beriev centre). More than 600 engineering changes took place in addition to airframe modifications, main ones being to use Soviet engines and equipment. Production continued until at least 1946, and possibly 1948. Number produced known to exceed 400, and may have exceeded 1000. (During the Second World War USSR also received under Lend-Lease 138 PBN-1 and 48 PBY-6A.)

DIMENSIONS Span 31,72 m (104 ft 1 in); length 20,68 m (67 ft $10\frac{1}{4}$ in); wing area 130 m² (1400 ft²).

ENGINES Two 14-cylinder two-row radials: GST, 950 hp M-87 or 87A; MP-7, 1000 hp M-62IR.

WEIGHTS Empty 6670 kg (14,705 lb); loaded (GST) 12,250 kg (27,000 lb), (MP-7) 11,800 kg (26,015 lb).

PERFORMANCE Maximum speed (GST) 329 km/h (204 mph) at medium height, (MP-7) 277 km/h (172 mph); ceiling (both) about 5400 m (17,700 ft); range (GST) 2600 km (1615 miles). Note: the GST was faster than any PBY but had much shorter range.

GST (No 2 aircraft)

O.K. *Antonov (left) with assistant A. Batumov*

Antonov

Oleg Konstantinovich Antonov was born on 7 February 1906 in Moscow. In 1921 he helped organize a branch in Saratov of the Moscow Glider Group, and two years later submitted a design in a light-aeroplane competition organized by K. K. Artseulov. In 1924 he built his first aircraft, the *Golub* (Pigeon) glider, which took part in the second national championships at Koktebel that year. Antonov became a student at the Leningrad Polytechnic Institute in 1926, and he continued glider design with the OKA-2 of which several were built at Saratov in 1926–1927.

Other gliders followed, as outlined on this page. In 1930 Antonov graduated, and was appointed first chief engineer and then chief designer at the newly founded Moscow Glider Factory. Many successful gliders were built here, as well as Antonov's first powered aircraft, the OKA-33 (LEM-2). In 1938 Antonov's application to the Jukovsky academy was refused. He then joined Yakovlev to assist on light aircraft. In 1939 he was detached to Saratov again and assigned the development of a STOL aircraft in the class of the German Fi 156. At about the same time his group began the design of one of the first troop-carrying gliders, the A-7. In 1943 Antonov had to rejoin the Yak OKB, as first deputy designer, and saw the war out on Yak fighters at Novosibirsk.

In 1945 he began recruiting people for his own OKB. This was established at Novosibirsk on 31 May 1946. He then moved to Kiev. This large establishment, built from scratch, became one of the best-equipped OKBs in the country, and from here came the An-2 and an impressive series of high-wing transports. Production of the latter is centred in eastern Siberia at Ulan-Ude, and even more distant Arsenyev, though limited production takes place at Kiev. The Saratov group continued as the leading organization on sailplanes, 36 types having flown by 1965. For many years first deputy designer at Saratov was A. Ya. Belolipetsky, but this group appears to be closed.

A-7

Antonov gliders

OKA-1 Nicknamed *Golub* (Pigeon), this simple glider refused to fly when it was assembled at the 1924 meeting at Koktebel, but later did achieve success. The designer flew it.

OKA-2 Built at Saratov 1926, and further examples in 1927.

OKA-3 Two-seat trainer, 1928.

OKA-5 Named Standart-1, competed outside USSR 1930.

OKA-7 Named Standart-2, small numbers exported.

OKA-6 Named *Lenin City*, won 1931 national contest.

PS-1,-2 Upar Advanced trainer, 140 built in early 1930s.

US-3 Standard primary glider, similar to Dagling; 2000 built.

RF series The Red Front series were the most important competition sailplanes in the pre-1941 era. The main types were the RF-5, RF-6 and RF-7, an RF-7 being flown 749 km in 8 h 35 min by O. Klepikov in 1939.

BS series BS (*Buskirovochny Serini*, towed-glider series) gliders were widely used by clubs and the VVS. The BS-3, BS-4 and BS-5 were used for 'trains' of towed gliders with as many as eight machines on a single cable.

US-4, US-5 and US-6 Standard training gliders of the late 1930s, the US-6 being a tandem dual machine. Like all previous Antonov gliders the structure was wooden, with a birch ply skin over the nacelle and fabric elsewhere.

A-2, Massovy 4 Competition gliders related to the RFs, 1939.

A-7 Also designated RF-8, because it was effectively a greatly scaled-up member of the RF family, the A-7 was the winner in December 1940 of a competion for a military assault glider. All-wood, with a fabric-covered wing (aft of the main spar) and control surfaces, it was remarkably refined, with the wing set into the top of the streamlined fuselage, glazed nose cockpit, two sets of double doors (forward on the left, aft on the right), main wheels retracted into recesses by handcranks, and ground-adjustable trim tabs on the rudder and both elevators. Normal load was six soldiers. Production from May 1941, 400 built. Some saw action behind the Nazi lines, towed by SB-2s.

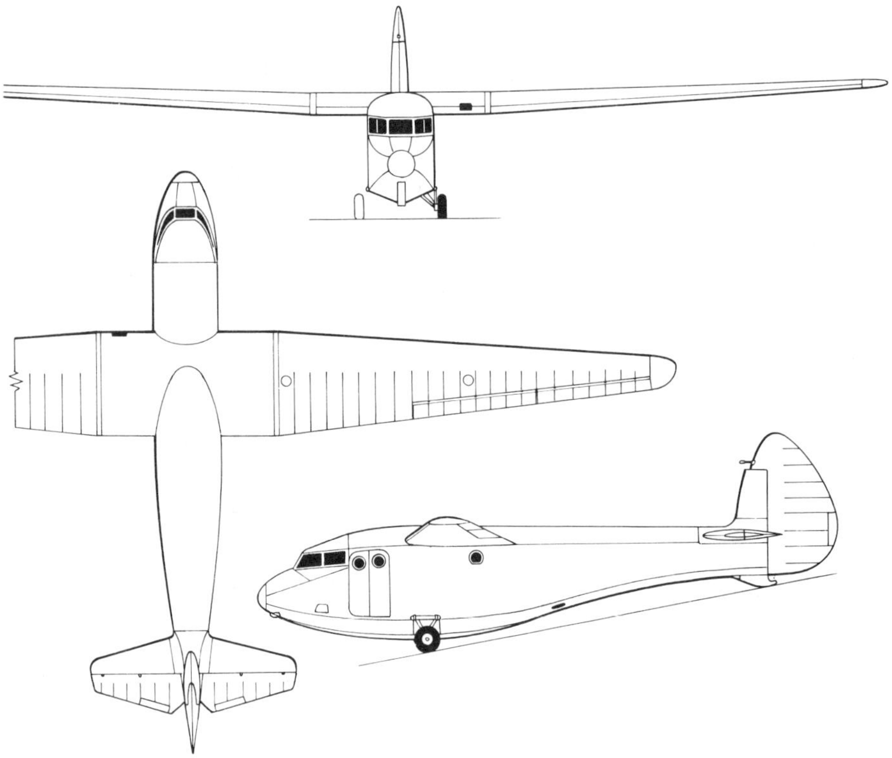

A-7

DIMENSIONS Span 19,0 m (62 ft 4 in); length 11,5 m (37 ft 8¾ in).
WEIGHT Laden 1100 kg (2425 lb).
SPEED On tow, 200 km/h (124 mph).

A-9 Originally designated RF-9, this was the ultimate RF design, published in 1939. Last of the wooden sailplanes, it had a centre section in the shoulder position and left and right outer wings with light-alloy spoilers on the upper surfaces. Deliveries from 1948; at least 50 produced, gaining national and international records. By 1951 wingtips turned sharply down, and in 1955 the **A-9bis** introduced a new wing with no centre section, higher aspect ratio, flaps, and under-surface spoilers.
DIMENSIONS (9bis): Span 16,5 m (54 ft 1½ in); length 6,4 m (21 ft 0 in); wing area 12.2 m² (131 ft²).
WEIGHTS Empty 320 kg (705 lb); loaded 420 kg (926 lb).
PERFORMANCE Glide ratio 29; sinking speed 0.65 m/s (2.13 ft/s).

A-10 A lash-up of the A-9 to carry a rear-facing passenger and thus qualify for Class D-2 FAI records. In 1952 a women's speed record was set in this class, and on 26 May 1953 pilot V. Ilchenko set a two-seat distance record with 829,8 km (515.6 miles) covered in 9 h 11 min.

A-11 First of a new family with all-metal stressed-skin construction and butterfly tail. Design leader A. Yu. Manotskov. Wing profile TsAGI R-IIIa; split flaps, drooping fabric-covered ailerons, and upper and lower spoilers. Later A-11s had a retractable landing wheel, but the prototype, flown 12 May 1958, retained the traditional rubber-sprung steel skid.

A-13 Whereas the 16,5-m A-11 was designed for competition, the A-13 was mass-produced (250-plus) for clubs. It was a short-span machine with TsAGI P-32-15 profile and no flaps. First flight 5 May 1958. In late 1960 a Lyul'ka TS-31 turbojet of 55 kg (121 lb) thrust was added to produce the A-13M, from which the An-13 lightplane (a one-off) was produced. The An-11 was a different ultralight with A-11 wings. In February 1962 the An-13 set speed records in Class C-1A including 192,56 km/h over 15/25 km and 196,776 km/h over 3 km. Data for the basic A-13.
DIMENSIONS Span 12,1 m (39 ft 8 in); length 6,0 m (19 ft 8 in); wing area 10,44 m² (112.38 ft²).
WEIGHTS Empty 254 kg (560 lb); laden 360 kg (794 lb).
PERFORMANCE Glide ratio (112 km/h) 26; sinking speed (97 km/h) 1,14 m/s (3.74 ft/s); limiting airspeed 400 km/h (249 mph).

A-15 First flown 26 March 1960, this competition sailplane was a major advance with longer span, better fuselage shape, NACA laminar section, Fowler flaps, and all-metal control surfaces. For the first time the competitor had complete equipment including water ballast. Heavy and strong, the A-15 was cleared for aerobatics to +5·3 g. It had good penetration but was outclassed by the opposition and was often damaged landing on rough fields. About 35 built; in summer 1960 set several speed and goal records.
DIMENSIONS Span 18,0 m (59 ft 0¾ in); length 7,2 m (23 ft 7½ in); wing area 12,3 m² (132·4 ft²).
WEIGHTS Empty 320 kg (705 lb); laden 420 kg (926 lb).
PERFORMANCE Glide ratio (97 km/h) 37; sinking speed 0,63 m/s (2.07 ft/s); limiting airspeed 250 km/h (155 mph).

KT Success with the A-7 resulted in a 1941 request to study the concept of the KT, *Kr'lya Tanka* (flying tank). The task was to see if it was feasible to fit wings to a light tank (the T-60 was the choice, though the T-26 was more numerous) and tow it like a glider, casting off at its destination for a free landing. The tank's own tracks were, if possible, to serve as the undercarriage. The T-60 was the first tank designed specifically for airborne forces, and it was hoped to tow them to partisan units behind enemy lines. (There was even a design for doing this with the T-34, using two L-760s as tugs!) Antonov's creation, with bureau designation A-40, and also known as the A-T, comprised biplane wings and a twin-boomed tail, made of wood with ply and fabric covering. Both wings had ailerons and 45° slotted flaps, and the flight controls were worked from the driving position of the tank. The wing/tail unit was to be jettisoned, by one lever, immediately on touchdown when the wings were still lifting. As for the tracks, there was argument about whether to declutch them or give the tank a special overdrive top gear to accelerate to take-off speed of 160 km/h (99 mph).

According to a Western report the tug was a Pe-8, and repeated attempts to become airborne were unsuccessful. All Soviet accounts state that a successful flight was made behind a TB-3 in 1942, the pilot being the famed glider pilot S.N. Anokhin. (According to Něměcek the flight took place in 1941, soon after the Nazi invasion, and Anokhin was arrested by the Russians as a German spy after landing!)
DIMENSIONS Span 18,0 m (59 ft 0¾ in); length of air portion 12,06 m (39 ft 6¾ in); wing area 85,8 m² (923·5 ft²).
WEIGHTS Air portion 2004 kg (4418 lb); T-60 tank 5800 kg (12,787 lb); combination 7804 kg (17,205 lb).

Powered aircraft

LEM-2 With bureau designation OKA-33, this was Antonov's first powered aircraft. It was built with Osoaviakhim funds in 1936 to create an efficient light transport for isolated communities. Called a 'powered glider', it was a completely new design, almost an all-wing aircraft but with two short booms carrying the tail. The key to efficiency was the wing, using Prof V. N. Belyaev's aerodynamics to obtain a larger inner section (centreline chord 6,7 m, 22 ft) and slender outer panels. Aerofoil section was PZ-2, derived from TsAGI R-11, construction being all-wood with ply skin. The engine had a long-chord NACA cowl and drove a U-2 (Po-2) propeller. Up to 1280 kg (2822 lb) of cargo could be loaded into the interior of the inner wing. N. I. Ferosyev made the first flight on 20 April 1937. Though described as the first efficient Soviet aeroplane, it was soon abandoned. It must have been grossly underpowered.
DIMENSIONS Span 27,6 m (90 ft 6½ in); length 10,6 m (34 ft 9¼ in); wing area 81,4 m² (876 ft²).
ENGINE One 100 hp M-11 radial.
WEIGHTS Empty 1640 kg (3616 lb); loaded 2920 kg (6437 lb).
PERFORMANCE Max speed 117 km/h (73 mph); cruising speed 100 km/h (62 mph); service ceiling 1500 m (4920 ft).

OKA-38 After the non-aggression pact with Nazi Germany in summer 1939 several German aircraft were supplied to the Soviet Union. The

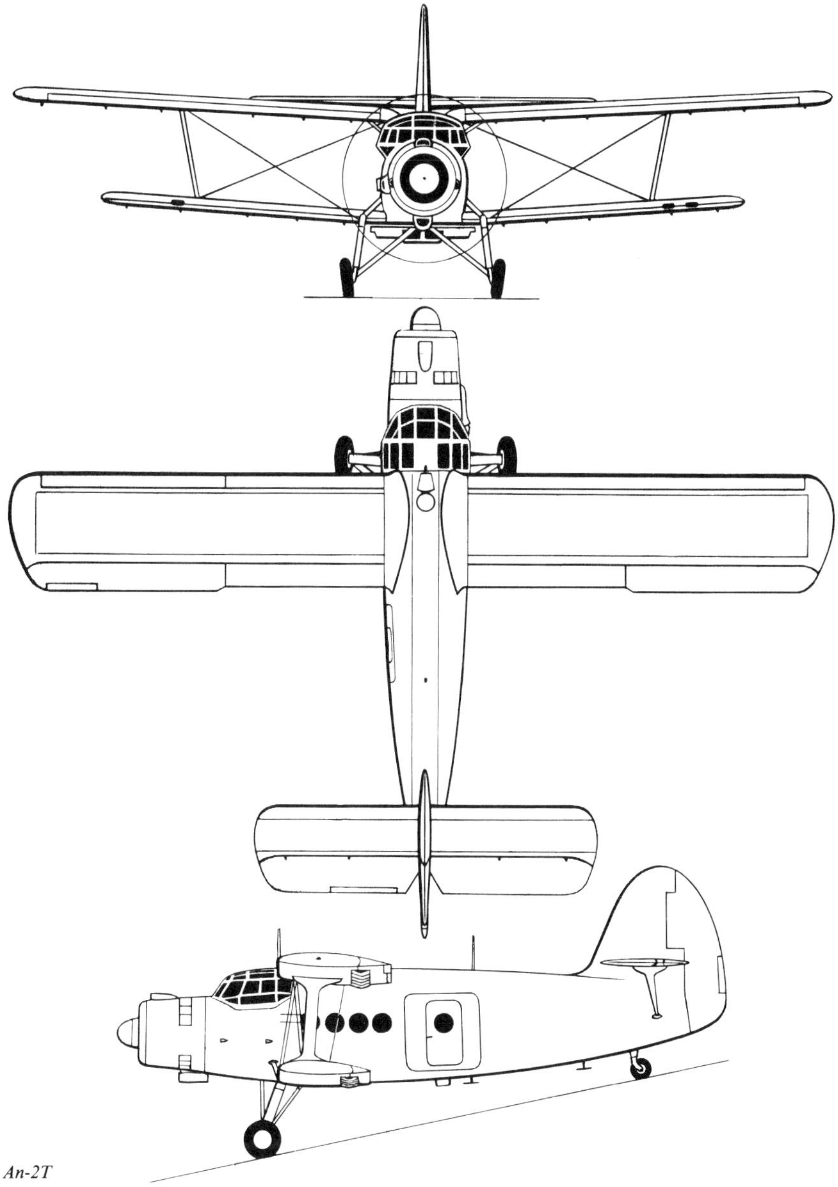

An-2T

Fieseler Fi 156C Storch light STOL aircraft was obviously relevant to Soviet requirements. Antonov was assigned the task of producing a Soviet equivalent, or making an exact copy. Antonov chose the latter, and though the welded steel-tube fuselage was unfamilar to his bureau it was copied exactly, the wooden wings presenting no problem. Having no Argus inverted-vee engines, the powerplant was changed to an MV-6, the Soviet-built French Renault Bengali 6Pdi. Prototypes of the OKA-38 (named *Aist* = stork) flew in 1940, and proved to be overweight. After further development a factory in newly annexed Lithuania (according to Něměcek, Estonia) was tooled up to produce the three-seat ShS (staff/liaison) transport and the N-2 casevac model equipped for two stretcher (litter) patients. The plant was overrun by the Nazis before the first aircraft came off the line.

DIMENSIONS span 14,28 m (46 ft $10\frac{1}{4}$ in); length 10,3 m (33 ft $9\frac{1}{2}$ in); wing area 26 m^2 (279·9 ft^2).
ENGINE One 220 hp MV-6 inverted six-inline.
WEIGHTS 'No 2' production, empty 981 kg (2163 lb); loaded 1343 kg (2961 lb).
PERFORMANCE cruising speed at sea level 173 km/h (107 mph); landing speed 60 km/h (37·3 mph); range 700 km (435 miles).

An-2 When photographs of this aircraft appeared in the West in 1947 it was regarded as an anachronism, out of date even as a prototype, because it was a biplane. In fact it was this hasty judgement that was in error, because the An-2 has outsold all other transport aircraft in history and all other aircraft of any type since the Second World War! Again, it is instinctive to assess single-engine biplanes as in the Tiger Moth or Stearman class, but this biplane has a cabin cross-section near that of a DC-3. Combined with STOL performance this has opened it up to 40 roles, again a world record.

It was the first task assigned to Antonov's reformed OKB, the requirement being a replacement for the Po-2, issued in May 1946 by the Ministry of Agriculture and Forestry. Studies begin with a larger version of the OKA-38 with ASh-21 engine, but the compactness of the biplane carried the day. In the Soviet environment

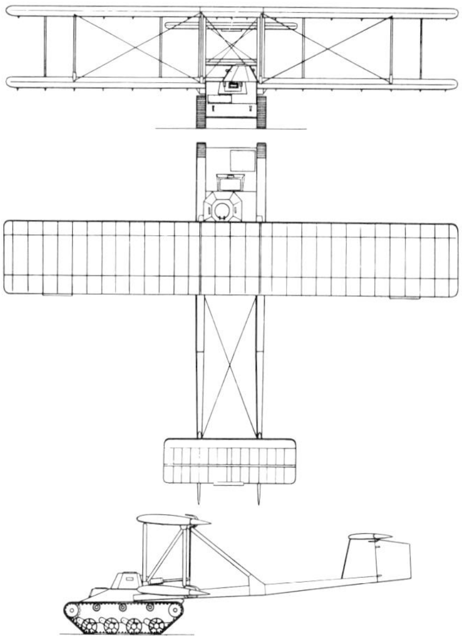

KT

it did not occur to Antonov that others might think a biplane passé; it was the smallest and lightest solution to the task, which as a result of long discussion grew to a machine much larger and more capable than the Po-2.

Though high-tensile (30KhGSA) steel was used for the welded forward fuselage carrying the engine and landing gear, it was decided to make the rest of the fuselage and fin as a stressed-skin unit, to give greater capacity and flexibility in providing door, window and other openings. The ruling interior section was fixed at 1,6 by 1,8 m (63 in wide, 70·9 in high), so that in the *Passarzhirski* role there is room for four rows of three seats, with an offset aisle. The wings, of TsAGI R-11 14% profile, are light alloy with I-spars at 15 and 60% chord, skin being stressed light alloy back to the front spar and fabric elsewhere. Upper wings have full-span slats. Both upper and lower wings are provided with electrically driven slotted flaps with travel of 45°, the upper wings also having drooping ailerons. Flight controls are manual, and the rudder, left aileron and elevator have electric trim-tabs.

At least two prototypes were built, designated **SKh-1** (rural economy 1), the first having the 760 hp ASh-21 and the second the 1000 hp ASh-62IR. In each case the propeller was the V-509A-D7 with four scimitar-shaped blades of 3,6 m (141·7 in) diameter and large round spinner. Six fabric tanks in the upper wing housed 1200 lit (264 gal) of fuel (91 octane). The engine was fitted with a 27V generator and an air compressor for charging a bottle in the rear fuselage at 49 bars (711 lb/in^2) for pressurizing the main landing-gear oleos according to terrain, and for operating the tailwheel lock; reduced to 9·8 bars (142 lb/in^2) it energizes the wheel brakes. Normal equipment includes blind-flying instruments, gyrocompass, radio compass, two radios, radioaltimeter and intercom. The side-by-side cockpit can have dual control, and its side windows oversail the fuselage to give view downwards. The centre and left windscreens are de-iced electrically, and the right panel uses engine-heated air which also heats the cabin, There is no airframe ice protection.

The first SKh-1, with ASh-21 engine, was flown on 31 August 1947 by N. P. Volodin. With this engine the payload was limited to 1300 kg (2866 lb), but with the ASh-62IR it could be raised to 2140 kg (4718 lb) in the first production version, the **An-2T** (*Transportny*), available from October 1948. The 2T remained in production at Kiev as a standard utility machine for Aeroflot and armed forces, supplemented from 1949 by the **An-2TP** for Aeroflot scheduled routes, with comfortable furnishing for 12 passengers, the **An-2P** with up to 14 lightweight seats in a soundproofed cabin, the **An-2S** ambulance version with six stretchers (three superimposed on each side of the aisle and an attendant) and the **An-2TD** for parachute training and operational parachute missions seating 12 and with special equipment. The first agricultural version was the **An-2Skh** with a 1400 lit (308 gal) copper tank in the fuselage for liquids or solids distributed via a spraybar system on six pylons under the lower wing or a 300 mm (11·8 in) diameter centreline duct. The eight-blade fan driving the pump was later replaced by a VD-10 with four variable-pitch blades. Operating at 155 km/h (96 mph) with swath width from 60 to 100 m (200–330 ft) the first SKh evaluated by G.I. Lysenko in 1948 on a collective farm near Kiev completed the monthly work quota in three days. In 1948 aerial pesticides were put down on 2·1 million hectares, but by 1963 the An-2SKh was annually doing nearly 26 million. A hectare, 10,000 m^2, is 2·47 acres.

Normally the SKh variant has a long-stroke landing gear, and like other versions can have two types of ski. In 1949 a seaplane, the **An-4**, was flown and given service designation **An-2V**. The dural floats reduce speed but according to OKB data do not change the empty weight. Most 2Vs are utility transports but in 1961 a water-bomber variant, the **An-2PP** (forest protection), was developed with pilot-activated sluices in the floats through which 1260 litres (277 gal) can be rammed in five seconds' taxiing, and then dumped over a fire. An earlier firefighting model, the **An-2L**, was a landplane carrying water in a fuselage drum or extinguishing chemicals dropped in frangible underwing bottles.

Two unusual early models were the **An-6** and **An-2F**. The former was a high-altitude model with ASh-62IR supercharged by a TK-19 turbo to maintain 850 hp to 9500 m (31,170 ft). This was flown by V. A. Didyenko on 21 March 1948 in the *Meteo* form subsequently designated **An-2ZA** (atmosphere sampling) with a heated compartment for a scientific observer faired into the fin. The **An-2F** *Fedya* was completely new aft of the wings, with a glazed rear fuselage tapering to a narrow boom precariously carrying a twin-finned tail. A dorsal cupola mounted a 12·7-mm UBT or 23-mm NS-23 cannon, aimed by hand. A small batch was evaluated in 1955 against unknown Su and Yak rivals, but the requirement was cancelled. An alternative designation was **An-2NRK** (night artillery correction), shortened to **An-2K**. Another oddball not given a designation was the special-chassis An-2 with six low-pressure tyres on the main gears for use from marsh, snow and sand. A field kit added the pair of extra sprung wheels ahead of and behind each existing main wheel, while the tailwheel was given a ski-like surround.

In 1959 general-aviation aircraft were assigned to Poland, and the last of about 5450

An-2T

An-2V

An-2M

An-2s built in the Soviet Union was completed in August 1960. Subsequently only a few An-2s have been made by the Antonov OKB, the most important being the **An-2M** (modified), flown on 20 May 1964. This incorporates 290 engineering changes aimed at improving utility. The agricultural hopper is of GRP (glass-reinforced plastics) and enlarged to 1960 lit (431 gal), and a 50 hp power take-off from the engine to a new pump almost doubles dispensing rate from the new spraying and dusting systems. The aircraft is equipped for one-man operation, instead of needing two crew, and the cockpit has air-conditioning and often a separate door instead of access via the hinged left half of the roof (Polish An-2s usually have access from the cabin). The structure incorporates metal bonding and spot-welding, brakes are pedal-operated, main wheels are further forward to preclude nosing over, quick-change arrangements allow for rapid conversion between roles, and the enlarged tail has increased tailplane span and a more rectangular vertical surface. Only a limited number of M-models have been built in Poland.

Since 1959 production of the An-2 has been centred at WSK-PZL-Mielec, where almost 10,000 were built by 1981. Mielec An-2s have their own designations, often different from the Soviet ones. In the late 1950s about 100, often with rectangular cabin windows, were produced at the DDR plant at Dresden. In 1957, China started building An-2s (Harbin C-5 or Y-5). It is no longer built there, but estimates of Chinese production range from 1500 to 3500, bringing the overall total to 17,000–19,000.

DIMENSIONS Span 18,18 m (59 ft 8½ in); length (tail down, most) 12,4 m (40 ft 8¼ in), (tail up) 12,74 m (41 ft 9½ in), (An-2V) 14,0 m (45 ft 11¼ in); height (tail down, most) 4,0 m (13 ft 1½ in); wing area (upper) 43,55 m^2 (468·8 ft^2), (lower) 27,96 m^2 (300·96 ft^2).

ENGINE 1000 hp Shvetsov ASh-62IR nine-cylinder radial.

WEIGHTS Empty (An-2T, An-2V) 3360 kg (7407 lb), (An-2SKh) 3440 kg (7584 lb), (An-2M) 3430 kg (7562 lb); loaded (An-2T and An-2M) 5500 kg (12,125 lb), (most other variants) 5250 kg (11,574 lb).

PERFORMANCE (typical): cruising speed 200 km/h (124 mph); max speed 250 km/h (155 mph); max take-off or landing run on soft ground 200 m (656 ft); service ceiling 4350 m (14,270 ft); range with max (700 kg) fuel 900 km (560 miles)

An-3 In 1959 Antonov studied versions of An-2 with a turboprop, advantages of which included a better power to weight ratio, less-flammable fuel and, especially, ample supplies of hot air for cold climates and of bleed air to drive air-cycle machines to cool interior at ambient temperatures up to 40°C. Studies in 1960s were for enlarged aircraft with 1500 hp TV-2-117, but final outcome was same-size project which can be produced by modifying gigantic existing An-2 fleet in Warsaw Pact countries. While WSK-PZL-Mielec has produced completely new M-15 turbofan-engined biplane (with Soviet assistance including Antonov engineer R.A. Ismailov) Antonov OKB has built single prototype (SSSR-30576) designated An-3 which by time this book appears will have been evaluated against M-15 to see if either or both is most cost/effective answer. A rough estimate suggests that converting existing An-2s to An-3 standard would cost one-sixth as much as building M-15s. Chosen engine is 940 shp Glushenkov TVD-10B, in production in Poland for An-28. This drives large slow-turning propeller optimised for operating speeds around 150 km/h (93 mph). Rest of the aircraft not greatly altered, but the payload is increased to 1900 kg (4188 lb).

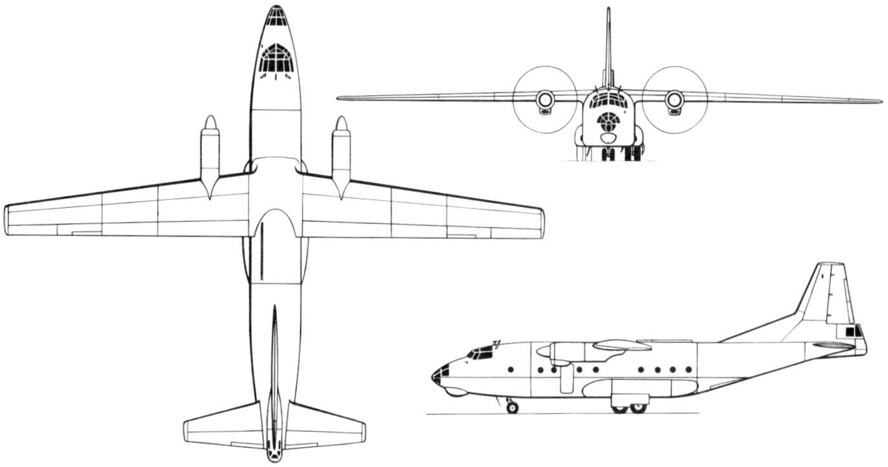

An-8

An-8 After the Second World War, the Soviet Union had a need for civil and military transport aircraft more capable than existing types such as the Li-2. Studies were made of the Tu-70 and Il-18(*), and of a C-97-type conversion of the much larger Tu-85, but what actually happened was that a 1952 joint requirement by the V-VS and Aeroflot was won by the Antonov OKB with a totally new design. It was a gigantic step for the bureau, which had no experience of large, highly stressed all-metal structures. In almost all respects the An-8 was a masterpiece, achieved at a time when the configuration that has since become standard was almost unknown (the C-130 had not appeared). Among basic features were an unpressurized hold 2,5 m (98·4-in) square in section, a full-width rear ramp/door, tandem twin-wheel main gears for unpaved airstrips retracting hydraulically into fuselage fairings, hydraulically driven double-slotted area-increasing flaps, manual flight controls, electro-thermal anticing of wings and tail, a glazed nose for contact navigation, and a chin radar for ground-mapping in bad weather and to assist accurate paradrops. Almost all An-8s were originally built with a hydraulic rear turret with a single NR-23 cannon. Crew comprised captain, co-pilot, navigator (nose), radio/radar operator (behind captain at lower level), engineer (behind co-pilot) and tail gunner. The wing, with aspect ratio of 11·7, was one of the most efficient in the world for subsonic transport in the first half of the 1950s, but the 5100 ehp Kuznetsov NK-6-TV2 single-shaft engines were immature when the prototype flew in 1955. Like many rear-loading transports the An-8 also suffered from rear-fuselage aerodynamic problems and eventually featured long strakes from the wing to just below the tailplane.

Batch of 100 delivered, with engine changed (see data), performance being little impaired and cowlings unchanged. Propellers were four-blade AV-68 with electric anticing. About 11000 lit (2420 gal) of fuel was housed in bag tanks in wing box. Normally the interior was arranged for cargo, with folding seats for handlers, but up to 48 troop seats could be installed. A few An-8s went to Aeroflot, both these and at least half V-VS aircraft later having turret replaced by fairing. In 1966 a military An-8 was monitoring Chinese nuclear-weapon fallout, and type continued to be seen occasionally in the 1970s. Nickname was *Keet* (Whale).

DIMENSIONS Span 37,0 m (121 ft 4¾ in); length (no guns) 30,74 m (100 ft 10¼ in); height 9,7 m (31 ft 10 in); wing area 117,2 m^2 (1262 ft^2).

ENGINES Two 4000 ehp Ivchyenko AI-20 single-shaft turboprops.

WEIGHTS Empty 21 250 kg (46,847 lb); max loaded 38 000 kg (83,774 lb).

PERFORMANCE Max speed 600 km/h (373 mph); long-range cruise 480 km/h (298 mph); field length 1000 m (ground run 700) (3280 ft); range with max payload 2280 km (1417 miles), with max fuel 3500 km (2175 miles).

An-10 Ukraina In 1955 Aeroflot issued a more challenging specification calling for 75 passenger seats in a pressurized fuselage. Antonov succeeded admirably in a minimum change revision of the An-8, main alteration apart from streamlined circular-section body being doubling number of engines. Wing modifications were minor, though 22 bag tanks were housed in main box to raise fuel capacity to 12,710 lit (2796 gal). Engines, four 4000 ehp Kuznetsov NK-4, driving AV-68 reversing propellers of 4,5-m (177-in) diameter (at first reverse-pitch was not permitted). The 2,5-m square cabin section had to be maintained, so circular profile drawn around outside to give 222 m^3 (7769 ft^3) of clear volume above floor. Cabin dP set at 0,5 kg/cm^2 (7·11 lb/in^2), though glazed nose retained. Cabin conditioning systems housed in main-gear fairings, of semicircular section unlike flat boxes of the An-8; left fairing also housed the APU, a new feature. Each main gear was a four-wheel bogie. Prototype, SSSR-U1957, flown by Ya. I. Vernikov and V. P. Vazin at Kiev on 7 March 1957. Shortly beforehand, tunnel testing had shown need for outer-wing anhedral, thus setting a fashion in Soviet high-

An-10A (definitive tail, no endplate fins)

wing transports. Flight testing revealed a need for improved stability and reduced rear-fuselage drag; palliatives included enlarging dorsal fin, adding rear ventral strakes and extra endplate fins on tailplane, and increasing outer-wing anhedral. Another major change was switch to Ivchenko's improved version of the NK-4 engine, AI-20, installed well below wing to give thrust-lines some 15 cm (6 in) lower. Another post-flight change was option of retractable skis with electric heating.

As originally built U1957 had 84 passenger seats in 14 triple-seat rows with a central aisle, with a 'children's playroom' at the rear. By the time Aeroflot services began in July 1959 the rear room was occupied by six revenue seats, and Antonov said the Ukraina (a name applied to all An-10s, not just U1957) was the most economic transport in the world. A year later the **An-10A** was disclosed, with a 2 m (78¾ in) fuselage plug allowing for two more seat rows and with normal accommodation for 100 passengers. The fuel capacity was increased (see data) and propellers were at last cleared for reversing. The 10A entered service in February 1960, and subsequently set the following world class records: 2000 km with 15 000 kg payload (723 km/h, 449¼ mph); 900-km round trip (760 km/h, 472¼ mph); and 500-km circuit (730·6 km/h, 454 mph). The An-10 and 10A were withdrawn in 1973 after a series of structural failures.

A single high-density aircraft, with OKB designation **An-16** and service designation **An-10V**, was flown in 1963. This was shown in a brochure by Antonov in 1958, the fuselage having a further stretch of 3 m (118 in).

DIMENSIONS Span 38,0 m (124 ft 8 in); length (An-10) 32,0 m (105 ft 0 in), (An-10A) 34,0 m (111 ft 6½ in); height 9,83 m (32 ft 3 in); wing area 119,5 m^2 (1286·3 ft^2).

ENGINES Four 4000 ehp Ivchyenko AI-20K single-shaft turboprops.

WEIGHTS Empty (10) 28 900 kg (63,713 lb), (10A) 29 800 kg (65,697 lb); max fuel (10) 12,710 lit = 9787 kg (21,576 lb), (10A) 13,900 lit = 10 700 kg (23,600 lb); max payload 14 500 kg (31,966 lb); max take-off (10) 54t (119,048 lb), (10A) 55 100 kg (121,473 lb).

PERFORMANCE Normal high cruising speed 680 km/h (423 mph); long range cruise 630 km/h (391 mph); typical take-off (paved surface) 800 m (2625 ft); range with max payload (10A) 1200 km (745 miles), (max fuel) 4075 km (2532 miles).

An-12 It was natural that Antonov should produce a cargo aircraft with full-section rear doors using basic airframe of An-10. Developed in parallel with the passenger machine, the NK-4-powered prototype An-12 flew in 1958 (date unknown). Antonov admitted several surprising defeats, one being to abandon pressurization of the cargo hold. Another was to use an integral rear ramp in only a few An-12s, standard model having left and right main doors hydraulically folded upwards, with rear door hinged up from rear edge in usual manner. Thus, though suitable for loading items from trucks, standard An-12 cannot handle vehicles without a separate ramp.

Though the An-12 has same basic airframe as An-10 there are many minor changes, most significant being greatly increased fuel capacity (see data) and much larger vertical tail which seems to work without auxiliary strakes or fins. At extreme rear a twin-NR-23 turret (almost identical with that of Tu-16) was supplied in batches to An-12 production line at Ulan-Ude. Usual Bee Hind direction radar for this turret is not fitted, but Gamma-A tail-warning radar is standard, while under-nose radar was updated to I-band set called Toadstool. Flight crew remained as before, with five forward and sixth in pressurized turret, and in some aircraft a 14-seat pressurized compartment was added behind flight deck for crews of AFVs, handling teams and other passengers. The 2,5 m square section allows such AFVs as the ZSU-23/4, ASU-57 and ASU-85, PT-76, and all the ICVs, APCs and scout cars. At Domodyedovo in 1967 a demonstration was put on by An-12s fitted with integral hinged ramps for delivery of such vehicles. Stan-

An-12B

dard **An-12BP** has no ramp and no pressurized passenger cabin, and with 100 paratroops aboard is restricted to 5000 m (about 16,400 ft) altitude, drop being made in under a minute with main doors raised on each side. About 800 BP are believed to have been delivered, all but about 50 to V-TA where for many years they have formed backbone of airlift capability. Two complete airborne divisions with equipment can be flown over 1200 km (746 miles). Electronically simplified export models went to nine air forces. Egypt used an An-12 to test E-300 turbojet. Many Indian An-12BPs became makeshift heavy bombers against Pakistan, carrying up to 16 tonnes of bombs mounted on pallets pushed out by handlers. Freight handling usually assisted by a 2300 kg (5071 lb) electric travelling crane able to reach anywhere in interior. Floor stressed to 1500 kg/m², but rear section inconveniently slopes down to door sill.

An-12BP entered service 1959, and within 18 months a civil version was supplied to Aeroflot. In 1965 a refined all-civil **An-12B** was exhibited with neat fairing in place of rear turret which had previously either been locally modified (in some cases as a toilet, not usually provided in the BP) or merely by having the guns and rear-fuselage magazine removed. Since 1961 the An-12B has been Aeroflot's main cargo transport, used by almost every directorate including Polar. Some have advanced skis fitted with braking and heating, a feature not seen on the An-12BP. Aeroflot received about 200 An-12Bs, and at least 12 civil examples were exported. They avoided structural problem of An-10 and were only gradually being withdrawn in early 1980s.

Large fleet of V-TA aircraft is being progressively replaced by Il-76, and was whittled down from about 1972 onwards by conversion of aircraft to other duties, mainly for EW (electronic warfare). An ECM variant (Cub-C) has been in use (and supplied to Egypt) since 1973, with several tons of electric-generation, distribution and control gear above the floor and the underfloor area devoted to palletized jammers for at least five wavebands. This was one of the first dedicated ECM platforms with central energy management, though details are unknown in the West, where number estimated at 30-plus. Dispensed payloads may be emitted through at least two aperatures. A less-common Elint (electronic intelligence) version (Cub-B) retains tail turret and uses underfloor region for from five to nine receiver aerials, main cabin being occupied by passive receivers, analysers, communications and recording equipment. Some of these EW versions, and all V-TA transports, are being given better radar in larger nose bulge (type unknown). Dedicated maritime reconnaissance version (Cub-D) with totally different sensors was first seen 1982.

DIMENSIONS As An-10A except overall length close to 37 m (121 ft 4 in) depending on variant.
ENGINES As An-10A.
WEIGHTS Empty (BP, typical) 28 000 kg (61,730 lb); max payload 20 tonnes (44,090 lb); max take-off 61 000 kg (134,480 lb).
PERFORMANCE Max speed (over 6000 m) 777 km/h (482 mph); cruising speed, up to 670 km/h (416 mph); take-off run on concrete 700 m (2300 ft); service ceiling 10,2 km (33,500 ft); range with max payload 3600 km (2236 miles); range with max fuel (18,100 lit, 3981 gal) 5700 km (3540 miles).

An-12BP

An-12 Elint-version (Cub-C)

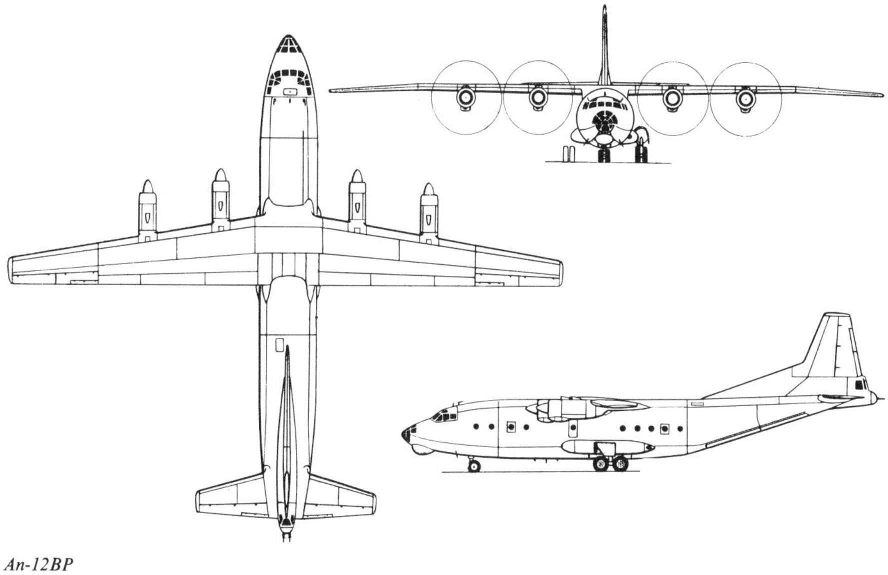

An-12BP

An-14 (prototype)

An-14

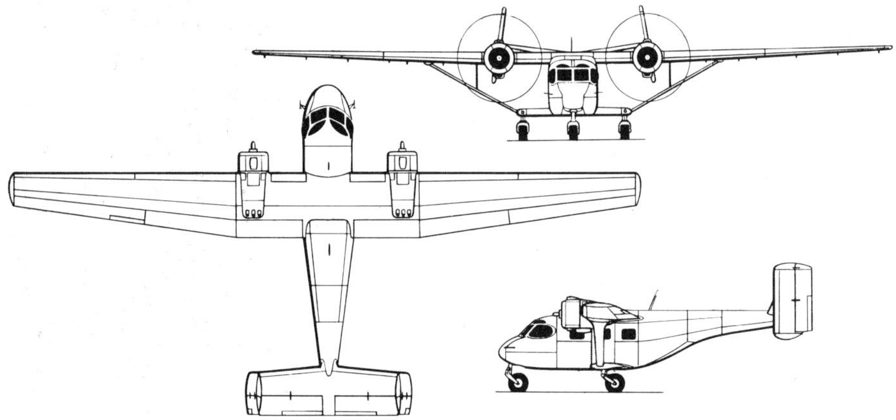

An-14

An-14 Named *Pchyelka* (Little Bee), the An-14 was planned around 1955 to meet an Aeroflot need for a light STOL utility aircraft smaller than the An-2 but more capable than the Yak-12 which it wished to replace. The answer was a stressed-skin high-wing monoplane with two radial engines, flown at Kiev by V. Izgeyim on 15 March 1958. There was a blaze of publicity; but over the subsequent eight years almost every part of the An-14 was redesigned, numerous ideas being tested on prototypes and rejected until eventually production An-14s became available from Progress Works at Arsenyev, near Vladivostok, entering service in the surrounding Far East Directorate and with the armed forces.

The original prototype (L-1958) had an untapered wing of 19,8 m (64 ft $11\frac{1}{2}$ in) span with full-span trailing surfaces hinged to brackets below the wing, the outer sections serving as slotted ailerons and the inner sections carrying hinged rear portions to form double-slotted flaps. Automatic slats were fitted outboard of the engines, which were 260 hp AI-14Rs. Tapered fins were mounted on the tips of a horizontal tailplane, and the cabin (about 3,1 m long by 1,53 wide and 1,6 m high, 122 × 50 × 63 in) was entered via rear ventral doors divided at the centreline and allowed to hang open on each side, with a folding central steps.

The production aircraft has a slender tapered wing, with powered slats inboard of more powerful engines driving V-530 constant-speed propellers usually with three blades. Rectangular fins are mounted on a dihedral tailplane, the nose is longer and, after trying other methods, the original rear door was made standard. A pneumatic system at 50 kg/cm^2 (711 lb/in^2) drives flaps, wheel brakes, inboard slats, engine starting and cabin heating. The nose gear freely castors 70° on each side. Alternative landing gears include skis and twin floats. Engine-heated air is supplied on demand to warm the cabin and the leading edges of the tail, the latter also having electric heater elements.

Dual control can be fitted, but usually the right cockpit seat is taken by a passenger, and the cabin can be furnished for six or eight passengers, six stretcher patients, 720 kg (1587 lb) cargo or 1000 lit (220 gal) of chemicals distributed via spraybars running along the aileron/flap brackets, down the struts and below the stub wings. There are several other special-role kits. About 200 An-14s are thought to have been built. The design influenced Chinese machines in this class.

DIMENSIONS Span 21,99 m (72 ft $1\frac{3}{4}$ in); length 11,44 m (37 ft $6\frac{1}{2}$ in); height 4,63 m (15 ft $2\frac{1}{4}$ in); wing area 39,72 m^2 (427·5 ft^2).

ENGINES Two 300 hp Ivchyenko AI-14RF radials.

WEIGHTS Empty (typical) 2000 kg (4409 lb); max take-off 3600 kg (7935 lb).

PERFORMANCE Max speed 222 km/h (138 mph); cruise 180 km/h (112 mph); landing speed 85 km/h (53 mph); take-off (concrete) 100 m (328 ft); range with max fuel (383 lit, 84 gal) 800 km (497 miles); range with max payload 650 km (404 miles).

An-22 Antei Appearance of this monster freighter at the 1965 Paris airshow caused surprise, but remarkable thing is that it did not materialize ten years earlier. The engine was

An-14 production at Arsenyev

An-22 (prototype)

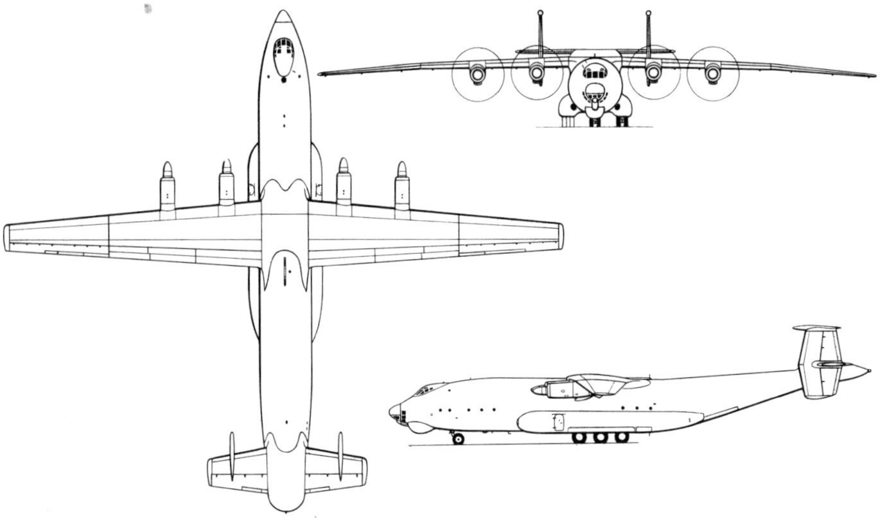

An-22 without tail turret

available, and big aircraft are not only part of the Soviet heritage but needed by the world's biggest country. The name, Antheus in English usage, is the giant son of Poseidon and Gaia. Antonov began serious work in early 1962 against a joint V-TA/Aeroflot requirement. Cargo-hold cross-section was selected at 4,4 m (14 ft 5¼ in) square, but again Antonov jibbed at attempting a pressurized fuselage, settling for a pressurized nose and forward fuselage accommodating 29 passengers only. This is separated by a pressure bulkhead with left and right doors from the main cargo hold, which has a floor of titanium with a non-slip surface and cargo locks, though no mechanical handling system had been seen on an An-22 by 1981, except for a typical Antonov overhead travelling crane. There are two rear doors, the forward section hydraulically locking at any height down to ground level (but it is not the patented swinging-link type) and the rear aft-hinged door containing on its underside (the outer skin) two rails which extend the travelling-crane tracks to the rear to assist picking up heavy cargo. Most An-22s have four travelling cranes driven by two winches each of 2500 kg (5511 lb) capacity. As in the An-12 two retractable jacks can support the fuselage near the main door sill. Available hold length is 33,0 m (108 ft 3 in). The rear doors can be opened for air-drops.

Normal crew access is via a door in the fairing for each main landing gear, stairs to the main deck, a pressure door to the passenger compartment, and stairs to the flight deck at the upper level. Normal crew is five, the navigator's glazed nose being retained. The first prototype, SSSR-46191, flown (possibly by I. J. Davidov) on 27 February 1965, was powered by NK-12MV engines driving the same AV-60N propellers as on the Tu-20, Tu-114 and Tu-126. Examination suggested that each engine exhausted through a single central stack containing a large heat exchanger for heating air rammed in through an inlet not present on the Tupolev aircraft and subsequently ducted along the wing and tail leading edges. The wing, loaded to an exceptional 0,725 tonnes/m^2 (148·5 lb/ft^2), is of typical gull-wing form. The main box forms integral tanks from tip to tip, housing 43 tonnes (about 55 800 lit, 12,285 gal). Structural parts in this wing and the main fuselage frames were made on a 75,000-tonne press and are of impressive size. Three frames lead down to the three tandem sets of levered suspension main gears, 12 wheels in all, hydraulically raised into large fairings which also house cabin-air systems, APUs and the pressure-fuelling couplings. The tyre pressures can be adjusted in flight and the nose gear is steerable. The double-slotted flaps are made in inner and outer sections of equal area, and all flight controls are manual, driven by Flettner tabs as on the Britannia. The twin fins are mounted so far ahead of the tailplane that one wonders how they stay on; the lower edges have no tail bumpers though they could touch the ground, and large bullet fairings (not quite so large on production aircraft) adorn their tops. The fairings are anti-flutter masses, but could serve also as electronics aerials or pitot heads, which are hard to find on An-22s. The prototype had no nose equipment beyond UHF and VHF blades, the radar being in the underside of the right main-gear fairing. This An-22 set 12 world load/height records in 1966, beaten by another An-22 a year later with 100 445 kg (221,440 lb) lifted to 7848 m (25,748 ft). Production aircraft have larger propellers (see data) and additional avionics, the main change being removal of the nav/mapping radar to below the nose and addition of a cloud/collision warning radar in the nose itself, retaining glazing for the navigator as on the Il-76. By 1974, when 100 An-22s were estimated to be in VT-A and Aeroflot service, military examples had a larger nav/mapping radar. Antonov had expected to build 30 per year, but it is doubtful if 200 in all have been built. Various stretched and double-deck variants, one with 724 seats, did not leave the drawing-board. Possibly half the An-22s are on strategic airlift with Aeroflot, especially in Siberia. Military examples can carry the T-62, T-72 or T-80 main battle tanks, and the twin-Ganef SAM transporter-vehicle.

DIMENSIONS Span 64,4 m (211 ft 3½ in); length 57,9 m (189 ft 11½ in); height 12,53 m (41 ft 1½ in); wing area 345 m^2 (3713·6 ft^2).

ENGINES Four 15,000 ehp Kuznetsov NK-12MA single-shaft turboprops driving mechanically coupled contraprops (as distinct from two independent contra-rotating propellers) of 6,2 m (20 ft 4·1 in) diam.

WEIGHTS Empty about 114t (251,325 lb); max take-off 250t (551,146 lb).

PERFORMANCE Max speed 740 km/h (460 mph); normal cruise 560/640 km/h (368/398 mph); take-off (concrete) 1300 m (4265 ft); range with max payload 5000 km (3107 miles); range with max fuel (and 45t payload) 10 950 km (6800 miles).

An-24 From 1955 Aeroflot recognised the need to replace the mass of Li-2s, Il-12s and Il-14s which handled its short-range routes, and in 1957 issued a specification for a 32-seater for operation in harsh conditions from primitive airstrips. Antonov's OKB was assigned the project in December 1957, and the first prototype An-24, L1959, was flown at Kiev by Y. Kurlin and G. Lysenko on 20 December 1959. A conventional high-wing twin-turboprop in the class of the F.27 and Herald, it exemplifies Russian disregard for operating economy, and concentration on a tough vehicle for a tough environment. Empty weight of a typical An-24 is more than 3 tonnes, or 25%, greater than that of its Western counterparts, though the latter carry greater

An-22 with three nose radars

An-24V (LAT Lebanon)

payloads further, with about 10% less power. The important point is that the An-24 met the need, and more have been made than of any other turboprop aircraft. It has been by far the most successful Soviet aviation export.

Ruling body section is 2,76 m wide by 1,91 m high (108·7 by 75·2 in), and pressure differential of 0,3 kg/cm² (4·27 lb/in²) is retained throughout the hold of cargo versions, unlike earlier An designs. Body section is formed from three circular arcs meeting at the dorsal centreline and at a chine low along each side. Extensive bonding (a copy, without licence, of CIBA/ARL methods) and spot-welding is used throughout, and for the first time great attention was paid not only to fatigue but also to corrosion. The body was tank-tested, and in 1961 a life of 30,000 h was stated. The wing has 2° anhedral on the outer panels, and the large machined skins are spot-welded, the outer wing boxes forming integral tanks. Four centre-section cells bring normal capacity to 5240 lit (1153 gal) and four additional centre-section cells give an option of 6220 lit (1368 gal). (Some 24s are believed to have the ten-tank system of the An-26.) A 155 kg/cm² (2200 lb/in²) hydraulic system drives the flaps, landing gear, nosewheel steering, wipers, feathering and, on cargo models, freight doors. The prototype had one track-mounted flap on each wing, double-slotted inboard of the nacelle whose rear portion travelled with the flap. Production aircraft have four flaps divided by longer nacelles. Flight controls are manual, with glassfibre servo and trim tabs, that on the rudder being a spring tab. Leading edges are de-iced by 10th-stage bleed air, which also drives air-cycle machines in each nacelle for cabin air. Windshield, inlet and propeller anticing is by raw AC. Twin-wheel landing gears have tyres variably inflatable to a maximum of 3·5 kg/cm² (49·8 lb/in²) and can free-fall.

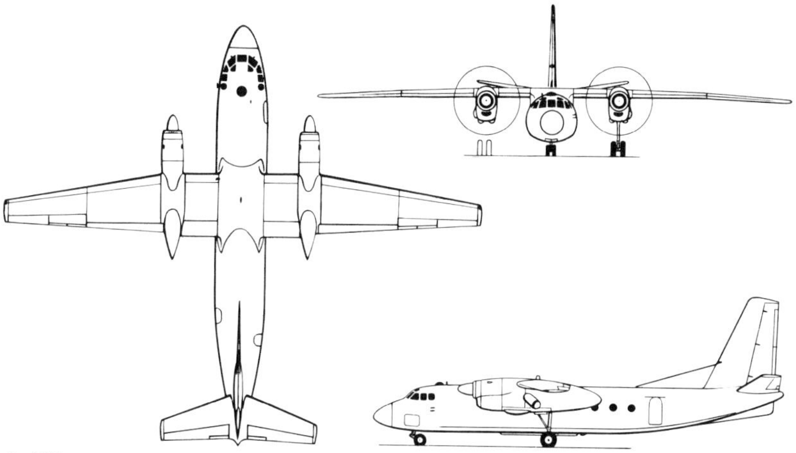

An-24V

Apart from the longer nacelles, production An-24s have a ventral fin, larger dorsal fin and longer nose. Cargo service began in July 1962, and 44-seat passenger service on 1 December 1963. By this time new An-24s were of the **An-24V** type seating 50 passengers in a fuselage having an extended (9·69 m, 381·5 in) cabin with nine instead of eight windows each side. The AI-24V engine introduced water injection, a TG-16 APU was fitted in the right nacelle and there were many detail improvements. By 1967 the inability of this aircraft fully to meet hot/high take-off demands had led to the An-24V Series II, with inboard flaps extended in chord (see wing area) and the AI-24T engine. Another customer option, available as a field modification, was to replace the TG-16 by the Tumanskii RU-19-300 turbojet, nominally rated at 1985 lb thrust but instead giving all the aircraft electric power on take-off plus about 480 lb thrust, and thus putting more power into the propellers.

An-24RV (Hang Khong Vietnam)

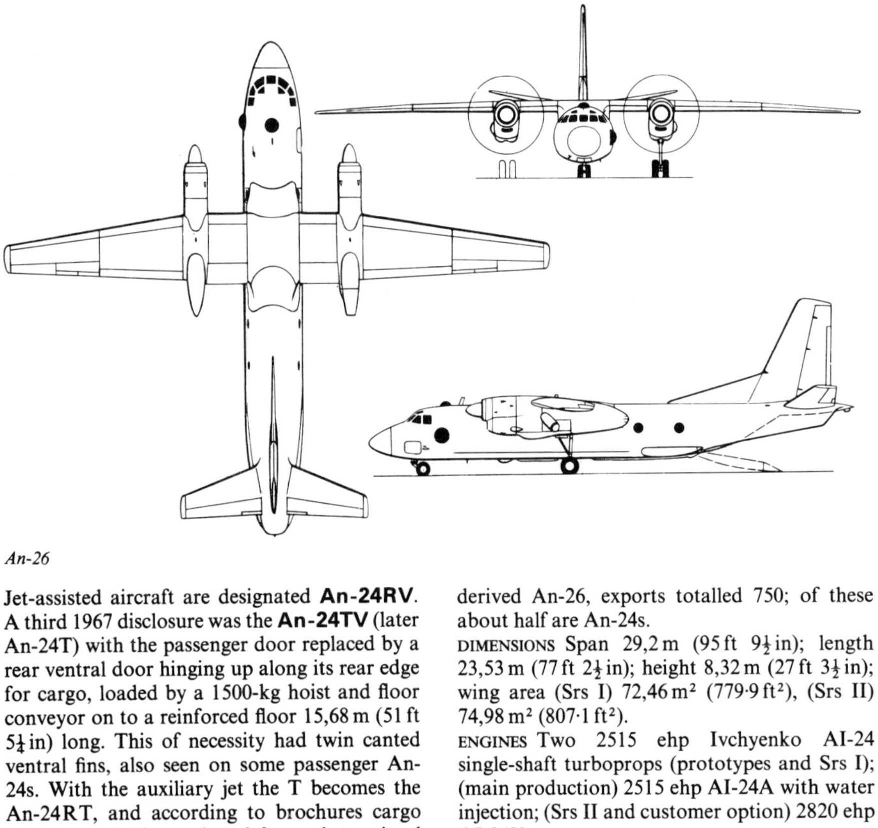

An-26

Jet-assisted aircraft are designated **An-24RV**. A third 1967 disclosure was the **An-24TV** (later An-24T) with the passenger door replaced by a rear ventral door hinging up along its rear edge for cargo, loaded by a 1500-kg hoist and floor conveyor on to a reinforced floor 15,68 m (51 ft 5¼ in) long. This of necessity had twin canted ventral fins, also seen on some passenger An-24s. With the auxiliary jet the T becomes the An-24RT, and according to brochures cargo versions could be equipped for rocket-assisted take-off; many 24Ts have an astrodome!

There are many special role kits including convertible schemes, executive furnishing, casevac with 24 stretchers and, in the **An-24P** (*Pozharny*), chemical packs, equipment and parachutists for fighting forest fires. Production, all apparently at Kiev, continued until 1978, when about 1100 had been produced. Including the derived An-26, exports totalled 750; of these about half are An-24s.

DIMENSIONS Span 29,2 m (95 ft 9½ in); length 23,53 m (77 ft 2½ in); height 8,32 m (27 ft 3½ in); wing area (Srs I) 72,46 m² (779·9 ft²), (Srs II) 74,98 m² (807·1 ft²).

ENGINES Two 2515 ehp Ivchyenko AI-24 single-shaft turboprops (prototypes and Srs I); (main production) 2515 ehp AI-24A with water injection; (Srs II and customer option) 2820 ehp AI-24V.

WEIGHTS Empty (24V) 13 300 kg (29,320 lb), (24T) 14 060 kg (30,997 lb); basic operating (24T) 14 698 kg (32,404 lb); max payload (V,RV) 5500 kg (12,125 lb), (T) 4612 kg (10,168 lb), (RT) 5700 kg (12,566 lb); max take-off 21 t (46,296 lb), (RV, RT) 21 800 kg (48,060 lb) to ISA + 30°C.

PERFORMANCE Max cruise 498 km/h (310 mph); normal cruise 450 km/h (280 mph); take-off run (concrete) typically 640 m (2100 ft); initial climb about 7·7 m/s (1515 ft/min); range with max payload (V, RV) 550 km (342 miles), with max fuel 2400 km (1491 miles).

An-26 First seen in 1969, this dedicated cargo derivative of An-24 was first Soviet aircraft to have pressurized cargo hold, with full-section rear door. It also introduced a novel door, patented by Antonov himself, which in addition to hinging down as a ramp can also be swung down on four parallel links to lie just below rear fuselage. Second position is for loading from trucks or for air-dropping. Door operation is hydraulic, if necessary by handpump which also builds up pressure in main system. Underside of rear fuselage sweeps sharply up to tailplane, but side profile is masked by deep glassfibre strakes on each side. Smaller strakes project along each side where door is suspended in air-drop position. Standard engine is VT, auxiliary RU-19A-300 (rated at 900 kg, 1984 lb) is always installed, there are two additional fuel cells giving capacity of 7100 lit (1562 gal), structure is restressed for operation at greater weights, main tyres are inflated to 6 kg/cm² (85·3 lb/in²), fuselage underskin is Bimetal (bonded ply of dural faced with abrasion-resistant titanium), and standard role equipment includes 2000 kg electric hoist, 4500 kg handling system flush with floor, 38 or 40 tip-up seats along walls, and retractable static lines for paratroops or cargo. Conversion to 24 stretchers takes 30 minutes. Most An-26s have bulged observation blister on left side of flight deck for contact navigation and precision drop guidance. In 1981 **An-26B** emerged, able to carry three standard cargo pallets, total 5,5 t (12,125 lb), with removable Rollgangs for pallet-positioning. About 650 in all had been delivered by late 1981, with production continuing. Used by Aeroflot (about 100) and at least 15 air forces.

DIMENSIONS As An-24 except length 23,8 m (78 ft 1 in).

An-28

ENGINES Two 2820 ehp Ivchenko AI-24VT single-shaft turboprops.
WEIGHTS Empty 15 020 kg (33,113 lb); normal payload 4500 kg (9921 lb); normal take-off 23 t (50,706 lb); max overload 24 t (52,911 lb).
PERFORMANCE Cruising speed 440 km/h (273 mph); take-off (concrete) 780 m (2559 ft); initial climb 480 m (1575 ft)/min; range with max payload (no reserves) 1100 km (683 miles), (max fuel) 2550 km (1584 miles).

An-28 This attractive light transport was one of the most delayed in Aeroflot history. Antonov mentioned a turboprop An-14A in the early 1960s, and in 1967 said his bureau was about to fly the An-14M with twin Astazou engines and 11 passenger seats. In the event the aircraft was completed with 810 shp Isotov TVD-850 engines, and with registration No 1968 was flown at Kiev by V. Tersky in September 1969. In 1973 the designation was changed to An-28, with a different tail and fixed landing gear. In 1975 development began with the TVD-10 engine, previously flown in the rival Be-30. The An-28 was selected over the Beriev, but because of delays large numbers of Czech L-410 transports preceded it into Aeroflot service, and have eaten into the export market.

As finally defined the An-28 has a fuselage larger than that of the An-14, with cabin 5,26-m (17 ft 3 in) long, 1,66-m (65·4-in) wide and 1·7-m (66·93-in) high. Normally there are five rows of seats, double on the left of the aisle; in high-density, double seats on each side of a central aisle allow 20 to be carried in some An-28s, plus one on the right cockpit seat. The stressed-skin airframe has much bonding and spot-welding. The high-aspect-ratio wing has automatic slats from tip to tip, and the slotted ailerons droop with the double-slotted flaps. Antonov explained with delight two novel safety features. Should an engine fail, an automatic spoiler extends ahead of the opposite aileron to restrict wing-drop and yaw. Should the pilot haul back too hard at low speeds the An-28 cannot stall, because of the wing slats combined with the horizontal tail of inverted section with a leading-edge automatic slat (which in addition collects ice rather than the tailplane should the de-icing fail, which is judged an advantage). Leading edges are heated by hot air from engine heat exchangers mixed with bleed air.

The cabin is unpressurized, and at the rear, in place of left/right clamshell doors of prototypes, is a swinging door electrically moved on four parallel links to lie just under the rear fuselage. A total of 1960 lit (430 gal) of fuel is housed in four integral wing tanks. The windshields, bulged cockpit side windows, engine inlets and AV-24AN propellers are anticed electrically. A simple 3-axis autopilot is standard, and Cat-III certification is planned. A wide range of role equipment is available including a 6/7-seat layout with four folding tables, military-style or freight interior with static line for six paratroops, fire-fighting models, casevac with six stretchers and five seated plus attendant, geological or photo survey, and agricultural with 800-kg (1764-lb) tank or hopper and centreline dispenser for solids or tip-to-tip spraybar.

With assignment of GA aircraft to Poland, PZL-Mielec was entrusted with production of the An-28 in February 1978. It was then expected that deliveries would begin in 1980, but 1982 is now the earliest date, with large-scale production (200 per year) not due until 1983.
DIMENSIONS Span 22,06 m (72 ft 4½ in); length 12,98 m (42 ft 7 in); height 4,60 m (15 ft 1 in); wing area 40,28 m² (433·6 ft²).
ENGINES Two 960 shp PZL-built Glushenkov TVD-10B free-turbine turboprops.
WEIGHTS Empty about 3500 kg (7716 lb); normal payload 1550 kg (3415 lb); normal take-off 5800 kg (12,785 lb), max overload 6100 kg (13,450 lb).
PERFORMANCE Max cruise 350 km/h (217 mph); normal cruise 300 km/h (186 mph); take-off run (normal weight, concrete) 180 m (590 ft); initial climb 12,5 m/s (2470 ft/min); range (15 pax) 660 km (410 miles), (max fuel) 1300 km (807 miles).

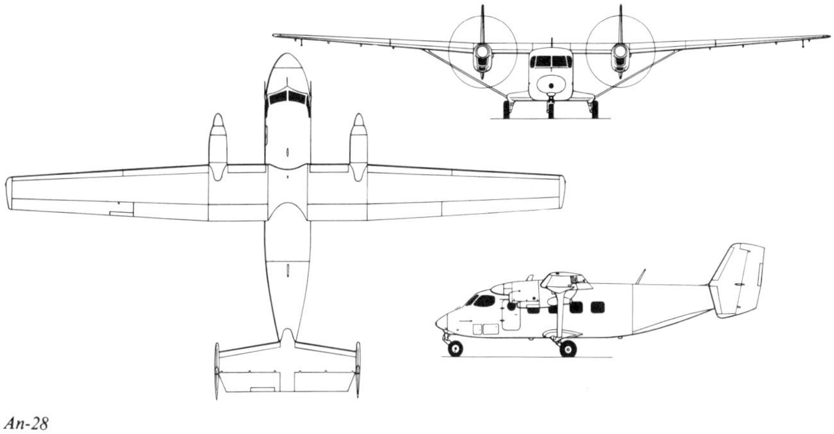

An-28

An-30 First flown in 1974, the An-30 is one of the few purpose-designed surveying and mapping aircraft. As well as optical cameras, it can be equipped with other sensors for all kinds of terrestrial mapping and prospecting, and its value in the largely unprospected Soviet Union is self-evident. Compared with the An-24T the An-30 has a new forward fuselage with an extended and glazed nose and flight deck raised by nearly 1 m (39 in) to give a capacious nose compartment for the navigator with access under the flight-deck floor. The pressurized main cabin houses special navigation equipment (not normally including doppler or inertial, but with VOR/DME), a flight-path computer, radio altimeter and various recording, display and communications sets. In the cartographic configuration there are five major cameras in floor installations, with at least one gyrostabilized. There is a wide range of cameras and mountings, usually with remote control of doors that open below each camera. Normal flight crew numbers five, plus two photographer/surveyors. Spare payload available, so fuel capacity has been further increased, to 6200 lit (1364 gal). A rear freight door similar to the An-24T is a customer option, as is conversion to freight transport with cover plates over the camera apertures. Details have yet to emerge of the other sensors that can be installed, but magnetometers, IR linescan, radiometers/bolometers, gravimetric sensors and lasers are all obvious possibilities. One awaits news of these, and of planned wet-lease of An-30s to other governments. One of the few known users in 1981 is the Romanian air force.

DIMENSIONS As An-24 except length 24,26 m (79 ft 7 in).

ENGINES As An-24RT.

WEIGHTS Basic operating (without role equipment) 15 590 kg (34,370 lb); typical camera installation 650 kg (1433 lb); max take-off 23 t (50,705 lb).

PERFORMANCE Max speed 540 km/h (335 mph); typical cruise at 6 km (19,685 ft) 430 km/h (267 mph); service ceiling 8,3 km (27,230 ft) (without APU operating, 7,3 km 23,950 ft); range with max fuel, no reserve, 2630 km (1634 miles) (oxygen for eight hours).

An-32 From the start of design of the An-24 O.K. Antonov has striven to improve performance from hot/high airfields, and instead of extending the small wing, or improving max lift-coefficient, has concentrated on power. With the An-32, announced May 1977, the already large engines were replaced by the most powerful variant of AI-20, an increase in propulsive power of some 100%. The thrust lines are 1,5 m (60 in) above the wing, much higher than required for fuselage clearance of the four-blade reversible propellers, which are AV-68 series increased in diameter to 4,7 m (15 ft 5 in). Modified tailplane, with span increased from 9,973 m (32 ft 8$\frac{3}{4}$ in) to 10,01 m (32 ft 10 in) and with fixed inverted slat along leading edge. Prototype, No 83966, otherwise had same airframe as An-26, though strengthened for greater thrust and weight, and with auxiliary turbojet replaced by TG-16M APU. The An-32 was said to have low-pressure tyres, though as it can operate at higher weights than An-26 (which has quite high tyre pressure).

In 1978 a drawing appeared in Czechoslovakia showing extended-chord outer wings with dogtooth discontinuities inboard, and two-section spoiler/lift-dumpers on the upper surface immediately ahead of outer flaps. At same time revealed that An-32 had been cleared to 1 tonne beyond design maximum weight of 26 tonnes, itself appreciably above that of other members of this family. Antonov had earlier stated An-32 was designed to operate from airfields at altitudes up to 4,5 km (14,750 ft) at up to ISA+25°C, and to fly 1100 km (683 mile) sectors with 3-tonne payload. India has placed the first export order for the An-32. It will replace Douglas C-47 and Fairchild C-119 transports.

DIMENSIONS As An-26.

ENGINES Two 5180 ehp Ivchyenko AI-20M

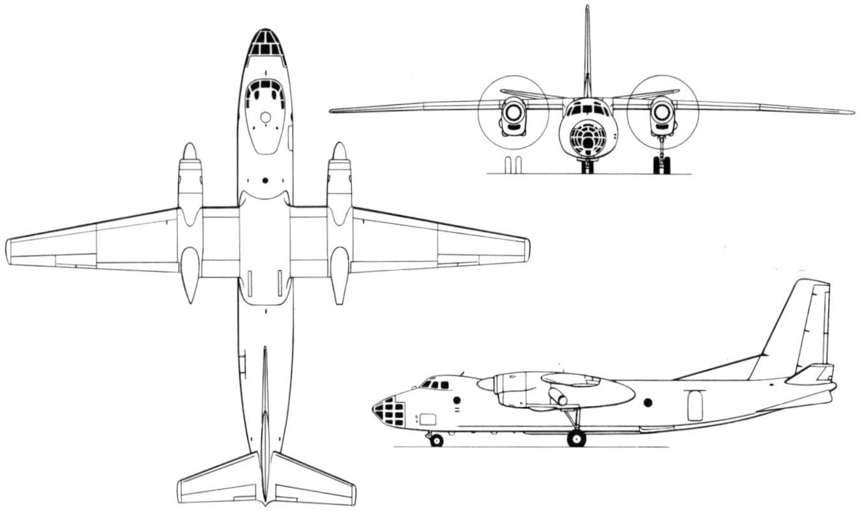

An-30

An-30

single-shaft turboprops.

WEIGHTS Empty estimated at 16 t (35,275 lb); max payload 6 t (13,228 lb); max take-off 27 t (59,524 lb).

PERFORMANCE Max cruising speed 530 km/h (329 mph); take-off (SL, concrete) 500 m (1640 ft); service ceiling 9,5 km (31,150 ft); range with 5-t payload (presumably no reserves) 1760 km (1094 miles).

An-72 This STOL airlifter is basically a smaller copy of the Boeing YC-14, though a simpler and more Russian aircraft. First flown at Kiev on 31 August 1977, the first prototype, No 19774, was the first jet built by Antonov's OKB. He insisted configuration was dictated by need to keep engines high above loose objects, and that USB (upper-surface blowing) was secondary. Little doubt USB was a prime objective, though Antonov had not by 1981 installed splitters to spread the turbofan efflux over a greater area of flap. (USB principle is based on self-attachment of jet, by Coanda effect, to upper surface of wing and flaps, even when latter are lowered). Geometrical similarity with YC-14 is near-total, though thrust-weight ratio corresponds to YC-14 in conventional, rather than STOL, operation.

An-72 designation is a typical Russian enigma. Designed to an Aeroflot study requirement, though it obviously has military potential. Larger than Antonov's twin-turboprops but smaller than An-12, ruling body cross-section is 2,2 m (86·6 in) square, width at floor being slightly less; available length is 9,0 m (29 ft $6\frac{1}{2}$ in). Pressure differential is higher than in other An types, for cruising at up to 10 km (32,800 ft). Rear fuselage upswept to high T-tail, broad underside comprising clamshell rear doors and main ramp/door of Antonov patented design, able to hinge as a ramp or swing down and forward on parallel arms under fuselage. Unlike other An types there is no retractable jack to support the rear fuselage. Main ramp/door bears pressure load, together with a small

An-32

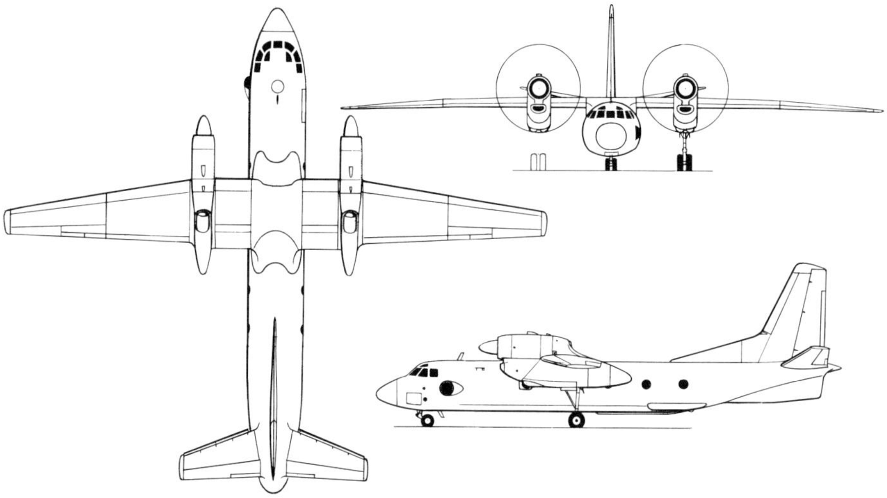
An-32

An-72 (No 2 aircraft)

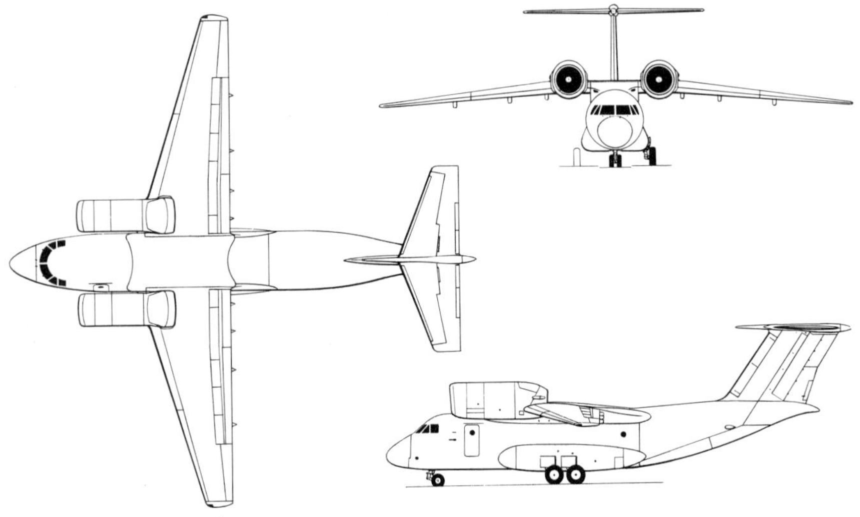

An-72 (original landing gear)

upward-hinged inner door, so that rear clamshells can be of light construction.

The wing, tapered on the leading edge, has thick machined skins, spot-welded, and startling anhedral of 10°. Engines are close alongside fuselage, with splayed and flattened nozzles blowing without turbulators or other guides across inner flaps, which are track-mounted double-slotted type. They must present a continuous upper surface in powered STOL mode, to keep flow attached, but Antonov has not revealed high-lift system in operation. Outer flaps are larger and triple-slotted. Ailerons, probably powered, are relatively small; and on each wing are five sections of spoiler, three of which give roll control; all five flick up on touchdown to act as lift-dumpers. The large tail has a double-hung powered rudder, downstream half being divided into upper and lower sections originally of equal area. The tailplane is fixed, and horn-balanced elevators each have two large tabs, and at rest hang trailing-edge down. Wing has powerful full-span slats, with hydraulic drive and variable profile, but tailplane just has a stainless-steel heated leading edge, like most Soviet transports. Entire wing box forms integral tankage; fuel is space-limited. Designed for rough strips, each main gear has tandem double (originally single) wheels on levered arms retracting upwards in the same way as those of An-8. Cabin conditioning, APU and refuelling sockets are in the large fairings, but though there is a prominent probe ahead of the fin/tailplane junction, this is for HF radio and a pitot head is hard to find. Avionic fit is comprehensive, and flight crew comprises just two pilots. Unlike earlier Antonovs, the flight deck has a central console with Western-style engine and flight-system controls between the pilots.

By mid-1979 Antonov had built two flight prototypes plus a static-test airframe, and 1000 hours had been flown in 300-odd flights. Antonov said programme was going 'better than the An-28,' and An-72 seems to be relatively troublefree despite reshaping rear fuselage of No 2 aircraft (SSSR-83966). The body now curves gracefully to a broad beaver-tail which finally turns slightly downwards. Canted ventral strakes are absent, and lower rear rudder is enlarged, root chord being greater. Production of either this aircraft or a near relative seems probable. In mid-1981 Antonov hinted OKB moving away from USB in favour of simpler and more conventional high-lift flaps.

DIMENSIONS Span 25,83 m (84 ft 9 in); length 26,58 m (87 ft 2½ in); height 8,24 m (27 ft 0½ in); wing area, about 110 m^2 (1200 ft^2).

ENGINES Two 6500 kg (14,330 lb) Lotarev D-36 three-shaft turbofans.

WEIGHTS Empty, in the region of 18 tonnes (40,000 lb); max payload 7500 kg (16,535 lb); max load 30,5 t (67,240 lb) (for operations from 1 km strip, 26,5 t 58,420 lb).

PERFORMANCE Max cruising speed 720 km/h (447 mph); take-off (max weight, concrete) 470 m (1542 ft); take-off (1-eng) 1200 m (3940 ft); range with max payload and 30-min reserve, 1000 km (621 miles); with max fuel and 30-min reserve, 3200 km (1990 miles).

Arkhangelskii

Aleksandr Aleksandrovich Arkhangelskii was born in December 1892, son of a professor at the University of Kazan. From 1911 he studied at MVTU under Zhukovskii. In the First World War he did tunnel tests and other work on Farmans and the underpowered *Svyatogor*. He joined TsAGI on its formation, and for the rest of his life worked closely with Tupolev. He handled much of the design of the ANT-3 and ANT-4, led the ANT-9 team, and was allowed to accompany Tupolev to the USA in 1932. On his return he plunged into the ANT-40, which became the SB-2 (described under Tupolev, though Arkhangelskii led the design). He also designed the vertical tail of the ANT-20. When Tupolev was arrested Arkhangelskii escaped suspicion, and became *de facto* head of the OKB; derivatives of the SB were entirely his creations. (For convenience most are covered in the Tupolev section, but the SBB, MMN and Ar-2 are included here.) When the new designation system was introduced in 1941 he was allowed the privilege of the SB-RK becoming Ar-2, but in the autumn of that year the OKB was evacuated and it reverted to Tupolev's name on the latter's release in 1942. Thereafter Arkhangelskii remained First Deputy Designer. He managed the definitive Tu-2S and led the structural team on the Tu-4 and its derivatives. He was effectively chief designer of all early Tupolev jet bombers, turboprop Tu-95, and derived civil transports. In 1945 he was elected to the Moscow Soviet, and in later life devoted much time to research and academic literature.

Ar-2 In 1937, with Tupolev behind bars, Arkhangelskii studied a second-generation development of the SB-2. His work centred on a more advanced wing, which by the use of better flaps could generate a much higher maximum lift-coefficient, and thus could be of reduced size. Combined with more powerful engines, in installations offering lower drag, the result was bound to be enhanced flight performance, keeping the bomber abreast of fighter speed and retaining its reputation, won in Spain, of being difficult to catch and shoot down. From the VVS came a fresh input: the impressive performance of another aircraft in Spain, the Ju 87A, led to a demand for a dive-bomber version of the SB-2.

By 1939 the design was ready, with an RK (slotted wing) having the inboard trailing edge in the form of large double-slotted flaps stressed for use as dive-brakes, as well as to keep down landing speed with a wing of only 40 m^2 area. Unfortunately the tight schedule forced this wing to be replaced by a simpler one closer to the original but nevertheless of new (NACA-22) cross-section, reduced span and area 8 m^2 less (it was aerodynamically related to that of colleague Petlyakov with the VI-100). Electrically actuated dive brakes were mounted under the leading edge (identical in geometry to those flown on the Ju 88 V7 and V8 in October 1938 and possibly known to Soviet intelligence). The structure was restressed, yet empty weight was actually reduced, compared with the SB-2bis or SB-3. The engines were the new M-105R, beautifully cowled and driving VISh-22Ye constant-speed propellers. To reduce drag the radiators were mounted behind the engines in the wing, fed by ram inlets in the leading edge outboard of the engines, the duct turning sharply inwards and then discharging warmed air rearwards through a grill in the upper surface. Because of the greater torque and thrust the chord of the fin and rudder were increased. Fuel capacity was 1490 lit, with provision for two strap-suspended overload cells of 370 lit each, a total of 2230 lit (490·5 gal), more than in standard SBs. Other changes included lengthened nacelles almost completely enclosing the retracted main wheels, a redesigned nose with central cupola mounting a ShKAS, and two more such weapons in a dorsal turret and rear ventral hatch. Normal bomb load was 6 × 100 kg, 2 × 250 kg or one of various 500-kg species, but loads up to 1500 kg could be carried with reduced fuel.

The prototype flew in 1940 as the **SB-RK** (even though the advanced wing had been dropped), redesignated Ar-2 the following year. Production was urgently put in hand, but only 200 had been delivered—direct to front-line units—when the factory had to be evacuated in about October 1941. No further production.

DIMENSIONS Span 18,5 m (60 ft 8½ in); length 12,5 m (41 ft 0 in); height 4,1 m (13 ft 5½ in); wing area 48,7 m^2 (524·2 ft^2).

ENGINES Two 1100 hp M-105R.

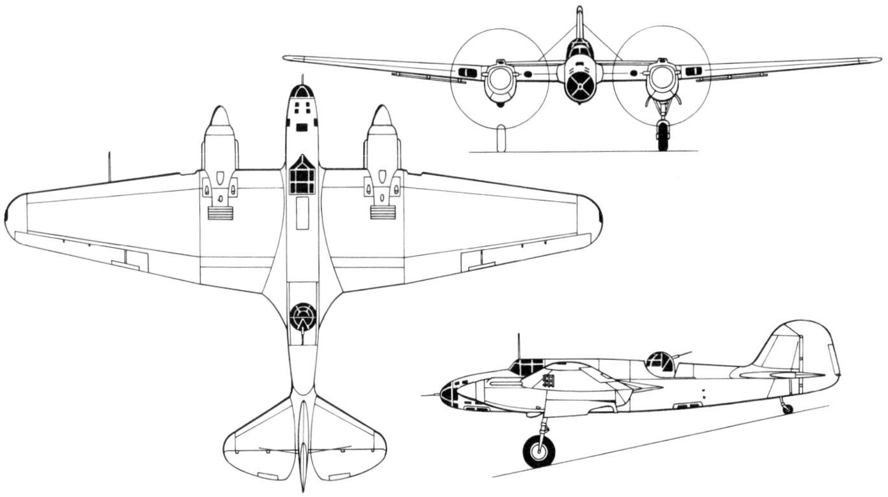

Ar-2

WEIGHTS Empty 4430 kg (9766 lb); normal gross 6650 kg (14,660 lb).
PERFORMANCE Max speed 480 km/h at 4,7 km (298 mph at 15,420 ft); cruise 410 km/h (255 mph); service ceiling 10,1 km (33,140 ft); range with 500 kg bombs, 1500 km (932 miles).

B Also called BB, this further development of the SB never got off the drawing board, but led to the SBB. Its main features were a better streamlined fuselage, smaller wing, turbo-charged engines and much higher performance. Intended to compete with the Pe-2.
DIMENSIONS Span 16,0 m (52 ft 6 in); length 12,27 m (40 ft 3 in); wing area 40,0 m^2 (430·5 ft^2).
ENGINES Two 1100 hp M-105R (2TK).
WEIGHTS Empty 4415 kg (9733 lb); loaded 5961 kg (13,142 lb).
PERFORMANCE Max speed 560 km/h at 5 km (348 mph at 16,400 ft); cruising speed 455 km/h (283 mph); range with max bombs 880 km (547 miles); service ceiling 14,1 km (46,260 ft).

MMN In 1939 Arkhangelskii produced a prototype designated MMN by putting a smaller wing and greatly modified fuselage on an SB-2bis. The wing was similar in span to that of the SB-RK but even smaller in area; curiously, the SB-2bis engine installation was retained, with radiators under the engines, though the engines were M-105s. The forward fuselage was almost perfectly streamlined, with a glazed upper portion (like a Japanese Ki-46-III), and the armament remained three SkKAS. The MMN was abandoned because of poor performance, high landing speed (160 km/h, 99·5 mph), and lack of development potential. Aeroflot used it subsequently as a trials and hack aircraft, calling it *Shchuka* (Pike).
DIMENSIONS Span 18,5 m (60 ft $8\frac{1}{2}$ in); length 12,78 m (41 ft $11\frac{1}{4}$ in); wing area 42,2 m^2 (452·2 ft^2).
ENGINES Two 1050 hp M-105.
WEIGHTS Empty 4820 kg (10,626 lb); fuel/oil 680 + 70 kg (1500 + 154 lb); normal loaded 6420 kg (14,153 lb).
PERFORMANCE Max speed 458 km/h at 4,2 km (285 mph at 13,780 ft); range 760 km (472 miles); service ceiling 9 km (29,530 ft).

Ar-2

SBB Derived from Type B, possibly borrowing from colleague Petlyakov, the SBB (high-speed short-range bomber) was the ultimate member of the SB family actually built. The wing was that of the B, and the engines were cooled by ducted radiators in the centre section with a leading-edge inlet and discharge grille in the upper surface behind the main spar. Oil coolers were outboard of the engines, so the arrangement was the reverse of that in the Ar-2. The fuselage was largely new. Crew comprised navigator (nose with ball-mounted ShKAS), pilot, and radio operator with ShKAS in a large glazed rear cockpit. New features were a twin-finned tail, with dihedral, and a retractible tail-wheel with twin doors. Wing profile was the popular NACA 22-series. Bombload was 880 kg, though 1000 could be carried for reduced range. The SBB was a handsome aircraft, flown in early 1941. After the Nazi invasion it was abandoned as offering no more than the Pe-2 and representing bad use of available resources.
DATA as for Type B, except engines without turbochargers, max speed 540 km/h (336 mph) and service ceiling 9,8 km (32,150 ft); these were flight-test figures.

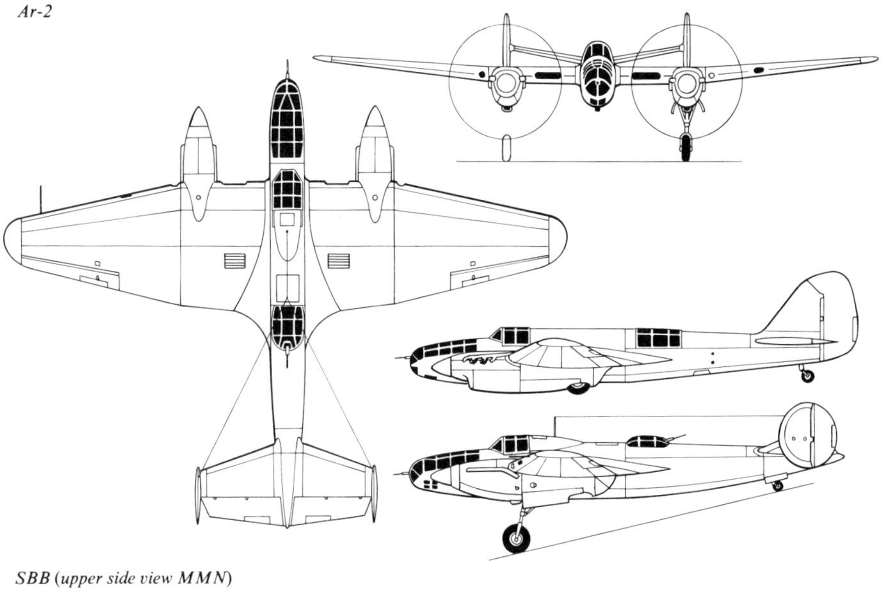

SBB (upper side view MMN)

Bartini

Roberto L. Bartini was born in Italy on 14 May 1897. In 1921 a founder of Italian Communist Party, and organized Milan workers into cells. Two years later Mussolini proscribed the party; Bartini, a qualified engineer, emigrated to the Soviet Union. He spent from 1924–1928 as an aviation engineer in the Red Army, and then joined the newly formed OSS 'Stal' OKB. By December 1930 he had shown such talent he was leading his own design group. He suffered political difficulties (apparently because he was of foreign birth) and in January 1938 was arrested. He escaped execution and was next heard of as a semi-free man with a 'special OKB' in Siberia in 1942. On his 70th birthday he received the Order of Lenin for services to aircraft design.

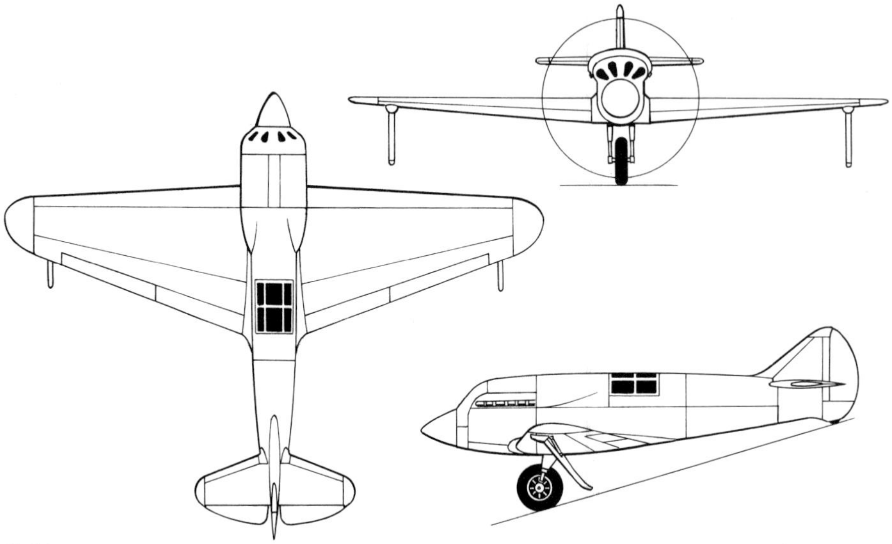

Stal-6

Stal-6 In the late 1920s Bartini had devoted great attention to steel construction, and in this experimental aircraft he went all out to create the fastest and most advanced machine possible. He put the proposal to TsKB in October 1930, but it was about 18 months before he obtained permission to build. The key to the design was a finely cowled water-cooled engine with surface-evaporation radiators in the double skin of the wings, an idea not uncommon at the time. Pilot view was bad, the fuselage rising over the engine to the same level as the top of the canopy so that there was no windscreen. Fuselage: steel tube and ply skin. The wings were of steel, with a double skin of Enerzh-6 back to the front spar to form the radiators. A pilot handcrank worked the large retractable landing wheel on the centreline and hinged sprung skids under the wingtips. First flight, autumn 1933, by A.B. Yumashyev who shared test-flying with P.M. Stefanovskii. First landing was in a cloud of steam, and cooling problems were as intractable as the bad view; but performance was exceptional.

DIMENSIONS Span 9,0 m (29 ft 6$\frac{3}{4}$ in); length 6,88 m (22 ft 6$\frac{3}{4}$ in); height 2,23 m (7 ft 4 in); wing area 14,3 m^2 (154 ft^2).
ENGINE 630 hp Curtiss V-1570 Conqueror V-12.
WEIGHTS Empty 850 kg (1874 lb); max 1080 kg (2381 lb).
PERFORMANCE Max speed 420 km/h (261 mph); max climb 21 m/s (4135 ft/min).

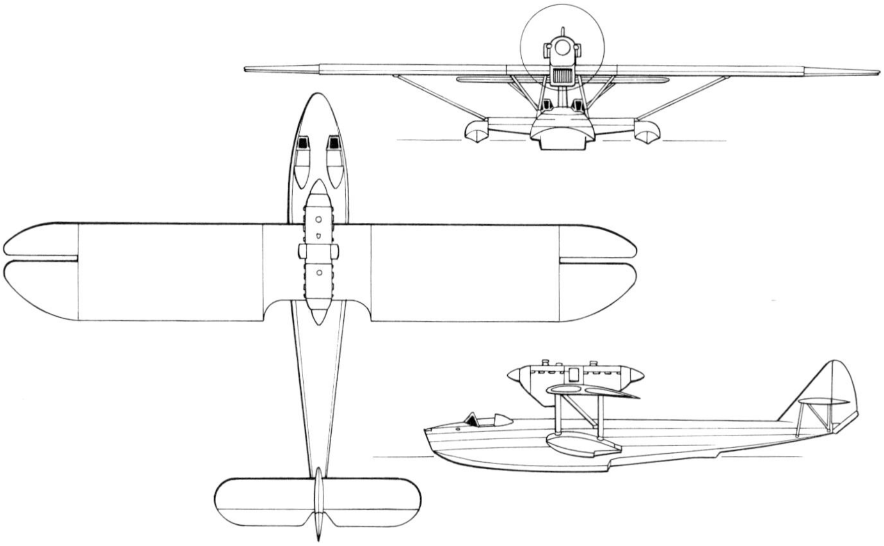

DAR

Stal-8 Petty jealousies plagued Bartini but he had a true friend in George Ordzhonikidze, who in winter 1932–1933 had agreed that the Italian could build a fighter derived from Stal-6, subject to the latter being a success. Stal-8 was almost the same airframe as Stal-6 but stronger for greater weight, and with a proper cockpit, 860 hp M-100A engine and two ShKAS in top decking. Design speed was 620 km/h (385 mph), appreciably faster than any other fighter of the day. Probably shortsightedly, VVS rejected the project (on grounds of vulnerability of cooling system) and the prototype remained about 90% finished in October 1934.

DAR Bartini was assigned in January 1934 to the ZOK NII GVF to lead the design of the *Dalnii Arkticheskii Razvyedchik* (long-range Arctic reconnaissance, the last word meaning a range of civil rather than military tasks). His

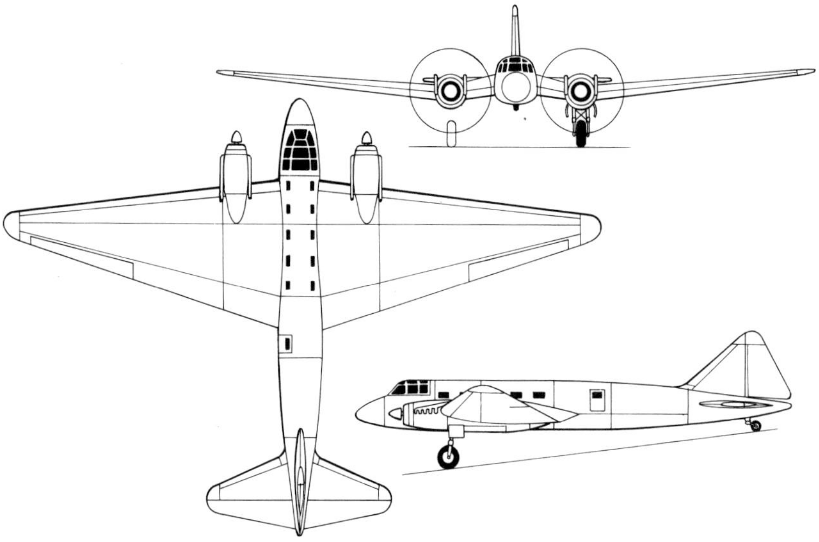

Stal-7

answer looked like a copy of the Wal, a machine familiar to the Soviet Union. In fact the DAR was entirely of stainless steel, and until a few months before first flight the intention was to shroud the tandem propellers to increase propulsive efficiency. The two engines were to be mounted in tandem in a centreline nacelle carried on struts above the hull, driving via coaxial shafts to two pusher propellers running in a large ring duct. Tests in a TsAGI tunnel confirmed the 'Bartini effect', but at an advanced stage of prototype erection (in the same hangar at the Andre Marti plant in Leningrad as the Sh-5) Bartini reluctantly bowed before the increased mass, vibration and sterilized area of wing, and switched to ordinary tandem engines. Highly stressed structure was Enerzh-6, with spot-welded skins, the trailing edge was hinged tip-to-tip to form slotted flaps, and the ailerons were patented pivoted wingtips made in front and rear sections. DAR was finished in late 1935 and launched at the small-boat port in Leningrad where famed Arctic pilot B.G. Chukhnovskii test-flew it in spring 1936 and was enthusiastic. Later it was fitted with a pair of steel-faced wooden skis, each 5,0 × 0,32 m, sprung by rubber bags along the sides of the hull, as previously tested on a Wal. Five ordered but no action taken to build; again a matter of personalities and politics as DAR was clearly sound, and better than a Wal (as it should have been, for it was 14 years later).

DIMENSIONS Span 27,4 m (89 ft $10\frac{3}{4}$ in); length 19,0 m (62 ft 4 in); wing area 100 m² (107·6 ft²).
ENGINES Tandem 860 hp Hispano-Suiza 12Ybrs V-12.
WEIGHTS Empty 4820 kg (10,626 lb); max 7200 kg (15,873 lb).
PERFORMANCE Max speed 240 km/h (149 mph); cruise 229 km/h (142 mph); range 2000 km (1243 miles); max endurance at reduced speed 20 h.

Stal-7 In 1934 Aeroflot issued a requirement for two modern transport aircraft, the larger to be a twin for 10/12 passengers. Two submissions were accepted for prototype construction, the ZIG and Bartini's Stal-7. The Italian was still heading the NII GVF team, and had already schemed a passenger transport to fly at 400 km/h in 1933. Design began in October 1934 and though of advanced form was to be a steel truss airframe with fabric covering. Great problems were met with the fuselage, which had 200 primary intersections between tubes of many cross-sections yet deflected excessively—especially in a bomber version which had to be studied in parallel to meet a Stalin decree. By 1935 the Stal-7 had become a light-alloy monocoque aircraft with a somewhat constricted body with sloping sides whose cabin was severely interrupted by the spars of the wing whose inner sections (of cambered profile with concave undersurface) sloped sharply up to pass through the fuselage in the mid-position. The one thing Stal-7 had was efficiency in speed, range and load (though a low wing and convenient cabin would hardly have hurt it). No fewer than 27 tanks of 7400 lit (1628 gal) capacity were installed, and flaps and gear were hydraulic. First flight spring 1937 by N.P. Shebanov, and measured tests showed better than predicted performance. A round-world flight was planned, but the aircraft crashed taking off on a full-load test. This resulted in Bartini's arrest. The aircraft was not repaired, under Yermolayev's direction, until 1939. On 28 August 1939 Shebanov, V.A. Matveyev and radio operator N.A. Baikuzov flew Moscow, Sverdlovsk, Sebastopol, Moscow (5068 km, 3149 miles) in 12 h 30 min 56 s, an average of 405 km/h (252 mph). Though the Stal-7 was obviously inconvenient as a passenger carrier, and the war halted the global-flight plan, its outstanding performance led to the DB-240 long-range bomber (see Yermolayev).

DIMENSIONS Span 23,0 m (75 ft $5\frac{1}{2}$ in); length 16,0 m (52 ft 6 in); wing area 72 m² (775 ft²).
ENGINES Two 760hp M-100 V-12, later (1939) 860 hp M-103.
WEIGHTS Empty 4800 kg (10,580 lb); fuel/oil 6000 kg (13,230 lb); max loaded 11 000 kg (24,250 lb).
PERFORMANCE Max speed 450 km/h (280 mph) at 3 km (9850 ft); cruise 360/380 km/h (224/236 mph); ceiling 10 km (32,800 ft); range 5000 km (3107 miles).

R Around 1942 Bartini was permitted to organise a special OKB in Siberia dedicated chiefly to jet interceptors. Chronologically the first design, never built, was this twin-jet flying wing, remarkably similar to Horten designs but with 35° sweep and with variable span and area achieved by telescopically extending the outer panels.

R-114 Project for vertically launched target-defence interceptor with 33° sweep and aerodynamics based on the R. Amazingly advanced for 1943 (pre-German data); 300 kg (661 lb) Glushko rocket, infra-red target tracker. Construction begun but not completed.

T-107 In 1944–1946 Bartini was switched to civil transport. Project for mid-wing double-decker with two ASh-82; recommended for manufacture 1945 but Il-12 chosen instead.

T-108 Unbuilt proposal for high-wing light cargo aircraft with twin 340 hp diesel engines.

T-117 Challenging project for high-capacity transport for main routes, begun in 1944. Schemed in two models, A for passengers, B for cargo. Latter with box fuselage and rear ramp/door, but model A chosen for construction with fully pressurized double-deck, double-bubble fuselage, both upper and lower lobes same size (1,45 m rad) giving body 5 m (16 ft 5 in) high and 2,9 m (114 in) wide. Packed with technically novel features, some even derived from Project R. Discontinued June 1948 when 80% complete, mainly because Tu-4 took all available engine production.

DIMENSIONS Span 35,0 m (114 ft 10 in); wing area 128 m² (1378 ft²).
ENGINES Two 2600 hp ASh-73.
WEIGHTS Empty 11 800 kg (26,015 lb); max loaded (crew 4, 80 passengers) 25 t (55,115 lb).
PERFORMANCE Estimated cruising speed 540 km/h (336 mph); ceiling 12 km (39,400 ft).

T-200 Heavy military transport with main cargo hold 5 m (16 ft 5 in) wide and 3 m (9 ft 11 in) high. Engines, four 2800 hp ASh piston engines (projected) and two 2270 kg RD-45 turbojets. Abounded in interesting features when final design submitted in October 1947, but Bartini's design OKB was closed the following year. In 1952 Bartini was appointed to strategic planning at the NII. In 1945–1961 he was author of five major projects—F, R, R-AL, Ye and A—with gross weights from 30 to 320 tonnes. Shavrov: 'These projects attracted much attention'.

Belyayev

Viktor Nikolayevich Belyayev was born in 1896. In 1920 he built a glider, unusual for the day in having wheels, and subsequently was accepted into TsAGI. There, among many other tasks, he built his own gliders in 1933, BP-2 and BP-3 (BP, tailless glider), which did well at Koktebel; a BP-2 (TsAGI-2) was towed behind an R-5 to Moscow. Subsequently Belyayev worked with Aviavnito and Aeroflot, OMOS, AGOS, KOSOS and the Tupolev OKB, gaining a reputation for versatility and for his technical papers. In 1934 he designed a transport with two tail booms each accommodating ten passengers (M-25 engines). His most important aircraft, DB-LK, was a military outgrowth of his 1934 transport, begun before he had a formal OKB (which dated from 1939). In 1940 he worked

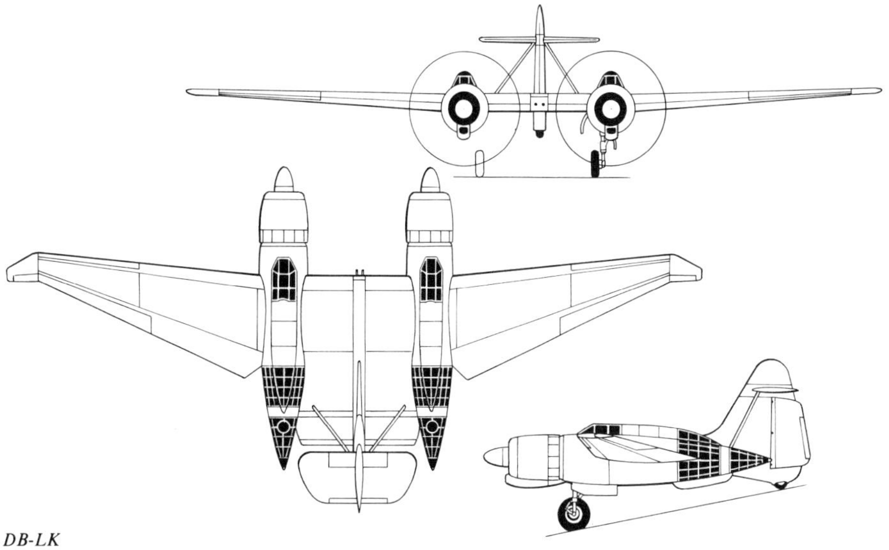

DB-LK

with V.I. Yukharin on a flexible-wing research aircraft with MV-6 engine.

DB-LK Ideal expression of Belyayev's search for inherently stable wing and superior geometrical efficiency. Initials stood for long-range bomber, flying wing, but it was far from being the latter. Two fuselages of minimum length joined by wing centre section of short span but large chord (5 m) and TsAGI MV-6bis (nothing to do with MV-6 engine) profile. Unrelated outer wings of Göttingen 387 profile, aspect ratio 8·2, swept forward 5°42′ at leading edge but with backswept tips, taper ratio 7. Frise ailerons with small extra sections on raked tips, slats on outer wings, 45° Zapp flaps. Five-spar light-alloy construction. Large strut-braced fin on centreline carrying near its top a very small (0,85 m²) tailplane to which were hinged relatively enormous (4,8 m² total) elevators with large tabs.

Crew of four: pilot in left fuselage, navigator in right, gunners in each tailcone, with access via roof hatches, to manage radio controls and two pairs of ShKAS. Two more ShKAS in leading edge on centreline, firing ahead with remote control within cone of 10°. Total 4500 rounds for six guns. Bomb load carried in fuselage immediately behind single-leg main gears: two FAB-1000 (1000 kg each), four FAB-250, two FAB-500 and two Der-19 or Der-20 containers, or 58 small bombs. (One drawing shows bomb bays in centre wing; another shows twin fins joining rectangular tailplane, neither according with aircraft as built.)

Prototype complete November 1939. Test pilot M.A. Nyukhtikov, lead engineer T.T. Samarin, test observer N.I. Shavrov. Ready for flight early 1940, with Mark Gallai joining team at this time. All-round performance outstanding, but project unable to displace Il-4 even in projected form with ASh-71 engines. (One report states incorrectly that DB-LK was viewed with distrust and 'did not fly until summer 1939'; at this time the prototype was still in the erection shop, and first flight was on schedule in 1940, according to Soviet records.)

DIMENSIONS Span 21,6 m (70 ft 10½ in); length 9,78 m (32 ft 1 in); height 3,65 m (11 ft 11¾ in); wing area 56,87 m² (612 ft²).

ENGINES Two 1100 hp M-88 in long-chord gilled cowlings driving 3,3 m (130 in) VISh-23D propellers.

WEIGHTS Empty 6004 kg (13,236 lb); fuel (3444 lit, 758 gal) 1048 kg (2310 lb); normal loaded 9061 kg (19,976 lb); max 10 672 kg (23,528 lb).

PERFORMANCE Max speed 395 km/h (245 mph) at sea level, 488 km/h (303 mph) at 5,1 km (16,730 ft); take-off speed 145 km/h (90 mph); landing speed 150 km/h (93 mph); max rate of climb 6,15 m/s (1210 ft/min); ceiling 8,5 km (27,890 ft); range with 1000 kg bombload, 1270 km (789 miles) at normal gross, 2900 km (1800 miles) at overload.

EI A typically advanced Belyayev design, EI (experimental fighter) was authorised August 1939 and prototype construction began the following year. It was a twin-boom pusher, planned for the new M-106 engine but carefully avoiding Stalin's personal involvement. The M-105 was intended to be fitted to the prototype, with wing-root radiators. Few details survive but it is known it was entirely of light-alloy stressed-skin construction, with the cockpit especially well streamlined into the nose. In the evacuation in October 1941 the prototype was destroyed, together with all drawings.

DIMENSIONS Span 11,4 m (37 ft 5 in); wing area 19 m² (204·5 ft²). No other data.

Bereznyak -Isayev

With designation **BI-1**, for the designers, the Soviet Union built the first rocket fighter in the world. Aleksandr Yakovlevich Bereznyak witnessed the tests of Dushkin's definitive rocket engine in 1939, and flight of RP-318 in early 1940. He discussed the practicability of a rocket-engined fighter with one of the lead engineers in Dushkin's group, Aleksei Mikhailovich Isayev. The latter had been a designer of RP-318 and was closely involved with Dushkin's next-generation engine, the D-1A. Fired with enthusiasm, Bereznyak went to V.F. Bolkhovitinov and in turn got the mercurial professor so convinced of the rightness of such a project that he took it to GUAP and to Stalin himself. He received permission to take Bereznyak and Isayev into his OKB and provide them with facilities and draughtsmen, and as the basic design had already been completed by Bereznyak it took a very short time in spring 1941 for drawings to be issued.

By this time the Kremlin had sanctioned construction of five prototypes of the BI-1 and of other rocket fighters (the letter was actually sent 9 July 1941) and working in shifts 24 hours a day the first unpowered machine was ready in 35 days. B.M. Kudrin was appointed test pilot, and made the first flight towed by a Pe-2 on 10 September 1941. He cast off and landed without incident. On 16 October the factory was evacu-

BI-1 (unpowered first prototype)

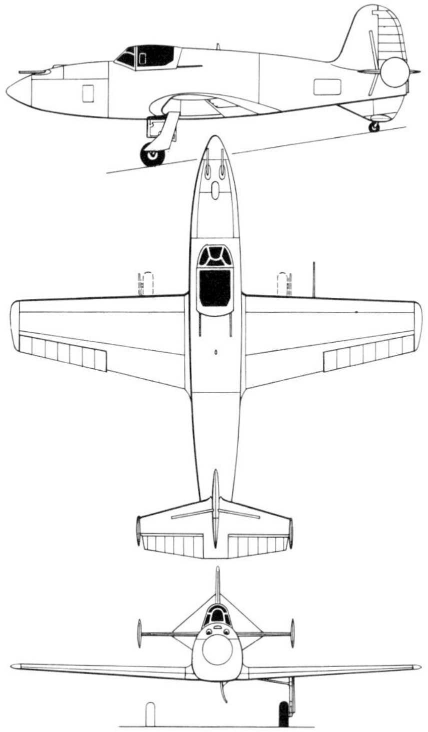

BI-1

ated (it eventually found a home in an incomplete building near Sverdlovsk) and because of illness Kudrin was replaced by G.Y. Bakhchivandzhi, an unusually technically qualified test pilot. The first engine was installed during January 1942, but was destroyed in an explosion on 20 February which injured Bakhchivandzhi and three technicians. Direct management was thenceforward exercised by VVS and TsAGI's Prof Puishnov, whose tunnels had been used to prove the aerodynamics a year earlier. Another pilot, K.A. Gruzdyev, was appointed to help Bakhchivandzhi, and on 15 May 1942 the latter made the first proper flight, in the third prototype, after a week of taxi and hop tests.

The BI-1 first flew on skis, attached to the original main legs and retracting inwards by compressed air which also worked the split flaps. The latter were almost the only metal parts of the airframe, structure being a smooth wooden assembly with painted fabric skin over moulded ply. Tailwheel mounted on ventral fin (BI-1 was prone to nose over) and tailplane carried end-plate auxiliary fins and on powered prototypes was braced by struts to both upper and lower fins. Nitric acid and kerosene fed from welded steel cylinders in centre fuselage by nitrogen bottles in nose, full-thrust endurance 80 sec. Armament of two ShVAK, each with 45 rounds, in upper nose above gas bottles. Canopy slid to rear, and radio installed.

Prolonged delays caused mainly by acid corrosion, with at least two minor spillages or explosions. By March 1943 seven BI-1s had been completed, making numerous towed flights, but powered flights 2 to 6 not accomplished until February/March 1943. On 21 March height of 3 km (9843 ft) reached in measured time of 30 seconds. On 27 March, on flight No 7, Bakhchivandzhi made high-speed run at low level and went straight into ground. TsAGI had not discovered existence of severe pitch-down at high speeds, and subsequently failed to find a solution. Production batch of 50 BI-1 abandoned, but prototypes continued active, modified with series of later Dushkin engines with large and small (cruise) thrust chambers, with aircraft designations BI-2, BI-3 and BI-7 (originally BI-1 Nos 2, 3 and 7). Pilots were Gruzdyev, Kudrin and M.K. Bazhkalov. Air force interest had waned in 1943, mainly because of the obviously long-term nature of development, but flying still going on at end of war. Handling excellent, but pilots understandably regarded propulsion as hazardous. At least one BI-1 preserved.

DIMENSIONS Span (Nos 1, 2) 6,48 m (21 ft 3 in), (No 3 and probably subsequent) 6,6 m (21 ft 8 in); length (1, 2) 6,4 m (21 ft 0 in), (3) 6935 m (22 ft 9 in); wing area (1, 2) 7,0 m^2 (75·3 ft^2).

ENGINE (3) One RNII (Dushkin and Shtokolov) D-1A-1100 bi-propellant rocket with sea-level thrust of 1100 kg (2425 lb).

WEIGHTS Empty (1) 462 kg (1019 lb), (3) 790 kg (1742 lb), (series) 805 kg (1775 lb); acid 135 kg (298 lb), kerosene 570 kg (1257 lb); loaded 1650 kg (3638 lb); max loaded 1683 kg (3710 lb).

PERFORMANCE Max speed (est) originally 800 km/h (497 mph), later (early 1943) 900 km/h (559 mph); time to accelerate 800 to 900 km/h, 20 s; take-off 400 m (1310 ft); initial climb 82 m/s (16,400 ft/min); landing speed 143 km/h (89 mph).

Beriev

G. M. Beriev reading Flight

Few Soviet constructors have had such a straightforward and successful career as Georgii Mikhailovich Beriev. A Georgian, he was born in 1902 and grew up in Tiflis (Tbilisi), and gained acceptance to Leningrad Polytechnic Institute in turbulent 1919. On graduation he joined Aviatrust, and when Richard was appointed to form a design group for marine aircraft, in 1928, Beriev was one of 20 qualified engineers assigned to him. In 1929 he was invited to form a design section for marine aircraft within TsKB in Moscow, and he went to Taganrog to undertake improvements to MBR-4 (license-built S.62). Soviet flying boats were not impressive, and in light reconnaissance and utility class the obsolescent Italian machine was only equipment available. Beriev sought permission to build an improved replacement, and this, MBR-2, launched his own OKB in 1932. Ever since (except for 1942–1945) it has been located at Taganrog, and from 1948 has had a monopoly of marine aircraft in the Soviet Union. His last known design was a landplane, the Be-30, and it was unsuccessful. He died in July 1979, and his OKB is believed to be inactive.

MBR-4 Though in no way a Beriev design, this flying boat did incorporate his work, undertaken at the Taganrog factory in 1930–1931. A single-engined pusher biplane, it was originally the Savoia-Marchetti S.62bis, which in turn had followed the S.16 as the most common imported light flying boat. After building 22 to the Italian design, a further 29 were built of the MBR-4 version. The specification is the same as for the S.62bis except for empty and gross weights being 200 kg greater and performance slightly worse. Presumably it carried more equipment.

DIMENSIONS Span 16,6 m (54 ft 5½ in); length 12,26 m (40 ft 2½ in); wing area 69,52 m^2 (748 ft^2).

ENGINE One 750 hp Isotta-Fraschini Asso V-12.

WEIGHTS Empty 2840 kg (6261 lb); fuel/oil 795+40 kg (1753+88 lb); loaded 4300 kg (9480 lb).

PERFORMANCE Max speed 220 km/h (137 mph); cruise 180 km/h (112 mph); range 900 km (560 miles).

MBR-2 This was at once Beriev's first and most important design, being one of a select number of flying boats to achieve a four-figure production total. Designation stood for *Morskoi Blizhnii Razvyedchik*, marine short-range reconnaissance. Beriev began the design at TsKB in May 1931, assisted by I.V. Ostoslavskii, M.P. Mogilyevskii and A.N. Dobrovolskii, and the prototype was built at the old Menzhinskii works in Moscow in 1932. Straightforward high-wing monoplane with wing thick enough to be cantilever (MOS-27 profile, 18% at root and 10% at tip). Structure entirely of wood except for light-alloy tail unit (based on MBR-4) and ailerons, with fabric covering. Skin mainly 3 mm ply elsewhere except for heavy sections along four hull chines, step and main frames. Hull interior unobstructed for easy access between pilot cockpit (one or two seats side-by-side) and open gun cockpits at bow and in rear fuselage. M-17b engine mounted on pylon chiefly of steel tubes and driving four-blade pusher propeller. Four tanks for 750 lit (165 gal) between wing centre-section spars at 18 and 50% chord. A.K. Belenkov designed a beaching chassis whose main vertical strut on each side clipped into a fixture under the front spar near the root, with a separate auxiliary two-wheel truck placed under the rear step. With small changes this chassis could be used as ski landing gear.

MBR-2 (prototype)

MBR-2

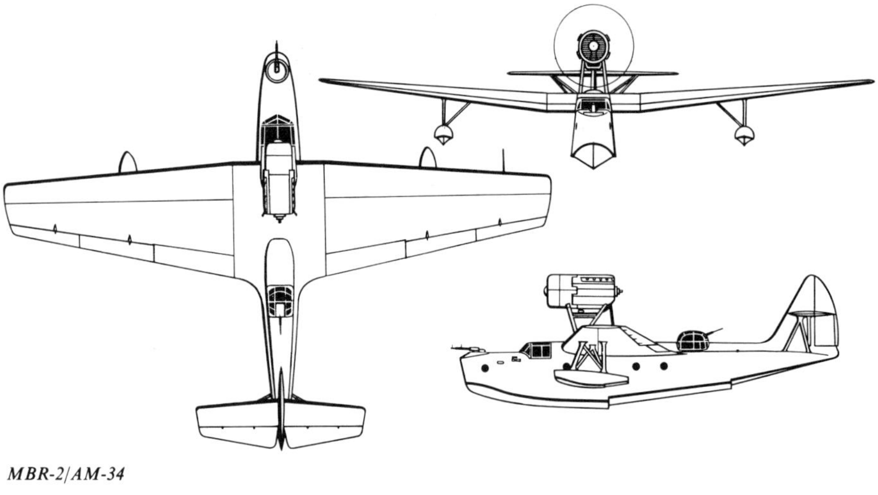

MBR-2/AM-34

Prototype taken in sections to Sevastopol and first flown there by B. Bukhgolts in October 1932. At about this time Beriev set up his own OKB at Taganrog, and all subsequent engineering and production was centred there. From the first it was evident MBR-2 was robust and efficient, and first version (about 100) was an armed MA variant. The first delivery took place in spring 1934, and the type was to serve for 30 years. Normal mission crew was three, the front gunner doubling as navigator although routine method was to keep coast in sight. Rear gunner, armed with one PV-1 like partner, manned radio which was standard in all MBRs. Max bombload 500 kg (1102 lb), tested on prototype, but normal load 300 kg (661 lb) carried externally under inner wings. Before end of 1934 Taganrog plant was also in modest production with civil version for Aeroflot, **MP-1** (*Morskoi Passazhirskii*). Central cabin with wall trim, soundproofing and thermal lining, and six seats (not made by OKB) for six passengers, boarding via hatch replacing rear cockpit of military version. Bow cockpit usually deleted and, thanks to better streamlining, speed higher than for original model. Another model was **MP-1T** freighter, identical to original military version but with armament provisions deleted. Later a flat floor was added in Aeroflot workshops.

In 1934 Beriev began a major improvement programme which resulted in the major production version; no separate designation, though sometimes called MBR-2 AM-34 from the new engine. This was installed in a completely different nacelle with a circular ducted radiator at the front in place of the car-type originally used. New propeller with two or four blades. Tail was redesigned, looking even more like that of S.62bis, and hull was made deeper, with larger enclosed cockpit and a retractable glazed turret for rear gunner, traversed by hand. Structure strengthened for greater weights and speeds, fuel load varying between 540 lit (original standard), 515 (MP-1), 580 (initial AM-34 batch), 670 (148 gal) and 886 (195 gal). Bomb load of 500 kg routinely carried, often as depth charges, and PV-1s replaced by ShKAS. This variant remained in production until 1942, when Taganrog had to be evacuated. By that time total production had reached 1300 of all variants, which were standard equipment with the 15th Reconnaissance Regt of the Red Banner (Baltic) Fleet, 119th Air Regt of the Black Sea Fleet, the 115th Aviation Regt in the Pacific Fleet and numerous utility, transport and training units. Several dozen M-17b-powered aircraft were rebuilt with new tails, and at least an equal number were converted as **BU** five-seaters for co-operation with fast patrol and torpedo boats.

The civil counterpart was **MP-1bis**, delivered from 1937. They quickly became the most important water-based transports, serving on short hauls from coastal bases and throughout the Siberian river system. In May 1937 an MP-1bis flown by woman-pilot P.D. Osipyenko set up several class records including climbs to 8864 m (29,081 ft), and to 7009 m (22,995 ft) with 1 tonne payload. On 2 July 1937 she flew with an all-women crew of three non-stop 2416 km (1501 miles) over the route Sevastopol, Kiev, Novgorod, Arkhangelsk in 10 h 33 min. The only other major variant was a single prototype flown in 1937 with M-103 engine. Significant increase in performance, but no spare engines

MBR-2/AM-34

available to support production.

DIMENSIONS Span 19,0 m (62 ft 4 in); length 13,5 m (44 ft 3¾ in); wing area 55 m² (592 ft²).

ENGINE One 500/730 hp BMW VIF (prototype), or 500/730 hp M-17b, or 750/830 hp AM-34B (MP-1bis) or AM-34NB (military). One aircraft, 850/1000 hp M-103. All V-12 water-cooled.

WEIGHTS Empty (prototype) 2450 kg, (M-17b) 2475 kg (5456 lb), (MP-1) 2640 kg (5820 lb), (MP-1T) 2525 kg, (AM-34NB) 2718 kg (5992 lb), (MP-1bis) 3119 kg (6876 lb); normal loaded (prototype) 3700 kg, (most variants) 4100 kg (9039 lb), (MP-1 overload) 4500 kg (9921 lb), (MP-1bis) 4640 kg (10,230 lb).

PERFORMANCE Max speed (prototype) 208 km/h, (M-17b) 203 km/h (126 mph), (MP-1) 214 km/h (133 mph), (AM-34NB) 238 km/h (148 mph), (MP-1bis) 260 km/h (162 mph), (M-103) 295 km/h (183 mph); typical cruise 160 km/h (100 mph); range (M-17b) 650 km (404 miles), (AM-34NB) 800 km (497 miles), MP-1bis 750 km (466 miles); normal endurance (typical) 5 h.

KOR-1

KOR-1 (Be-2) Under Stalin's first Five-Year Plan the Soviet Navy had to be dramatically overhauled and modernised, one provision being installation of (British) catapults on major surface vessels. No time to produce a new aeroplane for shipboard use; the Heinkel HD55 was adopted as the KR-1 (*Korabelnii Razvyedchik*, shipboard reconnaissance). Though adequate, the KR-1 was foreign and could be improved upon in many ways, and Beriev planned a successor as the Be-2 (bureau designation). Simple metal airframe with biplane wings folding to rear, with central float. Fuselage welded from steel tubes, with fabric covering apart from light-alloy engine cowl (with plated front with air cooling apertures ahead of cylinders) and front upper decking. Dural wings with two main spars and Warren-truss ribs, again with fabric covering, and hollow I-struts. Duralumin floats with flush riveting. Ailerons on upper wings, pneumatic landing flaps on lower. Tandem cock-

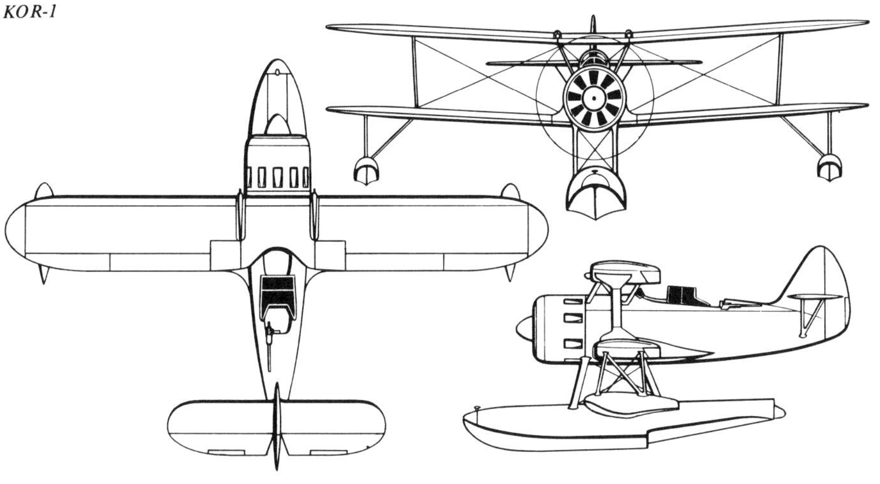

KOR-1

pits for pilot and observer/radio/gunner, with dual flight controls. Two windshields or, more often, glazed superstructure around front of large rear cockpit. Normally equipped with two forward-firing ShKAS in fairings above upper centre section with magazines under dural wing-skin covers, single ShKAS aimed by gunner, folding down into recess ahead of fin, and lower-wing racks for two FAB-100 bombs.

First flight, probably about April 1936; service delivery 1937. Considerable problems with seaworthiness, structural deflection afloat and during catapult shots, and also with engine overheating. Though production continued, at least 300 being built by 1940, the release for service use in 1937, with service designation KOR-1 was only partial. Most were used for shoreline patrol and customs duties. Beriev strove to rectify defects, and in 1939 obtained full release for the KOR-1 for naval aviation use without armament and with normal take-offs only. In 1939 a landplane version, with no separate designation, was also flown. Though this was ungainly, it was free from structural restrictions. Some were converted seaplanes. Both sea and land versions were still in service in June 1941, and the latter was pressed into use as a close-support and attack aircraft on the Romanian and Bessarabian fronts.

DIMENSIONS Span 11,0 m (36 ft 1 in); length 8,67 m (28 ft $5\frac{1}{2}$ in), (landplane) 7,2 m (23 ft $7\frac{1}{2}$ in); wing area 29,3 m^2 (315·4 ft^2).

ENGINE One 635/700 hp M-25 driving three-blade metal (Hamilton) propeller.

WEIGHTS (Seaplane) Empty 1800 kg (3968 lb); fuel/oil 293 kg (646 lb); loaded 2486 kg (5480 lb), overload with bombs 2686 kg (5922 lb).

PERFORMANCE (Seaplane) Max speed 245 km/h (152 mph) at sea level, 277 km/h (172 mph) at 2 km (6560 ft); climb 1 km (3280 ft) in 3·2 min; ceiling 6,6 km (21,650 ft); range 530/1000 km (329/621 miles) depending on fuel and overload clearance.

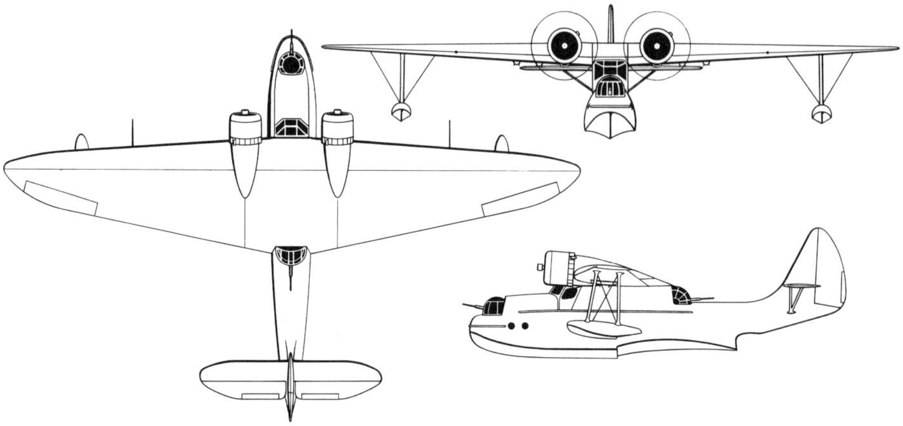

MDR-5

MDR-5 (No 2 aircraft)

MDR-5 Tupolev's structural designers and American imports had shown superiority of stressed-skin monoplane flying boats by the mid-1930s, and Beriev was one of those who responded to a 1936 demand for a Russian flying boat for long-range reconnaissance. MDR-5, *Morskoi Dalnii Razvyedchik* = Marine Long-range Reconnaissance, and also called **MS-5** (Marine Aeroplane 5), was a completely fresh design by Beriev's OKB though it was similar to the Sikorsky S-43 which Beriev inspected closely before beginning the design. He considered amphibian landing gear, but for the first MDR-5 provided only for beaching chassis with three twin-wheel units each independently attached to the hull.

Structure entirely duralumin, though control surfaces were fabric-covered. Crew of five comprised bow gunner, pilot, navigator, radio operator and observer/gunner. Wing of MOS-2718 profile with four spars and containing eight fuel tanks. Aspect ratio 7·96. Wing mounted on raised part of hull behind side-by-side cockpit (S-43 had wide but shallow hull and wing on pylon) with gun turret housing retractable ShKAS (usually a twin installation) at rear of this elevated portion. A second ShKAS in bow turret, traversed by hand. Eight racks under wing at extremity of centre section for total of 1000 kg (2205 lb) bombs, depth charges or other stores. Engines in long-chord cowlings with gills, driving VISh-3 three-blade constant speed propellers. Special effort made to minimise aileron span to increase size of electrically driven flaps, because wing loading was significantly higher than previous Russian practice.

Two prototypes built, the first flying in 1938. The second was an amphibian, with landing gear similar in geometry to that of the S-43. On test, the MDR-5 proved itself generally satisfactory, but the nose of the stabilizing floats had to be extended 0,3 m (1 ft) forwards to improve seaworthiness, and the amphibian variant was modified by making the wheels completely recessed when retracted. Had it not been for the MDR-6 this design would probably have been produced in quantity.

DIMENSIONS Span 25,0 m (82 ft $0\frac{1}{2}$ in); length 15,88 m (52 ft $1\frac{1}{4}$ in); wing area 78,5 m^2 (845 ft^2).

ENGINES Two 950 hp M-87A.

WEIGHTS Empty (flying boat) 6083 kg (13,410 lb); fuel either 1917 or 2135 kg (4226 or 4707 lb); loaded 8000 kg (17,637 lb), (max fuel and bombs) 9200 kg (20,282 lb).

PERFORMANCE Max speed 283 km/h (176 mph) at sea level, 345 km/h (214 mph) at rated height; landing speed 120 km/h (74·5 mph); ceiling 8150 m (26,740 ft); range (normal fuel) 2415 km (1500 miles).

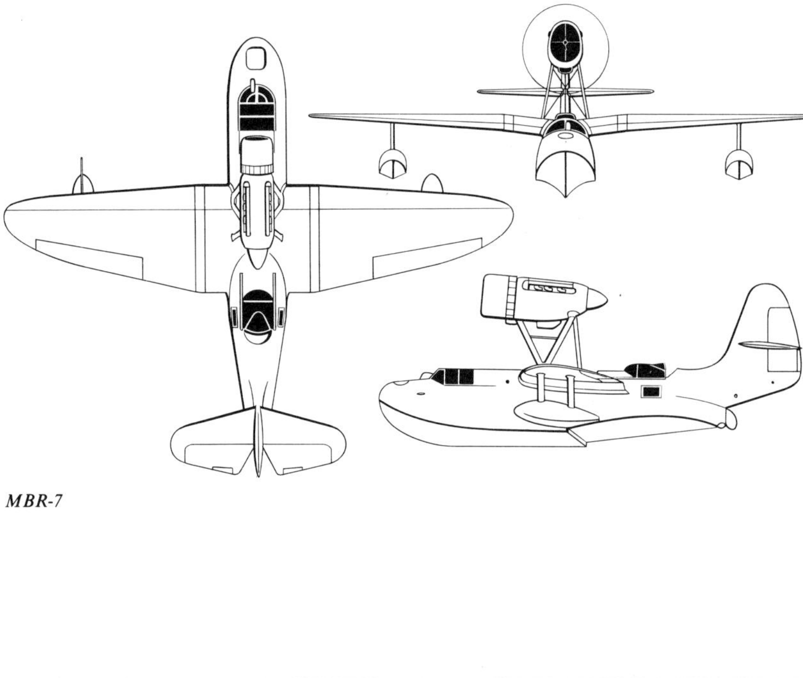

MBR-7

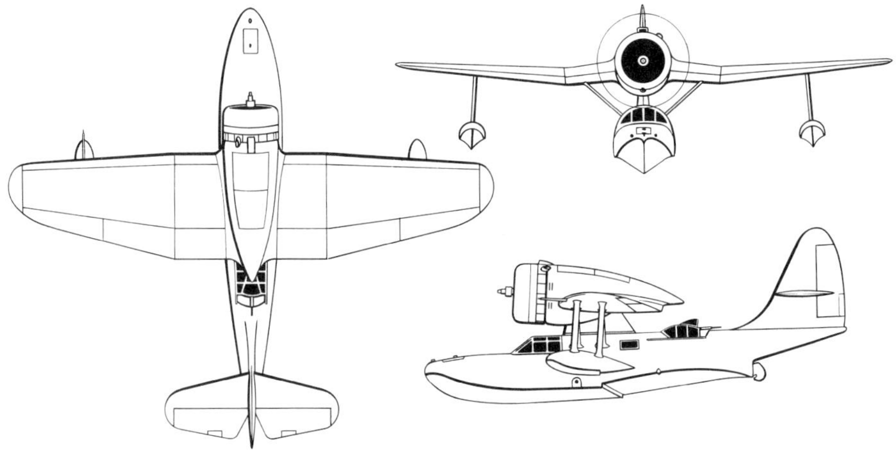

KOR-2, Be-4

KOR-2, Be-4

MBR-7 Also designated **MS-8** (Marine Aeroplane 8), this was a natural outgrowth of the M-103-engined MBR-2 which had flown in 1937. Though prospects of getting production engines were poor, Beriev completely redesigned the MBR-2 with a smaller and more modern airframe, improved not only aerodynamically but also hydrodynamically with a long planing bottom with a step amidships offering reduced drag, and a second step curving down right at the stern. Structure remained all-wood, the hull being covered with glued fabric without application of dope. Bow and tail duralumin, control surfaces with fabric covering, and steel pick-ups for beaching chassis which differed from that of MBR-2. Wing of gull form, with electrically driven flaps. Crew of two only, with glazing over pilot in single-place cockpit, and rear hull decking cranked by screwthread to form shield for observer/gunner with ShKAS. Another ShKAS fixed in nose, fired by pilot. Wing racks for normal bombload of four FAB-100 plus two FAB-50. Prototype built at Taganrog 1938, and flew early 1939. Handling at speeds over 200 km/h excellent, but as weight was only slightly less than MBR-2 and wing area had been cut to less than half, pilots found take-off and landing difficult. This was main reason for rejection. No bureau number known, though Be-3 would be logical.

DIMENSIONS Span 13,0 m (42 ft 8 in); length 10,6 m (34 ft 9¼ in); wing area 26 m² (280 ft²).

ENGINE One 960 hp M-103, driving large two-blade VISh-2PT constant-speed propeller.

WEIGHTS Empty 2418 kg (5331 lb); fuel 398 kg (877 lb); loaded 3168 kg (6984 lb), (overload, with bombs) 3600 kg (7937 lb).

PERFORMANCE Max speed 310 km/h (193 mph) at sea level, 376 km/h (234 mph) at rated height; climb 2·4 min to 1 km, 7·9 min to 2 km; ceiling 8500 m (27,890 ft); range 720/1215 km (447/755 miles) depending on fuel and overload.

KOR-2 (Be-4) Distressed at shortcomings of KOR-1, Beriev was determined to create a first-class replacement. Stressed-skin construction decided from outset of planning in August 1939, but increased size of monoplane caused arguments. Eventually Beriev achieved a span little greater than KOR-1, and go-ahead permitted before end of 1939.

Hull entirely duralumin, with efficient planing bottom similar hydrodynamically to MBR-7, with main V-step and curving pointed rear step followed by water rudder with attachment for beaching tailwheel. Side anchorages for beaching chassis (also study for amphibian, using an almost identical chassis as landing gear, retracting into hull recesses, not built). Crew of three: pilot and navigator/radio operator side-by-side (optional dual control) in enclosed cockpit, observer/gunner in glazed rear cockpit with pivoted rear hood forming windshield for gunnery. One ShKAS in rear cockpit, another fixed in bows aimed by pilot. In overload condition (one report states 'overload variant') provision for four FAB-100 or same mass (400 kg, 882 lb) of other stores on racks at extremities of centre section.

Centre section mounted on centreline pylon, braced by two struts each side and with 7° anhedral. Housed fuel tankage and electrically driven split flaps, with additional split flaps on outer panels which could be folded manually on skewed hinges to lie along rear hull with floats outward. Relatively large engine nacelle set at positive angle of 5°, with all-round cooling gills; nacelle interior layout similar to MDR-5 but extended to behind trailing edge. Fabric-covered control surfaces.

Prototype tested early 1941 and demonstrated excellent handling with no serious shortcomings. Tests included catapulting and armament trials, but interrupted by evacuation of test establishment at Sevastopol in late spring 1942. By this time the first two production aircraft were being tested by GUSMP pilot Malkov. Many (about 30) unfinished KOR-2s destroyed at Taganrog during evacuation. In 1943 production restarted in Siberia, at Krasnoyarsk, and small number delivered to completion in mid-1945. Described as 'average series', possibly 100. They served with the MA, including catapult duties on warships.

DIMENSIONS Span 12,0 m (39 ft 4½ in); length 10,5 m (34 ft 5¼ in); height (keel/fin-tip) 4,04 m (13 ft 3 in); wing area 25,5 m² (274·5 ft²).

ENGINE One 1000 hp M-62 driving VISh-105-62 or AV-24 three-blade c/s propeller.

WEIGHTS Empty 2082 km (4590 lb); fuel 315 kg (694 lb); loaded 2760 kg (6085 lb).

PERFORMANCE Max speed 310 km/h (193 mph) at sea level, 356 km/h (221 mph) at 4,7 km 15, 420 ft); climb 2 min to 1 km, 12 min to 5 km; ceiling 8100 m (26,575 ft); range 550/1150 km (342/716 miles) depending on use of overload fuel.

Be-8 There is evidence Beriev designed this neat utility transport amphibian during the war, but no attempt to build a prototype was made until his team returned to Taganrog in 1944–1945. Construction probably began the following year, and the first Be-8 flew in July 1947. Its design was reminiscent of the Be-4 (KOR-2) and possibly some portions may have been identical. The main differences were that the hull was wider and longer, the span considerably greater, and the engine less powerful.

Structure was dural stressed-skin throughout, though control surfaces fabric-covered. The wing had two main spars and housed four fuel

Be-8

cells. Flaps of the slotted type with electric drive. Pilot's cockpit seated two, with dual control. Main cabin heated by air from engine exhaust muffs, and could be arranged for 400 kg (882 lb) cargo, six passengers, or a wide range of special tasks including photo-survey, magnetometer prospecting and ambulance. The only known photographs show military markings but not the planned armament of one fixed and one movable guns. Though performance unspectacular, Be-8 fitted adequately into environment and Aeroflot requirement, and other reasons probably restricted production to only two aircraft, in addition to prototype.

In early 1950s the latter was chosen to test the hydrofoils being developed at TsAGI. These embraced both the surface-piercing (Supramar) type and also the broad, shallow depth-effect foils which were incorporated in *Meteor* and *Kometa* series of commercial hydrofoil ships.

DIMENSIONS Span 19,0 m (62 ft 4 in); length 13,0 m (42 ft 8 in); wing area 40 m² (430·6 ft²).
ENGINE One 700 hp ASh-21 driving AV-24 propeller.
WEIGHTS Empty 2815 kg (6206 lb); fuel 352 kg (776 lb); loaded 3624 kg (7989 lb).
PERFORMANCE Max speed 266 km/h (165 mph) at 1800 m (5900 ft); cruise 220 km/h (137 mph); ceiling 5,5 km (18,050 ft); range 1205 km (749 miles).

LL-143 Though Beriev's OKB worked under great difficulties at Krasnoyarsk, immense demands were made and the depleted team of experienced engineers were assigned the most challenging task ever put to Soviet designers of marine aircraft. The overdue need for a modern and capable long-range flying boat was to be met by this OKB, which called the aircraft LL-143 (Flying Boat, January 1943). It was to lead to the Be-6, by far the most capable and useful marine aircraft produced by Soviet designers apart from Beriev's later Be-12.

Beriev had sketched the gull-wing layout in 1942, and by April 1943 the first engineering drawings were issued. Stressed-skin duralumin structure throughout, except for fabric-covered control surfaces. Large and deep hull with transverse front step and curved V second step with water rudder synchronized with two main air rudders carried vertically (unlike generally similar Martin 162) on dihedral tailplane carried on shallow pylon above rear of hull. Skin plates

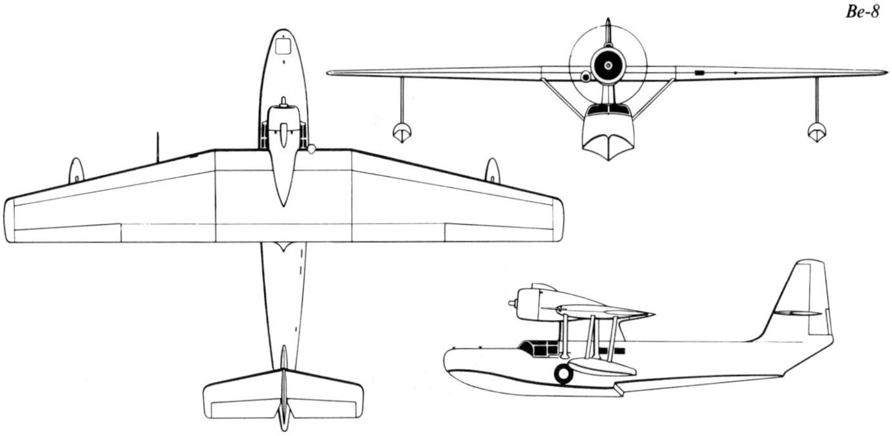

Be-8

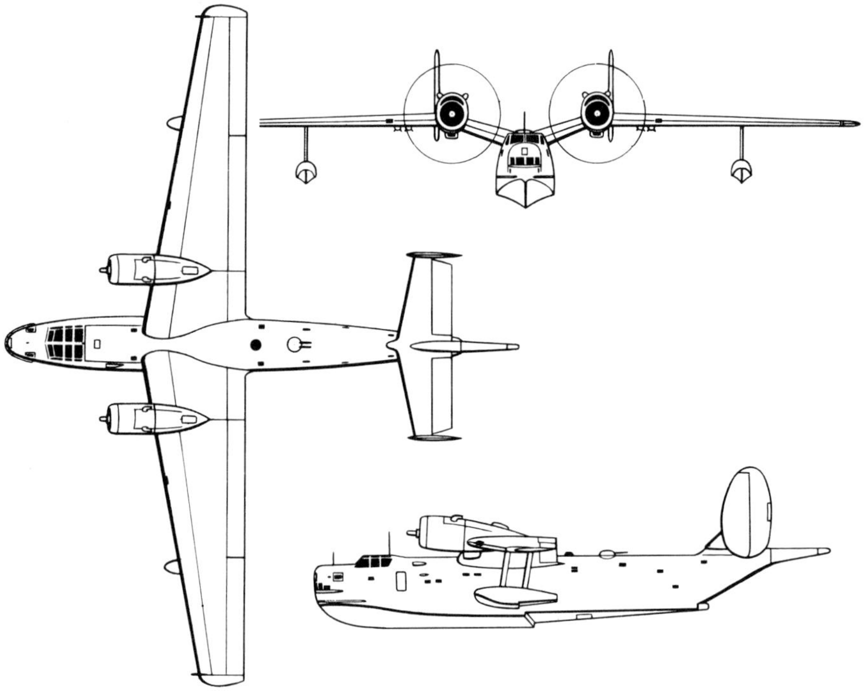

Be-6

Be-6

Be-6 on beaching chassis

flush-riveted to stringers on 44 frames, with planing bottom containing deep keel and transverse bulkheads (each with rubber-sealed hatch) forming eight watertight compartments. Provision for three-unit twin-wheel beaching chassis. Stabilizing floats on two fixed struts, two steps, divided into four watertight compartments; Beriev commented 'loss of float means loss of aircraft', explaining reluctance to adopt retractable floats. Wing built up on strong box with light leading and trailing structures, all riveted or bolted. Section NACA 23020 (root), 23010 (tip). Fuel in 22 flexible cells in wing box both in dihedral centre-section and horizontal outer panels. Flaps of TsAGI type (basically single-slotted) in three electrically driven sections each side. Aerodynamically balanced differential ailerons. Dual flight control by cables and push-rods, with AP-5 autopilot driving three power units in control circuits. Comprehensive ice protection: leading edges heated by hot air from combustion heaters, alcohol sprays for navigator's windows and propeller blades, and electric resistance mats for pilots' windscreens. Provision for crew of seven, plus reliefs. Other equipment described under production version.

LL-143 launched September 1945 and test-flown at Krasnoyarsk. By this time OKB moving back to Taganrog, and flight development at Taganrog and Sevastopol from 1947. While still in Siberia carried full armament: 12·7 mm UBT in nose, left/right beam, upper rear deck, immediately aft of rear step, and extreme stern, six guns in all. Underwing racks for various bomb-loads up to 400 kg (normal) or 4000 kg (8820 lb) overload.

DIMENSIONS Span 33,0 m (108 ft 2½ in); length 23,0 m (75 ft 5½ in); height 7,2 m (23 ft 7½ in); wing area 120 m² (1292 ft²).

ENGINES Two 2250 hp ASh-72 driving 5056 mm (199 in) V-3BA four-blade propellers.

WEIGHTS Empty 15 104 kg (33,298 lb); normal fuel 4300 kg (9480 lb) (overload fuel, 8600 kg); normal loaded 21 300 kg (46,958 lb).

PERFORMANCE Max speed 371 km/h (231 mph) at S/L, 401 km/h (249 mph) at 4,3 km; landing speed 140 km/h (87 mph); climb 21·5 min to 5 km; range (normal) 2800 km (1740 miles), (overload) 5100 km (3169 miles).

Be-6 The outstanding performance of LL-143 led to plans for a major production programme centred at Taganrog. With MA (now AV-MF) designation Be-6, the production machine had more powerful engines, a slightly modified wing box, redesigned bow with extended nose making room for eighth crew-member, interior provision for complete relief crew, 'balcony' flight-deck windows giving downward view, retractable radar in planing botton aft of main step, bow spray fences to reduce propeller erosion, provisions for carrying assault force of 40 commandos, and completely different defensive armament: nose, N-2 installation for NR-23 with 200 rounds; top deck, DT-V8 with two NR-23 with 500/550 rounds; tail, Il-K6-53Be with two NR-23 with 225 rounds each. Normal weapon load increased to 16 FAB-100, eight FAB-500, or AMD-500 (actual mass 550 kg) mines, two FAB-1500 or two 1100 kg torpedoes. Normal systems included two GSP-9000 engine-driven generators, M-10B1 APU driving GS-5000 generator, for 28·5 and 115 V systems; B-40 cabin heater, groups of eight KP-19 oxygen bottles; and comprehensive radio fit.

First flight February 1949 by M.I. Tsepilov, OKB pilot; state trials in same year. Few problems, and service delivery from 1950. Probably well over 200 built for service with all MA Fleets, as well as in paramilitary and Aeroflot service as utility transports. By 1954 modifications in progress, notably replacement of Ilyushin tail bar-

Be R-1

Be R-1

Be-10

bette by MAD stinger; replacement of nose guns by two different large radars for surveillance and possibly missile guidance (presumably in co-operation with warships); and conversion for dedicated transport duties. No EW variant known.

DIMENSIONS Span 33,0 m (108 ft 2½ in); length 23,565 m (77 ft 3¾ in); height (keel/fin-tips) 7,64 m (25 ft 0¾ in); wing area 120 m² (1,292 ft²).

ENGINES Two 2400 hp ASh-73 driving V-3BA-5 propellers.

WEIGHTS Empty (as delivered) 18 827 kg (41,506 lb); fuel 7400 kg + 500 kg oil (total 17,416 lb); normal loaded 23 456 kg (51,711 lb); max with bomb load 29 t (63,933 lb).

PERFORMANCE Max speed 377 km/h (234 mph) at SL, 414 km/h (257 mph) at 1,8 km; climb 20 min to 5 km; ceiling 6,1 km (20,000 ft); range 4800 km (2983 miles).

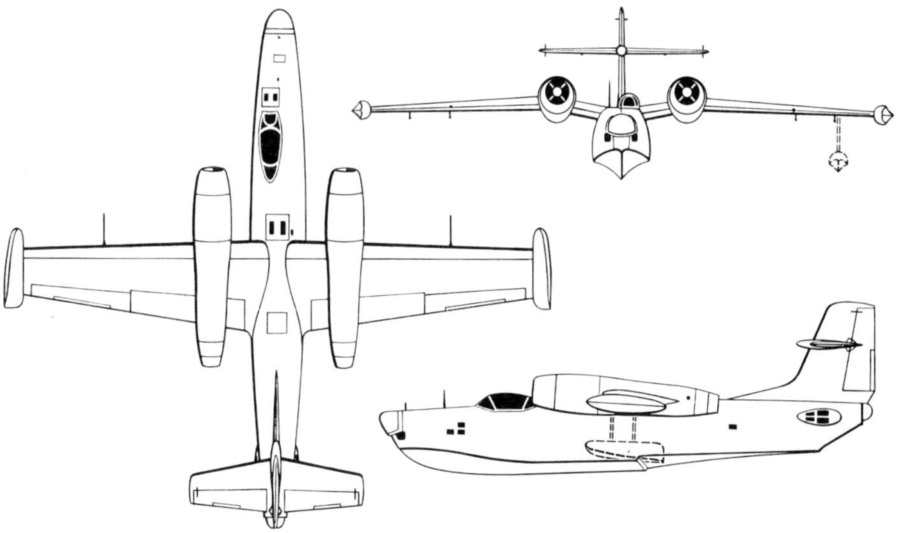

Be R-1

R-1 In 1946 Beriev studied LL-143 with two RD-45 turbojets and was sufficiently impressed to request permission to design a flying boat with such propulsion. R-1 (*Reaktivnii* 1, jet 1) purely experimental, not so much aerodynamic as structural and to explore possibilities. Much smaller than LL-143, but retaining gull wing to place simple engine nacelles as high as possible. Hull of high length/beam ratio with shallow front step and rear planing bottom tapered to point near stern. Duralumin throughout, including control-surface skins. Wing of NACA 23009 (9%) profile with machined skins and wing box forming integral tankage and Fowler flaps inboard and outboard of engines (all these new features drew on B-29 technology). Wing-tip floats on two struts retracted electrically to form wing-tips. Wing remarkably far back on hull. Fixed tailplane mounted high on large fin with bullet fairing. One-piece rudder and prominent elevator mass-balances, so manual flight controls. Crew of three, apparently without pressurization: nav/bomb-aimer entering through door in right side of hull to nose compartment with windows both sides, pilot in fighter-type cockpit on left side of hull, and rear gunner in stern compartment sighting through blister on each side to control electrically driven twin-NR-23 barbette. Two NR-23 fixed in bows aimed by pilot. Wing racks for 1000 kg weapon load. Scheme for internal weapon bay with watertight door(s) but doubtful if ever fitted.

Flown Taganrog by I.M. Sukhomlin 30 May 1952. By this time RD-45 engines replaced by VK-1s, set at 5° positive angle. Wing box passed below jetpipes without conflict, and engine performance close to optimum. Severe gas/water wake, but well away from rear hull and tailplane. Valuable lessons learned, especially with integral tankage and stability of hull at high planing speeds.

DIMENSIONS Span 21,4 m (70 ft 2½ in); length (no guns) 19,43 m (63 ft 9 in); wing area 58 m² (624 ft²).

ENGINES Two 2740 kg (6041 lb) VK-1 turbojets.

WEIGHTS Empty not published; loaded 17 t (37,478 lb).

PERFORMANCE Max speed 760 km/h (472 mph) at SL, 800 km/h (497 mph) at 7 km; ceiling 11,5 km (37,730 ft); range 2000 km (1243 miles).

Be-10 (M-10) Like some early jet bombers, this high-speed flying boat was a great technical achievement but a vehicle of doubtful military value. Reconciling the problems of range, fuel mass, take-off/landing speed and installed thrust were in the context of the 1950s impossible, but the Be-10 set several world class records and remains the fastest marine aircraft ever to have achieved operational status.

Little published about this aircraft, which appears to have Be-10 as OKB number and M (*Morskoi*, marine) as AV-MF designation. Service requirement pre-1958, probably specifying ASW, anti-ship attack and minelaying. Design combined features of previous Beriev boats with Tupolev Tu-16 style engine installation, using advanced Lyul'ka engine installed in nacelles under wing roots with engines mounted horizontal but toed-in towards rear; jetpipes then curved outwards to angle 7° on each side of centreline, total change in flow direction from inlet to nozzle being 12°. Capacious and deep hull with planing bottom scaled up from R-1, with large spray dam/fence right round bows and extending back almost to inlets. Main step of V form, rear step tapered to point at extreme stern with water rudder under keel at rear. Relatively small wings swept 50° at leading edge, with short horizontal centre section mounted above hull and outer panels with acute anhedral to bring tips close to stabilizing floats carried on very short pylons. Four large widely-spaced fences extending around undersurface at leading edge. Fowler flaps with internal rails, with inner ends of flaps outboard of large root fairings and jets. Cowling doors serve as servicing platforms.

Normal crew of three, two in pressurized drum in upper bows and gunner in pressurized tail turret. Navigator in nose with glazed visual bombing panel. No radar in aircraft publicly seen. Pilot cockpit on centre-line, with jettisonable canopy but normal access via steps from interior, main door on right side of hull. Rear turret has radar direction and probably twin-NR-23; superficially similar to that of Tu-16 but no side blisters. Some aircraft may have had to fixed NR-23 in nose, but uncertain. No details of offensive weapons, but carriage probably external. Wing box forms integral tankage, and probably additional overload tanks in hull. Possible communicating tunnel between front compartment and rear turret. Flight controls probably powered.

Engine selected 1958, when application described as reconnaissance flying boat. First flight prior to 1961. Four pre-production M-10s displayed publicly in 1961. World records: 7 August 1961, N. Andryevskii and two crew, 15/25 km speed 912 km/h (566·7 mph); 3 September 1961, G. Buryanov and two crew, 1000 km circuit with

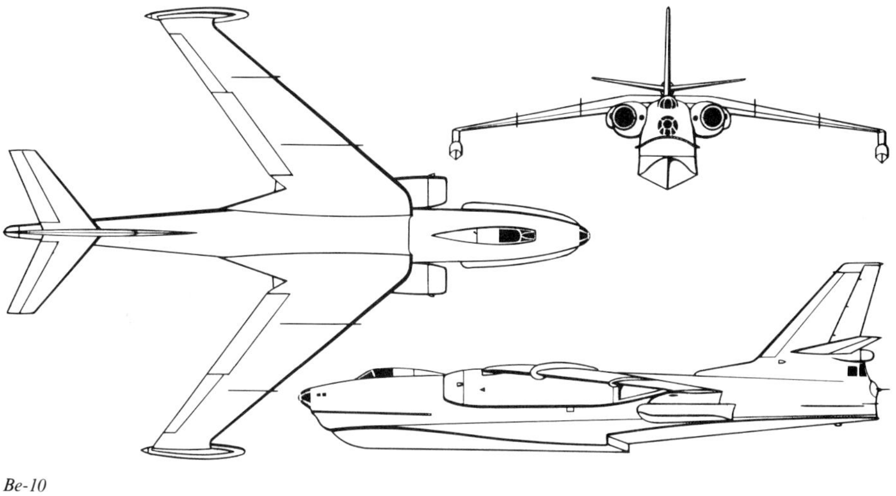

Be-10

M-12 (Be-6 monument believed at AV-MF base, Murmansk)

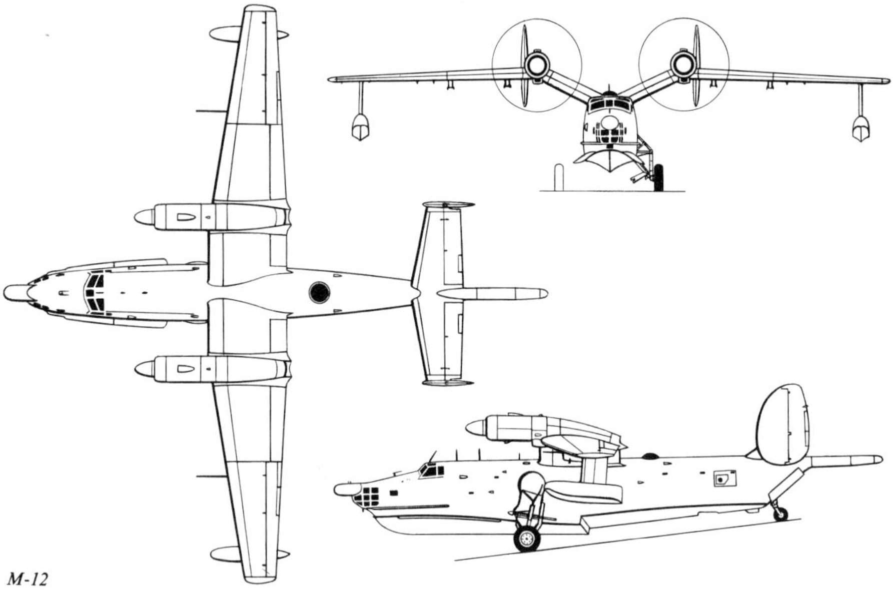

M-12

M-12s on airbase

5 tonnes payload at 875,86 km/hr (544·23 mph); 9/12 September 1961, Buryanov and crew, 12 733 m (41,775 ft) with 10 tonnes payload, various other altitude records up to 14 962 m (49,088 ft) with no payload. Total production, possibly only pre-production batch. Service experience unknown.

DIMENSIONS (Est) Span 25,0 m (82 ft 0 in); length 33,0 m (108 ft 0 in); wing area 130 m² (1,400 ft²).

ENGINES Two 6500 kg (14,330 lb) Lyul'ka AL-7RV turbojets.

WEIGHTS (Est) empty 24 t (52,900 lb); loaded 40 t (88,200 lb).

PERFORMANCE Indicated by record figures; range probably about 3000 km (1865 miles).

Be-12 (M-12) Chaika The last successful design from G.M. Beriev's OKB, this versatile amphibian was designed in parallel with the slightly larger and much heavier and faster Be-10. Unlike the latter it has enjoyed substantial production and a long service life in many roles, and no replacement is in sight.

Original AV-MF requirement probably dated about 1957, to replace Be-6. In practice roles varied including coastal patrol, multi-sensor reconnaissance, anti-ship, ASW, photo survey, Arctic support, submarine and surface warship co-operation, transport, search/rescue and electronic warfare. Hull essentially derived from Be-6, but stretched in length and with planing bottom nearer to Be-10. Small spray dam along each side of nose, V main step, tapered afterbody to pointed second step under stern with water rudder upstream. Retractable landing gear with main units hingeing up through 150° to lie in hull recesses, covered by door on inner side of leg in extended position; tailwheel retracting rearwards and upwards into diagonal stern compartment closed by twin doors. Tail little changed from Be-6, but wing entirely new with reduced span and area, thinner section (believed NACA 23010 at root) and Fowler flaps, probably driven electrically. Flight controls manual, with servo-tabs. Integral tankage along wing box inboard and outboard of engines; none in hull. Stabilizing floats on large-chord single struts. Engines carried on welded steel-tube trusses projecting up and ahead from wing box, with cowling panels forming servicing platforms and jetpipes curving across wing to nozzles at trailing edge.

Normal crew of most M-12s in MF service is five or six; captain, co-pilot/com-radio operator, navigator (in glazed nose), electronics operator, and one or two ASW sensor operators in rear compartment. Interior unpressurized. Internal weapon bay aft of step with watertight doors. Further aft are tubes and retrolauncher for sonobuoys housed in rear compartment. Further aft again is stowage area and, on left side, APU driven by gas-turbine whose exhaust heats leading edges of tail when not discharged through overboard stack. Extreme stern can house MAD stinger. Surveillance radar normally mounted in nose above navigator glazing, a later radar having a radome of wider oval section than drum of original A-304E ASW/nav set. Other emitters believed to include A-321A nav, A-322Z doppler, A-325Z nav, Cross Up beacon and IFF transponder, SRO-2 IFF and SRZ-2 interrogator (also used for rescue and ship homing), and no fewer than four radar altimeters (RV-UM, RV-3, RV-10 and RV-17 high-altitude). Individual aircraft have additional fits including tail-warning and passive receivers, and there is at least one dedicated EW variant. Weapons are also carried under the wing well outboard of the propeller discs, there being a minimum of one pylon on each side plus rocket rails. There is also a pure flying-boat variant, but this may have been merely to set records.

First flight believed 1960. Displayed publicly 1961 and large number (probably 200 or more) delivered from 1964. Serving in all fleet commands, number in active inventory in early 1980s being about 75. Small number based Egypt with Egyptian insignia early 1970s but no exports. M-12 holds all 21 FAI turboprop amphibian and all 19 turboprop flying-boat class records; ceiling given below and other figures include payload of 10,1 tonnes (22,266 lb) lifted to 2 km. The flying boat variant averaged 565,347 km/h (351·3 mph) over a 500 km circuit. Name *Chaika* (Seagull) is unofficial.

DIMENSIONS Span 29,71 m (97 ft 5$\frac{3}{4}$ in); length (with MAD) 30,17 m (99 ft 0 in), (new radar) 30,95 m (101 ft 6$\frac{1}{2}$ in); wing area 105 m² (1,130 ft²).

ENGINES Two 4000 shp Ivchyenko AI-20D turboprops.

WEIGHTS Empty (estimate) 18 t (39,680 lb); loaded 29 450 kg (64,925 lb).

PERFORMANCE Max speed at optimum height 608 km/h (378 mph); initial climb 912 m (2990 ft)/min; ceiling 12 185 m (39,977 ft); endurance at reduced speed 15 h; normal range 4000 km (2485 miles).

Be-30 A complete break with tradition, possibly reflecting absence of official interest in a new marine aircraft, this light airliner was designed in 1965–1966 to meet Aeroflot need for multi-role transport to replace An-2. Aerodynamically almost a scaled-down An-24 but with narrow slab-sided unpressurized fuselage. Structure all light alloy with extensive chemical-milling, bonding and spot-welding. Main wing box incorporates four integral tanks; secondary structure mainly honeycomb sandwich, both in wing and tail, though curiously also 'stiffened by stringers'. Intention from start to provide full de-icing, but systems unknown in first prototype flown by M.I. Mikhailov 3 March 1967 temporarily fitted with two 740 hp ASh-21. No photograph released. Second aircraft, (possibly first re-engined) SSSR-23166, fitted with imported Astazou XII turboprops; dates unknown but possibly flew mid-1967. By this time another (?) Be-30 completed with TVD-10 engines with three-blade propellers; no announcement of flying with any turboprop until 14 July 1968.

Unusual feature was high-speed shaft linking both engines so that drive to both propellers maintained following engine-failure; this is possible only with free-turbine engine, and thus not fitted to Astazou prototype. Shaft based on Br 941 system (Hispano-Suiza) connecting free-turbine rear extension shafts via bevel gears. Flight controls manual, tailplane fixed (unlike An-24, without dihedral) and flaps in four sections double-slotted hinged to deep underwing brackets. All leading edges de-iced by hot air (said to be bleed air on wings, and in one report on tail also, but this is not practical with such small engine mass-flow). Engine inlets are protected by bleed air; windshields are raw AC. Three-phase power at 200 V, probably also used for flaps and landing gear, nosewheel steerable and single-wheel main gears retracting rearwards into long nacelle extensions.

Fuselage only 1,5 m (59 in) wide, just sufficient for left/right passenger seats and central aisle. Door at left rear, with integral steps. Normal seating for 14, plus 15th passenger on right of pilot. Alternative schemes for casevac (nine stretchers plus six seated), photo-survey, geo-prospect, offshore/fishery patrol and executive/VIP. Options include autopilot, coupled ILS and roller-map display. Aeroflot service announced for summer 1970, but Czech L-410 purchased instead. Later An-28 also developed.

DIMENSIONS Span 17,0 m (55 ft 9$\frac{1}{4}$ in); length 15,7 m (51 ft 6 in); wing area 32 m² (344·5 ft²).

ENGINES Two 960 shp Glushenkov TVD-10B free-turbine turboprops driving AV-24AN three-blade reversing propellers.

WEIGHTS Empty 3360 kg (7407 lb); fuel 1000 kg (2205 lb); max payload 1500 kg (3307 lb); max loaded 5860 kg (12,919 lb).

PERFORMANCE Max cruise 480 km/h (298 mph); normal cruise 460 km/h (285 mph) at 2 km (6560 ft); take-off 250 m (820 ft); range with 1,25 tonne payload and 30-min reserve, 600 km (373 miles).

Be-32 In June 1976 a blurred photo was released of this prototype, seemingly indistinguishable from Be-30 despite announcement it could carry 18 passengers or 1900 kg (4185 lb) cargo. Flown by Ye. Lakhmostov to 3 km (9843 ft) in 2 min 25 s, and to 6 km (19,685 ft) in 5 min 8 s (records later broken by de Havilland Canada DHC-5D).

Be-30

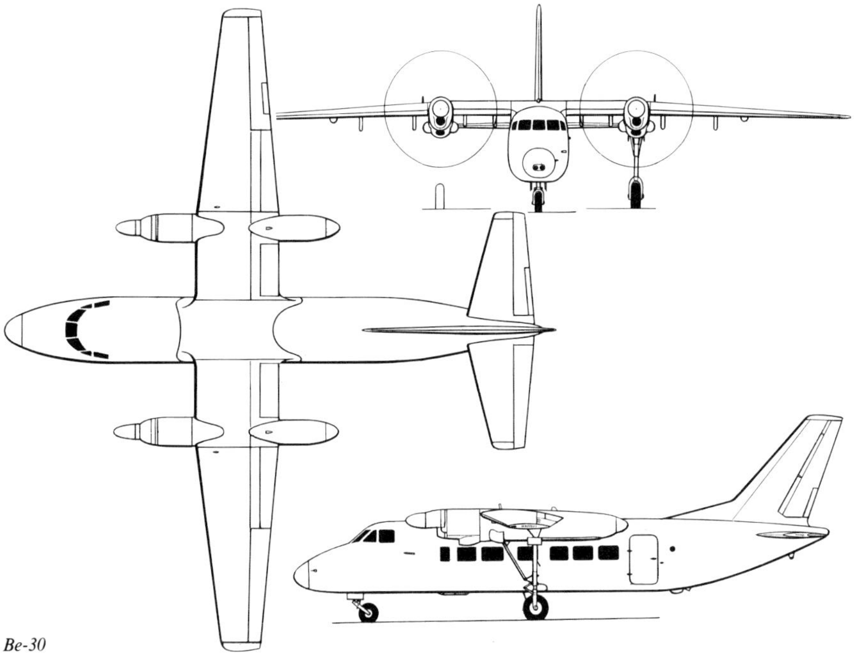

Be-30

Biesnovat

Matus Ruvimovich Biesnovat was born in about 1900 and in the mid-1930s was an engineer in Tairov's OKB. In 1938 he was permitted to form his own OKB, assigned the particular task of building a research aeroplane to test new wing profiles and planforms, new flight controls and new structural forms at the greatest flight speeds attainable. This aircraft was built, and from it was derived a fighter.

SK-1 Designation possibly from *Skorostnii Krylo*, high-speed wing. Smallest possible aircraft to take large V-12 fighter engine, and fitted with smallest possible wing for safe landing on Russian grass or board airstrips. Light-alloy stressed-skin construction, but fabric-covered control surfaces, all with 100% mass-balance. Direct manual flight control but trim tabs on rudder and elevators; no servo assistance. Wing of NACA 23014·5 profile. Single plate-web main spar and sheet skin, finally covered with thin layers of cork dust, marquisette openweave fabric and adhesive, polished off to mirror finish. Slotted split flaps of Vlasov (TsAGI) type. Minimum-drag cockpit with flush hood incorporating side windows, hinged up by hydraulic ram together with pilot seat to give view for landing. Minimum-drag engine installation with ejector exhausts, and pressurized (1,1 kg/cm^2) coolant system requiring radiator of only 0,17 m^2 frontal area, said to be half normal for chosen engine. Total fuselage frontal area 0,85 m^2. Hydraulic actuators for main and tail landing gears, with closure doors throughout.

Shavrov states SK-1 released for testing 1939, but latest Soviet accounts give date as January 1940. Again, Shavrov gives max speed as 577 km/h, 358 mph, unreasonably low and almost 100 km/h slower than known speed of SK-2 fighter which had same engine, armament, projecting canopy and higher gross weight. What is beyond question is that SK-1 flew well, did not frighten test pilot(s) and at high speeds demonstrated excellent handling and manoeuvrability.

DIMENSIONS Span 7,2 m (23 ft 7½ in); length 8,0 m (26 ft 3 in); wing area 9,5 m^2 (102 ft^2).
ENGINE One 1050 hp M-105 driving VISh-52 three-blade propeller.
WEIGHTS Empty 1505 kg (3318 lb); loaded 2100 kg (4630 lb).
PERFORMANCE Max speed probably not 577 but 677 km/h (421 mph); landing speed 165 km/h (102·5 mph).

SK-2 The success of SK-1 triggered immediate authorization for this fighter derivative. The airframe was the same except for use of a normal light-alloy wing surface, conventional cockpit with fixed seat and sliding canopy, conventional oil cooler and armament. The high-pressure water cooling system was retained, as was the small (unknown) fuel capacity. Pivoted tray above engine, able to rise 320 mm, carrying two 12·7 mm BS; some reports also mention one ShKAS, location not known. Flown by G.M. Shiyanov, October 1940. Exciting, but contained many unrectified defects which precluded any chance of displacing established fighters.

DIMENSIONS Span 7,3 m (23 ft 11½ in); length 8,28 m (27 ft 2 in); wing area 9,57 m^2 (103 ft^2).
ENGINE As SK-1.
WEIGHTS Empty 1850 kg (4078 lb); loaded 2300 kg (5071 lb).
PERFORMANCE Max speed 632 km/h (393 mph) at SL, 665 km/h (413 mph) at 5,5 km; climb 4 min 20 s to 5 km (16,400 ft); endurance at optimum slow cruise 45 min; take-off 350 m; landing 500 m.

SK-3 Designed as start for combat duty, advanced twin-engined low-wing two-seat fighter. Two AM-37 engines, 33,7 m^2 (363 ft^2) wing, four large-calibre fixed guns. Design speed 555 km/h at SL, 700 km/h (435 mph) at rated height. Project reassessed and terminated December 1940.

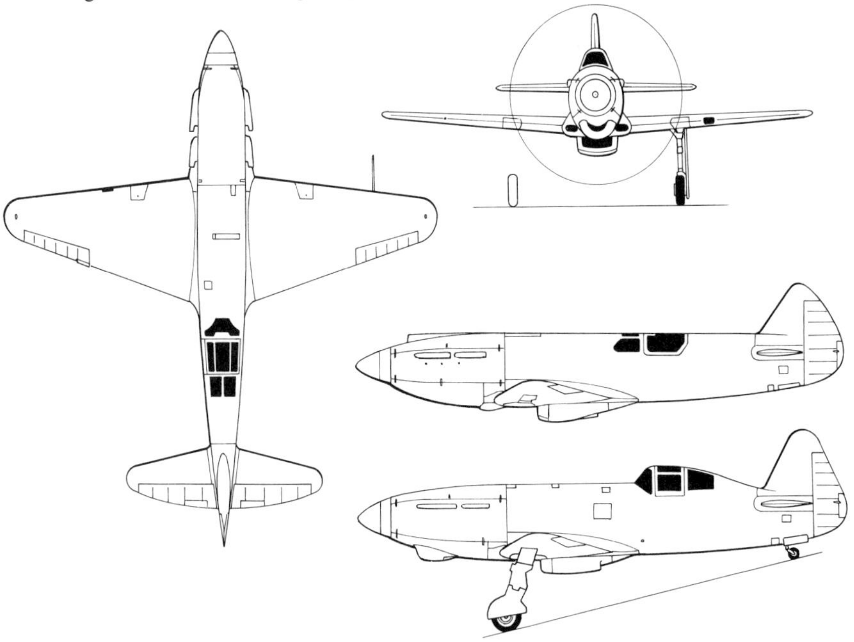

SK-2 (upper side view, SK-1)

BOK

BOK The Bureau Osovikh Konstuktsii (Bureau of Special Designers) was suggested in October 1930 on the initiative of P.I. Baranov. An integral element of TsAGI, it was charged with studying new aviation problems and producing aircraft of novel configuration or incorporating new technology. At the outset BOK was put in charge of Vladimir Antonovich Chizhevskii, with Nikolai Nikitovich Kashtanov as deputy. The bureau was opened on 1 January 1931 and in the course of its 10-year life included such designers as L.I. Sutugin, S.S. Krichyevskii, S.A. Lavochkin, B.I. Chyeranovskii, N.I. Kamov and A.Ya. Shcherbakov. Aircraft covered in numerical, not chronological, sequence.

BOK-1 Also designated **SS** (*Stratosfernii Samolyet*, stratospheric aeroplane), this was the first pressurized aeroplane to be designed in the world after the Ju 49. BOK was instructed that high-altitude flight was its No 1 priority, and its engineers visited Dessau to talk to the Ju 49 designers. On their return they designed the spherical gondola of the balloon SSSR-1 (exceeded 18 km in 1933), a feature of which was continuous recycling of purified atmosphere, oxygen and water vapour being kept at optimum proportions and carbon dioxide removed. This provided basis for design of 'hermetic cabin' for aeroplane to undertake research at up to 12 km (39,370 ft) to support major 1934 programme of Academy of Sciences.

To save time and effort the airframe was based on the RD (ANT-25), but cabin was completely new unit constructed separately. Cylinder of 2 cubic metres volume, constructed of riveted D1 light alloy 1,8–2 mm thick with sealing compound. Convex bulkheads front and rear, with main entry hatch in roof and emergency exit through porthole at rear into fuselage. Small glazed circular portholes, five for pilot and two for nav/radio/observer in rear seat. (This conflicts with several published descriptions based on misleading retouched photographs.) Design dP about 0,22 km/cm^2 (3·2 lb/in^2), holding interior at 8 km up to ceiling eventually reached of 14,1 km. Controlled leak through dump valve, made good by oxygen from bottles at flow rate keeping oxygen content roughly constant. Engine cooling circuit heated cabin to steady 15/18°C. Four small portholes illuminated unpressurized rear-fuselage.

Rest of aircraft basically RD but span reduced, structure restressed for lighter gross weight, fixed spatted landing gear with single wheels, and numerous minor changes especially to systems. Original M-34RN drove three-blade propeller. Shavrov: 'BOK-1 ready for flight test autumn 1936'; Němeček: 'Flown by I.F. Petrov summer 1936 at Smolyensk but replaced as test pilot in June 1936 by P.M. Stefanovskii'. Basic handling adequate but much trouble with condensation on portholes and final cure was added combustion heater, drawing air from outside cabin. Initial ceiling 10,7 km but after weight reduction (Němeček: 'and transfer to Moscow') worked up in stages to 13,1 km, and eventually

(1937) 14,1 km. In spring 1937 re-engined with M-34RNB with dual turbochargers and four-blade propeller. BOK disappointed with altitude performance of both engines, and even with new engine did not exceed 12 km. BOK-1 written-off after disintegration of turbo in October 1937.

DIMENSIONS Span 30,0 m (98 ft 5 in); length 12,86 m (42 ft $2\frac{1}{2}$ in); wing area 78,8 m² (848 ft²).
ENGINE One 725 hp M-34RN V-12 water-cooled; later 830 hp M-34RNB.
WEIGHTS Empty 3482 kg (7676 lb) (after engine change 3600 kg, 7937 lb); fuel 500 kg (1102 lb) (after engine change 1000 kg); loaded 4162 kg (9175 lb) (after engine change 4800 kg, 10,-582 lb).
PERFORMANCE Max speed 242 km/h (150 mph) at 4 km (after engine change, 260 km/h, 162 mph); endurance given as 4 h for each state. ceiling 14,1 km (46,260 ft).

BOK-2 Also called RK (*Razreznoye Krylo*, slotted wing), this was potentially a promising and possibly important aerodynamic research aircraft. Small wooden single-seater, with M-11 engine, designed by S.S. Krichyevskii in 1934 to test his wing comprising a main front portion and variable-incidence rear portion (too large to be called a flap) with intervening slot. BOK-2 flew successfully in 1935, being refined to achieve design objective of automatically adopting most efficient wing configuration. Intention was to add flaps (type unspecified) to hinged rear portion of wing. Difficulties with reconciling good results with theory and unfortunately BOK-2 languished inactive on death of designer later in 1935. All data lost.

BOK-5 A simpler but superficially similar research aircraft, this small tailless single-seater was the creation of V.A. Chizhevskii, who clearly thought BOK needed more unusual flying hardware. Virtually all-wing, and not significantly different from work of Chyeranovskii and others, though, because of small size, separate fuselage needed. Two main wing spars, each with tubular booms joined by two sheet webs. Light-alloy truss ribs, fabric covering. Dural monocoque fuselage, aluminium/fabric rudder and U-2 landing gear. Main feature trailing edge, comprising three sets of movable surfaces on each side, ailerons outboard, then flaps and elevators inboard. All sections interlinked by mechanism subject to much development. Each section comprised main member with $+3°/-5°$ movement and secondary trailing portion moved by pilot and acting as servo, balance and trimmer. Light-alloy tubular framework with 0,5 mm skin on main portion and fabric on trailing part. Wing profile TsAGI-890/15, with movable portions typically 21% chord. Structural load factor 8.

BOK-5 flew summer 1937; pilots Nyukhtikov and Stefanovskii. Stability and handling good, and of course with low wing-loading field performance excellent. NII VVS did official tests and agreed to support larger aircraft with speed 350 km/h (217 mph), but in 1938, Chizhevskii and several colleagues were arrested. Those left at BOK had no inclination to do anything difficult that might cause trouble with authorities; project for BOK-5 successor therefore withered.

DIMENSIONS Span 9,86 m (32 ft $4\frac{1}{4}$ in); length 4,365 m (14 ft 4 in); wing area 23,15 m² (249 ft²).
ENGINE One 100 hp M-11.

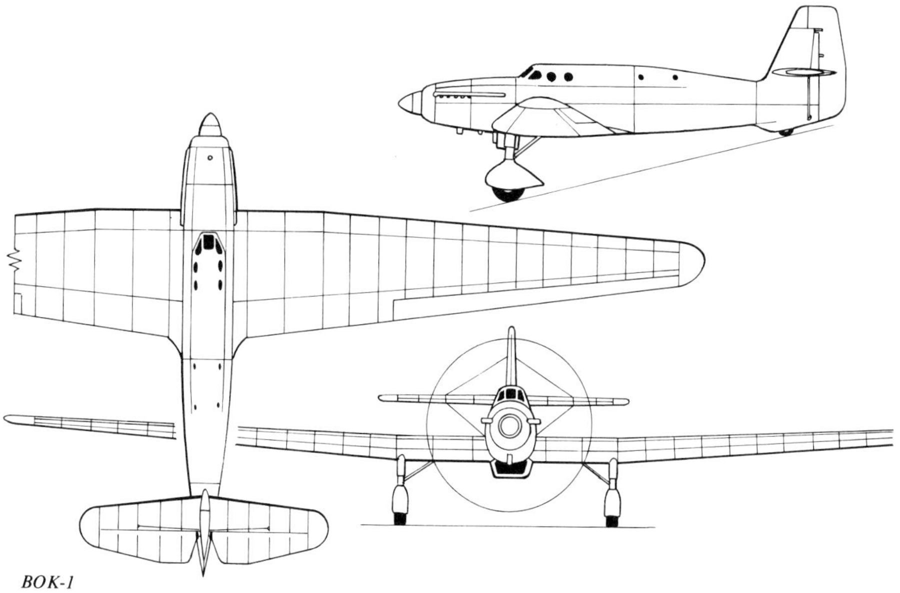

BOK-1

BOK-5

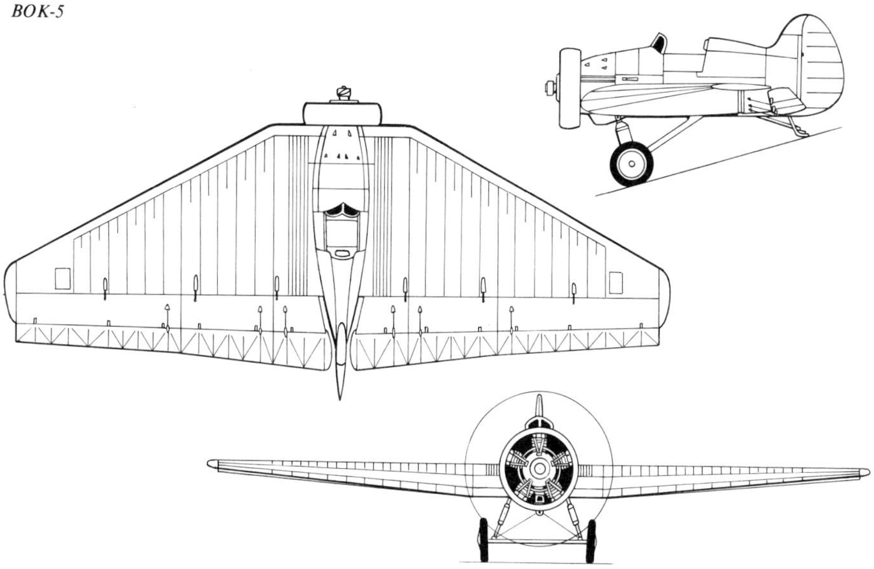

BOK-5

WEIGHTS Empty 596 kg (1314 lb); fuel 90 kg (198 lb); loaded 764 kg (1684 lb).
PERFORMANCE Max speed 174 km/h (108 mph) at SL; landing speed 85 km/h (53 mph); take-off/landing 120/200 m (394/656 ft); ceiling 4850 m (15,900 ft); range 600 km (373 miles), 4 h.

BOK-7 A natural derivative of BOK-1, this was likewise based on the RD and used the full wingspan. Structure basically as Tupolev aircraft, but tandem-seat GK (hermetic cabin) no longer a separate structure. Intended for long endurance (one report states 100 h, but actual figure probably nearer 75); much research done to perfect atmosphere recycling, maintenance of pressure (with PTsN auxiliary engine-driven compressor) and disposal of human waste products. In course of NII VVS studies possible pilots, including Gromov, Yumashyev, Danilin, Spirin, Baidukov and Belyakov, were made to undergo simulated missions to check on claustrophobic or endurance difficulties.

Fuselage largely new, with stressed-skin structure of smaller cross-section than RD or BOK-1. Central portion with thick riveted and bonded skins and hemispherical end-closures, for design dP of 0,28 km/cm² (3·98 lb/in²). No cut-outs except two projecting circular roof cupolas, each with hemispherical dural cover incorporating double-glazed portholes. Hatch closed by occupant screwing down peripheral wing-nuts in traditional marine style for porthole glass. Vision poor.

Official *Report of State Tests on BOK-7* dated 14 December 1936 must refer to underlying test programme; aircraft itself not flown until 1938 (Němĕcek states spring 1939, but there is evidence 1938 correct). Pilots I.F. Petrov and P.M. Stefanovskii, probably at Sverdlovsk. Records of measured performance lost, but much better than BOK-1 in most respects and particularly big jump in ceiling and practical cruise height. Intention at NII was to make round-world flight, and aircraft given VVS designation K-17 (K, *Krugosvyetnii*, round the world). Mission planned by NII commandant A.I. Filin, whose great experience included flight with RD to USA. In late 1939 or early 1940 Filin was arrested and shot, and flight never took place.
DIMENSIONS Span 34,0 m (111 ft 6¾ in); length 12,9 m (42 ft 4 in) wing area 87,0 m² (936·5 ft²).
ENGINE One 890 hp M-34FRN with two turbochargers.
WEIGHTS Empty 3900 kg (8598 lb); no other data survives.

BOK-8 The RD airframe was again used for this experimental aircraft intended to serve as the flying testbed for the Soviet Union's first remotely controlled armament system. The original scheme was worked out in the early 1930s by V.S. Kostishkin and K.V. Zhbanov, and the actual system was on a test rig by 1936. A Rezunov optical sight was linked to the gun(s) electromechanically, the main feature being angular synchros for traverse and elevation carefully designed for minimum error or lag. BOK-8 was built, and probably flew 1939, but details lacking. Experience gained put to use in design of SShA defensive armament system of Tu-4 in 1944–1947. BOK-8 data basically as for BOK-7.

BOK-11 As BOK had been working since the early 1930s on stratospheric-cruise aircraft it is remarkable that it took so long for VVS thinking to get around to such expertise being applied to a reconnaissance platform (nothing was done with ANT-49 either). Again the airframe was derived from that of the RD, but the engine was changed to the promising Charomskii diesel for maximum endurance. One report states three-man crew and remote-control defensive armament as developed on BOK-8, but this is probably in error. Two prototypes built, first made maiden flight 1940. Flight experience said to have been very satisfactory, but BOK closed within eight months and programme discontinued. VVS had no purpose-designed reconnaissance aircraft in 1941–1945 apart from conversions of combat machines.
DIMENSIONS As for BOK-7.
ENGINE One 1500 hp ACh-40 diesel.

BOK-15 Little information on this project for a further high-altitude reconnaissance aircraft powered by ACh-40 diesel. According to Němĕcek two built, with three-man crew but no armament.

Bolkhovitinov

Viktor Fedorovich Bolkhovitinov was born 1899. An impetuous character, he had a meteoric rise in the VVS. After passing numerous technical courses, appointed a lecturer at the Zhukovskii Academy (VVA) in 1932. In 1933 became head of VVIA, group of about 20 lecturers and engineers charged with actual design as an OKB, their first task being to plan a replacement for TB-3. About 1935 Bolkhovitinov became Professor of Aircraft Design at VVA, continuing in this post until 1946, when VVIA was closed. Last hardware programme BI. He died 1970.

DB-A Having planned a successor to TB-3 in 1934 Bolkhovitinov's small staff began serious engineering design at the end of that year. Structural leader M.M. Shishmaryev, aerodynamics Ya. M. Kuritskyes. DB-A (Long-Range Bomber, Academy) was an outstanding accomplishment, fully as advanced for its day as TB-3 had been. Duralumin stressed-skin throughout, except for fabric-covered control surfaces. Fuselage semi-monocoque, with numerous frames and stringers of Z and top-hat section. Main wing spars and ribs built-up trusses like TB-3 but with numerous stringers stiffening skins; wing verged on unacceptable complexity and weight. Fuel 14 000 lit (3080 gal) in 14 tanks. Deep wing spars above bomb bay almost barred access to rear fuselage. Bomb bay 6 × 2 m (236 × 79 in) with two doors each driven by two hydraulic jacks. Wing flaps of split type also hydraulic, on centre section and dihedral outer panel. Hydraulic retraction of mainwheels upwards into enormous trousers, with twin doors.

First aircraft built at a Moscow factory (believed Khodinka) and flown 5 March 1936 by N.G. Kastanayev and Ya.N. Moiseyev. This aircraft had radiators of inner engines in thin vertical strip on both sides of trousers; those of outer engines in ducts under rear of nacelle. Armament: 12·7 mm UBT in mid-upper turret and single ShKAS in nose and tail turrets and rear of each trouser fairing. Bombload 3 t (6614 lb); crew of seven.

DB-A (No 1 aircraft)

Second aircraft (designated **DB-2A**) cleared for increased weights and fitted with M-34RNV engines cooled by large radiators forming entire leading edge of each trouser and serving both engines on that side. Crew increased to eight and different armament: 20 mm ShVAK in nose and six ShKAS in mid-upper, tail and trouser positions (not known how ShKAS distributed). Bomb load increased to 5 t (overload). On 10 November 1936 DB-2A flown by M.A. Nyukhtikov and M.A. Lipkin to 7032 m with 10 t payload. Ten days later reached 4535 m with 13 t, both figures far better than existing world records. On 14 May 1937 pilots G.F. Baidukov and N.G. Kastanayev, with nav/radio L.L. Kerberom flew Moscow/Melitopol/Moscow 2003 km in 7 h 2 min 11·7 s with 5 t payload.

First aircraft painted red, with civil registration N-209, for non-stop flight over Pole to USA. Left Shchelkovo 12 August 1937 in command of S.A. Levanyevskii, with N.G. Kastanayev co-pilot, V.I. Levchyenko nav, G.T. Pobyezhimov and N.N. Godovikov engineers and N.Ya. Galkovskii radio. Refuelled Arkhangelsk and set off across Pole. Radioed crossing of 90° and after 14 h 32 min that No 4 engine stopped but gave ETA Fairbanks. Two further garbled messages. N-209 never seen again, and no trace ever found.

Despite this, DB-A an outstanding aircraft. Late 1937 order for 16 production aircraft, of which 12 delivered before decision taken to stan-

dardize ANT-42. Meanwhile in spring 1938 DB-2A re-engined with AM-34FRN/TK, Nyukhtikov handling high-alt test programme. Of production machines five actually served with DB regiment, seven being reserve or trials aircraft.

DIMENSIONS Span 39,5 m (129 ft 7 in); length 24,4 m (80 ft 0⅓ in); wing area 230 m^2 (2476 ft^2).

ENGINES No 1, four 970 hp AM-34RN V-12; DB-2A, 1000 hp AM-34RNV; (1938) 900 hp AM-34FRN/TK turbocharged.

WEIGHTS Empty (No 1) 15,4 t (33,951 lb), (others) 16 t (35,273 lb); fuel 10,2 t (normal); take-off with max fuel 26 t (57,320 lb). Note: weights as published indicate with bombload little fuel could be carried, max for DB-A being 22 t (48,500 lb) only. Subtracting 5 t bombs leaves only 1 t for fuel.

PERFORMANCE Max speed (No 1) 280 km/h (174 mph) at SL, 330 km/h (205 mph) at 4 km; (DB-2A) 335 km/h (208 mph) at 2 km; (TK engines) 356 km/h (221 mph) at 6 km; take-off 400 m; landing 300 m (landing speed given as 85 km/h, impossibly low?); range (load not stated) all in region of 4600 km (2858 miles).

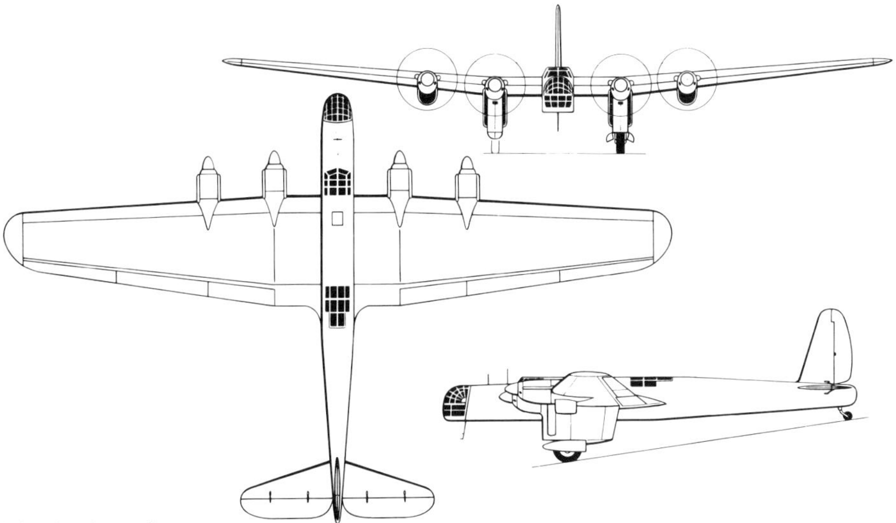

DB-A (No 1 aircraft)

S One of the more remarkable combat aircraft of the 1930s, this was intended as an ultra-fast bomber; indeed its design had more kinship with speed-record contenders than with existing bombers. The designation, said to stand for *Skorostnii* (Speedy), in fact stood for *Sparka* (Twin, Coupled). The powerplant (*Sparka*) was developed as a separate system, based to some degree on the Fiat A.S.6 of the Macchi M.C.72 racing seaplane. The Zhukovskii Academy OKB (VVIA) under Bolkhovitinov was enlarged to handle the problems of this tandem-engine system as well as the S aircraft.

The two M-103 engines were mounted in line. The front engine had an extended propeller shaft driving a three-blade propeller. The rear engine was geared to two high-speed (believed crankshaft speed) shafts carried in spherical bearings on the crankcase of the front engine finally driving gears to a second contra-rotating propeller immediately behind the first. The intention was not only that this should confer the highest possible speed but that the aircraft should be able to remain airborne after failure of either engine. It was not intended to take-off on one engine, however, and the wing was made small and heavily loaded in a further attempt to obtain the highest possible speed. It was accepted that the exceptional moment of inertia of the tandem engines, and the high wing-loading, would make S far from agile.

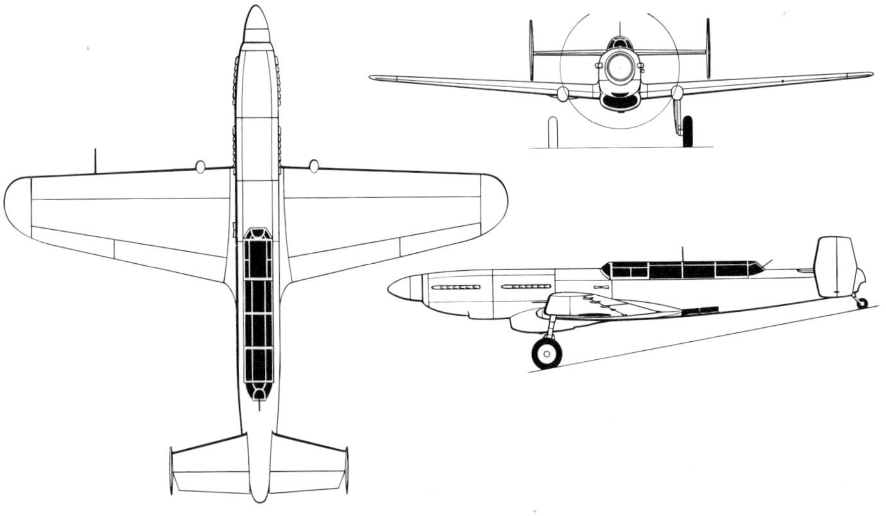

S

Stressed-skin light alloy, including control surface skins. Wing with main two-spar box with heavy upper and lower skins flush-riveted to machined plate spars with lightening holes along neutral axis. Fuselage from top, bottom and two side panels joined at four angle-section longerons. Structure described as original and progressive, and ten years later applied to Il-28. Flaps of Fowler type, driven electrically as was landing gear (wheels turned 90° on backwards-retracting main legs) and numerous other services (29 electric actuators). One actuator drove exit flap on enormous ducted radiator serving both engines. Twin-finned tail, variable-gear drive to elevators, and rudders each with separate trim and servo tabs and inset hinges. Differential ailerons with trimming built into circuit. Pilot and observer in tandem, latter having emergency dual control but seat normally facing to rear with manually aimed ShKAS (typical of S was electric interruption of firing when gun aligned with twin fins, field of fire generally being good). Later ShKAS replaced by much more powerful twin 12·7 mm UBT. Forward-firing guns in original design, not fitted. Internal bay immediately behind rear spar for up to 400 kg of various bombs, with twin electric doors.

Powerplant on test after two years of work in May 1938. Detail design of S begun early 1937, prototype construction July 1938. First flight about September 1939 by B.N. Kudrin. Official tests by Kudrin and A.I. Kabanov 1940. Performance exceptional (see data) but engine installation ceaseless mechanical failures and a hazard to flight. Nose-up attitude a problem even without simulated bombload (which was aft of CG) and in 1940–1941 Z.I. Itskovich, then at VVIA, redesigned wing with modified profile, leading edge and upper surface being covered by ply strips attached by 'secret riveting' and adhesive. Considerable improvement, but inability to solve mechanical problems with powerplant eventually resulted in decision to remove rear engine (probably late 1940). In winter 1940–1941 testing continued on non-retractable skis. Under powered with one engine and spare mass could not be used for fuel or bombs. Factory needed for Pe-2 production and development abandoned 1941.

DIMENSIONS Span 13,8 m (45 ft 3¼ in); length 13,2 m (43 ft 4 in) (with single engine 13,0 m, 42 ft 8 in); wing area 26 m^2 (280 ft^2).

ENGINE(S) Originally two 960 hp M-103 in tandem; later, one 960 hp M-103P.

WEIGHTS Empty not published; loaded 5652 kg (12,460 lb); (one engine) loaded 3676 kg (8104 lb).

PERFORMANCE Max speed 570 km/h (354 mph) at 4,6 km; (with one M-103P) 400 km/h (248·5 mph) at 4,4 km; range (two engines) 700 km (435 miles).

I Designation of experimental fighter/dive bomber conceived early 1940 and in prototype construction 1941. Scheme confirmed by VVS. *Sparka* installation of tandem M-107 engines, though prototype to use M-105 or M-103. Smaller derivative of S but with even more advanced features including Elektron (magnesium alloy) structure, integral tankage, tricycle landing gear and scheme for catapult launch. Lead designer A.M. Isayev. Project stopped at start of war, summer 1941.

D Project for impressive four-engined bomber with two *Sparka* tandem M-105 powerplants. Clean spindle-like fuselage with projecting gondola, mid wing and twin-wheel main gears. Max weight 28 t (wing loading 200 kg/m^2). Also passenger variant. Abandoned summer 1941.

Borovkov -Florov

In 1935 Aleksei Andreyevich Borovkov and Ilya Florentyevich Florov were young engineers at TsKB. In 1935 they proposed a new fighter biplane smaller than any previously attempted except with much less powerful engines. Their studies were so professional that Ya.I. Alksnis at VVS agreed at the end of 1935 to recommend an OKB be started, and this was set up under GUAP authority as OKB-7 early in 1936. Working closely with VVS staff the resulting aircraft, called I No 7211 (Fighter 7211), was flown successfully in 1937. It led to an outstanding series of tiny biplane fighters that saw action and came close to mass production.

7211 This beautiful prototype amply fulfilled designers' belief that large engine and heavy firepower could be packaged into significantly smaller airframe, whilst retaining good handling, agility and flight safety. Basis was diminutive fuselage, reminiscent of Gee Bee racer with pilot immediately ahead of fin in part-glazed cockpit. Forward fuselage welded truss of 30KhGSA steel, with dural skin panels; rear fuselage and tail wooden monocoque with ply skin similar to I-16. Identical upper and lower sets of outer wing panels, pinned at front and rear spars to carry-through structure under fuselage and to upper centre section, with considerable stagger. No interplane struts. Wings light-alloy stressed-skin, each with spars and ribs pressed from sheet and skin a sandwich stiffened by thin corrugated light alloy between smooth faces. Three hinged trailing surfaces on each panel, serving as ailerons and drooping as flaps, all worked without interplane connection. Long-chord NACA cowling with exhaust pipes grouped into ventral stack. Provision for four ShKAS with 2200 rounds total, two guns in top of fuselage and two in sides all firing through leading edge of cowling. (These guns are retouched out in most, but not all, 7211 photographs.)

Aircraft destroyed early in flight-test programme. According to Něměcek, first flight by P.M. Stefanovskii, and later testing carried out by 'E.J. Preman' who was killed as result of engine failure on approach. According to Shavrov, engine cut dead on first take-off on 21 June 1937, pilot being E.Yu. Preman. No 7211 reached calculated height of 23 m. No room to land ahead, and lost control on attempted turnback. Board of enquiry cleared aircraft of blame, and in March 1938 OKB-7 authorized to proceed with series of prototypes of fighter designated I-207.

DIMENSIONS Span 6,98 m (22 ft 10¾ in); length 5,88 m (19 ft 3½ in) (Shavrov states 6,35 m for No 7211 and I-207); wing area 18 m^2 (194 ft^2).

ENGINE One 800 hp M-85 assembled from imported GR14N parts; three-blade c/s propeller.

WEIGHTS Empty 1321 kg (2912 lb); loaded 1745 kg (3847 lb) (these probably without armament).

PERFORMANCE Max speed 365 km/h at SL, 416 km/h (258·5 mph) at 4 km; climb 4,6 min to 5 km; service ceiling 13 km; endurance 2 h/750 km; time 360° turn 14/15 s; take-off 150 m.

I-207 Four prototype and pre-production fighters were built using essentially same airframe as No 7211. According to Něměcek all specially designed to use two Merkulov DM-2 or DM-4 booster ramjets, but in known Soviet literature these were intended for last two aircraft only.

I-207/M-62, also called *Izdelye 7 No 1* (Product 7, No 1), little changed apart from close-fitting cowl with projecting fairings over cylinder-head rocker-boxes and prominent carb-air inlet at 12 o'clock position. VISh-26 two-blade propeller. Full armament from start of testing. Open cockpit; spatted landing gear without the transverse tie fitted to No 7211. First flight 20 April 1939; test pilots included P.M. Stefanovskii, L.M. Maksimov and N.I. Nikolayev. Second prototype, called *Izd. 7 No 2*, similar except fitted with M-63 in shuttered cowling without blister fairings. Direct-drive engine, VISh-26 propeller. Also flew first half 1939.

I-207M-63, first aircraft called *Izd.8, No 3*, ungeared engine with individual exhaust stacks, but retractable gear and provision for two bombs of 250 kg. Landing gear designed at OKB-7 but similar in principle to I-153 with legs folding to rear and wheels rotating 90°. Little advantage noticed. Bomb racks well outboard under lower wings (presumably same as planned location of ramjets). First flight autumn 1939, State tests 1940, when judged not good enough to warrant series production. Final I-207 was called *Izd.9, No 4* with geared M-63R driving three-blade VISh of 3 m diameter. Enclosed cockpit with canopy hinged to right side. First flight spring 1941. Nos 3 and 4 on VVS combat duty in late summer 1941.
DIMENSIONS As No 7211.
ENGINE See text.
WEIGHTS Loaded (7 No 1, No 2) 1950 kg (4299 lb; (8 No 3) 1850 kg (4078 lb); (9 No 4) 2200 kg (4850 lb).
PERFORMANCE Max speed at SL (1) 387 km/h, (2) 397 km/h, (3) 428 km/h, (4) 449 km/h; max speed at rated height (1) 436 km/h (271 mph), (2) 423 km/h (263 mph), (3) 486 km/h (302 mph), (4) 498 km/h (309 mph); climb to 5 km (1) 6·2 min, (2) 6·7 min, (3) 4·6 min, (4) not known; endurance 2 h (all); 360° turn (all) around 19 s; landing speed (all) 115 km/h (71·5 mph).

D Experimental single-seat fighter powered by combined 2000 hp M-71 piston engine in same duct as Merkulov ramjet with rear propulsive nozzle. High monoplane wing of gull form, span 14,8 (48 ft 7 in); leading edge swept (tapered) at 20°. Stressed-skin, tail (at least) having smooth skin stabilized by underlying corrugated structure. Armament two NS-37 and two ShVAK-20 (exceptionally heavy). Active project January 1941 but abandoned at end June 1941 (OKB-7 was in extreme Western USSR). Borovkov killed in aircraft accident 1945; Florov continued design (see later).

I-207/M-62

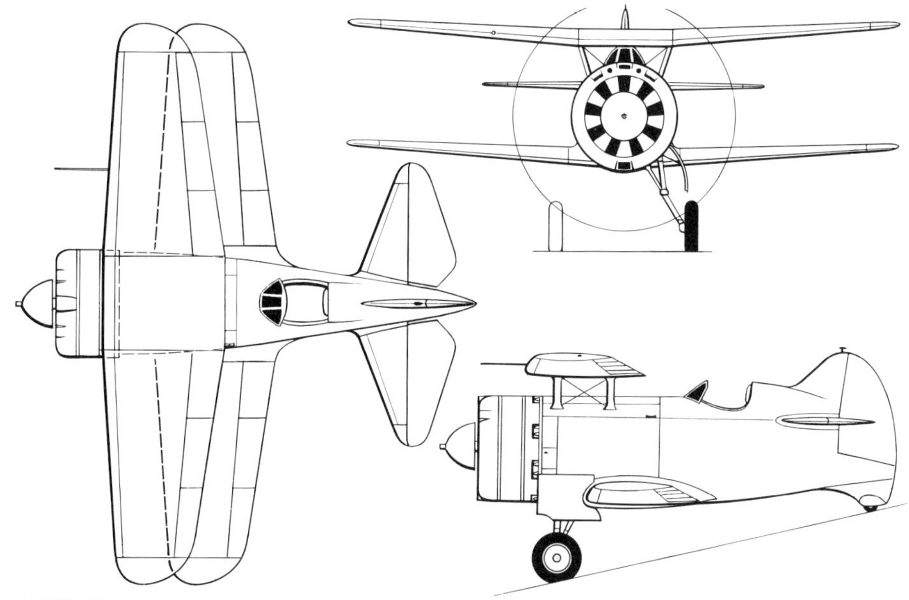

I-207/M-63

Bratukhin

Ivan Pavlovich Bratukhin was born in 1911. He concentrated entirely on helicopters from his student days, and was one of the pioneers in the TsAGI OOK (see later). As early as 1933 he was leader of OOK Brigade B, and made significant contributions to TsAGI helicopters from 5-EA onwards. During the purges of the late 1930s Bratukhin escaped arrest and inevitably moved up to replace those less fortunate, and in January 1940 was appointed first deputy designer in the newly formed OKB-3 at the MAI, under Yuryev. Only three months later Yuryev was replaced by Bratukhin, who ran the OKB for 11 years. It was closed in 1951, after which Bratukhin researched VTOL devices as a member of MAI's staff. Bratukhin is currently working at the Mozhaisky Institute in Leningrad.

Omega Also designated **2MG** (twin-engined helicopter), this ambitious project was authorised on 27 June 1941 (not 27 July as reported), and launched Bratukhin as creator of a long series of machines with two engine/rotor groups side-by-side. He was undoubtedly influenced by success of German Fw 61, and likewise included conventional tail, of T-configuration. Steel-tube construction with fabric covering. Lateral structures carrying engine/rotor units and fixed main landing gears were triangular spaceframes with two lower booms and one at top, with no covering. Fully articulated hubs of steel and light-alloy, carrying three duralumin blades, rotors being handed to rotate in opposite directions. Manual controls, driving swash-plates in fixed and rotating parts of head for collective and cyclic pitch control. Much research into optimum method, with differential collective to apply initial bank and then rudder, worked by pedals, to make turns. Emergency control for immediate autorotative setting of both rotors, but single-engine flight intended by connecting shaft between engines with universal joint on aircraft centreline. Final 0·231 gearbox to rotors (577 rpm). No centrifugal clutches. Three mechanical clutches, with overrunning capability, engaged by observer after both engines were running. First drive to associated rotor was clutched-in; then interlink left/right shaft. Fuel tanks behind engines. Observer behind pilot.

Helicopter ready for testing August 1941. Final design had no wheel or rotor brakes but trimming tailplane with pilot handwheel. Tentative hovering tests, interrupted by engine rough running and overheating. Six-month delay followed evacuation October 1941. Pilot K.I. Ponomaryev gradually made progress in 1942, discovering structural and control problems but remaining tethered until early 1943. Summer 1943 was hot and engines seriously overheated (original Renault not designed for prolonged high power, zero airspeed).
DIMENSIONS Diameter of each rotor 7,0 m (22 ft 11½ in); span between rotor axes 7,2 m (23 ft 7½ in); length (discounting rotors) 8,2 m (26 ft 11 in); disc area 76,96 m² (828 ft²).
ENGINES Two 220 hp MV-6 inline.
WEIGHTS Empty 1760 kg (3880 lb); loaded 2050 kg (4519 lb).

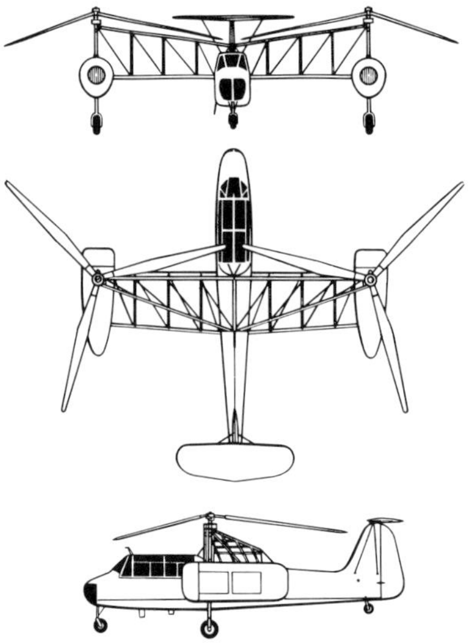

Omega 2MG

PERFORMANCE Max speed 116 km/h (72 mph) (one report states 186 km/h); range 250 km (155 miles).

Omega II Also sometimes called G-2 (helicopter 2), this was the original design with superior engines. Two Soviet radials were fitted in streamlined pods with fan-assisted cooling, and this not only cured the unreliability but increased performance. Drive ratio 0·32. According to one report outrigger structure now all welded tube instead of using diagonal lift wires, but photographs and patent drawings show all-tubular construction from original design. Rotor masts and outriggers stiffened, and dynamic parts (clutches and gearboxes) redesigned for long life. Test flown by Ponomaryev September 1944 with good results. Damaged January 1945, repaired and improved (drive ratio 0·283) and used again from July 1945, by this time for research and pilot training. With chief engineer D.T. Matsitskii as observer, gained height of 3 km. Demonstrated Tushino by M.K. Baikalov August 1946.

DIMENSIONS As 2MG.
ENGINES Two 330 hp MG-31F.
WEIGHTS Empty 1880 kg (4145 lb); loaded 2300 kg (5071 lb).
PERFORMANCE Max speed 150 km/h (93 mph); ceiling at least 3 km (9840 ft).

G-3 (AK) Third Bratukhin helicopter, based on G-2 but planned from outset for operational use by VVS as AK (*Artilleriskii Korrektirovshchik*, artillery correction). No significant differences apart from more powerful engine, available from many US Lend-Lease aircraft in absence of suitable indigenous power units. Two prototypes ordered 1944, flown 1945. On completion of State trials in 1945 batch of ten AK ordered. Confusion over whether any were completed; certainly not more than five flown, and most Soviet histories mention only original two prototypes as having flown. A single AK delivered to VVS with dual control for training helicopter pilots; one account states 1946, another 1948–1949.
DIMENSIONS As 2MG.
ENGINE Two 450 hp Pratt & Whitney Wasp Junior R-985-AN-1.
WEIGHTS Empty 2195 kg (4839 lb); loaded 2600 kg (5732 lb).
PERFORMANCE Max speed 170 km/h (106 mph); ceiling (hovering) 1,1 km (3608 ft), (forwards flight) 2,5 km (8200 ft).

G-4 First Soviet helicopter with engine designed for such duty. AI-26 radial by A.I. Ivchyenko produced in AI-26GR form with cooling fan and front gearbox giving vertical and lateral outputs for rotor and for transverse coupling shaft. Transmission provided with centrifugal clutch; overall drive ratio 0·27 (540 rotor rpm). Rotor diameter slightly increased, inbuilt twist of 6° 45′ along blade, and blade spar extruded instead of folded from sheet. Two prototypes, first flown October 1947 by M.K. Baikalov and second (one report states only this example had twisted blades) a month later. In January 1948 first G-4 damaged in course of exhaustive autorotational descents and dead-stick landings typically at 12 m/s descent along 15·5–16° glide path.

Omega G-4

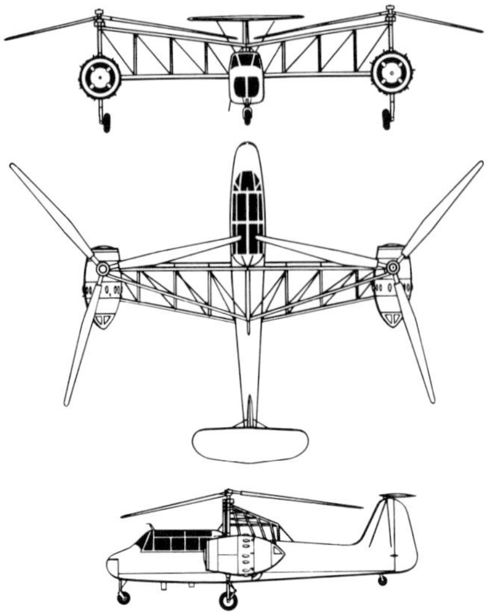

Omega G-4

Second G-4 first in Soviet Union to meet stipulated life for dynamic parts (in this case 100 h). Demonstrated at 1947 Aviation Day. Small series constructed 1947–1948, according to one account four flying out of ten ordered.
DIMENSIONS Diameter of each rotor 7,7 m (25 ft $3\frac{1}{4}$ in); span between rotor axes 7,6 m (24 ft $11\frac{1}{4}$ in); length (discounting rotors) 8,1 m (26 ft 7 in); disc area 93 m^2 (1002 ft^2).
ENGINES Two 500 hp AI-26GR.
WEIGHTS Empty 2364 kg (5212 lb); loaded 3002 kg (6618 lb).
PERFORMANCE Max speed 148 km/h (92 mph); hovering ceiling 2,4 km (7874 ft); range 233 km (145 miles). (Note: speed low in comparison with reasonable expectation and especially when compared with B-5.)

B-5 First helicopter designated for Bratukhin himself. Scaled-up derivative of G-4, with slightly more powerful model of same engines. Transmission and other dynamic parts identical. Same configuration but new airframe with lifting aerofoil wing instead of space-frame outriggers and large passenger fuselage. Latter designed as duralumin semi-monocoque (not steel-tube as has been reported) with level floor and door on right side. Total of eight seats, intended as two crew and three double passenger seats with aisle along right wall. Wings also of light-alloy stressed-skin construction with lifting profile to bear about 25% of weight in cruise. Fixed tricycle gear with bumper tailwheel. Single example only, completed 1947; only limited testing because of inadequate wing stiffness.
DIMENSIONS Diameter of each rotor 10,0 m (32 ft 10 in); other dimensions not known; disc area 157 m^2 (1690 ft^2).
ENGINES Two 550 hp AI-26GR(f).
WEIGHTS Empty 2932 kg (6464 lb); loaded 4032 kg (8889 lb).
PERFORMANCE Max speed claimed 236 km/h (147 mph) (disbelieved by author); ceiling (hovering) 2280 m (7480 ft), (forwards flight) 6400 m (21,000 ft); range 595 km (370 miles).

B-9 Ambulance/casevac derivative of B-5, with larger, more rectangular fuselage housing four stretchers in two layers on right and attendant on left. (Presumably door moved to left side.)

Wing changed to non-lifting symmetrical section but set at positive incidence. Single example completed 1947 but, because of aeroelastic difficulties with B-5, apparently never being flown (Shavrov states merely 'served perfectly as basis for long-range/long-term modifications').
DIMENSIONS Essentially as B-5.
ENGINES As B-5 or (Shavrov) AI-26GRF as B-10. No other data.

B-10 Also designated VNP (*Vozdushnii Nabludatyelnii Punkt*, aerial observation point), this could have been AK-2 because its original role was to replace the AK in artillery spotting. In fact by this time the basic Bratukhin helicopter had become rather larger and potentially more capable and VNP was to be a multi-role machine able to fly night recon, tactical supply and even casevac missions. Engines fully boosted AI-26 version, and dynamic parts essentially same as B-9. Wings of same plan and section as B-9 but with pair of bracing struts from bottom of two main-spar frames in fuselage to spar booms at 60% semi-span, and two further bracing struts from upper spar booms at same location to top of rotor masts. Fuselage entirely new: dural monocoque with glazed nose seating pilot on left and navigator on right under large observation dome; observer in tail again with large observation dome. New tail with variable-incidence tailplane mounted on fuselage carrying endplate fins (latter possibly rudders, but not described as such in literature). Usual four-wheel landing gear. Central fuselage available for additional loads: three passengers, or two stretchers (room for more but weight-limited) or 200 kg cargo or various radio or photographic equipment. Entrance door on left.

Single example built and flown 1947 (pilot not named). Behaviour satisfactory, and complete performance measurements taken. According to Němĕcek armament later fitted (ShKAS at both nose and tail) but hard to find evidence. According to Shavrov 1947–1948 saw general disillusionment with helicopters and especially with twin lateral rotor configuration because of lack of real progress with Bratukhin designs. This configuration subjected to fundamental reappraisal.
DIMENSIONS Essentially as B-5.
ENGINES Two 575 hp AI-26GRF.
WEIGHTS Empty 3019 kg (6656 lb); loaded 3900 kg (8598 lb).
PERFORMANCE Max speed 218 km/h (135 mph); ceiling as B-5; range 440 km (273 miles).

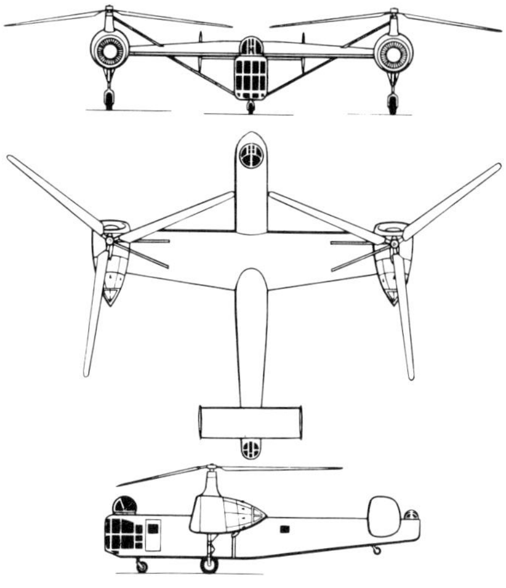
B-10

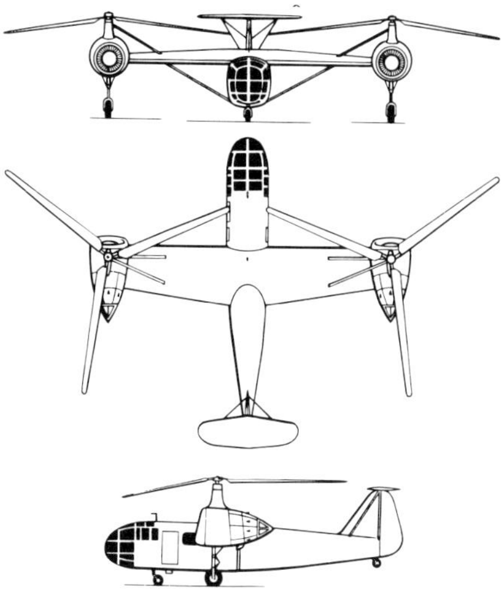
B-11

B-11 Last design authorized from OKB-3, solely to provide direct comparison with this configuration against Mil and Yak single-rotor submissions to VVS requirement for three-seat all-weather communications helicopter. Dynamic parts as before except for hydraulic rotor-hub dampers and faired masts with oil-cooler inlets. Wing of lifting section, set at zero incidence. Fuselage of improved form, with round instead of polyhedral top and bottom. Tail basically as B-5. Pilot in B-5 type nose, main cabin for two seats, with space at rear for freight or two stretchers (in lieu of passengers) loaded through enlarged door. Improved differential rotor controls with reduced friction.

Two prototypes completed in April 1948, respectively flying in June and September. Made good progress with measured performance, sustained (47 min) single-engine flight, autorotative landings and in eradication of various faults stemming mainly from vibration. One problem was lack of wing lift resulting from incidence setting, causing rotors to stall at high forward speeds. Further snag was hydraulic leak, difficult to rectify. On 13 December 1948 first machine shed blade from right rotor, killing Ponomaryev and I.G. Nilus. Numerous modifications suggested but B-11 really needed broader-chord blades and other major changes which did not receive support.
DIMENSIONS Rotors as B-5; length of fuselage 9,76 m (32 ft $0\frac{3}{4}$ in).
ENGINES Two 575 hp AI-26GRF.
WEIGHTS Empty 3398 kg (7491 lb); loaded 4150 kg (9149 lb).
PERFORMANCE Max speed 155 km/h (96 mph); range 328 km (204 miles).

B-11

B-12 Unbuilt project for single-rotor training helicopter with anti-torque tail rotor in various versions with M-14 (AI-14) or twin M-11 engines. Bratukhin also had studies for a 30-seat assault helicopter powered by two M-82FN engines and, after closure of his OKB, for a ramjet tip-drive helicopter which by 1955 got as far as running a full-scale rig using an engine salvaged from a G-4 to accelerate the test rotor to ramjet self-sustaining speed. This work was done at MAI, where one of the designer's last projects was for a piston-engined (later gas-turbine) convertiplane which formed the conceptual basis of the *Vintokryl* built at the Kamov OKB.

Chyeranovskii

Boris Ivanovich Chyeranovskii was born in 1896 and deeply interested in aeroplanes as a boy. Throughout his 64 years he concentrated on various forms of tailless machine, building more than any other designer in history and in general successful, though often at the expense of ease of handling. He was the pioneer of the so-called Parabola wing with curved leading edge. He was able to enter the Zhukovskii Academy in 1922, and in the same year proposed his first published design, a flying wing with aspect ratio 1·5. Many TsAGI aerodynamicists were convinced such a wing was useless but tests with model wings of aspect ratio 1·5, 3 and 6 did much to refute their predictions. Via the route of simple gliders in the Crimea Chyeranovskii progressed to aeroplanes, most of them constructed at the Academy but in some cases as projects of TsKB. He remained a loner, never really having an OKB, and it is sad that in the jet era when his tailless forms came into their own his failing health prevented construction. He died on 17 December 1960.

BICh-1 Simple tailless glider, the first Parabola actually constructed (1923). Thick (so-called 'inhabited') wing almost hid pilot. Aspect ratio 4. Trailing edge occupied by inboard elevators and outboard ailerons; rudder not necessary because turns possible on trailing-edge controls alone. All wood, fabric covering doped tight.

BICh-2 Refined successor, still with aspect ratio 4. Taken to Koktebel 1924 where made 27 flights at heights up to alleged 570 m.

BICh-3 Chyreranovskii's first aeroplane, based on previous gliders. Single-seater with cockpit faired into low vertical tail with rudder. Parabola type wing with ailerons, worked by differential bell-cranks, and elevators, all with inset hinges and aerodynamic balance. Single trousered wheel and wingtip skids. Test-flown and demonstrated by B.N. Kudrin at Moscow 1926. Rudder powerful because of slipstream, but on the whole BICh-3 not stable. Control improved by minor changes and final assessment was that aircraft safe.
DIMENSIONS Span 9,5 m (31 ft 2 in); length 3,5 m (11 ft 6 in); wing area 20,0 m² (215 ft²).
ENGINE One 18 hp Blackburn Tomtit driving 1400 mm propeller.

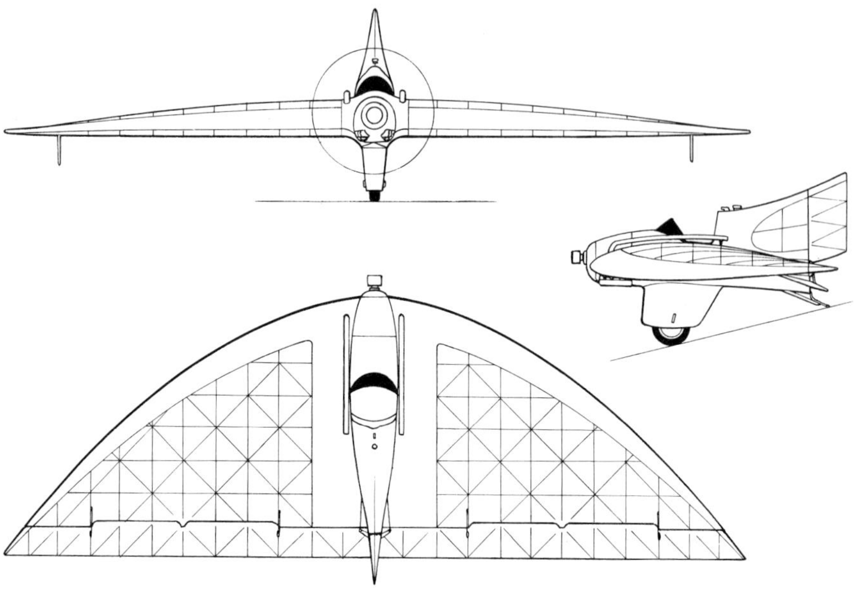

BICh-3

WEIGHTS Empty 140 kg (309 lb); fuel 10 kg (22 lb); loaded 230 kg (507 lb).
PERFORMANCE Max speed not known (probably about 140 km/h, 87 mph); landing speed estimated only 40 km/h (25 mph).

BICh-4 Last of original series, a flying-wing glider which dispensed with vertical surface entirely. Built 1927 but no further information.

BICh-5 Largest of the BICh series, this was to have been aerodynamically clean bomber with two BMW VI engines and retractable main wheels. No data but tested as model in tunnel 1928. Much research done on trailing-edge controls which became multi-segment elevons hung below trailing-edge with convex undersides. Work terminated 1929.

BICh-6 Not known.

BICh-7 Enlarged development of BICh-3, first flown 1929. Scale said to be 1·5 times on area basis, but in fact larger than this. No tail, but small rudders, without fins, on tips of wing. Centreline wheel, with skids under rudders. Two tandem open cockpits. Directional stability and control poor, and take-off almost impossible. Urgent modifications, first being conventional landing gear.
DIMENSIONS Span 12,2 m (40 ft 0½ in); length 4,7 m (15 ft 5 in); wing area 30,0 m² (323 ft²).
ENGINE One 100 hp Bristol Lucifer.
WEIGHTS Empty 612 kg (1349 lb); fuel 93 kg (205 lb); loaded 865 kg (1907 lb).
PERFORMANCE Max speed 165 km/h (102·5 mph); landing speed 70 km/h (43·5 mph).

BICh-7A Chyeranovskii completely rebuilt BICh-7 and the resulting BICh-7A did not fly until 1932. Enclosed tandem-seat cabin with fin and rudder downstream. No wing-tip surfaces. Normal landing gear with two wheels and tail-skid. Totally transformed, with good directional

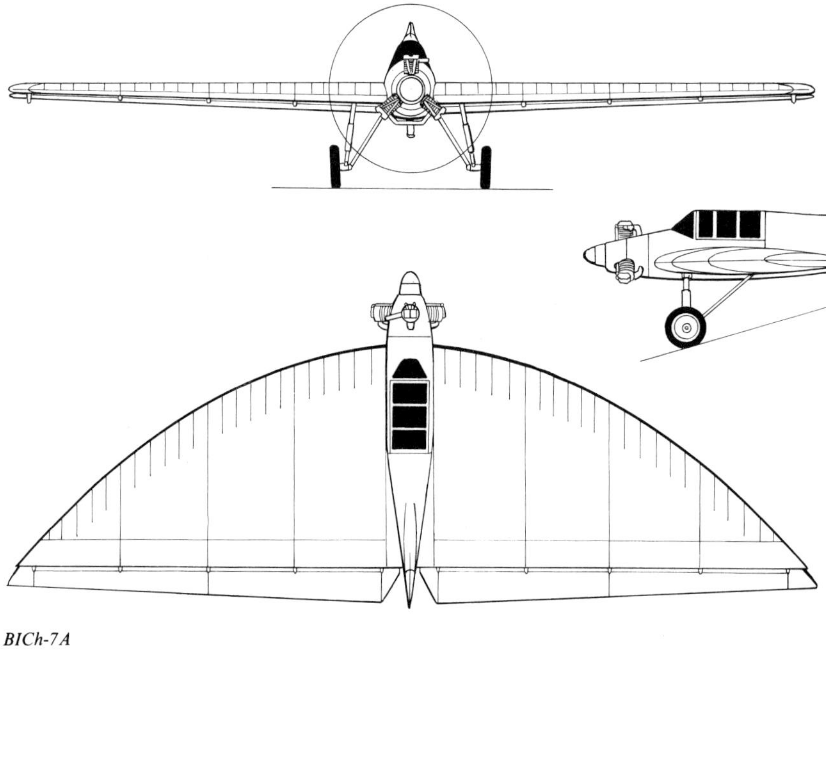

BICh-7A

stability, fine flying qualities and immediate response to pilot demand. Main problem was loss of speed in turn because large elevons caused high pressure on rudder. Test-pilot N.A. Blagin (later collided *Maksim Gorkii*) gradually improved by adding strips to elevons and setting at lower incidence. Control surfaces hung in Junkers double-wing style on five inset hinges below trailing edge of wing. Only other problem was vibration of engine, fault common to all Lucifers which had three Jupiter-size cylinders whose firing pulses could be strongly felt.
DIMENSIONS Span 12,5 m (41 ft 0 in); length 4,95 m (16 ft 3 in); wing area 34,6 m² (372 ft²).
ENGINE One 100 hp Bristol Lucifer.
WEIGHTS Empty 627 kg (1382 lb); fuel 93 kg (205 lb); loaded 880 kg (1940 lb).
PERFORMANCE Max speed 165 km/h (102·5 mph); landing speed 70 km/h (43·5 mph); range 350 km (217 miles).

BICh-10 Nothing is known of BICh-8 and BICh-9, and the BICh-10 never flew and led to BICh-14. BICh-10 was first Chyeranovskii twin, with two M-11 engines, tested as tunnel model 1933. Few changes led to:

BICh-14 (one modification was addition of Townend ring engine cowls) which was built at TsKB at Menzhinskii works and received additional designation **TsKB-10**. Built to double scale of BICh-7 on area basis, with twin engines on leading edge and from two to five seats in fuselage of same length as wing chord on centreline. Usual wood/fabric construction apart from light alloy in cabin and fin. Centre section of 3,3 m span and outer panels, with total of four spars and 60 ribs. Three surfaces on each side below trailing edge hung on four inset hinges. First flight at end 1934 by Yu.I. Piontkovskii. By 1936 BICh-14 tested at NII VVS, pilots including P.M. Stefanovskii, M.A. Nyukhtikov, and I.F. Petrov. General stability and control marginal. Trailing-edge aileron/flaps and inboard elevators of symmetrical section—largely ineffective. Considerable stick force needed to get tail down on landing. Rudder without slipstream and ineffective. Testing discontinued after 1937.
DIMENSIONS Span 16,2 m (53 ft 2 in); length 6,0 m (19 ft 9 in); wing area 60 m² (646 ft²).
ENGINES Two 100 hp M-11.
WEIGHTS Empty 1285 kg (2833 lb); loaded 1900 kg (4189 lb).
PERFORMANCE Max speed 220 km/h (137 mph); landing speed 70 km/h (43·5 mph); range 370 km (230 miles).

BICh-11 (RP-1) Designed 1931 in parallel with BICh-12, this tailless machine was first purpose-designed rocket aeroplane in world. All-wood flying wing, with vestigial central nacelle. Wing-tip rudders, trailing-edge ailerons and elevators. Originally centreline wheel, later changed for normal gear and tailskid. First tests as bungee-launched glider, on skis, early 1932. Intended to become RP-1 (*Raketnyii Planer*, rocket glider) with two of F.A. Tsander's OR-2 rocket engines rated at 50 kg (110 lb) thrust each. Ahead of each engine large lagged spherical tank of liquid oxygen and smaller capsule of gasolene. OR-2 never regarded as safe for installation, though run on bench 18 March 1933, so BICh-11 flown with small piston engine.
DIMENSIONS Span 12,1 m (39 ft 8½ in); length (rockets) 3,09 m (10 ft 1¾ in), (piston) 3,25 m (10 ft 8 in); wing area 20,0 m² (215 ft²).
ENGINE Intended two Tsander OR-2 rockets, finally one 35 hp ABC Scorpion.
WEIGHTS Only known figure: empty (rockets) 200 kg (441 lb).
PERFORMANCE No data.

BICH-12 Single-seat tailless glider using basically same wing as BICh-11. Flown on centreline ski early 1932.

BICh-16 More than any other country the Soviet Union has tried to build ornithopters (flapping-wing machines). Chyeranovskii schemed one in 1921 and finally got Osaviakhim support to build it in 1934 as BICh-16. Few details, but birdlike appearance: wood/fabric gull wing, tailless with central cockpit. Small auxiliary horizontal surface at rear to preserve stability in pitch. Pilot drove wings by means of pedals oscillating actuating rod projecting slightly forward of vertical on centreline below wing, joined on each side by pivoted links to wing spar at about 30% semi-span. How wing made flexible not recorded but probably two sets of pivots on each side. Pilot could walk aircraft on his own legs, and skid fitted to underside of central actuating rod. First tested August 1935 at Podlipki (Moscow) as glider with bungee launch, with lightweight (58 kg) pilot, R.A. Pishchuchyev. Stability unimpressive. Attempts to take-off by flapping unsuccessful, given up in 1938 after various modifications. No data.

BICh-17 Fighter described under Kurchyevskii.

BICh-18 Named *Muskulyet* (from muscle-power), this was another man-powered device but one with much better chance of success. Again supported by Osoaviakhim and assigned to unfortunate Pishchuchyev to fly, it was basically a high-performance sailplane in style, with nose cockpit and conventional tail. Wings in form of two pairs crossing over in X form on centreline so that lower right plane became upper left and vice versa. Both wings pivoted axially on centreline and driven by pedals and bell-crank linkage. Large portion of each wing freely pivoted to rear of main spar and able to flap up and down. Thus, as pilot pedalled, wings rocked in unison, tips never quite touching, oscillating rear portions giving forward thrust. Wing tips in form of ailerons. Light balsa wood structure. Flown 10 August 1937 at Poplipki off bungee launch without pedalling, gliding 130 m from release. On launch No 4 Pishchuchyev pedalled and accomplished six wing oscillations. Glide extended to 430 m, pilot reported noticeable forward thrust. Numerous demonstrations but sustained flight impossible.
DIMENSIONS Span 8,0 m (26 ft 3 in); length 4,48 m (14 ft 8½ in); wing area 10,0 m² (108 ft²).
ENGINE Pilot's muscle-power.
WEIGHTS Empty 72 kg (159 lb); loaded 130 kg (287 lb).
PERFORMANCE Max range attained 0,45 km.

BICh-20 Pionyer Chyeranovskii's smallest aeroplane, this also marked a shift away from the parabola wing to a short-span straight-tapered wing of almost delta shape. Trailing-edge ailerons and elevators now of inverted lifting profile. Short fuselage with pilot canopy in effect forming leading edge of fin. Latter broad, to house pilot, and relatively small, but effective because of slipstream. Extensively tested making turns of about 35° in horizontal flight at different heights; stability judged acceptable. Originally flown early 1938, on skis, and then re-engined in same year.
DIMENSIONS Span 6,9 m (22 ft 8 in); length (original) 3,5 m (11 ft 6 in), (re-engined) 3,56 m (11 ft 8¼ in); wing area 9,0 m² (97 ft²).
ENGINE First, one 18 hp Blackburn Tomtit; later, 20 hp Aubier-Dunne.
WEIGHTS Empty 176 kg (388 lb), (re-engined) 181 kg (399 lb); fuel 24 kg (53 lb), (re-engined) 26 kg (57 lb); loaded 280 kg (617 lb), (re-engined) 287 kg (633 lb).
PERFORMANCE Max speed 160 km/h (99 mph), (re-engined) 166 km/h (103 mph); ceiling 4 km (13,120 ft); range 320 km (199 miles); landing speed 49 km/h (30 mph).

BICh-21 Satisfactory behaviour of BICh-20 prompted Chyeranovskii to design a similar air-

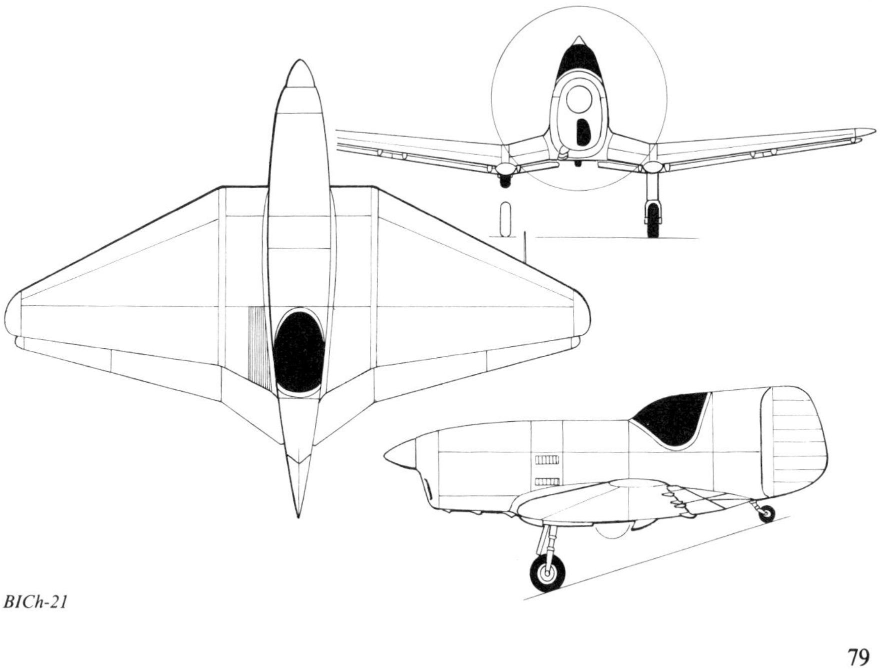

BICh-21

craft, but with a much more powerful engine, as an entrant in the Osoaviakhim all-union air race planned for August 1941. Minimum aircraft capable of taking chosen engine which filled fuselage back to rudder pedals, with hinged canopy forming leading edge of fin. Small fuel tanks in roots of 1,5 m centre section, anhedral with straight leading edge. Bolted-on outer sections with dihedral and sharp taper to round tips. Except for steel-tube and light alloy engine installation, structure all-wood, with polished surface. Ailerons and elevators of usual form below trailing edge. Pneumatically retracted landing gears, folding to rear with wheels partly exposed ahead of fairings under lowest part of wing. Ratier two-blade v-p propeller of 2 m diameter. BICh-21, also styled **SG-1** (*Samolyet Gonochnii*, racing aeroplane), was projected in 1938 but not completed until 1940 after numerous model tests at TsAGI. First flight June 1941, when results were good. In view of problems with SAM-13, widely expected to win race, but Nazi invasion came first.

DIMENSIONS Span 6,9 m (22 ft 8 in); length 4,4 m (14 ft 5½ in) (Shavrov's figure 4,7 m); wing area 9,0 m^2 (97 ft^2).
ENGINE One 220 hp MV-6 (Renault 6-inline).
WEIGHTS Empty 526 kg (1160 lb); fuel 37 kg (82 lb); loaded 643 kg (1418 lb).
PERFORMANCE Max speed 417 km/h (259 mph); landing speed 80 km/h (50 mph).

BICh-26 Between November 1947 and June 1948 Chyeranovskii ran what was in effect an OKB working on advanced jet fighters. BICh-24 and BICh-25 were the first Soviet variable-sweep designs, with plan shapes remarkably like those of modern combat machines, with pivots outboard. These were tunnel-tested but not built, and their place was taken by BICh-26, again with a most modern style of wing and tailless configuration remarkably like 1990s fighter projects. Powered flight controls of typical BICh form, light-alloy structure and pressurized cockpit. Design incomplete.

DIMENSIONS Span about 7,0 m (23 ft 0 in); length about 9,0 m (29 ft 7 in); wing area 27 m^2 (291 ft^2).
ENGINE One 2000 kg (4410 lb) AM-5 turbojet.
WEIGHTS Loaded 4500 kg (9920 lb).
PERFORMANCE Max speed Mach 1·7 at 7 km (22,960 ft); ceiling 22 km (72,000 ft).

Chyetverikov

Igor Vyacheslavovich Chyetverikov was born in 1904. In 1922 he was admitted to the LIIPS (Leningrad institute of aerial communication engineers) and succeeded in graduating in about 1927. He joined the TsKB in Moscow and in January 1931 was—surprisingly, in view of his limited experience—appointed head of the TsKB marine aircraft brigade, located at the Menzhinskii factory. Here he created a major flying-boat which, by all accounts, then had to be designed again by a more experienced team. In 1932 he moved to the NII GVF and worked in the OSGA brigade under N.M. Andreyev, where he achieved an original design that did not prove satisfactory. A year later he made a proposal to Glavsevmorput which immediately led to the establishment of his own OKB at Sevastopol in late 1934. Here he had another failure, but also one successful design. His only prototype after the Second World War was a failure, and his OKB was closed in 1948. He went back to Leningrad to lecture at the Mozhaiskii Academy.

MDR-3 Chyetverikov was appointed to TsKB marine division with one overriding commission: design a new long-range flying boat for MA. Absence of a Soviet aircraft in this class, other than prototypes, and supposed obsolescence of MDR-2, made the assignment urgent. This, coupled with Chyetverikov's inexperience, made him avoid as much innovation as possible; he sought to make use of existing designs, with minimal alteration.

On the face of it, he was both lucky and well-advised, because in a few weeks he had produced most of the engineering drawings for a fine modern boat that used few parts that were new. Designation: **No 11** (not TsKB-11). The hull was almost a direct scale of that of ROM-2, only major changes being to increase depth and thus allow wing to be mounted direct on hull, and to reduce drag by using curved instead of vertical steps in planing bottom. Complete wing borrowed from TB-5 heavy bomber, with span increased slightly by mating it to wider hull, added centre section having corrugated skin, and with powerplant nacelles attached above fourth rib on each side instead of below. Horizontal tail from same source. There was little that could go wrong with stabilizing floats (again based on existing designs), central fin carrying tailplane, rounded twin fins and rudders (which were original) and pylon-mounted tandem engine installations, each pair of engines sharing common large ducted radiator under front of nacelle.

Provision for crew of six. Dual flight controls in enclosed cockpit which, with position for navigators and gunners, and much on-board equipment, were also based on TB-5. Four pairs of DA guns in two tandem nose, dorsal and tail positions. Racks under centre section for two 250 kg (551 lb) bombs or equivalent.

Swift construction, first No 11 completed December 1931, and transported from Moscow factory to Sevastopol. First flight, by B.L. Bukholts, 14 January 1932. Test programme completed 25 March 1932. So far story sounds resounding success, and structurally and hydrodynamically No 11, by 1932 given service designation MDR-3, was excellent. Trouble lay in all-round poor performance, exemplified by take-off time on smooth water of 36 s, time to 2 km of 40 min, and ceiling of 2,2 km. In late 1932 project transferred to KOSOS TsAGI for improvement; it led to ANT-27, MDR-4.

DIMENSIONS Span 32,2 m (105 ft 7¾ in); length 21,9 m (71 ft 10½ in); wing area 153 m^2 (1649 ft^2).
ENGINES Four 680 hp BMW VI V-12.
WEIGHTS Empty 8928 kg (19,683 lb); fuel 3,3 t (7275 lb); loaded 13 973 kg (30,805 lb).
PERFORMANCE Max speed 210 km/h (130.5 mph); ceiling 2,2 km (7218 ft); range 1600 km (1000 miles); alighting speed 110 km/h (68 mph).

SPL (OSGA-101) According to Shavrov British trials convinced Soviet Navy it had to deploy aircraft aboard large cruiser submarines for open-sea recon. Chyetverikov had studied such an aircraft when he was at TsKB, and in early 1931 had placed a proposal for an SPL (*Samolyet dlya Podvodnikh Lodok*, aeroplane for submarine boats) on desk of TsKB head. No response for two years; then NII suddenly awarded 100,000 rubles for two prototypes of SPL. Chyetverikov decided to make the first a plain non-folding machine with landing gear, and this was designated OSGA-101. After testing, if it was successful, a foldable flying boat would be built as SPL.

OSGA-101 completed spring 1934 and first flown by A.V. Krzhizhevskii in July. Main hull and two-spar wing wooden, but tail (with twin fins to reduce height) carried on welded steel tubular booms. Engine, with Townend ring, carried on pylon above wing; two stabilizing floats of wood; landing gear comprised main wheels cranked by hand up under wing (though remaining fully exposed) and castoring tailwheel ahead of the water rudder. Enclosed cockpit seated two side-by-side with a third seat behind, in front of wing spar. Tail construction dural and fabric, flight-control cables running inside the tubular booms. Flight tests were satisfactory.

SPL which followed had almost same airframe but only two front seats, no landing gear, short-span wings folding about skewed hinges to lie alongside tail, and an unusual pivoted engine nacelle with bracing struts sliding along two upper tail booms (probably driven by hand-cranks and screwthreads) so that in folded position the nacelle lay between booms with

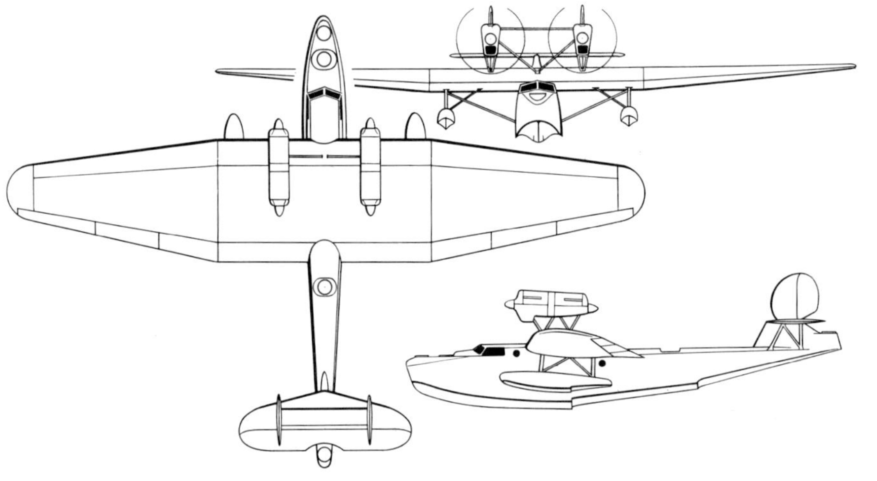

MDR-3

SPL

SPL with cowl removed

two-blade wooden propeller parallel with longitudinal axis. Folded (specification allowed four minutes for this) SPL fitted watertight cylinder 2,5 m (8 ft 2½ in) diameter and 7,45 m (24 ft 5¼ in) long. Withdrawal and preparation for flight was allowed five minutes. SPL completed in December 1934, taken to Sevastopol and flown by Krzhizhevskii early 1935, testing being completed 29 August. MA rejected it on grounds of inadequate seaworthiness, and never did acquire SPL-type aircraft. Prototype rechristened **Gidro-1** and given to Osoaviakhim, later setting up various class records.

DIMENSIONS Span (OSGA) 11,4 m (37 ft 5 in), (SPL) 9,5 m (31 ft 6 in); length (OSGA) 7,6 m (24 ft 11½ in), (SPL) 7,4 m (24 ft 3½ in); wing area (OSGA) 17,0 m² (183 ft²), (SPL) 13,4 m² (144 ft²).

ENGINE One 100 hp M-11.

WEIGHTS Empty (OSGA) 630 kg (1389 lb), (SPL) 592 kg (1305 lb).

PERFORMANCE Max speed (OSGA) 170 km/h, (SPL) 186 km/h; cruise (OSGA) 130 km/h (81 mph), (SPL) 183 km/h (114 mph) at 2,5 km; alighting speed (OSGA) 75 km/h, (SPL) 85 km/h; range (both) 400 km (248 miles).

ARK-3 In 1933 Chyetverikov roughed out a compact flying boat with tandem engines, with relatively high speed and long range, but was unable to build it. Off his own initiative he proposed to Glavsyevmorput that this organization, in charge of all northern sea transport, should adopt his design as multi-role vehicle for Arctic. He gained an order for a prototype, designated ARK-3 (*Arktichyeskii*, Arctic, 3). This set him up as constructor, with OKB at Sevastopol.

ARK-3 was straightforward design with dural hull and wooden wings of MOS-27 profile set at 5° incidence, Ailerons and tail, light alloy with fabric covering. Wooden underwing floats well inboard. Dual-control enclosed flight deck and two gunners or observers in bow and rear-hull cockpits. Design configured for minimum dimensions, but structural factor of safety 5·5.

Prototype completed Sevastopol January 1936 and flight test programme completed September. Modifications needed to bows and floats to give adequate seaworthiness, and engine pylon had to be strengthened, but measured performance good (later, 25 April 1937, A.V. Yershov took 1 tonne load to 9190 m) and second prototype authorized as ARK-3-2, original becoming ARK-3-1. Second aircraft more powerful, with longer hull and increased wing chord, and fitted with manual gun turret in bow and rear gun in sliding hatch installation. MA placed small production order for five, speedily implemented, but when first about to fly, on 14 July 1937, ARK-3-1 suffered catastrophe. Nowarra: 'suffered structural failure of hull in flight'; Nemecek, 'broke up in air as result of flaw in design of tail covering'; Shavrov, 'made heavy landing, engine collapsed and propeller killed pilot'. Precisely a year later ARK-3-2 also destroyed; Shavrov 'tail separated in flight in plane of rear gun installation'. Programme abandoned.

DIMENSIONS Span 20,0 m (65 ft 7¼ in); length (1) 14,0 m (45 ft 11 in), (2) 14,6 m (47 ft 11 in); wing area (1) 58,7 m² (632 ft²), (2) 59,5 m² (640 ft²).

ENGINES Two tandem radial driving two-blade Hamilton Standard v-p propellers: (1) 710 hp M-25, (2) 730 hp M-25A.

WEIGHTS Empty (1) 3242 kg (7147 lb), (2) 3642 kg (8029 lb); fuel/oil (1) 870 + 150 kg, (2) 820 + 160 kg; loaded (1) 4787 kg, overload 5800 kg (12,787 lb), (2) 5600 kg (12,346 lb).

PERFORMANCE Max speed at SL (1) 252 km/h (157 mph), (2) 260 km/h (162 mph); at rated

ARK-3

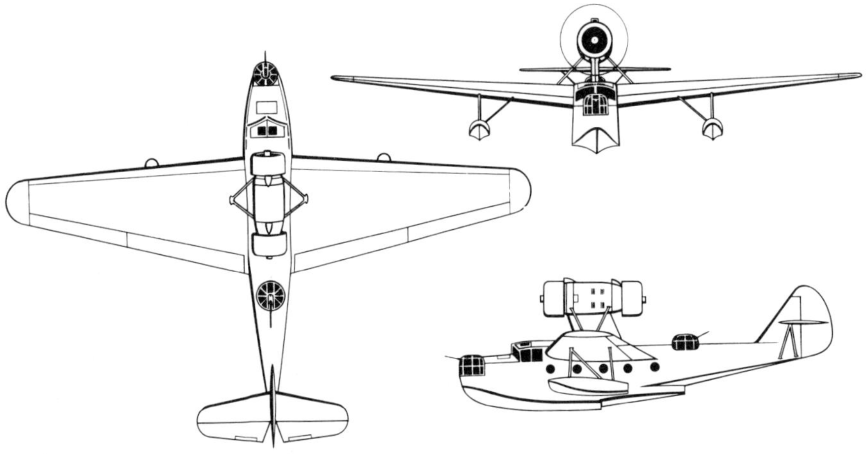

ARK-3

height (1) 308 km/h (191 mph), (2) 320 km/h (199 mph); climb to 1 km 3·5 min; endurance 7 h; time 360° turn 45 s; alighting speed 110 km/h (68 mph).

MDR-6 (Chye-2) Designed in 1936, this modern long-range military flying boat was a bold and original creation, and the designer's only real success. Quite shallow and streamlined hull, with gull wing and high-mounted engines to keep propellers out of spray. Structure light-alloy stressed skin, but fabric-covered flight control surfaces and some other parts. Skin plating of planing bottom and wing primary structure 2 mm, hull mainly 0·8 mm. Generally advanced flush riveting with dimpled holes. No flaps shown or mentioned in most literature, though certainly fitted; one report states full-span, with inset ailerons. Transverse main step, planing bottom tapered to a point at second step. Braced tailplane and fixed stabilizing floats. Fuel in wings. Normal crew only three: pilot, nav/gunner in front turret and radio/observer in rear dorsal turret. Spare seat on right of pilot cockpit. Armament: Shavrov 'three ShKAS'; Alexander 'one ShKAS and one UBT, or two pairs of ShKAS'; Němeček 'one ShKAS in nose turret, two UBT in dorsal'. Racks under wing for load of 400 kg, overload 1000 kg (12 stores total), with nose bombsight.

Prototype flown July 1937 with M-25 engines, replaced by M-25Ye and then by M-62. In early 1938 M-63 fitted, and this engine selected for 50 production examples, built at Taganrog 1939–40. Called Aircraft N, Letter *ash* (Ш). Entered service 1941 redesignated Chye-2 with Baltic Fleet, and in Black Sea from October 1941. Good service apart from hull weakness at Frame 10, severe vibration in plane of propellers and incomplete fuel-system drain and venting.

Taganrog/Sevastopol overrun early 1942 and no further series production. Designer strove ceaselessly to improve MDR-6, but instead of rectifying faults kept making major redesign to increase speed, which was not a requirement. **MDR-6B-1** designed autumn 1939 and flown December 1940, with dramatic reduction in span, normal slotted flaps inboard of ailerons, more powerful liquid-cooled engines, low-drag twin-finned tail and streamlined nose with hand-held ShKAS. Stabilizing floats of advanced design retracted inwards electrically into wing bays so that outer face of float/strut formed smooth bulge. Major structural redesign, especially of wing and planing bottom, latter also being of better hydrodynamic shape. Electric dorsal turret with two UBT. Provision for four stores of up to 250 kg each. **MDR-6B-2** completed June 1941, differed in having radiators built into wing box between spars instead of behind rear spar of dihedralled centre section (where precluded flaps). Both B-1 and B-2 departed for State trials 16 October 1941. B-2 more scope for development, but low priority.

Chyetverikov reluctantly gave up complex low-drag engine installation, which put propellers in bow spray, and in December 1943 at last flew **MDR-6B-3**, with simple SB-type engines with higher thrust lines and frontal radiators. Many other changes included third fin, fixed stabilizing floats and side blisters instead of turret. Large bow strake added, also seen on MDR-6 in combat service. **MDR-6B-4**, flown May 1944 and State trials December 1944 to July 1945, returned to retracting floats but of improved design, other changes including a hull of greater beam (2,2 instead of 1,9 m) and raised tail. Crew of four, armament three UBT and four FAB-250 bombs. Final aircraft was **MDR-6B-5**, flown 1946. Even more powerful engines, radiators in boxes under wing, forward hull further enlarged and lengthened 0,5 m, span 0,5 m greater, tail of greater span without central fin, fixed floats. Hand-held B-20 in nose (200 rounds) and SEB electric dorsal turret with twin B-20 (150 rounds each); four FAB-250 or two FAB-500. Called Aircraft B; State trials late 1946 but no report written.

DIMENSIONS Span 21,0 m (68 ft 11 in), (B-1 to B-4) 16,2 m (53 ft 2 in), (B-5) 16,7 m (54 ft 9½ in); length 15,7 m (51 ft 6 in), (B-5) 16,2 m (53 ft 2 in); wing area 59,2 m^2 (639 ft^2), (B-1 to B-4) 48,0 m^2 (517 ft^2), (B-5) 49,4 m^2 (532 ft^2).

ENGINES Two 750 hp M-25 or 25Ye driving two-blade Hamilton propellers, (Chye-2) 1000 hp M-62 or M-63, (B-1) 1050 hp M-105 with three-blade c/s VISh, (B-2) 1050 hp VK-105, (B-3, B-4) 1150 hp VK-105PF. (B-5) 1650 hp VK-107A with four-blade VISh.

WEIGHTS Empty 4087 kg (9010 lb), (Chye-2) about same, (B-1, -2, -3) all about 4250 kg (9369 lb), (B-4) 4700 kg (10,361 lb), (B-5) 5610 kg (12,368 lb); fuel/oil (most) 1570 + 110 kg, (B-5) 3250 kg total; loaded 6450 kg (14,220 lb), (Chye-2) 6500 kg (14,330 lb), (B-1 to B-3) 7200 kg (15,873 lb), (B-4) 8200 kg (18,077 lb), (B-5) 10 080 kg (22,222 lb).

PERFORMANCE Max speed 338 km/h (210 mph) at 3 km, (Chye-2) 350 km/h (217 mph) at 4 km, (B-1, -2) 454 km/h (282 mph) at 6 km, (B-3, -4) 430 km/h (267 mph) at 6 km, (B-5) 472 km/h (293 mph) at 7 km; climb to 5 km (Chye-2) 15 min; range (Chye-2) 2650 km (1647 miles); take-off and alighting runs, both 350/400 m.

MDR-6, Chye-2

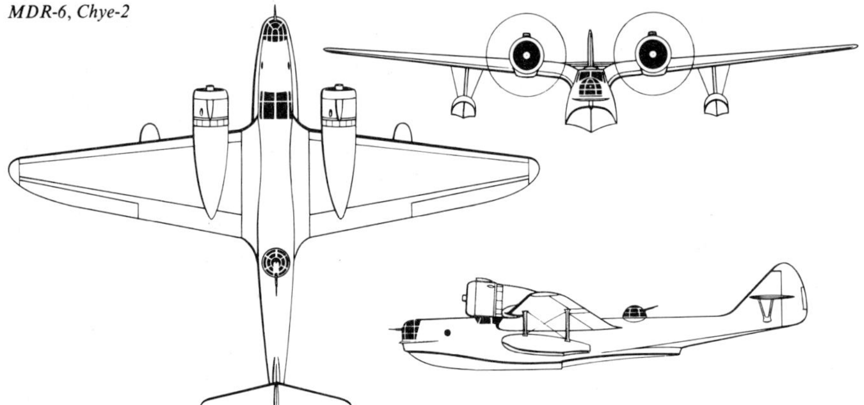

MDR-6, Chye-2

MDR-6B-1

MDR-6B-3

MDR-6B-4

U-1

TA Simple dural stressed-skin *Transportnaya Amfibiya* (transport amphibian), designed immediately after war. Spacious hull for crew of two and six to eight passengers (by modern standards room for more) and 1 tonne cargo. Fabric-covered control surfaces. Untapered wing of NACA-23015 15% profile with electric slotted flaps (30° takeoff, 50° landing), mounted on pylon and braced by N-struts. Stabilizing floats fixed near wing-tips. Electrically retracting landing gear, main units raised flush into sides of hull, Completed June 1947 and tested from airfield and water until November when main gear broke at take-off and TA landed on keel. Repaired but OKB closed before resumption of testing.

TA-1, second aircraft with semicircular wing-tips added and retractable stabilizing floats. Sliding (area-increasing) flaps and various other changes. Completed May 1948, State trial report 20 June but no production decision. **TAF**, *TA Fotografichyeskii*, photo variant with new outer wings of tapered and increased-span design (dimensions not known). Flew successfully late 1948 but OKB closed down shortly afterwards at end of year. Possibly TA was victim of circumstance and could have been cured of faults.

DIMENSIONS Span 17,2 m (56 ft 5¼ in), (TA-1) 17,8 m (58 ft 5 in), (TAF) over 17,8 m; length 14,0 m (45 ft 11 in); wing area 43,0 m² (463 ft²), (TA-1) 43,6 m² (469 ft²).

ENGINES Two 700 hp ASh-21 driving VISh propellers of 2,8 m diam with three scimitar blades.

WEIGHTS Empty 4658 kg (10,269 lb), (TA-1) 4510 kg (9943 lb), (TAF) 4268 kg (9409 lb); fuel/oil 550 + 55 kg; loaded 6255 kg (13,790 lb), (TA-1) 6107 kg (13,463 lb), (TAF) 5758 kg (12,694 lb).

PERFORMANCE Max speed 328 km/h (204 mph) at 1,7 km; range 700 km (435 miles), (TAF) 1200 km (746 miles, not explained on same fuel); take-off/landing runs 240/380 m on land.

Dudakov -Konstantinov

These two engineers are the only ones named in connection with the long and important Soviet career of the Avro 504—apart from Ilyushin who got it started. It is not known at what point they became involved with the U-1 programme.

U-1 In 1919 an Avro 504K of White (anti-Bolshyevik) forces was shot down and captured almost undamaged. Taken to Moscow by young S.V. Ilyushin, it was soon decided that this famous and highly developed machine was the best choice as standard trainer for the future Red air force, but it was not until 1923 that the drawings for the U-1 (*Uchyebnii*, training) had been completed at the Dux factory (GAZ-1). Manufacture began at the Red Airman plant, GAZ-3, in Petrograd (later Leningrad). There was no licence agreement for either the aircraft or its engine, the 110 hp Le Rhône rechristened M-2. A total of 664 U-1 trainers, all apparently similar to the original 504K, were built at GAZ-3 by 1931, together with a locally developed twin-float variant (73 built 1924-1930) designated **MU-1**. In 1927 the production factory completed full static testing and structural calculations for the U-1, the first time this had been done on any aircraft since the revolution.

MU-1 used floats based on the British design but modified in shape and construction. Originally strong but heavy (211 kg the pair) and with heavy steel-tube and wood struts. Later lighter (170 kg). Noteworthy that no satisfactory float version of U-2 (Po-2) was ever developed, and MU-1 remained in use until 1934. In 1931 a U-1 (land version) was fitted with the first assisted take-off powder rockets tested in the Soviet Union and possibly in the world. Pilot S.I. Mukhin was airborne in measured time 1·5 s. Popular name of U-1 was *Avrushka*. Several modified for special tests, but data basically as for standard Avro 504K.

Ekonomov

Pavel Ivanovich Ekonomov, professional aviation carpenter and joiner, was a prolific inventor and made various propositions while he was working at MAI in 1930s. In 1936 he constructed primitive but large rotary-wing craft with two contra-rotating sets of two-blade rotors (virtually large wings) of 22 m (72 ft) diameter. Thick wing profile, each with aileron. Called *Zhiroplan*; never completed.

Fedorov

Dmitrii Dmitriyevich Fedorov was born in Kungur in 1875. In 1897 he was arrested for distributing subversive literature and exiled, but managed to become trained aviation engineer in Germany. After 1917 revolution Fedorov returned to his native land and brought with him a design for a two-seat reconnaissance biplane. He managed to continue work at the Anatra

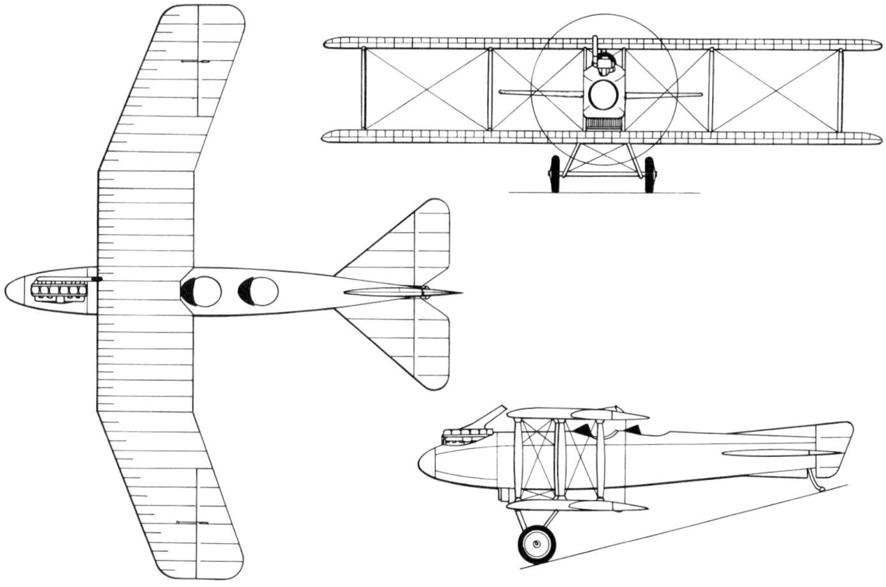

DF-1

factory at Odessa. When this was 'liquidated' he made his way to Factory No 15 at Simferopol (another report states 'aircraft repair plant of 4th Red Army', possibly same location). Here construction of his aircraft began with enthusiasm but difficulties appalling. Constructor became ill before work was finished, and died 22 December 1922.

DF-1 Tough two-bay biplane, of unusual form with large (5 m span) centre sections on upper and lower planes, 20° swept-back 3,5 m outer panels with transverse-axis ailerons, fuselage mounted on struts midway between wings, and long, shallow vertical tail. Incorporated some Farman and Nieuport parts, but essentially original. Mainly wooden, with truss fuselage and machined wood wing spars. First flown by engineer Pavel Pavlovich Uspasskii, who, with assistance of pilot Ryabovim, carried out test programme in May/June 1922. Aircraft proved most satisfactory, with straightforward take-off and good control, small difficulties easily improved. First reconnaissance aircraft built in Soviet Union, but impossible to build in quantity though a second was complete before Factory No 15 was shut.

DIMENSIONS Span 12,0 m (39 ft 4¾ in); length 10,0 m (32 ft 9¾ in); wing area 47,5 m² (511 ft²).
ENGINE 280 hp Maybach 6-inline.
WEIGHTS Empty 1000 kg (2205 lb); fuel about 500 kg; loaded 1700 kg (3748 lb).
PERFORMANCE Max speed 170 km/h (106 mph).

Florov

I.F. Florov survived 1941–1945 war, unlike co-designer Borovkov on BI-1, and in 1943 was designing completely new rocket aircraft. Though it owed much to BI-1, No 4302 was more refined and intended not for combat but for aerodynamic research.

No 4302 This aircraft was planned before any German data had become available, and wing and tail were aerodynamically conventional. Wing profile by G.P. Svishchyev at TsAGI, laminar acrofoil of 13% thickness with aspect ratio 5. Trailing edge incorporated three sliding (Fowler type) flaps on each side also used—possibly with spoilers—for lateral control. Tips turned 30° downwards. Manual tail controls with fixed endplate fins on tailplane. Pressurized nose cockpit with upward-hinged canopy. Jettisonable takeoff trolley and skid/tailwheel alighting gear, but prototype originally built with conventional fixed main landing gears for slow-speed test flying. Tailwheel and strut from La-5. Main tanks in fuselage for propellants in Enerzh 18-8 stainless steel, 3 mm thick, tightly wound with OVS wire (implying gas-pressure feed). Full power for 1 min, normal flight endurance 20 min.

Aircraft constructed from 1944; test pilot familiarization and ground testing 1946 and first flight 1947. Pilots (Heroes of the Soviet Union) Paxomov and Yakubov. Initial programme with fixed gear for sole purpose of testing rocket engine (ZhRD, aircraft also sometimes given this designation). Intention later to attain higher speeds. Initial flights up to 520 km/h at 5 km. Later high-speed programme cancelled at end 1947 because of greater potential of jet fighters.

No data except gross weight with original 1100 kg Isayev engine 2400 kg (5291 lb). Later intended to be fitted with Dushkin engine, see next entry.

No 4303 Second experimental aircraft, with ZhRD (rocket) by L.S. Dushkin, rated at 1140 kg thrust. Aircraft completed late 1947 as glider, but flight development never started and rocket engine never installed.

Golubkov

From the end of 1939 until late 1940 A.P. Golubkov was running his own brigade working on the project described below. Main objective was to produce drawings and mock-ups (engineering and systems and for choice of powerplants). Believed this project was passed over from Tupolev OKB with ANT number between 54 and 57. At end of 1940 Golubkov was pulled off this project and assigned wartime task of modifying foreign aircraft, including C-47, DB-7, and B-25. After war rejoined Tupolev to work on Tu-104.

SRB Few details available beyond designation (*Skorostnoi Razvyedchik-Bombardirovshchik*, high-speed reconnaissance-bomber. Twin-engined, stressed-skin, possibly a cousin of family that led to Tu-2 (speculation).

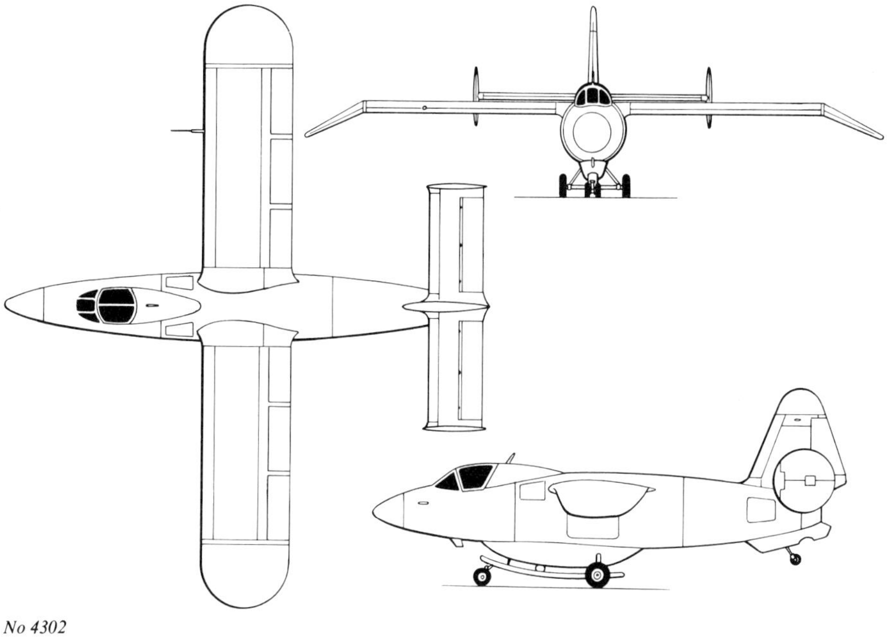

No 4302

Gorbunov

Vladimir Petrovich Gorbunov was chief of tech directorate of NKAP when he became partner with Lavochkin in I-22 and subsequent LaGG programme.

GSh This designation has been suggested, but not confirmed, for two-seat armoured attacker (BSh category) with one AM-37 engine. No details, but direct rival to Il-2. Success of latter caused project to be abandoned in 1942.

105 In 1941 Gorbunov decided, or was assigned, to make modifications to LaGG-3 to improve fighting capability. No possibility of switching to more powerful engine, so only possibility was to reduce weight, whilst also improving rear vision. Under designation No 105 (one report states I-105, and this is possible; also called LaGG-3 *Oblegchennyi* (lightened), work was completed and prototype flown autumn 1942. Careful refinement of airframe to reduce weight. Main alterations: cut-down rear fuselage with Yak-1M type canopy sliding to rear, removal of wing slats, aileron mass-balances and main-gear well doors, simplification of fuel and coolant systems, and reduction of armament to one B-20 and one BS. Total weight reduction 300 kg (661 lb), but though 105 proved major improvement, no production ordered in view of equally good rivals such as La-5 already available in quantity.
DIMENSIONS Span 9,8 m (32 ft 2 in); length 8,81 m (28 ft 11 in); wing area 17,5 m² (188 ft²).
ENGINE One 1260 hp M-105PF-1.
WEIGHTS Empty 2400 kg (5291 lb); fuel/oil 332 kg (732 lb); loaded 2865 kg (6316 lb).
PERFORMANCE Max speed (SL) 570 km/h (354 mph), (4 km) 623 km/h (387 mph); climb 6 min to 5 km; range 1100 km (684 miles).

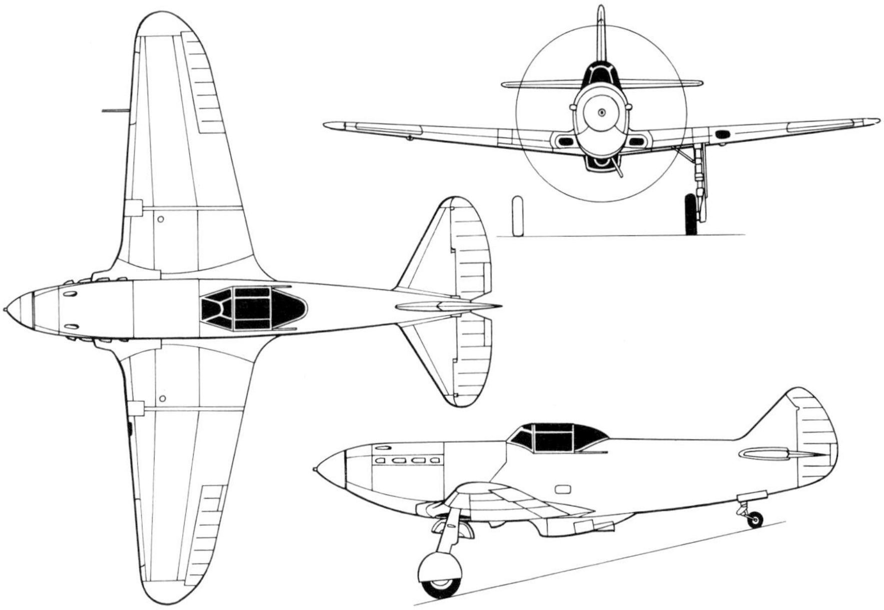

No 105

Gribovskii

Vladislav Konstantinovich Gribovskii was born 1909 and raised in Gatchina. Passionately interested in aviation, he wrote to first Russian glider pilot, Vyekshin, and pestered other pilots after he came to Petrograd during First World War. In 1919 he tried to get into an aviation school but eventually joined 2nd Petrograd Artillery School. He finally made it to theoretical aviation course in Moscow in January 1921. In 1922 he learned to fly at Sevastopol, and following year was back in Moscow training on Red fighters (mainly Nieuports). Attended first Soviet air firing school, was posted to Kiev, and in 1924 attended second all-union glider trials at Koktebel. This set him off designing his own machines, and though he continued in VVS until 1930, partly as instructor at air-firing school, he was increasingly involved in designing, helping Osoaviakhim and putting light aviation on map. In 1933 he finally became a full-time designer, leading Osoaviakhim Moscow KB (MKB). Altogether he created 14 aeroplane types and 17 gliders.

G-1 Originally glider, flown Koktebel 1925. Wood/fabric, mid-wing monoplane, cockpit ahead of wing above twin wheels.

G-2 Early (possibly first) Soviet sailplane, jointly with A.B. Yumashyev. Successful, led to small series G-2bis 1927–1931.

G-3 Project for four-seat transport glider. Studied as carrier for military airborne assault.

G-4 First aeroplane, never flown. Strut-braced high-wing monoplane, 30 hp Bristol Cherub, built Serpukhov 1926.

G-5 First aeroplane flown, at Orenburg 1928. Neat wooden low-wing monoplane, oval-section monocoque fuselage, wings and tail of high aspect ratio. Single open cockpit. No bracing struts except for landing gear.
SPAN 9,0 m (29 ft 7 in); length 5,1 m (16 ft 9 in); wing area 9,0 m² (97 ft²).
ENGINE One 18 hp Blackburn Tomtit.
WEIGHTS Empty 170 kg (375 lb); fuel 20 kg; loaded 270 kg (595 lb).
PERFORMANCE Max speed 130 km/h (81 mph); ceiling 4,5 km; range 350 km (217 miles)/3 h; landing speed 60 km/h (37 mph).

G-6 High-performance sailplane, developed with expert pilot V.A. Stepanchenok. Set record endurance 10 h 22 min.

G-7 Training glider, 1931.

G-8 Single-seat sporting and training aircraft. Streamlined monocoque fuselage skinned 1·5/2 mm ply, integral with low wing centre-section. Two-spar left/right wings with thin ply skin back to rear spar. Set structural pattern for subsequent designs. Several notable flights.
DIMENSIONS Span 8,0 m (26 ft 3 in); length 5,0 m (16 ft 5 in); wing area 9,0 m² (97 ft²).
ENGINE One 60 hp Walter NZ-60 4-inline.
WEIGHTS Empty 320 kg (705 lb); fuel 70 kg; loaded 483 kg (1065 lb).
PERFORMANCE Max speed 150 km/h (93 mph); climb 7 min to 1 km, 18 to 2; ceiling 3 km; range 550 km (342 miles)/4 h; take-off 85 m/12 s; landing 100 m/80 km/h/14 s.

G-9 Gribovskii's most important training glider, built in large series from 1932. Simple single seat. Conducted pioneer tests with air towing (U-1) 1933, and subsequently regular feature of Aviation Day show at Tushino with 11 in V-formation towed by each TB-1. One test after high release included 176 loops and ten spins of 1·5 to 6 turns, among other manoeuvres. In 1934 Simonov remained on tow 35 h 11 min; many other notable flights.

G-10 Another attractive single-seat sporting machine, built at GAZ-1 1933. Streamlined monocoque fuselage, two-spar wing mounted on shallow pylon and braced by V-struts, spatted main wheels. Provided useful data with both engines.
DIMENSIONS Span 8,4 m (27 ft 6¾ in); length 5,6 m (18 ft 4½ in); wing area 11 m² (118 ft²).
ENGINE One 65 hp M-23; later one 60 hp Walter.
WEIGHTS Empty 335 kg (Walter 330 kg, 726 lb); fuel/oil 75 + 10 kg: loaded 510 kg (Walter 505 kg, 1,113 lb).
PERFORMANCE Max speed 170 km/h (Walter 165 km/h, 102·5 mph); climb 5 min to 1 km, 11 to 2 km (Walter 13 min); ceiling 5,2 km (Walter 4,8); range 700 km (435 miles) (1300 km overload fuel); take-off 100 m/7 s; landing 80 m/67 km/h (42 mph).

G-11 Not known. This was VVS designation of later G-29.

G-12 First Soviet water-based glider; monoplane with parasol wing and planing hull. Built 1933 at No 19 Sadovo-Spasskaya Street, Moscow (basement was occupied by GIRD rocket team).

G-13 Not known.

G-14 Training glider, especially for aero-towing. Single centreline wheel, tandem seats. Manufacture passed to factory collective 'Aviakhim' with participation of Shcherbakov.

G-5

G-15 First touring aircraft, two seats side-by-side. Circular monocoque fuselage integral with centre section and fin. Outer panels ply-skinned back to rear spar, slotted flaps and slotted ailerons. Four fuel tanks between spars. Engine in long-chord NACA cowl. Fabric-skinned control surfaces. Trousered main gears. Built at glider works 1934; regarded as outstanding in concept and performance. In 1935 suffered engine failure when 100 km out from Moscow but made safe forced landing.
DIMENSIONS Span 11,0 m (36 ft 1¼ in); length 6,2 m (20 ft 4¼ in); wing area 14,0 m² (151 ft²).
ENGINE One 100 hp M-11.
WEIGHTS Empty 670 kg (1477 lb); fuel/oil 92 + 10 kg: loaded 940 kg (2072 lb).
PERFORMANCE Max speed 185 km/h (115 mph); ceiling 4,5 km (14,760 ft); range 1400 km (870 miles); landing speed 70 km/h (43·5 mph).

G-16 Refined glider flying boat, 1935. For first time (in world, probably) demonstrated practicability of aero-tow take-off from sea; flown by Gribovskii behind Sh-2 flown by L.G. Minov.

G-17/19 Not known, but one was project for canard with same wing as G-15.

G-20 Low-wing strut-braced trainer, with enclosed tandem cockpit. Wing R-II profile, variable chord and thickness with patented manual flaps. Inverted-vee steel struts braced wing and formed apex of crash pylon to protect front-seat occupant. Ground-adjustable braced tailplane. Spatted main wheels. Successful tests but much improved 1937 by switch to more powerful engine in same helmeted cowl. Subsequently trained some 70 pilots.
DIMENSIONS Span 9,7 m (31 ft 10 in); length 6,3 m (20 ft 8 in); wing area 13,2 m² (142 ft²).
ENGINE One 100 hp M-11; from 1937 one 150 hp M-11Ye.
WEIGHTS Empty 607 kg (1338 lb, (M-11Ye) 620 kg (1367 lb); fuel/oil 69 kg (M-11Ye, 100 kg); loaded 836 kg (1843 lb), (M-11Ye) 880 kg (1940 lb).
PERFORMANCE Max speed 209 km/h (130 mph), (M-11Ye) 235 km/h (146 mph); climb (original engine) 4·6 min to 1 km, 11·1 to 2; ceiling 3870 m (12,700 ft); range 400 km (overload fuel 1017 km, 632 miles); take-off 190 m/14 s; landing 70 km/h (43·5 mph).

G-21 Neat touring, sporting or ambulance aircraft, 1936. Low-wing cantilever monoplane, two- or three-seat enclosed cabin in wood monocoque fuselage. Spatted main gears on ends of centre section. Wing geometrically similar to G-15 with skin 1·5 mm ply round leading edge, then 1 mm to rear spar and fabric aft. Automatic slats, joined by steel tubes left/right wings, slotted ailerons. G-21 made several long-range flights with extra fuselage tank.
DIMENSIONS Span 11,0 m (36 ft 1¼ in); length 7,0 m (23 ft 0 in); wing area 14 m² (151 ft²).
ENGINE One 150 hp M-11Ye.
WEIGHTS Empty 705 kg (1554 lb); fuel/oil 105 + 10 kg; loaded 980 kg (2160 lb).
PERFORMANCE Max speed 220 km/h (137 mph); climb 5·6 min to 1 km; ceiling 4760 m (15,600 ft); range (normal fuel) 500 km (311 miles); landing speed 70 km/h (43·5 mph).

G-22 Extremely clean single-seat sporting aircraft, first flown 1936. All wood but fuselage of truss type (vertical sides) instead of monocoque. One-piece wing with single spar, ply ahead and fabric to rear. Frise ailerons hung on door hinges level with upper wing surface. Main gears with spatted balloon tyres. Several notable performances such as 164,94 km/h by Ekaterina Mednikova, women's record for class, 3 June 1938. In 1939 re-engined with Pobjoy and in 1940 with M-23.
DIMENSIONS Span 8,7 m (28 ft 6½ in); length 5,6 m (18 ft 4½ in) (varied slightly with engine); wing area 10,0 m² (108 ft²).
ENGINE One 50 hp Walter Mikron inverted 4-inline; (1938) 80 hp Pobjoy Niagara 7-cylinder radial; (1940) 65 hp M-23.
WEIGHTS Empty (Walter) 210 kg (463 lb); fuel/oil 35 kg; loaded 325 kg (716 lb).
PERFORMANCE Max speed 165 km/h (102·5 mph), (Pobjoy) 190 km/h (118 mph), (M-23) 170 km/h (106 mph); ceiling (Walter) 3 km (9842 ft); range 350 km (217 miles); take-off and landing both 80–85 m/10 s/55 km/h (34 mph).

G-23 Komsomolyets 2 Tandem two-seat low-wing machine completed February 1937 to evaluate GAZ-M-1 (Avia) car-derived engine. Spatted main gears (most of Gribovskii's aircraft also flew on skis in winter) but simple and no slats or flaps. Tested by NII VVS; speed commendable but climb abysmal. Nevertheless, flown by I. Grodzyanskii Moscow Tushino / Kharkov / Zaporozhye / Kerch / Zaporozhye / Kharkov / Orel / Moscow 2584 km in 21 h flying time. Second (1938) machine, **G-23bis**, totally different animal with M-11Ye radial and startling performance. On 23 July 1938 Grodzyanskii reached 7266 m; on 2 August N.D. Fedosyeev reached figure given in data. Late 1938 fitted with new GAZ-11 as **G-23bis-GAZ**.
DIMENSIONS Span 11,0 m (36 ft 1¼ in); length (M-11Ye) 10,5 m (34 ft 5½ in); wing area 15,0 m² (161 ft²), (M-11Ye) 14,9 m² (160 ft²).
ENGINE One 56 hp GAZ-M-60; (G-23bis) 150 hp M-11Ye; (bis GAZ) 85 hp GAZ-11.
WEIGHTS Empty 483 kg (1065 lb); fuel/oil 40 + 14 kg; loaded 713 kg (1572 lb); no figures for G-23bis.
PERFORMANCE Max speed 150 km/h (93 mph), (bis) 179 km/h (111 mph), bis-GAZ 160 km/h (99 mph); climb 19 min to 1 km, 58 to 2 (bis figures, 1·5 and 3·4!); ceiling 2480 m (bis 7985 m, 26,200 ft); range 450 km (280 miles); take-off (GAZ) 150 m/16 s; landing 90 m/10 s/65 km/h (40 mph).

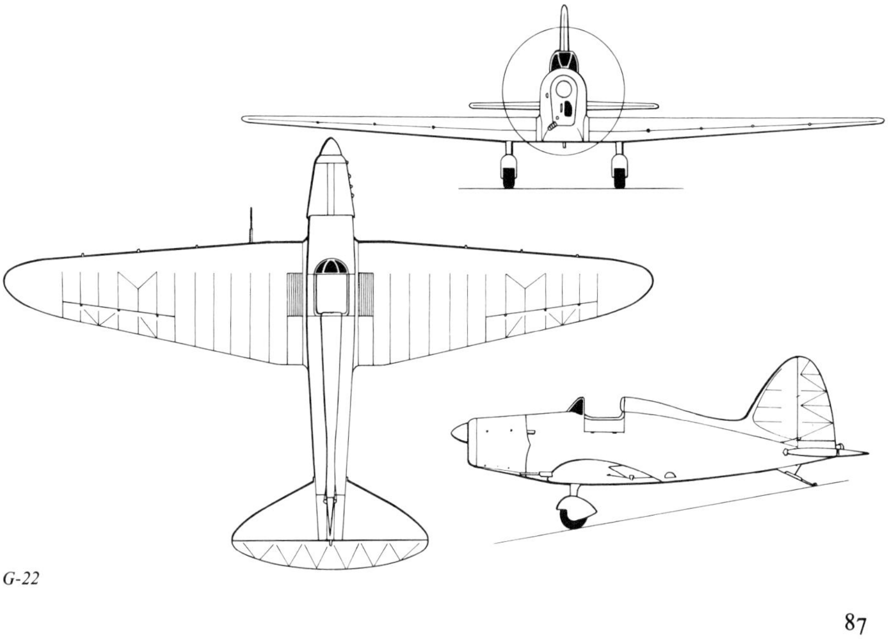

G-22

G-24 Not known.

G-25 Possibly Gribovskii's only biplane, this neat machine was built at MKB in 1937 to see to what extent a practical tandem trainer could be made smaller and more economical than U-2. Outstanding all round performance and manoeuvrability, but of course could not equal U-2 versatility in utility roles. Engine newly imported from Britain, not same as G-23bis. But when GAZ engine removed from G-23 in 1938 it was installed in G-25, which became **G-25bis**. Performance unacceptable, but MKB also received newly designed GAZ-11 of 85 hp and with this installed G-25bis flew reasonably well.

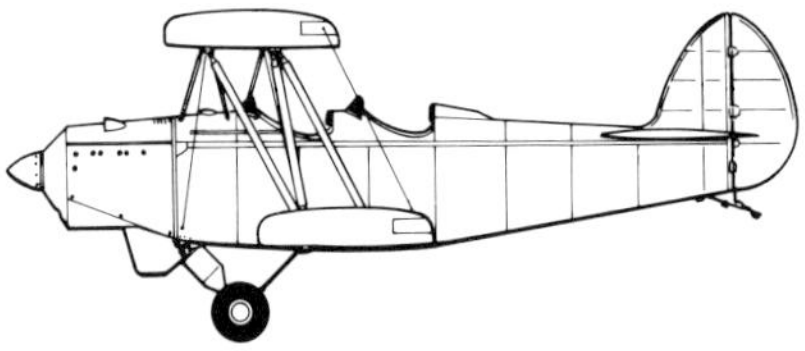

G-25

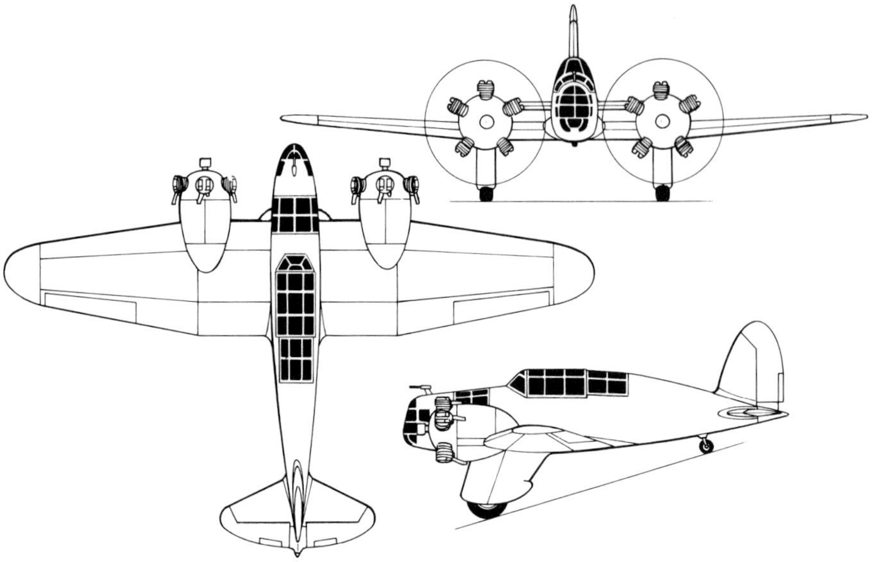

G-27

DIMENSIONS Span 9,0 m (29 ft 6½ in); length 6,4 m (21 ft 0 in); wing area 23,0 m² (248 ft²).
ENGINE (25) one 85 hp Pobjoy Niagara II 7-cylinder radial, (bis) one 85 hp GAZ-Avia-11.
WEIGHTS Empty (25) 430 kg (948 kg), (bis) 500 kg (1102 lb); fuel/oil 40 kg; loaded (25) 630 kg (1389 lb), (bis) 700 kg (1543 lb).
PERFORMANCE Max speed 170 km/h (106 mph), (bis) 165 km/h (102·5 mph); ceiling 3,5 km 11,480 ft); range 280 km (174 miles); take-off 40 m (bis, 80); landing 60 m at 55 km/h (bis, 80 m at 65 km/h).

G-26 Attractive low-wing sporting aircraft, structurally almost identical to G-22. Pilot in open cockpit further aft than in G-22 and design biassed heavily in favour of performance rather than simple training and aerobatics. G-26 not an aircraft for novice. Flew late 1938 on skis. Handling improved during 1939.
DIMENSIONS Span 7,7 m (25 ft 3¼ in); length 6,0 m (19 ft 9 in); wing area 9,0 m² (97 ft²).
ENGINE One 140 hp MG-40 inverted 4-inline.
WEIGHTS Not known.
PERFORMANCE Max speed 290 km/h (180 mph); range 350 km (217 miles).

G-27 In late 1930s Gribovskii campaigned—insofar as anyone could—for a modern crew trainer for VVS. He was concerned at inability of service to train bomber crews before they actually flew in advanced and costly machines such as SB and DB-3. He spent much time in 1938 designing safe and economical aircraft that could serve as three-seat crew trainer, light transport, ambulance, photo and for various other duties. It is curious that this useful aircraft, which could have been employed in large numbers as were Anson, Oxford, Beech 18 family and many other Western types, should never have been built in series. Structure wooden, with slim monocoque fuselage. Wing with rectangular centre section (1,62 m chord) with small (1,53 m²) pneumatic split flaps, two-spar all-wood outer panels with slotted ailerons, and tailwheel landing gear. At different times main gears were trousered (first flight), fixed unspatted, fully retractable and skis. Gibovskii designed a floatplane version, not built. Structural provision for nose machine gun and light bombs under centre section. Normal military crew three: nav/bomb in nose, pilot, and observer/radio in rear seat; could have dual control but rear-seat vision not good. Apparently many thought G-27 should have been mass-produced; one recent Soviet report suggests preoccupation with G-11 (G-29), supposedly needed more urgently, prevented this.
DIMENSIONS Span 10,6 m (34 ft 9½ in); length 6,99 m (22 ft 11½ in); wing area 17 m² (183 ft²).
ENGINES Two 100 hp M-11; 1941 re-engined with 150 hp M-11Ye.
WEIGHTS Empty 900 kg (1984 lb); fuel/oil 130 kg; loaded 1300 kg (2866 lb), (M-11Ye) 1430 kg (3153 lb).
PERFORMANCE Max speed 240 km/h (149 mph), (M-11Ye) 250 km/h (155 mph); ceiling 4 km (M-11Ye 5 km); landing speed 80 km/h (50 mph).

G-28 (TI-28) For many years it was believed that this speedy single-seater had been planned purely as entrant in August 1941 Osoaviakhim all-union air race. Named *Kryechet* (hawk, gerfalcon) and only recently has it become known that it was actually (or additionally) planned as a TI (*Trenirovochni Istrebitel*, trainer fighter), and received VVS designation TI-28. Structure was all-wood, with no fabric anywhere except on flight controls which were duralumin framed. Dural flaps, pneumatic operation. Fin integral with monocoque fuselage, with pilot behind wing under sliding canopy. Two-spar wing, RAF-34 section. Fixed landing gear with single cantilevered oleo struts on front spar, castoring tailwheel. Engine on steel-tube mounts with light-alloy cowl, driving two-blade propeller (described as fixed-pitch, but photos show Ratier v-p). Provision for reflector sight, one synchron-

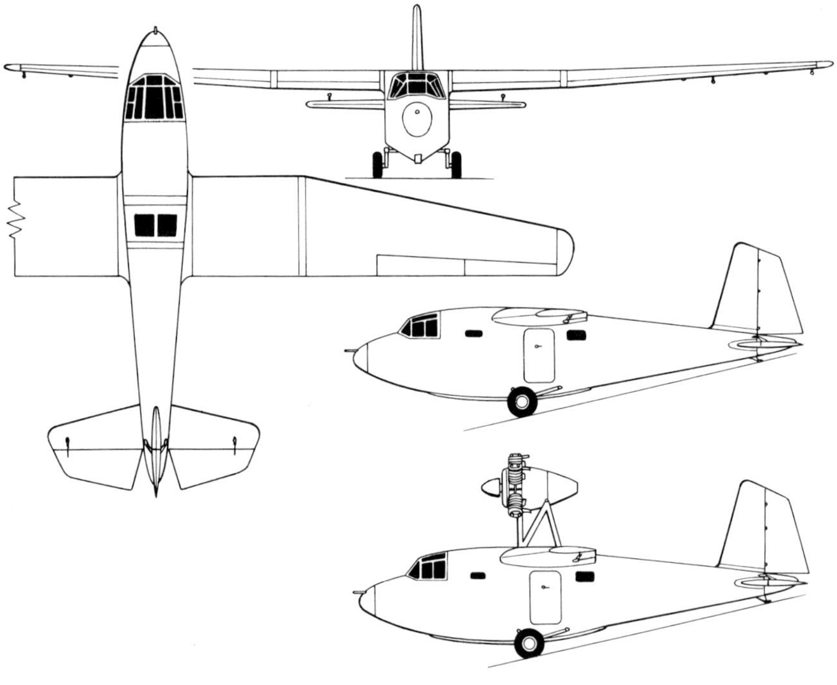

G-29, G-11, lower side view G-30, G-11M

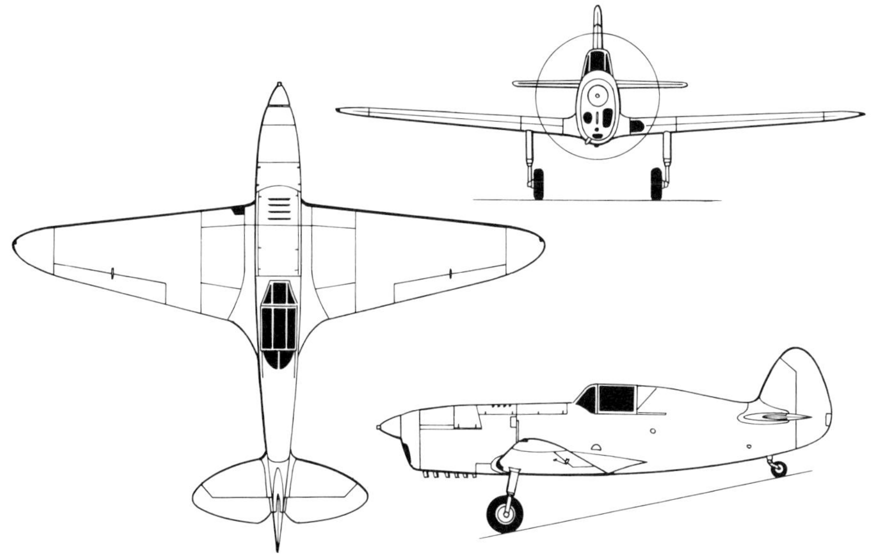

G-28

ized ShKAS with 400 rounds, combat camera in left wing root, and underwing racks for two bombs of 10, 25 or 40 kg. Flown by V. Gavrilov for MKB on 22 May 1941, just a month before invasion. NII VVS testing by M.M. Gromov, A.B. Yumashyev and P.M. Stefanovskii. Satisfactory, though Gribovskii wanted more powerful MV-6A engine for production version. Latter was unable to be implemented because of over-riding need to produce G-29 (G-11). Note: there is evidence original design was a racer, with retractable gear, intended for 400 km/h. Not yet explained why first aircraft, completed just before race, was a fixed-gear military prototype.
DIMENSIONS Span 9,0 m (29 ft 6¼ in); length 7,66 m (25 ft 1⅛ in); wing area 11,6 m^2 (125 ft^2).
ENGINE One 240 hp MV-6 inverted 6-inline.
WEIGHTS Empty 897 kg (1978 lb); loaded (no bombs) 1157 kg (2551 lb).
PERFORMANCE Max speed at SL 275 km/h, at 1,6 km 303 km/h (188 mph); climb 19·4 min to 5 km; service ceiling 6,6 km; range at 90% max speed 500 km (497 miles); time for 360° turn at height 20 s; landing speed with flaps 90,5 km/h (56 mph).

G-29 (G-11) Important type almost unknown until recently, G-29 was Gribovskii's largest aircraft and one of few to go into production. Designed 1940 in parallel with A-7, it was a large assault glider (though small in comparison with later KS-20, BDP and SAM-23) of wooden construction, intended for simple production by quickly trained labour. Frame-truss fuselage with vertical sides, but fish-like streamlined side profile. Two-spar wing with 6,3 m rectangular centre section mounted in high position with spars integral with fuselage frames. Outer panels tapered on leading edge, aspect ratio 10·8. Split landing flaps worked from air bottles with standby hand pump. Landing gear with two main wheels attached to fuselage frame and rear tailskid. Wheels to be jettisoned on operational mission, landing being made on skid on centreline of V-shaped bottom of fuselage. Single-seat cockpit in nose glazed with fixed panes of flat Plexiglas. Main cabin with accommodation for 11 troops or 1,1 tonne cargo, with door on left side and escape hatch in roof. Tow hook well back under nose; usual tug SB, DB-3, Il-4 or Li-2. Tested 1941 and NII VVS trials in same year by team of six led by V. Fedorov. Production as G-11 (VVS designation) begun late 1941; probably 100 built.
DIMENSIONS Span 18,0 m (59 ft 0¾ in); length 9,8 m (32 ft 1¾ in); wing area 30,0 m^2 (323 ft^2).
WEIGHTS Empty 1200 kg (2646 lb); loaded 2400 kg (5291 lb).
PERFORMANCE Max speed on tow or free 280 km/h; normal gliding speed 146 km/h (91 mph), with gliding angle 19·2 and rate of sink 2·2 m (7·2 ft)/s; landing speed 82 km/h (51 mph).

G-30 (G-11M) In 1942 Gribovskii decided (one report: 'was requested') to build power-assisted version of G-29. Airframe identical to glider but 100 hp M-11 engine on steel-tube pylon above fuselage, probably with fuel tank in nacelle. Tractor two-blade fixed-pitch propeller with spinner. Test-flown October 1942, and VVS designation G-11M assigned, but State trials never took place. One account states Shche-2 procured instead. Note: G-30 was not transport aeroplane but powered glider, and could hardly take-off loaded. Like Western aircraft (eg, Hamilcar X) it was intended to be able to return to base after delivering load.

G-31 In 1948, with deliveries of G-11 completed, Gribovskii designed two-seat training glider for instruction of military (G-11) pilots. Resulting G-31 was simple all-wood tandem-seater, with shoulder wing with flaps, tailplane mounted part-way up fin, and enclosed cockpits with hinged canopies. Jettisonable twin wheels and skid landing. Single prototype; no post-war requirement for glider pilots.

Dosav 1950 Gribovskii's last known design was light tourer for 1950 Dosav competition (see Avietka section). Most remarkably his offering was light-alloy stressed-skin. Low-wing side-by-side two-seater with enclosed cockpit, dual control, tricycle landing gear and 90 hp engine. No known designation.
DIMENSIONS Span 11,4 m (37 ft 4¾ in); length 7,05 m (23 ft 1½ in); wing area not known.
WEIGHTS Empty 502 kg (1107 lb); loaded 750 kg (1653 lb).
PERFORMANCE Max speed 195 km/h (121 mph); ceiling 5,4 km; landing speed 65 km/h (40 mph).

Grigorovich

Dmitrii Pavlovich Grigorovich was the most important constructor in Russia to have stayed in post-revolutionary Soviet Union and become a famed Soviet designer. Born 1883, he was a full-time student at Kiev polytechnic institute and graduated 1910. His first job was as a journalist on an aviation magazine in St Petersburg, but in January 1913 he was appointed works manager for newly opened aircraft plant of S.S. Shchetinin and M.A. Shcherbakov, second in Russia to build aircraft in series. Batches of Nieuport IV and Farman F.16 were produced, and under Grigorovich's direction the first strength calculations and static structural testing were completed in May/June 1913. He set up on his own by accident; the accident happened to D.N. Aleksandrov, whose flying boat suffered a crushed nose and other damage. Russo-Baltic Wagon Works (later producer of Sikorskii's IM series) quoted 6500 rubles for repair, and Lebed factory 6000. Grigorovich thought a fair price 400, and did the job. This was so extensive result was first Grigorovich aircraft, designated M-1. Long series of aircraft of many classes followed. He was original head of OMOS and later a renowned lecturer at MAI, but suffered period in wilderness under arrest in Hanger 7 at GAZ-39 in 1930–1933. He died in 1938, reportedly as result of illness. Many of his team swelled Lavochkin OKB.

M-1 Original Grigorovich flying boat, produced by not only repairing Aleksandrov's French-built machine (1912 Donnet-Levecque) but also altering it. Designation from *Morskoi* (marine). Original mixed-construction biplane boat with pusher engine, floats at ends of smaller lower wings and tailplane half-way up fin. Two seats in side-by-side cockpit ahead of wings. Provision for beaching trolley. Grigorovich cut 1 m off nose, redesigned wings closer to Farman F.16 profile and reduced height of step from 200 to 80 mm. Flew as M-1 autumn 1913; met requirements with improved flying qualities.
DIMENSIONS Span 9,5 m (31 ft 2 in); length 7,4 m (24 ft 6¾ in); wing area 18,2 m^2 (196 ft^2).
ENGINE One 50 hp Gnome.
WEIGHTS Empty 420 kg (926 lb); loaded 620 kg (1367 lb).
PERFORMANCE Not known.

M-2 Larger two-seater with more powerful engine, first flown 1914. Both wings extended in span, improved planing bottom, modified tail, and wing cellule raised 100 mm above hull. First flying boat in the Soviet Union produced in small series in proper erection berth locating all parts accurately.
DIMENSIONS Span 13,68 m (44 ft 10½ in); length 8,0 m (26 ft 3 in); wing area 33,5 m^2 (361 ft^2).
ENGINE Originally 80 hp Clerget, later 100 hp Gnome Monosoupape.
WEIGHTS Empty, not known; loaded 870 kg (1918 lb).
PERFORMANCE Not known.

M-3 Also called Shchetinin Third, built autumn 1914. Further development to wing profile, giving better flying qualities than M-2, but seaworthiness unacceptable. Data as M-2 with Gnome Monosoupape.

M-4 Developed winter 1914 and flown spring 1915; further modification to wing profile but main attention to hull. Concave step, small longitudinal angle at keel, stabilizing floats of revised form, tailplane set at positive incidence to lift in slipstream. Built at Sevastopol; four served Black Sea and Baltic.
Basically as M-3 and M-5.

M-5 First mass-production marine aircraft in the Soviet Union, also called *Morskoi* 5, Shchetinin 5 or ShchM-5. Numerous changes, mostly minor, but removed all previous shortcomings. Lower wing extended, wing cellule raised 150 mm above hull, tail of trapezoidal cross-section with sharper edges, step reduced to 70 mm on centreline and 140 at chines, and other alterations. Set pattern for ongoing family, steadily improved with years in numerous minor variants, many with bow gun and light bombs. About 300 built, saw extensive service in war, revolution and civil war, some remaining in use in late 1920s as dual trainer, reconnaissance and utility aircraft.
DIMENSIONS Span 13,62 m (44 ft 8¼ in); length 8,6 m (28 ft 2½ in); wing area 37,9 m² (408 ft²).
ENGINE One 100 hp Gnome Monosoupape; alternatively 110 hp Le Rhône, 130 hp Clerget (common for armed versions) or other rotaries.
WEIGHTS (typical) Empty 660 kg (1455 lb); fuel 140 kg; loaded 960 kg (2116 lb).
PERFORMANCE (typical) Max speed 105 km/h (65 mph); climb 9·6 min to 1 km; ceiling 3,3 km; endurance 4 h.

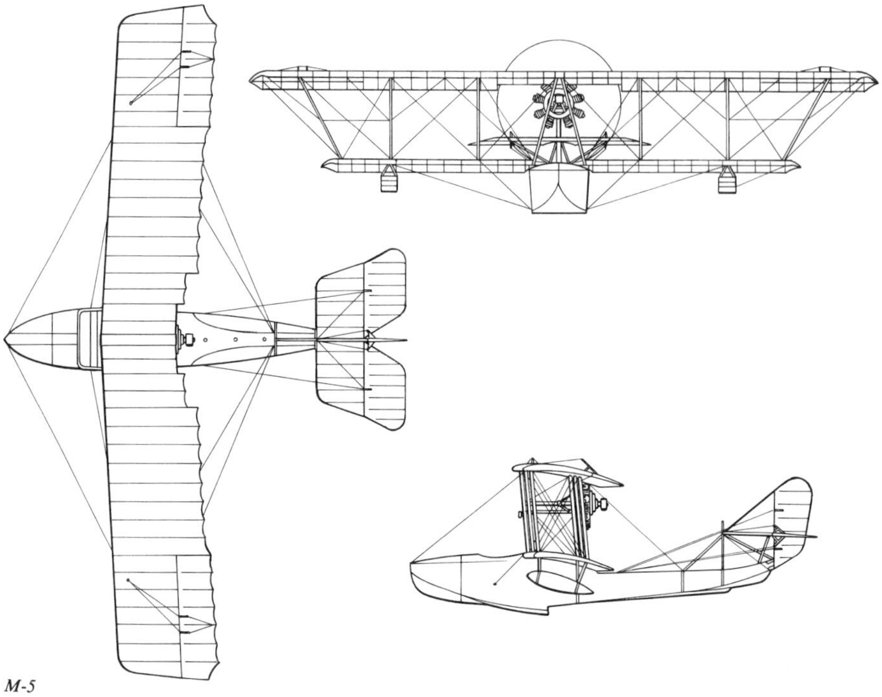
M-5

M-9

M-6 Essentially M-5 with 150 hp Sunbeam water-cooled engine and other changes; unsuccessful, especially in poor water take-off.

M-7 Essentially M-5 with rounded hull with larger keel longitudinal angle and raised step. Normal in flight, but water take-off described as heavy.

M-8 Even more rounded hull and higher step (150 mm) with moderately widened keel; water take-off unachievable.

M-9 Apart from MBR-2 and Be-6 this was most important flying boat ever produced by Russian designer. First flown December 1915, also known as *Morskoi*-9, *Morskoi devyati* (marine, ninth), Shchetinin M-9, ShchM-9 and ShchS. Basically as M-5 but larger wings and more powerful engine, usually water-cooled with two radiators hung between left and right inboard interplane struts on each side of engine. Hull of different cross section with planing bottom no longer of concave form with side skegs but of modern V-shape with 5° deadrise and outward-sloping lower hull provided with side strakes forward of step 1,5 m long and increasing in width to 100 mm at step. Large horn balance on rudder, usually provision for third crew-member and for gun in bows (7,7 mm Vickers, 7,5 mm Hotchkiss, 20 mm Oerlikon or 37 mm Puteaux), with light bomb racks under lower wings. Rounded top to hull giving egg-shaped appearance (M-5 said to look starved by comparison). Hull ply planking thicker than before, with several extra frames. Fuel pump driven by windmill. Generally tough and serviceable boat able to operate reliably in waves up to 0,5 m. First M-9 (at that time works drawings inscribed M-9bis, bis later removed) tested by making flight from St Petersburg to Baku 25 December 1915 to 9 January 1916. Production machines combat duty start of 1917, subsequently used for air combat as well as all other military duties. On 17 September 1916 made loop, later being looped twice with passenger on board. Spirited flying by crews resulted in numerous victories over German Albatros seaplanes and other enemies. Single examples had 140 hp Hispano-Suiza, 220 hp Renault or 225 hp Salmson (Canton-Unné) engines. Total production estimated at 500.
DIMENSIONS Span 16,0 m (52 ft 6 in); length 9,0 m (29 ft 6½ in); wing area 54,8 m² (590 ft²).
ENGINE Usually one 140 or 150 hp Salmson 9-cyl water-cooled radial.
WEIGHTS Empty (typical) 1060 kg (2337 lb); fuel 220 kg (485 lb); loaded 1610 kg (3549 lb).
PERFORMANCE Max speed 105 km/h (65 mph); climb 13 min to 1 km, 35 to 2; ceiling 3 km; endurance 5 h.

M-10 Small boat with Gnome-Monosoupape, built at Shchetinin plant without Grigorovich involvement.

M-11 Small flying boat fighter, also called Shch-I (Shchetinin-fighter), first flown summer 1916. Two-seater with pivoted bow gun (various but usually rifle-calibre) and also single-seat version with bow gun pivoted or, usually, fixed. Considerable armour round bow cockpit, pilot cockpit and front of engine, thickness up to 6 mm steel. In winter mounted on three skis for operation from snow or ice. At least 100 ordered and 60 delivered, most as single-seaters. Some believed disarmed and converted as tandem trainers prior to revolution.
DIMENSIONS Span 8,75 m (28 ft 8¼ in); length 7,6 m (24 ft 11¼ in); wing area 26,0 m² (280 ft²).
ENGINE One rotary, (two-seat) 100 hp Gnome-Monosoupape, (single-seat) 110 hp Le Rhône.
WEIGHTS Empty 665 kg (1466 lb) (single-seat

676 kg); fuel 90 kg (single-seat 106); loaded 915 kg (2017 lb) (single-seat 926).
PERFORMANCE Max speed 140 km/h (87 mph) (single-seat 148); climb 11 min to 1 km; ceiling 3 km; endurance 2·7 h.

M-12 Single-seat boat distinguished from M-11 by deeper nose and redesigned tail. At least one was fixed-gun fighter, but most had no gun or armour and used for civil utility duties and single-seat training. Data as M-11 except loaded weight 870 kg (1918 lb) and faster climb.

M-15 Larger tandem-seater designed for long-range reconnaissance, often as landplane with three skis. First flown May 1916; about 80 delivered, limiting factor being supply of engines. By 1917 used mainly for training; many survived revolution.
DIMENSIONS Span 11,9 m (39 ft 0½ in); length 8,4 m (27 ft 6¾ in); wing area 34,4 m² (370 ft²).
ENGINE One 140 hp Hispano-Suiza V-8.
WEIGHTS Empty 840 kg (1852 lb); fuel 184 kg; loaded 1320 kg (2910 lb).
PERFORMANCE Max speed 125 km/h (78 mph); climb 8·5 min to 1 km; ceiling 3,5 km; endurance 5·5 h.

M-12

M-16 Large two-seat reconnaissance aircraft designed for efficient operation on skis (nickname *Zimnyak*, from winter). Nacelle and tail similar to late Farmans. First flown December 1916 and 40 built 1917.
DIMENSIONS Span 18,0 m (59 ft 0¾ in); length 8,6 m (28 ft 2½ in); wing area 61,8 m² (665 ft²).
ENGINE One 150 hp Salmson.
WEIGHTS Empty 1100 kg (2425 lb); fuel 185 kg; loaded 1450 kg (3197 lb).
PERFORMANCE Max speed 110 km/h (68 mph); climb 15 min to 1 km; endurance 4 h.

M-20 Variant of M-5 with 120 hp Le Rhône; two-seat reconnaissance 1916. M-17 and 19 were related to M-15, no production.

MK-1 Complete break with previous designs, large *Morskoi Kreiser* (sea cruiser), built and tested late 1916. Fuselage of Sikorskii IM type mounted on large wooden float and carrying new biplane wings without sweepback (as on M-boats) but with swept-back aileron trailing edges giving large tip chord. Four-seat reconnaissance, with various planned armament. No production.
DIMENSIONS Span 30,0 m (98 ft 5 in); length 16,5 m (54 ft 1⅜ in); wing area not known (about 165 m² (1776 ft²).
ENGINES Two 220 hp Renault on inner interplane struts, one 150 hp Salmson (later 140 hp Hispano) on upper wing. No other data.

GASN Twin-float seaplane built 1916. Four-seat transport, name *Gidro-Aeroplan Spetsialno Naznachyeniya* (special destination). Mainly wood with fabric skin, struts steel tube with bolted or welded joints. First aircraft in which M.M. Shishmaryev assisted design. Flown A.E. Gruzinov 24 April 1917. Production interrupted by revolution.
DIMENSIONS Span 28,0 m (91 ft 10 in); length 14,1 m (46 ft 3½ in); wing area 150 m² (1615 ft²).
ENGINES Two 220 hp Renault.
WEIGHTS Not known except useful load 1450 kg (3197 lb).
PERFORMANCE Max speed 110 km/h (68 mph).

M-23bis After five years' interruption because of civil war, Grigorovich was able to resume manufacture in 1922 in GAZ-3, completing this flying boat in September 1923. It was a refined M-9 with smaller wings. Poor seaworthiness, and soon wrecked at Krestovskii seaplane base.
DIMENSIONS Span 12,5 m (41 ft 0¾ in); length 8,7 m (28 ft 6½ in); wing area 45,8 m² (493 ft²).
ENGINE One 280 hp Fiat V-12 water-cooled.
WEIGHTS Empty 1165 kg (2568 lb); loaded 1615 kg (3560 lb).
PERFORMANCE Max speed not known but about 165 km/h (102 mph).

M-24 Essentially refined M-9 with more powerful engine, first flown late 1923 from GAZ-3. Series of 40 built, but official testing of first, handed over April 1924, revealed various defects. After Grigorovich went to Moscow in mid-1923 aircraft was carefully redesigned and emerged mid-1924 as **M-24bis.** Series of 20 (some probably from original rejected batch) delivered up to 1926 and served with armament on coastal patrol.
DIMENSIONS Span 16,0 m (52 ft 6 in); length 9,0 m (29 ft 6½ in); wing area 55 m² (592 ft²).
ENGINE One 220 hp Renault, (M-24bis) 260 hp Renault.
WEIGHTS Empty 1200 kg (2646 lb); loaded 1650 kg (3638 lb) (M-24bis 1700 kg, 3748 lb).
PERFORMANCE Max speed 130 km/h (81 mph), (M-24bis 140 km/h, 87 mph); ceiling 3,5 km (bis 4).

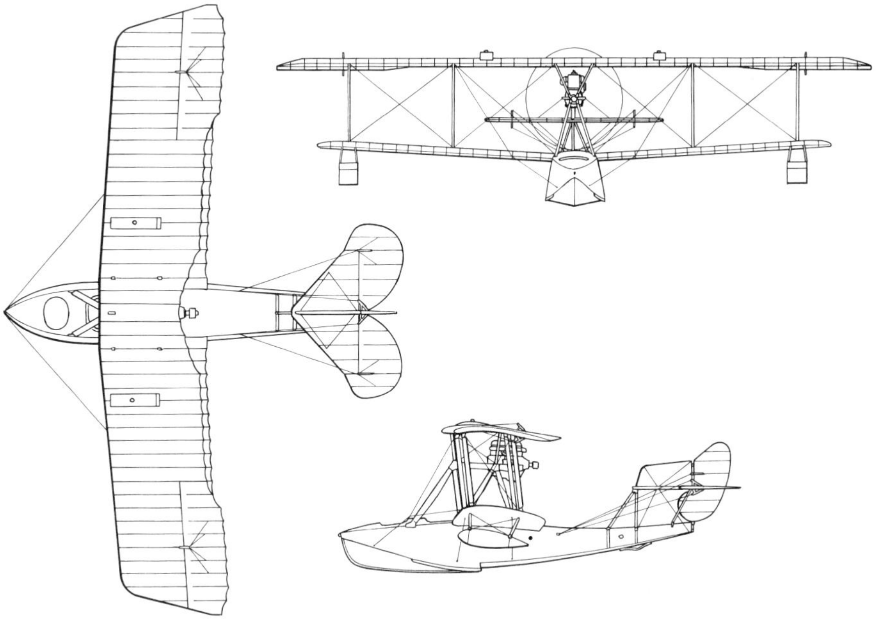
M-15

I-1 First Soviet *Istrebitel* (fighter), and first design by Grigorovich after transfer to Moscow as technical director of GAZ-1. Design group: A.N. Sedyelnikov, B.L. Korvin, A.A. Krylov, V.V. Kalinin and V.L. Moiseyenko. Neat biplane designed around Liberty engine, wood structure with fabric covering except light-alloy cowl and ply-skinned forward fuselage. Göttingen 436 aerofoil, RAF streamlined bracing wires, wooden interplane struts, radiator hung between landing gears as in water-cooled flying boats between interplane struts. Flown Khodinka early 1924. Radiator remounted hung under engine bearers. Stability and climb inadequate. No production.
DIMENSIONS Span 10,8 m (35 ft 5¼ in); length 7,32 m (24 ft 0¼ in); wing area 26,8 m² (288 ft²).
ENGINE One 400 hp Liberty V-12.
WEIGHTS Empty 1090 kg (2403 lb); fuel 220 kg; loaded 1490 kg (3285 lb).
PERFORMANCE Max speed 230 km/h (143 mph); ceiling 6 km (19,685 ft); endurance 2·5 h; range 600 km (373 miles).

I-2 Grigorovich refined I-1 to such extent I-2 emerged in autumn 1924 as largely new design. Wings of reduced chord without dihedral, cut-out in trailing edge, faired I-type interplane struts, more streamlined semi-monocoque fuselage of oval section, long-chord fin and larger rudder with horn balance and angular outline, improved engine cowl, two 7,62 mm PV-1 guns in sides of fuselage. Tested by A.I. Zhukov (photos show skis), who appreciated performance and handling but found cockpit narrow and visibility poor. Further major alteration resulted in **I-2bis**, with complete structural redesign of fuselage incorporating welded steel-tube truss with wooden secondary structure and skin. Guns moved to top of fuselage to make breeches accessible to pilot and improve cockpit comfort. Cockpit cut down and seat raised. Ailerons on lower wings only. Flown A.I. Zhukov early 1925 and soon cleared for service; first Soviet-designed fighter in production. GAZ-1 built 164, and GAZ-23 another 47 in 1926-1929. In 1926 airframe completely static-tested at Aviatrust. Several I-2bis modified with twin Lamblin radiators, becoming **I-2** or **I-2prim.**
DIMENSIONS Span 10,8 m (35 ft 5¼ in); length 7,32 m (24 ft 0¼ in); wing area 23,4 m² M(252 ft²).
ENGINE One 400 hp M-5 (Liberty).
WEIGHTS Empty (2) 1130 kg (2491 lb), (2bis) 1152 kg (2540 lb); fuel/oil 236 + 35 kg; loaded (2) 1530 kg (3373 lb), (2bis) 1575 kg (3472 lb).
PERFORMANCE Max speed (2) 242 km/h (150 mph), (2bis) 235 km/h (146 mph); climb (2) 2·1 min to 1 km, (2bis) 2·4 min; ceiling (2) 5,8 km, (2bis) 5340 m; range (2) 650 km (404 miles), (2bis) 600 km (373 miles); take-off (2) 120 m/8 s, (2bis) 160 m/11 s; landing (2) 190 m/15 s/95 km/h (59 mph), (2bis) 210 m/16 s/same.

SUVP (PL-1) Another break with tradition, this high-wing monoplane was a transport built for Ukrainian civil aviation authority, designation thus coming from *Samolyet Ukrvozdukhput*, PL-1 from *Passazhirskii Leningrad.* Almost entirely welded steel-tube fuselage structure, including wing struts and landing gear. Wing (Göttingen profile) and tail of wood, with fabric covering throughout. Door on left side for pilot in enclosed cockpit behind engine, three passengers or 210 kg cargo. Built at GAZ-3 and first flown autumn 1925. Successful, and served several years in Ukraine though believed only one built.
DIMENSIONS Span 13,7 m (44 ft 11½ in); length 8,4 m (27 ft 6¾ in); wing area 24,1 m² (259 ft²).
ENGINE One 100 hp Bristol Lucifer 3-cylinder.
WEIGHTS Empty 820 kg (1808 lb); fuel 120 kg; loaded 1150 kg (2535 lb).
PERFORMANCE Max speed 139 km/h (86 mph); climb 9 min to 1 km; ceiling 3050 m (10,000 ft); endurance 4·5 h; landing speed 70 km/h (43·5 mph).

MRL Another single-pusher biplane boat, this was designed in Moscow, though built at GAZ-3. Designation from *Morskoi Razvyedchik Liberty* (sea reconnaissance, Liberty). Single-bay biplane of familiar lines, with shallow V planing bottom extending to tail. Wings Göttingen 436, ply-covered leading edge, N-struts. Hull with layer of fabric between main planks and ply skin. Variable-incidence tailplane. Drawings and many design decisions by P.D. Samsonov and K.A. Vigand. First flown 1925. Unimpressive climb and long take-off. Basis for later MR-2.
DIMENSIONS Span 13,2 m (43 ft 3¾ in); length 10,6 m (34 ft 9¼ in); wing area 50,0 m² (538 ft²).
ENGINE One 400 hp Liberty V-12.
WEIGHTS Empty 1660 kg (3660 lb); fuel/oil 520 kg; loaded 2600 kg (5732 lb).
PERFORMANCE Max speed 185 km/h (115 mph); climb 11 min to 1 km; ceiling 3050 m (10,000 ft); range 950 km (590 miles); take-off 40 s; landing 15 s/95 km/h (59 mph).

MR-2 First aircraft designed at OMOS under Grigorovich's overall direction after its establishment in 1925. Improved MRL with later engine, increased-span upper wing, more rounded nose, lower-drag hull planking with aluminium rivets, triple or twin 5 mm steel bracing wires, generally increased dimensions. Latter

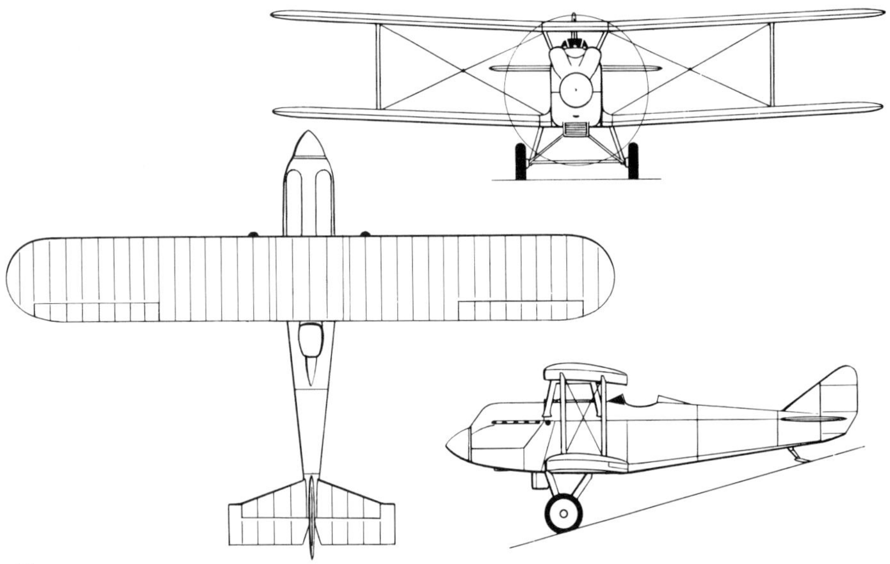
I-1

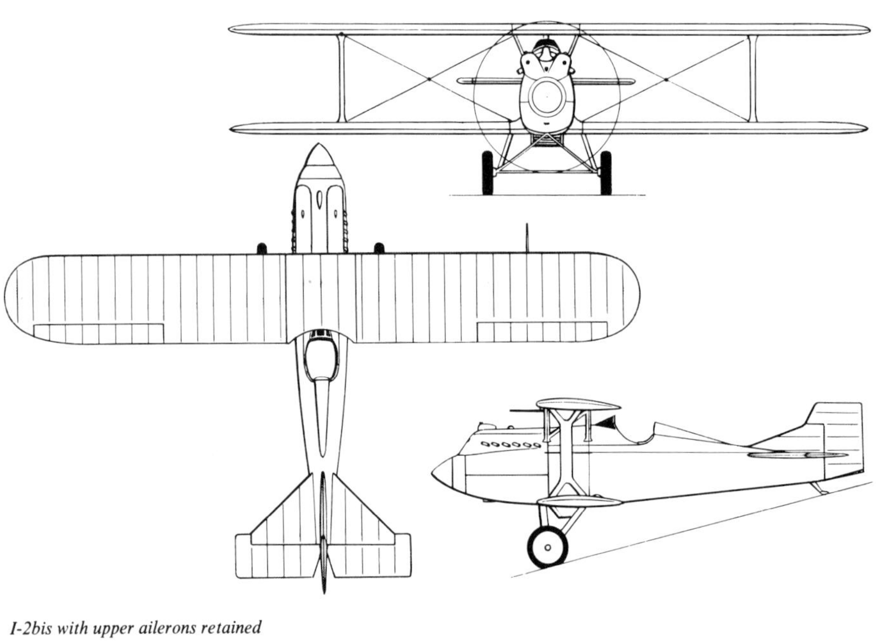
I-2bis with upper ailerons retained

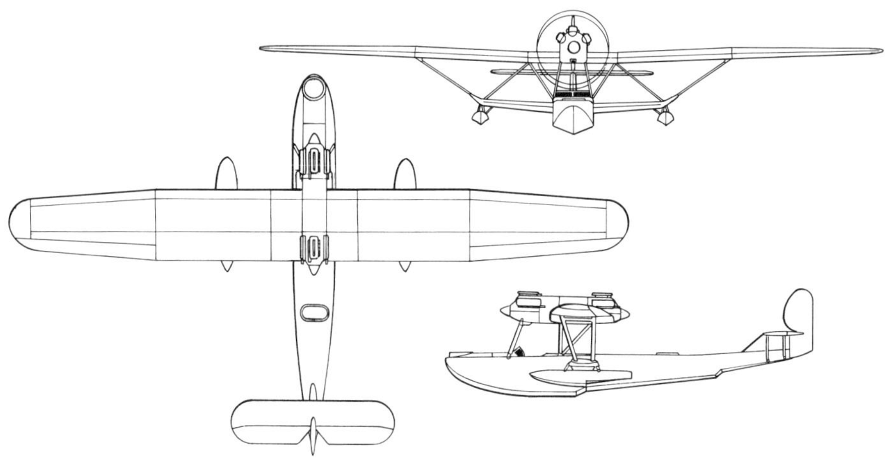

ROM-1

reduced performance despite extra power, but at least MR-2 could take-off reasonably and climb better. First flight at Leningrad 23 September 1926. NII UVVS pilot F.S. Rastegayev then took over; never flown flying boat before (ex-fighters) and crashed. Later discovered CG too far aft in any case. No production.

DIMENSIONS Span 15,6 m (51 ft 2¼ in); length 13,6 m (44 ft 7½ in); wing area 56,7 m^2 (610 ft^2).
ENGINE One 450 hp Lorraine-Dietrich V-12.
WEIGHTS Empty 1770 kg (3902 lb); fuel/oil 560 kg; loaded 2770 kg (6107 lb).
PERFORMANCE Max speed 179 km/h (111 mph); climb 7 min to 1 km; ceiling 4,2 km; range 900 km (559 miles)/5 h; take-off 25 s; landing 15 s/82 km/h (51 mph).

MUR-1 Traditional-style pusher boat but modernized and refined, though with Soviet-built rotary engine. Intended as dual trainer for all flying-boat pilots. Based on M-5/M-20 but with three-bay wings replaced by single-bay wings of reduced span but deeper aerofoil profile. Tail likewise of thicker aerofoil section and improved overall shape. Designation from *Morskoi Uchyebni Rhône*, designed 1925 and flown 1926 at Leningrad. Small series, replaced by MU-2.

DIMENSIONS Span 11,5 m (37 ft 8¾ in); length 8,0 m (26 ft 3 in); wing area 33,0 m^2 (355 ft^2).
ENGINE One 120 hp M-2 (Le Rhône).
WEIGHTS Empty 700 kg (1543 lb); fuel/oil 124 kg; loaded 1 t.
PERFORMANCE Max speed 129 km/h (80 mph); climb 8 min to 1 km; ceiling 3,5 km; range 360 km (224 miles); take-off 130 m/12 s; landing 100 m/10 s/70 km/h (43·5 mph).

ROM-1 Another completely new creation, this was Grigorovich's most powerful machine to date. His team at OMOS designed it in 1927 after studying Dornier Wal. Intended as long-range sea reconnaissance flying boat; designation from *Razvyedchik Otkrytogo Morya*, reconnaissance open sea. Same configuration as Wal but higher aspect-ratio wooden wing and stabilizing floats on tips of small lower wing with Warren interplane bracing. Hull of Kolchug aluminium, fully riveted, with skin thickness 2 mm at step, 1,5 mm over rest of bottom, sides and top 1 mm, fin 0,8 mm. Several AGOS planing-bottom schemes studied, final choice transverse step of 150 mm but angled at 45° instead of vertical. Crew of four; armament four guns (DA, later intended PV-1) in TUR-4 and TUR-5 installations in bow and dorsal, bomb load under lower wing with Sbr-8 sight in bows. First flight winter 1927, by L.I. Giksa. From late November moved to Sevastopol for more intensive testing by S.T. Ribalchuk. By autumn 1928 established modifications needed, resulting in ROM-2.

DIMENSIONS Span 28,0 m (91 ft 10⅓ in); length 16,0 m (52 ft 5¾ in); wing area 104,6 m^2 (1,126 ft^2).
ENGINES Four 450 hp Lorraine-Dietrich W-12 in tandem pairs.
WEIGHTS Empty 4518 kg (9960 lb); fuel/oil 775 + 185 kg; loaded 5830 kg (12,853 lb).
PERFORMANCE Max speed 165 km/h (102·5 mph); climb 10·1 min to 1 km; ceiling 3470 m (11,385 ft); range 800 km (497 miles); endurance 5 h; take-off 25 s; landing 13 s/85 km/h (53 mph).

ROM-2 (MDR-1) One fundamental defect of ROM-1 was CG too far aft, and a way to cure this was to replace tandem pairs of engines by two larger engines on leading edge. Though individually more powerful, these provided much less power in total than four previously used, and to credit of OMOS ROM-2 managed to have all-round higher performance than predecessor despite greater fuel capacity and increased gross weight. Important alteration concerned planing bottom, with much sharper V-angle (105° included at keel instead of 155°) curving round to deep downward-pointing chines on each side. Hull longer, steps vertical and second step moved slightly forward. Hull 16,45 m by 1,6 m beam and 2,1 m high. Wings little changed though span slightly reduced; two spars strengthened, ply skin back to rear spar. Lower wing Kolchug alloy, Göttingen 420 profile. Vertical tail redesigned with larger areas. Service designation MDR-1 from *Morskoi Dalnii Razvyedchik*, marine long-range reconnaissance. First flight 1929. Behaviour better than ROM-1 but State pilots still not satisfied, and ROM-2 failed structurally during rough landing in 1930. OMOS prepared design for ROM-2bis with slightly shorter hull and engines on N-struts above wing, but insufficient promise to be built.

DIMENSIONS Span 26,8 m (87 ft 11 in); length 17,4 m (57 ft 1 in); wing area 108,2 m^2 (1165 ft^2).
ENGINES Two 680 hp BMW VI (M-17) V-12.
WEIGHTS Empty 4150 kg (9149 lb); fuel/oil 830 + 90 kg; loaded 6587 kg (14,522 lb).
PERFORMANCE Max speed 180 km/h (112 mph); climb 7·0 min to 1 km; ceiling 4,5 km; range 900 km (559 miles); endurance 5 h; take-off 250 m/22 s; landing 170 m/15 s/95 km/h (59 mph).

MUR-2 Not a different aircraft type but an MUR-1 modified at Sevastopol 1930 by TsAGI engineer N.N. Podsyevalov with special planing bottom incorporating membranes, pressure, and force-sensing instrumentation.

MU-2 Improved successor to MUR-1 with much better engine (though less powerful), longer hull of metal construction, of superior form with V instead of concave planing bottom, longer bows, step moved to rear and other changes, slightly swept wings, redesigned vertical tail and longer stabilizing floats set at reduced angle. *Morskoi Uchyebnii* 2, side-by-side dual

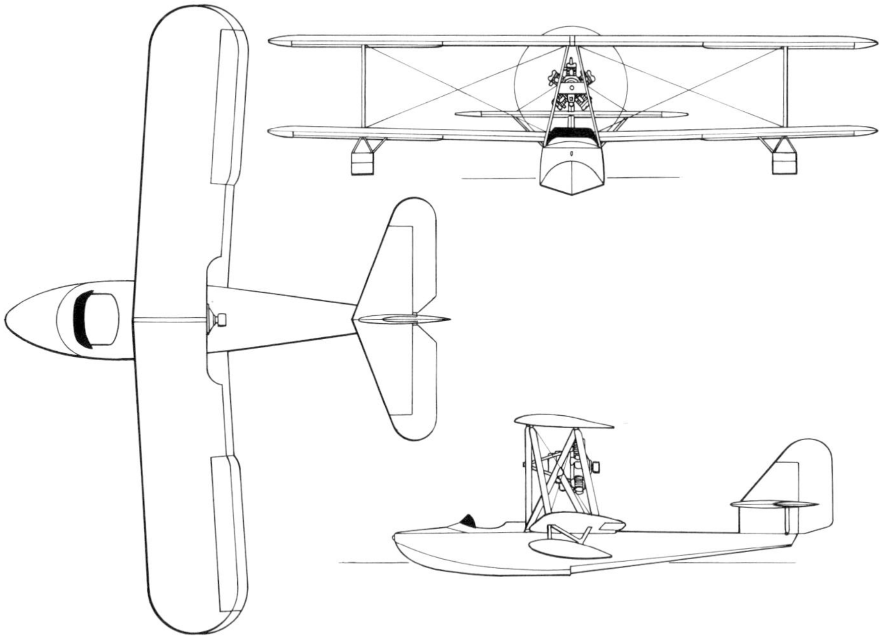

MU-2

trainer. Flown September 1929. No particular faults, but not accepted for production.
DIMENSIONS Span 11,8 m (38 ft 8½ in); length 8,6 m (28 ft 2½ in); wing area 35,6 m² (383 ft²).
ENGINE One 100 hp M-11.
WEIGHTS Empty 820 kg (1808 lb); fuel/oil 90 kg; loaded 1086 kg (2394 lb).
PERFORMANCE Max speed 136 km/h (84·5 mph); climb 10·8 min to 1 km; ceiling 3150 m (10,335 ft); range 380 km (236 miles); endurance 3 h; take-off 35 s; landing 12 s/70 km/h (43·5 mph).

MR-3 Another boat in classic Grigorovich tradition, this ought to have been a big success. Essentially an MR-2 with light-alloy hull and more powerful engine. Same requirements for crew of two/three with bow machine gun and light bomb or stores load. Minor improvements to planing bottom and tail as in other boats, Designed 1927, built 1928 and flown spring 1929. State trials by S.T. Ribalchuk at Taganrog July/August 1929. Major defects. Intended that MR-3 (alternative designation, MR-5) should be redesigned by P.A. Richard, but task later assigned to TsKB at Menzhinskii works and work done by I.V. Chyetverikov. Result was **MR-3bis**: same wings but wooden hull greatly improved hydrodynamic form, and other minor changes including Soviet-built M-17 instead of BMW VI (same engine imported). Tested on Moscow River but, though satisfactory, whole concept considered antiquated and NII UVVS trials not even bothered with. Chyetverikov later used hull as basis for parasol monoplane with M-17 engine, **MR-5bis**, which was remarkably successful and is said by TsKB to have provided basis for Beriev's MBR-2.
DIMENSIONS Span 15,6 m (51 ft 2¼ in); length 11,4 m (37 ft 5 in); wing area 52,0 m² (570 ft²).
ENGINE One 680 hp BMW VI (bis, 680 hp M-17).
WEIGHTS Empty 2027 kg (4469 lb), (bis) 2050 kg (4519 lb); fuel/oil 440+30 kg; loaded 3082 kg (6795 lb), (bis) 3100 kg (6834 lb).
PERFORMANCE Max speed 194 km/h (120·5 mph); climb 7·0 min to 1 km; ceiling 4 km; range 750 km (466 miles); endurance 4 h; take-off 35 s; landing 15 s/85 km/h (53 mph).

MM Project for a *Morskoi Minonosyets*, marine mine carrier. Monoplane with wooden wing (slightly scaled-down ROM-1), twin floats, twin tail booms and tandem Lorraine-Dietrich 450 hp engines above central nacelle. Construction begun 1928 but not completed.

MT Another unbuilt project of 1928, this was to be a *Morskoi Torpedonosyets*, marine torpedo carrier. Fuselage of ROM-1 mated to biplane wings with two BMW VI engines (both tractor). Probably carried single torpedo under wing root.

I-5 Though I-5 fighter is accepted as Polikarpov design, it is only fair to note that Grigorovich—oldest and most senior of designers kept in detention at VT at GAZ-39—himself handled much of design and, according to some reports, was ultimately responsible for all work carried out at VT.

TB-5 This heavy bomber was largest aircraft produced by internees at VT special detention group at GAZ-39, and it was wholly Grigorovich's design. Bureau number TsKB-8. Followed configuration popular at time (subsequently standard for large bombers of French Farman company). Designed to use 800/1000 hp FED X-24 water-cooled engine being developed by A.A. Bessonov; when this failed to materialise, reliable engines of much lower power were substituted.

Fuselage of welded steel tube with multiple stringers giving polyhedral cross section; fabric covering. Wings with large centre section without flaps, and tapered outer panels with slotted ailerons occupying entire trailing edge. Labour-intensive construction with three spars and many ribs built up as complex trusses from light-alloy tube and sections. Aerofoil R-II, 18% at root and 12% at tip. Light-alloy secondary structure and fabric covering. Tail similar structure, with aerodynamic and mass balance of control surfaces. Normal crew six, with enclosed pilot cockpit, navigator in forward fuselage and engineer/radio in mid-fuselage. Three gunners each with pair of PV-1, front gunner having enclosed turret traversing manually 220° (one of first on any bomber). Bombs up to total of 2,5 t (5511 lb) carried in internal bay between wing struts, from 15 to 65% of wing chord.

First flight by B.L. Bukholts, 1 May 1931.

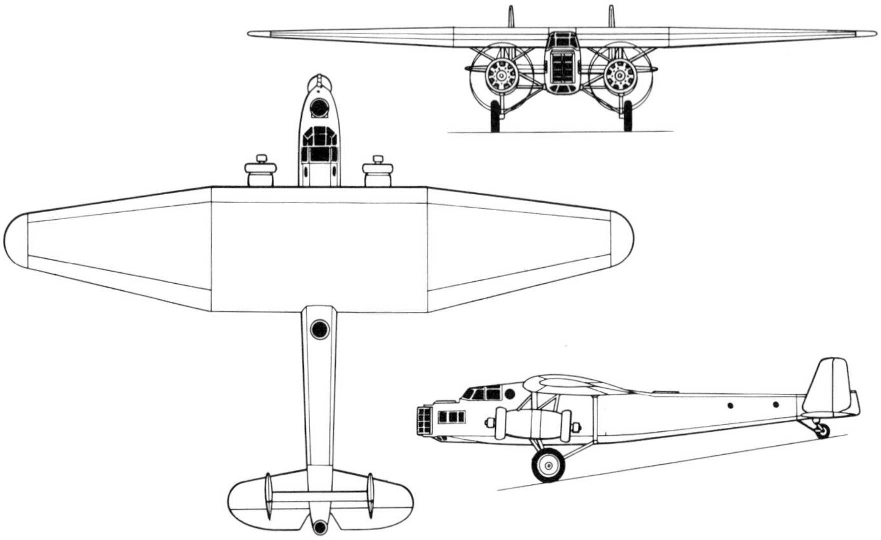

TB-5

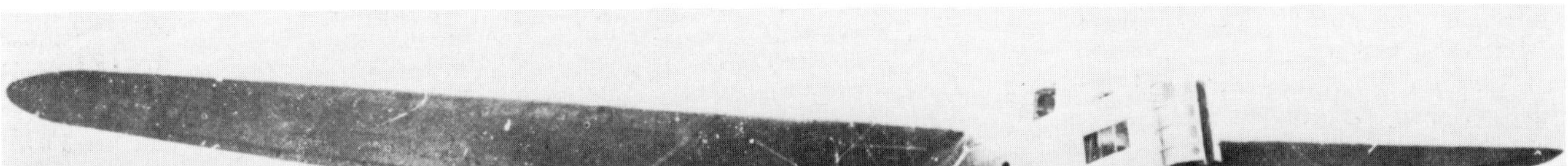

TB-5

Performance poor, because of low-powered engines and apparent inefficiency of tandem arrangement. Special Townend rings added to rear engines, and later also added to front pair. Directional stability marginal. Small improvements made and in late 1931 NII VVS trials in hands of M.M. Gromov and test crew. In spring 1932, with 12 on board, rear left engine broke away and hung dangling, making control impossible. A.V. Chyesalov escaped by parachute; no other parachutes on board. Gromov managed to get aircraft on ground in severe crash-landing, TB-5 bursting into flames.
DIMENSIONS Span 31,0 m (101 ft 8½ in); length 22,1 m (72 ft 6 in); height 5,8 m (19 ft 0¼ in); track 6483 mm (21 ft 3½ in); wing area 150,0 m² (1614·5 ft²).
ENGINES Four 450 hp Siemens/Aviatrust (Bristol licence) Jupiter VI.
WEIGHTS Empty 7483 kg (16,497 lb); fuel/oil 3300 kg; loaded 12 535 kg (27,634 lb).
PERFORMANCE Max speed 180 km/h (112 mph) at SL (possibly rather more at best height but not recorded); climb, no figures; ceiling 2,6 km (8530 ft); range not measured.

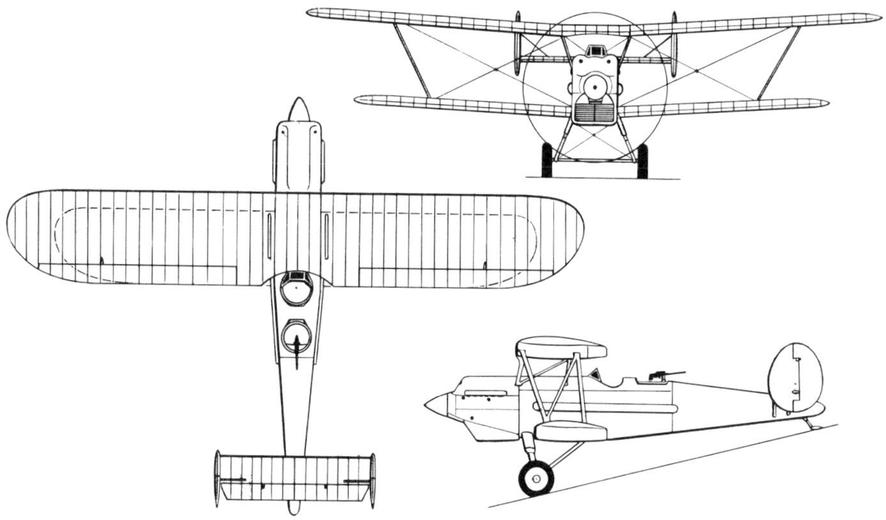

DI-3

DI-3

DI-3 Another design managed by Grigorovich during his period of detention at VT was this two-seat fighter, which is believed also to have had Bureau number TsKB-9. Preparation for production at GAZ-21 went ahead in parallel with design. Conventional except for twin-finned tail, adopted to improve field of fire of observer. Fuselage of welded chrome-molybdenum steel tube with wood secondary fairing structure. Wooden wings, control surfaces duralumin. Fabric covering throughout. Imported engine with underslung fixed radiator. Two PV-1 fixed in top decking, and pivoted DA in rear cockpit with long fairings along sides of fuselage for ammunition drums. First flown August 1931. Performance satisfactory and no shortcomings, but design rejected on grounds of excessive weight and inadequate manoeuvrability. Skis fitted winter 1931–1932.
DIMENSIONS Span 11,8 m (38 ft 8½ in); length 7,97 m (26 ft 2 in); wing area 30,1 m² (324 ft²).
ENGINE One 730 hp BMW VI z7,3 V-12.
WEIGHTS Empty 1487 kg (3278 lb); fuel/oil 200 + 25 kg; loaded 2122 kg (4678 lb).
PERFORMANCE Max speed 256 km/h (159 mph); climb 7·4 min to 3 km; ceiling 6,3 km; time for 360° turn 13 s; take-off 150 m/11 s; landing 225 m/17 s/98 km/h (61 mph).

I-9 Unbuilt heavy fighter design of 1932 with (according to Němĕcek two M-22) M-30, M-31, M-32, M-37 or M-38 engine.

I-10 Unbuilt high-speed fighter of Elektron (magnesium alloy) with new M-41 engine. Nêmêcek states high-wing monoplane.

LSh Though some reports assign this designation to one of purpose-built variants of Po-2 in 1942, it originally applied, with same meaning (*Legkii Shturmovik*, light assault aircraft) to design prepared under great pressure by TsKB under Grigorovich during latter's period of detention in 1929–1930. Bureau designation TsKB-5. To speed project, made use of as many parts as possible of R-5 aircraft, including complete wings, but with considerable local reinforcement. Welded steel armour around engine and tandem cockpits. Twin synchronized PV-1, two aimed by observer from rear cockpit and battery of four under fuselage firing down and ahead at angle set from 30° to 60°. LSh (sometimes reported as LSh-1) completed at end of 1930, but VVS had decided six months earlier not to buy this type, TSh series offering greater promise.
DIMENSIONS Span 15,45 m (50 ft 8¼ in); length 10,4 m (34 ft 1½ in); wing area 51,2 m² (551 ft²).
ENGINE One 680 hp M-17 V-12.
WEIGHTS Not reliably reported but empty/gross about 2000/3200 kg.
PERFORMANCE Max speed 225 km/h (140 mph).

TSh-1 Again based on R-5 airframe, with much alteration and reinforcement, this was a potent machine in TSh (*Tyazheli Shturmovik*, heavy attacker) category. With bureau number TsKB-6, three prototypes built 1930 under Grigorovich direction and all differing in important design features. Much thought given to steel armour in ruling thickness 6 mm and total weight typically 520 kg. In one prototype armour welded, second riveted and third bolted. Armour either mounted on auxiliary duralumin frames or attached to pine and thick ply structure with 35 mm gap. Severe problem accurately matching drawings to armour. Three engine cooling systems: water, fixed radiator; water, retractable; glycol (smaller radiator). Fuselage basically as LSh but lower wings further reinforced and carrying four underwing containers each housing pair of PV-1 and ammunition. Two synchronized PV-1, twin DA in rear cockpit, and in addition *Granatitsa* box from which 300 grenades dispensed. First flight, on skis, January 1931. Subsequent testing by B.L. Bukholts, Yu.I. Piontkovskii and M.A. Bolkovoinov, as well as NII VVS pilots. Fair behaviour but sluggish above 3,3 t, and chosen water cooling system caused overheating to engine and cockpit because of prolonged high power necessary. VVS rejected TSh-1 in favour of more efficient R-5 derivative, TSh-2.
DIMENSIONS Span 15,5 m (50 ft 10¼ in); length 10,56 m (34 ft 7¾ in); wing area 51,2 m² (551 ft²).
ENGINE One 680 hp M-17 V-12.
WEIGHTS Empty 2495 kg (5500 lb); loaded 3490 kg (7694 lb).
PERFORMANCE Max speed 200 km/h (124 mph); range, claimed 650 km (404 miles).

TSh-2 Basically TSh-1 with new lower wings of duralumin construction, greatly thickened immediately outboard of propeller disc to incorporate four PV-1 in each wing, with ammunition boxes all within wing. Twin DA in rear cockpit retained but synchronized PV-1 believed removed. Bureau number TsKB-21. First flown late 1931, and superior to TSh-1. Pre-series of ten built, but persistent troubles with accurate armour (repeated ten years later with Il-2) and M-17 deliveries prolonged project which was beginning to look dated. In 1932 one TSh-2 tested with M-27, of greater power and reduced tendency to overheat, but this engine never cleared for production.

DIMENSIONS, engine as TSh-1.

WEIGHTS Empty not known; loaded 3950 kg (8708 lb).

PERFORMANCE Max speed 213 km/h (132 mph); ceiling 4220 m (13,845 ft); range 650 km (404 miles).

ShON Prolonged insurrection caused by discontented *Bazmashii*—well armed and organized bands of horsemen in Turkestan—in late 1920s brought swift response from Moscow which wished to collectivize all Soviet peoples and crush all dissidents. ShON (*Shturmovik Osobogo Naznachyeniya*, attacker for special purposes) was ordered from TsKB in 1930, with designation TsKB-23; first example completed in April 1931. Basis again R-5, but folding wings to allow transport by rail and road. Much lighter than TSh series, with only light armour around vital areas and no weapons except four twin boxes of PV-1 as in TSh-1. Tested and found satisfactory early 1932, but *Bazmashii* eliminated by land forces before ShON reached Turkestan.

DIMENSIONS Span 15,5 m (50 ft 10¼ in); length 10,3 m (33 ft 9½ in); wing area 51,2 m² (551 ft²).

ENGINE One 680 hp M-17 V-12.

WEIGHTS Empty 1610 kg (3549 lb); loaded 3 t (6614 lb).

PERFORMANCE Max speed 225 km/h (140 mph); ceiling 6,1 km (20,000 ft); range 730 km (454 miles).

I-Z Yet another of combat landplanes assigned to Grigorovich during detention at VT, this was one of first Soviet monoplane fighters since original IL-400. Created specifically to carry large-calibre DRP (ARK) recoilless cannon designed by L.V. Kurchyevskii, who also participated in aircraft design. Project begun 1930 as TsKB-7, also called Project Z. To speed project, forward fuselage and engine same as second prototype (*Klim Voroshilov*) I-5; rest of fuselage dural monocoque. New low-mounted wings, of Göttingen-436 profile, mainly of Enerzh-6 stainless-steel lattice construction with torch-welded joints, ribbon bracing wires and underwing bracing by streamlined dural struts to landing-gear structure. Fabric covering throughout wing, rudder and braced horizontal tail mounted well up fin out of way of gun blast. Guns slung under wing attached to both spars. Single PV-1 in left side of fuselage for sighting purposes. First flown late summer 1931; bureau pilots B.L. Bukholts and Yu.I. Piontkovskii. Second prototype with modified wing structure flown 1932. Small series of 21 aircraft built as I-Z with minor alterations and, instead of helmeted Jupiter, with fully cowled M-22. Further 50 I-Z with wooden wings built at Kharkov 1934–1935, but service experience was limited because only at this late time did various shortcomings, notably difficult recovery from developed spin, become appreciated. Most I-Z used in development of later recoilless guns and fast-firing 20 and 37 mm cannon. One used in *Zvyeno* trials (see Vakhmistrov). Led to IP-1, see later.

DIMENSIONS Span 11,5 m (37 ft 8¾ in); length 7,65 m (25 ft 1¼ in); wing area 19,5 m² (210 ft²).

ENGINE One 480 hp M-22.

WEIGHTS Empty 1180 kg (2601 lb); fuel/oil 180 kg; loaded 1648 kg (3633 lb).

PERFORMANCE Max speed 259 km/h (161 mph) at SL, 300 km/h (186 mph) at 3 km; climb 14 min to 5 km; ceiling 7 km (22,970 ft); range 600 km (373 miles); endurance 2·5 h; take-off 110 m/8 s; landing 180 m/15 s/100 km/h (62 mph).

TSh-1

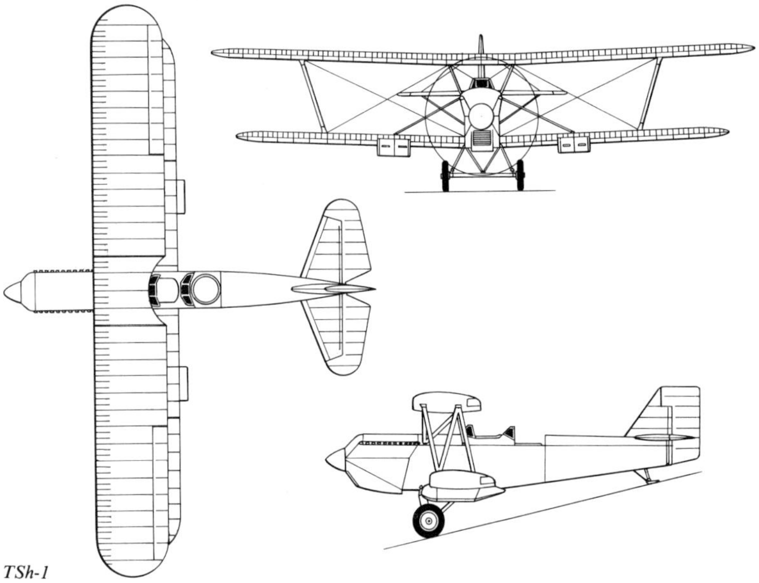

TSh-1

Stal-MAI This advanced structural essay resulted from Grigorovich's role as director and professor at MAI at end of 1931, after his release from detention. He organized a group of students to study airframe entirely of Enerzh-6 stainless steel, and investigate structural and manufacturing problems. Group led by P.D. Grushin and included M.M. Pashinin, L.P. Kurbala, V.A. Fyedulov and A.P. Shchyekin. Study concluded aircraft practicable in 1932, and became MAI project with Grigorovich supervising. Low-wing cantilever monoplane, tandem enclosed cockpits, fixed landing gear, one 725hp M-34R V-12 engine. Apart from fabric-skinned control surfaces, entire airframe of various steels, over 90% being Enerzh-6. Thickness remarkably low, typically 0,3 to 0,5 mm, much being sandwich stabilized by underlying corrugations of 80 mm pitch. Corrugations sometimes rounded, in some areas trapezoidal. Joints almost entirely welded, by torch and electric arc. Two-spar wing, front spar being at deepest part of profile at 28% chord and with corrugated-sheet web. Semi-monocoque fuselage with integral fin. First aircraft in world with such structure. Completed mid-1934 and first flown September 1934 by I.F. Kozlov and Yu.I. Piontkovskii. Failure of engine mounting on fifth take-off (Piontkovskii flying, Grushin passenger). Stal-MAI repaired but project discontinued. Few numeric details.

I-9 Project for fighter biplane with M-30, M-31, M-32, M-37 or M-38 engine of about 600 hp. Not completed, 1933.

I-10 Believed project for single-seat long-range fighter with two M-22 radials and cannon.

IP-1 (DG-52) First aircraft known with alternative designation for Grigorovich's own name. Basic designation from *Istrebitel Pushyechnii*, fighter, cannon). Refined development of I-Z designed in less haste, with much better aero-

I-Z (prototype)

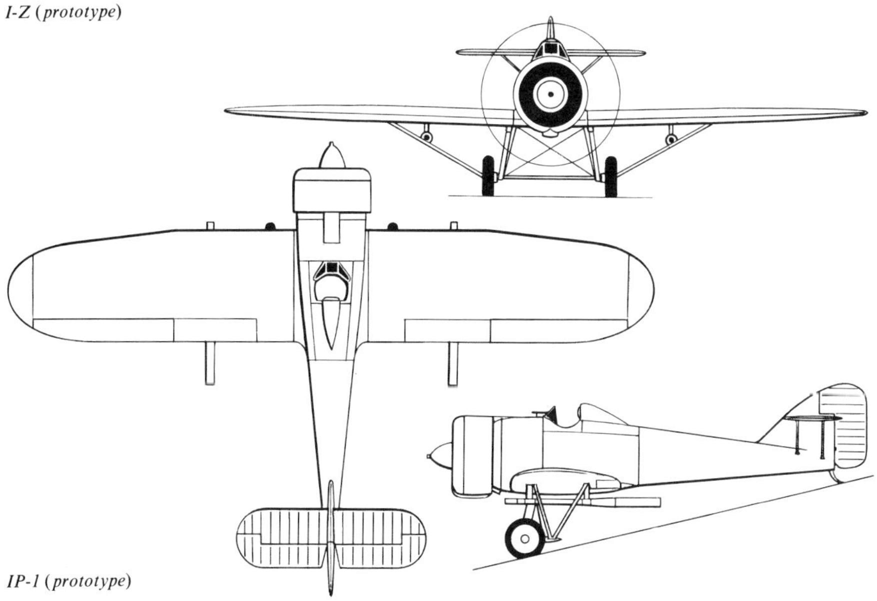

IP-1 (prototype)

I-Z (production)

dynamics and structure. All light-alloy stressed-skin construction, elliptical wing with centre section of 55% span carrying APK-4 recoilless cannon at extremities, with bolted wingtips outboard. Two spars built up from chrome-molybdenum tubes, with lattice and sheet ribs and 0,6 to 0,8 mm skin flush-riveted. Slotted flaps and ailerons. Circular-section monocoque fuselage with integral fin skinned in 1,0 to 1,5 mm sheet. Hydraulic operation of flaps and main landing gears folding backwards into underwing blisters. First prototype with imported Wright Cyclone and Hamilton propeller flown 1934. Tested with APK-4 with five rounds each, sighted by two synchronized ShKAS. Good aircraft but APK-4 eventually rejected and 200 production IP-1 ordered from Kharkov with armament of two 20 mm ShVAK in wing roots and six ShKAS in boxes at extremities of centre section in place of large recoilless guns, and with M-25 (licensed Cyclone). Change of armament moved CG to rear, and spin recovery difficult with full ammunition until large dorsal fin added. Actual production total only 90, 1936–1937.

DIMENSIONS Span 10,97 m (36 ft 0 in); length 7,23 m (23 ft 8¾ in); wing area 19,98 m² (215 ft²).
ENGINE One 700 hp M-25.
WEIGHTS (production) Empty 1200 kg (2646 lb); fuel/oil 275 + 25 kg; loaded 1880 kg (4145 lb).
PERFORMANCE Max speed 368 km/h (229 mph) at SL, 410 km/h (255 mph) at 3 km; climb 1·3 min to 1 km; ceiling 8,3 km; range 600 km (373 miles) (1000 km overload fuel); take-off 230 m/17 s; landing 175 m/11 s/97 km/h (60 mph).

IP-4 (DG-53) Family derived from IP-1. Original DG-53, 1934, smaller version of DG-52 with four 45 mm APK-11 sighted by two ShKAS. Intended M-25 but flown at end of 1934 with Cyclone. **DG-53bis** with M-25 and armament of two ShVAK and two ShKAS cancelled 1935 when nearly complete.

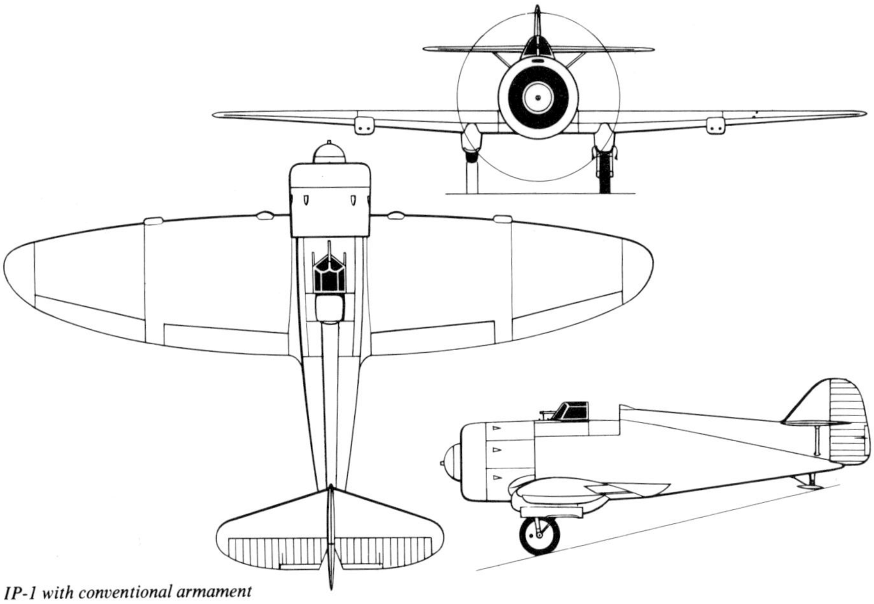

IP-1 with conventional armament

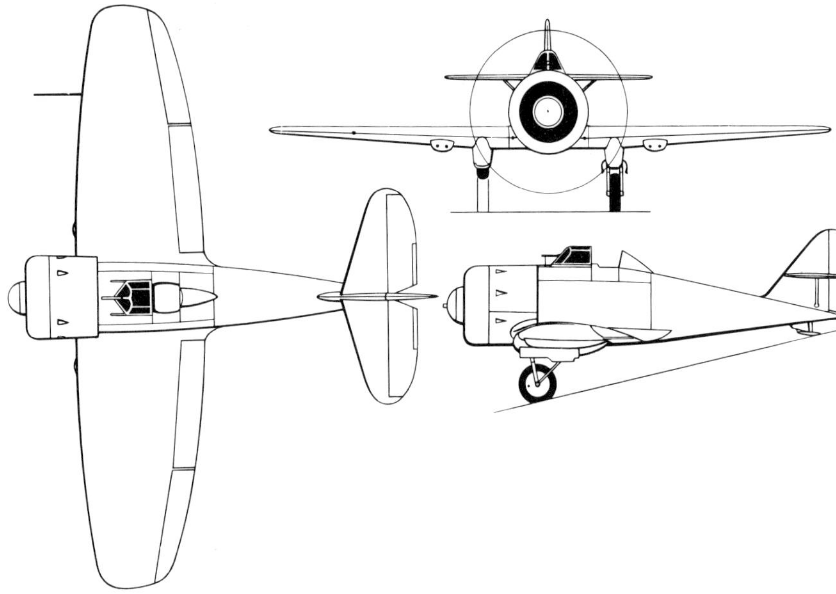

IP-4

DIMENSIONS Span 9,6 m (31 ft 6 in); length 7,08 m (23 ft 3 in); wing area 16,36 m² (176 ft²).
ENGINE One 640 hp Wright R-1820-F Cyclone.
WEIGHTS Empty 1080 kg (2381 lb); fuel/oil not known; loaded 1549 kg (3415 lb).
PERFORMANCE Max speed 382 km/h (237 mph) at SL, 435 km/h (270 mph) at 3 km; climb 1·1 min to 1 km; ceiling 8,3 km; range 600 km (373 miles) (830 km overload fuel); take-off 180 m/8 s; landing 200 m/97 km/h (60 mph).

IP-2 (DG-54) Uncompleted prototype of further development of IP-1 with different engine and devastating armament of either 12 ShKAS or two ShKAS and four ShVAK. Full data have been published including gross weight with 760 hp Hispano-Suiza 12 × brs of 1952 kg and calculated max speed of 519 km/h (322·5 mph). Cancelled 1936.

E-2 (DG-55) Also named *Kometa* (for its design inspiration was obvious) and *Dyevushkovaya Mashina* (Girls' Machine, for there were eight girls in design team at MAI, a clear majority). Though based on D.H.88 it used engines of low power and was in no sense intended as a racer but as an exercise in efficient long-range travel. Simple wooden construction, main wing box being skinned with 8-mm ply. Landing flaps of Zapp type, low hinge-moment allowing manual operation; landing-gear retraction also manual. First flight 1935; after test programme, passed to Osoaviakhim and used as courier.
DIMENSIONS Span 11,0 m (36 ft 1¼ in); length 7,9 m (25 ft 11 in); wing area 13,8 m² (148·5 ft²).
ENGINES Two 120 hp Cirrus Hermes inverted 4-inline.
WEIGHTS Empty 1051 kg (2317 lb); loaded 1546 kg (3408 lb).
PERFORMANCE Max speed 296 km/h (184 mph); service ceiling 5 km; range 2200 km (1367 miles); take-off 255 m/15 s; landing 310 m/23 s/102 km/h (63 mph).

LK-3 (DG-56) Project for *Legkii Kreiser* (light cruiser) with armament of eight ShVAK or other impressive alternatives; estimated speed 438 km/h with two 825 hp Hispano-Suiza 12Ybrs. Single-seat prototype begun 1935 but not completed; cancelled 1936.

PB-1 (DG-58) Last known programme by Grigorovich began as PB-1 (*Pikiriyushchii Bombardirovshchik*, dive bomber) in 1936. All-metal

IP-4, DG-53bis

G-37

stressed-skin with M-85 (GR 14K derived) and internal weapon bay. Special hydraulic perforated dive brakes. Main gears semi-retracted into underwing fairings. Crew of two in tandem. Estimated speed with full load 450 km/h (280 mph). In parallel schemed tactical reconnaissance aircraft with bureau designation **DG-58R** (also reported as 58bis). Grigorovich fell ill early in this programme and died in 1938.

Grokhovskii

Pavel Ignatyevich Grokhovskii was an enthusiastic pilot, parachutist and inventor. He succeeded in forming his own design group in Leningrad in 1931. By 1933 he had organized a bureau of experimental production at VVS RKKA, and in autumn 1934 he took over an experimental institute under GUAP authority to do RKKA work. His interest centred around air transport, and especially ways of carrying goods and assault troops in airborne landings. He was first to pioneer parachute delivery of large loads, and perfected at least one design of large cargo container with parachute system and cushion to reduce landing shock, dropped from TB-1s during 1934. He also managed development of carriage of tanks and other heavy loads under G-2s. In December 1936 there was sudden change in official policy; his institute—described as remarkably harmonious, with unusual team-spirit—was abruptly closed; last aircraft, G-38, was nearly complete.

Inflatable Throughout his brief design career Grokhovskii was working on inventions that many years later were to be picked up by workers in other countries. In 1950s ML Aviation (UK) and Goodyear (US) claimed originality in building ultralight aeroplanes made of rubberized fabric, unpacked from box and inflated under gentle air pressure. This is what Grokhovskii did in 1934. His first *Naduvatsya* (Inflator) was a glider, weighing 77 kg (170 lb) and packing into a box 1 × 1 × 0·5 m. Tested from Tushino January 1935, towed behind U-2. Inventor's intention was to build refined powered version.

Kukuracha Experimental lightplane built at Leningrad 1934–5 with wing swept at 35°, slightly swept trailing edge, wingtip rudders and no horizontal tail. Pusher 100 hp M-11 radial, speed probably not over 160 km/h (100 mph). Wood, ply and fabric, with single spar. Built by S.G. Kozlov, V.F. Bolkhovitinov and A.Ye. Kaminov with agreement of Grokhovskii. Structural failure on take-off.

G-26 High-speed aircraft in class of Stal-6. One 860 hp Hispano-Suiza 12Ybrs engine, all-metal stressed-skin construction, cantilever low wing, single retractable landing wheel (presumably plus outriggers on wings), single-seat enclosed cockpit. Designer B.D. Urlapov. Built 1935–1936 but never quite completed: politically afraid of failure.

G-31 Named for *Yakov Alksnis*, this was modification of (Grokhovskii) unbuilt G-31 glider but with a single engine and capacity to carry 20 people. Wooden glider with high aspect ratio and great span, with thickened centre section housing 18 passengers (assault troops or casualties) lying down as in G-61. Slim wooden monocoque fuselage with fully cowled engine and tandem cockpits for pilot and flight engineer. Designed by Grokhovskii and Urlapov. Built Leningrad 1935, later made flight to Moscow for production test, but general opinion doubted validity of concept.

DIMENSIONS Span 28,0 m (91 ft 10¼ in); wing area 70,0 m² (753 ft²).

ENGINE One 700 hp M-25.

WEIGHTS Empty 1400 kg (3086 lb); loaded 3200 kg (7055 lb).

PERFORMANCE Max speed 135 km/h (84 mph).

G-37 Probably Grokhovskii's best-known achievement, this interesting machine was also called ULK (*Universalnoye Letayushchyeye Krylo*, universal flying wing). Though original objective was versatile transport for airborne assault landings, its potential as a commercial cargo or even passenger carrier was obvious. Idea was that G-37 should pick up a pre-loaded container shaped to conform to rest of aircraft, deliver it and then collect a fresh container. (Same idea seen later in Fi 333, Miles M.68 and Fairchild XC-120.) To reduce time and cost Grokhovskii used the ANT-9 wing. On to this he built engines (in different installation from PS-9), stressed-skin tail booms and deep trousered landing gear. On centreline was a small nacelle for pilot and flight engineer, with special attachments on underside for payload pod. Tail was dural with fabric skin on rudders and elevators. Twin castoring tailwheels. Construction in hands of V.F. Rentel (see Krylov) at Grebno port, Leningrad. Completed 1934 (this organization did not number its projects in a consecutive manner). Test-pilot V.P. Chkalov satisfied, and G-37 later flew to Moscow in 2hr 50 min, average 250 km/h, then almost a record. No production—possibly because G-37 wing was outdated.

DIMENSIONS Span 23,7 m (77 ft 9¼ in); length 16,0 m (52 ft 6 in); wing area 84,0 m² (904 ft²).

ENGINES Two 680 hp M-17.

WEIGHTS Not known but probably about 3500/6000 kg.

PERFORMANCE Max speed 285 km/h (177 mph); ceiling 5,5 km (18,050 ft).

G-38 (LK-2) This fighter-bomber may have been influenced by contemporary (1934) French *multiplaces de combat*. The G-38 featured twin tail booms, a central nacelle for 2 crew and guns, and retractable landing gear. Mainly wood construction, except for stressed-skin metal nacelle and fabric-covered light-alloy control surfaces. Greatest possible combination of speed and firepower. Four ShKAS and two ShVAK firing ahead, two ShKAS aimed by gunner at rear of nacelle, various bombs hung under nacelle. Project begun September 1934. Grokhovskii led design, construction under P.A. Ivyensen and V.I. Korovin, static testing under M.V. Orlov and A.F. Yepishyev from GVF, with consultant professors A.K. Martinov and V.N. Belyaev. LK signified *Leningradskii Kombinat* (Leningrad Combine). G-38 virtually complete when institute abruptly closed in 1936.

DIMENSIONS Span 13,6 m (44 ft 7½ in); length not recorded; wing area 27,0 m² (291 ft²).

ENGINES Two 800 hp Gnome-Rhône 14Krsd Mistral Major.

WEIGHTS Empty 3090 kg, loaded 4500 kg (9921 lb).

PERFORMANCE (Est) Max speed 550 km/h (342 mph).

G-61 Not an aircraft but a standard 'people pod' attached under lower wing of R-5. Each container was flat streamlined wooden box of 4,3 cubic metres volume divided into four compartments each accommodating two occupants lying face-down and head-first. Loaded via hinged rounded leading edge. Complete aircraft load 16 persons (troops, casualties or rescuees), total aircraft weight 3800 kg. On 8 December 1936 Grokhovskii tested R-5 with full load: airborne 400 m/30 s; cruise 201 km/h (125 mph), ceiling 2,8 km. Each container weighed 200 kg (441 lb) empty. Later similar containers were used to rescue crew of icebound vessel *Chelyushkin*.

Groppius

Ye.E. Groppius is one of least-known Soviet constructors. In 1923 he was working on a canard (tail-first) machine, but this was never completed. His only product was a single moderately successful passenger biplane, designated for factory in which it was built.

GAZ-5 Two-bay biplane with a deep fuselage filling space between wings. Light-alloy nose covering engine, with Groppius cooling radiator underneath with regulator flaps. Wooden mid-fuselage with door on right and seats for four passengers. Behind cabin, open cockpit for pilot and mechanic side-by-side. Wings and tail fabric-covered and wire braced. Large horn balances on control surfaces, ailerons on all four wings. Designed 1923, construction begun early 1924, completed autumn 1924. Test-pilot Yefremov unimpressed by long take-off run, slow climb, and general unwieldiness. Shavrov states 'not accepted', but other reports say GAZ-5 was used for a time by Dobrolyet.

DIMENSIONS Span 11,2 m (36 ft 9 in); length 8,5 m (27 ft 10¾ in); wing area 35,0 m² (377 ft²).

ENGINE One 300 hp Hispano-Suiza 8fb V-8.

WEIGHTS Empty 1118 kg (2465 lb); loaded 1849 kg (4076 lb).

PERFORMANCE Max speed 165 km/h (102·5 mph); ceiling 300 m (984 ft).

GAZ-5

Groschyev

G.F. Groschyev was a designer of gliders in 1930s. **G-4** tested 1934 with 250 kg (551 lb) cargo, towed by R-5. Largest machine was **G-5**, one of submission for troop-carrying assault gliders in 1939. Shoulder-wing machine with monocoque fuselage of wooden construction, accommodating pilot in nose and five armed troops or 450 kg (992 lb) cargo. Not accepted.

Grushin

Pyetr Dmitriyevich Grushin first came into prominence working at MAI on construction of Stal-MAI under Grigorovich. This took from 1931 until 1934, by which time he was designing his own ultralight, named *Oktyabrnok*. He also produced a kind of simplified Link Trainer for blind-flying instruction, and an experimental high-pressure steam engine for aircraft propulsion which was tested in a U-2. In late 1941 he had to close his own KB and joined MiG OKB to design DIS.

Sh-tandem This typically bold Soviet prototype got its designation from *Shturmovik-tandem* (tandem attacker); other designations included Tandem-MAI and MAI-3, from institute where it was designed and built. Basic concept was excellent one of making aircraft close-coupled, with tanden wings and rear gun turret with unobstructed field of fire. Wing profile of TsAGI R-II series on both main wing and quasi-elliptical rear surface which could be regarded as tailplane or rear wing with 45% of area of main surface. Much argument over controls; final scheme put ailerons on main wing and elevators on rear surface, but alternative (intended to be flown) was two front ailerons and two rear elevons. Twin fins/rudders on underside of rear surface at 50% semi-span, leaving clear field of fire for turret through 250° azimuth. Pilot in enclosed cockpit with sliding canopy. Gunner in MV power-traversed turret (probably electrical) with ShKAS. Four ShKAS fixed in wings firing ahead. Bomb load 200 kg (441 lb). Basically wooden construction, fuselage being monocoque of *delta* (birch plies baked with Bakelite-type polymer). Main gears retracted into wing (poor-quality photos suggest inwards, but could have been to rear, with wheels turning 90° and standing proud of undersurface). Fixed tailwheel.

Prototype constructed in MAI production training school. First flown 5 December 1937,

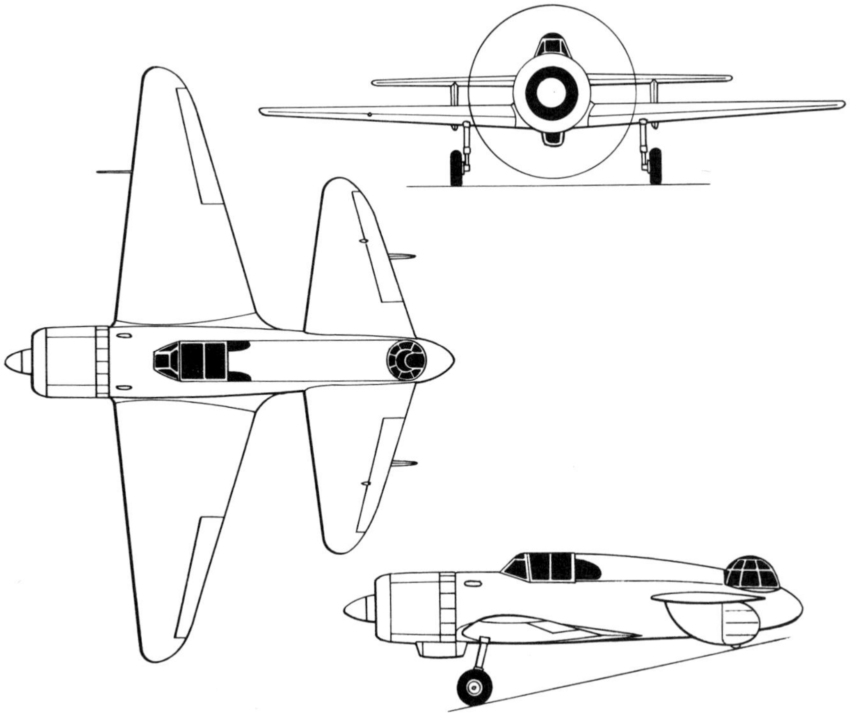

Sh-tandem

subsequently subjected to prolonged test-flight programme not completed until 1939. Test pilot P. M. Stefanovskii. Němĕcek suggests directional stability inadequate, but Soviet reports state designer's calculations were corroborated and that he then went on to design improved BB-MAI described below.
DIMENSIONS Span 11,0 m (36 ft $1\frac{1}{4}$ in); span of rear wing 7,0 m (23 ft 0 in); length 8,5 m (27 ft $10\frac{3}{4}$ in); wing area (combined) 30,4 m² (327 ft²).
ENGINE One 930 hp M-87.
WEIGHTS Only figure recorded is loaded, given variously as 2560 and 3088 kg (5644 or 6808 lb).
PERFORMANCE Max speed 406 km/h (252 mph) at SL, 488 km/h (303 mph) at 4,2 km; no other data.

BB-MAI (BB-2) No photograph appears to survive of this more formidable development of Sh-tandem, designed 1938 and built at MAI 1939–1941. Structure little changed though designed for higher weight and factor of +12, multi-layer *delta* wing skins being 25 mm thick between spar webs. Wing and tailplane (rear wing) areas much smaller, automatic slats on main wing, and rear surface skin never thicker than 5 mm, with 3 mm on 'tail parts'. Longer fuselage than Sh-Tandem, with tricycle landing gear and engine cooling radiator immediately ahead of nose leg. Fuselage *delta* bonded with VIAM V-3 adhesive. Main gears retracted inwards. For sake of extra speed, wing loading exceptional (ignoring rear surface, 230 kg/m²). Prototype completed after Nazi invasion and flown by A. N. Grinchik as fighting approached. Test programme abandoned, though BB-MAI could have been flown to East.
DIMENSIONS Span probably about 10 m; wing areas 15,2 m² (front) and 6,8 m² (rear) (164, 73 ft²).
ENGINE One 1050 hp M-105.
WEIGHTS Empty not recorded; loaded 2965 kg (6537 lb).
PERFORMANCE Max speed 508 km/h (316 mph); no other data.

Gr-1 (IS) Grushin's last known design, this was a break with past in configuration and structure, being of conventional layout and all-metal construction. Main wing box with two sheet webs and spars with steel angle booms, with intermeshing-comb (piano-hinge) joint between centre section and outer panels. Armoured cockpit for single pilot in nose, thinner armour over engines. Designation IS from *Istrebitel Soprovozhdyeniya*, escort fighter. Heavy armament of four ShKAS and two ShVAK, plus eight RS-82 or RS-132 rockets all firing ahead, plus bomb load under fuselage up to 500 kg (1102 lb). No information on landing gear. Prototype construction for nine months, with static testing complete by spring 1941. Evacuated October 1941 but wrecked in transit, causing immediate closure of OKB.
DIMENSIONS Span 15,8 m (51 ft 10 in); length, not recorded; wing area 42,0 m² (452 ft²).
ENGINES Two 1400 hp AM-37.
WEIGHTS Empty, about 4900 kg; loaded (normal) 7250 kg (15,983 lb), (max fuel and bombs) 7650 kg (16,865 lb).
PERFORMANCE (estimated) Max speed 480 km/h (298 mph) at SL, 645 km/h (401 mph) at 7,2 km; climb 9·8 min to 8 km; ceiling 11,7 km (38,385 ft); range 1380 km (857 miles), (max fuel 1890 km, 1,174 miles); landing speed 120 km/h (74·5 mph).

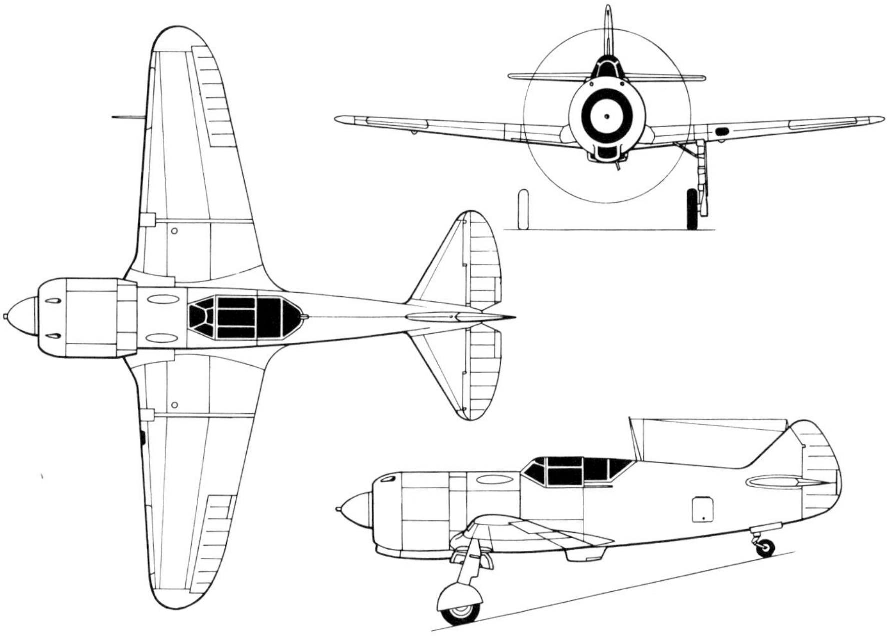

Gu-82

Gudkov

Mikhail Ivanovich Gudkov was a GAZ manager in September 1938 when he became one of three partners who created LaGG-3 (see Lavochkin). When LaGG OKB was evacuated to Gorkii in October 1941 Gudkov remained behind in Moscow. Discouraged by failure to improve LaGG-3, he had not only begun developments of his own but, without Lavochkin's approval, had at least a year earlier begun layout of a completely new fighter which became Gu-1.

K-37 Also known as **LaGG-3K-37**, this was first of Gudkov's several planned improvements to LaGG-3 to materialise. Intended primarily for anti-armour attack, it replaced usual 20 or 23 mm engine-mounted cannon by 37 mm weapon. Gun chosen was ShK-37, eventually rejected in favour of NS-37. This big gun rested between cylinder banks, but was so long that firewall, and thus oil tank and pilot's cockpit, had to be moved 35 cm to rear. (According to another report gun chosen was the NS-37, which fitted original length; maybe prototypes had different guns.) First prototype ready August 1941 and successfully tested (Němĕcek says flying did not begin). According to Soviet records three were completed and were shipped to front, no more being produced. Data as LaGG-3.

Gu-82 Lavochkin, Gorbunov and Gudkov all developed LaGG-3 with ASh-82 (M-82) engine. Gudkov's was designated Gu-82 (not as often reported LaGG-3/ASh-82) and was created hurriedly at GAZ-31, then evacuated to Tbilisi by taking production LaGG-3 and mating it, with minimal prior design effort and no tunnel testing, with existing ASh-82 installation complete with engine bearers and cowling. It came from an Su-4 (Shavrov) or Su-2 (Green/Swanborough). Trailing-edge cooling ring thermostatically adjustable. Oil cooler under fuselage at trailing edge. Venetian-blind shutters retained at front, rear modified by light sheet to conform to slimmer fuselage. Not a refined aircraft but minimum-change lash-up, though superficially adequate. Two ShVAK above engine. One only; second prototype never completed because of October 1941 evacuation. First Gu-82 did not fly until 1942 (according to one report February, another 'the following summer'). By this time La-5 had been accepted.
DIMENSIONS Span 9,8 m (32 ft 2 in); length 8,75 m (28 ft $8\frac{1}{2}$ in); wing area 17,51 m² (188·5 ft²).
ENGINE One 1330 hp M-82 (ASh-82).
No other data.

Gu-1 Gudkov had been convinced American Bell Airacobra was a sound concept, and in early 1940 studied a similar fighter with engine on CG, shaft drive to tractor propeller, and cockpit and guns in nose. Construction mainly wood, except forward fuselage of welded steel tube with removable dural skin panels, steel and dural centre-section spars and dural control surfaces. Wing profile 1V-10 Type V-2, automatic slats, hydraulic flaps and tricycle landing gear. Engine above wing with main radiators in wings, oil cooler under centre section. Drive via 120 mm ($4\frac{3}{4}$ inch) diameter shaft, single 37 mm Taubin cannon with 81 rounds (large capacity for this calibre) firing through reduction gear. Prolonged problems with engine and drive, and flight-testing did not begin until summer 1943. Mark Gallai quotes test pilot A. I. Nikashin (first to fly LaGG-1 and La-5) as being unhappy after taxi trials, saying 'It seems glued to the ground'. First flight 12 July 1943; long run, aircraft became airborne, reached about 200 m and then fell off in sideslip and crashed, killing Nikashin. General opinion was wing too small. Gudkov's bureau disbanded.
DIMENSIONS Not known.
ENGINE One 2000 hp AM-41.
WEIGHTS Empty 3742 kg (8250 lb); loaded 4610 kg (10,163 lb).
No other data.

Ilyushin

Sergei Vladimirovich Ilyushin was one of greatest Soviet designers, achieving not only success with widely contrasting aircraft but also having ability to command complete respect of Stalin and Politburo. He was appointed head of GUAP and could have reached high political office, but had wisdom and diplomacy to resign and stick to design. Born 31 March 1894 into a poor peasant family in Vologda district, he became a mechanic at Komandantskii airfield, St Petersburg, in 1916, working on IM bombers. Called into army and qualified as pilot 1917. An enthusiastic revolutionary, he managed to join Red Army and among many other important contributions realised Avro 504 would fill need for good standard trainer and got captured example to Dux factory (GAZ-1) so that it could be copied (as U-1). In 1922 he entered Zhukovskii Academy, and soon became leader of infant gliding movement, bringing his own designs to first six All-Union meetings at Koktebel. On graduation 1926 appointed to NTK-UVVS, soon becoming its chief. In 1932 took civilian appointment with TsAGI, quickly being appointed Tupolev's deputy at KOSOS. On formation of TsKB, appointed to run its brigade of method studies; after severe political vicissitudes he was given charge of long-range bomber brigade in TsKB – where one of first projects to mature was a fighter (I-21). In 1935 he appointed Vladimir Kokkinaki brigade test pilot, and worked closely with him for next 35 years. In late 1937 he was appointed to top job in aviation industry, Director of GUAP; he judged that at his KB he could do more worthwhile work and probably live longer, and he succeeded in returning there in February 1938.

On 21 April 1938 Ilyushin had to make a solo forced landing, commuting between TsKB and GAZ-18 at Voronezh in his Yakovlev AIR-11, which left his forehead scarred for life. Some 30 years later he started to relinquish control of his bureau to his deputy, Genrikh V. Novozhilov, who took over entirely in 1976 but retained founder's name on bureau. Awarded Order of Lenin and third Hero medal on 80th birthday, and died at 82 on 9 February 1977.

S. V. Ilyushin

TsKB-16 Never completed, project for flying-wing bomber with two M-34, assigned to department of V.V. Nikitin; soon replaced by conventional low-wing development with two M-85. This led in turn to TsKB-26 and TsKB-30, see later.

I-21 (TsKB-32) No original illustration survives of this unusual fighter, which like many others of its day was designed to use surface-evaporation cooling. According to Soviet records, engine fitted with special increasing (not reduction) gear to raise propeller to 2400 rpm from crankshaft speed of 1800 rpm; this is reverse of normal practice and is unexplained. Outstandingly clean design. Duralumin stressed-skin fuselage and tail. Wing, tapered only on leading edge and of RAF-38 section, built up from welded steel tube with flush-riveted metal skin, much of surface comprising stainless-steel radiator panels shaped to profile wherein steam from engine was condensed. Pipe connections to engine via four steel tubes forming main engine mounting. Engine-air and oil-cooler inlets in wing roots. Single-leg main gears retracted into centre section, probably to rear with wheels rotating 90°. Schrenk-type flaps. Retractable tailwheel. Probably cleanest fighter in world when first of two began flight testing late 1936. High wing loading (according to some published reports) combined with fancied vulnerability of cooling system to cause cancellation of 20 production aircraft ordered late 1936. (Note severe conflict of published data.)

DIMENSIONS Span (Shavrov) 10,0 m (32 ft $9\frac{3}{4}$ in), (Němeček) 9,2 m (30 ft $2\frac{3}{4}$ in); length 7,0 m (22 ft $11\frac{1}{2}$ in); wing area (Shavrov) 18,1 m² (195 ft²), (Němeček) 13,8 m² (148·5 ft²).

ENGINE One M-34RNF rated at (Shavrov) 1275 hp (Němeček) 810 hp.

WEIGHTS (Shavrov) Empty 1716 kg (3,783 lb); fuel/oil 150 + 20 kg; loaded 2125 kg (4685 lb); (Němeček) loaded 2000 kg (4409 lb).

PERFORMANCE (Shavrov) Max speed at SL 550 km/h (342 mph) (faster at best height); climb 4·6 min to 5 km; ceiling 12 km (39,370 ft); range 760 km (472 miles); landing speed 120 km/h (74·6 mph). (Němeček) max speed 520 km/h (323 mph).

TsKB-26 Precursor of what was to become most important family of Soviet long-range bombers of the Second World War, this efficient unarmed prototype was Ilyushin's first response to 1933 requirement for DB (long-range bomber) and used techniques explored when he was at KOSOS. Objective was at least to equal range performance of Tupolev aircraft whilst significantly increasing cruise speed. Wing structure not unlike Tupolev and his aides: efficient TsAGI profile with main spar built-up truss of 4 mm angle and U-sections, welded and riveted, with four angle booms, ruling material Cr – Mo steel. Single rivet in same material joining each spar boom at centre/outer panel joint, booms fitted inside each other. Ribs built-up trusses from U or top-hat sections. Skin, light alloy, flush-riveted. Fuselage of narrow oval section, constant over central length. Entirely wood, monocoque, ruling thickness 5 mm at front and 2,5 mm aft of wing and on fin. Most of structure glued *shpon*, finally covered with fabric and doped. Flight controls duralumin with fabric covering. Split flaps, rearward-retracting main gears, both pneumatic actuation.

Intended as prototype bomber, but devoid of military equipment. Nav/bomb in nose with hand-aimed ShKAS (not fitted), pilot in open cockpit (just room for man to squeeze past) and radio-gunner with manual turret (not fitted) with ShKAS. Stressed for external racks for up to 1 t (2205 lb) bombs (note: not internal). First flight February 1936. At May Day parade looped by Kokkinaki over Red Square. National records: 3 August 1936, 12 816 m with 500 kg payload; 21 August, 12 101 m with 1 t; 7 September, 11 005 m with 2 t. Also 26 August flew Moscow/Sevastopol/Sverdlovsk/Moscow 5018,2 km with 1 t payload in just 16 h. Outstanding aircraft with amazing altitude capability, but not an optimized bomber; so Ts-KB-30 built instead.

DIMENSIONS Span 21,4 m (70 ft $2\frac{1}{2}$ in); length 14,3 m (46 ft 11 in) (Shavrov: 13,7 m); wing area 65,62 m² (706 ft²).

ENGINES Two 765 hp Gnome-Rhône K14.

WEIGHTS Empty 4100 kg (9039 lb); max loaded (overload fuel) 9356 kg (20,626 lb) (Shavrov, 6 t, 13,228 lb).

PERFORMANCE Max speed 330 km/h at SL, 390 km/h (242 mph) at 3250 m; climb 15·1 min to 5 km; service ceiling 10 km (32,808 ft), ceiling in record weight-lifts 12 816 m (42,047 ft); normal

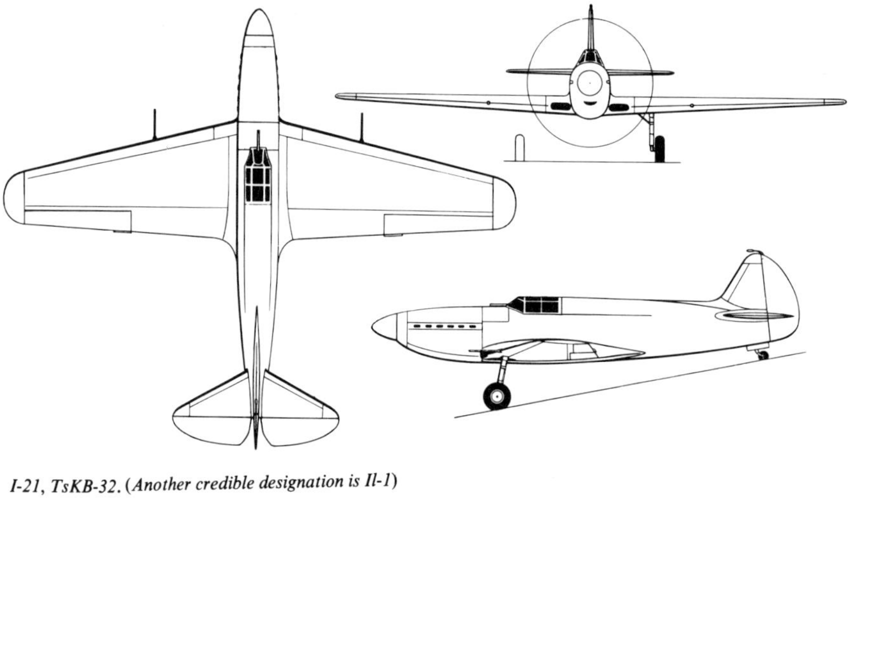

I-21, TsKB-32. (Another credible designation is Il-1)

DB-3B

range (800 kg fuel) 4000 km (2485 miles); landing speed 100 km/h (62 mph).

TsKB-30 Ilyushin deliberately designed TsKB-26 as a pure prototype of an efficient load-carrier. TsKB-30 was in contrast prototype of a DB (long-range bomber). Wing, landing gear and basic aerodynamics unchanged, but fuselage completely new with all-metal construction. Large number of oval frames and longitudinal stringers, many joints being welded. Skin thickness generally 0,6 mm, 0,4 on control surfaces. Rivets to 6 mm diameter in Cr-Mo steel parts, 2,6 and 3 mm dural in light alloy, exterior riveting being flush. More capacious nose and provision for bomb bay and armament. Single aircraft completed May 1936, painted red and named *Moskva* (Moscow). (According to Shavrov this aircraft was a series type DB-3B; most historians disagree and claim it was TsKB-30.) By time of first flight Stalin had been excited by looping of TsKB-26 and ordered DB-3, military designation of production TsKB-30, to be ordered as standard long-range bomber instead of DB-2 already tooled up. According to Němĕcek GAZ director refused; all that mattered was his output figure. It took intervention of Gen Alksnis, Voroshilov and Ordzhonikidze personally to get Stalin's order carried out. (In fact, no doubt DB-2 was superior, speed being some 100 km/h better.) DB-3B was designation of production development of TsKB-30, and it is possible that, as Shavrov insists, it was this second machine that did following record flights: flown by Kokkinaki and A.M. Bryandinskii, 27/28 June 1938, Moscow/Spassk-Dalnii (dry tanks, just short of Vladivostok), 7580 km, 24 h 36 min; 28/29 April 1939, flown by Kokkinaki and M.Kh. Gordiyenko, Moscow/USA attempt but autopilot failure, −54°C, adverse winds and fog at New York, eventually dry tanks and wheels-up landing on island of Miscou, New Brunswick, roughly 8000 km, 22 h 56 min.

DIMENSIONS Span 21,44 m (70 ft 4½ in) (Němĕcek, 21,4, same as TsKB-26); length 14,3 m (46 ft 11 in); wing area 65,62 m² (706 ft²).

ENGINES Two 800 hp M-85.

WEIGHTS Empty (Shavrov) 4200 kg (9259 lb), (Alexander) 5270 kg (11,618 lb); loaded (normal) (Shavrov) 6250 kg (13,779 lb), (Němĕcek) 9365 kg (20,646 lb), (Alexander) 7600 kg (16,755 lb); (max) (Shavrov, Alexander; not quoted by Němĕcek) 9700 kg (21,385 lb).

PERFORMANCE Max speed 335 km/h at SL, 409 km/h (254 mph) at 4,2 km; ceiling (Němĕcek) 5790 m (19,000 ft), (Shavrov, Ilyushin OKB) 9800 m (32,150 ft); range about 3500 km with 800 kg fuel, 8000 km with max; landing speed 105 km/h (65 mph).

DB-3 Though there was a separate prototype (possibly more) designated DB-3, first production bomber was designated **DB-3B.** As related above, only Stalin's personal insistence got this aircraft selected in preference to already-chosen DB-2; according to Sukhoi and Tupolev even this was not true, and DB-2 lost in normal NII VVS trials in late 1936. Certainly by December 1936 at least two DB-3B bombers were flying, and according to Shavrov long-range record-breaker *Moskva* was actually one of these, demilitarized. Production DB-3B identical in main features to TsKB-30, but equipped for crew of three, there being a rear turret with radio/gunner, nose occupant being nav/bomb. Pilot seat-back 9 mm armour. Six unprotected fuel cells, 2860 lit (629 gal). Semi-retractable skis in winter, attached by six bolts around normal wheels, plus small ski over tailwheel. Normal armament single ShKAS in nose (manual turret, 1100 rounds), mid-upper (manual turret, 1100 rounds) and rear ventral hatch. Sometimes one ShVAK in nose installation (not clear whether this replaced ShKAS in turret) and from 1939 single ShKAS with 300 rounds fixed in tip of tail firing aft. Internal bombload 1 t (typically ten 100 kg); with reduced fuel and/or increased gross weight up to 1500 kg (typically three 500 kg) on external racks. Engines in efficient long-chord cowls with twin exhaust stacks, no gills; VISh-23 propellers.

Production begun February 1937, and deliveries to VVS summer that year. By 1938 three production GAZ engaged in assembly, but manufacture was by previous standards complex and labour-intensive and rate of output ran behind target. Major redesign by KB January 1938 to remove difficulties, simplify structure and issue completely new drawings and data tables to speed production. Resulting aircraft **DB-3M** (*Modernizirovanni*, modernized). As in later batches of DB-3B, engine changed to M-87 or 87B. Second 1938 variant, usually with original engine, **DB-3T** torpedo version, with external centreline attachments for 45-12-AN torpedo and special sight in nose. Third 1938 variant was twin-float **DB-3PT** (*Poplavkovyi Torpedonosyets*, floatplane torpedo) with Type Zh floats and other small changes, as well as torpedo installation of DB-3T. Flew late 1938 but concept

DB-3M captured by Finland

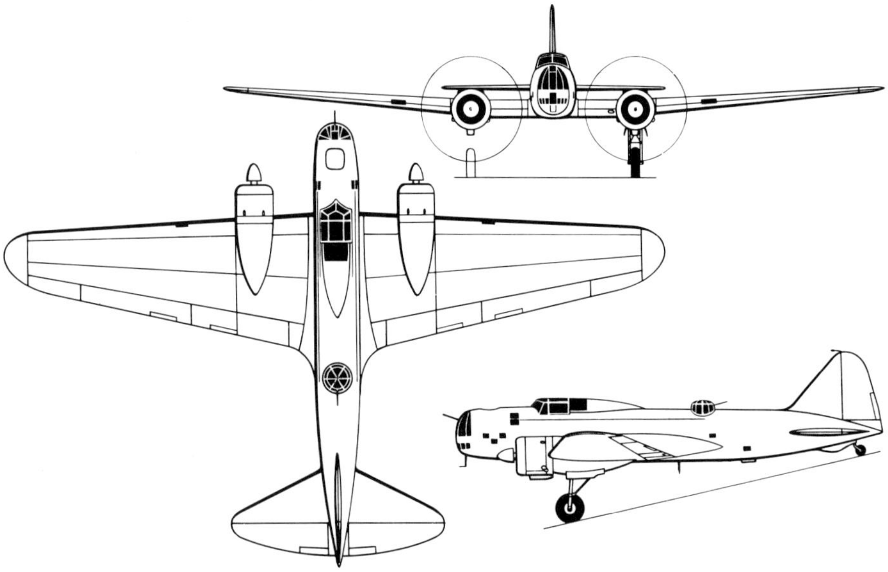

DB-3M

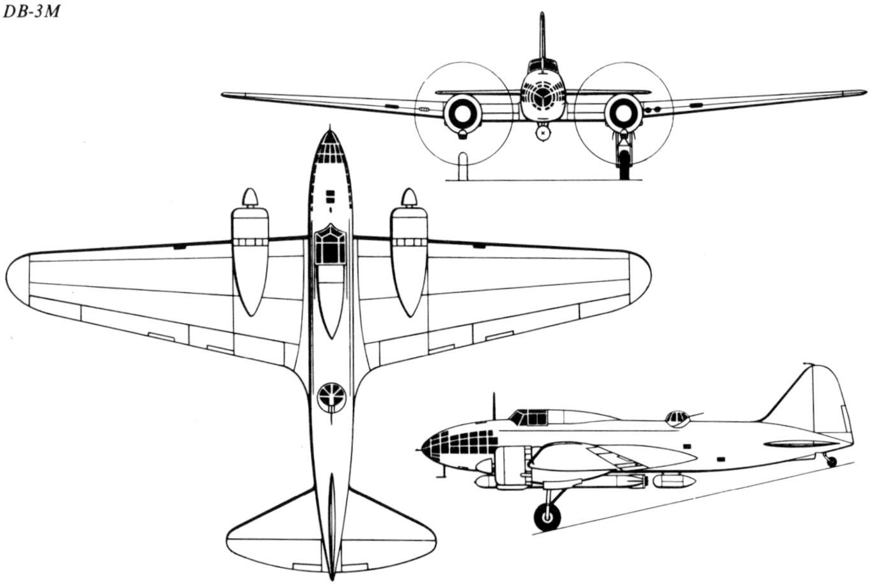

Il-4 with torpedo and rear external tank

judged obsolete and only torpedo landplane completed acceptance trials. Total of DB-3B, DB-3M and DB-3T, 1528 by 1940. Played major role in Winter War and in the Second World War, from 1942 mainly as trainer, transport and glider tug. Famed attack on Berlin 7 August 41 by DB-3 and 3M bombers of MA's 81st (1st Guards) Mine/Torpedo Regt, flying from Saaremaa, Ösel Island; repeated 7 September when Ösel far behind front.

DIMENSIONS Span 21,44 m (70 ft 4½ in); length 14,34 m (47 ft 0½ in); wing area 65,62 m² (706 ft²).

ENGINES Two 765/800 hp M-85; (late 3B, 3T and 3PT) 800 hp M-86; (final 3B and all 3M) 950 hp M-87B.

WEIGHTS Empty (3B, M-85) 4598 kg (10,137 lb), (3B, M-86; 3T) 4712 kg (10,388 lb), (3M) 5270 kg (11,618 lb), (3PT) 5630 kg (12,412 lb); normal loaded (3B, M-85) 6965 kg (15,355 lb), (3B, M-86; 3T) 7079 kg (15,606 lb), (3M) 7660 kg (16,887 lb), (3PT) 7550 kg (16,645 lb).

PERFORMANCE Max speed typically 330 km/h (205 mph) at SL, 395 km/h (245 mph) at 4 km, (DB-3M, 440 km/h, 273 mph; 3PT, 343 km/h, 213 mph); climb typically 2·5 min to 1 km; ceiling 8,8/9,7 km (3PT, 7570 m); range 3800/4000 km (2360/2485 miles); take-off typically 350 m/14 s; landing 460 m/120 km/h (74·5 mph).

DB-3f While production of DB-3M was in full swing at last, in 1939, Ilyushin completely redesigned structure to make it easier to produce and maintain. Resulting DB-3f (*forsirovannii*, forced or intensive) also incorporated a redesigned nose, more powerful engines in a better installation and other visible changes, but greatest change was modern airframe. Ilyushin later credited Li-2 (DC-3) with opening Russian eyes to superior structures. Could not do multi-spar wing, but 3f represented 'leap into modern era'. Dualumin sheet spar webs, four rolled angle booms, vertical reinforcing angles at intervals with easy riveted joints; frames and ribs single items each side of spar(s) produced with flanged lightening holes on imported rubber presses. No welding, no tubes, no U-sections, no internal rivets, no layers of strips, no manual assembly, and no fitting with hand tools. Welded steel tube never again used structurally by this KB except for engine mountings, landing gears and similar local concentrated loads. Reduction of some 70% in numbers of wing parts and man-hours, and lesser gains elsewhere. Airframe weight fractionally higher than 3M, but stronger and greater capability with more power and fuel. First 3f flown January 1940 with M-87B engines and VISh-23 propellers, but M-88 standard for production later in year. Fuel capacity increased to 3855 litres (848 gal), mainly by addition of four leading-edge cells making total of ten. Production aircraft plumbed for external overload tanks under fuselage, see Il-4.

DIMENSIONS As Il-4.

ENGINES Two 1000 hp M-88.

WEIGHTS Empty close to 5300 kg (11,684 lb); loaded 7933 kg (17,489 lb) with 750 kg fuel (1050 lit).

PERFORMANCE Max speed 360 km/h at SL, 447 km/h (278 mph) at 7 km; ceiling 10 050 m; range (max fuel) 3300 km (2050 miles).

Il-4 In late 1940 designation of DB-3f was changed to Il-4. (Designation of DB-3B and M not changed.) Three factories built this aircraft as standard long-range bomber and torpedo aircraft of Soviet Union 1940–1944, total deliveries being widely reported as 5256. Structure already described under DB-3f. Light-alloy flight controls with fabric covering. Split flaps inboard of large ailerons with trim tabs. Flaps, landing gear and wheel brakes all pneumatic actuation, with emergency hand pump. Fuel system, six wing cells (self-sealing from late 1942 cutting normal fuel from 1440 to 1425 kg (about 2000 lit) plus four long-range cells in leading edge, and two overload external tanks under fuselage centreline each of 400 lit (88 gal, 290 kg). At max weight Il-4 could operate with external bomb load or torpedo plus rear external tank at highest weight quoted below. Normal engine from late 1940 M-88B at 1100 hp driving VISh-23, updraught carburettors, twin exhaust stacks, adjustable cooling gills (Bristol copy) and oil cooler in wing with leading-edge inlet outboard of engine. Normal crew four because of lower-rear gun and improved working space in nose. Normally two men in nose, with much improved glazing and reduced drag: nav seated at chart table with view of ground, and separate bombardier/front gunner. In action nav could squeeze past pilot to man rear gun on pintle mounting with left/right hinged glazed doors projecting into slipstream. Original armament three ShKAS as before, but with nose gun in ball mount at tip of nose. Later dorsal turret of modified type with BS or UBT with 500 rounds. Alternative installation, used in service in small numbers, with two ShVAK, nose cannon with 120 rounds, turret with 240. Normal bombload 1 t in internal bay. Max bomb load 2700 kg

Il-4 with 45-36-AN torpedo

(5952 lb), not permissible with max fuel. By late 1942 standard fuel system reduced to six tanks, simpler system reducing switching errors, normally just 1425 kg, 2000 lit. All self-sealing, and armour 6 to 9 mm now added to shield gunner in turret as well as original pilot's 9 mm. Standard provision for torpedo of 940 kg (2072 lb), either 45-36-AN for low-level release or a 45-36-AV for high dropping. No separate designation for torpedo aircraft. No ice protection, but experimental installation of underslung fuel-burning heater (reduced speed 7 km/h) to warm rear cabin and leading edges of wing and tailplane. Tough service resulted in local strengthening of fuselage longerons, tail, nose and engine cowls. Small series said in some Soviet

Il-4s

reports to have been powered by M-82 (ASh-82) at 1400 hp rating. Many Soviet accounts make no mention of fact that, at least in 1942, there was major effort to reduce light-alloy consumption and Il-4 produced (without designation change) with wooden nose, and/or fuselage deck and/or outer wing complete, with small penalty in weight and speed. Il-4 was standard long-range bomber of VVS and MA. Operational from 11 August 1941 with DA, two *eskadrilii* formed from crews of 22, 40, 53 and 200 BAP. Berlin attack of 7 August was by DB-3 force of AVMF. Il-4 was most common tug for A-7 glider. From 1946 many converted for photo and geophysical survey.

DIMENSIONS Span 21,44 m (70 ft 4½ in); length 14,8 m (48 ft 7 in); wing area 66,7 m² (718 ft²).
ENGINES Two 1100 hp M-88B.
WEIGHTS (typical 1942) empty 5800 kg (12,787 lb); fuel 1425 kg; normal loaded 9139 kg (20,148 lb), (max) 10,3 t (22,707 lb).
PERFORMANCE (at normal gross) max speed 335 km/h (208 mph) at SL, 420km/h (410/440) (261 mph) at 6 km; climb 12 min to 5 km; service ceiling 9,4 km; range 3800 km (2,361 miles) with max fuel, usually about half this; take-off 420 m/20 s; landing 220 m/18 s/105 km/h (65 mph).

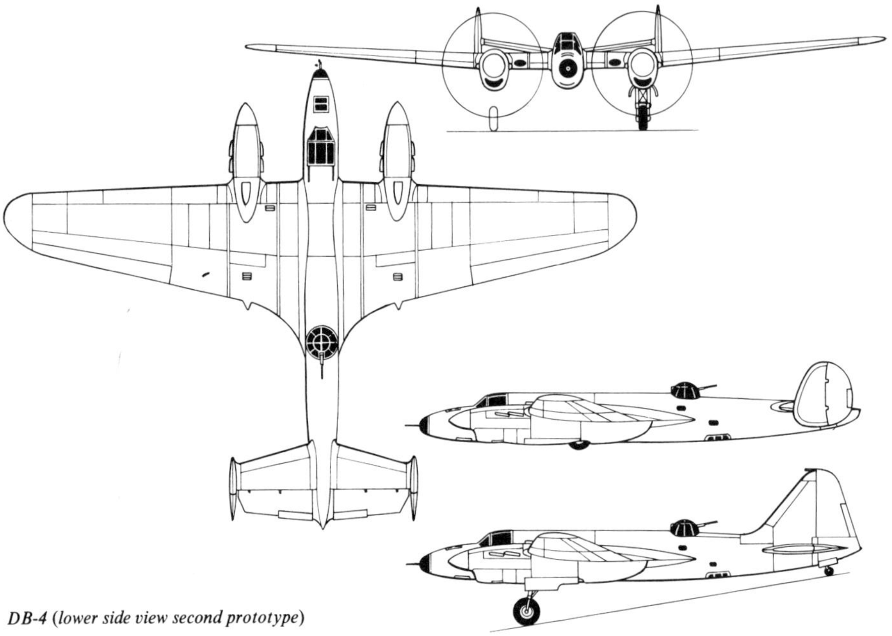
DB-4 (lower side view second prototype)

DB-4 (TsKB-56) In parallel with DB-3f Ilyushin's brigade planned a superior long-range bomber which, while using a slightly modified form of same wing, would use more powerful engines and have larger bomb bay. Structure entirely light-alloy, stressed-skin, with wing based on that of DB-3f but modified by different engine installations. DB-3f landing gear, retractable tailwheel with doors. Twin-finned tail, four-section split flaps. Crew four; in war either pilot or nav could fly aircraft, other two being turret gunner and radio/ventral gunner. ShKAS or ShVAK in nose, twin ShKAS or one ShVAK in dorsal turret, ShKAS in DB-3f type lower rear position. Deep bomb bay with two doors, normal capacity 1600 kg, maximum 2000 kg. Designed for M-120 engines, but delays with these resulted in temporary use of AM-37, in long nacelles with glycol radiators under engines and oil coolers in centre section inboard of engines. Factory tests started by Kokkinaki December 1940, and following NII trials given designation DB-4 early March 1941. Second prototype built with single fin and planned for M-71 aircooled radials, but this too had to be powered by AM-37. Early testing encouraging, but Ilyushin KB had to concentrate on Il-2 and Il-4, and production of even interim Mikulin V-12 engines would not suffice for production programme as well as meet needs of MiG-3 and Il-2. Test flying continued only to improve technology of engine installations (for example, for Il-6) and assist Il-4 programmed modifications.

DIMENSIONS Span 21,44 m (70 ft 4½ in); length 14,88 m (48 ft 10 in); wing area 66,7 m² (718 ft²).
ENGINES Actually fitted, two 1350 hp AM-37.
WEIGHTS Empty 5782 kg (12,747 lb); loaded (normal) 9 t (19,841 lb), (max) 11 325 kg 24,967 lb).
PERFORMANCE Max speed 447 km/h at SL, 560 km/h (348 mph) at 7 km; service ceiling 9 km; take-off 350 m; landing 360 m/130 km/h (81 mph); range 2500 km with 1 t bombload.

Il-6 Possibly first aircraft to have borne a designation for Ilyushin from outset, this was second major attempt to develop a successor to Il-4. Work began February 1942, objective being to use as many Il-4 parts as possible whilst greatly increasing range with 2 t bombload. Early in project decision taken to use completely new wing; prior to start ACh-30B diesel had been selected because of promise of significantly lower fuel consumption and demonstrated efficiency (albeit with poor reliability) in Yer-2. During 1942 design inevitably moved away from Il-4 until final drawings showed noticeably larger and heavier aircraft. Stressed-skin, flush-riveted externally, with fabric-skinned controls. Split flaps divided by large nacelles into four sections; operation of flaps and large main landing gear derived from that of Il-4 but with hydraulic power. Fuselage similar in layout to Il-4 but only rear portion actually same. Cross-section slightly increased to ease access between nose and rear, because of six crew two had to move aft to man guns in combat. Design armament five ShVAK: nose, dorsal turret, two beam windows and rear aft position (different from Il-4 with cannon faired largely external and with restricted cone of fire). Starting with Il-4 as basis kept wing in low position with restricted bomb bay, internal limit being six 500 kg or one 2 t bomb; overload bomb load 3 t (6614 lb), mainly external. Two torpedoes alternative. Wing totally new with excellent structure (DC-3 influence with multiple spars), aspect ratio 7·98, thickness/chord 16% at root and 12 at tip. Effort made to incorporate thermal de-icing for wings and tail, and to minimize pilot effort with accurate aileron and rudder trimmers. First Il-6 flown by Kokkinaki August 1943 and put through NII trials by A. Grinchik later 1943. Altogether four examples flown, but programme terminated early 1944. Problem with high wing loading no longer serious, but engine development was protracted and Ilyushin himself commented on lack of confidence in propulsion.

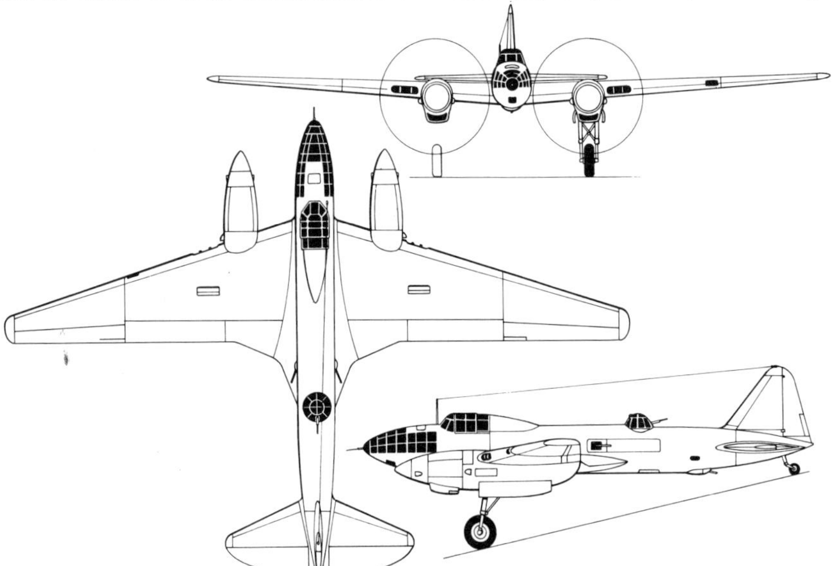
Il-6

DIMENSIONS Span 26,0 m (85 ft 4 in); length 16,47 m (54 ft $0\frac{1}{2}$ in); wing area 84,8 m^2 (913 ft^2).
ENGINES Two 1500 hp ACh-30B diesels.
WEIGHTS Empty 11 690 kg (25,772 lb); normal gross 16 650 kg (36,706 lb), max with 3 t bombload 18 650 kg (41,116 lb).
PERFORMANCE Max speed 368 km/h at SL, 464 km/h (288 mph) at 5,5 km; climb 28 min to 5 km; service ceiling 6,2 km (20,340 ft); design range 4000 km (2485 miles) with 1 t bombload; take-off 730 m; landing 650 m.

BSh-2 Also designated **TsKB-55** and **DBSh,** BSh-2 (*Bronirovannii Shturmovik*, armoured assaulter) was a single-engined armoured attack aircraft whose design was begun by Ilyushin's KB in 1938. Ilyushin took it upon himself to write appreciation of need to produce modern armoured attack aircraft, less vulnerable than existing biplanes and twin-engined bombers, and sent copies to Stalin and various officials on 27 January 1938. At this time he was still fighting to get out of his official post as Director of GUAP, which he contrived to do a month later. This made Stalin angry (he had torn up an earlier request), and Ilyushin was in a most insecure position when he returned to his KB in February 1938. Less than two months later he had Politburo go-ahead on BSh-2, and had agreed to fly a prototype by November 1938. Within days he was seriously hurt in his crash of AIR-11, and programme foundered. He tried to direct his staff from hospital, and returned to GAZ-39 earlier than he should. Basic design was conventional low-wing machine with single engine and tandem seats for pilot and radio/gunner (hence designation DBSh, *Dvukhmestnii BSh*, two-seat armoured assaulter). Armament forward-firing guns in wing, bombs in cells in inner wing, defensive gun in rear cockpit. Landing gears retracting backwards into fairings under wing. Choice of engine a severe compromise: final selection was AM-35, which offered just about adequate power but was large and heavy, and rated for best power at heights far above BSh levels. Main concern was armour, and like contemporary Su and MiG rivals basic philosophy was to fight crippling payload problems by making armour integral with airframe and bear flight loads. Unfortunately this pious hope difficult to achieve because main stresses elsewhere, and heaviest armour not called upon to carry severe loads except underside of engine cowl. From start severe problems with making accurate armour according to drawings, so that bolt and rivet holes matched up. This (far from new) problem resulted in decision to build first prototype as non-flying engineering mock-up. AB-1 (see note on armour in section on materials) used on engine cowl, 4 mm around front and 5 mm on lower sides and underside; also used 7 mm thick for rear bulkhead behind second crew-member. Carefully shaped before case-hardening and then held by 5 mm or 6 mm steel rivets to underlying dural airframe. Top of engine cowl, 5 mm dural sheet. Rough estimate of extra weight of protection, 700 kg. Rest of aircraft mixed construction. Rear fuselage and fin, wood monocoque, mostly from birch *shpon* (laminates 0,8 mm by 100 mm, glued into curved panels 5 mm thick). Wings and tail light alloy, flight controls being fabric-covered. Second BSh-2 made first flight of type on 30 December 1939. Kokkinaki pleased, but performance marginal. Armament four ShKAS in wings (later, about May 1940, increased to two ShVAK with 210 rounds each and two ShKAS with 750 each) plus one ShKAS at rear, with bombload of 400 kg and possible overload of 200 kg carried externally under fuselage. KB tests completed 26 March 1940 and NII testing 1/19 April. After years of failure there seemed here to be germ of successful machine, despite unimpressive take-off climb, speed, range and longitudinal stability. Ilyushin sensed VVS would ask for second crew-member to be removed to restore performance nearer specification, and began **TsKB-57** as single-seater. Heated correspondence ensued, finally settled by Politburo in November 1940 accepting VVS position and noting VVS belief that single-seat BSh-2 would be protected by friendly fighters. Ilyushin did not believe this to be practical, but single-seater flew October 1940, leading to Il-2.
DIMENSIONS Span 14,6 m (47 ft $10\frac{3}{4}$ in); length 11,6 m (38 ft $0\frac{3}{4}$ in); wing area 38,5 m^2 (414 ft^2).
ENGINE One 1350 hp AM-35.
WEIGHTS Empty 3625 kg (7992 lb); fuel/oil 315 + 30 kg; loaded 4735 kg (10,439 lb).
PERFORMANCE Max speed 362 km/h (225 mph) at SL, 422 km/h (262 mph) at 4,8 km; climb 11·5 min to 5 km; range 618 km (384 miles); take-off 340 m; landing 250 m/135 km/h (84 mph).

Il-2 Originally designated BSh-2, with KB designation **TsKB-57,** this aircraft entered an arena filled with uncertainty. Two-seater had failed to meet official requirements, as had a profusion of other armoured attack aircraft, and even Ilyushin was far from popular with Stalin and Politburo for his rejection of Directorship of GUAP, year's delay in appearance of prototype, and its failure to meet specification. Yet this aircraft, in almost all numerical values so close to Britain's disastrous Fairey Battle, was destined to become perhaps most famous aircraft ever built in Soviet Union, to play as great a part in winning the Second World War as any other type of weapon, and to be built in larger numbers than any other aircraft in history.

It derived directly from TsKB-55, which in autumn 1940 merged into it. At least one of two TsKB-55 prototypes was quickly modified with rear cockpit replaced by an additional fuel tank, giving a much-needed extension in range, with a wooden fairing behind canopy. Meanwhile, according to recent evidence, production of two-seater, with four SkKAS firing ahead, actually began at GAZ-18 in late 1940 and was supplemented by a factory in Leningrad (author doubts this), both continuing to build two-seater until autumn 1941. If so, such aircraft were probably used for NII trials and development of combat techniques. Designation BSh-2 was not changed to **Il-2** until April 1941. A month earlier Ilyushin had been awarded a Stalin Prize 2nd Class for BSh-2, indicating Stalin's anger with its designer, which had been compounded by

Il-2

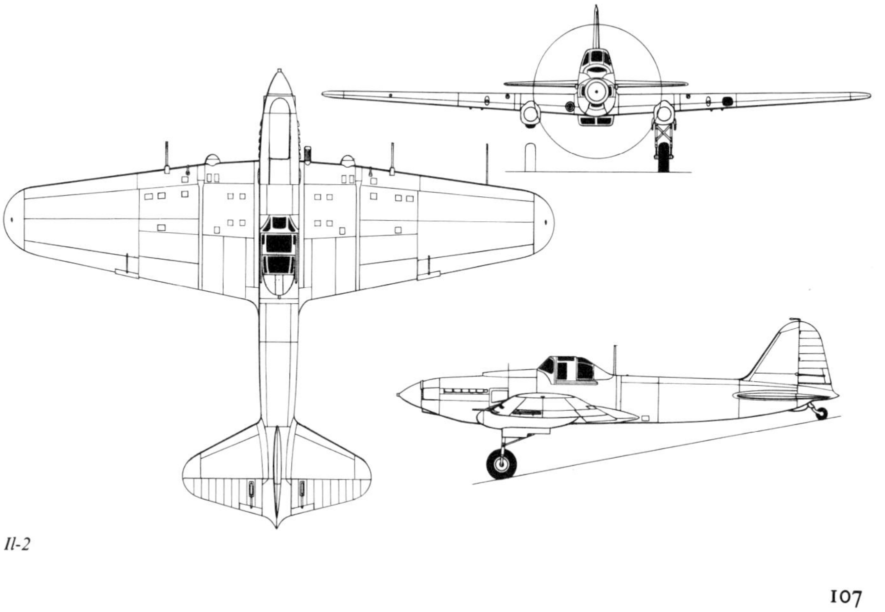
Il-2

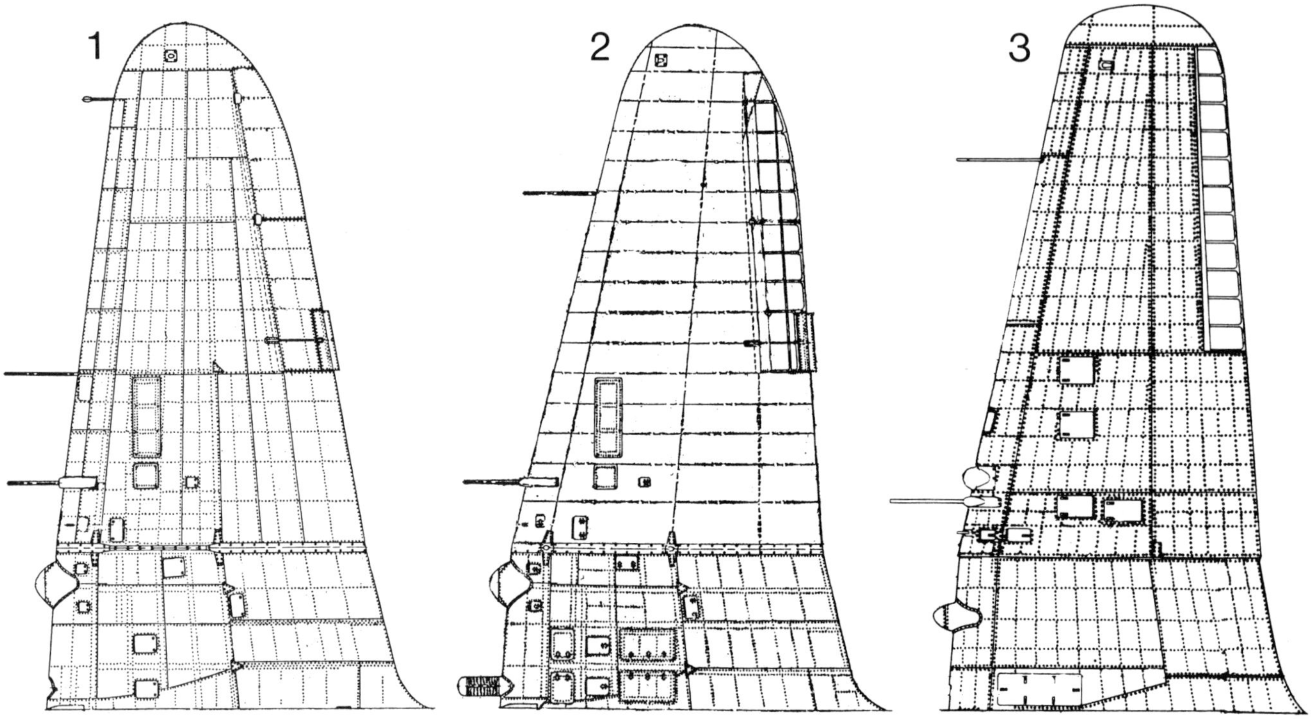

Based on recent Soviet drawings, these three wing-plan views show: 1, Il-2; 2, Il-2 Type 3M; 3, Il-10

Two interesting views of an identical formation of Il-2 Type 3Ms. A sorry-looking chunk of 'Berlin' is superimposed on both photographs, and spurious markings appear on the lead-aircraft (right)

slow build-up to production. GAZ-18 explained that it could not get enough supplies of preformed armour from Kirov Works, Leningrad. Asked reason, and totally unable to meet rapidly rising demand for armour from all users, Kirov Works director, Zazulskii, was unwise enough to produce a Voronezh drawing covered with doodles by Ilyushin after a long meeting, and explain that he 'could not work from such shoddy blue-prints'. Stalin flew into a rage, threatened Ilyushin by telephone, and summoned Zazulskii and Director of GAZ-18, Shenkman, to Moscow. Delegation from Voronezh were soon able to set picture straight; Zazulskii was fortunate to keep his job, and even his life, and there was no more trouble with armour (one wonders whose supplies suffered in consequence).

Main new feature of Il-2 was more powerful engine, though installationally similar. First batches had AM-35A or AM-37, but AM-38 soon standard. VISh-23 propeller with Hucks starter dogs, three blades, 3,4 m (133·8 in) diameter. Engine 175 mm shorter, fuel cells rearranged to make best use of space and final configuration four cells of total 470 kg (653 lit, 144 gal) instead of 315 kg in TsKB-55. Longitudinal stability improved by sweeping back outer wings 5° (putting CG at 30·2% chord) and increasing tailplane area 3·1%. Wing centre-section, two spars with 30KhGSA stainless-steel booms and dural plate webs, inter-spar box forming two bomb cells on each side, each with two doors pulled open manually against springs. Six bolted joints to outer wing, of wholly light-alloy construction. Split flaps on centre section and outer panels, same pneumatic actuation (pressure 35 to 50 at, 515 to 735 lb/in^2) as landing gear. Latter labour-intensive but twin shock-struts considered more reliable (though rejected later in Il-10). Main tyres 888 × 260 mm, 2,9 at pressure (42·6 lb/in^2) for soft fields; Il-2 seldom seen on skis. Retraction to rear, with wheel protruding to allow belly landing with little damage. Landing-gear fairings sometimes used to transport people, gear being left extended. Armament and armour as TsKB-55 except that VVS dissatisfaction resulted in rear bulkhead, now moved up behind pilot, being of 12 mm thickness. In addition to two ShVAK and two ShKAS, and 400 kg bombs, rails added under outer wings for six (mid-1941 eight) RS-82 or four RS-132 rockets. Provision for four Der-50 boxes for total of 200 PTAB-2,5 (2,5 kg) anti-armour bombs in wing bomb cells.

TsKB-57 first flew 12 October 1940. State trials 28 February to 20 March 1941, resulting in 54 mostly minor modifications including enlarged radiators in both engine-coolant and oil-cooler circuits, raised seat and improved rear view through wholly transparent Plexiglas rear canopy fairing, extension of rear (now 13 mm) armour upwards to meet this fairing, addition of 65 mm bullet-proof front windscreen, and removal of skin above tailwheel to improve access. Standard armament two ShVAK and two ShKAS, plus rockets/bombs already mentioned. Urgent mass-production at GAZ-18 augmented by two additional Zavods, identity uncertain but from GAZ-22, 30, 38 and 39. GAZ-18 believed initially to have supplied parts for assembly by other two. Production build-up in 1941 believed: March, 2; April, 24; May, 74; June, 159; and at full rate of about 300 monthly by August. March 1941 first recipient unit 4th Light Bomber Regt, 4th Division, in Ukraine; severe attrition from use of R-Z pilot techniques, incorrect maintenance procedures (no manuals yet) and overwhelming difficulty of harassed technical staff. On 22 June (war) most of regiment's pilots still unsure how to fly Il-2, let alone use armament; and soon demonstrated that policy of fighter protection from stern attack was incapable of fulfilment. Shortcomings in aircraft included failure of glued joints made in winter, and general weakness in rear fuselage, overcome by addition of four steel angle-section longerons by A.K. Belyenkov at repair works, subsequently standard on production aircraft.

By end of 1941 GAZ-18 had been evacuated to Kuibyshyev and production of group had been slow to pick up. Despite heavy losses, almost wholly from fighters, effectiveness of Il-2 indisputable. Stalin sent telegram December 1941 to factories, 'Il-2 is as needed by Red Army as air or bread . . . I demand production of more Il-2s; this is my last warning!' January 1942 high-level conference not only increased production resources but changed engine to AM-38F, effective about May 1942, which enabled important changes to be made in armour and firepower. Many field conversions had already been made as two-seaters, mechanics manning twin ShKAS or a UBT in local lash-up to provide desperately needed rear defence. **Il-2M** (*Modifikatsirovannii*) restored rear gunner, isolated from pilot behind fuel tank but with intercom, firing one UBT. Main forward guns changed to VYa-23, better able to penetrate enemy armour. Rocket installation standard eight RS-82 or four RS-132. Normal bombload increased to 600 kg. Outer wings restored to original sweep angle and temporarily made of wood to save aluminium; entire rear fuselage and fixed tail surfaces also wood, with changes in armour around cockpit. Main armour case-hardened in 4,5,6,8 and 12 mm thicknesses, with vital areas *bochka* (barrel) sandwich of armour plus 5 mm dural. Total mass of armour now typically 990 kg, academician Ye-O. Paton having solved problem of good welding. Il-2M reached production (allegedly Stalin loath to introduce it because of effect on output) third quarter 1942, and in action that winter at Stalingrad.

Autumn 1943 outer wings again revised to 15° leading-edge angle, which remained standard through subsequent improvements. Longitudinal control again improved by elevator mass balances inside tailplane. Gradual restoration of lighter and less damage-prone dural structure in outer wings and tail. Batches of American Cr-Mo steel tested for landing gears but found 'too brittle and not shock-resistant'. During 1944 **Il-2 Type 3,** originally test-flown December 1942, entered production with engine uprated to 1770 hp, duralumin outer wings and tail, 45 improvements to reduce drag including greater precision in fitting adjacent sheets of armour, detail changes to canopy and stronger springs to shut bomb doors tightly. **Il-2 Type 3M** further improvement, on field testing 20 June to 16 December 1943 and standard in 1944. Thanks to aerodynamic refinement could still take-off in 364 m with much heavier armament. Main guns NS-OKB-16 of 37 mm calibre, each with 32 rounds; could defeat PzKW VI Tiger. Ability to carry 32 RS-82 in two-stage zero-length installation. Total production by November 1944 believed to be 36,163.

Several non-standard models tested. **Il-21, IB,** (*Istrebitel Bombardirovshchik*) with one seat, strengthened wings, no bombs, reduced armour, two VYa-23. About 760 kg lighter but when tested 1943 too slow to catch German bombers. **Il-1** described separately. **Il-2T** carried 533 mm torpedo on centreline; served in small numbers with Black Sea Fleet. **Il-2U** (also designated torpedo on centreline; served in small numbers with Black Sea Fleet. **Il-2U** (also designated **UIl-2**, Il-2 *Uchyebnii*) tandem dual trainer with different rear cockpit and canopy, two ShKAS, two RS-82, 200 kg bombload; would have saved many lives and aircraft in 1941, but not tested until 1943 and built in small numbers only. **Il-2/ASh-82** (also called **Il-4**) tested September 1941, NII tests by M. Nyukhtikov February 1942—in parallel with rival Su-6; about 400 kg lighter and flew well, but no reason to disrupt production and ASh-82 in great demand.

ENGINE One Mikulin V-12, until 1942 1665 hp AM-38, then 1720 hp AM-38F, from December 1943 1760/1770 hp AM-38F.

WEIGHTS Empty (1940) 3792 kg, (1941) 4350 kg (9590 lb), Type 3) 4525 kg (9976 lb); fuel/oil

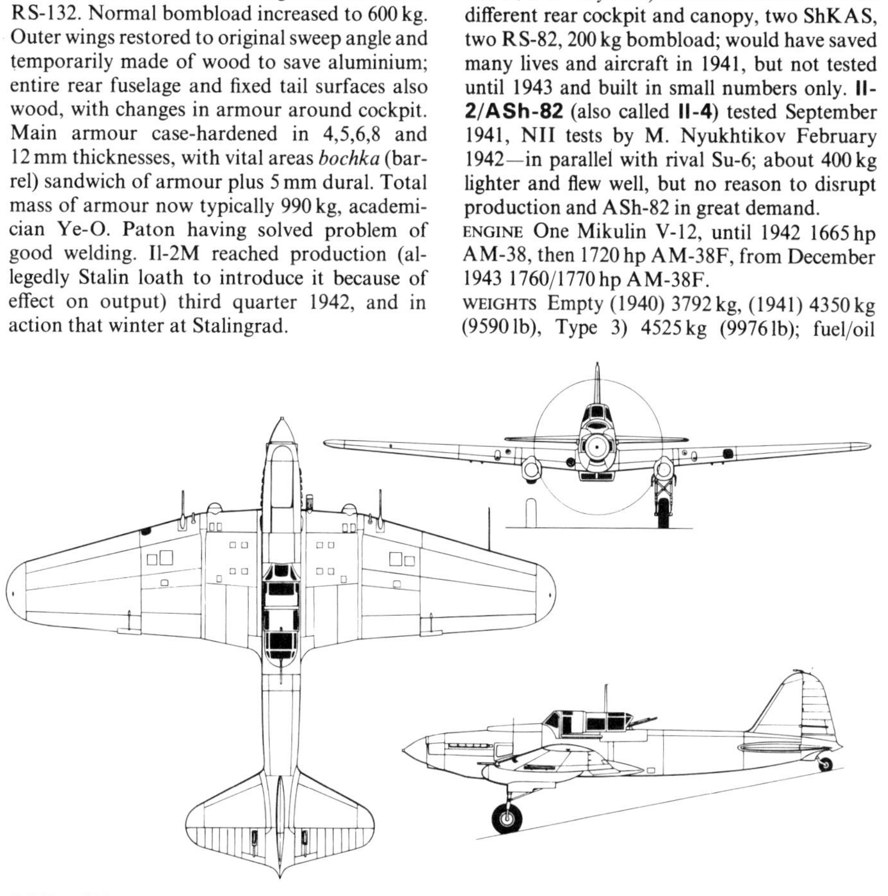

Il-2 Type 3M

(1941) 470+40, (1942 on) 535+50; loaded (1940) 4988 kg, (1941) 5750 kg (12,676 lb), (1942, -2M) 6060 kg (13,360 lb), (Type 3) 6360 kg (14,021 lb).
PERFORMANCE Max speed at SL (1940) 422 km/h, (1941) 433 km/h (269 mph), (1942–44, typical) 390/403 km/h (242/250 mph), (at best height, typical) 415 km/h (258 mph); ceiling (typical) 6 km; range 765/800 km (say, 480 miles); take-off (Type 3) 395 m; landing (1940) 260 m/135 km/h, (Type 3) 535 m/145 km/h (90 mph).

Il-1** Rather uninspired single-seat fighter derived from Il-2 by reducing dimensions and fitting more powerful engine with four-blade propeller. Reported (not by Ilyushin KB) to have been produced solely to provide competition for Su-7, and to have been halted on failure of that aircraft. Il-1 used 67% standard Il-2 parts but with reprofiled canopy (clear-view sliding, resembling Fw 190), smaller outer wings, shorter fuselage and retractable tailwheel. Armament two VYa-23, each with 150 rounds, and quite heavily armoured for *Shturmovik* role. First flown 19 May 1944; Kokkinaki satisfied, but soon evident performance totally inadequate, especially at height.
DIMENSIONS Span 13,4 m (43 ft 11½ in); length 11,1 m (36 ft 5 in); wing area 30,0 m² (323 ft²).
ENGINE One 2000 hp AM-42.
WEIGHTS Empty 4285 kg (9447 lb); loaded 5320 kg (11,728 lb).
PERFORMANCE Max speed 525 km/h (326 mph) at SL, 580 km/h (360 mph) at 2,5 km; climb 8·3 min to 5 km; service ceiling 8,6 km (28,215 ft); time 360° turn 21 s; range 1000 km (621 miles).

Il-8 Kremlin conference of January 1942 launched several Il-2 offshoots, including Il-1, Il-8, Il-10 and Il-16, all of them major redesigns. Il-8 was least modified, chief alteration being more powerful engine with cleaned-up installation identical to that of Il-1, four-blade propeller with anticing, oil cooler radiators in wing roots, improved belly radiator, and new landing gear with single air/oil shock strut retracting rearwards carrying large low-pressure tyred wheel turning 90° to lie inside wing. Armour similar to late Il-2, but extended rearwards to enclose gunner. Outer-wings and tail of duralumin. Two-seat cockpit further forward than in Il-2, improved aerodynamic form, and radio mast on windscreen frame. Armament two VYa-23 and two ShKAS in wings (some reports state two VYa and two ShVAK) and one UBT aimed by backseater; bombload up to 1 t. Flown by Kokkinaki April 1944 and subjected to NII trials, but Il-10 a superior aircraft.
DIMENSIONS Span 14,6 m (47 ft 10¾ in); length 12,9 m (42 ft 4 in); wing area 39,0 m² (420 ft²).
ENGINE One 2000 hp AM-42.
WEIGHTS Empty 4900 kg (10,802 lb); fuel/oil 670 kg; loaded 7660 kg (16,887 lb).
PERFORMANCE Max speed 428 km/h (266 mph) at SL, 472 km/h (293 mph) at 2,5 km; service ceiling 6,4 km; range 980 km (609 miles); take-off 435 m; landing speed 136 km/h (84·5 mph).

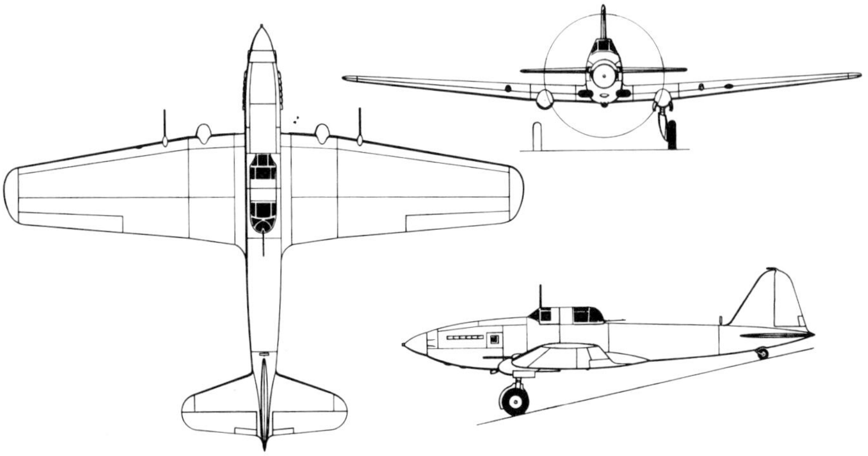
Il-8

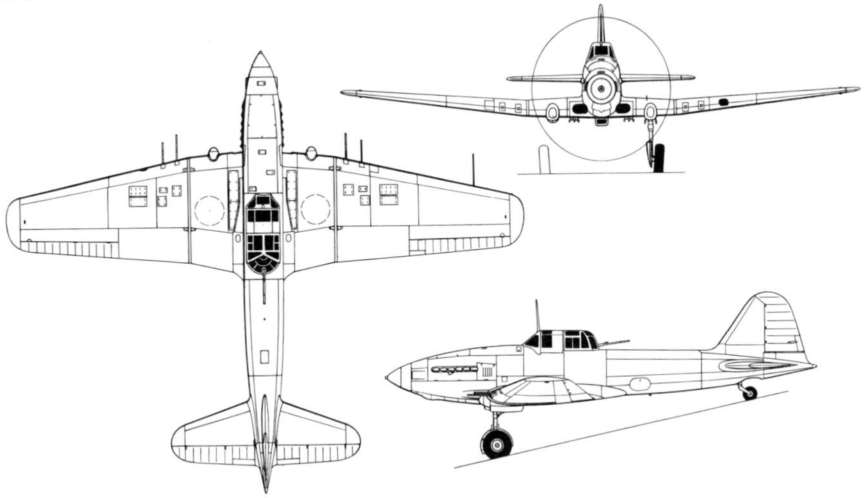
Il-10

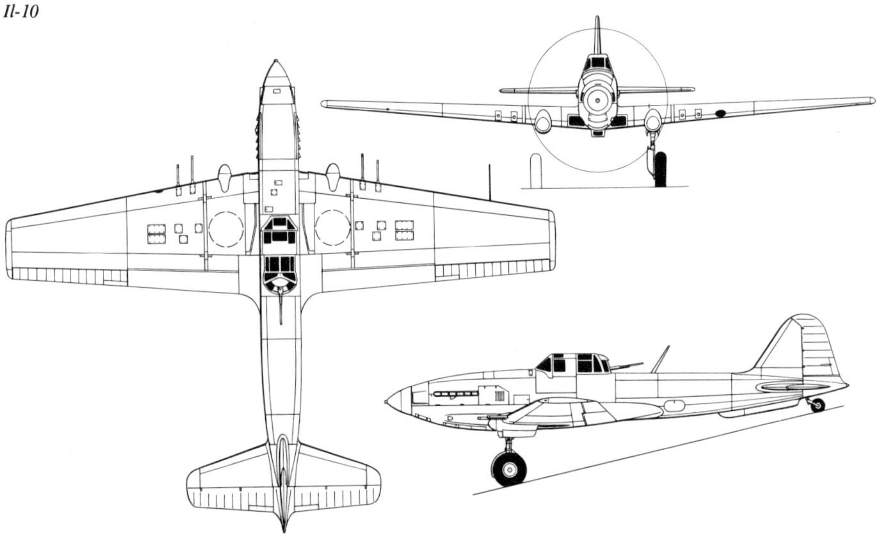
Il-10M

Il-10 This second-generation *Shturmovik* used airframe of Il-1** and thus had little in common with Il-2 except basic layout. AM-42 engine with three-blade AV-5L-24 propeller with Hucks dogs. Light-alloy construction throughout, except for armour which was identical with Il-8. Modern pressed-sheet and rolled sections in centre section, with improved weapon bays and rearwards-retracting landing gear with pneumatic actuation as in Il-8, with single shock struts. Low-pressure tyres 900 × 300 mm. Flaps extended beneath fuselage. Stressed-skin outer wings of reduced span and area, and with spars swept slightly back to move centre of pressure aft. One-piece Frise aileron. Improved tail, light-alloy structure with fabric-covered movable surfaces, rudder having horn (as on Il-1) instead of external mass balance, slightly greater height of vertical tail, horizontal tail of reduced chord but much greater span and area. Retractable tailwheel. Same crew compartment as Il-8. Original armament two VYa and two ShKAS on first test flights in April 1944, changed during KB testing to two NR-23 and two ShKAS, with further changes to two NS-OKB-16 (37 mm)

Il-10U, BS-33

and two ShKAS or four NR-23. Large access doors for speedy replenishment of magazines, unlike Il-2. Normalbomb load 400 to 600 kg, with up to 100 kg size in each centre-section cell, plus eight RS-82. Excellent gunner's cupola with B-20 EN cannon with 150 rounds and improved protection, headroom and visibility. Factory tests followed by NII trials by A.K. Dolgov from 9 June 1944. Outstanding aircraft in all respects, superior to Il-8 or Su-8, and ordered into production in place of Il-2 on 23 August. First Il-10 with troops in October. Enthusiastic reception, and from start availability and effectiveness much higher than Il-2. Unlike Il-2 also produced as dual trainer variant **Il-10U** or **UIl-10** from outset, usually with no armament except two ShKAS and almost same canopy as Il-2U.

In 1951 small number made of **Il-10M** with completely different wing. Single structure from tip to tip, with structural joint between centre section and outer panels but no change in taper or dihedral and with one-piece flaps from aileron to centreline. Clark-YH profile, thickness 18% at root and 12% at broad square tip. Span and area slightly greater than Il-10. Ailerons and horizontal tail redesigned, aerodynamics of wing and horizontal tail being scale (analog) of Il-20, then already abandoned. Slightly longer fuselage and improved vertical tail. Normal armament four NR-23 and one UBT. At least one Il-10M fitted with Glushko RD-1X3 rocket, with smaller rudder above thrust chamber and extra ventral strake ahead of tailwheel (this aircraft preserved at Monino). Total production of Il-10 put at 4966, concluded in 1949 or 1950. In 1950 drawings and tooling were transferred to Czech Avia works which built a further 1200 designated **B-33** and (trainer) **BS-33**. It has been suggested some of Czech production was of Il-10M type.

DIMENSIONS Span 13,4 m (43 ft 11½ in), (10M) 14,0 m (45 ft 11¼ in); length 11,1 m (36 ft 5 in), (10M) 11,8 m (38 ft 8½ in); wing area 30,0 m² (323 ft²), (10M) 33,0 m² (355 ft²).

ENGINE One 2000 hp AM-42.

WEIGHTS Empty 4680 kg (10,317 lb), (10M) 5570 kg (12,280 lb); fuel/oil 535+50 kg (10M, 580+80); loaded 6535 kg (14,407 lb), (10M) 7320 kg (16,138 lb).

PERFORMANCE Max speed 507 km/h (315 mph) at SL (10M, 476 km/h), 551 km/h (342 mph) at 2,8 km (10M, 512 km/h); climb 9·7 min to 5 km (10M, 12·7 min); service ceiling 7250 m (23,790 ft) (10M, 7 km); range 800 km (497 miles); take-off 475 m (10M, 410 m/18 s); landing 460 m/148 km/h (92 mph) (10M, max landing wt) 500 m/19·4 s/179 km/h.

Il-16* Last of direct descendents of Il-2, this two-seat *Shturmovik* was designed to use Mikulin's AM-43 engine of 2200 hp, with four-blade propeller slightly larger than that of Il-1 and Il-8. Design very close to Il-10. Shavrov records that wing was fractionally smaller, and that structure was weak, 'especially in tail'. Three prototypes built early 1945; began KB testing August, soon discontinued because of clear suitability of Il-10. Other observers claim there was severe vibration in engine, causing switch to AM-42, and need to lengthen rear fuselage to correct CG position; Něměcek even reports production was begun along with prototypes and halted only at 53rd aircraft.

DIMENSIONS Span 13,4 m (43 ft 11½ in); length (originally) 11,2 m (36 ft 9 in); wing area 30,0 m² (323 ft²).

ENGINE Originally one 2200 hp AM-43, later 2000 hp AM-42.

WEIGHTS Not reliably reported (Něměcek, 4200/6180 kg).

PERFORMANCE Not recorded.

Il-12 By 1943 total lack of modern Soviet transport caused Kremlin to issue a requirement, basic task being replacement of Li-2. Priority at that time lower than for *Shturmoviks* but sizeable team was put on Il-12 immediately. Competitors were Bartini T-117 and Yermolayev Yer-2-ON. Like Yermolayev Ilyushin intended to use Charomskii diesel, but changed his mind on closer acquaintance in Il-6. From outset his structure was based on Li-2 (DC-3), extending to three spars, Clark YH aerofoil inboard, multiple stress-bearing stringers, and hydraulic secondary power. Straightforward, except for tricycle landing gear, then uncommon in Soviet Union. Rectangular centre-section with chord greater than root of outer wing where section changed to K-4. Flight controls of D4 dural with fabric covering. Ailerons 29% aerodynamic and 100% mass-balanced; elevators 26% balanced and rudder 23·6%, with Flettner (servo) and electric trim tab. Fuselage circular section but unpressurized, multi-stringer semi-monocoque with skin 0,6 to 2,0 mm. Flush riveting on most exterior surfaces. Wing aspect ratio 9·75, dihedral 2° from root. All-dural split flaps, hydraulic actuation to 45°. Landing gear with single legs (total about-face from Il-2) but twin wheels (900 × 300 mm tyres) on main units. Hydraulic retraction with pneumatic emergency, assisted by free-fall and air drag on main gears. Castoring nose gear, retracted to rear. Highly developed engine installation (basically Tu-2) available, initially with exhaust stack each side, cooling fan and oil cooler in leading edge of wing with discharge along interior to provide ice protection. Four-blade AV-9E-91 propellers with autofeathering (direct copy of wartime Hamil-

Il-12 (CSA, Czechoslovakia)

ton). Rubber-boot, near Goodrich copy, deicers on tailplane. Also based on US technology were rubber shock mounts for engines and detail design of fuel cells, normal capacity 4170 lit (2935 kg) in four tanks in centre section, with two in each outer wing in the two inter-spar boxes to bring max capacity to 6020 lit (1324 gal). AP-42A autopilot.

First flown by V.K. Kokkinaki, assisted by his brother Konstantin, 9 January 1946. Generally satisfactory but CG so near main gears that tail bracing strut was added for support on ground. Many minor faults, directional stability requiring dorsal fin. Aeroflot service August 1947 with 27 passengers, door on right at rear. Faults led to stronger nose leg, ASh-82T engines, and above all proper ice protection with large engine exhaust heat-exchangers (oil coolers moved to cowl), electric heating of tail and windscreen, and alcohol slingers for propellers. Resulting extra weight 260 kg, reducing speed 15/20 km/h. Previously marginal engine-out performance became unacceptable, and immediate solution was to restrict weight to 16 t and 18 passengers. Aircraft uneconomic by Western standards (empty weight similar to 48-seat CV-240) but tough and simple and estimated 1500 built 1946–1949 (it is believed, at Khodinka) of which more than half military. Developed model often called **Il-12B.** Freight version with 2,2 m wide rear door on left side and 3,5 t payload designated **Il-12T.** Arctic/Antarctic version with skis and additional ice protection, no separate designation. Military assault transport **Il-12D** (*Desantnyi*) with turret mounting ShKAS (later UBT), glider tow cleat and canvas seats for theoretical 37 paratroops (in practice 30 or less). Some military casevac versions with 16 stretchers and six seated. Normal crew four (two pilots, nav and radio); same in civil use plus stewardess. Exports to CSA, LOT and CAAC.
DIMENSIONS Span 31,7 m (104 ft 0 in); length 21,31 m (69 ft 11 in); wing area 103 m² (1109 ft²).
ENGINES Two 1850 hp ASh-82FN; some later batches 1900 hp ASh-82T.
WEIGHTS Empty (civil) 11 045 kg (24,350 lb); fuel/oil 3130 kg; loaded (if unrestricted) 17 250 kg (38,029 lb).
PERFORMANCE (nominal) Max speed 366 km/h at SL, 407 km/h (253 mph) at 2,5 km; climb 15 min to 5 km; service ceiling 6,5 km (21,325 ft); range 1500 km (932 miles); endurance 4·5 h; take-off 475 m; landing 563 m/128 km/h (79·5 mph).

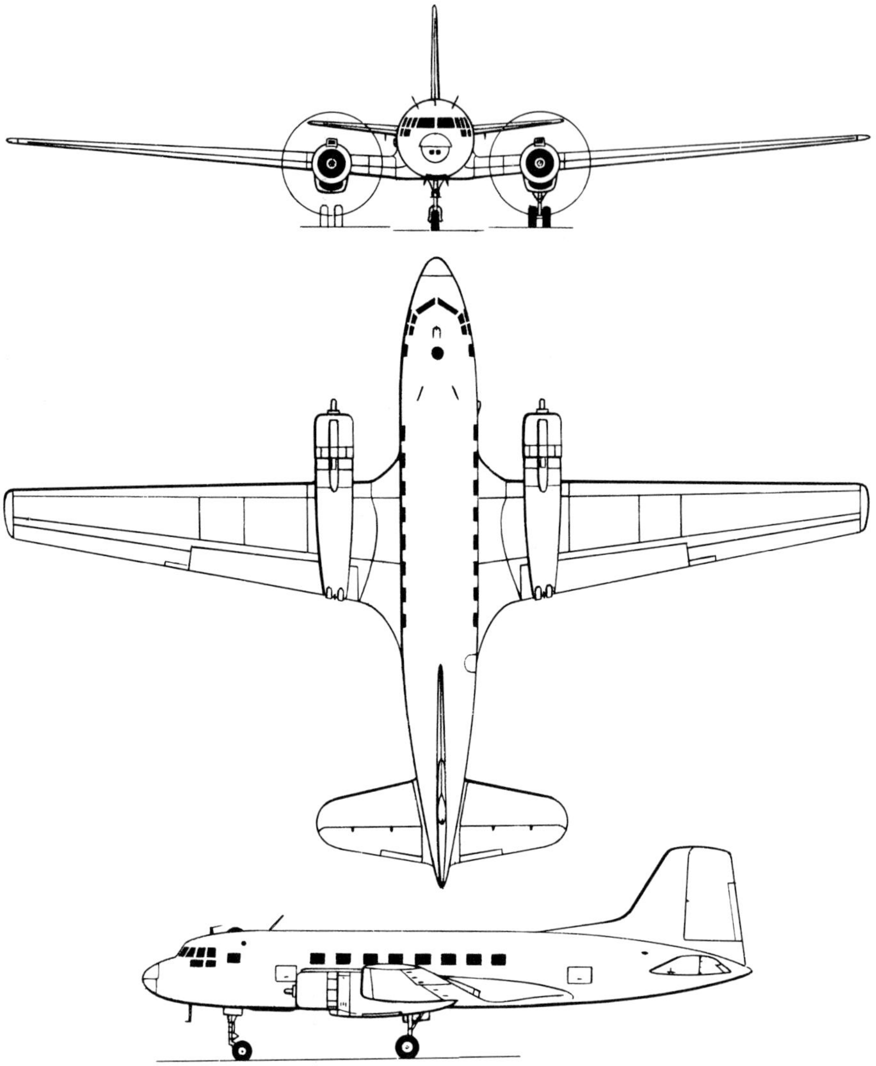

Il-14M

Il-14 Ilyushin was determined to rectify underlying deficiencies of Il-12, and this turned out to be major redesign. Only parts left were fuselage and landing gear, and even these were substantially modified. Wing was entirely new, same span but straight taper root to tip entirely on trailing edge without broad centre section; aerofoil SR-5, slightly deeper section than on Il-12, aspect ratio increased to 10. Engine installations aerodynamically cleaned up, ASh-82T (*Transportnii*) standard, with slightly reduced fuel consumption and 500 h overhaul period to reduce failure-rate. AV-50 propellers, with feathering time reduced from 18 to 4 or 5 s. Fuel confined to four outer-wing cells. Exhaust system copied from CV-240 with twin stacks taken across wing to ejector nozzles above trailing edge. Improved thermal anti-icing (again based on CV-240) making reduced demand on engine power and, with other changes, greatly improving performance in adverse conditions and especially with one engine out. Latter regime also improved by new vertical tail of increased area. Large wing-root fillet extended forwards around leading edge. Flaps of slotted type. As in practice eight rows of passenger seats never fitted to Il-12, cabin windows reduced to seven each side. First Il-14 flown 20 September 1950. Prolonged trials, with inability to carry desired payload; released for production late 1953 and estimated 2200 built at Khodinka finishing 1 January 1958.

Original **Il-14P** seated 18 passengers (660 kg loaded weight per passenger compared with 314 for Li-2). Theoretical load could be 40 (ten rows of four), and Aeroflot strove to increase load actually carried with safe performance. Soon after start of service new sprayed film (with RA-6 adhesive) used to seal fuel cells against seepage. Many other minor modifications, and three Soviet variants: **Il-14M** (*Modifikatsiya*) with 1 m longer fuselage to seat up to 40 (actual number 24, then 30, finally 32); **Il-14T** freighter with large 2,2 m door on left, cleared to same 17,5 t weight as 14M; **Il-14D** (*Desantnyi*) assault transport with longitudinal bench seats along sides (but no turret); and **Il-14F** photo mapping and survey variant. From 1955 Avia in Czechoslovakia and VEB in Dresden DDR received drawings and assistance with tooling, but full production delayed until transfer of jigs from Khodinka in 1958. Several local improvements in these foreign models, Avia building 200 and VEB 80. Il-14 was one of first Soviet aircraft to be exported in large numbers all over world. Large numbers remain in use, and as late as 1976 a squadron of ECM/Elint rebuilds (designation not known) went into use with VVS in DDR.
DIMENSIONS Span 31,7 m (104 ft 0 in); length 21,31 m (69 ft 11 in), (14M, 22.31 m, 73 ft 2¼ in); wing area 100 m² (1076 ft²).
ENGINES Two 1900 hp ASh-82T.
WEIGHTS Empty 12 080 kg (26,631 lb), (14M, 12,7 t, 28,000 lb); fuel/oil 2760 kg; loaded 17 250 kg (38,030 lb), (14M, 14T, 17,5 t, 38,-580 lb).
PERFORMANCE Max speed 393 km/h at SL, 430 km/h (267 mph) at 2,4 km; climb 8·5 min to 5 km; service ceiling 7,4 km (24,278 ft) range, typically 1500 km (932 miles) with 26 passengers, 400 km (248·5 miles) with max payload of 3,3 t; endurance 4·5 h; take-off 485 m; landing 480 m/135 km/h (84 mph).

Il-18* Also called **SPD**, transport for 66 passengers and 900 kg baggage. Physically largest task attempted by Ilyushin, and rivalling anything tackled in USSR in 1945, this was a crash

*Il-18**

*Il-20**

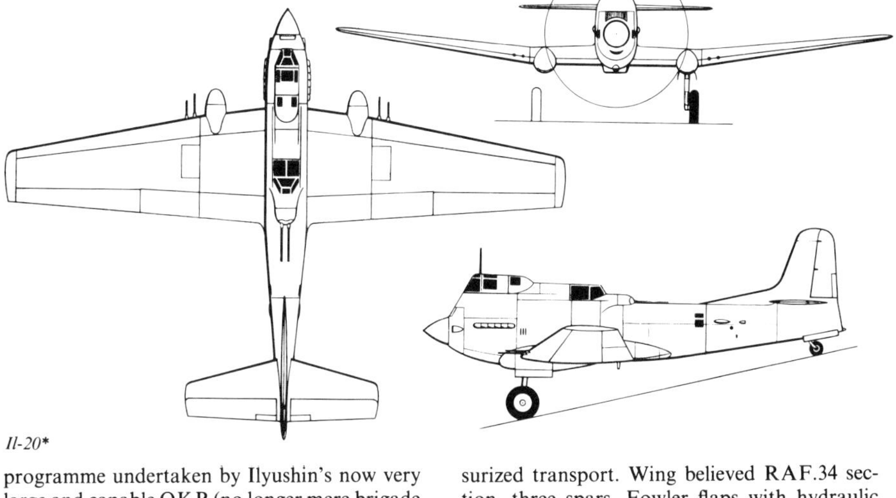

*Il-20**

programme undertaken by Ilyushin's now very large and capable OKB (no longer mere brigade within TsKB) as soon as European war over. Using same engine as Tu-70, but without turbochargers, driving same propellers, objective was to build large and capable long-range pressurized transport. Wing believed RAF.34 section, three spars, Fowler flaps with hydraulic operation, hydraulic landing gear with twin main wheels retracting forwards, twin steerable nosewheels retracting to rear. Circular-section fuselage with detail design closely similar to Tu-70 and possibly identical (diameters apparently same). Designed for pressurization but not known if system fitted. Large flight deck faired into nose as in Boeing 377 (flown November 1944); provision for flight crew of five plus two cabin crew. Passenger cabin built as separate tube of constant section with ten circular windows each side, normal seating 60 (not 66 in practice) in ten rows of six (triple seats). Tail similar to scaled-up Il-12. Flight controls manual, probably fabric-covered surfaces, two-section ailerons with Flettner servo tabs. All leading edges de-iced by pneumatic rubber boots. No details of systems, but fuel mass (see data) significant. Single prototype, first flown 30 July 1947. No evidence of dissatisfaction, and performance excellent, but despite national need for capable transport Il-18, like Tu-70 and Tu-75, was incapable of being properly used. Reluctantly recognized it would take years to bring airfields, ground services and engineering staff to level demanded by aircraft of this class. Development discontinued soon after first flight.

DIMENSIONS Span 41,1 m (134 ft 10 in); length 29,86 m (97 ft 11½ in); wing area 140,0 m^2 (1507 ft^2).

ENGINES Four 2300 hp ASh-73.

WEIGHTS Empty 28 490 kg (62,809 lb); fuel/oil 14 010 kg; loaded 42 500 kg (93,695 lb).

PERFORMANCE Max speed 588 km/h (365 mph) at SL, probably more at best height but not measured; typical cruising speed 520 km/h (323 mph) at height; climb 8 min to 5 km, 13·9 to 8 km; service ceiling 10,7 km (35,105 ft); range 6200 km (3853 miles) with reduced payload; max endurance 13 h; landing speed 170 km/h (106 mph).

Il-20* One of ugliest post-war aircraft, this *Shturmovik* was a multi-purpose attacker for use against all surface targets including shipping, though it carried no sensors. Aerodynamically it was direct scale-up of Il-10M, but by chance its configuration (except for unconventional location of pilot) and shape was a close parallel to Douglas AD Skyraider. All light-alloy stressed-skin, Clark-YH wing profile, landing gears similar to Il-8/10/16, retractable tailwheel with doors. Most powerful Russian V-12 engine, with large but shallow belly radiator and leading-edge oil coolers. Pilot's cockpit directly above engine

Il-22

with 6 to 9 mm armour covering entire nose; engine also helped protect pilot. Sliding and jettisonable armoured canopy; poor view to rear but superb view ahead, immediately behind four-blade propeller. Second crew-member radio/gunner with remote electrical control of power-driven turret with two 23 mm guns (Shavrov, NA-23 (*sic*); Němeček, two 20 mm). Turret and ammunition filled fuselage cross-section immediately to rear of gunner; armour unknown. Internal cells for four 100 kg bombs or equivalent; max load an additional pair of 500 kg or equivalent hung externally. Underwing racks for eight RS-82. As far as known, only one prototype, NII trials 1948. Dubbed *Gorbun* (Gorboon), hunchback. Engine undeveloped and general performance, except range, inferior to Il-10. Judged obsolescent and discontinued in favour of Il-40; yet basic aircraft might with development have proved as versatile as Skyraider?

DIMENSIONS Span 17,0 m (55 ft 9 in); length 12,59 m (41 ft 3⅔ in); wing area 44,0 m² (474 ft²).

ENGINE One 2700 hp M-47F.

WEIGHTS Empty 7500 kg (16,534 lb); fuel 800 kg; loaded 9800 kg (21,605 lb).

PERFORMANCE Max speed 515 km/h (320 mph) at SL, falling off with height; climb 8 min to 5 km; service ceiling 7750 m (25,430 ft); range 1680 km (1044 miles).

Il-22 Though, like most other high-speed aircraft of its day, a traditional airframe with jet engines, this light bomber is notable on several counts. It was first four-jet aircraft after wartime Ar 234C to fly in Europe. It was first jet bomber in Soviet Union, four years earlier than Britain's Canberra. It was almost first aircraft to fly with engines designed by A.M. Lyul'ka's KB (just pipped to post by Su-11), and started a partnership between Ilyushin and engine designer that endured through several generations of successor bombers. Design started summer 1945. Configuration and systems details strongly influenced by German work, especially Ar 234C and He 343. Shoulder-high unswept wing of laminar profile skinned with long stretch-pressed panels; in later version to form integral tankage, but most fuel still in fuselage, bringing total capacity to 11 250 lit (2475 gal), though Shavrov gives mass (see data) corresponding to only 8560 lit. Engines hung in well-separated single pods at easy height above ground yet low enough not to damage flaps. Crew of five in circular-section fuselage, occupied portions being pressurized: nav/bomb in nose, with two NS-23; pilot on left side of nose; electronics operator or co-pilot on right side of nose; with nose radar (not fitted); radio/gunner in dorsal turret at rear of nose compartment, with twin B-20; and tail gunner in Ilyushin K-series power turret of Tu-4 type with twin NS-23. Large bomb bay under wing with capacity for 2 t (4410 lb) or (overload) single 3 t bomb, twin doors opening into slipstream. Tricycle landing gear with steerable twin-wheel nose unit retracting to rear and large single mainwheels retracting into recesses in sides of fuselage beside bomb bay. Access between front crew and tail gunner not possible in prototypes. Four-section Fowler flaps, metal-skinned manual flight controls, secondary power systems included pneumatic and electric. First flight 24 July 1947. Took part in Tushino parade 3 August 1947. Both Kokkinaki brothers flew Il-22, but programme terminated 22 September 1947. Deficiencies: long take-off, poor speed, short range.

DIMENSIONS Span 23,06 m (75 ft 8 in); length 21,05 m (69 ft 0¾ in); wing area 74,5 m² (802 ft²).

ENGINES Four 1300 kg (2866 lb) Lyul'ka TR-1 turbojets.

WEIGHTS Empty 14 950 kg (32,959 lb); fuel 6160 kg; loaded 24 t (52,910 lb).

PERFORMANCE Max speed 656 km/h at SL, 718 km/h (446 mph) at 7 km; climb estimate 8·6 min to 5 km; service ceiling 11 km; range estimate 865 km (537 miles); endurance 1·4 h; take-off 2 km; landing speed 190 km/h (118 mph).

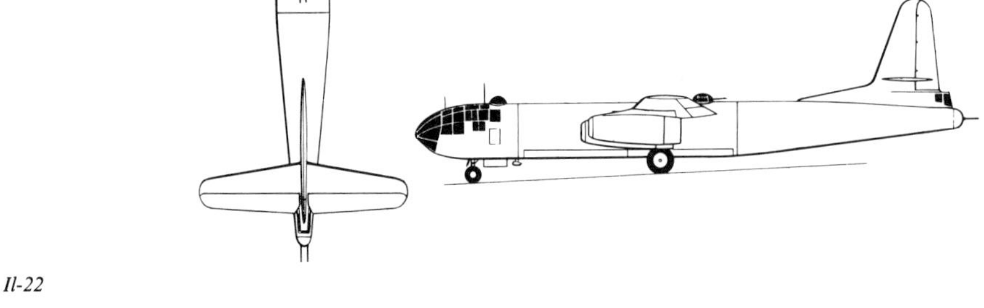

Il-22

Il-28

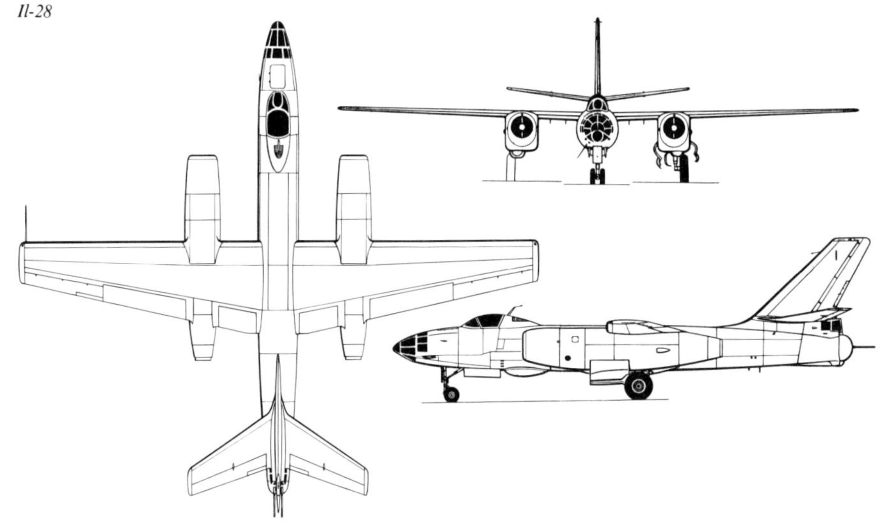

Il-28

Il-24 In 1947–48 Ilyushin produced drawings for this improved Il-22 with four RD-500, and main landing gears, in twin underwing pods.

Il-28 Often regarded as Soviet counterpart of Canberra, this tactical bomber was begun as project 18 months later than British aircraft, in December 1947, and flew nine months earlier. Ilyushin was under pressure to match timing of Tupolev's sequence of rival prototypes with a single superior aircraft. Result looked like Tu-14 but had smaller fuselage and 35° swept tail. (Canberra had broader wing and better aerodynamics, giving superior load, height and manoeuvrability.) Like Soviet rivals, Ilyushin had to instal his own (then-standard Il-K6 tail turret, severely penalizing small aircraft. Key to whole design was imported Nene (RD-45); nacelle and landing gear virtually common to this aircraft and Tu rivals. Third contemporary was Su-10.

Wing superior to that of Il-22, TsAGI SR-5S profile, ruling t/c ratio 12%, set at 3° incidence but only 0°38′ dihedral. All taper on trailing edge, aspect ratio 7·55. Two-spar construction in D-16T, skins up to 4 mm. Like entire airframe, structurally divided into upper/lower (or left/right) halves to speed manufacture and installation of systems and equipment, completed halves then being joined, usually by bolting via small hand-aperatures with flush-screwed doors; weight penalty 1·5% but saved time. Slotted flaps inboard and outboard of nacelles, hydraulic actuation to 50° by AK-150 pump on each engine. Landing gears retracted pneumatically (55 kg/cm^2), main wheels with tyres 1150 × 355 mm, folding forward and turning 90° to lie flat under jetpipe. Nose gear twin steerable tyres 600 × 180, later (1951) 600 × 155V, retracted rearwards. Small fuselage, no access between crew. Pressurized nose and tail compartment, system operated above 2 km to 0·4 ata (5·8 lb/in^2) with filtered main bleed air; ATIM-X and ANZM insulation for heat and noise. Fuselage frames and stringers pressed or rolled, skin 1,0 or 1,5 mm, flush-riveted. Fixed tailplane with 7° dihedral mounted on fin, all swept 35° to avoid control problem at max dive speed. Flight controls manual, light-alloy skin, electric trim. Nav/bomb in nose, jettisonable roof entry hatch, upward-ejection seat. Pilot on centreline immediately to rear, canopy hinged to right, upward ejection. Radio/gunner access/escape via hinged ventral hatch, with potentiometer/hydraulic steering of K6 armament (twin NR-23, 450 rounds each). Pilot gyro sight for twin fixed NR-23 in nose, 200 rounds each. Normal bombload 1 t in internal bay with twin doors opening hydraulically into airstream; oveload one 3 t FAB-3000. Normally no wing stores or wing fuel: soft fuselage cells, three ahead of wing and two behind, for 7908 lit (1740 gal), with option (1951 on) of two 333 lit tip tanks (not with 3 t bomb). Crew seats armoured 6/10/32 mm, mass 454 kg, and glazing 102 mm thick (forwards) and 68 mm (laterally).

First flight V.K. Kokkinaki 8 July 1948 (often reported as 8 August), well behind Tu-73. Final crucial evaluation was against Tu-78 in October; Marshal Vershinin ordered three test crews to fly both bombers and all favoured Il-28. Stalin ordered that 25 should participate in 1950 May Day; panic ensued, superimposed on major on production planning and numerous (mostly minor) modifications including VK-1 engine. First VVS regiment complete September 1950.

Standard M-9 (Norden) sight, ventral radar for nav/bombing and adequate electronics. **Il-28T** (*Torpedonosyets*) with two short 553 mm torpedoes in weapon bay and different radar and radio. **Il-28U** dual trainer without radar or armament but additional pilot cockpit in nose. **Il-28R** (R did not stand for *Razvyedchik*, recon) with auxiliary tip tanks. Also (without known separate designation): reconnaissance version with 4 or 5 cameras and often a second radar in place of weapon bay; electronic platform with ECM or Elint installations; target-towing version without armament; unarmed met reconnaissance version with atmospheric sensors; unarmed multi-sensor version for sampling nuclear tests; unmanned RPV used chiefly as missile target; and unarmed civil transport (see Il-20**) used by Aeroflot. Production estimated at 3000, of which over 1500 exported to WP air forces, China (500+) and at least 15 other countries. Many saw action (Nigeria, Egypt, Vietnam, North Korea, Iraq, Yemen, Syria). Small number built in Czechoslovakia as **B-228**, and at least 1500 in China as B-5, not included in above total.

DIMENSIONS Span 21,45 m (70 ft 4½ in); length 17,45 m (57 ft 3 in) (also reported as 17,65 m, 57 ft 10¾ in); wing area 60,8 m^2 (654 ft^2).

ENGINES Two 2700 kg (5952 lb) VK-1A turbojets.

WEIGHTS Empty (1951) 12 890 kg (28,417 lb); fuel/oil 6400+200; loaded 18,4 t (40,564 lb); max 21,2 t (46,737 lb).

PERFORMANCE Max speed 786 km/h (488 mph) at SL, 902 km/h (560 mph) at 4,5 km; climb 6·5 min to 5 km; service ceiling 12,3 km (40,350 ft); range (max fuel) 2400 km (1490 miles), endurance 4·2 h; take-off and landing both 960 m (3150 ft); landing speed 185 km/h (115 mph).

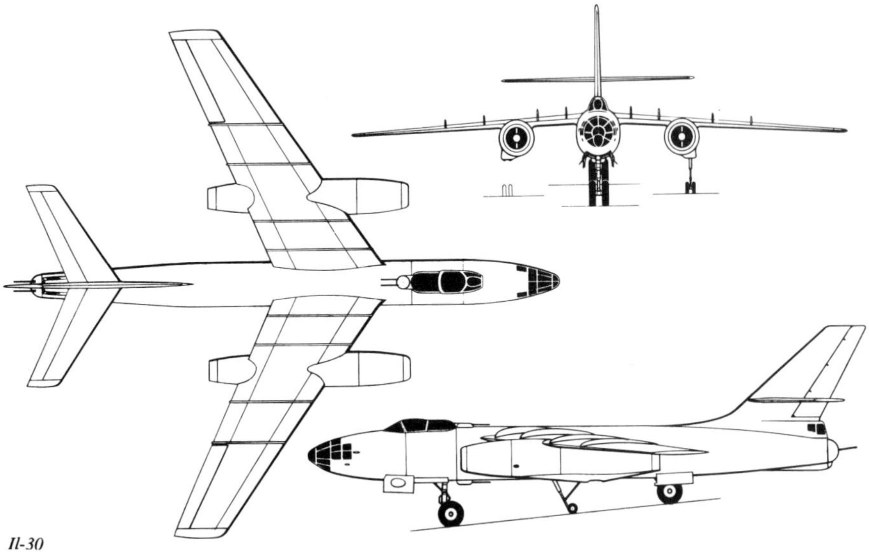

Il-30

Il-30

*Il-20*** *(newspaper matrices being unloaded)*

Il-20** Designation of unarmed civil Il-28 used by Aeroflot as express transport from 1955. Some were flown to get crews and ground facilities used to jets, while small fleet carried mail and freight, especially matrices for *Pravda* and *Izvestiya* newspapers published in Sverdlovsk, Novosibirsk and other distant cities. Data as Il-

Il-16** Project for 56-passenger transport with four turbojets, 1955. To cruise 800 km/h for 1600 km. Rejected by Aeroflot in favour of Tu-104.

Il-30* A logical successor to Il-28, this was first bomber in USSR to exceed 1000 km/h. Also one of first designs to escape from Nene-derived propulsion, and marked second major link with Lyul'ka KB for advanced axial engine. As noted in section on engines, this was first to be designated for Lyul'ka; as AL-5 first ran as complete engine 1950. Il-30 twin-jet bomber was first application, and engine is believed never to have flown in testbed prior to start of flight testing of Il-30 in spring 1951. Little known of Il-30 apart from what can be deduced from single photograph. Strongly based on Il-28 and some parts probably identical. Wing of reduced span, larger root chord, swept 35° at leading edge; eight large fences. Fuselage fractionally longer, with wing root further forward than in Il-28 but weapon bay unchanged. Bicycle landing gear; twin-wheel main units widely spaced, front unit being steerable hydraulically and retracting forwards, twin doors bulged to accommodate tyres; small twin-wheel outriggers retracting under engines. K-16 tail turret, front crew as Il-28. There is persistent report that Il-30 had a fourth crew member (presumably a gunner) and upper and lower remote-control gun turrets, each with twin NR-23, ahead of wing. This would ruin payload/range performance, displace valuable fuel and radar and dramatically increase weight and field length. Barbettes cannot be seen in photograph, but presumably same as Tu-4 or Tu-73. Unlike Il-28, wings of Il-30 were probably used for fuel, almost certainly as integral tankage using B-29 technology. Field-length problem may have been chief reason for early rejection of this aircraft; fuel capacity for range quoted must have been roughly 4·2 times that of Il-28, giving impossible fuel mass of some 27 t (59,500 lb), leading one to doubt range figure! With four crew and three twin-cannon turrets fuel capacity cannot have exceeded 14,000 lit (10 t, 22,000 lb). This gives gross weight probably near 28 t (61,700 lb), with range of about 1200 km (750 miles).

DIMENSIONS Span 16,5 m (54 ft 1½ in); length 18,0 m (59 ft 0⅔ in); wing area, not recorded but about 49 m² (530 ft²).

ENGINES Two 4500 kg (9920 lb) Lyul'ka AL-5 turbojets.

WEIGHTS Not recorded, but see above.

PERFORMANCE Max speed 1000 km/h (621 mph) at height; climb 4 min to 5 km; service ceiling 13 km (42,650 ft); range, claimed to be 3500 km with 2 t bombload, but see above.

Il-32* About two years after end of the Second World War, Aviation of Airborne Troops issued requirement for transport glider larger than any it then possessed. Specified payload 3,5 t (7716 lb), light vehicles and artillery to be readily loaded and disembarked. In competition with Yak-14, Ilyushin OKB produced Il-32. Typical high-wing glider with large box-like fuselage, but most unusual feature was light-alloy stressed-skin construction. Main hold square section, unlike Yak; and broad two-pilot cockpit was part of sideways-hinging nose (powered, probably, by compressed-air bottles). Tricycle landing gear jettisoned on operational mission, with belly skids. Rear fuselage, with braced tail, hinged sideways (this may have been manual) to give both-ends access. Accommodation for two pilots and 35 armed troops or 3,5 t freight. Rejected; possibly in part because of costly construction. According to Shavrov carried 7 t (15,432 lb) payload and built in small series in 1950. No data.

Il-34 At least one Il-32 was converted into a powered aircraft. Two piston engines were installed in wing nacelles; type believed to be 730 hp ASh-21 with fixed-pitch two-blade propellers.

Il-40 Last of armoured *Shturmoviks*, this prototype of 1953 was a strange amalgam of old and new parts. Among old, but highly developed, parts were armoured tandem-seat crew compartment, and weapons comprising devastating forward-firing guns, rear guns for defence and internal bomb cells. Wing design close analogue on reduced scale of Il-30, though with much thicker profile (root t/c 17%). Tail likewise derived from that of Il-28, and twin-NR-23 tail barbette related to bureau's K6, though much further from controlling radio/gunner. Engine installation unique: two of Mikulin's new small axials, widely separated on each side of fuselage, but fed by long circular ducts diverging from close double-barrel nose. Fuel between and under crew and in tapering nose and rear fuselage. Tricycle landing gear believed to comprise single-wheel nose gear retracting to rear and main units retracting forwards into bulged compartments, leg being faired beneath main wing box (it is believed wheels turned 90°). Forward guns, four NS-37; position not known, depending on whether bomb cells were in inner wing or fuselage (Něměcek, 1500 kg, 3307 lb, internal; one Western report states bombload was external). Wing swept about 30° on leading edge, four large fences, metal-skinned control surfaces (probably manual). Several prototypes built and apparently no significant shortcomings (though lack of agility compared with MiG-17). It was dramatically superior performance of latter which finally convinced VVS that day of specialized armoured attacker was over. Though normal fighter/bomber was not armoured, its speed and agility helped protect it, and unlike Il-40 it did not need escort but could match any hostile interceptor. Emergence of USAF AX requirement, met by A-10 Thunderbolt II, caused reawakening of interest in jet *Shturmovik*.

DIMENSIONS Not recorded, but span and length probably each about 15 m (50 ft).

ENGINES Two 2700 kg (5952 lb) Mikulin AM-5F turbojets.

WEIGHTS Not recorded but empty about 5700 kg (12,600 lb) and loaded in region of 11 t (24,250 lb).

PERFORMANCE Max speed 964 km/h (599 mph) at height; service ceiling 11,6 km (38,060 ft); range (clearly not at low level) 1000 km (621 miles).

Il-46 This straight-wing bomber was a better concept than Il-30, which used same engines but was too small and must have been far removed from what VVS wanted in range and field length. First official demand for medium bomber larger and more capable than first-generation Tu-73/Il-28 is believed to have been dated January 1950. Prototype Il-46 flew on 15 August 1952. Such progress was made possible by fact most of it was familiar ground: Il-46 was essentially a scaled-up Il-28, using improved model of Il-30's engine. Structurally conventional, except one of first Ilyushin aircraft known to have machined wing skins. Almost certainly integral tankage, though most fuel still in fuselage. Latter same layout as Il-28 but slightly larger cross-section and considerably longer; removal of main gears from fuselage left capacity for double-size weapon bay (max 6 t, 13,228 lb) and fuel tankage of about 20 000 lit (4400 gal), which roughly tallies with published weights. Crew as in Il-28, and same armamemt of two fixed NR-23 and two more in rear turret. Wing and tail close analogues of Il-28 but wing had area-increased flaps (and some evidence of drooped leading edge) and vertical tail proportionately larger. Nacelles refined derivatives of Il-30. Tricycle landing gear; steerable twin-wheel nose unit retracting to rear, and main gears comprising inner and outer units, each with single wheel and leg, respectively retracting to front and rear with wheel turning 90° to lie under jetpipe (designed to land with any one of four main gears

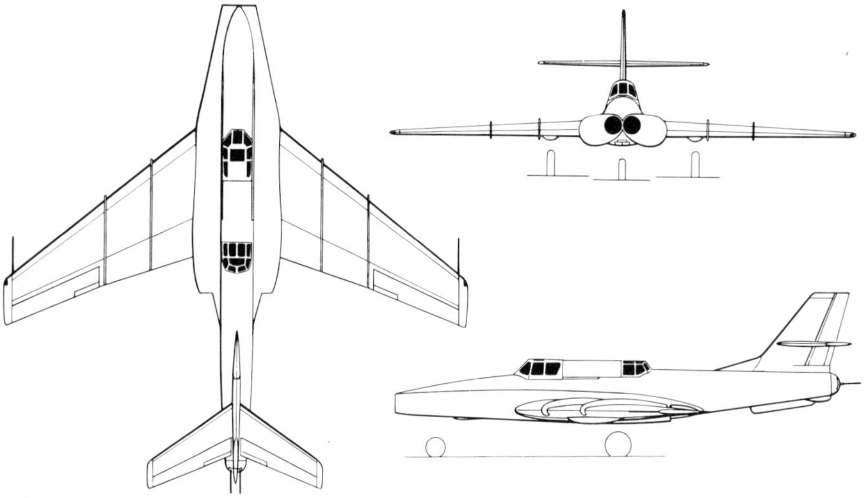

Il-40

not extended). No information on electronics, but under-fuselage radome larger than that of Il-28, and at one time an electronic pod (presumably for front and rear radar warning) was fitted to top of fin. Flight controls almost certainly remained manual. There may have been only a single prototype, and though it was doubtless an excellent aircraft it was not in same class as Tu-88. Ilyushin schemed a swept Il-46, designation not known.

DIMENSIONS Span 30,0 m (98 ft 5 in); length 27,0 m (88 ft 7 in); wing area, not recorded but close to 87 m² (938 ft²).

ENGINES Two 5000 kg (11,023 lb) thrust Lyul'ka AL-5 turbojets.

WEIGHTS Empty 24 565 kg (54,156 lb); loaded 42 t (92,593 lb).

PERFORMANCE Max speed 928 km/h (577 mph) at 3 km; service ceiling, greater than the 12,3 km reported; range 4950 km (3076 miles) with 3 t bomb load.

Il-54 Another logical development, made possible by further impressive turbojet progress by Lyul'ka, this high-speed tactical bomber has been described as rival of Yak-28, but latter was half the weight. True rival to Il-54 was again a Tupolev prototype, Tu-98. Requirement believed issued 1953, and configuration that of Il-30 with more sweep (Ilyushin hoped to exceed Mach 1 in dive) and better use of internal volume. Thanks to powerful new engine, with transonic upstream stages on compressor, it was possible to match greater sweep with greater weight; published figure is remarkably low. Following Yakovlev, outrigger gears put on wingtips, retracting into small fairings; main gears were remarkably far apart, and fuselage sag must have been major structural problem compounded by large bomb bay amidships. Large doubler plates riveted on outside between main gears. Wing with straight taper root to tip, 55° leading-edge sweep, details of movable surfaces unknown but

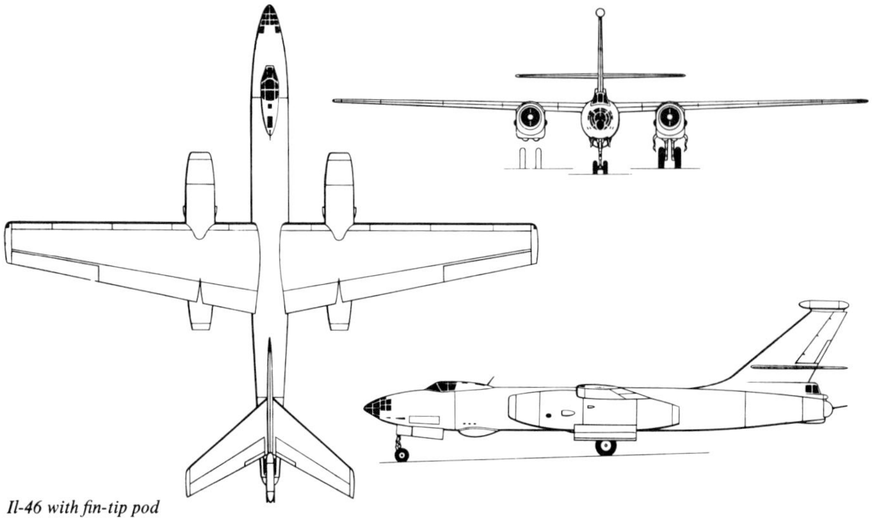

Il-46 with fin-tip pod

Il-46

Il-54

only four fences, inboard pair being interpreted by some as aligned with engine pylons. Oblique ventral fins low on sides of rear fuselage. Vertical tail fin extended in dorsal spine to ram inlet near wing trailing edge. Bombload not known but believed same weapon bay as Il-46 with 3 t normal, 6 t max. No evidence of fixed nose guns but defensive turret (believed twin NR-23) retained at tail, with gunner. Two crew in forward fuselage; like Il-46, pilot canopy metal to rear, transparent hood hinging to right. Large optically flat panel under glazed nose, bulge (presumably radome) between front gear and weapon bay. First flight early 1955; Kokkinaki praised engines, and photographs of him with Novozhilov was first to show today's OKB General Constructor in limelight with a new prototype. Neither Il-54 nor Tu-98 accepted; Il-54 displayed to West at Kubinka (then described as supersonic) August 1956.

DIMENSIONS Span 17,8 m (58 ft 4$\frac{3}{4}$ in); length 21,8 m (71 ft 6$\frac{1}{4}$ in); wing area, close to 50 m^2 (540 ft^2).

ENGINES Two 6500 kg (14,330 lb) thrust Lyul'ka AL-7 turbojets.

WEIGHTS Empty, not recorded but close to 20 t (44,000 lb); fuel, probably about 6 t; loaded 29 t (63,916 lb).

PERFORMANCE Max speed at SL 1150 km/h (715 mph), possibly more at height; service ceiling reported as 13 km, probably higher; range 1400 km (870 miles), probably with 3 t bombload.

Il-18** This passenger transport was built to 1953 Aeroflot demand for modern 75-passenger aircraft able to fit into environment of primitive unpaved airfields and sparse or absent navaids. Made possible by approaching maturity of rival turboprops, Kuznetsov NK-4 and Klimov VK-2. Latter discontinued 1953, and NK-4 chosen for Il-18 (note: Il-18 is service designation; OKB designation unknown, and thus confusion with earlier transport with OKB designation Il-18).

Straightforward design with constant circular-section pressurized fuselage and straight-tapered unswept low wing. TsAGI SPS-series profile with thickness 15% at root and 13% at tip. Three spars, thus two inter-spar boxes root to near tip with flush-screwed machined (not integrally stiffened) skins. One-piece double-slotted flap on each side, electric drive via ball-screwjacks to 30°. Fuselage diameter 3,5 m, simple monocoque but during prototype construction modified to incorporate Western fail-safe principles with more than 150 doublers or rip-stops adding 270 kg. Nose made as secondary structure riveted to front of pressure hull with obvious discontinuity at joint. Max dP 0,5 kg/cm^2 (7·1 lb/in^2). Manual flight controls, all stressed-skin construction with aerodynamic and mass balance and electric trim, plus spring tab on rudder. Tricycle landing gear. Twin-wheel nose unit steerable ±45° retracting forward into unpressurized nose. Main gears with four-wheel bogies, tyres (production) 930 × 305 mm at 8 kg/cm^2 (114 lb/in^2), retracting forwards after bogie has rotated 90° front-upwards so that bogie lies horizontally under jetpipes ahead of wing box. Hydraulic (210 km/cm^2, 3000 lb/in^2) retraction, steering and brakes, latter with one-shot emergency by dry nitrogen. Engines with axially hinged cowl doors, ventral oil coolers and jetpipes carried across wing to

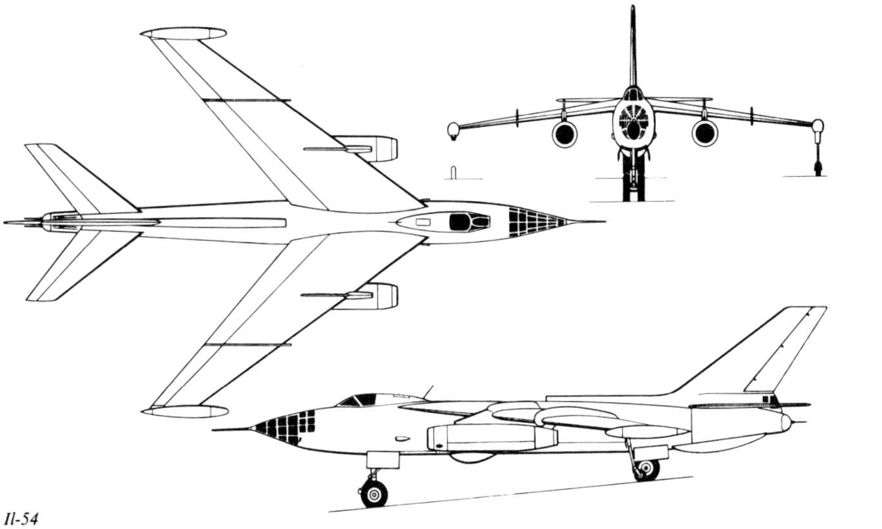

Il-54

Il-18D (CSA, Czechoslovakia)

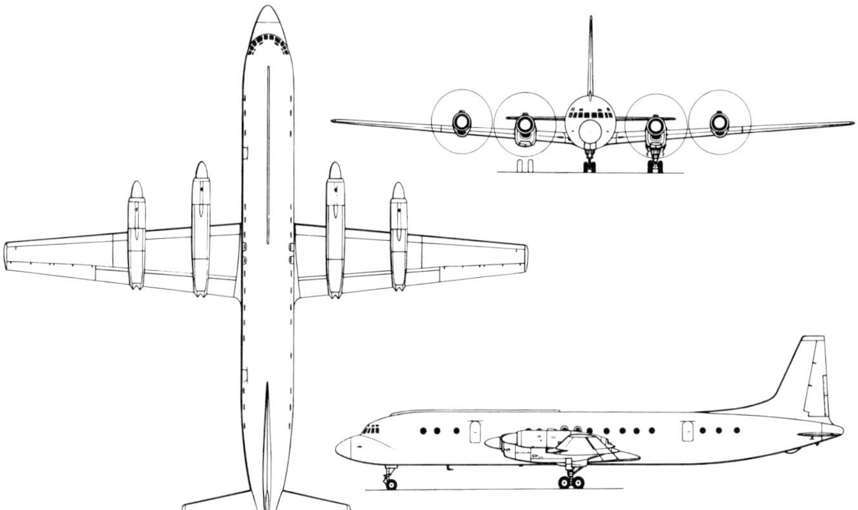

Il-18D

Il-18D freighter conversion

Civil Il-18 EW test-bed with SLAR, cameras, and IRLS

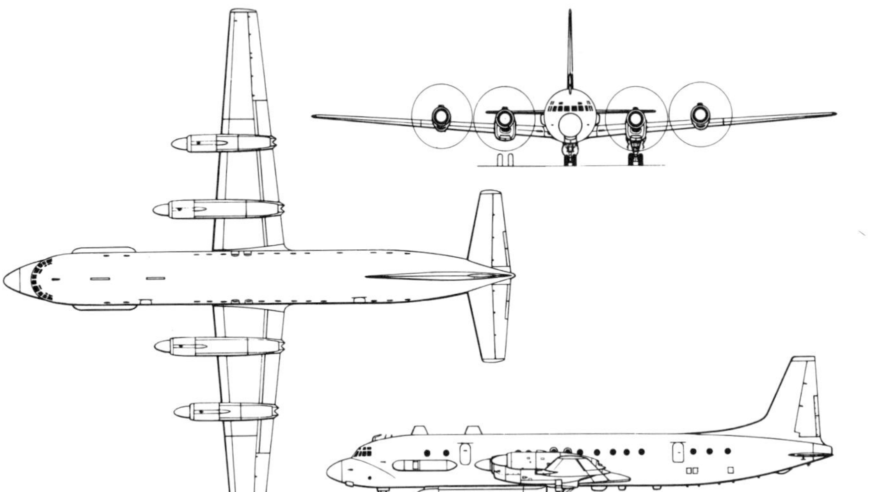

Il-18 EW conversion, Coot-A

trailing edge. AV-68I four-blade 4,5 m (14 ft 9 in) reversing propellers. Basic tankage 20 flexible cells in front and rear wing boxes from root to aileron, total 16 400 lit (3607 gal). Auxiliary integral tanks in outer wings, total 7300 lit (1606 gal). Total 23 700 lit (5213 gal); later Il-18D adds four centre-section cells bringing total to 30 000 lit (6599 gal). Ice protection totally electrical, supplied by two STG-12 (12 kW) starter/generators on each engine; total 96 kW at 28·5 V. Most heater elements (wing, tail, engine inlets, propeller blades and flight-deck windscreens) supplied as raw AC. Weather radar type *Emblema* (Emblem); navaids include Decca with Flight Log display.

Prototype L-5811 named *Moskva* (Moscow), NK-4 engines, flown 4 July 1957. This instrumented aircraft and five 75-seat development aircraft performed well and few modifications needed. Flat pressure bulkhead inserted behind flight deck, locked in flight. Normal flight crew five: two pilots, nav, radio, engineer. Original production aircraft Il-18, NK-4 or AI-20 engines, 75 seats, two pressurized underfloor holds (cramped) and unpressurized rear hold, access external only. From 21st aircraft gross weight raised from 57,2 to 59,2 t, engine standardized as AI-20K (refined NK-4 by Ivchyenko, see engine section), pressure-fuelling from inner nacelles as well as gravity overwing, nine extra seats, designation **Il-18B.** This was standard at entry to service 20 April 1959. By 1961 **Il-18V** had rearranged interior seating 80 to 100. In 1964 **Il-181** introduced AI-20M engine, gross weight 64 t, rear pressure bulkhead moved aft (from frame 56 to 62, eliminating rear hold) to increase max seating to 122, and four fuel cells in wing under passenger floor added 6300 lit (1386 gal) additional fuel. Entered service 1965 redesignated **Il-18D.** Produced alongside **Il-**

18Ye, same except for absence of additional fuel cells.

Production at GAZ-30 estimated at about 800, completed about 1970. At least 130 exported, and possibly one-quarter military including nearly all early models (ex-Aeroflot). Safety record initially poor, and TBO and utilization disastrous by Western standards; but a tough and valued aircraft which with all Aeroflot directorates had carried over 250m passengers in 14m hours by 1981. Same aircraft basis of Il-38 described separately. From about 1974 substantial number converted as civil freighters at GAZ-402, several features borrowed from Vanguard/Merchantman conversion. Since 1978 EW (electronic warfare) version also seen, possibly ex-civil or military transports; designation unknown. This model has large canoe pod about 10,25 m (33 ft 8 in) long under forward fuselage (probably SLAR), smaller long pod (about 4,4 m, 14 ft 5 in) on each side of fuselage aft of flight deck (IRLS and/or other radar), four large blade aerials on top and below fuselage on centreline, dielectric bulge (doppler?) under belly, five small projections along vertical centreline of aft fuselage, and at least nine additional aerials flush with fuselage skin. Some aerials are probably digital communications to send data gathered by various sensors; others are part of relay system linking satellites, ships or missiles.

DIMENSIONS Span 37,4 m (122 ft 8½ in); length 35,9 m (117 ft 9 in); wing area 140 m² (1507 ft²).
ENGINES Initial, alternate 4000 ehp NK-4 or AI-20 turboprops; first production standard 4000 ehp AI-20K; (from Il-18B) 4250 ehp AI-20M.
WEIGHTS Empty (Il-18B) 30,2 t (66,578 lb), (Il-18V) 31,5 t (69,444 lb), (Il-18Ye) 34,63 t (76,345 lb), (Il-18D) 35 t (77,160 lb); max payload (V onwards) 13,5 t (29,762 lb); max loaded (B) 60 t (132,275 lb), (V, Ye) 61,2 t (134,921 lb), (D) 64 t (141,093 lb).
PERFORMANCE Max cruise (typical) 685 km/h (426 mph) at 8 km; high-speed cruise (typical) 625 km/h (388 mph) at 8 km; take-off ISA (V) 1200 m (3937 ft), (D) 1450 m (4757 ft); landing (typical) 800 m/200 km/h (124 mph).

Il-38 First reported 1970 but believed to have flown at least three years earlier, this ASW and maritime patrol aircraft uses what appear to be wings, tail, engines and landing gear of Il-18 (**) and also a fuselage of same diameter and with structurally same nose. To an extraordinary degree CG has shifted so that, while forward fuselage is actually shorter than in transport, rear fuselage is over 8 m (26 ft) longer, with MAD boom resulting in substantial increase in length overall. This extension could not be demanded by internal volumetric requirement. Apart from small (mainly avionic) changes, distinguishing features are in new fuselage, which is pressurized but has weapon bay ahead of wing box with two conventional outward-hinging doors. Ahead of this is search radar with radome similar to that of Ka-25 (Hormone-B) helicopter, but radar is not same. There is also shallow rear weapon bay beneath wing. These bays appear to house all dropped stores, there being no evidence of underwing hardpoints or rear-fuselage sonobuoy tubes. Offensive armament of torpedoes, depth bombs and possibly various missiles may total 5 t but is probably less. Interestingly, Il-38 duties now shared by ASW version of An-12. Crew put at four (flight) plus eight (tactical), with main processor ahead of wing and rear given over to accommodation and domestic areas. Fuselage almost windowless, especially in later aircraft. Forward fuselage has bulged observation window, long external service fairing and external air inlet/outlet (diesel sniffer or APU?). Many puzzling features, notably lack of sensors and use of internal bay for dropped sonics. Another is believed range (see data) yet weapon bays preclude underfloor fuel and transport already used available wing volume; one supposition is that wing is restressed for this duty and is now integral tank root to tip. Numbers believed fewer than 100 including small forces based in Egypt and Libya and three (six planned) with Indian Navy 315 Sqn.

DATA Generally as Il-18 except length 39,6 m (129 ft 10 in); weights probably higher than Il-18, and reported able to sustain 645 km/h (400 mph); range suggested 7240 km (4500 miles).

Il-38

Il-62 First large intercontinental jet transport built in the Soviet Union. The Il-62 followed British Super VC10 almost exactly in configuration, capability and engineering design, but is fractionally larger (it is identical with Super VC10 as originally planned in 1959) and in flight development rectification of faults resulted in introduction of new features. Basic airframe conventional, but largest use of integrally stiffened panels and large forged frames at time of design (1960). Wing swept 35° at ¼-chord, primary box with four spar webs to aileron, two to tip. Built as centre section with trailing edge at 90° to fuselage, and two outer panels. Single flap on centre section and another on outer panel; single-slotted type, not track-mounted, driven electrically (DC early, raw AC on 62M). Ahead of outer-wing flap, two spoiler sections, 211 kg/cm² (3000 lb/in²) hydraulic, for letdown/lift-dump only. Outboard, three-section manual aileron with spring tabs and electric trim. T-tail with electrically driven tailplane, manual elevators with separate manual and autopilot tabs,

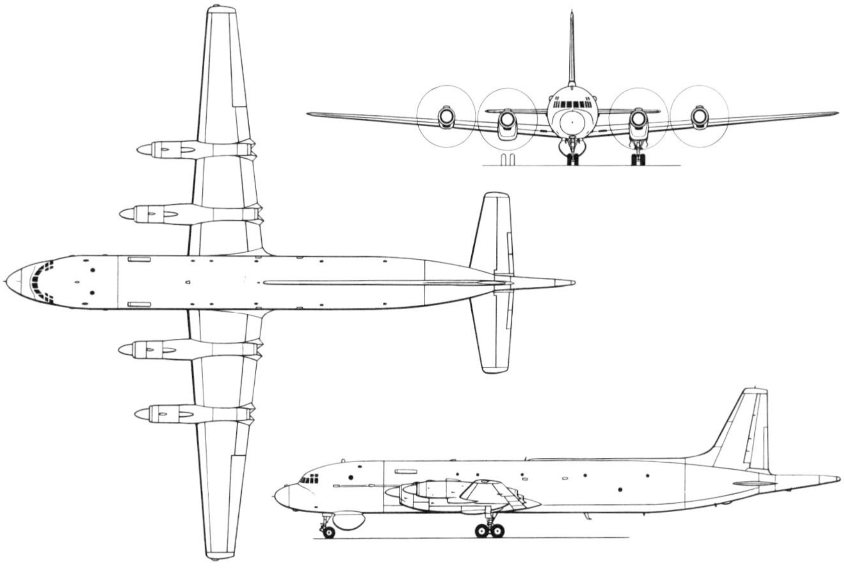

Il-38

Il-62s

two-section manual rudder with spring and trim tabs and with yaw damper (series type). Fuselage almost circular section (external width 4,1 m, height 4,2) with fail-safe rip-stop structure designed for 25,000 h. Max dP 0,63 km/cm² (8·96 lb/in²), vertical-elliptical windows almost identical to VC10 structure, floors mainly metal/foam sandwich. Landing gear hydraulic, steerable twin-wheel nose unit retracting forwards and main bogies with four 1450 × 450mm tyres (9,5 kg/cm², 135·1 lb/in²) and anti-skid hydraulic brakes inwards under passenger floor. Emergency braking parachute. Twin-wheel vertical rear support strut extended hydraulically to apron after parking. Electrics, originally eight 18-kW generators, most (including all 62M) now generated as raw AC, four 40-kVA. Fuel in seven integral tanks (three in centre section), total 100k lit (21,998 gal), four underwing sockets and eight overwing gravity fillers. All leading edges and engine inlets de-iced by hot air from bleed system; electric windscreens. Cabin environmental inlets at wing roots. TA-6 gas-turbine APU in tailcone.

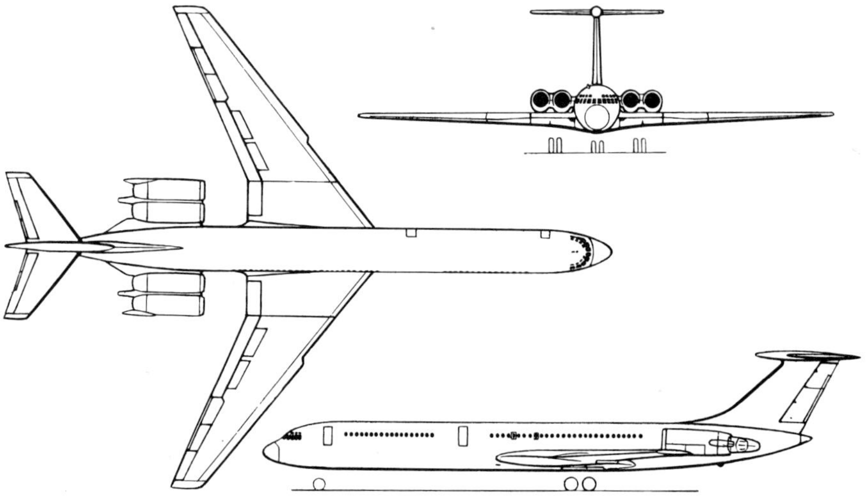

Il-62

First prototype No 06156 flown unknown date January 1963. Engines (temporary) Lyul'ka AL-7 turbojets; dorsal spine from fin to wing leading edge, second dorsal service fairing from roof of flight deck half-way to wing and shorter but fatter axial fairing along nose on each side of nose-gear compartment. Unconfirmed report this or other early Il-62 also flew with AM-3M engines. Second prototype and three pre-production, latter without nose fairings but at least initially with AL-7 engines. Numerous aerodynamic and systems changes, including major increase in span and chord of drooped outer leading edge, addition of six small fences and small wingtip fairings (incorporating fuel vents and possibly other items) and progressive introduction of NK-8-4 turbofan engine with cascade-type reversers on outboard engines. Prolonged development, first Aeroflot service 10 March 1967 with production Il-62 built at Kazan. Basically good long-range aircraft, with exports to CSA, LOT, Interflug, Tarom, Cubana and CAAC. Flight crew five, normal seating for up to 186 (usually 163) in triple units with baggage/cargo under floor ahead of and behind wing and (unpressurized) rear fuselage, total 48 m³ (1694 ft³). In 1970 improved Il-62M-200, later called just **Il-62M**, with different engines, clamshell reversers on outers only, 5000 lit (1100 gal) fin tank, no fences or tip fairings, differential spoilers for roll augmentation, containerized baggage/freight, modern pilot yokes

Il-76 production interior and ramp

Il-76 (first prototype)

Il-86 at Mineralnye Vody during route-proving trials

instead of large ram's horns with 360° nose-gear steering wheels, generally updated avionics and emergency equipment. Entered service early 1974. Followed 1978 by **Il-62M**K with longer-life airframe cleared to higher weights, wider bogies (lower-pressure tyres, improved brakes), auto spoiler on touchdown, better interior arrangement giving 195 seats yet wider aisles for service carts. Total production all versions at least 135, possibly continuing at low rate 1981.

DIMENSIONS Span 43,2 m (141 ft 9 in), (with tip fairings 43,3/142 ft 0$\frac{3}{4}$ in); length (fuselage) 49,0 m (160 ft 9 in), (overall) 53,12 m (174 ft 3$\frac{1}{2}$ in); wing area 279,6 m^2 (3010 ft^2).

ENGINES (initial production) four 10,5 t (23,150 lb) thrust NK-8-4 two-shaft turbofans, (62M) 11 t (24,250 lb) D-30KU.

WEIGHTS Empty (equipped) (early) 67,8 t (149,470 lb), (production) 69,4 t (152,998 lb), (62M) 71,6 t (157,848 lb); max payload 23 t (50,700 lb), (62M) 23 t, (62MK) 25 t (55,115 lb); max take-off (early) 157,5 t (347,222 lb), (production) 162 t (357,143 lb), (62M) 165 t (363,757 lb), (62MK) 167 t (368,166 lb).

PERFORMANCE Normal cruise 820/900 km/h (510/560 mph, max M 0·846); range (max payload, 1 h reserve) 6700 km (4160 miles), (62M) 7800 km)4846 miles); max climb (62, SL) 1080 m (3540 ft)/min; FAR take-off field length (62, ISA, SL) 3250 m (10,660 ft).

Il-76 Possibly first aircraft from OKB in which Ilyushin played no direct part, this impressive freighter again bears close resemblance to Western type (C-141), wing design, propulsion geometry and flight control being virtually identical, though hold is wider and higher and engines more powerful. Designed from mid-1960s as replacement for An-12 for V-TA and Aeroflot, basic requirement being 40 t cargo carried 5000 km in 6 h. Short-field capability of Il-76 significantly better than Lockheed C-141.

Wing built in five sections, centre section being width of fuselage and structurally part of it, rest of wing −4° anhedral and 25° sweep at $\frac{1}{4}$-chord with joint outboard of outer engines. Main box multi-spar integral tank with integrally stiffened skins. Each wing has five sections of hydraulically-powered slat, inboard and outboard hydraulically-powered triple-slotted flap, eight sections of hydraulically-powered spoiler (four ahead of each flap) used for roll augmentation, letdown and lift-dump, and one-piece ailerons with hydraulic boost. Powered tailplane, tabbed elevators, one-piece rudder without tab, with hydraulic boost. All flight controls, manual reversion. Fuselage diameter unreported but about 4,9 m (193 in), almost circular section, pressurized throughout to 4,5 kg/cm^2 (6,4 lb/in^2). Crew door each side at front, hydraulically powered for escape at high IAS. Rear door large left/right halves, hinged outward hydraulically, with upward-hinged rear central portion and downward-hinged ramp able to lift 30 t load placed on it. Hold 3,46 m (136·2 in) wide, 3,4 m (133·9 in) high and 20 m (65 ft 7$\frac{1}{2}$ in) long (24,5 m, 80 ft 4$\frac{1}{2}$ in, including ramp). Titanium floor, optional or folding roller conveyor panels, overhead electrical mechanical handling (2,5 and 3 t capacity) with computer control for correct load distribution. One emergency escape window each side. Flight compartment for two pilots, radio and nav, plus supernumerary and two freight handlers. Nose glazed for contact nav, heavy dropping and similar tasks. Very comprehensive avionics including weather radar in nose and nav/mapping radar under nose. High-flotation landing gears: steerable nose unit with left/right pairs of wheels retracts forward; four main gears, each with left/right pairs of wheels, retract inwards with rotation 90° so that all four axles lie fore/aft, all hydraulic actuation. Main tyres (16) 1300 × 480 mm, tyre pressure variable in flight 2,5/5 kg-cm^2 (36/72 lb-in^2), all doors closed with gear extended to keep wells clean on snow, water, sand. All engines fitted with lateral clamshell reversers. Entire wing box forms six integral tanks, total 81 830 lit (18,000 gal). APU in left landing-gear fairing; environmental-system inlets in wing roots, and hot-air leading-edge de-icing throughout, with electro-thermal glazed panes.

First prototype No 86712 flown by Eduard Kuznetsov from Khodinka 25 March 1971. Five pre-production, one civil and remainder military with twin-NR-23 rear turret with pressurized gunner's compartment and main aft-facing radar at base of rudder. Comprehensive avionics, including computer for flight management and Cat III landing and full range of military equipment for com, EW and special nav. In 1975 series production at GAZ-30 designated **Il-76T** with outer-wing fuel and minor changes including gross weight increased from 157 to 170 t. Majority military, with about 150 delivered to V-TA since 1974. Important Aeroflot airlifter for trunk routes (from 1979) and underdeveloped regions with about 40 civil Il-76T delivered since 1976. In 1975 set 25 FAI records including 70 121 kg raised to 2 km, 70 t to 11 875 m, 60 t round 2000 km circuit at 856,697 km/h, 40 t round 5000 km at 815,968 km/h, and record group parachute jump from 15 386 m. Export of military **76M** version to Iraq (guns removed but turret remained), Czechoslovakia and Poland and civil 76T to Interflug and Libyan Arab, Iraqi and Syrian Arab Airlines. Evaluated as standard tanker with three hosereels, reported chosen for service in this role with ADD and AV-MF (not normally fitted with probe). Quick-change interior possible with installation of up to three 20 m modules each with 30 seats or provision for stretcher patients or other loads. Paratroops and heavy dropping via main rear aperture. From 1979 believed same aircraft with extended forward fuselage basis of Mainstay AWACS platform to replace Tu-126.

DIMENSIONS Span 50,5 m (165 ft 8 in); length 46,59 m (152 ft 10$\frac{1}{2}$ in); wing area 300 m^2 (3229 ft^2).

ENGINES Four 12 t (26,455 lb) Soloviev D-30KP turbofans.

WEIGHTS Empty not published but about 75t (165,344 lb); normal fuel 58 536 kg; max payload 40 t (88,185 lb) but record flights with over 70 t; max take-off 170 t (374,785 lb).

PERFORMANCE Max speed 850 km/h (528 mph);

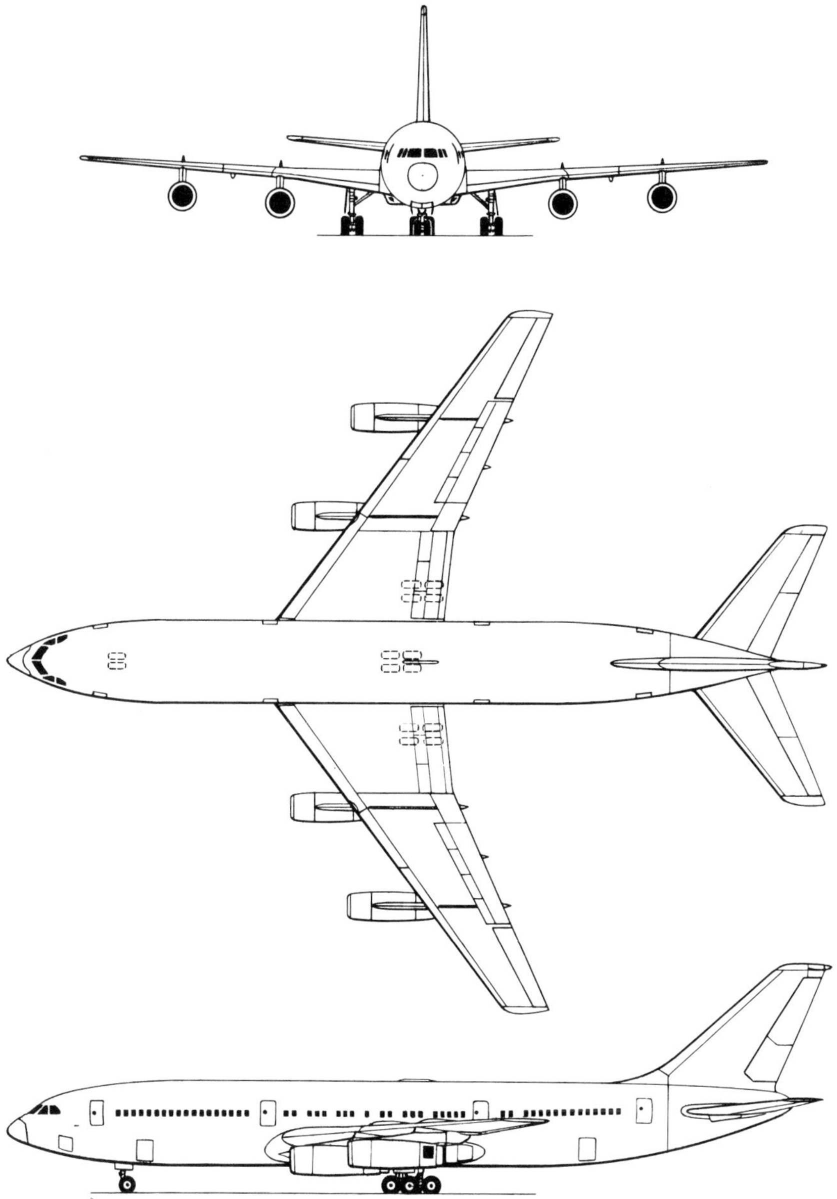

Il-86

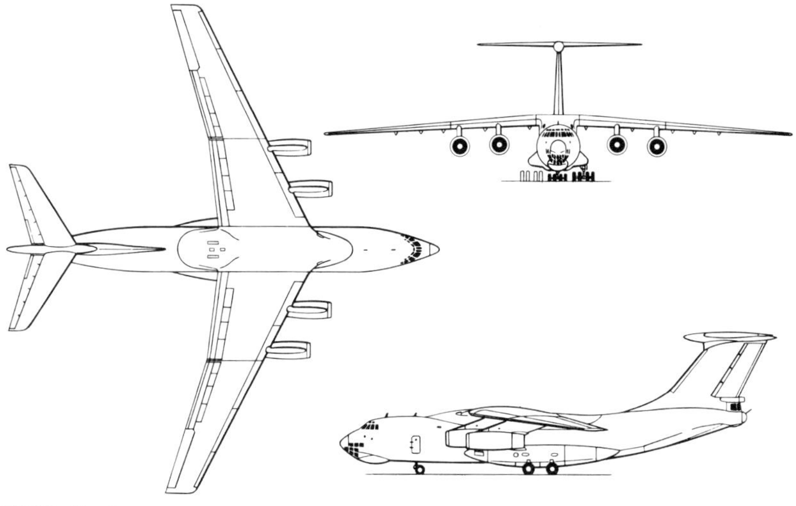

Il-76T (military)

cruise 750/800 km/h (466/497 mph); ceiling, see records, 15 386 m is 50,479 ft; range with 40 t cargo 5000 km (3107 miles), max fuel 6700 km (4163 miles); take-off 850 m/210 km/h; landing 450 m/220 km/h (137 mph).

Il-86 Result of longest and most detailed parametric evaluation of any Soviet aircraft, Il-86 is high-capacity passenger carrier for Aeroflot trunk routes. Not expected to be built as dedicated V-TA aircraft, but large civil fleet will fulfil airlift role if necessary. Basic requirement was ability to use airfields with poor runway and few terminal facilities. Original Il-70, 72 and 74 projects disclosed 1967–1970, growing from 150 to 250 and then to 350 seats. In 1971 Novozhilov revealed Il-86 as medium-range aircraft with large circular-section fuselage, T-tail, low wing and four rear-mounted D-30 engines, to fly 1976. Ilyushin OKB brochure mid-1972 showed changed layout with underwing engines of different type.

Approximately size, weight and power of medium-range DC-10-10 but with traditional 707-type layout and low-bypass engines. Wing closely similar to Il-76 but swept 35° at $\frac{1}{4}$-chord. Two-part hydraulic slat on each leading edge (notch to clear inner pylon). Small upper-surface fences aligned with pylons. Hydraulic double-slotted flaps on centre section and outer panels; inboard end of outer flap made separately and max angle reduced to avoid inner jet. Hydraulic spoilers, two ahead of inboard flap and four ahead of outer, for roll augmentation, letdown and lift-dump. Hydraulically boosted outer-wing ailerons. Flight controls, no manual reversion. Low-mounted powered tailplane with slight dihedral; elevators and rudders in two parts each boosted by separate hydraulic circuits (quad hydraulics 211 kg/cm^2, 3000 lb/in^2, each energized by separate engine-driven pump). Circular fuselage barrel sections of 6,08 m (239·37 in) diameter (studies also made at 5,64 and 6,58 m). Early studies often double-deck; selected configuration has upper deck for passengers, with floor of CFRP/honeycomb sandwich (various Western specimens imported during development). Lower deck 8 to 16 LD-3 containers plus carry-on baggage and coats of passengers boarding or leaving via three powered stairways. Three further internal stairs to main deck, typically furnished with 5,7 m interior width for up to 350 passengers in three triple seats with 550 mm aisles. Enclosed baggage lockers. Four Type A ICAO doors each side at upper level for emergency escape with inflatable slides (and to mate with loading bridge where available). Ten principal doors at lower level, three for passengers, three for cargo and four to systems compartments. Steerable twin-wheel nose gear retracts forwards; DC-10-30 arrangement of main gears but all being four-wheel bogies (tyres 1300 × 480 mm), two retracting inwards and centreline gear forwards. All landing gears made at Kuibyshyev, hydraulic operation. Integral tankage in wing box; details not known by 1983 but capacity about 80 000 lit, 17,600 gal. All engines hung on pylon struts aligned with fences and flap tracks, and equipped with left-right clamshell reversers also said to serve as noise-attenuators. APU in tailcone (occupied by parachute in prototype). First aircraft fitted with novel airframe de-icing (developed on other Ilyushin aircraft since 1963) using flex leading-edge skin periodically pulsed by giant electrical currents for a few millisec. Flight deck for two pilots and engineers, with nav if required. Weather radar, doppler, VOR/ILS and computer for Cat IIIA.

Prototype No 86000 flown by E. Kuznetsov from 1820 m runway at Khodinka 22 December 1976. 86002, flown 24 October 1977, described as first production Il-86. Prototypes assembled from parts made elsewhere (eg, tail at Kiev). Production wing movable surfaces, tail surfaces, engine pods and pylons all made by WSK-Mielec, Poland. Hoped to begin scheduled services in time for Moscow 1980 Olympics, but in fact start was delayed to 26 December 1980. Optional variant without three ground-level stairways, with 25 extra (total 375) seats and 7% better economics. Range short of specification, and considerably less than equivalent Western aircraft; but latter are not tailored to such austere airstrips. Evaluation predicted of future military command-centre version.

DIMENSIONS Span 48,06 m (157 ft 8¼ in); length 60,21 m (197 ft 6½ in); wing area 320 m² (3444 ft²).
ENGINES Four 13 t (28,660 lb) thrust Kuznetsov NK-86 turbofans.
WEIGHTS Empty, not disclosed; max fuel 86 t; max payload 42 t (not with max fuel); max take-off 206 t (454,145 lb).
PERFORMANCE Normal cruise 900/950 km/h (560/590 mph); range (max payload) 3600 km (2237 miles), (max fuel) 4600 km (2858 miles); published field length 2,6 km (8530 ft); approach speed 260 km/h (162 mph).

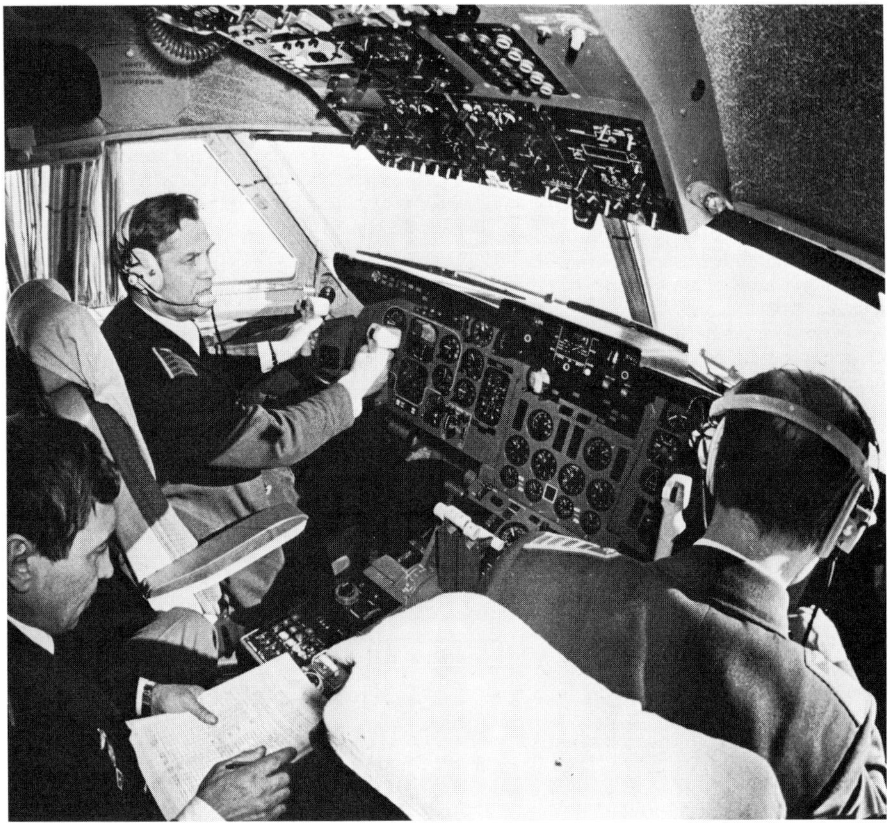
Il-86 flight-deck

Isacco

Vittorio Isacco was Italian designer who worked on a helicopter in USSR 1932–1936. In 1936 he was arrested and worked in a Special KB, possibly at GAZ-39.

I-4 Also called **Isacco-4** and *Gyelikogyr*, this unusual helicopter was only Isacco design actually to be completed. Fuselage of KhMA welded steel tube with fabric covering. Tail, pilot-operated vertical and horizontal surfaces of light alloy, fabric covering. Tailskid and wide-track fixed main wheels. Cabin amidships for pilot and five passengers. On nose, main propulsion engine. Four-blade lifting rotor, each blade having constant profile with light-alloy ribs (welded from 12 × 10 mm ellipitical tubing) located at intervals along light-alloy box spar with two main webs and upper/lower booms, fabric covering overall. Blades supported at rest by bracing ties from central cabane pyramid. Pilot controls to ailerons on pairs of arms behind outer trailing edge for cyclic/collective pitch control. Rotor driven by separate engines on tip of each blade. I-4 begun late 1932 and built at ZOK NII GVF. Prof. B.N. Yuryev acted as consultant. Designer's calculations found unreliable, delaying completion until 1935. Ground tests in that year caused deformed dural trunnion on engine, remanufactured in steel, but went on to discover severe blade flutter resulting in departure of one of tip engines and severe straining of whole machine. Never flew, and final conclusion was that tip-mounted engine idea was not practical.

DIMENSIONS Diameter of four-blade rotor 24,4 m (80 ft 0⅔ in).
ENGINES One 300 hp Wright J-5 radial driving four-blade propulsion propeller; four 120 hp D.H. Gipsy III each driving small four-blade propeller.
WEIGHTS Loaded 3 t (6614 lb): also reported (Něměcek) 3,5 t (7716 lb).
PERFORMANCE Did not fly.

Junkers

Though strictly German designs, aircraft built at Fili by Junkers company 1923–1927 qualify for brief inclusion as they were designed in Soviet Union and had no counterparts outside that country. Part of design work done at AB Flygindustri at Linhamm, Junkers' other foreign subsidiary.

Ju 20 Basically same as **A 20** but BMW instead of Mercedes engine. Duralumin low-wing monoplane, pilot and one/two passengers. Fili-built aircraft all military, 20 twin-float seaplanes used by MA (Baltic and Black Sea Fleets) to 1930, then transferred to White Sea; also 20 landplanes for Red Army. Many famous flights including first to Soviet Arctic (B.G. Chukhnovskii, 1924). In 1925 K.A. Vigand installed 310 hp Junkers L-5 in one. Standard military type to 1930 re-engined with M-6, aircraft redesignated **R-2**.

DIMENSIONS Span 17,8 m (58 ft 4¾ in); length 8,3 m (27 ft 2¾ in); wing area 32 m² (344 ft²).
ENGINE One 185 hp BMW IIIa 6-inline, later 300 hp M-6.
WEIGHTS (landplane) Empty 1113 kg (2454 lb); loaded 1593 kg (3512 lb).
PERFORMANCE (landplane) Max speed 181 km/h (112·5 mph); climb 10·7 min to 2 km, 43 min to 5 km; range 570 km (354 miles).

Ju 21 Though today known thus in Soviet Union, correct designation **H 21**. Cantilever parasol monoplane, military reconnaissance, pilot and observer/gunner in tandem cockpits. Typical corrugated skin except over fuselage-side fuel tanks which formed large bulges. First flown late 1922, about 100 built at Fili by late 1925. Fixed Vickers and movable DA guns, light bombs (usually splinter anti-personnel) and fixed and hand-held cameras. Widely used in suppressing peasants resisting collectivization, especially in Turkestan.

DIMENSIONS Span 13,3 m (43 ft 7⅔ in); length 7,8 m (25 ft 7 in); wing area 21,7 m² (233·6 ft²).
ENGINE One 185 hp BMW IIIb.
WEIGHTS Empty 913 kg (2013 lb); fuel 180 kg; loaded 1350 kg (2976 lb).
PERFORMANCE Max speed 179 km/h (111 mph); climb 4·5 min to 1 km, 9·7 to 2 km; service ceiling 5,6 km; endurance 2·5 h.

Ju 22 Correct designation **H 22**; single-seat fighter derived from H 21; only three built.
Data as H 21 except much lighter, loaded weight 850 kg (1874 lb); speed 250 km/h (155 mph); two fixed guns.

Ju 13 Soviet designation for large number of F 13 transports, also used on floats or skis in military roles.

PS-4 Soviet designation of W 33 transport. At least 70 built at Fili with Junkers L-5 engine, widely used in Siberia and Arctic on floats and skis to 1941, seven with Dobrolyet, 10 with TsARB and 25 military.

JuG-1 Military variant of G 24 trimotor transport (also built at Fili), this was landplane bomber called K 30C by Junkers and **R-42** by VVS. According to Něměcek, also known as **TB-2** despite confusion with Polikarpov bomber. Between 30 and 80 built, in Sweden and at Fili, plus smaller number of twin-float seaplanes designated **R-42M** (*Morskoi*) and **R-42T** (*Torpedonosyets*) used by MA for recon, torpedo dropping and utility transport. One, armament removed, used by Chukhnovskii to direct icebreaker *Krasin* to wreck of Nobile's airship *Norge* north of Spitzbergen, 1928. Others, armament removed and with civil radio, operated by Aeroflot 1930–1931 from Lena, Yenesei and other Siberian rivers. Similar float lengthened used on first TB-1 seaplanes.
DIMENSIONS Span 29,9 m (98 ft 1 in); length (landplane) 15,2 m (49 ft 10½ in), (seaplane) 15,5 m (50 ft 10¼ in); wing area 94,6 m² (1018 ft²).
ENGINES Three 310 hp Junkers L-5.
WEIGHTS Empty (land) 3860 kg (8510 lb), (sea) 4400 kg (9700 lb); fuel/oil 1035 kg; loaded 6,5 t (14,330 lb).
PERFORMANCE Max speed (land) 190 km/h (118 mph), (sea) 175 km/h (109 mph); climb (land) 7·5 min to 1 km; service ceiling (land) 4,5 km; endurance 5 h.

Kalinin

Konstantin Alekseyevich Kalinin was born 1890. In the First World War he enlisted in army and trained as pilot, seeing action from 1916 on German front. He fought with Reds in civil war, both as pilot and plant engineer, and in 1923 appointed director of *Remvosdukhozavod* 6 (Aircraft Repair Factory 6) at Kiev. Here he had plenty of good aircraft-quality wood, and large amounts of steel tube from wartime Voisins. From 1925 he designed aircraft, setting up GROSS at Kharkov and becoming one of first well-known Soviet designers. He had the pick of graduates of Kharkov Aviation Institute, and his team soon included I.G. Nyeman, Z.I. Itskovich, A.Ya. Shchyerbakov and V.Ya. Krylov, all of whom achieved fame on own account. His aircraft began with series of civil transports characterized by high wing of elliptical planform and wooden construction, mounted on welded steel-tube fuselage. Later he designed two remarkable bombers, but a third was never finished. Shavrov's semi-official account blandly states Ilyushin's DB-3 was better, so work on last bomber, K-13, was discontinued. He omits to state that in spring 1938 Kalinin was arrested on fraudulent charge of conspiracy and spying and put to death. Many hundreds of aviation designers were arrested at this time but Kalinin was one of few famous OKB leaders to be executed.

K-1 Also designated **RVZ-6** or *Remvosdukhozavod*-6 (from factory), K-1 set pattern for most of Kalinin's subsequent designs. Given that he had to use available materials and ancient (ex-Voisin) engine, hard to see how result could have been improved upon, and from mid-1920s Kalinin was rightly regarded as source of most economic transports in USSR. Strut-braced high-wing monoplane. Wing of elliptical shape, aspect ratio 7, a basic outline Kalinin adhered to rigorously in successive variations. Centre section same width as fuselage and integral with it in welded steel tube. Left and right wings of wood built up on two spars with truss ribs and fabric covering. Two struts each side of steel tube with ply fairing. Fuselage and fin welded from steel tube, first Soviet metal truss fuselage. Engine cowl removable aluminium panels. Skin covering aluminium back to rear of cabin, fabric thereafter. Single door on left for pilot (enclosed cockpit with glazed front and side windows in line with wing leading edge) and four passengers. Main gear, wire-spoked wheels with fabric or metal covering, sprung on steel struts by rubber cords. Engine with ventral water radiator, tall exhaust stack and fuel tank under cockpit floor. K-1 built under Kalinin's direction by RVZ-6 workers led by D.L. Tomashyevich, A.N. Gratsianskii and A.T. Rudyenko. First flight 20 April (Něměcek, 26 July) 1925, successful. September 1925 flew to Moscow to conclude series of State tests. Acknowledged suitable for civil air fleet after being re-engined (see data). Decision to adopt Kalinin designs laid foundation for his own OKB at Kharkov initially named GROSS or GROS (*Grazhdanskoye Opytnoye Samolyetstroenie*, civil experimental aeroplane works), later a production factory.
DIMENSIONS Span 16,76 m (54 ft 11¾ in); length 10,72 m (35 ft 2 in); wing area 40,0 m² (430·5 ft²).
ENGINE Built with 170 hp Salmson RB-9 (data for this engine); later fitted with 240 hp BMW IV.
WEIGHTS Empty 1452 kg (3201 lb); fuel/oil 170 + 20 kg; loaded 1972 kg (4347 lb).
PERFORMANCE Max speed 161 km/h (100 mph); cruise 130 km/h (81 mph); climb 12·3 min to 1 km; service ceiling 3 km; range 600 km (373 miles)/4 h; take-off 120 m; landing 180 m/70 km/h (43·5 mph).

K-2 With support initially from Ukraine government, GROSS was established and developed this refined K-1 with BMW engine. Solitary Kalinin all-metal design of this period, using welded-steel truss structure with skin of corrugated *Kolchug* aluminium, except for fabric flight control surfaces. First flight 1926. Four passengers and pilot. Successful performer, and several built and used by Ukrvozdukhput. But this construction was labour-intensive and heavy, and Kalinin never again departed from simple and cheap wooden wing for his civil transports.
DIMENSIONS Span 16,7 m (54 ft 9½ in); length 11,17 m (36 ft 7¾ in); wing area 40,0 m² (430·5 ft²).
ENGINE One 240 hp BMW IV.
WEIGHTS Empty 1600 kg (3527 lb); fuel/oil 200 + 20 kg; loaded 2236 kg (4929 lb).
PERFORMANCE Max speed 170 km/h (105·6 mph); cruise 140 km/h (87 mph); climb 12 min to 1 km; service ceiling 3,5 km; range 650 km (404 miles); take-off 220 m; landing 200 m/75 km/h (46·6 mph).

K-3 Variant of K-2 specifically built for ambulance duty. Cabin for doctor and either two stretcher patients or four seated. Long door on left side for loading stretcher. Equipment called 'very complete', and special hanging-strut suspension for superimposed stretchers devised by Dr A.F. Linhart (in Russian, Lingart), Czech-born 'father of Soviet aerial ambulances'.
DIMENSIONS, engine As K-2.
WEIGHTS Empty 1560 kg (3439 lb); fuel/oil 265 kg; loaded 2300 kg (5071 lb).
PERFORMANCE As K-2 except range 730 km (454 miles).

K-4 With this 1928 machine Kalinin improved same basic design into versatile aircraft which at last weaned away Ukrvozdukhput from Dornier equipment and also sold in three versions, respectively for passengers, photography/survey and ambulance. Refined structure was lighter than K-3, so that even with BMW engine aircraft could carry four passengers, baggage and mail. Photo version with two or three operators in cabin to manage two fixed cameras (normally vertical) installed above hatches in floor. This model used for survey by Ukrainian government and Ukrvozdukhput. Ambulance version al-

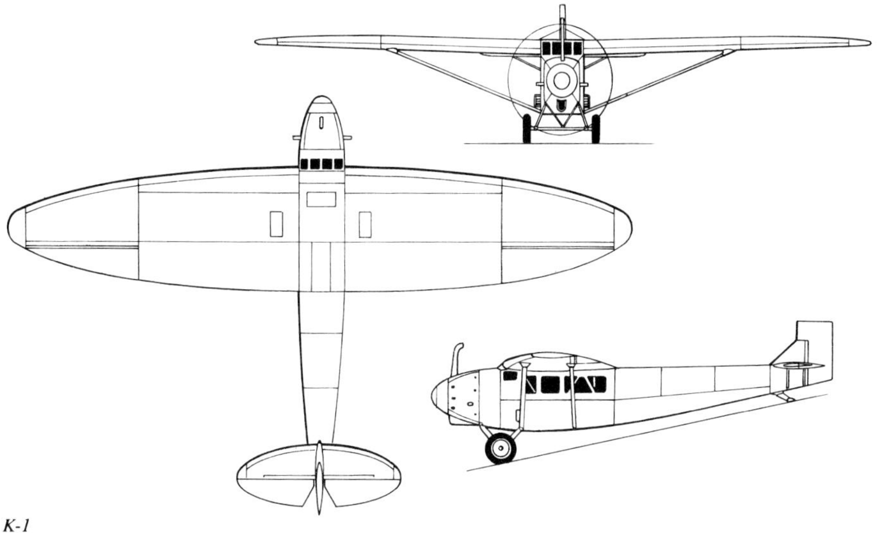

K-1

BMW-powered K-4

most same as K-3 except for more powerful engine not fitted to other variants. First of this version exhibited at ILA Berlin 1928 (note: Shavrov gives this date, but elsewhere dates ambulance model as 1929, possibly indicating had not flown when exhibited). Total of 22 of three models built, all sold. One, *Heart of Ukraine*, made record flight August 1928 Kharkov, Moscow, Irkutsk, Moscow, Kharkov; pilot M.A. Chyegirev, nav I.T. Spirin.

DIMENSIONS Span 16,75 m (54 ft 11½ in); length 11,35 m (37 ft 3 in); wing area 40,0 m² (430·5 ft²).
ENGINE (most) one 240 hp BMW IV; (ambulance) 300 hp M-6.
WEIGHTS Empty (passenger) 1540 kg (3395 lb), (others) 1400 kg (3086 lb); fuel/oil 320 kg; loaded (passenger) 2350 kg (5181 lb), (photo) 2040 kg, (ambulance) 2240 kg.
PERFORMANCE Max speed (passenger) 173 km/h (107·5 mph), (others) 175 km/h; climb (passenger) 7 min to 1 km (others 5·4 min); service ceiling 4,5/5,5 km; range 1040 km (646 miles); take-off (passenger) 270 m, (others) 160 m; landing 200 m/73 km/h (45 mph).

K-5 Growing demand for air transport in Ukraine encouraged Kalinin to build larger, resulting in K-5, most popular and important of all his 13 designs. Consistent low price and operating economy put K-5 in fully competitive position with any foreign transport (position not equalled again in the Soviet Union) and finally enabled German equipment to be replaced not only in Ukraine but throughout Aeroflot. Basic requirement to carry eight passengers 800 km at over 150 km/h. Wing exact scale of earlier designs. Fuselage welded KLMA steel tube, dural skin from nose to rear of cabin, then fabric at rear and on tail. Enclosed cockpit for pilot and flight mechanic, one set of flight instruments but dual controls. Spoked main wheels (usually with light disc fairing), 1100 × 250 mm tyres; alternative skis but not floats. Tailplane adjustable in flight ±5° from datum. Compressed-air starting system for main engine (note: this probably refers to Bristol patented gas starting for Jupiter, made as M-22). First flight 1929 with M-15 engine. Insufficiently powerful, and early forced landing spurred switch to M-22, with which large-scale production organised, 260 examples being delivered by 1934. Most passenger aircraft with eight dural seats, with superimposed upholstery. Some had carpet and curtains. Good results, but (though Bristol had special installation department which under Freddie Mayer longed to hear from distant customers) Kalinin did not know how to instal engine to get good airflow, cool cylinder heads and low drag. Experiments with Townend rings 1933, followed by decision to fit more powerful watercooled M-17F. First K-5 with this engine crashed following in-flight failure of nose rib. Prolonged problem with CG and weight of M-17F, and either range or payload had to be cut. Original M-22 aircraft continued to serve in large numbers throughout USSR until 1941, together with 'several tens' with M-17F and reduced payload.

DIMENSIONS Span 20,5 m (67 ft 3 in); length (M-15) 15,87 m, (M-22) 15,7 m (51 ft 6 in), (M-17F) about 16,5 m (54 ft 1½ in); wing area 66,0 m² (710 ft²).
ENGINE (prototype) one 450 hp M-15, (most) 480 hp M-22, (rebuilds) 730 hp M-17F.
WEIGHTS (prototype) empty 2275 kg; fuel/oil 500 + 50 kg; loaded 3750 kg; (M-22) empty 2400 kg (5291 lb); fuel/oil 400 + 40 kg; loaded 3925 kg (8653 lb); (M-17F) empty 2740 kg (6041 lb); fuel/oil 550 + 50 kg; loaded 4030 kg (8884 lb).
PERFORMANCE Max speed (M-15) 190 km/h, (M-22) 185 km/h (115 mph), (M-17F) 209 km/h (130 mph); cruise (M-22, M-17F) 169 km/h (105 mph); climb 8 min to 1 km; service ceiling 4,5/5 km; range 820/960 km (500/600 miles); take-off about 200 m/20 s; landing 250 m/19 s/75 km/h (47 mph).

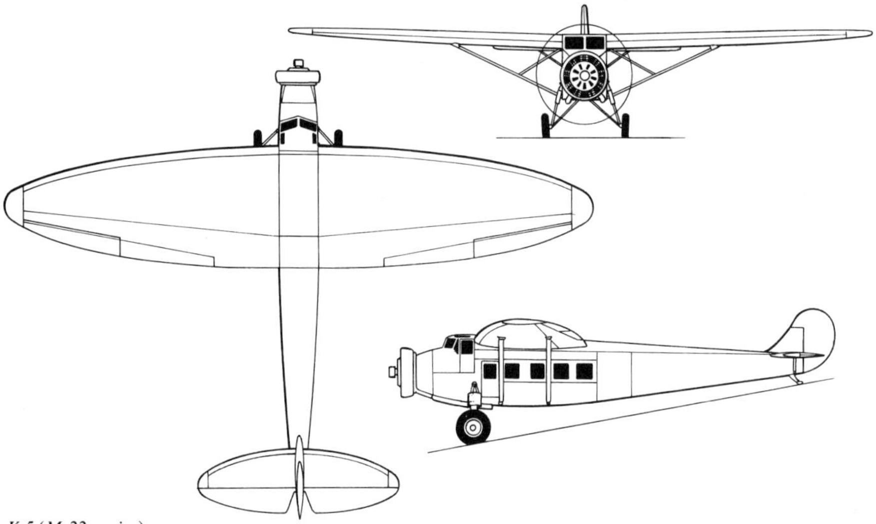

K-5 (M-22 engine)

K-6 Derivative of K-5 for urgent dense cargo, notably mail and matrices for printing of national newspapers in places distant from Moscow. Wing basically that of K-5 but left and right panels joined to new small centre section held on two quad cabane struts above slim fuselage. Latter had modified structure, with thin seam welds and rectangular section just adequate for two pilots and box of freight, with same tankage as M-17F K-5. Main landing-gear shock struts attached further up sides of fuselage. Engine not M-22 but supplied by Gnome-Rhône. Front cabin two pilots, rear cargo floor 4 m (157·5 in) long to adjust CG. First flight August 1930; no particular fault but no production.

DIMENSIONS Span 20,0 m (65 ft 7½ in); length 15,0 m (49 ft 2½ in); wing area 64,0 m² (689 ft²).
ENGINE One 420 hp GR9 (Bristol Jupiter IV).
WEIGHTS Empty 1720 kg (3792 lb); fuel/oil 500 + 50 kg; loaded 2820 kg (6217 lb).
PERFORMANCE Max speed 210 km/h (130 mph); cruise 170 km/h (105·6 mph); climb 5 min to 1 km; service ceiling 5,6 km; range 1250 km (777 miles); landing speed 70 km/h (43·5 mph).

K-7 Marking a complete and dramatic break with his successful past, this giant aircraft was one of most impressive achievements of whole pre-1939 era, and nearest thing to true 'flying fortress' ever flown. Basic concept was ultimate extrapolation of elliptical wing to very largest size possible. At this size wing depth became large enough for 120 passengers to occupy cabins in wings without affecting space required for fuel. Kalinin was convinced he could out-do Junkers whose G 38 could seat six of its 34 passengers in leading edge of wing. By early 1930 he had roughed out remarkable aircraft with six tractor engines and one pusher, twin tail booms and ability to carry 120 passengers or 7 t of cargo. Prolonged discussions ensued, reaching Kremlin, and in 1931 Kalinin received permission to build K-7, but only as heavy bomber. Even more unusual features then appeared.

Wing of elliptical shape, aspect ratio 6·2, TsAGI R-II profile with mean thickness of 19% rising to 22% at centreline, giving depth of 2,33 m (91·7 in) on chord of 10,6 m. Two main

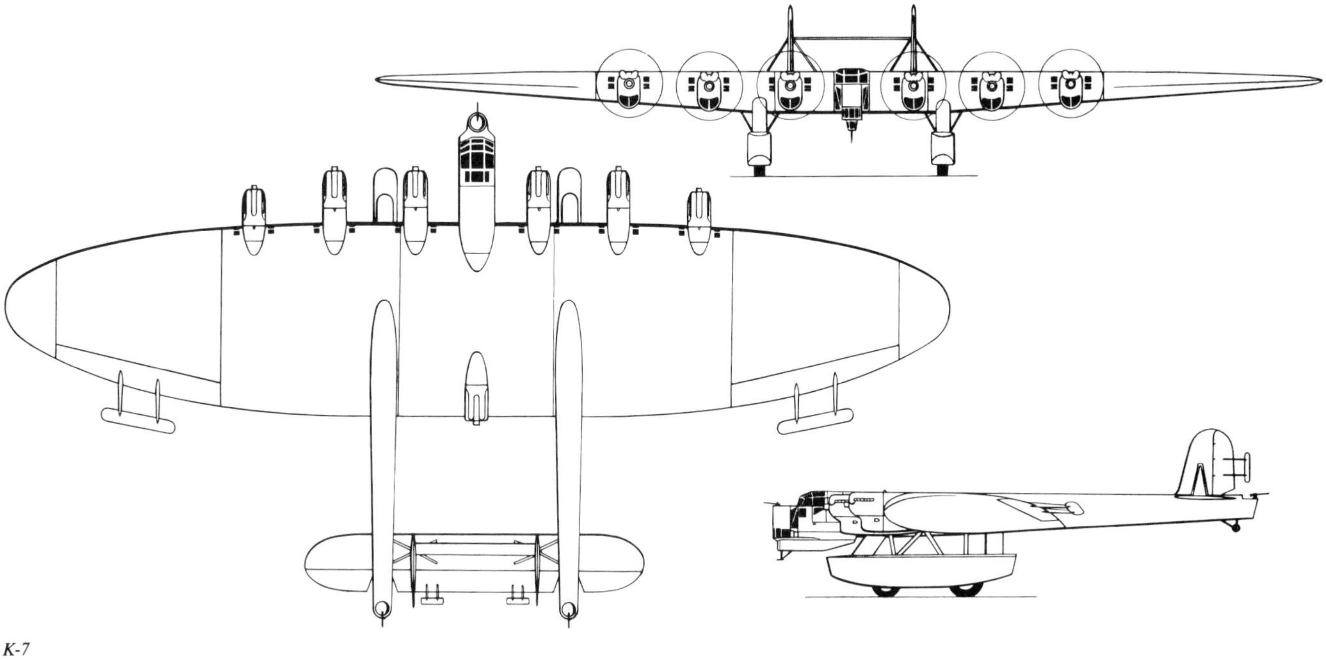

K-7

and two subsidiary spars built up from KhMA steel tube (first deliveries from new V.I. Lenin works opened at Dniepropetrovsk). Lattice girder ribs, multiple spanwise stringers. Rectangular centre section skinned in D1 dural, rest in fabric. Small front nacelle on centreline, all dural construction. Twin tail booms of triangular cross-section (flat top, apex down) of KhMA steel tube, fabric covering. Distance between boom centrelines 11 m (36 ft 1¼ in). Carried monoplane tailplane on which were two fins/rudders 7 m (22 ft 11½ in) apart, fins braced by small auxiliary tailplane at higher level. All flight controls driven manually by large servo surfaces carried downstream of trailing edge on pairs of struts. Six tractor engines on leading edge of wing, one pusher on trailing edge at centreline. Each engine with ventral radiator, two-blade propeller. Aircraft supported by large columns (rear vertical, front sloping) aligned with fourth/fifth rib on each side which also carried tail booms, outboard of engines 3 and 5. These columns linked aircraft to gondolas of all light-alloy construction housing gunners, bombs, entry doors and landing gear comprising one front wheel and side-by-side rear wheels in each gondola, with pneumatic brakes. Stairway in front column, ladder in rear column, to hatches in wing. Inflight access to all engines. Fuel 9130 lit (2008 gal) in relatively insignificant metal tanks in wing. Minimum crew 11: two pilots, nav/bomb, radio/gunner (nose 20 mm gun), engineer, four gunners (each twin DA) in cockpits at front and rear of gondolas and two gunners (each 20 mm) at tips of tail booms. Maximum-bomb load 14,6 t (32,187 lb); overload 19 t (41,887 lb), evenly divided between bays in centre of each gondola, with twin doors. Complete intercom throughout aircraft.

K-7 completed at Kharkov summer 1933. First engine run 29 June; soon discovered severe vibration, especially of booms and tail, at particular engine speeds. Though problem clearly resonance, only solution was local reinforcement, achieved by welding on extra steel angle sections to reduce motion to minimum. Taxi tests 9 August. First flight 11 August, satisfactory (no military load) but pilots would have preferred geared engines and larger propellers. Flying continued, causing immense interest around city, until within a month of completion of factory tests. On ninth flight, 21 November 1933, during speed tests at 100 m, sudden vibration in tail broke right tail boom; aircraft went straight into ground and burned. Pilot M.A. Snyegirev and 13 crew and one passenger killed; five crew survived.

This put blight on twin booms and on Kalinin. Latter was sent to new GAZ at Yoronezh where at end 1933 plan organised under P.I. Baranov to build two more K-7s with various structural changes including stressed-skin booms of rectangular section. In 1935 work halted when first was 60% complete; basic concept no longer competitive.

DIMENSIONS Span 53,0 m (173 ft 10$\frac{5}{8}$ in); length 28,0 m (91 ft 10$\frac{1}{2}$ in); wing area 454 m² (4887 ft²).
ENGINES Seven 830 hp M-34F.
WEIGHTS Empty 24,4 t (53,792 lb); fuel/oil 6500 + 600 kg; normal loaded 38 t (83,774 lb), (max bombload) 42,4 t (93,474 lb), (overload) 46,5 t (102,513 lb).
PERFORMANCE Max speed 225 km/h (140 mph); long-range cruise 180 km/h (112 mph); service ceiling 4 km (13,123 ft); normal range 1600 km (994 miles).

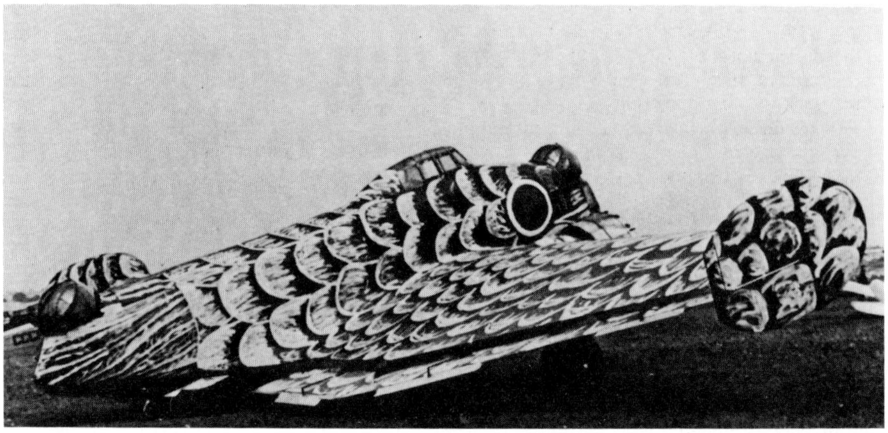

K-12, VS-2 in Firebird livery

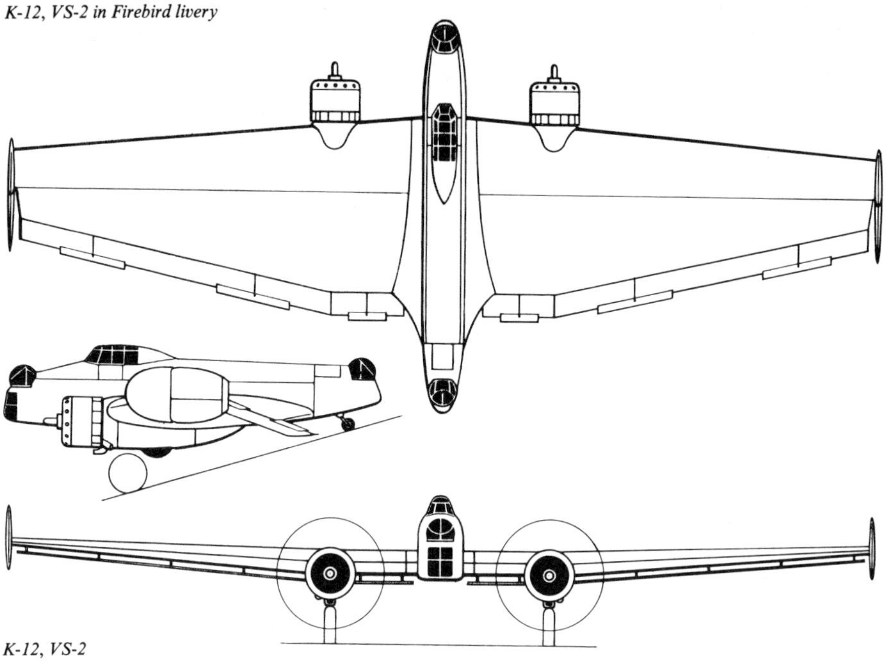

K-12, VS-2

K-9 While K-7 was in design, Kalinin as light relief essayed simple tandem-seat sporting and liaison aircraft. Parasol monoplane with usual construction for fuselage, but elliptical wing and tail of mainly metal construction and arranged to fold for convenience. Skewed hinge at rear spar folded outer wings down and to rear with upper surface facing outward. Cockpits wide apart, separated by large chord of wing. Welded steel-tube main gears, with vertical rubber-sprung shock struts well away from fuselage, braced by diagonal to top fuselage longeron. For its power this was overdesigned and too large; would have been better with M-11 engine. Test-flown 1932.

DIMENSIONS Not accurately recorded, but span about 11 m (36 ft) and length about 7,5 m (24 ft).
ENGINE One 60 hp Walter NZ-60 five-cylinder radial.
WEIGHTS Empty 550 kg (1213 lb); fuel/oil 60 kg; loaded 770 kg (1698 lb).
PERFORMANCE Max speed 120 km/h (74·5 mph); endurance 3 h; landing speed 60 km/h (37 mph).

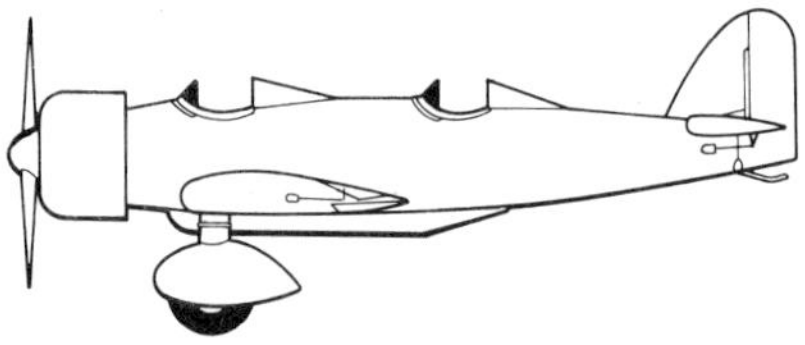

K-10

K-10 This attractive cantilever low-wing machine used many wing, fuselage and tail parts almost identical to those of K-9, but result was dramatically superior because of greater power. Welded truss fuselage made integral with centre section carrying cantilever landing gears with spatted wheels. Left and right wings arranged to fold manually in same way as on K-9, with skewed hinge at top of rear spar and with trailing edge inboard of aileron previously folded up across wing to provide clearance. Engine fully cowled in long-chord cowl, rare for M-11 in 1932, driving 2,3 m two-blade propeller with spinner. Though built as civil sport aircraft, entered as military trainer in competition with AIR-9 (winner) and Gribovskii G-20. After this contest, proposed as agricultural machine for seeding and pollination (presumably also spraying/dusting); with ventral tank. Popular machine, flown September 1932, but no production.

DIMENSIONS Span 10,7 m (35 ft 1$\frac{1}{4}$ in); length 7,03 m (23 ft 0$\frac{3}{4}$ in); wing area 18,0 m² (194 ft²). No other data.

K-11 Believed designation of tailless glider of 9 m (29 ft 7 in) span built in 1934 as first stage of three-stage development of ultra-fast tailless bomber (see K-12). Completed 100 flights and confirmed stability and control of chosen configuration would be satisfactory.

K-12 (VS-2) One of most extraordinary aircraft of its day, this tailless bomber was second stage in development by Kalinin of a super-fast bomber with flying-wing configuration. Total break with designer's traditions, except structurally. Objective was eventual bomber, possibly propelled by rockets, in which crew and all other items would be inside wing of perfect aerodynamic form. Having proved basic flight characteristics with K-11, K-12 was to be undemanding, and quite slow, experimental bomber to about half linear scale of eventual machine. On this scale not practical to bury everything in wing, so short central fuselage for crew of three. Wing of R-II profile, unswept with straight main spar and multiple auxiliary spars, stringers and built-up truss ribs. Structure welded KLMA steel throughout (ruling section elliptical, 10 × 8,5 mm) with fabric covering. Welded steel-tube fuselage in three sections, main joints and joints between wings and centre section being bolted. Scheibe-type rudders on vertical hinges at wingtips. Double-wing trailing edge with servo-operated ailerons outboard and elevators inboard, all of inverted R-II profile. Crew of three, pilot in enclosed cockpit and two gunners each with ShKAS in manually rotated turret at nose and tail. Internal bay for 500 kg bombload. Main gears retracted backwards into engine nacelles. No attempt at large bombload or long range: two small wing tanks totalled 700 lit (154 gal).

First drawings late 1934. First flight December 1936 by P.M. Stefanovskii. Long take-off and in air demonstrated poor stability and control (much worse than glider), and rudders zero or negative effectiveness at low speeds. Prolonged attempts to improve behaviour yielded slow results. Worse, though no attempt at high performance, latter seemed worse than conventional aircraft of equal power. Tailless bomber abandoned, but K-12 (service designation **VS-2** from *Vystablyat samolyet*, demonstration aircraft) was painted bright red/yellow feathers and named *Zhar Ptitsa*, Firebird (Phoenix) and participated in Tushino show 18 August 1937.

DIMENSIONS Span (Shavrov) 20,9 m (68 ft 6¾ in), (Němĕcek) 18 m; length (Shavrov) 10,3 m (33 ft 9½ in), (Němĕcek) 8 m; wing area (Shavrov) 72,7 m^2 (783 ft^2), (Němĕcek) 72,5 m^2.
ENGINES Two 480 hp M-22.
WEIGHTS Empty 3070 kg (6768 lb); fuel/oil 500 kg; loaded 4200 kg (9259 lb).
PERFORMANCE Max speed (Shavrov) 218 km/h (135 mph), (Němĕcek) 240 km/h; service ceiling 7170 m (23,524 ft); range (Shavrov) 110 km (probably misprint), (Němĕcek) 700 km (435 miles); take-off given by Shavrov as 700 m and also as 300 m.

K-13 Kalinin assigned **K-14** to his planned futuristic flying-wing bomber, and designed K-13 as interim conventional bomber, made of usual welded KhMA steel tube. Biplane tail with twin fins/rudders to give optimum angle of fire for spherical tail turret. Other guns in glazed nose and positions on top of wing. Underwing braking flaps (this could mean for landing or dive-bombing). Begun 1936 and approaching first flight when Kalinin arrested; OKB disbanded. No data, except two M-34 engines

Kamov

N.I. Kamov

Nikolai Ilyich Kamov was born 1902 in Siberia. Graduated from Tomsk Technical Institute 1926 as locomotive engineer, but two years later joined OMOS, qualified as pilot, and worked on ROM-1 and other flying boats under Grigorovich. In 1929 joined forces with another engineer to produce first Soviet autogyro (KaSkr-1, below). In 1931 joined OOK at TsAGI where his greatest achievement was leader of 3rd Brigade which created A-7 (see TsAGI). Throughout second half of 1930s worked at BOK. In 1940 set up A-7/A-7bis production works at Smolensk, but his AK design had to be abandoned because of war. In 1945 he was again able to set up his own KB (OKB from 1948) with completely new co-axial lightweight helicopter, Ka-8. From this stemmed major family of co-axial helicopters, initially piston-engined under chief engineer Vladimir Barshyevskii and from 1960 turbine-engined with greatly expanded design team (reported to be located at Ulan-Ude). Chief deputy M.A. Kupfer, but when Kamov died 24 November 1973 his place was taken by S. Mikheyev. OKB retains Kamov's name, and continues to work not only on helicopters but also on aerosleighs.

KaSkr-1 Taking designation from its creators, Kamov and Nikolai Kirillovich Skrzhinskii, this autogyro was painted red and named *Krasnii Inzhyener* (Red Engineer). Its inspiration was Cierva C.8 Mk III, whose detail design was in some parts copied exactly. Like Cierva, its designers used existing Avro 504 fuselage, in this case from U-1 production line. U-1 also supplied landing gear and most of flight control system, but Kamov and Skrzhinskii designed own rotor (four braced blades), small wings and other parts. First ground running test 1 September 1929. Rotor began to spin, but control system ineffective and subjected to major changes. U-1 rudder changed for larger surface; then torque of engine/propeller almost overturned machine, rectified by hanging 8 kg weight under right wingtip. Test pilot I.V. Mikheyev (father of present KB chief) unable to fly aircraft because of lack of power. Rebuilt as KaSkr-2.

DIMENSIONS Diameter of four-blade rotor 12,0 m (39 ft 4¾ in); length 8,8 m (28 ft 10½ in); solidity 0·106 (later 0·127); rotor speed 115 rpm.
ENGINE One 120 hp M-2 rotary.
WEIGHTS Empty 750 kg (1653 lb); loaded 950 kg (2094 lb).
PERFORMANCE Achieved speed 90 km/h (56 mph); design endurance 1·5 h.

KaSkr-2 Major reconstruction of KaSkr-1 with much more powerful engine in helmeted cowl forming part of new light-alloy front end. Other minor changes including rudder of better shape. Flown 1930; one photograph shows it on skis in winter 1930–1931. Pilot D.A. Koshits flew KaSkr-2 on 90 occasions by late 1931, reaching figures given below. Pioneer Soviet autogyro, leading quickly to 2-EA and A-4 at TsAGI.

DIMENSIONS Diameter of four-blade rotor 12 m (39 ft 4¾ in); length 9.0 m (29 ft 6¼ in); solidity 0·127; rotor speed 135 rpm.
ENGINE One 225 hp Gnome-Rhône Titan 5-cylinder radial.
WEIGHTS Empty 865 kg (1907 lb); loaded 1100 kg (2425 lb).
PERFORMANCE Speed 110 km/h (68 mph); altitude 450 m (1476 ft); endurance 28 min.

AK Discouraged by atmosphere of fear at TsAGI which stultified design, Kamov took job of chief designer in factory at Smolyensk opened 1939 to make production autogyros (beginning with A-7-Za). Obtained permission to undertake fresh design and drew simple observation machine with pusher engine and two seats side-by-side doors. Tricycle gear, single fin/rudder on struts from rotor head and main gears, no wings. Delayed by evacuation July 1941 but work restarted at new facility in Lake Baikal region 1942. Abandoned 1943 because of termination of interest by VVS.

DIMENSIONS Rotor diam 13,5 m (44 ft 3½ in); length not known.
ENGINE One 220 hp MV-6.
WEIGHTS Empty 1026 kg (2262 lb); loaded 1317 kg (2903 lb).
PERFORMANCE (est) Max speed 176 km/h (109 mph); ceiling 4,7 km (15,400 ft).

Ka-8 Official disinterest in autogyro made Kamov switch to helicopters, and he decided to build one-man *Vozdushnii Mototsikl* (flying motorcycle) for civil or military use. Main design effort on coaxial rotors, each with three built-up wooden (mainly spruce) blades of NACA-230 profile with glued construction and fabric covering. Metal root held in hub with drag and flapping hinges driven by superimposed swashplates moved directly by pilot. Rest of airframe welded steel tube, with pilot and fixed fin at rear and engine and fuel tank at front, resting on two pontoons of rubberized fabric. Reported to have taken 18 months before permission granted to organise small informal group and build Ka-8 (said originally to have been designated K-17). First flown 1947, pilot Mikhail Gurov. Generally satisfactory but original BMW engine insufficiently powerful and developed into later M-76 with hemi heads, higher compression and, ultimately, special doped fuel causing short plug life. Handlebar flight control replaced by vertical collective and cyclic levers, pontoons tapered front to rear, and fin changed to rudder driven by pedals. At least three built, one displayed from truck at 1948 Tushino show.

DIMENSIONS Rotor diameter 5,6 m (18 ft 4½ in); length (ignoring rotor) 3,62 m (11 ft 10½ in); solidity (each rotor) 0·04; rotor speed 475 rpm.
ENGINE Originally 27 hp BMW flat-twin, modified into 45 hp M-76.
WEIGHTS Empty 183 kg (403 lb); loaded 275 kg (606 lb).
PERFORMANCE Speed 80 km/h (50 mph); ceiling (hover) 50 m; (in forward flight) 250 m (820 ft).

Ka-10 Success of Ka-8 enabled Kamov to open his own OKB in 1948, by which time he had completed drawings for this improved and enlarged (but still single-seat) machine. Structure similar but refined. Engine completely new, designed by Ivchyenko for this application with two stages of reduction gearing, freewheel with centrifugal clutch and improved power split between rotors. Electric started and engine-driven cooling fan. First hover by D.K. Yefremov September 1949. Four built, at least three bought by AV-MF and displayed on Navy Day. Prolonged engineering improvements, mainly concerned with hubs and control system but also including revised blade profile and twist and twin fins, led to **Ka-10M** of 1954. At least eight (Němĕcek, 12) of this model, some doing sea duty as spotters for whalers, icebreakers and Coast Guard. Basically, however, performance too limited to be of lasting value.

DIMENSIONS Diameter of two three-blade rotors 6,12 m (20 ft 1 in); length (ignoring rotors) 3,70 m (12 ft 1¾ in); height 2,5 m (8 ft 2½ in); solidity (each rotor) 0·037; rotor speed 410 rpm.
ENGINE One 55 hp AI-4V.

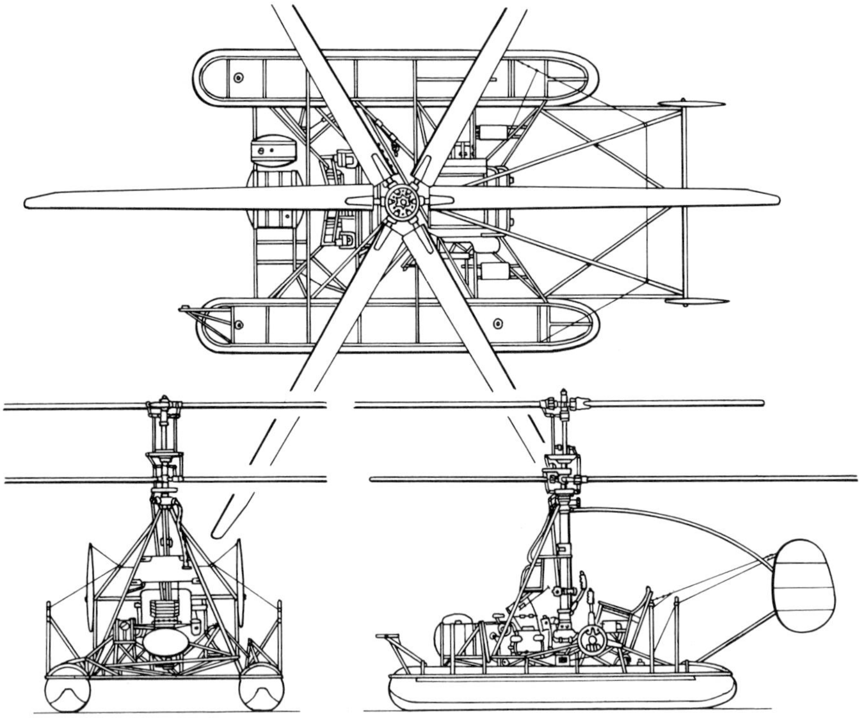

Ka-10M

Ka-18

WEIGHTS Empty 234 kg (516 lb); loaded 375 kg (827 lb).
PERFORMANCE Speed 90 km/h (56 mph); ceiling (hovering) 500 m, (in forward flight) 1 km (3300 ft); range 95 km (59 miles).

Ka-15 It was clear by 1950 that, while Kamov's basic engineering was sound and coaxial configuration resulted in compact helicopter (good for shipboard operations), Ka-10 was totally inadequate. Ivchyenko was already preparing much more powerful radial engine, and AV-MF wrote outline requirement for larger two-seat helicopter with enclosed cabin and much greater endurance. As far as possible Ka-15 built on previous experience. Rotor hubs and blades scaled up but compared with Ka-10M only significant change was low-density foam filling of blades between ribs and taper of blade towards tip. Basis of airframe welded steel tube, with covering of ply or dural removable panels and thin plastics glazing and sliding side doors round side-by-side cockpit ahead of rotor, with engine behind. Latter mounted with crankshaft horizontal, driving cooling fan, 90° angle drive to rotor via overrunning clutch, and DC generator/starter. From engine to tail, stressed-skin dural construction, with fixed tail comprising braced tailplane and two endplate fins toed in at front (parallel on some Ka-15s), with pedal-driven rudders for yaw control (poor in hover). First flight by V.V. Vinittskii early 1952. Rather slow development, but probably in production 1955 and subsequently some hundreds built in several versions. Most fitted with two main and two nose landing wheels, plus tail bumper; nose wheels castoring and main wheels braked. At least one with pontoons and one with three skis. AV-MF versions (designation unknown) used for communications, training and shipboard spotting and utility; also demonstrated with two side-mounted depth charges. Civil **Ka-15M** wi-

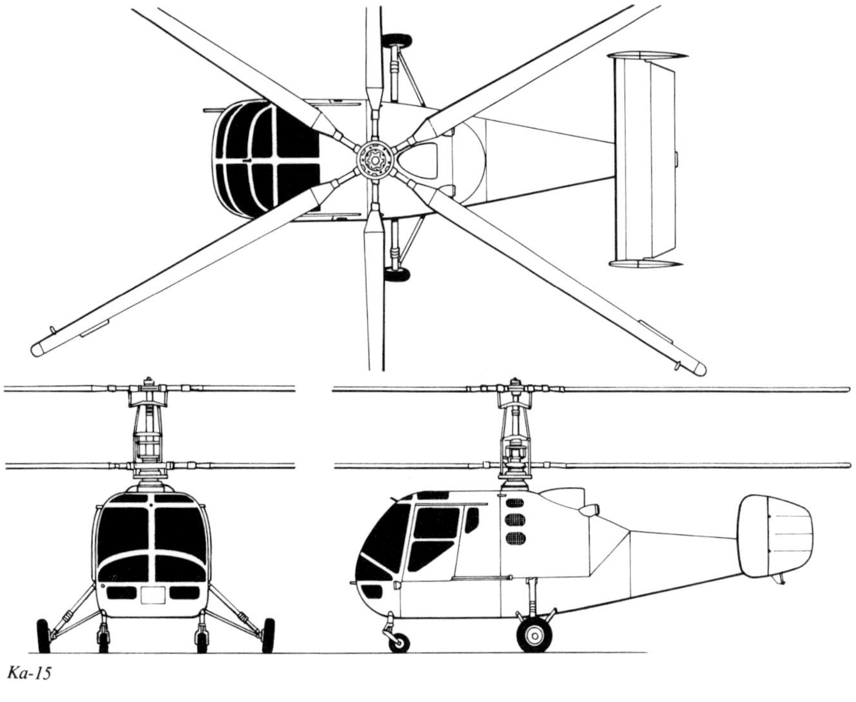

Ka-15

Ka-15S (two stretchers)

Ka-22

dely used as transport (one passenger inside, mail or other cargo in external side containers), forestry/pipeline patrol, ambulance (two external stretcher containers) and agricultural (320-lit tank for liquids or solids dispensed via long spraybars). Set two records including 170,455 km/h over 500 km circuit. Civil 15M exported to about 12 countries. Not known with slung load, guns or AI-14V F engine.

DIMENSIONS Diameter of three-blade rotors 9,96 m (32 ft 8 in) (also reported as 9,97 m); length (ignoring rotors) 5,95 m (19 ft 6¼ in); rotor speed 330 rpm.

ENGINE One 255 hp AI-14V.

WEIGHTS Empty (15M) 968 kg (2,134 lb); loaded (15M) 1370 kg (3020 lb) (naval given as 1134 kg, surely incorrect).

PERFORMANCE Max speed 150 km/h (93 mph); ceiling (hover) 800 m, (forward flight) 3 km (9842 ft); range (15M, normal) 290 km (180 miles).

Ka-18 Utilizing what appear to be unchanged rotor and dynamic components, this is a stretched Ka-15 with longer fuselage of all stressed-skin construction, though retaining original steel-tube basis. Much roomier cockpit with hinged side doors and loading hatch on right side of nose for stretcher carried internally on right of pilot. Dual control with side-by-side pilots in training role. One rear passenger behind pilot (doctor in aeromedical role) or without stretcher two rear passengers; alternatively 200 kg cargo. Nose no longer transparent; doors hinged at rear; 176 lit (38·7 gal) fuel in floor tanks; extended rear fuselage and fins/rudders of much greater chord; whole aircraft cleaned up aerodynamically. Alcohol de-icing of blades and windscreen, exhaust heater muff feeds hot air on demand to cabin. First flown early 1957. State trials completed 1958, but recognised that extra airframe and equipment weight reduced payload to slightly less than Ka-15, and most production

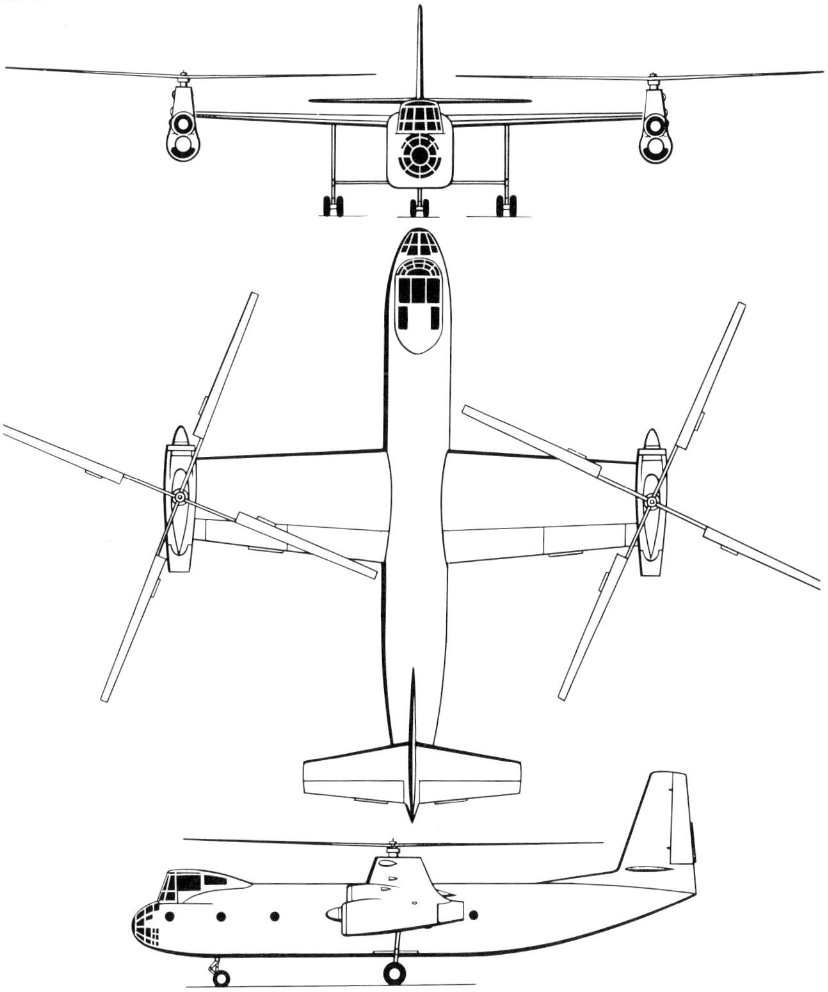

Ka-22

therefore fitted with AI-14VF engine with supercharger (data for this version). Production for AV-MF, VVS and Aeroflot, but probably fewer than 200. Production Ka-18 subtypes (designations unknown) feature detachable blades, blind-flying instruments and provision for two 70-lit long-range tanks at expense of payload.
DIMENSIONS As Ka-15 except length (ignoring rotors) 7,03m (23 ft 0¾ in).
ENGINE (prototypes) as Ka-15, (production) one 280 hp AI-14VF.
WEIGHTS Empty (production, typical) 1032 kg (2275 lb); loaded 1502 kg (3311 lb).
PERFORMANCE Max speed (prototypes) 145 km/h, (VF engine) 160 km/h (99 mph); ceiling (forward flight) 3,5 km (11,483 ft); range (three passengers, 130 km/h cruise) 300 km (186 miles).

Ka-22 Named *Vintokryl* (screw-wing) this was a major surprise at 1961 Tushino show. Utterly unlike any previous Soviet aircraft, though in helicopter mode using configuration of Bratukhin, Ka-22 was never publicly recorded in detail, but must have begun as project in mid-1950s. Single example seen was wearing military national marking on tail. Basically compound helicopter (also called convertiplane) with complete engine/rotor/propeller group on each tip of conventional wing. All-metal airframe, stressed-skin covering, but Kamov hinted that steel-tube foundation was retained in fuselage. Large fuselage with unobstructed interior providing room for estimated 80 to 100 troops, about 70 civil passengers or light vehicles loaded via rear ventral ramp-door. Glazed nose for nav, high flight deck for two pilots and radio/engineer. High-mounted wing with slight taper, outboard tabbed ailerons and inboard flaps which were not lowered in hovering displays. Conventional aeroplane tail, used only in aeroplane mode. Power group comprising turboshaft engine with drive capable of being progressively clutched to either four-blade propeller or four-blade rotor, latter being used for vertical flight and propellers for cruise, with lift shared between wing and windmilling rotors. Selected engine normally has rear drive from free turbine; installation probably has engine mounted in normal sense, with rear jetpipe and air from inlet ducted round underside of cowling, driving at rear to high-speed shaft to reduction gearbox under rotor shaft, from which front drive goes to propeller. Upper circular inlet feeds fan-assisted oil cooler. Fixed tricycle landing gear with twin main wheels. Superficially rotors and hubs resembled those of Mi-4 and Yak-24, but with trailing-edge tabs inboard; handed, left rotor being clockwise seen from above. First flight 1960 or 1961. Public display (confident) Tushino 9 July 1961, D.K. Yefremov. Same pilot, assisted by V.V. Gromov, set world 15/25 km record 7 October 1961 at 356,3 km/h (221·4 mph), with spatted landing gears, followed by record lift on 24 November of 16 485 kg (36,343 lb) to 2 km. Only one Ka-22 seen, and no news since 1961.
DIMENSIONS (estimated) Diameter of each four-blade rotor 20 m (65 ft 7½ in); span (between rotor centrelines) 20,4 m (67 ft); length (ignoring rotors) 22,5 m (73 ft 9¾ in).
ENGINES Two 5500 shp Soloviev D-25V (TV-2BM).
WEIGHTS Not known but empty probably about 12 t (26,455 lb) and loaded (normal) about 20 t (44,000 lb), (record) at least 28,5 t (62,830 lb),

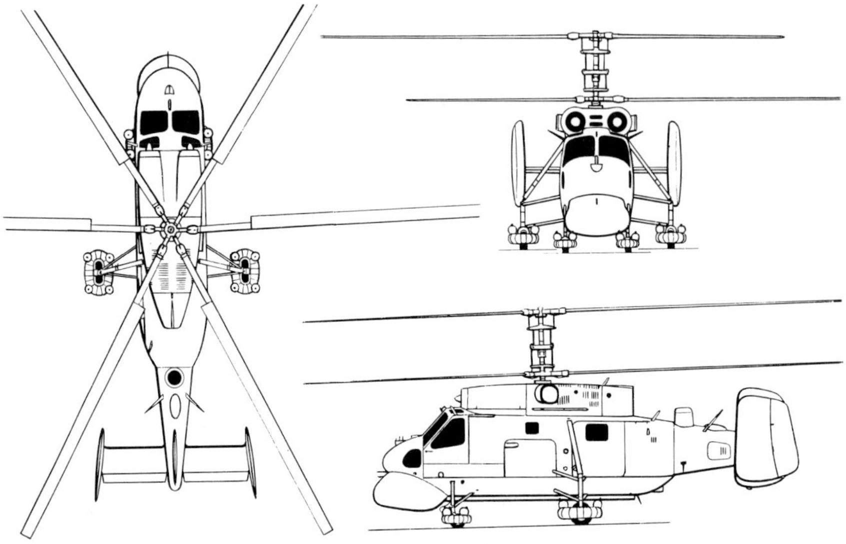
Ka-25 Hormone-A showing flotation gear

Ka-25 Hormone-B from the Leningrad

Ka-25 Hormone-C, note sonobuoy dispenser

almost certainly needing long take-off run.
PERFORMANCE Not known, see records.

Ka-25 Great increase in ASW (anti-submarine warfare) effort from 1957 was reflected in urgent requirement for dedicated shipboard ASW helicopter. Though Mil competed, compact Kamov formula appeared superior and first of three prototypes displayed at 1961 Tushino show with dummy missiles on lateral pylons of pattern not fitted to production helicopter; probably erroneously reported as 'Ka-20'. State trials eventually successful, and production decision probably not later than 1962, with deliveries late 1965. Larger and much more powerful than previous (Ka-15 and Ka-18) designs, powered by free-turbine engines mounted above unobstructed cabin forming compact group with superimposed rotors with flapping and drag hinges (lubricated), aluminium blades with nitrogen-pressure crack warning, hydraulic control, alcohol deicing and auto blade folding. Forward-facing electrically heated inlets, lateral plain (no IR protection) exhausts, and rear drive to rotors and to large cooling fan for oil radiator served by circular aft-facing inlet above rear fuselage. Airframe entirely dural stressed-skin, mainly flush-riveted but incorporating some bonding and sandwich panels. Main fuselage devoted to payload: side-by-side dual control nose cockput with sliding door on each side, main cabin 1,5 m wide, 1,25 m high and 3,95 m long with sliding door on left and access at front to cockpit, and much of underfloor volume being fuel (possibly integral tankage). Boom at rear carries all-metal tail with upper and lower central fin and toed-in fins and rudders on end of tailplane provided with elevators. Two front and two main landing gears each with single wheel, all with fittings for four optional rapid-inflation buoyancy bags for emergency water landing. Nose wheels castor, main wheels with brakes and in most examples can be raised in flight out of field of view of nose radar. Flight equipment comprehensive including autopilot and various radio navaids for overwater use (except, it is said, night and adverse-weather sonar dipping). Three main AV-MF versions identified, with many subvariations. One (NATO Hormone-A) is ASW with crew of four, radar (Big Bulge I/J-band), A-346Z datalink, SRO-2 IFF and SRZ-2 interrogator, RV-3 radio altimeter and Tie Rod electro-optical sensor, plus towed MAD, dipping sonar and (not always fitted) aerial blade above tail boom, faired pod at base of ventral fin and other unidentified equipment. Some have Home Guide quad *Yagi* array on nose. In most aircraft linear weapon bay along ventral centreline for short 553 mm torpedo, nuclear depth charge or other stores; some carry weapons in long ventral box beneath fuselage. External side attachments for fuel drums, sonobuoy dispenser or pylons for 'fire and forget' missiles (not positively identified by mid-1983). Optical tip-up seats along cabin walls for 12 passengers in lieu of weapons. Hormone-B is EW variant with larger Short Horn J-band radar, A-346Z tied in with SSN-3 Shaddock (and possibly other) missile for midcourse guidance and Mushroom radar in rear cabin floor; no weapons. Utility variant identified early 81, with simplified avionics. Total production, believed all Ulan-Ude, about 460 ending 1975 for AV-MF, plus small number exported to India, Syria and Jugoslavia. First seen on Kresta I

Ka-25 Hormone-C, SAR

Ka-25K

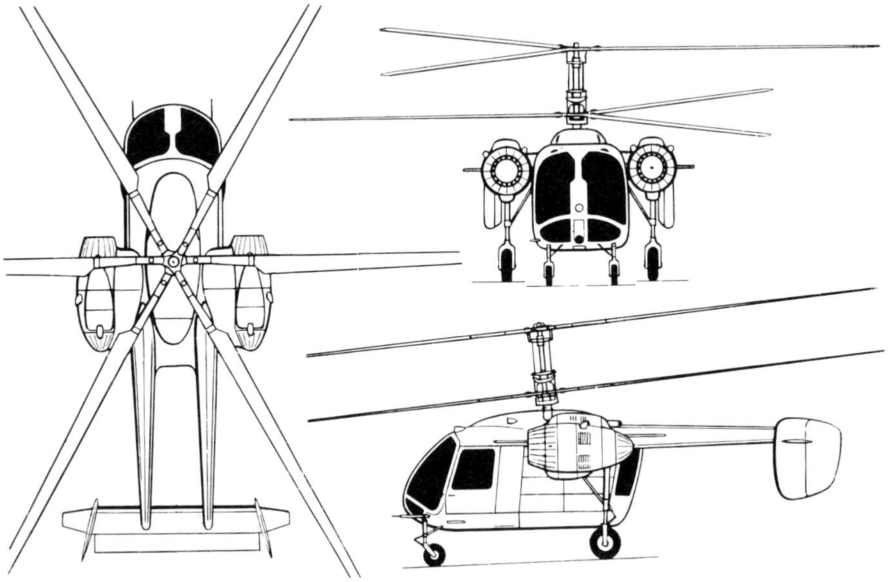
Ka-26

Ka-26 equipped for spraying/dusting

Ka-32? ASW helicopter aboard Udaloy

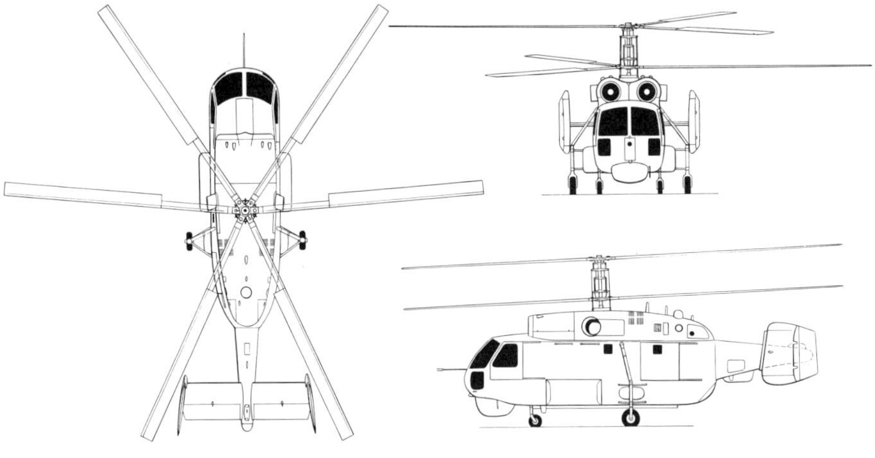
Ka-32 (provisional)

cruisers; *Moskva/Leningrad* usually 16 A and 2 B; *Kiev* 27 A and 3 B; many other ships including Kresta IIs, Karas and BPKs.

Ka-25K civil *Kran* (crane) version shown at 1967 Paris air show but no production. Undernose gondola, provisions for 2 t slung load and 250 kg capacity electric winch in cargo compartment; other minor differences including electrically deiced blades and longer nose (and, of course, no naval avionics).

DIMENSIONS Diameter of each three-blade rotor 15,74 m (51 ft 7¾ in); length ignoring rotors 9,75 m (31 ft 11¾ in); height overall 5,37 m (17 ft 7½ in).

ENGINES Two 900 shp Glushyenkov GTD-3; post-1971 believed 990 shp GTD-3BM.

WEIGHTS Empty about 4765 kg (10,505 lb); loaded 7,5 t (16,535 lb).

PERFORMANCE Max speed 209 km/h (130 mph); cruise for range 193 km/h (120 mph); service ceiling 3,5 km; range (internal fuel) 400 km (249 miles).

Ka-26 One of few successful Soviet aviation exports, this versatile utility helicopter is refined and cheap to buy. Announced 1964, first flight 1965. Coaxial rotors with mast inclined 6° forwards and GRP blades (first in Soviet Union and among first in world) with alcohol deicing. Hydraulic control, manual reversion. Light-alloy stressed-skin airframe with external ribbing for skin stability (used on lesser scale on Ka-25). Piston engines mounted with crankshafts horizontal on tips of stub wings attached to roof structure linking nose cockpit and tail boom. Fully glazed cockpit with sliding door on each side equipped for pilot on left; optional passenger or second pilot on right. Engines cooled by fans and driving via right-angle boxes and overrunning clutches giving twin-engine safety. Two castoring nose wheels and two braked main wheels, tyres 595 × 185 mm. Twin tail booms mainly GRP construction carrying aeroplane-type tail with two vertical surfaces toed in 15°. Payload attached externally in space under rotor. Options include six-seat cabin (warmed like cockpit by combustion heater); same-size compartment for two stretchers, two seated casualties and attendant, with medical equipment; fire-protection model with six firemen and/or chemicals; 900 kg ag-hopper dispensing 1·2 to 12 lit or kg per second via spraybars or dust-spreader; cabin equipped for aerial survey (AFA-31 camera and operator); or geophysical compartment with EM-pulse generator feeding large ring emitter and with towed receiver 'bird' whose cable is sheared if overloaded. About 600 Ka-26 produced by 1977; production possibly continuing. Widely used on wheels, skis or pontoons on land and from ships for many utility tasks, one of which is clearing river ice in spring by landing demolition teams at selected spots. Total hours 0·5 million mid-81. Exports, mainly civil, to at least nine countries.

DIMENSIONS Diameter of each three-blade rotor 13,0 m (42 ft 8 in); length ignoring rotors 7,75 m (25 ft 5 in); height overall 4,05 m (13 ft 3½ in)

ENGINES Two 325 hp M-14V-26.

WEIGHTS Empty (basic) 1950 kg (4299 lb), (with passenger cabin) 2100 kg (4630 lb); payload typically 1 t; loaded (max, all models) 3,25 t (7165 lb).

PERFORMANCE Max speed 170 km/h (106 mph); cruise 110 km/h (68 mph); service ceiling

3 km; range (7 pax, 30 min reserve) 400 km (249 miles), (max with auxiliary tankage) 1200 km (745 miles).

Ka-126 Photograph of this twin-turbine version of Ka-26, or possibly a mock-up, was published early 1981. Basic helicopter appears unchanged from 1980 production Ka-26, with short tailplane. Instead of large piston-engine nacelles, slim turboshaft units are mounted close beside top of fuselage, with rear drive gearbox on same outriggers as main legs. Engine type not announced; Polish-built Isotov GTD-350 would be suitable but would not fit cowling shape and single outboard exhaust stack. OKB's chief designer, S.V. Mikheyev, announced machine in 1979 but no further information available by early 1983.

Ka-32 An example of this helicopter, intended for all-weather ice reconnaissance from ice-breakers, was to be put on display in Moscow in late 1980 in advance of its entry to service. Had not appeared at end of 1982. Range 185 km (115 miles) with slung load 5 t (11,020 lb).

Ka-32? Possibly also designation of new ASW helicopter revealed September 1981. Two (one AV-MF, the other civil Aeroflot markings) were observed operating from new warship *Udaloy*. Probably same type as exhibit listed above, for which Ka-32 is announced designation. Configuration as Ka-25 but scaled up to more power and much greater payload. Slightly larger rotors and completely new fuselage offers much more room for sensors and operators. Cockpit similar to Ka-25 now in extreme nose, with relatively small radar below. Ventral bay for anti-submarine torpedoes or other weapons, side bulges probably main fuel tanks, sliding doors for flight crew and ASW operators, no inflatable pontoons on landing gears and no central fin. Compatible with lifts of ASW cruisers. Speculation that roles could include AV-MF amphibious assault, resupply and logistic transport, civil transport and flying-crane duty. NATO code name Helix. Data estimated.

DIMENSIONS Diameter of two three-blade main rotors 16,75 m (54 ft 11½ in); fuselage length 11,9 m (39 ft 0 in); height 5,5 m (18 ft 0 in).
ENGINES Two turboshafts each of about 1500 shp (possibly Isotov TV2 or TV3).
WEIGHTS Empty about 5500 kg (12,1255 lb); maximum 11,5 t (25,353 lb).
PERFORMANCE Similar to Ka-25; see previous entry for Ka-32 payload/range.

Kazan KAI

Kazan Aviation Institute has since 1934 been one of most important SKBs, though no designs appeared between 1937 and 1956. In 1934–1937 KAI designs were created under supervision of S.P. Gudzik by team led by Zyeliman Isaakovich Itskovich, who had been one of Kalinin's designers in 1927–1930 and then worked at KhAI. After 1937 work lapsed until in 1956 a fresh SKB was formed under M.P. Simonov to create sailplanes and light aircraft.

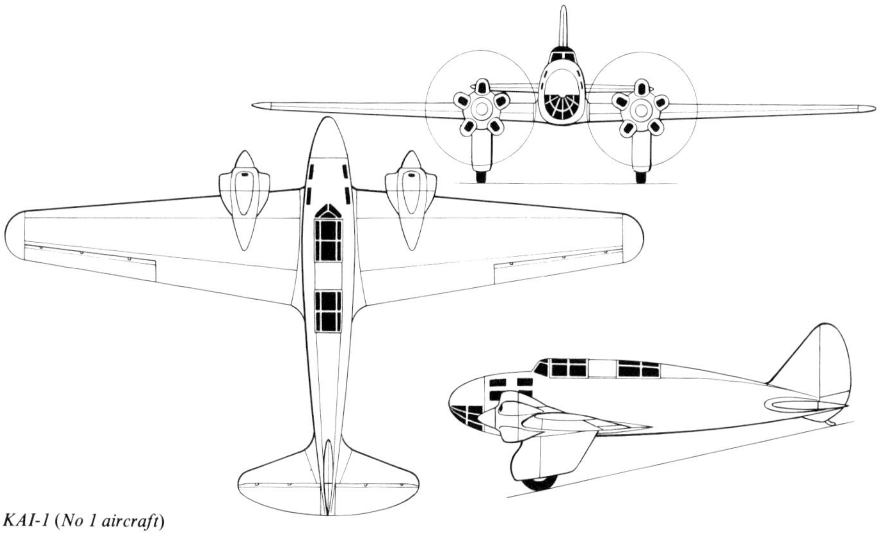

KAI-1 (No 1 aircraft)

UPB

KAI-1 First of Kazan designs, this light twin was a clean cantilever monoplane intended for touring, with pilot and five passengers. Shavrov believes built for local passenger services. Glazed nose for fifth passenger because of intention also to make military version with nav/bomb in nose. Other three passengers in cockpits beside and behind pilot (2 by 2) with two sliding canopies. Structure wooden. Two-spar wing of R-II profile, 14% at root but only 6% at tip, attached to fuselage by four steel fittings. Ailerons of symmetric profile mounted just above level of trailing edge. Zapp-type landing flaps, pulled down against air load by cables; one of first flap installations in country. Monocoque fuselage, elliptical section 1,2 × 0,94 m, ply skin 1,5 to 2,5 mm thick. Tail with tailplane incidence adjustable in flight. Engines with Townend ring cowls on first KAI-1, individual helmeted cylinder fairings on second. Trousered main gears. Second aircraft had additional features for use as bomber crew trainer, smaller wing area (not explained), normal ailerons and only three (occasional four) seats. First KAI-1 flown November 1934 by B.N. Kudrin, who was favourably impressed. Recommendation for production of VVS trainer version followed, not implemented.
DIMENSIONS Span 12,6 m (41 ft 4 in); length 7,9 m (25 ft 11 in); wing area (No 1) 22,3 m² (240 ft²), (No 2) 20,6 m² (222 ft²).
ENGINES Two 100 hp M-11.
WEIGHTS Empty (No 1) 780 kg (1720 lb), (No 2) 855 kg (1885 lb); fuel/oil 200 + 20 kg; loaded (No 1) 1310 kg (2888 lb), (No 2) 1395 kg (3075 lb).
PERFORMANCE Max speed 218 km/h (135·5 mph); climb 3·5 min to 1 km; service ceiling (No 1) 4,8 km (15,750 ft); range (No 1) 1000 km (621 miles)/5 hours; landing speed 70 km/h (43·5 mph).

UPB Third KAI-1 was given this designation from *Uchyebno Perekhodnoi Bombardirovshchik*, training transitional bomber; *perekhod* could mean interim or temporary but in this context meant intermediate stage of training. Almost identical in most respects to KAI-1 No 2 but equipped as dedicated military trainer. Three seats: pilot, nav/bomb in nose and radio/gunner in rear cockpit with hand-aimed DA with 200 rounds. Internal cells in fuselage between wing spars for up to 160 kg of various light bombs hung vertically. First UPB tested by B.N. Kudrin from 11 May 1935; second by A.A. Ivanovskii from 23 July. Good results, and decision to build initial series of 25; but no spare capacity could be found. Third UPB had retractable landing gear.
DIMENSIONS Span 12,65 m (41 ft 6 in); length 7,98 m (26 ft 2¼ in); wing area (No 1) 20,6 m² (222 ft²), (No 2) 20,8 m² (224 ft²).

ENGINES Two 100 hp M-11.
WEIGHTS Empty (No 1) 825 kg (1819 lb), (No 2) 922 kg (2033 lb); fuel/oil (No 2) 130 + 16 kg; loaded (No 1) 1250 kg (2756 lb), (No 2) 1400 kg (3086 lb).
PERFORMANCE Max speed (No 1) 245 km/h (152 mph), (No 2) 232 km/h (144 mph); climb to 1 km (No 1) 1·6 min, (No 2) 3·0 min; service ceiling (No 1) 5,7 km, (No 2) 5,3 km; range (No 2) 1000 km (621 miles); endurance 5 h; take-off 160 m/15 s; landing 120 m/12 s/73 km/h (45 mph).

KAI-2 Attractive dural stressed-skin trainer for combat pilots, with full aerobatic and inverted-flight capability. Low wing with main gears retracting inwards into fuselage immediately behind radial engine cowl. Single seat in enclosed cockpit. No photograph and few details of design, because engine failed to arrive and aircraft never flew.
DIMENSIONS Span 9,0 m (29 ft $6\frac{1}{4}$ in); length 6,5 m (21 ft 4 in); wing area 13,0 m^2 (140 ft^2).
ENGINE One 200 hp MG-21.
WEIGHTS Empty 750 kg (1653 lb); fuel/oil 80 + 10 kg; loaded 960 kg (2116 lb).
PERFORMANCE Not measured, but calculated endurance 2 h.

DKL Last of Itskovich's designs at KAI, this 10-seat passenger transport got its name from *Dvukhmotornyi Krayevoi Linyeinyi*, twin-engined regional liner. Generally similar to RAF-11, and using identical wheel or ski landing gear, but with low/mid wing to leave room for bomb bay (500 kg of various bombs) in projected military version. Cargo hatch 2,2 × 1,2 m in roof of fuselage. All-metal stressed-skin construction, pneumatic-actuated flaps. Prototype flight-tested at KAI from August 1937, with improving stability and control resulting from minor changes. Lack of interest, because too close to RAF-11 and Yak UT-3, and eventually flying halted through lack of finance.
DIMENSIONS Span 15,05 m (49 ft $4\frac{1}{2}$ in); length 9,1 m (29 ft $10\frac{1}{4}$ in); wing area 33,0 m^2 (355 ft^2).
ENGINES Two 300 hp MG-31.
WEIGHTS Empty, not recorded; loaded 3 t (6,614 lb).
PERFORMANCE Max speed 360 km/h (224 mph); service ceiling 6,5 km (21,325 ft); range with 10 passengers 790 km (491 miles).

KAI-6 First known post-war design, primary glider tested 1956.

KAI-7 Project for wooden flying-wing glider with twin fins.

KAI-8 Duralumin competition sailplane, 1957.

KAI-9 Single-seat primary training glider.

KAI-11 Duralumin primary glider, forward-swept wings with full-span fabric-covered ailerons, 1957.
DIMENSIONS Span 9,43 m (30 ft $11\frac{1}{4}$ in); length 5,1 m (16 ft $8\frac{3}{4}$ in); wing area 10,2 m^2 (110 ft^2).
WEIGHTS Empty 70 kg (154 lb); loaded 142 kg (313 lb).
PERFORMANCE Max tow 140 km/h (87 mph); sink 1,1 m (3·6 ft)/s.

KAI-12 Named *Primoryets*, basically all-metal derivative of Czech LF-109 tandem-seat training glider. Flown 1957, made in very large numbers.
DIMENSIONS Span 13,42 m (44 ft $3\frac{1}{2}$ in); length 7,77 m (25 ft 6 in); wing area 20,2 m^2 (217 ft^2).
WEIGHTS Empty 253 kg (558 lb); loaded 433 kg (955 lb).
PERFORMANCE Max tow 140 km/h (87 mph); sink 1,29 m (4·23 ft)/s.

KAI-13 Named *Letayushchaya Koltso* (flying platform); single piston engine, tested 1958.

KAI-14 Famed dural stressed-skin Standard-Class sailplane, forward-swept wing, butterfly tail. Participated in 1965 World Championships.
DIMENSIONS Span 15,0 m (49 ft $2\frac{1}{2}$ in); length 5,82 m (19 ft 1 in); wing area 9,0 m^2 (97 ft^2).
WEIGHTS Empty 195 kg (430 lb); loaded (no water) 260 kg (573 lb).
PERFORMANCE Max dive 250 km/h (155 mph); sink 0,58 m (1·9 ft)/s.

KAI-15 Tailless ultralight; 1960.

KAI-16 Ultralight single-seat aerobatic or tandem trainer.

KAI-17 Dural side-by-side training glider with tandem-wheel gear. Built in large numbers from about 1962.
DIMENSIONS Span 13,0 m (42 ft $7\frac{3}{4}$ in); length 6,22 m (20 ft $4\frac{3}{4}$ in); wing area 17 m^2 (183 ft^2).
WEIGHTS Not published.
PERFORMANCE Max tow 140 km/h (87 mph); sink 1,09 m (3·58 ft)/s.

KAI-18 An-2 type aircraft, not built.

KAI-19 Advanced open-class sailplane, stressed-skin structure with foam-filled movable surfaces and chemically-etched skins. T-tail, elec-retracted wheel, split trailing-edge airbrakes, 70 lit water. Set 92,562 km/h (57·515 mph) round 300-km circuit 1 August 1964.
DIMENSIONS Span 20,0 m (65 ft $7\frac{1}{4}$ in); length 7,96 m (26 ft $1\frac{1}{3}$ in); wing area 14,0 m^2 (151 ft^2).
WEIGHTS Empty 334 kg (736 lb); loaded (no water) 414 kg (913 lb).
PERFORMANCE Max dive 250 km/h (155 mph); best glide ratio 45; sink 0,59 m (1·94 ft)/s.

VTOL Undesignated full-scale model (possibly actual aircraft) of experimental single-seat VTOL aircraft exhibited 1967, no announced designation. One 210 hp M-337 (Czech inverted 6-inline) engine driving two four-blade lift/thrust ducted rotors, pivoting 90° on each side of short fuselage, and ducted four-blade propeller at tail (no other tail surfaces).

KB-2

With title more like designation of an aircraft, *Konstruktor Byuro 2* was active in Leningrad 1934–1938. Full title was KB-2 OVI RKKA (*Otdel Voyennikh Izobretennii* RKKA, department of air invention of RKKA). Formed by three designers, G.M. Zaslavskii, A.S. Bas-Dubov and G.M. Syemenov. Two types, few details.

PI Designation from *Pushechnii Istrebitel*, gun-fighter. Twin-boom pusher with single-seat enclosed cockpit in nose together with two PV-1. Unusual side radiators with engine-driven cooling fan(s). In each wing root, special drum for firing six RS (RS-82?) rockets. Prototype construction discontinued 1936.
DIMENSIONS Span close to 11 m; wing area 17 m^2.
ENGINE One 830 hp M-34R.
WEIGHTS Loaded about 2,5 t (5511 lb).

1967 VTOL, Pegasus badge may suggest name

MPI Designation from *Morskoi Poplavkovyi Istrebitel*, sea floatplane fighter. Conventional configuration with monoplane wing, single seat and central float retracted against fuselage in flight. Project design late 1935, prototype construction August 1937, but never completed. No data.

KB-7

This *Konstruktor Byuro* was organized 1936 from a previous design brigade supervised by A.I. Polyarn in order to create aircraft and rocket vehicles to fly in stratosphere. Funding partly Osoaviakhim. Head of KB, L.K. Korneyev, his deputy Polyarn. So far ahead was its thinking, it does not seem actually to have been able to produce much except paper projects. These included five types of liquid (mainly Lox/alcohol) rockets, **R-03** to **R-07**, with several variations. Another family of engines included ANIR-5 and ANIR-6 and ENIR-7, and there were several variations of these. Vehicles included winged aircraft and ballistic vehicles, among latter being two-stage **R-10c** to reach 100 km height. **R-05v** was a fighter to climb at 40/50 m/s to a height of 50 km with a cruise engine and two solid boost motors for launch. On a more practical note KB-7 also designed, and apparently built, research rockets for Soviet geophysical institute, programme directed by academician O.Yu. Schmidt.

Kharkov KhAI

Indisputably, *Kharkovskii Aviatsionni Institut* established itself as leading aviation institute in the Soviet Union for aircraft design. Its KB was opened in 1930 under Iosif Grigoryevich Nyeman, and until 1941 produced several major types of advanced conception. In 1958 KhAI reopened its KB as student bureau (SKB) confined to ultralight aeroplanes and helicopters.

KhAI-1 With this trim passenger transport Nyeman's design team hit headlines from start. Though KhAI-1 was based squarely on Lockheed's Orion it was nevertheless major achievement and first in country with retractable landing gear and, except for He 70, probably first transport outside USA to demonstrate 300 km/h cruise. Clean low-wing monoplane, entirely of wooden construction with whole surface fabric-covered and finally doped (silver/red). Monocoque fuselage of elliptical section made chiefly from glued *shpon* in 0,5 mm thickness in five or more layers. Integral centre-section with bolted joints to two-spar wings with 1,5 and 2 mm ply skin. Thin ply skin also on ailerons and tail surfaces. Engine in Townend-ring cowl driving two-blade aluminium propeller. Main gears pulled inwards by cables from cockpit hand-wheel until latched under fuselage. Pilot in open cockpit (retouched to look enclosed in some photos); six passenger seats on right of cabin, each with window; central aisle, five windows and door on left. First flight of prototype L-1351 by B.N. Kudrin 8 October 1932. Permission for series production given for use on routes to Ukraine and Crimea from Moscow. Production KhAI-1 reached 324 km/h when tested (state trials) November 1934 by S.I. Taborovskii. Ultimately 43 KhAI-1 delivered 1934-1937, all with enclosed cockpit and sliding hood; used on various routes beginning Moscow/Simferopol. In 1935 military variant **KhAI-1B** (also called KhAI-1VV, from VVS) produced for bomber training; two-seater with 200 kg load of practice bombs hung vertically in fuselage and one fixed and one movable machine guns, two examples converted from production passenger aircraft.
DIMENSIONS Span 14,85 m (48 ft 8⅝ in); length 10,26 m (33 ft 8 in); wing area 33,2 m² (357 ft²).
ENGINE One 480 hp M-22.
WEIGHTS Empty 1630 kg (3593 lb), (−1B) 1724 kg (3801 lb); fuel/oil 310 kg; loaded (both) 2,6 t (5732 lb).
PERFORMANCE Max speed 324 km/h (201 mph); econ cruise (civil) 258 km/h (160 mph); climb 12 min to 3 km; service ceiling 7,2 km (23,620 ft); range 1130 km (702 miles); endurance 4·6 h; take-off 330 m/14 s; landing 240 m/18 s/85 km/h (53 mph).

KhAI-2 A complete contrast, this ultralight trainer was named *Blokha* (Flea), but had nothing in common with Mignet Fleas. Designed under military-glider engineer P.I. Shishov. Tandem open cockpits under parasol wing, mainly wood construction, twin main wheels with nose and tail skids, nose skid being used for bungee launch. Power in cruise from small engine by local engineer P. Labur. Built at Kharkov Young Pioneers Palace in 1936. Successful, but no official interest in production.
DIMENSIONS Span 13,0 m (42 ft 8 in); length 6,2 m (20 ft 4 in); wing area 16,0 m² (172 ft²).
ENGINE One 14 hp Labur 2-inline aircooled.
WEIGHTS Empty 200 kg (440 lb); fuel/oil 10 kg; loaded 370 kg (816 lb).
PERFORMANCE Max speed 80 km/h (50 mph); landing speed 50 km/h (31 mph).

KhAI-3 Named for *Sergei Kirov* and also known as *Aviavnito-3*, this unconventional transport was a project of Aviavnito brigade and designed under supervision of Aleksandr Alekseyevich Lazarev. It was one of numerous *Planerlyet* motor-glider transports of period (1936) intended to reduce costs. Basic concept: all-wing machine with two axial gondolas each with six seats in line, first seat in right unit being for pilot. Engine mounted on truss pylon above wing on centreline in first drawings, but finally placed on leading edge. All-wing idea adhered to closely, with no other parts except fin/rudder and land-

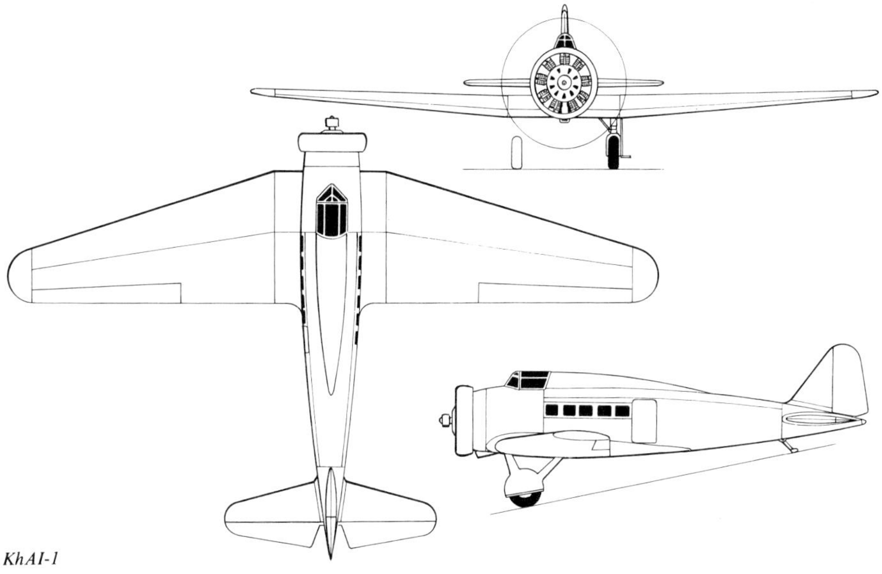

KhAI-1

ing gear. Tapered only on leading edge, giving effective 16° sweep on ¼-chord. Profile V-106 throughout, thickness 14% on centreline and 7% at tip. Rectangular centre section 5 m chord and 4 m span made of welded KhMA steel tube; four spars and six ribs, with covering of 0,5-mm dural. Outer wings, each 9,2 m root to tip, all-wood structures with 8° washout carrying inner and outer trailing-edge controls all driven by single pairs of cables to operate as ailerons or elevators. Flat turns in gliding flight by large rectangular interceptors (operating as airbrakes) near wingtips, opened differentially by pedals; pedals always operated rudder on centreline, with area (inc fin) of 2 m^2. Engine on steel tubes off front spar. Four pairs of wing-root attachments. Tailwheel landing gear, main tyres 800 × 150 mm, ground angle 15°. Four fuel tanks between gondolas for 8 h endurance. First flight 14 September 1936; pilots V.A. Borodin and E.I. Schwartz, prototype having dual control from front of both gondolas. First flight with sustained turns 27 September; results discouraging, with great difficulty in getting good turn no matter how elevons, rudder and interceptors were used or not used. Prolonged effort improved control considerably; stability always satisfactory. No production, though at conclusion of SNII GVF trials overall assessment was positive.

DIMENSIONS Span 22,4 m (73 ft 6 in); length 6,8 m (22 ft 3¾ in); wing area 78,6 m^2 (846 ft^2).
ENGINE One 100 hp M-11.
WEIGHTS Empty 1440 kg (3175 lb); fuel/oil 200 kg; loaded 2200 kg (4850 lb).
PERFORMANCE Max speed 135 km/h (84 mph); cruise 115 km/h (71·5 mph); climb 25 min to 1 km; ceiling 2 km; range 850 km (528 miles); take-off 210 m; landing speed 60 km/h (37 mph).

KhAI-4 Institute's numbering was not consecutive; this small experimental machine antedated KhAI-3 and was probably intended to assist in proving tailless configuration. Single example, named *Iskra* (spark, flash of light) and also *Osoaviakhimovyets Ukrainy* for local branch of Osoaviakhim which helped finance KhAI-4. All-wood tailless tandem-seat ultralight, with relatively high power (same engine as 12-seat KhAI-3). Designers: P.G. Benning, A.A. Lazarev and A.A. Krol, determined despite great difficulties to master difficult layout. Wing tapered on leading edge carrying normal ailerons outboard (65% semi-span) with elevons inboard. All surfaces driven together by handwheel as in KhAI-3; fore/aft pilot input moved inner surfaces only. Fins and rudders on wingtips, with separate pedal control. Streamlined but stumpy central nacelle with enclosed tandem cockpits and pusher engine, uncowled. Short landing gears with balloon tyres; described as first nosewheel-type in USSR but drawings show trad layout with main wheels under leading edge and third wheel under engine. Many elements of KhAI-4 similar in concept to KhAI-3. First flight October 1934 by B.N. Kudrin; inadequate elevon moment to lift nose to take-off angle of attack. Left ground at about 180 km/h; trajectory in undulating flight, Kudrin explaining difficulty controlling in longitudinal plane. Severe problems with ineffectiveness of fin also, and concluded that drastic and unconventional measures needed to achieve positive take-off and controlled flight. Acknowledged dangerous, and after third flight KhAI-4 grounded.

DIMENSIONS Span 12,0 m (39 ft 4½ in); length 4,2 m (13 ft 9¾ in); wing area 21,25 m^2 (229 ft^2).
ENGINE One 100 hp M-11.
WEIGHTS Empty 550 kg (1213 lb); fuel/oil 120 kg; loaded 850 kg (1874 lb).
PERFORMANCE Max speed at SL 180 km/h (112 mph); est service ceiling 3,25 km; design range 600 km (373 miles); landing speed 100 km/h (62 mph).

KhAI-5 (R-10) One of few Soviet aircraft of its day to become known to outside world, this undistinguished machine was one of several competing in 1936 for Ivanov specification for light tactical attack and reconnaissance aircraft for VVS. KhAI-5 was essentially derivative of KhAI-1, with closely related airframe made from wood. Its design was completed well before Ivanov requirement was issued, and in many respects successor to KhAI-1B (–1VV) and a running-mate to KhAI-6, which appeared a year earlier, in 1935. KhAI-6 was one of many Soviet aircraft to use F-series Cyclone engine, and this was again adopted for KhAI-5, in long-chord cowl with radial air shutters at front, driving two-blade Hamilton propeller. Monocoque fuselage with integral centre-section carrying two-spar wings. Unlike KhAI-1 and KhAI-1B, fitted with split flaps; power system (believed electric) worked flaps and KhAI-1 type landing gear. Pilot and radio/gunner widely separated, pilot with sliding canopy and optical sight for two ShKAS in top decking and gunner in power-driven turret aft of wing with single ShKAS (turret design, I.V. Vyenevidov and G.M. Mozharovskii); internal bomb bay for 300 kg bombload (eg, six FAB-50). Small series put in hand at Kharkov 1935 with US engine, and thus three available for NII VVS testing 1936. Generally satisfied VVS demands, but Ivanov competition still held to bring in rival designs. I.G. Nyeman, lead designer of KhAI-5, produced a specially modified version designated Ivanov to fly against ANT-51, Polikarpov Ivanovs and DG-58bis; this prototype built September 1937 and flown April 1938. Long before this, in June 1937, original KhAI-5 had been accepted and ordered into production as R-10 (R, *Razvyedchik*, reconnaissance). Later Ivanovs were undoubtedly better, but R-10 met requirements and was available, whereas rivals were much later in timing. Decision often thought precipitate, and ascribed to Stalin personally. In 1938–1940 Kharkov factory made 490, the first 180 with engine given in data and final 310 with M-62 engine driving VISh-6 pro-

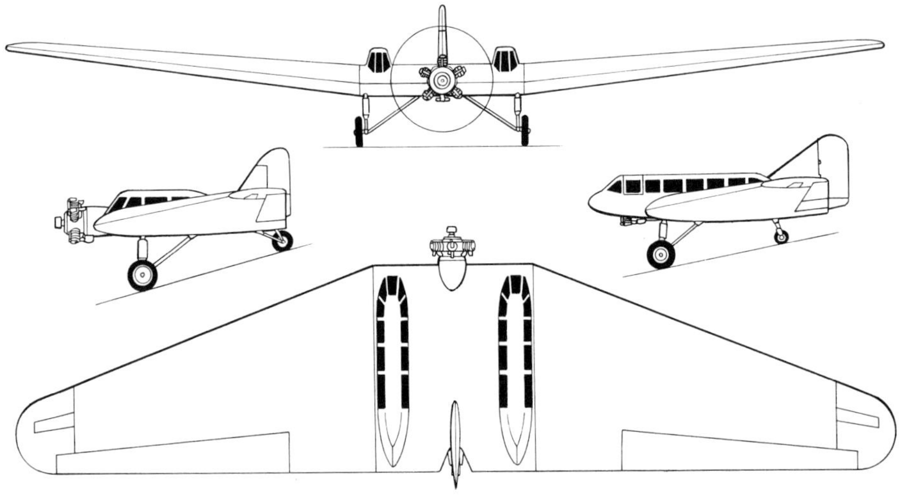

KhAI-3 (side elevation on right as modified)

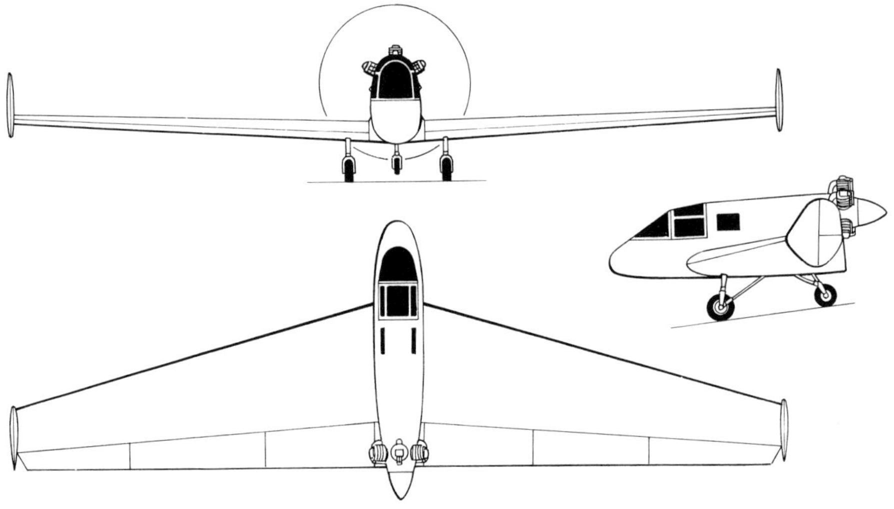

KhAI-4

R-10/KhAI-5

peller (no data for this version). Series aircraft had radio, 8 mm armour on back of pilot seat, heater muff to warm cockpit and blind-flying instruments. Obsolescent in 1939 but saw action on skis in Winter War. In 1940 at least 60 survivors passed to Aeroflot, redesignated **PS-5**, cleared to 2880 kg with three passenger seats and mail or spare parts.

DIMENSIONS Span 12,2 m (40 ft 0⅔ in); length 9,4 m (30 ft 10 in); wing area 26,8 m² (288 ft²).
ENGINE One Wright Cyclone: (prototypes) 710 hp Cyclone SGR-1820-F3; (production R-10) 730 hp M-25B. (later) 830 hp M-62, no data for this.
WEIGHTS Empty (KhAI-5) prototypes 1650 kg (3638 lb), (R-10) 2135 kg (4707 lb); fuel/oil 260 + 30 kg; loaded (KhAI-5) 2515 kg (5545 lb), (R-10) normal 2875 kg (6338 lb), overload 3200 kg (7057 lb).
PERFORMANCE Max speed at SL 345 km/h, (at height) KhAI-5, 388 km/h (241 mph) at 2,5 km, R-10, 370 km/h (230 mph) at 2,9 km; climb (both) 2·4 min to 1 km; service ceiling (R-10) 7,1 km (23,300 ft); range (KhAI-5) 1450 km, (R-10) 1300 km (808 miles); take-off 300 m/15 s; landing 240 m/15 s/93 km/h (58 mph).

KhAI-6 Though produced under I.G. Nyeman's direction at same time as KhAI-1VV and KhAI-5, this unarmed reconnaissance aircraft was a completely different design intended to lead to new family of higher performance. First Kharkov essay in light-alloy stressed-skin construction for certain details including control surfaces (fabric covering) and Zapp-type flaps. Main airframe wood, with monocoque fuselage and two-spar outer wings. Pilot close behind engine and observer/gunner well to rear with opening hatch (note: though called gunner in contemporary accounts, no gun) and remote control of twin or triple cameras covering ground up to 50 km from track. Test-flown by B.N. Kudrin 1935; good behaviour and demonstrated record speed for class. No production because of acceptance of more versatile R-10 using same engine.

DIMENSIONS Span believed 9,3 m (30 ft 6 in); length not known; wing area 14,0 m² (151 ft²).
ENGINE One 710 hp Wright Cyclone SGR-1820-F3.
WEIGHTS Empty not recorded; loaded 1730 kg (3814 lb).
PERFORMANCE Max speed 429 km/h (267 mph) at 2,3 km; no other data.

KhAI-8 This successor to KhAI-3, designed by small group under A.A. Lazarev, was never completed. Prototype begun 1937. Efficient passenger transport of *Planerlyet* (glider) character, same dimensions as KhAI-3 with two six-seat payload pods (called gondolas, as in KhAI-3) with M-11 on nose of each.

KhAI-51 This is covered under KhAI-52.

KhAI-52 Last of Institute's pre-war designs, KhAI-51 was a refined development of KhAI-5/R-10 family almost identical to Ivanov prototype completed April 1938. According to Shavrov, wing had D-16 dural plate spar webs covered with glued ply, with ply skin. Differed also in heavier armament comprising seven ShKAS with 3,500 rounds (presumably six fixed and one at rear) and 400 kg (882 lb) bombload. Prototype flown 1939, but deferred in favour of more powerful KhAI-52, designed under A.A. Dubrovin. Institute attempted to get main R-10 orders switched to this much superior machine, and did succeed in getting order for small series in 1939.

DIMENSIONS Span (51) 12,2 m (40 ft 0⅔ in), (52) 13,42 m (44 ft 0⅓ in); length (51) 9,4 m (30 ft 10 in), (52) 9,6 m (31 ft 6 in); wing area (51) 26,8 m² (288 ft²), (52) 26,73 m² (287·7 ft²).
ENGINE (51) one 830 hp M-62, (52) 900 hp M-63.
WEIGHTS Empty (51) 2380 kg (5247 lb), (52) 2546 kg (5613 lb); fuel/oil (52) 520 + 53 kg; loaded (51) 3220 kg (7099 lb), (52) 3376 kg (7443 lb).
PERFORMANCE Max speed (51) 358 km/h (222 mph), (52) 410 km/h (255 mph) at 4 km; climb (51) 16 min to 5 km; service ceiling (51) 8,8 km (28,870 ft); range (51) 1000 km (621 miles); no other data.

KhAI-17 Resurrected as a student SKB in 1957 or 1958, KhAI continued to number projects out of chronological order. This was first of attractive series of pusher ultralights of late 1960s designed by student team assisted by O.K. Antonov as advisor. KhAI-17 set pattern with cantilever low wing, nosewheel fixed gear, enclosed cockpit (single-seat) and pusher propeller above single tail boom. Wooden construction except for fabric rear of main spar and on all control surfaces. High aspect ratio; whole trailing edge slotted ailerons or manual slotted flaps. Flown on 30·5 hp M-61K geared to four-blade propeller on 30 April 1967.

KhAI-18 Immediate successor to KhAI-17, planned as more powerful two-seater; dropped in favour of KhAI-20.

KhAI-19 Completely fresh start after war, believed first project of SKB, designed late 1950s by group led by V. Reshetnikov and flown with Dosaaf support 1962. Conventional low-wing single-seater, all-wood except fabric aft of spar and on control surfaces. Rubber bungee shock absorption, steerable nose gear immediately aft of unusual four-blade two-position propeller driven via reduction gear. Trailing edge entirely slotted ailerons and manual slotted flaps. Successful; probably cannibalized to build KhAI-17.

DIMENSIONS Span 7,5 m (24 ft 7¼ in); length 5,2 m (17 ft 0¾ in); wing area 9,55 m² (103 ft²).
ENGINE One 30·5 hp M-61K.
WEIGHTS Empty 200 kg (441 lb); loaded 312 kg (688 lb).
PERFORMANCE Max speed 140 km/h (87 mph); claimed range on 27 lit (5·9 gal) 600 km (373 miles).

KhAI-20 Final form of rebuilt KhAI-17, by group led by V. Lyushin, with much more powerful engine (from Meta-Sokol and installed with Czech two-blade propeller hub with blade angles reversed as pusher). First flown 1968.

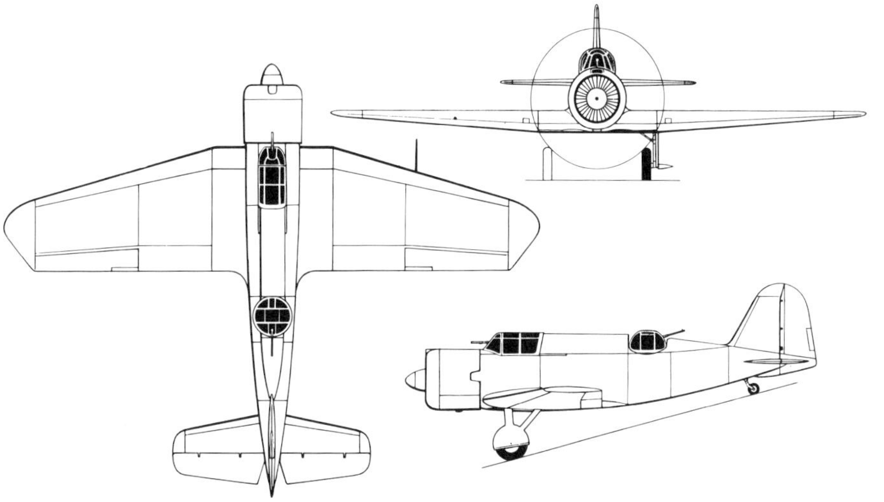

R-10

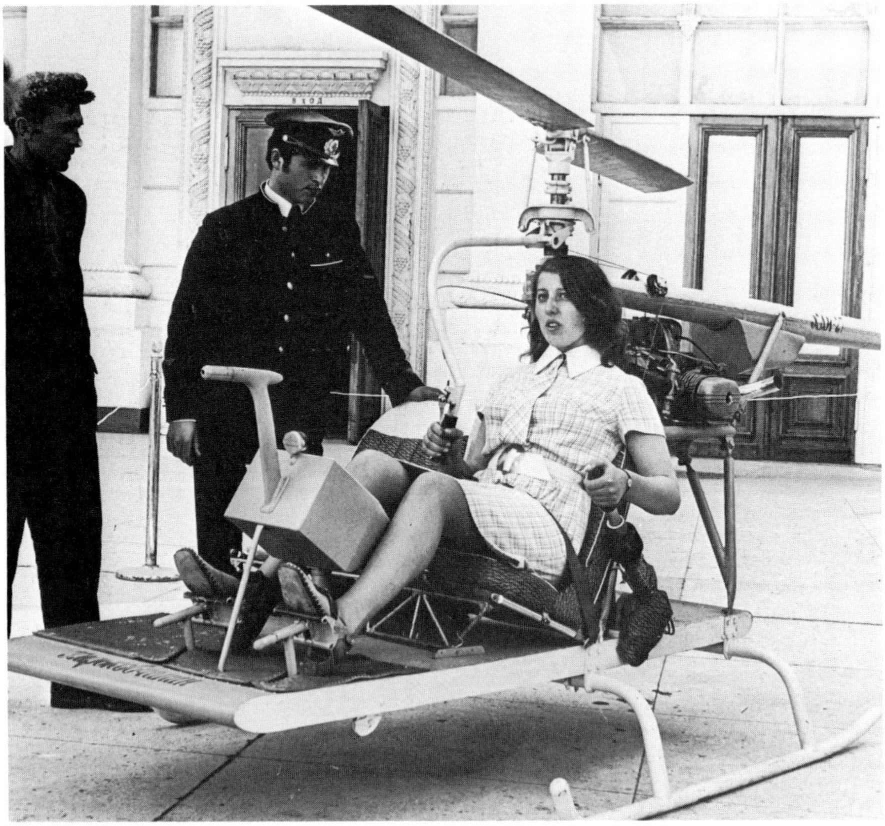

KhAI-27 with designers

KhAI-21

DIMENSIONS Span 10,44 m (34 ft 3 in); length (inc nose probe) 6,8 m (22 ft $3\frac{3}{4}$ in); wing area not recorded.
ENGINE One 140 hp Avia M-332 inverted 4-in-line.
WEIGHTS Not recorded.
PERFORMANCE Max speed reported 180 km/h (112 mph), should have been much higher; take-off and landing reported 180 m; no range or ceiling quoted.

KhAI-21 Single-seat ultralight Rogallo-wing aircraft, M-61K engine.

KhAI-24 Most ambitious Kharkov SKB project, commissioned by Estonian Ministry of Power. Tandem-seat cabin autogyro designed by group under B. Mysov. Mixed construction with three-blade articulated rotor and light-alloy boom carrying twin-fin tail. Tricycle gear, nose unit mounted off steel-tube bearers for same engine as KhAI-20 driving same tractor propeller. Completed 1965; no information on production.
DIMENSIONS Main rotor 9,96 m (32 ft 8 in); length (ignoring rotor) 7,8 m (25 ft 7 in).
ENGINE One 140 hp (derated to 115 hp) Avia M-332.
WEIGHTS Empty 614 kg (1354 lb); loaded 800 kg (1764 lb).
PERFORMANCE Max speed 150 km/h (93 mph); cruise 100 km/h (62 mph); min speed 40 km/h (25 mph); range not recorded.

KhAI-22A Single-seat ultralight helicopter, exhibited 1968. Welded tube airframe with tricycle gear, carrying flat-twin engine (probably M-61K from KhAI-17) at front. Stabilizer bar at 90° to main two-blade rotor.
DIMENSIONS Main rotor 5,4 m (17 ft $8\frac{1}{2}$ in).
WEIGHTS Empty 130 kg (287 lb); loaded 220 kg (485 lb).
PERFORMANCE Max speed 100 km/h (62 mph); ceiling (forward flight) 2 km (6560 ft).

KhAI-27 Fresh attempt at light helicopter; not a rebuild. Flat platform with skid gear supporting side-by-side seats, left having collective on left, cyclic passing in front of pilot and back over head to hub of new two-blade rotor without stabilizer bar, pedals to tail rotor carried on light-alloy tube. Same engine but relocated behind occupants' shoulders under tail boom. Exhibited 1970. Loaded about 300 kg; no performance data.

Khioni

Vassili Nikolayevich Khioni was born 1880 and qualified as engineer 1905. In the First World War he was a lead designer at Anatra works at Odessa, assisting in several of that company's designs. He died in 1930.

VKh Anadva Neat twin-engined twin-fuselage combat aircraft similar structurally to Khioni Anadye series but larger. Also named *Dvukhvostka* (twin-tail) and Anatra-Khioni No 4. Mainly wood, part ply covering especially on fuselages. Five seats, two pilots with dual control, two rear gunners (one nav/bomb, one observer) and third gunner in nacelle on upper wing. Small bombload. Completed 30 June 1916

VKh Anadva

and flown 9 July 1916. Next aircraft more powerful, see Anasalya below.
DIMENSIONS Span 19,0 m (62 ft 4 in); length 7,7 m (25 ft 3¼ in); wing area 62,0 m² (667 ft²).
ENGINES Two 100 hp Gnome Mono rotary.
WEIGHTS Empty and loaded not recorded; fuel/oil 160 + 45 kg; useful load 600 kg (1323 lb).
PERFORMANCE Endurance 3 h; no other data.

VKh Anasalya Also called Anadva-Salmson, second VKh series with more powerful engines and minor airframe changes. First flight 5 may 1917. Order for 50 for EVK (squadron of flying ships, then equipped exclusively with IM-series Sikorskis); October Revolution came before deliveries began.
DIMENSIONS Span 19,1 m (62 ft 8 in); length 8,1 m (26 ft 7 in); wing area 62,0 m² (667 ft²).
ENGINES Two 140 hp Salmson M9 water-cooled radials.
WEIGHTS Empty 1280 kg (2822 lb); fuel/oil 180 + 30 kg; loaded 1930 kg (4255 lb).
PERFORMANCE Max speed 140 km/h (87 mph); climb 7·6 min to 1 km; service ceiling 4 km (13,120 ft); take-off and landing 60 m (200 ft).

Khioni No 4 Construction interrupted by Civil War, but by 1921 Khioni had completed this improved VKh (not same aircraft as 'Anatra-Khioni No 4') with more powerful engines (water radiators on upper wing) and considerably greater fuel capacity. Built Odessa and successfully flown to Moscow where based at Central Aerodrome; damaged by taxiing Nieuport early 1922 but repaired. From late 1922 'several tens' of successful test flights by K.K. Artseulov and P. Stolyarov. In 1923 handed to Serpukhov gunnery and bombing school.
DIMENSIONS As VKh Anasalya.
ENGINES Two 160 hp Salmson P9 water-cooled radials.
WEIGHTS Empty 1300 kg (2866 lb); fuel/oil 410/40 kg; loaded 2160 kg (4762 lb).
PERFORMANCE Max speed 140 km/h (87 mph); climb 7·7 min to 1 km; service ceiling 4,4 km (14,440 ft).

Khioni No 5 Named *Konyek-Gorbunok* (hunchback hobbyhorse), neat single-engined biplane built Odessa 1923, at former Anatra plant redesignated Air Repair Factory 7. Tandem-seat dual trainer, tested at both Odessa and Moscow. Modified with tank of insecticide powder for anti-locust patrol (believed first agricraft in world) and 30 delivered by 1928.
DIMENSIONS Span (upper) 11,46 m (37 ft 7¼ in); length 7,8 m (25 ft 7 in); wing area 37,0 m² (398 ft²).
ENGINE One 100 hp Fiat 6-inline water-cooled.
WEIGHTS Empty 700 kg (1543 lb); fuel/oil 110 kg; loaded 975 kg (2149 lb).
PERFORMANCE Max speed 122 km/h (76 mph); climb 9·8 min to 1 km; service ceiling 3,5 km (11,480 ft); range 480 km (298 miles).

Kochyerigin

Sergei Aleksandrovich Kochyerigin was born in 1893. In 1914–1915 he trained as military pilot and fought with Imperial Air Service, almost entirely on seaplanes and flying boats. In 1917 appointed test pilot at Moscow Central Aerodrome. This brought him into contact with N.N. Polikarpov who appointed him, with A.A. Krylov, chief deputy for aircraft design at OOS on its formation at GAZ-25 in spring 1926. Just four years later he went with Polikarpov to TsKB on its formation, being appointed head of Reconnaissance Aircraft brigade. He led design of several combat aircraft in pre-war era from KB at Moscow Menzhinskii factory, but never succeeded in opening his own OKB and faded from scene after his first fighters failed to be accepted in 1941–1942. He died in 1953.

LR Though a modification of ubiquitous R-5 this was such a major redesign it deserves separate inclusion here. LR (sometimes called LR-1) from *Legkii Razvyedchik*, light reconnaissance. Also designated TsKB-1 as first numbered project at TsKB. Requirement was R-5 replacement with more engine power and reduced weight, able to manoeuvre like contemporary fighter at speed as close as possible to 300 km/h. Authorized January 1932 together with A.N. Tupolev rival which was never built. Basic design similar to R-5 and used many common parts, but sig-

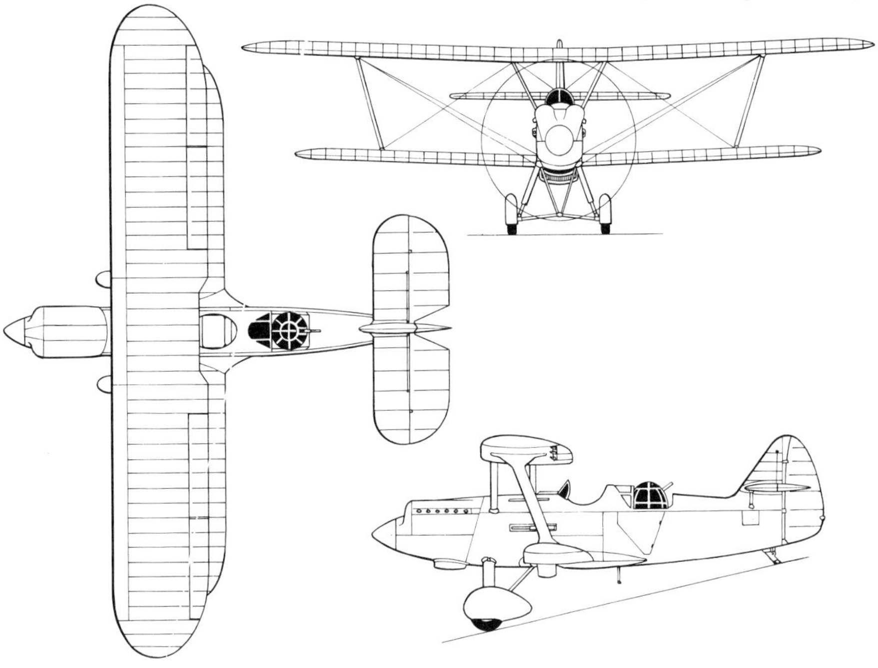

LR

LR (No 1 aircraft)

nificantly smaller. Wooden wings, Göttingen 436 section, 11% thick. Single I-type interplane struts. Fuselage truss welded Cr-Mo steel tube, dural sheet and panels forward, from cockpit to tail light dural sheet and fabric. Tail and ailerons, dural with fabric covering. Two-spar braced tailplane unusually high on fin, adjustable angle in flight. Landing gear as R-5 but air/oil shock struts filled with 90/10 mix glycerine/alcohol. State trials on skis, but wheels had disc brakes, first in USSR. Pilot cockpit open, with left wall folding down for access. Observer/gunner with light-weight glazed turret rotating 360° (one ShKAS) with jettisonable door on left side. Single synchronized PV-1 fired ahead by pilot with optical sight. Bombload 200 kg, usually 2 × 100, 4 × 50 or 8 × 25. First flight June 1933 and NII State tests early 1934. Two built (see data). Production decision in favour of R-Z.

DIMENSIONS Span (upper) 13,0 m (42 ft 7¾ in); length 8,64 m (28 ft 4¼ in); wing area 36,52 m^2 (393 ft^2).

ENGINE One 750 hp M-34, (No 2 prototype) 815 hp M-34N.

WEIGHTS Empty 1734 kg (3823 lb), (No 2) 1812 kg; fuel/oil 275 kg, (No 2) 300 kg; loaded 2426 kg (5348 lb), (No 2) 2626 kg.

PERFORMANCE Max speed 271 km/h (168 mph) at SL, (No 2) 314 km/h (195 mph) at height; climb 2 min to 1 km; service ceiling 7,4 km (24,278 ft), (No 2) 9,1 km; range 800 km (497 miles); take-off 210 m/13 s; landing 250 m/18 s/94 km/h (58 mph).

TSh-3 Also designated TsKB-4, this was one of first armoured *Shturmoviks* (designation from *Tyazhelyi Shturmovik*, heavy armoured attacker) and was unusual for its day (1932) in being a monoplane. Designed to meet requirement of VVS by Kochyerigin staff led by M.I. Guryevich (later partner of Mikoyan), with overall support of S.V. Ilyushin, at time head of TsKB. Remarkably well armed and protected, but thus heavy and rather unwieldy. Construction mainly metal and fabric. Two-spar low-mounted wing tapered from second main rib each side inwards to root in plan chord and thickness as well as towards tip. At second rib, two compression struts bracing wing to top of fuselage. Duralumin truss/plate spars and ribs, fabric covering. Struts, steel tubes, faired with thin dural. Long-span two-part slotted ailerons drooping neutral point 15° to serve as flaps on landing. Basic fuselage and tail structure of welded steel tube, fabric covering, with duralumin keel girder and bulkheads, especially supporting structure for armour. Forward fuselage enclosed by box of bolted armour sections. Frontal thickness 8 mm, complete underside and side 6 mm, top 5 mm across fuel tank. Water radiator and piping protected by 6 mm armour (radiator retractable). Trousered main gears, wheels 900 × 200 mm, rubber shock-absorption, disc brakes. Crew of two in tandem, both fully armoured. Ten ShKAS installed in wing, firing from leading edge in two batteries of five immediately beyond propeller disc. Inner wing also contained six cassettes (three each side) each containing six frag bombs; additional hardpoints under outer wings for four 100 kg or (eventually) eight RS-82 when available. First flight by V.K. Kokkinaki spring 1934. Probably best of current TSh prototypes but, though met specified 1932 performance, was judged rather sluggish by 1934 standards. Real problem was disenchantment in basic concept, so will to improve TSh-3 with more powerful engine was lacking.

DIMENSIONS Span 16,5 m (54 ft 1½ in); length 10,75 m (35 ft 3¼ in); wing area 45,04 m^2 (485 ft^2).

ENGINE One 830 hp M-34F.

WEIGHTS Empty 2665 kg (5875 lb); fuel/oil 230 + 30 kg; loaded 3557 kg (7842 lb).

PERFORMANCE Max speed 247 km/h (153·5 mph) at SL, about same at height; climb 10·7 min to 3 km; service ceiling 5,8 km (19,030 ft); range 470 km (292 miles); endurance 2·5 h; landing speed 95 km/h (59 mph).

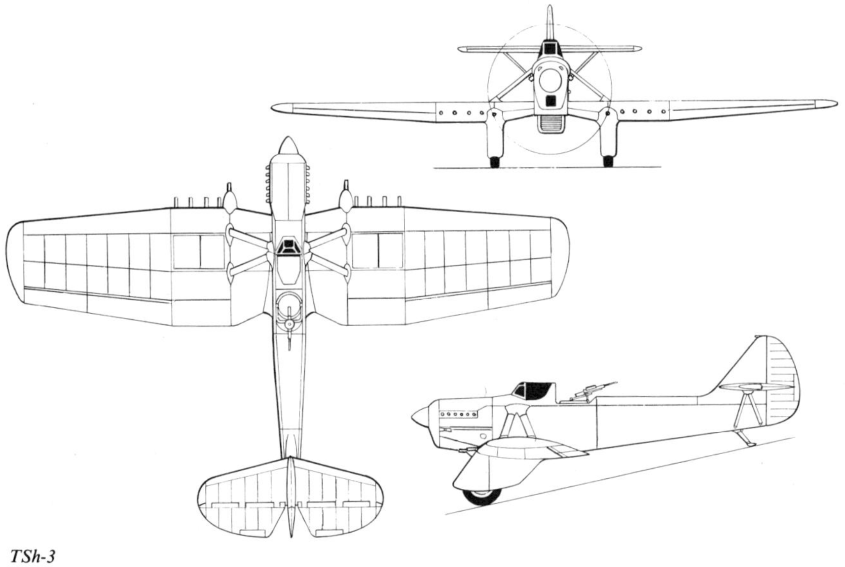

TSh-3

LR-2 Projected further development of LR begun late 1933, for flight late 1934. AM-34RN engine, variable-pitch propeller, fully enclosed crew compartment (but apparently no turret) and cantilever main gears with spatted wheels. Prototype never completed.

DI-6 One of the few Soviet aircraft of pre-war era to become known outside the Soviet Union, this two-seat fighter was a typically advanced design (comparing favourably with contemporary Hawker Hind) but saw action only after it had become obsolescent. Design by Kochyerigin in partnership with Vladimir Panfilovich Yatsyenko as **TsKB-11**, started November 1934. Wire-braced biplane with N cabane struts but I interplane struts. Fuselage welded KhMA steel tube, with integral cabane struts and upper centre section. Wings otherwise wooden, two-spar, with ply leading edge and fabric covering. Slotted ailerons with inset hinges. Interplane struts D6 dural with central spar and riveted aerofoil. All tail and control surfaces D6 dural with fabric covering. Fuselage covered in D6 removable panels back to cockpit, fabric aft. Welding by hydrogen, first Soviet use of technique. Engine of prototype imported Wright SR-1820-F3 (Wright 720 hp, Soviet figure 630 hp) in NACA cowl with Eclipse-Pioneer electric starter and driving adjustable metal propeller (later, two-position Hamilton). Main gears with welded KhGSA struts hinged to both spars of lower wing, retracted inwards by cable pull on unlatched lateral bracing struts whose upper ends slid up vertical guide. Wheels 750 × 125 mm, Dowty internally sprung (produced later without licence). Single fuel tank of riveted D1. Pilot and observer back-to-back, former in open cockpit with optical telescope sight and observer with side and top glazing. One ShKAS with 750 rounds in dural fairing under each lower wing, one ShKAS with 750 rounds in rear cockpit. Four bomb beams in fuselage (Der-32,

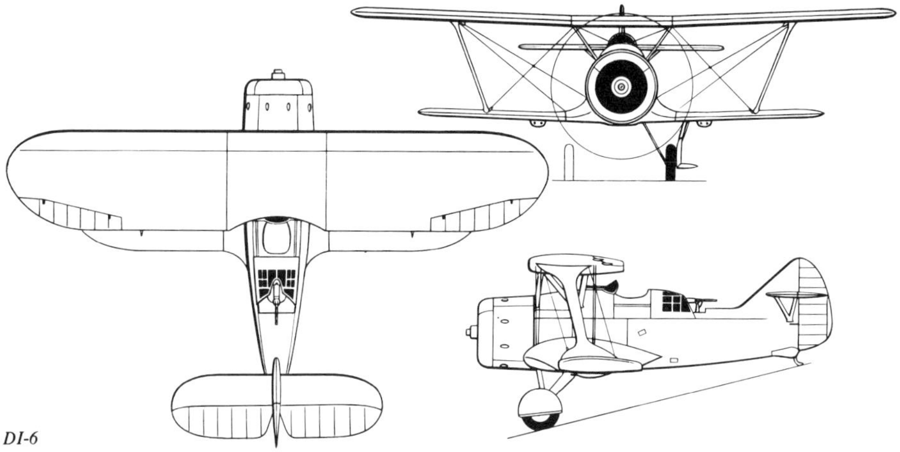

DI-6

TsKB-11 (DI-6 prototype)

DI-6

Esbr-3) each for one or two bombs of 8 or 10 kg. State trials by Fedorov and Stepanchenok 27 May to 21 November 1935. TsKB-11 ordered in series of 200 as DI-6 (*Dvukhmestnyi Istrebitel*, two-seat fighter). Delay in M-25 production, so no issue to VVS until spring 1937. One regiment engaged in fighting with Japanese in Khalkin-Gol and related regions 1938–1940. Many destroyed on ground 22 June 1941; few participated in Winter War or Second World War.

Second prototype completed as **TsKB-11Sh**, later redesignated **TsKB-38**. *Shturmovik* with 8 mm armour around crew and two pairs of PV-1 (not ShKAS) under lower wings. Judged rather ponderous but produced as **DI-6Sh**, 60 delivered in parallel with DI-6, completed October 1938. **DI-6MMSh** ((*Malya Modifikatsika Shturmovik*) with experimental M-300 engine; single aircraft completed except for engine 1940 (other modifications unknown) but engine not cleared for flight. **DI-6bis**, also called *Samolyet 21* (aeroplane 21), intermediate trainer with simple fixed landing gear (speed reduced 25/30 km/h) and dual flight controls (obtained, with instruments, from damaged UTI-4s); some dozens thus modified 1950–1941. **DI-6OS** (*Opyshyennyi Stabilizator*, trimmed stabilizer) single aircraft with flight-adjustable tailplane. **DI-6DU** (*Dvoinyi Upravlenii*, war control) with no rear gun and dual control (not same as DI-6bis) for air fighting and bombing instruction; small series of rebuilds.

DIMENSIONS Span 10,0 m (32 ft $9\frac{3}{4}$ in); length 7,0 m (22 ft $11\frac{1}{2}$ in); wing area 25,15 m² (271 ft²).
ENGINE One 700 hp M-25; (6bis) 750 hp M-25V.
WEIGHTS Empty (series) 1360 kg (2998 lb), (6Sh) 1434 kg (3161 lb); fuel/oil 172 + 20 kg (6Sh, 162 + 20); loaded 1955 kg (4310 lb), (6Sh) 2115 kg (4663 lb).
PERFORMANCE Max speed 324 km/h (201 mph) at SL, 372 km/h (231 mph) at 3 km; climb 4·9 min to 3 km; service ceiling 7,7 km (25,260 ft); range 500 km (311 miles); time for 360° circle 12 s; take-off 200 m/10 s; landing 250 m/25 s/95 km/h (59 mph).

SR Believed to be first prototype built to meet January 1934 NTK specification for SR (*Skorostnoi Razvyedchik*, fast reconnaissance) aircraft. Launched as **TsKB-27**, tandem two-seat mid-wing monoplane to undertake fighter and light bombing missions also. Unexpected, mixed construction with well-streamlined wooden monocoque fuselage. Wings metal with two truss spars hydrogen-welded and riveted from KhMA steel tube, dural ribs (some truss, some flanged sheet) and skin of D6 in 0,6 to 1,5 mm, countersunk flush riveting. All-dural Zap flaps. Ailerons and tail, D6 and fabric; elevators and rudder with trim tabs. Main gears with tall single struts off front spar carrying internally sprung wheels with 800 × 150 mm tyres, twin lateral bracing struts broken and pulled in by hydraulic system energized by compressed-air cylinder recharged by pump on engine, wheels housed in fuselage. Engine in NACA cowl driving three-blade metal propeller, ground-adjustable in first TsKB-27, v-p in others. Armament, two ShKAS in rear cockpit with sliding canopy and pintle mount (some reports claim 20 mm cannon firing ahead, not mentioned in Soviet literature); internal bay with two hand crank doors for up to 400 kg (882 lb) various bombs. Three prototypes built 1935–1936. Prolonged difficulty with land-

SR (cowling panels removed)

ing gear retraction, and general policy was to leave extended, cutting speed to just 100 km/h short of requested 460 km/h. But basic aircraft promising (460 km/h was attained in clean condition, see data, but argument over interpretation of figures). KB authorized to proceed with further model, R-9.

DIMENSIONS Span 12,0 m (39 ft 4½ in); length 9,9 m (32 ft 5¾ in); wing area 24,15 m² (260 ft²).
ENGINE One 670/780 hp Gnome-Rhône 14Krsd Mistral Major.
WEIGHTS Empty 1862 kg (4105 lb); fuel/oil 260 + 30 kg; loaded 2649 kg (5840 lb).
PERFORMANCE Max speed 380 km/h (236 mph) at SL, 460 km/h (286 mph) at 4 km; climb 2·2 min to 1 km; service ceiling 9 km (29,530 ft); range 840 km (522 miles); take-off 350 m; landing 380 m/104 km/h (65 mph).

R-9 Experience with SR enabled Kochyerigin brigade quickly to produce good multi-role aircraft for reconnaissance, fighting and bombing duties. Airframe essentially same as TsKB-27 and no separate KB number issued. Crew remained widely separated, but observer was given remarkable low-drag turret for single ShKAS, possibly hydraulic drive and advanced for period. Modified rear fuselage and broad rounded vertical tail. Forward firing guns added in wings: two 20 mm ShVAK and two ShKAS. Fixed landing gear with oleo-pneumatic shock struts (not sprung wheels) cantilevered from fuselage and with leg fairing and spat; 750 × 250 mm balloon tyres. Improved bomb bay but same maximum load of four FAB-100. Production engine to be M-86, but prototype flown December 1936 with one of first Tumanskii-produced M-85s in Bristol-type cowl with front collector ring and rear gills; Hamilton three-blade propeller. Generally judged better than R-10, but latter already ordered.

DIMENSIONS Span 12,0 m (39 ft 4½ in); length 10,0 m (32 ft 9¾ in); wing area 24,15 m² (260 ft²).
ENGINE One 800 hp M-85.
WEIGHTS Empty 1940 kg (4277 lb); fuel/oil 260 + 30 kg; loaded 2730 kg (6019 lb).
PERFORMANCE Max speed 366 km/h (227 mph) at SL, 447 km/h (278 mph) at 4,5 km; climb 2·2 min to 1 km; service ceiling 8350 m (27,395 ft); range claimed 1300 km (808 miles); take-off 360 m; landing 400 m/105 km/h (65 mph).

LBSh Also called just **Sh**, this was a *Legkii Bronnirovannyi Shturmovik*, (light armoured at-

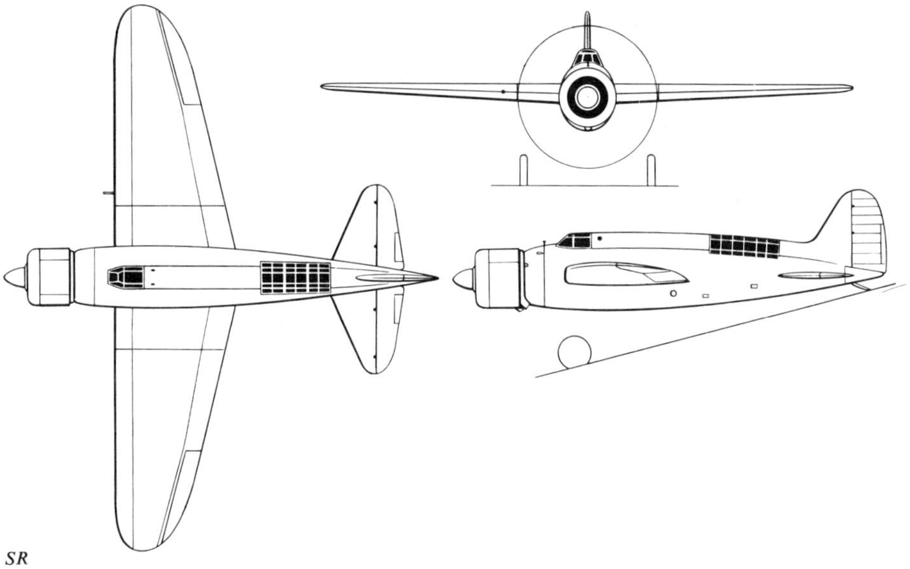

SR

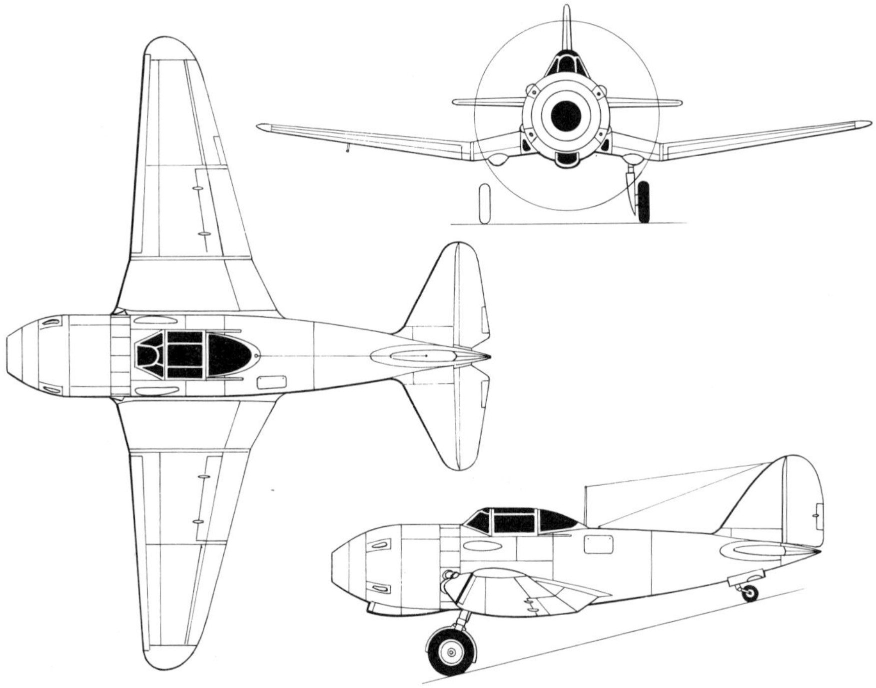

OPB-41

tacker) derived from R-9. Not certain if prototype ever completed. Similar but, because of delay of two years, more powerful engine was available to combat weight (240 kg, 529 lb) of considerable armour up to 8 mm round cockpits and other vital areas. VISh-22Ye propeller, armament same as R-9. Dimensions as R-9.
ENGINE One 950 hp M-87A.
WEIGHTS Empty not recorded; loaded 3450 kg (7606 lb).
PERFORMANCE Max speed 350 km/h (217 mph) at SL, 439 km/h (273 mph) at 4,5 km; climb 2·3 min to 1 km; service ceiling 9820 m (32,220 ft); range 1300 km (808 miles); landing speed 115 km/h (71·5 mph).

BSh-1 In 1936 Kochyerigin's brigade was assigned task of overseeing investigation of imported Vultee V-11 all-metal attack bomber and making recommendations on possible modifications. Detailed and well-documented reports, agonizing indecision centreing on intense technical interest, lower rear defence with third crew-member but several manufacturing difficulties. Eventually series of 36 (some reports state 31) constructed as BSh-1 (armoured attacker 1). Different licensed Cyclone model, Hamilton propeller, only two crew so no lower rear gun, but ShKAS in rear cockpit and four more fixed in wings, bombload 250 kg (551 lb). Landing gear retracted reliably, impressing Kochyerigin, but VVS trials caused many arguments and final outcome was rejection in December 1938, same month as delivery of 36th aircraft. Early 1939 decision to pass whole batch to Aeroflot, which soon put them into service as **PS-43** mail aircraft on such routes as Moscow to Kiev and to Tashkent. Some, possibly all, were commandeered during Second World War as military liaison aircraft, a few still being in VVS service in this role in late 1947.
DIMENSIONS Span 15,24 m (50 ft 0 in); length 11,35 m (37 ft 2¾ in); wing area 35,67 m² (384 ft²).
ENGINE One 750 hp M-62IR.
WEIGHTS Empty 2911 kg (6418 lb) (V-11 typically 5100 lb); loaded 4056 kg (8942 lb).
PERFORMANCE Max speed 339 km/h (211 mph); service ceiling 7,3 km (23,950 ft); range 913 km (567 miles) (most V-11s much greater).

OPB-41 Designation *Odnomestnyi Pikiruyushchii Bombardirovshchik*, single-seat dive bomber. Kochyerigin himself led design. Looked like fighter and was planned around one of most powerful engines in world in mid-1938. Essentially attempt to build Ju 87 that could take care of itself in combat. Mainly metal stressed skin, forward fuselage being duralumin monocoque and two wing spars having plate webs and rolled T or L booms. Rear fuselage wood monocoque. Inverted gull wing with anhedral centre-section leaving room for wide but shallow bomb bay beneath. Root section NACA-230, 14% thick. Main gears hydraulically retracted to rear in centre-section, legs faired but wheels (tyres 750 × 250 mm) fully housed after rotating 90° and largely enclosed by plate on leg. Retractable tailwheel. Outer wings with full-span slats, D6-skinned ailerons and upper and lower dive brakes (90°) immediately ahead of hydraulic slotted flaps. Fin and tailplane wood, rudder/elevators D6 with fabric. Large engine in very advanced installation with ducted spinner previously investigated by TsAGI for I-190 and I-185R; three-blade propeller (3,1 m, 122 in), ejector exhausts, ventral oil cooler, electrically driven gills. According to one record all fuel in fuselage (capacity limited, see weights). Single-seat cockpit with sliding canopy and good rear view. Two BS with 440 rounds (upper) and two ShKAS with 1700 rounds in sides, firing through front of cowl. Normal bombload one 500 kg (1102 lb), carried on special mechanism to ensure clean separation without hitting propeller. First prototype test-flown 1941, while estimates made of 584 km/h with ASh-82A and 593 km/h with ASh-71 which were more fully-developed engines. Promising, but unreliability of engine, poor short-term prospect of engine maturity and adequacy of mass-produced Pe-2 killed OPB-41 at time when numbers and timing mattered more than performance. Note: This aircraft often called just OPB, and in some Russian literature **OKB-5**.
DIMENSIONS Span 10,4 m (34 ft 1½ in); length 8,28 m (27 ft 2 in); wing area 18,0 m² (194 ft²).
ENGINE One 1500 hp M-90.
WEIGHTS Empty 2806 kg (6186 lb); loaded 3842 kg (8470 lb).
PERFORMANCE Max speed (500 kg bomb) 600 km/h (373 mph) at 5,7 km (18,700 ft); service ceiling 9,9 km (32,480 ft); range (500 kg bomb) 660 km (410 miles); landing speed (full flaps and slats) 123 km/h (76·5 mph).

Kolpakov

Leonid Dyementyevich Kolpakov-Miroshnichyenko qualified as engineer before turn of century, and in First World War worked at Lebed company where he led design of several aircraft incorporating numerous innovations. Chief among latter was complete installation for machine-gun in cabin aircraft, for which he received royalty of 50R per ten sets supplied to Lebed production. Own designs follow.

K-1 In full, Kolpakov-1, outwardly conventional tandem two-seat reconnaissance biplane with 110 hp Austro-Daimler 6-inline, flown 1916. Unusual in that entire wing cellule variable incidence 7° pivoting about lower front spar; manual screwthread.

Lebed XIV Also called Lebed-Grand, three-bay biplane called *Bolshoi Istrebitel*, large fighter. Two 150 hp Salmson, streamlined near-circular section fuselage with gunners in nose and aft of unequal-span wings, pilot in line with leading edge. Three guns in all, speed 140 km/h (87 mph). Ordered 1916, flown first half 1917.

LB-2LD Designation from *Lyegkii Bombardirovshchik* (light bomber) with two Lorraine-Dietrich engines. Development of Lebed-Grand, but unable to be drawn, far less built, until after civil war. Two-bay biplane with crew of four. All wooden construction except for struts which were steel tube. Fabric covering, except for occupied part of fuselage which was oval-section plywood semi-monocoque. Design load four guns and 500 kg (1102 lb) of bombs. Intended engines never installed, and those fitted were only half as powerful. Prolonged difficulties with structural strength and deflection in flight, during test programme begun spring 1926 by K.K. Artseulov and Ya.G. Paul. Careful static test showed need for detailed reinforcement, and as R-1 and TB-1 formed adequate team there was no need for production, and rectification never carried out.
DIMENSIONS Span 23,0 m (75 ft 5½ in); length 16,0 m (52 ft 6 in); wing area 140 m² (1,507 ft²).
ENGINES Two 240 hp Fiat A-12.
WEIGHTS Empty 3200 kg (7057 lb); loaded approx 6200 kg (13,670 lb).
PERFORMANCE No figures except max speed 150 km/h (93 mph).

Kolyesnikov

Dmitri Nikolayevich Kolyesnikov was involved in design of several gliders from about 1930, and in RMK-1 powered aircraft (with Romyeiko-Gurko). Later designed aircraft below with P.V. Tsybin.

KTs-20 Few details survive of this troop-carrying assault glider built 1940 to same requirement as SAM-23. (Some reports state 1943 but original Soviet sources give earlier date.) Designed to carry 20 armed troops (some recent sources give number as 16). Cantilever high-wing monoplane (recent sources say 'braced') of all-wood construction (recent sources 'mixed construction'), ply skin back as far as main spar. Ruling hold cross-section 1,75 m (69 in) square, with nose manually hinged to right for loading small vehicles or artillery up portable ramps. Door on left side of forward fuselage. Two-seat pilot cabin at upper level ahead of leading edge. Span about 22 m (72 ft), length about 15 m (49 ft). Landing at 85 km/h (53 mph) on combined wheel and skid gear. Built in small series (recent reports, 'did not reach series production'). No further data or photograph, and not known if direct ancestor of Tsybin Ts-25.

Komta

After 1917 Revolution, only air services in Soviet Union were operated by IM-type bombers converted for transport operations by DVK (*Divisionye Vozdushnii Korablei*, flying ships division, successor to Tsarist EVK squadron of flying ships which had operated same aircraft as bombers). Clear need for transport aircraft led to formation in spring 1920 of KOMTA (or KOMPTA), *Kommissii po Tyazheloi Aviatsii*, commission for heavy aviation. Chairman Prof N.Ye. Zhukovskii, most famous Soviet aerodynamicist and founder of TsAGI. Members B.N. Yuryev, V.P. Vyetchinkin, V.A. Arkhangyelskii, V.L. Moiseyenko, V.L. Aleksandrov, A.A. Baikov, M.V. Nosov, A.M. Chyeremukhin, K.K. Baulin and A.N. Tupolev. DVK engineers under Aleksandrov submitted proposal for transport based on IM but KOMTA

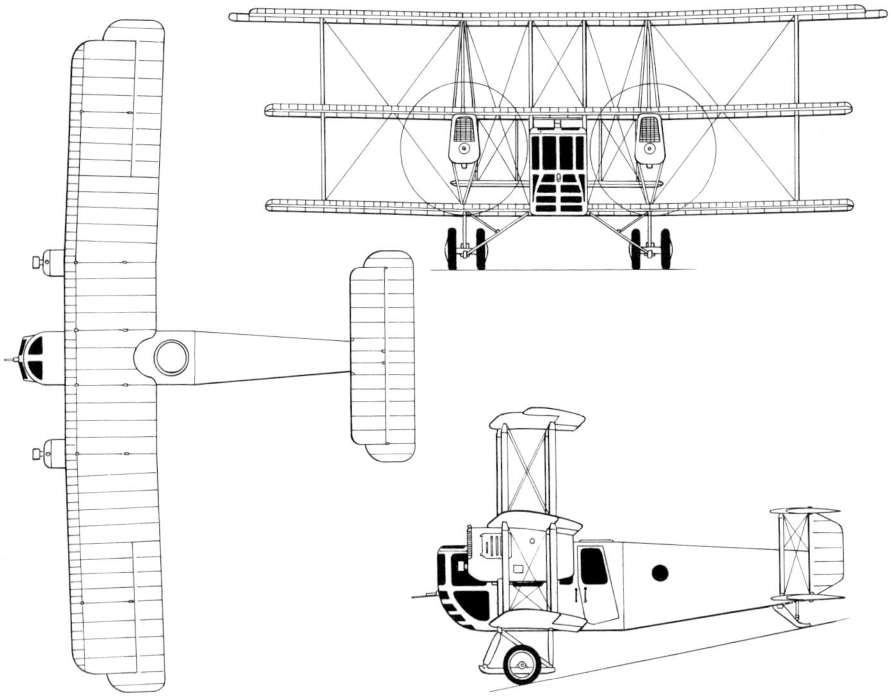

Komta

decided outdated and planned its own aircraft.

Komta No separate designation, though sometimes rendered *Kometa* (Comet). Planned as triplane for compactness and large yet robust lifting area; Zhukovskii 'raised no objection'. Several configuration studies and model tests in first Soviet wind tunnel in summer 1920. Influenced by contemporary Bristol Braemar, Tramp and Pullman, though Komta much smaller. Eventually engines not in fuselage but on wings, direct drive to large two-blade propellers. Old wartime engines, but available from stock and reliable. Structure almost identical in principle to IM-series, with wooden parts joined by small pressed and/or welded mild-steel fittings which also anchored bracing wires. Fabric covering overall. Wing profile better than IM as result of tunnel tests, but underside still concave. Nine ailerons, biplane tail with two tailplanes and elevators (large horn balances like ailerons) and four rudders (no fins). Tailskid and either four main wheels or two skis. Internally wire-braced fuselage with up to 10 seats, normally two pilots and six/eight passengers, all boarding via door on left. Parts made by DVK at Sarapul and assembled at Aviarabotnik, Moscow. Complete March 1922. Test flown by DVK commander V.M. Remezyuk. Could hardly fly, partly lack of power but mainly CG too far aft. Major reconstruction followed, in course of which engines were moved forward 1 m (39 in). Second series of flights by A.M. Chyeremukhin autumn 1923, and by A.I. Tomashyevskii and B.N. Kudrin spring 1924. Inadequate performance, and no production. Parked (gate guardian) at front of Serpukhov air-firing school.

DIMENSIONS Span 15,0 m (49 ft 2½ in); length 9,7 m (31 ft 10 in); wing area 91,0 m^2 (979·5 ft^2).
ENGINES Two 240 hp Fiat A-12.
WEIGHTS Empty 2650 kg (5842 lb); loaded 3550 kg (7826 lb).
PERFORMANCE Max speed 130 km/h (81 mph); ceiling 600 m (1968 ft).

Korolyev

Sergei Pavlovich Korolyev was born 30 December 1906 at Zhitomir. After basic technical-school training he entered aircraft design in 1927, gaining admission to both top aviation schools in Moscow: Bauman Higher Technical School and Moscow School of Aviation. He designed and built light aircraft which flew 1930, in which year he graduated from both schools. By 1930 also qualified pilot with national reputation on gliders. Never lost interest in aeroplanes and gliders (eg, SK-7) but was so excited by Tsiolkovskii's writings that he began studying rocketry and was appointed head of MosGIRD (Moscow group for study of rocket propulsion). When Marshal M.N. Tukhachyevskii ordered setting up of RNII on 21 September 1933 Korolyev was appointed deputy chief, and six months later became first head of its winged-aircraft department. In 1942 made deputy chief designer at GDL-OKB. He made it a point of being as closely involved as possible with hardware, and not only flew as flight engineer but twice piloted such aircraft as Pe-2R and La-120R. In 1945 appointed faculty member at Kazan University, and at Bauman school, and from this time onwards became not only chief designer of GDL-OKB's large rocket engines but leading technical architect of Soviet Union's immense ICBM and space programmes. He died, laden with honours, on 14 January 1966.

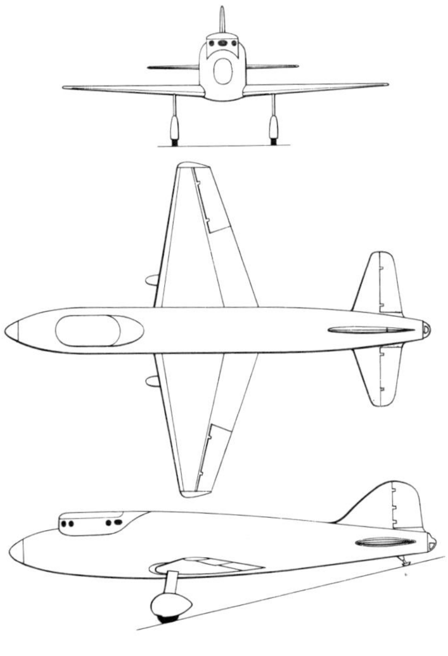

Korolyev design for rocket aircraft to follow RP-318

SK-4 Dubbed *Dalnyego Deistviya*, long-range action, this was intended to be efficient cruising tandem two-seater. Wood construction, monocoque fuselage with 1,5 mm ply skin, and entire braced high wing with aspect ratio 8·17 was also covered with thin ply. Dual control. Six small tanks for 12 hour endurance. First flown 1930; programme halted after pilot-error crash.

DIMENSIONS Span 12,2 m (40 ft 0¼ in); length 7,1 m (23 ft 3½ in); wing area 15,3 m^2 (165 ft^2).
ENGINE One 60 hp Walter.
WEIGHTS Empty 335 kg (739 lb); fuel/oil 190 kg; loaded 690 kg (1521 lb).
PERFORMANCE Max speed 150 km/h (93 mph).

SK-7 Korolyev could not resist becoming involved with rash of motor-glider transports of 1936. This, joint project with P.V. Flerov, had cantilever low wing of span smaller than most. Conventional layout with pilot ahead of five passenger seats, trousered main gears and separate belly cargo compartment. Built at OSGA SNI GVF, work discontinued late 1937 when almost complete.

DIMENSIONS Span 20,7 m (67 ft 11 in); length 9,0 m (29 ft 6¾ in); wing area 39,2 m^2 (422 ft^2).
ENGINE One 100 hp M-11.
WEIGHTS Empty 780 kg (1720 lb); fuel/oil 180 kg; loaded 1660 kg (3660 lb).
PERFORMANCE Max speed calculated 128 km/h (80 mph).

RP-318 In amongst SK-4 and SK-7 were Korolyev's gliders, and one of these, SK-9, formed basis for one of world's first rocket aircraft, designed 1936 to test ORM-65 engine. This engine was developed under V.P. Glushko, burning RFNA (red fuming nitric acid) and kerosene. SK-9 was two-seat glider originally flown 1935. To fly rocket engine it was converted as single-seater, with quite complicated propellant and control system: vertical D1 tank behind seat for 10 kg kerosene, with two vertical stainless-steel tanks total 40 kg of RFNA between wing spars. Thrust chamber at extreme tail, below cut-back rudder. Further details of ORM-65 in Engines section. No 1 engine fired 20 times on bench, nine in Korolyev's Type 212 winged missile and 21 times in RP-318, latter from February 1937. RP-318 flown as towed glider several times, but no attempt to fly on rocket power until modified ORM-65, with improved 'man-rated' installation, had been

cleared in static testing. First rocket flight 28 February 1940, pilot V. P. Fyedorov. Towed by R-5 pilot Fikson, passengers Pallo and Shchyerbakov (later head of own OKB). After 31 min cast off at 2600 m at 80 km/h; after 5–6 seconds speed 140 km/h and pilot then climbed at 120 km/h for 110 seconds gaining 300 metres. Photo taken by Shchyerbakov. Subsequently RP-318 flown several times, finally with propellants for 30 min.
DIMENSIONS Span 17,0 m (55 ft 9¼ in); length 7,44 m (24 ft 5 in); wing area 22,0 m² (237 ft²).
ENGINE One RDA-1 (ORM-65 derived) rocket, thrust 70–140 kg, normal 100 kg (220 lb).
WEIGHTS Empty 570 kg (1257 lb); propellants and gas feed 75 kg; loaded 700 kg (1543 lb).
PERFORMANCE Speed held to 140 km/h (airframe limit).

Kozlov

Sergei Grigoryevich Kozlov was professor at Zhukovskii VVA throughout first half of 1930. He supervised design of three challenging aircraft, though none was completed.

Gigant Needing no translation, this was first of truly giant bombers to be projected in the Soviet Union, followed later by those from TsAGI Tupolev KB. Apparently no record of team members, but begun as full-scale Academy project December 1931. No known numerical designation. Structure basically welded KhMA steel, fabric covering, with some duralumin skin. Mainly enormous wing, with spars so long and deep (3 m) that hinges were inserted to give pin instead of rigid joints (presumably calculations were too onerous). Engines strung along front spar inside wing, in nose-to-nose pairs, each driving gearbox to vertical shaft to tractor propeller on vertical pylon, three propellers above each wing. Short central nacelle for crew of 18–22 with 15 guns and large bombload. Tail carried on twin booms. Static testing of twin-engine group (called *Sparki*, twin) suddenly broke gearbox and front drive-shaft, money running out thereafter in 1933.
DIMENSIONS Span greater than 60 m (197 ft); wing area approx 600 m² (6500 ft²).
ENGINES Six pairs of coupled 730 hp M-17F.
WEIGHTS Loaded, more than 40 t.

PS Designation not explained, because full name was *Nyevidimyi Samolyet*, invisible aircraft. Full Academy project of 1935. AIR-4 was used as basis, entire surface being covered with Rodoid, patented French organic-glass material. Objective was to create aircraft whose approach would be almost imperceptible. Just how aircraft invisible not explained, though intention obviously to make it transparent. Apart from existence of inevitably opaque structure, engine, occupants and other parts, great difficulty found in getting effective result, and cowling, wheels, cabin and struts were not successfully made transparent. As far as possible opaque parts painted silver-white. Rodoid glass sheet then attached by eyelets and aluminium rivets. First flight 1936. Eventually results considered to have achieved 'measure of importance'. Seen from ground, flying PS not seen at first glance as were other aircraft, and often noticed only when observer knew just where to look (height, and accuracy of binaural hearing direction, are in quantified records). Prolonged trials with observers from above as well as below, at varying distances. Effect of Rodoid-type skin deteriorated by cracks, and aircraft performance also suffered slightly. Eventually discontinued, but certainly only prolonged officially supported project of type ever undertaken.

EI Sometimes called **EOI** (*Eksperimentalyni Odnomyestnyi Istrebitel*, experimental single-seat fighter). Project by Zhukovskii academy 1939, Kozlov assisted by M. M. Shishmaryev (landing gear), D. O. Gurayev (deputy chief constructor), V. S. Chulkov (wing) and S. N. Kan and I. A. Sverdlov (calculations). Main feature that low wing of 9,2 m span had variable incidence, driven by irreversible Acme-thread on rear spar about ball-bearing trunnions on front spar roots. Spars mixed steel booms and duralumin webs with glued birch *shpon* covering. Fuselage oval-section duralumin monocoque. Engine 1650 hp M-107. Prototype built at outside factory. Severe technical difficulties, project ran late and on 16 October 1941 prototype and drawings destroyed and factory evacuated.

A.A. Krylov

Aleksei Aleksandrovich Krylov is one of least-known constructors. No relation to V. Ya. Krylov.

R-II Also known as **P-1** (*Perekhodnyi Pyervyi*, interim No 1), this pedestrian two-bay biplane was strictly First World War technology and used one of the old wartime engines which at start of design in 1923 were all that were available. R-II for *Razvyedchik* (reconnaissance) No 2, intended as replacement for R-1 (D.H.9) which itself confusingly had variant designated R-II. Mostly wood/fabric, but metal-covered nose. Two seats in tandem, intended to carry free machine-gun and synchronized gun firing from left side. Few details survive. Interest lapsed after first flight in 1925 because offered no advantage over existing R-1.
DIMENSIONS Span 11,5 m (37 ft 8¾ in).
ENGINE One 260 hp Maybach Mb IVA 6-inline.
WEIGHT Loaded 1650 kg (3638 lb).
PERFORMANCE No data.

Krylov R-II

V. Ya. Krylov

This designer worked at GVF Leningrad in 1930s, and collaborated with other constructors on two successful light marine aircraft.

AT-1 Joint project with I.N. Vinogradov for three-seat sporting and light transport aircraft 1935. Low-wing cantilever monoplane with trousered main gears and fully cowled engine driving propeller with spinner. Mixed construction. Fuselage built on Warren-braced truss of welded steel tube with metal and plywood covering. Centre-section welded steel tube, duralumin covering. Outer wing panels of R-II-C profile 16% at root, 10% at tip, three (probably wooden) spars, ply covering. Split flaps between ailerons including underside of fuselage. Prototype professionally built at Moscow aviation technical secondary school. Completed late 1935 and made more than 30 flights.
DIMENSONS Span 11,8 m (38 ft 8½ in); length 7,0 m (22 ft 11½ in); wing area 22,0 m² (237 ft²).
ENGINE One 100 hp M-11.
WEIGHTS Empty 750 kg (1653 lb); fuel/oil 72 + 12 kg; loaded 1070 kg (2359 lb).
PERFORMANCE Max speed 180 km/h (112 mph); service ceiling 4 km; range 450 km (280 miles); landing speed 60 km/h (37 mph).

ASK Designation from *Amfibiya Severnogo Kraya* (amphibian for northern territory), sponsored autumn 1935 by Glavsevmorput. Cantilever monoplane with twin boat hulls and tractor engine on pylon above wing at centreline. Design led by Krylov in partnership with I.M. Zharnylskii, G.I. Bakshayev and L.S. Vildegrub. All-wooden construction. Two-spar wing with ply-covered centre-section and fabric outer panels. Hulls stoutly built with multiple frames and bulkheads but without internal stringers, though strong keel. Two steps on concave planing

Krylov-Rentel MA-1

bottom giving weak wake. Ply skin basically 3mm thick, increased to 6mm over planing bottom and 8mm at steps. Twin booms carrying three-finned tail. Pilot in open cockpit in small nacelle ahead of leading edge on centreline. Each hull equipped for three passengers, front seat having direct view ahead, or 600 kg cargo. Landing wheels on inner sides of hulls, raised backwards except when needed. Some photographs retouched to show gears pivoted below wing, but leg pivot was on side of hull, with bracing strut to underside of wing at front spar. Skid at rear of each planing bottom. Construction began a year after start of design and ASK flew spring 1935, test pilots B.V. Glagolyev and P.P. Skarandayev. Satisfactory, but one landing gear broke in October 1936 and ASK beset by several other troubles culminating in complete write-off in flood of autumn 1937.

DIMENSIONS Span 20,8 m (68 ft 3 in) (not 17,4 m); length 12,9 m (42 ft 4 in); wing area 66,4 m² (715 ft²) (not 46,4 m²).

ENGINE One 480 hp M-22.

WEIGHTS Empty 2450 kg (5401 lb); fuel/oil 400 kg; loaded 3450 kg (7606 lb) (not 4 t).

PERFORMANCE Max speed 215 km/h (133·5 mph); climb 7 min to 1 km; service ceiling 4,1 km (13,450 ft); range 700 km (435 miles); endurance 4 h; take-off 300 m/20 s; landing 170 m/9 s/95 km/h (59 mph).

MA-1 Designation from *Mestnaya Amfibiya*, regional amphibian, this was GVF project undertaken from 1938 jointly by Krylov and Vladimir Fedorovich Rentel. Straightforward transport with echoes of ASK in hull shape and landing gear. Cantilever high wing with 30° dihedral gull centre-section integral with hull and outer panels with spars at 15 and 60% chord of wood construction with ply skin 2 mm to rib 9 on each side and then 1,5 mm to rib 20 at tip. Ailerons and tail control surfaces light wood/fabric built up on ply-sheathed nose box. Fin and high braced tailplane ply skinned. Particularly effective flaps of ply construction hinged to multiple brackets to descend to 60° whilst also increasing wing area (no evidence of tracks or projecting hinges in photographs). Single-step hull skinned in 3 mm ply (4 or 5 mm near step), sides braced by diagonal truss frames, finally covered with fabric and doped. Light and compact landing gear (though narrow track) with wheels or skis raised pneumatically to lie along sides of hull. Simple Townend-ring cowl mounted on N-strut pylon above centreline and driving fixed-pitch tractor propeller, soon replaced by 2,74 m VISh (Hamilton). Stabilizing floats later fitted on two struts well inboard from tips, not installed in most photographs. Prototype No 3 completed December 1939 equipped for two pilots side-by-side and four passengers with separate doors to cockpit and cabin. Successful early flying on skis from January 1940; later in year floats installed and tested from Leningrad Old Port. September 1940 flown to Moscow by A.V. Krzhizhyevskii with flight engineers A.M. Tyetyeryukov and V.V. Zhivoglyadov. Demonstrated against Sh-7 4 October at Khimki River station for Aeroflot, where a fast or badly judged landing broke landing gear on airstrip causing severe gash in planing bottom. Repairs stopped by war.

DIMENSIONS Span 14,0 m (45 ft 11¼ in) (Němeček 13 m); length 11,82 m (38 ft 9¾ in) (Němeček: 9,4 m); wing area 29,6 m² (319 ft²) (Němeček: 23,6 m²).

ENGINE One 330 hp MG-31F.

WEIGHTS Empty 1450 kg (3197 lb); fuel/oil 220 kg; loaded 2200 kg (4850 lb).

PERFORMANCE Max speed 210 km/h (130 mph) at SL; climb 4 min to 1 km; service ceiling 4,3 km (14,100 ft); range 700/1200 km (435/746 miles); endurance given as 4 h (low); take-off 215 m/11·5 s; landing 107 m/10·2 s/84 km/h (52 mph).

Kurchyevskii

L.B. Kurchyevskii was designer of APK series of large-calibre cannon (see Armament section). In 1935 Marshal Tukhachyevskii got him to organize a USP (control of special work) within NKTP for construction of fighters armed with these guns. He issued invitations to aircraft constructors to join USP: B.I. Chyeranovskii, S.A. Lavochkin and V.B. Shavrov (whose resulting Sh-3 is described under his own heading). All were at work by spring 1935, but a year later Kurchyevskii was arrested and USP closed.

IL Designated from *Istrebitel Lavochkina*, (Lavochkin's fighter); joint project with S.N. Lyushin (deputy) and also called **LL** from both designers. Appearance similar to IP series but with pilot low in fuselage seeing through periscope. Seat and hinged windscreen raised for landing or for better view in emergency. Prototype built, but no photograph or data. Mock-up inspected at outset 12 January 1936 by Gen Ya.I. Alksnis of VVS, who often visited to see progress. Eventually concluded problems were not worth solving, and VVS did not approve seat-raising method proposed.

BICh-17 Chyeranovskii's fighter (see BICh) followed typical *parabola* lines, with extremely stumpy fuselage with 480hp M-22 on nose. Gull wing with 5° dihedral to mid-span, then anhedral to tip. Inboard of highest point on each wing was 80 mm APK, just beyond propeller disc and with rear barrel dividing flaps into inner and outer sections. Wooden construction, ply/*shpon* skins, twin-wheel main gears retracting inwards. Enclosed cockpit faired into squat fin as usual. Discontinued when 60% complete when USP terminated as aircraft works February 1936. By that time it had several other projects including BICh-type fighter with DRP guns and another APK-armed fighter begun by P.D. Grushin at MAI.

LAK

Brief mention deserved of important Lithuanian SSR glider group Litovskaya Aviatsionnaya Konstruktsiya, begun 1969 by Balis Karvyalis (chief designer), Vitautas Pakarskas (director) and Bronyus Oshkinis. First product was **BRO-11** (1954 design by Oshkinis), followed by **BK-7** (confusingly, earlier Lithuanian glider series by Boris Kaunas stopped at BK-6) from which stemmed large and well-documented series of competition sailplanes of glassfibre/epoxy construction culminating at time of writing in **LAK-12.** Good reputation, several designs including BRO-11 and BRO-11M produced in numbers for Dosaaf training.

Laville

André Laville was one of three French designers invited to work in USSR by Aviatrust in 1928. First employment was with fellow-countryman P.A. Richard at OPO-4 where he drew plans for two-seat fighter based to some degree on Nieuport-Delage designs on which Laville had worked a year previously. When Richard began to find political troubles in 1930 he left OPO-4 and in August began to organize his own Buro Novyikh Konstruktsii (bureau of new designs), BNK, in Moscow. BNK folded 1933, Laville going to factory work for NII GVF. In 1935 he became Russian correspondent for Paris newspaper, and returned to France January 1939. He is seldom mentioned in accounts of his aircraft.

DI-4 Two-seat fighter derived from design prepared at OPO-4. Parasol wing strut-braced to main gears, twin lateral Lamblin radiators and twin-finned tail for good field of fire to rear. Wing profile MOS-27, gull-winged and increasing in thickness from fuselage to standard 16% over horizontal outer portions. Excellent pilot view, first fuselage-joined gull wing in USSR All-duralumin construction, ruling skin thickness 0,5–0,6 mm. Finely streamlined monocoque fuselage and cantilever tail, with special features ensuring stability of Y-strut under each wing and smoothness of tail skins. Four PV-1, two synchronized and two aimed from rear cockpit. Prototype completed early 1933. Factory test-flying by B.L. Bukholts and Yu.P. Piontkovskii, State trials by K.K. Popov. Altogether DI-4 did quite well, only adverse comment being marginal yaw stability 'and effectiveness of tail generally, but reason for rejection was absence of other production requirement for US engine (Laville might have selected available engine; in any case, engine type could have been changed).

DIMENSIONS Span 13,3 m (43 ft 7⅝ in); length 8,5 m (27 ft 10⅝ in); wing area 23,9 m² (257 ft²).

ENGINE One 600 hp Curtiss Conqueror V-12.

WEIGHTS Empty 1448 kg (3192 lb); fuel/oil 200 + 30 kg; loaded 1949 kg (4297 lb).

PERFORMANCE Max speed 266 km/h (165 mph) at SL, 238 km/h (148 mph) at 5 km; climb 7·4 min to 3 km; service ceiling 6440 m (21,130 ft); range 500 km (311 miles); endurance 2 h.

PS-89 (ZIG-1) This attractive passenger airliner was designed by Laville immediately after DI-4, as major project of NII GVF in about May 1933 immediately upon closure of BNK. Cantilever low-wing monoplane, all-duralumin construction with flush-riveted stressed-skin covering except for fabric flight-control surfaces. Designed for highest possible performance, surpassing that of contemporary biplane fighters, yet with maximum security (eg, well-established engines and fixed landing gear). Wing of aspect ratio nearly 11, with three spars, multiple stringers and power-driven landing flaps (shown as split type in drawings). Well-streamlined fuselage with three long but shallow windows each side, squat vertical tail and tailplane braced by double struts. Well-cowled engines with underslung radiators, faired into trousered main gears. Equipped for two pilots and 12 passengers in six pairs facing each other across small tables. Prototype construction assigned to GAZ-89, major aircraft-repair works known as *Zavod Imyennyi Goltsman* (works named for Goltsman), or ZIG, hence designation. Ready for trials spring 1935, after final inspection and refinement by A.V. Kulyev. Factory tests began satisfactorily, but on 27 November 1935 tailplane broke away while gliding in to land (there were rumours of sabotage) and aircraft dived in, killing pilot Ablyazovskii, Kulyev and crew of four engineers. Remarkably, work was allowed to continue, and Aeroflot bought six ZIG-1 with designation PS-89 (*Passazhirskii samolyet*, factory 89). Production aircraft supervised by Pyetr Ivanovich Eberzin, and first was tested spring 1937. All delivered by late 1938 and four proving flights made on Moscow-Simferopol route. Results described as perfect, and PS-89 thereafter established excellent record in several thousand hours' regular line operation. (3-view, see page 152.)

DIMENSIONS Span (Shavrov, Něměcek) 28,11 m (92 ft 2⅝ in), (several other sources) 23,1 m (75 ft 9¼ in); length 16,245 m (53 ft 3½ in); wing area 72 m² (775 ft²).

ENGINES Two 730 hp M-17F.

WEIGHTS Empty 5 t (11,023 lb) (one German source: 4,9 t); fuel/oil 800 + 60 kg; loaded 7,2 t (15,873 lb) (German source 7,1 t).

PERFORMANCE Max speed 284 km/h (176 mph) at SL; cruise 244 km/h (152 mph); climb 5,7 min to 1 km; service ceiling 4,4 km (14,435 ft); range 1300 km (808 miles); take-off 23 s; landing speed 95 km/h (59 mph).

LAK-12 (in rear, Blaniks)

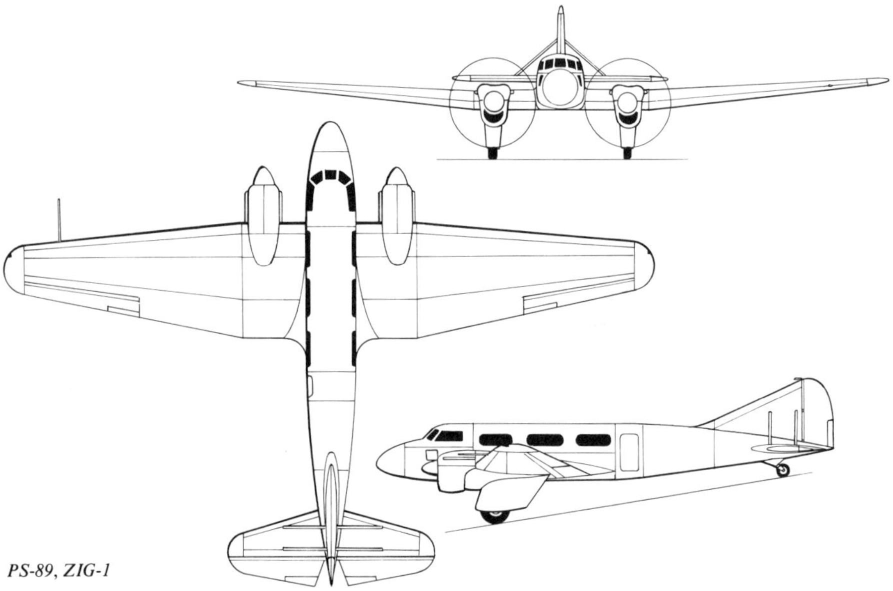

PS-89, ZIG-1

Lavochkin

Syemyen Alekseyevich Lavochkin was born Smolyensk 11 September 1900. After revolution joined Red Army, but in 1920 gained admission to Moscow technical high school to study engineering, later specializing in aviation and assisting in stressing ANT-3 and ANT-4 at TsAGI. Graduation 1929, joined Richard at TsKB, moving to BOK in 1931. In late 1934 collaborated with BRIZ of Glavsevmorput on design of boats and other craft and became increasingly involved with *Kaplyurit*, invention of BRIZ's O.F. Kaplyur, plastic-impregnated plywood reinforced with internal steel gauze. Within a few months assigned to Kurchyevskii's USP to build IL (LL); on closure of USP in 1936 assigned to GUAP as senior engineer. Intimate contact several programmes while spent much time at factory of Leontii Iovich Ryzhkov (products, propeller blades and skis) studying *delta-drevesiny* developed mainly by Ryzhkov from 1930 as tough fire-resistant material made from compressed plastic-impregnated laminates of birch (similar to UK's Jablo and Rotol densified woods). By August 1938 Lavochkin convinced such materials could be of great strategic importance for military aircraft, reducing drain on steels and light alloys without seriously compromising aircraft performance. Teamed up with V.P. Gorbunov and M.I. Gudkov (both mentioned previously) to build *delta* fighter, and received permission by M.M. Kaganovich, GUAP Commissar, to open OKB. Effective 15 September 1938, in premises vacated by liquidated Silvanskii OKB. Lavochkin attended Kremlin conference January 1939 called to discuss strategy for future combat aircraft and received permission to build prototype designated I-22. At same time production base granted, and this was found in GAZ-301, former Moscow furniture works used as OKB-301 by A.A. Dubrovin, developing Caudron fighters, and also for manufacture of Yak BB-22 fuselages. Dubrovin went to improve R-10 at Kharkov, deputy A.G. Brunov joined new MiG bureau and LaGG (Lavochkin, Gorbunov, Gudkov) OKB-301 expanded mainly by hiring design engineers from BNK (Laville) and Grigorovich bureau. Subsequent fighters described below. Success of La-5 and derivatives brought Lavochkin three Orders of Lenin, but from 1945 his large and famous OKB was consistently placed second in competitions with other bureaux, notably MiG, and achieved merely long succession of prototypes. But for its eminence OKB would have been closed; as it was, it withered but survived until Lavochkin's death on 9 June 1960.

S. A. Lavochkin

I-22/LaGG-1 First LaGG fighter, originally called *Frontovaya Istrebitel* (frontal fighter) to fly tactical missions against air and ground targets at medium heights. Conventional in all respects except materials, and exceptionally tough and simple. Ruling material not *delta* but birch ply and *shpon*, though similar to *delta* in processing and called bakelite-ply. Fuselage narrow oval section, 13 main frames, triangular-section stringers, integral fin and centre-section of 3,17 m span. Engine mounting welded steel tube. Skin thickness 9,5 mm forward tapering to 3,0 mm at fin and tailpiece. Wings with two box spars, close-spaced ribs and bakelite-ply skin mainly 3 mm thick. Duralumin flight-control surfaces with fabric covering. Duralumin split flaps driven hydraulically to 15° or 50° (landing). Main landing gears with 650 × 200mm tyres retracted inwards hydraulically, wheels housed in lee of engine air ducts in roots. Retractable tailwheel, twin doors. Engine with Hucks starter dogs, also compressed-air starter in production aircraft. VISh-61P propeller with three blades 3 m (118 in), 58/230°. Ventral oil cooler, main radiator well aft under fuselage at trailing edge with manual shutter. Fuel 340 lit (74·8 gal) in three inter-spar tanks of AMTs (aluminium/magnesium alloy) overlain by four layers of phenol-formaldehyde resin-impregnated fabric and with short-term possibility of feeding engine exhaust above fuel to give inert atmosphere (prolonged use softened metal of tanks). Spartan cockpit with no gyro instruments or radio but 10 mm seat armour. Plexiglas glazed canopy manually sliding to rear. Simple telescopic sight, later replaced by PBP-1a reflector sight. Armament arguable: most Soviet sources state one ShVAK firing through propeller hub and two ShKAS in top decking, but Western sources state one VYa-23 with 80 rounds and two UB (causing bulges) each with 220 rounds. (Note: VYa was not cleared for production until mid-1940.) First flight by A.I. Nikashin 30 March 1940. Generally unimpressive, with sluggish climb and acceleration, though speed fractionally better than rival I-26. Short on range, and, most important of all, manoeuvrability poor and aircraft dangerous to novice, especially one used to I-15. Crash programme to rectify faults launched as **I-301**; production I-22 nevertheless went ahead at GAZ-301 as LaGG-1, though number delivered not large (about 100).

DIMENSIONS Span 9,8 m (32 ft $1\frac{3}{4}$ in); length 8,81 m (28 ft 11 in); wing area 17,51 m^2 (188·5 ft^2).

ENGINE One 1050 hp M-105P.

WEIGHTS Empty 2968 kg (6543 lb); fuel/oil 250 kg; loaded 3380 kg (7451 lb).

PERFORMANCE Max speed 500 km/h (311 mph) at SL, 605 km/h (376 mph) at 4,95 km; climb 6·2 min to 5 km; service ceiling 9 km (29,530 ft); range 556 km (345 miles); take-off 23·5 s; landing speed 143 km/h (89 mph).

LaGG-3 While manufacture built up on LaGG-1, improved prototype **I-301** (named for factory) hastily contrived with assistance from VVS and TsAGI to rectify worst faults. New outer wings with inter-spar tank of 61 lit (13·4 gal); detail analysis of structure to reduce weight (almost 200 kg pared off); outer wings incorporated internal slots, later replaced by automatic slats; armament standardized as one ShVAK with 120 rounds and two ShKAS each with 325; provision for attachment beneath each wing of three RS-82 rockets or one 100-lit (22-gal) drop tank; system of internal pendulum

LaGG-3

weights inserted in elevator circuit; upper and lower mass-balance fitted to rudder; and intention to fit PF engine when available. First I-301 flown by Nikashin 14 June 1940. Major all-round improvement and, following Nikashin's non-stop flight Moscow/Kursk and back with 15% fuel remaining on 28 July 1940, decision taken to organize production as LaGG-3 at four plants: No 301, No 31 at Taganrog (which for some months became centre for fighter development), No 21 at Gorkii and No 153 (former tractor works) at Novosibirsk. Thanks to this plan production built up impressively, 322 LaGG-3s being delivered in first half 1941 and 2,141 in second half (far outstripping Yak-1 output). But fatalities and write-offs in training were high, morale of LaGG pilots low (initials said to mean *Lakirovannii Garantirovannii Grob*, varnished guaranteed coffin) and defects still numerous. Radio at last installed, hydraulics made reliable, brakes made controllable, canopy more transparent, rudder lower mass balance removed and later replaced by horn, elevators properly balanced and pendulum masses removed, bullet-proof windscreen fitted, and inert-gas tank system made operative. Training eventually removed grosser faults in piloting technique, and various armament schemes fitted, such as VYa or ShVAK plus one/two ShKAS or one/two UB. Field mods resulted in other schemes such as five UB, two of them in underwing gondolas. Night-flying equipment added to some, and also reconnaissance version with AFA-1 camera built in small numbers. Late 1941 main OKB evacuated to GAZ-21 at Gorkii and GAZ-31 evacuated to Tbilisi, but GAZ-153 ordered to switch to Yak-1 instead. LaGG-3 remained inferior combat aircraft, its main asset being toughness. Much of trouble lay in shoddy workmanship by untrained personnel who had had no prior contact with modern technology. Total deliveries 6528 LaGG-1 and LaGG-3 by August 1942, from when all airframes received M-82 engine.

This remarkable total does not include prototypes, which included several produced at Gorkii or Tbilisi in attempts to rectify faults. Both Gorbunov and Gudkov produced improved prototypes, described separately. Lavochkin's own efforts included prolonged attempts to reduce weight and even greater efforts to find a better engine. **LaGG-3** *Dubler* (understudy) fitted with VK-105PF-2 engine in 1943; one VYa-23 and one BS. Gross 2875 kg and max speed 618 km/h (384 mph) at 3400 m, not good enough when tested in early 1944 by I.M. Dzyuba and discontinued. **LaGG-3F** or No 107 major modification at Tbilisi summer 1942, with prototype M-107 engine; potentially outstanding but test pilot G. Mishchyenko suffered engine failure on every one of 33 flights and with other snags resulted in abandonment of project by 1943. By this time Lavochkin had also tried small Bocharyev ramjets on wingtips, but while these increased max speed by 30 km/h when operating (with penalty in already short range) they reduced cruise and unboosted maximum speeds by 50 km/h and also impaired manoeuvrability.

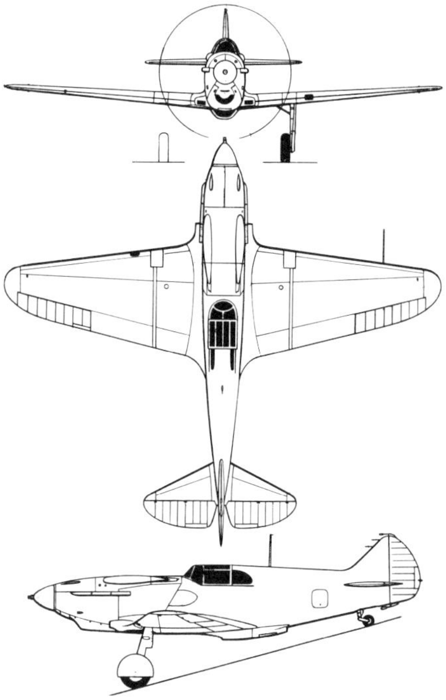

LaGG-3 (early production, 23-mm and two 12.7-mm guns)

DIMENSIONS Span 9,8 m (32 ft 1¾ in); length 8,81 m (28 ft 11 in) (8,82 with VYa-23); wing area 17,51 m² (188·5 ft²).

ENGINE One 1210 hp M-105PF.

WEIGHTS Empty 2620 kg (5776 lb); fuel/oil 332 or 347 kg; loaded (Shavrov) 3076 kg (6781 lb), (Něměcek) 3150 kg (6944 lb), (Alexander) 3190 kg (7032 lb).

PERFORMANCE Max speed 495 km/h (307 mph) at SL, 575 km/h (357 mph) at 5 km (Něměcek 535 km/h, Green 570, Alexander 560); climb 5·8 min to 5 km; service ceiling 9,7 km (31,824 ft); range (Shavrov) 1000 km (621 miles), (Něměcek) 570 km (354 miles), (Green) 556 km (345 miles), (Alexander) 650 km (404 miles); take-off 20 s; landing speed 139 km/h (86 mph).

La-5 Within a year installation of M-82 radial engine in LaGG-3 had transformed sadly defective fighter into one of most effective of the Second World War, and also transformed Lavochkin's status. There had been real danger in 1942 of Lavochkin's OKB being closed; most of its top engineers had been posted elsewhere, and it had become a small downcast team no longer welcome at Tbilisi.

Original reason for alternative engine was to safeguard major combat-aircraft programmes against shortage or serious trouble with existing engine. In about August 1941 instruction sent to La, MiG and Yak OKBs to fit recently qualified M-82 radial to their production fighters. Gudkov did this independently (q.v.). Lavochkin had more direct assistance from A. D. Shvetsov's engine KB and unlike Gudkov did not attempt a minimum change crash conversion but the best M-82 installation possible. Work began late September 1941 at Tbilisi. Major problems were: greater weight of engine (about 850 kg compared with 600), compounded by reduction of some 70 kg at rear by removal of water-filled radiator, duct fairing, control flap and piping; greater engine width of 1260 mm compared with 777; and lower thrust-line. On credit side was reduced length of engine which greatly eased problem of CG shift and promised to overcome major cause of poor manoeuvrability. With Shvetsov instal-

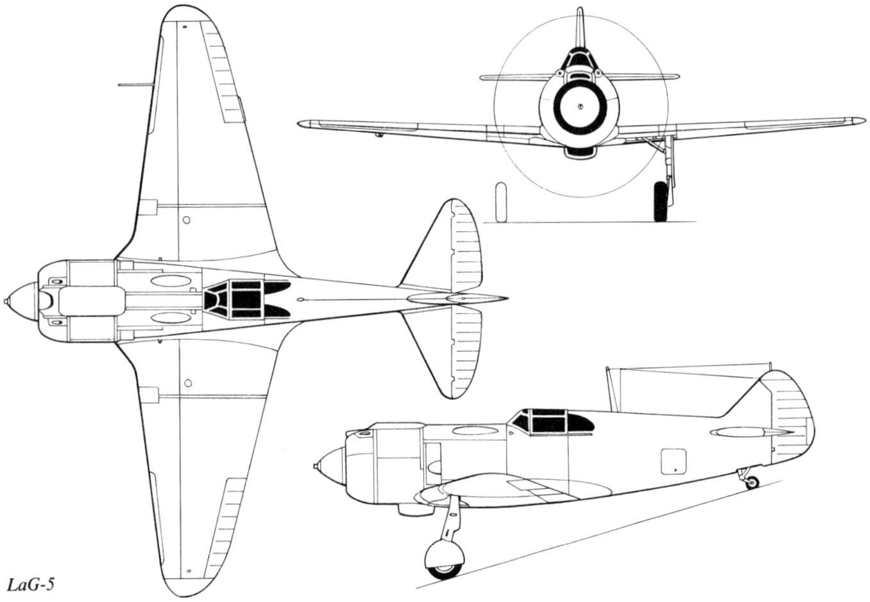

LaG-5

lation engineer Valedinskii, Lavochkin's designers created outstanding installation with tightly fitting cowling with central fairing over reduction gear, radial controllable cooling-air vanes behind large spinner and exhaust pipes collected in left and right groups of seven discharging past hinged door controlling exit airflow. Inlet to supercharger on top, oil cooler underneath. VISh-105V propeller, three blades, 3,1 m (122 in) diam, hydraulic control and feathering, with Hucks dogs on drive shaft (engine also equipped with compressed-air starter). First conversion (in some sources, because Gorbunov still with OKB, called LaG-5) with some compromises including double skin behind engine, both old and new profiles. Seat armour 10 mm, armament two ShVAK each with 200 rounds. Tankage as LaGG-3, five cells totalling 462 or 464 lit (102 gal), rest of aircraft also almost unchanged. Completed in small OKB shop outside main Tbilisi factory December 1941; thereafter GAZ manager so anxious not to compromise himself he refused to allow it inside a hangar. His cool attitude, combined with severe winter and various teething troubles, delayed first flight until March 1942. OKB test pilot G. Mishchyenko not happy with take-off or landing, general control balance or harmonization, but pleased with climb and speed. Initial testing mixed results, and produced numerous detail changes such as ailerons with slightly skewed axes and progressively greater chord on underside only, from tip to inner end, giving more aerodynamic balance. When NII pilots I. Ye Fedorov and A. I. Nikashin flew La-5 in late March they were impressed, and Nikashin told Stalin personally. Result was crash programme of State trials, by NII team led by Col I. V. Frolov and comprising pilots A. Yakimov and A. Kubishkin and engineers V. Saginov and A. Frolov. Begun April 1942, and resulted in priority directive in July for maximum-rate production of La-5, with M-82 also fitted to all available LaGG-3 airframes. (When Yakovlev arrived at GAZ-153 in late 1942 he found scores of incomplete LaGG aircraft, some mere bumps in snow and many not even discovered until following spring; even these were later turned into La-5s.) Control of GAZ-21 was restored to Lavochkin, previous manager now obsequious, and both this and Gorkii expanded to boost production. First ten La-5s completed in three weeks, for service test while flying operationally on war front. Performance far short (up to 50 km/h) of that expected; Lavochkin called to Kremlin after TsAGI team had reported reason was chiefly high drag of crude hand-made cowlings. Stalin told designer such things were his responsibility, Malyenkov adding that his 'future performance will be scrutinized closely'. Worse, two wings broke off, one in shallow dive and other on landing approach: in this case cause found to be hammering wing-attach bolts into under-sized holes! Vibration traced to unbalanced propellers, and cannon mounts redesigned to reduce vibration when firing. With these snags overcome special trials regiment formed September 1942, at Stalingrad; La-5 was universally acclaimed.

Entry over high cockpit sill awkward. Still no gyro instruments and only small inaccurate compass, but RSI-4 single-channel radio standard, with good press/speak button on throttle. No cockpit heating, poor view to rear (or ahead when taxiing) and PBP-1a sight a simple lens with just two deflection rings; for accurate shooting pilot had to be dead astern target. Need to watch cylinder-head temperature constantly; especially in early days heads commonly flew off cylinder when overheated. General flight handling superb, easily superior to Bf 109G or Fw 190 and including loop or Immelmann begun at mere 300 km/h (186 mph)! Good recovery from stall or spin, no special limitations and only real problem tendency to bounce on landing (instructors said 'ignore it', but many pilots instinctively added power, causing torque to invert aircraft). Another problem was short range. Five tanks but outers never used in front line, and Lavochkin again called to Kremlin where he reported he could not increase range. Stalin, by now well-disposed to Lavochkin, asked designer to think about it; by early 1943 L.A. Zaks at Tbilisi had managed to get full original tank capacity into three tanks in centre section (464 lit), with 160 kg reduction in empty weight. In December 1942 M-82F (ASh-82F) had replaced original engine, aircraft being designated **La-5F**. At end March 1943 important direct-injection ASh-82FN became standard, for first time eliminating engine-cut under negative-g and also giving more power; resulting **La-5FN** distinguished by full-length engine air duct starting at cowl lip. Another important change, introduced soon after completion of last La-5 based on a LaGG airframe (about November 1942), was improved rear view from cut-down rear fuselage and glazed rear canopy with 75 mm bulletproof glass transversely. Many aircraft had fixed tailwheel for simplicity. Few departures from standard twin-ShVAK armament; some lightened by twin-UBS, and several experimental fits at NII. Underwing loads 200 kg bombs (various) or four/six RS-82. To reduce training losses tandem dual **La-5UTI** produced August 1943, tested 3 to 30 September. (Note: dual two-seaters had been made by field conversion as early as about November 1942, but these poorly engineered.) UTI had tandem sliding canopies, rerouted tail controls and radio mast, relocated battery and, usually, only one ShVAK. By summer 1943 UTI had FN engine and interspersed with La-5FN on assembly lines which by this time included not only Tbilisi and Gorkii but also Yaroslavl and a GAZ in Moscow area. Early 1943, several **La-5TK** with turbocharger, no series output. Final change in production was

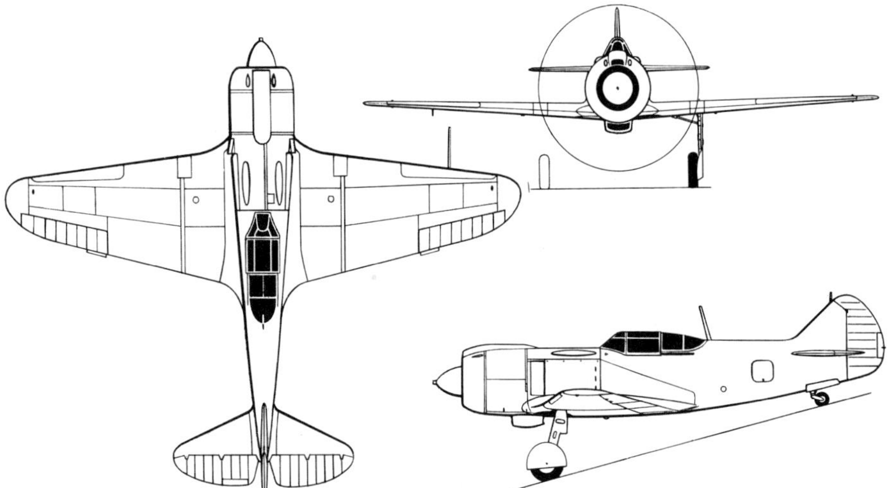

La-5FN

La-5FN

La-5UTI (early conversion on production line)

La-7

introduction of new wing with D1 duralumin spar webs and 30KhGSA booms in May 1944, sub-type called **La-5FN Type 41**; at same time this wing was also fitted to parallel fighter with improved fuselage, La-7. Smaller spar dimensions saved 172 kg structure weight and enabled internal fuel to rise to 560 lit (123 gal). Despite La-7, last La-5FN did not leave factory until late 1944. Total production estimated 9920. Popular name *Lavochka*.

DIMENSIONS Span 9,8 m (32 ft 1¾ in); length 8,71 m (28 ft 7 in) (FN engine, 8,67 m, 28 ft 5⅓ in; UTI same); wing area (1942) 17,37 m^2, (1943) 17,27 m^2 (186 ft^2), (FN) 17,59 m^2 (189 ft^2).

ENGINE (prototype) one 1330 hp M-82, (1942 production) 1480 hp M-82A, (F) 1540 hp ASh-82F), (FN) 1630 hp ASh-82FN, (TK) 1850hp ASh-82FNV.

WEIGHTS Empty (1942) 2789 kg (6149 lb), (FN) 2605 kg (5743 lb); fuel/oil (typical) 370 kg; loaded (various) 3265/3402 kg (7198/7500 lb).

PERFORMANCE Max speed (SL, typical) 562 km/h (349 mph), (altitude) (prototype) 604 km/h, (1942 pre-production) 554 km/h (344 mph) at 6,5 km, (November 1942 production) 603 km/h (375 mph) at 6,5 km, (FN) 648 km/h (403 mph) at 6,5 km (21,325 ft), (UTI) 600 km/h at 3,5 km; climb (early production) 6·2 min to 5 km, (FN) 5·0 min to 5 km; service ceiling (early) 9,6 km (31,500 ft), (FN) 11 km (36,090 ft); range (early) 655 km (407 miles), (FN) 765 km (475 miles); time 360° turn (early) 24 s, (FN) 18 s; landing speed (typical) 148 km/h (92 mph).

La-7 By late 1943 it was clear light-alloys would not be in short supply; TsAGI meanwhile ran major tunnel programme on La-5FN to find aerodynamic improvements. These were main inputs to Samolyet 120 (also called **La-120**, first of published designations, begun at 105 and 107, of Lavochkin OKB prototypes). Aircraft No 120 also incorporated many minor improvements schemed by OKB but ignored through overriding wish not to interfere with production.

Main change was new wing, mentioned at end

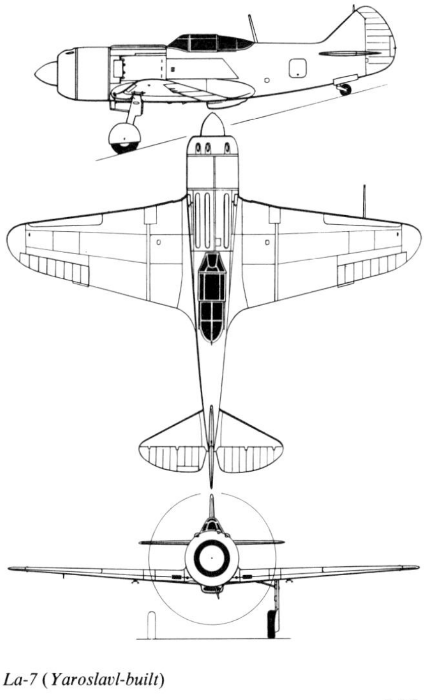

La-7 (Yaroslavl-built)

of La-5, with metal spars. Webs D17-T, booms Chromansil (virtually KhGSA) steel rolled to u.t.s. 130 kg/mm^2. Centre-section joint ribs duralumin, otherwise ribs and skin unchanged. Centre-section leading edge straight taper from root (slightly sharper angle than outer wing). Numerous refinements to fuselage aerodynamics, especially engine installation. Supercharger inlet moved from above cowl to left wing root, with equal-size auxiliary inlet in right root. Oil cooler relocated at trailing edge. New cowling, improved production method, with light but stiff left/right panels hinged at upper centreline exposing entire engine when opened and locked by struts. VISh-105V-4 propeller, same size but improved blades and Hucks dogs eliminated. Improved PBP-1B(V) reflector sight and more comfortable cockpit with heating from exhaust muffs, better radio tuning and gyro-horizon. Armament arguable. Shavrov: three ShVAK, though many only two ShVAK; later batches two or three of new B-20. Green: designed for three B-20 but insufficient supplies to equip all, so this armament on Yaroslavl output only, Moscow La-7 having twin ShVAK. All guns in top of fuselage, third gun on left of centreline, all cooled by ram air from small wing-root inlets. Prototype No 120 built at SKB (Yaroslavl) under S.M. Alekseyev and flown 19 November 1943 by N.V. Adamovich. Outstanding aircraft, hardly any snags, and put through NII trials January/April 1944, VVS service May 1944, used by most of famous IAPs and several top-scoring aces. Dual **La-7UTI** often had one gun and oil cooler under engine. Production terminated early 1946 at 5753.

Many modifications and experimental versions. **La-7TK** on factory test July 1944 with ASh-82FN/TK-3 (same power but maintained to 8 km) giving better climb and high-altitude performance. Destroyed when one of two turbos disintegrated. **La-7ASh-71** with new 2000 hp engine, weights 2849/3505 kg, factory test 1944. **La-7ASh-83** with new 1900 hp lightweight engine, weights 2522/3140 kg, max speed 725 km/h (450·5 mph) at 7,4 km; built with two NS-23, devastating new gun, completed December 1944, factory test completed 12 September 1945. **La-7R** ultra-high-altitude interceptor with V.P. Glushko's RD-1 liquid rocket engine in tail below taller vertical tail with cut-back rudder. Acid (170 lit)/kerosene (90 lit) tanks behind radio bay; armament two B-20. Ground tests 1944, eventually 15 flights by G.M. Shiyanov (first flight, last week of 1944) and A.V. Davydov. RD-1KhZ fitted in modified aircraft with ASh-83FN called **La-120R;** Tushino flypast with rocket firing 18 August 1946. **La-7S** flown by Davydov September 1946 with two underwing VRD-430 ramjets boosting speed 64 km/h. **La-7PuVRD,** also called **PVRD,** and in some reports described as **La-126PVRD,** with two underwing ramjets also; some reports state VRD-430, others give designation D-10. Speed 800 km/h (497 mph) at 8 km. **La-126** fitted with TsAGI laminar-section wing with 2° more dihedral, less taper, trailing-edge root further forward; all-metal stressed-skin throughout with several major junctions cast in Elektron magnesium alloy. Many other changes including modified canopy; armament four NS-23 with 290 rounds. Factory test by Davydov, Fedorov and A.A. Popov complete 10 January 1945; led to La-9.

La-9 *La-126 (PVRD)*

DIMENSIONS Span 9,8 m (32 ft $1\frac{3}{4}$ in); length (all except La-126) 8,6 m (28 ft $2\frac{1}{2}$ in), (La-126) 8,64 m (28 ft $4\frac{1}{4}$ in); wing area (except La-126) 17,59 m^2 (189 ft^2), (La-126) 17,50 m^2.

ENGINE One 1850 hp ASh-82FN (special variants, see text).

WEIGHTS Empty 2,6 t (5732 lb), (TK, 2711 kg; UTI, 2625 kg); fuel/oil 326 kg (UTI, 443 kg; 7R, 604 kg); loaded 3260 kg (7187 lb), (TK, 3280 kg; ASh-71, 3505 kg; UTI, 3293 kg; 7R, 3498 kg).

PERFORMANCE Max speed 600 km/h (373 mph) at SL, 680 km/h (423 mph) at 6,8 km (22,300 ft), (TK, 676 km/h at 8 km; La-120, 725 at 7,4; UTI, 648 at 3; -7R, 752, later 795 at 6,3; -120R, 805); climb 4·5 min to 5 km; service ceiling 10,7 km (35,105 ft), (TK, 11,8; -7R, 13); range 635 km (395 miles), (UTI, 675 km; La-120, 800); time 360° circle 19 s; take-off 340 m; landing 510 m/ 152 km/h (94 mph).

La-7UTI (oil cooler was often moved forward under engine)

La-9 About mid-1944 enlarged OKB at Tbilisi began complete redesign of fuselage, changing not only shapes but also starting afresh with duralumin stressed-skin structure. Many other airframe changes, wing being basically that of La-126 but with new tip of rectilinear form with improved ailerons of almost constant reduced chord and simpler aerodynamic balance. Improved engine installation with better cooling baffles (closer fins on cylinders, no change in engine designation) and exhaust arrangement and with supercharger duct inlet moved from wing roots to top of cowl. Redesigned wider canopy with frameless hood and deeper rear fuselage giving greater comfort and better all-round view. D/F radio behind seat with loop behind rear armoured glass plate. Better tank arrangement making full use of metal wing structure, outer-wing supplementary cells raising total capacity to 825 lit (181·5 gal). Larger reshaped vertical tail and new rectilinear horizontal tail of increased span with spring tabs in rudder and left elevator. Overall structure weight actually slightly less than La-7, allowing for devastating armament of four NR-23 with 300 rounds. Unarmed **La-130** prototype flown 16 June 1946, on NII test October. Few snags, and production authorized November 1946; because of end of war and imminent jet fighters numbers small by comparison with previous programmes, and gradually run down from 1947. Some early batches retained armament of three of four ShVAK and many had one of left-side NR-23 removed leaving three (often retaining blister fairing for missing gun). Total production, possibly 1000 including **La-9UTI** dual trainer with one NR-23 first flown January 1947, NII test June and built in small numbers from August 1948. Several experimental variants. **La-138** fitted with two PVRD-430 ramjets in same installation as La-7S, complete end 1946 and factory test March/April 1947; boosted speed 107/112 km/h at expense of high fuel consumption and severe drag when not operating. **La-9RD** fitted with two RD-13 pulse-jets attached to same wing hardpoints but with different pylons extending ahead of leading edge. Batch of at least nine aircraft converted, first flying second half 1947; formation demonstration at Tushino but vibration severe and soon abandoned despite temporary boost of 127 km/h.

DIMENSIONS Span 9,8 m (32 ft 1¾ in); length 8,63 m (28 ft 3¾ in); wing area 17,72 m² (191 ft²).
ENGINE One 1850 hp ASh-82FN.
WEIGHTS Empty 2638 kg (5816 lb), (UTI, 2554 kg; RD, 3150 kg); fuel/oil 595 kg; loaded 3676 kg (8104 lb), (UTI, 3285 kg; RD, 3815 kg).

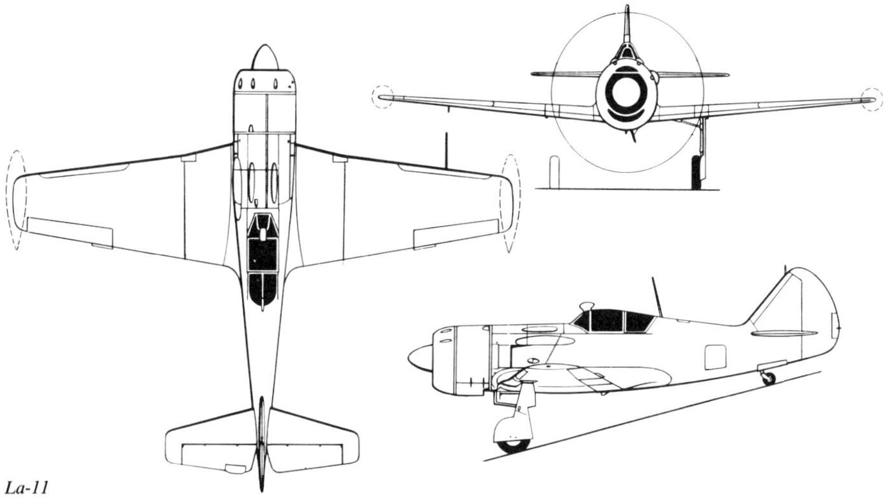

La-11

La-11

PERFORMANCE Max speed 600 km/h (373 mph) at SL (UTI, 558 km/h), 690 km/h (429 mph) at 6250 m (20,500 ft) (UTI, 659 km/h); climb 4·8 min to 5 km (UTI, 5 min); service ceiling 10·8 km (35,433 ft); range 1735 km (1078 miles) (UTI, 940 km); take-off 345 m; landing 490 m/146 km/h (91 mph).

La-11 Final piston-engine La, begun 1946 as long-range escort with provision for two 137,5 lit (30·25 gal) drop tanks on wingtips, giving total fuel 1100 lit, more than three times LaGG-1. Armament three NS-23 (not NR-23), lower right position and blister removed; three magazines 225 rounds. Only other significant change relocation of oil cooler in bottom of deeper oval cowling. Prototype **La-140** flown Col A.G. Kochyetkov, NII chief of fighter testing, May 1947; NII trials August and immediate order for large-scale production (much greater number than La-9). Entered service 1948 and subsequently used by virtually all communist air arms well into 1950s. First known to West 18 May 1949 when defector landed at Tüllinge, Sweden; substantial numbers encountered with N Korean and Chinese air forces in Korean war 1950–1953. Small number also built of tandem dual **La-11UTI**.

DIMENSIONS Span 9,8 m (32 ft 1¾ in); length 8,63 m (28 ft 3¾ in); wing area (no tip tanks) 17,72 m² (191 ft²).
ENGINE One 1850 hp ASh-82FN.
WEIGHTS Empty 2770 kg (6107 lb); fuel/oil 880 kg; loaded 3996 kg (8810 lb).
PERFORMANCE Max speed 562 km/h (349 mph) at SL, 674 km/h (419 mph) at 6,2 km; climb 5·0 min to 5 km; service ceiling 10 250 m (33,630 ft); range 2550 km (1584 miles); endurance 6·3 h; time 360° circle 19·5 s; take-off 345 m; landing 505 m/149 km/h (92·6 mph).

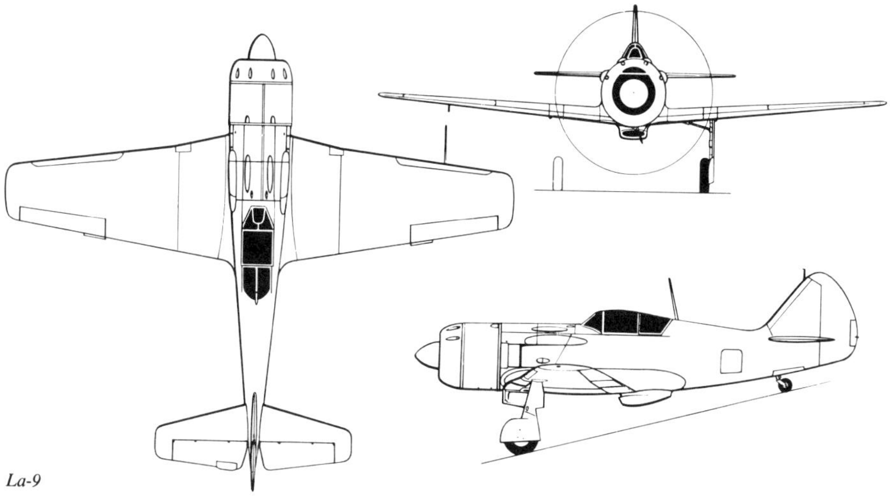

La-9

La-150 Lavochkin's OKB was assigned urgent task of building a jet fighter at meeting with Stalin February 1945 also attended by rivals

La-150F

La-152 temporarily fitted with third NS-23 cannon

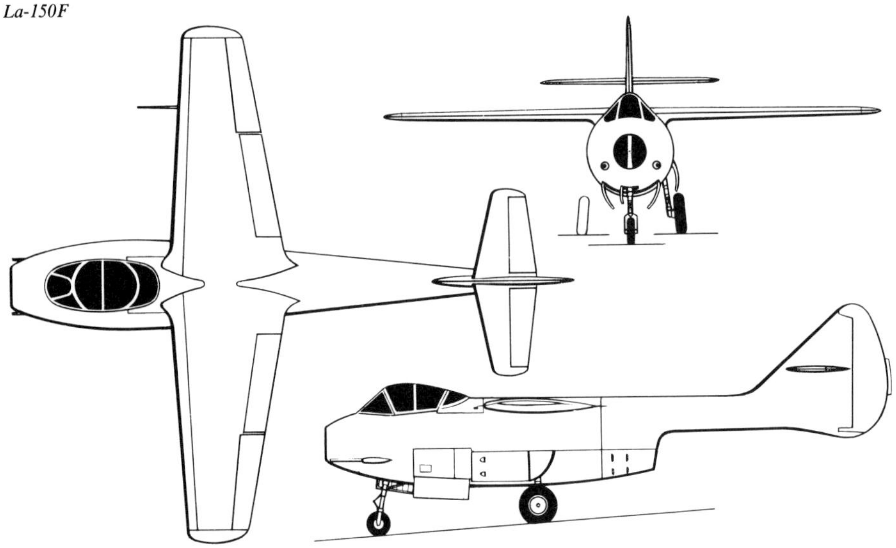

La-150

Mikoyan/Guryevich, Sukhoi and Yakovlev. Assignment: build fighter around single RD-10 (Jumo 004B). Work began immediately, though much talent still applied to La-9 and La-11 series. Like MiG and Su OKBs decision taken to start with clean sheet of paper using no major part of existing fighters. Configuration, not influenced by German work, finally settled as pod/boom with tricycle gear, nose cockpit and high wing. All-metal stressed-skin airframe. Wing with TsAGI laminar section, 12% root 9·5% tip, two spars with five fuel cells in inter-spar box 770 lit (169 gal); slotted hydraulic flaps, manual ailerons, fixed leading edge without slats. Wing attached to two strong frames also carrying engine at positive angle 3° and main landing gears, of 1823 mm (5 ft 11¾ in) track, with 825 × 200 mm tyres, retracted about skewed hinges to lie under front of engine. Nose inlet immediately bifurcated to ducts along sides of fuselage, passing unpressurized cockpit with conventional seat. Nose gear retracted to rear (according to Alexander, wheel rotating 90° to lie flat). Large tail with fixed tailplane and left/right elevators mounted quite high on fin entirely ahead of mass/horn-balanced rudder. Entire lower part of fuselage unstressed access panels round engine and armament of two NS-23 with projecting barrels installed below ducts and beside nose-gear compartment. Five prototypes built (for planned 7 November 1946 parade), first being complete in September 1946; first flight A.A. Popov, subsequent testing also by I.Ye. Fedorov, M.L. Gallai, N.I. Zvonaryev and A.G. Kochyetkov, continued until April 1947. Many shortcomings including high airframe weight, generally sluggish acceleration, poor stability and tail oscillation traced to inadequate stiffness of tail boom. Second prototype completed as **La-150M** (*Modifikatsirovanni*) with wingtips turned down at anhedral of 30° and extended to preserve original span, stronger and stiffer tail-boom, greater fuel capacity, repositioned equipment, low-pressure main tyres, and guns with shorter barrels. Empty and gross weights rose appreciably and performance fell further; first flight December 1946, testing stopped September 1947 by which time La-150 no longer active project. Final three prototypes again modified to **La-150F** (*Forsirovannii*) with primitive afterburning engine; on factory test July to September 1947. First Soviet afterburning aircraft, one of first in world.

DIMENSIONS Span 8,2 m (26 ft 10¾ in); length 9,42 m (30 ft 10¾ in); wing area 12,15 m² (131 ft²).
ENGINE One 900 kg (1984 lb) thrust RD-10, (La-150F) 1100 kg (2425 lb) RD-10F.
WEIGHTS Empty (150) 2059 kg (4539 lb), (150M) 2369 kg (5,223 lb); fuel/oil (150) 553 kg, (150M) 623 kg; loaded (150) 2961 kg (6528 lb), (150M) 3338 kg (7359 lb), (150F) 3340 kg.
PERFORMANCE Max speed (150) 840 km/h (522 mph) at SL, 850 at 5 km, (150M) 760 at SL, 805 km/h (500 mph) at 5 km, (150F) 950 km/h (590 mph) at SL; climb to 5 km (150) 4·5 min, (150M) 7·2 min, (150F) 6·0 min; service ceiling (150 and M) 12,5 km (41,000 ft), (F) 13 km (42,650 ft); range (150) 700 km (435 miles); endurance 0·8 h; field length over 1 km.

La-152 Though officially a modification of La-150 this was in effect a different fighter, with totally redesigned fuselage with cockpit above mid-mounted wing and engine in nose. Main aerodynamic change was new wing of mean 9·1% thickness, with improved sealed and internally balanced ailerons and structurally innovative. Rear fuselage of more conventional form, giving no aeroelastic problems. Broad cockpit above wing, later (about January 1948) with primitive ejection seat, fitted to all subsequent prototypes. Engine in extreme nose with no inlet duct and short tailpipe. Main landing gear not greatly changed from 150 series but folding rearwards immediately beneath wing root with different doors. Deep forward fuselage with NS-23 on each side, engine attached to frames 1 and 4, nose gear to frame 2 and longitudinal walls of compartment, and guns to 3 and 5. Factory test October 1946 to August 1947. Undistinguished but no major snag.

DIMENSIONS Span 8,2 m (26 ft 10¾ in); length 9,4 m (30 ft 10 in); wing area 12,15 m² (131 ft²).
ENGINE One 900 kg (1984 lb) thrust RD-10.
WEIGHTS Empty 2310 kg (5093 lb); fuel/oil 563 kg; loaded 3239 kg (7141 lb).
PERFORMANCE Max speed 730 km/h at SL, 778 km/h (483 mph) at 5 km; climb 6·5 min to 5 km; service ceiling 12,5 km (41,000 ft); range 500 km (311 miles); endurance 0·9 h.

La-154 Further modification of 152 for research purposes with new wing of different profile but superficially resembling 152. Limited flying from late 1946 because of greater potential with afterburning engine in 156.

DIMENSIONS Span 8,5 m (27 ft 10⅔ in); length 9,1 m (29 ft 10¼ in); wing area 13,24 m² (142·5 ft²).
ENGINE One 900 kg (1984 lb) RD-10.
WEIGHTS Empty 2400 kg (5291 lb); loaded 3500 kg (7716 lb).
PERFORMANCE Max speed 900 km/h (559 mph)

La-156

at 5 km; climb 4 min to 5 km; service ceiling 12,5 km (41,000 ft); range 500 km (311 miles).

La-156 Essentially 154 with afterburning engine, installed at angle 5°40′ with better secondary airflow than La-150F. Additional NS-23 installed on right side, subsequently retrofitted to La-152. Tail areas: horizontal 2,3 m², vertical 2,2. First La with ejection seat from outset. First flight S.F. Mashkovskii February 1947, subsequently factory tested by I.Ye. Fedorov to late March. NII testing 5 September 1947 to 31 January 1948. Best La jet to date, but recognized outdated by swept wing aircraft.

DIMENSIONS Span 8,52 m (27 ft 11½ in); length 9,12 m (29 ft 11 in); wing area 13,32 m² (143·4 ft²).

ENGINE One 1100 kg (2425 lb) RD-10F.

WEIGHTS Empty 2398 kg (5287 lb); fuel/oil 743 kg; loaded 3521 kg (7762 lb).

PERFORMANCE Max speed 845 km/h at SL, 905 km/h (562 mph) at 2 km; climb 4·0 min to 5 km; service ceiling 12,7 km (41,670 ft); range 660 km (410 miles); endurance 1·2 h.

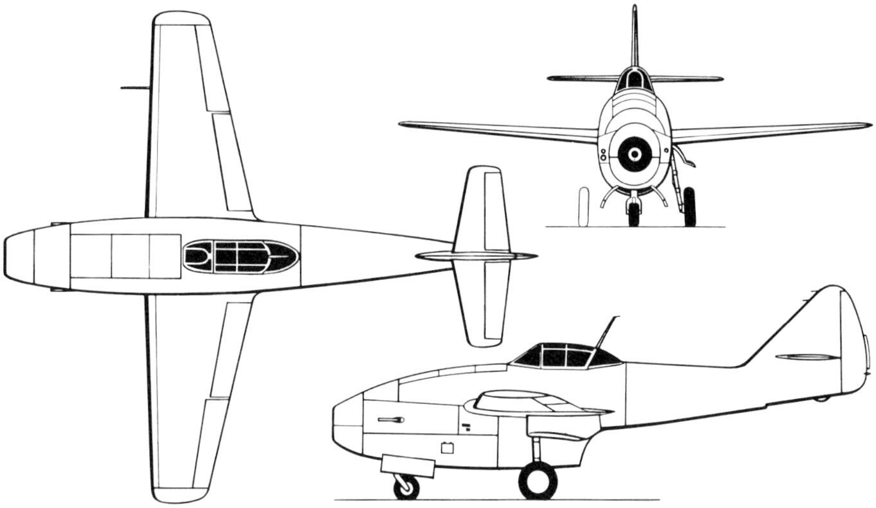

La-156

La-174TK Confusingly numbered out of sequence, this was basically a 156 with even thinner wing (TK, *Tonkoye Krylo*, thin wing) and at last a different (but still obsolescent) engine. Purely experimental, and 6% wing believed to be thinnest flown in world at that date (certainly on a fighter); but intended as basis for direct rival to Yak-23. Last attempt to use straight wing, prototype being flown January 1948 more than nine months after swept La-160. Apart from thin wing, main change was bulging forward fuselage to house plenum chamber of UK-imported engine, installed at 6°20′ angle and necessitating repositioning armament (Shavrov, two N-37; Alexander, three NS-23) in bottom of forward fuselage. Engine right at front, with bullet fairing over forward wheelcase and accessories. Nose gear bay now with single door. Great advance on 156 but slower than less-powerful 160 so straight wings finally abandoned.

DIMENSIONS Span 8,64 m (28 ft 4¼ in); length 9,41 m (30 ft 10½ in); wing area 13,52 m² (145·5 ft²).

ENGINE One 1590 kg (3500 lb) thrust Rolls-Royce Derwent V.

WEIGHTS Empty 2310 kg (5093 lb); fuel/oil 945 kg; loaded 3315 kg (7308 lb).

PERFORMANCE Max speed 970 km/h at SL, 965 km/h at 3 km; climb 2·5 min to 5 km; service ceiling 13 km (42,650 ft); range 960 km (597 miles); endurance 1·5 h.

La-160 Nicknamed *Strelka* (Arrow), this was first Soviet swept-wing aircraft, but otherwise was member of old Jumo-engined family and retained a lengthened version of same fuselage as 154/156 though with reinforced canopy and windscreen for higher indicated airspeeds. Wing swept 35° on leading edge, with TsAGI profile 9·5% thick making use of German data and with German aerodynamicists involved. About 2° anhedral, two fences on each side extending to trailing edge, believed first on any aircraft. No details of flight controls or flaps. Despite substantial rearwards shift in centre of lift CG was brought forwards by extending nose and fitting armament of two heavy NS-37 as far forward as possible above nose with barrels projecting far ahead of inlet. Yet again a new nose gear, hinged right at front with square door ahead of leg;

La-174TK

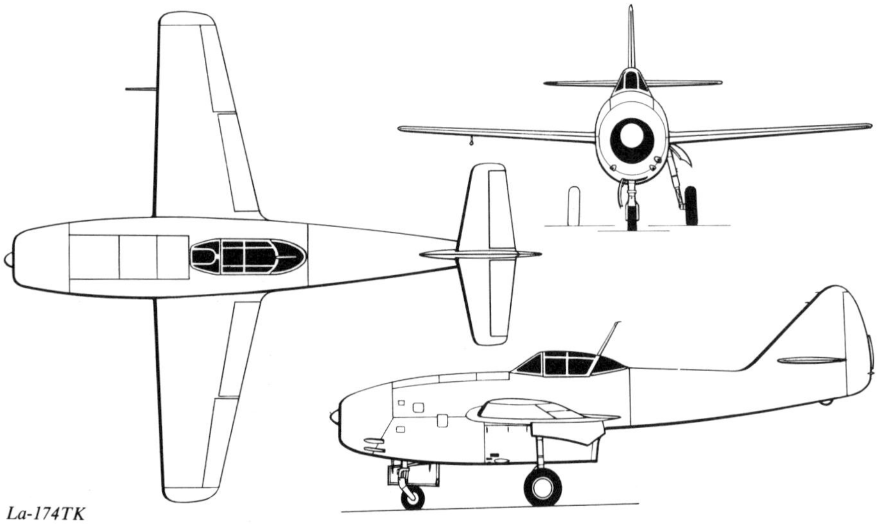

La-174TK

main door closed on ground. Restressed tail, of reduced thickness and with 35° swept tailplane. Longer fuselage accommodated part of increased fuel capacity of 1528 lit (336 gal) (another report gives value slightly less). Programme regarded as of greatest importance; probably several La-160s built. First flown 24 June 1947; tested four months by team including Fedorov and Mashkovskii in wide programme investigating stability and control. Remarkably few modifications needed, and M 0·92 reached on level; clearly showed swept wing at that time was superior, but La-160 recognized as not definitive fighter because of inadequate engine. Lavochkin OKB built up important team on afterburners and their installation headed by I.A. Merkulov (ramjet engineer, joined OKB April 1945) and deputy V.I. Nizhnyego, La-160 being a major vehicle for research.

DIMENSIONS Span 8,95 m (29 ft 4⅓ in); length 10,06 m (33 ft 0 in); wing area 15,9 m² (171 ft²).

ENGINE One 1100 kg (2425 lb) RD-10F.

WEIGHTS Empty 2738 kg (6036 lb); fuel/oil 1100 kg; loaded 4060 kg (8951 lb).

PERFORMANCE Max speed 900 km/h (559 mph) at SL, 1050 km/h (652 mph) at 6 km; climb not recorded; service ceiling 11 km (36,090 ft); range (Shavrov) 500 km, possibly pessimistic.

La-168 As early as July 1947 Lavochkin OKB had recognized need to rethink entire fuselage arrangement, and began study of straight-through fuselage with nozzle at tail. Later Yak OKB was to find Yak-25* with this layout inferior in most respects to Yak-23, which was adopted in place of La-174TK, but La calculations indicated straight-through fighter would be superior. Result was La-168, by far the best La jet to date. Wing larger than La-160 and more sharply swept with leading edge 37°20', but profile same and no change in 2° anhedral and location and shape of fences. Substantial fuel capacity in wing, and three further cells in new fuselage giving total of 1230 lit (270·6 gal), to which could be added a further 610 lit (134 gal) in two flush underwing drop tanks. High performance expected from permission to use Nene engine, installed in rear fuselage which could be removed (possibly together with jet-pipe) in about 15 min to expose engine. Nose inlet immediately bifurcated along each side past forward-mounted pressurized cockpit with same canopy as La-160. Landing light in duct bifurcation leading edge. Almost same main landing gears as earlier La jet fighters but retracting forwards between engine ducts; long nose gear retracting to rear, door on left of bay remaining open on ground. One of few advanced features was use of Fowler flaps, installed neatly and running out on tracks inside upper surface of wing to 20° take-off, and 58° landing. All flight controls hydraulically boosted with internal balance; no tabs except projecting behind ailerons, and high-mounted tailplane fixed. Ventral fin with steel bumper. Effective airbrakes on each side of rear fuselage, operated hydraulically like landing gear and flaps. Armament one N-37 and two N-23 in lower part of nose. Built in parallel with smaller, lower-powered La-174D. First La-168 flown by Fedorov 22 April 1948, by which time MiG-15 already accepted for production, yet another blow for Lavochkin. Unlike third rival, Yak-30, La-15 proved to be generally better than early MiG-15, and almost 1000 lb lighter, but decision had been taken and thus no Nene-derived engine available.

DIMENSIONS Span 9,5 m (31 ft 2 in); length 10,56 m (34 ft 7¾ in); wing area 18,08 m² (194·6 ft²).

ENGINE One 2270 kg (5000 lb) thrust Rolls-Royce Nene I.

WEIGHTS Empty 2973 kg (6554 lb); fuel/oil kg; loaded 4412 kg (9727 lb).

PERFORMANCE Max speed 1000 km/h (621 mph) at SL, 1084 km/h (674 mph) at 3 km; climb 2·0 min to 5 km; service ceiling 14 570 m (47,800 ft); range 1275 km (792 miles); endurance 2·2 h; take-off and landing both 500 m (1640 ft).

La-15 Apparently on his own initiative Lavochkin built a second prototype, designated **La-174D** (no relation to La-174TK), slightly smaller than 168 and tailored to Derwent engine. Running a few months later in timing, it was refined and attractive aircraft with slightly better systems than 168 and comparable performance

La-160

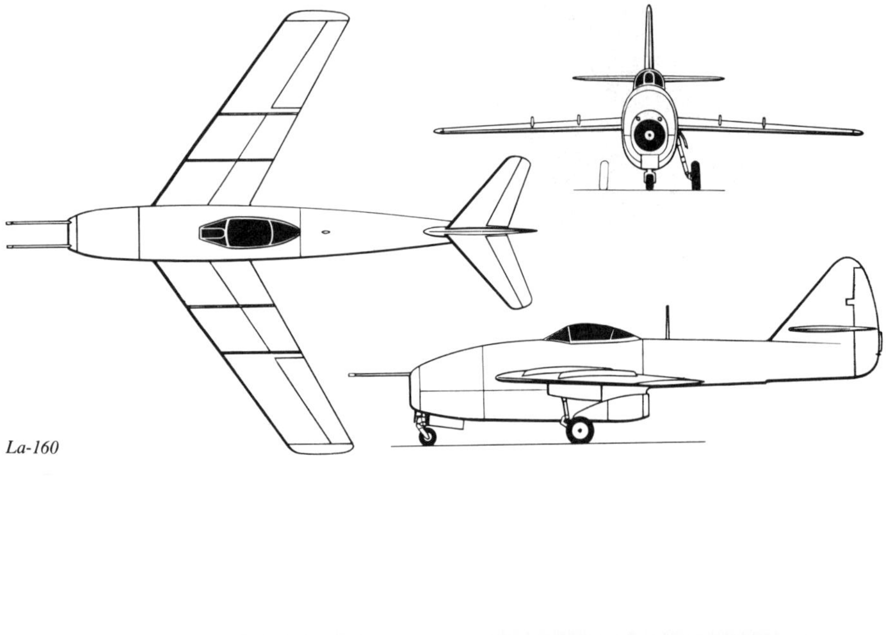

La-160

(thrust/weight ratio declined to 0·428 from Nene-powered prototype's 0·515). Aerodynamically La-174D almost an exact scale (Russian, *analog*) of 168 except for vertical tail being fractionally larger, not smaller, to improve on 168's slight tendency to snake and Dutch-roll. Fuel capacity 1110 lit (244 gal) plus 605 lit (133 gal) in two drop tanks, giving exceptional range for so small and light an aircraft. Armament three NS-23, one on left of nose and two on right. First flight on British engine (possibly taken from La-174TK) August 1948. Though not really required, all-round performance so good that 174D ordered into production for VVS as La-15 early October 1948, with first delivery as early as February 1949. Total believed 500, built as a single batch as a different GAZ directed by A.K. Belyenkov. Production La-15 powered by RD-500 (locally modified Derwent), armed with two NS-23, and not normally fitted with drop tanks; training sorties at varying heights limited to 45 to 50 min. Most regiments employed in frontal ground-attack role, though no record of weapons other than guns. Popular in service, and wing singled out for strength and torsional stiffness which removed all flight limitations. (Note: performance very close to early Hunter with 100% greater thrust, and much better than Meteor with two of same engine.)

In 1949 two prototypes built of **La-180** tandem dual trainer version. Same overall length despite two capacious tandem cockpits, so fuel reduced and brochure endurance 1·5 h. Armament one 12·7 mm BS. NII testing completed September 1949 and, though flying qualities not as good as for single-seater, accepted as **La-15UTI** fighter-trainer and produced in series (again believed 500). Both variants did not begin to be withdrawn until 1954.

DIMENSIONS Span 8,83 m (28 ft $11\frac{2}{3}$ in); length 9,56 m (31 ft $4\frac{1}{3}$ in); wing area 16,16 m^2 (174 ft^2).
ENGINE One 1590 kg (3500 lb) thrust RD-500.
WEIGHTS Empty 2575 kg (5677 lb), (UTI) 2805 kg; fuel/oil 1110 kg (UTI) 800; loaded 3708 kg (8175 lb), (UTI) 3730 kg (8223 lb).
PERFORMANCE Max speed 900 km/h (559 mph) at SL, 1026 km/h (638 mph) at 3 km, (UTI) 1010 km/h (628 mph); climb 3·1 min to 5 km; service ceiling 13,5 km (44,290 ft); range 1170 km (727 miles), (UTI) 1150 km; endurance 2·1 h, (UTI) 1·5 h; take-off and landing both 740/760 m (UTI 900 m take-off).

La-176 Hectic pace of fighter development continued with this advanced derivative of La-168 flying in September 1948. Experimental frontal (tactical) fighter, with first wing in world swept 45°, with same 9·5% profile as before but three fences (outer fences ahead of ailerons). Several other engineering or aerodynamic changes including variable-incidence tailplane with dihedral and long ventral fin. Armament one N-37 and two NS-23. First flight September 1948 by Fedorov (now Hero of SU); subsequent testing also by Capt O.V. Sokolovskii. According to Soviet historians Mach 1 was exceeded by former pilot in dive on 26 December 1948, first in Europe. Some dispute about this, instrument error being mentioned, but there is no doubt La-176 was transonic in dive, Mach 1 often being confirmed by sonic bang in early 1949, first bang being by Sokolovskii. Despite fame brought to OKB, it again lost out, this time to rival MiG-17; third rival was Yak-50. Prototype

La-168

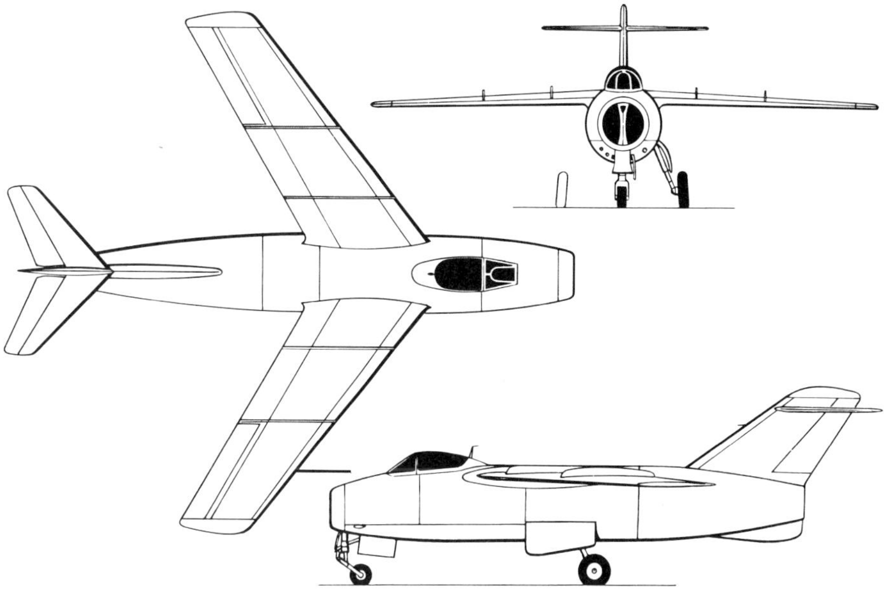
La-168

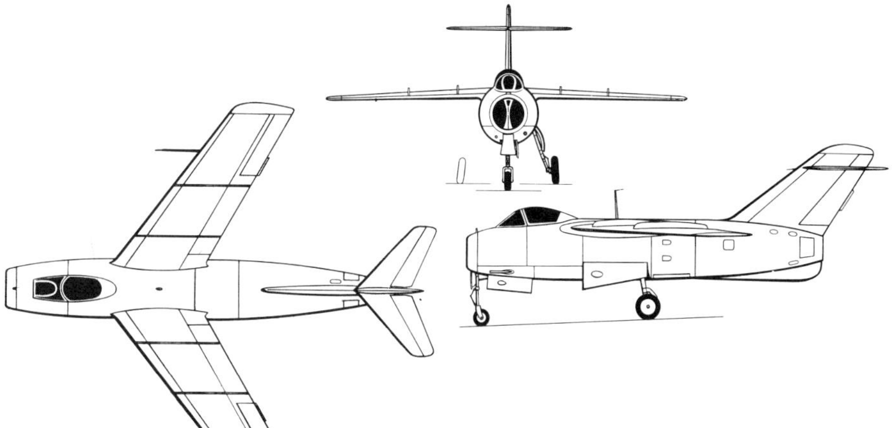
La-15

La-15UTI

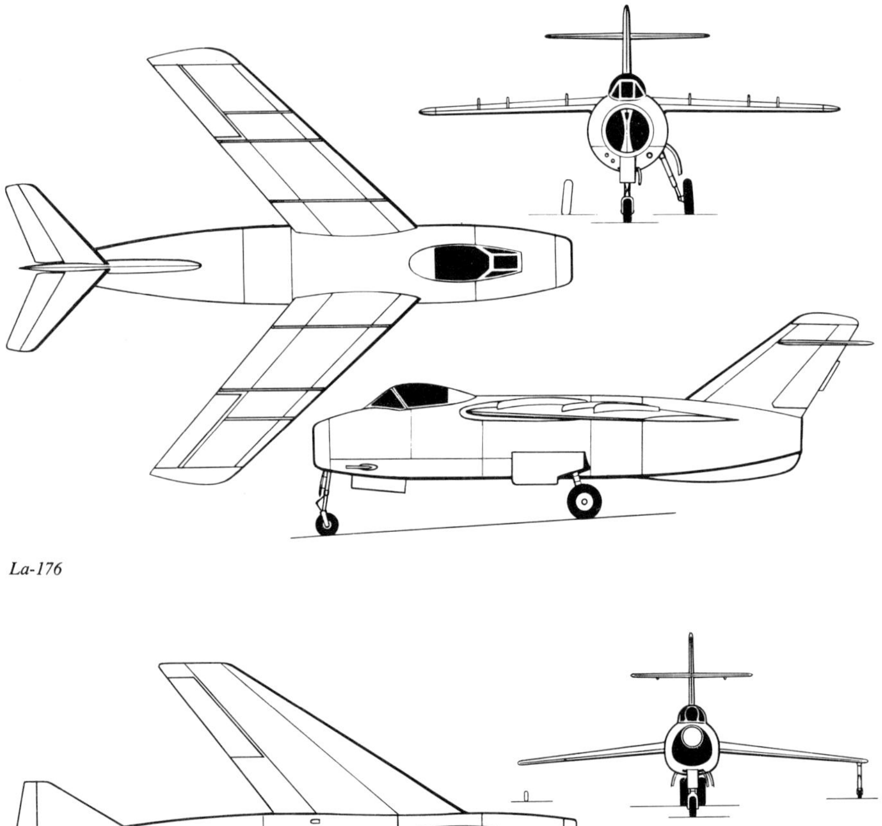

La-176

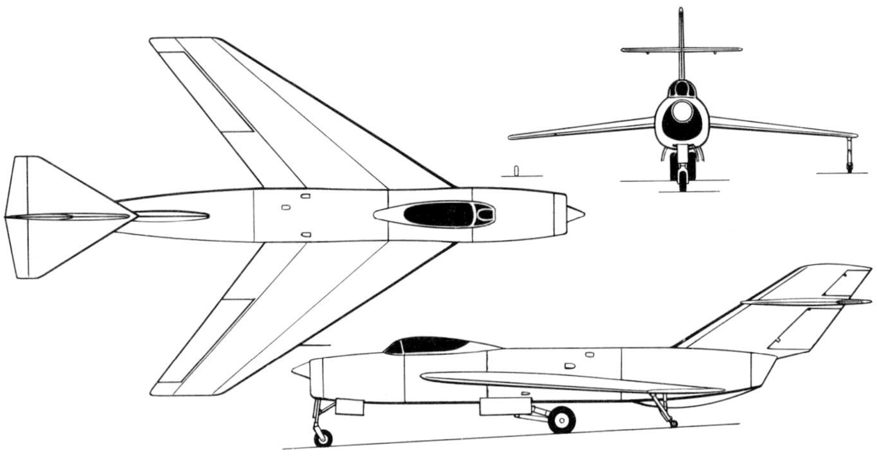

La-190

lost later 1949 when canopy locks failed near Mach 1, Sokolovskii being killed.

DIMENSIONS Span 8,59 m (28 ft 2¼ in); length 10,97 m (36 ft 0 in); wing area 18,25 m² (196·4 ft²).

ENGINE One 2270 kg (5000 lb) thrust RD-45; later 2270 kg VK-1.

WEIGHTS Empty 3110 kg (6858 lb); fuel/oil 1165 kg; loaded 4631 kg (10,209 lb).

PERFORMANCE Max speed 995 km/h at SL, 1105 km/h (687 mph) at 8 km; climb 1·8 min to 5 km; service ceiling 15 km (49,200 ft); range 1000 km (621 miles); endurance 1·5 h.

La-190 Considerable further advance beyond La-176 begun in 1949 to meet NII requirement of October 1948 for genuine transonic fighter for service in early 1950s. Concept modified about 1950 to interceptor with at least some night and all-weather capability. Virtually all-new and challenging, so joint research programme with TsAGI. First aircraft, with rival Yak-1000 and Il-30 bomber, to use powerful new Lyul'ka axial AL-5 turbojet; considerably larger and heavier than predecessors. Aerodynamics planned for established local supersonic flow, with free-stream Mach number of unity. New wing with leading-edge sweep 55°, 6·1% thickness (presumably mean value) and almost entire inter-spar box integral tankage with machined upper and lower skins. No fences. Details of flight controls unknown but comprised ailerons, high horizontal tail surface of low aspect ratio and divided rudder, all surfaces fully powered by irreversible dual-tandem actuators (believed first in country). Wing fitted with flaps, suggesting ailerons were outboard. Near-circular section fuselage with nose inlet to left and right ducts passing under wing on each side of compartments for steerable aft-retracting nose gear and large levered-suspension main gear with twin wheels side-by-side just aft of CG, retracting forward. Wingtip outrigger gears, probably retracting inwards. Ventral fin broadened into twin-door compartment for braking parachute, no bumper strip. Internal fuel 2100 lit (462 gal), two 300 lit (66 gal) drop tanks. Radome (probably empty)

La-200A

above inlet, armament two N-37 in lower front fuselage. Prototype complete February 1951; flight date not recorded. Generally, high performance and at low/medium altitude stability and control satisfactory. But many serious problems, most important being unreliability of engine which caused flight testing to be discontinued. Again La-OKB had lost out, this time to MiG-19. One claim to fame: Mach 1·03 in level flight (believed 11 March 1951), first fighter in world to do so.

DIMENSIONS Span 9,9 m (32 ft 5¾ in); length 16,35 m (53 ft 7¾ in); wing area 38,93 m² (419 ft²).
ENGINE One 5 t (11,023 lb) thrust AL-5.
WEIGHTS Empty 7315 kg (16,127 lb); fuel/oil 2100 kg (max 3750); loaded 9257 kg (20,408 lb).
PERFORMANCE Max speed 1190 km/h (739·5 mph) at 5 km; climb 1·5 min to 5 km; service ceiling 15,6 km (51,180 ft); range 1150 km (715 miles); take-off 620 m.

La-200 Another large and difficult programme that was to lead to yet another failure to find a production aircraft, this was an all-weather interceptor designed to the first properly schemed requirement for a post-war interceptor to be issued in Europe, in January 1948. Supersonic performance not demanded, but severe range requirement which later was greatly extended. Because of nature of design problems, and past failures because rivals had faster timing, decision taken to adhere as far as possible to known technology, with established structure and aerodynamics scaled up in size, and using two of Nene-derived engines. Wing of established 9·5% profile, 40° on leading edge, almost untapered, with two full-chord fences inboard of ailerons. Fowler flaps, fixed leading edge. Conventional swept tail with fixed tailplane high on fin. All flight controls hydraulically boosted but not fully powered. Because of increased size of fuselage pressurized cockpit wide enough for pilot and radar operator side-by-side in ejection seats under large aft-sliding canopy; instrument and navaid fit no longer inferior to Western standards, and included ILS and imported Zero Reader (subsequently made without license for other aircraft). Two engines installed in tandem, one in tail and other in forward fuselage exhausting in familiar La way under wing via steeply inclined jetpipe with almost horizontal nozzle section. All air aspirated via annular nose inlet with radome for *Izumrud* (Emerald) AI radar in centre. Large proportion of fuselage thus taken up by bifurcated ducts, those for rear engine being quadrant section filling space above wing outboard of cockpit. Lower part of nose occupied by three N-37 (two on right side); upper part with radar accessed by opening large doors on inner and outer sides of engine ducts. Next section, ahead of cockpit, with further doors to plenum chamber of forward engine. Landing gears broadly as in ealier La jets but with sturdy levered-suspension main units each with twin side-by-side wheels. Outstanding achievement in internal capacity of 2800 lit (616 gal), chiefly in integral-tank wings, supplemented by two 1120 lit (246 gal) underwing drop tanks. Several innovations in manufacture (to USSR) including heavy stretch-formed plate, copies of patented (eg, Camloc) Western fasteners and rain-resistant radome.

Prototype flown 9 September 1949 by S.F. Moshkovskii and A.F. Kosaryev. Phase I testing complete February 1950, Phase II in October 1950. Several alterations, but aircraft acceptable and in all respects dramatically in advance of Western counterparts. Held Mach 0·946 and reached 1·01 in dive. Final NII report April 1951 recommending production; but thwarted by issue in November 1950 of much more severe demand for range of 3500 km, carrying much heavier long-range radar. Another blow was successful demo of *Izumrud* in MiG single-seaters already in service, and La-OKB for a time thought new long-range demand could not be met. After much study decision taken to build **La-200B** (La-200A interim project not built). With slightly more powerful version of same engine redesign of forward fuselage and slight increase in length provided room for considerable additional fuel as well as bulky Scan Three radar with 995 mm dish (OKB not saddled with development of large radome). In revised scheme front engine fed from its own chin inlet and short duct to plenum chamber. Rear engine fed by two 'elephant ear' inlets on sides of nose via ducts curved in behind radar and new

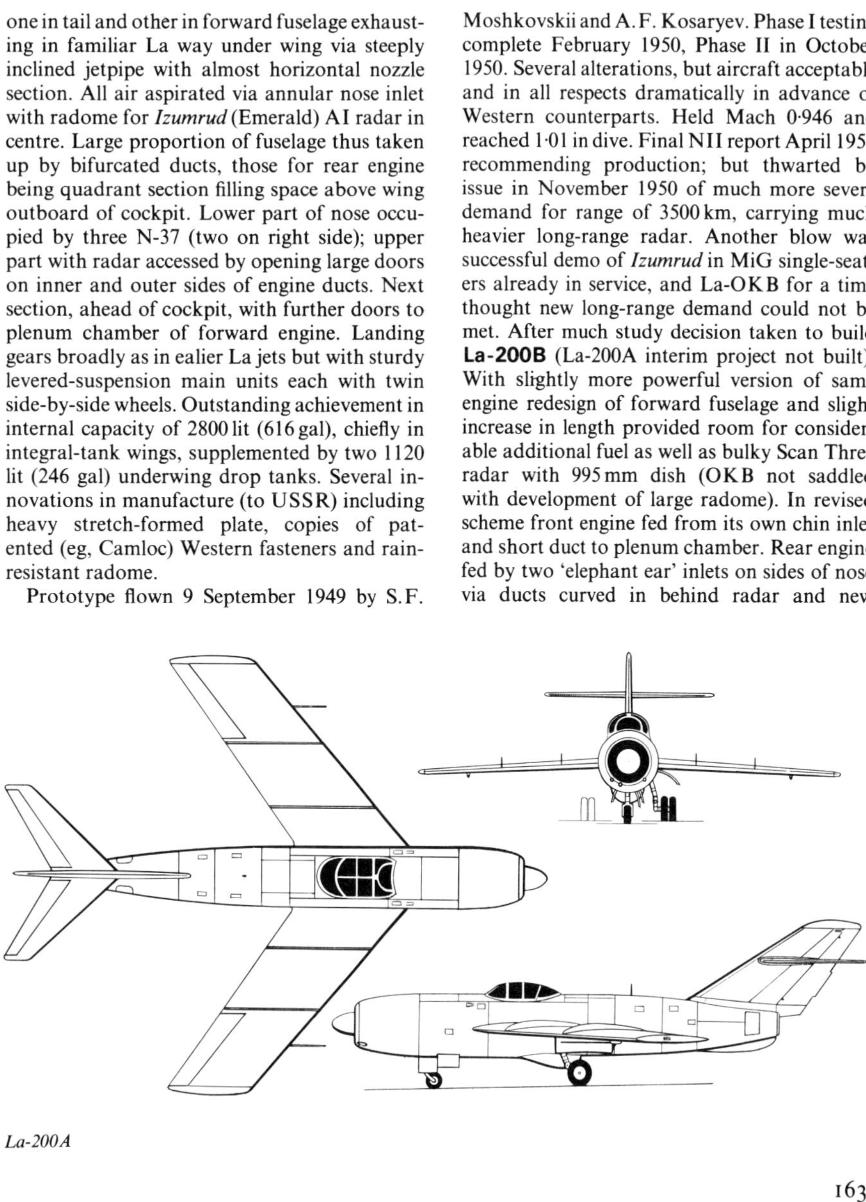

La-200A

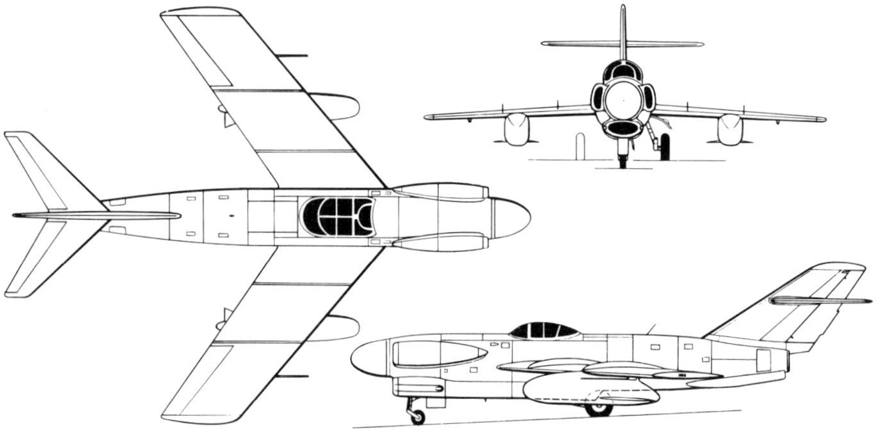

La-200B

La-200B

forward-fuselage tank; additional fuel in rear fuselage assisted by smaller compartments for single-wheel main gears tailored to paved surface only (first time in USSR). Biggest fuel increase of all, wings restressed (small changes needed) to carry giant 2650 lit (583 gal) drop tanks to bring max fuel to 8100 lit (1782 gal). These tanks probably never fitted; La-200B seen only with original small tanks. Final change was to remove third gun to save weight and free additional fuselage space. First flight by A.G. Kochyetkov 3 July 1952; mock-up radar fitted until 10 September when major system test programme involving 109 flights with radar began under M.L. Gallai. At end of day, lost out to Yak-25, later concept designed to meet November 1951 from scratch.

DIMENSIONS Span (200) 12,92 m (42 ft 4⅔ in), (200B) 12,96 m (42 ft 6¼ in); length (200) 16,59 m (54 ft 5¼ in), (B) 17,32 m (56 ft 10 in); wing area (200) 40,18 m^2 (432·5 ft^2), (B) 40,0 m^2.

ENGINES (200) two 2270 kg (5000 lb) thrust VK-1, (B) 3100 kg (6834 lb) VK-1A.

WEIGHTS Empty (200) 7675 kg (16,920 lb), (B) 8810 kg (19,422 lb); fuel/oil (200 internal) 3890 kg, (200 max) 7 t, (B int) 3903 kg, (B max) 11,25 t; loaded (no external fuel) (200) 11 565 kg (25,500 lb), (B) 12 700 kg (28,000 lb), (B max fuel) 19 350 kg (42,659 lb).

PERFORMANCE (no external fuel) Max speed (200) 964 km/h (599 mph) at SL, 1062 km/h (660 mph) at 5 km, (B) 1030 km/h (640 mph) at 5 km; climb (200) 2·6 min to 5 km, (B) 2·8 min; service ceiling (200) 15 150 m (49,700 ft), (B) 14 135 m (46,375 ft); range (200) 1165 km int fuel, 2000 km max, (B) 960 km int fuel, 2800 km (1740 miles) max.

La-250 Dubbed *Anaconda*, this large and powerful all-weather interceptor was the straw that broke the camel's back of La-OKB. Representing much greater engineering effort even than La-190 or 200, it was built to meet far-sighted requirement of January 1954 calling for new class of super-interceptor to fly great distances at high altitudes and strike from above with missiles. Necessitated large and powerful aircraft, with unprecedented fuel capacity for fighter. Solution was conventional configuration with enormous fuselage of almost constant section riding on 57° delta wing and tailplane both in mid position. Extensive machined and chem-milled plate, metal honeycomb in movable surfaces, all tankage integral. Small leading-edge notch/fence at mid-span. Two movable trailing-edge surfaces on each wing, combined flaps and drooping ailerons, with independent slab tailplanes used for pitch and roll. No spoilers. All surfaces fully powered with duplex systems, no manual reversion. Complex flight systems with pitch/yaw dampers and supervising autopilot to assist interception (probably linked with radar). Latter unknown, but filled large nose. Engines side-by-side fed by straight through ducts, area-ruled in plan, through which passed wing box with streamlined aerofoil fairing. Fixed lateral inlets with small centrebody to focus oblique shock on lip inclined in vertical plane to angle for Mach 1·5, in first aircraft

La-250 (No 4 aircraft, preserved)

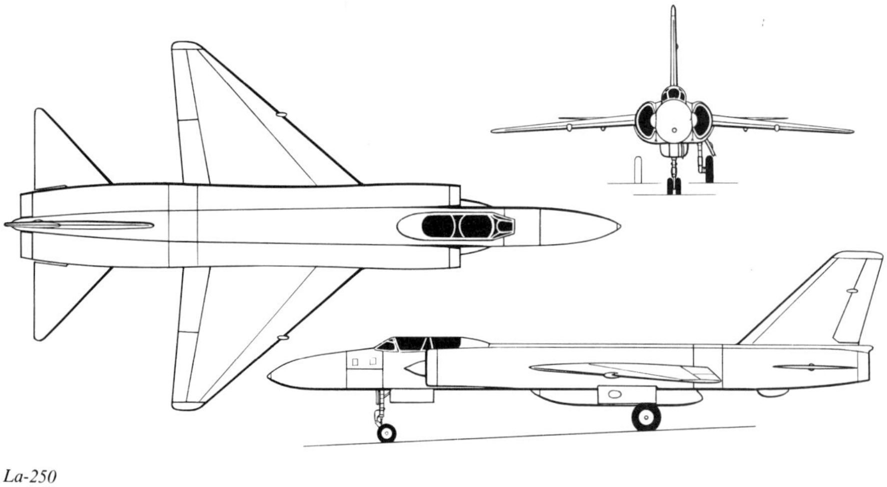

La-250

extended forwards to nose. No knowledge of armament, but to be all-missile. Single-seater, but in view of magnitude of test programme four aircraft built (one static test, three flight) and flight articles completed with temporary second cockpit for radar operator/test observer. First flown by A.G. Kochyetkov on 16 July 1956; even he had severe difficulty and totally lost control on take-off, but without serious injury to occupants. Prolonged investigation showed cause to be roll-coupling of long heavy body and small wings, giving moment of inertia in ratio 8:1. Coarse control to lift nose was not needed in roll, where response too rapid. Result was first Russian electronically modelled systems rig for La-250 flight control. When completed, tried by Gallai, Bogorodskii, Vasin, Garnayev and Shiyarnov; not one could fly it. Gradually system was made controllable, with electronic shaping of signals for correct response; at same time two remaining aircraft redesigned with inlet ducts cut back to give acceptable view downwards on each side. Second prototype with new flight controls successfully flown by Kochyetkov spring 1957. With colleague Bogorodskii put through intense test programme ('several tens' of flights) until another emergency arose 28 November 1957 when Kochyetkov had total engine failure after airfield had suddenly been blanketed by fog. Third aircraft severely damaged 8 September 1958 after another total propulsion failure (caused by 'trivial production defect'). Yet another incident was loss of wheel on take-off, aircraft sliding almost to far end of runway on wingtip. This appears to have been repaired No 3, brought up to final standard and given number 04, now preserved at Monino. Altogether, despite great promise of *Anaconda*, unreliability of engine and seemingly endless succession of hair-raising incidents led to termination of programme before death of Lavochkin on 9 June 1960, though Shavrov suggests his demise contributed to decision.

DIMENSIONS Span 13,9 m (45 ft 7¼ in); length 25,6 m (83 ft 11¾ in); wing area 80,0 m² (861 ft²).

ENGINES Two 6,5 t (14,330 lb) thrust AL-7F (afterburning, fitted at end of programme, raised thrust to 9t, 19,840 lb).

WEIGHTS Empty about 15 t (33,070 lb); loaded approximately 30 t (66,000 lb).

PERFORMANCE Max speed (afterburner) over 2000 km/h (1243 mph) at 5 km; service ceiling est 18 km (59,000 ft).

Lisunov

Boris Pavlovich Lisunov was engineer assigned to supervise technical side of licence agreement with Douglas Aircraft for DC-3. He was permitted to go to Santa Monica where between November 1936 and April 1939 he went over every part of DC-3 and its tooling and in-service support. Primary reason was use as civil aircraft by Aeroflot; subsequently Lisunov managed development of many other models by V.M. Myasishchyev, I.P. Tolstikh and I.P. Mosolov.

Li-2 Original Soviet designation **PS-84**, passenger aeroplane 84 (from GAZ-84, Khimki, where production laid down). Despite wish to avoid changes, 1293 engineering change orders on original Douglas drawings involving part design, dimensions, materials and processes. Engine installation totally different even from Cyclone-powered DC-3; original ASh-62IR driving VISh-21, changed 1940 to AV-7N (or AV-7NE) later AV-161. Hucks-dogs on all standard models. No cooling gills, many later fitted with front baffle in winter to reduce cooling airflow. Baggage doors on left but main passenger door moved to right (only seven windows). Span slightly reduced, airframe locally reinforced and thicker skin in many vulnerable places adding to empty weight. Main-gear radius arms welded 30KhGSA steel tube, and provision for skis or wheels (1200 × 450 mm). Performance appreciably below that of R-1820 or R-1830 DC-3. PS-84 in Aeroflot service June 1940. In October 1941 GAZ-84 evacuated to Tashkent. By this time military versions, and all variants redesignated Li-2. Basic passenger model **Li-2P**. Freighter **Li-2G** (*Grazhdanskii*, civil) and military **Li-2T** (*Transportnyi*) with cargo floor, tie-downs and door on left side 1,52 × 1,63 m (59·8 × 64·2 in). Front left window deleted from -2T and left and right windows added behind flight deck as standard on all models. Option on -2T mid-upper turret, either MV with one ShKAS or VUS with one UBT. Two ShKAS aimed by hand from pintle mount on each side at rear, with inwards-hinged doors. Bombload under centre-section, typically four FAB-250, total 1 t. Optional provision for up to six RS-82 under each outer wing. Normal crew four and normal troop load 20. Proportion designated **Li-2D** (*Desantnyi*, airborne assault) with glider tow hook and paratroop gear. From early 1944 (or late 1943) commonly glazed front left (crew) door with bulged top panel for observing paradrop DZs. **Li-2R** with alternative large projecting 'gondola' windows on right side of flight deck, often equipped for survey (R, *Razvyedchik*, reconnaissance); related variant for casevac role with provision for 15 stretchers. **Li-2PG** convertible pax/freighter (civil) and **Li-2DB** with supplementary long-range tanks. Non-standard models fitted with various engines, often as testbeds; AM-88 and AsH-82 fitted to small numbers of production aircraft. One (1943) tested S.A. Mostovogo's caterpillar track landing gear. Last known variant **Li-2V** (1956) with TK-19 turbochargers on engines for use in Arctic met research at over 8 km, invariably on skis. Total production about 2930. Most variants had different designations in Czechoslovakia and some other countries.

DIMENSIONS Span 28,81 m (94 ft 6¼ in); length 19,65 m (64 ft 5⅜ in); wing area 91,33 m² (983 ft²).

ENGINES Usually two 900 hp M-62.

WEIGHTS Empty around 7,7 t (16,975 lb); loaded not over 11 280 kg (24,867 lb).

PERFORMANCE Max speed about 280 km/h (174 mph); service ceiling 5,6 km (18,370 ft); range (normal fuel) 2500 km (1553 miles).

Li-2 (pre-war civil PS-84)

Maksimov

Dmitri Sergeyevich Maksimov collaborated with aerodynamicist Ivan Ivanovich Drakin working under Bartini on Stal-7. In 1937 they formed own KB, growing by 1940 to 70 persons, at Gorkii Aeroflot repair works to build SPS.

SPS-89 SPS, *Skorostnoi Passazhirskii Samolyet*, fast passenger aeroplane; 89 from GAZ-89 Gorkii where centred. Triggered by study of DC-3 and intended as PS-89 replacement. Slim constant-section fuselage for 17 passengers and crew of three; two M-100 or M-103 on low wing, twin fins, tailwheel landing gear. Begun late 1937; in April 1940 GAZ handed to Yermolayev for new OKB. SPS not affected, but following further study of project and PS-84 (Li-2) in service, decision to abandon.

Mikhelson

N.G. Mikhelson was a First World War designer who joined with several other partners over many years to create diverse types which, though often successfully flown, saw no production. In 1930s he worked at GAZ-3 where, in addition to types described, he produced several light projects including PSN (specially allocated glider); he also designed Nikitin MU-4.

MK-1 Ryibka Name meaning Little Fish, joint project with Mikhelson responsible for management and drawings, M.M. Shishmaryev for calculations and V.L. Korvin for manufacturing. Begun as project at former Anatra works at Taganrog 1 May 1921. Single-seat fighter seaplane, designed for UVVS competition. Single-bay biplane of wooden construction with fabric wings and tail and birch-ply semi-monocoque fuselage of excellent profile with fully cowled engine. Radiator in upper centre-section. Single main spar in each wing and single interplane strut each side. Four-blade propeller with large spinner. Completed as twin-float seaplane spring 1923 and made 'fairly good' test flights, major problem being indifferent float design. Later flew better as landplane. Few details and no subsequent series production.
DIMENSIONS Span about 10 m; length about 8 m; wing area in region of 35 m².
ENGINE One 200 hp Hispano-Suiza (judged inadequate for 1920s).
WEIGHTS Probably about 1200 kg loaded.
PERFORMANCE Max speed (landplane) 190 km/h (118 mph).

U-3 Development of U-2 by Mikhelson in partnership with A.I. Morshchikhin. Project started at *Krasnyi Lyetchik* plant (GAZ-3) 1934. Intended to be superior for flying instruction to U-2(AP), with more power and various detail features considered advantages (eg, seven-sided Townend ring cowl made of Enerzh-6 stainless). Flown on factory test 1935 but consensus was U-3 offered nothing not available more cheaply from U-2; in any case engine not produced in quantity.
DIMENSIONS Span 11,0 m (36 ft 10⅔ in); length 8,4 m (27 ft 6¾ in); wing area believed 30 m² (323 ft²).
ENGINE One 200 hp M-48.
WEIGHTS No data.
PERFORMANCE max speed 210 km/h (130 mph).

U-4 Second attempt to find superior replacement for U-2. Described (Shavrov) as smaller, but in fact same size and dramatic 20 km/h speed increase obtained entirely by careful aerodynamic refinement. Slimmer streamlined fuselage, different wings (same as U-3), spats and many other changes including fully cowled engine. Tested A.A. Ivanovskii 1936. Satisfactory aircraft, but again offered no advantage over U-2 for instruction and both costly and more fragile.
DIMENSIONS Span 11,0 m (36 ft 10⅔ in); length 8,1 m (26 ft 7 in); wing area 30,0 m² (323 ft²).
ENGINE One 100 hp M-11.
WEIGHTS Empty 750 kg (1653 lb); fuel/oil 90 + 10 kg; loaded 1016 kg (2240 lb).
PERFORMANCE Max speed 170 km/h (105·6 mph); climb 29·6 min to 3 km (U-2, 40–48 min); service ceiling 4 km; range 550 km (342 miles); endurance 4 h; take-off 130m/11 s; landing speed 70 km/h (43·5 mph).

RV-23 Designation from *Rekord Vysoty*, record height, major project by Mikhelson at GAZ-3 to gain world seaplane height record, with much-modified U-2! Single-seater with greatly extended span, restressed airframe and much more powerful engine. New wing centre-section of 7,1 m span, outer panels 2,8 m longer each side. Forward fuselage redesigned to mate with engine installed in I-15 type cowl driving special large-blade propeller. Supplementary tanks ahead of enclosed cabin and beneath upper wing. Wooden floats on faired steel-tube struts. Completed August 1937 and tested by F.F. Zhyerebchyenko from Moscow reservoir. On 9 September reached 11280 m; 23 October reached 11 869 m; finally (no date) 13 430 m. Later taken to Sevastopol for continued testing by Polina (Paulina) Osipyenko, after which decision to build small series.
DIMENSIONS Span 17,0 m (55 ft 9¼ in); length 9,8 m (32 ft 1¾ in); wing area 51,7 m² (556·5 ft²).
ENGINE One 710 hp Wright Cyclone SGR-1820-F3.
WEIGHTS (landplane) empty 994 kg (2191 lb); fuel/oil 130 + 20 kg; loaded 1244 kg (2743 lb).
PERFORMANCE Max speed (seaplane) 105 km/h (65 mph) (Shavrov, possibly an error), (landplane) 130 km/h (81 mph); long-endurance climb, same figure; ceiling 14 km (45,930 ft); landing speed 90 km/h (56 mph).

MP Designation from *Morskoi Podvesnoi*, naval suspended; radical high-performance torpedo carrier projected by Mikhelson/Morschikhin at Leningrad 1936. Original idea by N. Valko based on Vakhmistrov (q.v.). Reasoning was that high-performance aircraft able to attack heavily defended ship would lack range; but if carried to target under parent aircraft with just sufficient fuel for return trip it could be smaller and more agile. Moreover, it could be water-based yet carry torpedo under or recessed in keel because it would not have to take off by itself. Krasnyi Lyetchik plant took on construction job to drawings by M/M team, with assistance from Vakhmistrov. Apart from being designed to hang (in flight of two, possibly three, aircraft) under large carrier aircraft, MP was itself unconventional. Cantilever low-wing monoplane single-seater (pilot needed to navigate only on return trip) with powerful water-cooled engine. Mixed construction, mainly welded Cr-Mo tube fuselage with dural covering, wing all-metal but structure unknown. Tough planing bottom from bow (under nose of engine) to second step aft of wing, with large recess to accommodate torpedo (553 mm with twin fins, Type 45-36-AN). Aircraft armed and hung under parent aircraft by single locking attachment above CG in front of inverse-raked windscreen. Near target, engine started; release controlled by MP pilot. After high-speed low-level attack, return

Mikhelson U-3

to base and water landing, engine being tilted 20° upwards on long mounting beams to raise propeller clear of water. Wings designed to serve as sponsons giving lateral stability. Unfortunately, not sufficiently thought through and so many unresolved snags that in late 1937 V.V. Nikitin had to step in to finish job. Ready for flight 1938, but political atmosphere so frightening nobody dared to sanction flight testing in case anything went wrong.

DIMENSIONS Span 8,5 m (27 ft 10$\frac{3}{4}$ in); length about 8,0 m (26 ft 3 in); wing area 20,0 m² (215 ft²).

ENGINE One 860 hp Hispano-Suiza 12Ybrs.

WEIGHTS Empty about 2200 kg (4850 lb); loaded 3200 kg (7055 lb). No other data.

MiG

A. I. Mikoyan

Unlike most of great names in aircraft manufacturing, this OKB has shown little versatility: its products have been almost without exception fighters. It did not exist until immediately before the Second World War and was never eminent until long after that conflict, when its second major type of jet fighter appeared in the Korean war. Since then its designs have been so constantly in news that it has become most famous aircraft-manufacturing organization in world, known to more people than Boeing.

Artyem Ivanovich Mikoyan was son of carpenter in Sanain (now Tumanyan), born 5 August 1905. Began work as turner at Rostov about 1922, then joined Red Army and entered Frunze Military Academy. Moved to Zhukovskii VVA 1930, designed *Oktyabrnok* (see Avietka) year before 1937 graduation. Joined TsKB Polikarpov brigade on I-153. Mikhail Iosifovich Guryevich born into more academic family near Kursk, 12 January 1893. Kharkov University, l'Academie de l'Aéronautique (Paris) and Kharkov tech institute; graduated 1923. Joined TsKB, and in 1928 appointed engineer-constructor with Richard's KB, working on TOM programme. In 1931 reorganization, appointed deputy chief in Kochyerigin's brigade; led engineering design of TSh-3. In 1936–1938 worked at Douglas under Lisunov on DC-3 programme. When NKAP Project K issued early 1938 Mikoyan and Guryevich decided to collaborate and try to create winning design for this important new fighter to meet UVVS demand. Original scheme Mikoyan's but detail design equally shared. Proposal submitted to GUAP late 1938. Go-ahead at Kremlin meeting early 1939; permission to form OKB, numbered from GAZ-155 (director, P.A. Voronin; chief engineer, P.V. Dyemyentyev). OKB-155 organized chiefly under Mikoyan and became effective October 1939. Chief deputy constructors Guryevich and V.A. Romadin, with tech staff drawn mainly from TsKB and Polikarpov brigade but also from closed KB-2 and stillborn KB-3; section heads A.G. Brunov, I.Z. Matyuk, N.I. Andrianov, Ya.I. Selyetskii and others.

Subsequent work detailed here. Several important designers joined OKB in 1940–1941, notably P.D. Grushin, followed by R.A. Belyakov who rose to fame with swept-wing jets. In 1950s OKB responsible for design of several of Soviet Union's first large ASMs (air/surface missiles), with surface-launched variants forming sub-office still important in this field. Guryevich suffered failing health and retired 1964, Mikoyan (by then twice Hero of Soviet Union) establishing precedent of keeping partner's name on masthead now invariable throughout all major OKBs. Guryevich lived until 21 November 1976, but Mikoyan collapsed and died in harness 9 December 1970, since when Rostislav A. Belyakov has been chief constructor.

Type 65 Heavy TSh-class armoured attacker with AM-37 engine. Faster than rival BSh-2, all-metal stressed-skin, but few details. Design begun at OKB-155 November 1939 as one of two launch projects. Work pressed ahead rapidly, and two prototypes taking shape when GUAP decided Ilyushin's design promising and unassailable in timescale. Type 65 terminated autumn 1940. Sometimes called MiG-6 in Western accounts; unlikely, as never accepted for service.

MiG-1 Second launch project was high-altitude fighter. Again, design begun November 1939 after long prior parametric study. Two versions:

I-61 with AM-35A engine, **I-63** with AM-37. (Hence '65' designation of parallel programme.) First drawings released for I-61 on 15 November, and manufacture of three prototypes begun immediately. I-63 withered and AM-37 never used in this programme. Project redesignated **I-200** on 21 January 1940. Rapid progress and first flight by A.N. Yekatov 5 April 1940.

Very mixed construction but conventional layout. Fuselage back to behind cockpit of welded 30KhGSA steel tube (110 kg/mm²) with duralumin skin, mainly in form of removable panels held by unlicensed Dzus fasteners. Rear fuselage and tail, wooden monocoque with four main longerons and bakelite-ply skin comprising five 0,5 mm layers of *shpon*. Highly tapered single-spar (plus front/rear auxiliary spars) wing of Clark-YH profile, 14% at root, 8% at tip. Centre-section span 2,8 m, no dihedral, duralumin 2 mm webs with heat-treated 30KhGSA booms, 13 dural pressed ribs and five stringers above and five below with flush-riveted skin. Outer wings 6° dihedral, wooden construction with main structure 14 or 15 mm *delta*, main spar 115 mm tapering to 75 mm, auxiliary spars and stringers carrying five layers bakelite-ply 2,5–4 mm applied diagonally and bonded with casein glue. Flying-control surfaces duralumin with AST-100 fabric. All-dural Schrenk-type flaps driven pneumatically to 18° and 50°. Main-gear shock struts with usual 70/30 glycerine/alcohol filling, 270 mm stroke, 600 × 180 mm tyres, pneumatic retraction inwards with electromechanical signalling, bays closed by doors on legs with 90° hinged lower segments to cover retracted wheels. Tailwheel retracting with twin doors. Engine resting on 30KhGSA welded mounts, glycol radiator (40-lit system, unpressurized) under fuselage at wing trailing edge, supercharger inlets both wing roots, oil cooler in duct each side of cowl, compressed-air starting, no Hucks dogs on Elektron (Mg-alloy) spinner of 3,0 m VISh-22Ye three-blade propeller. Three main tanks, all AMTs aluminium: 150-lit (33 gal) protected tank behind main spar in left and right centre-section, third tank (Shavrov 150 lit, Alexander 110 lit, Green 109 lit) in fuselage between engine and cockpit. First series all provision for underwing drop tanks (seldom fitted). Simple cockpit, 13 instruments, no armour (9 mm armour later), Plexiglas canopy hinged to right (thus always closed in flight), RSI-3 single-channel radio occasionally installed. KPA-3bis oxygen, GS-350 generator, 12A-5 battery. Armament one UBS (300 rounds) and two ShKAS (375 rounds, later 750) all above engine, plus FAB-100 or two FAB-50 bombs.

First prototype unarmed. Immediately evident excellent speed, but handling totally unacceptable; high wing-loading, tendency to stall/spin, hopeless longitudinal stability and poor manoeuvrability, and dangerous except to skilled high-speed monoplane pilot. Yekatov soon killed by engine failure on approach, replaced by A.G. Kochyetkov, fellow VVA student of Mikoyan and after the Second World War chief test pilot for Lavochkin. Urgent programme to redesign and rectify most faults; meanwhile first series of 100 accepted as MiG-1 and manufacture assigned GAZ-1. Output slowed by constant modification (only 20 by end of 1940) and VVS debut inauspicious with extreme difficulties and numerous accidents. Canopy unpopular, often removed. Some ShVAK instead of UBS, others twin UBS and no ShKAS, and at least one with original armament plus two UBS in underwing gondolas. Attrition so high few survived to face Nazi onslaught June 1941.

DIMENSIONS Span (Shavrov) 10,2 m (33 ft 5$\frac{1}{2}$ in), (most other sources) 10,3 m (33 ft 9$\frac{1}{2}$ in); length 8,16 m (26 ft 9$\frac{1}{4}$ in); wing area 17,44 m² (187·7 ft²).

ENGINE One 1350 hp AM-35A.

WEIGHTS Empty 2630 kg (5798 lb); fuel/oil (internal) 266 kg; loaded (prototypes) 3071 kg, (MiG-1) 3100 kg (6834 lb).

PERFORMANCE Max speed (prototypes) 508 km/h at SL, 648 km/h (403 mph) at 7 km, (MiG-1) 480 km/h (298 mph) at SL, 628 km/h (390 mph) at 7 km; climb 5·3 min to 5 km; service ceiling 12 km (39,370 ft); range (max int fuel) 730 km (454 miles); take-off 355 m; landing 410 m/144 km/h (89·5 mph).

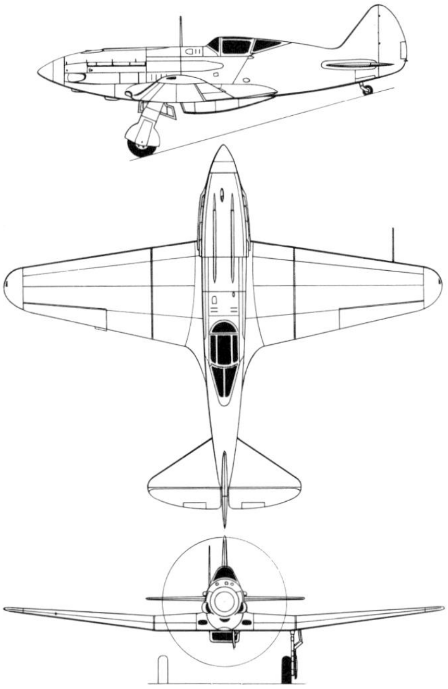

Late production MiG-3

MiG-3 abandoned at captured airfield, summer 1942

MiG-3 without rocket rails

I-211, Ye

MiG-3 Urgent rectification of MiG-1 faults involved major TsAGI tunnel programme, and extensive engineering changes. Major change addition of 250 lit (55 gal) tank under cockpit; drop-tank plumbing removed. Supercharger inlets moved 100 mm forward, radiator given revised duct to enlarged tube-plate matrix mounted further forward, second oil tank added, propeller changed to VISh-61SH, 35° pitch range. Main tyres enlarged to 650 × 200 mm, wheel-bay doors removed, tailwheel fixed, 9 mm seat armour standard, all tanks with cool exhaust-gas inerting, outer wing dihedral increased to 7°, new canopy sliding to rear, and reprofiled and glazed rear fuselage deck to improve rear view. Standard armament one UB plus two ShKAS, from mid-1941 plus four FAB-25, two FAB-100 or six RS-82 (intended primarily air-to-air) under outer wings. Same gun variations as MiG-1, plus other field conversions. RSI-3 radio increasingly fitted but still no gyro instruments nor fuel gauge. Some reports call modified aircraft **I-201**, but invariably referred to by service name, MiG-3, effective from 101st aircraft off GAZ-1 line (February 1941). Considerable improvement, but still dangerous to novice. Rapid build-up in output at GAZ-1 and another factory, continuing until spring 1942 at 3322. Main faults manoeuvrability (partly because long and heavy engine), poor firepower and great challenge to almost all its pilots who at first resisted leaving I-153 or I-16 and after June 1941 had to fight at low level where MiG at great disadvantage. By 1942 used mainly rear-area defence; persistent rumour converted to reconnaissance role appears unfounded.

By 1942 decision to terminate AM-35A output, because high-alt fighter seldom needed (but see later MiG programmes) and this helped AM-38 output for Il-2. Alternative engine therefore sought. Original I-63 programme with

AM-37 terminated late 1941 when decision not to produce engine in quantity, single airframe thus left without powerplant. October 1941 decision to fit M-82, shorter and (taking into account liquid cooling system of AM-35A) considerably lighter, thus allowing armament to be increased. Resulting **I-210** or **MiG-3M-82** with three UBS completed December 1941, flown January 1942 by V.Ye Golofastov and I.G. Lazarev. Atrocious aircraft with poor control, severe vibration and speed only 565 km/h and service ceiling 8,7 km! Decision then taken to design properly engineered MiG-3/M-82 derivative as **I-211**; first MiG prototype given shorthand identification of one letter, in this case E (*Ye*). With Shvetsov engine bureau assistance beautiful installation achieved, closely resembling La-5, with internal supercharger-duct inlet and oil-cooler ducts in wing roots. Cockpit widened and moved 245 mm back, fin chord extended forwards, horizontal tail span increased slightly and raised 200 mm higher, many other changes including redesigned main gears, retractable tailwheel and armament two ShVAK synchronized in centre-section. While MiG-3 production finished early 1942 low-rate output continued of ten I-211 (no longer called *Ye*) but despite excellent performance (speed 670 km/h, service ceiling 11,3 km) no advantage over La-5 and poorer manoeuvrability. **MiG-3U** (*Ulushchennyi*, improved) built early 1943 with duralumin monocoque rear fuselage and tail, largely 30KhGSA/duralumin wings, wider cockpit, 440 lit fuel, two wing ShVAK; AM-35A retained. Speed 656 km/h at 7 km, no production despite range increase. I-230 series described separately.

DIMENSIONS Span (Shavrov) 10,2 m (33 ft 5½ in), (most other sources) 10,3 m (33 ft 9½ in); length (Shavrov and all other Soviet sources) 8,255 m (27 ft 1 in), (some Western sources and Němeček) 8,15 m (26 ft 8¾ in); wing area 17,44 m^2 (187·7 ft^2).

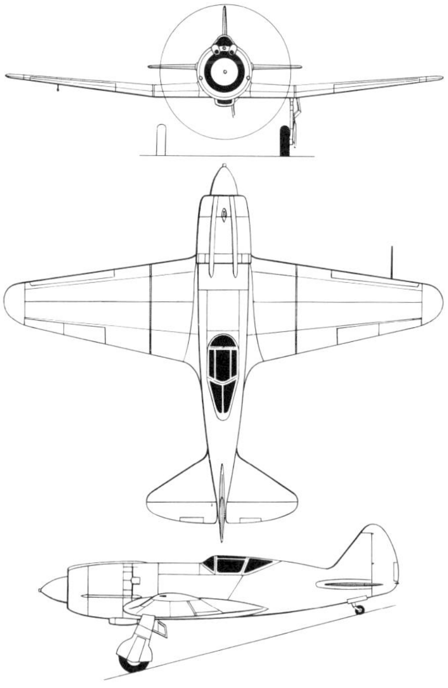

I-210

ENGINE One 1350 hp AM-35A.

WEIGHTS Empty 2595 kg (5721 lb); fuel/oil 463 + 56 kg; loaded 3350 kg (7385 lb).

PERFORMANCE Max speed 505 km/h (314 mph) at SL, 640 km/h (398 mph) at 7 km; climb 5·7 min to 5 km; service ceiling 12 km (39,370 ft); time for 360° turn 26·5 s; range (max) 1195 km (743 miles); endurance 3 h; take-off 345 m; landing 410 m/144 km/h (89·5 mph).

I-220, A, MiG-11 Ultra-high-altitude reconnaissance of western Soviet Union by Ju 86P from late 1940 triggered early 1941 requirement for VP (*Vysotnyi Pyerekhvatchik*, high-altitude interceptor). I-220, Aircraft A, assigned to MiG bureau to result in major programme progressing in stages, little commonality with MiG-3. First experimental aircraft introduced airframe with long-span wing of of TsAGI laminar profile 20,44 m^2 area, steel/dural spar, dural extruded stringers and dural skin over centre section, mainly wood outer panels. Two large sections of Schrenk flap each side and outer panels with full-span dural automatic slats. Fuselage longer than MiG-3 but mixed construction; tail all light-alloy to simplify production, with bolted joints. Wide cockpit with sliding canopy. All air inlets in centre-section leading edge. Main cooling radiators rectangular matrices along spar with air exit via variable shutter in upper surface at 52 to 57% chord. Oil coolers inboard with auxiliary inlets at root to serve carburettor and, eventually, pressurized cockpit. Completely new main gears with levered-suspension legs giving 515-mm wheel travel for soft ride on rough surfaces; new-design retractable tailwheel. All fuel tanks soft rubberized-fabric self-sealing cells, between wing spars (4) and in fuselage (2). AM-39 engine selected at start but not then cleared for flight; with a few minor changes, first aircraft completed with AM-38F and flown 21 (or 27) January 1943 by A.P. Yakimov. Second Type A fitted with AM-39 but without turbocharger and flown by A. Zhukov about 5 July 1943. Later fitted with four-blade propeller. Heavy armament, four ShVAK with 600 rounds all in fuselage. Service designation MiG-11, though no production; service test not until 14/24 July 1944.

DIMENSIONS Span 11,0 m (36 ft 10⅔ in); length 9,50 m (31 ft 2 in); wing area 20,44 m^2 (220 ft^2).

ENGINE (1) One 1700 hp AM-38F, (2) one 1700 hp AM-39.

WEIGHTS Empty (1) about 3050 kg, (2) about 3200 kg; fuel/oil 346 kg; loaded (exact figs) (1) 3574 kg (7879 lb), (2) 3730 kg (8223 lb).

PERFORMANCE Max speed (both) 572 km/h (355 mph) at SL, (1) 652 km/h (405 mph) at 2,6 km, (2) 697 km/h (433 mph) at 11,5 km; climb 4·5 min to 5 km; service ceiling (1) 9,5 km (36,090 ft); range 960 km (600 miles) at hi-alt; field length 330 m.

I-221, 2A, MiG-7 Considerably further advanced high-altitude interceptor with new longer-span wing of 22,44 m^2, NACA-234 laminar profile. Aspect ratio 7·5, thickness 14% root, 10% tip. Duralumin stressed-skin fuselage and wing throughout. Engine with two TK-2B turbos, armament (not fitted at first flight) only one BS and one ShKAS. Flown P. Zhuravlyev 2 December 1943. Engine and turbos unreliable, but much valued data.

DIMENSIONS Span 13,0 m (42 ft 7¾ in); length 9,55 m (31 ft 4 in); wing area 22,44 m^2 (241·5 ft^2).

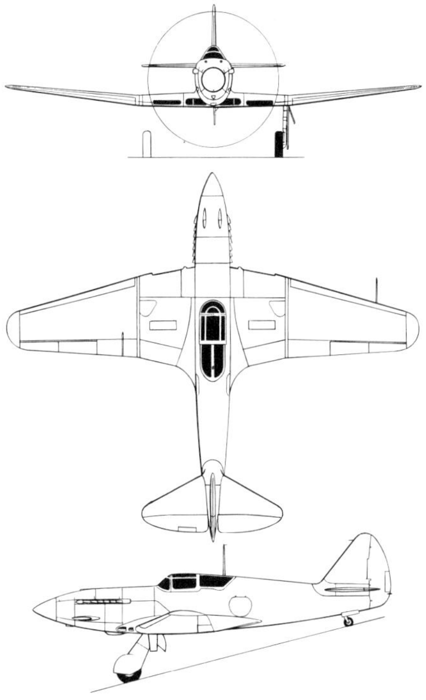

I-220

ENGINE One 1550 hp (SL) AM-39A.

WEIGHTS Empty about 3200 kg; fuel/oil 340 kg; loaded 3,8 t (8377 lb).

PERFORMANCE Max speed 690 km/h (429 mph) at 13 km; climb 4·6 min to 5 km; service ceiling not recorded; range 1000 km (620 miles).

I-222, 3A, MiG-7 Fitted with advanced form of Shchyerbakov-type pressure cabin, developed from types fitted to I-153 and I-16. Wooden rear fuselage and outer wings (Shavrov), same geometry as I-221 (2A). Cockpit welded dural, pressurized from engine turbos and with hot-air demisting and inflatable seal around sliding canopy of new profile with slightly lower top to

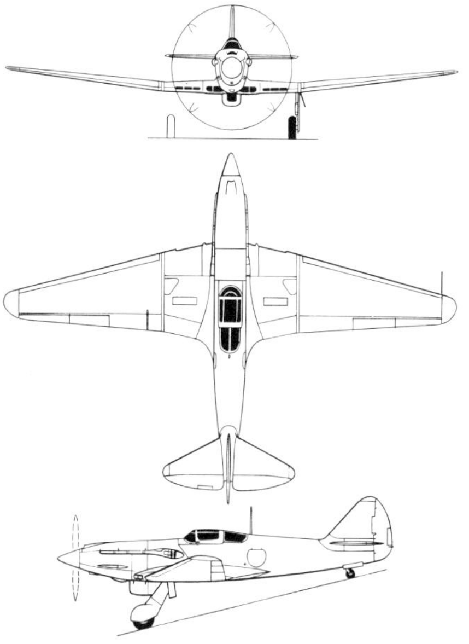

I-222

I-224, 4A

rear fuselage. Water and oil radiators of modified design in centre section, large belly inlet for first stage of cooling and engine/cabin air. New fully high-rated engine with two TK-300B turbos, driving propeller with four blades. All tanks self-sealing bags. Cockpit with bulletproof screens and pressure bulkheads of 8 or 9 mm armour. Two ShVAK in sides of fuselage, with 200 rounds. Completed late April 1944, flown A.P. Yakimov 7 May. Intended production (as MiG-7) countered by poor engine reliability and dwindling need.
DIMENSIONS Span 13,0 m (42 ft 7¾ in); length 9,60 m (31 ft 6 in); wing area 22,44 (some reports 22,38) m² (241·5 ft²).
ENGINE One 1900 hp AM-39B.
WEIGHTS Empty about 3,3t; fuel/oil 300 kg; loaded 3790 kg (8355 lb).
PERFORMANCE Max speed 691 km/h (429·3 mph) at 13 km; climb 5·5 min to 5 km; service ceiling 14,5 km (47,575 ft); range about 700 km (435 miles); landing speed 169 km/h (105 mph).

I-224, 4A, MiG-7 Last of MiG series of long-span stratospheric interceptors, with more powerful engine with same two turbos (all original reports state two TK-300B but photographs and drawings show one only, on right side). Deeper, narrower ventral radiator duct. AV-9L-26 propeller with four paddle blades of 0,4 m chord. Two ShVAK as in I-222. On factory test autumn 1944; achieved outstanding altitude and range.
DIMENSIONS As I-222.
ENGINE One 1800 hp (SL), 2000 hp (rated height) AM-39FB.
WEIGHTS Empty about 3,3 t; fuel/oil 355 kg; loaded 3780 kg (8333 lb).
PERFORMANCE Max speed about 545 km/h at SL, 693 km/h (431 mph) at 13 km; climb 4·0 min to 5 km; service ceiling 14,1 km (46,260 ft); range 1400 km (870 miles).

I-225, 5A Last of wartime MiG fighters, this outstanding aircraft represented a translation from high-altitude series to meet normal medium-altitude demands. Chief engineer Type 5A, A.G. Brunov. Great engine fitted—fundamentally better Mikulin design than 39—gave such high performance that aircraft 5A not only achieved highest speed of any Soviet piston-only fighter but also satisfactory high-altitude performance. Basically same wing as 2A to 4A, but span reduced back to 11 m. Engine fitted with single TK-1A, and driving three-blade propeller. Unpressurized cockpit with light sliding canopy. Vertical tail of reduced chord. Shallow ventral radiator and minor clean-up of exterior, though engine needed deeper front cowl. Two ShVAK, 200 rounds. First flight 14 March 1945. All-round highest performance of any Soviet piston-engined fighter, but war won and future lay with jet.
DIMENSIONS Span 11,0 m (36 ft 10⅞ in); length 9,50 m (31 ft 2 in); wing area 20,4 m² (219·6 ft²).
ENGINE One 1900 hp (SL), 2200 hp (rated height) AM-42FB.
WEIGHTS Empty 3395 kg (7485 lb); fuel/oil 350 kg; loaded 3978 kg (8770 lb).
PERFORMANCE Max speed 560 km/h (348 mph) at SL, 726 km/h (451 mph) at 10 km; climb 4·0 min to 5 km, 8·8 to 10 km; service ceiling 12,6 km (41,350 ft); range 1300 km (808 miles); landing speed 173 km/h (107 mph).

I-225, 5A

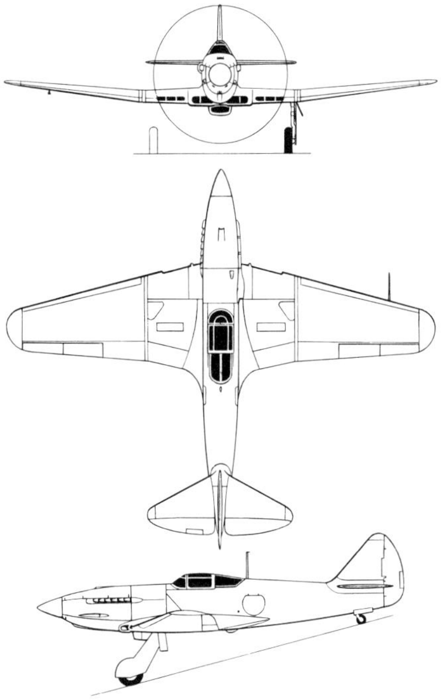

I-225, 5A

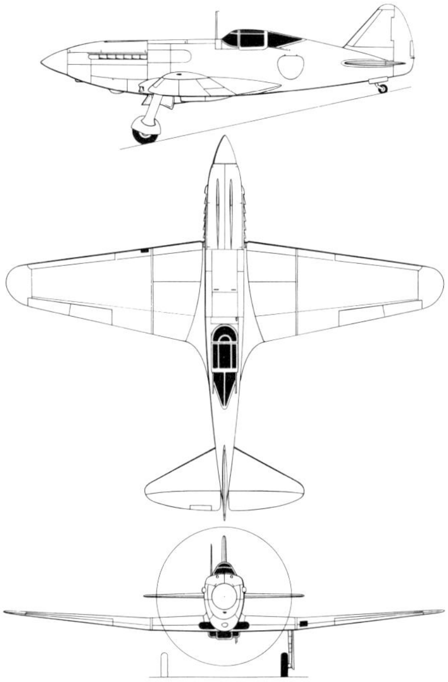

I-231

I-230, D Though widely described as specialized high-alt fighter, this was merely next generation after MiG-3, using as many MiG-3 parts as possible for general air fighting at all altitudes. Geometrically similar to MiG-3 but greatly improved aerodynamically, and with steel/dural main spar to tips and mainly light-alloy outer wing generally. Improved balanced ailerons and automatic leading-edge slats. Longer and better-profiled fuselage, and same tail as I-211(*Ye*) with 200 mm-higher tailplane of increased span. New cockpit with gyro instruments, major advances in equipment, push-button gun/radio/radiator controls and toe brakes. All-round good view from new sliding canopy and rear glazing (except on ground). Revised landing gear and doors, retractable tailwheel. Engine air inlets in roots, water and central oil radiators in wide but shallow group under wing. Intended for AM-39, actually completed with (Shavrov) AM-35, (recent Soviet reports) AM-38F, because AM-35A no longer in production. Armament two ShVAK with 370 rounds. Called Aircraft D (*Dalnostnyi*, long-range), or **MiG-3D.** First flight late 1942. Few records but apparently good aircraft. According to recent Soviet publications, test squadron (Guards IAP sub-unit) successfully used 12 MiG-3D in defence of Moscow first quarter 1943. AM-39 at last available late 1942 and MiG OKB produced further improvement, **I-231**, also called Aircraft **2D** or **MiG-3DD**, 'doubly-extended range'. Apart from more powerful engine and slightly greater fuel capacity other differences included sharply tapered top to rear fuselage, horizontal tail in original position and modified grouped radiator installation for even lower drag. Outstanding aircraft when tested 1943 (one Soviet report states July) but no production. Shavrov gives shortage of AM-39s as sole reason.

DIMENSIONS Span 10,2 m (33 ft 5½ in); length (both) 8,62 m (28 ft 3⅓ in); wing area 17,44 m² (187·7 ft²).

ENGINE (D) one 1350 hp AM-35A, (2D) one 1700 hp AM-39.

WEIGHTS Empty (D) 2612 kg (5758 lb), (2D) 2,7 t (5952 lb); fuel/oil (D) 324 kg, (2D) 333 kg; loaded (D) 3260 kg (7187 lb), (2D) 3287 kg (7247 lb).

PERFORMANCE Max speed (D) 660 km/h (410 mph) at 6 km, (2D) 707 km/h (439 mph) at 7 km; climb (D) 5·2 and (2D) 4·5 min to 5 km; service ceiling (D) 12 km, (2D) 11,4 km; range (D) 1300 km (808 miles), (2D) 1350 km (839 miles).

DIS, MiG-5 Presence of P.D. Grushin in OKB enabled separate design brigade to be formed for completely different project. August 1940 decision to produce rival to Polikarpov TIS; launched as DIS (also called **DIS-200**, not explained), *Dvukhmotornyi Istrebitel Soprovozhdyeniya*, twin-engined fighter escort. Capable machine with large wing and considerable power, but single-seater. Fuselage slim monocoque of *delta drevesina*, eight layers of *shpon* and bakelite-ply skin. Centre-section slight anhedral (1·5°, much less than many Western representations), duralumin spar webs and pressed ribs, 30KhGSA steel booms and main outer-panel joints, dural skin flush-riveted. Wooden outer wings, two main spars tip to tip with multiple stringers. Light-alloy twin-finned tail with all control surfaces fabric-covered. Four protected tanks in centre-section and two in fuselage, total 2675 lit (587 gal). Engines in large underslung nacelles with chin radiators but leading-edge supercharger inlets. Main gears with 950 × 300 mm tyres on inner sides of single cantilever shock struts (possibly rotating 90° during retraction). Retractable tailwheel. Two flying prototypes authorized, first with armament of one VYa in underside of nose (magazine behind and below seat) plus two BS and four ShKAS in wing roots (magazines ahead of spar box). Advanced all-glazed canopy with jettisonable sliding mid portion. Armour up to 9 mm in front, rear, sides and underside of seat. First flight summer 1941, soon after May 1941 decision to allocate service designation MiG-5 and broaden capability to include attack, reconnaissance and torpedo roles. Generally good performance but landing unacceptable and modified with improved slotted flaps and automatic leading-edge slats outboard of propeller discs. Second DIS completed with improved low-drag engine (believed to be AM-37) installation with close-fitting cowl, exhaust led above wing and main radiators in sides of nacelle with vertical variable exit shutters under trailing edge. Heavier armament: two VYa instead of one, plus existing wing-root guns, and centreline attachment for 1 t bombs (eg, two FAB-500) or torpedo. Flown August 1941, data for this. OKB evacuated Kuibyshyev October 1941, programme lapsed, but early 1942 at least one additional DIS built with radial engines, more internal fuel and various minor changes such as extended tailcone. Recent Soviet accounts hint several such constructed; Western accounts (not Soviet) claim ShKAS were moved from wing to nose but not substantiated and from appearance not enough room. VVS reluctant to order fresh type for which need had lapsed; Pe-2 worked unescorted and handled DIS type offensive missions.

DIMENSIONS Span 15,10 m (Shavrov, 15,3) (49 ft 6½ in); length (AM-35A) 10,875 m (35 ft

DIS (No 3 aircraft)

8¼ in), (ASh-82) 11,85 m (38 ft 10½ in); wing area 38,9 m² (418·7 ft²).

ENGINES (1, 2) Two 1350 hp AM-35A (Shavrov, 1400 hp AM-37), (3) two 1540 hp ASh-82F.

WEIGHTS Empty not recorded; fuel/oil (1) 1920 kg; loaded (1) 8060 kg (17,769 lb), (3) est Shavrov at 8 t, probably nearer 10 t.

PERFORMANCE Max speed (1) 610 km/h (379 mph), (2) 630 km/h (391 mph), (3) 604 km/h (375 mph); climb (1) 5·5 min to 5 km; service ceiling (1) 10,8 km (35,435 ft); range (1) 2280 km (1417 miles), (3) 2500 km (1553 miles).

I-250, N This unusual little interceptor was, with Su-5, unique example of crash programme for combat aircraft designed for speed at all costs, to meet potential challenge of German jets. Programme begun about March 1944 at personal order of Stalin (who criticized industry for not having jets already). Only turbojet, Lyul'ka VRD-2, still under development; alternative was to use most powerful piston engine in conjunction with VRDK (*Vozdushno-Reaktivnyi Dvigatyel Kompressornyi*, air-reaction engine compressor). This developed from about 1942 by TsIAM team led by K. V. Kholshchyevnikov, and comprised externally driven compressor feeding fresh air through water-cooled radiator of main engine to combustion chamber housing group of seven fuel burners; from here propulsive jet accelerated through variable rear nozzle, capable of being faired over in cruising flight. Basic airframe advanced all-metal stressed-skin construction. Wing of quite large span, two-spars and plate ribs, TsAGI-1A root (low-lift) changing to TsAGI-1V (hi-lift) at tip, 10% thickness throughout to preserve aileron control and avoid tip stall. Frise ailerons, TsAGI slotted flaps. Fuselage appeared stumpy because of large VRDK air duct from nose, under engine and cockpit, to tail. Engine air drawn from inlet above main intake, immediately behind spinner of 3,1 m three-blade propeller. Drive from rear wheelcase to compressor of VRDK via pilot-controlled clutch. At max forward speed combined propulsion equivalent to 2,800 hp at 7 km height. Fuel (same for both units) in inner and outer wings and ahead of cockpit. Latter unpressurized with sliding canopy. Main landing gear derived from I-220 series with levered-suspension legs with shock-absorber in front of leg. First I-250 apparently fitted with retractable tail-skid beneath propelling nozzle incorporating left/right clamshell shutters actuated by pilot. One NS-23 firing through propeller hub, two UBS with 200 rounds in top decking. This prototype also had large side inlet behind propeller and duct entering fuselage above wing on left, possibly on both sides. These may have been main VRDK ducts in this aircraft. First flight by A.P. Dyeyev 3 March 1945. Preliminary trials completed May, showing excellent speed, higher than Su-5 and only marginally below Me 262 at medium/low altitudes. Dyeyev killed June 1945 in experimental MiG, possibly this aircraft or refined second prototype. Latter generally cleaned up with single inlet at nose and improved tail with better clamshells and small ventral fin accommodating retracted tailwheel. New armament of three lightweight B-20, two on left of engine and one on right. According to Shavrov I-250, also called N, built in small production series for VMF with armament of four B-20, two on each side; used by Northern and Baltic Fleet fighter units until 1950, as **MiG-13.**

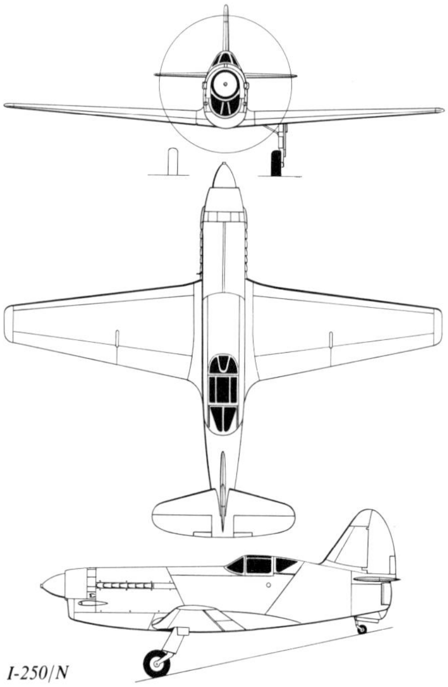
I-250/N

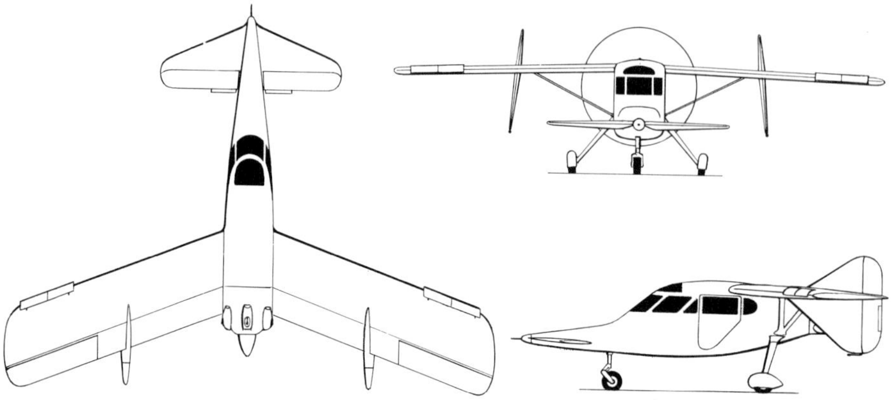
Utka, often called MiG-8

DIMENSIONS Span 11,05 m (36 ft 3 in); length 8,75 m (28 ft 8½ in); wing area 15 m² (161 ft²).

ENGINES One 1650 hp VK-107R with shaft drive to VRDK rated at 300 kg (661 lb) thrust for 10-minute periods.

WEIGHTS Empty not recorded; fuel/oil 570 kg; loaded 3680 kg (8113 lb).

PERFORMANCE Max speed 825 km/h (513 mph) at 7,8 km (25,590 ft); (on VK-107R only about 700 km/h (435 mph); climb 4·6 min to 5 km; service ceiling 11,9 km (39,040 ft); range (max, VK-107R only) 1800 km (1118 miles); landing speed 150 km/h (93 mph).

Utka, MiG-8 This unconventional canard (tail-first) aircraft, named *Utka*, Duck, was built in MiG OKB and assigned bureau number which made it sound like production type. Part of design assigned to VVA students under Col (later Prof) G.A. Tokayev; no connection with MiG OKB's normal work, except in important respect that it confirmed low-speed behaviour of slightly swept wings and one of unusual configurations which might be suitable for future jet fighter. High wing with two triangular Scheibe fin/rudder surfaces tested at 55% span and on wingtips. Clark-YH, 12% t/c, constant chord, two spars, strut-braced, sweep 20°, anhedral − 2°, tested wide variety of flap, slat and wingtip configurations. Three-seat cabin with pilot in front. Extended nose carrying fixed tailplane and tabbed elevators. Fixed tricycle gear (nose 300 × 150, main 500 × 150 mm), mainwheel spats later removed. Pusher two-blade fixed-pitch 2,35 m propeller driven by M-11 with experimental helmeted cowl. Construction wood throughout, with most of wing and control surfaces fabric. Flown end 1945 by A.I. Zhukov, no problem but prolonged tinkering with aerodynamics.

DIMENSIONS Span 9,5 m (31 ft 2 in); length 7,1 m (23 ft 3½ in); wing area 14,71 m² (158 ft²), foreplane 9,75 m².

ENGINE One 110 hp M-11F.

WEIGHTS Empty 642 kg (1415 lb); fuel/oil 140 kg; loaded 1150 kg (2535 lb) (Němĕcek, 997 kg).

PERFORMANCE Max speed 205 km/h (127 mph) at SL; endurance 5 h; take-off 238 m.

I-270, Zh Aware of Me 163B in early 1944, at least two OKBs, including MiG, prepared prelim studies for copy, using Dushkin/Glushko rocket engines, but no prototype construction. After the Second World War considerable Junkers data available on Ju 248 programme (Me 263), including one intact prototype, believed only one completed. Decision taken to build Soviet aircraft in same class, but with more conventional aerodynamics (not known whether Ju 248 flown). MiG OKB assigned task and quickly produced good design, believed joint Grushin/Guryevich. All-metal stressed-skin, fuselage based on Ju 248 but better shape, longer nose and longer pressurized cockpit with hinged canopy, smaller unswept wings with slotted flaps inboard of ailerons, larger vertical tail with mass-balanced rudder and T-type 30°-swept tailplane with mass-balanced elevators. Engine pump-fed nitric acid and kerosene, with main and upper auxiliary (cruise) chambers respectively giving 4¼ and 9 min endurance under power. (Note: GRD OKB exhibited main chamber only and never publicized this engine, unlike RD-1 family.) Landing gears strong resemblance Ju 248, but aircraft Zh longer, smaller wing, similar empty weight but smaller propellant tankage so lower gross weight. First Zh pointed nose with German windmill-driven generator, all-silver, reported (Shavrov and others) to have two NS-23 with 80 rounds. Believed destroyed in ground test, mid-1946. Second aircraft with no windmill and rounded nose painted

with red trim. Successfully flown V.N. Yuganov later 1946. This aircraft also written-off during testing; no serious expectation of production.
DIMENSIONS Span 7,75 m (25 ft 5 in); length 8,77 m (28 ft 9$\frac{1}{4}$ in); wing area 12,0 m^2 (129 ft^2).
ENGINE One RD-2M-3V bi-propellant rocket, SL rating 1450 kg (3197 lb).
WEIGHTS Empty 1900 kg (4189 lb); propellants 2120 kg (4674 lb); loaded 4120 kg (9083 lb).
PERFORMANCE Max speed 1000 km/h (621 mph) at height (possibly est, not actually achieved); climb 3·0 min to 5 km, 7·23 to 10 km; service ceiling 18 km (59,055 ft); endurance (Shavrov) 4·3 h, must be error, even with gliding, more like 20 min.

MiG-9, I-300, F Design of Soviet turbojet fighter began at MiG OKB early 1944. Aircraft F planned as minimum-risk fighter to be powered by two Lyul'ka VRD-3 (later called S-18 and also TR-1), each rated 1250 kg thrust, installed side-by-side in bottom of fuselage fed by nose inlet and with nozzles under rear fuselage. Unswept wing closely related to I-250 (aircraft N). Work pressed ahead despite major problems, under chief engineer Aleksei Timofeyevich Karyev, in competition with Su-9 which had underwing engines. Worst worry was engine, judged to lag airframe timing by up to a year, because, though several prototype engines on testbed, reliability very poor. Then February 1945 Kremlin meeting attended by all Fighter OKB leaders at which Stalin instructed crash programme to build fighters using German turbojets, BMW 003 (later called RD-20) and Jumo 004B (RD-10). La and Yak told to use single engine, and fit two NS-23; MiG and Su told to use twin engines and add N-37 to armament. Three prototypes of each, to fly at earliest date. (After end of the Second World War pressure eased, and despite valuable data from flight-testing of Me 262 original flight expectation of summer 1945 slipped by nine months). MiG OKB took decision, whilst not terminating original aircraft, to redesign front fuselage of F to take allocated BMW 003A, slimmer and lighter but only 800 kg thrust each. To preserve CG guns fitted far forward, together with unpressurized cockpit with excellent armour and sliding canopy. Two-spar wing of TsAGI-1 series profile, ruling thickness 9%, slotted flaps, Frise ailerons. Good fuselage with ample tankage above mid wing and simple ground-level access to engines, guns, radio and other items. Only unusual feature 15-mm air-gap sandwich

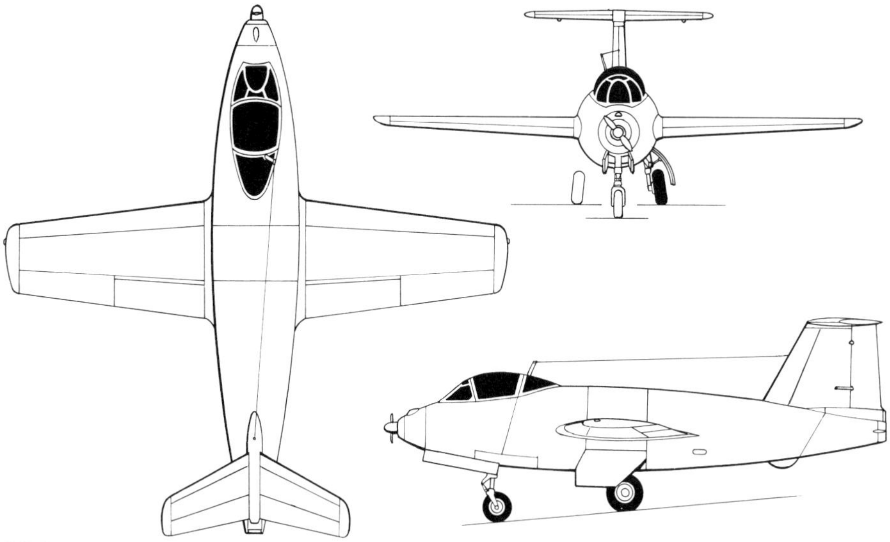
I-270/Zh

of stainless steel, with corrugated core, formed into curved panels above jet nozzles. Duralumin flight controls with 0,3/0,5 mm skins, manual system. Tricycle landing gear with typical MiG levered-suspension throughout, though with lower arms trailing leg instead of leading it as in OKB's previous fighters. Main gears retracted outwards into inter-spar box with bay closed by wing-mounted doors. Castoring nose gear with shimmy-damper, retracting to rear between engine ducts. Hydraulic actuation for all main powered items, single circuit but pump on each engine. Fuel 1595 lit (351 gal) in four fuselage and six wing cells, all protected rubberized fabric. Wing piped for two 235 lit (52 gal) underwing tip tanks fitted from fourth aircraft. Armament fitted from No 1 (called **F-1**), one NS-37 with 40 rounds and two NS-23 with 160 total. No wing stores.

First I-300, aircraft F-1, sent with special test team (OKB pilot A.N. 'Lesha' Grinchik, chief engineer Karyev and mechanics V.V. Pimyenov and A.V. Fufurin) to NII flight test centre at Chkalovskaya. There met Yak team with Yak-15; tossed coin on 24 April 1946 and Grinchik made first Soviet jet flight, unambitious short sortie to feel behaviour. Only real problem severe buffet traced to steel sandwich immediately above jets. On 20th flight, 11 June, aileron separated during high-speed pass (fatigue of compensation lever) and F-1 dived straight into ground. F-2 flown G.M. Shiyanov 11 August preceded by F-3 M.L. Gallai 9 August. F-3 fly-past with Yak-15 Tushino 18 August; following day Mikoyan summoned to Kremlin and told to have 15 in October Revolution parade! Sent to production factory, with *Commissar* P.Yu. Dementyev, where some 60,000 sets of drawings hastily prepared and financial inducements offered to workers who thereupon built all 15 by hand without production tooling or properly organized procedure. (All 15 aircraft ready, but fly-past cancelled by fog.) NII trials December 1946; May 1947 accepted as MiG-9, becoming with Yak-15 first Soviet production jet. According to Gallai, who had hair-raising experiences with I-300 testing, handling unexpectedly pleasant and no problem to average pilot, provided he allowed 12-15 seconds for opening throttle and could manage high idling thrust by cutting one engine dead on touchdown. Number built probably 1000, not including tandem dual trainer, which added about 80. Trainer requirement **I-301T** led to prototypes FT-1 (flown December 1946) and FT-2, with 260 lit less fuselage fuel and tandem cockpits. Production trainer designated **MiG-9UTI**, sometimes written UTI MiG-9. About 1947 used for first test in USSR of ejection seat from jet aircraft. In 1946 original programme yielded I-305, Aircraft **FL**, powered by TR-1 engines. **MiG-9FF** with RD-20F engines, same 800 kg rating.

MiG-9

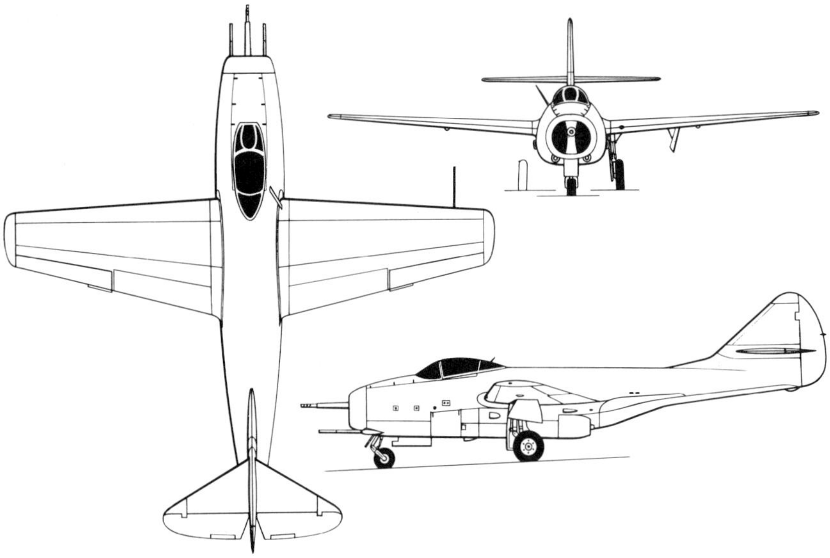

MiG-9

MiG-9PB, larger underwing (slipper) tanks. **MiG-9B** *Babochkoi* (Butterfly) with totally redesigned nose and inlets avoiding ingestion of gun gas. **MiG-9FR** final (1947) refined version, redesigned nose of better profile, pressurized cockpit, ejection seat, rearranged guns (two 23 on left, 37 on right) and more powerful engines. According to Shavrov, mass-produced; most other writers dispute this. Single example built of **MiG-9FN** with single R-R Nene 2 engine, completed March 1947 but never flown because of extreme pressure on demonstrably superior I-310, Aircraft S. Wide parallel studies for swept and RD-500 (Derwent) versions.

DIMENSIONS Span 10,0 m (32 ft 9⅔ in); length 9,75 m (31 ft 11¾ in) excl guns; wing area 18,2 m² (196 ft²).

ENGINES Two 800 kg (1764 lb) thrust RD-20; (FR) 1000 kg (2205 lb) RD-21.

WEIGHTS Empty (F) 3330 kg, (series) 3540 kg (7804 lb), (FR) 3570 kg, (UTI) 3584 kg; fuel/oil (F) 1334 kg, (series) 1762, (FR) 1300, (UTI) 847 + 35); loaded (F) 4860 kg, (series) 5501 kg (12,127 lb), (FR) 5070 kg, (UTI) 4762 kg.

PERFORMANCE Max speed (F) 860 km/h at SL, 910 at 5 km, (series) 865 at SL (537 mph), 910 at 5 km (565 mph), (FR) 965 km/h at 5 km (600 mph), (UTI) 910 km/h (565 mph); climb to 5 km (F) 4·5 min, (series) 6·2, (FR) 2·7, (UTI) 5·0; service ceiling (F) 13 km, (series) 12,8 (42,-000 ft), (FR, UTI) both 13 km; range (series) 1100 km (684 miles), (others) 800 km (497 miles); time 360° turn 37 s; take-off 760 m;, landing 1060 m/170 km/h (106 mph).

MiG-15, S, I-310 One of most famous aircraft of all time, this simple fighter was not only traumatic shock to Western intelligence when encountered in combat in Korea in November 1950 but also marked first occasion on which speed of design and development bettered that of any Western rival. Programme begun by Kremlin meeting March 1946 attended by all major fighter constructors, charged with design of high-altitude day interceptor able to operate from rough strips, reach Mach 0·9, have good manoeuvrability at high (over 11 km) altitude and flight endurance at least 1 hour. Swept wing taken for granted, and OKBs told to work closely with TsAGI where swept wings studied at least from 1935 (though not necessarily for high-Mach use). MiG OKB studied forward-swept wing also, as flown by Tsybin. Aircraft S planned on basis of mid-mounted swept wing on shortest circular-section fuselage with large T-tail, configuration studied from late 1945 in many German reports and judged to offer best compromise. Engine choice between two competing designs of 2 t (4410 lb) thrust: axial derived from German (mainly BMW) work, similar to first Atar, and large centrifugal based on known external appearance of Rolls-Royce Nene and designated VK-1PO (VK from Maj-Gen V.Ya. Klimov, PO from 'first consignment'). Though latter was crude and generally outside prior Soviet experience MiG OKB told to go ahead, and fuselage sized to 1,45 m diameter in consequence. (No doubt whatever that details and drawings of Nene were soon expected to be obtained by Soviet intelligence.) Design well advanced in September 1946 when, under terms of trade agreement, UK agreed to export Nene to USSR. Ten engines shipped at once, 15 in March and more later. First engine carefully stripped and issue of Russian production drawings began as early as 30 October at No 45 factory in Moscow, a large production plant headed by Klimov and to which design staff were specially sent on 21 September from Factory No 117 (Leningrad), Klimov's main design office. VK-1PO terminated and replaced by RD-45, designated after Moscow factory. MiG OKB received accurate installational drawings in February 1947.

Aircraft S, also with prototype number I-310, simple all-metal stressed-skin. Wing swept 35° at ¼-chord, one main spar at ¼-chord with sheet web of D16-T (ruling material throughout airframe) and booms machined from V-95. Two rear spars, 21 stringers and 20 ribs, flush-riveted skin 2 mm between spars, 1 mm elsewhere. Section TsAGI S-10s at root, high-lift SR-3 at tips, 11% thick throughout; anhedral -2°, MAC 2,12 m, aspect ratio 4·85, taper ratio 1·61. Anti-flutter masses (each 30 kg) in tip leading edge, powered ailerons (sealed and internally balanced), fixed leading edge, hydraulic Fowler-type flaps of 2,36 m², driven to 20° take-off and 55° landing. Main structural junctions 30KhGSA steel. Fuselage diameter 1,45 m, frontal area 1,16 m² (1,35 including canopy), length 8,08 m, fineness 5·57. Pressurized cockpit ahead of wing with rear-sliding canopy and ejection seat. Plain nose inlet to duct bifurcated past cockpit and again above and below unbroken wing centre-section to plenum chamber behind wing. Nene 2 engine carried on 30KhGSA tubular truss off strong frame at rear spar to which entire rear fuselage and tail secured by four large quick-detach bolts. Vertical tail 4,0 m² swept 56° with main spar 30KhGSA carrying 3,0 m², 40°-swept horizontal tail 1582 mm above fuselage centreline with incidence ground-adjustable only. Manual tail surfaces with trimmers. Rear-fuselage airbrakes, 0,48 m² each, swinging out and slightly down under hydraulic rams. Tricycle landing gear with levered-suspension legs throughout, nose unit retracting forwards into lower part of duct bifurcation and main gears with 660 × 160 mm tyres retracting inwards to lie entirely within wing between spars; actuation, like flaps and airbrakes, hydraulic, with compressed-air standby. Kerosene T-1 fuel in main protected flexible cell behind cockpit between air ducts and in rear fuselage, total in I-310 1512 lit (332·7 gal). Later provision for two 250 lit (55 gal) slipper underwing tanks. Full armament on first I-310: one NS-37 with 40 rounds and two NS-23 with 80 rounds each, mounted as single unit in quickly removed pack under nose, winched up and down on two pairs of cables.

Various rumours: that first prototype was

I-310, S

built with dihedral, flew on 2 July 1947 and later crashed; that I-310 first flew with slats, later removed and replaced by four fences; that it had only two NS-23, and NS-37 was added later; that rear fuselage was originally longer and was later cut back with short jetpipe, and more fin sweep to preserve tail moment-arm; that airbrakes were tried on wing and elsewhere before rear-fuselage finalized; and that horizontal tail was originally at top of fin. No evidence for most of these suggestions. Numerous photographs indisputably showing I-310 all show configuration closely resembling production aircraft, even with standard 100 mm-high fences. This aircraft first flew, in hands of Viktor Nikolayevich Yuganov, on 30 December 1947. Only major engineering modifications resulting from early test-flying were to cut back length of jetpipe 0,32 m, on suggestion of Kalikhman's team from TsIAM, and to increase sweep of tailplane slightly (from 35°) and effect small modification to wing trailing edge on suggestion of TsAGI aerodynamics team (S.A. Khristianov, G.P. Svishchyev, Ya.M. Syerebriiskii and V.V. Struminskii).

Performance of OKB on this programme far ahead of rivals, and spring 1948 (believed 21 March) aircraft S confirmed as production fighter designated MiG-15. Development under leading engineer A.A. Andryeyev, with OKB test pilots I.T. Ivashchyenko and S.N. Anokhin. First pre-production MiG-15 received for NII testing 10 May 1948. RD-45 engine fitted, full armament and operative systems and equipment including Russian ejection seat, RSI-6M radio and British-derived gyro gunsight. Test programme under Col Grigori Sedov begun on S-02 on 27 May 1948, with S-01 joining on 5 July. Added equipment included landing light at top of inlet bifurcation with combat camera at 12 o'clock (top of inlet lip), steel blast skin round underside of nose, remote-indicating gyrosyn compass, and full-length trailing-edge tab on lower rudder. All-round extremely good report, with dives to Mach 0·92; but many shortcomings including serious tendency to stall/spin in tight turn, poor behaviour at any high angle of attack (even low speed) and progressively worse buzz and snaking as Mach number rose beyond 0·88. Latter was fixed as service release limit, and airbrake was tied to Mach instrumentation to open automatically at 0·9 – 0·91. Cleared for issue to PVO (newly formed) October 1948. All production MiG-15s powered by improved RD-45F of same thrust.

NII urged development of **ST(I-312T)** trainer, and resulting tandem dual **MiG-15UTI** (also called UTI MiG-15) designed from August 1948 with reduced fuel, with rear cockpit above wing with sliding canopy and front (pupil) cockpit with canopy hinged to right. Armament (not always fitted) one UBK-Ye with 150 rounds or one NR-23 with 80. Available for issue early March 1949, subsequently retained in production long after termination of single-seat models. Next came three simultaneous developments, SD/SP/SI (described later), plus single research aircraft designated **MiG-15LL** (*Letayushchye Laboratorii*, flying lab) with reduced sweep upper fin and added ventral fin giving much greater side area, fully powered rudder, increased-chord horizontal tail and many other flight-control changes. MiG-15LL project under I.M. Pashkovskii and M.I. Masurskii, aircraft flown A.M. Tyuteryev 21 September 1949 and soon held Mach 0·985; on 18 October reached confirmed Mach 1·01 in dive from 12,2 km and valuable in development of flight controls including yaw dampers and all-flying tailplane. **MiG-15SD**, basic improvement with VK-1 engine and 92 engineering changes, flown September 1949 and produced in place of original MiG-15 as **MiG-15bis**. Airframe carefully analysed and structure weight reduced by 90 kg. Wing trailing edge given riveted 'knife' strip 40 mm wide, and 30 mm strip on right aileron. Modified wing spars with single main spar branched into Y at 9th rib to twin steel root attachments, rear member at 90° to fuselage axis. Perforated flaps, elevator balance increased to 22%, and in course of 1950 major changes included improved aileron booster in left leading edge, new design of airbrake hinged further forward and with increased area, landing light moved to left wing root and fast-firing NR-23 instead of NS-23 guns. Basis for all post-1949 production, but variants of original MiG-15 included: **MiG-15PB** (*Podvesnyi Bakami*, underwing tanks) with slipper tanks of 600 lit (132 gal) each; initial **MiG-15P** with pre-production *Izumrud* radar; **MiG-15SV** with NS-37 and two NR-23 as on bis; and several pilotless variants (believed all rebuilds). For **SI** see MiG-17.

During 1949–1950 (MiG-15 and MiG-15bis) additional equipment included new avionics: RSIU-3M VHF com, MRP-48 series beacon receiver, ARK-5 radio compass, RV-2 or RV-10 radio altimeter (dipole aerial under left wingtip, and usually right wing root) and SRO-1 IFF (post aerial above fuselage). **MiG-15SP-1** prototype single-seat all-weather interceptor with large nose radar (probably same set as MiG-17SP-2 and I-320) and armament of one NS-37 and (Shavrov) one NS-45; flown with near-bis airframe late 1949. Small numbers built of less-ambitious **SP-5** (dual) and **MiG-15bisP** (single-seat) *Izumrud*-equipped interceptors, usually with two NS-23 or, from late 1950, NR-23. **MiG-15bisS** escort with 600-lit slipper tanks. **MiG-15bisR** photo-reconnaissance variant with two (rarely one) vertical cameras under cockpit floor projecting into external fairing box related model made in Poland). **MiG-15bisSB**, also called **ISh** (*Istrebitel Shturmovik*), dedicated ground attack with a.t.o. rockets and braking 'chute (one seen with blown flaps); four underwing hardpoints for tanks, and (usually) inner axial beams carrying tandem bombs or rocket pods. Single **MiG-15U**, also called **SU**, with lateral engine inlets and pair of NS-37 mounted on transverse pivots in completely new 'solid' nose firing round vertical arc of 60° (+5° to −55°), mainly for ground attack.

Production from at least two factories, more than half total being from Kuibyshyev. Despite MiG-17, production continued at high pressure to late 1951 (UTI continuing thereafter), supplemented by licence-manufacture in Czechoslovakia as S-102 and S-103 (bis), Poland as LIM-1 (few) and LIM-2 (bis) and Hungary as *Jaguar*. Total at least 5000, plus several thousand UTI made under licence as CS-102 and LIM-3 (many UTI may be converted fighters, but most were not). China built spares from 1959 and later complete major airframe assemblies for bis and UTI.

DIMENSIONS Span 10,08 m (33 ft 1 in) (SI-2 45°, see MiG-17); length (most) 10,04 m (32 ft 11¼ in), (production bis) 10,86 m (35 ft 7½ in), (UTI, SP-1) 10,1 m (33 ft 1⅝ in); height 3,7 m (12 ft 1⅝ in); wing area 20,6 m² (221·75 ft²).

ENGINE One R-R Nene type centrifugal turbojet: (I–310) 2270 kg (5000 lb) Nene 2, (MIG-15 and UTI) 2270 kg RD-45F, (bis and SP-1) 2700 kg (5952 lb) VK-1.

WEIGHTS Empty (I-310) 3330 kg, (MiG-15) 3382 kg (7456 lb), (P/B) 3416 kg, (UTI, Shavrov) 3500 kg (7716 lb), (UTI, Němĕcek) 3340 kg (7363 lb), (one actual UTI of LSK) 3747 kg (8260 lb), (bis) 3681 kg (8115 lb); fuel/oil (I-310) 1245 kg, (MiG-15) 1210 kg (2668 lb), (bis) 1173 kg internal, 1837 max (2586/4050 lb); max (I-310) 4840 kg, (MiG-15) 4806 lb (10,595 lb), (P/B) 5260 kg, (UTI) 4850 to 5415 kg (10,692/11,938 lb), (bis) clean 5044/5069 kg (11,120/11,175 lb), max 6045 kg (13,327 lb).

PERFORMANCE Max speed (I-310) 1042 km/h, (MiG-15) 1050 km/h (652 mph) at SL and 1030 at 3 km, (UTI) 1015 km/h (631 mph) SL to 5 km, (bis) 1076 km/h (669 mph) at SL and 1044 km/h (649 mph) at 3 km; climb (I-310, MiG-15) 2·3 min to 5 km and 7·1 to 10 km, (bis) 2·1/5·5 min to same heights, (UTI) 2·6/6·8 to same heights; service ceiling (MiG-15) 15,2 km (49,869 ft), (UTI) 14 825 m (48,638 ft), (bis) 15,5 km (50,853 ft); range (MiG-15) 1420/1920 km on internal/max fuel (882/1193 miles), (UTI) 950/1340 km (590/833 miles), (bis) 1330/1860 km

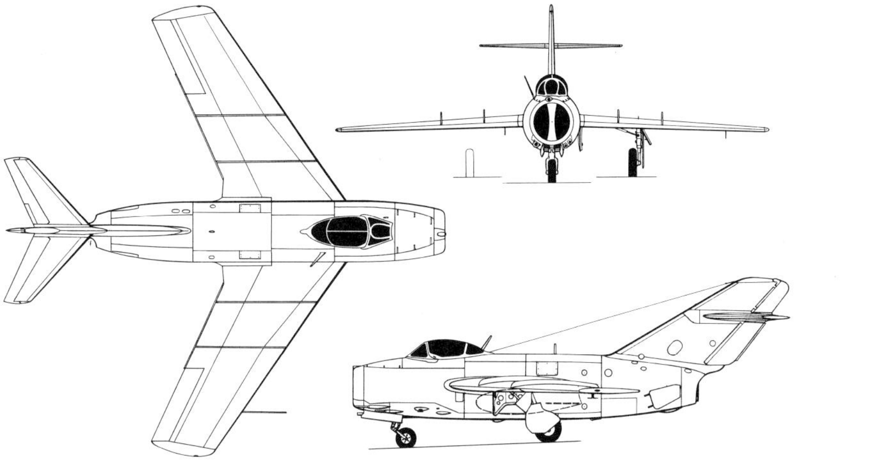
MiG-15bis

(826/1156 miles) (all ranges at econ cruise at 12 km); time 360° turn at 12 km, 32 s; take-off (MiG-15 and UTI) 570/600 m (1870/1969 ft), (bis clean) 500 m (1640 ft), (bis max wt) 1,2 km (3937 ft); landing 740 m (2428 ft)/160 km/h (99 mph), (bis clean) 880 m (2887 ft)/178 km/h (111 mph).

MiG-17, SI MiG OKB decided in January 1949 to transfer substantial part of aerodynamics personnel to plan improved S designated **SI (I-330)** as successor to MiG-15 rectifying faults. Authorization to build SI March 1949. Few details of this aircraft beyond wing sweep 45°. Completed December 1949 and first flown 13 January 1950 by I.T. Ivashchyenko. Good results, and February (believed 21 February) SI-01 reported to reach 1114 km/h at 2,2 km (M 1·03 approx, according to Soviet air-temp figs). Most Soviet records support this, though instrumentation is disputed, and certainly no later MiG-17 was level-sonic. In March sudden in-flight emergency at near Mach 1 destroyed SI-01, killing Ivashchyenko. Second SI generally known as MiG-15bis/45° but also reported as SI-2 (not SI-02). Design considerably further refined in extensive tunnel testing, and first flight at least six months after SI-01 (date not known).

Wing entirely new. Ruling section TsAGI S-12s at root, SR-11 at tip, 10% thickness. Root chord increased from 2,75 to 3,2 m mainly by extending leading edge forward. LE sweep increased from 35° to 45° out to semi-span and thence 42° to tip; TE sweep zero to second main rib on each side, thence increased from original 25° to 40° to tip. Tip rounded, with chord increased from 1,5 to 1,7 m. Anhedral increased from −2° to −3°. Trailing edge fitted with chord-extending sharp strips as on MiG-15bis from kink to aileron, width 35 mm. Fences 100 mm high at trailing-edge kink (inboard of inner MiG-15 fence) and inboard of aileron (outboard of outer MiG-15 fence); later third 100 mm fence added ahead of aileron. Pitot boom on left as well as right wing, almost at tips. Hydraulic perforated Fowler-type flaps, 20° for take-off, 60° for landing. Rear fuselage lengthened 90 cm (35·4 in) from rear plenum-chamber frame (rearmost point at full 1,45 m diam) giving gentler taper. Vertical tail increased in height to give more pointed tip and area increased from 4,0 to 4,26 m², tip now being fixed dielectric aerial with inset rudder balance. Horizontal tail increased in sweep (LE from 42° to 48° and TE from 25° to 32°) increasing area from 3,0 to 3,11 m² with more pointed tip; still a fixed surface with ground adjustment, manual elevators now with inset balances. Construction as MiG-15 but D16 changed to D16-AM alloy. Main tyres reduced diam 660 to 600 mm, but track increased from 3,81 to 3,85 m. Improved cockpit instrumentation and new ejection seat with faceblind actuation influenced by Martin-Baker patents. Main fuel tank of multilayer rubberized fabric 1250 lit (275 gal) between ducts above wing; supplementary metal tank of 160 lit (35 gal) under jetpipe immediately behind engine. Standard guns, one N-37 with 40 rounds, two (optional three) NR-23 each with 80. Underwing load two 400 lit (88 gal) drop tanks and two bombs of up to 250 kg, or 12 combinations of other stores.

Test team led by G.A. Sedov included S.N. Anokhin, K.K. Kokkinaki and P.I. Kazmin. Excellent aircraft with few shortcomings, only visible alteration being addition of ventral strake/fin and further improvement of airbrakes to initial standard 0,88 m² driven to 55°. NII testing completed 20 June 1951 and production authorized as MiG-17. Cleared to 12 g at max weight 6072 kg (endurance 2 h 53 min). Deliveries from about October 1952. By 1953 production also begun on **MiG-17P**, flown as prototype in 1951. New nose with *Izumrud* S-band (now E/F band) fixed-scan radar in bulged upper inlet lip (ranging) and circular fairing on inlet splitter (conical scan), with combat camera relocated on right side of nose. Length increased 0,27 m to house racking, with obtrusive viewing scope with large hood of firm rubber normally very close to pilot's right cheek and demanding new windscreen sloped at 60° with extra horizontal frame. Limited all-weather capability and greater weight cut performance (initial climb reduced from 47 to 37 m/s); main *Izumrud* production waited for afterburning VK-1F engine, first flown in MiG-17 in 1951. Production day fighter with VK-1F replaced MiG-17 in production following completion of NII testing in April 1953, designated **MiG-17F**. Production rate increased by switching over all MiG-15 resources except UTI; public display by MiG-17F squadron at Tushino 20 June 1953. This version distinguished not only by cutback rear fuselage exposing variable nozzle but also by new larger airbrakes pulled open by jack on horizontal centreline of fuselage on outside of brake, instead of pushed by jack on inside. Very large-scale production of MiG-17F, backed up by about one-sixth as many **MiG-17PF** with after burning engine and improved RP-5 *Izumrud* working on S and X bands and with normal armament three NR-23 only. In 1953 prototype **MiG-17PFU** deleted guns and added four ARS-212 beam-riding AAMs (so-called AA-1 Alkali) carried on large individual pylons under inner wings ahead of landing gear. This was first missile-armed aircraft in Soviet Union, several hundred delivered from 1956 for training and indoctrination and with a number of first-line regiments in PVO in late 1950s.

At least three variants remained prototypes. **SN** (OKB designation) was ground-attack model flown in November 1953, with completely new nose resembling earlier SU at least 1 m longer and of streamlined form, plenum chamber being aspirated by plain side inlets about 1 m ahead of leading edge (sidewalls upstream concave to bring ducts into original lateral location on each side of fuel tank). In nose were installed two NR-23 in installation designated TKB-495; guns could be hydraulically elevated or depressed ±40° with barrels moving in large boxed-in slits with sliding seal strips to alleviate high drag. Third such installation by Soviet designers (Iordan 1916, M.V. Kombain 1940); aiming system unknown. Probably one only, and possibly early SI rebuilt (not afterburning). **MiG-17SP-2** (OKB designation SP-2), 1951 prototype with unknown highpower search radar (probably related to I-320, La-190, Yak-50 and Su-15) for full night and all-weather interception. Nose closely resembled SP-1 (MiG-15 airframe) but armament two NR-23. Third experimental variant **SR-2** photo-recon prototype of 1953. Redesigned fuselage with large (Shavrov 1 m², another report 1,15 m²) airbrakes, increased tankage and frameless canopy, and two reconnaissance cameras in heated and shuttered compartment between armament of two NR-23. Recent reports have also unearthed I-340 (SM-1) as halfway stage to MiG-19 with twin AM-5 engines.

Total Soviet production probably about 6000, ending about 1958. Subject of major license production and development programme in Poland as LIM-5P (MiG-17F), with locally developed LIM-5M STOL tactical model with brake chute, a.t.o. lugs and extra bomb pylons. Also extensively modified LIM-6 with twin-wheel main gears for soft surfaces, retracting into enormous wide-chord deep inboard wing housing same fuel as drop tanks (not built in series). Further extensive programme in China as F-4 (MiG-17F and also locally designed tandem trainer) and F-5 (MiG-17PF). Polish production possibly 1000, Chinese at least 2000. Czech designation S-104, all Soviet built. Basic MiG-17F served with 30 air forces, about 21 still using it in 1982.

DIMENSIONS Span 9,63 m (31 ft 7 in); length (SI) 11,09 m, (MiG-17, MiG-17F) 11,26 m (36 ft 11⅓ in), (PF, PFU) 11,68 m (38 ft 3¾ in); height 3,8 m (12 ft 5⅔ in); wing area 22,6 m² (243·26 ft²).

ENGINE (SI, MiG-17, MiG-17P) 2700 kg VK-1A, (all subsequent) VK-1F rated at 2600 kg

SI-01

MiG-17F (Chinese F-4)

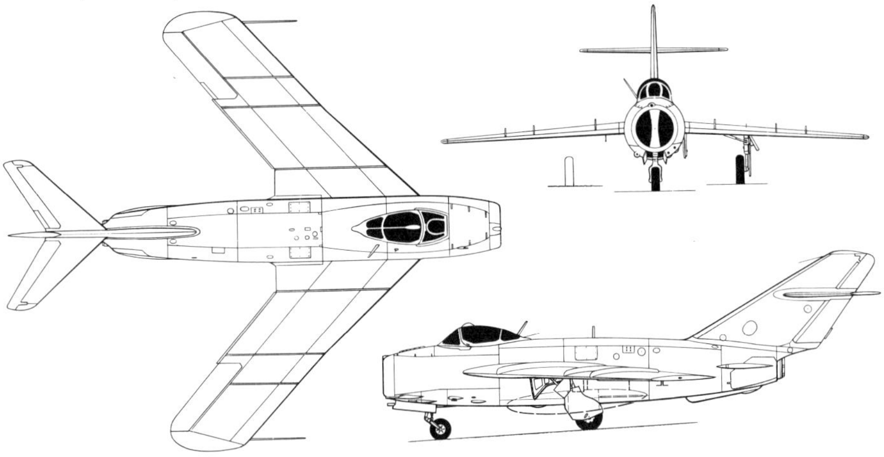

MiG-17F

MiG-17PF

(5732 lb) dry and 3380 kg (7451 lb) with afterburner.

WEIGHTS Empty (SI) 3798 kg, (F) 3930 kg (8664 lb), (PF) 4182 kg (9220 lb), (PFU) 4065 kg (8962 lb); max fuel (SI) 1173/1837 kg, (17, 17P) 1210/1867 kg, (F) 1155/1810 kg, (PF, PFU) 1143/1792 kg; max loaded (SI) 6072 kg, (17) 5932 kg, (P) 6280 kg, (F) 6075 kg (13,393 lb), (PF) 6330 kg (13,955 lb), (PFU) 6552 kg (14,444 lb).

PERFORMANCE Max speed (SI) 1070 km/h SL to 5 km, (17) 1114 km/h at 2 km, (F) 1145 km/h (711 mph) at 3 km, falling to 1071 km/h (626 mph) at 10 km, (PF) 1121 km/h at 4 km, (PFU) 1107 km/h at 4 km; climb to 5 km (17) 2 min, (17F) 2·6 min cold, 1·8 afterburner, (PF) 3·1/1·9, (PFU) 3·3/2·0; to 10 km (17) 5·1, (F) 5·8/4·1, (PF) 7·6/4·5, (PFU) 7·9/4·8; service ceiling (afterburner where fitted) (17) 15,6 km, (F) 16,6 (54,460 ft), (PF) 15,85, (PFU) 15,65; range max ext fuel at 12 km econ cruise (17) 2150 km, (F) 1980 km (1,230 miles), (PF) 1930, (PFU) 1850; take-off (17) 805 m, (F) 590 m, (PF) 730 m; landing (17) 885 m/170 km/h, (F) 850 m/170 km/h (106 mph), (PF) 910 m/190 km/h.

I-320, R Inability of single-engined aircraft to carry powerful all-weather radar (as fitted to SP-1, SP-2 and several types by rival OKBs) led to specification for larger twin-engined aircraft. Issued to OKBs January 1948, made explicit demands on designers that were hard to reconcile. Aircraft R was delayed by overloading of design engineers and prototype designated I-320 flew 1950. Most aerodynamics were scaled-up S (MiG-15) rather than SI (17), and VK-1 was not available at first flight which was made by A.A. Vernikov with Ye.F. Nashchyekin as flight engineer. Side-by-side ejection seats in wide cockpit with windscreen 105 mm thick with electric heating. Large nose inlet with radar above, bifurcated past nose gear bay with twin lower ducts feeding front engine and upper ducts feeding engine in MiG-15 style rear fuselage. Two flexible fuel tanks in front and rear fuselage,

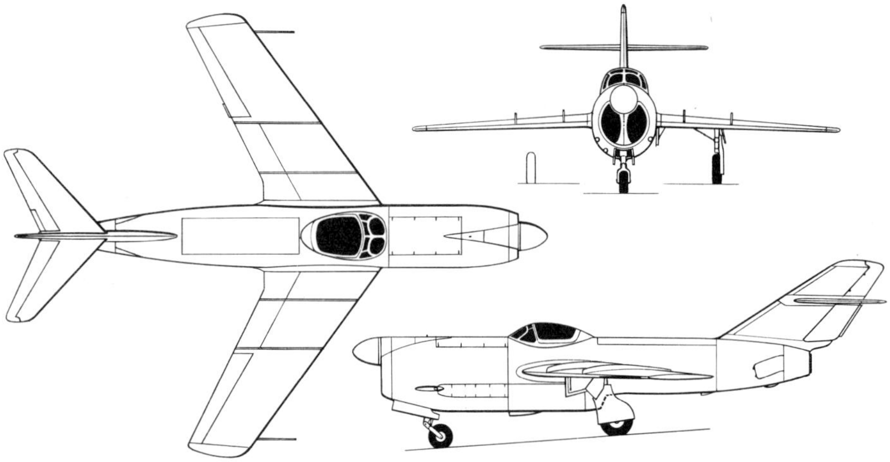

I-320, R

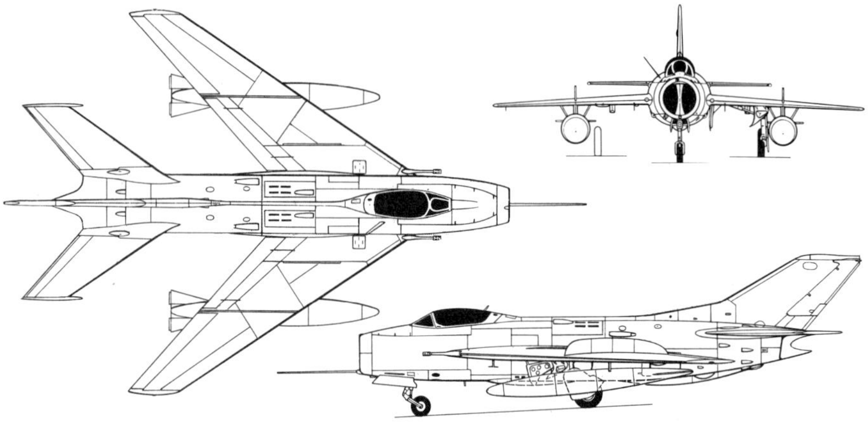

MiG-19S

total 3175 lit, 698 gal. Armament three N-37 each with 50 rounds. Not a bad aircraft (better than La-200), good report written by NII pilot Yu.A. Antipov. About mid-1951 fitted with VK-1 engines and ammunition increased 10 rounds per gun. Second prototype **R-2** with minor changes extensively tested by Antipov followed by M.L. Gallai, S.N. Anokhin and others. **R-3** built with strengthened wing with third fence each side for higher performance with VK-1F engine, but not flown. Programme eventually led to Yak-25, with *Izumrud*-equipped MiG-17PF as inadequate stop-gap.

DIMENSIONS Span 14,2 m (46 ft 7 in); length 15,77 m (51 ft 9 in); wing area 41,2 m² (443·5 ft²).

ENGINES R-1, originally, two 2270 kg RD-45F, later (and R-2) 2700 kg (5952 lb) VK-1.

WEIGHTS Empty (R-1) 7367 kg (16,241 lb), fuel/oil 2230 kg (note: published internal fuel weighs 2540 kg); max 10 265 kg (22,630 lb).

PERFORMANCE Max speed 1060 km/h (RD-45F) at 14,5 m (659 mph); climb not recorded; service ceiling 15 km (49,200 ft); endurance on internal fuel 3 h; landing speed 200 km/h (124 mph).

MiG-19, I-350 and I-360, SM First truly supersonic fighter developed in Europe, and probably in world (as noted, uncertainty about first-flight dates), MiG-19 was structurally and aerodynamically a remarkable achievement. Though accepted as Soviet counterpart of North America F-100 it has been undervalued by Western writers, who have paid it scant attention compared with MiGs that preceded and followed it. Even Soviet Union pushed ahead to Mach 2 and tailed deltas, leaving it to Chinese and their foreign customers to discover that as an air-combat fighter this now old design is hard to equal, besides serving as basis for Chinese attack bomber in class of Buccaneer.

MiG-19S

MiG-19PM

Following abject failure of La-190 and Yak-1000, Stalin personally ordered fresh specification for advanced yet practical supersonic fighter, and this was issued autumn 1950. In this year Guryevich's failing health caused him progressively to abandon active management, and SM family was first without his full-time participation. Basic design notable for amazing wing, with higher aspect ratio than F-100, much greater sweep, plain leading edge and conventional outboard ailerons, yet aeroelastically stiff and efficient from Mach 1·4 down to 230 km/h. Design accepted at Kremlin 30 July 1951, and I-350 (SM-01) prototype built forthwith. Mikoyan had wide choice of engines. SM-01 flew in 1952 (October, probably) with single AL-5 or -5F. SM-02, I-360, flew at end of 1952 with twin AM-5 in wider but shallower rear fuselage fed by same inlet ducts. (Note: this engine had no connection with any design by V. Klimov bureau and was redesignated RD-9 by its designer, Tumanskii, following Mikulin's blacklisting in 1956.) Polish report illustrated third 1952 prototype, **I-370** with two VK-7F. AL-5 was unreliable, and AM-5 was adopted for SM-03 (**I-350M**) and subsequent prototypes. According to one report I-350M flew in 1952 also, and another gives its engines as TR-3A (a service designation), but it is this aircraft that was flown by G.A. Sedov on 18 September 1953 to mark start of true MiG-19 development. There is evidence I-350 (S-01) and I-360 (S-02) both had high tailplanes; in two reports S-02 is said to have crashed following tailplane flutter.

Wing profile S-12s at root, SR-7s at tip, ruling thickness 8·24%, sweep 55° at ¼-chord (58° at leading edge), anhedral-4°30′ (zero on I-350M and predecessors), basic material D16-T with one extremely strong spar at 90° to fuselage axis running from left to right leading edges at mid-span and also carrying main gears. Spar booms and major joints 30KhGSA. Machined skins, max thickness 4,8 mm (more than double MiG-15 or MiG-17). Ribs and aileron hinges at 90° to leading edge. Hydraulic Fowler flaps running aft on two tracks with pneumatic emergency actuation. Hydraulically boosted ailerons with inset hinges and manual reversion, left aileron with trim tab. Fixed leading edge. Fuselage made in front and detachable rear sections with joint immediately behind trailing edge. Inlet duct bifurcated at nose to pass each side of cockpit and above and below aerofoil fairing main spar. Twin hydraulic airbrakes on flanks aft of wing. Entire rear fuselage removable for access to engines, ventilated by four upstream and four downstream ram inlets standing proud of skin. Ventral keel and tail bumper. Vertical and horizontal tail based on MiG-15LL but with increased areas and control power. Wide track (4,15 m) landing gear with levered-suspension legs. Production tyres 660 × 220 mm (main), usually 883 kPa (129 lb/in²), 500 × 180 mm (nose). Main gears inwards, non-steerable nose gear forwards, hydraulic with pneumatic emergency. Pneumatic brakes with back-up system. Braking parachute pneumatically released from bay beneath afterburners. Duplicate hydraulic systems, 207 MPa (3000 lb/in²) with main system from right engine serving gear, flaps and engine nozzles and left engine handling flight-control with back-up from right. Production aircraft, two main rubberized-fabric fuel cells aft of cockpit and two shallow curved cells under jet-pipes, total 2170 lit (477 gal). Provision for 800-lit (176 gal) drop tank under each wing. Armament one N-37 on right of nose and one NR-23 in each wing root, with steel skin on adjacent wall of fuselage. Hardpoint for various loads to 250 kg under each wing inboard of tank. Cockpit with faceblind ejection seat, reflector sight with depressed reticle for air/ground, environmental system packaged in upper mid fuselage behind tanks, fluid windshield anti-icing, aft-sliding canopy later fitted with electro-thermal anti-icing. Standard equipment VHF, radio compass and radio altimeter, large upward-hinged instrument boom at 6 o'clock on nose.

Mach 1·1 routinely exceeded during 1953, but with unacceptable control problems and aerodynamic buffet, mainly at tail. Several prototypes investigated all-flying tail of various areas and at two different heights on rear fuselage, together with various fence, nozzle fairing and canopy profiles. From December 1953 pre-series batch **MiG-19F**, first with service designation, with afterburning engines and at least one of these with *Izumrud* radar and with combat camera relocated from top to right of nose. First 19F set claimed national speed record 1650 km/h. Production of MiG-19F authorized 1954 with AM-5F engine, large pen-nib rear fuselage fairings and 280 mm full-chord fences at flap/aileron junction. Cleared to use 12° flap to enhance manoeuvre at up to 797 km/h IAS. Severe attrition, partly attributed to persistent elevator shortcomings, resulting in priority programme to fit slab tailplane with pendulum type gear-ratio control. About one year of intense effort resulted in **MiG-19S** (*Stabilizator*), first true production model, with enlarged slab tailplane outboard of fixed root fairing and with anti-flutter masses faired ahead of tips. Electro-mechanical signalling via added dorsal spine from canopy to fin to surface power units, with low-rate electric back-up in event of total loss of both hydraulic systems. Additional airbrake added under belly, causing bulge, and all-speed spoilers for enhanced roll control. Aircraft examined against NACA Area Rule and found to conform excellently. Revealed in flypast of 48 (mix of S and earlier aircraft including prototypes) at Tushino 1955 Aviation Day.

Limited production from 1955 of **MiG-19PF** with RP-5 *Izumrud* (nose boom moved to right wingtip), IFF (first SRO series) and Sirena tail-warning, reported developed with Czech industry assistance. New standard canopy of reduced height with electric demist. In 1956 armament changed to three NR-30, with enlarged steel skin areas beside longer barrels with muzzle brakes. Improved retractable landing lamp under nose with taxi headlight on nose gear; latter steerable on some PF interceptors. Engine designation changed to RD-9B in 1956 and, following refinements to TBO, starting, and DC generation to RD-9BF in 1957. Aircraft designation changed to **MiG-19SF.** Small batch built of **MiG-19PM** with same AAM installation (four K-5M on individual wing pylons) as MiG-17PFU, with Scan Odd radar and no guns and different sight system from MiG-19PF. Alleged more than one prototype tandem dual **MiG-19UTI** trainer, but not adopted by Soviet armed forces. Production complete about 1959, possibly 2500 delivered of which 90% MiG-19S or SF. Supplied to Czechoslovakia as S-105 and to Poland as LIM-7.

Several other non-series versions. **MiG-19R** photorecon aircraft with two cameras in nose between ducts, replacing nose gun. **MiG-19SV** specialized target-defence interceptor (one report states two N-37 guns). **SM-10** (1955) with probe for inflight refuelling. Five examples built of **SM-30** (1956) off-airfield variant with catapult launch and soft-field gear. **SM-12** (1956) with redesigned MiG-21 nose with conical centrebody. **SM-12PM** (1957) with redesigned fuselage with MiG-21 nose housing R1L radar and ducts feeding two RS-26 afterburning turbojets; 1720 km/h. **SM-12PMU** (1958) with two RSM-25 turbojets and belly pack containing RU-01S rocket engine and propellants. Whereas SM-12PM was armed with two K-5M, -12PMU unarmed; latter reached 24 km alt. **SM-50** (1959) with original nose, S-type airframe, RD-9BM engines and belly pack housing U-19 rocket engine and propellants; 1795 km/h, almost 24 km alt.

Outside scope of this book, important production programme in China of variants designated F-6 and (two-seat) TF-6, with many local changes.

DIMENSIONS Span 9,20 m (30 ft 2¼ in); length (S) 12,6 m (41 ft 4 in) (14,9 m, 48 ft 10½ in, with probe), (PM, PMU) 13,25 m (43 ft 8½ in); wing area 25,0 m^2 (269 ft^2). Note: persistent Polish and other reports giving span 11,1 m, length 13,7 m and wing area 23 m^2 are not borne out by Soviet sources.

ENGINES Two Tumanskii (Mikulin OKB) afterburning turbojets: (19) 2175/3040 kg (4795/6702 lb) AM-5F; (19S) 2600/3250 kg (5732/7165 lb) RD-9B; (SF, PF, PFM) 2600/3300 kg (5732/7277 lb) RD-9BF series.

WEIGHTS Empty (SF) about 5760 kg (12,-700 lb), (PF) 6050 kg (13,338 lb); loaded (SF, clean) 7600 lb (16,755 lb), (PF) not known; max (SF) 9100 kg (20,062 lb).

PERFORMANCE Max speed (SF, PF) 1452 km/h (902 mph, Mach 1·36) at 10 km; initial climb (SF) 115 m/s (22,635 ft/min); service ceiling 17,9 km (58,725 ft), reached in 8 min 12 s; combat radius (hi, tanks) 685 km, (426 miles); ferry range 2200 km (1366 miles); take-off (max fuel) 515 m (1690 ft); landing (chute) 600 m (1970 ft)/ 235 km/h (146 mph).

SM-30 on launcher

SM-12PM

SM-12PMU

MiG-21 Probably best-known Soviet aircraft, and built in larger numbers than any other warplane since the Second World War, the MiG-21 series has sustained a programme which for long life and number of variants has no equal in history. Original planning by Mikoyan but from 1964 programme increasingly taken over by present OKB head Rostislav A. Belyakov, who assumed General Constructor title on Mikoyan's death in 1970.

Official requirement for short-range interceptor issued autumn 1953. Stipulated features included ability to carry limited all-weather radar and AAMs with secondary guns and bombs, to operate under RSIU (Markham) secure ground control, and to have highest possible flight per-
series has sustained a programme which forir combats studied, and range was discounted (as it was with parallel specification for larger aircraft with AL-7 engine). Sole engine chosen by Mikoyan OKB was new two-spool R-11, marking cementing of bond between airframe and engine bureau that has been maintained to this day. Prolonged TsAGI aerodynamic research threw up two rival configurations, both with low mid-mounted wings and swept slab tailplanes but differing in wing plan, one being same as MiG-19 and other a pure delta with 57° leading edge. (Sukhoi adopted both configurations.) For reasons of timing first prototype, designated **Ye-50**, with MiG-19 type wing, was completed in mid-1955 prior to availability of flight-cleared R-11 and was therefore fitted with single RD-9Ye (max afterburner 3800 kg) plus S-155 rocket engine in fairing at base of vertical tail. Two NR-30 guns fitted. Flown V.P. Vasin about November 1955; gross weight 8,5 t, max speed 2460 km/h (Mach 2·3), twice as fast as any other European aircraft except FD.2 and certainly world's fastest fighter. OKB chief pilot G.A. Sedov assigned to **Ye-4** and **Ye-5** tailed deltas (regarded as leading contenders), G.K. Mossolov and V.A. Nyefyedov being chiefly concerned with rival **Ye-2** with MiG-19 type wing. Ye-4 flown by Sedov December 1955, first aircraft properly regarded as MiG-21, but still with RD-9Ye engine. By this time OKB had commissioned largest experimental lab in industry, under A.V. Minayev, to solve aerodynamic, systems, structural and manufacturing problems. R-11 engine available spring 1956 and Sedov assisted in its flight development. First R-11

Ye-2

prototypes designated **Ye-2A** (flown Nyefyedov about May 1956) and **Ye-5** (flown Sedov, 16 June), both with three large fences on each wing. Both made flypast at 1956 Aviation Day, Tushino. Intensive testing, with no clear advantage; Ye-5 did not exhibit predicted margin in speed, and this was traced to air spillage from inlet. It offered slightly greater internal fuel and better turn radius; after development reached almost exactly 2000 km/h compared with 1940 for Ye-2A. Delta wing chosen about December 1956. Production authorized as MiG-21, and OKB built pre-production prototype **Ye-6** incorporating all results of testing to date for prolonged task of perfecting propulsion and flight control which were clearly still unacceptable. Ye-6, outwardly a MiG-21 except for six fences, and with two instead of three NR-30, built under chief engineer I.I. Rotchik and assigned to Nyefyedov, who made first flight (probably late 1957). Excellent results, but on about eighth flight total engine failure near Mach 2 was followed by loss of control just before touchdown and Nyefyedov died from injuries. Cause was inlet/engine mismatch and compressor stall, inability to relight because starting fuel tank was overheated and contained only vapour, and slow switchover to stand-by electric tailplane drive as hydraulic pressure was lost on approach. Brunov proposed revision of electric stand-by, but Mikoyan instead threw this system out (while leaving it on series MiG-19) and accepted Belyakov's proposal of fully duplex hydraulics with maximum (but not total) redundancy. Mossolov handled subsequent flight-control development, and Kokkinaki greatly improved propulsion with three-position translating inlet centrebody and suction relief doors just below extended leading-edge root. Initial MiG-21 cleared for production 1958 (date uncertain).

Wing profile TsAGI S-12 series with thickness 4·2% root and 5·0% tip; anhedral −2°. Main spar at 33·3% chord, three auxiliary spars at 90° to fuselage with left/right wings attached to frames on each side (no centre section). Ruling material D16-T with machined but not integrally stiffened skins nowhere thicker than 2,5 mm; booms V-95 or VM-65 and joints 30KhGSA with ML5-T4 at other stress concentrations. Fowler flap 0,935 m² each side driven hydraulically with actuator and track fairing above flap tip with take-off setting 24·5°, landing setting 44·5°. Fully powered tabless ailerons with small fence upstream near tip. One-piece fuselage, engine removed to rear on internal rails. Canopy one piece hinged at front with integral windscreen, ejected with seat to provide airblast protection. Flight-control push/pull rods in small dorsal spine to input power units for rudder (0,965 m²) and slab tailplanes (4,45 m², A6A 6% profile, 55°) with anti-flutter masses on tips. Air ducts on each side past main tanks of T-6 aluminium (235, 660 + 60, 265, 200 and 2 × 240 lit)

SM-50

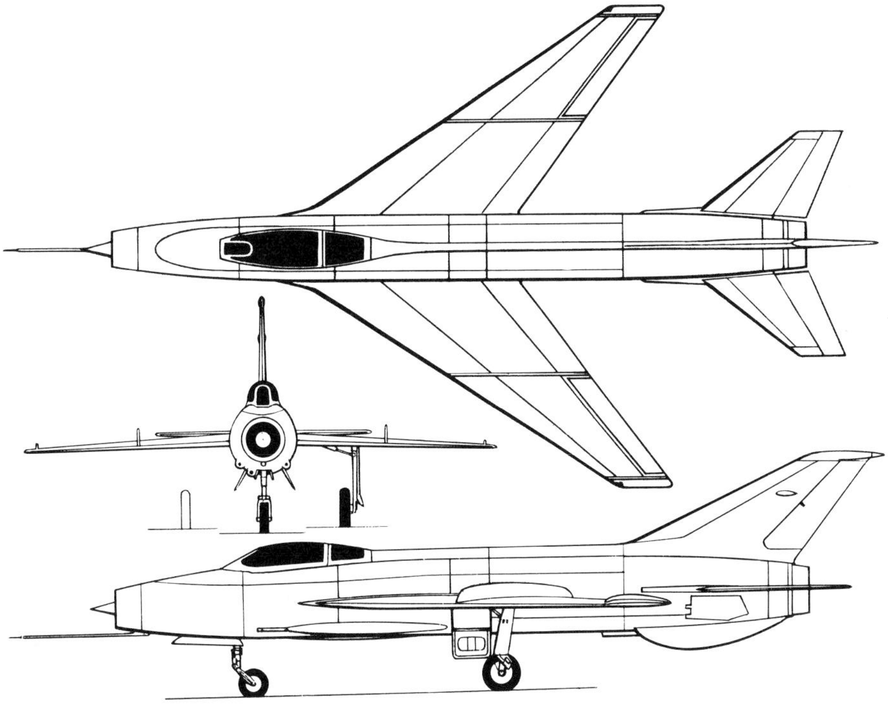

Ye-2A

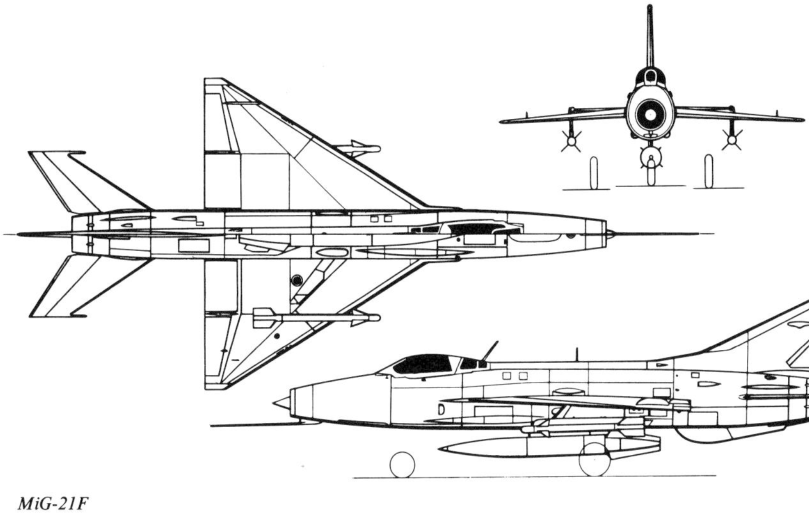

MiG-21F

MiG-21F-5 (Jugoslavia)

supplemented by 175 lit in each leading edge and 110 lit behind main gears, total 2470 lit of which 2340 (515 gal) usable; also provision for 490 lit (108 gal) on centreline pylon. Small fuselage airbrakes under leading-edge wing roots and ahead of ventral fin. Main gears 660 × 200 mm, 1,01 MPa (147·6 lb/in²), nose 500 × 180 mm; steering by differential use of air-bottle mainwheel brakes, nose gear also being braked, and hydraulic retraction with mainwheels pivoting 87°. Track 2,692 m, wheelbase 4,810. Drag chute in left flank of rear fuselage beside single centreline ventral fin replacing twin canted ventrals of prototypes. Two NR-30 well aft on flanks of mid-fuselage, wing pylons for two K-13A clear-weather AAMs or two UV-16-57 or other ordnance. Deliveries late 1958. Engine life 100 h, and residual problems with flight controls included complex airspeed/alt instrument used to indicate to pilot when to change tailplane gear ratio and autostab (finally on pitch/roll only, with q-feel).

Ye-6T led to **MiG-21F**; late 1959 with more powerful engine (F-1 on), broader fin with improved Sirena TWR (F-13 on), and (except for batch for India) righthand gun only. F-13 and certain later models license-produced in Czechoslovakia without rear-vision windows. **Ye-7** prototype of **MiG-21PF**; introduced less tapered forward fuselage with inlet diameter increased from 690 to 910 mm with large centrebody housing R1L search/track radar and pitot boom above instead of below nose, boundary-layer discharge above/below nose, new canopy with reduced wave-drag and enlarged aft fairing into spine to house saddle tank increasing internal fuel to 2850 lit (626 gal); guns, gun blisters and rearview windows removed, simpler and more effective forward airbrakes, enlarged main tyres (0,785 MPa, 115 lb/in² for soft fields) necessitating large blisters above and below wing root, primary VHF blade moved to mid-spine and secondary blade deleted, and, in all but first few PF, fin same as late F-series and more powerful engine. Many variants, PF-17 introducing brake 'chute re-positioned in bullet fairing at base of rudder and an earlier PF having provision for a.t.o. rocket-bottles flanking rear airbrake. **Ye-7SPS** prototype Tushino 1961 had SPS, blown flaps, plain hinged flaps of larger chord than Fowlers with no tracks but large actuator fairing on underside at mid-span, reducing landing speed. Later (PF-31?) broad fin with straight leading edge and GP-9 belly pack housing twin GSh-23, with predictor sight and electrical ranging. **MiG-21PFS** production aircraft with SPS and all other updates, some also introducing R2L radar. **MiG-21FL** export PF-31 with R2L but without SPS, a.t.o. or some classified avionics. **MiG-21PFM** combined all PF-31 improvements plus blown flaps with new canopy with conventional fixed windscreen, canopy hinged to right and improved ejection seat with ground safety pins instead of spring-loaded arming handle made safe by opening canopy on ground. Large VHF/UHF dielectric aerial at top of fin as on some late PF/PFS. Last model made in Czechoslovakia.

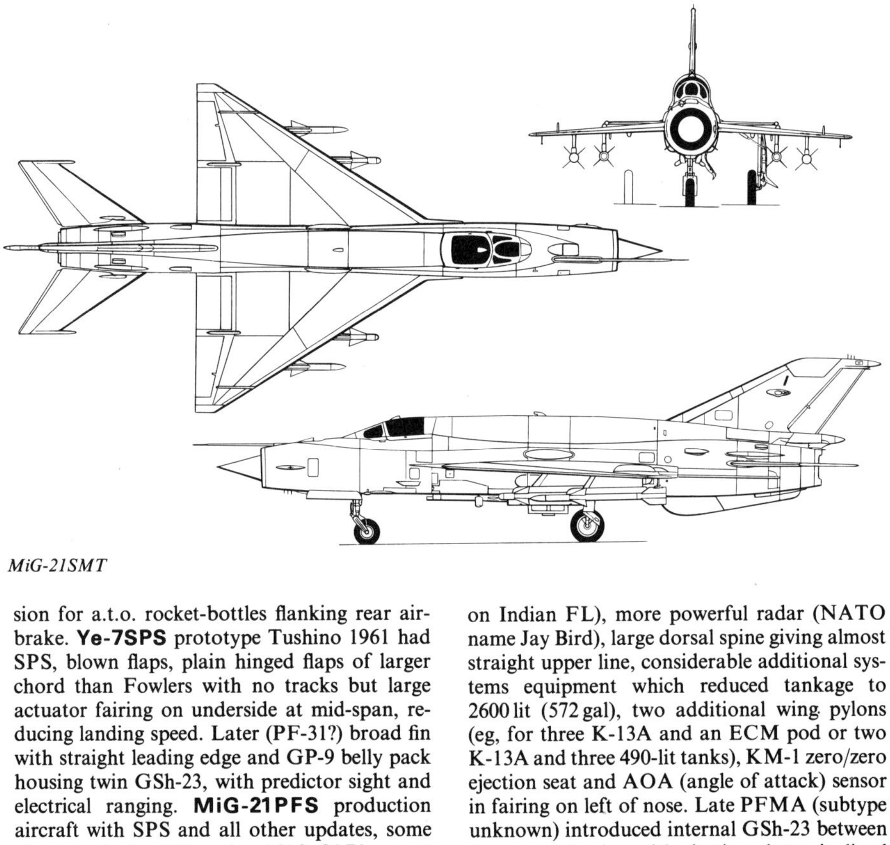

MiG-21SMT

About 1965, **Ye-9** led to **MiG-21PFMA** multi-role variant, R-11-300 engine (also used on Indian FL), more powerful radar (NATO name Jay Bird), large dorsal spine giving almost straight upper line, considerable additional systems equipment which reduced tankage to 2600 lit (572 gal), two additional wing pylons (eg, for three K-13A and an ECM pod or two K-13A and three 490-lit tanks), KM-1 zero/zero ejection seat and AOA (angle of attack) sensor in fairing on left of nose. Late PFMA (subtype unknown) introduced internal GSh-23 between forward airbrakes with ejection chutes inclined each side of centreline store, as well as compatibility with radar-homing K-13 variant. **MiG-21M** export PFMA with internal gun. **MiG-21R** produced in several subtypes beginning with internal optical cameras in projecting box under cockpit floor in place of internal gun, and in more common variant having centreline pod housing forward and oblique cameras and IR linescan. All R variants can have ECM pods on wingtips and those in VVS service have extra flush aerial in spine ahead of fin.

MiG-21MF, flown about 1967 and delivered

1969–1970, introduced R-13 engine with greater airflow (necessitating debris guard below suck-in auxiliary inlets) but reduced weight. Structure strengthened for M 1·06 at sea level. Internal gun standard, and rear-view mirror in top of canopy. **MiG-21RF** reconnaissance variant of MF. **MiG-21SMT** with dorsal fairing continued to brake-chute housing to reduce drag and, by repositioning equipment, houses added 300-lit (66-gal) tank. **MiG-21bis** flown about 1971 introduced totally re-engineered airframe, dramatically simplifying and lightening structure while giving increased fuel capacity in integral tanks while accommodating more equipment in larger dorsal spine and for first time taking into account fatigue over long period of service. About 1975 bisF introduced new R-25 engine, installationally interchangeable despite slightly greater airflow and much higher afterburning thrust. Two-axis instrumentation boom first seen on some PFMA made standard. Still hamstrung by basic inability to use more than $\frac{2}{3}$-fuel without CG shifting too far aft for safe flight, as well as poor look-down capability and ineffective AAMs, though two Aphid added inboard from early 1980.

First tandem dual trainer prototype **Ye-6U** June 1960, leading to **MiG-21U** of about 1962 with two canopies hinged to right, no guns, large PF type main tyres and inlet/fin of F. Main trainers **U-11** and later sub-types with broad fin, Sirena and upper brake chute pod. **MiG-21US** with blown flaps and instructor retractable periscope. **UM** trainer counterpart of MF with R-13(SPS), four pylons and AOA sensor. Almost all trainers have two-axis vanes on nose boom.

Major license-production by HAL in India under following designations: 21F, Type 74; PF, Type 76; FL, Type 77; M, Type 96; MF and bis, over 100 but not yet published; U, Type 66. Small-scale production of a literal Chinese copy of the F began as the F-8 and was later updated to PF and M standards whilst taking in local modifications. Many of the worldwide users of MiG-21 versions have introduced non-Soviet equipment, most notably Ferranti and Smiths Industries nav and Hudwac systems. Late model Soviet MiG-21s now have datalink.

Numerous experimental variants. **Ye-33,** MiG-21U used for climb/altitude records with women pilots. **Ye-66,** pre-production 21F-13 used by Mossolov for 15/25 km record at 2388 km/h on 31 October 1959, and by Kokkinaki for 100 km circuit at 2148 km/h on 16 September 1960. **Ye-66B**, record version 1974 with twin rockets. **Ye-66A,** research aircraft for PF but with added belly pack housing U-2 rocket engine, height record 34 714 m by Mossolov 28 April 1961. **Ye-76,** PF for women's records including 500 km circuit at 2062 km/h by M. Solovyeva 16 September 1966. STOL versions **Ye-8** with powered foreplane (intended to lead to **MiG-21Sht** attack model) and **MiG-21DPD** with two lift jets in added fuselage bay at CG, with rear-hinged dorsal door and controllable transverse louvres below nozzles, wide-track fixed main gears and no armament, demonstrated at Domodyedovo July 1967. **A-144**, or MiG-21 *Analog*, major redesign to test scaled tailless delta wing of Tu-144; chief engineer I.V. Frumkin, test pilot O.V. Gudkov assisted by Shchyerbakov, Fyedotov and Ostapyenko.

MiG-21bis with AA-2A and AA-8 AAMs

MiG-21VD V/STOL

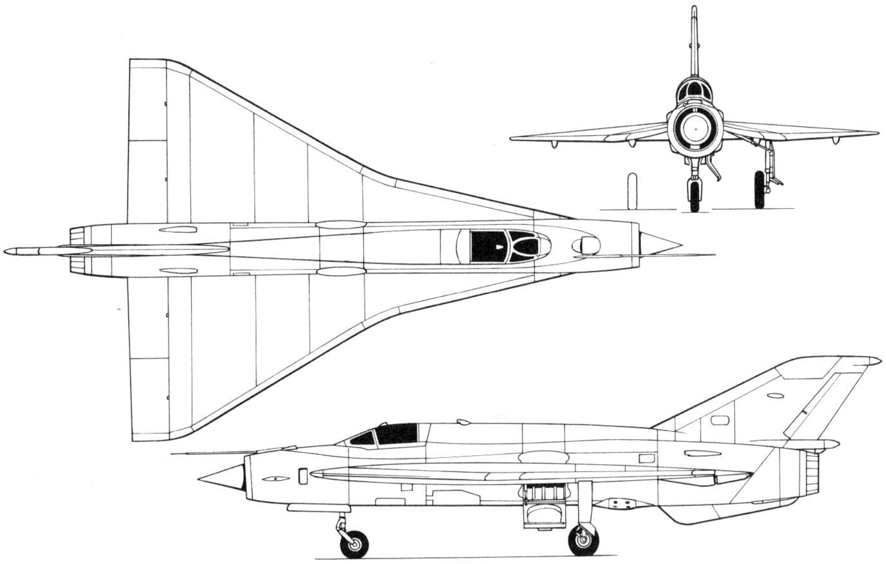

A-144, MiG-21 Analog

MiG-21 now active manufacturing programme ten years longer than Po-2. Number built not less than 11,000.

DIMENSIONS Span 7,15 m (23 ft 5$\frac{1}{2}$ in); length (with probe, all variants very close) 15,76 m (51 ft 8$\frac{1}{2}$ in), (F, ignoring probe) 13,46 m (44 ft 2 in), (PF onwards) about 14 m (45 ft 11 in); height 4,1/4,5 m depending on type; wing area 23,0 m^2 (247·6 ft^2).

ENGINE (prototypes) Tumanskii RD-9Ye; (21) one 3900/5100 kg (8600/11,240 lb) Tumanskii R-11 two-spool afterburning turbojet, (F) 4310/5750 kg (9502/12,676 lb) R-11F, (PF) R-11F2S with increased augmentation to 5950 kg (13,117 lb), (PFM, FL) F2S-300 with further boosted afterburning rating of 6200 kg (13,-668 lb), (MF) 5100/6600 kg (11,240/14,550 lb) R-13-300, (bis) 5800/7500 kg (12,790/16,535 lb) R-25 series.

WEIGHTS Empty (F) 4980 kg (10,979 lb), (bis) 6200 kg (13,670 lb); loaded (clean) (Ye-6) 7050 kg, (F) 7370 kg (16,248 lb), (MF) 7900 kg (17,416 lb), (bis) 7960 kg (17,550 lb); max (F) 8630 kg (19,026 lb), (MF) 9400 kg (20,723 lb), (bis) believed to be 10 t (22,046 lb).

PERFORMANCE Max speed at SL (up to M) 1100 km/h, (MF onwards) 1300 km/h; max speed at 11/18 km, typically 2125 km/h for R-11 aircraft, 2230 km/h (M 2·1) for later; initial climb (F) 132 m/s (25,900 ft/min), (bis, clean and 50% fuel) 295 m/s (58,000 ft/min); service ceiling (all) about 17,5 km (57,400 ft); range with max fuel econ cruise at 11 km (F) 1670 km (1038 miles), (MF) 1790 km (1112 miles), (bis) about 1590 km (988 miles); typical hi-lo-hi mission radius 220 km (137 miles) in 45 min; take-off (typical) 800 m (2625 ft)/350 km/h (217 mph); landing (typical, blown flaps) 550 m (1800 ft)/265 km/h (165 mph).

Ye-152A

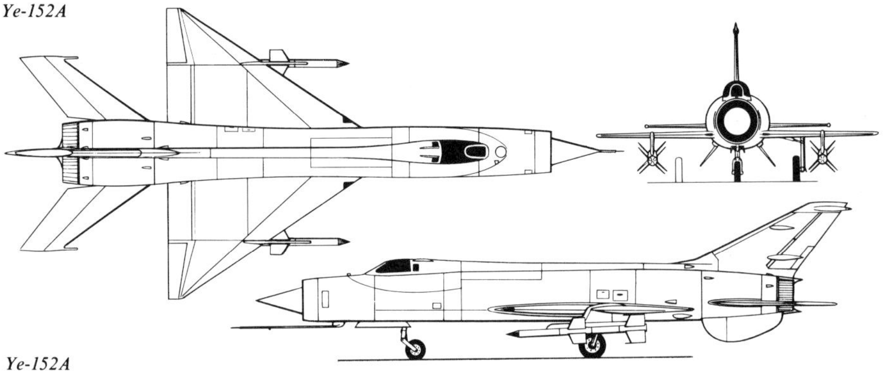

Ye-152A

I-3 family Despite engineering workload on bomber-launched missiles and on what became MiG-21, OKB challenged Sukhoi for almost parallel programme for larger aircraft of roughly twice gross weight based on VK-3 engine and intended (unlike smaller partner) to yield both tac fighter/bomber and all-weather interceptor. Requirement times parallel, and first submission made December 1954. First to fly was **I-1 (I-370)** with 60° wing and VK-3 engine in November 1956. From this stemmed single- and twin-engined aircraft embracing swept and tailed-delta forms scaled directly from MiG-21 aerodynamics.

I-3U, I-380, was swept-wing aircraft with added section at root giving kinked trailing edge; Fowler flaps, powered ailerons (with single deep full-chord intermediate fences) and two NR-30 in wing near roots. Large canopy hinged at front and serving as blast shield for seat as on early MiG-21. Plain nose inlet with rounded exterior but sharp lip, with small pointed centrebody on splitter. Wing almost in mid-position with about −2° anhedral, slab tailplanes slightly higher at mid position and apparently with no fixed root section. Main gears with levered-suspension pointing forwards, nose unit levered aft. Subtle area-ruling, small rear ventral keel. Cooling inlet at front of small dorsal spine, and instrumentation booms on nose and both wingtips. This prototype fighter/bomber superficially resembled rival Sukhoi S-22 which beat it. **I-3P,** also with number in I-380 series, was radar-equipped interceptor using same airframe, also flown 1956. This lost to similar but cheaper Su-9. I-7 series again used same airframe but with AL-7F of higher thrust, requiring usual large rectangular bleed exhaust in fuselage, **I-7K** of January 1957 reaching highest speed of any pure-turbojet aircraft of era.

DIMENSIONS Span 9,3 m (30 ft 6$\frac{1}{8}$ in); 16,73 m (54 ft 10$\frac{3}{4}$ in); wing area 27 m^2 (291 ft^2).

ENGINE (3) one 8400 kg (18,518 lb) VK-3, (7) one 9300 kg (20,500 lb) AL-7F.

WEIGHTS Empty (est) 8,5 t (18,750 lb); loaded (3U) 10 t (22,050 lb), (7K) 10,7 t (23,589 lb).

PERFORMANCE Max speed (3U) 1960 km/h (1218 mph, M 1·84), (7K) 2500 km/h (1,553 mph, M 2·35); service ceiling (3) 18 km (59,000 ft), (7) 22,5 km (73,800 ft); range (both) 1800 km (1120 miles).

I-75 OKB built several I-7 prototypes including I-7D, P and U in addition to I-7K using original I-3 airframe. These led in 1957 to fully equipped all-weather interceptor **I-75F** using slightly enlarged airframe which also incorporated first switch from guns to AAMs. Improved area-ruling assisted by dorsal spine and giving increased volume at rear for fuel. Still retaining forward-hinged ejectable canopy, but shallower and more rounded wing fences and other aerodynamic improvements including less-tapered nose to accommodate prototype X-band radar (predecessor of *Uragan* series), inlet sharp-edged 1,2-m diameter. Flown with large wing pylons carrying either K-8 or K-9 AAMs, one of these being precursor of Anab. Full mission electronics including SRO-3 above nose, but (unique among I-3, -7, -150 families) no instrumentation boom. Suck-in auxiliary nose inlets forming complete ring. Lyul'ka collaborated but never mentioned his association with Mikoyan, unlike his work with Sukhoi.

DIMENSIONS Span 9,97 m (32 ft 8$\frac{1}{4}$ in); length 16,96 m (55 ft 7$\frac{3}{4}$ in); wing area 29 m^2 (312 ft^2).

ENGINE One 8,4 t (18,518 lb) AL-7F, later replaced by fully rated 9 t (19,840 lb) AL-7F.

WEIGHTS Empty 8800 kg (19,400 lb); loaded 11 380 kg (25,088 lb).

PERFORMANCE Max speed 2300 km/h (1430 mph, M 2·17); service ceiling 21 km (68,900 ft); range 2000 km (1240 miles).

Ye-150 family Though retaining almost unchanged TsAGI tailed-delta configuration adopted for Ye-6 and related small (MiG-21 size) family, this series extrapolated shape to speeds well in excess of 2000 km/h and introduced titanium and steel in rear fuselage and, in final Ye-166, in leading edges and other areas. Original Ye-150 of 1958 was powered by complete propulsion system, from inlet to nozzle, perfected with I-7K but with important difference that new and shorter Tumanskii engine was installed. Easily fastest fighter in world. Radar (unknown) linked to autopilot as in rival P-1 to provide automatic trajectory control. Armament two K-8 or K-9, no guns. **Ye-152** of 1959 introduced 'improved sight system' and was first capable of true all-weather operation (assume means first in USSR). Fuselage of these aircraft broadly similar to I-7 and I-75 series except wing spar frames much further forward. Other changes included shorter canopy though still frameless and separating forwards to protect pilot on ejection, improved spine utilization, thinner but stronger vertical tail with two power-unit fairings and five flush aerials, two large canted ventrals and (at least on Ye-150) no small fence ahead of aileron as in 'small' series deltas. One AAM, believed K-9, was called Awl by NATO but never built in series. Final member of family, **Ye-152A** (1959) had modified fuselage with twin engines of same type as fitted to production MiG-21F, first of 13 different MiG deltas to have twin engines. Considerable tankage between ducts and engines. Demonstrated Aviation Day Tushino 1961, with aerodynamic model AAMs. Other member of Ye-150 family was Ye-152M, which spawned the record-breaking Ye-166.

DIMENSIONS Span 8,97 m (29 ft $5\frac{1}{8}$ in); length (150) not known but similar to 152A, (152A) 19,8 m (64 ft $11\frac{1}{2}$ in); wing area 28,2 m^2 (304 ft^2).

ENGINE(S) (150) one 9,5 t (20,943 lb) R-15, (152) 10,22 t (22,530 lb) R-15A; (152A) two 5,75 t (12,676 lb) R-11F.

WEIGHTS Empty, not known; loaded (152A) 14,2 t (31,300 lb).

PERFORMANCE Max speed (150) 2900 km/h (1800 mph, M 2·73), (152A) 2500 km/h (1550 mph, M 2·35); service ceiling (150) 25 km (82,000 ft), (152A) 21 km (68,900 ft); range (150) 1500 km (932 miles), (152A) 2300 km (1430 miles).

Ye-166 Completely uncompromised high-speed aircraft for research into structure and aerodynamics for 3000 km/h flight, OKB's answer to national requirement also met by Sukhoi T-37 series and having most immediate application to Ye-266 (RSR, see Tsybin, having already been cancelled). Special high-augmentation AL-7 (called for record purposes TRD type P-166) with optimized inlet having translating centrebody with Oswatitsch profile (four cone angles) and upstream boundary-layer perforations ejecting dumped air through aft-facing nozzles above and below nose. Suck-in auxiliary doors well downstream. Convergent/divergent nozzle of diameter 50% greater than inlet capable of giving correct operation at Mach 3. Minimal canopy followed by large fuel-filled dorsal fairing leading into enlarged wet (integral-tank) fin later fitted with leading-edge camera and carrying small powered rudder. Large ventral fin on centreline, small fences at mid-span on underside of wing only, faired aileron power units (thickness even less than on MiG-21), slab tailplanes as far aft as possible behind nozzle, new main gears without levered suspension, AOA sensor on each side of nose, and long instrument boom attached as on Ye-152A. Major problem clearly to accommodate enough fuel to reach full speed potential, and fuselage so full of fuel that – despite use of high-pressure tyres demanding rigid pavements – wheel bays cause bulges. Carried VVS insignia. Set 100 km circuit record at 2401 km/h, A. Fyedotov 7 October 1961; 15/25 km record 2681 km/h, G. Mossolov 7 July 1962 (full-rated engine); sustained alt 22,67 km, P. Ostapyenko 11 September 1962.

Ye-166

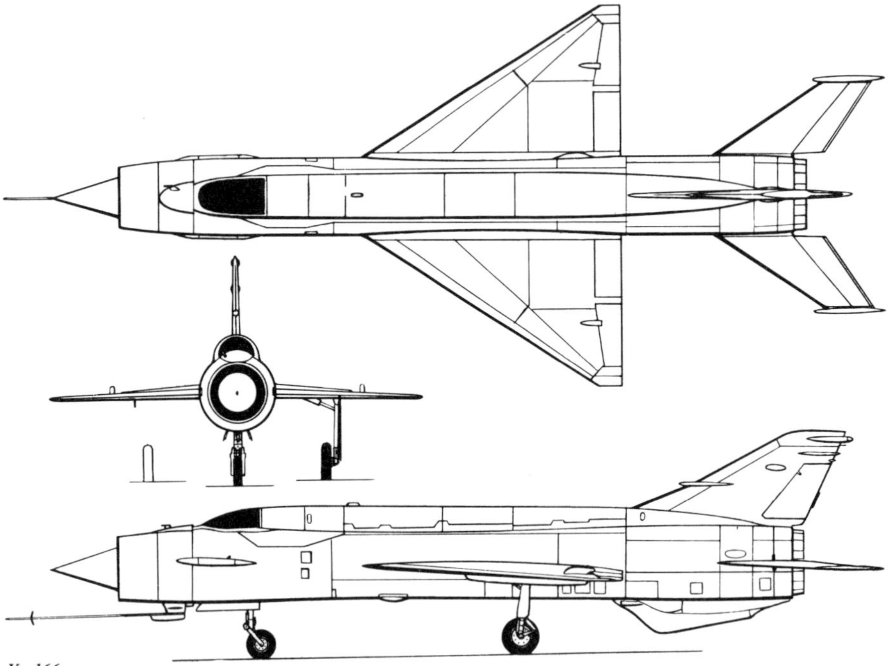

Ye-166

DIMENSIONS Span 8,97 m (29 ft 5⅛ in); length about 18,0 m (59 ft); wing area about 29 m² (315 ft²).
ENGINE One advanced AL-7F rated at 10 t (22,050 lb) static but with afterburner giving much greater thrust augmentation at Mach numbers near 3.
WEIGHTS Empty probably in neighbourhood of 8,5 t (18,750 lb); max probably near 20 t (44,000 lb).
PERFORMANCE Max speed 3000 km/h (1864 mph, M 2·82); service ceiling 25 km (82,000 ft); endurance 12 min at max power.

MiG-23 First major programme in which Belyakov played central managerial role, this successor to MiG-21 was carefully planned over many years to avoid earlier type's severe shortcomings in range/endurance, radar performance, firepower and weapon load. After many parametric studies decision taken about 1963 to eschew small air-combat fighter in favour of formidable air/ground attack aircraft with fighter variant tailored more to all-weather interception than close combat. As in earlier programmes very extensive TsAGI and OKB research led to totally new configuration with high-mounted variable-sweep wing of high aspect-ratio in final arrangement so similar to NASA/GD aerodynamics of F-111 it was probably plagiarized. V/STOL rejected at outset for many reasons (P. 1127 formula studied at length, and in late 1970s picked up again, but posed high risk and long timescale in class of engine missing from USSR entirely). STOL aircraft with lift jets offered less but was capable within timescale and cost, and so prototype built in parallel.

Lift-jet aircraft, believed **Ye-23** (several reports, **Ye-230**), built in parallel with VG prototype **Ye-231**. Maximum commonality except in inlet design, where OKB chose to explore two arrangements both new to bureau. Ye-23 had semicircular side inlets with translating half-Oswatitsch centrebodies, boundary layer ejected above and below inboard of duct, and with suck-in auxiliary doors downstream above wing leading edge. Wing similar to MiG-21 (though estimated by some at over 9 m span, and in some Western drawings shown with reduced LE sweep) but without fences and mounted in mid position; blown flaps used at 25° in low-speed flight regime as in jet-lift MiG-21. Same lift-engine bay as in MiG-21 with two (believed Koliesov) jets fed by rear-hinged dorsal louvred door and discharging through grid of pilot-controlled transverse louvres to deflect jets for thrust during accelerating transition. Completely new tail with broad fin having three LE sweep angles and small powered rudder above pod for cruciform drag chute. Trapezoidal left/right tailerons driven together for pitch and differentially for

Ye-23 V/STOL (believed Ye-230)

roll, without fixed root portions or tip anti-flutter masses. All tail surfaces cropped at tips at Mach angle. Small ventral strake on centreline incorporating aerial and steel tailskid. Main gears related to Ye-166 but larger tyres at normal pressure, bays sealed by doors on leg and on fuselage (latter remaining open with gear down). New aft-retracting twin-wheel steerable nose gear with surrounding debris and mud guard. Nose configured for large radar.

This interesting aircraft, almost certainly powered by an AL-7F-1, was exhibited at Domodyedovo 9 July 1967 in company with jet-lift MiG-21 and its rival, VG prototype Ye-231. Latter had not only most of new features of Ye-23 apart from lift jets but also introduced totally new wing. Almost identical to NASA F-111 in shape of broad upper surface and glove, outer-panel shape and sweep range, but outer panels much simpler with fixed leading edge and plain trailing-edge flaps. Large fixed glove with no variable surfaces. Lateral inlets similar to F-4 Phantom but lacking lower-lip droop, with great vertical depth and large inboard splitter plate perforated for sucking out boundary layer and with variable wall ramp angles. Two suck-in auxiliary inlet doors in each duct under wing glove. New main gears with unusual transverse folding legs of V-95/30KhGSA steel and duralumin forgings pulled inwards to bays in sides of fuselage at point where ducts curve in to engine bay behind main fuselage tanks. Large ventral fin folded to right on extension of landing gear. Tailplane high on rear fuselage, surrounded by four airbrakes. Otherwise design similar to Ye-23.

Prolonged development largely due to Tumanskii's new family of turbofan engines, much shorter and lighter than AL-7 series, which he was eager to get into programme to continue his monopoly position with Mikoyan. Jet-lift never serious contender, and VG formula swept board among builders of combat aircraft, being chosen for all new-generation jets by Sukhoi and Tupolev also. To avoid gap in manufacture decision taken to build substantial pre-production series with AL-7F-1 and many of these were issued to a complete fighter regiment in 1971. Designation MiG-23. Believed to have no spoilers, and lacking many features of true production variants. First of new family of engines, R-27, cleared for flight in single-engined fighters late 1968 and resulted in **MiG-23M** production aircraft in 1971. Compared with MiG-23 this was notably different internally and externally. Because of shorter and lighter engine, wings re-

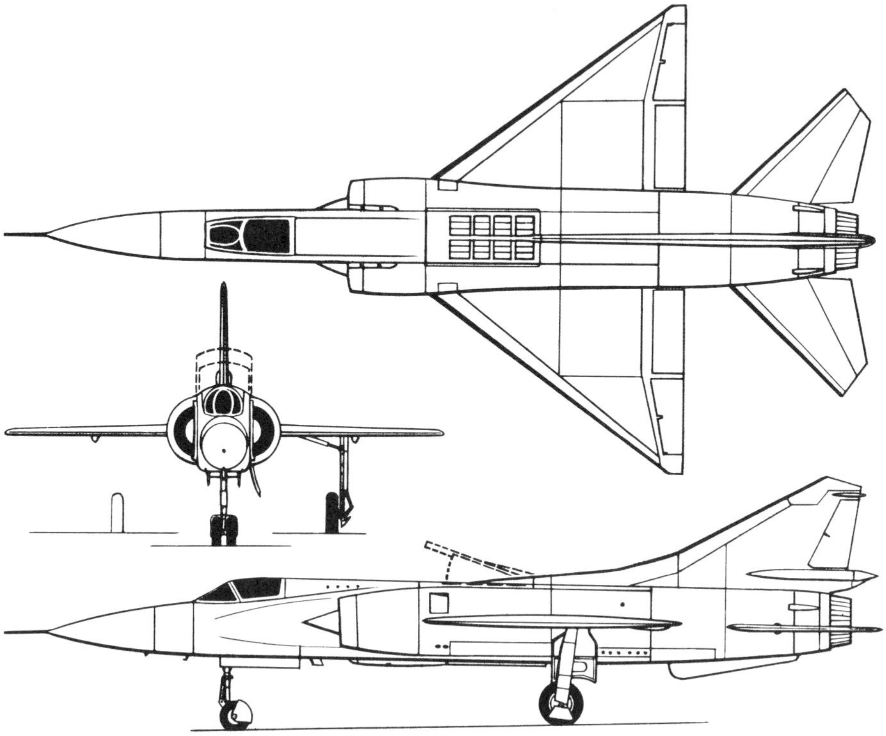

Ye-23 V/STOL (believed Ye-230)

Ye-23 prototype (believed Ye-231)

MiG-23MF with AA-7 and AA-8 AAMs

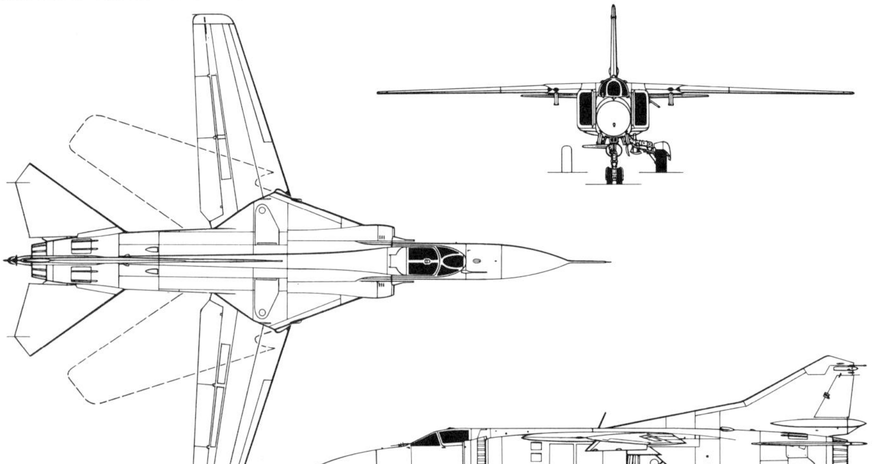

MiG-23MF

positioned 610 mm further forward on smaller fixed gloves, shifting c.p. forward by about same distance to line up with new CG position. Keeping tail in same place, rear fuselage was reduced in length 1,06 m, further reducing drag, weight and body loads. Third major change was greatly to extend wing chord at leading edge, inboard end forming a slot against leading edge of glove at min sweep of 17° and at greater angles forming extremely large dogtooth. Outer two-thirds of extra leading edge carries powered flap, drooped in hi-lift regime. Following is description of basic 23M.

Single-seat air-combat fighter with secondary air/ground capability. Wing carry-through box mainly of V-95 steel carrying large-diam Teflon-coated pivot bearings very similar to F-111. Glove LE sweep 72° with forged D16-T rib and spar. Outer wings basically SR12s/SR7 profile, thickness about 10% at min sweep of 17° (severe limitation on IAS and manoeuvre at this setting); alternative sweep settings of 45° and 72°. Main box integral tankage, five spars and machined/etched skins. Inboard, centre and outboard slotted flaps occupy entire TE, dural honeycomb construction, all driven together in hi-lift regime, two outers operable at 45° and outers alone at 72°. Ahead of flaps on upper surface are two spoiler sections on each wing used as primary roll control in hi-lift regime; said to be used as lift dumpers after touchdown, but such use not observed. At high speeds primary roll control by tailerons (small lines on TE of these surfaces in 3-view drawing are static wicks). Pressure-balance perforations in underskin beneath engine. Fuel 5750 lit (1265 gal) in integral wings, gloves, between ducts, under jetpipe and in dorsal fin. Hardpoints on centre-line and under outer wings plumbed for 800 lit (176 gal) drop tanks (wing pylons fixed and usable only at 17°). Basic armament GSh-23L on centreline installed as single pack with ammo tank of about 400 rounds. Pylon under glove for AAM, FAB-500, UV-16-57 or similar store on each side; similar pylons well inboard under inlet ducts. AAM originally K-13A; AA-2-2 Atoll (radar-guided) also carried. Since 1977 AA-7 Apex and AA-8 Aphid becoming predominant. Radar called High Lark by NATO, J-band, 90-cm phased-array reflector, search to 85 km, track from 55. Laser ranger ahead of nose gear, doppler ahead of laser and ILS (Swift Rod) in front of that with yaw sensor sometimes replacing it. Second ILS aerial at tip of fin, together with SO-69 Sirena 3 tail-warning; forward-sector SO-69 receivers in pods at outer ends of LE of gloves (in some aircraft one of these pods is optical target tracker), and SRO-2 IFF rods ahead of windscreen.

Deliveries from about 1972. In about 1975 succeeded (except for export) by **MiG-23MF** with R-29 engine. In parallel with original 23M deliveries made of **23U** tandem dual two-seater with full combat capability and weapons but reduced fuel and with periscope for instructor. Two-seater's radar normally smaller (probably Jay Bird), and ILS aerial closer to nose in consequence. Larger environmental system in deeper spine behind rear canopy, both canopies upward-hinged at rear. Later two-seater is **MiG-23UM**, but all believed to have R-27 engine; some may be ECM platforms. Original standard export aircraft (true designation not yet known) combined 23M airframe with small radar and ILS, buts neither doppler nor laser.

Slightly later than original 23M, work devoted to attack/interdiction variant resulted in two parallel models. **MiG-23BM** introduced new forward fuselage — aircraft popularly called *Utkanos*, duck nose — with no radar but improved forward view from deeper windshield and quarter-lights above sharply sloped upper profile. Raised seat and canopy, additional cockpit armour, and totally different avionics including LRMTS (later ranger/marked-target seeker) in 'chisel' nose, terrain-avoidance radar, doppler and CW (continuous-wave) target-illuminating radar with twin aerials in blisters on flanks of nose between doppler and nose gear. Glove aerials normally ECM or IR seeker (left) and missile guidance (right). Landing gear with tyres of increased diam and width, for soft-surface operation, resulting in bulges on nose doors and a major bulge of fuselage walls near trailing edge. R-29 B engine, same ratings as-29. Provision for two a.t.o. rocket units aft of main gears (some reports claim these on all variants). Extremely wide range of ordnance to 4,5 t on tandem ejector racks on centreline, under ducts (further out than in fighter) and gloves. BM, originally thought only export variant, entered service about 1974. At about same time production began of dedicated attack variant with different propulsion system optimized to low-level range and acceleration, at cost of reduced high-Mach. Engine (designation unknown) with increased by-pass ratio and simple afterburner with short pipe and two-position nozzle. Fed by plain inlets with bulged outer lips and small fixed splitter plates, and with nozzle about 0,4 m shorter. Basic designation **MiG-27**. Thick cockpit side armour, new six-barrel gun, normal bombload 16 FAB-250 or equivalent. **MiG-23BN** combines attack *Utkanos* with engine installation and gun of MF; exported and licensed to India. NATO Flogger-G is MF with simpler avionics and smaller dorsal fin. Flogger-H is BN with twin nose blisters. Flogger-J is MiG-27 with revised sensors (nose with upper lip and chin blister) and wing LE root extensions. Since 1980 all tailerons have kinked TE and reduced chord outboard, all models plumbed for three 800-lit drop tanks and all equipped to carry two pods with 23 mm guns able to fire obliquely down. No FR probe or two-seat MiG-27 yet seen.

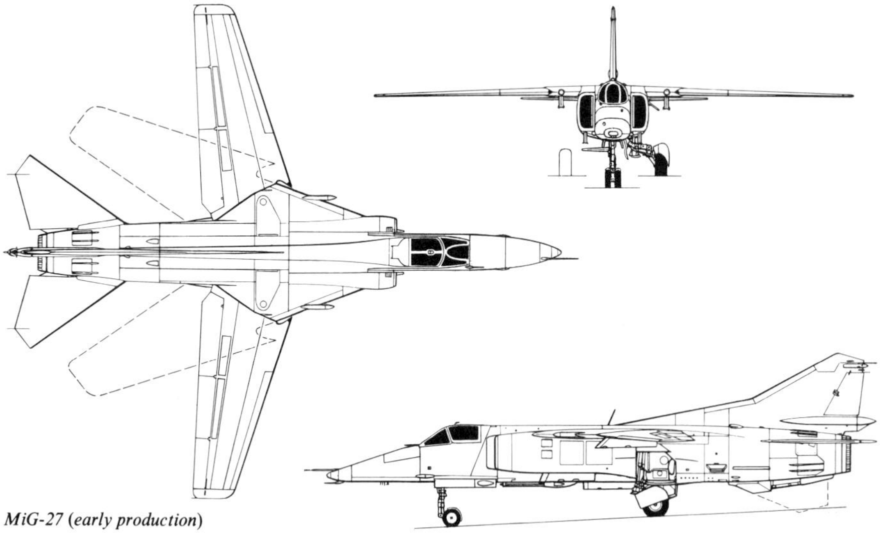

MiG-27 (early production)

Despite size, cost and challenge to user, MiG-23 family already (1983) used by 18 countries and probably produced at higher rate than any other combat aircraft. Deliveries mid-1983 almost certainly over 4000, including 1600+ with FA and 500+ fighters with PVO. A çarrier-based version is predicted.

DIMENSIONS Span 14,25/8,17 m (46 ft 9 in/26 ft 9½ in); length with probe (23) 18,8 m (61 ft 8¾ in), (23M, MF, U) 18,15 m (59 ft 6½ in), (BM, MiG-27) 16,8 m (55 ft 1⅔ in); wing area (17°) 27,26 m^2 (293·4 ft^2).

ENGINE (Ye-23, 231 and MiG-23) one 7/10 t (15,432/22,046 lb) AL-7F-1 afterburning turbojet; (M, U, export models) one 7/10,2 t (15,432/22,485 lb) R-27 two-spool afterburning turbofan, (MF, BM) one 8/11,5 t (17,635/25,350 lb) R-29 or (BM), R-29B, (MiG-27) one R-29 derivative of ratings est by author at 7,25/9 t (16,000/20,000 lb).

WEIGHTS Empty (MF) est 11 t (24,250 lb), (27) 10 790 kg (23,787 lb); fuel (all) 4600 kg (10,140 lb); gross (27 clean) 15,5 t (34,170 lb), (MF with AAMs only) est 16t (35,275 lb); max (BM, two tanks and six FAB-500) 20,1 t (44,312 lb), (27) about 20t, (MF) est 18,9 t (41,670 lb).

PERFORMANCE Max speed at SL (M,U) about M 1, (MF, BM) M 1·1, (27) M 0·95; max dash at height (fighters, AAMs only) 2450km/h

MiG-23 variant Flogger-G

MiG-23MF (kinked taileron TE), with AA-7 and AA-8 AAMs

MiG-27 (Flogger-D) with gunpods

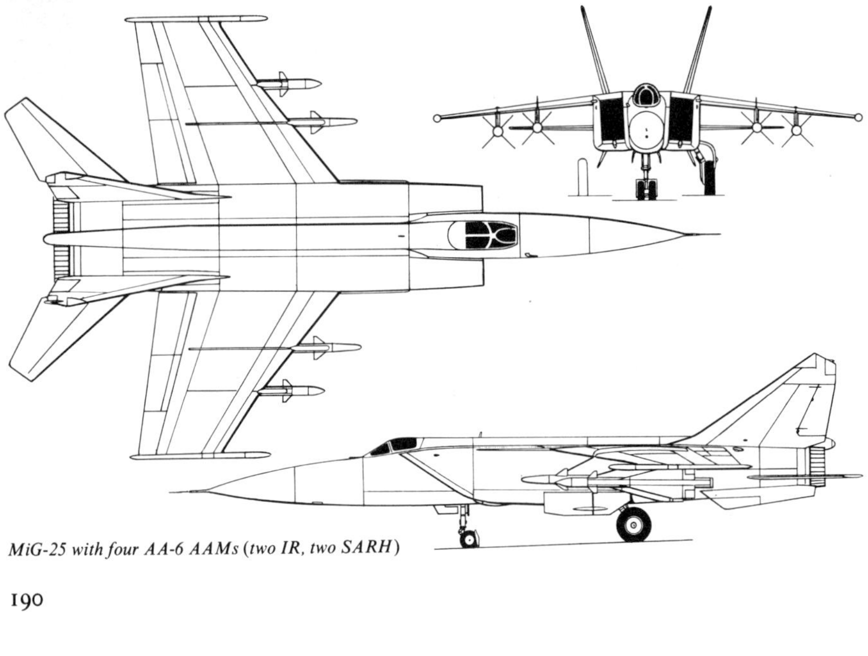

MiG-25 with four AA-6 AAMs (two IR, two SARH)

(1522 mph, M 2·3), (27) est 1700 km/h (1055 mph, M 1·6); climb, no data; service ceiling est 18,3 km (60,000 ft); typical combat radius (hi-lo-hi, centreline tank) 950 km (590 miles); ferry range (3 tanks) 2500 km (1550 miles); take-off (all, clean gross) 800 m (2625 ft)/330 km/h (205 mph); landing 800 m/280 km/h (174 mph).

MiG-25, Ye-266 About 1958 Mikoyan OKB, apparently without competition, instructed to propose highly specialized aircraft to reach highest possible speeds and heights. Prime requirement was defence against B-70 (Mach 3 at over 70,000 ft); secondary application as recon platform and possibly EW. Emphasis on state-of-art technology to reduce risk, timing and cost and provide workable interceptor to meet B-70 in-service date of about 1964. No attempt to produce fighter, but a straight-line interceptor operating under close ground control throughout mission and carrying long-range radar and AAMs. Major problems included radar power/range, need for new longer-range AAM, lack of national capability in Mach 3 airframe aerodynamics and structure, and impossibility of reconciling range demand with aircraft drag and performance. Predictably, Tumanskii assigned engine, simple single-spool turbojet similar to cancelled British Gyron, with large afterburner and convergent/divergent nozzle much greater in diameter than inlet.

Design settled about 1960, and prototype (probably **Ye-26** or **266**) flown about 1964. First of modern fighters with configuration pioneered by Vigilante with high wing and wide boxy fuselage mainly comprising inlet ducts and engines. Wing of unknown profile 4·4% thick, aspect ratio 3·3, LE sweep 40° to outer pylon, 38° thence to tip. Leading edge plain folded titanium-alloy sheet, otherwise structure argonarc-welded nickel steel heat-treated after assembly. Three main spars forming main box joined by welded skin of thin steel forming unstressed integral tank, outer skin then being welded above and below with typically 3 mm gap. Plain inboard ailerons and plain flaps, not honeycomb construction. Fuselage likewise basically arc-welded Ni-steel with welded-in thin steel tanks (2) along centreline aft of cockpit as far aft as engine fuel manifolds, plus saddle tanks (4) at sides aft of main gears extending above duct and compressor. System capacity 17 900 lit (3938 gal). Pressurized and inerted by dry nitrogen; no inflight-refuelling probe. Large inlet ducts with sharp lips cut back at Mach angle, lower lip hinged at rear and positioned by electric jackscrew, inner wall curved (not parallel to outer), top of duct with front and rear variable ramps driven hydraulically. Large rectangular boundary-layer exits in top skin. Four transverse pivoted vanes across duct midway between throat and engine driven by same electronic control system governing other variable-geometry features. Ring of bleed ducts immediately ahead of engine inlet feeding extra secondary flow past engine and around primary nozzle. Water/methanol coolant piped from leading edge along outside of duct to inlet. Conventionally built canted vertical tails and slab tailplanes (not tailerons) with titanium leading edges, Ni-steel structure and some dural at rear. All flight controls powered by duplex hydraulics. KM-1 seat, canopy hinged to right, avionics ahead of and behind cockpit, rear dorsal spine terminating in housing

MiG-25 (Libyan, with AA-6 radar AAMs)

MiG-25R

for dual brake chutes. Airbrake beneath jetpipes between canted ventral fins with retractable sprung tailskids. All landing gears retract forwards, main tyres 1200 × 340 mm, hi-press, twin-wheel nose unit steerable with debris deflector. Extensive dielectrics for all predictable avionics, 600 kW J (formerly X) band radar with 85 cm phased-array aerial and 90-km lock-on, anti-flutter pods at wingtips housing Sirena 3 and ECM, plus CW illuminators pointing ahead. Entered service mated to RSIU electronic environment 1970, but with AA-5 Ash AAMs. Definitive AA-6 Acrid (IR and radar) available from about 1974.

From 1971 VVS received **MiG-25R** basic reconnaissance variant. New nose of similar profile housing one vertical and five oblique cameras, small SLAR on right, doppler and ground-mapping ventral radars and Jay Bird radar in nose. Different outer wing with constant 42° sweep, reduced span and changed tip pods. In 1975 later 25R (designation unknown) for Elint. No cameras, comprehensive passive sensors and large SLAR further aft on right of nose. From 1973 dual trainer **25U** with pupil in added nose cockpit replacing radar; same wing and fuel capacity as original 25. **Ye-266** OKB designation for prototype used for many impressive records including 1000 km circuit with 2 t payload at 2320 km/h (Fyedotov 16 March 1965), 500 km circuit at 2981 km/h (Komarov 5 October 1967), time-to-height records eg, 4 min 3·86 s to 30 km (Ostapyenko 4 June 1973), alt 35,2 km (Fyedotov 25 July 1973). **Ye-133** for women's records. From May 1975 **Ye-266M** with more powerful engines, 30 km in 3 min 9·7 s and 35 km in 4 min 11·3 s and alt of 37,65 km (Fyedotov 31 August 1977). Defector Lt V. Belyenko who flew 1974-built MiG-25 to Japan 6 September 1976 said over 400 then delivered and mentioned uprated interceptor said to be **MiG-25MP** (Foxbat-E). Same engines as Ye-266M, look-down radar, new AAMs (six AA-X-9) and internal gun. Two-seat Foxhound is revamped MiG-25MP with alleged anti-cruise missile capability. MiG-25s exported to India, Libya, and Syria.

DIMENSIONS Span (25) 13,95 m (45 ft 9 in), (R) 13,4 m (43 ft 11½ in); length 23,82 m (78 ft 1¾ in), (ignoring probe) 22,30 m (73 ft 2 in); height 5,60 m (18 ft 4½ in); wing area (25) 56,0 m^2 (603 ft^2).

ENGINES Two Tumanskii R-31 single-spool afterburning turbojets rated at 9,3/12,3 t (20,500/27,120 lb); (266M, 25MP) two R-31F rated at 14 t (30,865 lb) with max augmentation.

WEIGHTS Empty (25, equipped) 20 t (44,090 lb), (R) 19,6 t (43,210 lb); fuel 14 322 kg (31,575 lb); max (25 normal) 35 t (77,160 lb), (25 overload with four AA-6) 37 t (82,500 lb), (R) 33,4 t (73,635 lb).

PERFORMANCE Max speed, M 0·85 at SL, M 2·8 at height with AAMs (theoretical 3·2 clean, see records); initial climb 208 m/s (40,950 ft/min); service ceiling 24 km (78,740 ft); ferry range 2575 km (1600 miles); mission radius (25 all-hi, all dash) 400 km (249 miles), (R) about 950 km (590 miles); take-off 1380 m; landing 2180 m/290 km/h.

MiG-29? A new air combat fighter prototype was observed by US satellite not later than January 1977 at Ramenskoye and given DoD designation Ram-L. From available information suggested VVS designation MiG-29 will probably prove correct, though prototypes presumably have Ye-numbers.

Configuration strongly resembling MiG-25 and McDonnell Douglas F-15, though much smaller. Dedicated air combat fighter with look-down, shoot-down radar with track-while-scan, and stand-off engagement capability against multiple targets. Internal multi-barrel cannon and six to eight pylons for AAMs or other ordanance. Features include almost unswept wing with Lerx, twin canted fins and tail, variable-incidence inlets and teardrop canopy raised above fuselage giving 360° view. Initially biassed to air-to-air combat but with considerable strike potential (probably in slightly different (two-seat?) version with modified radar and software, more armour, and increased gross weight). AAMs obviously might include AA-7, AA-8, and AA-X-9. Design optimized for agility, with SEP, turn radius and turn rate comparable with any Western fighter. Long gestation period suggests major technological innovations including composite (plastic) primary structure, all-digital avionics and quad FBW with relaxed static stability. Data are speculative.

DIMENSIONS Span 10 m (32 ft 10 in); length 17 m (55 ft 9 in); wing area 35 m (377 ft).

ENGINES Two augmented turbofans (R-25s?) with max rating in 7,7-t (17,000-lb) class.

WEIGHTS Empty 8,8 t (19,400 lb) loaded (clean) 12,5 t (27,560 lb); max, attack mission 16 t (35,270 lb).

PERFORMANCE Max speed about M 1·2 at SL, over M 2 at height and probably M 2·5 (2655 km/h, 1650 mph); service ceiling about 21,3 km (70,000 ft).

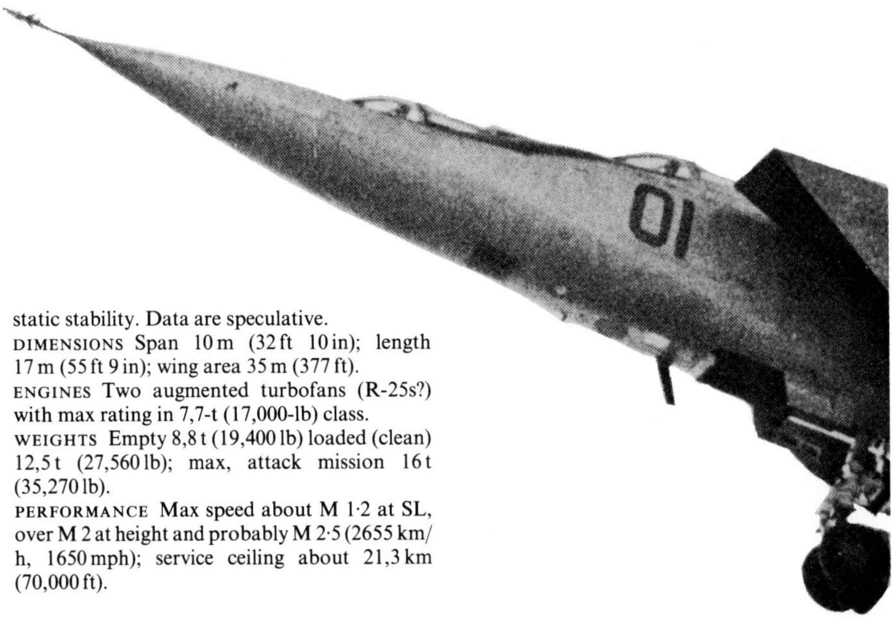

MiG-25U

Mil

M.L. Mil

Mikhail Leontyevich Mil was Siberian, like Kamov, born son of mining engineer at Irkutsk 22 November 1909. Siberian Tech Inst, Tomsk, from 1926; Don Poly Inst, Novochyerkassk, 1928, transferring to Novochyetkassk Aviation Inst, graduating 1931. In 1929 through Osoaviakhim assisted with KaSkr-1. From 1931 in Izakson's brigade at TsAGI and played leading role in A-15 autogyro. Deputy chief designer to Kamov 1936. Served at front with A-7 autogyros 1941–1943. In 1945 head of rotating-wing lab at TsAGI; formed own OKB 1947. Twice awarded Order of Lenin. Died 31 January 1970. Present OKB General Constructor Marat N. Tishchyenko.

Mi-1, GM-1 First project of OKB, this was (remarkably, in view of widespread prior rotary-wing efforts) first Soviet helicopter of now-classic layout with single main rotor and anti-torque tail rotor. Original designation GM-1 (*Gelikopter* Mil); design begun September 1947 and prototype completed exactly a year later. Three-blade main rotor, blades based on A-15 and related autogyros, mixed steel/ply/fabric NACA-230 profile, fully articulated hub with friction dampers, normal speed 232 rpm. Fuselage light alloy, except for welded steel-tube basis of mid-section housing engine with crankshaft horizontal and cooling fan, driving through angle box to transmission with centrifugal clutch and rotor brake. Four-seat cabin with left/right hinged doors. Fuel in welded aluminium tank 240 lit (53 gal) behind engine and, from about 40th production, provision for external supplementary tank of 160 lit (35 gal) on left side. Tail rotor with three wooden blades. Fixed nosewheel-type landing gear with brakes, plus long rear skid to protect tail rotor. First flight M.K. Baikalov (ex-Bratukhin) September 1948. Both first two GM-1 lost, second killing Baikalov after weld failure in tail-rotor bearing. Project taken over by Mark Gallai and V.V. Vinitskii, followed in summer 1949 by NII testing by G.A. Tinyakov and S.G. Brovtsyev, reached height 6800 m and speed 190,5 km/h. Production authorized as Mi-1. Eight took part in 1951 Aviation Day display. Civil and military variants including ambulance with left/right stretcher pods externally, agricultural **Mi-1NKh** with two 500 lit (110 gal) hoppers (note: solids only, liquid being weight-limited to smaller capacity) and many specialized models, with optional pontoon landing gear. From about 40th Mi-1 tail fitted with 0,32 m^2 adjustable stabilizer (tailplane). From 1957 new blades with extruded steel-tube spar. By this time basic model called **Mi-1T**, pilot and two passengers plus radio and fluid de-icing; also dual **Mi-1U** trainer. In 1961 Mi-1 *Moskvich* with all-metal blades of almost untapered plan, hydraulic con-

Mi-1

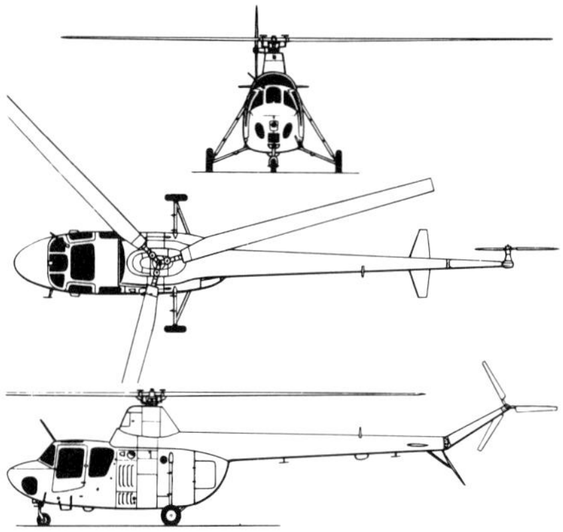

Mi-1T

trols and better standard of equipment and soundproofing. Name dropped and improvements (initially at request of Aeroflot) mostly standardized. Variant with four-blade rotor (erroneously dubbed Mi-3 in West) remained prototype. From 1954 Mi-1 built in Poland by WSK-Swidnik as SM-1, engine likewise as Lit-3. Series production tapered off in USSR (some hundreds) but continued in Poland until 1965 (over 1700).

DIMENSIONS Diameter of main rotor 14,346 m (47 ft 0¾ in); length (ignoring rotors) 12,1 m (39 ft 8⅓ in); height 3,3 m (10 ft 10 in).

ENGINE One 575 hp AI-26V radial.

WEIGHTS Empty (depending on model) 1760/1890 kg (3880/4167 lb); loaded (normal) 2470 kg (5445 lb), (max) 2550 kg (5622 lb).

PERFORMANCE Max speed (Shavrov) 190 km/h (118 mph), a fair figure though set 100-km circuit record 1959 at 210,535 km/h; cruise 140 km/h (87 mph); hover ceiling 1200 m at gross wt; range 360 km (224 miles) (max 590 km with aux tank).

Mi-1 Moskvitch

Mi-2 Chronologically later than Mi-4 and Mi-6, Mi-2 was planned 1958–1959 as modernized turbine derivative of Mi-1, just as Mi-8 was to Mi-4. Originally Mi-1 dynamic parts retained and mated with completely new fuselage, all light-alloy monocoque with steel forgings at concentrated loads, with twin turboshaft engines above cabin ahead of gearbox. Structural basis deep floor box carrying wheel or ski landing gears and housing flexible fuel cell of 600 lit (132 gal). Normal accommodation for pilot and passenger (on right) with main cabin for 700 kg (1543 lb) cargo or seat unit for three passengers facing forward and three facing aft, with eighth passenger seat on right opposite rear door. Option of four stretchers and attendant, or slung load of 1,2 t (2645 lb) or two 600 lit ag containers. All versions plumbed for two 250-lit (55-gal) auxiliary tanks on sides. First flight of **V-2** September 1961. Subsequently developed as production Mi-2 with improved bonded/welded fuselage, simpler and more reliable hub with hydraulic instead of friction dampers, bleed-air anticed intakes, new tail rotor with bonded-metal honeycomb blades and electrothermal de-icing on all rotor blades. Whole programme transferred to WSK-Swidnik in Poland in January 1964. All production and development subsequently at WSK (outside scope of book), involving 12 series versions including search/rescue and anti-armour. Total over 3970 mid-1982, two-thirds for USSR.

Mi-2 crop duster

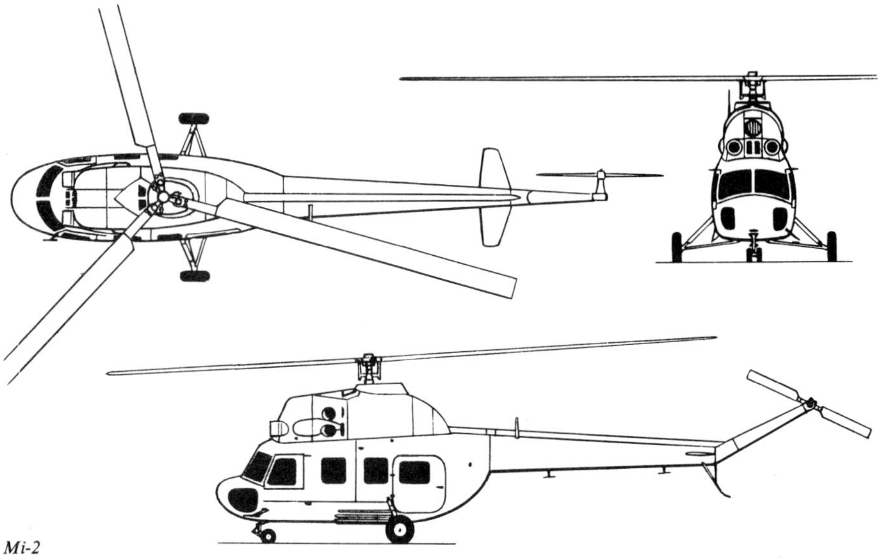

Mi-2

Mi-4 (Finnish air force)

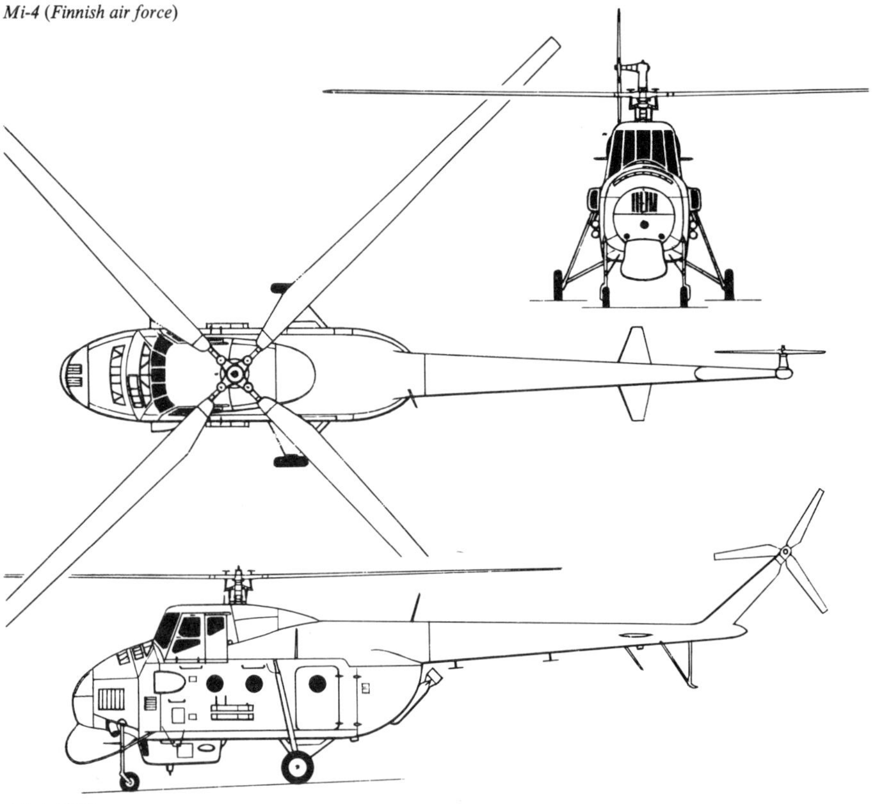

Mi-4 ASW

DIMENSIONS Diameter of main rotor 14,56 m (47 ft 9¼ in); length (rotors turning) 17,42 m (57 ft 2 in), (ignoring rotors) 11,94 m (39 ft 2 in); height 3,75 m (12 ft 3½ in).
ENGINES Two PZL-built Isotov GTD-350 (431 shp) or GTD-350P (444 shp) free-turbine turboshafts.
WEIGHTS Empty (passenger) 2402 kg (5295 lb); loaded 3,55 t (7826 lb); max (not ag versions) 3,7 t (8157 lb).
PERFORMANCE Max speed (except ag) 210 km/h (130·5 mph), (ag models) 155 km/h (96·5 mph); cruise 190 km/h (118 mph); SL max climb 4,5 m/s (885 ft/min); hover ceiling OGE 1 km (3280 ft); service ceiling 4 km (13,125 ft); range (max payload) 170 km (105 miles), (ferry, no reserve) 797 km (495 miles).

Mi-4 Second challenge to OKB, this was dramatic leap in capability and resulted from Kremlin meeting of constructors September 1951 at which Stalin insisted on sudden great advance in Soviet helicopters. All backed away except Mil and Yakovlev; on following day these two were given one year to design, build and fly prototypes, Mil's assignment being single-engined 12-passenger machine. No prototype, but small batch from start. Strong influence of American S-55, but much larger and in fact more powerful even than later S-58. Mil had prepared outline design beforehand which he produced at Kremlin; basically scaled-up rotors of Mi-1 with added fourth main-rotor blade, and S-55 configuration. Rotor axis inclined forwards 5°. Fuselage light-alloy semi-monocoque with extensive use of magnesium. Engine installed at 25° in nose accessible through upper/lower hinged nose doors and left/right hinged side doors. Cooling fan and centrifugal clutch immediately to rear of engine, with inclined shaft between pilots to main gearbox. Separate cooling systems for oil radiator and hydraulics for flight control. Straight tail boom with adjustable stabilizers, deep skid/bumper and narrow fin carrying tail rotor on right, as in all early Mil helicopters, with three bakelite-ply blades. Main fuel tank welded aluminium, 1000 lit (220 gal), behind gearbox; optional aux tank 500 lit in hold or externally. Quad landing gear with pneumatic-braked mainwheels and castoring nosewheels; optional pontoons for water. Main hold 4,15 m (13 ft 7⅓ in) long, about 1,8 m (71 in) square section. Max internal load 1740 kg (3836 lb) including small vehicles loaded through left/right rear doors and clip-on ramps. Slung load to 1,3 t (2866 lb). Alcohol de-icing of blades and windscreens as on Mi-1. First flight delayed several weeks by blade flutter in ground-running from 14 April 1952. First flight May, Vinitskii assisted by Brovtsyev. Remarkably few subsequent snags and NII testing completed before end of year. Main production model military Mi-4, with increased-diam main rotor, aluminium cargo floor, bulged circular windows with gun ports, ventral gondola for nav/observer, and tactical avionics. From 1954 **Mi-4P** civil variant with large rectangular windows, spatted wheels (often later removed), no gondola, and interior heated, soundproofed and equipped for ten passengers (each 20 kg baggage)/wardrobe and toilet Small batch of **Mi-4L** (*Lyuks*, de luxe) six-seaters. Some civil and mil equipped for casevac with eight stretchers and attendant. **Mi-4S** multi-role ag variant for spraying (1600 lit,

Mi-6A (civil)

352 gal) with wide spraybars, dusting (1 t, 2205 lb) or forest fire-fighting. Urgent development of improved metal blades 1954–1960 culminating in dural blade with extruded spar and honeycomb box trailing sections. Magnesium fuselage skins replaced by aluminium, and better flight control and avionics. April 1956 various records including 500 km circuit at 187,254 km/h, and later 1012 kg lifted to 7575 m (24,850 ft). About this time AV-MF received ASW version (designation not known) with chin radar (also fitted to various military variants), short but deeper gondola, towed MAD at rear and sonobuoys on external rack on right side. High-altitude (2-speed supercharged) model 1965, armed tactical variant with gun turret and air/surface rockets 1968, and EW platform first seen 1977 with two pairs of lateral *Yagi* arrays and other aerials mainly for communications jamming. Production ceased about 1969 with over 3500 delivered, of which 650–700 exported. In addition about 1000 license-built in China from 1959 for civil, army and navy use including tac attack, SAR and ASW; Chinese designation H-5, at least one re-engined with PT6T-6 Turbo Twin-Pac.

DIMENSIONS Diameter of main rotor (initial) 17,22 m (56 ft 6 in), (series) 21,0 m (68 ft 11 in); length (rotors turning) 25,02 m (82 ft 1 in), (ignoring rotors) 16,79 m (55 ft 1 in); height 5,18 m (17 ft 0 in).

ENGINE One 1700 hp ASh-82V two-row radial.

WEIGHTS Empty (with gondola) 5390 kg (11,883 lb); fuel/oil 750 kg; max loaded 7,8 t (17,196 lb).

PERFORMANCE Max speed 210 km/h (130·5 mph); cruise 160 km/h (99 mph); service ceiling 5,5 km (18,050 ft); range with 11 pax and 100 kg cargo or baggage 250 km (155 miles).

Mi-6 Heavy transport helicopter, built to meet combined military/civil requirement of 1954, possibly greatest single advance in history of rotary-wing aircraft. By far largest helicopter of its day, and also fastest; pioneered large turbines, use of lifting wings and (with wings removed) heavy crane role. From it stemmed series

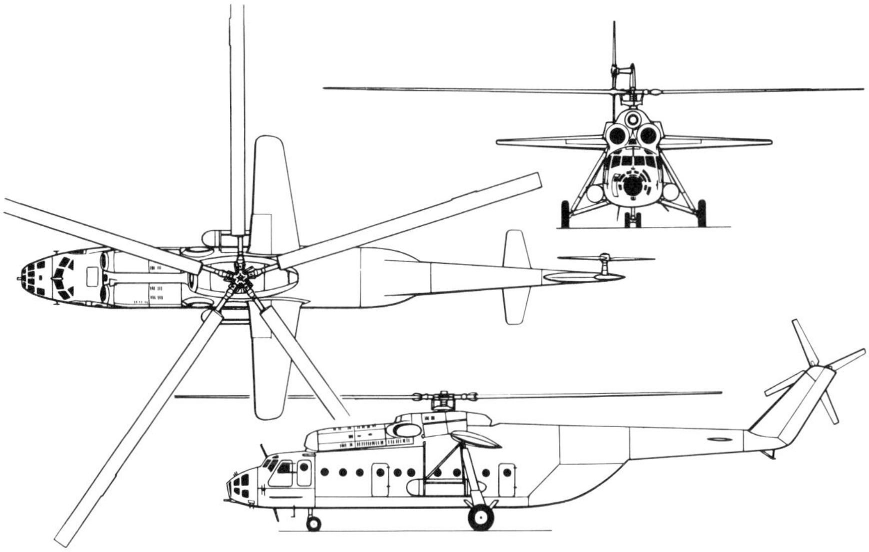

Mi-6

of equally successful crane helicopters and today's much more powerful Mi-26.

Prime original requirement was VVS need for VTOL airlift to complement An-12 and carry similar-size items (two lifts with Mi-6 equal one full load of An-12). Main Aeroflot need was strategic airlift in Siberia and other developing regions, though passenger version also built. Cargo hold cross-section smaller than An-12, width 2,65 m and height 2,5 m at rear reduced over front half to 2,01 m. Other basic factor was engine/gearbox, sized to give twin-engine safety in this application. Solovyev bureau designed new gas-generator for D-25 engine, and adopted free turbine to give speed flexibility and easy starting, and eliminate clutch. Engines same each side except for handed jetpipes. Trolley APU driven by 100 hp AI-8 turbine carried on board for ground power and to supply engine-mounted 12 kW starter/generators. Each engine also drives 90 kVA alternator feeding 360V at 400 Hz, partly radio but mainly for heavy electrothermal load anticing engine inlets and main-rotor blades. Left/right engines attached flexibly to sub-structure above forward fuselage with drive shafts at rear to R-7 gearbox, formidable package roughly 2 m square and 3 m (10 ft) high weighing 3,2 tonnes not including oil system and housing four sets of large gearwheels reducing speed 69·2 times. Box also drives oil cooling fan served by central intake ahead of rotor hub and three hydraulic systems (11,77/15,2 MPa, 1705/2205 lb/in^2) for flight control. Rotor axis angled forward 5°. Five blades, final standard based on extruded cold-rolled tubular spar 40KhNMA steel with screwed-on aerofoil sections in short lengths made from 2 mm D19A-M dural giving profile TsAGI-modified NACA-230M with thickness 11% from root to tip. Normal speed 120 rpm. AV-63B four-blade tail rotor with blades of bakelite ply on steel spar, electrothermal anticing changed to alcohol late in production. Conventional stressed-skin fuselage and tail boom. Wing of TsAGI P35 profile, 15% root and 12% tip, set at 14°15′/15°45′ incidence to provide 20% gross lift in cruise;

Mi-6P

removed in crane role. Horizontal stabilizer 4,87 m^2 trimming $-5°/+13°$. Fixed landing gear, main tyres 1320 × 480 mm, 0,686 MPa (99·5 lb/in²), pneumatic brakes, dual-pressure legs interconnected across aircraft to damp ground resonance. Nose gear free castoring, twin tyres 720 × 310 mm. Cargo via left/right full-section rear doors/ramp with hydraulic drive. Hold length 12 m, volume 80 m^3 (2825 ft³), floor stressed to 2 t/m^2 and electric winch (800 kg pull) multiplied by pulley-blocks. Slung cargo to 8 t, internal overload 12 t (26,450 lb). Flight deck with two jettisonable doors each side for two pilots, nav (glazed nose), radio and engineer; electrothermal window anti-icing, three-channel autopilot. Normally tip-up seats along main hold, max 65; up to 90 passengers with clip-on central seating. Max fuel capacity 17 250 lit (3794 gal) comprising eleven fuselage tanks total 8250 lit and four overload (ferry) drum tanks of 2250 each, two in cabin and two external. Engine side panels form maintenance walkway, closed hydraulically.

Five development aircraft, first flight R.I. Kaprelyan September 1957 without wings. Many subsequent records by Brovtsyev, N. Lyeshin, V. Kolosychyenko, B. Galitskii and other pilots, including 20 117 kg useful load lifted to 2738 m by Kaprelyan 1961, and speed over 100 km circuit of 340,15 km/h (211·35 mph) with specially prepared aircraft. Pre-series of 30 followed by **Mi-6A** production believed terminating 1981 with over 800 delivered. Almost all standard utility variant. Optional casevac interior for 41 stretchers, two attendants and associated equipment such as oxygen. Firefighting installations of at least two types with provision for spraying or dumping over fire, wings removed. No ag version revealed. Some military variants fitted with gun aimed by nav, normally DShK. Single **Mi-6P** with 80 airline seats and extra windows all of large rectangular shape.

DIMENSIONS Diameter of main rotor 35,0 m (114 ft 10 in); length (rotors turning) 41,739 m (136 ft 11½ in), (ignoring rotors) 33,179 m (108 ft 10½ in); height 6,71 m (22 ft 0 in), (tail rotor turning) 9,86 m (32 ft 4 in); span 15,3 m (50 ft 2½ in); wing area 35,0 m^2 (376·7 ft²).

ENGINES Two 5500 shp D-25V (service designation TV2-BM) free-turbine turboshaft.

WEIGHTS Empty (6A) 27 240 kg (60,055 lb); fuel (normal) 6315 kg; loaded (9016 kg payload) 44 t (97,002 lb); limit for normal VTO 42,5 t (93,695 lb).

PERFORMANCE Max speed (normal) 300 km/h (186 mph); max cruise 250 km/h (155 mph); climb at 40,5 t, 9·7 min to 3 km, 20·7 to 4,5; service ceiling 4,5 km (14,750 ft); range with 8 t payload at 1 km econ cruise 600 km (373 miles), (4,5 t and external tanks) 1050 km (652 miles), (ferry) 1450 km (900 miles).

V-7 Few details available of this experimental tip-drive helicopter completed by Mil OKB 1959. Pilot and three passengers in stressed-skin nacelle with three doors, tail on tubular boom, skid landing gear and kerosene tank in roof. All-metal blades (possibly related to final Mi-1 but shorter) carrying subsonic tip ramjets of roughly 220 mm (8.6 in) diam and giving about 30 kg thrust each. Hub of design unlike other Mil helicopters. Inclined drive shaft to tail rotor. Believed never flew with more than pilot on board, and never publicized.

DIMENSIONS Diameter of two-blade main rotor 11,6 m (38 ft 7 in); length not recorded.

ENGINES Two AI-7 ramjets (possibly based on Merkulov designs), each rated at 56 hp.

WEIGHTS Empty 730 kg (1609 lb); loaded 835 kg (1841 lb).

Mi-8 Great success of large free-turbine Mi-6 naturally spurred development of smaller and more versatile machine, and V-8 (series designation Mi-8) was designed on basis of Mi-4 and retaining existing rotors, transmission (except clutch and fan) and tail boom. Fuselage pod much larger, and because of high installation of engine wholly available for payload. Light-alloy

Mi-8T (Finnish air force)

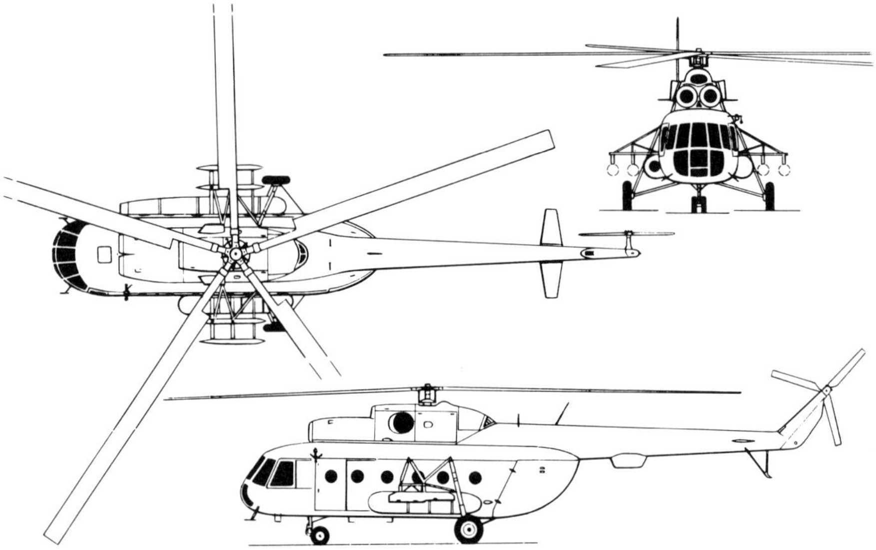

Mi-8T

semi-monocoque with nose cockpit for two pilots, with jump seat between for engineer. Main cabin 6,42 m (later 6,36 m, 20 ft 10¼ in) long, 2,2 m (later 2,34 m, 7 ft 8¾ in) wide and 1,82 m (later 1,80 m, 5 ft 10¾ in) high. Engine KB under S.P. Izotov assigned development of new free-turbine engine which, like that for Mi-6, was a conservative design and eschewed performance in favour of robust reliability. Drive via VR-8 two-stage gearbox reducing engine input (max 12,000 rpm) to rotor speed 192 rpm. Engine not flight-cleared when prototype approaching completion, and to begin flight development prototype V-8 fitted with large Solovyev engine, almost certainly D-25 derated to suit transmission limit of 2700 shp. Began flying early 1961 and no serious problems. Appreciated modern rotor needed and this was then designed, with five blades of better structural design than previous Mil rotors. NACA-230 profile, entire leading edge extruded aluminium-alloy spar with rear formed from 21 honeycomb-stabilized sections screwed on. Production spar gas-pressurized to warn of fatigue crack, and balance tab added to trailing edge. New hub scaled from that of Mi-6, with irreversible hydraulic control. Axis inclined forwards 4°30′. New blades of similar construction also designed for three-blade tail rotor. All blades with electrothermal anticing. Before these blades were ready, TV2-117 engine became available, at rating of 1400 shp, installed in second prototype flown 17 September 1962, still with Mi-4 dynamic parts. New rotor hub and blades first flown 1964, but several pre-production Mi-8s flew with old rotor which caused prolonged difficulties. About 1966 standard engine uprated to 1500 shp as TV2-117A. Small internal fuel bag of 445 lit (98 gal), main supply in external drum tanks housing (L) 745 lit (164 gal), (R) 680 lit (149·5 gal); provision for one or two similar tanks in cabin raising max ferry fuel to 3700 lit (814 gal). Right external tank faired at front into large cabin heater on production aircraft (heater sometimes not installed). Main and standby hydraulics at 4,4/6,38 MPa (640/925 lb/in²), lower than Mi-6 and Mi-10. DC starter/generators, but main anti-icing load AC at four voltages from 7·5 to 208. Comprehensive instruments (duplicated) and avionics including autopilot giving stabilization about all axes and set hover height or IAS. Main gear with tyres 865 × 280 mm, pneumatic brakes, twin steerable nosewheels locked central in flight.

Production authorized 1966. Basic utility variant **Mi-8T**, civil or military, with circular windows, aluminium cargo floor, rear full-width doors and hook-on ramps and hold thereby reduced in length to 5,34 m (17 ft 6 in). Capacity 23 m³ (812 ft³). Optional 24 tip-up seats along walls, 200 kg (441 lb) electric winch with pulley-blocks, sling for external load of 3 t (6614 lb) and max internal load 4 t (8820 lb). Optional rescue hoist, electric 150 kg (330 lb), above sliding jettisonable front left door. Military variants usually with doppler in box under tail boom, and following options: external stores rack each side of cabin for four UV-32-57 rocket packs or other loads; EW payloads (four suites identified), carried mainly externally; DShK in nose and ten external ordnance pylons, six below (typically 192 rockets) and four above (AT-2 Swatter); six AT-3 Sagger missiles; and mine-sweeping and MCM (mine countermeasures) gear. Mi-8 (without T suffix) is civil (rarely military) passenger version with large rectangular windows, comfortably furnished interior for 28/32 passengers with baggage compartment and toilet, airstairs in rear clamshell and often with spatted mainwheels. **Mi-8 Salon** is luxurious executive model normally for 8/11 passengers and restricted to 10,4 t. Ambulance interior for 12 stretchers and attendant, plus oxygen. Several projects including utility amphibious version and two commercial models with retractable landing gear, one stretched with seven windows each side, believed not built. Most successful European helicopter, and certainly more widely used than any other of same size and power with at least 29 customer air forces and many civil operators. Production total 8100. Progenitor of Mi-14 and -24, with new dynamic parts fed back to Mi-8 to produce Mi-17.

Mi-8

DIMENSIONS Diameter of main rotor 21,29 m (69 ft 10¼ in); length (rotors turning) 25,24 m (82 ft 9¾ in), (ignoring rotors) 18,31 m (60 ft 0¾ in); height 5,65 m (18 ft 6½ in).
ENGINES Two 1700 shp TV2-117A free-turbine turboshaft.
WEIGHTS Empty (8) given as 7417 kg to 1973, 6799 kg (14,990 lb) since, (8T) given as 7161 kg to 1973, 6624 kg (14,603 lb) since; fuel 724 kg (1596 lb); loaded 11,1 t (24,470 lb); max for VTO 12 t (26,455 lb).
PERFORMANCE Max speed 260 km/h (161 mph) at 1 km (250 km/h at SL); cruise 225 km/h (140 mph) at normal gross, 180 km/h at max; service ceiling at normal gross 4,5 km (14,764 ft); range 28 pax plus 20 min reserve 500 km (311 miles); ferry range 1200 km (745 miles).

Mi-10 It was logical to mate dynamic parts of Mi-6 with rest of helicopter tailored to crane role, lifting bulky external load and positioning over short ranges. Decision to build January 1959, using max commonality with Mi-6A. Prototype **V-10** flown 1960 (Green 'early', Alexander 'towards end'), in VVS markings. Almost standard Mi-6A rotors, transmission and engine installation, but main-rotor axis inclined forwards only 1°30′. New fuselage with shorter nose, different flight deck with no eye-brow windows but deep bulged side windows and single door each side well aft (under engine compressors), two pilots and engineer but no nav so no nose compartment. Slim fuselage with

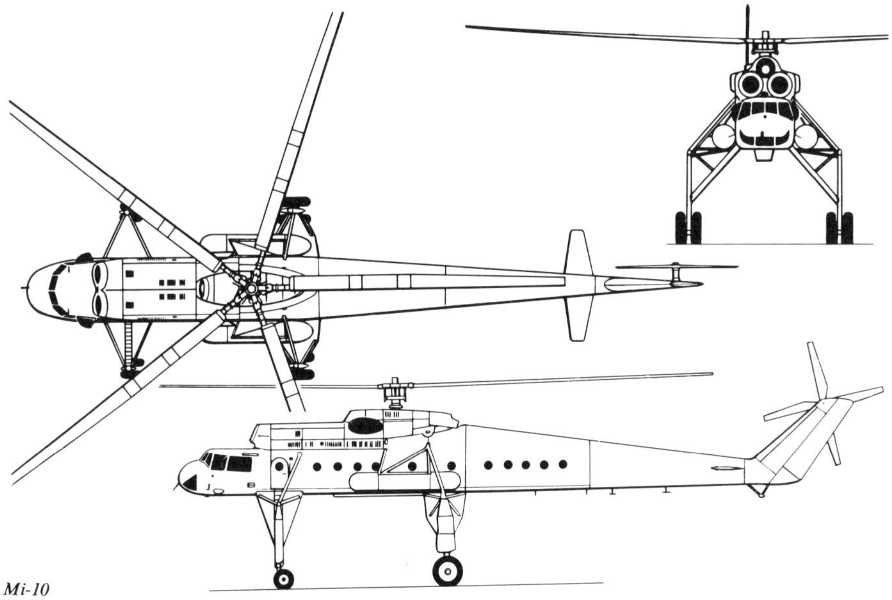
Mi-10

Mi-10 with emergency—escape trapeze wires

cabin 14,04 m (46 ft 0¾ in) long, 2,5 m (8 ft 2½ in) wide and 1,68 m (5 ft 6 in) high for cargo and with 28 tip-up wall seats. Almost straight bottom line; top of rear fuselage slopes down to bring tail fin and rotor much lower than in Mi-6A. Tall quad landing gears with two pairs 1230 × 260 mm main tyres and two pairs 950 × 250 mm nose tyres (Alexander 'steerable', *Jane's* 'castoring', latter appears correct), all fixed and with flight-crew steps in left front leg fairing, in some Mi-10s both front legs. Development aircraft had trapeze wires from above flight deck to front wheels for emergency crew escape in low hover. To counter side-thrust at tail and torque effects right legs 300 mm (11·8 in) shorter than left, crew cabin being canted to keep it laterally level on ground. Fuel in two external pods (3500 lit, 771 gal each) plus internal service tank (731 lit, 161 gal); total 6184 kg (13,633 lb). Optional ferry tanks in hold, total 2400 lit (528 gal, 1920 kg, 4233 lb). Provision for pressure-fuelling from ground whilst hovering. Internal cargo loaded via rear right door with 200 kg electric hoist. Main load slung externally. Ground clearance 3,75 m (12 ft 3½ in) at full load. Normal procedure to taxi over and straddle load which can measure 20 m by 10 m (actual Mi-10 track and wheelbase, measured from strut centrelines, 6,92 and 8,29 m). Two load-carrying systems: 500-kg winch through floor hatch, and group of four swinging struts picking up corners of load with hydraulic grips controlled from cockpit or remote panel in cabin via TV from two locations. Load can be mounted on special platform 8,53 × 3,54 m (27 ft 11¾ in × 11 ft 7⅓ in) with or without wheels. AI-8 turbine APU permanently installed for electric/hydraulic power without main engines. Anticing as Mi-6A. Can make running take-offs and landings at 100 km/h. Total estimated 1981 at 55–60 including civil (about 20), military and exports.

Mi-10K (*Korotkonogii*, short-legged) presaged by special Mi-10 flown 1965 with single centreline nose gear and single spatted main gears of min length and weight, used to lift 25 105 kg (55,347 lb) to 2840 m (G. Alferov, 28 May 1965). This was later restored to Mi-10 standard but OKB was then about to fly Mi-10K designed specifically for slung loads, displayed in action March 1966 (first flight not known). Four short landing gears reducing door sill height from almost 4 to 1,8 m. New crew compartment with single pilot at original level and second in central all-glazed gondola facing aft with full controls for helicopter and load. Larger internal fuel cells, giving total with two external tanks of 9000 lit (1980 gal). Tail bumper and much narrower tail fin. Cleared for production October 1969 but no production Ks seen.

DIMENSIONS Diameter of main rotor 35,0 m (114 ft 10 in); length (rotors turning) 41,89 m (137 ft 5½ in), (ignoring rotors) 32,86 m (107 ft 9¾ in); height (10) 9,8 m (32 ft 2 in), (10K) 7,8 m (25 ft 7 in).

ENGINES As Mi-6A; 1966 report of 6500 shp D-25VF but not known to have been installed.

WEIGHTS Empty 27,3 t (60,185 lb), (K) 24 680 kg (54,410 lb); max payload (10, platform) 15 t (33,070 lb), (10, slung) 8 t (17,637 lb), (10K, slung) 11 t (24,250 lb), (10K, D-25VF engines) 14 t (30,865 lb); max 43,7 t (96,340 lb), (K) 38 t (83,775 lb), (K, VF engines) 41 t (90,389 lb).

PERFORMANCE Max speed (10, max wt) 200 km/h (124 mph); cruise (10, max wt) 180 km/h (112 mph), (K, empty) 250 km/h (155 mph), (K, slung load) 202 km/h (125 mph); authorized height limit 3 km (9843 ft); range (typical load) 250 km (155 miles), (max ferry) 795 km (494 miles).

V-12 By far largest helicopter ever built, this was unusual extrapolation of Mi-6 a decade later to match greater fixed-wing airlift of An-22 and Il-76. To avoid immense task of developing new set of rotors, reduction gears and transmission, decision taken to double up Mi-6 dynamics and use two sets of Mi-6 engines, gearboxes and lifting rotors. After much study, assisted by TsAGI, decision to use rotors side-by-side, handed to rotate in opposite directions (right is original, left rotor has mirror-image blades). Rotors overlap; it has been assumed diam same as Mi-6 but engines are more powerful and overlap (3 m calc on basis of overall 'span') is given as 5,05 m, leading to belief diam actually slightly larger; reinforced by reduced rpm of 112 instead of 120. Rotors linked by transverse shafting. Axes inclined forwards 4° 30′. Engine/rotor groups carried on wings of light-alloy stressed-skin construction with 8° dihedral, sharp inverse taper and set at incidence 7° root 14° tip. Braced at root and tip to main landing gears with torque reacted by horizontal bracing to rear fuselage. Inner/outer trailing-edge flaps fixed in up position after flight trials. Fuel in outer wings and two external tanks; optional ferry tanks in cabin. Fixed twin-wheel landing gear with main tyres 1750 × 730 mm, pneumatic brakes, and steerable nose tyres 1200 × 450 mm. Large stressed-skin fuselage with crew door each side, three sliding side doors and full-section rear clamshell doors and ramp with left/right twin-wheel ventral bumpers. Aeroplane tail with fin, tabbed rudder, dihedralled tailplane with tabbed elevators, and endplate fins mounted vertically but toed-inwards. Flight deck for pilot (left) with engineer behind and co-pilot (right) with elec-syst operator behind. Upper flight deck for nav with radio operator behind. Hydraulic flight control with emergency manual reversion. Autopilot with

Mi-10K

V-12

three-axis autostab; mapping radar under nose, AI-8 turbine APU for ground power and engine start. Main cabin 28,15 m (92 ft 4 in) long, 4,4 m (14 ft 5 in) square. Overhead gantry crane with four 1 t hoists. Tip-up seats along sides (50 to 120). First flight 10 July 1968; this V-12 destroyed in non-fatal heavy landing 1969. Second flown by V.P. Koloshchyenko to 2255 m on 6 August 1969 with payload 40 204,5 kg (88,636 lb). Extensive demo including flights to West but, apart from scale model showing minor changes in 1972, no further work (prototype preserved at Monino); replaced by Mi-26.

DIMENSIONS Span over rotors 67,0 m (219 ft 10 in); length 37,0 m (121 ft 4½ in); height 12,5 m (41 ft 0 in) (Soviet figures, close approximations).

ENGINES Two pairs of 6500 shp D-25VF.

WEIGHTS Empty not disclosed; normal payload 25 t (55,115 lb) VTOL, 30 t (66,140 lb) STOL; loaded (normal) 97t (213,850 lb), (max) 105 t (231,480 lb).

PERFORMANCE Max speed 260 km/h (161 mph); cruise 240 km/h (149 mph); service ceiling 3,5 km (11,480 ft); range with max payload (payload given as 35,4 t, not explained) 500 km (311 miles).

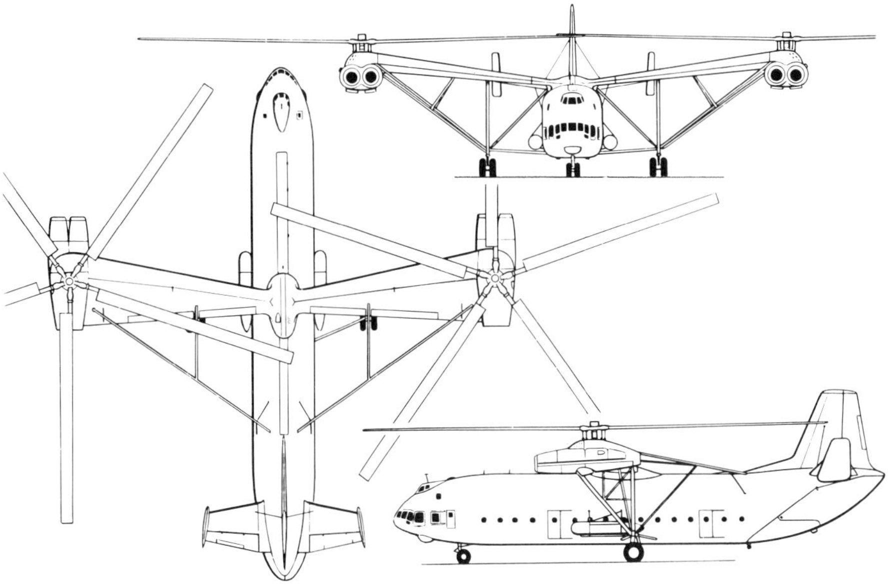

V-12

Mi-14, V-14 Original V-14 first of derived offshoots of Mi-8 with significant but subtle differences. Like many as yet unbuilt or unseen projects such as retractable-gear airline transport and cargo version with full-width rear ramp/door V-14 introduced more powerful TV3 engine which originally was derated to provide constant power of 1800 hp at all airfield heights and air temperatures. This fitted slightly more compact engine bay but drove almost unchanged main rotor. Other differences include improved main gearbox, larger tailplane (stabilizer) and tail rotor moved to left side of fin. Transport version introduced retractable tricycle landing gear with main units having twin wheels retracting forwards into sponsons on sides of rear fuselage. Nose gear similar to Mi-8 but retracting into fuselage. Only member of this family so far seen is an Mi-14 naval patrol and ASW helicopter used by AV-MF in shore-based ASW (in emergency in SAR) role with watertight boat hull but not normally intended for off-water operation. In this variant features include keels on rear sponsons, large undernose radar, fuel drums removed (fuel in sponsons behind main gears), no rear clamshell doors, internal tactical compartment with crew of five, towed MAD bird, doppler under tail boom (as well as small protective bumper pod under tail, surmised by some as 'tail float') and several EW aerials. No weapons externally and probably carried in internal bay. About 25 built annually since 1976, majority probably with five-blade main rotor. Almost certainly used by AV-MF and probably other military and civil operators in dedicated SAR and transport versions.

DIMENSIONS Essentially same as Mi-8.

ENGINES Two 1900 shp TV3-117.

WEIGHTS Empty (est) 8,5 t (18,700 lb); loaded (est) 13 t (28,660 lb).

PERFORMANCE Not significantly different from Mi-8.

Mi-17, V-17 This helicopter was natural result of combining new dynamic parts of V-14 series with original V-8. Design similar to Mi-8 except five-blade main rotor and generally modernized airframe. Flight deck updated, jump seat for third occupant, main cabin improved and slightly enlarged to 5,34 × 2,34 × 1,8 m all usable. Normal seating up to 24, though still only 12 stretchers. Engine installation with deflectors and ejectors for sand, dust, ice or other foreign objects, auto synchronization of inputs with main rotor speed (engine-out emergency rating 2200 hp either engine) and pneumatic supply from APU for air-turbo starters. Mi-8 fuel system almost unchanged with cabin heater at front of right external tank. Various civil and military sub-variants, most with clamshell rear doors and full all-weather and IFR capability.

DIMENSIONS Diameter of main rotor 21 294 mm (69 ft 10¼ in); length (rotors turning) 25 262 mm (82 ft 10½ in), (ignoring rotors) 18 424 mm (60 ft 5½ in); height (main hub) 4755 mm (15 ft 7¼ in), (tail rotor) 5521 mm (18 ft 1¼ in).

ENGINES Two 1900 hp TV3-117MT.

WEIGHTS Empty 6790 kg (14,969 lb); normal loaded (4-t payload) 11,1 t (24,471 lb), (max) 13 t (28,660 lb).

PERFORMANCE Max speed (13 t) 250 km/h (155 mph); cruise 240 km/h (149 mph); service ceiling (11 t) 5 km (16,400 ft), (13 t) 3,6 km (11,800 ft); hover ceiling (11 t, OGE) 1760 m (5775 ft); range 5% reserve (11 t) 495 km (307 miles), (max wt) 465 km (289 miles); ferry range (cabin tanks) 950 km (590 miles).

Mi-18 Announced 1981, no details disclosed.

Mi-24, A-10 Developed during mid-1960s, this family of helicopters has so far appeared only in military versions which, in numbers and capability, are most important in world. Prototype flying while Mil was still alive, but entire programme stands to credit of Tishchyenko. Like V-14, this family was derived from Mi-8, but with new engines and with very little commonality except to V-14. Altogether Mi-24 reinforces view that, despite inflation, Soviet procurement tailors new hardware to mission even when a 95% platform already exists. Basic mission was to carry squad of eight combat-equipped troops and powerful external weapons. Resulting Mi-24 subsequently used as basis for new family with different forward fuselage dedicated to night and all-weather gunship role but retaining original cabin. Compared with Mi-8, basic dynamic parts generally uprated yet reduced in size. Main-rotor speed higher, putting equal or greater engine power through substantially smaller disc with no increase in blade number, chord or solidity. New hub, with basis of machined titanium forging, though retaining full articulation and deliberately not adopting elastomeric bearings. Blades believed still NACA-230 series but glass-fibre skins and new form of (probably extruded steel) spar. Electrothermal anticing on leading edges, balance tabs on trailing edge. Tail rotor moved to left of tail fin on all except prototypes and pre-production machines. Same large stabilizer (slab tailplane) as V-14 family, but large swept vertical tail of new design, offset to left. Engine installation of reduced bulk, especial care taken to reduce height to minimise drag and using a new compact gearbox. Tricycle landing gears retract rearwards, main units with low-pressure tyres turning almost square-on to legs to be stowed transversely in narrow bays, and twin nosewheels believed to be steerable (in later versions on longer leg and not retracting fully). Engines exhaust left/right through large stacks (closer to inlet than on Mi-8) with no IR suppression. Circular inlet at upper level for fan-assisted oil cooler. No details of fuel system,

Mi-14

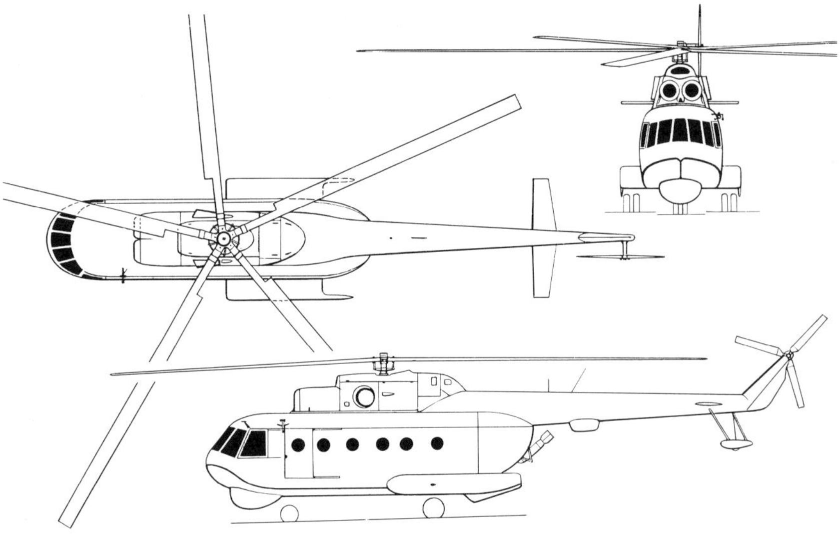

Mi-14

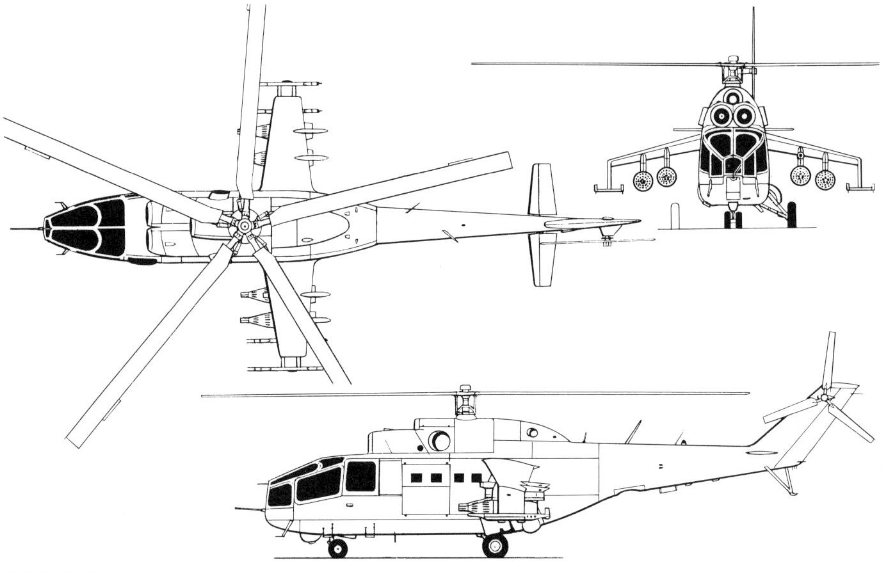

Mi-24 Hind-B

Mi-24 Hind-B

but no external tanks and fuel probably beneath cabin floor or aft of rotor mast above cabin ceiling. Exceptionally comprehensive avionics including full-authority autopilot, stab-augmentation system, ADF, pictorial map display and air/army communications. Original Mi-24 flight deck for gunner/nav and forward observer in front of pilot and co-pilot, with sliding door (wholly occupied by bulged side window) on left and upward-hinged glazed forward roof panel. Optically flat front window for aiming DShK from nose. Main cabin for eight troops with door on left divided into upper and lower hinged sections opening outward. Large lifting wing with spars passing above rear of cabin with pronounced positive incidence and anhedral, no movable surfaces, equipped with two underwing stores hardpoints on each side plus pylons at tips. (In early Mi-24s these wings were horizontal and had no tip pylons.) Aircraft of this standard delivered 1972 or earlier (first-flight date unknown) and production subsequently maintained at est 15 to 20 monthly. Next model had tail rotor switched to left side as on Mi-14, extra titanium armour and six pylons each side. Typical weapon load for these models four UV-32-57 rocket pods on wing pylons and four AT-2 Swatter missiles on tip rails. Third variant (1975) without under-nose magnifying optical sight, nose gun or outer anti-tank missile rails and used primarily as assault troop and supply transport.

Second major family (still Mi-24, despite many reports of Mi-27 or Mi-28) entered service late 1975, showing design early 1970s and prototype not later than 1973. New forward fuselage made largely of titanium armour accommodating crew of only two. Pilot with door on right and large optically flat windscreen with wiper in fixed bubble canopy. Weapon operator lower in nose with canopy of curved armourglass hinged to right and kick-steps on left side of nose. Flat bulletproof windscreen, right side of frame mounting SRO-2 series IFF pod aerials and long precision air-data boom with accurate pilot system and two-axis wind-vanes. Under nose two large bulges, left for LLTV and right for radar (at least one Mi-24 with FLIR, but this not expected in production by Western observers, without any reason given). Under nose on centreline hydraulic barbette mounting gun with four 12,7 mm barrels. Some sub-types replace this with six-barrel 23-mm gun of greater long-range hitting power. Laser ranger on tip of left wing or on left inboard pylon. Same wing ordnance as other variants and same tail-boom avionics including GIK-1 gyrocompass and RV-5 radar altimeter (doppler not usually fitted). Latest models of Mi-24 gunship sub-types

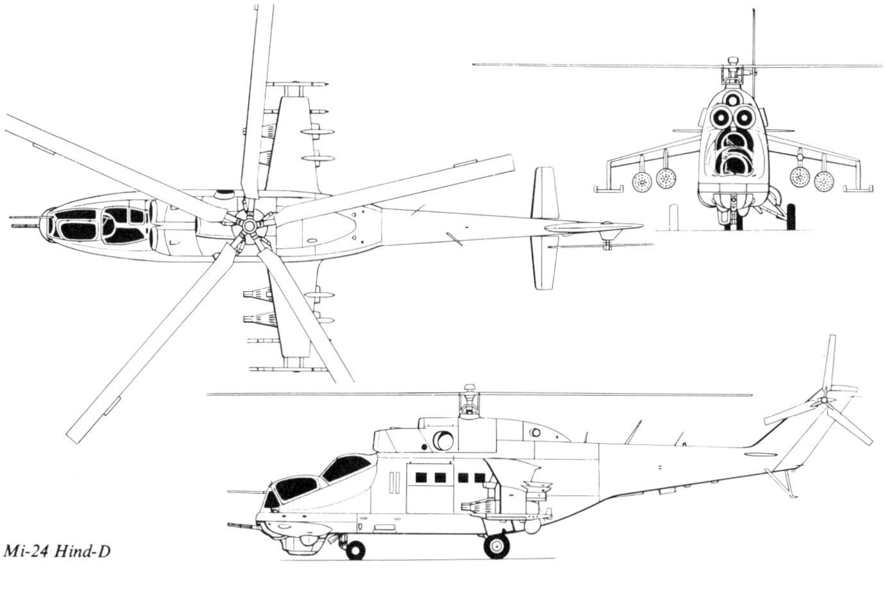

Mi-24 Hind-D

Mi-24 Hind-D

include additional sensors and laser-homing AT-6 Spiral anti-armour missiles launched from eight pylon-mounted tubes. By mid-1983 over 2100 Mi-24s in service, and large and increasing numbers exported. Mi-24s have been used operationally by Iraq in the Gulf War against Iran. Soviet forces in Afghanistan have made extensive use of this imposing gunship, particularly against the feared Majahedin guerillas.

DIMENSIONS Diameter of main rotor (est) 17,0 m (55 ft 9 in); length (ignoring rotors) 17,0 m (55 ft 9 in); height 4,25 m (14 ft 0 in.).

ENGINES Believed in all sub-types two 1700 hp TV2-117A.

WEIGHTS No data, but empty est 6500 kg (14,330 lb) and normal loaded (all known sub-types similar) about 10,5 t (23,150 lb).

PERFORMANCE Max speed, with max load at least 290 km/h (180 mph) and has set records at speeds to 334,5 km/h (207·8 mph); max climb 15 m/s (2950 ft/min); ceiling, range, no data but potentially greater than Mi-8.

Mi-26 By 1970 it was clear V-12 was major error. Mil died aged 61 at height of troubles, and successor Tishchyenko at once decided to start with clean sheet of paper. GUAP agreed this course, despite extra time needed and, esp, need to create completely new dynamic parts on much greater scale in order to achieve desired load-carrying ability with conventional helicopter lifted by single main rotor. Everything possible done to reduce risk, even at cost of greater time or less-competitive final result. From start **V-26** planned for military and airline tasks, but chief duty support of exploitation of Soviet Union's undeveloped regions where environment severest in world and reliability essential in week-long operations away from main base. Lotaryev KB already working on new D-136 free-turbine engine, vital to success and efficiency of new helicopter. Final breakthrough was Mil OKB's reluctant decision to handle design and development of new main gearbox itself, finding no external bidders.

GUGVF laid down severe numerical requirements, one of which was empty-weight fraction of 0·5, figure missed by large margin with V-12. This worked against low-risk approach, yet Tishchyenko's team spent fruitful three years in detail examination of engineering, and result is excellent compromise. V-26, designated **Mi-26** in production, is similar in configuration to Mi-6 but totally different dynamic parts, different structure and modern flight deck and avionics. Main rotor with eight blades surprisingly accomplished within smaller diameter than Mi-6 and Mi-10 despite handling twice engine power. Prolonged research on blades led to compromise with extruded high-tensile steel spar forming nose carrying 26 glass-fibre trailing-edge secctions (called *Kolpachok*, cap). This hañdled power with eight blades, with adequate autorotative inertia and sufficient torsional stiffness. In-flight vibration one-tenth that of Mi-6. No expected corrosion problem. For 7,61-m tail rotor Kamov experience with GRP used to underpin all-GRP blades, five used, again with constant profile.

Main hub machined from titanium forging, largest on any helicopter. Test hub made with elastomeric bearings and may introduce later, but standard production hub has trad articulation in lubricated bearings. Main gearbox handles twice power and twice torque of R-7 box used in previous generation. Max torque is 90 000 kg-m (650,992 lb-ft). Despite this it is smaller, and only slightly heavier at 3,5 t (7716 lb). Engines identical except for handed jetpipes, and have large FOD deflectors upstream of airframe inlets to avoid ingestion of ice and birds. Dust and sand removed by centrifugal separators in each duct. Cowl panels fold down to form work platforms. Ahead of rotor is large oil radiator in duct with powered compressor to increase airflow. Gas-turbine APU under flight-deck floor instead of in cabin, and all fuel in eight integral tanks beneath main cargo floor, instead of in drums internally and externally. Bleed-air inlet anticing, rest of helicopter de-iced by pulsed raw AC electric power.

Stressed-skin pod/boom fuselage with much lower % weight than Mi-6. Conventional flush-

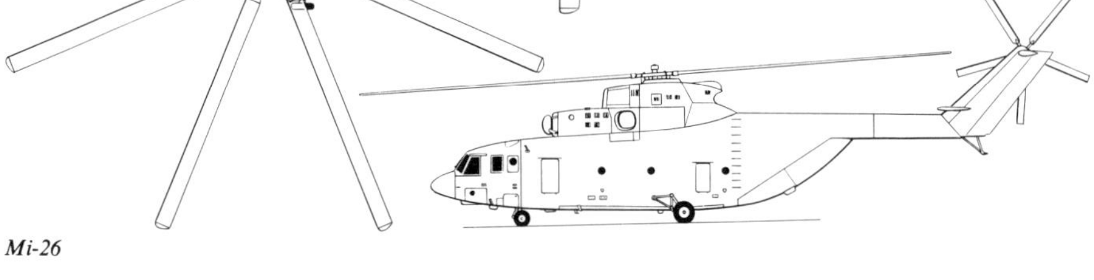

Mi-26

riveted construction with frames notched to receive close-pitched stringers. Cross section similar to Il-76T (3,2 m square) with strong titanium floor all at one level over usable length of 15 m. Left/right rear clamshell doors opening downwards, with vehicle access up left/right hinged ramps positioned according to vehicle track. Doors closed hydraulically, with hand-pump for use on ground. Normally interior bare and unlined, but with fold-down wall seats for handling crews. No passenger windows but two Type A doors on left side. Rear internal ladder giving access to tail boom. External step/handholds aft of rear side door for access to top of boom, tail and rotor pylon. Large cambered fin with ground-adjustable tailplane (stabilizer) short way up leading edge, with tail rotor on right. Twin steerable nosewheels, twin mainwheels with low-pressure tyres and hydraulic brakes on trailing-link levered suspension from bottom of fuselage frames, long tail bumper. Provision for lifting wings but, though flight-tested, not normally fitted. Single 30-t cargo hook under CG for external slung load; interior cargo handling by two 2,5-t electric hoists running full length of hold on tracks along upper sides (not a gantry).

Spacious flight deck at main floor level with large windows bulged at sides for direct view of slung load or ground below, augmented by TV cameras under tail looking obliquely forwards, at front of hold looking aft and looking vertically down through floor hatch at slung load. Pilot (left) and co-pilot with TV screen, doppler-driven moving-map display giving accurate blind nav and drift in hover, autopilot and stab-augmentation system. Nav to rear (right) handles all basic nav problems, radio and advanced mapping/weather radar in nose. Flight engineer behind on left manages systems. Central jump seat for loadmaster or supernumerary.

First V-26 flown in hover 14 December 1977 and began full translational flying 21 February 1978. Fourth aircraft, production Mi-26, exhibited at Paris June 1981, flown by chief test pilot Gurgen R. Karpetyan. Mi-26 already cleared for series production and expected to play central role in exploitation of undeveloped regions. Long-term study of even more capable successor.

DIMENSIONS Diameter of main rotor 32,0 m (104 ft 11$\frac{3}{4}$ in); length (ignoring rotors) about 35 m (115 ft); length overall, approx 37,8 m (123 ft 10 in).

ENGINES Two 11,400 shp D-136.

WEIGHTS Empty equipped 28,2 t (62,169 lb); normal payload (excl fuel) 20 t (44,090 lb); normal loaded 49,5 t (109,127 lb); max loaded 56 t (123,457 lb).

PERFORMANCE Max speed at SL 295 km/h (183 mph); normal cruise at max wt 255 km/h (158 mph); hover ceiling OGE at max wt 1,8 km (5900 ft); normal operating ceiling 4,5 km (14,760 ft), (has lifted 15 t to 5 km); range with 20 t payload 800 km (497 miles).

Moiseyenko

Born about 1890, Viktor Leonidovich Moiseyenko was cadet in Czarist army 1913, and became pilot of IM-class bombers, rising to be flight commander in post-revolutionary DVK 1919. He then enjoyed 30 years as a chief regional supplier of aircraft bought-out components and accessories.

2U-B3 Few details available of this interim training aircraft, built at GAZ-1 1925. Many details said to be copied from P-2, built at same time, though Polikarpov transport was much larger. Designation from 2-*Uchyebnii* BMW-III (2nd training type, BMW III engine). Originally designed as equal-span biplane with N struts, upper wing removed and finally completed as steel-braced low-wing monoplane. Engine 185 hp BMW IIIa, with metal cowl. Forward fuselage wire-braced wooden with ply skin. Tandem dual cockpits. Landing gear 'U-2 type' (that aircraft did not exist, means trad rubber-sprung pyramid). Tested late 1926 and flew adequately but no production. One report states because of P-2 meeting need, but this was a transport; may mean P-2 took up all available GAZ facilities. No other data.

Mi-26 (No 4)

Moskalyev

Aleksandr Sergeyevich Moskalyev was one of indefatigable Soviet constructors who, despite having no assured finances and no production base, yet managed to build an impressive run of aircraft. Many were of outstanding merit. By sheer enthusiasm on part of pilots who flew them, some gained production orders; many more Moskalyev aircraft would have served their country had not GUAP Commissar Kaganovich been antagonistic and done all he could to hamper work of this dedicated and good-natured enthusiast. Born 1898, Moskalyev qualified at Univ of Leningrad and then joined *Krasnyi Lyetchik* plant as stressman in Grigorovich KB, being assigned to structure of I-2bis. He showed promise and made major contribution to improved I-2bis radiator installation. Continued post-grad studies at Lensovyet Tech Inst as external student, whilst beginning design of SAM-1 and -2 described below. Successful flight of second of these resulted in its designer being sent in 1933 to vast newly built GAZ-18 at Voronezh, where under impossible conditions in makeshift shed he created further designs which included tailless configurations as well as conventional production transports. He also engineered 1935 and later TB-3 for production, designed installation of Charomskii diesel in RD, and made many contributions to other constructors' aircraft. In 1936 he was permitted to organize his own OKB, No 31, but with no official support. Following year appointed Director of Voronezh Aviatekhnikum (air commercial school). Partly through aiming too far ahead of available technology OKB was shut 1946, Moskalyev becoming lecturer at VVA (facilities went to Chyetverikov). Now works at MAI.

SAM-1 Designation from *Samolyet* A. Moskalyev (aeroplane, A. Moskalyev). Single-seat gull-winged monoplane fighter, design speed 345 km/h. Prototype begun 1930 but M-34 engine never made available.

SAM-2, MU-3 Designation from *Morskoi Uchyebnyi*, marine trainer. Simple wooden biplane flying boat with side-by-side open cockpit and pusher engine based on Grigorovich MU-2 and resulting from Moskalyev's work for that KB. Designed using many MU-2 components by group including N.G. Mikhelson and O.N. Rozanov and completed about February 1931. Improved planing bottom, smaller wings and much lighter. State tests spring 1931 resulted in selection of Sh-2 instead.

DIMENSIONS Span about 10,5 m (34 ft 5⅓ in); length about 8,0 m (26 ft 3 in); wing area about 28 m² (300 ft²).

ENGINE One 100 hp M-11.

WEIGHTS Empty 650 kg (1433 lb); fuel/oil 90 kg (198 lb); loaded 920 kg (2028 lb).

PERFORMANCE Max speed SL 132 km/h (82 mph); climb 10 min to 1 km; service ceiling 2,3 km (7550 ft); range 400 km (249 miles), 4 h; take-off 400 m/30 s; landing 100 m/10 s/65 km/h (40 mph).

SAM-3 Designed 1931, this seemingly efficient 12-passenger transport was intended to run shuttle service over 27 km route Leningrad–Kronstadt (island). Never completed.

SAM-4, Sigma First and most radical of Moskalyev's tailless designs, on drawing board at Leningrad early 1933. Serious attempt to exceed Mach 1, with Glushko rocket. Pure ogival (Gothic) delta, no protruding surfaces except fins/rudders at tips; elevons at trailing edge, pilot prone. Collaboration with V.P. Glushko at GRD, but obvious that ORM series engines far from yielding sufficient thrust. Decision 1934 to shelve and build piston-engined fighter to test aerodynamics (SAM-7). No other data.

SAM-5 Most important of SAM series, made Moskalyev famous and led to numerous aircraft in several variants. High-wing monoplane transport, designed in light duralumin construction. First project at Voronezh, built under great difficulty by team with no experience of stressed-skin structures. First prototype, supported by Osoaviakhim funds, was clearly a botch-up sprinkled with manufacturing errors caused by bad hand-workmanship. Potentially dangerous in view of exceptionally thin material gauges. Fuselage skinned with 0,3 mm sheet stiffened by single beads (longitudinal corrugations) at pitch of 15 cm; wings and tail 0,3 mm corrugated sheet. Accommodation (Shavrov and other Soviet sources) five-seat, (Něměcek and Western descriptions) pilot and five passengers. Enclosed cockpit under leading edge, entry door on right, cantilever wing but braced tailplane, uncowled engine, spatted main gears attached only to fuselage. Inspected and approved by S.P. Korolyev for Osoaviakhim, but no production.

Moskalyev recognized Voronezh team then incapable of satisfactory dural construction, and his small brigade – L. Polukarov, Ye. Serebryanskii, M. Shubin and B. Dyakov – redesigned whole aircraft in wood. Result was **SAM-5bis**, completed late 1934. Same dimensions but slightly narrower fuselage and two bracing struts under each wing. Wheel spats removed, and other simplifications. Dramatic reduction in empty weight, and disposable load better than 45% of gross weight. Much of skin fabric, but ply over leading edge and front half of fuselage. Spring 1935 completed NII testing by P.M. Stefanovskii, who was impressed by handling and recommended series production. Several excellent flights by pilot N.D. Fikson and mechanic A.S. Buzunov: 21 September 1936 flew 1600 km Voronezh/Moscow/Kharkov/Voronezh in 12 h; 21/22 October flew 3200 km Sevastopol / Genichyesk / Mariupol / Rostov / Stalingrad / Astrakhan / Stalingrad/ Kazan/ Gorkii in 25 h 05 min. Eventually GAZ-18 given order for 37, almost all of ambulance version with long stretcher door on left side. Carried three patients plus attendant; allegedly often flew with six adults on board. Ambulance had no separate designation; delivered 1937–1938 and served into the Second World War with GVF.

Final model of immediate series was **SAM-5-2bis**, with reduced span and great attention to drag reduction, all bracing struts being removed from wing, tailplane and main landing gear. Wing profile R-II, thickness 14%. Rubber bungee sprung cantilever main-gear legs of curved 10 mm ply forming rigid streamline section, extremely successful. Fuel tanks between two spars of wing outside cabin area. NII tests early 1937 by pilot V. Borodin and leading engineer M.P. Mogilyevskii. On 23/24 September 1937 pilot A.N. Gusarov and mechanic V.L. Glebov set FAI distance record 3513 km Moscow/Krasnoyarsk non-stop in 19 h 59 min. Moskalyev then fitted MG-21 engine and Borodin reached 8 km (class ht record). In summer 1939 supercharged M-11FN installed, driving metal propeller, and B.K. Kondratyev reached 8,9 km. Meanwhile VVS did thorough testing and in 1938 ordered 200 SAM-5-2bis ambulances, but none delivered: Shavrov, for diverse reasons; Něměcek, because Kaganovich countermanded the order.

DIMENSIONS Span (5, 5bis) 12,5 m (41 ft 0 in), (5-2, 5-2bis) 11,49 m (37 ft 8¼ in); length (5, approx) 8,0 m (26 ft 3 in), (5-2) 8,02 m (26 ft 3¾ in); wing area (5) 24,0 m² (258 ft²), (5-2) 21,8 m² (235 ft²).

ENGINE One 100 hp M-11; 5-2bis later fitted with 200 hp MG-21 and 200 hp M-11FN.

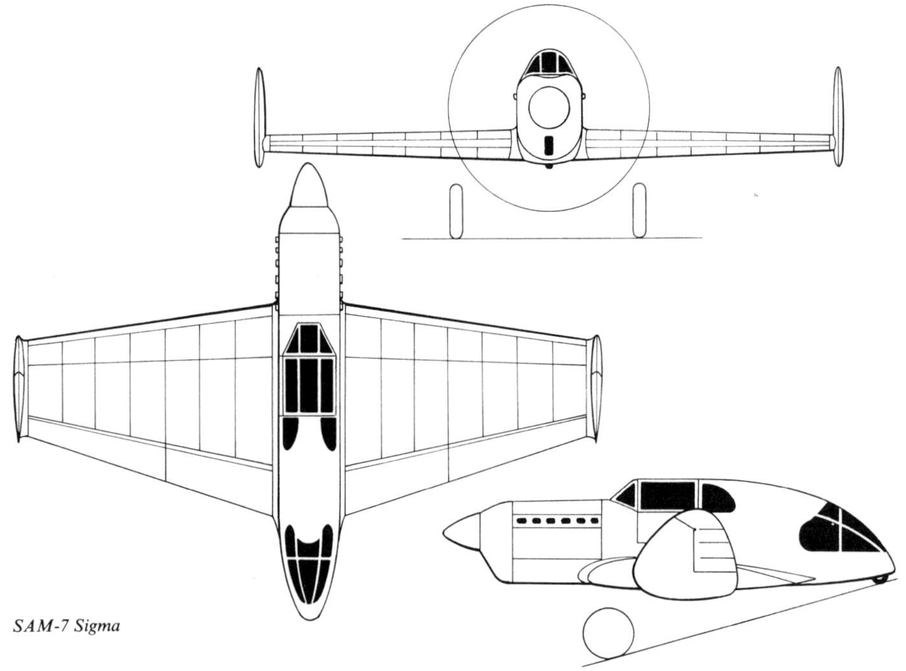

SAM-7 Sigma

WEIGHTS Empty (5) 626 kg, (bis) 580 kg, (bis-ambulance) 710 kg (1565 lb), (5-2bis) 656 kg (1446 lb); fuel/oil (bis amb.) 146 + 19 kg, (2bis) 90 + 14; loaded (5) 1106 kg, (bis) 1070 kg, (bis amb.) 1219 kg (2687 lb), (2bis) 1160 kg (2557 lb).
PERFORMANCE Max speed (5) 175 km/h, (bis) 185 km/h, (bis amb.) 173 km/h (107·5 mph), (2bis) 204 km/h (127 mph); cruise 140 km/h (87 mph), (2bis) 175 km/h (109 mph); climb 7 min (bis amb., 11) to 1 km; service ceiling 3,7 km (bis amb., 2,8); range (5) 1760 km, (bis amb.) 900 km, (2bis) 515 km; take-off (bis amb.) 13 s/150 m; landing 16 s/250 m/70 km/h.

SAM-6 Small single-seat research aircraft to investigate single-wheel landing gear, planned for tailless fighter. Moskalyev was unable to obtain information on parallel Bartini research with Stal-6 and later Stal-8 fighter. SAM-6 wooden with open cockpit, and conventional tail added for prudence. Scheibe-type vertical surfaces on wingtips with skids providing lateral support on ground. Built 1933 but flown on ski early 1934 with fair success. Later trousered wheel tested. By end 1934 modified into **SAM-6bis** with conventional gear (two trousered wheels) and tandem enclosed cockpits for pilot and passenger.
DIMENSIONS Span 8,0 m (26 ft 3 in); length 4,5 m (14 ft 9 in); wing area 12 m² (129 ft²).
ENGINE One 65 hp M-23.
WEIGHTS (bis) Empty 380 kg (838 lb); fuel 50 kg; loaded 500 kg (1102 lb).
PERFORMANCE Max speed 130 km/h (81 mph); service ceiling 3 km; range 200 km (124 miles); landing speed 55 km/h.

SAM-7 Sigma As major interim step along long road to ultimate *Sigma* (SAM-4) Moskalyev designed piston-engined two-seat fighter intended to offer superior speed and manoeuvrability and, from tailless layout, perfect rear field of fire. All-metal stressed-skin construction with two-spar wing R-II profile 12%, with CG 13/15%. Smooth skin 2/2,5 mm, fixed leading edge, trailing-edge inboard elevators and outboard ailerons with neat drives from stick via push/pull rods and bell-cranks. Scheibe fin/rudder on each wingtip. Moskalyev wanted Hispano 12Ybrs but had to settle for direct-drive M-34 with four-blade wooden propeller, probably from TB-3. Cooling by surface radiators, supplemented at low speeds by retractable radiator similar to that on Stal-6. Single-strut main gears pivoted to front spar and retracting inwards, small wheel at extreme tail. M-34 prohibited *moteur canon* so armament two fixed ShKAS above engine and one (option two) aimed by rear gunner. No good photograph and, though completed and flown October 1935 (Shavrov 1936), fin/rudder shape differs in all six known Soviet drawings. Dimensions are Shavrov's and conflict with other Soviet sources. Aircraft judged dangerous, with fast landing and difficult to keep straight on ground. Never reached maximum speed.
DIMENSIONS Span 9,46 m (31 ft 0½ in); length 7,0 m (22 ft 11½ in); wing area 20,0 m² (215 ft²).
ENGINE One 750 hp M-34.
WEIGHTS Empty 940 kg (2072 lb); loaded 1480 kg (3263 lb).
PERFORMANCE Max speed (est) 435 km/h (270 mph) at SL, 500 km/h (311 mph) at height; ceiling est 9,2 km; range est 800 km; landing speed 138 km/h (86 mph).

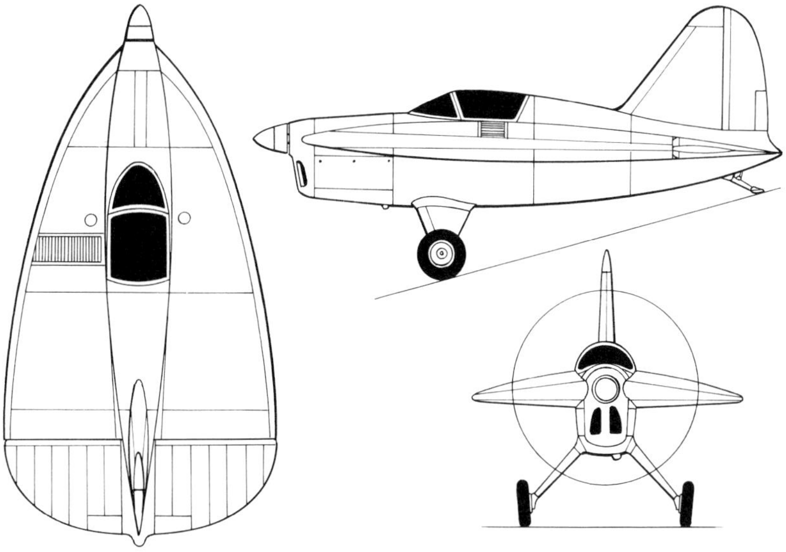

SAM-9 Strela

SAM-9 Strela SAM-8 not known. SAM-9 *Strela* (arrow) was major step towards supersonic gothic delta SAM-4, and in recent years hailed (justifiably) as aerodynamic pioneer of today's SSTs. Again failing to get 760 hp HS12Y engine Moskalyev had to settle for low-powered Renault; and permission to build such radical machine granted only in late 1936 after prolonged aerodynamic testing by TsAGI which, taking cue from Kaganovich, failed either to comprehend or show interest in concept. Wooden construction with high surface finish, fabric-skinned control surfaces. Wing root extended entire length of aircraft except for spinner; aspect ratio 0·975, aerofoil RAF-38 with Moskalyev's local modifications. Pilot in small enclosed cockpit with linkage to two large trailing-edge elevons. Cantilever fixed main gears as on SAM-5-2, and tailskid. Prototype also known as **Aircraft L**, built in first 70 days of 1937. V.P. Gorski tested model in tunnel at TsAGI, and N.S. Rybko then made first flight at Voronezh. Controllable, but demanded intense concentration and 20° attitude on approach then novel and frightening. Flown by A.N. Gusarov and further flying then at TsAGI field in Moscow by Rybko and A.P. Chyernavskii (Něměcek, B.N. Kudrin also). Moskalyev's unofficial status and supposed fantastic ideas warped judgement, especially with opposition of Kaganovich; new style of flying slender delta was proclaimed dangerous, and project banned mid-1937.
DIMENSIONS Span 3,5 m (11 ft 5¾ in); length 6,15 m (20 ft 2 in); wing area 13,0 m² (140 ft²).
ENGINE One 140 hp Renault MV-6.
WEIGHTS Empty 470 kg (1036 lb); fuel/oil 60 + 10 kg; loaded 630 kg (1389 lb).
PERFORMANCE Speed reached at SL 310 km/h (193 mph); height reached 1,5 km; take-off 200 m; landing 100 m/102 km/h (63 mph).

SAM-10 Conventional low-wing 5/6-seater developed from SAM-5-2bis and using actual rear fuselage, tail and wing panels from earlier high-wing machine. Wooden, with ply sides to fuselage as far back as rear of cabin, fabric elsewhere. Light-alloy cowl over experimental engine driving two-blade Ratier propeller. Light-alloy cabin roof frames with Celluloid windows. Trousered main gears with 470 × 200 mm tyres and air/oil shock struts. Two-spar wing with ply skin, panels removed by unscrewing beneath tankage. Outstanding performance on SNII GVF testing 5 June to 9 August 1938, and ordered as passenger and ambulance aircraft. Thwarted by unavailability of engine. Two **SAM-10bis** built with MV-6 but this Renault-derived engine likewise failed to get into production.
DIMENSIONS Span 11,49 m (37 ft 8¼ in); length 8,5 m (Shavrov 8,1) (27 ft 10⅝ in); wing area 21,35 m² (Shavrov 21,8) (230 ft²).
ENGINE (10) One 220 hp Bessonov MM-1; (10bis) 220 hp MV-6.
WEIGHTS Empty (10) 866 kg (1909 lb), (bis) 873 kg (1925 lb); fuel/oil 150 + 20 kg; loaded (10) 1436 kg (3166 lb), (bis) 1448 kg (3192 lb).
PERFORMANCE Max speed (10) 311 km/h at SL, 336 km/h (209 mph) at 1,7 km, (bis) 262 km/h at SL, 275 km/h (171 mph) at 1,5 km; climb (10) 2·7 min to 1 km, (bis) 3·2 min; service ceiling (10) 7,1 km, (bis) 5910 m; range (10) 1000 km (621 miles); take-off (10) 95 m/7 s, (bis) 100 m/9 s; landing (10) 120 m/9 s/87 km/h (54 mph).

SAM-11 Yet another adaptation of SAM-5-2bis components, this amphibian was built 1939 and used same wings, tail and engine as SAM-10, plus SAM-5-2bis main landing gears. Wooden boat hull seating pilot and three passengers. Main gears hinged to strong sidewalls and manually cranked up so that wheels lay in recesses in wing. Fixed tailwheel at second step in keel. Tractor engine caused severe turbulence which made tail ineffective; after severe struggle pilot lost control and aircraft badly damaged in crash on first flight. Rebuilt as **SAM-11bis** with MV-6 engine in better nacelle. Test flown Sept/October 1940 by P.V. Yakovlev and A.N. Gusarov; flew satisfactorily but after NII testing at Sevastopol both VMF and VVS decided payload too small.
DIMENSIONS Span 11,49 m (37 ft 8¼ in); length 8,74 m (28 ft 8 in); wing area 21,35 m² (Shavrov 20,2) (230 ft²).
ENGINE (11) One 220 hp MM-1; (bis) 220 hp MV-6.

WEIGHTS Empty 1094 kg (2412 lb), (bis) 1030 kg; fuel/oil 95 + 10 kg; loaded 1400 kg (3086 lb), (bis) 1350 kg (2976 lb).
PERFORMANCE Max speed (SL) (11) 225 km/h, (bis) 217 km/h; max speed at 2,4 km (both) 240 km/h (149 mph); service ceiling (11) 4,7 km, (bis) 5,6 km; take-off (bis) 200 m/16 s; landing (bis) 110 m/9 s/85 km/h (53 mph).

SAM-12 Tandem dual trainer of conventional layout, low wing, tricycle landing gear, wooden construction, enclosed cockpits. Designed for MM-1 but converted to MV-6 and believed completed late 1940. Features included Ratier v-p propeller, split flaps and steerable nosewheel, but no record of flight test.

SAM-13 Persisting in MV-6 (Renault) engine, Moskalyev designed this fighter from scheme of 1937, inspired by Fokker D.23, but was unable to build until 1939. Rather 'hot' design with small wing. Push/pull aircooled engines with pilot between under rear-sliding hood. Twin tail booms 2,38 m apart carrying wide-chord tailplane with vertical tail on centreline. Fully retractable tricycle landing gear, nose gear with trailing levered-suspension and shimmy damper. All-wooden construction except for welded chrome-steel engine mountings, ply skin throughout, two-spar wing set at +2° incidence with split flaps, all flight controls with aerodynamic and static balance. Four ShKAS, two above front engine and two at outer ends of centre section beyond front propeller disc (2,2 m diam). First factory test flight late 1940 by N.D. Fikson. Poor handling and, because of error in drawings, nose gear failed to retract fully; but speed still reached 560 km/h. Rapid rectification of faults, and LII testing spring 1941 under M.L. Gallai. Promising, and entered for summer-1941 high-speed race, but after invasion work halted and SAM-13 destroyed prior to evacuation of OKB to Omsk *oblast* (possibly Irtysh).
DIMENSIONS Span 7,30 m (Shavrov 6,7) (23 ft 11½ in); length 7,68 m (Shavrov 7,4) (25 ft 2⅔ in); wing area 9 m² (96·9 ft²).
ENGINES Two 236 hp Renault MV-6.
WEIGHTS (Shavrov, remarkably low) Empty 754 kg (1662 lb); loaded 1183 kg (2608 lb).
PERFORMANCE Max speed (est) 463 km/h (288 mph) at SL, 680 km/h (423 mph) at 4 km (latter unreasonably high, and Něměcek's 509 km/h unreasonably low); service ceiling 10 km; range 850 km (528 miles); landing speed 125 km/h (78 mph).

SAM-14 Substantially modified SAM-5-2bis built for Aeroflot 1939. Utility transport retaining simple features but more powerful engine. Wing of R-II section, 14% thick, fabric covering, wood truss fuselage with ply skin from nose to rear of cabin, fabric at rear. Ventilated cabin for pilot and five passengers, two doors on left, Kalman wing flaps, trimmers on control surfaces. NII testing November 1939 to June 1940; GVF order rescinded by Kaganovich.
DIMENSIONS Span 11,49 m (37 ft 8⅓ in); length 8,06 m (26 ft 5⅓ in); wing area 21,86 m² (235 ft²).
ENGINE One 140 hp MV-4 inverted 4-inline.
WEIGHTS Empty 765 kg (1687 lb); fuel/oil 95 + 10 kg; loaded 1280 kg (2822 lb).
PERFORMANCE Max speed 196 km/h (122 mph) at SL, 170 km/h at height; service ceiling 3360 m; range 550 km (342 miles); take-off 240 m/17 s; landing 190 m/15 s/68 km/h (42 mph) with flaps.

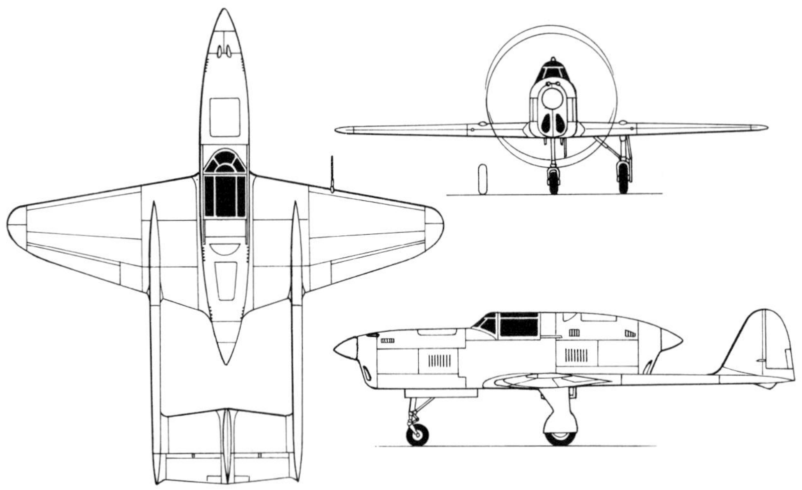
SAM-13

SAM-16 SAM-15 not known. SAM-16 small twin-engined three-seat wooden reconnaissance flying boat, with engine nacelles central on gull wing. Wing profile NACA-230, 16% at root and 12% at tip, slotted flaps and slotted ailerons. Stabilizing floats on neat fixed single struts. Twin-step hull with pilot cabin ahead of leading edge and two ShKAS in glazed turrets in bow and between wing and twin-finned tail. In erection shop June 1941, destroyed prior to evacuation.
DIMENSIONS Span 15,5 m (50 ft 10¼ in); length 12,03 m (39 ft 5¾ in); wing area 32,15 m² (346 ft²).
ENGINES Two 330 hp MG-31F.
WEIGHTS Empty 2160 kg (4762 lb); fuel/oil 390 + 30 kg; loaded 3 t (6614 lb).
PERFORMANCE Max speed (est) 362 km/h (225 mph); service ceiling (est) 4,6 km (15,000 ft); alighting speed 100 km/h (62 mph).

SAM-18 SAM-17 not known. SAM-18bis under construction 1941 as civil/military amphibian version of SAM-16.

SAM-19 Yet another use for well-proven SAM-5-2bis wing, light attack aircraft (*Shturmovik*), project dated 1942. High wing on central nacelle, pilot cockpit with side door, tricycle landing gear, pusher 330 hp MG-31F on pylon above wing at centreline, and twin tail booms.

SAM-22 Project for slow economical transport seating 16 passengers, with single pusher 140 hp M-11F on pylon above high wing; 1943.

A-2bis Modernized version of Antonov A-2 training glider; 1942.

AM-14 Modernized A-7 assault glider, designation from Antonov/Moskalyev; dated 1943.

SAM-23 Evacuated OKB in Omsk region concentrated on assault trooping pods (DK, *Desantnyi Kabine*), seating 10 (DK-10) or 16 (DK-16) men, carried by retired DB-3 bombers, and also on large assault gliders. Only completely new aircraft design to fly was SAM-23, inspired by Go 242 assault glider and with same config uration but larger. Wooden construction, with box-section tail booms off high wing, and upward-hinged rear to give full-section access to 16-seat nacelle, with hinged ramp for small vehicles. Max tow 241 km/h (150 mph), gliding speed after cast-off 172 km/h (107 mph). Prototype flown behind DB-3 May 1943, but no production.

SAM-24 Derivative of SAM-23 with two M-11F engines; not flown.

SAM-25 This was main powered aircraft built by Moskalyev-led assault-transport group in evacuated OKB-31. In all respects outstanding,

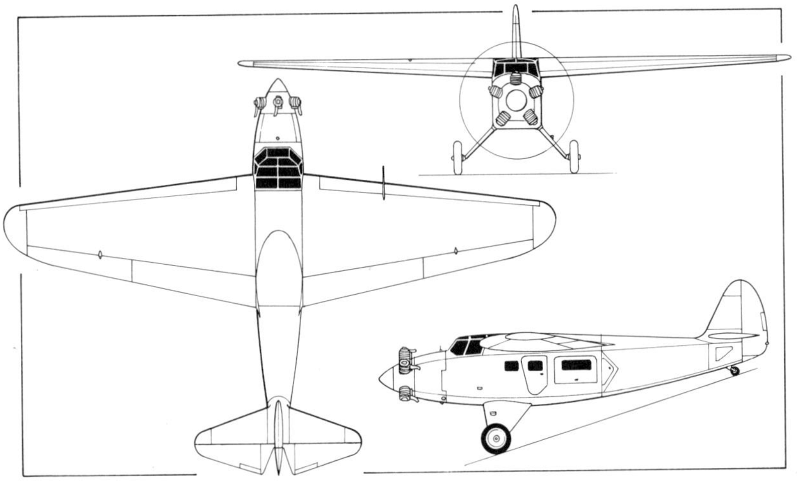
SAM-25

updated SAM-5-2bis with cleaned-up airframe designed 1942 to meet military/civil need for passenger, cargo, ambulance and assault utility transport. Wooden construction retained but refined and simplified further, but with addition of automatic slats, drooping ailerons and slotted flaps. On left side main entry door, wide stretcher (litter) hatch and rear door/window for photography. Tabbed rudder/elevators. Tested at Omsk-district OKB mid-1943, followed by NII testing by A. Dabakhov during which flown in stages to Moscow and then back non-stop. Arguments over production; impossible during war, but recent info suggests series built 1946 for GVF.

DIMENSIONS Span 11,5 m (37 ft 8¾ in); length 8,02 m (26 ft 3¾ in); wing area 21,9 m^2 (236 ft^2).
ENGINE One 140 hp M-11F.
WEIGHTS Empty 720 kg (1587 lb); fuel/oil 140 + 10 kg; loaded 1280 kg (2822 lb).
PERFORMANCE Max speed 200 km/h (Shavrov), 220 km/h (recent Soviet reports, 137 mph) at SL, less at height; service ceiling 4850 m (15,900 ft); range 1760 km; (1094 miles) take-off 150 m; landing speed 65 km/h (Shavrov), (62 km/h, 38·5 mph, recent reports).

SAM-26 Largest SAM design, mid-wing assault glider of 1942 seating 102 troops on two decks; rear ramp for vehicles. Not completed.

SAM-28 Improved SAM-22 with deeper fuselage and tricycle landing gear; not built.

SAM-29 RM-1 Final SAM project, in detail design 1944. Ultimate *Strela* rocket fighter with ogival (gothic) delta wing blended into needle fuselage, no horizontal tail but large vertical tail, tricycle landing gear. Dushkin RD-2M-3V rocket engine of 2 t SL thrust (more at altitude). Despite support of S.P. Korolyev project collapsed through being ahead of its time in immediate post-war era. OKB shut January 1946, but studies continued to 1948.

Mozharovskii -Venyevidov

Georgii Mironovich Mozharovskii and Ivan Vasilyevich Venyevidov were specialists in aircraft armament from 1926–1950. Their work encompassed design and development of turrets, ammunition supply systems, sights and various dropped stores. From 1940 they were also engaged in design of an aircraft.

MV Kombain Named (Combine) because of its versatility, this was to be a single-seat single-engined *Shturmovik* (armoured attacker). Engine, 1600 hp AM-38, driving pusher propeller at rear of central nacelle. All-metal construction, low wing, twin tail booms. Forward-firing armament two or four ShVAK at front of tail booms, projecting ahead of leading edge, two or four ShKAS in nose on pivoted mounts to fire from 0° to −20° (20° downwards). Heavily armoured enclosed cockpit. Small compartments for fragmentation bombs. Tricycle landing gear with all units retracting to rear. Radiator under wing with engine-driven fan in cooling duct. Sponsors collected good team but lacked design, calculation and test skills. Money voted and substantial personnel assigned to project, but design never completed. VVS NII mock-up conference late March and early April 1941. Decision to terminate in view of success of BSh-2 (Il-2). No other data.

Myasishchyev

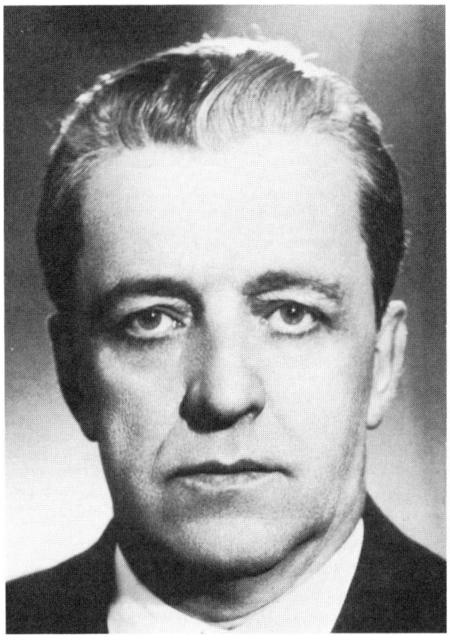

V. M. Myasishchyev

Vladimir Mikhailovich Myasishchyev was born 1902, pupil of Zhukovskii at MVTU in 1918–1921. With several friends, some later famous, joined TsAGI 1921 and from 1924 assigned increasingly important roles in ANT designs including flush radiators of R-6, rear fuselage of TB-3, TB-4 and ANT-20 and entire design of DIP. Accomplished designer of metal structures and led move away from traditional Tupolev truss/corrugation to smooth stressed-skin. At Douglas 1937 helping translate DC-3 drawings. Arrested 1938 and imprisoned at TsKB-29 as chief of KB-102 brigade. Produced DVB-102, delayed by evacuation October 1941 to Irtysh, and additionally in late 1943 assumed responsibility for Petlyakov programmes in succession to Putilov. OKB closed 1945; Mya became lecturer at MAI but obsolescence of Tu-4 and need for completely new strategic bomber prompted Stalin to call him back in 1949. Charged with first intercontinental jet bomber, in 1950 assigned new OKB and factory base at GAZ-23. Lenin Prize 1957. OKB closed finally 1960; Mya appointed Director of TsAGI. Retired 1967 and died 14 October 1978.

DVB-102 First Myasishchyev design not to bear another OKB's designation, DVB-102 title from *Dalnyi Vysotnyi Bombardirovshchik* (long-range high-altitude bomber) numbered in same series as Petlyakov 100 and Tupolev 103 from NKVD-run Special Brigades. Project authorized to meet VVS need late 1939; design started early 1940. Prototype construction begun late April 1940, with airframe in static test summer 1941. Late August 1941 factory evacuated and prototype seriously delayed, finally being completed with numerous modifications. An advanced and efficient design. All stressed-skin, with high-mounted gull wing of aspect ratio 8·2, thickness 14·5% root and 10% tip, three spars inboard and two to tip, max skin thickness 3 mm, held by countersunk screws for access to large integral wing tanks filling whole inter-spar box. Pioneered construction in upper/lower halves, joined on neutral axis (later used on Il-28). Three TsAGI flap sections each side, electric actuation along steel tracks inside wing. Circular-section fuselage 1,6-m diameter with pressure cabins in nose and rear for crew of four: nav/bomb (glazed nose with hand-aimed ShVAK), pilot (fully glazed canopy over cockpit offset left of centreline), and two rear gunners with sealed sight blisters and remote-directed barbettes with electric drive. Rear armament (Shavrov) one ShVAK and one BS firing above at rear, and similar pair below; later changed to two BT and one ShKAS, and later ShVAK cannon being exchanged for NR-23. Recent Soviet account states rear installation was integrated system DUS-1 with single UBK above and ShKAS below (evidence of ShVAK). Weapon bay for 28 combinations of bombs and other stores with individual weight to 2 t; normal load 2 t for long range, overload to 4 t. Bomb doors hydraulically retracted up inside fuselage. Tricycle landing gear with single legs and twin main wheels, hydraulic retraction (nose to rear, main forwards) and pneumatic brakes. Twin fins at 90° to tips of tailplane with 11° dihedral. Design engines two M-120TK in long enclosed cowls with fan cooling and extension shafts to AV-9L-80 four-blade propellers. Engine not cleared for flight in time, and prototype eventually flown February 1942 by V.I. Zhdanov with conventional ASh-71s, retaining wing-duct oil coolers. (Curiously, only known photos show M-120TK installation.) A successful development with Zhdanov later assisted by F.F. Opadchii and flight engineer I. Kvitko. Opadchii reached 11,5 km, and in August 1943 Zhdanov carried max bombload Omsk/Kazan/Moscow with ASh-71s. B-29 adopted while engines still having teething troubles.

DIMENSIONS Span 25,16 m (82 ft 6½ in); length 18,90 m (62 ft 0 in); wing area 78,3 m^2 (843 ft^2).
ENGINES Two 2500 hp M-120TK; originally flown with 2100 hp ASh-71.
WEIGHTS Empty (ASh-71) 9895 kg (21,814 lb); fuel/oil 3800 + 250 kg; loaded 15,5 t (34,171 lb), (max) 17,8 t (39,242 lb).
PERFORMANCE Max speed 445 km/h (271 mph) at SL, 565 km/h (351 mph) at 9,5 km; climb 13·5 min to 5 km; ceiling 11,5 km (37,730 ft); range with 2 t bombs 2230 km (1386 miles, intended to be 4000 km); take-off 15,5 t 640 m/12 s; landing 750 m/145 km/h (90 mph).

M-2 Designation of second DVB-102 completed 1943 with fully developed ASh-71F engines, retaining wing-duct oil coolers and with lighter rear armament of one BT above and one below. Nose lengthened to provide improved accommodation for pilot (metal rear to canopy) and nav/bomb (larger glazed area in front and fewer but larger side windows). Sparse data but,

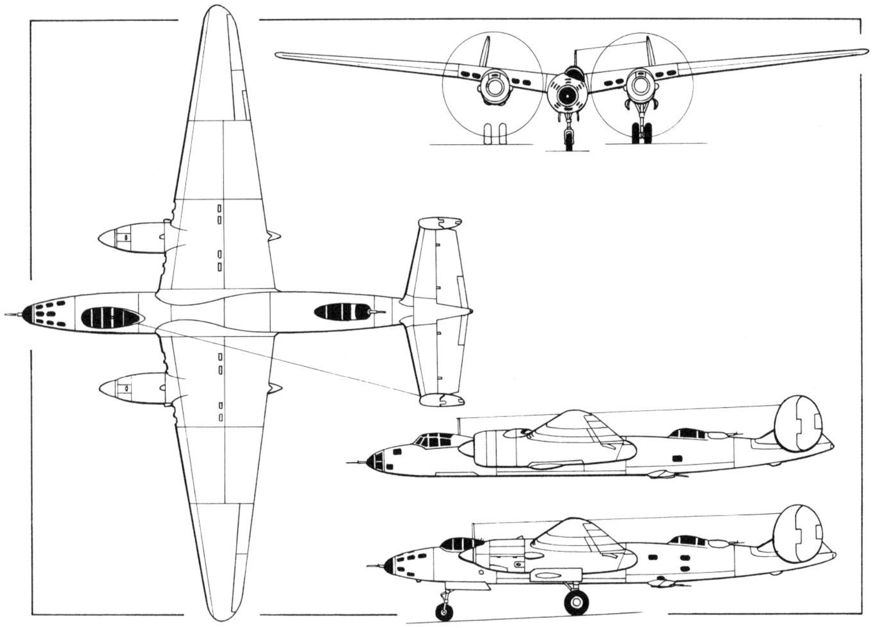
DVB-102 (upper side view M-2 with ASh-71 engines)

despite larger size, higher performance than first aircraft.
DIMENSIONS Span 25,32 m (83 ft 0¾ in); length 19,50 m (63 ft 11¾ in); wing area 78,8 m² (848 ft²
ENGINES Two 2200 hp ASh-71F.
No other data.

DB-108, VM-16 Myasishchyev's involvement with Pe-2 from start of programme made him natural choice to manage derivatives after Petlyakov's death. Pe-2VI (see Petlyakov) was entirely Mya's responsibility, and served as basis for several further mid-wing designs of outstanding performance. Designation **DB-108** from *Dnyevnoi Bombardirovshchik*, day bomber, and VK-108 engine, latest of Klimov series. Built in three variants all extremely clean stressed-skin, with beautiful engine installation with usual VK-108 side and upper exhausts, four-blade propellers, glycol radiators in controllable centre-section ducts, oil coolers and supercharger inlets in tapered outer wings. Basic variant designated **VM-16** from constructor's initials, two-seat bomber with bomb bay under wing with two doors for load of 2 t (4410 lb), with later testing of two 1 t bombs under wings, with modified tailplane. Second crewman manned nav station in nose, visual bombsight and also sight system in right seat beside pilot facing aft controlling remote-aimed gun in extreme tail (UBS, later ShVAK). This OKB-43 system defective and second aircraft, **VM-17** dive bomber, had third crewman controlling radio and upper rear 20 mm gun. Prolonged testing on ground rigs 1944, but VM-16 completed with tail guns and flown 30 December 1944. VM-17 first flown June 1945, tested with various dive brakes. Third aircraft, **VM-18**, four-seater with gunner in rear fuselage manning DUS-1 system, upper UBS and lower ShVAK, with another UBS in rear of crew compartment. VM-17 had 20 mm aimed from nose by nav/bomb, but VM-18 replaced this with fixed B-20 firing ahead. VM-18 fuselage lengthened to accommodate 3 t bombload internally, with two FAB-500 under wings as overload. Could not equal parallel Tu-2 developments, but led to long-span SDB (20,6 m, 48 m²) and long-range DIS fighters with 37 or 45 mm guns in place of bombload.

DIMENSIONS Span 17,8 m (58 ft 4¾ in); length (16, 17) 13,47 m (44 ft 2¼ in), (18) 15,02 m (49 ft 3¼ in); wing area 43·1 m² (463·9 ft²).
ENGINES Two 1800 hp VK-108.
WEIGHTS Empty (16) 6922 kg (15,260 lb); loaded (16) 9400 kg (20,723 lb), (17) 9990 kg (22,024 lb), (18) 10 530 kg (23,214 lb).
PERFORMANCE Max speed (16) 575 km/h at SL, 700 (435 mph) at 6 km, (17) 545/670 km/h, (18) 542/660 km/h; service ceiling (16) 12 km, (17) 10 km; range (16) 2250 km with 2 t bombload, (18, load unstated) 2000 km; take-off (16) 500 m; landing (16) 145 km/h (90 mph).

VB-109 Promise of continuing development of V-12 engine by Klimov led to this VB (day bomber) with number matched to new engine. Project design early 1944. Almost same airframe as DB-108 but increased normal gross weight, greater power transmitted through paddle-blade propellers (similar to those of MiG I-224 and relatives) and simpler armament of one fixed and one (dorsal) ShVAK. Bombload 4 t max. Shchyerbakov pressure cabin intended, but not fitted to prototype. Still only two seats. High performance, but according to Něměcek caught fire on first flight spring 1945 and written off.
DIMENSIONS Span 17,8m (58 ft 4¾ in); length 14,17 m (46 ft 6 in); wing area 43,1 m² (464 ft²).
ENGINES Two 2073 hp VK-109.
WEIGHTS Empty, not recorded; loaded 11 060 kg (24,383 lb).
PERFORMANCE (Est) Max speed 720 km/h (447 mph) at 9 km; service ceiling 12 550 m (41,175 ft); range with 2 t bombs 2200 km (1367 miles); take-off (11,06 t) 820 m.

SDB Prototype *Skorostnyi Dnyevno Bomardirovshchik* (high-speed day bomber) abandoned January, 1945 when partly-finished. Basically DB-108 but substitution of primary structure to increase range; another report states greater wing area, probably by extending span. Gross weight no less than 13,5 t, and speed on VK-108 engines 660 km/h at 5,8 km. Long span, more weight and less speed are reverse of normal in deriving SDB from high-altitude aircraft. No other data.

DIS Last of Mya's aircraft to fly from his wartime OKB, *Dalnyi Istrebitel Soprovozhdeniya* (long-range fighter escort) was squarely based on Pe-2, with low wing, three seats and VK-107A engines. Compared with VB series much slower, extra crew and longer range, all surpris-

DVB-102

M-4 Bison-B

ing. Heavy armament: two ShVAK in nose, two NS-37 or NS-45 in ventral box and pivoted 20 mm (type unstated) at upper rear. Almost every part of rest of airframe occupied by flexible fuel cells for long range. One crew-member managed 'two locating installations', suggesting AI radar. Heated but unpressurized cabin, full de-icing of wing, tail, windshields and three-blade propellers. First flight January 1945, though project abandoned late 1944.

DIMENSIONS Span 17,99 m (59 ft 0¼ in); length 13,83 m (45 ft 4½ in); wing area 43,4 m² (467 ft²).
ENGINES Two 1700 hp VK-107A.
WEIGHTS Empty 6991 kg (15,412 lb); fuel (max) 3 t; loaded 9850 kg, (max) 11,7 t (25,794 lb).
PERFORMANCE Max speed 628 km/h (390 mph) at 5,8 km; service ceiling 9,6 km (31,500 ft); range 1700 km (max 4000 km); landing speed 140 km/h.

DVB-202 Prototype construction abandoned May 1945 of last DVB, totally new design with four ASh-72TK (turbocharged), three pressure cabins as on B-29, tricycle landing gears and multiple remote-control cannon barbettes. Gross weight 45 t with max bombload 16 t.

DVB-302 Projected development of DVB-202, late 1944; not built.

RB-17 Projected jet bomber (*Reaktivnyi Bombardirovshchik*) with four RD-10 engines, to fly 3000 km at 8 km at 800 km/h at 16,4 t with 1 t bombs. OKB closed with this incomplete.

M-4 One of greatest engineering achievements of early 1950s, this was outcome of Stalin's late-1949 instruction that Myasishchyev should design a modern bomber able to fly missions to North America. In fact task then impossible except with propellers, which Tupolev chose for parallel Tu-95. Myasishchyev reluctantly agreed to use jets, only available engine eventually becoming AM-3. VVS interpreted range requirement as ultimate still-air 16 000 km (with bomb load of 5 t), and this was judged by OKB as beyond state of art. According to Mikulin it was thought marginally possible with eight AM-3 in aircraft weighing well over 250 t but, though Mya carried out design study, this was considered impractical within timescale. (Mikulin implied Myasishchyev chickened out of giant aircraft and built bomber capable of realization at early date, possibly hoping for better engines in course of time.)

Original design aerodynamically assisted by TsAGI; designation **TsAGI-428** often said to be applied to prototype but not found in any Soviet source. Typical 1950 aerodynamics with basic 35° sweep on wing of high aspect ratio for range and engines buried in roots. Wing posed severe structural problems. Original wing, flown on several prototypes, had TsAGI S-12/SR-7 profile, LE sweep 37° 30′ to structural joint well outboard of engines (end of centre section perpendicular to LE) and thence 35° to tips; TE almost straight and unswept to well outboard of engines, then 35° to point in line with LE kink and finally 27° to tip. This wing replaced by wing of unknown deeper (up to 20% t/c) profile, giving better aeroelastic properties for much-reduced weight. Myasishchyev now credited with early supercritical form. Trailing-edge kink removed, and thickness reduced to about 14% over outer panel, with pronounced washout. Single spar at 30% chord, many stringers, max skin thickness 12 mm on original wing but reduced on production wing. Considerable wing fuel, believed integral on production wing. Aspect ratio 8·6, extremely high for wing of such sweep and yet ailerons conventional and powered. Hydraulic double-slotted flaps outboard of engines. Plain split flaps curved round below jetpipes. Single fence aligned at flap/aileron junction. Fuselage circular section with pressurized nose compartment for six of original crew of seven: pilot, co-pilot, nav/bomb (glazed nose), radar/EW and two gunners (at rear of compartment with three sight stations with blisters at sides and upper centreline); third gunner in pressurized tail turret. Original armament eight NR-23 in twin turrets at tail, lower rear, lower forward and upper forward, last three being barbettes electrically directed from forward sight stations. In some aircraft one NR-23 fixed on right of nose firing ahead. Mid/high (shoulder) wing filling upper two-thirds of fuselage depth. Central weapon bay for up to 9 t free-fall bombs, double laterally-folding doors. Front and rear main gears with bogie trucks carrying four 1550 × 480 mm tyres, front truck steerable. Small outrigger gears with twin wheels folding forwards into wingtip pods. Fuel cells above both main gear bays. Variable-incidence tailplane with dihedral mounted part-way up fin. Engines in separate nacelles close to fuselage mounted below centreline of wing but with large multiple spectacle frames carrying wing loads and with bottom halves unbolted for engine change. Airframe mainly bleed-air de-iced, but electro-thermal glazing.

Last drawing sent to production 1 May 1952. Prototype flown late 1953 and made fly-past over Red Square 1 May 1954. Primitive engines could never be improved sufficiently to meet range requirement, but production authorized 1955 and M-4 believed entered ADD service early 1956. Total production of original version about 200. Popular name *Molot* (hammer). Soloviev KB eventually produced much more advanced D-15 engine, flown in 1957 and adopted for M-4. Aircraft **201-M**, set load/height records 16 September 1959 flying from 'Podmoskovnoye' with crew of six under Nikolai Goryanov: 10 t payload lifted to 15 317 m (50,253 ft) and 55,22 t (121,480 lb) to 2 km. Another M-4, aircraft **103-M**, possibly third of original AM-3 prototypes set 1000 km circuit record with 27 t payload at 1028 km/h (638·77 mph).

By early 1960s, major rejuvenation programme. Not known if any production from new (Myasishchyev OKB then closed) but most existing aircraft remanufactured for new career in different roles associated with AV-MF maritime operations. All rebuilt aircraft believed powered by AM-3, with outer jetpipes splayed outwards and inner nozzles curved in plan. In all cases lower rear gun barbette removed, and fixed gun removed from nose. Original weapon bay of bomber (called Bison-A by NATO) rebuilt to house inflight refuelling hosereel, hydraulic drives and transfer fuel, with further augmented fuel in front and rear fuselage. Some rebuilt ahead of flight deck with radar filling nose in place of glazed nav station, and FR probe added above. Progressively further avionic items added

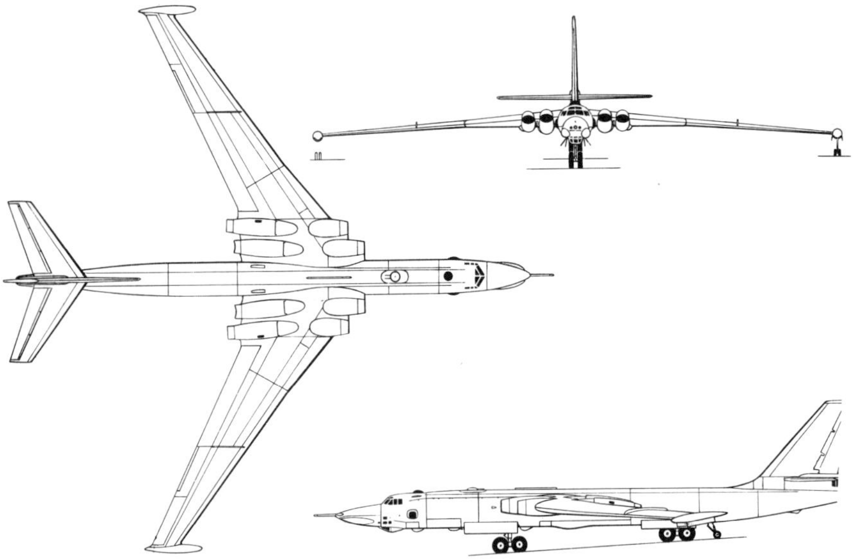

M-4 Bison-C

to this model (Bison-B) used for multi-sensor reconnaissance with tanker capability. Except for first, original nav/bombing radar under nose replaced by observation compartment with three windows each side and ventral blister with large forward windows. By 1980s possibly as many as 23 avionic items, including 12 Elint/EW receivers, warning radars and allegedly a cruise-missile guidance capability. Final known variant, called Bison-C, with a third new nose, extended and fitted with probe at tip above radar (believed to be Puff Ball, AS-2 guidance) and with large reconnaissance installation filling compartment ahead of nose gear, with flush aerial around lower half fuselage. All current M-4s have Bee Hind tail radar, AM-3 engines, rear turret and evidence of structural strengthening by doubler plates. Average airframe time now about 5000 h.

DIMENSIONS Span (A) as built 50,48 m (165 ft 7½ in); (201-M,B,C) 52,5 m (172 ft 3 in); length (A, as built) 47,2 m (154 ft 10 in), (B) 49,54 m (162 ft 6⅓ in), (C) consistently given as 53,4 m (175 ft 2⅓ in); wing area (A, as built) 309 m^2, (D-15 engines, all models) 320 m^2 (3,444 ft^2).

ENGINES Four Mikulin AM-3 turbojets, initially 8700 kg (19,180 lb) AM-3D, later 9500 kg (20,943 lb) AM-3M, (201-M) four 13 t (28,660 lb) D-15 two-spool turbojets.

WEIGHTS Empty (A) est 70 t, (C) given as 90 t (198,500 lb); normal loaded (A) 160 t (352,730 lb), (C) 165 t (363,760 lb); max (C) 210 t (462,963 lb).

PERFORMANCE Max speed (all) about 620 km/h (385 mph) at SL, 1000 km/h (621 mph) at height; typical cruise 835 km/h (519 mph); service ceiling (C) 17 km at normal gross, 13 km at max; endurance 15 h; range (A) about 10 700 km (6650 miles), (B) 12 500 km (7767 miles), (C) at max weight 18 000 km (11,185 miles).

M-50 One of most breathtaking aircraft of its day, M-50 was second attempt to build jet bomber beyond state of art, in this case one capable of supersonic speed. Based on same TsAGI tailed-delta aerodynamics as several fighters. Bold yet uninspired design with enormous area-ruled fuselage riding on tandem bogie landing gears reminiscent of M-4 but with front gear much taller, shoulder-mounted cropped-delta wing carrying four engines, and crew of three in pressurized nose compartment. No known defensive armament but weapon bay between landing gears has larger cross-section than in M-4 because, while fuselage diameter is same, wing thickness is much less. Wing t/c about 5%, structure rectilinear with four transverse spars and seven main axial ribs each side, swept 50° inboard and 41° 30′ outboard, fixed leading edge, trailing edge with inboard flaps of unknown type, outboard ailerons. Swept slab tailplanes with anti-flutter pods mounted on upswept rear fuselage. In first M-50 four engines believed hung under wing on pylons, inner pylon struts forming upper-surface fences back to aileron. Outrigger gears with twin wheels (same wheels/tyres as M-4) on tall long-stroke leg retracting rearwards into underside of wingtip. Dorsal spine from canopy to fin. Cockpit with V-windscreen, tandem ejection seats and entry via door in fuselage. Pointed nose with instrument probe. First-flight date given as 1957 (Green), 1958 (Alexander), 1960 (1981 East German account) and even 1961. Several aircraft built with various changes before final machine (with 12 painted on fuselage and called **M-52** in some Soviet reports) appeared at Aviation Day flypast 1961. This aircraft had afterburners on inner engines (though all engines given as 14-t thrust each in recent East German report) and

M-52 with Ye-6T development aircraft

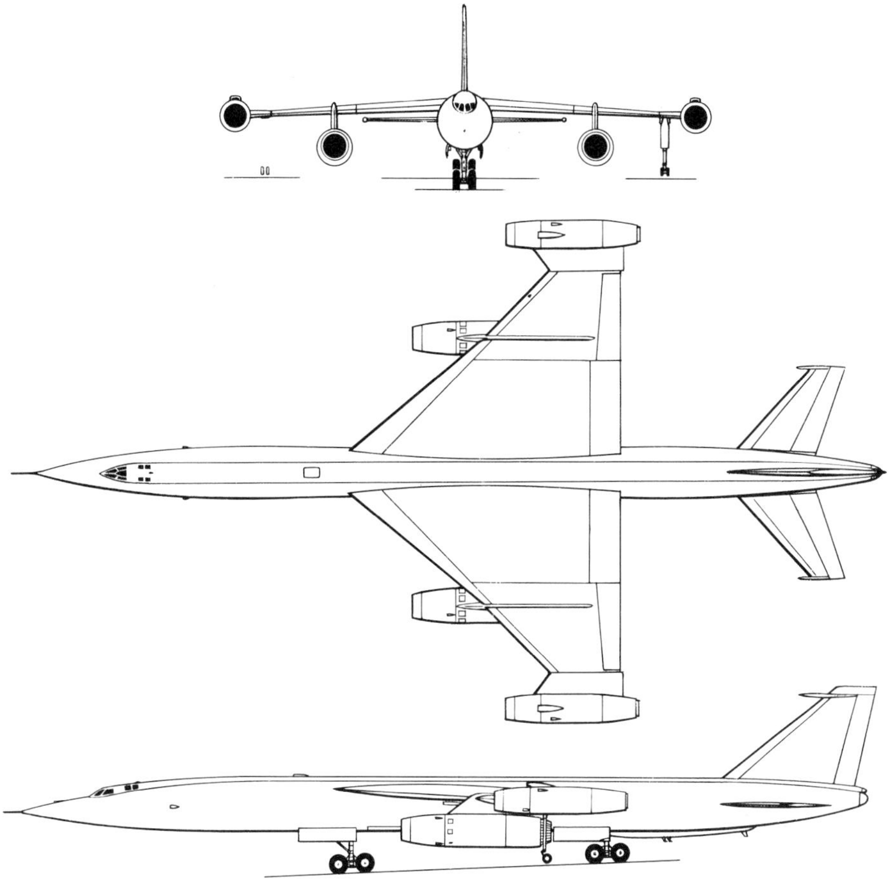

M-52 (No 4 aircraft, preserved)

outer engines on pylons arranged horizontally beyond wingtips. Same aircraft now preserved at Monino. Not known to have carried weapons, operational avionics or inflight-refuelling probe. Following data generally based on aircraft No 4 (numbered '12').
DIMENSIONS Span over engine pods 37,0 m (121 ft $4\frac{3}{8}$ in); length 57,0 m (187 ft 0 in); wing area 280 m² (3000 ft²).
ENGINES Four Koliesov ND-7F or VD-7F turbojets, rated dry at 13 t (28,660 lb) thrust each; with afterburner probably about 18 t (40,000 lb).
WEIGHTS Empty 74 500 kg (164,240 lb); max loaded 200 t (440,900 lb).
PERFORMANCE Max speed at height 1950 km/h (1212 mph, M 1·83); service ceiling at 157 t gross 20 km (66,000 ft); max range (subsonic, no payload) 6000 km (3730 miles).

NIAI

In September 1930 Leningrad LIIPS formed educational institute, UK GVF (training combine of civil air fleet). In turn this formed NIAI (*Nauchno-Issledovatelskii Aero-Institut*, scientific research aero institute) in 1931. This attracted good design engineers, and after appearance of LK-1 it was reorganized in 1934 into OKB, O in this case standing for *Osoboye* (personal). Brigades led by Lisichkin, Bedunkovich, Krylov, Domrachyev and, later, Bakshayev. NIAI liquidated 1938, but construction of experimental aircraft continued by GVF group at Leningrad to 1941.

Grigorii Ivanovich Bakshayev was born in 1918. On leaving school he joined the Leningrad institute of aerial communication (LIIPS), and gained experience in aircraft engineering. His first responsibility was for parts of the ASK amphibian.

LK Bakshayev's first lead assignment was a simple tandem two-seat cabin monoplane, *Leningradskii Komsomolyets* (Leningrad young communist). Mixed construction with welded truss fuselage and two-spar wooden wing with duralumin slats and flaps. Fixed endplates on wings with patented spoiler (interceptor) type ailerons carried on rotating brackets and projecting above the outer wings. Prototype built April to July 1936. Following successful flight tests in August, it is presumed to have flown to Moscow. One built.
DIMENSIONS Span 10,0 m (32 ft $9\frac{3}{4}$ in); length 6,5 m (21 ft 4 in); wing area 15,5 m² (167 ft²).
ENGINE 100 hp M-11 radial.
WEIGHTS Empty 740 kg (1631 lb); fuel/oil 120 kg (265 lb); max 1100 kg (2425 lb).
PERFORMANCE Max speed 175 km/h (109 mph); landing 75 km/h (47 mph); range 750 km (470 miles).

LIG-8 Development of LK with restressed structure and wider fuselage accommodating five-seat cabin. Test-flown 1937 and built in small numbers.
DIMENSIONS Span 10,0 m (32 ft $9\frac{3}{4}$ in); length 6,6 m (21 ft 8 in); wing area 15,5 m² (167 ft²).
ENGINE 300 hp MG-31 radial.
WEIGHTS Empty 1000 kg (2205 lb); fuel/oil 220 kg (485 lb); max 1600 kg (3527 lb).
PERFORMANCE Max speed 245 km/h (152 mph); landing 100 km/h (62 mph); range 800 km (497 miles).

RK Also designated **LIG-7**, this research monoplane was Bakshayev's first project at the Leningrad GVF, which he joined in 1936. Influenced by the contemporary interest in variable-geometry wings, he sought to prove a different principle from other VG designers. Like the *Matroshka* (set of dolls, each fitting tightly inside the next) he designed a wing around which was a set of telescopic larger wings with which wing area could be reduced for high speed or increased for take-off and landing. The RK (*Razdvizhnoye Krylo*, extending wing) was a simple low-performance tandem-seat cabin machine of mixed construction, with a wire-braced low wing of constant M-6 profile. Around each half-wing were arranged five telescoping ply aerofoils (TsAGI-846 profile) normally housed in the fuselage. The observer had a handcrank

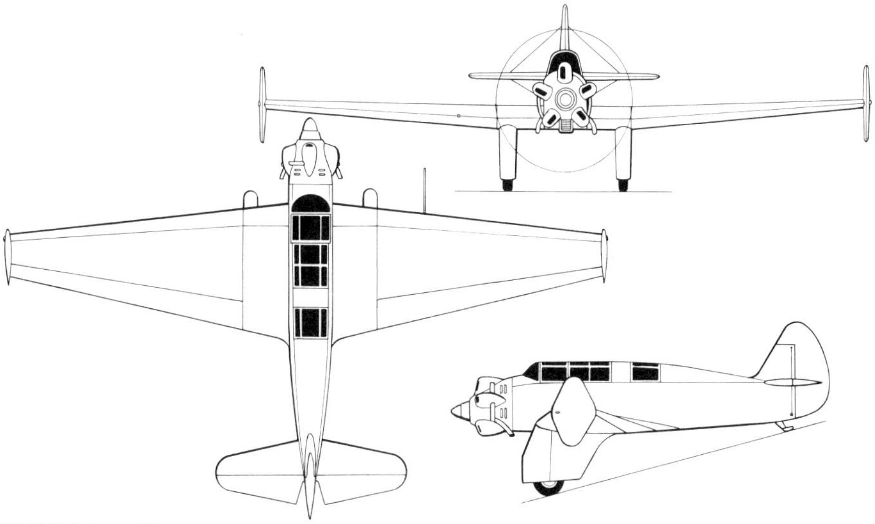

NIAI-Bakshayev LK

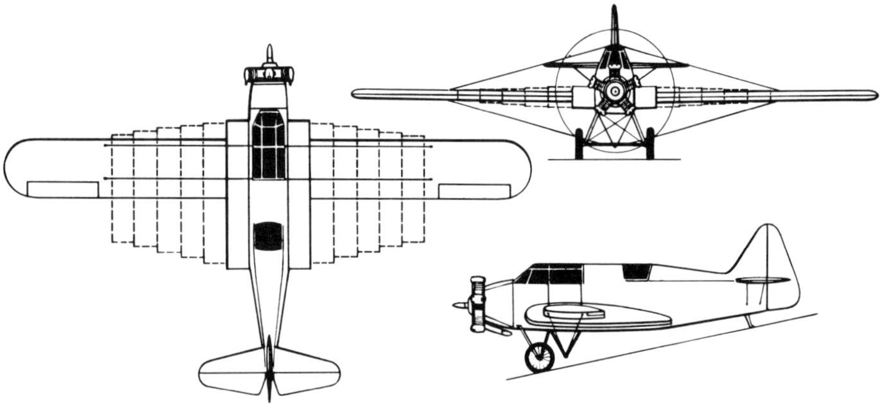

NIAI-Bakshayev RK/LIG-7

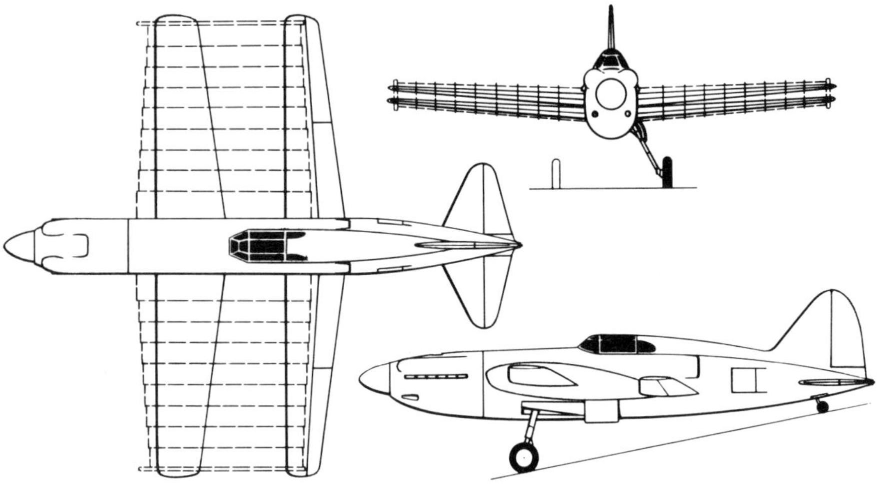

NIAI-Bakshayev RK-1

with which he could pull out the outermost section on each side more than half-way to the tip, where bracing wires were attached. Each section had a span of 460 mm and pulled out the one behind it. Extension or retraction took about 40 seconds. Trials in 1937 paved the way for fighter application of RK principle.

DIMENSIONS Span 11,3 m (37 ft 0¾ in); length 7,34 m (24 ft 1 in); wing area variable 16,56–23,85m² (178·25–256·72 ft²).
ENGINE One 100 hp M-11.
WEIGHTS Empty 667 kg (1470 lb); loaded 897 kg (1978).
PERFORMANCE Max speed 150 km/h (93 mph); landing (small wing) 250 m/18 s/100 km/h, (big) 110 m/9 s/70 km/h.

RK-I Also known as RK-800, this was to be the definitive application of the telescopic wing to a combat aircraft (RK-I from variable-wing fighter). For the first and probably only time it used tandem wings as the supports and guides for telescopic sections which, when extended, multiplied wing area by nearly 2·4. The wings were light alloy and steel, with spot-welded 30KhGSA stainless skins, the rear wing having flaps and ailerons. Fuselage, light-alloy monocoque. There were nine sections of 'large wing' on each side, housed with main gear in fuselage. Large pipes between engine and coolant radiators on each side of rear fuselage for minimum drag. Stalin was enthusiastic and insisted on use of most powerful engine available. Original design of October/December 1938 based on M-105 was replaced by enlarged aircraft with M-106, retaining same armament of two ShVAK and two ShKAS all in nose. In definitive form large wing was extended hydraulically in 14 seconds, first section forming a large endplate at the tip and the rear of each duralumin segment running in tracks ahead of rear-wing ailerons and flaps. TsAGI tunnel-tested a 1:5-scale model, and a full-scale rig assisted development of extensible wing hardware. Prototype complete early 1940, but engine in serious difficulty. Nobody dared to fit any engine other than the type Stalin had suggested, and RK-I languished in erection shop. Bakshayev probably later joined Bartini's 'Special OKB' to work on Project R.

DIMENSIONS Span 8,2 m (26 ft 10¾ in); length 8,8 m (28 ft 10½ in); wing area (high speed) 11,9 m² (128 ft²), (landing) 28,0 m² (301 ft²).
ENGINE One 1600 hp M-106 V-12.
WEIGHTS Max loaded 3100 kg (6834 lb).
PERFORMANCE (Est) max speed 720 km/h (447 mph).

LK-1, NIAI-1 Designated from *Leningradskii Kombinat*, and also called *Fanera-2* (Plywood No 2). Designed by Alexei Ivanovich Lisichkin and Vladimir Fedorovich Rentel. Basically simple all-wood passenger aircraft but with thick inboard wing integrated into lifting fuselage to seek reduced drag. Wing with one main spar, large ailerons, no flaps, spar carried across cabin forming support for two rear pasenger seats. Two front seats (pilot on left) with view ahead through sloping Celluloid front windows; rear passengers with three large windows on each side sloping 60° in hinged frames serving as doors. Trad pyramidal main gears and tailskid. Rudder and possibly all control surfaces fabric covered. Prototype flown May 1933, and good behaviour (though obviously pilot had asymmetric view ahead). Autumn 1933 A. Ya. Ivanov flew to Moscow where NII trials resulted in order for 20 series examples. Several saw transport service in Arctic with Aeroflot. Some operated on skis, and at least one (**NIAI-1P**) had twin floats. Series aircraft had revised wing root and rear fuselage, and redesigned much taller but shorter-chord vertical tail.

DIMENSIONS Span 12,47 m (40 ft 11 in); length (landplane) 8,87 m (29 ft 1¼ in); wing area 27,6 m² (297 ft²).
ENGINE One 100 hp M-11.
WEIGHTS Empty (prototype) 730 kg, (production) 746 kg (1645 lb); fuel/oil (production) 170 kg; loaded (prototype) 1035 kg, (production) 1160 kg (2557 lb).
PERFORMANCE Max speed (prototype) 157 km/h, (production) 154 km/h (96 mph); climb 10 min to 1 km; service ceiling (prototype) 3950 m, (production) 3370 m (11,000 ft); range (prototype) 770 km, (production) 850 km (528 miles); take-off 200 m/7 s; landing 120 m/12 s/65 km/h (40 mph).

LK-1 (production aircraft)

LK-4, NIAI-4 Designed by Anatolii Georgievich Bedunkovich, engineer-colonel who wrote many instructional books and among other designs produced AB-55 engine (55 hp, 1930) using Anzani cylinders dating from 1910. LK-4 was neat trainer which, as explained, was 'four aircraft in one'. Original machine, flown early 1934, had spatted main wheels. Wooden sesquiplane with ply leading edge and forward fuselage, fabric elsewhere. Two tandem cockpits with dual controls, slotted ailerons (Shavrov: and flaps). Engine in Townend-ring cowl. Later spats removed and new leading edge to upper wing with large plywood slats. Flown in four configurations. **LK-4-I,** slatted upper wing with twin parallel bracing struts each side, cantilever lower wing (upper wing 13 m², lower 7 m²). **LK-4-II,** different upper leading wing edge without slats, upper wing moved aft and lower wing forward. Flew faster but landed faster, spun more easily and simpler to perform aerobatics. **LK-4-III,** parasol monoplane with lower wing removed, faster still but required harsher control. **LK-4-IV,** low-wing monoplane with original lower wing replaced by upper, with twin bracing struts to top of fuselage. Fastest of all, but control described as 'more complicated'. Simple aircraft to make, and propeller and instruments standard U-2. NII testing late 1934 resulted in recommendation for start of series production. This never materialized, though in different configurations LK-4 successful in various light aircraft competitions 1934–1936.

DIMENSIONS Span 9,0 m (29 ft 6¼ in) (lower wing of LK-4-I, LK-4-II) 5,7 m (18 ft 8½ in); length 7,07 m (23 ft 2¼ in); wing area (LK-4-I, LK-4-II) 20,2 m² (217 ft²), (LK-4-III, LK-4-IV) 13,0 m² (140 ft²).

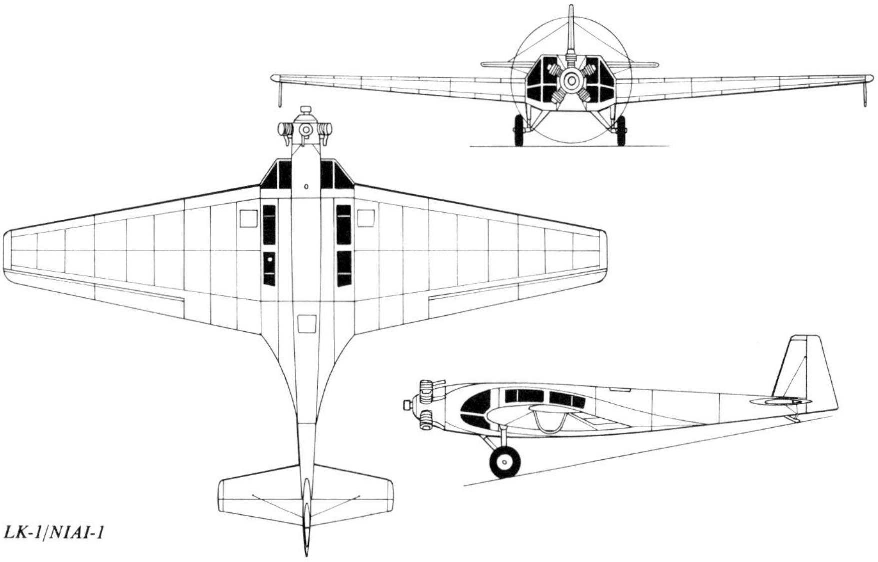

LK-1/NIAI-1

ENGINE One 100 hp M-11.

WEIGHTS Empty (I) 565 kg (1246 lb), (II) 558, (III) 517, (IV) 510; fuel/oil 45 kg; loaded (I) 790 kg (1742 lb), (II) 783, (III) 742, (IV) 735.

PERFORMANCE Max speed (I) 157 km/h (97·5 mph), (II) 168, (III) 177, (IV) 180; climb to 1 km (I, II) 6 min, (III) 5, (IV) 4·5; service ceiling (I, II) 3300 m, (III) 4500, (IV) 3815; range (I) 250 km, (II) 280, (III, IV) 300; take-off (I) 70 m, (II) 80, (III) 90, (IV) 130; landing (I) 100 m/60 km/h, (II) 150/70, (III) 170/80, (IV) 220/90.

P-3, LIG-5 Success of LK-4 prompted this faster and more powerful machine in LIG (Leningrad Institute GVF) series. Wooden, mainly ply covering, fully cowled engine. Three basic configurations, **P-3DP, P-3OB** and **P-3ON**. DP (*Dvukhmestnyi Polutoplan*), two-seat sesquiplane for training pilot/observer of R-5 and similar aircraft. Full combat equipment including fixed and free ShKAS, radio and recon camera. **OB** (*Odnomestnyi Biplan*), single-seat biplane for training pilots for I-15 and other biplane fighters. Upper centre-section removed together with side cabane struts, interplane slanting struts and bracing wires, leaving diagonal struts to upper plane only. Rear cockpit faired over. **ON** (*Odnomestnyi Nizkoplan*),

LK-4, NIAI-4

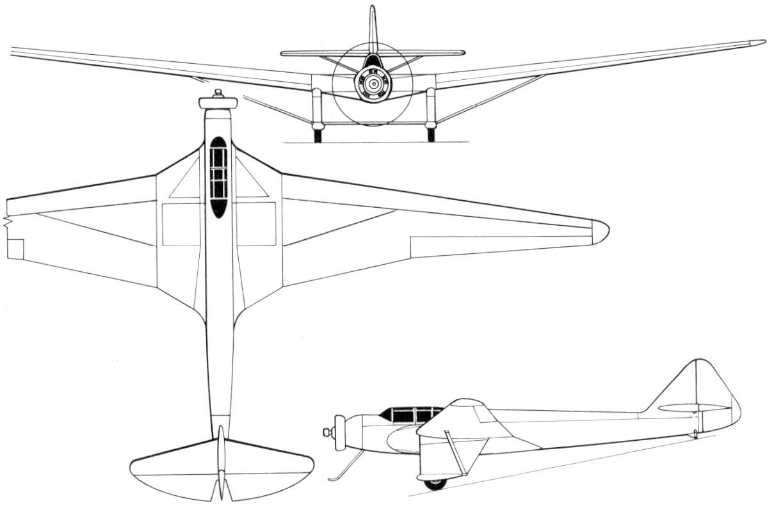

LEM-3, LIG-6

single-seat low-wing monoplane for training pilots of I-16 and similar low-wing fighters. Cantilever low wing only, and smaller horizontal tail. Aircraft did well in testing from late May 1936, and completed factory testing February 1937. To Moscow for NII tests, with expectation of major production; crashed by pilot error, not repairable.

DIMENSIONS Span (DP) 10,6 m (34 ft 9⅓ in), (others) 9.0 m (29 ft 6⅓ in); length 7,5 m (24 ft 7¼ in); wing area (DP) 30m² (323 ft²), (OB) 26,0 m² (280ft²), (ON) 14,0 m² (151 ft²).

ENGINE One 330 hp MG-31F.

WEIGHTS Empty (DP) 1100 kg (2425 lb), (OB) 960, (ON) 850; fuel/oil (DP) 220 kg, (others) 110; loaded (DP) 1560 kg (3439 lb), (OB) 1260, (ON) 1150.

PERFORMANCE Max speed (DP) 210 km/h (130 mph), (OB) 220 km/h, (ON) 280 km/h (174 mph); range (DP) 500 km (373 miles), (OB) 280, (ON) 300; landing speed (DP) 80 km/h, (OB) 75, (ON) 100.

LEM-3, LIG-6 Another of LIG series, this also had designation in LEM series (initials coined from Lev Pavlovich Malinovskii, director of NTU-GVF in 1930s) of *motor planer* (powered gliders). No NIAI number known. Designed by Yuri Vladimirovich Domrachyev in partnership with Leonid Sergeyevich Vild'grub. Remarkable use of horsepower: Soviet sources agree accommodation in enclosed cabin for two pilots side-by-side and eight passengers in four double seats behind. Access by hinged glazed roof panels with small windows. In addition, four cargo compartments in wing. All-wooden construction, with fabric-covered control surfaces. Wing braced by struts from main spar to main gears with horizontal strut between legs (drawings show trousered gears, not flown). Townend-ring engine cowl, U-2 propeller. First flight 1936, completed factory tests early 1937 and flew to Moscow for NII testing (implication in 1979 account flew non-stop in 12 h with passenger-cabin tanks) but suffered forced landing on arrival.

DIMENSIONS Span 26,0 m (85 ft 3⅔ in); length 13,3 m (43 ft 7⅔ in); wing area 57,0 m² (613 ft²).

ENGINE One 100 hp M-11.

WEIGHTS Empty 1050 kg (2315 lb); fuel/oil 170 kg; loaded 2 t (4409 lb), (overload) 2240 kg (4938 lb).

PERFORMANCE Max speed (Shavrov) 122 km/h (76 mph), (Něměcek) 135 km/h (84 mph); cruise (Shavrov) 100 km/h (62 mph); ceiling (Shavrov) 2,2 km, (Něměcek) 3,2 km; range (Něměcek) 800 km (497 miles); landing speed 55 km/h (34 mph).

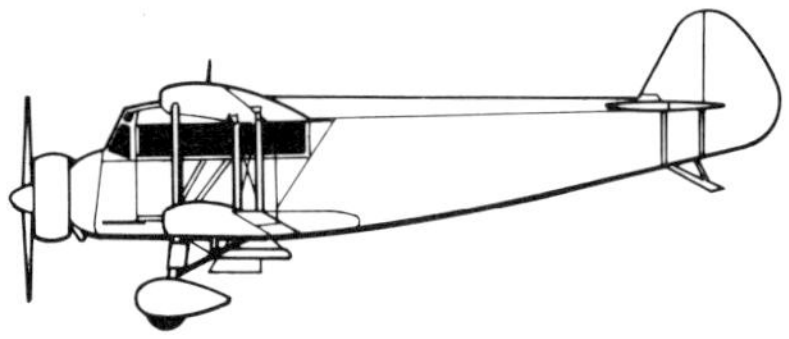

SKh-1, LIG-10

SKh-1, LIG-10 Another of LIG series, this was ancestor of An-2 and designed by Bedunkovich for same wide spread of duties. Designation *Syelskolkhozyaistyennyi*-1, agricultural-1. Two-bay biplane with equal-size wooden/fabric two-spar wings, R-II section 12%, four slotted ailerons and slotted flaps, hinged to centre section and folding to rear. Fuselage welded from mild-steel tube, fabric covering. Tail wood and fabric, with pilot control of tailplane incidence. Large cabin with pilot high up for good view through all-round Celluloid windows. Dural fuel tanks filling upper centre section outboard of fuselage. Accommodation for eight persons (front left seat for pilot, or side-by-side dual control); casevac with four stretchers, 690 kg cargo, or 600 kg ag-chemicals with ventral spreader for solids (no record of liquid spraying). Prototype flown 1937; prolonged testing in many roles including full season seed-sowing and casevac role throughout Finnish war 1939–40. Early 1941 decision to produce in series, but thwarted by evacuation of chosen factory.

DIMENSIONS Span 12,8 m (42 ft 0 in), (folded 5,85 m); length 10,7 m (35 ft 1¼ in), (Něměcek, 10,75); wing area 41,17 m² (443 ft²).

ENGINE One 330 hp MG-31F.

WEIGHTS Empty 1215 kg (2679 lb); fuel/oil 175 kg (later 275, with reduced payload); loaded 2150 kg (4740 lb).

PERFORMANCE Max speed 182 km/h (113 mph); climb 5·6 min to 1 km; service ceiling 3,8 km (12,500 ft); range 420 km (long-range tanks, much greater); take-off 210 m/19 s; landing 180 m/18 s/65 km/h (40 mph).

Nikitin

Vasilii Vasilyevich Nikitin was born 1901 and studied at an institute of architecture. No formal engineering training yet learned how to design aircraft and, again without instruction, how to fly them. Began designing details under D.P. Grigorovich 1922, assisting N.N. Polikarpov 1925–1929 and in 1930–1936 at TsKB. Designed and built his own aircraft 1933–1939, whilst continuing to assist others. At OKB-30 in 1938–1940. From 1941 manager of repair factories, and assisted TsAGI build new wind tunnels. Converted captured Ju 52/3m into flying lab for TsAGI and rebuilt several Douglas Boston/A-20 into six-passenger staff transports. Post-war deputy to N.I. Kamov, dying in this post 1955.

NV-1 Single-seat sporting aircraft inspired by US racers. Wooden wing with bracing struts to fuselage and to trousered main gears. Fuselage welded from mild-steel tube, duralumin tail, fabric covering throughout. Control by push/pull tubes. Unsprung main legs except for low-pressure tyres. First flight by V.P. Chkalov September 1933. Nine flights but difficult to fly and regarded as little practical use.

DIMENSIONS Span 6,4 m (21 ft 0 in); length 4,25 m (13 ft 11⅓ in); wing area 6,85 m² (73·7 ft²).

ENGINE One 100 hp M-11.

WEIGHTS Empty 350 kg (772 lb); fuel/oil 70 kg; loaded 510 kg (1124 lb).

PERFORMANCE Max speed 232 km/h (144 mph) at SL; service ceiling 4,8 km (15,750 ft); range 850 km (528 miles); landing speed 95 km/h.

NV-2 Single-seat sporting and training aircraft, again with M-11 in full-length NACA cowl but still driving U-2 propeller. Wooden construction with monocoque fuselage with wall-thickness 2 mm made from glued layers of 0,5 mm birch *shpon*. Wing with 2 mm ply back to rear spar, fabric covering overall. Single-leg main gears retracted backwards into underwing fairings. Built 1935 with Osoaviakhim funds at OKB-30 and proved to have excellent flying qualities, partly stemming from superb finish.

DIMENSIONS Span 8,6 m (28 ft 2¼ in); length 6,15 m (20 ft 2 in); wing area 11 m² (118 ft²).

ENGINE One 100 hp M-11.

WEIGHTS Empty 385 kg (849 lb); fuel/oil 250 + 25 kg; loaded 750 kg (1653 lb).

PERFORMANCE Max speed 230 km/h (143 mph) at SL; service ceiling 5,8 km (19,000 ft); max endurance 10 h; landing speed 75 km/h.

NV-2bis, UTI-5 Original NV-2bis built at OKB-30 in 1938, essentially an NV-2 with more powerful MG-11 and slight local strengthening. Successfully tested; small series of ten ordered by VVS but abandoned when plant assigned to produce UT-2. Nikitin then built further prototype called UTI-5 (NV-2bis/MG-31) to order of UVVS as training fighter. This was an NV-2bis with further increase in power, restressed airframe and other changes, plus synchronized ShKAS with 250 rounds. Hinged glazed canopy, fully retracting main gears and metal propeller with spinner. Flown early 1939 and tested by more than 40 pilots including representatives of VVS, NII, GVF and Osoaviakhim. Excellent

aircraft, much better finished than I-16; 200 (Shavrov, 20) ordered by VVS but never produced.
DIMENSIONS Span 8,0 m (26 ft 3 in); length 6,15, (20 ft 2 in), (UTI-5) 6,3 m (20 ft 8 in); wing area 11,0 m² (118 ft²).
ENGINE One 165 hp MG-11, (UTI-5) one 300 hp MG-31.
WEIGHTS Empty 435 kg (959 lb), (UTI) 560 kg (1235 lb); fuel/oil 250+25 (UTI, +30) kg; loaded 800 kg (1764 lb), (UTI) 950 kg (2094 lb).
PERFORMANCE Max speed 260 km/h (162 mph), (UTI) 350 km/h (217 mph); service ceiling 7 km (23,000 ft), (UTI) 8 km (26,250 ft); endurance 7h, (UTI) 4·5 h; range 800 km (497 miles), (UTI) not known; landing speed (both) 75 km/h.

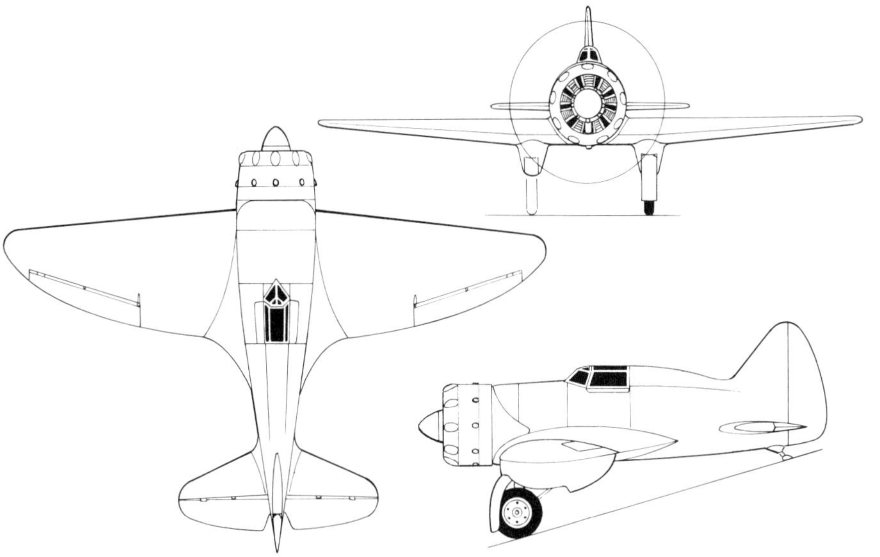

NV-2bis

NV-4 Grumman-inspired biplane amphibian with two seats in tandem enclosed cockpits. Fuselage circular-section monocoque glued from layers of 0,5 mm *shpon*, with ply and dural panels at front, and integral wooden float carrying main gears retracted by hand-crank. Two-spar wooden wings with ailerons (upper only) and landing flaps (lower only). Wooden stabilizing floats, without step, beneath lower planes in line with N interplane struts. Equipped for night flying. Completed 1936 and flown by Nikitin, but had to be shelved through pressure of other work.
DIMENSIONS Span 10,5 m (34 ft 5⅓ in); length 8,7 m (28 ft 6½ in); wing area 28,5 m² (307 ft²).
ENGINE One 100hp M-11.
WEIGHTS Empty 825 kg (1819 lb); fuel/oil 90+15 kg; loaded 1090 kg (2403 lb).
PERFORMANCE Max speed 160 km/h (99·5 mph) at SL; ceiling 3,5 km (11,500 ft); endurance 4 h; landing speed 65 km/h.

MU-4 Small training amphibian designed by N.G. Mikhelson working with Nikitin at OKB-30. Mainly wooden, but dural struts and fabric on rear of wings and on control surfaces. Single-bay biplane, side-by-side dual-control cockpit with glazed hinged canopy, tractor engine on upper wing, and air/oil shock struts on main gears manually retracted along sides of hull. First MU-4 completed 1936 and flew well, but after prolonged testing crashed because of failure of glued joint between wooden boss, carrying main engine controls, and side of hull! Nikitin supervised construction of second MU-4, without such flaw, but Sh-2 was already in production fulfilling same objectives.
DIMENSIONS Span 12,0 m (39 ft 4½ in); length not known; wing area 33,0 m² (355 ft²).
ENGINE One 165 hp MG-11F.
WEIGHTS Empty 900 kg (1984 lb); fuel/oil 80+20 kg; loaded 1200 kg (2646 lb).
PERFORMANCE Max speed 168 km/h (104 mph); no other data.

MU-5 Development of MU-4 with MV-6 (Renault) inline engine of 222 hp. Construction abandoned 1938.

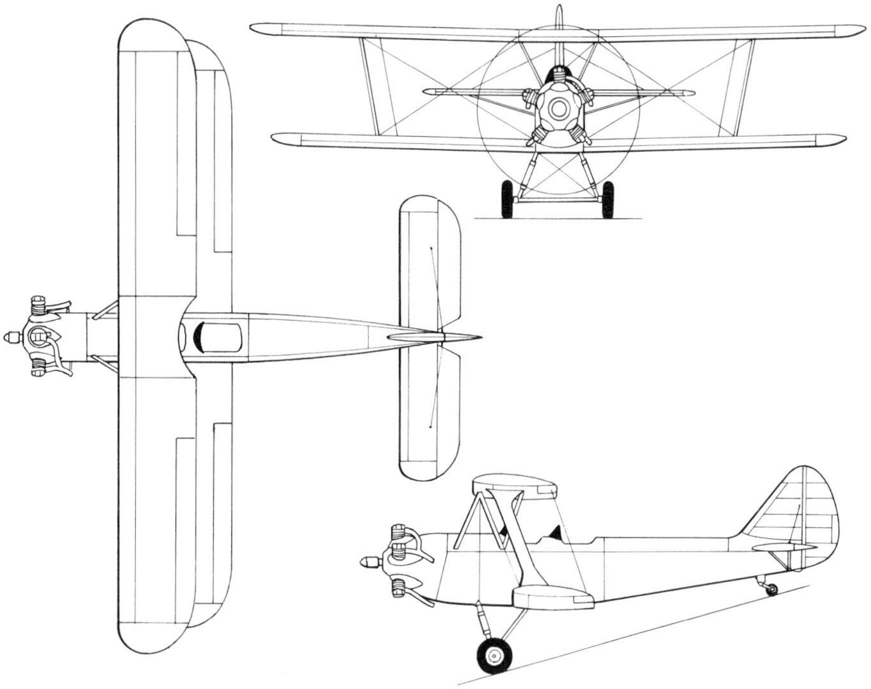

NV-5, U-5

NV-5, U-5 Simple tandem dual biplane trainer, smaller in dimensions than U-2, with I-type single interplane struts and small (500 mm) semi-balloon tyres. Various other refinements, such as rubber shock-isolating engine mounts. Mixed construction, fuselage truss welded 30KhGSA steel tube with ply covering, wooden wings and fabric-covered control surfaces. Design prompted by Osoaviakhim/Aviavnito competition in late 1934 for safe aeroplane. First NV-5 flown early 1937 and won first prize. This machine had MG-40 engine driving an efficient Kuznetsov propeller, plain U-2 type ailerons and tail skid. Subsequently fitted with slotted ailerons and tailwheel. Made 250 flights in hands of 15 pilots, with wheel and ski landing gear. In 1938 first **NV-5bis** flown, with regular production engine in place of Kossov's experimental MG-40. Even better than NV-5 and drawings prepared for production for Osoaviakhim and, later, UVVS. In late 1938 U-5 produced as prototype and four series examples. M-11 and M-11G engines, simplified fuselage, wing of TsAGI-876 profile with flat underside (instead of Göttingen 436), control-surface frames of dural, control system by push/pull rods and aluminium propeller. Prolonged testing by 60 pilots, all satisfied. In 1939 one U-5 fitted with ShKAS on lower right wing outside propeller disc and four RS-82 rockets under lower wings. Later in 1939 one prototype and four series **U-5bis** built with minor strengthening and MG-11F engine. In all, UVVS tested 12 examples of U-5 family but retained U-2 and UT-2 as mass training types. U-5/LSh described separately.
DIMENSIONS Span (NV-5) 9,82 m, (U-5 family) 9,84 m (32 ft 3⅓ in); length (NV-5) 7,7 m, (U-5) 7,62 m (25 ft 0 in); wing area (NV-5) 25 m², (U-5) 25,53 m² (275 ft²).
ENGINE (NV-5) one 140 hp MG-40, (5bis) 165 hp MG-11F, (U-5) 100hp M-11 or 115hp M-11G, (U-5bis) 180hp MG-11F.
WEIGHTS Empty (NV-5) 612 kg, (U-5) 700/711 kg, (U-5bis) 773 kg (1704 lb); fuel/oil (all) 75+12 kg; loaded (NV-5) 850 kg (1874 lb), (5bis and U-5) not known, (U-5, M-11G) 974 kg, U-5bis) 1036 kg (2284 lb).

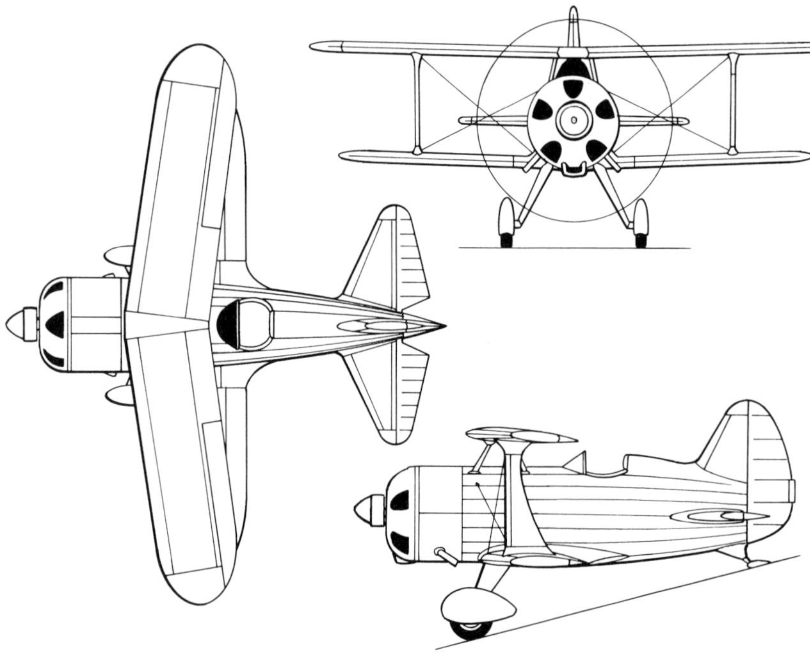

NV-6/UTI-6

PERFORMANCE Max speed (NV-5) 202 km/h, (5bis) 220 km/h, (U-5) 170 km/h, (M-11G) 181 km/h, (U-5bis) 205 km/h (127 mph; climb to 1 km, (NV-5, 5bis) 3 min, (U-5) 5 min, (U-5bis) 3·8 min; service ceiling (NV-5) 6 km, (U-5) 3,75 km, (U-5bis) 4,5 km; endurance (NV-5) 5·5 h, (5bis) 4h, (U-5) 3 h, (U-5bis) 2·5 h; take-off (NV-5) 120 m, (U-5) 70 m/9 s; (U-5bis) 70 m/7 s; landing (NV-5) 110 m/60 km/h, (U-5) 65 m/10 s/60 km/h, (U-5bis) 120 m/10 s/70 km/h.

LSh, U-5/MG-31 Though a U-5 derivative, this variant sufficiently different for separate treatment. Built 1942 at request of Moscow defence HQ in MVO front-line repair shops where Nikitin was chief of design and technology. Much more powerful, structurally strengthened, and new upper wing cannibalized from I-153 but with roots slightly shortened to preserve original span. Large glazed cockpit with pilot in bucket seat and longitudinally arranged plank (*sic*) on which two passengers sat astride at rear. Tough aluminium cockpit able to take weapons and heavy supplies without damage. Outstanding aircraft with STOL and good range and speed. No available capacity for production, but sole LSh (*Legkii Shtabno*, light staff aircraft) became famous from Leningrad to Caucasus, making over 600 operational missions often over ground battles and frequently riddled with holes.

DIMENSIONS Span 9,84 m (32 ft 3⅓ in); length 7,75 m (25 ft 5¼ in); wing area 25,53 m² (275 ft²).

ENGINE One 330 hp MG-31F.

WEIGHTS Empty 880 kg (1940 lb); fuel/oil 250 + 30 kg; loaded 1400 kg (3086 lb).

PERFORMANCE Max speed 272 km/h (169 mph); cruise 240 km/h (149 mph); range with reserves 1000 km (620 miles) in 4·5 h; take-off 40 m/6 s; landing 130 m/11 s/71 km/h.

IS-1

NV-6, UTI-6 Last of Nikitin's pre-war sporting machines, this nimble biplane was tailored for aerobatics, then an unusual design objective (1939). Fuselage truss of welded KhMA steel tube taken from NV-1, together with complete wooden lower wing and dural/fabric tail. New upper wing of slightly greater span and 8° sweepback on leading edge, single large-chord streamlined interplane struts. Cantilever main legs with spatted balloon-tyred wheels. Engine with M.A. Kossov's special carburettor for sustained inverted flight. No engine available until December 1940, when Nikitin and V.V. Shyevchyenko carried out test flying with ski gear. Excellent results, but TsAGI refused permission for NII testing on pretext static testing had not been done (though airframe designed to basic factor of 13). War prevented further work on this attractive machine.

DIMENSIONS Span 7,0 m (22 ft 11½ in); length 5,8 m (19 ft 0⅓ in); wing area 14 m² (151 ft²).

ENGINE One 165 hp MG-11F.

WEIGHTS Empty 560 kg (1235 lb); fuel/oil 80 + 20 kg; loaded 750 kg (1653 lb).

PERFORMANCE Max speed 270 km/h (168 mph); service ceiling 4,5 km (14,750 ft); endurance 2·5 h; take-off 50 m; landing 170 m/75 km/h.

IS-1 Soviet designers such as Bakshayev and (working in France) I. Makhonine were pioneers of polymporphic (variable-shape) aircraft. In 1938 Nikitin's test pilot, Vladimir Vasilyevich Shyevchyenko, began to investigate practicability of making a biplane which, after taking off from short field, could retract lower wing and turn into fast monoplane fighter. Nikitin assisted, and in 1939 Shyevchyenko built working model at MAT. Crucial factor was relative insensitivity of underside of aerofoil to cavity big enough to receive smaller wing retracted into it from below. Effect further reduced by fact that almost half lower wing could fold into recess in side of fuselage, reducing disruption of upper plane in biplane regime. In mid-1939 OKB-30 was organized for design task, with NII sponsorship, engineering strength gradually growing to reach 60. IS-1 (*Istrebitel Skladnoi*, folding fighter) based on I-153 in size, power and style, but with fuselage truss, wing spar booms and basic structure of lower inner wing and landing gears welded from 30KhGSA Cr-Mo steel tube. Rest of structure D16 duralumin, with flush-riveted dural skin except fabric control surfaces, driven by push/pull rods. Main landing gears attached to outer ends of inner section of folding lower wing, with single leg in trunnion on third rib and dural sheet fairing over leg and wheel. After take-off pilot selected single retraction lever to 'chassis up' position. Pneumatic retraction of main gears inwards, legs and front half wheels (700 x 150 mm tyres) lying ahead of recesses forming inboard lower leading edges. Selection of 'wing fold' position could be made at any time; in theory IS-1 could fight as biplane, gaining in turn radius but slower than monoplane. To fold wing, further pneumatic actuator mounted vertically near CG pushed upwards to break lower-wing bracing strut on each side and pull wings inwards and upwards. Instead of allowing lower wingtips to scrape along underside of upper wing, linkage held lower-wing outer section horizontal, this section being housed in underside of gull-type upper plane. On extension, actuator had to push lower wings

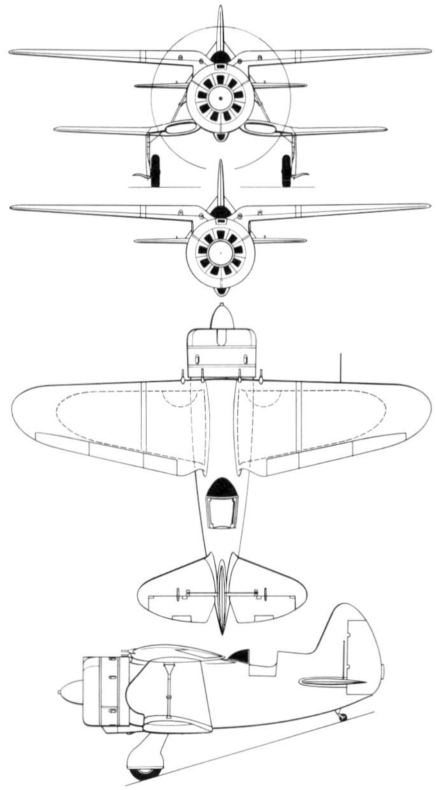

IS-1 (lower front view as monoplane)

down despite lift. Armament four ShKAS with 1000 rounds in inboard part of upper wing. Fuel in centre fuselage. Fabric-covered tail, fixed tailwheel, open cockpit with deep screen and down-folding side door. Imported three-blade 2,8 m Hamilton propeller. First flight 6 November 1940, on wheeled landing gear (skis would have precluded wing fold). Satisfactory, but by this time performance poor in comparison with monoplane fighters. Completed factory tests, and G.M. Shiyanov tested IS-1 at LII. NII did not bother to test IS-1, and reported designation I-220 not discovered in Soviet literature.

DIMENSIONS Span 8,6 m (28 ft 2½ in), (lower, extended) 6,72 m; length 6,79 m (22 ft 3¼ in); wing area 20,83 m² (224 ft²), (lower 7,83 m², upper 13,0 m²).

ENGINE One 900 hp M-63.

WEIGHTS Empty 1400 kg (3086 lb); loaded 2300 kg (5070 lb).

PERFORMANCE Max speed 453 km/h (281 mph); climb to 5 km, 8·2 min; service ceiling 8,8 km (28,870 ft); range 600 km (373 miles); landing speed 115 km/h.

IS-2 Though Nikitin had reached conclusion IS was not worth while, construction of second airframe had been put in hand parallel with first, and this was completed with various improvements. Engine was changed for GR14-derived M-88 of reduced diameter in long-chord cowl with gills, driving VISh-61 series propeller. Outer ShKAS replaced by two BS. Revised vertical tail of almost circular shape. Retractable tailwheel, and possibly other modifications. Wing retraction mechanism in this aircraft was faultless, but result still inferior to simple monoplanes. IS-2 flew in early 1941 (believed February). Testing discontinued spring 1941.

DIMENSIONS As IS-1 except length 7,1 m (23 ft 3½ in).

ENGINE One 1150 hp M-88.

WEIGHTS Not known.

PERFORMANCE Max speed 507 km/h (315 mph).

IS-4 No information on IS-3, but IS-4 was ultimate folding fighter, designed amidst arguments over validity of concept in 1940. Soviet accounts either omit IS-4 or describe it as design only, while Western accounts state prototype was flown summer 1941 (implying quick engineering development and construction). Heavier and better-streamlined derivative of IS-2, with liquid-cooled engine (M-120 chosen, but AM-37 accepted instead). Sliding hood over cockpit, and tricycle landing gear enabled main gears to be moved back into ideal position at thickest part of lower wing, thus allowing normal leading edge. Same armament as IS-2: two BS, two ShKAS. No information on radiator, and omitted from Western drawings. Following data from Western (Green/Swanborough) account:

DIMENSIONS As IS-2 except considerably longer, and lower wing same area but extended span to 7,1 m (23 ft 3½ in).

ENGINE One 1400 hp AM-37.

WEIGHTS Loaded (est) 2900 kg (6393 lb).

PERFORMANCE (est) Max speed 720 km/h (447 mph), (as biplane) 436 km/h (271 mph); service ceiling 12,5 km (41,000 ft); landing speed 107 km/h.

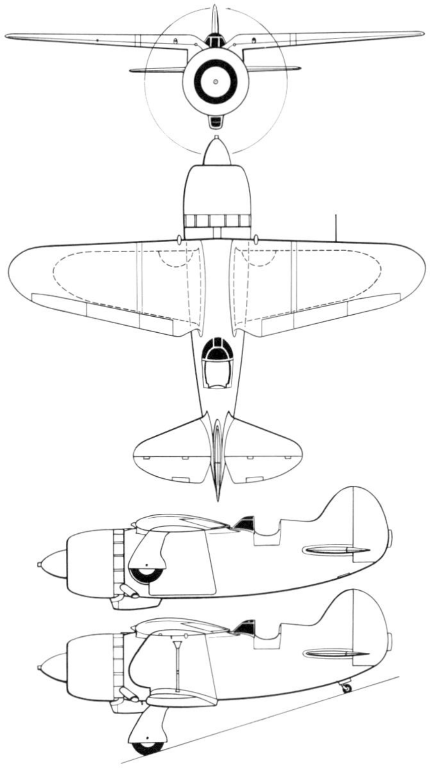

IS-2 (front view and upper side view as monoplane)

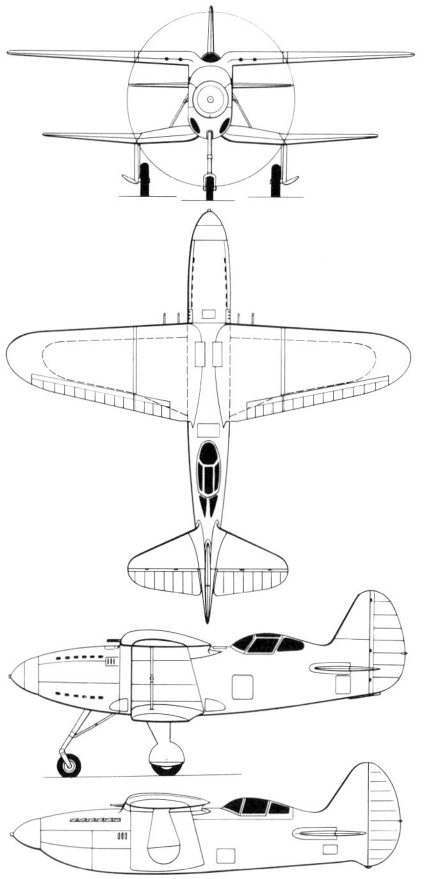

IS-4 (lower side view as monoplane, AM-37 engine)

IS-2

OMOS

This organization was founded in Leningrad 1925; *Otdel Morskogo Opytnogo Samolyetostroyeniya* (Dept of Experimental Marine Aircraft Design). Headed by D.P. Grigorovich, deputy A.N. Syedelnikov, other engineers included Korvin, Gimmelfarb, Shavrov, Samsonov, Mikhelson and Vigand. Products described under constructors.

KR-1 Only OMOS product not assigned to particular constructor, this reconnaissance flying boat was Heinkel HD 55 assembled under licence and fitted with Soviet engine and equipment. In 1930 purchased two Heinkel ship catapults and 30 HD 55 airframes. Wood hull and fin, fabric wings and tail surfaces. Stressed for operation from skis but otherwise not amphibious. Tractor engine between folding biplane wings, pilot under engine, and observer/gunner aft of wings with DA-2. Aircraft assembled at OMOS 1930–1931 and served from surface warships and shore stations until 1938. Designation from *Korabelnyi Razvyedchik*, fleet reconnaissance.

DIMENSIONS Span 14,0 m (45 ft 11$\frac{1}{4}$ in); length 10,4 m (34 ft 1$\frac{1}{2}$ in); wing area 56,9 m^2 (612 ft^2).

ENGINE One 480 hp M-22.

WEIGHTS Empty 1550 kg (3417 lb); fuel/oil 450 + 50 kg; loaded 2200 kg (4850 lb).

PERFORMANCE Max speed 194 km/h (120·5 mph); climb to 1 km, 4 min; service ceiling 4,8 km; endurance 5$\frac{1}{2}$ h; range 800 km (497 miles); alighting speed 80 km/h (50 mph).

OMOS KR-1

OOS

In 1920s national shortage of both aluminium and necessary electric power for smelting prompted growing research into steel as material for primary airframe structure. Work centred at VVA under Zhukovskii, where in 1928 special *Stal* (steel) group formed. In 1929 this was headed by Aleksandr Ivanovich Putilov, enticed away from TsAGI where for almost ten years he had managed design of fuselages and landing gears in brigade under Tupolev. With Prof S.G. Kozlov and VVA lab chief P.N. Lvov, Putilov drafted detailed programme for research into high-tensile and special steels (chiefly *Enerzh*-6), welding methods, and overall plan for future research. In 1930 programme took shape under OOS (*Otdel Opytnogo Samolyetostroeniya*, section for experimental aircraft construction). After some months outgrew VVA lab and relocated in former Dobrolyet hangar (preferable, as OOS ostensibly civil, with admin by GVF). Later, probably late 1932, expanded into large new OKB offices at GAZ-81, Tushino. Aircraft designated Stal, from material used; but some Stal aircraft not OOS but by other constructors (see Bartini, Grigorovich) and even Putilov's later designs are often ascribed to him rather than to OOS.

Stal-2 First product of OOS (no record of Stal-1). Conventional cabin monoplane seating pilot (plus optional extra passenger) in front and four passengers in main cabin, with door on left. Structure entirely of stainless steel, chiefly *Enerzh*-6, with fabric covering. Sections never thicker than 1 mm and ranging down to 0,1 and 0,15 mm for ribs and other detail components. Joints spot and seam-welded, but wing spar built up from sheet rolled into complex U-sections resembling those of Petlyakov. Upper/lower booms each based on single rolled U-section riveted inside larger section with two Us, and finally capped by outer three-U section, booms connected by pairs of diagonal struts each stiffened by being pressed to dished section. Supply

Stal-2 prototype

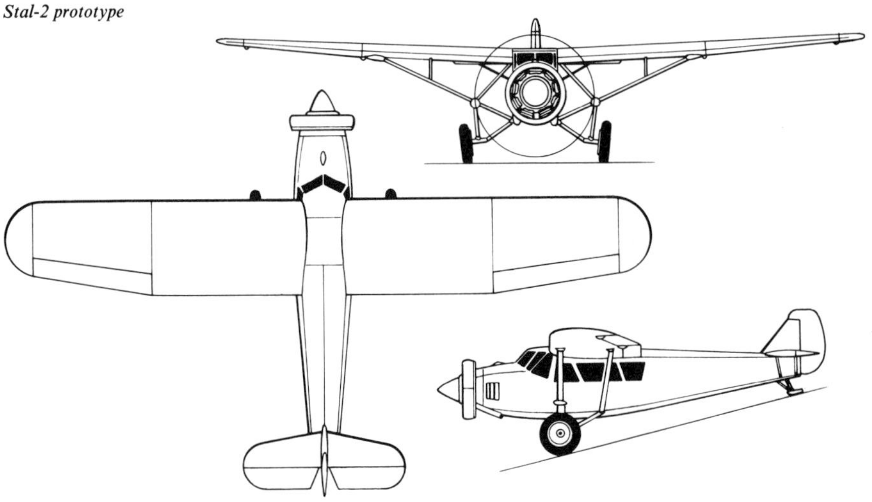

Stal-2 series

of *Enerzh*-6 slow and costly (same price as silver) until bulk purchase of similar 18-8 stainless from Sweden 1932, and import of Krupps rolling mill same year. Low-rate production begun. First Stal-2 flown successfully 11 October 1931 and production ordered from GAZ-81. Manufacture still labour-intensive, and first production aircraft delayed until early 1934. Shavrov: Wright engine, plus small number also with M-26 or MG-31; Němeček: first fitted with M-26, then MG-31. Single **Stal-2bis** with Frise ailerons. Total production 111 by late 1935, many remaining in use during Second World War.
DIMENSIONS Span (Shavrov and some others) 16,2 m (53 ft $1\frac{3}{4}$ in), (Němeček and other sources) 15,2 m (49 ft $10\frac{1}{2}$ in); length (Shavrov) 9,7 m, (Němeček) 9,5, (recent Soviet account) 9,74 m (31 ft $11\frac{1}{2}$ in); wing area (Shavrov) 31 m² (333·7 ft²), (Němeček) 32 m².
ENGINE One radial, uncowled: (prototype) 300 hp Wright J-6, (series) 300 hp M-26, then (most) 300 hp MG-31, driving aluminium propeller.
WEIGHTS Empty 1030 kg (2270 lb), (Němeček 1170 kg); fuel/oil 290 kg; loaded 1800 kg (3968 lb), (Němeček) 1900 kg).
PERFORMANCE Max speed 200 km/h (124 mph); cruise 170 km/h (105·6 mph); climb to 1 km, 4 min; service ceiling 5760 m (18900 ft); endurance 5 h; range (Shavrov) 750 km (466 miles), (Němeček) 700 km; take-off 130 m/11 s; landing 140 m/12 s/70 km/h (43·5 mph).

Stal-3 Enlarged successor to Stal-2 with refined but simplified structure cutting man-hours dramatically. Structure weight reduced from 43 to 41% and design load factor raised. Pilot and (normally) co-pilot with dual control in front, six passengers in main cabin of increased cross-section. Slotted ailerons and manual slotted flaps, engine in Townend-ring cowl, spatted wheels fitted with brakes, or streamlined skis. Prototype tested 1933, series production ordered and 79 delivered 1935–1936. Several fitted with water-cooled M-17. Important Aeroflot aircraft until summer 1941, thereafter continuing on utility duties, some impressed into VVS.
DIMENSIONS Span 17,02 m (55 ft 10 in); length (prototype) 10,8 m (35 ft $5\frac{1}{4}$ in), (production) 10,68 m (35 ft $0\frac{1}{2}$ in), (M-17, 11,3 m); wing area 34,8 m² (374·6 ft²).
ENGINE One 480 hp M-22; some 680 hp, M-17.
WEIGHTS Empty (production) 1672 kg (3686 lb); fuel/oil 440 kg; loaded 2817 kg (6210 lb).
PERFORMANCE Max speed 237 km/h (147 mph); climb to 1 km, 5 min; service ceiling 5340 m (17,520 ft), (prototype 6550 m); range 940 km (584 miles); take-off 280 m/16 s; landing 230 m/15 s/88 km/h.

Stal-5 Impressive flying-wing schemed by A.I. Putilov in 1933, to reach ultimate transport efficiency. Payload (normally 18 passengers) in broad centre section, carrying two long but shallow vertical tails at extremities with hinged rear part of wing forming rectangular elevator between them. Tapered outer wings with slotted flaps and ailerons. Two main and two tail wheels, all retractable. Fully glazed cockpit in leading edge on centreline. Structure entirely *Enerzh*-6 with skin of bakelite-ply on centre section and fabric elsewhere. Also planned **KhB** version (*Khimichyeskii Boyevik*, chemical fighter) for spraying war gases. In 1934 complete wing spar made for static test, and flying scale

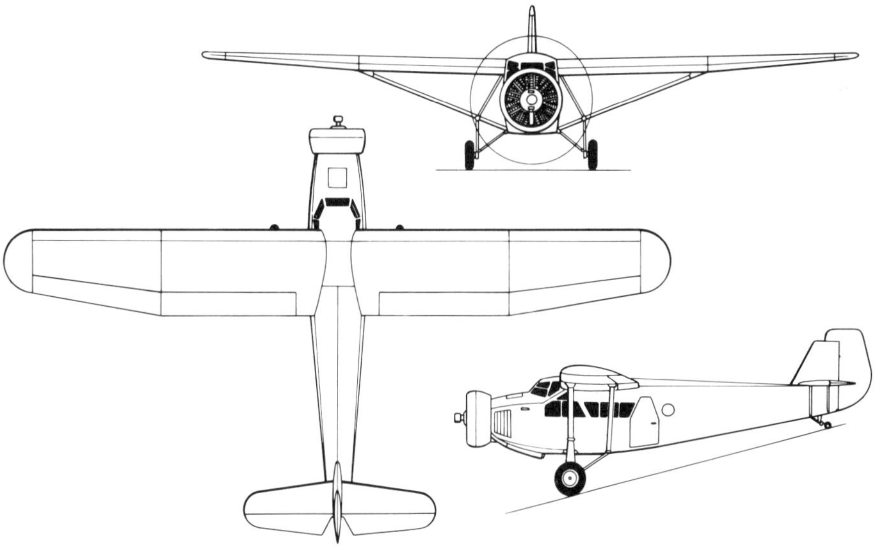

Stal-3

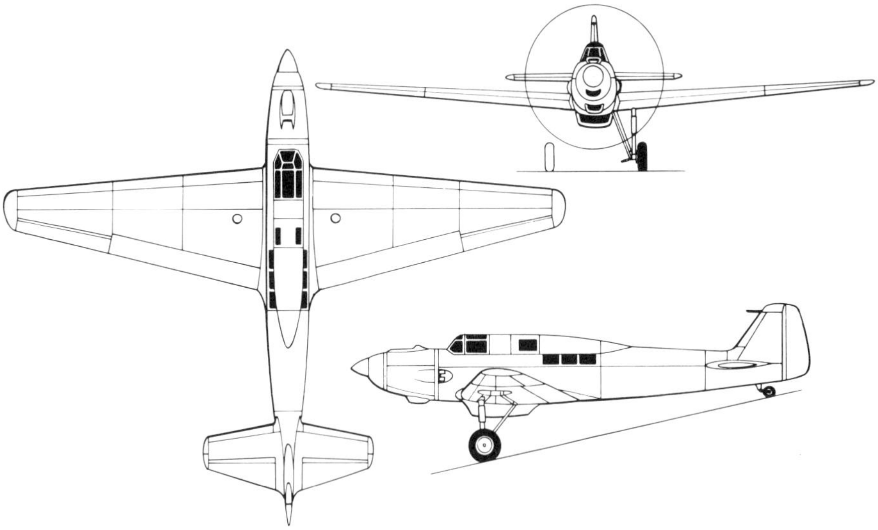

Stal-11

model (span 6,0 m, wing area 15,0 m², two 45 hp Salmson) flown late 1935 by V.V. Karpov and Ya.G. Paul. Stability and control response poor, and after some tinkering project abandoned.
DIMENSIONS Span 23,0 m (75 ft $5\frac{1}{2}$ in); length 12,5 m (41 ft 0 in); wing area 120 m² (1,292 ft²).
ENGINES Two 900 hp M-34F.
WEIGHTS (est) Empty 5,5 t (12,125 lb); loaded 8 t (17,640 lb).
PERFORMANCE No data.

Stal-11 High-speed light transport intended primarily to carry pilot and four passengers, mail and baggage, but also planned as military recon aircraft. Mixed construction: fuselage built on truss of *Enerzh*-6 with bakelite-ply skin, wings of high-speed TsAGI profile with all-wood construction around two spars with sheet webs, built-up ribs, multiple stringers and exceptionally smooth skin. Engine (HS 12Y derived) with detachable metal cowl, belly radiator and two-blade v-p propeller. Main landing gears retracted outwards into wings, with bays sealed by hinged doors on inside of legs. Exceptionally large slotted flaps (actuation probably pneumatic), of TsAGI type, which could be depressed to 60° with slot progressively closing. Modified Frise ailerons. Prototype completed autumn 1936 and tested on wheels and also on fixed skis. In 1937 tested as reconnaissance version. Flown approximately 300 times, but no further action. Performance good, but expensive to make and maintain.
DIMENSIONS Span 15,0 m (49 ft $2\frac{1}{2}$ in); length 12,5 (41 ft 0 in); wing area 31,0 m² (333·7 ft²).
ENGINE One 860 hp M-100A.
WEIGHTS Empty 1830 kg (4034 lb); fuel/oil 380 kg; loaded 2,7 t (5952 lb).
PERFORMANCE (wheels) Max speed 430 km/h (267 mph); cruise 370 km/h (230 mph); service ceiling 8 km (26,250 ft); range with full payload 1000 km (621 miles); landing speed 80 km/h (50 mph).

Aviatourist Smaller edition of Stal-11 intended for long-range racing, with D.H. Comet configuration. Two crew in tandem enclosed cockpit, and two 130 hp Gipsy Major engines on wing of 10,18 m² area. Structure mainly bakelite ply. Airframe ready late 1936, but despite visit to Stag Lane in England engines never received and project eventually abandoned.

Pashinin

Mikhail Mikhailovich Pashinin was unknown until recently. Even now career details lacking, beyond fact he was a deputy designer to Polikarpov on fighters of 1930s. In 1938 combat reports from Spain and Siberian frontier prompted him to plan modern fighter able to dive at highest possible airspeed.

I-21, IP-21 Authorized at Kremlin meeting January 1939; number assigned by NII even though previously used for defunct Ilyushin TsKB-32. Conventional low-wing monoplane, mixed construction. Wing of NACA-0012 (symmetric) profile tapering to 0009 at tip. Wide (3 m) centre section, no dihedral, 30KhGSA steel tube, ribs D16, aluminium-riveted 3/1,75 mm wood-ply skin. Outer panels dihedral and sharp taper, all-wood with ply skin. Forward fuselage welded KhGSA steel tube, removable dural skin panels. Rear fuselage, monocoque of wood *shpon*, 3 mm thick tapering to 1,5 mm over tail surfaces made as one unit. Unarmoured cockpit with hinged canopy. Three retractable landing wheels, each main gear folding to rear with wheel rotating 90° to lie just ahead of split flap. Oil cooler under engine and main radiator under wing on centreline. Carburettor air via wing-root inlets. Intended engine M-107, not developed in time; all known prototypes with M-105 or 105P. First prototype fitted with BT-23 firing through propeller hub, two ShKAS above. Construction finished 1 May 1940, first flight P. M. Stefanovskii 18 May. Despite severe handling problems NII tests began 5 July and continued with four further prototypes all with modifications to improve handling. Second I-21 had taller vertical tail and greater 'sweep' on outer wings. Factory testing shared with S. Suprun who recommended reduced span and greater dihedral; new wing on third aircraft flown January 1941, but NII claimed to notice no improvement. Believed there were variations in armament, height of radiator and arrangement of exhaust stacks. Many details exactly as I-16, and consensus of opinion was that I-16 was safer than I-21! Abandoned April 1941.

DIMENSIONS Span (Shavrov 1 and 2 prototypes) 11,0 m, (3rd prototype) 9,43 m (30 ft 11¼ in); length 8,73 m (28 ft 7¾ in); wing area (long span) 15,8 m² (170 ft²).
ENGINE One 1050 hp M-105P.
WEIGHTS No data except first prototype loaded 2670 kg (5886 lb).
PERFORMANCE Max speed (No 1) 488 km/h at SL, 573 km/h (356 mph) at 5 km, (No 2) 506 km/h at SL, 580 km/h (360 mph) at 4750 m; climb to 5 km (No 1) 6 min; service ceiling (No 1) 10,6 km (34,777 ft); time 360° turn 25/26 s; landing speed (No 1) 165 km/h (102·5 mph).

S-82 Two-seat multi-role attack aircraft with long range and mixed propulsion, schemed 1946 and basis of sudden expansion of Pashinin OKB 1947 onwards. All-metal stressed-skin, low-wing monoplane with powerful piston engine in nose, with two turbochargers (and intended to drive five-blade propeller), and turbojet in rear fuselage with wing-root inlets. Turbojet used only for take-off and combat. Crew in central pressurized tandem cockpits designed by V. B. Shavrov. Heavy armament (details lacking). Prototype construction 1947, but Pashinin did not expand manufacturing strength and in 1948 work abandoned and OKB closed.

DIMENSIONS Span 21,2 m (69 ft 6⅔ in); length 18,0 m (59 ft 0⅔ in); wing area 61,5 m² (662 ft²).
ENGINES One 2000 hp ASh-73TK (two TK-19) and one 2270 kg (5000 lb) thrust RD-45 turbojet.
WEIGHTS Empty about 9 t (19,840 lb); fuel/oil 4400 + 300 kg; loaded 15 t (33,070 lb).
PERFORMANCE Max speed (est) 870 km/h; endurance on piston engine 10 h.

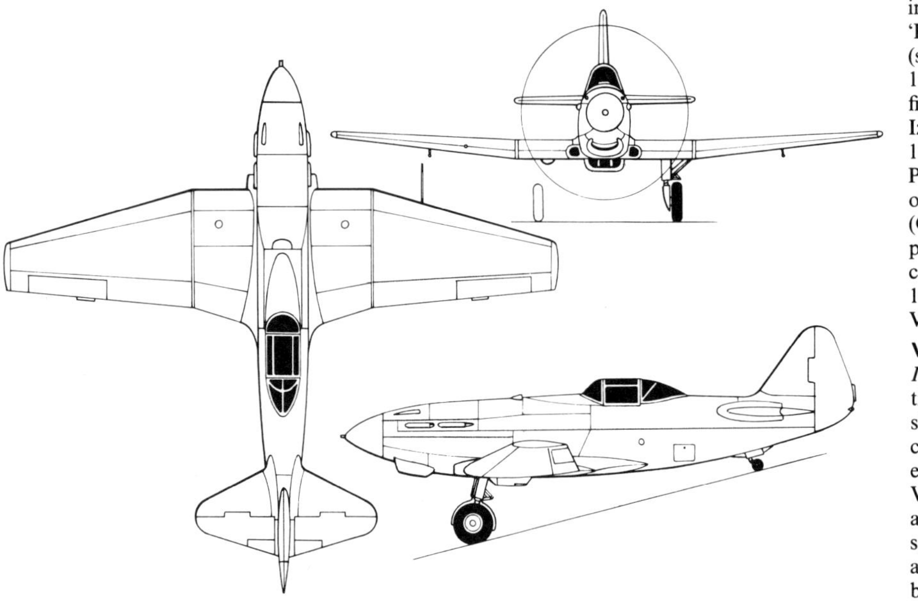

I-21, IP-21

Petlyakov

V. M. Petlyakov

Vladimir Mikhailovich Petlyakov was born 27 July 1891 at Sambek (now Novoshakhtinsk), near Rostov. Studied at Taganrog Tech and from 1911 under Zhukovskii at MVTU, subsequently staying on as lab assistant. Close collaboration with Tupolev but did not join TsAGI until 1921, cutting teeth on numerous (mainly Tupolev) projects including hydroplanes, aerosleighs and airship. Appointed to 1922 committee on Kolchug structures, and from 1923 leader of AGOS brigade responsible for wing design. With Junkers tuition became world leader on light-alloy (Kolchug) wings, and managed wing programme of TB-1, TB-3 and many other AGOS and KOSOS designs prior to 1935. In Tupolev's absence in USA managed entire design of TB-4 and ANT-20, and June 1936 appointed chief designer of ZOK to manage ANT-42 (later Pe-8). Arrested 1937, possibly implicated in charge of assisting Tupolev pass 'Pe-2 type' plans to Germans as basis of Bf 110 (see Tupolev). Imprisoned at TsKB-29, GAZ-156, and assigned task of creating high-altitude fighter as leader of brigade KB-100, with A. M. Izakson as deputy. Aircraft Type 100, later VI-100, led to smashing success with Pe-2 and to Petlyakov's release and reinstatement as leader of OKB July 1940. Based mainly at Kazan (GAZ-125); killed 12 January 1942 when second production Pe-2, used as OKB liaison transport, caught fire in air. A. M. Izakson took over April 1942, soon followed by A. I. Putilov and, in 1943, V. M. Myasishchyev. OKB closed 1946.

VI-100 First assignment of KB-100, *Vysotnyi Istrebitel* (high-altitude fighter) 100. Conventional configuration but extremely advanced design, with turbocharged engines and pressure cabin (by M. N. Petrov's brigade). Stressed-skin except for fabric-covered control surfaces. Wing VVS profile, designation derived from V-series aerofoil at root and VS on outer panels, two spars, Schrenk-type flaps in four sections. These and almost all other movable items positioned by alleged 50-odd electric actuators in extensive 28V DC electrical systems suggested and man-

VI-100

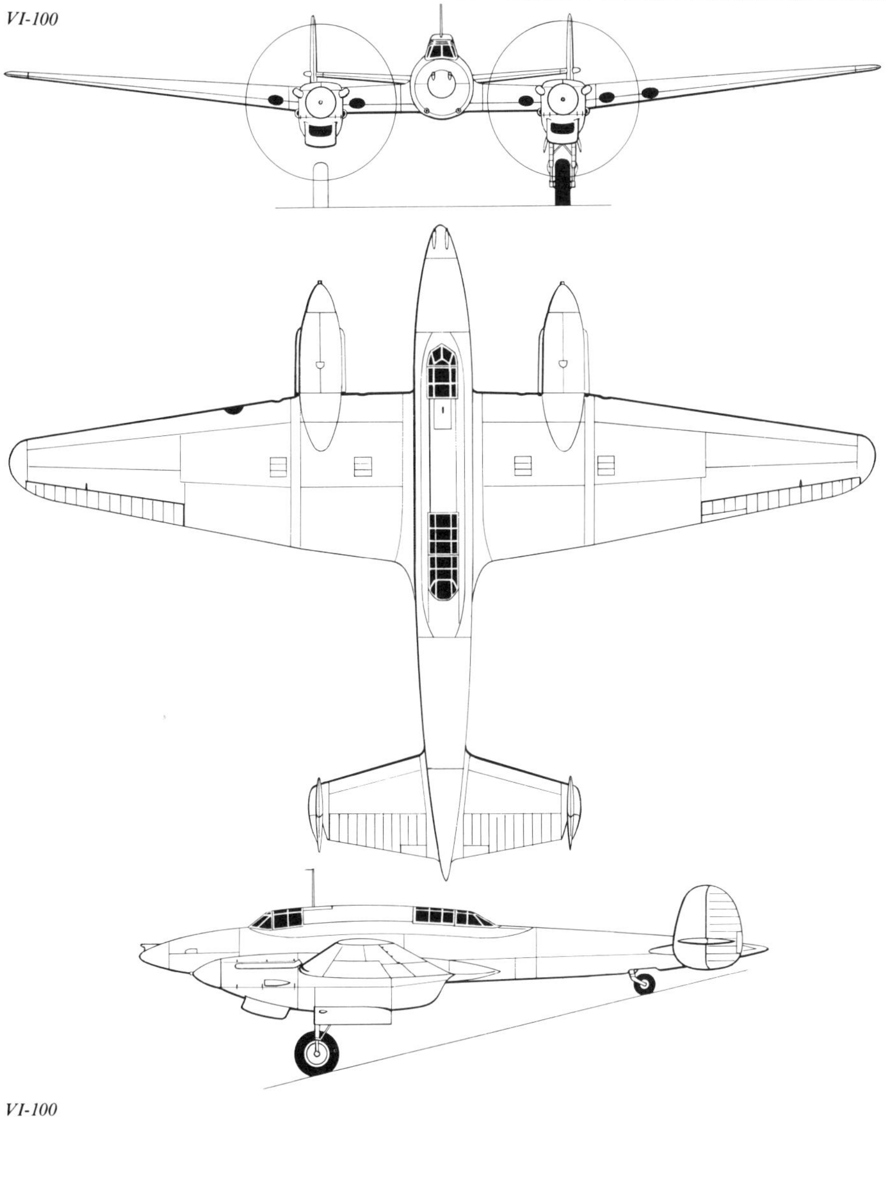

VI-100

aged by K.V. Rogov; no hydraulics. Radiators in ducts inside wing, two per engine, exit in upper surface. Entire nose occupied by four ShVAK with 600 rounds, pressure cabin to rear above leading edge. In event pressure cabin delayed and not installed in prototype, completed instead with widely spaced pilot and observer cockpits, each with rapid emergency escape via ventral hatches also serving as normal entry doors. Single ShKAS in rear cockpit. Impossible to reconcile conflicting reports and three-view drawings which show dissimilar aircraft. Shavrov: VI-100 prototype commenced December 1939, completed quickly and flown April 1940. Another Soviet report: first flown 22 December 1939. Green/Swanborough: first flight 7 May 1939. Only agreement is P.M. Stefanovskii pilot, I.V. Markov flight engineer. Called *Sotka* (little hundred); main problem on first flight incorrect shock-strut damping, resulting in pilot in desperation flinging aircraft at ground in 'pancake' landing after prolonged bouncing (Soviet 'pancake' normally = belly landing). According to Shavrov No 100 flew six weeks, with modified shock struts, including 1 May 1940 flypast over Red Square. No major shortcoming but complex and expensive, and late May decision to build in series as three-seat bomber with even heavier armament; Arkhangyelskii, Ilyushin and Yakovlev gave up engineers to expand KB-100 to 300 personnel. New designation PB-100 (*Pikiruyushchii Bombardirovshchik*, dive bomber). Pressure cabin abandoned, and twin TK-3 turbos replaced by twin TK-2. Petlyakov wanted to retain two separate pressure cabins, but final arrangement seated pilot ahead of wing, optional nav/bomb prone beneath floor, and radio/gunner aft of wing. Two armament schemes, one with four ShKAS in nose and two pairs (above/below) at rear, alternative with two ShVAK (on right) and two ShKAS (on left) under fuselage in shallow box on pivots to angle all four downwards in attack role. Bombload 1 t, 600 kg in internal bay (Shavrov, between; Green/ Swanborough, behind wing spars). According to recent Soviet articles outer wings redesigned with equal taper to adjust c.p. to new CG position. Single PB-100 completed from second VI-100 and flown soon after first, early June 1940 (Green/Swanborough, 22 December 1939). On 23 June decision to mass-produce as Pe-2 with small modifications, without further prototype. July, OKB released from detention; January 1941, Petlyakov awarded State Prize.

DIMENSIONS Span 17,16 m (56 ft 3¾ in); length (excl guns) 12,6 m (41 ft 4 in); wing area 40 m² (431 ft²).

ENGINES (VI) two 1050 hp M-105/2TK-3, (PB) two 1050 hp M-105/2TK-2.

WEIGHTS Loaded (VI) 7260 kg (16,005 lb), (PB) 7200 kg (15,873 lb).

PERFORMANCE Max speed (VI) 630 km/h (391 mph) at 10 km, (PB) 535 km/h (332 mph) at 6 km; speed at SL (both) 455 km/h (283 mph); climb to 5 km (VI) 6 min; (PB) 6·8 min; service ceiling (VI) 12,2 km, (PB) 12 km; range (VI) 1500 km; landing speed 206 km/h (128 mph).

Pe-2 Outstanding tactical bomber, using almost same airframe as PB-100 but with replanned accommodation, M-105R engines without turbos, different nacelles, hydraulic gear retraction, larger vertical tails and improved crew and tank protection. Structure rationalized to reduce construction man-hours. Fuselage skin 1,5/2 mm flush-riveted. Wing with two spars of D16 sheet with 30KhGSA tube booms, pressed ribs, skin 0,6/0,8 mm flush-riveted. Dihedral 7° outer panels only. Schrenk flaps driven electrically to max 45°. Welded-steel Venetian-blind dive brake under each wing with AP-1 (*Avtomat Pikirovaniya*) auto dive control, latter feature later removed and pilot control substituted. D16 tail with fabric movable surfaces, 8° dihedral, elevators +31°/−18°, rudders ±25°. Five rubberized-fabric fuel tanks inerted by cooled exhaust gas. Initially 440 lit (97 gal) fuselage, 180 lit (39·6 gal) each centre section, 143 lit (31·5 gal) each outer panel. Later 518 lit (114 gal) fuselage, others as before, plus two 53 lit (11·6 gal) in wing box in fuselage, plus two 107 lit (23·5 gal) outboard of original outer-wing cells, total 1484 lit (326·5 gal). Comfortable pilot cockpit with large multi-pane canopy housing pilot on left side with walkway and entrance floor hatch with integral steps on right. Nav/bomb swivel seat at rear on right, with hand-aimed ShKAS firing above to rear, moving near target to prone bombing position in nose. Two ShKAS fixed in sides of nose aimed by pilot. Radio/gunner isolated aft of fuselage tank in compartment with roof hatch, two lateral windows and periscopic sight to hand-aimed ShKAS in rear ventral position retracted when not in use. Normal bombload four FAB-100 in compartment between wing spars with two hinged doors. External racks under centre section for four FAB-250. Provision for FAB-100 in rear of each nacelle with twin bomb doors. Landing gear only hydraulic item, main tyres 900 × 300 mm, pneumatic brakes, fully retractable tailwheel with twin doors. First production drawings released to GAZ-22 7 July 1940, first Pe-2 off line flew 18 November 1940. By 22 June 1941 deliveries 458 with about 290 operational. October 1941 GAZ-22 evacuated to Kazan; later GAZ-125 merged to augment output.

Pe-2 became standard tactical bomber of VVS progressively from late April 1941, commonly called *Peshka* (pawn, but meaning also 'little

PB-100

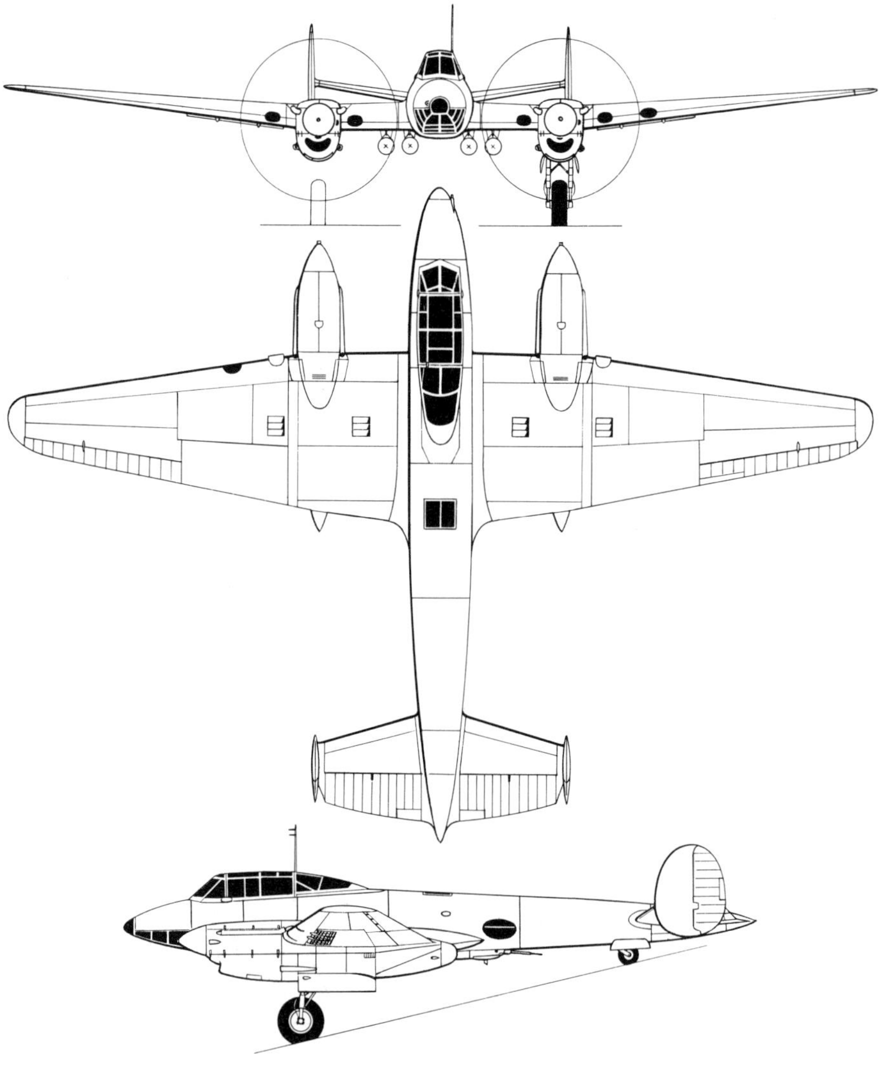

Pe-2 (early production)

Pe'). **Pe-2M** (*) flown October 1941 with VK-105TK engines and internal bay for two/four FAB-500, later automatic slats; soon dropped. **Pe-2Sh** (*Shturmovik*) flown same month with battery of two ShVAK and one UBS under fuselage for ground strafing; later (early 1942) second Sh flown with PB-100 type installation of box housing pairs of guns at front and rear (ShVAK on right, ShKAS on left) all pivoting together to any angle up to −40°. **Pe-3** flown early 1941, day/night interceptor with VK-105RA engines, crew two (pilot/nav both on left side back-to-back) with fuel tanks instead of bombs and heavier gun armament. Prototype (believed February 1941) two ShVAK and two UBS in nose, two UBT aimed by navigator. Also one prototype (called Pe-2) with original nose ShKAS plus two ShVAK and two UBS, plus ventral hatch for UBS and belly gondola for two FAB-100. Decided to produce Pe-3 to intercept bombers, with two ShVAK, two UBS and two ShKAS in nose and MV-3 dorsal turret (one UBT); dive brakes removed. Only 23 built (prior to 22 June 1941) when discontinued. Need for night fighter in late summer met by urgent **Pe-3bis**, modified on Pe-2 production line with one ShVAK, one UBS and three ShKAS in nose, plus combat camera. From early August 1941 some 300 built as alternate aircraft on line. Many later fitted with two ShVAK, three UBS and two ShKAS and some with VK-107A engines. Most with internal bay for three FAB-100 and outer-wing rails for eight RS-82. Some fitted with vert/oblique reconnaissance cameras as **Pe-3R** fighter/reconnaissance with Northern Fleet. January 1942 trials with Pe-2 (no special suffix) with retractable skis, presumably as previously tested on PB-100. **Pe-2MV** with two ShVAK and two UBS firing forwards in belly gondola, no bomb bay but MV-3 turret. Spring 1942 standard aircraft **Pe-2FT** (*Frontovoye Trebovaniye*, front-line request) with MV-3 turret, second ShKAS for radio/gunner (fired through left or right oval beam window which now opened); dive brakes removed, reduced nose glazing, and in 1943 progressively higher proportion with VK-105PF (priority supplied for Yak fighters) as standard. **Pe-2 Paravan** with clumsy nose boom carrying cables for deflecting balloon cables. **Pe-2FZ** (*Frontovoye Zadaniye*, front-line task) with redesigned cockpit and nav in FZ turret (two UBS), no nose accommodation; small series 1943. Pe-2 (no suffix known) flown with ASh-82FN engines, heavier but small gain in speed (547 km/h) and ceiling 9,1 km; also said by Shavrov to have revised wing profile reducing landing speed to 200 km/h. **Pe-2VI** (high-altitude fighter, as in VI-100), another mid-1943 conversion with pressure cabin at last delivered, this time by A.I. Putilov (now head of OKB), and special engine superchargers by V.A. Dollezhal; NII-tested, and basis of further developments (see Myasishchyev). Pe-2s flown in 1943 with various field modifications, especially to armament. **Pe-3M** two-seat fighter 1943 with PF engines, 700 kg bombs as well as two ShVAK, three BS and two DAG-10; 545 km/h. **Pe-2S/Pe-2UT/UPe-2** flown July 1943 and made in large numbers; instructor cockpit with poor view in place of fuselage tanks, retaining full bombload and in many cases even having two UBS as well as two ShKAS firing ahead. **Pe-2B** many structural and systems improvements, three UBT and one

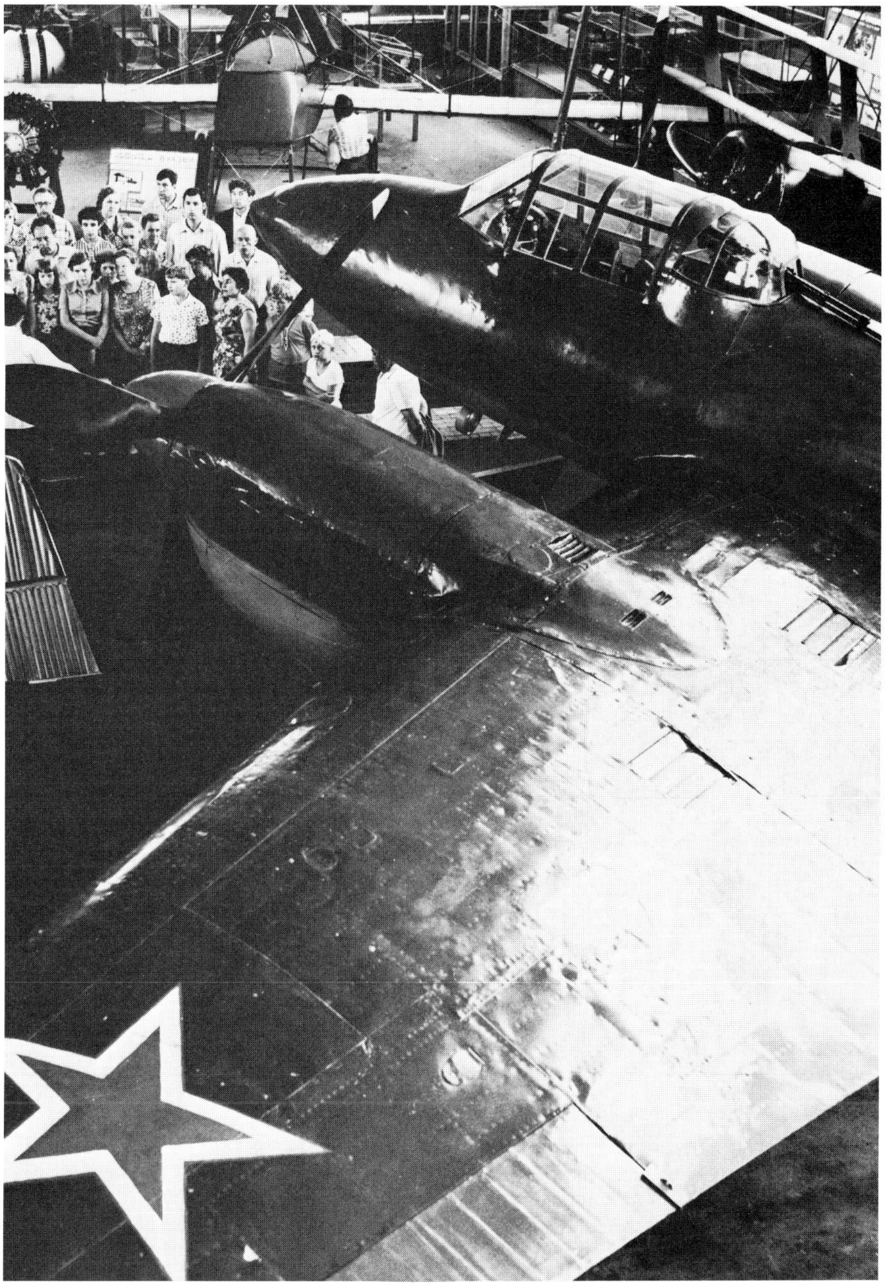

Pe-2 FT in Monino museum

Pe-2VI

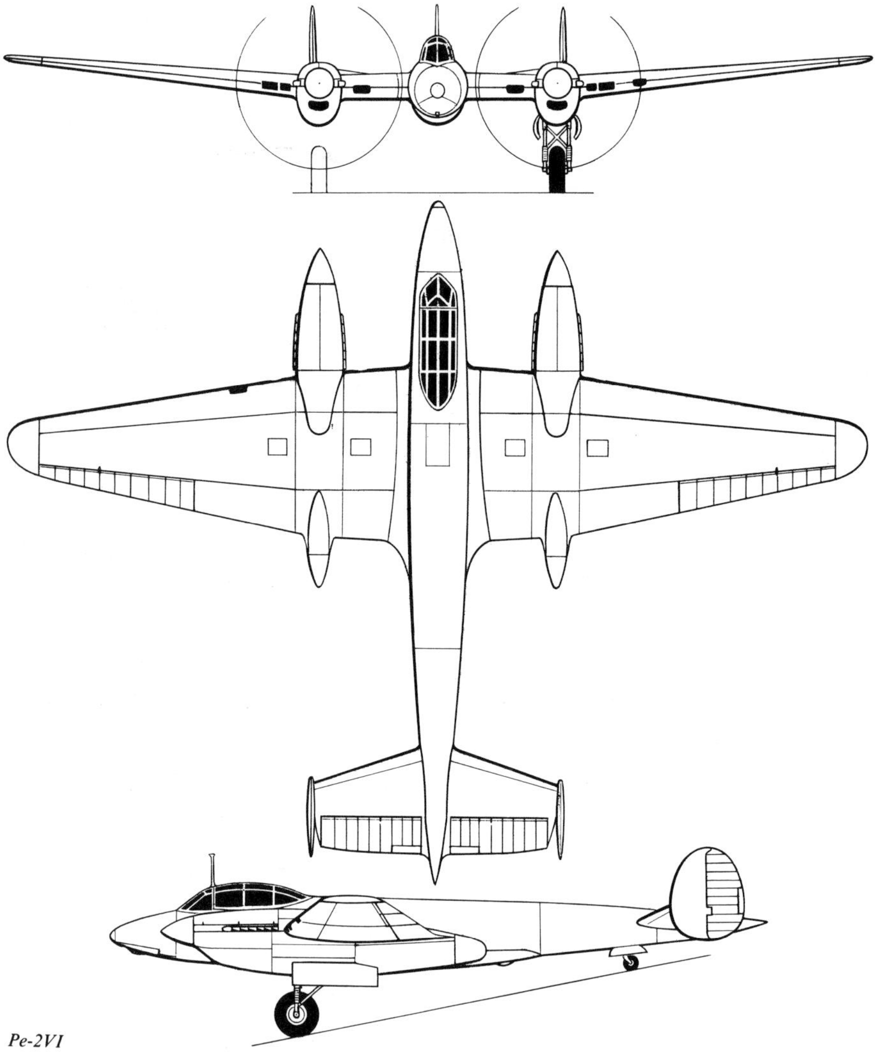

Pe-2VI

ShKAS, increased weight, tested late 1943 and in production as standard bomber 1944. **Pe-2R** (*) three-seat day reconnaissance with three/four cameras, three BS, PF engines, 580 km/h at 7603 kg and good climb despite extra tankage. **Pe-2R** (**) likewise 1944, VK-107A, three ShVAK, long-range (2000 km) tanks, 630 km/h. **Pe-2K** with wings, nacelles and landing gear of Pe-2I, and PF-1 engines. **Pe-2RD** with Korolyev/Glushko RD-1 rocket in tail, tested 1943–1945. (Projected Pe-3RD with RD-1 in each nacelle, 785 km/h fighter, incomplete.) **Pe-2D** three-seat bomber with VK-107A engines, three BT and one DAG-10, 600 km/h at 8750 kg in September 1944. **Pe-2M** (**) also September 1944 with VK-107A, 2 t bombload and three ShVAK with 520 rounds, 9400 kg yet 630 km/h. Never built, **Pe-2DV** with increased span, extra fuel, ASh-82 engines and pressure cabin.

Under Myasishchyev, **Pe-2I** followed Pe-2VI as two-seat bomber; new airframe with mid-wing NACA 23012, 18 m span, deep bomb bay for 1 t, 1 t also under centre section, one UB in nose and one in tailcone with limited aiming by nav back-to-back with pilot. VK-107A engines, 3 t fuel, superb aerodynamic finish, speed in May 1944 656 km/h at 8983 kg, ceiling 11 km, range 2275 km. Production planned but abandoned early 1945.

Total Pe-2 series output 11,427, completed first quarter 1945. Many post-war modifications. Czech designation, **B-32**; UT = CB-32.

DIMENSIONS Span 17,16 m (56 ft 3⅔ in), (from 2FT onwards) 17,11 m (56 ft 1⅔ in); length (standard) 12,78 m (41 ft 11 in); height (standard) 3,42 m (11 ft 2⅔ in); wing area 40,5 m^2 (436 ft^2).

ENGINES (2, 3) two 1100 hp M-105RA, (most) two 1260 hp VK-105PF, (I, M**) two 1650 hp VK-107A.

WEIGHTS Empty (initial 2) 5950 kg, (FT, typical) 6200 kg; fuel (2) 1070 kg; max (2) 7536 kg (16,614 lb), (FT) 8520 kg (18,783 lb).

PERFORMANCE Max speed (SL, typical of all) 450 km/h (280 mph), (2) 540 km/h (336 mph) at 5 km, (FT) 580 km/h (360 mph) at 4 km, (UT) 508 km/h at 3,6 km; climb to 5 km (2) 9·3 min; service ceiling (2) 8,8 km (28,870 ft); range with 1 t bombs (2) 1315 km (817 miles); landing speed 230/240 km/h (about 146 mph).

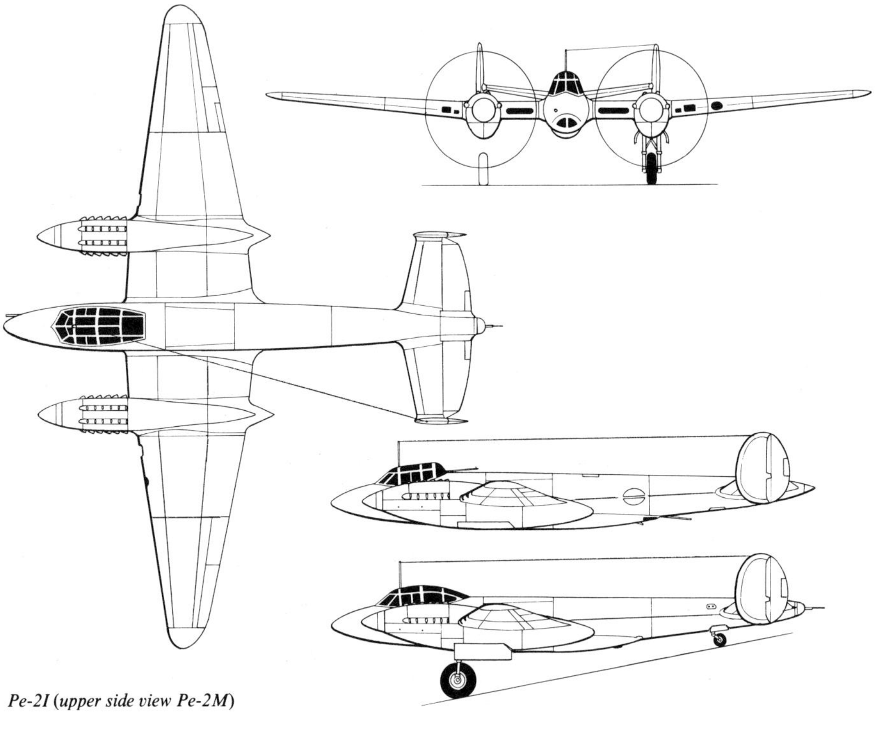

Pe-2I (upper side view Pe-2M)

Pe-8, ANT-42, TB-7 Only Soviet heavy bomber of Second World War. Requirement for successor to TB-3 issued mid-1934, in parallel with rival DB-A and much larger TB-6. Basic KOSOS concept by A.N. Tupolev as conventional stressed-skin aircraft similar in size to TB-3 but with central ATsN (*Agregat Tsentral-novo Nadduva*) supercharger installation in fuselage feeding four wing engines. Work assigned to Petlyakov brigade, with co-ordinating design role by Iosif Fomich Nyezval.

Ruling structural material D16 duralumin, general form as SB (ANT-40) with same stress limits and factors but twice linear scale. Main exception, two wing spars of trad Petlyakov truss-girder type but for first time made from 30KhGSA. Basic method rolled strip re-rolled to U-section and assembled by bolts, rivets and some welding; truss ribs, stringers and secondary structure entirely riveted. Wing profile TsAGI-40, root t/c 19%, tip 15·5. Mean chord 5,35 m, CG at 28·4% empty and up to 34% loaded. Fuselage oval section with main longerons tubular including four of 30 KhGSA; rest con-

Pe-8 at Tealing, Scotland, 20 May 1942

ventional D16 riveted structure with all exterior riveting round- or pan-head. First use of large plastic templates in lofting, and tooling more extensive than on any previous Soviet aircraft. Fabric-covered flight-control surfaces, all manual and with trim tabs on rudder and both elevators. Sharply tapering split flaps driven hydraulically to 45°. Long-span ailerons carried on eight brackets on underside of wing. Main gears with 1600 × 500 mm tyres retracting hydraulically to rear, with bay closed by twin doors leaving part of tyre showing; fixed tailwheel with tyre 700 × 300 mm. Fuel in protected tanks of welded AMts aluminium, originally 18 between spars and in leading edge all outboard of fuselage. In production aircraft extra 1440 lit (317 gal) tank in centre section bringing total to 15 600 lit (3432 gal), over 50% more than Lancaster. Engine cooling system self-contained in each nacelle with radiator beneath each engine. Three-blade Hamilton-derived VISh-2 constant-speed propeller of 3,9 m diam. Exhaust from each cylinder bank piped to single stack discharging above wing. Large internal bomb bay beneath wing with two doors driven hydraulically on swinging links. Two flare chutes in rear fuselage. Two pilots in tandem at upper level on left of centreline with passageway on right to steps leading to glazed nose with very large ventral gondola for bomb-aimer.

First ANT-42 completed 9 November 1936, lacking ATsN installation and armament and with twin bracing wires from tailplane to fin on each side. Fuel capacity in this prototype 8,25 t, bombload 5 t (overload including two 500 kg under inner wings), equipped empty weight 18 t. First flight M.M. Gromov 27 December 1936, using wheel landing gear (retractable skis later). Damaged in heavy landing (different pilot) but GAZ tests completed 20 March 1937. NII testing 11 August/28 October 1937. Nemecek: ATsN fitted between GAZ and NII tests; Green/Swanborough no ATsN until ATsN-2 installed after October 1937, second series (GAZ/NII in parallel) trials being flown 6 March/30 April 1938. Rudder horn balance replaced by deeply inset hinges. Engine cooling system redesigned with both engines on each side cooled by two staggered radiators in single duct under inboard engine, with upper/lower exit shutters in nacelle wall downstream. Large ATsN-2 blocked off upper deck on right side behind pilots, with ram inlet handling entire airflow for four engines, single large blower driven from M-100 by step-up gears (25,000 rpm caused bearing problems), and aluminium pipes feeding air to engines. Single exhaust stack emerged from blister on right side of fuselage. Best speed 403 km/h at 8 km, intended adequate to avoid interception. By this time Petlyakov in detention and programme managed by Nyezval; main VVS proponents also removed, Marshal Tukhachyevskii executed and Gen Alksnis died in prison. Nevertheless second prototype ANT-42 authorized early 1936 and flown 26 July 1938. Many improvements including full armament. MV electric dorsal and tail turrets each with one ShKAS and 200 rounds; tail traverse ±60°, elevation ±60°, dorsal 360° traverse and elevation +60°/−20° (max depression firing diagonally). Nose turret single (later twin) ShKAS, no data. Elec turret in rear of each inboard nacelle with single BT with 220 rounds, access via crawlway from fuselage and emergency escape via roof hatch. Tailplane braced each side by single cable. Engines of FRNV type with all four radiators inboard. ATsN-2 driven by M-100A instead of M-100. Added centre-section fuel tank. Normal bomb load six FAB-100 or four FAB-250 with full fuel; overload two FAB-2000. Better tank protection, and 9 mm armour to pilot seats and some other areas. Crew 11 including five gunners.

Pre-series of five aircraft authorized April 1937, but increasing disinterest in heavy bombers culminated in Kremlin meeting to halt programme early 1939. Aleksandr Filin, chief NII-VVS, succeeded in reversing decision and production authorized as TB-7 at GAZ-22. Main further change rejection of ATsN installation, requiring substitution of supercharged AM-35 main engines. Other changes twin nose guns, redesigned nose with no ventral gondola but extensive ventral and side glazing, twin aerial masts (nose and amidships) canted to left, new amidships compartment for commander and radio operator with two left-side windows, later MV-6 dorsal turret with large fairing (retracted by handcrank) surrounding stowed gun, deeper rear fuselage with side door, unbraced tailplane mounted lower on fuselage, and VISh-24 constant-speed propellers. One report states airframe de-icing, no details. Tanks given additional rubber protection and inerted by piping in cooled exhaust. Normal equipment two radios, intercom, beacon receiver and D/F loop. Max fuel 13,12 t in 19 tanks. Deliveries from May 1940, five (pre-production) with AM-35, subsequently AM-35A.

Nyezval sought alternative engines and examples flew with AM-37, M-105, M-82 (ASh-82) and mix of two AM-37 and two M-82. October 1940 decision to standardize on ACh-40 diesel, without change in designation, trading

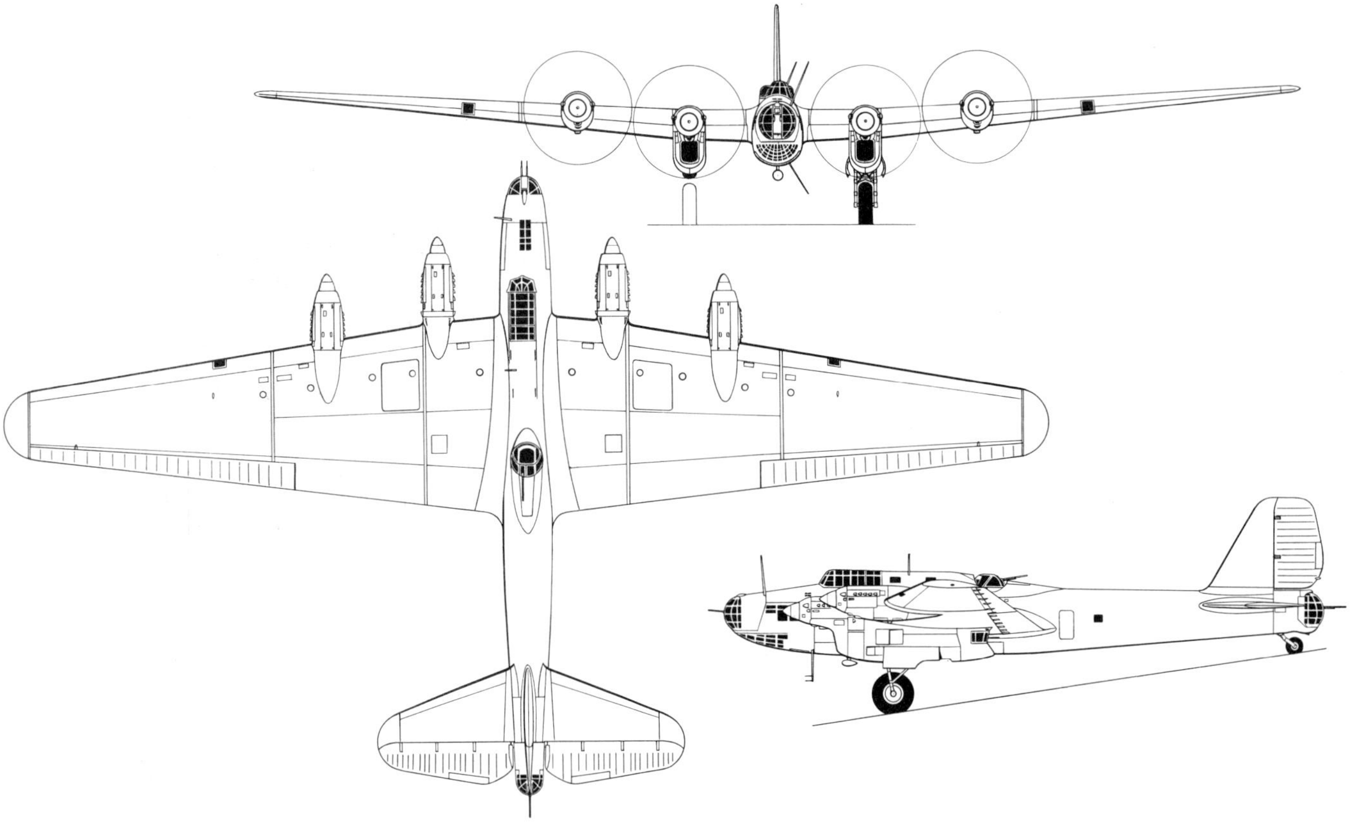

Pe-8 with AM-35A engines

flight performance for much enhanced range/endurance, original objective of speed/height giving immunity to interception being recognized as no longer attainable. Severe engine unreliability, not improved by switch to production version of related engine designated ACh-30B (regarded as not ready for production by Charomskii engine KB). Production continued at low rate with AM-35A, designation switching to Pe-8 in 1941. VVS formed 332 BAON (special-purpose bomber regt) May 1941; CO, Maj (Col in July 1941) V.I. Lebedyev, tracked down locations of bombers (24 delivered) and had them re-engined with diesels. Despite severe engine problems unit became operational as 412 Avn Regt of newly formed 81st Air Div, under Brig (later Maj-Gen) M.V. Vodopyanov, who led attack on Berlin night of 7/8 August 1941. Of 18 made ready, one crashed from engine failure after take-off, one was shot down by friendly fighters/flak on outward journey, at least three had engine-failure prior to target, 11 bombed Berlin, and six regained base (Pushkino), one after forced landing and refilling tanks with buckets! All others made forced landings with engine failure. This terminated diesel conversions, and accelerated switch to ASh-82. GAZ-22 evacuated October 1941 and production abandoned at this point at 79th aircraft. Last 25 (Green/Swanborough, last dozen or so) examples had pointed nose with hand-aimed ShVAK. By end of 1942 at least 48 re-engined with ASh-82FN, retaining deep inner nacelle with turret at rear even though main radiators removed. Single aircraft (said to be No 66, but original nose and still with AM-35A), flew Moscow/Murmansk/Tealing/Prestwick/Reykyavik/Washington and back on 19 May/13 June 1942 on diplomatic mission, first Soviet aircraft seen in West since 1937. Surviving aircraft, ultimately nearly all with ASh-82FN, intensively used in close-support night bombing and occasional strategic attacks, from February 1943 with FAB-5000NG bomb (11,023 lb) for special point targets. CO was A.E. Golovanov, former chief pilot GVF and later Col-Gen and first commander of ADD when formed 5 March 1942.

Post-war about 30 Pe-8 used as special trials aircraft, engine testbeds and, often civil-registered and sometimes on skis, with several Aeroflot directorates. Two played central role in setting up *Nordpol* Arctic station 1952, finally bringing expedition home in non-stop 5000-km flight to Moscow. None preserved, but 1980 discovery of little-damaged specimen near Khatanga has prompted restoration for eventual exhibition at Monino.

DIMENSIONS Span (ANT-42) 39,01 m (127 ft 11¾ in), (production) 39,1 m (128 ft 3¼ in); length (ANT-42) 23,4 m (76 ft 9¼ in), (production) 23,59 m (77 ft 4¾ in); height 6,2 m (20 ft 4 in); wing area (ANT-42) 188,4 m² (2,028 ft²), (production) 188,68 m² (2031 ft²).

ENGINES (ANT-42) four 930 hp M-34FRN + 850 hp M-100A driving ATsN, (production) four 1350 hp AM-35A; conversions to 1500 hp ACh-30B and 1700 hp M-82/ASh-82FN.

WEIGHTS Empty (ANT-42) 18 t (39,680 lb), (production) 18 420 kg (40,608 lb); fuel/oil (production) 13 120 + 670 kg; max loaded (ANT-42) 32 t (70,547 lb), (production) 31 420 kg (69,268 lb); ASh-82FN and 5 t bomb 36 t (79,365 lb).

PERFORMANCE Max speed at height (ANT-42) 403 km/h (250 mph) at 8 km, (production) 427 km/h (265 mph) at 6360 m, (ACh) 393 km/h, (ASh-82) 450 km/h (280 mph) at 9 km; climb to 5 km (production) 14·6 min; service ceiling (ANT-42) 11 km, (production) 8,4 km (27,560 ft); range with 2 t bombs (production) 4700 km (2920 miles) (ASh, about same with 4 t bombs), (ACh) 7820 km (4849 miles); take-off (production) 2,3 km at max wt over 15 m screen; landing 580 m/165 km/h (102 mph).

Polikarpov

Nikolai Nikolayevich Polikarpov was, with Tupolev, most famous Soviet designer before the Second World War. In general he concentrated on small aircraft, while Tupolev built large ones; in particular Polikarpov created roughly 99% of Soviet trainer, fighter and reconnaissance aircraft up to 1941. Born 8 July 1892 at Georgyevsk (now Livensk) east of Saratov. Graduated as mech and aero engineer early 1916 from St Petersburg Poly Inst, working until 1918 at Russo-Baltic Wagon Works (RBVZ) on IMs and other aircraft. In turmoil of civil war only surviving aircraft factory was former Duks plant, subsequently GAZ-1, whence Polikarpov went in 1918 and was appointed chief engineer. Supervised Spad S.VII production and then conversion of D.H.9a into important R-1 programme. First original design IL-400/I-1 (1922).

N.N. Polikarpov

R-1

In 1926 appointed Director of OSS, with V.M. Olkhovskii deputy and including many later famous such as P. F. Fedorov, A.A. Dubrovin, M.M. Shishmaryev, V.V. Nikitin, V.P. Yatsenko, A.G. Brunov, S.O. Zonshain, M.K. Tikhonravov, V.P. Nyevdachin, V.F. Savelyev, I.V. Venyevidov, L.D. Kolpakov-Miroshnichyenko, K.A. Petrov, S.A. Kochyerigin and A.A. Krylov. Wrote *The Manoeuvrability of Powerful Fighters* (1927). In 1929 arrested and, with his staff, set to work (alongside Grigorovich and his staff) in Hangar 7 at GAZ-39, pioneering VT 'internal prison' type of design office. Created I-5 but not released until 1933, when sent to GAZ-36 as chief landplane designer of TsKB. Following immense success of U-2, R-5, I-15 and I-16, numerous crashes of later prototypes brought retribution to colleagues, but Polikarpov enjoyed Stalin's protection and was still at desk when collapsed and died 30 July 1944. Soon afterwards U-2 redesignated Po-2 in his honour, but OKB abruptly shut with important projects incomplete.

R-1, R-2 Possibly fair to regard as first mass-produced aircraft of Soviet Union, derived by Polikarpov from D.H.4 and D.H.9. Several flyable examples of both, captured 1917–1921, and greatly admired. Embryonic VVF clamoured for more, and Polikarpov's main task at Duks factory from late 1918 was examining D.H.4 and preparing Russian drawings. No Rolls-Royce engines, so designed installation of Fiat A-12 (240 hp) and oversaw production of 20 examples 1920–1921. In 1922 Polikarpov switched to D.H.9a type airframe, powered by captured Mercedes D.IV(a) (260 hp), receiving designation R-1 (*Razvyedchik*, recon, type 1); 100 built 1922–1923, some dozens using British (Airdisco) airframes purchased as job lot. By 1923 Duks factory organized as GAZ-1 and in 1923–1924 delivered 130 R-2 (also written R-II) with 220 hp Siddeley Puma. By early 1924 Polikarpov had completed design of definitive R-1 with numerous detail improvements, powered by M-5 (copy of Liberty 12) and normally armed with fixed Vickers (PV-1) with 200 rounds, single (sometimes twin) DA in rear cockpit with 500 rounds and up to 400 kg (882 lb) bombs. Data below for this standard R-1, of which 2800 produced by GAZ-1 and GAZ-10 by 1931, outnumbering all other Soviet aircraft of period. Despite superior R-3 (ANT-3) R-1 continued mass-production because approx half as costly. Many famous flights, notably M.M. Gromov with M.A. Volkovoinov Moscow–Pekin 10 June/13 July 1925 with other aircraft including an R-2. Batch of 20 with 240 hp BMW IVa. Polikarpov also designed twin-float **MR-1**, with wooden floats, 124 built 1927–1928, in addition to prototype **PM-2** (R-1 with Myuntsel all-metal floats, 1927).

DIMENSIONS Span 14,02 m (46 ft 0 in); length 9,24 m (30 ft 3¾ in); wing area 44,54 m² (479 ft²).
ENGINE One 400 hp M-5.
WEIGHTS Empty 1450 kg (3197 lb); fuel/oil 327 + 40 kg; loaded 2200 kg (4850 lb).
PERFORMANCE Max speed 185 km/h (115 mph); climb to 1 km, 4·5 min; service ceiling 5 km; range 700 km (435 miles)/5 h; take-off 250 m; landing speed 90 km/h.

IL-400, I-1 Prime need of VVF was for fighter, and especially for national design capability. Project for Soviet single-seat fighter begun early 1922 at about time factory organized as GAZ No 1. Polikarpov decided to use Liberty engine (later made as M-5) and unbraced low-wing monoplane configuration. Assistance by I.M. Kostkin, head of technical section at GAZ-1, and A.A. Popov, head of manufacturing. Wooden construction with four main fuselage longerons, secondary fairings giving rounded top/bottom and 3/5-mm ply covering; wing with two box spars, lattice ribs and ply back to front spar, fabric elsewhere. Aerofoil RAF-derived, 20% root and 15% tip, set at −3° and with zero-lift angle of −7°. D.H.9a radiator and propeller. Wire-braced main gears and curved tube skids to protect wingtips. First flight 23 August 1923 (Shavrov, May); K.K. Artseulov could not prevent aircraft rearing up to about 20 m, with stall and fall in flat attitude. Discovered c.g. much too far aft (52% MAC) and aircraft redesigned as **IL-400B** or **IL-400bis**. New wing of same span but reduced area (Shavrov, increased span and area) with different section only 16/10% thick and with sheet ribs and covering of 0,8 mm Kolchug aluminium with beaded corrugations (possibly in line with ribs); probably this covering back to front spar only, but no information. Likewise redesigned horizontal tail, in-

MR-1

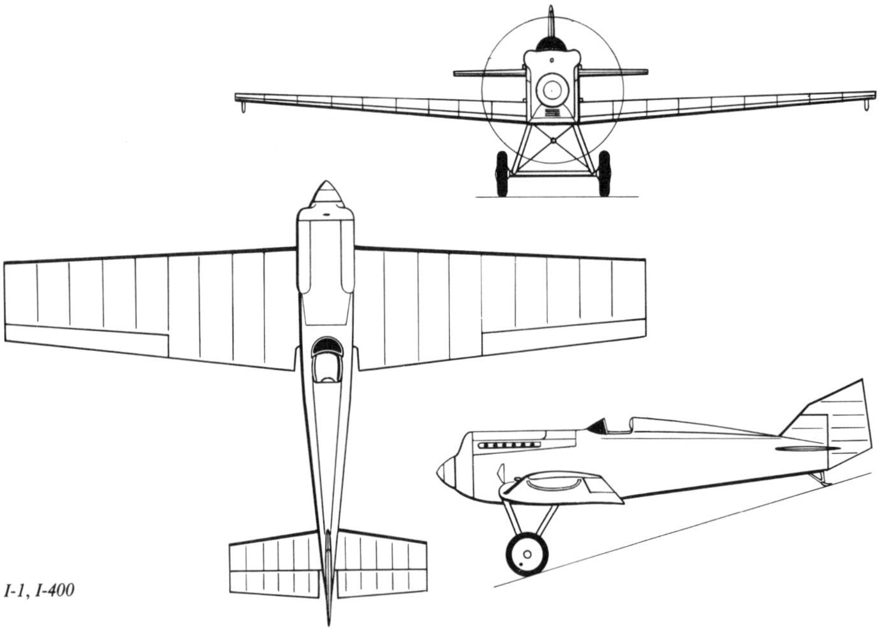

I-1, I-400

creased area and same metal skin. Engine moved forward, and frontal radiator replaced by ventral Lamblin. First flight spring 1924; following tests by A.I. Zhukov and A.N. Yetkatov, IL-400B passed for production as I-1. Next aircraft still a prototype, metal skins replaced by plywood and static tests carried out to establish safe factor of 10. Lamblin replaced by deep honeycomb radiator obliquely under nose, two PV guns mounted on forward fuselage (location apparently not recorded) and fuel tanks (plural) welded from Kolchug following discovery of suitable flux by alloy's inventors (see materials section). Total 33 I-1 ordered, but much variation; even first 13 had three variants, and welded tankage soon dropped. All 33 sent to NOA where prolonged tests showed recovery from spin often difficult; 23 June 1927 M.M. Gromov escaped by parachute first time in USSR, while A.I. Sharapov later in 1927 hit ground in flat spin and survived by sheer luck. Thus, though fast and in many respects advanced fighter, I-1 never in VVF service.

DIMENSIONS Span 10,8 m (35 ft $5\frac{1}{4}$ in); length (400) believed 7,3 m (23 ft $11\frac{1}{3}$ in), (400B) believed about 8 m (26 ft 3 in); wing area 20 m^2 (215 ft^2).

ENGINE One 400 hp M-5.

WEIGHTS (400B) Empty 1112 kg (2451 lb); fuel/oil 230 kg; loaded (Shavrov) 1510 kg (3329 lb), (Něměcek) 1530 kg.

PERFORMANCE Max speed 264 km/h (164 mph); climb to 1 km, 1·9 min; service ceiling 6750 m (22,150 ft); range 650 km (404 miles)/ 2·5 h; take-off 7s; landing speed 105 km/h.

PM-1, P-2 Need for Soviet transport prompted this beautifully executed sesquiplane, basic design of which was due to Aleksandr Aleksandrovich Syemyenov. All-wood construction; monocoque fuselage of glued *shpon* with integral fin, two-spar wings attached above and below main fuselage frames and joined by single streamlined I-type interplane struts, fabric covering aft of front spars and on movable control surfaces. Open cockpit for pilot (room for co-pilot but believed seat not installed) and comfortable cabin for five passengers (believed two pairs plus single at rear). Honeycomb water radiator extended by hand wheel and chain on sliding mounts ahead of main gears. Aircraft completed after three months' work and named PM-1 (*Passazhirskii* Maybach). First flight A.I. Zhukov 10 June 1925 (same day as start of group flight to Pekin in which PM-1 had hoped to participate). No problems, and all tests soon completed. Production of ten begun for Deruluft, and after public demo 26 July first PM-1 flew to Leningrad and in early August began service Moscow/Berlin. On one of first Deruluft flights suffered crash in Germany due to (Shavrov) engine shut-down, (Něměcek) structural failure of engine mount. Decided Maybach was outdated engine, aircraft not repaired, series cancelled, Kalinin monoplanes showing more promise.

DIMENSIONS Span 15,5 m (50 ft $10\frac{1}{4}$ in); length 11,0 m (36 ft 1 in); wing area 38,5 m^2 (414 ft^2).

ENGINE One 260 hp Maybach IVa.

WEIGHTS Empty 1380 kg (3042 lb), (Něměcek 1350 kg); fuel/oil 440 kg; loaded 2360 kg (5203 lb).

PERFORMANCE Max speed 180 km/h (112 mph), (Něměcek, 170); climb to 1 km, 8 min; service ceiling 4,1 km (13,450 ft); range 1200 km (746 miles), (Něměcek 800 km); take-off 22 s; landing 15 s/90 km/h (56 mph).

2I-N1, DI-1 Designations from 2-seat fighter, Napier No 1 and, later, two-seat (*Dvukhmyestnyi*) fighter No 1. Outstanding aircraft in both aerodynamic and structural design, and powered by most impressive available imported engine. Fuselage monocoque of glued *shpon*, oval section with multiple layers built up to thickness 4 mm over forward section tapering to 2 mm at tail. This fuselage by Vladimir Denisov, specialist in wooden monocoques through VT prison period and into late 1930s. Sesquiplane wings without internal bracing wires, with two wooden spars, ribs of 3-mm ply with large lightening

PM-1, P-2

holes capped by ply strips 23-mm wide, plus multiple stringers 10 × 10 mm, with 1,5-mm ply skin. Only known photo shows single V interplane strut (suggesting single spar in bottom wings) but in Shavrov's book this photo crudely retouched to show in addition two parallel diagonal struts in Warren style linking lower wing (apparently at junction of interplane strut) to top of cabane struts; no reason known for this artistic addition. All struts streamlined sections in Kolchug alloy, with steel Rafwires for external bracing. Aerofoil to fair main-gear axle; aircraft also flown with braced skis. Shavrov states aircraft well-designed and also on vibration (first time in USSR); meaning not apprehended; it was static-tested, but vibration/resonance testing was then unknown. One fixed PV and one DA on ring mount in rear cockpit. First flight 12 January 1926, excellent; Polikarpov as observer on flight 4 and flight 8 (ceiling climb). On flight 9, 31 March 1926, V.N. Filippov, with test observer V.V. Mikhailov, made speed runs over measured kilometre at Central Airfield. At max speed at 100 m covering ripped off right upper wing, upper surface first, then lower; lower right wing then also collapsed. Both crew killed. Cause eventually judged to be bad glueing of skin, with large areas of rib cap and stringer not glued at all, and many panel pins had missed underlying structure. Omission of bradawl holes in skin (usual practice to enable internal pressure to balance that outside) had resulted in pressurization on ceiling climb, forcing skin off wing, suction at high speed finally pulling it off. The crash of such advanced aircraft shocked entire industry, six months elapsing before resumption of designing and with many subsequent aircraft (I-3, U-2, DI-2 and even R-5) being over-strength.

DIMENSIONS (Shavrov) 12,0 m (39 ft 4½ in), (Něměcek) 11,5 m (37 ft 8¾ in); length (Shavrov) 9,75 m (32 ft 0 in), (Něměcek) 8,62 m (28 ft 3⅓ in); wing area (Shavrov) 27,15 m^2 (292 ft^2), (Něměcek) 27,7.

ENGINE One 450 hp Napier Lion.

WEIGHTS Empty 1153 kg (2542 lb); fuel/oil 547 kg; loaded 1,7 t (3748 lb).

PERFORMANCE Max speed 268 km/h (166·5 mph); climb to 1 km, 1·8 min; service ceiling 7,1 km (23,300 ft); range 800 km (500 miles)/3 h; time turn 360°, 12 s; take-off 100 m/7 s; landing 200 m/16 s/92 km/h.

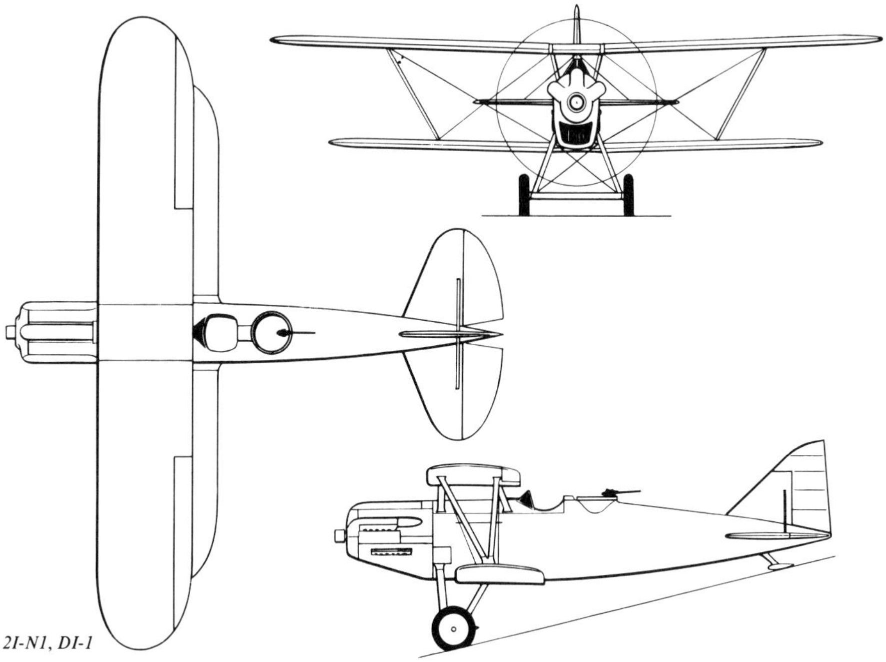

2I-N1, DI-1

Po-2 (Jugoslav, circa 1951)

U-2, Po-2 Though not famous outside the Soviet Union, this aircraft was possibly built in greater numbers in more variants than any other in history. Designed as simple biplane trainer, its robust reliability led to adaptation to countless other duties and continued production 1927–1944 in USSR, 1948–1953 in Poland and assembly from parts in USSR up to at least 1959. Number of recorded variants including one-off modifications exceeds 80, and total number built estimated at 29,000/41,000 (no accurate figure possible but between these limits).

In 1926 VVF used assortment of aircraft as trainers in addition to U-1, and wished to establish single Soviet type with reliable engine around which uniform syllabus could be written. As newly appointed head of OSS, Polikarpov instructed to build required aircraft. Emphasis on simplicity and cheapness resulted in compromised design in which aerodynamics and performance played little part. Long project definition with NTK UVVS (S.V. Ilyushin) resulted

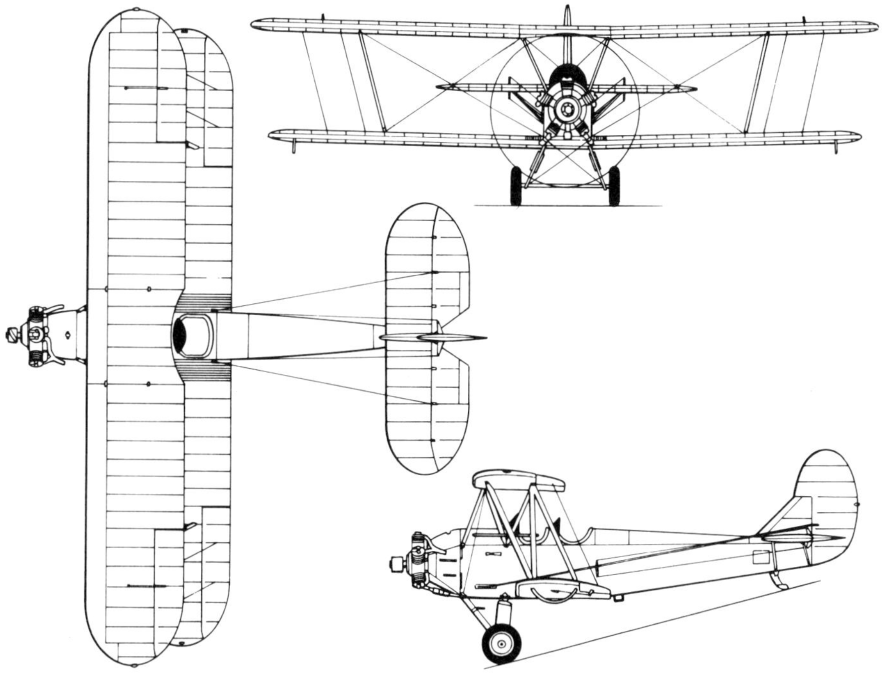

U-2, Po-2 (typical production 1935–1945)

Typical M-11 engine-installation in Po-2

in decision to use new M-11 engine, to eliminate previously important training stage of prolonged taxiing exercises in aircraft with wing skin removed, and to make maximum use of concept of interchangeable parts. Decision to follow U-2 phase with more powerful P-2 intermediate trainer led to stipulated speed not exceeding 120 km/h. Result was ugly single-bay biplane with four identical rectangular wings (upper span greater because of centre section) each 14% thick with constant-section spars, all ribs identical, and same hinged surface used as rudder, elevators and ailerons. This prototype, later called **TPK** (thick wing section), completed about February 1927. Tough and simple, but performance so poor it became a problem (speed reached 142 km/h, but climb to 1 km took 11·5 min, and to 2 km 29 min), and payload could not exceed 120 kg. Static tests showed excessive factor of 17.

Aircraft completely redesigned to have efficient structure without such emphasis on simplicity. Wings with rounded tips, all wings still interchangeable but of 8·1% TsAGI-541 profile resembling Clark Y with flat underside. Pine box spars, ply ribs and caps, rectangular strip stringers and leading-edge rib caps, and fabric covering. Fuselage pine truss with wire bracing, front part covered with removable 1 mm ply panels mainly held by screws, rear with fabric. Periphery of wings and tail surfaces dural tube, tail ribs ply, fabric covering. All struts originally streamlined-section dural tube, later (probably in 1929) replaced for cheapness by round mild-steel tube with downstream fairing of wood attached by doped fabric. Tailplane normally braced by two struts with screwed end-fittings adjustable for length. Rotating Y-forked bolt on fin spar enabled tailplane incidence to be altered on ground. All fittings mild steel, and casein glue used throughout. Engine hung on large ring stamped from dural plate 4-mm thick held on steel pipes with pinned forked end-fittings. In 1930 changed to copy of Sh-2 engine mount (made at same plant) of simple welded steel tubing. Pin-jointed main gears with rear struts sprung by 16 m on each leg of 13-mm bungee; spoked wheels with 700 × 120 mm tyres. Ash tail-skid joined to rudder by twin torque-springs. Skis, main 2200 × 334 × 264 mm, tail 500 × 204 mm. Engine, originally in streamlined cowl leaving cylinders only exposed, in production U-2 completely exposed but with four panels to rear held by cable and spring and released almost instantly for access to rear of engine. Many variations, and crankcase often covered by locally made cowl in winter.

First improved U-2 flown by M.M. Gromov 7 January 1928. Acclaimed for good qualities, especially positive longitudinal stability and absence of vices. Spun only with difficulty, and immediately recovered by releasing or centring stick (not necessarily good quality in primary aircraft). Prototype on skis completed state tests in ten days; then exhibited at Berlin. Series production 1930 at new *Krasnyi Lyetchik* factory, believed supplemented by GAZ-25, total about 13,500 by 22 June 1941.

First main variant **AP** (*Aeropyl*, air dust) or **AO** (*Aeroopylitel*, air duster), flown October 1930. First production aircraft designed for agaviation, front seat moved 250 mm forward, space behind occupied by tank (usually aluminium but type and capacity varied) for up to 250 kg (551 lb) chemicals dispensed across 10 m swath by dural sheet box-venturi, usually assisted by four-blade windmill and impeller. Production 260 by 1932 and 1235 by 1940.

U-2M, MU-2, seaplane variant designed at TsKB by S.A. Kochyerigin. MU, *Morskoi Uchyebnii*, marine trainer. Central float wooden, single step, dual tandem steel-tube struts with wire bracing; N-strutted wing-tip floats. Tested Moscow River spring 1931; poor performance and handling. Subsequently floatplane variants produced by V.B. Shavrov, N.G. Mikhelson, A.Ya. Shchyerbakov and S.A. Mostovozh, none being fully successful despite fitting 115 hp M-11D engine.

U-2 Siemens Single aircraft re-engined 1931 with 125 hp Siemens Sh 14 for Arctic service. Equipped with skis, radio and extra gravity fuel tank on centre section.

U-2KL Designated from name of factory; two aircraft completed with large rear cabin with bulged streamlined hinged canopy with Celluloid windows, flown early 1932.

U-2SP, SP Designation from *Spetsprimeneniya*, special purposes. Incorporated structural modifications of AP, but instead of tank had two open rear cockpits (often one large one) without instruments or controls and with easily removable seats. Great success and 861 built 1934–1939, most for Aeroflot for utility transport.

U-2S, S-1, SS Designation from *Sanitarnyi Samolyet*, ambulance aeroplane. Following proposal by Dr A.F. Lingart, one aircraft completely rebuilt 1932 with forward cockpit as on AP and SP, with closed cubicle to rear for doctor and compartment for stretcher patient between that and fin, covered by top decking folded to right (when closed, interior dark except later when Celluloid portholes added). Doctor could speak to patient and touch patient as far as waist. Batch of 100 built 1934–1936.

U-2G Designation from Gorzhan, name of pilot who suggested radically different flight-control interface in cockpit. No modification to control surfaces but rudder linked to modified control column with ram's horm spectacles operating in three senses, pedals being removed. Tested by NII GVF (Shavrov, GFV, probably misprint) summer 1934.

U-2 V-tail (no designation known). Single aircraft tested 1934 by K.A. Kalilyets and A.A. Ivanovskii fitted with V-tail, or *typa babochki* (butterfly); twin oblique tail surfaces with included angle 140°; ply skin on wood (no mention of dural periphery) with fabric to rear of spar. Described as 'no worse than U-2' but no production. Similar tail later on R-5.

E-23 Designation from *Eksperimentalnyi*, special training and research variant designed 1934–1935 by N.G. Mikhelson for sustained inverted flight. Wings of symmetric profile 9% thick, with flaps on lower wing. Modified fuel system and experimental carburettor for aerobatics. Flown May 1935, successful but many manoeuvres called for more power. No production.

SPL Designation from *SP Limuzin*, Sp by 1935 also coming to mean *Svyazno Passazhirskii*, liaison passenger. Development of original SP with two passengers in more comfortable cabin with hinged lid, exhaust muff heating, Celluloid windows and wicker chairs. SPL usually also fitted with Townend Ring or NACA cowl and often with spats. Oil company Bashnyeft adopted their own model; features attributed to engineer Barsuk. Shavrov says no production, but Bashnyeft had several.

U-2 Grushin No designation known for beautifully styled improved version produced at MAI under P.D. Grushin in 1935. NACA cowl, smoothly faired cockpit canopy, spatted wheels on streamlined struts and two 55-lit supplementary tanks. Whole aircraft brightly doped. Weight increase only 27 kg; speed increase 20 km/h.

U-3, U-4, RV-23 These major rebuilds are described under designer, Mikhelson.

U-2UT Designation from *Uchyebno-Trenirovochnyi*, educational training. First change in

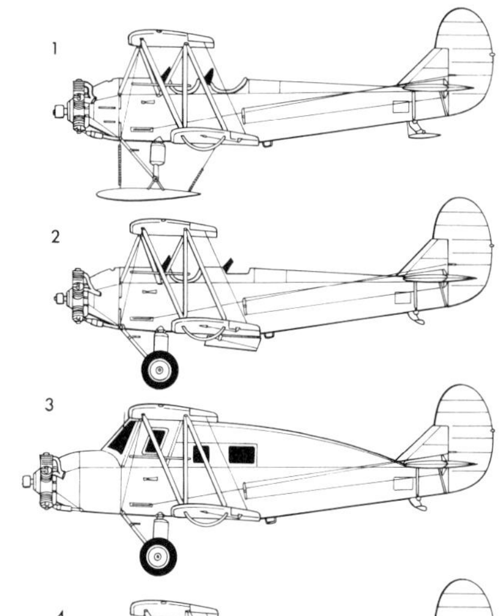

Po-2 variants: 1, standard aircraft on skis (GAZ-25 pattern); 2, U-2AP/Po-2A; 3, U-2L (Rafaelyants); 4, U-2KL (several variations); 5, Po-2L; 6, U-2M; 7, typical of many Po-2S and ShS

Po-2S (civil, 1954)

basic series, in January 1941, with switch to M-11D as standard. Few UT built, distinguished by individual helmets over cylinders and enclosed canopy over rear cockpit. From 1946 usual engine became M-11K.

U-2LPL, LPL Designation from *Lyezhachi Polozheni Lyetchik*, prone-position pilot. Need for prone piloting first argued 1935 for ultra-fast aircraft; then decided useful for air-combat manoeuvres. Eventually U-2 rebuilt with new rear cockpit accommodating pilot lying on front in inclined position, with chin-rest and soft pad against forehead (latter suggests difficulty with vision; no illustration found though may be in Dosaaf atlas 1952). Pilot Bragin did NII VVS testing from 1939, results suggesting excellent idea for record-breaking or interceptor-type aircraft. Provided background for test flights on Type 346 (ex-DFS) in 1950.

Po-2A Following Polikarpov's death in 1944 aircraft redesignated Po-2, and Po-2A agricultural variant remained in production throughout war and in Poland to 1953, post-war models having M-11K. Improved (V.F. Stepanov AOD-S3) dispenser increased swath width to 30 m, and raised working rate from 17 to 30 hectares/h. Production (with AP) 8980.

Po-2VS Basic VVS front-line aircraft, VS (*Voiskovoi Seriya*, military series) often impressed ex-GVF SP with three open cockpits. Standard Soviet military liaison aircraft, also built from new and issued to all senior officers of all services, large numbers with prison and labour-camp commandants and local military governors. Inventory of 1945 showed over 9200 in liaison duty. Many locally modified with extra tank on centre section, enclosed transparent canopy (often from other aircraft), slats and/or flaps (variant by M.M. Kulik), various engine cowls and external payload panniers.

LSh *Lyegkii Shturmovik* (light attacker), some hundreds of existing (mainly pre-1941) aircraft converted in various workshops as close-support aircraft; alternative designation **U-2VOM-1**. Normally equipped with ShKAS aimed by observer in rear cockpit, 120 kg of bombs and four RS-82 on underwing rails. Even without armour usually weighed 1,4 t, sluggish performance. Established great reputation; German troops said to believe LSh would look into each window to see if invaders inside houses.

Po-2SP No relation to previous SP, but designation again from *Spetsialno Primeneniya*, special tasks: photography, survey, instrumentation, post-war magnetometer survey etc.

LNB *Lyegkii Nochnoi Bombardirovshchik*, light night bomber, wartime production version based on emergency conversions in late 1941. Most two-seat (some single-seat) with two FAB-100 or similar 200 kg (441-lb) bombload. Invariably dull black overall, silencer on exhaust pipe and if possible with engine idling in target area. Target illuminated by flares or, according to many contemporary reports, searchlight carried by companion LNB. Large number used against Luftwaffe airfields and front-line troops.

NAK, Po-2NAK *Nochnoartilleriskyi Korrectovovshchik*, night artillery correction, local reconnaissance in dull black with observer equipped with army radio to report on effects and accuracy of gunfire. Possibly pre-war rebuilds.

Po-2P Designation from *Poplavkii*, floats; small number of Shchyerbakov seaplane variants (including at least one with twin floats) built or converted after 1941. Probably all unarmed.

Po-2L, RAF-2 Variant by A.N. Rafaelyants built 1943 with deep fuselage filling space between wings. Believed flown with M-11D but later had 145 hp M-11F. L possibly stood for *Limuzin*, though photo known with cargo being loaded. Probably single example.

Po-2ShS *Shtabnoi Svyaznoi*, staff liaison, variant produced in some numbers from 1942 or 1943. Polikarpov design, with new fuselage providing glazed cabin for four occupants, usually pilot and three passengers.

Po-2S Generalized designation for wartime ambulance variants, both rebuilds and new production, virtually all with M-11D. S-1 described earlier. **S-2** (1939) first with M-11D. **S-3** (1940) first with lower wings restressed for two patient pods (called *Kasseta*, drums, hence designation **SKF** or **Po-2SKF**). Original pod (1941) by A.Ya. Shchyerbakov accommodated patient semi-reclining ahead of and below lower leading edge. Improved type (1944) by G.I. Bakshayev resembled box-like drop tank into which stretcher slid from end. Most variants could seat third patient or doctor in rear cockpit. Large number of pre-war S-1 and S-2 continued in use, with many variations (rear decking hinged on left, or hinged up from front, or in front/rear sections, latter being fixed and stretcher slid in via front half, thick centre-section fuel tank, and glazed canopy in sections over patient and doctor/pilot). Po-2S remained in production in Poland post-war.

Po-2GN *Golos Nyeba*, voice from sky, psy-war variant of 1944 with 80-W amplifier and loudspeakers broadcasting messages usually direct from microphone in rear cockpit; same with silenced exhaust as LNB.

Popularly called *Kukuruznik* (corn-cutter), Po-2 is still in use in USSR and possibly other countries. Variant similar to LNB used by North Korea 1950–1953. License production in Poland 1948–1953 as **CSS-13** (trainer) and **CSS-S-13** (ambulance).

DIMENSIONS Span (TPK) 11,0 m, (standard) 11,4 m (37 ft 4$\frac{3}{4}$ in); length (TPK) 8,1 m, (standard) 8,17 m (26 ft 9$\frac{2}{3}$ in), (E-23) 8,2 m, (MU, Po-2M) 9,19 m (30 ft 1$\frac{3}{4}$ in); wing area (TPK) 34 m^2, (standard) 33,15 m^2 (356·8 ft^2).

ENGINE (pre-1941) one 100 hp M-11, (1941–1946) usually 115 hp M-11D, (post-1946) usually 115 hp M-11K or (rarely) 140 hp M-11F or other.

WEIGHTS (TPK) empty 758 kg; fuel/oil 95 kg; loaded 1013 kg; (standard, 1930) empty 635 kg (1400 lb); fuel/oil 71 + 10 kg; loaded 890 kg (1962 lb); corresponding weights for (AP) 656/35 + 12/1000, (SP) 662/90 + 12/1000, (S-1) 710/90 + 12/1050, (E-23) 752/116/1043, (SPL) 721/90 + 12/1063, (MU, M) 949/90 + 12/1350, (VS) 754/90 + 12/1023–1195, (LNB) 798/90 + 12/1400 max.

PERFORMANCE Max speed (TPK) 142 km/h, (std 1930) 156 km/h (97 mph), (AP, S-1, typical) 140 km/h (87 mph), (M) 144 km/h (89·5 mph), (LNB) about 130 km/h (81 mph), (post-war, typical) 150 km/h (93 mph); climb to 1 km (TPK) 11·5 min, (std 1930) 5·6 min, (SP) 9 min, (AP) 10 min, (S-1) 11 min, (M) 15 min, (LNB) probably unattainable, (post-war, typical) 6 min; service ceiling generally 3/4 km; range (TPK) 350 km, (std 1930) 400 km (249 miles), (AP) 200 km, (SP, S-1) 550 km, (SPL) 468 km, (post-war, typical) 500 km; take-off (TPK) 100 m/10 s, (std 1930) 70 m/8 s, (AP, SP, S-1) 120/130 m, (M) 315 m; landing (TPK) 85 m/9 s/65 km/h, (std 1930) 120 m/11 s/65 km/h (40 mph), (most later) 150/155 m/67 km/h (42 mph).

P-2 Designation from *Perekhodnyi*, intermediate; trainer intermediate between U-2 and R-5, and intended to train pilots and observers. Typical OSS biplane with strong resemblance to U-2 and R-5. Single-bay wing box with four identical wings with 25° stagger, joined by N-struts and long diagonal spanwise strut (teardrop section 100 × 40 mm) instead of bracing wires, with objective of eliminating time-consuming rigging by adjusting wire tensions. Construction same as U-2 and R-5, no forward-firing gun but DA on Scarff ring fired by observer. Water radiator retractable, similar to PM-1. Four identical interlinked ailerons, braced tailplane, rubber-sprung main gears, aluminium engine cowl and pointed propeller spinner. Prototype completed autumn 1927, while U-2 being redesigned, and flight tests satisfactory, resulting in order for 55 (probably regarded as initial batch), delivered from *Krasnyi Lyetchik* plant 1928–1930. It was then discovered diagonal struts serious mistake. Handling was unpredictable, and many aircraft reluctant to recover from spin. Over 200 test flights devoted to this problem alone, and with most aircraft repeated test flights needed to get setting of wing box right, with laborious adjustments to N-struts and diagonal struts. Many P-2s modified with conventional wing-box bracing wires. Eventually so

Po-SKF on skis

P-2

I-3

many adjustments made to wings that entire wing box separated from one aircraft in flight, test-pilot B.L. Bukholts escaping by parachute. Training schools hardly used P-2, preferring R-1 (esp 240 hp BMW IVa model) with armament removed.
DIMENSIONS Span 10,4 m (34 ft 1½ in); length 7,84 m (25 ft 8¾ in); wing area 28,0 m² (301 ft²).
ENGINE One 300 hp M-6.
WEIGHTS Empty 1 t (2205 lb); fuel/oil 200 kg; loaded 1470 kg (3241 lb).
PERFORMANCE Max speed 206 km/h (128 mph); climb to 1 km, 3·3 min; service ceiling 5680 m (18,635 ft); range 800 km (500 miles)/4 h; take-off 80 m/7 s; landing 150 m/13 s/85 km/h.

I-3 First Soviet fighter preceded by lengthy planning and careful design by substantial team. Polikarpov had devoted long attention to rival claims of water-cooled engines (long, heavy, but streamlined if one ignored radiator) and air-cooled radials (short, light, but higher drag). Balance favoured radial, esp for agile fighter, but OSS decided to build example of each. Water-cooled fighter was I-3, plans being approved 14 May 1927 but 2I-N1 crashing soon afterwards, resulting in urgent reappraisal and redesign with factors of safety afterwards seen to be excessive. Fuselage with pine truss framework, four longerons and 13 frames with integral fin, with light fairing structure to support semi-monocoque oval-section covering of *shpon*, from 0,5 mm glued veneer built up to thickness 5 mm forward and 3 mm near tail. Wings of Clark Y profile with two spars of pine/ply box type, ply ribs with ply caps and pine stringers, internal wire bracing, ply and fabric covering. All struts dural teardrop section with adjustable screwed end-fittings. All control surfaces dural framework with fabric covering, tailplane adjustable incidence in flight, elevators with large cut-outs though at 0° missed rudder. Elevator push/pull rods, cables to other controls, ailerons differential Frise type. Pin-jointed main gears with multi-laminate rubber shock-absorption, tyres 800 × 150 mm, skis R-1 type 2,73 × 0,34 m (area 1,86 m²). CG at 26% MAC. Radiator plain rectangular matrix extended from belly. Two synchronized PV-1 (Vickers in first prototype). Armament by Aleksandr Nadashkevich, responsible for armament of all subsequent Polikarpov aircraft. First flight 4 May 1928, second aircraft three months later. Good performance (283 km/h with high-speed prop but long take-off) and fair manoeuvrability. Fuel consumption 142 l/h. NII tests late 1928 resulted in order for substantial number, believed 400. Most had imported engine, licensed M-17 later substituted.
DIMENSIONS Span 11,0 m (36 ft 1 in); length 8,01 m (26 ft 3¼ in); wing area 27,85 m² (300 ft²) (Něměcek, 27,34).
ENGINE One 500/730 hp BMW VI 7,3z.
WEIGHTS Empty 1,4 t (3086 lb); fuel/oil 210 + 33 kg; loaded (Shavrov, whose figures do not tally) 1846 kg (4070 lb), (Něměcek, whose figures are doubtful) 1863 kg.
PERFORMANCE Max speed (standard prop) 278 km/h (173 mph) at SL; time to 1 km, 1·8 min; service ceiling 7,2 km (23,620 ft); range 585 km (364 miles) (Shavrov gives endurance 2 h, must have been much greater); take-off 150 m/12 s; landing 250 m/18 s/100 km/h (62 mph).

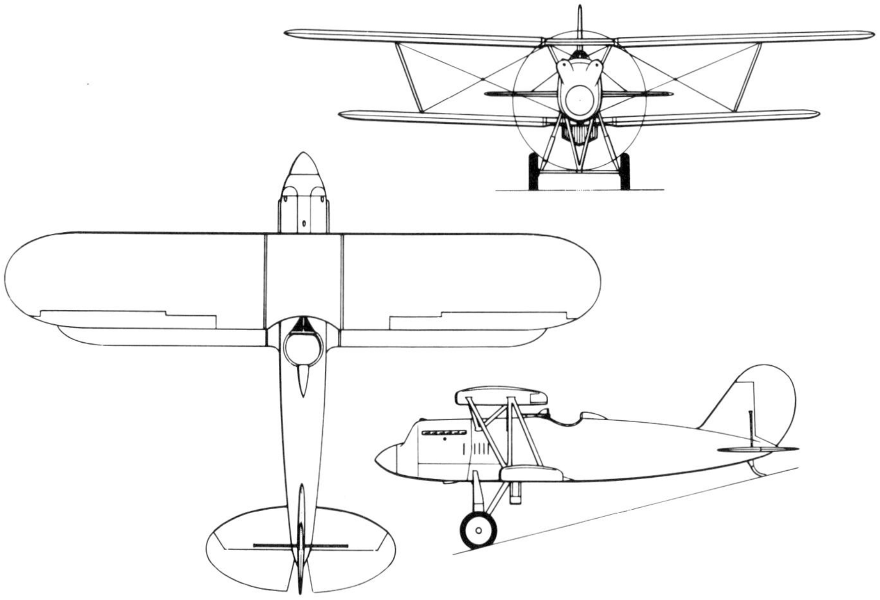

I-3

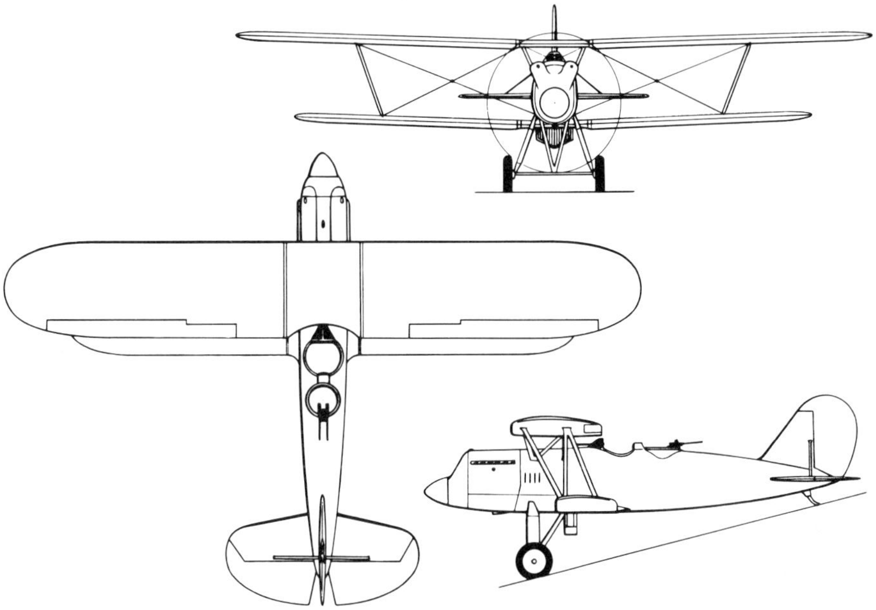

D-2, DI-2

D-2, DI-2 Designation from *Dvukhmyestnyi* (two-seat), slightly enlarged derivative of I-3 with extra cockpit for observer. Most parts of airframe identical, but wings joined to slightly extended centre-sections, fuselage lengthened by one frame and rudder increased in area (Shavrov adds that 8° cut-out provided in elevators but this was already on I-3 to cater for full-rudder up-elevator case). Two synchronized PV-1 and twin DA on Scarff ring for observer. Estimated performance not outstanding, but intended for small-series production in view of lack of indigenous aircraft in class. Prototype complete 1929 (no data). On early (not maiden) flight horizontal tail separated in flight (Shavrov, while diving), ascribed to flutter; test-pilot A.V. Chyekarev killed. Programme abandoned, and greater effort on DI-3.
DIMENSIONS Span (Shavrov) 11,8 m (38 ft 8½ in), (Něměcek) 12,5 m (41 ft 0 in); length 8,2 m (26 ft 10¾ in); wing area 31,8 m² (342 ft²), (Něměcek 31,2).
ENGINE One 500/730 hp BMW VI.
WEIGHTS Empty 1557 kg (3433 lb); fuel/oil 210 + 33 kg; loaded 2122 kg (4678 lb), (Něměcek 2075).
PERFORMANCE Max speed 256 km/h (159 mph), (Něměcek 272); climb to 1 km, 2·2 min; service ceiling 6,3 km (20,670 ft); range 510 km (317 miles); time 360° circle, 14 s; take-off 180 m/14 s; landing 250 m/18 s/100 km/h.

TB-2 Recognizing importance of heavy bomber, and obsolescence of Junkers R-42 and Tupolev TB-1, OSS was instructed 1927 to design modern bomber to replace these and also imported Farman F 62. Project begun as **L-2**, Kolpakov-Miroshnichyenko playing leading role. Major changes resulted in delay, but prototype finally appeared spring 1930. Sesquiplane of neat design and, according to contemporary

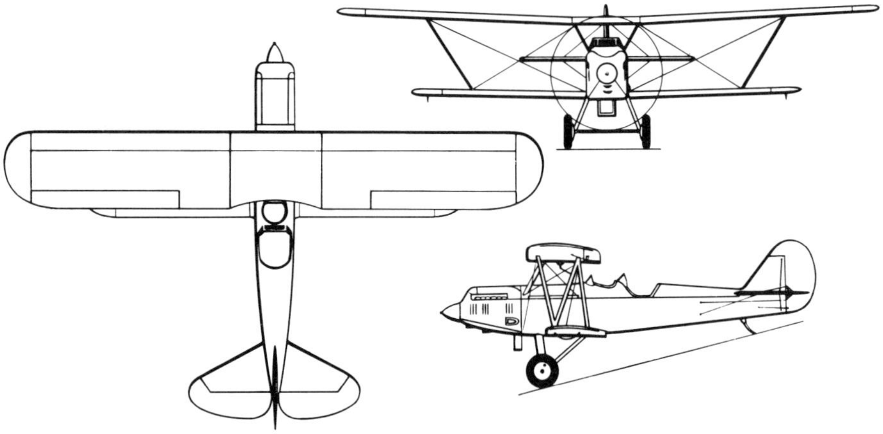
R-5 (typical production)

article, finished to high standard. Areas of upper/lower wings in ratio 2·6:1; profile modified Clark Y, t/c 16%. Wooden construction with two box spars, ply ribs and ply covering back to rear spar. Engine nacelles directly on top of lower wing. Upper wing mounted on reverse-N cabane and no other wing struts except single diagonal pair from lower spars just outboard of engines to upper spars well outboard. Much neater than most contemporary biplane bombers and satisfactory in practice. Struts steel tubes with wooden fairings. Box-like wooden fuselage with ply skin but softened (unlike Farman) by smooth rounded edges to reduce drag. Simple single tail, all control surfaces dural/fabric. Main gears beneath engines with rubber springing and small mudguards. Plain matrix radiators manually extended upwards into airstream just behind engines. Crew five, including three gunners (one with radio) each manning pair of DA, presumably one nose, one dorsal and others either beam windows or ventral. Bombload reported as 800 kg and also as 1 t (1764/2205 lb). On test TB-2 flew well and in some respects exceeded est figs, but by 1930s regarded as obsolescent and decision taken to put all trust in ANT-6. Něměcek: it was planned in production version to locate gunners in rear of extended nacelles.

DIMENSIONS Span 27,0 m (88 ft 7 in); length 17,6 m (57 ft 9 in); wing area 128 m^2 (1,378 ft^2).
ENGINES Two 500/680 hp BMW VI.
WEIGHTS Empty 4220 kg (9303 lb); fuel/oil 1 t; loaded 6770 kg (14,925 lb).
PERFORMANCE Max speed 216 km/h (134 mph); climb to 1 km, 3·2 min; service ceiling 6,8 km (22,300 ft); range 1200 km (746 miles) (presumably with bombs), (Němĕcek 1400); take-off 210m/18 s; landing 170 m/15 s/86 km/h (53 mph).

R-5 Like British Hart family and Dutch C.V this two-seat biplane served in vast numbers in a host of variants as VVF's standard tactical reconnaissance and attack aircraft, and in countless variety of other roles including over 1000 as civil transports. Design process exceptionally long (1925–1928) and included exhaustive statistical research and calculations never before attempted. Intended to replace R-1 but Polikarpov intended basic aircraft to be versatile. When prototype being built, structure restressed to higher factors as result of 2I-N1 crash, yet % airframe weight remained exceptionally low (in production such tight control exercised at GAZ-1 that empty and equipped weight of original batches hardly varied from 1969/2169 kg, former figure barely half permitted gross weight.

Close kinship with U-2, P-2, I-3 and D-2. Sesquiplane wings of modified Clark Y profile, t/c 10%, CG from 24·5% empty to 33·5/35·8% normal (bomber higher than reconnaissance) and reaching 40% with dry tanks. Two box spars each wing with 5 mm ply webs, 30 mm pine booms and box width 80 mm (upper wing), 55 mm (lower wing). Ply ribs with strip capping and oval lightening holes providing spaces for diagonal internal bracing wires. Multiple pine stringers, ply skin to front spar, fabric behind. All struts dural tube of streamlined section with adjustable machined fork ends. Streamlined external bracing wires (lift, pairs No 12; landing, individual No 11; cabane, Nos 10 and 7) all with 12 mm threaded end-fittings. Wooden fuselage truss with four longerons and 12 frames, diag side bracings and light secondary fairing to give round top, skin of ply panels 3 mm at front and 2 mm at tail. Wooden tail, but periphery of wings and all control surfaces dural, with fabric covering. Dual flight controls by cable, differential ailerons on upper wings only, 32° up and 10°30′ down. Engine mounted on frame of dural box sections joined by riveted arch frames below and with main side ties steel/dural pipes with machined end-fittings adjustable for length. Two main fuel tanks of galvanized iron in centre-section feeding via copper pipes. Brass honeycomb radiator well ahead of main gears extended by chain drive from front cockpit. Two-blade wooden 3350 mm propeller with spinner and Hucks dogs. Main gears with pin joints and front strut sprung by rubber laminates, wheels spoked to 1933 and disc subsequently (Shavrov's mention of disc brakes is mistake), tyres 900 × 200 mm. Four known patterns of ski; floats discussed later. Normal armament one sychronized PV-1, one (from 1934 usually twin) DA; 250 kg bombs on wing racks, (bomber version) overload up to 400 kg bombs. Throughout construction casein glue used, mild-steel fittings (most with two or three parts flame-welded) and galvanized iron screws and pins.

Prototype flown 1928, probably before October. Satisfactory, but prolonged testing and discussion prior to launch of series production. First R-5 (*Razvyedchik*, reconnaissance) appeared from GAZ-1 late 1930, and production continued as main occupation of GAZ-1 until 1937; total including variants more than 6000 of which 4995 were basic R-5 or P-5.

R-5 reached VVS early 1931, subsequently equipped over 100 regts up to close of Second World War and seeing especially intensive duty in Spain, at Khalkin-Gol and in Winter War. In 1941–1944, most subjected to various mods including fitting heavier guns, RS-82 launch rails, special communications and various kinds of role eqpt including searchlight, side stepladder, loudspeaker and glider tow hook. Important *Kasseta* (people containers) described later.

R-5Sh *Shturmovik* (attacker) first major variant, 1931. Merely used payload to carry more weapons. First example had two PV-1 in box above each lower wing and Der-5 box for 240/500 kg small bombs under fuselage, retaining existing guns. By 1933 in production with M-17B, eight PV-1 in two quads (later eight ShKAS) and minor changes.

R-5a, MR-5 Original designation for *Morskoi Razvyedchik*, marine reconnaissance. Twin-float seaplane; floats wooden with 21 frames and eight bulkheads arranged along two keelsons as on

R-5 with rocket rails

P-5 in Turkestan, 1933

Sh-2 and finally covered with fabric and varnished. Attached by 12 struts of dural tube streamline-section with wire bracing. Enlarged fin, hand-crank starter attachments on each side of engine and other minor changes. Project of V.B. Shavrov and D.A. Mikhailov, prototype flown April 1931. Adequate but performance capable of improvement. Often called **MR-5bis** (because of abandoned Chyetverikov MR-5) and Samolyet **No 10.**

P-5 Designation from *Passazhirskii*, but usually used to carry 400 kg mail/cargo. From about mid-1931 R-5 supplied to GVF as standard aircraft off GAZ-1 line but with armament removed. Aeroflot workshops increasingly devised ways of improving this transport version which by 1940 numbered over 1000. At first rear seat and control column removed and cargo not even secured. Later rear cockpit reconstructed without instruments and enlarged into cockpit for two passengers in wicker chairs with baggage. Smaller number rebuilt with enclosed rear cabin for two – possibly more – passengers with at least three types of lid or glazed roof (see *Limuzin* and PR-5). Aeroflot was also only known user of seaplane version, **P-5a**; believed small numbers. Important addition to P-5 was use of underwing *Kasseta* (drum or casket) designed by D.S. Markov, P.I. Grokhovskii (which see) and others. Some had lifting profile and thus could accommodate 1,3-t load in single container. As noted under Grokhovskii, that designer flew a P-5 with 16 adults, including seven in each *Kasseta*. Smaller *Kasseta* model played central role in dramatic rescue of *Chyelyuskin* expedition from Arctic ice in 1934, P-5s and other transports being on skis. P-5 important well into the Second World War, outlasting P-Z.

R-5L, Limuzin Developed at TsKB by A.N. Rafaelyants and B.L. Bukholts as comfortable transport with pilot in front and cabin for two passengers behind. Dural framed canopy with Celluloid windows and passenger door with airstairs in left side. First factory-built *Limuzin*, flown late 1931.

R-5D Designation from *Dalnost*, distance; long-range example of late 1931 with large fuselage tankage which cracked open in flight (safe forced landing without fire).

R-5PS Author's shorthand for *Povorotnyim Stoika*, rotating struts (may have been actual designation). Front interplane struts broad surfaces of aerofoil profile, chord 200 mm, mounted in bearings and separately controllable by pilot either to weathercock freely or be pulled almost broadside to airflow. Followed TsAGI research into spin-recovery. Tested on R-5 and also on I-5 with dire results, causing death of R-5 test-pilot M.A. Bolkovoinov September 1932.

R-5M-34 Standard R-5 used 1932 as flight test-bed for first M-34 engine. No major problem.

R-5RK Author's shorthand for *Razreznyim Krylo*, slotted wing. TsKB discussed concept

P-5a with MP-6 beyond

SSS (top) and R-5 V-tail (believed designated R-5TB)

1930, and assigned execution of full-scale flight test to L.I. Sutugin. Picked R-5 and rebuilt by S.A. Kochyerigin's brigade 1932. Meanwhile TsAGI tested many tunnel models to get best results. Upper wing effectively in three parts on each side of unmodified centre section: leading-edge forming automatic slat, chord 227 mm; main fixed wing; full-span ailerons and flaps, all slotted, with manual actuation. Rest of aircraft little altered apart from slight increase in area of tail surfaces. Two aircraft built, one for pure research and other with armament and reconnaissance cameras. Both flown 1932 and programme completed following year. No serious problems and STOL performance exceptional with 20° angle of attack sustained at 70 km/h (43·5 mph). After prolonged exploration discovered various problems, and concluded no justification for change in basic aircraft.

R-5T Designation from *Torpedonosyets*, redesign as single-seat torpedo carrier at TsKB in 1932 under V.V. Nikitin. Main modification redesign of main landing gear with two separate units each with diagonal side strut pin-jointed under fuselage longeron and with air/oil shock strut almost vertical from bottom of this strut to spar of wing, which had to have additional diagonal upper bracing strut to fuselage upper longeron. Torpedo crutch geometry resulted in increased landing attitude of 17° with torpedo on board. Idea put forward by A.I. Grebenyev at GAZ-1 in 1933 and results were fully satisfactory. Batch of 50 R-5T built 1935 serving at Far East MA.

P-5L Another *Limuzin* built at GAZ-1 in 1933 similar to R-5L but without airstairs. Several produced from new, called 'first production Limousine'.

SSS, R-5SSS Designation from *Skorostnoi Skoropodyemnyi Skorostrelnyi* (speedster, high-speed lift, fast-shooter). Major revision of R-5 by D.S. Markov and A.A. Skarbov for increased performance. M-17F with improved cowl (same propeller), air/oil shock strut landing gears with streamlined casings and spats, detail attention to joints and finish, streamlined cockpit, many exterior rivets made flush on metal areas (cowl). Increased armament of two ShKAS or one ShKAS and one PV-1 firing ahead (in *Shturmovik* variant, four additional ShKAS on lower wings). Made vital injection of increased performance (25/30 km/h, extra 2 km alt) leading to introduction of R-Z described separately. SSS built in small series for reconnaissance, light bomber role and as *Shturmovik*; probably about 100.

R-5 V-tail V-type (butterfly) tails studied at VVA since 1929 and designs worked out in detail by Yezhi Rudlitski, Polish engineer. In 1934 plans made to fly on U-2 and R-5, latter being joint effort by VVA and GAZ-1, with aerodynamics by EAO TsAGI under Prof A.N. Zhuravchyenko. Two tail surfaces, 140° angle, RAF-30 section, 12%, wooden fixed portions with dural/fabric movable surfaces geared to work together as elevators or differentially as rudders. Flight tests from summer 1935 by M.M. Gromov, K.K. Popov and I.F. Kozlov. Handling little different from series R-5, though pedals heavier, qualities poorer at point of landing or in tight turn, and spin characteristics worse.

R-5 Jumo, ED-1 Possibility of using Jumo-4 (Soviet designation for Junkers Jumo 205 opposed-piston two-stroke diesel) in VVS derivative of ANT-25 led to import of several engines and modification of an R-5 as flying testbed. Deep cowl, four-blade propeller (as used on G 38) and large radiator under belly of aircraft. Rear cockpit greatly enlarged, and equipped comfortably for two test observers. Aircraft flown October 1935, designation from *Eksperimental Dvigatyel*. Made over 200 flights, one by A.I. Zhukov lasting 12 h 01 min.

R-5USh Author's shorthand for *Ubirayemy shassi*, retractable gear. Another one-off at TsKB by Markov and Sharbov, this R-5 was rebuilt with completely different main gears retracting inwards into thickened inboard lower wing as on DI-6. Flown 1935.

R-5G Author's shorthand for *Gusenichnyi*, caterpillar tracklaying; R-5 tested tracked main gears designed by Chyechubalin 1935, but overall considered clumsy.

PR-5 Final modernized transport version, built 1936 by A.N. Rafaelyants. Completely new semi-monocoque fuselage with pilot in high front cockpit with glazed canopy and four-passenger cabin occupying enlarged cross-section immediately below and behind. Pilot access from above via hinged canopy, passengers via door with airstair on left. Tested spring 1936 at GVF repair field Bykovo, and found CG too far aft, adjusted by altering wing stagger; upper wing moved 100 mm to rear. Result called **PR-5bis**, CG never aft of 36% MAC and no problems. Small production series built by conversion and used by Aeroflot at least through 1941.

ARK-5 Following proposal by polar pilot M.V. Vodopyarnov, two R-5s rebuilt for Arctic use. Streamlined ply containers for payload faired into sides of fuselage and lower wing; enclosed cockpit with heating. On 26 March 1936 Vodopyarnov and Makhotkin flew these aircraft to Novaya Zemlya and Franz-Josef Land.

PR-12, R-Z, P-Z Described separately.

LSh, TSh-1, SHON Described under Grigorovich.

LR, LR-2, TSh-3 Described under Kochyerigin.

DIMENSIONS Span (upper) 15,5 m (50 ft 10¼ in), (lower) 12,0 m (39 ft 4½ in); length 10,555 m (34 ft 7½ in); wing area 50,2 m² (540 ft²).

ENGINE One BMW V-12: (prototype) 680 hp BMW VI, (main series to 1933) 680 hp M-17B, (post-1933) 715 hp M-17F, except most P-5 still M-17B.

WEIGHTS Empty (1930 reconnaissance) 1969 kg (4341 lb), (R-5a) 2330 kg, (RK) 2184 kg, (P-5) 2040 kg, (PR) 2118 kg, (PR bis) 2200kg; fuel/oil (standard) 400 + 30 kg, (P-5) 500 kg, (PR) 585 + 50 kg; loaded (prototype) 2955 kg, (1930) 3247 kg (7158 lb), (Sh) 3410 kg, (5a) 3230 kg, (1934) 2997 kg (6607 lb), (P-5, PR, bis) up to 3350 kg (7385 lb).
PERFORMANCE Max speed (1930) 228 km/h (142 mph), (Sh) 202 km/h, (5a) 198 km/h, (RK) 205 km/h, (1934) 244 km/h (152 mph), (P) 215 km/h, (PR, bis) 233km/h; cruise (P-5) 165 km/h (102·5 mph); climb to 1 km (1930) 2·1 min, (1934) 2·5; service ceiling (1930) 6,4 km (21,000 ft), (1934) 5940 m (19,490 ft), (5a) 4350 m, (P-5) 5,8 km; range (1930) 800 km, (1934) 1000 km, (5a) 700 km, (P-5) 1200 km; time 360° circle (reconnaissance, typical) 17 s; take-off (typical) 300 m/25 s (1934, 22 s); landing 220 m/18 s/95 km/h (59 mph).

R-Z Sufficiently different from R-5 to merit separate treatment, this final version had strange designation. Letter Z does not exist in Cyrillic alphabet, but same sound represented by letter з, and possible designation came from Russian word meaning enclosed which begins with this character. As letter Z unknown to Russians, written in Soviet Union R-Zet, phonetic rendition.

R-Z developed at instigation of A.M. Byelinkovich, director of GAZ-1, under chief engineer Ye.P. Shyekunov. Design by TsKB's D.S. Markov and A.A. Skarbov, and based on their earlier SSS. Main change was more powerful engine, but engine mounts and propeller believed unchanged. Larger and more efficient radiator relocated behind landing gear. Redesigned fuselage with modern wood monocoque structure, deeper section with larger cockpits and larger tanks. Glazed sliding canopy over pilot cockpit and fixed glazed fairing over gunner. Redesigned tail of larger area with balanced surfaces without horns. Centre section of upper wing without trailing-edge cutout. Low-pressure tyres 800 × 200 mm, with spats on first R-Z, thereafter left open. Wheel brakes (no details). Covering of fabric given only two (instead of three) coatings of coloured dope, to reduce weight. Structure generally refined to reduce weight without sacrificing strength.

First flight January 1935; handling soon improved to point where superior to R-5, and accepted for VVS service. Total 1031 built at GAZ-1 terminating spring 1937. (Same factory then license-built batch of Vultee BSh.) Armament usually same as R-5 in VVS: fixed PV, one or two movable ShKAS, six wing bombs eg two FAB-125 and four FAB-50. Prolonged service in Spain, nicknamed *Rasante* (ground-shaver) and in conflict with Japan. Still numerous in Winter War; first three BSh-2 (Il-2) regts converted from R-Z, finding great difficulty with modern monoplane.

R-ZSh Single *Shturmovik* prototype with four ShKAS on lower wings outboard of propeller disc. Believed later test-bed for heavier and more unconventional armament schemes.

P-Z, Pe-Zet Commercial variant of R-Z, believed all conversions though according to Aeroflot additional aircraft built as such. First in service 1936, few changes apart from more powerful engine and removal of armament, payload 275 kg. Used for carriage of mail and (usually two) passengers facing each other. Substantial number in use by 1937. Reliable, and majority still in use during the Second World War.

PT Single aircraft attempted reconstruction to improve commercial transport performance (T, *Transportnyi*). Streamlined rectangular-section cargo box on each side above lower wing, 1,5 m^3 each. Upper wing moved back 50 mm (half as far as PR-5), lower wings fitted with flaps (believed slotted), rear-fuselage top raised, tail extra bracing wires and more powerful radio. Payload 494 kg but poorer flying qualities.

R-ZR, *Rekordnyi* Single R-Z with armament removed and many detail improvements to reduce drag. Built on instigation of pilot V.V. Shyevchyenko and constructor V.V. Nikitin. Great attention to superb ('lustrous') finish. Flown by Shyevchyenko to 11,1 km on 8 May 1937.

R-Z GK Shorthand for *Gruzovymi Kassetami*, various transport R-Z with streamlined payload containers on and beneath lower wings.

DIMENSIONS Span (Shavrov) 15,5 m, (Něměcek) 15,45 m (50 ft 8¼ in), (Green/Swanborough) 15,2 m; length 9,72 m (31 ft 10¾ in), (Něměcek, 10,6); wing area 42,52 m^2 (458 ft^2), (Něměcek, 50,2).
ENGINE One 850 hp M-34N, (PZ, PT) 820 hp M-34NB.
WEIGHTS Empty 2007 kg (4425 lb), (PZ) 2154 kg, (PT) 2345 kg; fuel/oil 584 + 55 kg; loaded 3150 kg (6944 lb), (Něměcek) 3,7 t (8157 lb), (PZ) 3161 kg, (PT) 3575 kg.
PERFORMANCE Max speed 276 km/h at SL, 316 km/h (196 mph) at 3,5 km, (PT) 296 km/h at 3,5 km; cruise (PT) 213 km/h (132 mph); climb to 3 km, 6·6 min, (PT) 13·9 min; service ceiling 8,7 km (28,550 ft), (PZ) 9150 m, (PT) 6240 m; range 1000 km (621 miles), (PZ) 1130 km; time 360° turn, 18 s; take-off 270 m/15 s, (PT) 300/18; landing 220 m/14 s/105 km/h, (PT) 195 m/11 s/97 km/h.

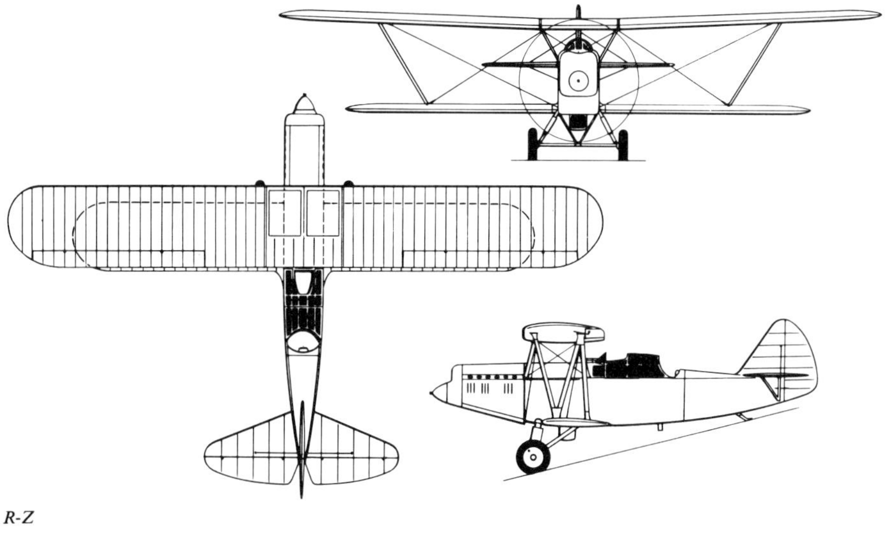

R-Z

I-6 As soon as I-3 was released to manfacturing, OSS began design of rival single-seat fighter with air-cooled radial. Polikarpov drew first three-view September 1928 and all brigades assisted with detail design 1929. Thanks to short and relatively light engine, overall dimensions appreciably less than I-3, and weight only 69% as much. Nevertheless trad OSS structure retained: two-spar wooden wings with dural periphery and fabric covering, streamlined-section dural tube struts, oval-section monocoque fuselage of glued layers of *shpon*, 2,5 to 5,0-mm thick, dural movable control surfaces with fabric covering, and rubber-sprung landing gear. Original engine mount by I.A. Tavastshyern rejected in favour of welded steel tube, with dural outer cowl leaving cylinders open at front but faired by individual part-helmets at rear. Wooden propeller with spinner and Hucks dogs. Though hard to believe, photographs (all retouched) show diagonal interplane struts as on 2I-N1 and P-2. OGPU, possibly following someone 'informing' against Polikarpov, decided work was taking too long and had constructor arrested September 1929. By this time prototype almost complete, and in Polikarpov's absence completion delayed to following spring. Two examples built, first flying 30 March 1930 and both in May Day parade. On 15 June test-pilot A.D. Shirinkin left I-6 by parachute (Shavrov 'without valid cause'). Eventually (1931) about a year spent comparing remaining I-6 with I-5 and latter chosen mainly on account of four guns, fractionally better time for 360° turn and supposed tougher structure. Polikarpov never officially informed of I-6 results until his release in 1933.
DIMENSIONS Span 9,7 m (31 ft 10 in) (lower, 7,5); length 6,78 m (22 ft 3 in); wing area 20,5 m^2 (221 ft^2), (Něměcek, 21,6).
ENGINE (1) Gnome-Rhône Jupiter VI, (2) M-22.
WEIGHTS Empty (Shavrov) 868 kg (1914 lb), (Něměcek) 980 kg; fuel/oil 180 kg; loaded (Shavrov) 1280 kg (2822 lb), (Něměcek) 1420 kg.
PERFORMANCE Max speed 280 km/h (174 mph), (Něměcek, 290); climb to 1 km, 1·5 min; service ceiling 7,5 km (24,600 ft), (Něměcek, 8,9); range 700 km (435 miles); time 360° circle, 15 s; take-off 90 m/7 s; landing 200 m/15 s/95 km/h).

I-5 Chief Soviet fighter of its day (first half of 1930s), this agile machine had extraordinary beginning. Assigned to AGOS TsAGI under first five-year plan, drawn up by Aviatrust 1927 and accepted 22 June 1928. To be mixed-construction, metal-framed fuselage, fighter otherwise similar to OSS-designed I-6 with wood monocoque fuselage, and likewise powered by Jupiter VI for which Aviatrust was then negotiating licence (with Gnome-Rhône, not Bristol, which helped trigger final break between Bristol and improper French licensee). Tupolev gave priority to ANT-6 and proposed I-5, with AGOS number ANT-12, lagged. Several obvious choices open to OGPU, then managing aviation industry; none taken, and instead strange decision to arrest designer of successful rival I-6! September 1929 both top constructors at OSS, N.N. Polikarpov and D.P. Grigorovich, arrested and told to build I-5 quickly. After disorganized autumn special *Vnutrenniya Tyurma* (internal prison) established November at Hangar 7, V.R. Menzhinskii factory (GAZ-39). First week December work started, records still unable to show exactly what happened. Tupolev told author 1957 'VT was special small KB set up to finish ANT-12 in shortest time'. Shavrov 'Polikarpov proposed revision of I-6 with different structure; this idea not accepted by Grigorovich'. Něměcek 'Polikarpov produced fresh sketch; Grigorovich then took over real design work'. In view of amazingly short timescale - partly due to 20-h working day, closely supervised by guards, until late January - balance of probability is that I-6 was indeed used as basis.

Fuselage truss gas-welded from standard steel tubing, as used in contemporary engine mounts, with light dural frames and stringers to give streamline form for fabric covering. Rest of airframe similar, or identical, to I-6, except for shape of fin/rudder, use of normal wing bracing wires (front lift wire going to anchor at main-leg attachment), small increase in span upper wing and revision of landing-gear pivots and bracing wires. Design completely finished in two months and approved 28 March 1930; prototype must then have been under construction, (Shavrov) 'took only one more month'. First flight **VT-11** by B.L. Bukholts 29 April 1930. This had supercharged Jupiter VII in completely helmeted cowl; doped silver and with VT badge proudly painted on rudder. Second had large faired rubber shock-absorbers on main legs, unblown Jupiter VI and was doped red, with fuselage emblazoned *Klim Voroshilov* who watched it fly. Third fitted with second licensed Jupiter VI (M-15) 'Gift No 16'.

Pilot opinions very favourable (but so they were on I-6) and construction described as refined and light. Prolonged evaluation against I-6, both in flight and to determine manufacturing problems, future service reliability and other aspects. Menzhinskii plant kept building I-5, gradually improving design by introducing Townend-ring cowl, crankcase fairing with cooling holes, dural propeller with pitch adjustable on ground, improved landing gear (some with spats), pilot headrest and fairing, pitot/static head on upper right wing and stronger tailskid. Seven aircraft produced by September 1930, and from No 10 armament increased from two synchronized PV-1 with 1200 rounds to four guns (two each side of fuselage) with 4000 rounds, or two guns and two 20 kg bombs. In 1932 preparations for production at GAZ-21; special group under I.M. Kostkin to prepare drawings. Final NII testing of definitive I-5 by V.A. Stepanchenok, A.F. Anisimov, I.F. Petrov, I.F. Kozlov and others. Series manufacture late 1932, deliveries from February 1933 (long and unnecessary gap bridged by I-7, under Heinkel licence) with est 800 built by late 1935. By this time no longer competitive. Standard advanced trainer 1936-1941.

VT-11 (No 1 aircraft)

VT-11 (No 2 aircraft)

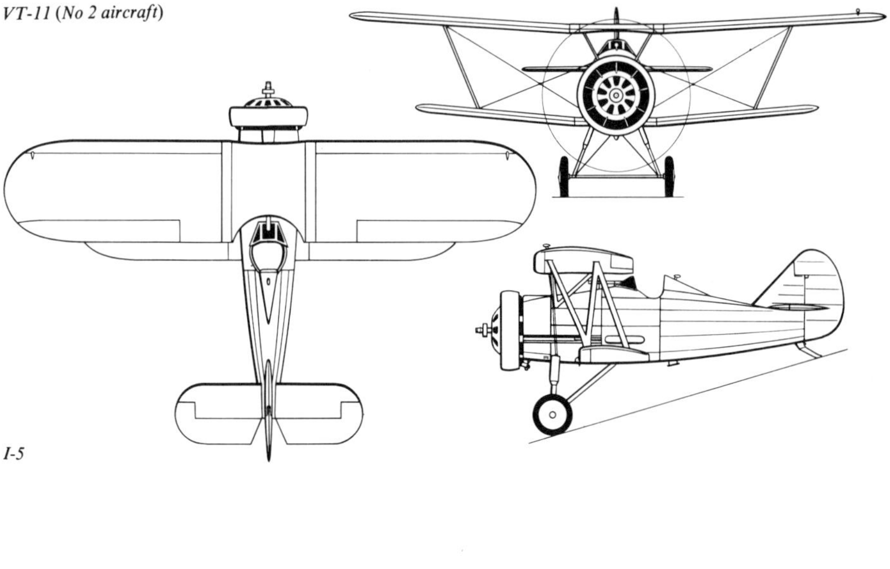

I-5

I-5

I-7

Many local modifications including reinforced plate under rear fuselage for *Zvyeno* parasite experiments, fitting of MF radio with wire aerial stretched from oblique mast ahead of upper centre-section, fitting of generator, battery and nav lights (widely installed), LSh light *Shturmovik* variant with four guns, and three types of skis. Factory-built **UTI-1** trainer with second cockpit (original moved forward) with dual control; 20 built 1934 but not used by VVS.
DIMENSIONS Span (upper) 10,24 m (33 ft 7⅛ in), (lower) 7,4 m (24 ft 3⅓ in); length 6,78 m (22 ft 3 in); wing area 21,25 m^2 (229 ft^2).
ENGINE (VT-11) 450 hp GR Jupiter VII, 525 hp Jupiter VI, (I-5) first with 450 hp M-15, (production) 480 hp M-22.
WEIGHTS Empty (VT-11 No 1) 919 kg, (production) 934 kg (2079 lb); fuel/oil 180 kg; loaded (VT) 1331 kg, (production) 1355 kg (2987 lb).
PERFORMANCE Max speed (VT) 273 km/h (238 at SL), (production) 278 km/h (173 mph) at SL, 252 km/h at 2 km, (Něměcek) 286 at SL; climb to 1 km, (VT) 1·4 min, (production) 1·6; service ceiling (VT) 7,8 km, (production) 7,5 km (24,600 ft); range 660 km (410 miles); time 360° circle, (VT) 14 s, (production) 10/11 s; take-off 100 m/8 s; landing 200 m/15 s/95 km/h (59 mph).

I-7 VT had largely completed design of I-5 by spring 1930 and played major role in studying further fighters. I-9 and I-10 (see Grigorovich) not built, partly owing to absence of engines, and long evaluation of I-5 led to such desperate need for newer fighter in squadrons that Heinkel HD 37c adopted and built under license as I-7, with existing licensed BMW engine. Few changes apart from PV-1 guns and Russian radio (same aerial installation as I-5). Regarded as stop-gap, yet many survived alongside I-5 and were withdrawn only upon debut of I-15.
DIMENSIONS Span 10,0 m (32 ft 9⅔ in); length 6,95 m (22 ft 9⅔ in); wing area 26,7 m^2 (287 ft^2).
ENGINE One 715 hp M-17F.
WEIGHTS Empty 1296 kg (2857) lb); fuel/oil 200 kg; loaded 1729 kg (3812 lb).
PERFORMANCE Max speed 290 km/h (180 mph) at SL; climb to 1 km, 2 min; service ceiling 7,2 km (23,620 ft); range 700 km (435 miles); time 360° circle, 12 s; take-off 90 m/7 s; landing 160 m/13 s/96 km/h (59·7 mph).

I-11 Unbuilt Polikarpov (VT) monoplane single-seat fighter with emphasis on speed rather than manoeuvrability (in conformity with 1932 VVS doctrine of fighter force made up of agile biplanes collaborating with fast monoplanes). One 800 hp M-34F; metal airframe.

I-13 Unbuilt project of 1932 for agile biplane fighter with Wright Cyclone. Led to I-15.

I-15, TsKB-3, Chaika Polikarpov's final months in detention were spent examining ways of improving I-5, then (January 1933) still not in full production. He returned to TsKB with detailed three-view of new fighter remarkably similar to definitive I-5 but with gull-type upper wing (hence nickname *Chaika*, seagull) to improve pilot forward view. Desired engine, Wright Cyclone F-series.

Design undertaken as TsKB-3. Wings almost identical to I-5 except for welded steel-tube basis of inboard sections of upper wings, inclined at 30°. I-type interplane struts of KhMA tube with light dural fairing. Fuselage truss of gas-welded KhMA tube with light secondary structure of rolled dural L-sections to give streamline form. Skin of removable D1 panels back to windscreen, fabric to rear. Large Frise-type ailerons on upper wings only, differential action. All control surfaces D6, with fabric covering. Most outstanding feature was cantilever main legs, each of machined steel tube with lower portion sliding in upper and located by internal slot 1,5 × 12 mm section with up to 190 mm stroke, with air/oil shock-absorbing. Wheels fitted with disc brakes and tyres 700 × 100 mm; or skis 1650 × 370 mm.

Prototype fitted with Cyclone SGR-1820-F3 driving Russian dural two-blade propeller with ground-adjustable pitch. Two synchronized PV-1 with 2000 rounds, optional overload of two 20-kg bombs. First flight by Valerii P. Chkalov, October 1933. Excellent handling, set record for 360° circle (just over 8 s). Factory testing took 26 days, and NII tests barely another month, resulting in immediate series production as I-15. License for Cyclone and initiation of production as M-25 took four years (1932-Oct 1936), so GAZ-21 had no option but to build I-15 with M-22, with much-reduced performance. Engine installation almost same as I-5 with Townend-ring cowl and ground-adjustable dural propeller. After building 404 aircraft production switched in 1936 to using imported Cyclone F3 engines (16:11 reduction gear) with important addition of Hamilton bracket-type two-pitch propeller, no change in designation. First of 59 of these, completed as **TsKB-3bis** prototype in November 1935, flown by V.K. Kokkinaki on 21 November in specially lightened condition to 14 575 m (47,818 ft). Cyclone

I-15 (red prototype with spats)

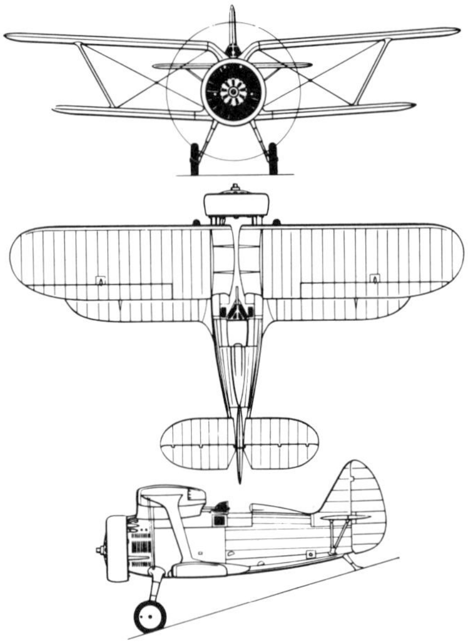

I-15

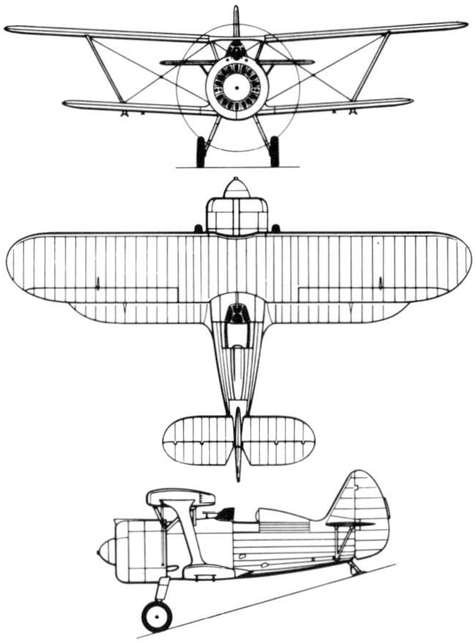

I-15bis, I-152

in short-chord cowl with carb intake at top and individual exhaust pipes discharging behind cowl all round. Final 270 fitted with almost identical installation of M-25, AV-1 (licensed Hamilton) propeller, and with four PV-1 (two in each side of fuselage as in some I-5) with 3000 rounds, and fuselage fuel tank reduced in capacity from 310 to 210 lit. Production completed 1937.

I-15 saw extensive service in Spain, China, at Khalkin Gol, Nomonhan and in Winter War, many remaining operational in June 1941. Gull wing was not universally liked, and in early 1936, following tests by TsAGI, 12 I-15 built with normal upper centre section. In 1938 about 40 built (author believes not extra aircraft but conversions) with normal guns replaced by two BS. In same year, following long research, TsKB's A.Ya. Shchyerbakov fitted rubber-sealed pressure cabin to production I-15, with circular pilot windows. At same time I-15 studied as light attack (LSh) aircraft; stoutly promoted by Chkalov, but DI-6 accepted instead, and this version believed not flown.

DIMENSIONS Span 9,75 m (31 ft 11$\frac{7}{8}$in); length 6,1 m (20 ft 0 in); wing area 21,9 m^2 (236 ft^2).

ENGINE (TsKB-3 and 59 built) one 710 hp Cyclone SGR-1820-F3, (404 prod.) 480 hp M-22, (270 built) 710 hp M-25.

WEIGHTS Empty (TsKB-3) 965 kg, (production, M-22) 1106 kg (2438 lb), (M-25) 1272 kg (2804 lb); fuel/oil 177 kg; loaded (-3) 1374 kg, (M-22) 1415 kg (3119 lb), (M-25) 1681 kg (3706 lb).

PERFORMANCE Max speed (-3) 369 km/h (229 mph) at 2130 m, (M-22) 320 km/h (199 mph), (M-25) 365 km/h (227 mph); climb to 1 km, 1·1 min (all); service ceiling (M-22) 7520 m (24,670 ft), (others) 9,8 km (32,150 ft); range (typical) 550 km (342 miles), less with four guns (Němeček, 725 km); time 360° circle, 8/8·5 s; take-off 70 m/4 s; landing 70 m/6 s/90 km/h.

I-15bis, I-152 Gull wing of I-15 pleased many pilots but some complained view worse than before; following VVS tests with 12 un-gulled aircraft Polikarpov brigade, about this time given status of OKB, effected major revision of I-15 as **TsKB-3 ter**, later I-152 and more commonly I-15bis. New upper wing with 0,6 m^2 greater area, normal centre section, simplified and restressed structure and profile of Clark-YH type. Front lift wires duplicated in tandem. Improved and more powerful engine, in totally different long-chord cowling developed at TsIAM with shuttered front, large removable side panels with apertures for individual exhaust stacks and ducted oil cooler at top. AV-1 propeller usually with spinner. Improved landing gear and brakes, and tyres now 120 mm wide. Pilot given 9-mm back armour. Empty weight 350 kg greater, but performance generally improved. Four PV-1 (often later replaced by ShKAS) with 2600 rounds or two BS, bombload up to 150 kg. First flight believed January 1937. Succeeded I-15 at GAZ-21 and output stepped up (probably by bringing in GAZ-156 also) so that 2408 were delivered within two years, ending early 1939. Together with I-15 total of 550 supplied to Republican Spain, where dubbed *Chato* (flat-nosed) by Nationalists. Fair results against Nationalist fighters, C.R.32 possibly having edge in manoeuvrability but I-15bis excelling in dive/climb and firepower. Many served in Far East, proving generally inferior to Ki-27, and in Winter War; over 1000 operational in June 1941.

I-152TK Single 1939 aircraft fitted with two TK-3 turbochargers driven by exhaust (4$\frac{1}{2}$ cylinders to each turbo, top pipe being divided) from otherwise standard M-25B. Speed 435 km/h at 6 km. Empty weight increased by 140 kg.

I-152GK Single 1939 aircraft rebuilt with improved Shchyerbakov pressure cabin, of rubber-sealed aluminium shaped to fit profile of rear

I-15bis, I-152

I-152DM (ramjets)

I-152GK (pressure-cabin)

fuselage. Cabin weighed 78 kg, but no details of any in-flight pressurization. Described as first really successful Soviet GK (*Germetichyeskoi Kabine*, hermetic cabin).

DIT Single 1938 I-152 rebuilt as two-seat *Shturmovik* with modified armament. Believed only two-seat biplane built by this OKB after 1934. Only 10 kg heavier empty and 22 kg heavier loaded, and speed actually higher at 327/379 km/h. No change in length.

DIMENSIONS Span 10,2 m (33 ft 5½ in); length (Shavrov) 6,2 m (20 ft 4 in), (Něměcek) 6,33 m (20 ft 9¼ in); wing area 22,5 m² (242 ft²).

ENGINE One 750 hp M-25B.

WEIGHTS Empty 1310 kg (2888 lb), (Něměcek, 1320); fuel/oil 177 kg; loaded 1730 kg (3814 lb), (Něměcek, 1900).

PERFORMANCE Max speed 321 km/h (199 mph) at SL, 370 km/h (230 mph) at 3 km, (Něměcek, 375); climb to 1 km, 1·1 min; service ceiling 9 km (29,530 ft); range 530 km (329 miles), (Něměcek, 450, errs on low side); time 360° circle, 10·5 s; take-off 170 m/9 s; landing (Shavrov) 237 m/15 s (not explained why so much greater than I-15, nor why DIT landing 420 m/30 s)/110 km/h (68 mph).

I-153 Again dubbed *Chaika*, but hardly ever called **I-15ter**, this final member of Polikarpov biplane family was probably best of all biplane fighters but represented too-prolonged attempt to perpetuate concept of agile if slow fighter in age of more powerful stressed-skin monoplane. Soviet Union lacked aircraft in class of early Bf 109 and had no way of knowing I-153 would be outclassed in nation's hour of dire need. Indeed I-153 stemmed from Kremlin meeting with Stalin and VVS at which results of Spanish war were examined and firm decision made to press ahead with improved biplane because of apparent superiority of Fiat biplane over I-16. This meeting late July 1937, when Bf 109B-1 already showing superiority in Spain. In August Polikarpov drew up plans and I-15ter approved 11 October 1937. Programme assigned to A.Ya. Shchyerbakov.

Remarkably few changes apart from reversion to gull wing and introduction of retractable main landing gear. Principal air/oil shock strut braced laterally by diagonal strut, both pivoted to fuselage to retract directly to rear, wheel rotating 90° to lie flat in well in lower wing and with tie-rod to doors on ventral centreline hinged outwards to cover legs. Actuation by cockpit handcrank, bevel and screwjack acting on mid-jointed rear bracing struts. Tyres further widened to 150 mm. Instead of skid, fixed tailwheel with solid tyre, castoring within small limits set by rudder position. Engine-driven generator, battery and nav lights standard, and radio in a proportion of series aircraft. Standard armament four ShKAS with 2600 rounds. Additional pre-production aircraft with four BS or two ShVAK, extremely powerful for 1938. Four racks under lower wing each stressed for FAB-50 or various other stores to same 200-kg total such as 25-kg anti-personnel bombs. First flight summer 1938, and NII tests with several aircraft completed in autumn. Series production organized at GAZ-156 under Artem I. Mikoyan, soon supplemented by GAZ-1 to rate of 48 per week.

First deliveries to Far East, where 70 IAP were in action 25 July 1939. Though not totally outclassed by lower-powered (650 hp) Ki-27 it was clear I-153 was becoming obsolescent. In absence of alternative, production was continued with improved version, **I-153BS.** Designation from four BS guns, but main advantage in combat was M-62 engine giving substantially more power at altitude and thus better climb, high-alt speed and ceiling. This version available from spring 1939, small number also being produced of **I-153P** (*Pushyechnyi*) with two ShVAK in place of four BS. Following service trials I-153 also cleared mid-1939 to launch up to eight (six more common) RS-82 from rails beneath lower wing. From early in production of M-62 model lower wing was plumbed to allow inboard racks to carry two 100-lit (22-gal) drop tanks, first in regular use in world. Production finally tapered off in November 1940, total deliv-

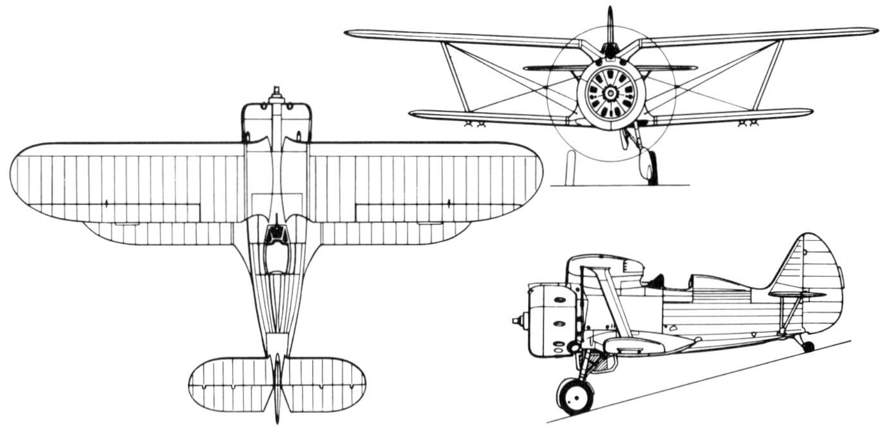

I-153

I-153 with retractable skis

eries 3437. Severe attrition second half 1941 but large number in front-line service 1943, mainly close-support role. Finnish Ilmavoimat used at least 14 captured examples re-equipped with Browning guns and German radio, eight surviving war!

I-153V Single aircraft with definitive Shchyerbakov pressure cabin. Capsule of minimum-leak regenerative type, of welded AMts-L0,8 aluminium with all apertures sealed by rubber. Much-improved glazing with large slabs of curved 6-mm Plexiglas in heavily framed hinged hood giving view not much inferior to that in normal enclosed cockpit. This cabin weighed 45 kg, and empty weight of I-153V was 190 kg heavier at 1538 kg. Designation from *Vysotnyi*, height.

I-153V-TKGK Single aircraft fitted late 1939 with M-63 engine with twin TK-3 turbochargers as well as flexible rubberized-fabric GK (pressure cabin) by Polikarpov KB. At 1,9 t this was lighter than 1959 kg of I-153V, though empty weight must have been appreciably more. Shavrov does not explain why speed at best height should have been same as regular 153BS, ceiling same and rate of climb worse, despite highly blown 930 hp engine.

I-153DM Designation from *Dopolnityelnyi Motor*, supplementary motor; aircraft used by Merkulov at Central Airfield September 1940 to test two 400-mm DM-2 ramjets, and (October) two 500-mm DM-4. On 27 October 440 km/h reached at 2 km with ramjets burning.

I-190 Described separately.

DIMENSIONS Span 10,0 m (32 ft 9½ in); length 6,17 m (20 ft 2⅞ in); wing area 22,14 m² (238 ft²).

ENGINE (Initial) one 750 hp M-25V, (1939) 850/1000 hp M-62.

WEIGHTS Empty (typical of all) 1348 kg (2,972 lb); fuel/oil 150 + 19 kg; loaded (normal) 1859 kg (4098 lb), (max) 2110 kg (4652 lb).

PERFORMANCE Max speed (clean) (M-25) 365 km/h at SL, 415 km/h (258 mph) at 3 km, (M-62) 366 km/h at SL, 444 km/h (276 mph) at 4,6 km; time to 1 km, (M-25) 1·1 min, (M-62) 0·8 min; service ceiling (all) about 10,7 km (35,100 ft); range (typical, clean) 480 km (298 miles), (drop tanks) 880 km (550 miles); time 360° circle, 11·4/12·4 s; take-off (M-62) 106 m/6 s (clean), 360 m/19 s (max wt); landing 150 m/10 s/110 km/h (68 mph).

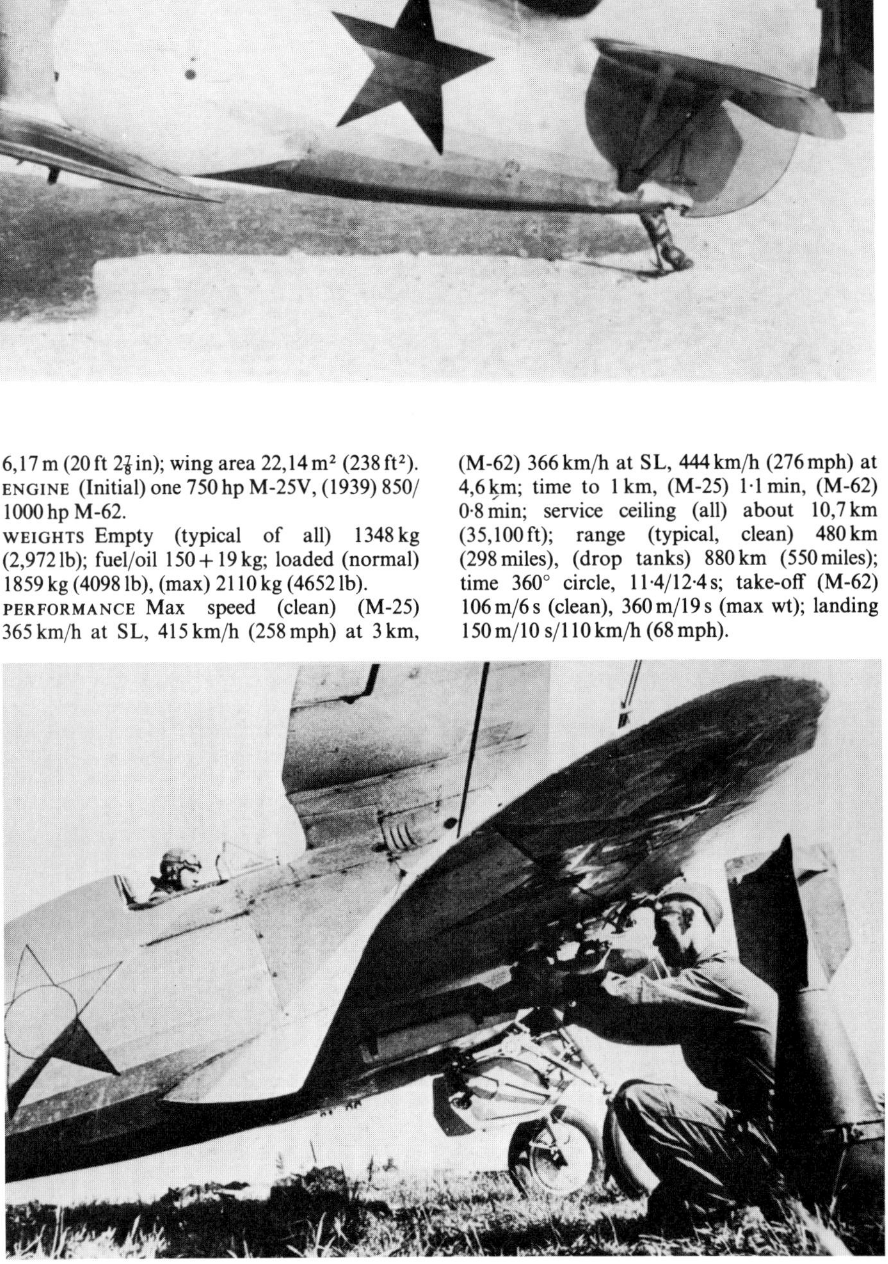

I-153 with four FAB-50 bombs

I-16, TsKB-12 While Polikarpov and aides were in detention in early 1932 NII concluded two-year study with strategic decision to use mix of agile (biplane) fighters and fast (possibly monoplane) fighters. Much argument over practicability of monoplane, especially one without bracing struts. When Polikarpov regained freedom in early 1933 he had already decided top priority was to make up for lost time on new monoplane fighter to compete with KOSOS ANT-31, then about to fly. TsKB-12 project launched about beginning of March 1933 and pressed ahead with same intensity as prevailed in VT prison. Resulting design was stumpy close-coupled monoplane of mixed construction, with pilot well aft as in I-15 and facing same problem of delay with licensed Cyclone engine. Though far from faultless it overtook ANT-31 to become leading Soviet fighter of rest of 1930s. Unfortunately it was still chief VVS and MA fighter in June 1941, when obsolescent.

Wing of largest practicable area (higher aspect ratio than in many published three-views), modified TsAGI R-II profile, t/c 16% at root, set at +3° in low-mid position with large root fillet. Centre section with two spars, widely separated, of riveted KhMA steel tube (from 1936, KhGSA) built up into strong truss, with ribs of truss type built up from riveted dural box sections, with flush-riveted dural D1 skin. Main wing panels with spars of D6 sheet webs riveted to KhMA tube booms and truss ribs riveted from D6 box and angle sections, with skin of flush-riveted 0,5-mm D1 back to front spar and fabric aft. Fuselage of trad multi-layer *shpon*, 4 mm at front and 2,5 mm towards tail, built up with casein glue on carcase made in left and right halves each with four pine longerons and 11 half-frames. Very large slotted ailerons of D6 with fabric covering, with differential push/pull rod actuation and drooping 15° for landing. Entire tail of D6, mainly pressed from sheet with lightening holes, with fabric covering; surfaces unbalanced and driven by cables (rudder) or rods and bell-cranks (elevators). Fixed tailskid but fully retractable main gears, with air/oil sprung legs braced by rear strut both pivoted to fold inwards under pull of cable from cockpit screwjack (there was prolonged study of pneumatic and hydraulic actuation). Tyres 700 × 100 mm, wheels with brakes (originally manual, later pneumatic). Only available engine M-22, but for first time installed in long-chord cowl with optimized cooling-air slot at rear. Usual perforated crankcase fairing, standard 2,8 m ground-adjustable duralumin propeller without spinner. Single aluminium fuselage tank of 425 l (93·5 gal). Rather narrow cockpit with folding left sidewall and seat adjustable for height only (as in I-15). Glazed aluminium/glass canopy with integral vee-windscreen, sliding forwards assisted by bungee cords to overcome drag in flight. Aldis-derived CP optical sight integral with windshield. Two ShKAS each with 900 rounds in centre section beyond propeller disc.

I-153DM (ramjets)

First prototype airframe 445 kg, engine and equipment 450 kg, gross weight 1311 kg. Doped red overall and flown by Valerii P. Chkalov 31 December 1933. Adequate handling; performance fair considering low power. Second (*dubler*) prototype, **TsKB-12bis,** flown 18 February 1934 with imported Cyclone F3 driving 9 ft 2 in (2794 mm) Hamilton two-pitch propeller. Intensive factory and NII trials quickly established TsKB-12 as fit for production as I-16, but not easy to fly. Marginally stable about all axes, no trimmers, and in glide tended to stall, also tending to stall/spin in hard manoeuvres; severe vibration from engine, great difficulty in cranking up landing gear (44 turns, progressively harder) and gear tended to jam when part-extended prior to landing (cable shears later standard kit in cockpit), shock struts undamped and landing dangerous even on rare smooth field, landing speed high and wing dropped if speed allowed to bleed off, and with M-22 high power needed whenever gear extended, and throttle still well open as flown on to ground. Despite this, considered best available fighter 1934, and ordered into production at GAZ-1 and GAZ-21 about late May 1934. Subsequent models given *tip* (pronounced teep, = Type) numbers, reflecting justified belief there would be many future variants.

I-153V (pressure-cabin)

I-16 tip-1 Often called **I-16M-22,** this was original production version, flown late 1934 and displayed in two flights of five in May Day parade 1935. Such pressure was put on introduction of more powerful versions that few Type 1 built (Green/Swanborough, fewer than 30). But by late 1935 substantial number with M-22 engine delivered as two-seat trainers:

UTI-2 Originally I-16 *tip*-1 with armament removed and fuselage redesigned by A.A. Brovkov to accommodate pupil in rear cockpit moved 450 mm to rear and instructor in added front cockpit. Slightly revised structure and modified fuel tank of almost unchanged capacity despite reduced length of tank. Both cockpits open, with separate windscreens.

UTI-3 New-build aircraft with UTI-2 fuselage and simple fixed landing gear almost identical to original but with retraction mechanism removed and wells plated over. From early 1936 many fitted with blind-flying canopy of plywood for rear cockpit, manually sliding to rear and with black curtain hanging across at front to pass over pupil's head.

I-16 tip-4 First main production model, closely resembling TsKB-12bis and powered by imported engine driving imported Hamilton propeller. Cowl and engine installation similar to *tip*-1 though cowl extended 405 mm aft. Landing gears fitted with extra wheel doors, with hinged lower portion, to cover wheels in flight. Many hundreds delivered 1934–1935.

I-16 tip-5 First variant with licensed M-25 engine driving AV-1 propeller. Seat fitted with 8 mm back armour as on final batch of *tip*-4. Attachment added under each outer wing for FAB-100, total bombload 200 kg (441 lb). Replaced *tip*-4 in production July 1935.

UTI-4 Two-seat conversion of *tip*-5 with essentially same fuselage as UTI-3 and often with standard retı actable landing gear. By late 1935 every fourth I-16 was dual-control, often also known as **I-16UTI** (*Uchyebno-Trenirovochnyi Istrebitel*, training fighter). Small number of dual trainers also built with later engines, or produced by field conversion of subsequent fighter models.

I-16Sh, TsKB-18 Single 1935 *tip*-1 modified for *Shturmovik* role with four ShKAS (Shavrov, or PV-1) and 100-kg bombload. First Soviet aircraft with bucket seat for seat-pack parachute incorporating rear and bottom armour; further armour ahead of pilot.

I-16P Single *tip*-5 with F3 Cyclone modified in 1935 with heavier armament; designation from *Pushyechnyi*, cannon. Two ShKAS in top of fuselage, and at extremities of centre-section two unsynchronized ShVAK with 150 rounds each. Racks under outer wings for six Der-31 bomb containers. First installation of wing cannon (Shavrov), but took two years of testing before production.

I-16 tip-6 Standard 1936 production with locally reinforced airframe, adding about 50 kg to structure, and more powerful M-25A engine.

SPB, TsKB-29 Designation from *Skorostnoi Pikiruyushchnyi Bombardirovshchik*, fast dive bomber. I-16 *tip*-5 with pneumatic system added for retraction of landing gear and operation of dive brakes added in place of inboard section of aileron on restressed wings which were also provided with racks for two FAB-250. Initial tests with two FAB-100 May 1936; full bombload used in connection with air-launched *Zvyeno* trials (see Vakhmistrov). Guns, two ShVAK in outer centre section. No production but unknown number of field conversions in 1941–1942.

I-16 tip-10 Standard 1937 model, produced in larger quantity than any other. M-25V engine, further local strengthening to structure, armament four ShKAS, extra pair being added under fairings in top of fuselage each with 650 rounds. Fixed windscreen, otherwise open cockpit, with simple reflector sight. First variant with retractable skis (previously in winter I-16s had used skis with legs locked down); new I-16 model had skis mounted on hinges on existing landing gears with small tie-rod to keep skis in unchanged attitude during retraction to lie flat under wing with toe in deep recess under engine (legs being flush as usual). According to VVS combat performance almost same as with wheeled gear, whereas fixed skis had reduced max speed 60/80 km/h.

I-16P, TsKB-12P Further cannon-armed prototype, 1938, based on *tip*-10 with ShVAK each with 150 rounds in outer centre-section. In this installation they were mounted much further forward, most of barrel projecting from leading edge. After refinement accepted as production armament. Same aircraft also tested four ShVAK (possibly two in fuselage in place of ShKAS but no details).

I-16 tip-17 Standard 1938 model introducing two fuselage ShKAS and two wing ShVAK, as previously tested. M-25V unchanged, but structure further improved with wing spars of KhGSA stainless steel and tailskid replaced by wheel with solid rubber tyre. Because of greater weight, new main gears introduced two-stage shock struts with steel main legs 80 mm diameter reflector sight improved and in some aircraft armour 9 mm instead of 8 and of larger area. With improved landing gear, cleared to 1925 kg with extra BS gun in pod on ventral centreline (just cleared by wheels or skis) and two 100-kg bombs. First variant armed with RS-82 rocket, usually six (rarely eight) on underwing racks; RS-82 trials with earlier models 1936, operational on *tip*-17 early 1939 and in action against Japanese August 1939.

I-16TK Several, possibly many, I-16s fitted with TsIAM turbochargers. First was this *tip*-10 with two TK-1 turbos, and engine driving AV-1 hydromatic with 30° pitch range; rated height increased from 2,9 to 7,25 km.

I-16 tip-18 Standard 1939 aircraft, introducing M-62 engine with two-speed supercharger. Modified exhaust system discharging through three holes on each side, alternately with single and paired pipes for nine cylinders. Propeller AV-1 or VISh-6A, smaller fuselage tank of 255 lit (56 gal) for highest flight performance, made up by plumbing for optional pair of 200-lit drop tanks as on I-153; otherwise as *tip*-10 with four ShKAS with 3100 rounds.

I-16 tip-24 Final major production version, second half 1939, similar to *tip*-10 or *tip*-18 but with M-63 engine, driving VV-1 or VISh-6 propeller. Wing stiffened by increasing number of ribs, increasing gauge of leading-edge metal skin to 0,6 mm and adding 3 mm ply between spars on both upper and under surfaces, retaining outer layer of fabric. Drop tanks in this model cleared to 254-lit (55·9-gal) size. Diverse weapons fitted, including four ShKAS, two ShKAS and two wing ShVAK, and four ShKAS plus single BS between fuselage guns on upper centreline. Underwing loads six RS-82 or bomb loads up to two FAB-250 (500-kg, 1102 lb). In addition, PBP-1 or RBP-1a reflector sight, RSI-1 or RSI-3 HF radio and oxygen increasingly made standard.

I-16 tip-28 to tip-30 Closely related to *tip*-24 but with direct-drive M-63 engine. Production of *tip*-24 terminated spring 1940, but in autumn 1941 urgent need for numbers resulted in further 450, mainly *tip*-28 to *tip*-30, produced with old tooling. Total production thus increased to: (single-seat) 7005, (two-seat) at least 1639 built as UTI-4 and small number of earlier models. Various popular names, notably *Mosca* (fly), also adopted officially by Republican Spain. Called *Rata* (rat) by Nationalists, yet this hostile epithet caught on in West and in the Second World War regarded almost as official designation! Well-documented operational history includes dive-bombing by SPB conversions (see Vakhmistrov) and deliberate ramming attacks. Generally replaced by later fighters by late 1943; several preserved.

DIMENSIONS Span (Green/Swanborough) 8,88 m (29 ft 1⅔ in), (other sources) 9,0 m (29 ft 6⅓ in); length (TsKB-12) 5,9 m, (−1 to −6) 6,0 m (19 ft 8¼ in), (−10, −17) 5,98 m (19 ft 7½ in), (M-62) 6,04 m (19 ft 9¾ in), (M-63) 6,13 m (20 ft 1⅓ in); wing area 14,54 m^2 (156·5 ft^2).

ENGINE One radial, (prototype, −1) 480 hp M-22, (−4) 710 hp Cyclone F3, (−5) 700 hp M-25, (−6, −12) 730 hp M-25A, (−10, −17) 750 hp M-25V, (−18, some −24) 920 hp M-62, (−24 and later) 1100 hp M-63.

WEIGHTS Empty (UTI-2) 1030 kg, (−5) 1200 kg (2646 lb), (−6) 1260 kg (2778 lb), (−10) 1350 kg (2976 lb), (−17) 1495 kg (3296 lb), (−18) 1428 kg (3148 lb), (−24, M-63) 1490 kg (3285 lb); fuel/oil (UTI) 155 + 16, (most) 183 + 25, (−24) 280 kg, (−24, M-63, internal) 190 + 30; max loaded (UTI) 1,4 t, (−4) 1420 kg

I-16 tip-10

I-16 tip-17 on retractable skis. This twin-cannon example captured by Finland

(3131 lb), (−5) 1460 kg (3219 lb), (−6) 1660 kg (3660 lb), (−10) 1715 kg (3781 lb), (−17) 1810 kg (3990 lb), (−18 1830 kg (4034 lb), (−24, M-62, normal) 1912 kg (4215 lb), (−24, M-63, max) 2095 kg (4619 lb).
PERFORMANCE Max speed (TsKB-12) 359 km/h, (UTI, typical) 364 km/h, (M-22, wheels) 360 km/h, (−4, −5) 395 km/h (245 mph) at SL, 455 km/h (283 mph) at 4 km, (−10, −17) about 385 km/h at SL, 440 at 5 km; (−18) 411/464 km/h (255/288 mph), (−24, either engine) 440/489 km/h (273/304 mph), M-25A aircraft with fixed skis) 354/385 km/h, (SPB) 350 km/h; climb to 1 km (−5) 1·3 min, (−18) 1·8 min; service ceiling (typical) 8,6/9,1 km, (−18) 9470 m (31,000 ft), (−24, M-63) 9,7 km (31,825 ft); range (typical) 820 km (500 miles), (−24) 700 km; time 360° circle (early) 15 s, (late models) up to 18 s; take-off (early) 230 m/13 s, (−18) 320 m/15 s, (−24, max wt) 450 m/22 s; landing (typical) 280 m/18 s/100 km/h (early) to 130 km/h (late models).

I-17 To provide advanced fighter with water-cooled engine for comparison with I-16 Polikarpov's TsKB collective designed **TsKB-15** in first half 1934, building prototype very quickly in summer and starting flight testing (V.P. Chkalov) on 1 September. Technology as TsKB-12 (I-16) with wooden *shpon* monocoque fuselage and KhMA steel/D6 dural wing with D1 skin back to front spar and fabric to rear. Bulky V-12 engine, then subject of licence negotiation, carried on mounting fabricated from dural box sections, with D1 skin panels. Large metal two-blade propeller, said to be two-pitch but unknown type. Large unducted radiator extended by manual cranking from belly. Main gears similar to I-16 with manual cranking but retracting outwards from pivots near wing roots. Provision for two ShVAK (then still experimental) and two ShKAS in centre section outboard of propeller disc, plus 50-kg bombload (almost certainly 2 × 25-kg). Forward-sliding canopy with integral windscreen with Aldis sight. Attractive aircraft, with cockpit nearer CG than in other Polikarpov fighters, but Chkalov found cockpit narrow and shock struts stiff in their cylinders, and on demo before VVS delegation one leg failed to extend. Nevertheless, designation I-17 allotted, and second prototype authorized. This was modified, designated **TsKB-19.** New wide-track landing gear retracting inwards with pneumatic (30 s at, 440 lb/in^2) operation. Licensed M-100 engine driving 3,6 m (11 ft 10 in) licensed French propeller with ShVAK firing through hub. Four ShKAS in outer centre-section. Wing of reduced aspect ratio, with shorter ailerons and Zapp-type flaps. Racks under outer wings for two 50-kg bombs. Unique coolant system with two equal-size radiators packaged in short ducts mounted on sliding semi-retractable pylons containing piping. One radiator for water, other half-water, half-oil. Excellent aircraft, faster than any I-16, better handling and good gun platform. Exhibited Paris Salon 1936. Third prototype built, **TsKB-33,** with surface-evaporation steam cooling using 7 m^2 (75 ft^2) of smooth D1 double skin along wing leading edges (details show intimate knowledge of British R-R Goshawk system). Armament reduced to three ShKAS to keep weight to 1935 kg and cooling system thought vulnerable. Perhaps unfortunately, Chkalov was by late 1935 preoccupied with planned RD record flight, improved I-16 was considered adequate and programme lapsed.

I-17Z Development for launching from TB-3 *Aviamatka* (see Vakhmistrov) with only 9 m^2 wing and no landing gear except emergency skid; three ShVAK or one ShVAK and two ShKAS, est speed 575 km/h, to hook back on parent aircraft after combat. Not built.

TsKB-25 Projected development of I-17 with M-34RNF or GR14Krsd, studied late 1935.

TsKB-43 Projected development of TsKB-19 with HS12Ybrs and four ShKAS plus 100 kg (two FAB-50) bombs; est speed 520 km/h, again December 1935. Significance of these fighters was that they could have led by 1941 to large number of aircraft as formidable in air combat as Bf 109, Hurricane or Spitfire, greatly reducing VVS/MF attrition in 1941–1942.

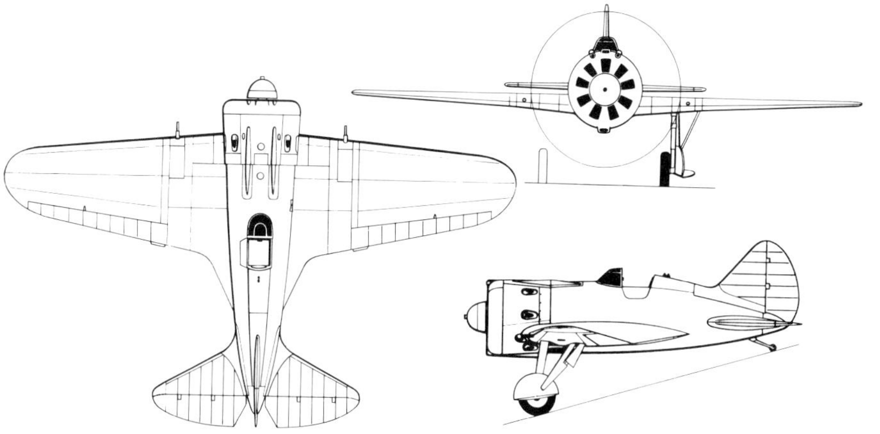

I-16 tip-24

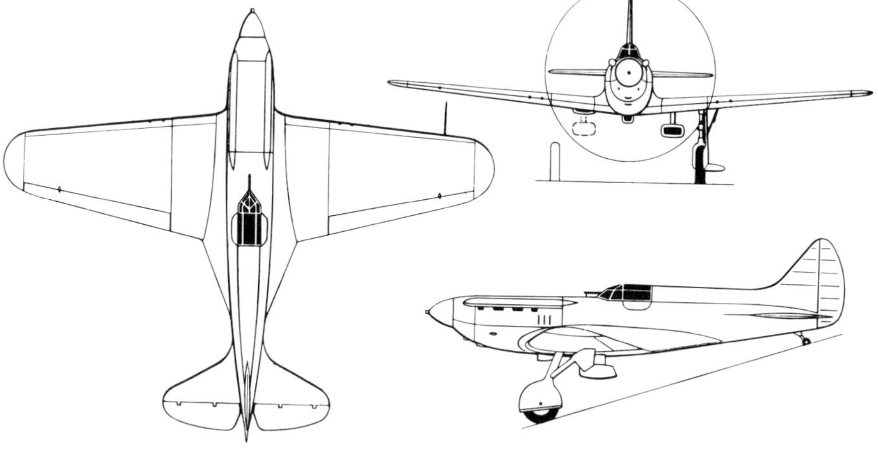

I-17 (No 2 aircraft)

I-17 (No 2 aircraft)

DIMENSIONS Span (1) 10,2 m (33 ft 5½ in), (2) 10,0 m (32 ft 9¾ in); length 8,8 m (28 ft 10½ in); wing area (1) 17,7 m² (190 ft²), (2) 17,9 m² (193 ft²).
ENGINE (1) One 760 hp Hispano-Suiza 12Ybrs, (2, 3) 750 hp M-100.
WEIGHTS Empty (2) 1620 kg) (3571 lb); fuel/oil 155+35 kg; loaded (1) 1655 kg (3649 lb), (Něměcek, 1930 kg), (2) 1950 kg (4299 lb), (Něměcek, 1930).
PERFORMANCE Max speed (1) 424 km/h at SL, 455 km/h (283 mph, Shavrov's low figure) at 3 km, (Něměcek, 487), (2) 'near 500 km/h', (Něměcek, 491 km/h, 305 mph); climb to 1 km, 1·1 min; to 5 km, 6·3; service ceiling (1) 9260 m, (2) 9,9 km (32,480 ft), (Něměcek, 11 km for both); range, not quoted by Shavrov, (Něměcek, 790 km/491 miles for both); time 360° circle, 16 s; take-off 240 m/13 s; landing 280 m/24 s/127 km/h.

Ivanov Stalin's personal telegraphic code-name was used for major 1936 VVS competition for TTT aircraft (*Taktiko-tekhnichyeskiye Trebovaniya*, tactical-technical requirements), a fast reconnaissance *Shturmovik*. Won by existing KhAI-5 as R-10, but several other later contenders, TsKB entrant having no known designation other than name of competition. Exceedingly like later Su-2 but lighter and different systems. Fuselage oval-section wood monocoque put together from left/right halves, *shpon* skin 3 mm front and 2 mm rear. Light-alloy wing first to have T-section booms of 30KhGSA stainless steel; rest of structure mainly D6 with 0,8 mm flush-riveted skin. Control surfaces D6 with fabric, all with trimmers. First Polikarpov levered-suspension landing gear, pneumatic retraction back into wing with wheels rotating 90°; tailwheel also retractable. Engine in long-chord cowl with pilot-operated gills, driving 3,0 m three-blade constant-speed propeller with spinner. First of two prototypes with four synchronized ShKAS in forward fuselage, two BK and one ShKAS in wing (inboard end of outer panels), one BS in manual dorsal turret and one ShKAS in retractable lower rear position. Remarkable bomb load, 400 kg in fuselage bay and 500 kg under wings. Design first quarter 1937, start of construction 4 July 1937, first flight February 1938. Better than R-10, but by then too late; flying qualities unimpressive but judged amenable to improvement. Tested until August as reconnaissance/bomber; second *Ivanov* not tested.

DIMENSIONS Span (Shavrov, table) 14,0 m (45 ft 11¼ in), (Shavrov, drawing) 14,3 m (46 ft 11 in); length (Shavrov, table) 9,4 m (30 ft 10 in), (Shavrov, drawing) 10,25 m (33 ft 7½ in); wing area 28,07 m² (302 ft²).
ENGINE One 830 hp M-62.
WEIGHTS Empty 2662 kg (5869 lb); fuel/oil 540 kg; loaded 3930 kg (8664 lb).

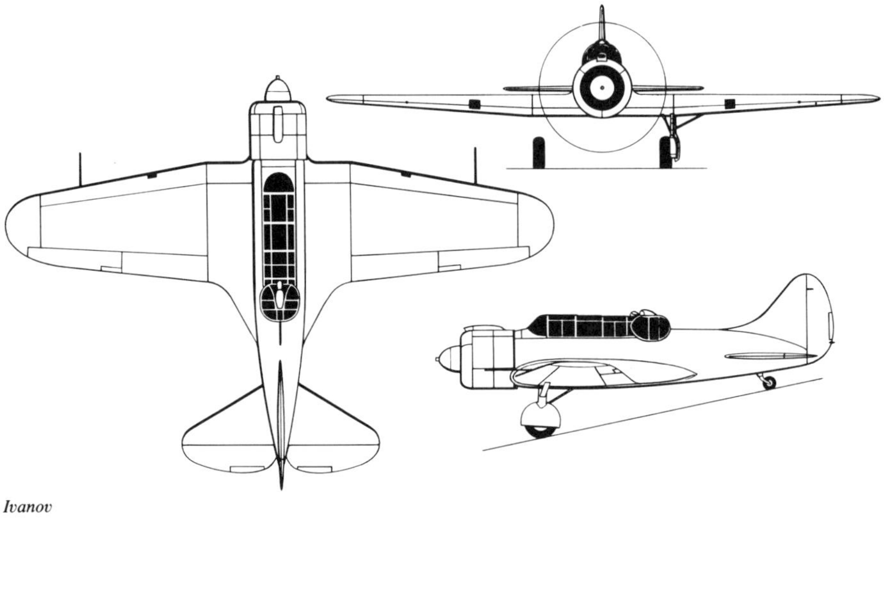

Ivanov

PERFORMANCE Max speed 410 km/h at SL, 425 km/h (264 mph) at 3 km; no other data.

VIT, SVB, MPI-1 By mid-1930s VVS deeply concerned to rationalize tactical combat aircraft and introduce types more effective against armour and other hardened targets. Decided conventional fighter useless unless cleared to bomb in vertical dive; heavy forward-firing guns also needed. In 1936 (Něměcek, May 1935) Polikarpov OKB instructed to prepare project design, and this materialized (date probably June 1936) as **TsKB-44.** Accepted and single prototype authorized. Intended as multi-role aircraft, reflected in three closely related variants: **VIT-1** (*Vozdushnyi Istrebitel Tankov*, aerial tank fighter), SVB (*Samolyet Vozhdushnogo Boya*, aircraft for air combat) and MPI-1 (*Mnogotsyelovoi Pushyechnyi Istrebitel*, multi-role cannon fighter; according to Něměcek M for *Mnogomyestnyi*, multi-seat). Potentially important and advanced aircraft which with successful development could have led to highly effective family for Second World War. Aerodynamically clean twin-engined low-wing machine but retaining mixed structure with fuselage monocoque of *shpon*, made in left/right halves completely assembled with systems and equipment before mating along centreline. Wing design probably same as VIT-2 described below; same span and almost same area, with large root fillets. Rectangular centre section carrying engines, tapered outer panels with 4° dihedral. Two spars with truss structure built up from welded KhMA stainless-steel tube. Multiple lattice ribs again with diagonal tubular or channel truss-members entirely from rolled sections of duralumin. Flush-riveted D1 skin. Tail likewise all-duralumin (first aircraft from KB, one of first in world, with metal-skinned control surfaces); surfaces aerodynamically balanced and fitted with trim tabs. Pneumatically driven split flaps and rearwards-retracting twin-leg main gears, fixed tailwheel. heavily armed. Pilot in wide cockpit above leading edge with rearward-sliding canopy and reflector sight for four ShK-37 in wing roots. Observer/nav in nose (which is shown 'solid' in Něměcek drawing) with hand-aimed (±10°) ShVAK-20. Radio operator in manual dorsal turret with ShKAS. Up to 600 kg bombs in fuselage weapon bay and two FAB-500 on external underwing racks (max bombload 1,6 t, 3527 lb). Aircraft described as exceptionally good finish, first flown by V.P. Chkalov summer 1937. By this time KB could see several improvements in construction, allied with more powerful engine, and had started fresh prototype.

VIT-2, TsKB-48, basically same airframe as VIT-1 but more power and even heavier armament. Wing of Clark-YH profile, 14% root and 6·35% tip, aspect ratio 6·67, improved four-part flaps. Redesigned fuselage with large fuel tank separating pilot from radio/gunner now aft of wing with hand-aimed ShVAK. Larger glazed area in nose, same hand-held ShVAK. In wing roots, two ShK-37 and two ShVAK. Addition of retractable lower rear installation of two ShKAS, presumably also managed by radio operator. Same bombload as VIT-1. Revised twin-finned tail, main gears with large dural fairings forming underside of nacelle when retracted, highly efficient coolant radiators just outboard of engines under wing ahead of flaps

VIT-1 model

(similar but horizontal arrangement later introduced on Messerschmitt Bf 110). First aircraft tested full-scale in large new TsAGI tunnel. First flown by Chkalov 11 May 1938; soon afterwards fitted with VISh-61 constant-speed 3,3-m propellers. Statically tested to design factor of 10·9 (VIT-1 was designed to excessive factor of 13). Factory testing by B.N. Kudrin and NII testing September 1938 by P.M. Stefanovskii. Generally excellent aircraft; decision to build in series, but with some armament removed in order to increase speed and ceiling.

VVS regarded chief role of aircraft as fast dive bomber. Něměcek implies VIT prototypes were fitted with rear-fuselage 'disc-like dive brakes' and reports 'oscillations at higher vertical dive speeds', but no dive brakes are mentioned in any Soviet account. Probably it would have been wise to have built VIT-2 in series; as it was, modification to SPB wasted time and brought end to promising family.

OKB had detailed proposal for special long-range aircraft derived from VIT-2, with armament replaced by fuel tankage. May have been designated **DDI,** though not a fighter; wing span increased and crew two pilots only, in tandem. Range 7900 km (4900 miles) at 350 km/h, 6200 km at 500 km/h. Never built.

DIMENSIONS Span 16,5 m (54 ft $1\frac{2}{3}$ in); length (MPI-1) 11,85 m (38 ft $10\frac{1}{2}$ in), (VIT-2) 12,25 m (40 ft $2\frac{1}{4}$ in); wing area (1) 40,4 m², (2) 40,76 m² (439 ft²).

ENGINES Two Klimov V-12: (1) 960 hp M-103, (2) 1050 hp M-105.

WEIGHTS Empty (1) not known, (2) 4032 kg (8889 lb); fuel/oil (2) 780 kg; loaded (1) (Shavrov) 6453 kg, (Něměcek) 5453 kg, (2) 6302 kg (13,893 lb).

PERFORMANCE Max speed (1) 450 km/h at SL (faster at height, no data), (2) 486 km/h at SL, 513 km/h (319 mph) at 4,5 km; climb, no data; service ceiling (2) 8,2 km (26,900 ft); range (Shavrov) not quoted for MPI-1, 565 km (VIT-2), (Něměcek) 1000 km for both; take-off (1) 390 m, (2) 450 m/22 s; landing (1) 460 m, (2) 400 m/150 km/h.

SPB, D Designation also written **SPB(D),** but in two recent Soviet references D is omitted. Designation from *Skorostnoi Pikiriyuschii Bombardirovshchik* (fast dive bomber) plus D for *Dalnost* (distance) because of exceptional fuel capacity. This was final outcome of promising VIT family, and it represented amazing change in VVS ideas. Instead of guns, this aircraft carried fuel, so it was actually heavier than before. However, by refining the design aerodynamically, it flew faster than VIT-2. Outwardly SPB looked much more like predecessor, though fuselage smaller and more streamlined, wing longer span, and low aspect ratio tail surfaces. Structurally it was totally new aircraft, finally rejecting mixed construction and old-fashioned truss construction, welded joints, closed riveted sections, and tubes and built-up profiles as basic structural members. Instead it was truly modern stressed-skin, with all spar booms rolled or extruded, webs made from plate and all ribs and frames pressed from sheet. Many parts made by rubber press, and estimated man-hours in production of bare airframe only 35% of VIT-2. Reluctantly adhered to three-seat layout, with nav/bomb in nose (single UB), and radio/gunner at back with single UB raised from retracted

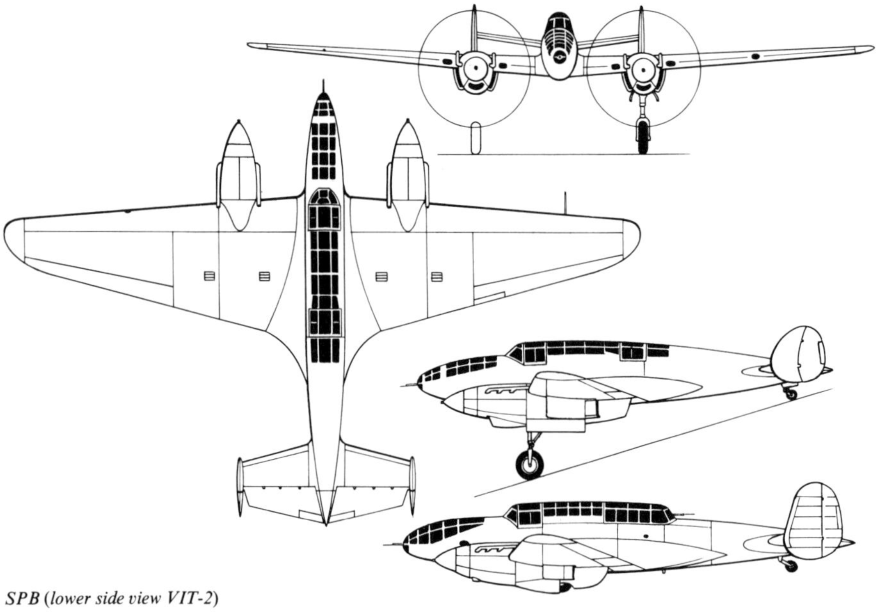

SPB (lower side view VIT-2)

position and aimed from rear cockpit after sliding canopy forward, and periscopic sight to paired ShKAS extended from floor of rear compartment as in VIT-2. No fixed guns, and all offensive reliance placed on bombs: 800 kg in fuselage bay and 700 kg under wings (less than VIT-1). Improved single-leg main gears retracting into nacelle bays with twin doors, improved pedal-actuated brakes, fully retractable tailwheel, oil coolers in wings each side of engine, and deep but narrow radiator in duct on each side of nacelle. CG at 24·8%, 31·3 max wt. Design structural factor 11, just higher than VIT-2. TsAGI tunnel drag only 88% that of VIT-2. Fuel capacity much greater, from range data, but no details and Shavrov's weights do not tally with this. In conformity with VVS demand OKB built five SPB(D), first flown spring 1940 (by B.N. Kudrin, according to recent account, but Shavrov says P.G. Golovin). On 27 April 1940 Golovin killed when SPB(D) refused to recover from spin. Second reared up in diving test and whole machine disintegrated, killing M.A. Lipkin. Investigation revealed failure to fit leading-edge balance weights to ailerons. Third suffered runaway of rudder trim, but Kudrin managed to land undamaged. Fourth put in TsAGI tunnel for research into flight qualities, but whole project terminated before end of 1940,mainly because of proven excellence of Petlyakov's No 100. Most KBs would have been shut, but Polikarpov was favoured by Stalin and only chief project engineer, N.A. Zhemchuzin, was imprisoned.

Termination halted work on **SPB(P)**, twin-float version with reversing propellers (first in world) to assist water manoeuvres; speed 435 km/h at 7 t gross. **SPB(BSB)** was 1938 project for reconnaissance-bomber version with M-88 engines, 1,5 t bombload, 535 km/h and range 2900 km at 6,5 t wt, with ceiling 11 km. **PB-1** was dive bomber of 1939–1940 with two M-71, single ShKAS in nose and BT dorsal. Also **SPBM-71** high-level bomber, 643 km/h (400 mph), 1939–1941. **E, E-2,** dive bomber of 1940 with two M-37, 3,3-t bombload, 622 km/h.

DIMENSIONS Span 17,0 m (55 ft $9\frac{1}{4}$ in); length 11,18 m (36 ft $8\frac{1}{8}$ in); wing area 42,93 m^2 (462 ft^2).

ENGINES Two 1050 hp M-105.

WEIGHTS Empty 4480 kg (9877 lb) (author believes this should be 4080); loaded 6850 kg (15,100 lb).

PERFORMANCE Max speed 490 km/h at SL, 520 km/h (323 mph) at 4,5 km; service ceiling 8,2 km; range 2200 km (1370 miles); take-off 500 m/25 s; landing 450 m.

I-180 Kremlin meeting spring 1938 took decisions on future fighter programme, strongly influenced by Spanish experience. C.R.32 continued to suggest need for agile biplane, but prime need was improved monoplane fighter(s) clearly superior to Bf 109B and successors. I-16 *tip*-10 was considered markedly superior to German fighter, and situation (wrongly) assessed as not urgent. Decision taken to build new fighters in two stages: first generation with 14-cylinder Tumanskii (GR14-derived) engine, I-180 monoplane and I-190 biplane; second stage with 18-cylinder Shvetsov or Tumanskii of much greater power, I-185 monoplane and I-195 biplane. Especially in case of monoplane, development was complicated; Soviet and Western reports are totally incompatible and in most cases latter must be inaccurate. Following is based on Shavrov, but modified in light of later Soviet accounts.

I-180 Several variants of I-16 on drawing board (Western accounts, that of OKB's D.L. Tomashyevich) in 1937–1938 with advanced all-metal structure with plate spar webs, T and L-section booms and stringers and frames and ribs rubber-pressed from sheet. Engine M-87A, systems as I-16. Structural detailing as in OKB's *Ivanov*, but this had been hand-built prototype and OKB gave in to pressure from GAZ production engineers who argued against structure with which they had no experience. Polikarpov reluctant, stating mixed I-16 construction was already obsolete, but I-180 abandoned.

I-180-1 Selected I-180 on 14 June 1938 from original studies but redesigned with traditional I-16 structure with wood monocoque fuselage. Wing Clark-YH profile, built-up KhMA tube spars and D6 lattice ribs, D1 sheet leading edge with adhesive tape edges securing fabric attached over rest of wing. Control surfaces D6 and fabric; three-strut main gears folding inwards pneumatically, protected AMTs fuel tank, three-blade VISh-23-4 constant-speed propeller, M-87A in extended I-16 type cowl 1310 mm diameter and 1260 mm long, four ShKAS in fuselage, bombload 40 kg or overload 200 kg. Flown at Central Aerodrome by V.P. Chkalov 15 December 1938; engine left uncovered all night in −24°C and, after listening to engine, Chkalov rashly decided to fly, suffered engine seizure in circuit and cartwheeled avoiding obstructions. Chkalov, national hero, killed; while body lay in state, many in OKB arrested including Tomashyevich, as well as Usachyev, director GAZ-156, and Belyaikin, director GAP.

I-180-2 Second prototype, generally similar but modernized form of mixed construction with fewer built-up lattice members in wings though retaining wooden *shpon* fuselage. Wing span and area increased, few other changes apart from M-87B with two-speed supercharger. Flown 30

I-180S

March 1939 by S. Suprun. In May, pilot Tomas Suzi suffered engine failure at 10 km and dived into ground almost vertically (no reason found). (Long Soviet reports on this, yet totally different stories in West of both aircraft and pilot.)

I-180-3 Polikarpov got GAP to prevail over GAZ production director and modern stressed-skin construction finally accepted, with simple presswork from sheet. Spar booms machined T-sections in KhGSA. Engine M-88R, more powerful and with geared VISh-23 series propeller, in improved installation with ejector exhausts grouped at rear. Impressive armament, two packages each of one BS and one ShKAS, firing between upper cylinders of engine (author's note: no space between cylinders of this two-row engine, later drawings of I-185 show guns just above cylinder heads). Bombload as I-180-1. Flown 25 February 1939, factory testing by Ye.G. Ulyarkhin and intention to begin series production August, but in early summer NII pilot A.G. Proshakov made badly executed flick roll and aircraft broke up (again Western accounts bear no relation whatever to this). Decision to continue production, with minor revisions to airframe and strengthened landing gear, and add wing drop tanks for *Shturmovik* role.

I-180S Designation from *Seriynyi* (series); similar to I-180-3 except for redesigned wing with higher aspect ratio. Retrograde decision to restore I-16 type wing construction at request of GAZ-156. New four-point pick-up for complete powerplant and armament group. Production organized on flow-line basis and first three of initial batch of ten completed December 1939. Passed production testing and all ten cleared for service, three participating in 1 May 1940 fly-past.

I-180Sh Designation not *Shturmovik* but *Shassi* (landing gear); this component redesigned with single cantilever shock-strut instead of triangulated pattern (called pyramid-type in Russian) used on all previous I-16 and I-180 fighters. Discontinued January 1940 when it was recognized I-180 family no longer competitive, and requiring less wing area and more power to meet more stringent demands for performance and firepower. Urgent redesign to second stage of development with new 18-cylinder engine resulted in I-185 series.

DIMENSIONS (180, 180-1) 9,0 m (29 ft 6⅓ in), (-2, -3, S) 10,1 m (33 ft 1⅔ in); length (180, -1, -2) 7,0 m (22 ft 11½ in), (-3, S) 6,9 m (22 ft 7⅔ in); wing area (180, -1) 16,51 m^2 (178 ft^2), (-2, -3) 17,17 m^2 (185 ft^2), (S, Sh) 16,1 m^2 (173 ft^2).

ENGINE (180, -1) one 950 hp M-87A, (-2) 950 hp M-87B, (-3, S, Sh) 1000 hp M-88R.

WEIGHTS Empty (180-1) 1696 kg, (-2) 1802, (-3) (Shavrov, disbelieved by author) 1686, loaded (-1) 1805 kg (3979 lb), (-2) 2175 kg (4795 lb), (-3) 2440 kg (5379 lb), (S) 2675 kg (5897 lb), (Sh) 2600 kg (5732 lb).

PERFORMANCE Max speed (180-1, est) 557 km/h, (-2) 540 km/h (336 mph), (-3) 455 km/h at SL, 571 km/h (355 mph) at 7,1 km, (S) 470 km/h at SL, 585 km/h (364 mph) at 7,1 km; time to 5 km (-1, -2) 6·3 min, (-3) 5·6 min, (S) 5·0 min; service ceiling (-1, -2) 10,25 km, (-3) 11,6 km, (S) 11,05 km; range (-3, S) 900 km (559 miles); time 360° circle (-1, -3) 16 s (-2) 20 s; landing speed (-3) 115 km/h, (S) 120 km/h.

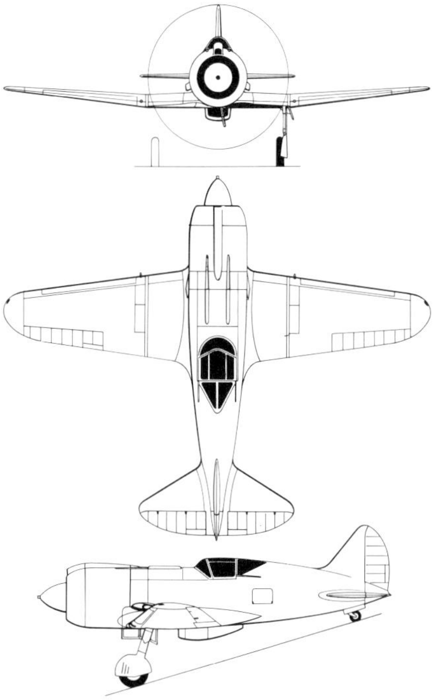

I-180S

I-185 Despite accidents Polikarpov OKB had by 1940 built fast and simple fighter ready for service; but it had been overtaken by rivals both at home and abroad. To achieve superiority in 1941 needed more power, higher wing loading and heavier armament, and though based on I-180 resulting I-185 was virtually fresh design. New wing with NACA-230 profile with thickness 14% on centreline, 12·2% at end of centre section and only 8% at tip. Further increased aspect ratio of 6·18. Improved structure yet still of mixed type, built to factor of 13. Light-alloy stressed-skin wing, large four-section pneumatic split flaps, large automatic leading-edge slats added on outer panels (after much argument over Bf 109). Dihedral 3° on outer panels only. Flight controls D6 and fabric, fully balanced with trimmers on left aileron, left (later both) elevator and rudder, control by cables from pedals and rods/bell-cranks elsewhere. Fuselage *shpon* monocoque with integral fin, wide cockpit with broad shallow windscreen, central canopy sliding to rear and Plexiglas rear section. Oil cooler in duct under fuselage at trailing edge. Large engine installed as complete unit on welded 30KhGSA tube mounting. Protected fuselage tank of 650 lit (143 gal). Single-leg main gears with track 2,7 m, shock-strut stroke 305 mm, tyres 700 × 220 mm, retracting inwards pneumatically. Fully retracting tailwheel with doors.

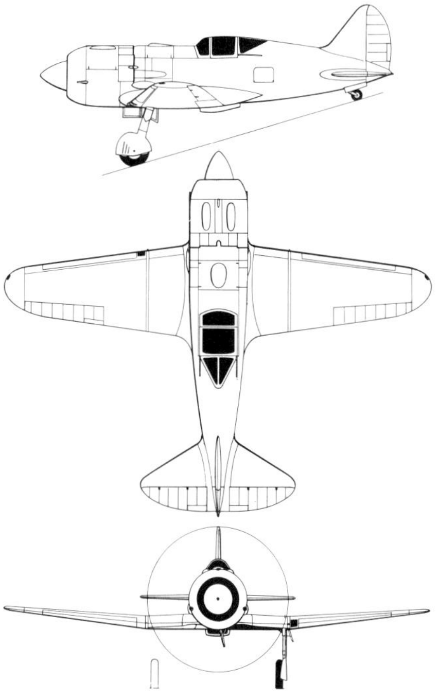

I-185, R4

First I-185 called Aircraft **R, No 02**, Project **I-188** and **I-185M-90**. Shavrov claims, despite wooden fuselage, structure thoroughly modern 'without regard to traditional experience of factory' and ideal for mass-production. No information on any aircraft called No 01 (Western accounts call first I-185 No 01, in conflict with all Soviet histories). This prototype built with amazing speed, 25 January to 10 March 1940, and tested in TsAGI tunnel to investigate advanced engine installation pushed by Polikarpov rather against wishes of Tumanskii. Giant propeller spinner forming front of fuselage with 205 mm central aperture for cooling air, as in preceding I-190. Western accounts claim fan cooling, no mention found by author in Soviet records. Close-fitting cowl with pilot-adjustable gills on each side to expel cooling air past grouped exhausts to give positive thrust. Armament, two ShKAS and two BS as on I-180S, but installation revised because of larger engine and guns probably never fitted. Wing racks for two FAB-250. Shavrov, because M-90 was never received, 02 completed with M-81 instead; Western accounts, aircraft scrapped April 1940. No record of flight test.

Second I-185, Aircraft **RM, No 03**, Project **I-187**, designed from start for first big Shvetsov engine, M-81. First Russian installation with air-tight cowl, with conventional large spinner and carefully designed cooling to give thrust from side slits discharging exhaust and cooling air. Same armament and airframe as first aircraft. Reported flown 10 March 1940, but this was also completion date for No 02. Engine down on power and unreliable, and neither engine nor aircraft taken further. Remaining three of five prototypes fitted with M-82 and (two aircraft) M-71.

Third I-185, called **ID** (possibly *Istrebitel Dvigatel*), earmarked for M-82A in installation generally similar to M-81 but modified by completely new cannon armament in advanced installation supervised by A.G. Rotenberg at Polikarpov OKB and K.A. Bortnovskii at Shpitalnyi OKB. Recognized any malfunction of synchronization would destroy aircraft, and great care in engineering this system for three ShVAK, one on upper centreline and others low on sides, with 500/540 rounds. Wing racks for four FAB-100 and (this word in all but one Soviet accounts, author suggests 'or') eight RS-82. Shavrov gives weight breakdown of this prototype airframe as: fuselage 211 kg, wing 410 kg, tail 49 kg; CG at 24·1% MAC with limits 20·8 to 25·7. No first-flight date found but probably May 1941. On 5 June Ye.G. Ulyakhin made first firing tests in air, and then Nazi invasion halted work for many months, and OKB evacuated October to Novosibirsk. Picked up again in new year (first with M-71 aircraft, described below) and M-82A aircraft put through NII testing 13 June to 5 July 1942. Recommendation for production, but not built because of existence of La-5 and severe shortage of duralumin. In July 1941 drawings of engine and armament installation passed to La, MiG and Yak OKBs on orders of NKAP.

Fourth prototype, in Western accounts called R4, completed after evacuation with M-71 engine, installation similar to M-82A though larger oil cooler and minor changes and 3,4-m ABV-118 propeller. Completely new wing with single spar, with T-section booms machined from 30KhGSA and twin sheet webs, landing light in left leading edge, wing set at +1°30′. Smaller main tyres only 650 mm diam. Armament returned to two BS (200 rounds each) and two ShKAS (700 each), plus 4 × FAB-100, two FAB-250 or eight RS-82. First flight not recorded, but NII tested 10 February to 28 March 1942. At that time possibly fastest Soviet fighter but numerous modifications requested by VVS, embodied in final prototype.

I-185E (*Etalon*, standard) incorporated completely redesigned fuselage of reduced cross-section giving better appearance and reducing drag (similar to La-9 and -11), though still wood. Improved engine installation, cowl sealed with diameter 1314 mm and length 1545, better profile and reduced pressure-loss in cooling engine. CG at 23·6% (limits 21·1/25·8) with armament three ShVAK with 560 rounds, plus 500 kg various bombs or eight RS-82. First flight April 1942 and completed NII testing October. In VVS opinion, best fighter in world (probably fastest) and in late 1942 gained excellent reputation when subjected to further testing with 728 IAP on Kalinin front. Sadly, this aircraft crashed, killing V.A. Stepanchyenok, as result of sudden engine failure at low altitude 5 April 1943. Polikarpov kept drawing improved versions, but this once-famed fighter designer built no new fighter during the Second World War, thwarted by unreliability or unavailability of engines and existence of La-5 meeting need.

DIMENSIONS Span 9,8 m (32 ft 1¾ in); length (M-90, M-81) 8,00 m (26 ft 3 in), (M-82, M-71) 8,05 m (26 ft 5 in); wing area 15,53 m^2 (167 ft^2).

ENGINE (02) one 1500 hp M-90, (RM) 1200 hp M-81, (ID) 1600 hp M-82A, (R4, E) 1700 hp M-71.

WEIGHTS Empty (ID) 2437 kg, (R4) 2595 kg, (E) 2760 kg (6085 lb); fuel/oil (ID, R4, E) 480 + 56 kg; loaded (R) 2708 kg (5970 lb), (RM) 3119 kg (6876 lb), (ID) 3329 kg (7339 lb), (R4) 3485 kg (7683 lb), (E) 3650 kg (8047 lb).

PERFORMANCE Max speed (R, est) 715 km/h, (RM) no data, (ID) 547 km/h at SL, 626 km/h (389 mph) at 6,5 km, (R4) 560 km/h at SL, 680 km/h (423 mph) at 6,1 km, (E) 577 km/h at SL, 685 km/h (426 mph) at 6,1 km; climb (ID) 6 km in 5 min, (R4, E) 4,7 km in 5 min; service ceiling (all) 11 km; range (typical, all) 800 km (500 miles); time 360° circle (all) 22 s; take-off (typical) 300 m; landing 370 m/132 km/h (82 mph).

I-190 No photograph appears to survive of this final Polikarpov biplane fighter, two of which were built in 1939. Natural outgrowth of I-153, these prototypes used virtually same airframe though restressed for increased weight and speed with more powerful two-row engine. Novel feature, later seen in other aircraft, was ducted propeller spinner shaped to form front of fuselage, with internal airflow to cool engine. Second prototype had flexible rubber-sealed pressure cabin (Něměcek, in addition twin turbochargers for engine). Numerous features in I-190 resulted from combat experience in Spain and at Khalkin-Gol, objective continuing to be highest possible manoeuvrability at all heights rather than sheer speed (latter being perogative of partner-monoplanes). Armament, (1) four ShKAS, (2) two ShVAK and two ShKAS, in each case with underwing bombload of up to 200 kg. First flight early summer 1939 (before 1 June). Factory and NII testing completed when one I-190 (believed first) crashed in winter 1940–1941, when being flown by Ye.G. Ulyakhin. Project then halted.

DIMENSIONS As I-153 except length 7,65 m (25 ft 1 in).

ENGINE One 950 hp M-88, (second aircraft, possibly 900 hp M-88TK).

WEIGHTS No data.

PERFORMANCE Max speed (first I-190) 490 km/h (304 mph); service ceiling (first) 12,4 km, (second) possibly 13,3 km; no other data.

I-195 Final biplane project of summer 1940, never built. Considerably heavier and more powerful, large wing area, armament included two ShVAK, enclosed cockpit (not pressurized) and with ducted spinner.

DIMENSIONS Longer than I-190; wing area 28,0 m^2.

ENGINE One 1500 hp M-90.

WEIGHTS Loaded 2916 kg (6429 lb).

PERFORMANCE Max speed (est) 580 km/h (360 mph).

ODB Little known of this *Odno-dvigatyel Bombardirovshchik* (single-engined bomber) with engine in fuselage on CG with shaft drive to two tractor propellers on wings. OKB figs: 1400 hp AM-37, gross weight 5300 kg with 2 t bombs, max speed 585 km/h, range 880 km. Single seat, probably dive bomber, odd propulsion adopted to minimize drag and put pilot in nose. Active in first half of 1941, abandoned on OKB evacuation.

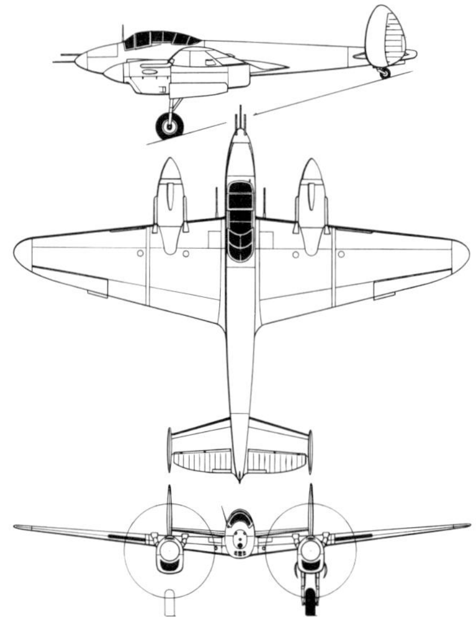

TIS, MA

TIS Designation from *Tyazhelyi Istrebitel Soprovozhdeniya*, heavy fighter escort. Appearance of large twin-engined fighters in other countries, especially Bf 110, caused urgent reappraisal and issue of VVS requirement (according to 1980 account, mainly to escort TB-7). Urgent demand could have been met by Yak Ya-22, but this became bomber. Polikarpov received parallel assignment 5 September 1938, but in this OKB work was much slower, and prototype did not appear until two years after Yak aircraft because engines were not ready.

First aircraft, also called Aircraft **A** or **TIS(A)**, started serious design early 1939, as parallel project to VIT/SPB series. Similar aerodynamically, and, though smaller, TIS more powerful and startlingly heavier (empty weight almost equal to loaded weight of heavily armed VIT-2). Heavy structure partly because of design load factor of 12 and large, heavy engines. Wing made as broad centre section and bolted outer panels, profile NACA-230, thickness 14·1% on centreline, 12·85% at joint and 7·8% at tip, dihedral 7° from roots, aspect ratio 6·9, taper ratio 4·06, incidence 1°30′. Modern wing structure with dural plate webs to two spars and ribs pressed from sheet with lightening holes. Light-alloy monocoque fuselage with streamlined form, cockpit well ahead of wing for pilot and aft-facing radio/gunner back-to-back under sliding canopies. Protected tanks in centre fuselage and inner wing for 2430 lit (534·5 gal) fuel. Metal-skinned balanced ailerons, but fabric-covered elevators and rudders all with trimmers. Automatic leading-edge slats, four-section split flaps divided by long nacelles. All three landing gear units fully retractable with doors, pneumatic actuation. Main coolant radiators under engines, oil coolers in wing with ram inlets above leading edge on engine centreline to duct air over front spar, down through cooler and out through louvred exit in upper surface adjacent to rear spar (Western drawings show wing radiators). Heavy armament of four ShKAS with 3000 rounds in nose, two ShVAK with 1600 rounds in wing roots and with backseater manning upper and lower ShKAS each with 750 rounds. Weight of fire 5,12 kg/s. Racks under centre section for two FAB-500 or equivalent bombload. According to most recent account TIS(A) also fitted with two BS with 400 rounds in wing roots immediately inboard of cannon; these now shown in Soviet drawings, but no known photograph showing wing guns clearly.

Aircraft complete 30 April 1941 but (possibly lack of engines) did not fly until September, and only one or two flights possible before evacuation. Flying not resumed until 1943; contrary to Western accounts aircraft handled well and showed fair performance and no shortcomings. Reason given for no production is discontinuation of TB-7 (Pe-8) and small part played by these aircraft, good results from Il-2 and Pe-2, and long range of Yak-9DD rendering large escort unwanted. Bf 110 no longer impressive, Battle of Britain experience proved that twin-engined fighters distinctly passé in bomber escort role.

OKB did, however, assemble second aircraft from parts brought to Novosibirsk during evacuation. **TIS(MA)**, or **MA**, designated

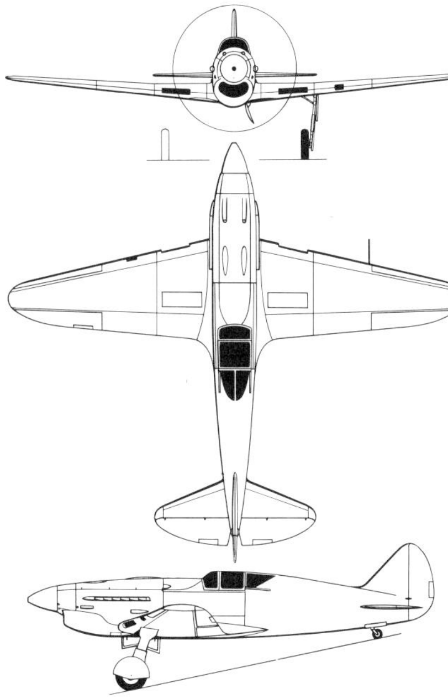

ITP, M

from *Mnogotsyelevoi* (multi-role) version of aircraft A. Made use of more powerful engines which had become available, replacing intended AM-38s. New installation in shorter nacelles with carb inlet at top just behind spinner, oil cooler underneath with exit on each side, and main radiator flat matrix in wing with leading-edge inlet and undersurface exit (not known how air duct passed front spar). Exhaust discharged through pipes leading over top of wing, as on Aircraft A. This second aircraft regarded as *Shturmovik* and tank-killer (Shavrov, as interceptor of fast bombers). No data on bombload but guns were two BS in nose (according to Western accounts, plus one ShVAK; not in Soviet accounts though projection from tip of nose looks more like ShVAK than pitot head) plus two heavy cannon in wing roots; aircraft was flown with two NS-37 and then with two NS-45, completing firing trials. At rear, just upper ShKAS; lower gun not mentioned. First flight late 1943. Four contrasting reasons given for no production, two of more plausible being diminishing need and death of Polikarpov.

In 1941 OKB studied derivative of TIS with spring-powered ejection seat for pilot (no mention of other crew member). Seat was tested on ground rig.

DIMENSIONS Span 15,5 m (50 ft $10\frac{1}{4}$ in); length (A) 11,70 m (38 ft $4\frac{2}{3}$ in), (MA) slightly longer; wing area 34,85 m² (375 ft²).

ENGINES (A) two 1400 hp AM-37, (MA) two 1900 hp AM-39.

WEIGHTS Empty (A) 5,8 t (12,787 lb), (MA) 6281 kg (13,847 lb); fuel/oil (A) 1750 kg; loaded (A) 7840 kg (17,284 lb), (MA) 8969 kg (19,773 lb).

PERFORMANCE Max speed (A) 490 km/h at SL, 515 km/h (320 mph) at 1,5 km, (MA) 502 km/h at SL, 635 km/h (395 mph) at 7,4 km; time to 5 km (A) 7·3 min; service ceiling (A) 10 250 m (33,630 ft), (MA) 11 km; range (A) 1720 km (1070 miles); take-off 435 m; landing 236 m/150 km/h.

ITP, M Polikarpov OKB began work November 1940 on ITP (*Istrebitel Tyazhelyi Pushechnyi*, fighter with heavy cannon) and to broaden scope of engine experience and acquire direct comparison with I-180 chose liquid-cooled M-107P. Totally fresh design but still mixed construction with wood *shpon* fuselage and integral fin. Ahead of firewall, engine mount structure welded 30KhGSA with dural cowl panels. Wing NACA-230 series, made as centre section 3,22 m span (0° dihedral) and outer panels (5°30′ dihedral). Two spars with T-booms of 30KhGSA, structure otherwise dural with flush-riveted stressed skin. All flight control surfaces fabric covered. Same landing gears as I-185, these and tailwheel retracted pneumatically and same system drove split flaps extending in two sections on each side of centreline under fuselage. Automatic leading-edge slats. Neat coolant radiator blocks in wing immediately aft of front spar with leading-edge inlet to duct passing over retracted main legs and through truss section of front spar; exit on underside immediately ahead of rear spar. Inlet under engine for oil cooler and carburettor. Tankage between spars immediately outboard of outer-section root, capacity 624 lit (137 gal). Cockpit, rear fuselage and tail similar to I-185 but with rudder extended to bottom, so cut-outs in elevators.

First ITP and second (static-test) airframe half-finished in October 1941. OKB decided to leave programme in Moscow at GAZ-156 where aircraft became **M-1** because of start of work of more powerful second flight article M-2. First flight October 1942 by A.I. Nikashin, with encouraging results apart from frequent engine failures. This aircraft was armed with one ShK-37 firing through propeller hub, with 40 rounds, and two ShVAK in sides of fuselage with 400 rounds; underwing racks for four FAB-100 and (Shavrov) or (Ponomaryev) eight RS-82.

Second ITP, **M-2**, was begun as static-test specimen but in 1942 completed with different engine and subjected to brief initial factory flight programme by N.V. Gavrilov from 23 February 1943. Heavy gun removed and replaced by third ShVAK on upper centreline as in I-185, weight and CG change being minimal. For various reasons speed about 40 km/h below calculation, but M-2 nevertheless impressive and several recent accounts give no hint of problems. Need for such aircraft diminishing and work was not at high pressure, ceasing on closure of OKB after founder's death.

DIMENSIONS Span 10,0 m (32 ft $9\frac{2}{3}$ in); length (M-1) 8,95 m (29 ft $4\frac{1}{3}$ in), (M-2) 9,2 m (30 ft $2\frac{1}{4}$ in); wing area 16,45 m² (177 ft²).

ENGINE (-1) one 1650 hp M-107PA, (-2) 1800 hp AM-39.

WEIGHTS Empty (-1) (Shavrov) 2960 kg, (Ponomaryev) 2598 kg (5728 lb), fuel/oil 449 kg; loaded (-1) 3570 kg (7870 lb).

PERFORMANCE Max speed (-1) (Shavrov) 568 km/h at SL, 655 km/h (407 mph) at 6,3 km, (Ponomaryev) 541 at SL, 645 at 6,3 km; (est figs for -2) (Shavrov) 540 at SL, 650 at 2,5 km, (Ponomaryev) 600 at SL, 650 at 2,5 km; time to 5 km (-1) 5·9 min; service ceiling (-1) 10,4 km (34,000 ft), (-2) 11,5 km (37,750 ft); range (-1) 1280 km (795 miles), (-2) 980 km (610 miles); take-off 350 m; landing 375 m/130 km/h.

VP,K (*Vysotnyi Perekhvatchik*, high-altitude interceptor) programme began in 1942 and embraced aircraft M (Mikoyan) and K (Polikarpov). Aircraft K was being built March 1943, using ITP tail and landing gear with different fuselage with pressure cabin and new high aspect ratio wing of greater span but fractionally reduced area. Appreciably lighter, partly because design factor only 10·5, despite heavy engine turbocharged by two TK-300B and two powerful 23 mm guns, in top of fuselage (intended for new NS-23 but had to be designed for heavy VYa as being available). Prototype left unfinished after Polikarpov's death.

DIMENSIONS Span 11,0 m (36 ft 1 in); length 9,2 m (30 ft $2\frac{1}{4}$ in); wing area 16,2 m² (174 ft²).

ENGINE One 1900 hp AM-39A with turbos.

WEIGHTS Empty 2727 kg (6012 lb); fuel/oil 550 + 55 kg; loaded 3320 kg (7319 lb) (these are Shavrov's figures and are clearly faulty, leaving minus 12 kg for ammo and pilot).

PERFORMANCE Max speed 500 km/h at SL, 714 km/h (444 mph) at 14 km; time to 5 km,

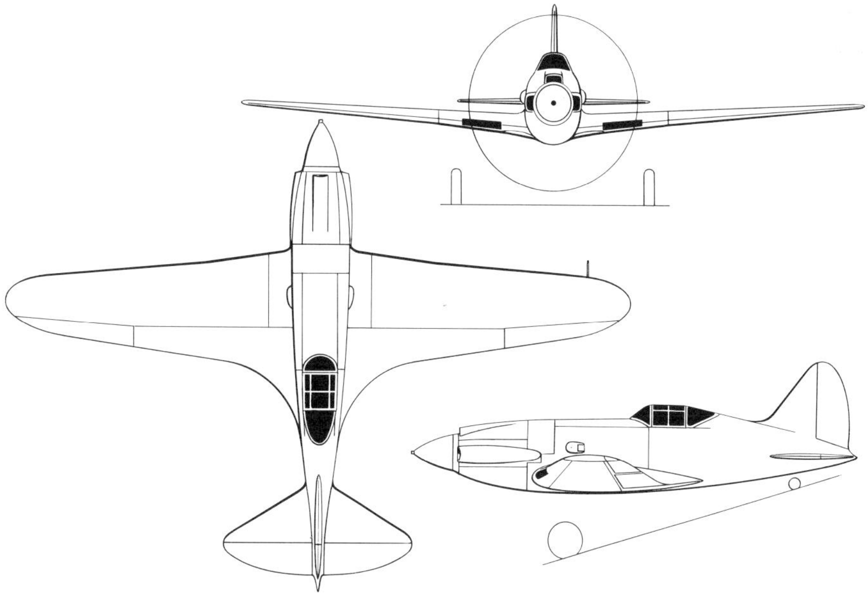

VP, K

NB, T

3·5 min, to 14 km, 18 min; service ceiling 14,05 km (46,000 ft); landing speed 150 km/h (estimated data.).

NB, T Little known about circumstances in which OKB became charged with developing Aircraft T, *Nochnoi Bombardirovshchik* (night bomber). VVS had no known specific requirement before or after 22 June 1941 and OKB had no bomber experience since TB-2 and was already heavily committed. Start probably dated from winter 1941–1942 and configuration possibly inspired by Do 217, especially insistence on cavernous internal bomb bay. Immense effort on minimum structure weight, success achieved shown by achieved weight of 2853 kg compared with max loaded weights up to 18 850 kg. This done despite, or because of, complex mixed construction with several materials in close proximity. Wooden fuselage, mainly *shpon* layers built up to 5,5 mm forward and 4 mm at tail, with frames of glued box section with inner/outer rings 17 × 4 mm and webs 1,5 mm ply. Whole mid-section affected by bomb-bay aperture and cut-out for wing, so stiffened by framework of welded 30KhGSA tube with diagonal struts and even network of bracing wires adjusted for tension. Wing shoulder-high, NACA-230, 16% centreline, 15·1% root, 8% tip, aspect ratio 7·96, taper ratio 3·47. Single, strong main spar with largest sections of 30KhGSA then attempted, machined to form upper/lower T booms joined by double webs of 1,5/2 mm D16. Lighter pressed-plate nose spar and rear spar carrying movable surfaces. Ribs of centre section (joint just outboard of nacelles) pressed from D16 plate; outer-panel ribs built up from wood trusses with ply sheet each side. Centre-section skin flush-riveted D1; outer panels skinned with ply of varying thickness. Area-increasing slotted flaps of all-dural construction divided by long nacelles with electric actuation to 42°. Automatic leading-edge slats on outer panels, all-dural. Most unusually, all control surfaces wooden structure, fabric covering, push-rod actuation. Tailplane with 7° dihedral with twin fins, all dural structure with plywood skin. Landing gears with two shock struts, 460 mm stroke, 1200 × 450 mm tyres for soft surfaces, pneumatic retraction to rear into bays covered by doors, separate actuator for fully retractable tailwheel. Hydraulic wheel brakes. Six protected fuel tanks in centre section and optional four in outer wings, all linked into system with electric valves to maintain trim and feed either engine from any tank. Engines originally (January 1942) to be ASh-82A, then ASh-71 chosen and finally ASh-82FNV. Efficient close cowls, fully sealed with electric gills and other cooling valves. Unspecified de-icing for wing/tail leading edges, carb inlet and AV-5-167 propellers. Crew of five in heated cockpits, with pilot reflector sight for fixed UB, dorsal turret for UBT and lower rear UB. Bomb bay with racking for many arrangements of bombs up to 2-t size to total mass 5 t (11,023 lb). Twin doors positioned manually via ratchet mechanism. Advanced flight system with autopilot and pneumatic inputs to command desired heading and attitude, with heading command input by nav/bomb in nose during bombing run. Design load factor 6·18, CG 22·9% with limits 18·6/26%.

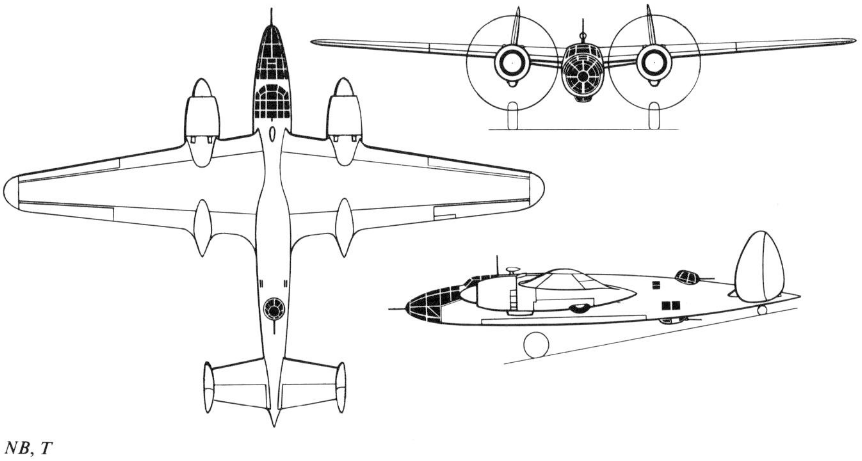

NB, T

FNV engines only installed at last moment, prior to first flight 23 May 1944. Promise of outstanding aircraft, see data from measured GAZ testing completed August. By this time OKB was being closed, and need for piston-engined bomber met by B-29.

DIMENSIONS Span 21,52 m (70 ft $7\frac{1}{4}$ in); length 15,29 m (50 ft 2 in); wing area 58,1 m^2 (625 ft^2).

ENGINES Two 1700 hp ASh-82FNV.

WEIGHTS Empty 6128 kg, fully equipped 6767 kg (14,918 lb) (Něměcek 6747); fuel/oil (normal) 2760 kg; loaded (design) 10 340 kg, (normal, no outer-wing fuel) 12 640 kg; (first flight) 14 060 kg, (max actually flown) 14 640 kg (32,275 lb), (proposed overload) 18 850 kg.

PERFORMANCE Max speed 436 km/h at SL, 515 km/h (320 mph) at 6,2 km; climb to 5 km, 12 min; service ceiling 6150 m (Něměcek 8,8 km, 28,870 ft); range with 3 t bombload 3030 km (1883 miles); take-off 660 m; landing 570 m/122 km/h (76 mph).

BDP Polikarpov himself oversaw design in 1941 of assault glider to compete with A-7 and G-11, but this BDP (*Boyevoi Desantnyi Planer*, troops assault glider) probably never flown. Same basic design used to meet 1942 requirement but considerably modified as **BDP-2,** also called **S-1,** and flown in four weeks. Wooden construction with rounded monocoque fuselage of glued *shpon* and wooden box spar (two in centre-section, one in outer panels) in wing with ply-skinned leading edge, fabric elsewhere. Fully balanced ailerons, Schrenk flaps worked by compressed-air bottle or cockpit handpump. Two pairs of wheels, low-pressure tyres 700 × 220 mm, dropped after take-off (tug, SB-2, Il-4, Li-2) with landing on large left/right skids. Interior cross-section 1000 × 610 mm, max 20 troops and kit, but 12 more common. Glazed nose cockpit for single pilot. No provision for large cargo. Evaluation quantity built, no production.

DIMENSIONS Span 20,0 m (65 ft 7½ in); length 13,5 m (44 ft 3½ in); wing area 44,7 m^2 (481 ft^2).
WEIGHTS Empty 1923 kg (4239 lb); loaded 3 t (6614 lb).
PERFORMANCE No data.

MP Like other constructors Polikarpov fitted prototype BDP-2 with engines in 1943. Believed single aircraft converted, designation from *Motor Planer*. Standard M-11F engines with steel-tube mounts on leading edge, aluminium pressed fairings over crankcase and 2,35 m (Po-2) propellers. Aluminium tanks adjacent to engines for 7 h flight. Several (Shavrov, various) windows arranged to open for firing DP machine guns, and 12 sheets of armour for protection against small-arms fire. One reason given for no production is availability of Shchye-2.
DIMENSIONS As BDP-2.
ENGINES Two 145 hp M-11F.
WEIGHTS Empty 2,3 t (5071 lb); fuel/oil 365 kg; loaded 3,7 t (8157 lb).
PERFORMANCE Max speed 172 km/h (107 mph) at SL; practical ceiling 2 km (6500 ft); range 930 km (580 miles) at 130 km/h (81 mph); landing speed 98 km/h (61 mph).

PB Unbuilt project for *Planer Bombardirovshchik* (glider bomber). Schemed 1942 with single pilot and 2 t bombload internally. Not a suicide aircraft and intended for operation at appreciable heights, but no details.

D Aircraft D was unbuilt wartime project for five-seat liaison aircraft with comfortable cabin; 145 hp M-11F, empty/gross 798/1375 kg, speed 250 km/h, ceiling 3,75 km, climb to 2 km in 17·5 min.

Malyutka Name meaning *Little One*, a simple rocket interceptor in same class as No 302 and BI-1 and overseen by Polikarpov himself from start in 1943 at Novosibirsk. Intended for target defence, with endurance under power 8 to 14 min. Clean low-wing aircraft with wood *shpon* fuselage and dural stressed-skin wings and tail. Pilot in pressurized nose cockpit, tricycle landing gear actuated like flaps by air bottles (probably with recharging handpump) and armament of two 23 mm cannon on sides of nose. Construction of prototype begun early 1944 but Polikarpov's rapidly failing health delayed completion, and abandoned with his death.
DIMENSIONS Span 6,4 m (21 ft 0 in); length 6,3 m (20 ft 8 in); wing area 10,0 m^2 (108 ft^2).
ENGINE One NII-1 two chamber rocket, 1,2 t (2645 lb) thrust SL.
WEIGHTS Empty 818 kg (1803 lb); propellants 1 t; loaded 2550 kg (5622 lb).
PERFORMANCE Design speed 875 km/h (544 mph); climb to 5 km, 1 min.

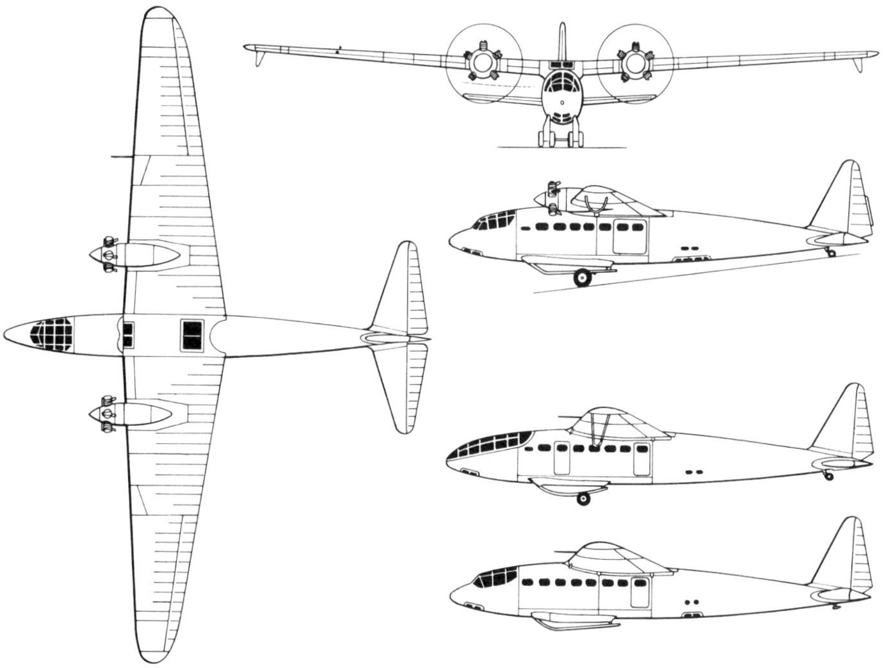

MP (middle side view BDP prototype; lower BDP production)

MP

Porokhovshchikov

Aleksandr Aleksandrovich Porokhovshchikov has been described as first Soviet constructor of aircraft. Despite First World War, civil war and War of Intervention throughout, he built numerous aircraft used as standard trainers by Imperial Air Service, Red Army and even other East European countries. All were simple biplanes, broadly derived from Caudron designs, with tractor or pusher engines but always with tail carried on pusher-type structure, with short central nacelle.

P-IV First flight 27 February 1917. Pusher engine, nacelle with pupil seated ahead of instructor. Major production from May 1917.
DIMENSIONS Span 10,2 m (lower wing 8,8); length 7,3 m; wing area 33,1 m^2.
ENGINE Usually 50 hp Gnome or 80 hp Le Rhône, but other rotaries also.
WEIGHTS Empty 340 kg typical; loaded around 605 kg.
PERFORMANCE Max speed (80 hp) 120 km/h; climb to 1 km, 9 min; service ceiling 3 km; endurance 4 hr; landing speed 60 km/h.

P-IVbis Similar to P-IV but part-cowled tractor engine and side-by-side seating. Produced in small numbers from February 1920, with major sections made by A. R. Rubenchik.
DIMENSIONS As P-IV.
ENGINE One 80 hp Le Rhône.
WEIGHTS Empty 398 kg; fuel/oil 72 + 24 kg; loaded 660 kg.
PERFORMANCE Max speed 112 km/h; climb 1 km in 9·5 min; ceiling 3 km; endurance 4·6 h; landing speed 60 km/h.

P-IV 2bis Basically P-IVbis with tandem seating as in P-IV.
DIMENSIONS As before but wing area 32,8 m^2.

ENGINE One 80 hp Le Rhône.
WEIGHTS Empty 400 kg; fuel/oil 72 + 24 kg; loaded 662 kg.
PERFORMANCE Max speed 113 km/h; otherwise as P-IVbis.

P-V Two-seater based on Nieuport IV, advanced trainer with relatively high wing-loading, ailerons upper wings only, 80 hp Le Rhône.

P-VI Strengthened P-IV type with 110 hp Le Rhône (most common), 80 hp Le Rhône or 120 hp Anzani. Side-by-side seating. No ribs or covering in upper centre-section to give upward view, this series built 1921. **P-VIbis** with covered centre-section, 40 built 1923.
DIMENSIONS As before but wing area (VI) 32,0 m², (bis) 33,1.
ENGINE Usually 110 hp Le Rhône.
WEIGHTS Empty 420 kg; fuel/oil 96 kg; loaded 682 kg.
PERFORMANCE Max speed 120 km/h; climb to 1 km, (VI) poor, (bis) 8·0 min; ceiling (VI) barely 200 m, (bis) 3,5 km; endurance 3·3 h; landing speed 62 km/h.

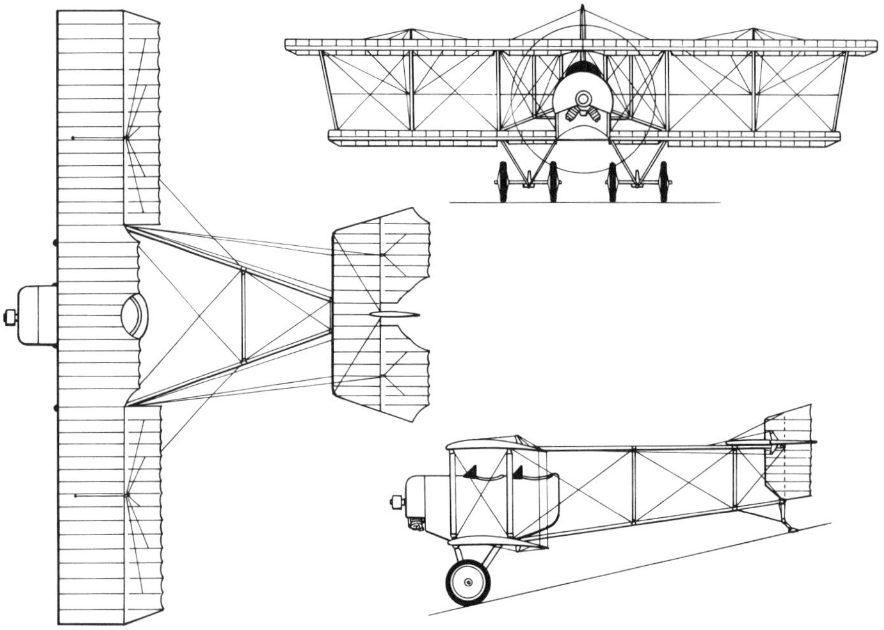

P-IVbis

Rafaelyants

Aram Nazarovich Rafaelyants was born 1897 and qualified at VVA 1927. For 30 years (about 1929–1959) chief engineer of GVF (Aeroflot) aircraft repair and modification shops at Bykovo, on Volga. Designer of several important modifications including improvements to early German transports, PR-5 and other variants derived from R-5, modified Li-2, and U-2L derived from U-2. Post-1945 leader in turbojet test equipment. He died 1960.

RAF-1 Ultralight built and flown 1925; simple wood/fabric low-wing monoplane of exceptionally clean design. Flew well.
DIMENSIONS Span 9,4 m (30 ft 10 in); length 5,5 m (18 ft 5½ in); wing area 12,6 m² (136 ft²).
ENGINE One 18 hp Blackburn Tomtit.
WEIGHTS Empty 175 kg (386 lb); fuel/oil 20 kg; loaded 273 kg (602 lb).
PERFORMANCE Max speed at SL 105 km/h (66 mph); ceiling reached 3250 m (10,700 ft); landing speed 47 km/h (29 mph).

RAF-2 Cantilever low-wing monoplane two-seater, built 1926. This was a failure, span and drag being too great for engine, flight only just being accomplished. Constructor never fitted a more powerful engine.
DIMENSIONS Span 12,0 m (39 ft 4½ in); length not recorded; wing area 20 m² (215 ft²).
ENGINE One 60 hp Airdisco Cirrus.
WEIGHTS Empty 435 kg; fuel/oil 50 kg; loaded 645 kg.
PERFORMANCE Poor.

RAF-11 By far largest of RAF's aircraft projects, this twin-engine transport was designed mid-1930s and built 1937–1938. All-wood, with *shpon* monocoque fuselage of fine aerodynamic form and single-spar cantilever wing with ply covering back to spar and fabric elsewhere. Well-engineered, and twin-leg main gears retracted to rear under power of hydraulic system, with pump on each engine; pneumatic (presumably bottle) system provided for emergency extension against air drag. Split flaps, hydraulic actuation with pneumatic standby. Also flown with retractable skis. Flight deck with windows large for period, passenger cabin seating six (three on each side, beside windows) with door at rear on right. Measured performance safe but unimpressive. Rafaelyants spent 18 months refining aircraft, dramatically reducing weight (and slightly reducing fuel capacity, and fitting more powerful engines) and in 1940 tested resulting **RAF-11bis.** Outstanding machine, flown with abandon ('like fighter') by many pilots. NII GVF recommended production early 1941 for second-class Aeroflot routes, and also as interim civil crew trainer, but this had not been organized when Nazis invaded.
DIMENSIONS Span 15,0 m (49 ft 2¼ in); length (11) 10,86 m (35 ft 7½ in), (bis) 10,1 m (33 ft 1⅔ in); wing area 30,0 m² (323 ft²).
ENGINES (11) two 300 hp MG-31, (bis) 330 hp MG-31F.

RAF-11

WEIGHTS Empty (11) 2,5 t (5511 lb), (bis) 2097 kg (4623 lb); fuel/oil (11) 400 + 56 kg, (bis) 380 + 40 kg; loaded (11) 3270 kg (7209 lb), (bis) 3 t (6614 lb).
PERFORMANCE Max speed (11) 289 km/h (180 mph) at SL, (bis) 294 km/h (183 mph); cruising speed 257 km/h (160 mph); climb to 1 km (bis) 3·5 min; service ceiling (bis) 4,5 km (14,750 ft); range (11) 1000 km, (bis) 930 km (578 miles); take-off (bis) 355 m/18 s; landing (bis) 290 m/18 s/107 km/h (66·5 mph).

Turbolyet Inspired by Rolls-Royce TMR (Flying Bedstead) this VTOL device was designed in partnership with Prof V.N. Matveyev and team at LII and first hovered under tethers early 1957. Publicly flown free October 1957. Engine single AM-3 (RD-3) mounted vertically with special bearings and oil system, bellmouth inlet pointing upwards and bleed pipes to four reaction control jets on long outrigger arms. Four vertical sprung legs, three fuel tanks around engine and pilot cabin with strong crash-proof roof structure. Most flying done by helicopter pilot Yu.A. Garnayev. Later used for research into jet deflection and engine noise. Played small preliminary role in development of control systems for Yakovlev VTOL aircraft.

Richard

Paul Aimé Richard was one of several foreign (in this case French) designers to work in the Soviet Union. Invited to do so by Aviatrust 1928, arriving in August that year. Worked at MOS VAO at GAZ-28 while organizing his own KB at OPO-4 as part of TsKB. Team included I.I. Artamonov (head of manufacturing), D.M. Khomskyi (head of technical section), P.D. Samsonov (projects), S.A. Lavochkin (calculations), fellow-countrymen Augé and Laville, and many other engineers including G.M. Beriev, D.A. Mikhailson, G.M. Mozharovskii, N.K. Skrzhinskii, N.I. Kamov, A.L. Gimmelfarb, M.I. Guryevich, S.P. Korolyev, I.V. Chyetverikov and V.B. Shavrov! Projects included two-seat fighter, (later basis for Laville's DI-4), monoplane reconnaissance flying boat (later used by Beriev as starting point for MBR-2), parasol-winged military flying boat with two M-17 engines on wing, four-engined transport flying boat of stressed-skin construction, and studies for flying boats of 100 and 200 tonnes. When TOM failed to win production order he returned to France, late 1931.

TOM-1 Designation from *Torpedonosyets Otkrytogo Morya* (torpedo carrier, open sea). Up-to-date and relatively clean design with cantilever mid wing with twin engines neatly faired in, riding on twin floats each with tandem struts with diagonal wire bracing, single fin carrying high tailplane with N-struts and well-streamlined fuselage. Duralumin construction throughout. Wing with St Cyr 60 (French) profile and high aspect ratio (9·075), two built-up truss spars with T-section rolled/machined booms, ribs pressed from sheet and stringers spaced at 100 mm. Fuselage with pressed open-section frames and L stringers at 150-mm spacing. Entire skin (no data on whether this includes control surfaces) smooth dural sheet 0,5-0,6-mm, in places flush-riveted. Slotted flaps power-driven to 40°. Three PV-1 guns in nose and dorsal gunners' cockpits and sliding (retractable) lower rear turret. Torpedo in internal bay under wing with manually operated doors. Prototype launched Sevastopol 1 January 1931 and tested until August. Pilots N.I. Kamov and N.A. Kamkin favourably impressed, but series production rejected on grounds that TB-1P was adequate (and, doubtless, that TOM-1 would be expensive and structurally difficult to build and maintain).
DIMENSIONS Span 33,0 m (108 ft 3¼ in); length 19,0 m (62 ft 4 in); wing area 120 m² (1,399 ft²).
ENGINES Two 680 hp BMW VI (in 1933 re-engined with similar M-17).
WEIGHTS Empty believed 4929 kg (10,866 lb); fuel/oil 1300 + 100 kg; loaded 8030 kg (17,703 lb).
PERFORMANCE Max speed 210 km/h (130·5 mph) at SL; patrol speed 171 km/h (106 mph); service ceiling 5,5 km (18,000 ft); range (Něměcek) 1500 km (932 miles); take-off 25 s; alighting speed 80 km/h (50 mph).

Romeiko -Gurko

RMK-1 Second of constructor's designs. According to Něměcek designation was GMK-1. One of fashionable crop of *planerlyet* powered-gliders intended 1936 to achieve lowest-cost air transport. High wing pusher with tail carried on slim lower boom on centreline. Engine installation essentially U-2 in reverse. Welded AMTs fuel tank in nacelle ahead of engine. Fixed spatted main gears braced to fuselage. Well-glazed fuselage nacelle with pilot on centreline at front and six passengers in three rows (or 1 t cargo) with door on left. Shavrov, construction not completed, but recent suggestions RMK-1 flew late 1936.
DIMENSIONS Span 28,0 m (91 ft 10¼ in), (Němě-cek, 30 m); length 12,4 m (40 ft 8¼ in); wing area 64,0 m² (689 ft²).
ENGINE One 100 hp M-11.
WEIGHTS Empty 1170 kg (2579 lb); fuel/oil 230 kg; loaded 2,5 t (5511 lb).
PERFORMANCE Max speed (Shavrov) 110 km/h (68 mph), (Něměcek) 130 km/h (81 mph); cruising speed 90 km/h (56 mph); practical ceiling (Něměcek) 2,5 km (8200 ft); range (Něměcek) 1000 km (620 miles); landing speed 56 km/h (35 mph).

RG-1 Designation has appeared in West and 'RGP' in East Europe; neither found in Soviet source. Unconventional high-speed passenger/mail aircraft designed (believed in GVF workshops) about 1934. Mixed-construction, braced low-wing monoplane with large water-cooled engine on CG driving tractor propeller via extension shaft under pilot's seat. Rather cramped rear cabin for 1 t mail or cargo but room for only four passengers, two at front facing aft and two in tandem on right at rear facing forward; door or left. Trousered main gears, wing with split flap(s). Entered for Aviavnito competition, high-speed section, but judges said 5/6 passengers were stipulated and they criticized passenger accommodation and alleged rear CG position. Not flown, no data.

Samsonov

Pyetr Dmitriyevich Samsonov was (possibly apprenticed) at Shchyetinin works in the First World War. In 1925 appointed joint head, with V.B. Shavrov, of manufacturing at OMOS. With K.A. Vigand handled drawings and cal-

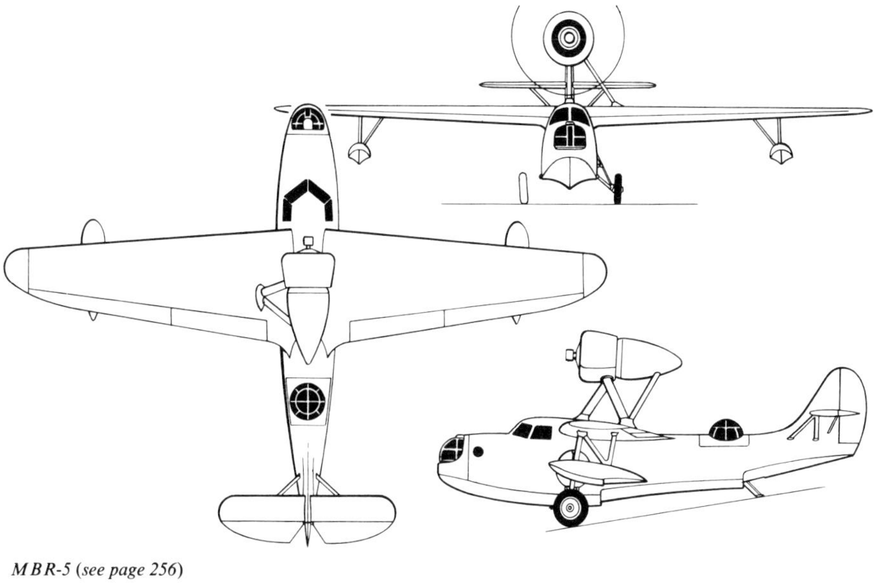

MBR-5 (*see page 256*)

culations for MRL-1 and several other Grigorovich boats.

MBR-5 Funded as possible successor to MBR-2. Clean amphibian of mixed construction. Two-spar wings of MOS-27 profile joined on centreline, structure similar to DB-3B with spars welded from KhMA tube and light ribs built up from riveted dural box, tube and angle sections. Spars joined by diagonal struts of welded KhMA tube braced with double steel tapes. Fabric covering, varnished. Wooden hull with two-step planing bottom without inner keelson, wide-spaced frames and close-pitch stringers carrying ply skin and varnished fabric covering. Control surfaces dural with fabric covering, actuation by cables throughout, pilot control of tailplane incidence via screwjack in wood fin integral with hull, wings with slotted flaps. Main landing gears with compressed-air shock struts also arranged when required to unlatch sprung locks and raise gear into well in side of hull. Retractable tailskid. Engine in NACA cowl carried on N-strut on centreline with V side-brace struts on left only. Oil cooled in nine-tube ring radiator round nacelle. DA gun in bow and dorsal turrets (manual drive), four FAB-50 in enclosed underwing fairings, radio and reconnaissance camera. First flight August 1935; good performance but caught fire when moored and then (Shavrov) major malfunction. NII tests followed at Sevastopol, during which MBR-5 met with accident; repairs started but in September 1936 work abandoned.
DIMENSIONS Span 15,4 m (50 ft 6⅓ in); length 11,2 m (36 ft 9 in); wing area 32,5 m^2 (350 ft^2).
ENGINE One 710 hp Wright Cyclone SGR-1820-F3.
WEIGHTS Empty 2060 kg (4541 lb), (Něměcek, 2150); fuel/oil 441 kg; loaded 3100 kg (6834 lb), (Něměcek, 3400).
PERFORMANCE Max speed 256 km/h (159 mph) at SL, 306 km/h (190 mph) at 1,8 km; climb, 8 min to 3 km, 18 to 5; service ceiling 7,5 km (24,600 ft); range 750 km (466 miles), (Něměcek, 800); alighting speed 110 km/h.

MDR-7 No photograph found of this important reconnaissance flying boat whose design was offered to MA 14 October 1938 and accepted. Clean high-wing cantilever monoplane, all-metal stressed-skin construction, excessive wing-loading (188 kg/m^2) to obtain speed much higher than normal for class. Long-life (DC-3 inspired) wing with five sheet-web spars root to tip, made as centre section and tapering outer panels. Upper surface strengthened by corrugated inner skin between second and third spars to act as tank bay. Skin thickness 0,6/1,2 mm. Automatic slats ahead of slotted ailerons, slotted flaps and pneumatically retracted wing-tip floats folding into outer side of streamlined engine nacelles. Two-step planing bottom to streamlined hull, first step V in plan on first of three prototypes, transverse on others, and rear step tapering to knife edge. Keel of twin dural webs, angle at bottom 30° and not concave as in MBR-2 and many other boats. Relatively thin hull skin spot-welded to numerous stringers. Twin fins on tailplane with slight dihedral. Engines in low-drag cowls driving VISh-23-3 three-blade two-pitch propellers. Novel riveted aluminium tanks with varnished fabric tape along joints. Crew 3 or 4, flight controls cable-operated, armament two BS in dorsal turret, two ShKAS (location not stated) and underwing racks for twin FAB-100. Comprehensive radio and photo equipment. First MDR-7 flown from large reservoir by T.V. Ryabenko 25 July 1940. Pilot had no trouble until end of brief flight when turned in to land; at about 100 m aircraft slipped in sideways, broke up on impact. (Probably did not allow for wing loading, even at light weight.) Second flown spring 1941, twice and at high power, by I.M. Shyevnin. Concluded not enough wing (long and part-controversial report); flying stopped and third machine not flown, though completed with increased span and fixed tip floats and with engine nacelles completely reshaped.
DIMENSIONS Span 18,0 m (59 ft 0⅔ in); length 14,0 m (45 ft 11 in); wing area 40 m^2 (430·5 ft^2).
ENGINES Two 1100 hp M-88.
WEIGHTS Empty 5100 kg (11,243 lb); fuel/oil 1100 + 140 kg; loaded 7500 kg (16,534 lb).
PERFORMANCE Max speed at SL 395 km/h (245 mph); intended range 1000 km (621 miles); take-off 27 s; alighting 20 s/163 km/h (101 mph).

Shavrov

Vadim Borisovich Shavrov was born 7 November 1898, served in Red Army after revolution and qualified as engineer 1923. In 1925 joined OMOS on its formation, being assigned joint responsibility with P.D. Samsonov for manufacturing. Had idea for smaller and simpler machine, a U-2 style amphibian able to do small utility tasks from fields or rivers. With Osoaviakhim funds designed Sh-1 and built prototype in own small flat in Leningrad. Great success, and derived Sh-2 made in large numbers. In 1935 appointed to USP (NTK) under L.V. Kurchyevskii to build Sh-3. In 1936 assigned to build flying boat for Far East and amphibian for Glavsevmorput, but increasingly involved in administration, teaching and writing. Design consultant to ESKA-1 (Avietka section). By far most important historian of Soviet aircraft, published articles in aviation press and two hardback books, latter dealing with periods up to 1938 and 1938–1950. Manuscript covering 1950–1960 was well advanced when he died 23 December 1976.

Sh-1 Shavrov gradually formulated outline design for this simple light amphibian soon after beginning work at OMOS but failed to get it adopted as official OKB project. Bold decision to try and build it himself and in 1927 approached Osoaviakhim and eventually obtained financial backing on extremely modest scale. Managed to obtain enthusiastic support of Viktor L'vovich Korvin (see MK-1 under Mikhelson) and mechanic N.N. Funtikov, and drawings mainly completed by time actual construction began on 16 April 1928. Major airframe parts sized to fit into one-room flat and go downstairs, one result being division of wing into three equal-span sections. Simple wooden construction, with two-spar wing carried on four pairs of mild-steel tube struts forming two inverted pyramids all meeting at two points at upper sides of wood-planked hull, with two added bracing struts to rear. Outer wings cantilever. Small lower wings also cantilevered and carrying stabilizing floats. Landing gear with spoked main wheels cranked up around sides of hull. Simple wood/fabric tail, and engine mounted on front of wing with no pretence at cowl or nacelle, with fuel tank in wing. Cockpit with side-by-side seats and small space at rear for third occupant. Whole design rather compromised by limited funds, and limited objectives matched to adverse environment. Parts assembled at Grebno Port and, without landing gear, launched 4 June 1929 and tested on water by L.I. Giks (Hicks). First flight 21 June, and subjected to serious measured testing by B.V. Glagolyev 1 to 8 July. Landing gear then installed and on 6 August took off from water and landed on Leningrad airfield. On 31 August flew from water at Grebno Port to Moscow Central Aerodrome where on instructions of P.I. Baranov of VVS Sh-1 was put through official NII

Sh-1 being assembled (Shavrov in suit)

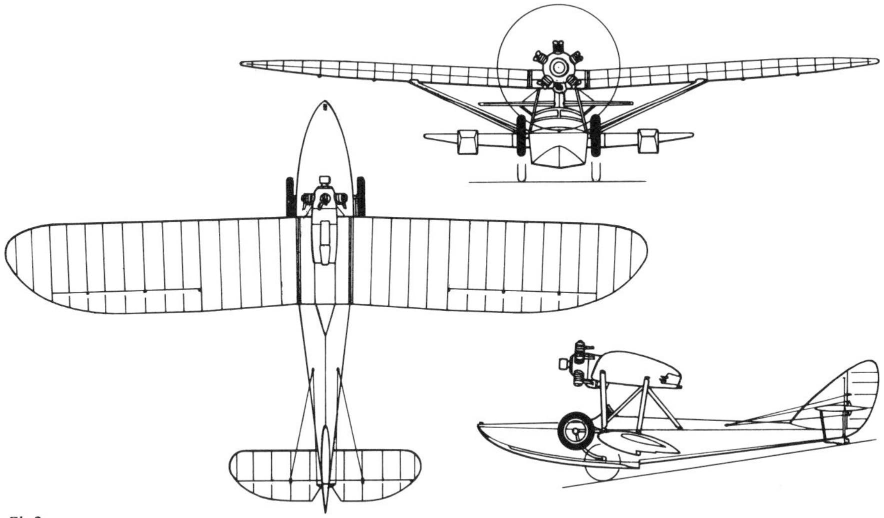

Sh-2

testing by Glagolyev, M.A. Korovkin and A.V. Chekaryev from Central Aerodrome and Moscow reservoir. As result Shavrov was asked to build improved version with more power (original engine was all he could manage, not what he wanted). Original machine, first amphibian in the Soviet Union and also first to have wooden structure protected by layer of varnished fabric, continued to be popular at aero club at Leningrad until no less a pilot than V.P. Chkalov demolished it (without injury to himself or mechanic Ivanov) flying in severe snowstorm on 26 February 1930.

DIMENSIONS Span 10,7 m (35 ft 1¼ in); length 7,7 m (25 ft 3⅛ in); wing area 20,2 m² (217 ft²).
ENGINE One 85 hp Walter 7-cylinder radial.
WEIGHTS Empty 535 kg (1179 lb); fuel/oil 60 + 7 kg; loaded 790 kg (1742 lb).
PERFORMANCE Max speed 126 km/h (78 mph); climb to 1 km, 17·5 min; ceiling 2470 m (8100 ft); range 400 km (249 miles); take-off 200 m/20 s; landing 100 m/12 s/65 km/h.

Sh-2 Shavrov's simple homebuilt was right vehicle at right time, and when refined into uncompromised design with M-11 engine it sustained major production run, all built at *Krasnyi Lyetchik* factory. Sh-2 was similar to original machine except for different centre section, proper engine nacelle, increased dimensions and redesigned wing/hull struts and horizontal tail. Hull of pine, with some parts ash, with 25 frames (four being bulkheads) and numerous stringers, cross sections milled (planed) to 12 × 15 up to 15 × 35 mm. Ply skin 2,5 to 3 mm, with 6 mm at single step of simple planing bottom. Completed hull covered with casein-glued fabric, with top coat of varnish (then novel, but found to give long-term protection). Small lower wing of same construction and protective covering with two spars and watertight ply skin and incorporating two streamlined-box stabilizing floats. Wing redesigned with smaller centre-section, made of duralumin to avoid danger from fire, and manually folding outer panels. Two built-up box spars with overlapping ply webs with grain at 45°. Built-up truss ribs, with ply skin over leading edge to front spar (dural on centre section) and fabric elsewhere. Slotted ailerons 'slanting construction'. Aft of rear spar centre-section hinged upwards to allow outer panels to fold to rear, trailing edges fitted with simple latch to link folded wings. Welded mild-steel tube engine mount with dural nacelle and crankcase fairing. Two-blade wooden propeller, often 2,35-m U-2 type but occasionally with spinner and sometimes metal blades. Mild-steel wing/hull struts rearranged in conventional diagonal pairs aligned with spars, lower front attachment being disconnected to fold wing. Two extra near-vertical struts, with streamlined fairings, from nacelle to top of main landing gears and incorporating lower front wing-strut anchors at lower ends. Landing gear with light disc wheels and 700-mm tyres joined by axle across hull requiring circular-arc slots in sides of hull (not cutting main longitudinals) for manual retraction by handcrank and worm drive. Tailplane with two bracing struts each side, elevators with previous horn balances deleted. Fuel tank in centre section for 330 lit (72·6 gal), and 30-lit oil tank in nacelle. Pilot and passenger or mechanic side by side, rear seat for third (at a pinch, fourth) occupant.

First Sh-2 test-flown from airfield by Glagolyev 11 November 1930, and four days later (with Shavrov) made first test from water, successfully landing in 0.8-m waves in blinding snowstorm. Subsequently tested NTK UVVS at Sevastopol and 12–17 June 1931 by NII GVF in Leningrad. Result was production from 1932 to 1934 totalling (Shavrov) several hundred, (Simakov) about 300, (Něměcek) over 700. Standard utility transport with many Aeroflot directorates (Shavrov mentions Northern, Siberia and Far East), often on skis and including 16 **Sh-2S** (*Sanitarnyi*, sanitary ie, casevac) carrying one or two stretcher patients in open rear compartment with attachment notches. Duties of Sh-2 included frontier and fisheries patrol, reconnaissance for icebreakers and Arctic expeditions, civil utility transport, military liaison and above all training. In 1939 Aeroflot shops began assembling additional Sh-2s from spare parts, and by 1940 were building from scratch, Shavrov stating this added further several hundred. Něměcek suggests more were built post-war, but according to Shavrov and other writers these were rebuilt aircraft with various improvements and later engines, usually M-11L. Certainly majority of **Sh-2bis** (post-war designation) had compressed-air engine starting, some had ring cowl and considerable proportion glazed cabin instead of open cockpit. Survivors continued in use until at least 1964.

DIMENSIONS Span 13,0 m (42 ft 7¾ in); length 8,2 m (26 ft 10¾ in); wing area 21,75 + 2,95 = 24,7 m² (266 ft²).
ENGINE Originally one 100 hp M-11; later 115 hp M-11L or other version.
WEIGHTS Empty 660 kg (1455 lb), (no landing gear) 620 kg, (Sh-2S) 680 kg; fuel/oil 87 + 15 kg; loaded 937 kg (2066 lb), (Sh-2S) 1 t (2205 lb).
PERFORMANCE Max speed 139 km/h (86 mph); cruise 120 km/h (75 mph); climb to 1 km, 8·3 min; service ceiling 3850 m (12,600 ft); range up to 1300 km (800 miles); endurance up to 11 h; take-off 100 m/10 s; alighting 100 m/10 s/60 km/h (37 mph).

Sh-5 In 1928 head of Soviet cartographic and geophysical committee made enquiry about use of specially designed aircraft for photography and aerial surveying. Early 1929 special committee organized under Academician A.Ye. Fersman to study possibilities, and quickly concluded that special aircraft could photograph large areas and greatly speed up mapping of vast unmapped regions of Soviet Union. Shavrov was requested to supply report outlining possibilities and how demand could best be met. He recommended large enough cabin for full photographic equipment (including, according to non-Russian reports, developing and printing on board). Emphasized need for large (144°) field of view, need to keep landing gear out of field of view of cameras, absence of good airfields and probable desirability of amphibian. Eventually, early 1930, decision to build aircraft. Further committees April/June 1930 decided two versions, **FS-1** landplane and **FS-2** flying boat (FS, *Fotosamolyet*, photo aircraft). Committees by this time included NII AFS and NTK UVVS, while aircraft itself, Sh-5, assigned to Richard OKB, and on that bureau closing, March 31, to TsKB. Project ostensibly handled by Shavrov, assisted by K.A. Vigand for calculations, but too many people involved for fast progress. June 1931 development assigned to Marine Section at GAZ-28 (former Richard OKB) and construction to ZOK NII GVF, already overloaded with nine prototypes including DAR and several for Grigorovich and AGOS. Single Sh-5 slowly built, Shavrov having chosen amphibian from outset but having to increase engine power from 300 hp each to meet progressively greater demands. Capacious fuselage and vertical tail made of gas-welded KhMA steel tube with fabric covering. Planing bottom, scaled from Sh-2, and underwing floats wood with glued fabric, varnished. Wing of MOS-27 profile, constant 16% thickness, with two widely spaced spars, made like horizontal tail from D1 dural with fabric covering. Struts steel tube with D1 fairings. Engines in Townend-ring cowls on D1 pylons/nacelles above wing. Metal propellers with ground adjustment of pitch. Main landing gears with air/oil shock struts pivoted to KhMA tubular struts between hull, floats and wing, main legs drawn up by cables from cockpit windlass to horizontal position for alighting on water. First flight eventually accomplished 19 March 1934, on skis (like wheels, retractable for alighting on water). Flight testing satisfactory, but by this time Sh-5 was outdated and no longer excited original sponsors. At end of 1934 one

Sh-5

landing-gear strut broke because of manufacturing defect and aircraft never repaired. Surveying continued to be done mainly by R-6.

DIMENSIONS Span 24,0 m (78 ft $8\frac{7}{8}$ in); length 15,0 m (49 ft $2\frac{1}{2}$ in); wing area 73,1 m² (787 ft²).

ENGINES Two 480 hp M-22.

WEIGHTS Empty 3470 kg (7650 lb), (as FS-1 landplane 3150 kg); fuel/oil 500 kg (FS-1, 800); loaded 5 t (11,020 lb).

PERFORMANCE Max speed 213 km/h (132 mph), (FS-1, 225 km/h); climb to 1 km, 5 min; service ceiling 4,9 km (16,000 ft); range 800 km (500 miles), (FS-1, 1200 km); take-off 250 m/16 s; landing 240 m/16 s/80 km/h.

Sh-3 In 1935 Shavrov accepted invitation of L.V. Kurchyevskii to join NTK, and was permitted to form his own small team to build aircraft of his choice. Sh-3 unusual light transport amphibian with attractive lines. Cantilever low-wing monoplane with four landing wheels on oleo struts retracting into twin floats. Mixed construction, fuselage all-dural monocoque with oval section and almost headroom to walk upright at centreline. Dural centre-section integral with fuselage, dural struts and floats, wooden outer wings. Floats replaceable by wheels or skis. Enclosed cockpit at front for single pilot, space behind for two passengers or light cargo or mail. Windshield and door quickly jettisonable. Intention later to produce **Sh-3S** for stretcher patients and other variants such as **Sh-3F** for photo-survey. Seen as fast modern successor to Sh-2, though with efficient slotted flaps to keep down landing speed and thus increase utility in undeveloped regions. Whole project had to be dropped when NTK closed February 1936, with prototype in early stage of construction.

DIMENSIONS Span 14,0 m (45 ft $11\frac{3}{16}$ in); length 7,8 m (25 ft 7 in); wing area 24,0 m² (258 ft²).

ENGINE Originally one 120 hp Cirrus Hermes inverted 4-inline, later to be 100 hp M-11.

WEIGHTS Empty 720 kg (1587 lb); fuel/oil 150 kg; loaded 1070 kg (2359 lb).

PERFORMANCE Designed for 5-h endurance; never tested.

MDR-7 On termination of NTK work Shavrov was asked by Siberian Far East district of MA to design long-range reconnaissance flying boat. Agreement reached to use maximum (possibly 60%) of parts of Ilyushin DB-3B bomber, including wing, powerplant installation, tail, control system, equipment and armament. Visited Ilyushin OKB and design of aircraft begun January 1937, sponsored by V.K. Blyukher and F.A. Ingaunis of Far East and GAZ director K.D. Kuznetsov. Detailed tank-test model made and run in TsAGI water channel to prove hydrodynamic qualities. Good-looking aircraft resembling PBY but with smaller wing and deeper but narrower hull. Terminated at end of 1937 mainly because of existence of MDR-6. No explanation given of MDR-7 designation, subsequently used by different KB (Samsonov). No data, though clearly span and engines as DB-3B.

Sh-7 In late 1938 Shavrov began design of this neat light transport amphibian for Glavsevmorput and Aeroflot. Cantilever high wing of NACA-230 series, 16% root and 12% tip, two spars with elliptical-tube booms of 30KhGSA in centre section and dural outer panels, and double spar webs in DL-0,8 sheet. Ribs mainly dural truss construction from channels 12 × 10 × 0,5 mm. Fabric covering, with slotted ailerons drooping 15° when slotted flaps driven to 50°. Tail mainly from dural tube and rolled sections, with fabric covering. Flight controls dual in side-by-side flight deck with cable operation. All dural hull with full-length one-step planing bottom, with pedal-controlled rear water rudder and tailwheel. Skin mainly 1 mm, 1,5 at step, 0,8 at rear, not flush-riveted. Dural wire-braced underwing floats. Main landing gears with oleo shock struts carrying wheels or skis (latter I-15bis type) with breaking strut cranked up by hand until wheel housed in recess in side of hull. Two seats in cockpit and four in cabin, all using left/right cockpit doors. Circular roof hatch at rear of cabin at trailing edge for gun position, emergency escape or loading cargo. Two welded AMTs aluminium fuel tanks in centre section, oil tank in pylon-mounted nacelle. Originally designed for 220hp MV-6 but more powerful engine substituted during prototype construction in 1939. Original propeller from Stal-2, later a three-blade VISh fitted.

Sh-7

Sh-7

Fully equipped for open-sea operation, night flying and radio navigation, and military version with TT-1 ring mount for ShKAS with 300 rounds. Launched spring 1940 for water tests and flown by Ye.O. Fyedorenko 16 June 1940. Completed factory tests September and then SNII GVF testing, with December 1940 recommendation for production with MG-31F and small increase in wing area. Production prevented by war, but prototype (No 359) busy throughout war on urgent cargo along Volga linking Saratov, Stalingrad, Astrakhan etc.

DIMENSIONS Span 13,0 m (42 ft 7¾ in); length 9,4 m (30 ft 10 in); wing area 23,3 m² (251 ft²).
ENGINE One 300 hp MG-31, later 330 hp MG-31F.
WEIGHTS Empty 1230 kg (2712 lb); fuel/oil 320 kg; loaded 1,9 t (4189 lb).
PERFORMANCE Max speed 218 km/h (135·5 mph) at SL, 184km/h at height; climb to 1 km, 5 min; service ceiling 2960 m (9700 ft); range 920 km (572 miles); take-off 280 m/25 s; alighting 210 m/20 s/90 km/h (56 mph).

Shchyerbakov

Aleksei Yakovlyevich Shchyerbakov was Ukrainian, born 1902, admitted Kharkov Tech (not Aviation) Institute 1924, two years later additionally joining design team at Kalinin OKB, graduated Kharkov 1929, remained with Kalinin until 1935 when to OSK in Moscow to specialize in high-altitude flight. Became national, if not world, leader in pressure-cabin technology, flexible GK (*Germetichyeskoi Kabinyi*) designed for Gribovskii G-14 sailplane, I-15 series, I-16 series and two unbuilt prototypes, and in addition welded aluminium ('hard') type for I-153 in design of which he played major role. In 1938 led group under Korolyev in research/test of RP-318 and in flight test of PVRD under wings of I-15bis. In 1941 managed design and mass-production of underwing *kasset* people-containers for U-2 and R-2, 1942 designed floatplane variant of U-2 (never previously successful), 1943 own OKB at Chkalov to build Shchye-2, whilst also working at Myasishchyev OKB on GKs for Pe-2, Yak-7B and La-5. Last project VSI VTOL fighter.

IVS Designation from *Istrebitel Vyisokoskorostnyi*, high-speed fighter. Project of 1937, eventually received positive VVS decision 29 September 1940, but prototype discontinued at Nazi invasion. Mid-mounted M-120 engine with shaft drive under floor of front cockpit to 0·666 gearbox for tractor propeller, plus auxiliary boost PVRD at tail. Glycol radiator under fuselage ducted to main PVRD duct. Hard-type pressure cabin, tricycle landing gear, nose armament one ShVAK (Shavrov erroneously 'ShKAS') and two BS. Design speed 700 km/h, rising to 825 with PVRD; corresponding ceilings 12 and 14 km.

SP Few details survive of *Stratosfernyi Planer*, stratospheric glider, second project of 1937. Supported by VVS rather than civilian funds, possibly intended clandestine recon. Span in neighbourhood of 30 m, believed single-seat GK (pressure cabin) and intended to be towed by high-performance aircraft to max height and then soar to still-greater altitudes. No mention of auxiliary rocket or other propulsion; intended operating height 15 km (49,200 ft).

Shchye-2, TS-1 Often written Shche-2; (2 because it is not a fighter). Alternative designation from *Transportnyi Samolyet*, transport aeroplane. Design undertaken to meet urgent need recognized about July 1942 for utility transport to carry items in front-line areas and between factories and repair shops. Shchyerbakov was chief engineer and GAZ director, and also head of central office at NKAP for aircraft repair. U-2 and R-5 used in large numbers to carry many items, latter being able to carry fighter wings slung under lower wing, but neither could carry engines. Desperate need to fly engines such as ASh-82 and AM-37, weighing up to 1 t when packed, to front-line repair units whose location moved almost daily in regions devoid of usable roads. Such aircraft also useful for general front-line supplies, support of partisans and regular duties such as passenger and casevac missions. Financial cover obtained from MA naval aviation September 1942, design completed in six weeks and prototype TS-1 started before end of year. As far as possible non-strategic materials, and airframe designed for lightness even at cost of labour-intensive construction. Intended engine MG-31 no longer available, and much less powerful M-11 accepted despite poor performance (judged not dangerous, and still adequate for need).

Wing R-II profile, 10% root to 6% tip, with single box spar and built-up truss ribs, glued and pinned joints. Slotted ailerons and flaps. Streamlined oval-section fuselage with built-up frames and even stringers made as light box sections with booms 4 × 8 mm and webs of 1-mm ply made up to box with section 10 × 30 mm. Wooden twin-finned tail, whole airframe fabric covered and spray-doped. Aluminium sheet floor to accept high point loads, steel-tube strut bracing high wing on each side, braced fixed landing gear with La-5 shock struts, tyres 600 × 180 mm, alternative skis 2400 × 620 mm. Castoring tailwheel with 300 × 125 mm tyre or 800 × 380 mm ski. Prototype and nearly all later aircraft initially built with spats, often later removed. Engines on welded mild-steel frame with rubber mounts. Prototype uncowled, most production with cowling. U-2 type propeller. Fuel in four welded AMTs tanks, total 850 lit, in centre section. Single door in left side 1,43 × 1,64 m with metal-clad frame. Design structural load factor 5·85.

Often reported first flight 1942 but this

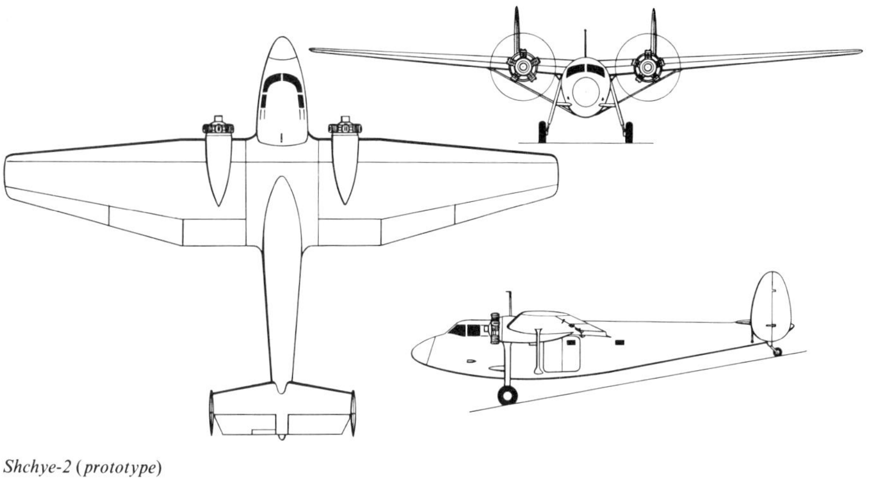
Shchye-2 (*prototype*)

appears erroneous. No mention in Soviet accounts of flight test until start of flight programme 17 April 1943 (V.P. Fyedorov). Immediately proceeded to NII testing, and decision to produce in series taken August. Production begun in Shchyerbakov OKB with designation Shchye-2. Series aircraft flown from 1 August 1944 and total of 550 built by 1946. First production aircraft made 20 full-load flights on route Chkalov/Kuibyshyev/Moscow and demonstrated service life of 1000 hours. Series aircraft widely used as 16-passenger transport, ambulance (11 stretchers), assault transport (nine paratroops) or as 5-pupil navigator trainer. Several experimental models including light (3,4 t max) variant with same tail but wing cut down to 55 m^2, and another flown with General Motors diesels from US armoured vehicle. OKB deputy chief, M.V. Lyapin, suggested twin-boom version with third M-11D at rear of cargo nacelle; not built. Final (1945) model **Shchye-2SKh** (ag) with main-gear legs 450 mm longer and tyres 800 × 260 mm. Not accepted because of extremely poor performance and time 85 s to make 360° turn. By Western standards basic type grossly underpowered, but it was easy to fly and at 3 t (ie, with little payload) could even remain above stall with one engine stopped at about 80 km/h.

DIMENSIONS Span (TS-1, bulk production) 20,54 m (67 ft $4\frac{2}{3}$ in), (1945 and SKh) 20,484 m (67 ft $2\frac{1}{2}$ in); length 14,27 m (46 ft $9\frac{3}{4}$ in); wing area 64,0 m^2 (689 ft^2), (1945, Skh) 63,88 m^2 (687·6 ft^2).
ENGINES Two 115 hp M-11D.
WEIGHTS Empty (TS-1) 2210 kg, later 2235 kg (4927 lb), (Něměcek) 2365 kg, 2270 kg, (SKh) 2,5 t; fuel/oil (TS) 370 + 40 kg, (1943–1945) 300 + 40 kg, (SKh) 100 + 30 kg; loaded (TS) 3,3 t, 3,4 t (7496 lb); max overload (not SKh) 3,7 t (8157 lb).
PERFORMANCE Max speed (TS) 168 km/h, (1943–1945) 155 km/h (96 mph); cruise 140 km/h (87 mph); climb to 1 km, 13–17 min, (Skh) 24 min; service ceiling 2–3 km; range 980 km (600 miles) with 1 t load; take-off 350 m/19 s; landing 170 m/15 s/70 km/h (43·5 mph).

VSI Conceptually years ahead of its time, this was world's first project for vectored-thrust jet VTOL. Designation as for same designer's earlier IVS but words rearranged: high-speed fighter. Streamlined fuselage accommodating retracted tricycle landing gear, broad but low T-tail, high wing of low aspect-ratio carrying tip pods housing engines. Each pod rotated through up to 120° to provide lift, thrust or braking force, with 'gas rudder' in each jet to give control in hover and in forward flight. Scheme submitted in 1946 brochure using two Nene (RD-45) in fighter weighing 4 to 5 t. More detailed design 1947 following closure of OKB. Favourable appraisal by B.N. Yuryev and V.S. Puishnov of VVIA (VVS engineering academy) and also from VVS central command. Decision to build flight test rig, but designer no longer in MAP system so construction begun at VVIA. Large rig with hovering vehicle of welded KhMA steel tube part-skinned in stainless sheet, supported on cables from four large towers and with underground tunnels for efflux gas. Only available engines German BMW 003); hovering begun 1948 but work soon halted, conflicting reasons given by different sources.

Sheremetyev

B. N. Sheremetyev was an important sailplane pilot/designer in the inter-war period. Among his powered aircraft were a *Blokha* (Flea) and Sh-13, described in Avietka section.

Shishmaryev

Mikhail Mikhailovich Shishmaryev was one of earliest Russian designers with major programmes at Shchyetinin factory during the First World War. After Revolution he became major-general and professor at VVA.

GASN Designation from *Gidroaeroplan Spetsialno Naznachyeniya* (seaplane for special duties), incorrectly claimed (Shavrov and others) as world's first torpedo seaplane. Alternative designation **SON** (aeroplane for individual duties). Large three-bay biplane with twin floats and three-finned biplane tail, mixed construction with three-spar wings, steel-tube struts throughout (many with fabric fairings) and ply-skinned forward fuselage for nose observer/gunner, two pilots side-by-side and second gunner behind wings. Rubber shock-absorbers in float struts. Engines between wings on inclined groups of four struts aligned with float attachments, upper LE cut away near props. Torpedo hung under centreline, provision for several bombs under central lower wing. Ten ordered but only one completed at Shchyetinin works 1916–1917, first flown 24 August 1917 by Lt A.Ye. Gruzinov. Outstanding on water; in air CG too far aft. Rectified but damaged 24 September when float broke. Derelict until 1920, then restored but 4 Nov 20 forced landing and frozen-in 2 km from shore.

P. O. Sukhoi

DIMENSIONS Span 28,0 m (91 ft $10\frac{1}{3}$ in); length 14,2 m (46 ft 7 in); wing area 150 m^2 (1615 ft^2).
ENGINES Two 220 hp Renault.
WEIGHTS Not known but weapon load 1450 kg (3197 lb).
PERFORMANCE Max speed 110 km/h (68 mph).

R-III First flown 1925, this was a minimum-change rebuild of R-1 (ie, neé D.H.9a) with fuselage attached between upper wings instead of lower, and different cabane struts joining bottom of fuselage to lower wings. Involved exceptionally long-strut main gears and also slightly increased ground angle. Idea was to improve field of view in reconnaissance role. Some accounts suggest more than one R-III built, but R-1 remained sole recon aircraft in service units. No data (very similar to R-1 since regular wing panels, engine and fuselage retained).

Silvanskii

A.V. Silvanskii is a blurred figure, hardly taken seriously by Shavrov and other historians yet responsible in 1938–1939 for small fighter aircraft.

IS Designation from *Istrebitel Silvanskii*, designed at OKB formed at GAZ where Silvanskii worked, no indication of how funded. Partners V.D. Yarovitskii and Yu.B. Sturtsel. Aircraft described as similar to I-16 but with slimmer M-88 engine and short single-strut landing gear; criticisms unbelievable, including inadequate recess for retracted wheel which accordingly ruined wing profile, and inadequate ground clearance for propeller. Eventually Silvanskii cropped 100 mm off each propeller blade. Thus, aircraft could hardly take-off and could not climb, but undeterred designer (refused flight-test facilities at factory) brought IS to Moscow and prevailed upon LII to carry out test programme. Unnamed pilot struggled into air and at full power found aircraft on point of stall at 300 m; managed to effect landing, claiming IS would not fly. Silvanskii bankrupted, and industry delegation banned him from further design. No data.

Sukhoi

Pavel Osipovich Sukhoi was one of greatest Soviet designers, but his early work never carried his name and his first 20 years as independent designer were heartbreakingly unrewarding, successive excellent designs for various reasons failing to be selected for production. Today his name is commemorated in about half of Soviet tactical airpower. He was born 10 (22 in old calendar) July 1895 at Glubokoye, Byelorussia. Studied from 1905 Gomel Gymnasium, Moscow University (1914, briefly) and at Moscow Highter Tech School MVTU under Zhukovskii (later Prof at VVA). Commissioned in the First World

War, then managed to survive revolution to join Red Army. In 1920 joined TsAGI, initially in capacity of student but, after demonstrating to Tupolev considerable design ability, as junior member of AGOS. First assignment, December 1924, design ANT-4 tailskid. Subsequently led one of three great AGOS (later KOZOK) TsAGI brigades with entire responsibility under Tupolev for ANT-5 (I-4 fighter) and at least eight other designs described under ANT designation (see Tupolev). Last was ANT-51 Ivanov, at new Komsomolsk GAZ, and here in December 1938 (Shavrov, end of 1939) Sukhoi invited to form own OKB. Returned to Moscow and took over premises of defunct BOK, initially to develop ANT-51 into BB-1. Subsequently OKB was consistently beaten by rivals, usually for reasons other than technical excellence, and was closed by Stalin 1949. Sukhoi assigned as assistant to Tupolev. On Stalin's death Sukhoi applied to GUAP and was permitted to re-open, expanding continually from then until present day. Profusion of research and experimental prototypes in late 1950s led to several major production aircraft which underpinned important families still being built. Sukhoi died September 1975, just after 80th birthday, and OKB leadership passed to Ye.A. Ivanov (General Constructor), Ye.S. Felsner and N.G. Zyirin, retaining original General Constructor's name on masthead.

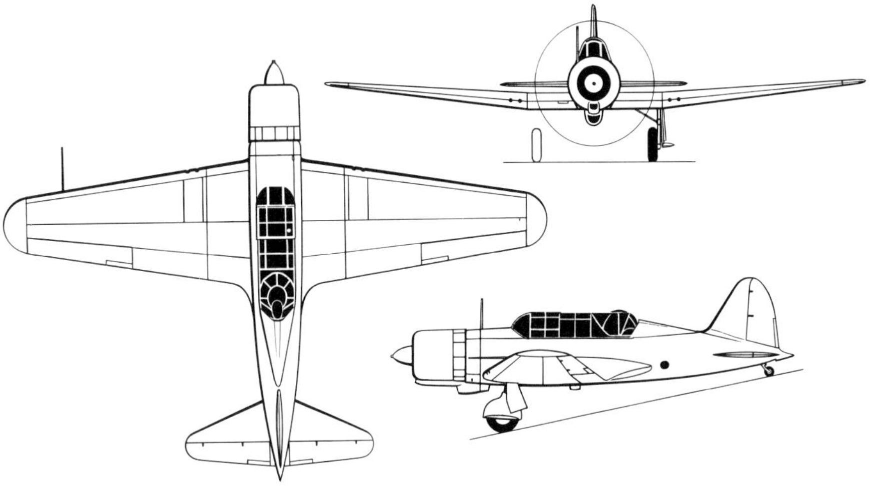

Su-2

Su-2, BB-1 Designation BB from *Blizhnii Bombardirovshchik*, short-range bomber, Su-2 adopted under new 1941 system (2 because bomber, thus an even number). Based on ANT-51 (see Tupolev) designed by Sukhoi brigade 1937 and flown 1937. In 1938 at Komsomolsk-na-Amur improved to meet later requirements with M-87A engine and increasingly referred to not as ANT-51 but as Sukhoi Ivanov. After 1938 formation of Sukhoi OKB two prototypes completed, with M-87A and M-87B engines. Both flown Komsomolsk and called Ivanovs. By this time Sukhoi setting up OKB in former BOK facilities and prepared design for intended mass-production version with even more powerful M-88 engine, increased bombload of 600 kg and many other changes including decreased usage of aluminium.

Wing little changed but restressed for increased weights, profile TsAGI B-series, 15·25% root and 8% tip. Centre section 3940 mm, outer panels with taper on both edges, dihedral uniform from roots. Two spars with D16 sheet webs and 30KhGSA booms, smooth flush-riveted dural skin with screwed fairing strip over centre/outer wing joint. All-dural split flaps in four sections driven pneumatically to 55°. All three units of landing gear retractable, main gears with 750 × 250 mm tyres, pneu brakes, single shock struts on outer side of wheels, fully housed between wing spars pulled up by pneu cylinder 300 × 125 mm diam, no standby, tailwheel semi-retracted to rear with own actuator, steering ±42°. Fuselage wooden semi-monocoque with 20 frames and bakelite-ply skin, with integral fin. Control surfaces dural with fabric covering, tailplane all-dural set at −5°, trimmers all-dural, elevators with inset hinges. Advanced engine installation in long-chord cowling with variable gills, opening in three petals (lower incorporating carb-air duct) with oil cooler immediately to rear and driving 3,25-m VISh-23-7 hydraulic propeller. Fuselage tank 425-lit, outer-wing tanks 140-lit each. Crew of two in tandem under larged glazed canopy, pilot high above bomb bay and radio/gunner in manual turret with RSB radio, AFA-13 camera installation and single ShKAS with 650 rounds. Four fixed ShKAS, 650 rounds each, in inboard outer wings. Internal bomb bay with left/right doors housing four FAB-100 (or 30 × 8, 20 × 15, 20 × 20, 12 × 25 etc); wing racks for two bombs up to 250 kg (overload) or 14 containers or ten RS-82 or eight RS-130. Both cockpits well-protected with 9-mm armour.

State trials autumn 1940, order for immediate production at three GAZ at high rate. Report (Němeček) 100 delivered by 22 June 1941 contrasts with 640 by 1 September and possibly erroneous. In VVS service quite popular because no vices and comfortable, but performance unimpressive and from spring 1941 engine changed to M-88B and much done to reduce weight, even by reducing armament (only two wing guns and max 400 kg bombs). Faster, and in summer often used as single-seat fighter with four or six wing guns because of heavy attrition of fighters. This was most numerous variant, though still easy meat for a Bf 109 and severe losses among all Su-2 regiments. One report designates M-88B aircraft **Su-2M** (*Modifikatsirovannyi*), most with two ShKAS in turret. Evacuation of factories October 1941 reduced output, but at least one GAZ in East continued producing until 1942, last 200 (possibly many more) having M-82 engine, first fitted about October 1941 but no known separate designation. M-82 aircraft heavier, faster and less pleasant to fly, especially suffering from directional instability despite increase in height of vertical tail. Total production probably more than 2000 but many lost to fighters and ground fire and generally withdrawn from front-line units by early 1943. A few still in use at end of war in utility, target-tug and training roles.

DIMENSIONS Span 14,3 m (46 ft 11 in); length (M-88) 10,25 m (33 ft 7½ in), (M-82) 10,46 m (34 ft 3¾ in); wing area 29,0 m² (312 ft²).

ENGINE (2) One 950 hp M-88, (M) 1000 hp M-88B, (final series) 1400 hp M-82 (ASh-82).

WEIGHTS Empty (1939) 2918 kg, (1940 production) 2930 kg (6459 lb), (M-88B) 2970 kg (6548 lb), (M-82) 3273 kg (7216 lb); fuel/oil (most) 580 kg, (lightened 1941) 550; loaded (1939) 4345 kg, (1940) 4360 kg (9612 lb), (M-88B) 4375 kg (9645 lb), (M-82) 4700 kg (10,362 lb).

PERFORMANCE Max speed (typical, all M-88, 88B) 375 km/h (233 mph) at SL, 460 km/h (286 mph) at 5 km, (M-82) 430 at SL, 486 km/h (302 mph) at 5,8 km; climb to 4 km (typical) 8·2 min; service ceiling (most) 8,8 km, (M-82) 9,0 km; range (most) 1200 km (746 miles), (M-82) 1100 km (683 miles); take-off (1940) 380 m/20 s; landing 425 m/22 s/130 km/h (81 mph).

Su-2

ShB This single prototype was modified from one of Su-Ivanovs in spring 1940 as *Shturmovik Bombardirovshchik*, armoured attack bomber. Main change new main gears retracting to rear with wheels rotating 90° on legs to lie horizontally in wing. Bright-metal area of skin behind cowling on each side (exhausts remained distributed round cowl), much larger area of armour on underside, max bombload 600 kg. No production because inferior to Il-2.
DIMENSIONS As Su-2.
ENGINE One 980/1000 hp M-88A.
WEIGHTS Empty 3100 kg (6834 lb); fuel/oil 580 kg; loaded 4,5 t (9912 lb).
PERFORMANCE Max speed 370 km/h (230 mph) at SL, 460 km/h (286 mph) at 4 km; no other data.

Su-4 Aware that underlying reason for vulnerability of Su-2 was lack of power, Sukhoi studied every available high-power engine and in late 1941 received permission to build prototype with most powerful of Shvetsov's engines then running, M-90 (later ASh-90). Like ShB resulting Su-4 dropped reconnaissance role, in this case being classed as LB (light bomber). Powerful engine of smaller diam than alternatives, and excellent installation achieved with adequate cooling and low drag. Three-blade propeller retained though larger blades; deep carb-air duct and oil cooler on underside. Main gears as Su-2 (photo often said to be Su-4 shows ShB with different landing gear). Outer wings structurally redesigned with existing steel/dural spars but wooden ribs and ply skin to conserve scarce metals. No wing racks, sole bombload in unchanged internal bay. Two BS in wing (Shavrov, in centre section, almost certainly error), each 400 rounds; two ShKAS in turret (apparent improved fairing of turret is probably artist retouching of photographs). Same taller vertical tail as Su-2/M-82. Flown December 1941, NII tests completed April 1942. Western historians state no production, reason given being unreliability of engine. Shvetsov confirmed no M-90 production, which certainly in 1942 had experimental status, yet Shavrov claims Su-4 produced in series and used in action during the Second World War. To make confusion worse Shavrov's data table gives engine as 1250 hp ASh-82 and gives speeds as 460 km/h at SL and 486 km/h at height (3 km). Doubling engine power must have had significant effect on flight performance, but no reliable data found. Unlikely Su-4 was in fact produced in quantity.
DIMENSIONS As Su-2 except length 10,79 m (35 ft 4¾ in).
ENGINE One 2100 hp M-90.
WEIGHTS Empty 3192 kg (7037 lb); fuel/oil 525 kg; loaded (Shavrov) 4620 kg (10,185 lb).
PERFORMANCE Not reliably known; Shavrov gives figures for M-82 Su-4, though SL speed 459 km/h (285 mph) and time 10·5 min to 6 km may be correct.

Su-1, I-330 Sukhoi was invited to Kremlin meeting on new fighters in early 1939 and immediately gave positive response, suggesting his OKB produce interceptor for high-altitude performance. Aircraft **330** (presumably I-330, but I inserted only in Western accounts) studied with pressure cabin but built without it. Main feature was twin TK (turbochargers) and large cannon firing through propeller hub. Straightforward low-wing aircraft with mixed construction similar to Su-2 family. Fuselage wood semi-monocoque, skinned in bakelite-ply 5/2,5 mm with integral fin. Neat sliding canopy, with rear fairing of teardrop shape but opaque. Engine cowl dural with Dzus fasteners, TK flush on each side of fuselage surrounded by square of stainless-steel skin. Single-spar centre-section and outer wings, profile not known, dihedral c/s 0°, outer 5°. Thick sheet spar web, heavy machined D16 T-section booms, pressed-sheet ribs, numerous angle-section stringers, flush-riveted D1 skin. Single-strut main gears retracted to rear, wheels pivoting 90° on legs. Four-section split flaps. Tailwheel retracting to rear with two doors, small portion of tyre showing. Duralumin tailplane with stressed skin, duralumin flight control surfaces with fabric covering (but all-dural trim tabs on rudder, both elevators and left aileron). Push/pull rods for ailerons and elevators, cables for rudder. No information on fuel tankage. Engine (which did not have electrically driven two-stage supercharger, as has been reported, but was itself standard M-105P) carried on welded 30KhGSA truss with glycol header tank behind standard VISh-61P propeller, main radiator being in streamlined duct under rear fuselage; carb-air ram inlets on each side of fuselage above TK installations, with aluminium ducts thence to normal mechanically driven supercharger on engine. Design armament, one BT-23 with 80 rounds between cylinder blocks and two ShKAS with 400 rounds each in top of fuselage. All known photographs appear to show spinner with no central hole, but this may be result of retouching. Project authorized spring 1939, and at this time also given designation Su-1, ahead of normal usage of such designations. First flight late 1940 (one account, October), showed considerable promise. General handling good and easy to land (despite narrow track). With turbos operative general performance surpassed that of all other available fighters, especially in manoeuvrability at 10-km level, while landing speed was half that of Pe-2 family. Only fault was serious: TK-2 installation suffered from endless difficulties and failures, and when OKB evacuated decision taken reluctantly to terminate work on programme. Su-3 was variant.
DIMENSIONS Span 11,5 m (37 ft 8¾ in); length 8,42 m (27 ft 7½ in); wing area 19,0 m² (204·5 ft²).
ENGINE One 1100 hp M-105P with twin TK-2.
WEIGHTS Empty 2495 kg (5500 lb); fuel/oil 255 kg; loaded 2875 kg (6338 lb).
PERFORMANCE Max speed 500 km/h at SL, 641 km/h (398 mph) at 10 km; climb to 5 km, 4·9 min; service ceiling 12,5 km (41,000 ft); range 720 km (447 miles); take-off 220 m; landing speed 111 km/h (69 mph).

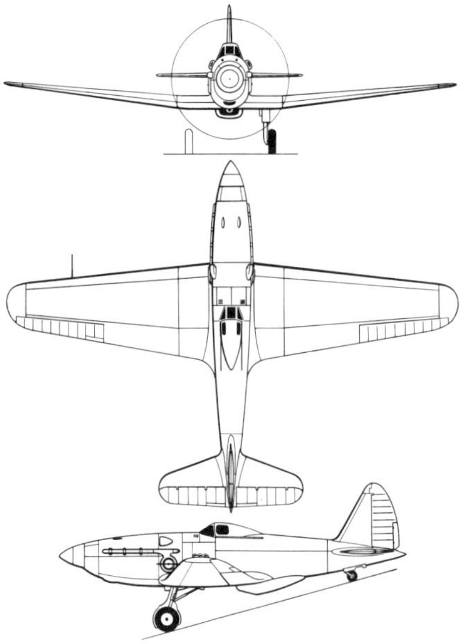

Su-1

Su-3 With such low landing speed, Sukhoi decided to clip wing-span for more speed, at same time designing to higher factor of 13·5 and removing dive limits. Structure, engine and armament basically unchanged from Su-1 but fuel capacity slightly reduced, possibly suggesting tankage in outer wings. Recent Soviet account mentions altered radiator, and drawing suggests main radiator was in shorter duct and that oil cooler was moved to below leading edge (in Su-1 not visible at this location and presumably in main duct). Prototype **I-360** authorized in parallel with I-330 in 1939. Redesignated Su-3 and almost complete at evacuation; taken to Novosibirsk, flown and put through LII testing 1942. Expected speed increase not achieved (no reason given) and turbos still unreliable. Programme terminated late 1942 and Su-3 handed to NII VVS. Ponomaryev comments these two Sukhoi fighters, whose handling was exemplary, were valuable in assisting TK development for other aircraft.
DIMENSIONS As Su-1 except span 10,1 m (33 ft 1⅝ in); wing area 17,0 m² (183 ft²).

Su-1

ENGINE One 1100 VK-105P with twin TK-2.
WEIGHTS Empty 2480 kg (5467 lb); fuel/oil 240 kg; loaded 2860 kg (6305 lb), overload 3 t (6614 lb).
PERFORMANCE Max speed 500 km/h at SL, 638 km/h (396 mph) at 10 km; climb to 5 km, 5·5 min; service ceiling 11,9 km (39,000 ft); take-off (Shavrov) as Su-1, 220 m; landing speed 122 km/h (76 mph).

Su-6 Though it had misfortune to have to compete with Il-2 at every stage of development, this armoured *Shturmovik* was not a parallel design but much later project begun at Sukhoi OKB June 1940. Authorization as Aircraft **81**, also called **OBSh** (experimental armoured attacker). Far from being delayed by engine, as often suggested, prototype construction was rapid and OBSh made first flight about mid-April 1941 with designation Su-6. Closely followed by almost identical second machine called A, or **Su-6(A)**. Having carefully studied earlier Ilyushin, Sukhoi adhered to single-seat formula but adopted most powerful available aircooled engine and designed improved scheme of armour. Basic airframe typical Sukhoi with metal wings and wood fuselage. Wing TsAGI B-series profile, similar thickness to Su-2 but reduced chord giving t/c 18% root and 8% tip. Single spar with booms made up of centre channel and two side angles all 30KhGSA steel joined by close Warren truss of D16 channels, riveted gusset joints. D16 truss (inboard) and pressed-sheet ribs, flush-riveted skin. Centre section 3285 m, dihedral 0°, outer panels dihedral 8°. Hydraulic split flaps, auto slats over 50% of leading edge, landing light left LE inboard of slat, large pitot boom cantilevered ahead from below outer left wing. Fuselage almost scaled-up I-330 with semi-monocoque structure covered with bakelite-ply; integral wood fin. All flight control surfaces D1 with fabric covering, fully balanced with inset hinges, those of ailerons being beneath lower surface on brackets. All-D1 trim tabs on rudder, both elevators and left aileron. Single-strut main gears with hydraulic retraction to rear, leg and wheel rotating through 90°. No bay doors on first two aircraft, same leg fairing as Su-4. Tyres 800 × 260 mm, pneumatic brakes. Tailwheel 300 × 125 mm with separate retraction cylinder folding leg to rear with lower part of tyre projecting below tailcone. Excellent engine installation in long-chord cowl with electric gills, AV-5-4A propeller 3250-mm diam, with Hucks dogs. Short carb-air ram inlet above cowl, oil coolers in centre section outboard of landing-leg well fed by kinked duct from LE root and with exit in upper surface. Self-sealing fuel tank 667 lit in centre section between landing gears with 2-mm armour. Same thickness around engine, with 4-mm around cylinders, sides and underside of fuselage, 6-mm upper sides of cockpit, 8-mm seat armour and 12-mm behind pilot's head and back. Armoured glass 50-mm pilot windscreen, 28-mm sides, added late 1941. Armament two BT-23 with 230 rounds (VYa to be used when available) and four ShKAS with 1500 rounds all in outer wings. Internal bomb bay with twin hydraulic doors, normal load four FAB-100. Underwing racks for ten RS-82 or RS-132 (latter remarkable, but in all Soviet accounts).

Second aircraft was similar but main gears with no fairings retracting into bay with twin doors. Both completed factory testing prior to evacuation. In early 1942 OKB instructed to prepare two-seat variant as insurance against problem with Il-2 and to sustain programme in view of fact in most respects Su-6 was superior to Il-2, presenting smaller, faster and more agile target capable of carrying at least as much firepower. In recent account Ponomaryev comments that NII pilots and engineers strongly recommended Su-6 produced in place of Il-2, but no chance of disrupting production. Evacuated OKB did, however, get go-ahead on two-seater, called **2A** or **Su-6(2A)**, never written Su-6-II except in Western accounts. Extended mid-fuselage with radio/gunner with UBT with four magazines each of 49 rounds, standing between outward-canted noses of four FAB-100 in revised bay divided along outer sides of fuselage but with same doors (relocated) and unchanged sighting for dive or level bombing. (Note: on Su-2 bombs were below pilot, not aft of gunner.) Heavier forward-firing armament of

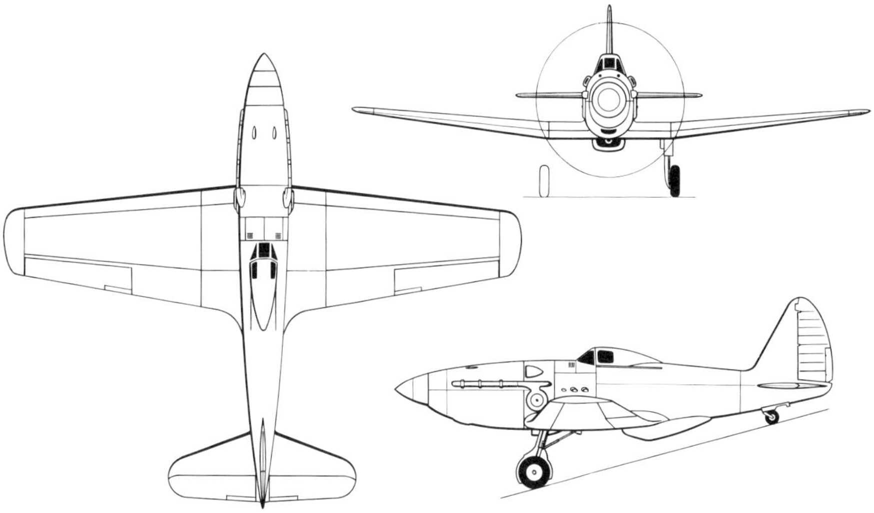

Su-3

Su-6 (*A*)

Su-6 (*2A*)

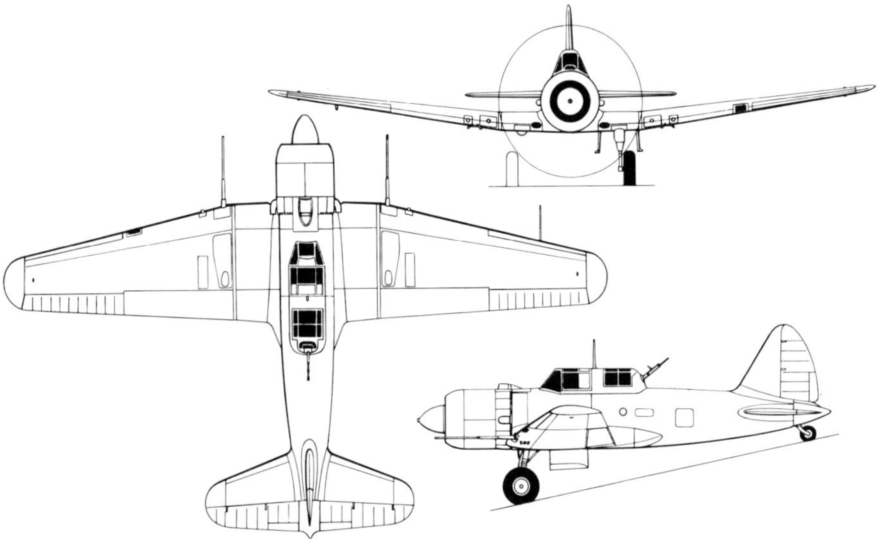

Su-6 (2A)

two 37-mm OKB-16 or 11-P-37 each with 45 rounds, plus two ShKAS with 1400 rounds used mainly for sighting. Underwing racks for (Shavrov) 200-kg (Ponomaryev) up to 500-kg bombs, but rockets reduced to six. Tailwheel tyre 400 × 150 mm. With more powerful engine performance not markedly affected, and according to Shavrov range considerably increased. Armour up to 643 kg with 8 mm round gunner, 12-mm at rear and 65-mm gunner's oblique rear window. Aircraft 2A flown 14 November 1943, NII tested by September 1943. All-round better than Il-2M3 and OKB won State Prize, but no disruption of Il-2 production.

Final Su-6 launched together with Il-8 and Il-10 at 1942 meeting to decide next-generation *Shturmovik* to replace Il-2. Sukhoi went ahead with totally different Su-8, but also pulled out one more stop with Su-6 programme. Adopting liquid-cooled engine (also chosen by rival) he at last increased wing area and produced best aircraft of series, called **2A(M-42)**. New wing with trailing edge at 90° to aircraft axis, slight increase in span, tip t/c 6·25%, additional 2,6 m² area (all to rear of spar, with increased-chord flap and aileron) but still less than three-quarters area of Il-2. Big engine carried in left/right trusses of welded 30KhGSA with four pin-jointed but undamped pick-ups on main longerons. Underslung radiator, carb-air inlet projecting at top, oil coolers in outer centre section as before but with discharge from lower surface. Four-blade 3,4 m AV-9L-172 propeller, Hucks dogs shown on Soviet drawings but not visible in photographs. Believed greater fuel capacity but no info (Shavrov quotes vastly greater disposable load but shorter range). Aircraft 2A(M-42) flown December 1943 and completed NII testing second quarter 1944, but by this time Ilyushin had superior aircraft.

DIMENSIONS Span (except AM-42) 13,5 m (44 ft 3½ in), (AM-42) 13,58 m (44 ft 6¾ in); length (SA) 9,133 m (29 ft 11½ in), (2A) 9,243 m (30 ft 4 in), (M-42) 9,5 m (31 ft 2 in); wing area (except AM-42) 26,0 m² (280 ft²), (AM-42) 28,6 m² (308 ft²).

ENGINE (A) one 2000 hp M-71, (2A) 2200 hp ASh-71F, (2A/M-42) 2000 hp AM-42.

WEIGHTS Empty (A) 3727 kg (8216 lb), (2A) 4137 kg (9120 lb), (AM-42) 4370 kg (9634 lb); fuel/oil (A) 480 kg, (2A) 570 kg, (M-42) believed greater, despite reduced range; loaded (A) 5250 kg (11,574 lb), (2A) 5534 kg (12,200 lb), (M-42) 6,2 t (13,668 lb).

PERFORMANCE Max speed (A) 496 km/h (308 mph) at SL, 527 km/h (327 mph) at 2,5 km, (2A) 480 km/h (298 mph) at SL, 514 km/h (319 mph) at 2,5 km, (M-42) 492 km/h (306 mph) at SL, 521 km/h (324 mph) at 1,5 km; climb to 3 km, (A) 7·3 min, (2A) 8·2 min, (M-42) 8·5 min; serviceceiling(A)notinSovietsources,(Něměcek) 7,6 km, (2A) 8,1 km (26,575 ft), (M-42) 8 km (26,250 ft); range (A) not reliably recorded, probably about 850 km but (Shavrov) 576 km, (Něměcek) 450, (2A) 973 km (605 miles), (M-42) 790 km (490 miles); take-off (A) 520 m, (2A) 410 m, (M-42) 540 m; landing (A) not recorded, (2A) 730 m/146 km/h, (M-42) 660 m/150 km/h (93 mph).

Su-8 January 1942 Kremlin conference on Shturmoviks also demanded next-generation machines. AM-42 Su-6(2A) was regarded by Sukhoi as interim, and it was his idea to build large long-range aircraft. Little evident need at time; it was only from late 1944 that Nazi retreat became so fast that close-support air units could not keep up, and short range/endurance of Il-2 became a problem. Sukhoi said he predicted this situation and that Kremlin meeting concurred, authorizing two prototypes designated **DDBSh** (*Dvukhmotornyi Dalnii Bronirovannyi Shturmovik*, twin-engined long-range armoured attacker; according to Shavrov, second D = *Dvukhmyestnyi*, two-seat). OKB called new project Aircraft **B**. Exceedingly impressive aircraft, with two of most powerful available

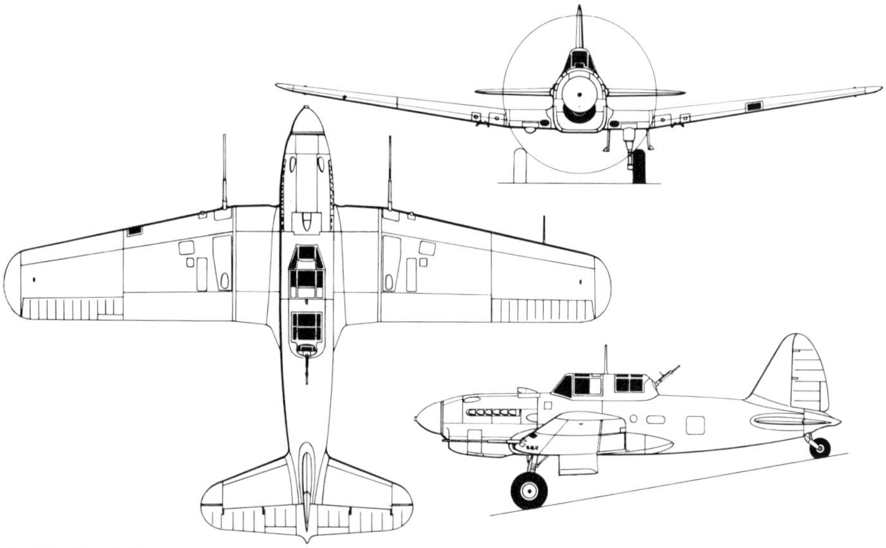

2A (M-42 engine)

2A (M-42 engine)

engines, capacious tankage and devastating armament. Slim fuselage with pilot and radio/gunner separated by large central fuel tank, low wing and twin-finned tail. Mixed construction, with complex fuselage having entire front-end *bronyekorpus* (armour-body) with five thicknesses up to 15 mm. Mid-section duralumin stressed-skin with armour slabs for second crew-member, mainly bolted and carrying share of flight loads. Rear fuselage wood semi-monocoque with skin of bakelite-ply. Wing modified NACA-230, 14% root and 7·5% tip, single straight spar tip to tip (broken with precision-bolt joints at ends of centre section) with D16 plate web(s) and upper/lower booms of machined 30KhGSA channel and angle sections. Rest of rectangular centre section duralumin with flush-riveted skin. Outer panels with 3° dihedral and taper almost entirely of wood, with truss/ply ribs and casein-glued ply skin. Hydraulic slotted flaps and all tail and flight control surfaces duralumin with D1 flush-riveted skin. Main gears with 950 × 300 mm tyres on single shock struts retracting hydraulically into nacelle bays with twin doors, wheels rotating 90°. Fully retractable tailwheel. Engines in efficient cowls with carb-air and oil-cooler ducts in LE immediately outboard, individual exhaust stacks and three-blade propeller of VISh-105 series with root cuffs. Total fuel capacity 3300 lit (726 gal) including centre-section cells inboard of engines. Primary armament large ventral box housing (first aircraft) four 11P-37, (second) four OKB-16-45, each with 50 rounds in clips loaded by radio/gunner (OKB-16 had rig with auto feed, not installed in aircraft). In addition four (some sources, eight) ShKAS in outer wings firing ahead, used air/air and for air/ground sighting. Glazed nose, according to some accounts used by pilot to sight forward-firing guns, all angled slightly downwards and with sight allowing for this. Author believes fired straight ahead. Glazed nose and same sight system, probably reset to different trajectory, also used by pilot to aim bombs. Normal load four FAB-150 in four cells in wing aft of main spar between engines and ShKAS batteries. Overload 1400 kg including external beneath wing (probably inboard of engines). Upper rear defence single UBT aimed by radio/gunner. Lower rear ShKAS at rear of ventral gun box also aimed by backseater via unusual sight system (no details). Total 5900 rounds weighing 232 kg for all guns (interpreted by some as all machine guns ie, not including four large cannon). Heaviest forward-firing firepower of any Second World War aircraft, with over 1 t/min for big guns alone. Total mass of armour on first aircraft 1680 kg. Designated Su-8 before completion, first aircraft on factory test late 1943, second joined early 1944. Both outstanding with superb handling even at full load, but prevailing mood was war could be won with existing equipment. (Il-10 thought to meet immediate needs). In fact Su-8 range and endurance would have been useful in final year of war. Land armies advanced over 1500 km and were often 150–200 km ahead of nearest close-support air unit.

DIMENSIONS Span 20,448 m (67 ft 1 in), (Shavrov 20,5, Alexander 20,2); length 13,58 m (44 ft 6¾ in), (Shavrov 13,5); wing area 60,0 m² (646 ft²).

ENGINES Two 2200 hp ASh-71F.

WEIGHTS Empty (1st) 9180 kg, (2nd) 9208 kg (20,300 lb); fuel/oil 2370 kg; loaded (1) 12 425 kg, (2) 12 413 kg (27,366 lb); max 13,3 t (29,321 lb).

PERFORMANCE Max speed 500 km/h (311 mph) at SL (Něměcek 485), 550 km/h (342 mph) at 4,6 km; climb to 3 km, 7·3 min, to 5 km in 9 min; service ceiling 9 km; range with full weapons 1500 km (932 miles) (Něměcek 1100 km); take-off 400 m; landing 470 m/140 km/h (87 mph).

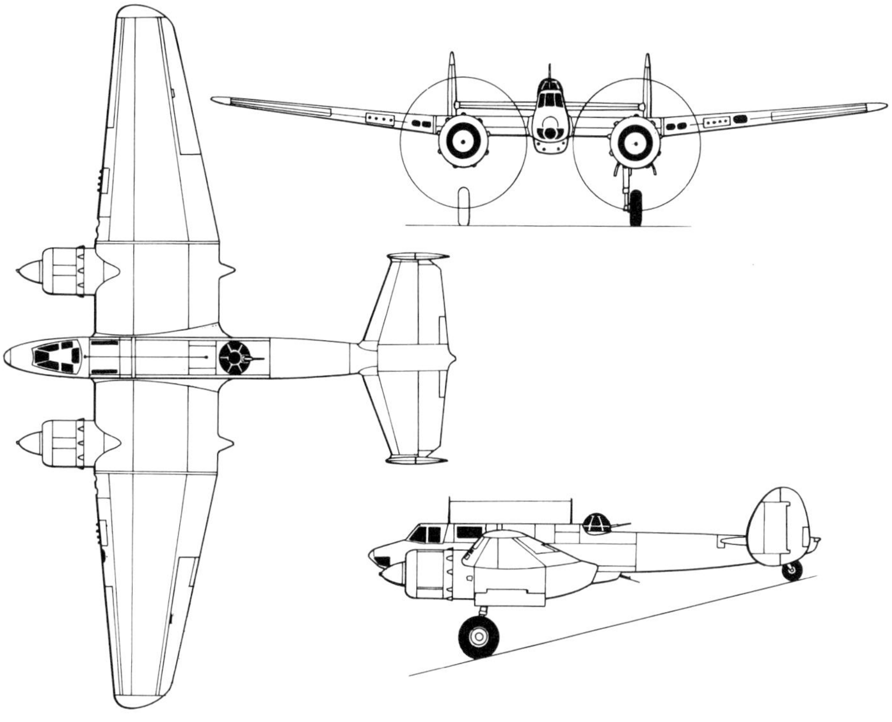

Su-8 (eight wing guns)

Su-7* Chronologically earlier than Su-5, this experimental mixed-power high-altitude interceptor used airframe of Su-6(A). Few changes to airframe but local strengthening to ultimate factor of 13·5 and all armour removed except normal fighter armour (probably 9-mm) around seat. Same tankage, self-sealing and inerted, but added cell in rear fuselage for nitric acid. Few changes to cockpit (not pressurized) but new canopy with full glazing and more acutely raked windshield. History confused, because while neither Shavrov nor Něměcek mentions more than one prototype, photographs show four different build-standards of at least two different aircraft! Even armament said to differ: (Shavrov) three 20-mm cannon with 370 rounds, no information on gun type or disposition; (Něměcek) two VYa-23, with drawing showing installation at inboard ends of outer wing panels. All agree engine was changed to ASh-82FN, but only one known photo confirms Shavrov statement that engine had two TK-3 turbochargers. This photo shows undoubted ASh-82FN installation with internal carb-air inlet, and four-blade propeller. It also shows long fairing at tail, projecting far behind rudder, for rocket engine in almost same installation at La-7R of same timescale. Other photos show Su-7* with ASh-71F installation, three-blade propeller and projecting carb-air inlet at rear of cowl; in this condition Su-7 had rocket fairing removed, leaving blunt open end just aft of rudder hinge. Third, most puzzling picture shows one of original M-71 installations with long carb-air duct from front of cowl, three-blade propeller and normal tail without rocket. Almost certainly this was how Su-7* was originally built and flown in 1944 (Green/Swanborough, late spring). Landing gear as on original Su-6(SA) with fairings on legs/wheels but no wing-hinged doors (incorrectly shown on Czech 3-view). No guns in wings at this time, but three ShVAK might have been installed in fuselage without interfering with left/right turbos. Rocket not installed until 1945, by which time main engine was undoubtedly ASh-82FN with four-blade propeller. Total rocket burn time about 4min. Su-7* obviously too large to be superior dogfighter and described in official document as experimental interceptor. Even with both engines operating performance (as re-

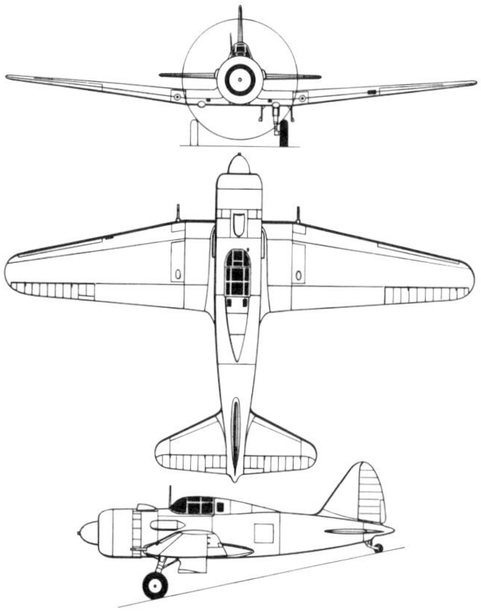

Su-7 (without rocket)*

corded) unimpressive, and no evidence of VVS interest. Aircraft appears to have been built simply because airframe and rocket were available, and evidence suggests airframe was actually that of first Su-6 reconstructed. Also suggests that no serviceable Su-1 or Su-3 was in existence, because that would have been better basis for mixed-power interceptor?

DIMENSIONS Span 13,5 m (44 ft 3½ in); length (no rocket) 9,14 m (29 ft 11¾ in), (with rocket) 10,03 m (32 ft 10¾ in); wing area 26 m^2 (280 ft^2) (incorrectly given as 16 m^2 in Czech accounts).

ENGINES One 1850 hp ASh-82FN with two TK-3 plus (1945) Glushko RD-1-KhZ of 300-kg thrust at SL.

WEIGHTS Empty, not recorded (given by Němeček as 2600 kg, more than 1 t less than Sa-6SA, unbelievable); fuel/oil 480 + 50 kg plus 180 kg nitric acid; loaded 4360 kg (9612 lb).

PERFORMANCE Max speed (both engines) 480 km/h at SL, 680 km/h (423 mph) at 4,5 km, 705 km/h (438 mph) at 7,5 km; service ceiling 12,75 km (41,830 ft); range (Němeček) 990 km (615 miles); take-off 350 m piston engine, 290 m both; landing speed 120 km/h (74·5 mph).

Su-5 Second of OKB's experimental interceptors of 1944, Su-5 was rival to MiG N (I-250) as mixed-power aircraft able to dogfight German jet and rocket aircraft. Prototype authorised as **I-107** early 1944, using same combination of engines as I-250: modified VK-107A with step-up (13:21) geared drive to compressor in separate large fuselage duct for TsAM (Kholshchyevnikov) VRDK boost propulsion burning same fuel from seven ducted combustors and discharging through stainless-steel welded pipe and variable-area nozzle with hydromechanical actuation. Main-engine exhaust discharged straight overboard, but carb-air supplied via left/right pipes taken from high-pressure area downstream of VRDK compressor. Airframe entirely duralumin, including flight-control surface skins. Wing with single spar with heavy plate web, profile TsAGI 1B10 inboard 16·5% at root, changing to NACA-230 outboard mainly 11%. Structurally in three sections each side, one bolted joint outboard of main gears and other at flap/aileron junction. Main gears with track 3,15 m, tyres 650 × 200 mm, retracting inwards hydraulically ahead of spar. Fully balanced Frise ailerons. Hydraulic split flaps driven to 54°. Fully retractable 300 × 125 mm tailwheel

*Su-9**

with asbestos insulated well. Four-blade 2890 mm propeller without Hucks dogs, 646 lit fuel in wing aft of spar (gravity fillers near outer ends of centre section), oil cooler in left centre section immediately behind spar fed by large shallow duct from leading edge, curved over retracted main leg and exhausting via guide-vanes

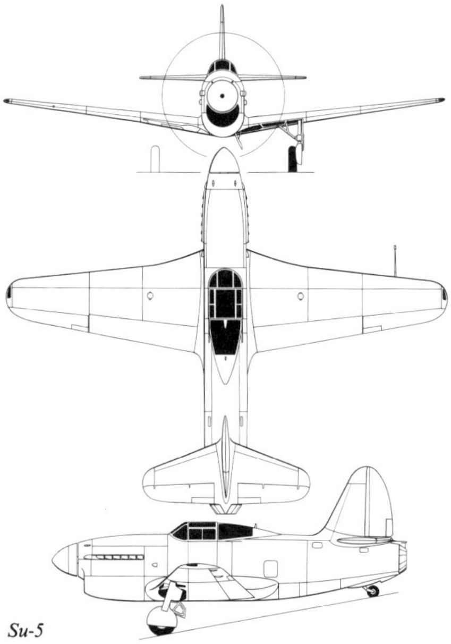

Su-5

Su-5

in bottom skin ahead of flap. Spring-tab flight controls, with trimmers using same tabs by biassing neutral position. Armament one NS-23 with 100 rounds firing through propeller hub plus two UBS with 400 rounds in top of fuselage. Pilot seat 10 mm armoured, canopy sliding back over glazed rear fairing, gyro sight, HF radio with wire aerials to fin including IFF. Su-5 with matt-painted finish on factory test, believed Novosibirsk, using wheeled landing gear April/June 1945. Almost all flying by G. Komarov. Satisfactory aircraft, but no production requirement in view of unquestioned superiority of turbojet. Did not fly after 15 July 1945. Three-view in Simakov's book shows ram inlets projecting on each side of rear fuselage, not shown in Soviet detail plans or photos.

DIMENSIONS Span 10,562 m (34 ft 7⅝ in); length 8,51 m (27 ft 11 in) (8,21 m often quoted is error); wing area 17,0 m^2 (183 ft^2).

ENGINES One 1650 hp VK-107A (modified) plus VRDK giving high-alt boost equivalent to 900 hp for max 10 min.

WEIGHTS Empty 2954 kg (6512 lb); fuel/oil 465 kg; loaded 3804 kg (8386 lb).

PERFORMANCE Max speed 810 km/h (503 mph) at 7,8 km (Simakov, 815 km/h); speed at 4350 m (est) 768 km/h, (measured) 793 km/h (493 mph); Shavrov gives time to 5 km as 5·7 min, most unimpressive; service ceiling 1205 km (39,550 ft); range 650 km (400 miles); landing speed 140 km/h (87 mph).

UTB This low-powered (700 hp ASh-21) trainer derivative of Tu-2 was developed by P.O. Sukhoi's OKB. See under Tupolev, page 319.

Su-9* OKB's first jet was straightforward fighter/bomber authorized as two flight prototypes plus static-test airframe May 1944. OKB designation Aircraft **K.** General appearance strikingly similar to Me 262, and underwing engine nacelles almost identical apart from having longer inlet ducts making engine nose bullet less visible. All-dural airframe with flush riveting or bonding throughout. Wing of TsAGI S-10 series, no attempt at sweepback, ruling t/c 10%, single main spar, fuel both inboard and outboard of nacelles with two gravity fillers. Fixed leading edge but trailing edge slotted flaps inboard of nacelles and novel airbrakes between nacelles and ailerons divided into upper (large) and lower (smaller) surfaces pulled apart to 88° and stressed to 900 km/h IAS. Fin integral with oval-section monocoque fuselage, carrying fixed tailplane. Eight published three-views fail to show cut-out at roots of elevators to allow rud-

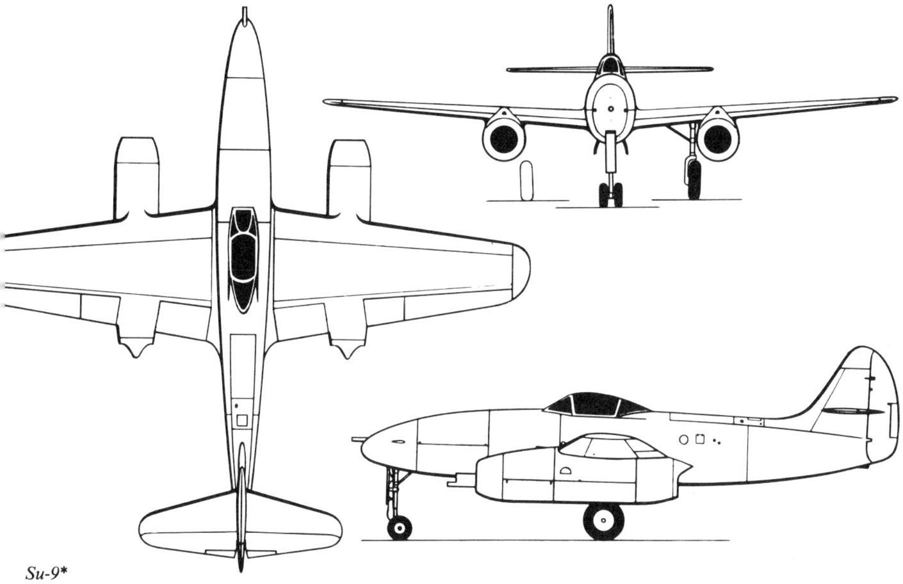

*Su-9**

der movement. All flight control surfaces metal-skinned and hydraulically boosted, with 12:1 gear ratio manual reversion (judged unacceptable for combat but adequate for landing). Airbrakes, flaps and landing gear also hydraulic, with single system but pump on each engine. Other new features included cockpit with completely transparent enclosure (with frameless blown Plexiglas main canopy sliding to rear), provision for two U-5 solid a.t.o. rockets on lower sides of lower rear fuselage (each 1150 kg for 8 s), cordite-fired Ye-24 ejection seat, toe-operated wheel-brakes, and braking parachute streamed from compartment immediately ahead of rudder. Nose gear with twin wheels, retracting to rear into bay with twin doors, main gear with wide track (3,51 m) and large low-pressure tyres retracting inwards behind spar with entire face of each main wheel/tyre visible (one Western 3-view shows tyres almost touching; of course they were separated by width of fuselage). Three protected flexible fuel cells in fuselage supplementing those in wing, total 2430 lit (535 gal); no provision for drop tanks. Armament one NS-37 or N-45 with 30 rounds plus two NS-23 with 200 rounds each. Racks under centre fuselage for FAB-500 or two FAB-250 (latter believed in tandem). First flight, G. Komarov, summer 1946 (often said 18 August). Factory testing showed excellent handling, fully up to standard of Me 262 (which was superb) but lacking German type's dangerous character at low speeds or with engine out. Testing included gun-firing and steep dive bombing using airbrakes. Rate of roll higher than MiG-9 (I-300) despite wing-mounted engines, and much better range, endurance (1 hr 44 min with fuel for spare circuit at base) and ammo capacity. Despite stigma of similarity to Me 262, so good that NII recommended series-production but no GAZ capacity available. Believed one example rebuilt as Su-11. Other prototype flown publicly in Tushino parade 3 August 1947.

DIMENSIONS Span 11,20 m (36 ft 9 in); length 10,55 m (34 ft 7¼ in); wing area 20,2 m^2 (217 ft^2).

ENGINES Two 900 kg RD-10.

WEIGHTS Empty 4060 kg (8951 lb); fuel 1750 kg max; loaded (normal) 6,1 t, (max) 6380 kg (14,065 lb).

PERFORMANCE Max speed 847 km/h (526 mph) at SL, 900 km/h (559 mph) at 8 km; climb to 5 km, 4·2 min; service ceiling 12,75 km (41,830 ft); range 1140 km (708 miles); take-off 350 m; landing speed 150 km/h (93 mph).

Su-11* Several observers believe sole Su-11, known to OKB as Aircraft **LK**, was rebuild of one Su-9. At one time thought to have RD-500 (Derwent) engines, in fact first association of OKB with A. Lyul'ka, whose TR-1 was chosen. Larger engines required completely different installation, engine being on welded-steel truss close ahead of front spar, jetpipe close beneath lower wing skin, enclosed by vast nacelle which for min drag extended well above top of wing as in Meteor. TsAGI did tunnel work, fair results though no change in Mach, hence now faster at SL. Aircraft marginally heavier and, despite expected lift from nacelles, decision taken to make wing slightly larger. Only other significant change was pressurized cockpit and fractionally reduced fuel of 2335 lit (514 gal). Single LK, by this time called Su-11, flown by OKB October 1947 (another report 'late 1947'). Factory test completed April 1948 but no production. TR-1 was faulty engine, and in any case aircraft outclassed by MiG-15. Still handicapped by superficial suggestion of copying Germans, even Yakovlev telling Stalin Me 262 layout undesirable and very dangerous to fly (would be judged merely good bit of fiction had Yakovlev not included it in one of his books!).

DIMENSIONS Span 11,8 m (38 ft 8½ in); length 10,55 m (34 ft 7¼ in); wing area 21,4 m^2 (230 ft^2).

ENGINES Two 1300 kg (2866 lb) TR-1.

WEIGHTS Empty 4495 kg (9910 lb); fuel 1782 kg; loaded 6350 to 6877 kg (15,161 lb max).

PERFORMANCE Max speed 940 km/h (584 mph)

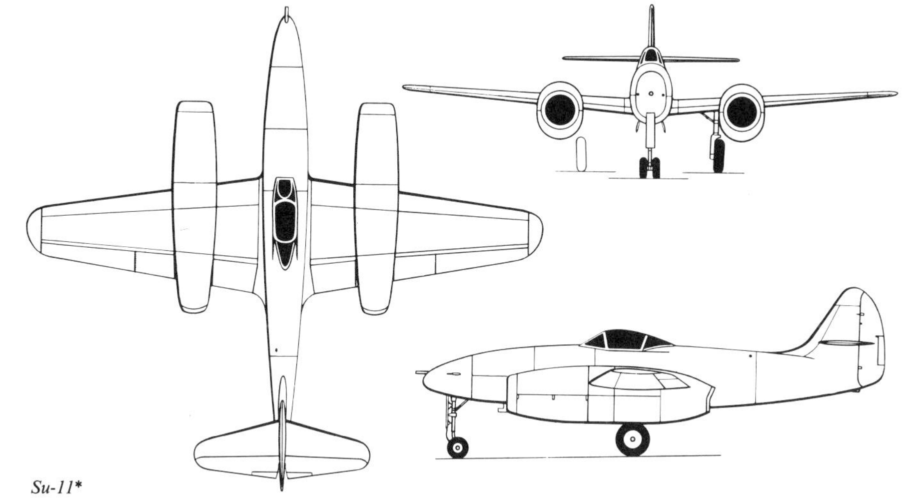

*Su-11**

*Su-11**

*Su-11**

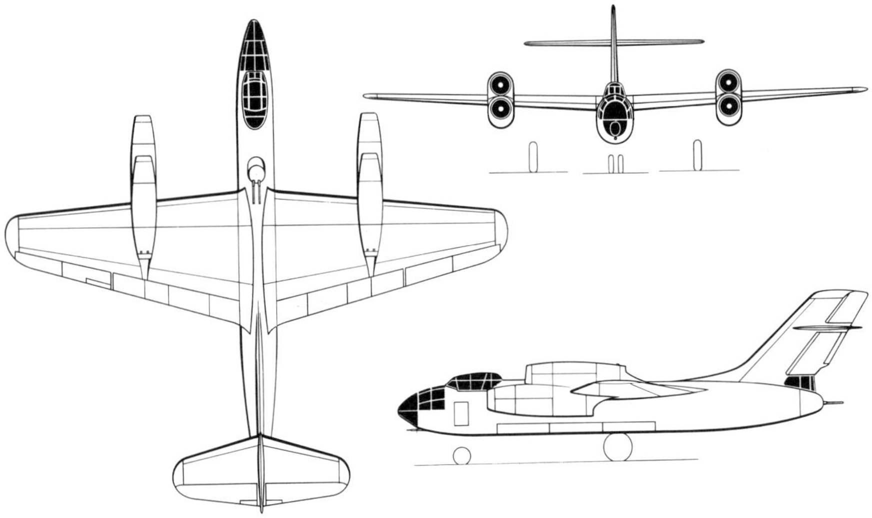

Su-10

at SL, 910 km/h (565 mph) at 3 km; climb to 5 km, 3·2 min; service ceiling 13 km (42,650 ft); range 900 km (560 miles); take-off 320 m; landing speed 150 km/h (93 mph).

Su-13 Final member of OKB's fighter family with twin wing-mounted engines, this prototype, Aircraft **KD**, had airframe generally as Su-11 but with swept tailplane (believed variable incidence for trimming) and 1590 kg RD-500 engines. Designed to push further up Mach scale than Su-11, despite apparently retaining original wing. Single KD under construction 1947 but never completed because recognised as having no chance of series production. No data.

Su-10 First large bomber designed under Sukhoi supervision since 1934, this four-jet day bomber was major challenge and abounded in interesting features only now becoming known. Single prototype authorized 1946 as Aircraft **Ye**, actual construction begun 1947. Large finely streamlined fuselage of circular section with pressurized nose compartment for nav/bomb in glazed nose, pilot on upper centreline under large canopy, radio/gunner back-to-back with pilot, and observer/gunner in pressurized compartment at tail. All-dural construction with flush riveting or (new techniques) bonding. Unswept wing with main box enclosed by two spars with heavy plate webs and machined stretched skins forming integral tank over most of span, except between engines and fuselage where large cut-outs for retracted main gears. These required so much space engines had to be well outboard, and four turbojets installed in superimposed staggered pairs, each engine on welded 30KhGSA spaceframe carried off main box and with large dural nacelle of removable panels. Fixed leading edge, large Frise ailerons and large one-piece Fowler flaps driven hydraulically on internal rails to 32°. Main gears retracted inwards, no details but usually shown on 3-views as having single main wheels. Short twin-wheel nose gear retracting forwards under pressure floor. Large bomb bay occupying full cross-section of lower half fuselage, max capacity 4 t (8818 lb), doors opened hydraulically inside fuselage. All flight controls hydraulically boosted including upper/lower rudders on fin swept at 45° on LE carrying high horizontal tail as far to rear as possible. Four flexible fuel cells in fuselage bringing total capacity to 8350 lit (1837 gal) at which bombload not normally above 1500 kg. Fixed NR-23 in nose, twin NR-23 in dorsal turret and twin NR-23 in tail turret; no inflight access between tail gunner and forward compartment and no control authority by either gunner over other pair of movable guns. (Note: Něměcek states guns were B-20.) Provision for four U-5 solid a.t.o. rockets on lower sides of rear fuselage, retractable tail bumper and tail braking parachute. Ejection seats for three forward crew, rear gunner with single-lever escape via ventral slide complete with seat. Programme abandoned 1948; prototype airframe passed (unflown) to VVS for instructional purposes, serving until 1958 as vehicle for teaching bomber and jet-transport pilots taxiing and ground manœuvring.

DIMENSIONS Span 20,6 m (67 ft 7 in); length 19,55 m (64 ft $1\frac{2}{3}$ in); wing area 71,3 m² (767·5 ft²).

ENGINES Four 1500 kg (3307 lb) TR-1A.

WEIGHTS Empty 13 436 kg (29,621 lb); fuel 6 t; loaded (normal) 21 138 kg (46,600 lb), (max, with a.t.o.) 23 845 kg (52,568 lb).

PERFORMANCE New speed (est) 810 km/h at SL, (Shavrov) 850 km/h (528 mph) at 8 km, (Něměcek) 940 km/h at SL; service ceiling (est) 12 km; range (Shavrov) 1500 km (932 miles), (1981 East German) 2000 km, (Něměcek) 900 km.

Su-12 This multi-role tactical aircraft was inspired by Fw 189 but on much more powerful scale. Unfortunate for OKB, such aircraft might have been useful in the Second World War and could have proved valuable in many post-war situations, but it was launched June 1946 just as such heavy piston-engined combat aircraft were appearing outmoded. Project called Aircraft RK, from *Razvyedchik Korrektirovshchik* (reconnaissance and artillery spotting), but Su-12 design grew to have crew of four and appreciable offensive power. Modern all-metal stressed-skin structure almost entirely D1 and D16 and with flush-riveted exterior skins throughout. Unswept wing built as rectangular centre section and tapered outer panels with 6·5° dihedral, NACA-230 section 14% t/c at root and 9·25% at tip. Single straight spar at 40% chord with heavy plate web and extruded/machined booms. Pressed-sheet ribs, L-stringers and 0,6 mm or 1,0 mm skins. Hydraulic slotted flaps pivoted on brackets well below lower surface in four sections inboard and outboard of tail booms, outer sections stressed as airbrakes. Manual flight controls with D1 skin over leading edge back to spar, fabric to rear; servo tab on right aileron, elec trimmer on left. Central crew nacelle with wing in low/mid position, housing pilot on left,

Su-12

nav on right in small seat with tall vertical armoured back, radio/gunner at rear of compartment with seat and radio behind pilot and vertical pillar/saddle on centreline for aiming electric-powered mid-upper turret with twin B-20E with 200 rounds each, observer/gunner seated on centreline at rear of nacelle with control of rear B-20E with 200 rounds, recon camera in floor and various army liaison subsystems. Fourth B-20E fixed firing ahead with 100 rounds. Eight FAB-100 or various alternative weapon loads carried in bays with twin doors in tail booms at trailing edge, elec door operation and release. Neat engine installations, filtered/de-iced carb-air inlets above, ducted oil coolers below, four-blade AV-9VF-21K propellers 3,6 m diam. Two 440-lit wing tanks and two 180-lit tanks between engines and front spar, total 1240 lit (273 gal). Nacelle protected by 28 pieces of armour from 2 to 12 mm, weighing 450 kg. Armour-glass 15 mm to 90 mm thick over most glazed areas. All three units of landing gear retracting hydraulically, main units with straight single oleo legs with fork-ends and 900 × 300 mm tyres folding to rear and tailwheel with levered suspension and 420 × 185 mm tyre retracting sideways to right into slightly bulged tailplane bay, all bays fully closed by doors. Su-12 first flew December 1947 and was so trouble-free it completed NII testing late February 1948 and was recommended for production. This was eventually countermanded in belief concept was outdated. (Recent Moscow article says Su-12 took part in 1947 Tushino flypast; conflicts with published first-flight date.)

DIMENSIONS Span 21,576 m (70 ft 9½ in); length 13,053 m (42 ft 9·9 in); wing area 52,44 m^2 (564·5 ft^2).

ENGINES Two 1850 hp ASh-82FN (designed for 2100 hp ASh-82M).

WEIGHTS Empty 7552 kg (16,649 lb); fuel/oil 1820 kg; loaded 9510 kg (20,966 lb).

PERFORMANCE Max speed 460 km/h (286 mph) at SL, 531 km/h (330 mph) at 5,3 km; time to 5 km, 5·3 min; service ceiling 11 km (36,000 ft); range at 1 km alt, 1140 km (708 miles); take-off 220 m; landing 320 m/125 km/h (78 mph).

Su-15* The VVS requirement for a modern jet all-weather interceptor, issued January 1948, is known to have resulted in La-200, MiG I-320 and Yak-25 two-seaters with powerful radar. To slightly earlier timescale Sukhoi OKB built Aircraft **P**, 293rivalling radar-equipped models of MiG bureau in 1947–1949 timescale yet having same twin-engine staggered configuration as La-200 and I-320. This configuration did not originate with Sukhoi OKB and may have been TsAGI shape. It was allied with 35° swept wing and swept tail, all new to OKB, yet Sukhoi beat all others in timing with Aircraft P which was rolled out at Novosibirsk 25 October 1948. Stressed-skin aircraft with D16 airframe incorporating 30KhGSA details at joints and stress concentrations. Wing built around main two-spar box incorporating integral tankage, four full-chord fences, outboard balanced hydraulically boosted ailerons, inboard hydraulic Fowler flaps, 0° dihedral. Plain nose inlet divided by vertical centreline splitter acting as structural support to underside of pressurized upper compartments for radar and (left of centreline) pilot. Right-hand air duct for second engine carried behind wing centre-section on main fuselage frames in sealed plenum box, removable upwards. Fixed rear fuselage carrying twin airbrakes and swept, hydraulically boosted tail surfaces, fin carrying electrically trimmed tailplane well above fuselage. Front engine at bottom of fuselage, fed by left duct, immediately behind box for rearward-retracting levered-suspension nose gear and attached to fuselage frames ahead of wing with surrounding plenum box and short jetpipe under wing. Simple single-strut main gears with single wheels, hydraulic retraction inwards into wing. Photos appear to show wheels housed in wing at root, most undesirable structurally; it is possible wheels were in fuselage beside jetpipe, leaving main underskin uncut except for bay for leg. Cordite ejection seat with faceblind, heated windshield and sandwich type canopy sliding electrically to rear, no data on pilot access (no visible kick-in steps on either side of nose). Small radar, almost certainly same as La-200A and MiG I-320. Armament two N-37 each with 55 rounds in lower forward fuselage, magazines beside nose-gear compartment. Two rear-fuselage sockets for U-5 solid a.t.o. motors. Entire top of fin dielectric material for various antennae. Flight testing delayed by prolonged ground systems test of this relatively complex aircraft, finally begun 11 January 1949 and handled by G.M. Shiyanov and S.N. Anokhin. Excellent performance, but prototype lost

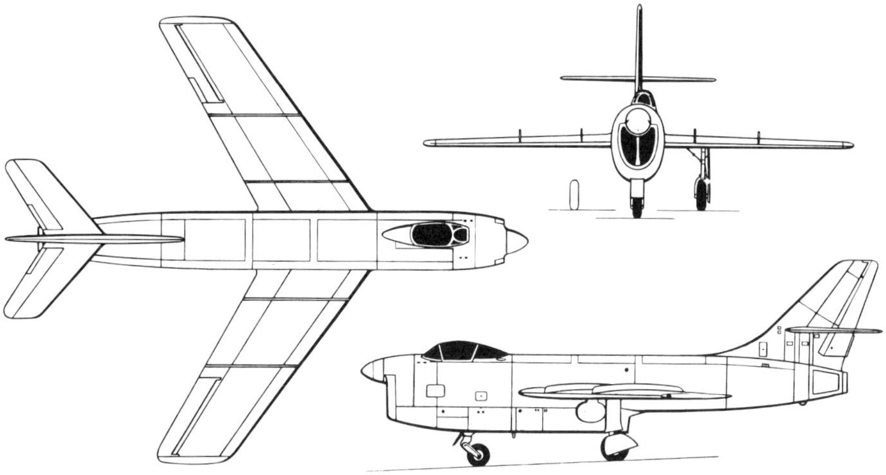

*All three illustrations show Su-15**

3 June 1949, following severe flutter and structural failure, Anokhin ejecting successfully.
DIMENSIONS Span 12,87 m (42 ft 2⅝ in); length (Shavrov) 15,44 m (50 ft 7⅞ in), (Simakov, disbelieved by author) 13,55 m; wing area 36,0 m² (387·5 ft²).
ENGINES Two 2200 kg RD-45F.
WEIGHTS Empty 7409 kg (16,334 lb); fuel 2760 kg; loaded 10 437 kg (23,009 lb).
PERFORMANCE Max speed 1032 km/h (641 mph, M 0·888) at 4550 m, 985 km/h (612 mph, M 0·926) at 10 950 m; climb 40 m/s, time to 5 km 2·5 min; service ceiling est 15 km; range internal fuel 1050 km (652 miles); no other data.

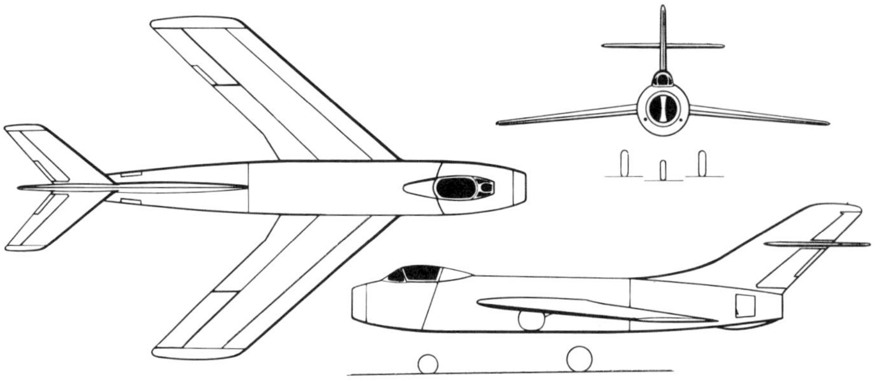
*Su-17**

Su-17* Few details yet available of this bold attempt at supersonic day fighter, started 1948 as Aircraft **R**. Configuration reminiscent of US Navy/Douglas D-558-I and D-558-II though OKB had little knowledge of US types and were supported mainly by TsAGI. Similar philosophy to Yak-1000 to same requirement, with emphasis on length at expense of frontal area. Straight-through tubular fuselage with plain nose inlet bifurcated past cockpit and nose gear and then occupying full body cross-section above wing before reaching engine in rear fuselage. Mid-mounted wing, TsAGI-9030 profile root, SR-3-12 at tip, ¼-chord sweep 50°, four full-chord fences, outboard ailerons, inboard Fowler flaps. Large acutely swept vertical tail carrying 50°-swept horizontal tail without dihedral ⅔-way up. All flight controls hydraulically boosted, rudder and elevator power units being first fully powered irreversible type in Soviet Union. Hydraulic speed brakes on sides of rear fuselage. Tricycle landing gear with nose unit folding to rear and main gears folding inwards with wheels inside fuselage below centre-section. Engine without afterburner carried on truss to rear of centre-section, rear fuselage being removable. Integral tankage in wings, additional cells behind wheel bays and beneath engine. Small rear underfin incorporating tail bumper and box for braking parachute. Novel jettisonable nose incorporating pressurized cockpit housing cordite ejection seat. Sukhoi did not consider seat sufficient at anticipated IAS (1200 km/h) and arranged entire nose to separate by explosive bolts at diagonal plane behind rear bulkhead, pilot using seat to escape cabin when at safe lower altitude. Něměcek drawing shows holes in face of fuselage suggesting guns were to rear of jettisonable nose, though this hard to credit. Guns were to be two N-37, each with 40 rounds. Regarded as important programme, three prototypes (two flight, one static test) and GAZ production capacity reserved. By 1949 OKB had become candidate for closure, in wish to reduce number of OKBs, and loss of Su-15* precipitated 'liquidation'. OKB shut on Stalin's personal recommendation 1 November 1949, with first Su-17* approaching completion.
DIMENSIONS Span 9,95 m (32 ft 7¾ in); length 15,25 m (50 ft 0⅜ in); wing area 27,5 m² (296 ft²).
ENGINE One 4,6 t (10,140 lb) TR-3 without afterburner.
WEIGHTS Empty 6240 kg (13,757 lb); fuel 1 t; loaded 7390 kg (16,292 lb).
PERFORMANCE (Est) Max speed 1252 km/h (778 mph, M 1·022) at SL, 1207 (M 1·048) at 5 km and 1152 (M 1·07) at 10 km; climb to 10 km, 3·5 min; service ceiling 15,5 km; range 1080 km.

S-1 From December 1949 Sukhoi and about half his design engineers were assigned to Tupolev OKB to work on that group's programmes. Sukhoi himself was allowed complete work-freedom and chose to continue to explore possibilities for supersonic fighter. No regrets over elimination of Su-17* and no attempt to develop it further. Much of 1950 spent in aerodynamic and structural research, in close collaboration with TsAGI, and played central role in arriving at two rival configurations of tailed 60° (or 62°) swept wing and tailed 60° (or 57°) delta. Tupolev had right to regard Sukhoi as his assistant, as he had been 20 years earlier, but was wise enough to let him make fighter project studies having no relevance to Tupolev programmes. Immediately on Stalin's death in 1953 Sukhoi applied for permission to reopen OKB and this was granted. In direct competition with MiG OKB permission given to pursue two families of experimental fighter prototypes, **S** (*Strelovidnyi*, sweptback) and **T** (*Treugolnyi*, triangular, ie delta). New numbering sequence started, so fighter (odd) numbers were duplicated.

S-1 was first of 62° swept series, broadly similar to rival MiG I-380, both using AL-7 family of engines which were destined to find main production application in Sukhoi fighter/bombers from both S and T series. Clean straight-through low/mid-wing aircraft in many respects extrapolated from Su-17* but with no common parts. Wing approximately SR-3 series profile, t/c 5·7% root and 4·7% tip, two-spar box with machined skins and heavy transverse spar at 90° to fuselage linking front spars on each side and providing chief bending input to forged/machine root rib as well as rear mount trunnion for main landing gear. Root rib distributing wing loads into three machined/forged fuselage frames (no centre section carry-through structure). Direct pitot nose inlet with conical centrebody translated in/out to adjust supersonic airflow (first in USSR). Air ducts bifurcated past presssurized cockpit (with air-conditioning by engine-bleed bootstrap cycle) and forward-retracting nose gear, to engine occupying rear fuselage with compressor face just behind rear-spar frame. Original scheme was detachable rear fuselage but in some prototypes choice was to withdraw engine on internal rails through rear aperture. Wide-track levered-suspension main gears, wheels and doors rotating over 50° to lie flat in wing ahead of spar. Braking parachute (ribbon canopy) in box under rear fuselage. S-1 flown by G. Kochyetkov mid-1955, and subsequently factory-tested by Mikhailin and Korovushkin, and NII-tested late 1955 with promising results. At least five S-1 prototypes investigated belly/rear-fuselage speed brakes, various armament configurations (mainly boxes of spin-stabilized rockets but including NR-30 guns in wing roots and in lower fuselage), different inlet systems with centrebody or top-lip radar, afterburning engine (from about January 1956) and slab tailplanes (again from about January 1956). OKB claimed first use of slab tail in USSR, disputed by today's MiG OKB, with automatic bias to trim out nose-down effect of wing flaps. Sukhoi later gave perfection of supersonic inlet system as main achievement of S-1. At conclusion of programme in 1957 Korovushkin set national speed record with special AL-7F-1 engine of 2170 km/h, Mach 2·05. (MiG never went for record with I-7K, then flying.)
DIMENSIONS Not recorded, but extremely close to Su-7 series.
ENGINE One 6500 kg AL-7; later various afterburning AL-7 rated at up to 8 t (17,640 lb).
WEIGHTS Originally 7850 kg (17,306 lb) empty and 12 t (26,455 lb) loaded.
PERFORMANCE Max speed 1800 km/h (1118 mph, M 1·7) at 10 km (record was with non-standard engine); other data not reliably recorded but similar to Su-7.

Su-7 One of most important families of tactical fighter/bombers of past 20 years, this series began as production offspring of S-1 and because of configuration lacked sufficient internal fuel capacity. Inability to carry heavy weapon-load with external fuel and ECM, compensated by superb handling and general robust simplicity. Even today, firm favourite with Indian and Egyptian aircrew, who still praise high penetration speed and low-level stability. Dogged persistence of Soviet method, and of Sukhoi OKB in particular, gradually transformed basic Su-7 (notably with variable geometry) into formidable Su-17**/Su-20/Su-22 still in production 27 years later!

Prototypes of this family designated **S-2**, introducing slab tailplanes with anti-flutter rods. Pre-production aircraft, **S-22** (2 model 2). All (about 20) had airframe derived from S-1 but with area ruling, ARZ-1 q-feel system driving tailplanes, four rear-fuselage airbrakes, improved kinked trailing edge to wing with tracked inboard flap giving slight increase in area, less-tapered nose handling greater airflow, auxiliary suck-in inlet doors in sides of nose, KKO-2 gaseous pilot oxygen, clamshell canopy, box for 3,95-m ribbon parachute under rear fuselage, SRD-5 radar in translating inlet centrebody, and armament of two NR-30 in wing roots each fed from 70-round box curving round entire space between fuselage skin and engine air duct as far as upper centreline of aircraft, in addition to retractable box of 32 spin-stabilized rockets in place occupied on S-1 by belly speed brake. Internal fuel 2940 lit (646·7 gal) in integral wings plus fuselage cell. Provision for two 600 lit drop tanks on side-by-side pylons on each side of rocket box. Decision to build in series as Su-7 (odd ie, fighter number) taken after evaluation against MiG I-3U, with broadly similar potential, about January 1958. Production launched 1958 but by this time decision to use Su-7 not as fighter but as FA attack aircraft. According to Něměcek small number of Su-7 were delivered as fighters.

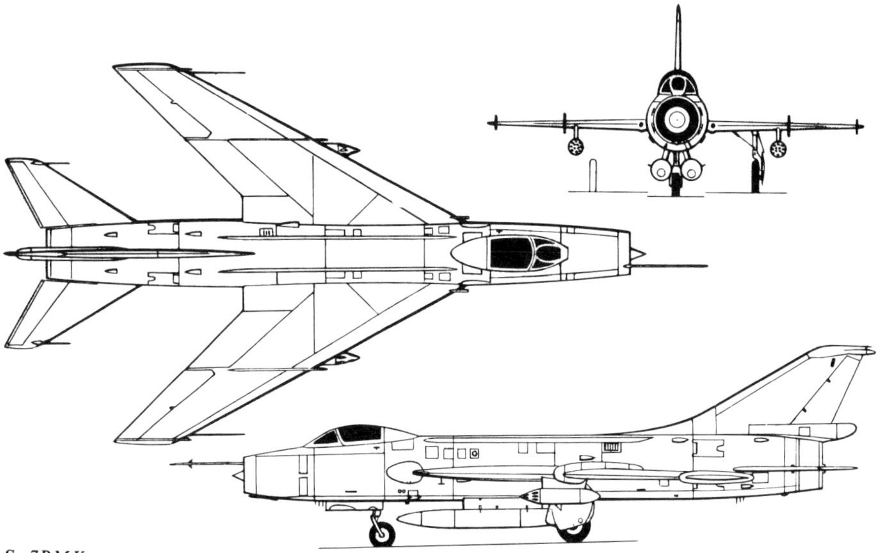
Su-7BMK

Except for first (fighter) batch, initial production model, made at Novosibirsk, was **Su-7B** with 9 t afterburning engine (distinguished by six projecting ram inlets to cool rear-fuselage liner), removable rear fuselage, four wing fences (outers at tip), four pylons (two fuselage, two wing) all plumbed and stressed for 600 lit tanks, four rear-fuselage airbrakes stressed to 1200 km/h IAS, steel anti-blast panel in fuselage beside gun muzzles and improved avionics including SRO-2 IFF and both VHF and UHF com radio. VVS service entry 1959. Produced in several sub-variants, later Su-7B variants (eg, Su-7B-20) having instrument boom moved from top to upper right of nose and fuel pipe/cable fairing ducts added on each side of fuselage between main avionics bay and tail. At early stage, possibly from original S-1, provision for two SPRD-110 a.t.o. rockets on lower sides of rear fuselage. At least 12 known subsequent standards of build, some associated with known suffix letters. **Su-7BKL** (KL, *Koleso-lyzhnyi* wheel/ski) introduced new landing gears with strengthened legs, longer stroke levered-suspension main gears, steel soft-field skids outboard of mainwheels, enlarged nosewheel tyres (bulge on nose-gear doors) and increased braking capacity, as well as twin braking parachutes streamed on separate cables from new compartment in fairing at base of rudder. **Su-7BM** introduced

Su-7BKL using assisted take-off rockets, skis visible

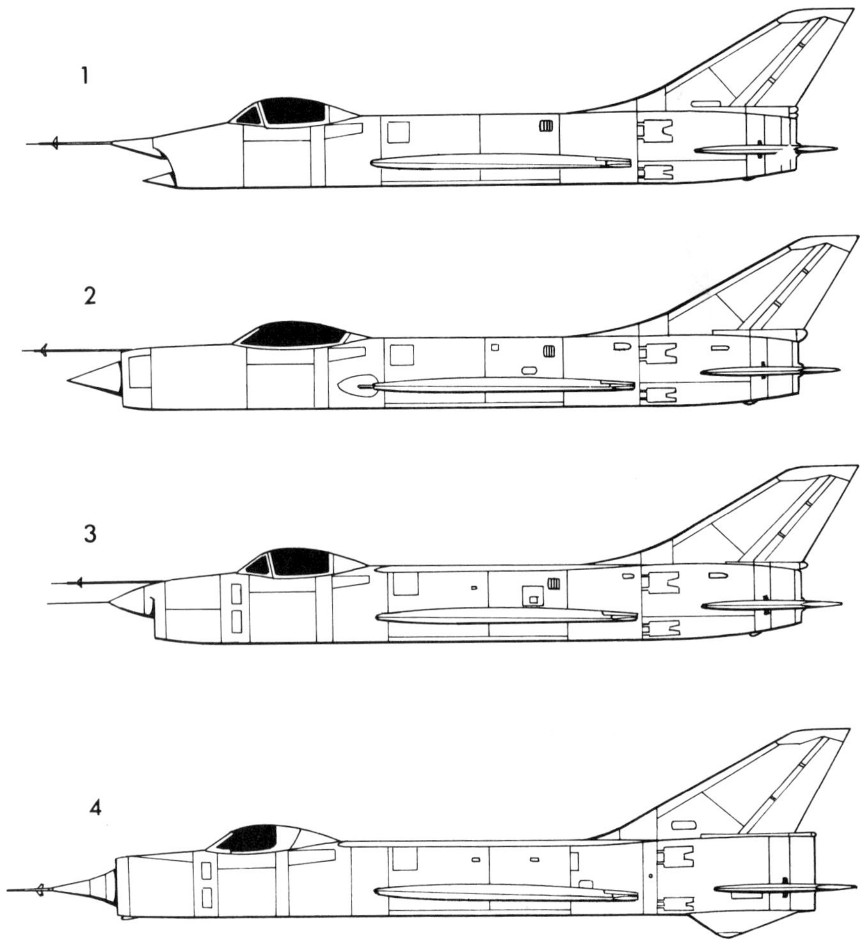

Sukhoi delta prototypes: 1, PT-7 (rectangular inlet, variable lips); 2, PT-8; 3, T-3; 4, T-37 (see page 274)

AL-7-F1 engine, and by 1962 original nose boom carried yaw/pitch vanes and served improved weapon-delivery system with ballistic computer. By 1965 standard model was **Su-7BMK** with further enhanced avionics (including Sirena 3 rear-warning radar), larger gun-blast panels and two additional stores pylons to rear of main gears. Max theoretical weapon load 4 t (4 × 750 kg + 2 × 500 kg) but this cannot be used in combat where drop tanks and ECM-pod limit ordnance to 1 t (2 × 500 kg). All basic Su-7 variants retain outstanding handling and fair reliability but are severely restricted by fuel (low-level afterburner endurance 8-min) and also to reported vulnerability to small-calibre gunfire. Modifications since 1970 include rocket-boosted KM-1 seat, rear-view mirror and updated British (Smiths/Ferranti) nav/attack fits for some export customers.

Though not seen in West until 1966 Sukhoi said tandem dual models **Su-7U, UM, UKL** and **UMK** were produced in parallel with single-seaters with same suffix letters. Su-7U family represented careful exercise in repackaging because fuselage structure lengthened only 300 mm, rear cockpit fitting into tapering space between inlet ducts (they rejoin ahead of front spar) previously occupied by fuel. Both canopies clamshells, rear cockpit having its own small left/right windshields giving diagonal view forwards, plus periscope below 600 km/h. Dorsal spine for aerodynamic reasons (no fuel inside). Seats with electromech interlock.

Final, major advance to Su-7 family was VG prototype **S-22I**, believed to be single aircraft but also having service designation **Su-7IG** (*Izmeneniya Gayometriya*, variable geometry). Described further under Su-17.

DIMENSIONS Span 8,93 m (29 ft $3\frac{9}{16}$ in); length (from nosecone) 16,6 m (54 ft $5\frac{1}{4}$ in), (from instrument boom) 17,37 m (57 ft 0 in), (two-seat) 17,7 m (58 ft $8\frac{1}{2}$ in); wing area 27,6 m^2 (297 ft^2).

ENGINE (7, 7B, 7KL, all U subtypes) one 9 t (19,840 lb) AL-7F afterburning turbojet; (all M subtypes) one 9810 kg (21,627 lb) AL-7F-1.

WEIGHTS Empty (BMK, typical) 8620 kg (19,040 lb); int fuel/oil 2350 + 65; normal loaded 12 t (26,455 lb); max 14,8 t (32,630 lb).

PERFORMANCE Max speed (clean) 1700 km/h (1055 mph, M 1·6) at 11 km, in max cold thrust at SL 850 km/h (530 mph); max SL climb (clean) 150 m/s (29,500 ft/min); service ceiling (clean) 15,15 km (49,700 ft); combat radius (hi, two tanks) typically 320 km (200 miles); ferry range (four tanks) 1450 km (900 miles); take-off (two tanks only) 880 m/375 km/h (max, hot day) 2,4 km; landing speed 305 km/h (189 mph).

T-3 series OKB devoted more attention to supersonic air inlets than any other group in 1950s. No fewer than 12 different arrangements built and flown, five of them in delta prototypes all regarded as interceptors, in contrast to 62° swept aircraft which were for ground attack. First of *Treugolnyi* (triangular) family to be built was T-3, designed from late 1954 and flown by Kochyetkov early 1956. Two participated in 1956 Tushino Aviation Day fly-past, together with an S-1. Original T-3 had AL-7 without afterburner and chin inlet with broad elliptical simulated radome above, believed all fixed-geometry. Second had S-1 type circular inlet with conical centrebody. This was start of inlet research, partly to support OKB's aircraft and partly national effort under contract to TsAGI, extending up to present day. Pilots included V. Ilyushin, Korovushkin, Mikhailin, Adrianov, Kozlov and, by 1967, Kukushyev. So far as known, all interceptors from OKB have geometrically similar wings, TsAGI S-12 series profile, t/c believed 5·5%, LE sweep 57°, dihedral 0°, incidence + 1°30′. Forged/machined rib at mid-span separating plain rectangular flaps from tapered irreversibly powered ailerons. Outboard, five D16 sheet spars meeting at or near tip. Inboard, four heavy forged/machined spars all at 90° to root, meeting fuselage much further back than wing of S series. Space ahead of first spar, and between second and third, integral tankage. Between first and second, bay for levered-suspension main gears with geometry different from Su-7, pivoting directly inwards without need for rotation on leg and with completely different doors. Tyre smaller and higher pressure than Su-7. Nose gear similar to Su-7 family but also with smaller high-pressure tyre. Fuselage generally similar to S family but inlet ducts brought together immediately behind cockpit, which, with absence of guns, leaves room for much greater internal fuel capacity (initial production aircraft 3300 kg). Slab tailplanes initially same as S series, later became structurally different but with similar anti-flutter rods. As far as known, no fence on any T-series wing.

Comparative evaluation against S-1 and TsAGI tunnel testing confirmed delta offered marginally higher flight performance (difference less than prediction, as with MiG OKB) at cost of longer field length and less-pleasant handling at low speeds, with particular back of drag-curve problem (when falling airspeed causes increased drag) which with early AL-7 was dangerous. Decision taken to select tailed delta for interceptors operating from PVO bases with good runways. Major effort on inlets and radar, though (Piotr Butowski reports) OKB also investigated different methods of pilot escape. One of first prototypes to follow T-3 series was **PT-7** (P possibly from *Perekhvatchik*, interceptor), in which better inlet efficiency was sought by making inlet two-dimensional, with upper and lower horizontal wedges with variable angle and throat area. PT-7, flown before September 1956 believed first of T family to have four rear-fuselage airbrakes. This inlet not pursued (never expected to) because of difficulty of accommodating radar. Bifurcation past cockpit reduced efficiency gain from favourable arrangement of inclined shocks, but results were better than T-3. More practical arrangement was tested in **PT-8** of 1957. This had afterburning AL-7F fed by circular nose inlet with large conical centrebody scheduled by automatic engine/inlet airflow matching system, together with at least two large suck-in auxiliary doors to increase mass flow on takeoff. It was first OKB aircraft with dog-tooth leading edges. Conical body was sufficiently large to house specified radar of RL series then completing development, later called Spin Scan by NATO. It was expected a larger radar might become available, and to accommodate this and provide data on lateral inlets **T-49** was flown early 1957 with nose radome and sharp-edged oval side inlets with translating centrebodies. As far as known, final T-series research prototype was **T-5** of 1957–1958 with twin engines. As flown, T-5 had lateral inlets similar to T-49 but OKB also drew twin-engined T-5 (believed **T-53)** with nose inlet and ducting similar to MiG Ye-152A.

DIMENSIONS Span 8,43 m (27 ft 7⅞ in); length, excl nose boom (T-3, PT-7) 16,75 m (54 ft 11½ in), (PT-8) 18,0 m (59 ft 0½ in); wing area 24,2 m² (260 ft²).

ENGINE (T-3) one 6500 kg (14,330 lb) AL-7, later 9 t (19,840 lb) AL-7F with afterburner; same for most other variants except T-49 with twin engines (probably Tumanskii, type uncertain).

WEIGHTS No accurate data.

PERFORMANCE No accurate data but T-3 max speed was about 1500 km/h with afterburning engines while fastest variant (PT-8) just reached 2000 km/h (1243 mph, M 1·88).

Su-9

Su-9, Su-11**** By 1957 an interceptor had been designed as **T-40** series, matched with AL-7F engine fed by circular nose inlet with R1L radar housed in centrebody and two suck-in auxiliary doors on each side. Airframe had been designed for easy series production from outset, and main new feature incorporated in T-40 series of pre-production prototypes was armament. T-3 series did carry various armament schemes including either guns or rockets, and PT-7 possibly had box of rockets; PT-8 reverted to wing-root guns in addition to box of rockets, this possibly accounting for considerable body length. Final decision was to use guided missiles only, and T-40 was first of T-series to have wing pylons. As in earlier MiG-17PFU and MiG-19PM sole armament comprised four K-5 (AA-1 Alkali) radar-guided AAMs carried on individual pylons projecting ahead from leading edge, each with command

Su-9s

rod aerial pointing forward. Unlike S family (and Su-7*) canopy arranged to slide to rear, with hot-air and elec demisting. Cordite-powered seat (later, KM-1 retrofitted), SRO-2 IFF, VOR, VHF/UHF com, SOD-57 ATC/SIF transponder and/or rear-warning radar in pod above jetpipe, combat camera below nose. Provision for two 600 lit drop tanks on side-by-side belly pylons. Ground-power receptacle at left leading-edge root for electric starting, usual AL-7F compressor bleed through large rectangular vent in upper left of mid-fuselage. Engine change via internal rails in fixed rear fuselage. Irreversible flight controls almost indentical to S family.

T-40 flown not later than October 1958 and production aircraft designated Su-9** entered PVO service about mid-1959 (both Moscow and Baku districts). In parallel, first unarmed and specially prepared member of later series, **T-431** used 1959 by V. Ilyushin and other OKB pilots to set various records, allegedly still with 9 t engine which had been superseded in other OKB prototypes. Records included alt 28 852 m (94,659 ft) in Moscow district 4 July 1959. With 10 t engine, Kozlov set 500 km circuit speed of 2337 km/h (1452 mph) on 25 September 1962, and Ilyushin sustained 2100 km/h at 21 170 m over 15/25 km course on 4 September 1962. Much earlier Su-9** prototype, **T-405** with 9 t engine, flown by Adrianov May 60 over 100-km circuit at 2092 km/h. Total production of Su-9 at least 1000 including tandem dual **Su-9U** trainer with same radar, reduced internal fuel and addition of external service fairings from cockpit to tail. One report (P. Butowski) states that from start of Su-9** production there were in addition a special high-altitude variant and a remotely piloted unmanned version for use in air-defence research and as missile target.

Aviation Day at Tushino in July 1961 included several OKB research prototypes including **T-43** series (first being T-431 already mentioned) for next production version Su-11 with different armament. Development of large and powerful Uragan 5B radar, matched with AA-3 Anab missile, naturally led to T-43 series aircraft with new front fuselage lengthened to accommodate this radar as well as secure digital data-link and other updates including full Sirena 3 and ILS. Larger scanner resulted in centrebody of almost doubled cross-section, in turn requiring almost untapered aircraft nose to handle airflow. Remarkably, added side area and mass at nose could be balanced merely by tailoring AAM installation further aft than before, without increasing moment-arm or area of fin. Normal armament two AA-3 Anab AAMs, one with SARH (semi-active radar homing) and other with IR (infra-red). Fired separately or in close pair depending on target, cloud, rain and other factors. Alternative armament two close-range AA-2 Atoll, likewise locked-on by same nose radar but not requiring target illumination. Aircraft has ability to carry two AA-2 as well as two AA-3 but both pairs not seen together. This aircraft also introduced AL-7F-1 engine to interceptor series, with external service fairing along fuselage, KM-1 rocket seat, rapid engine start and improved cockpit instrumentation and displays. VVS designation Su-11**, replaced Su-9** in production about 1966 and combined output of both estimated 1980 at 2000, and completed. Dual Su-11** has not been seen, neither have these interceptors served with other WP air forces or export customers. From early 1970s many converted as RPV drones and targets (one estimate, 250-plus).

DIMENSIONS Span 8,43 m (27 ft 7⅞ in); length, excl nose boom (Su-9) about 16,5 m (54 ft 1⅔ in), (Su-11) 17,4 m (57 ft 1 in); wing area 26,2 m^2 (280 ft^2).

ENGINE (Su-9**) one 9 t (19,840 lb) AL-7F; (Su-11**) one 10 t (22,046 lb) AL-7F-1.

WEIGHTS Empty (Su-9**) about 8800 kg (19,400 lb), (Su-11**) 9100 kg (20,060 lb); internal fuel 3300 kg; loaded (Su-9**) about 12 t (26,450 lb), (Su-11**) 12,3 t (27,120 lb); max fuel and AAMs (both) 14 t (30,900 lb).

PERFORMANCE Max speed (both, clean) 1915 km/h (1190 mph, M 1·8) at 11 km; service ceiling 17 km (55,700 ft); combat radius (hi, with AAMs) 460 km (290 miles); ferry range 1100 km.

P-1 By 1956 OKB had roughed out a scheme for interceptor using semi-automatic collision-course attack, as pioneered by Hughes Aircraft. This called for radar of much greater power than any then in imminent prospect, and size of radar virtually dictated lateral inlets. These were flown on T-49 already mentioned, and T-5 explored use of twin engines. P-1 (*Perekhvatchik*, interceptor) programme was definitive programme to use collision-course radar and battery of rockets as alternative to guided AAMs for blind all-weather interception. Basic aircraft geometric scale of T series and incorporating dog-tooth and drooped outer leading edge originally flown on PT-8. Extremely large nose to accommodate X-band radar (precursor of *Uragan* series but with larger-diameter dish), and crew of pilot and radar observer/nav in tandem, with clamshell canopies level with top of fuselage downstream. Inlets almost same as T-49, with variable area by translating centrebodies. At least two P-1 built, first flown 1957. Only known photograph shows single-engined aircraft, believed AL-7F-1, but field performance must have been poor with single engine. Intention was to use twin engines (not necessarily AL-7 series) in production aircraft, taking full advantage of available capacity for fuel between widely spaced inlet ducts. Nose gear retracted to rear, unlike all other S and T aircraft, leaving large bay immediately ahead occupied by two boxes each with 25 S-5 rockets of 57-mm calibre. At appropriate moment in interception sequence rockets were fired via spring-loaded doors on sides of nose, pulled open by jacks but closing automatically. Termination of programme ascribed to problems with engine, but same engines used in all other OKB aircraft. Field length was certainly excessive, though no measured data available.

DIMENSIONS Span about 10 m (32 ft 10 in); length 21,75 m (71 ft 4⅓ in); wing area approx 36 m^2 (387 ft^2).

ENGINE(S) In first P–1, probably one 10 t AL-7F-1; others, believed two 9 t AL-7F.

WEIGHTS Not known but approx 1·6 times weight of T-series and Su-9.

PERFORMANCE Intended speed 2050 km/h (1274 mph, M 1·93): service ceiling 19,5 km (64,000 ft); range with full fuel at least 2500 km (1550 miles).

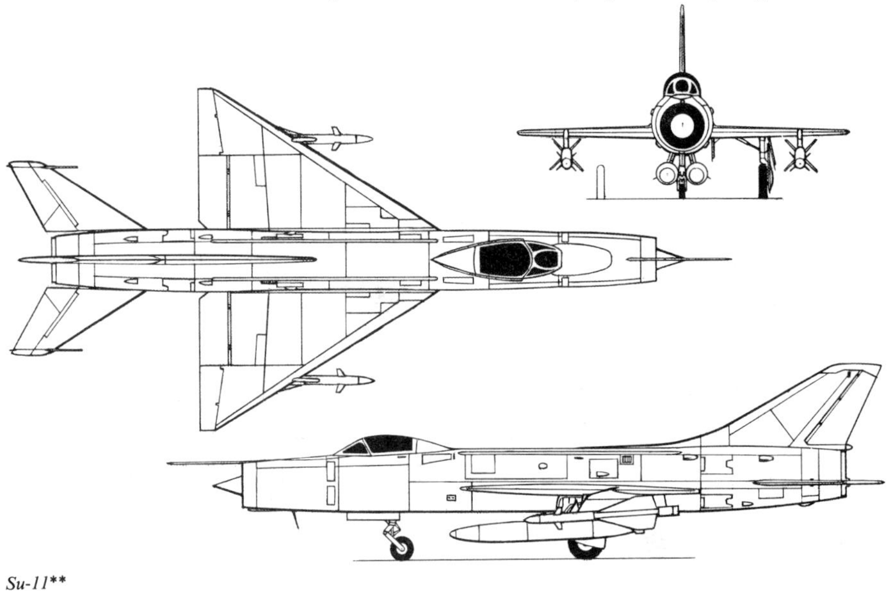

*Su-11***

T-37 General demand for Mach 3 technology in 1957, spurred by prospect of having to intercept B-70, resulted in immediate response from Sukhoi OKB. Like MiG team, answer was single-seat research aircraft adhering to proven tailed-delta configuration but with completely new propulsion system dominated by advanced fully variable inlet and nozzle. Basic engine of unknown type but believed same as MiG Ye-166, namely P-166 type derivative of AL-7F-1 with new enlarged afterburner terminating in variable con/di nozzle of diam considerably greater than rest of engine and giving approx doubled thrust at Mach 3 at high altitude. Basic aircraft using much T-series structure but with rear fuselage, wing LE and certain details in titanium and ti-alloys, new to Soviet industry. Almost untapered nose based on PT-8 but with larger lip diam and different form of centrebody with Oswatitsch profile and multiple bleed holes (no radar, of course), translated over greater travel. Small pressurized cockpit with V-windscreen and small clamshell canopy. Wing with dogteeth of PT-8 type, slab tailplanes apparently below usual equatorial position, usual petal airbrakes but extra canted ventral fins with drag

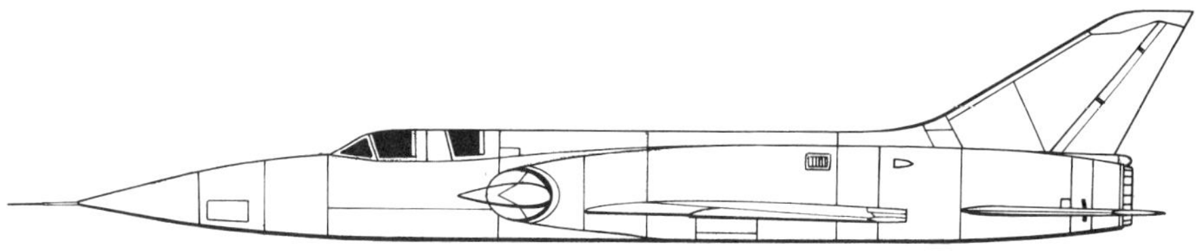

P-1

chute in box between them. Landing gear of Su-9** geometry but high-pressure tyres allowing increased internal fuel capacity (no details but probably about 50% greater than regular T-series aircraft). Sukhoi hinted at numerous innovations in T-37, including sandwich and stainless honeycomb secondary structures. First, possibly only, T-37 flown 1960 and completed OKB testing in hands of Ilyushin and several other pilots. No further information, and not known why never used to attack FAI records unless incapable of beating Ye-166.

DIMENSIONS Span, probably 8,43 m (27 ft $7\frac{7}{8}$ in); length, excl nose boom, about 17,75 m (58 ft $2\frac{3}{4}$ in); wing area, probably 24,2 m^2 (260 ft^2).

ENGINE Believed one AL-7F-1 with M 3 afterburner and nozzle, giving unchanged SL 10 t rating but much greater performance at high-Mach.

WEIGHTS No data, but probably similar to Su-11.

PERFORMANCE Design max speed 3000 km/h (1864 mph, M 2·82); design service ceiling 25 km (82,000 ft).

Su-15** Though scare of B-70 evaporated, clear need to upgrade all-round performance of PVO interceptors translated into challenging requirement of 1962 for genuine all-weather aircraft with speed of Mach 2·5 and with automatic direction on to target (incorrectly described as world pioneering accomplishment). MiG response was Ye-23/231 series with aerodynamics versatile enough also to serve as FA attack-bomber. Sukhoi took conscious decision not to go for VG wing (but see Su-17**) and instead to rely on long PVO runways and to extrapolate existing T-series into more powerful twin with completely new weapons and radar. Little was new, side inlets and twin engines having flown in 1958 on T-5 and engine believed to be Tumanskii (new to OKB in jet era) already well developed and used in large numbers. Aerodynamics drawn in part from T-37, which like Ye-166 was never intended as anything but pure research aircraft.

Code-letter for this programme not yet known, only designation published being VVS Su-15** for service use. First prototype, possibly painted black and flown by V. Ilyushin at 1967 Aviation Day, probably flew 1964 and development apparently free from major difficulty. Numerous major parts similar (not identical) to T-series, including whole wing and tail surfaces, though restressed for increased flight temperatures and loads. Engines shorter than AL-7 and neatly accommodated in removable rear fuselage though giving obvious area-ruled effect (all production S and T aircraft complied with area rule, but less obviously) and requiring anhedral -9° on tailplanes. Tankage between ducts with bleed pipe emerging above fuselage forming dorsal spine. Wing not identical with T series but slightly reduced LE sweep (est 53°) to give fractionally greater span. Profile and structure believed unchanged, though flaps of powerful Fowler type, fences added ahead of inner ends of ailerons and landing gear modified to bear greater loads and retract with wheels in lower duct fairings. Cockpit basically as Su-11** but with major changes in systems (no details). Internal fuel capacity at least 50% greater than for typical T-series; probably about 5 t (6950 lit, 1530 gal). Vertical rectangular inlets with inner splitter plate separated from fuselage skin by boundary-layer space, variable ramp angle and throat area, vertical suck-in auxiliary door in outer wall.

Ten development aircraft at Aviation Day July 1967 but VVS entry (except service-test unit) believed delayed until after 1970. OKB meanwhile produced several variants. Original pre-production Su-15** believed powered by R-11F2 engines, Uragan 5B radar in unusual conical radome and same pair of SAHR/IR Anab AAMs as Su-11**. In addition to reported 'squadron' of black examples, one early PVO unit in Moscow district 1967 formed display team with scarlet Su-15s**, believed named Golden Hawks (AAMs were carried). At least one pre-production aircraft had large fairing at top of fin, widely reported as non-standard rear-warning radar (standard fit on all versions is Sirena 3). Experimental V/STOL version **Su-15VD** (*Vertikalnye Dvigatel*, vertical engines) demonstrated 1967 with new double-delta wing with outer panels outboard of fence at 70% semi-span of extended span resulting from reduced LE sweep of 37°, and new centre fuselage with tankage replaced by three Koliesov lift jets in bay sealed in flight by louvred rear-hinged upper doors and airtight left/right lower doors as in similar conversions of other fighters. Alternative designation **Su-15DPD** (*Dopelnitelnye Pod'yomnye Dvigatel*, supplementary lifting engines). Reduced take-off landing run to 300 m but gravely reduced endurance and never intended for service use but for evaluation against VG wing used on frontal attack aircraft.

Main production version, called Flagon-D by NATO, introduced improved form of double-delta wing with added constant-chord section at kink giving mild LE dogtooth and useful extra span and area for increased lift in all regimes (same as control fins of US AIM-9L missile). New engine fitted for this first major production version, at first thought to be R-13F2 but now believed to be R-13F-300 to give required thrust for exceptional climb and altitude performance. Modified inlet with perforated splitter plate with separate upper/lower slots, electhermal anticing of upper lip, titanium in rear fuselage with 20 ram-air inlets including large ducts each side of fin root, integral-tank fin with four avionic aerials at tip, Sirena 3 (radar warning) receiver aerials at fin tip (150° rear) and LE both wings (110° sectors to front), curved SOD-57M ATC/SIF aerial under nose with SRO-2M IFF immediately ahead, long nose boom with multiple pitch/yaw transducers providing data for fire-control computer (normal pitot on left wing outboard of kink), landing gear with tyre bulges on all four bay doors, optional rear-view mirror on sliding canopy, AAM pylons at wing kink (usually IR on left, SAHR on right) and twin body pylons for 800-lit tanks. Body pylons can carry AA-2 or AA-8 AAMs or 23 mm gun pods.

From early in production (1966) tandem dual aircraft, presumed **Su-15U**, with pupil cockpit added ahead of original and displacing major avionics bay aft of radar. New canopies, both aft-hinged clamshells, instructor cockpit with separate small windshields and roof periscope. Weapons retained, though relocated avionics reduce fuselage fuel. From 1973 possibly more powerful model (**Su-15F** or **MF**?) with deeper inlet ducts; this may have signalled introduction of R-13F2-300 or related engine. From 1975 conical radome replaced by ogival shape with

Su-15VD

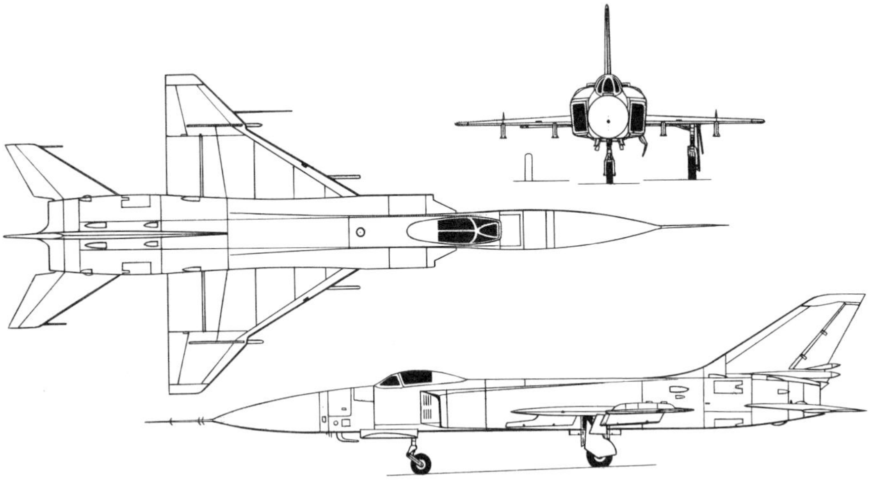

Su-15 Flagon-F

reduced drag and greater volume leading to speculation on enlarged radar scanner and possible later radar related to Fox Fire (but AA-6 Acrid AAM not observed on this aircraft). Probable look-down, shoot-down retrofit. Today Su-15** deliveries total at some 1500, of which at least 1000 in PVO polks. Never supplied to any other operator, but in 1971 small unit detached to Egypt. Extremely effective and undoubtedly equipped with various later AAMs than those seen in West, and guns, though Anab used for training. OKB had desk-top models in mid-1970s of aerodynamically advanced derivatives (foreplanes, twin canted fins) presumably intended for close air combat as well as stand-off interception.

DIMENSIONS Span (pre-production) about 9,3 m (30 ft 6 in), (production) about 10,6 m (34 ft 9½ in); length, excl nose boom, about 19 m (62 ft 4 in), overall about 21 m (68 ft 10½ in); wing area about 36 m² (388 ft²).

ENGINES Not known, but believed originally two 6600 kg R-11F2, then 7200 kg R-13F2 or R-13F-300 (initial production), and in current variants 7,5 t R-13F2-300 afterburning turbojets.

WEIGHTS Not known but empty est for current Su-15 at 11,5 t (25,350 lb); internal fuel est 5 t; combat est 17 t (37,480 lb); max fuel plus AAMs, est 19,2 t (42,330 lb).

PERFORMANCE Max speed (at height, dash, clean) 2755 km/h (1712 mph, M 2·59), (with AAMs) 2450 km/h (1520 mph, M 2·3); outstanding rate of climb, time to 11 km at combat wt 2·5 min; service ceiling 20 km (65,600 ft); radius (AAMs and internal fuel) 725 km (450 miles); range with two tanks est 2415 km (1500 miles); field length about 2 km; landing speed 300 km/h (186 mph).

Su-17, Su-20, Su-22** From 1960 OKB, with TsAGI and rival OKBs, studied variable-sweep wing with outboard pivots following publication of UK/NASA geometry that solved previous problems. Not warranted for interceptors but valuable for support aircraft with primary air/ground capability. OKB elected to follow cautious and protracted programme based on existing and notably deficient Su-7 series, introducing half-hearted VG (variable-geometry) wing with pivots at 50% semi-span and large fences shielding inner wing which apart from structural redesign was little changed. This semi-VG wing tested on **S-22I**, also called **Su-7IG** (*Izmenyayemaya Gayometriya* = VG) early 1966, demo at Aviation Day July 1967. Despite limited nature of new wing, gains so valuable that VVS decided on series production, together with more powerful engine. Resulting Su-17** entered service 1971 as dedicated support (battlefield ground attack) aircraft despite retention of odd-number designation. Basic wing believed unchanged S-22 series profile but enlarged and structurally different 5,22-m centre section including swept inboard TE with broad area-increasing flaps, outer TE being swept at original angle. Fence on upper surface to 50% chord aligned with outer end of inboard flap. Two axial stiffeners, probably also serving as fences, over upper skin outboard of kink from 30% chord to TE. At outer end of centre section, giant fence combined with stores pylon. Pivoted outer wings driven by irreversible screwjack and balance

Su-15 Flagon-D

links between LE limits 28° and 62°, latter lining up with centre section to give wing similar to S-22 series except larger. LE almost full-span powered slat, TE slotted irreversible ailerons (almost identical S-22 series) and inboard slotted flap usable only at 28° sweep. Fuselage derived from S-22 series but slightly enlarged duct and nozzle for more powerful engine installationally interchangeable. Internal fuel increased by dorsal spine derived from Su-7U. Updated avionics with SRD-5M radar, nose pivot and separate long air-data sensor boom plus anticed alpha (AOA) sensor on left of nose serving ASP-5ND computerized fire-control, 360° Sirena 3 system with receiver aerials at base of rudder and in each LE between fences, SOD-57 above jetpipe, flush SRO-2M IFF and usual HF/VHF/UHF radio. Tubular container for twin braking parachutes replacing flat-sided tapering type. Twin NR-30 usual, plus eight stores pylons, two tandem pairs on fuselage and four under fixed wing, total load 5 t (achievable in practice) with combat radii some 30% greater than Su-7 with 2 t. Late VVS aircraft carry AS-7.

Immediately released for export as Su-20 (air/ground designation now also used by VVS). Equipment standard generally below that of VVS Su-17 and speculation that some customers have AL-7F-1 engine. In 1976 **Su-17M** introduced augmented avionics: laser ranger and marked-target seeker in inlet centrebody with window on underside, terrain-avoidance radar at front of new under-nose pod and doppler at rear of pod, all necessitating 0,38-m (15-in) extension of nose ahead of cockpit. No change in fin area to compensate, but 1977 export counterpart, Su-22 **(S-22M-18)**, did introduce enlarged dorsal fin with squared top; supplied to Peru with reduced navaids, aft-sector-only Sirena 2 and IFF incompatible with that country's SA-3 missiles. Also supplied (different avionics) to Algeria, Egypt, Iraq, Vietnam. Su-22 also replaced multiple ram inlets around engine by just two (new) inlets, as well as unexplained asymmetric increase in rear-fuselage diam. **Su-22U** mated this new back-end with nose resembling Su-7UMK without ventral avionics or extended length. Possibly final member of family, Su-20 or **Su-20M**, introduced 1979 with similar fuselage change as on MiG-21 family: enlarged dorsal spine probably giving more internal fuel, reduced drag and, unusually, inclined cockpit and forward fuselage for better forward view (especially in **Su-20U** two-seat version). Enlarged rear fuselage for R-29B engine. New fin (possibly integral tank) with greater height and simpler structure, plus centre line ventral-fin with SRO-2M aerials once more projecting immediately downstream. Left gun often omitted in late variants. Nose as in original Su-17** without extension or ventral avionics, though laser retained. Two-seat Su-20U normally has right gun only (like many Su-7UMK and Su-22U) though blast panel retained, and new canopy scheme tailored to min drag, instructor having small clamshell canopy opaque except for square pane on each side and with flush metal skin in place of left/right windshields of earlier two-seaters. Internal fuel about 5000 lit (1,100 gal) and external load believed to allow six × 500-kg plus two 800-lit tanks on outer pylons. First export customer (reported designation Su-22) Libya with AA-2 Atoll shoes, but VVS believed to carry various advanced tactical

Su-7IG

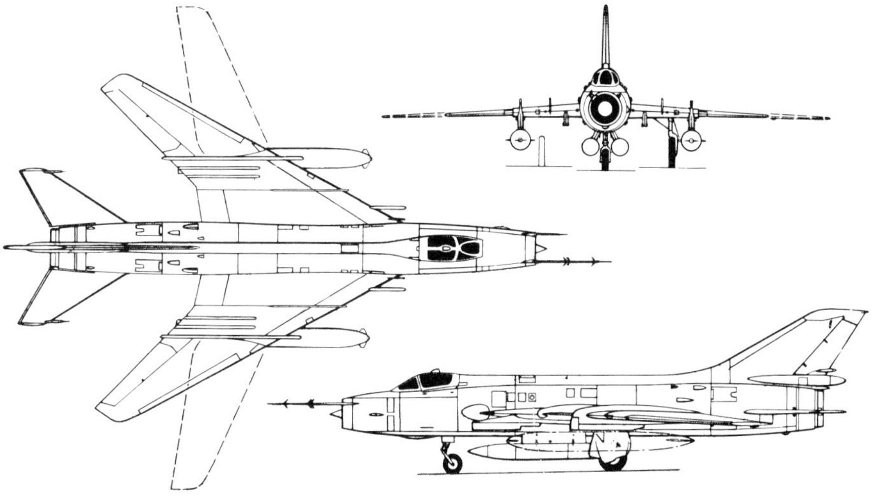

Su-17 Fitter-C

Su17M displayed at Kubinka with 6 FAB-500s, 2 smaller FABs (outboard), rolls of gun ammunition (either side of nosewheel), and K-13A AAMs (fins visible bottom left)

ASMs including AS-7 and AS-9. Supplied 1980 to India and exports 1981 Czech, E Germany, Syria, N and S Yemen. Production of all swing-wing variants about 1500 by 1981, including 800 in FA polks, with output then continuing at 15 to 18 monthly. Data are estimates.

DIMENSIONS Span (62°) 10,6 m (34 ft 9½ in), (28°) 14,0 m (45 ft 11¼ in); length, excl nose booms (22I) 16,6 m, (Su-17**) 16,9 m (55 ft 5¼ in), (17M, 22, 22U) 17,3 m (56 ft 9 in), (20, 20U) 17,2 m (56 ft 5 in); wing area (62°) 37,2 m² (400 ft²), (28°) 40,1 m² (432 ft²).

ENGINE (22I) One 10-t AL-7F-1; (some export Su-20 and most Su-20U and Su-22U) one 10 t AL-7F-1; (other Su-17**s) 11,2 t (24,690 lb) AL-21F-3; (most Su-22s) one 11,5 t (25,350 lb) R-29B.

WEIGHTS (Su-20M, est) Empty 9800 kg (21,600 lb); internal fuel 3950 kg; loaded (clean) 13,95 t (30,750 lb); (max) 18,3 t (40,340 lb).

PERFORMANCE Max speed (all AL-21 variants, clean) 2300 km/h (1429 mph, M 2·16), max at SL just over M 1; SL rate of climb (clean gross) 230 m/s (45,276 ft/min); service ceiling 18 km (59,000 ft); combat radius (2 t bombs, two tanks) 435 km (270 miles) lo-lo-lo, 675 km (420 miles) hi-lo-hi; ferry range (four tanks) 3000 km (1860 miles); take-off (17 t) 620 m; landing 600 m/ 265 km/h.

Su-22? Fitter-J (Libya)

Su-24 USAF TFX competition exerted great influence on VVS procurement and in late 1960 decision taken to instruct Sukhoi OKB to prepare Soviet counterpart. Predictably this followed GD/Grumman design much closer than Boeing, and – to some degree by chance – avoided most of the painful difficulties encountered by U S aircraft. Detailed design complete by 1965 (Butowski) and OKB given go-ahead on one static-test and several flight prototypes (designation unknown). First flight about 1969 and following careful refinement initial VVS service entry followed 1974.

Much larger and more capable than any previous Soviet tactical aircraft, combining great penetrative capability with heavy and varied weapon load and exceptional radius at all flight levels. Few new features in fuselage, but wing of true IG (VG) form with no fixed portion except triangular glove carrying outboard pivots. Geometry exact scale of TsAGI-researched configuration also used by MiG OKB, with full-span LE slats on outer sections, full-span three-piece slotted flaps, and spoilers also serving as lift-dumpers on landing. In this configuration wing is mounted high but (unlike US aircraft) not forming unbroken upper surface; dihedral 0° and sweep pilot-selectable to 16°, 45° or 68°. Single fin, high-mounted slab tailerons (further from wing than US aircraft) providing all-speed roll control backed up by spoilers at low speeds, twin canted ventral fins. Propulsion by modern augmented turbofans using long inlet ducts with slightly inclined wedge inlets as explored on Su-15**. Extensive internal tankage, mainly integral, between and above ducts, in fin and in glove, total est 13 000 lit (2859 gal), plus various external tank options including two of 2000-lit each on glove pylons. No FR probe seen but plumbing believed provided pending FA tanker. External weapons on four body pylons, two under gloves and two auto-swivelling pylons under outer wings, total load 8 t (17,635 lb) including every tactical store. Underside of fuselage flat for large stores load and houses two recessed items in large fairing on left and small on right: author believes both are guns, left being Gatling-type. Large doors under guns serve as airbrakes. Exceptionally large multi-mode radar (almost certainly pulse-doppler) dictating fuselage width and thus facilitating pilot and navigator seated in side-by-side KM-1 seats under wide clamshell canopy. Landing gears all with twin levered-suspension wheels, all retracting forwards into fuselage (main gears without compromising body weapon carriage, unlike US aircraft). Nose unit steerable, with debris guard. Tyre pressure matched to unpaved surfaces, and field length likewise matched to off-base rough airstrips. Main-gear doors form airbrakes, opened separately. Twin braking parachutes above jetpipes, possibly thrust reversers, four rear-fuselage airbrakes. By far most comprehensively equipped tactical aircraft in VVS inventory, with digital computer flight-control and weapon-aiming (USAF: can deliver ordnance in all weather within 55 m of target) and advanced internal ECM and EW systems. Main radome also houses terrain-following radar with auto-control of vertical profile. Nav systems include doppler, VOR and ILS, and laser ranger and marked-target seeker is combined with CW illuminator and command aerial for AA-2 and AS-7; other weapons include AA-8 and AS-9, AS-11 and AS-12.

Since 1975 programme managed by General Constructor Ye. A. Ivanov. Basic support/escort (ie, interdiction) aircraft produced as Su-24 for FA and possibly AVMF. Numerous derived versions include dedicated multi-sensor reconnaissance and long-range all-weather interceptor, both believed to have tandem seating, but no evidence of production yet. Original aircraft produced at estimated 100 per year for seven years, all for VVS. Data are accurate.

DIMENSIONS Span (68°) 10,0 m (32 ft 9¾ in), (16°) 17,25 m (56 ft 7 in); length, with short nose probe 20,5 m (67 ft 3 in); wing area (68°) 42,0 m² (452 ft²), (16°) 46,4 m² (500 ft²).

ENGINES Believed two 8,6/12,5 t (18,960/ 27,500 lb) R-29B augmented turbofans.

WEIGHTS Empty 18,1 t (39,900 lb), (equipped)

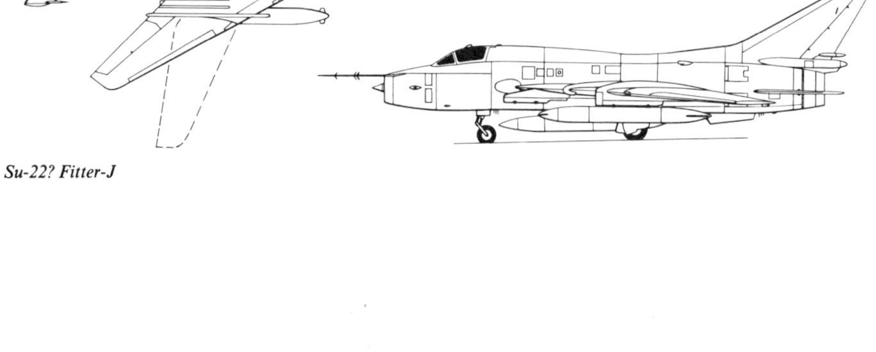

Su-22? Fitter-J

Su-24 with wings at intermediate sweep

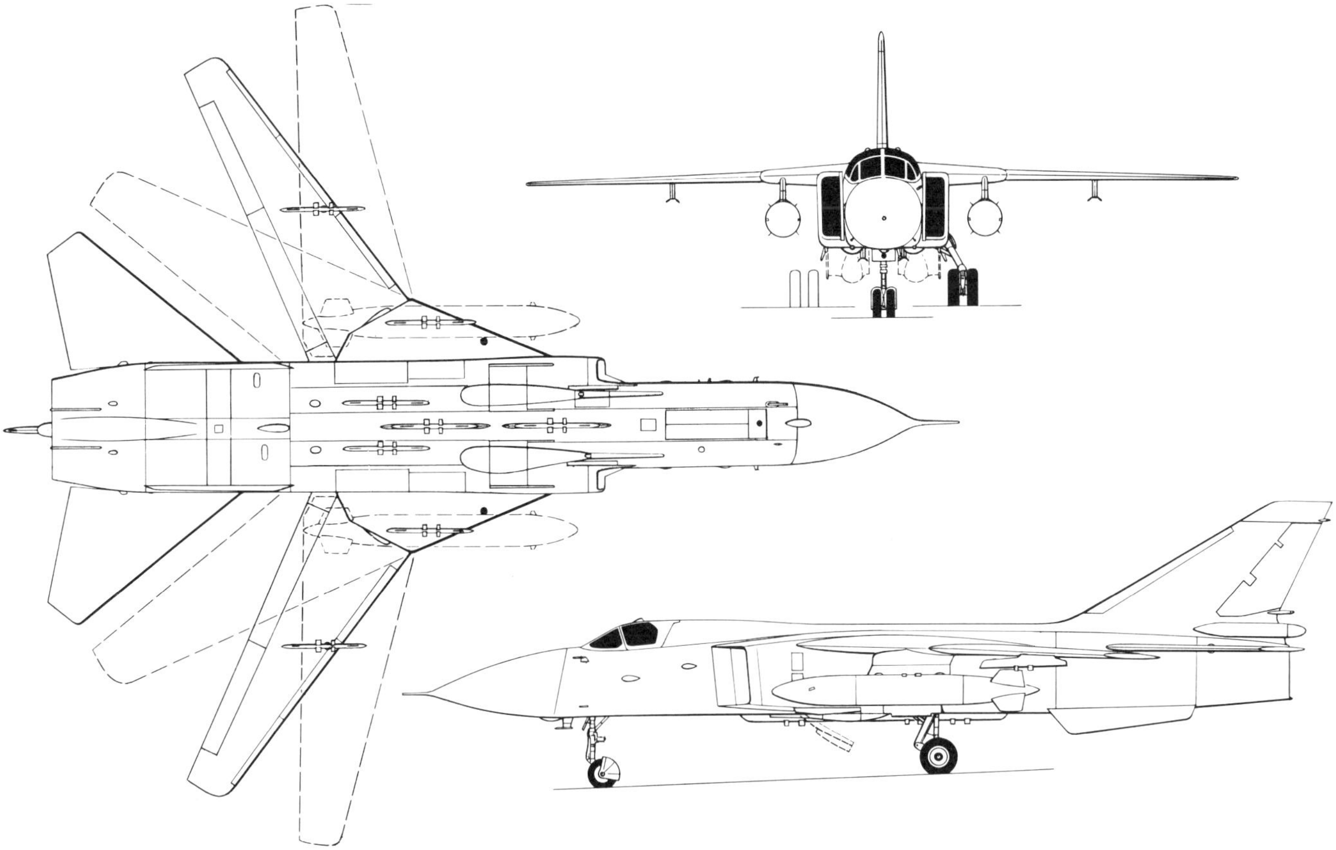

Su-24

Su-24 (wings at 16°)

Above, below: Su-25 in Afghanistan

19 t (41,887 lb); internal fuel 10,4 t; loaded (clean) 27,2 t (60,000 lb); max loaded 39,5 t (87,081 lb).

PERFORMANCE Max speed (clean) 1470 km/h (913 mph, M 1·2) at SL, 2560 km/h (1590 mph, M 2·4) at over 11 km; cruise with max weapons 955 km/h (M 0·9) at 11 km; combat radius with 3,5-t weapons and two 2000-lit tanks (Lo-Lo-Lo) 560 km, (Lo-Lo-Lo, 8 t weapons) 322 km (200 miles); (Hi-Lo-Hi) 1700 km; ferry range 6400 km (4000 miles); service ceiling 18,5 km (60,700 ft); field length (not max wt) 800 m; landing speed 240 km/h (149 mph).

Su-25? Dedicted subsonic ground attack aircraft which possibly marks a rejuvenation of the Soviet *Shturmovik* concept. Reminiscent of Northrop A-9 (losing AX contender, fly-off won by Fairchild A-10), but likeness probably only superficial. Formidable aircraft with one or more large calibre multi-barrel cannon under-nose and 10 hardpoints spread under wings and fuselage. Extensive armour protection assumed, and other survivability features include widely-separated engines, commanding pilot view (possible 360° bubble canopy), and high degree of control system redundancy.

Shoulder-mounted, long-span, high aspect ratio wing swept-back around 20° with slight anhedral. Fixed geometry engine intakes at wing-roots; integral tankage and wingtip sensor pods of unknown type/function. Single fin, tail-plane appears to have no anhedral, but likely to be all-moving to sustain good manoeuvre performance with heavy warload. Main gear retracts into fuselage between powerplants and fuel. According to *Jane's*, wing span 15,5 m (50 ft 10 in), length 14,5 m (47 ft 6 in). Assumption of turbofan engines could be premature – dry-rated turbojets in 4535 kg (10,000 lb) thrust-class equally credible. What is indisputable is that this aircraft exists in considerable numbers and has been in active service in Afghanistan since late 1981. There is no obvious reason to assign it to the Sukhoi OKB, and it would be just as reasonable to conclude that the design was by Yakovlev. Certainly the Sukhoi bureau is unlikely to have been responsible for all the aircraft mentioned on this page. No other data as this book went to press.

Su-27? Since 1981 this has been given (by US DoD and others) as new multirole fighter in class of F-15, allegedly with two engines and variable sweep wing. Other Western designations Ram-J and Flanker. No other data.

Su-18? This is a possible designation for large bomber designed to cruise at Mach 3 as counter to XB-70 in 1960 era. Photo (see this page), displayed at Frunze Central House of Aviation and Cosmonautics, Moscow, in special 1982 exhibition of Sukhoi OKB. No positive evidence aircraft actually flown.

Su-18?

SYeN

This group, *Samolyet Yefremov ili Nadiradzye*, was formed 1939 by Nikolai Ivanovich Yefremov and Aleksandr Davidovich Nadiradzye to work on large inflated air bags used as landing gear for water, ice or snow. Called air cushions, but today this has meaning associated with powered air supply in ACV technology. Some of SYeN air bags were true cushions, notably one flown 1940 on UT-2 in which 25 hp motorcycle engine was used to drive blower to inflate bag and create 'sliding cushion' beneath suitable also for dry land. No data, but bag was rubberized fabric and attached under centreline by dural struts giving adequate stability without wing-tip support. First flight I.I. Shyelyest, other flights by M.M. Gromov, A.B. Yumashyev and A.P. Chyernavskii. NKAP then authorized advanced air-cushion installation for Pe-2, with one under each nacelle connected by elastic muffs to engine-driven blowers. Aircraft completed 20 June 1941, two days before invasion, and never flown. SYeN had original designs for air-cushion aircraft but war halted operations.

Tikhonravov

Prof Mikhail Klavdiyevich Tikhonravov was member of staff at NII; some reports state RNII.

302, I-302 This experimental mixed-power interceptor was advanced project authorized by NKAP 1940 despite radical nature. Take-off by rocket, in tail of fuselage, and cruise on two VRDP (ramjets) under wings. Wooden construction, low wing of high aspect-ratio for fighter (7·3) with two spars and laminar profile. Wood monococque fuselage with integral fin, four 20-mm ShVAK in nose, pilot in pressurized cockpit, hydraulically retractable tailwheel landing gear. Intended to have wing racks for bombs and RS-82 rockets. Ramjets not Merkulov but by brigade led by Vladimir Stepanovich Zuyev. Delays with propulsion led to construction of Aircraft 302P, glider for low-speed flight test, with VRDP mounts faired over. Two built 1942 at VVA by authority of A.G. Kostikov of NKAP as stepping-stone to interceptor despite decision in that year not to pursue such aircraft. One airframe static-tested at TsAGI, second flown spring 1943 under tow by Pe-2; pilots included S.N. Anokhin and M.L. Gallai. Terminated by declining need and poor progress of chosen VRDP; Western accounts give crash of rival BI as true reason.

DIMENSIONS Span 11,4 m (37 ft 4¾ in); length about 8 m (26 ft 3 in); wing area 17,8 m² (192 ft²).
ENGINES One 1,5 t (3307 lb at SL) NII-3 rocket engine, two Zuyev ramjets of unknown thrust. No other data.

Tokayev

Utka research aircraft is described as MiG-8, see page 172.

Tomashyevich

Dmitrii Lyudvigovich Tomashyevich was born in Ukraine about 1898, serving in the First World War and subsequent Red Army as engineer and finding work on RVZ-6 on its establishment in 1923. Picked out by Kalinin as senior assistant and played active role in K-1 and K-2 whilst also attending Kiev Poly Inst for formal qualification. KPIR-5 lightplane was diploma project. Moved to TsKB 1931, and on Polikarpov's release from prison 1933 joined his brigade as senior deputy constructor. Chief designer on I-180 programme, and on Chkalov's death in first I-180 immediately imprisoned. Assigned to Special Prison KB-29 January 1939 to lead Group 101, to create Fighter No 101. Abruptly terminated and assigned to assist Tupolev on No 103. In October 1941 moved to Siberia and placed in charge of own semi-free KB at GAZ-266 in Siberia (Kulomzino, suburb of Omsk). Here produced Aircraft 110 and Pegas.

KPIR Successful firstborn of Tomashyevich was a neat cantilever monoplane of wood and fabric construction. Full designation was **KPIR-5**, though forerunners never built. Initials stood for Kiev Polytechnic Institute, where Tomashyevich built it as a diploma project in 1926–1927.

DIMENSIONS Span 12,0 m (39 ft 4½ in); length 7,0 m (22 ft 11½ in); wing area 19 m² (204·5 ft²).
ENGINE One 27/35 hp ABC Scorpion.
WEIGHTS Empty 233 kg (514 lb); fuel/oil 20 kg (44 lb); loaded 403 kg (888 lb).
PERFORMANCE Max speed 95 km/h (59 mph); landing speed 45 km/h (28 mph).

110 Often called **I-110** in West, this fundamentally conventional fighter was designed for simple field maintenance, as shown by removal of four bolts to release entire powerplant group complete with cowl, and provision of small hinged panels in top cowl for crane hooks. Mixed construction saving scarce alloys. Wing NACA-23 profile with tapered centre-section 3,6 m, dihedral 0° and outer panels dihedral 8°30′. Main spar D1 and 30KhGSA booms, front and rear secondary spars and truss/sheet ribs all-dural, but wing skin birch *shpon*. Fuselage steel-tube (mainly 30KhGSA) at front, with D1 cowl, but aft of main spar birch *shpon* monocoque. Wood fin and tailplane carrying control surfaces of D1 and fabric. Eight fuel tanks, four in centre section and four in outer wings, all claimed self-sealing against fire up to 12,7-mm calibre. Single-strut main gears, all three units fully retractable. Extremely large (29 m²) radiator under engine in pressurized glycol circuit with integral oil radiator, all auto-controlled with elec-driven flaps at rear of duct and removed as part of complete powerplant. Large glazed areas over cockpit with central hood sliding to rear. Standardized instrument panel with quick elec-vacuum/pressure connections removable as one unit. Armament, one ShVAK firing through hub of 3,2-m three-blade propeller and two UBS (alternatively ShKAS) in top decking; belly rack for bomb or other store to max 500 kg. Previously thought completed 1943, now known P.M. Stefanovskii made first flight December 1942 and was generally satisfied. Handling fair, and performance adequate though severely compromised by extra weight of easy-maintenance and quick-build features such as making every dimension exact multiple of 10 mm. Major reasons for abandoning idea of recommended production was unavailability of engine and lack of production capacity for airframe.

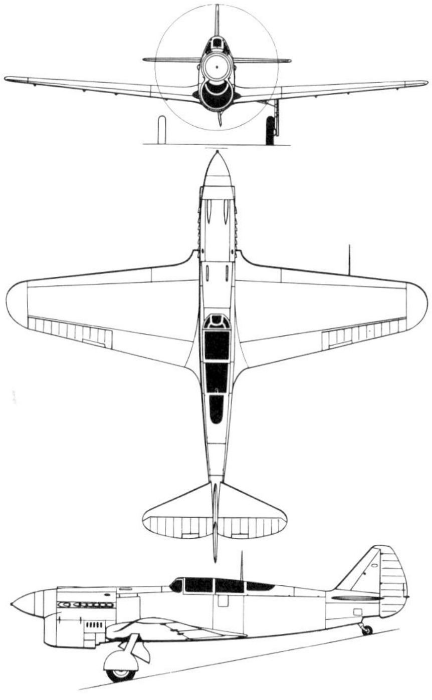
Type 110

DIMENSIONS Span 10,2 m (33 ft 5½ in); length 9,91 m (32 ft 6⅛ in); wing area 18,73 m² (202 ft²).
ENGINE One 1400 hp VK-107.
WEIGHTS Empty 3285 kg (7242 lb); fuel/oil 410 + 35 kg; loaded 3980 kg (8774 lb).
PERFORMANCE Max speed 508 km/h at SL, 610 km/h (379 mph) at 6,2 km; time to 3 km, 4 min, to 7 km, 7 min; service ceiling 10 km (32,800 ft); max range 1050 km (652 miles).

Pegas Successful use of U-2 (Po-2) variants as night bomber and close-support attack aircraft spurred launch of this much better light tactical attack aircraft making small demands on either construction workers or pilots, and sacrificing performance for simplicity and utility. Despite poor performance everything possible done to ensure survivability against ground fire (rifle-calibre for transparencies and 12,7 or 20-mm for vital areas) and ability to regain base and be quickly repaired. Authorized August 1942 and first of five prototypes flying before end of year. Severely angular low-wing machine with two Po-2 engine/propeller groups. Aerodynamics ignored except to allow flight by unskilled pilot at angle of attack up to 20°. Construction almost entirely wood, mainly pine frames and birch ply skin. Two-spar wing with fixed slots over outer sections, large ailerons but no flaps. Option of removable or jettisonable upper plane as in British Hillson scheme of same era. Fuselage built up on four pine longerons with ply skin except mild-steel armour over nose and cockpit. Armoured glass windscreen giving view 55° downwards directly ahead. Engines uncowled though with small dural shield above cylinders and exhausts piped around rear and over leading edge. Galvanized-iron fuel tanks forming nacelles jettisonable but leaving small emergency armoured tank giving several minutes' supply. Fixed tailwheel landing gear with rubber shock-absorption, first flight made on wheels but skis soon substituted. All-wood tail. Armament two VYa-23 and one UBS side-by-side in nose with breeches in cockpit. Alternative load, two 250-kg or one 500-kg bomb under fuselage, or fragmentation bombs. Original intention was mass-production at same airframe price as Po-2, using all locally available materials. First flight about same time as Aircraft 110, at end 1942. Stefanovskii and several other pilots carried out NII testing February 1943 and found aircraft safe but overweight. Recommendation that examples be tested at Kursk front came to nothing, partly because of sheer distance of OKB.

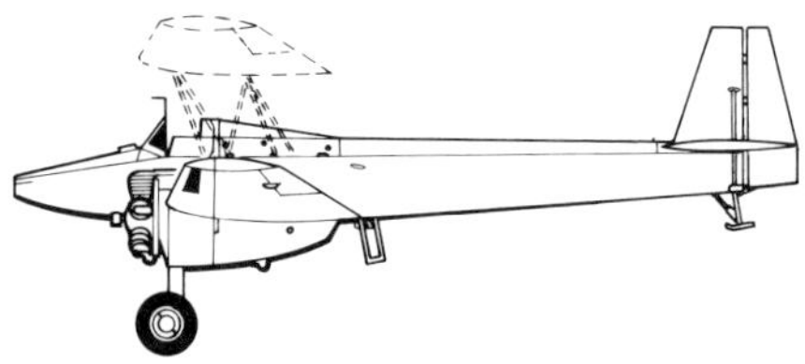

Pegas (Aircraft 01, showing slip-wing, never fitted)

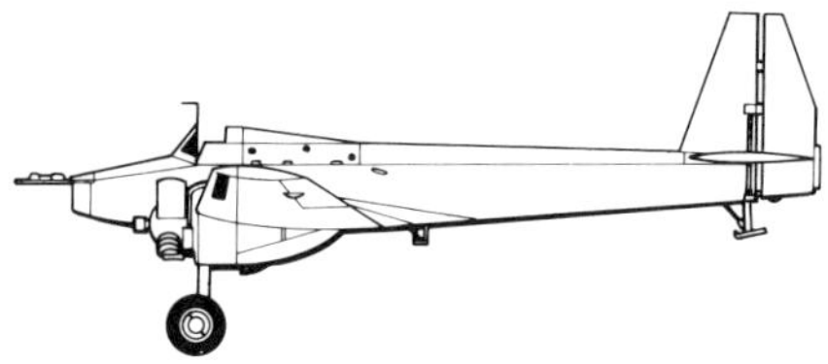

Pegas (Aircraft 03)

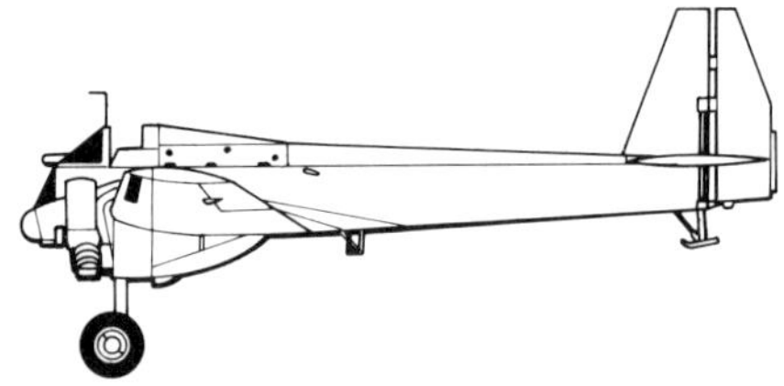

Pegas (Aircraft 04)

MG-31 engine was suggested but programme was dropped spring 1943 because of declining need for such emergency solutions.

DIMENSIONS Span 12,63 m (41 ft 5¼ in); length 8784 mm (28 ft 9⅞ in); wing area 26,6 m² (286 ft²).

ENGINES Two 140 hp M-11F.

WEIGHTS Empty 1800 kg (3968 lb); loaded (normal) 2150 kg (4740 lb), (max) 2320 kg (5115 lb). Shavrov's max wt does not allow for 500-kg bomb.

PERFORMANCE Max speed 172 km/h (107 mph) at SL, (max wt) 167 km/h (104 mph); initial climb 2 m/s (400 ft/min); service ceiling 2,62 km (8600 ft); range 400 km (249 miles); landing speed 80 km/h (50 mph).

TsAGI

National aero and hydrodynamic research organization, TsAGI sponsored several aircraft design groups including AGOS, KOSOS (both described mainly under Tupolev) and several others covered under individual constructors. ZOK (*Zavod Opytnyi Konstruktsii*, factory for experimental prototypes) in addition built pioneer autogiros and helicopters which, even if directed mainly by designers featured elsewhere, were known as TsAGI programmes and are dealt with here as coherent families involving several chief designers: Yur'yev, Chyeremukhin, Bratukhin, Kuznetsov, Skrzhinskii, Mil and Kamov.

Helicopters

1-EA First helicopter to fly in the Soviet Union, brain-child of TsAGI Prof Boris Nikolayevich Yur'yev, who from 1909 had striven to build such machine and under Zhukovskii had been first employee of TsAGI and chief architect of its original test facilities. In 1925 he organized a *vertolyet* (helicopter) group at TsAGI and in 1927 tested a 6-m two-blade rotor driven by 120 hp M-2. In 1928, from at least four project studies, design picked for 1-EA (*Eksperimentalnyi Apparat*) and machine built at ZOK under G.Kh. Sabinin. Chief designer Aleksei Mikhailovich Chyeremukhin and Aleksandr Mikhailovich Izakson. Fuselage welded from M1 mild-steel tube forming spaceframe resting on tailwheel landing gear with rubber springing. Twin engines at centre with reduction and bevel gears to vertical shaft to main rotor and side-by-side pairs of 1,8-m anti-torque rotors at nose and tail. Chief development task was finding best structure for main rotor blades, an all-metal blade being rejected in favour of one with dural spar, wood ribs and stringers and ply/fabric skin. Four-blade main rotor with 5° coning angle driven at 153 rpm. Cyclic and collective controls described as similar to those of today, and pedal control of nose/tail rotors from pilot seat just ahead of engines. Chyeremukhin elected to fly 1-EA himself, making first tethered run August 1930. No disasters and by 1932 reliable flights of up to 12 min; 1 August 1932 same pilot reached 160 m, 3 August 230 m, 5 August 285 m and on 14 August 605 m (one Western accounts says lost control in descent and crashed). Soviet Union not FAI member and did not announce achievement, world record remaining 18 m (d'Ascanio). 1-EA continued to fly until at least 1934.

DIMENSIONS Main-rotor diam 11,0 m (36 ft 1 in); length (over nose/tail rotors) 12,8 m (42 ft 0 in); height (main rotor lifting) 3380 mm (11 ft 10¾ in).

ENGINES Two 120 hp M-2.

WEIGHTS Empty 982 kg (2165 lb); fuel/oil 70 + 13 kg; loaded 1145 kg (2524 lb).

PERFORMANCE Max speed reached 30 km/h; max ht 605 m (1985 ft); endurance 14 min.

3-EA Second helicopter built 1933 for training pilots. Similar to 1-EA and same data. Never flown except on tethers.

5-EA Broadly similar to predecessors, incorporated new rotor proposed by I.P. Bratukhin with three large blades with articulated roots which provided lift, and three smaller blades with rigid attachment which provided control. Some accounts incorrectly state large and small rotors superimposed; all blades were in same plane, large and small alternating. This rotor worked, yet 5-EA appears not to have reached any considerable height or endurance (Western figures 13 miles and 1200 ft not confirmed in Soviet accounts). 5-EA flew from 1933 until late 1935 and was instrumental in providing research basis for machine with more powerful and more modern engine.

DIMENSIONS Main-rotor diams (large blades) 12,0 m (39 ft 4½ in), (small) 7,8 m (25 ft 7 in); length of fuselage 11,0 m (4,5 ahead of main axis, 6,5 to rear) (36 ft 10¾ in); length over nose/tail rotors, as 1-EA; height 3105 m (10 ft 2¼ in).

ENGINES Two 120 hp M-2.

WEIGHTS Empty 1047 kg (2308 lb); fuel/oil 70 + 13 kg; loaded 1210 kg (2668 lb).

PERFORMANCE Max speed 20 km/h; alt not over 40 m; endurance 8½ min.

11-EA Designed 1934, this used Bratukhin's rotor with alternate large articulated blades and small rigid blades but scaled up to absorb power of large US water-cooled V-12 engine. Latter mounted in nose of steel-tube fuselage covered in fabric for streamlining, with tandem cockpits at rear behind main rotor pylons. Engine arranged facing to rear with reduction gear driving second reduction gearbox at foot of rotor shaft. Auxiliary drive from rear wheelcase to three-blade cooling fan drawing air through main radiator on nose. Rotor torque reacted by two 2250-mm three-blade propellers near tips of small fixed wing. Complete aeroplane flight controls – ailerons, elevators, rudder – in addition to improved cyclic/collective controls on main rotor. Intention was to test as helicopter and later arrange for drive to main rotor to be disconnected and aircraft flown as autogyro, with all power used for forward propulsion via propellers, with aeroplane flight control. 11-EA was completed summer 1936 and completed tethered testing on a platform, using front cockpit as observer and rear as pilot, though dual controls provided. Considerable difficulties with distribution of power, main blade construction and maintenance of steady height whilst varying push/pull power of propellers. Late 1937 wave of arrests removed Chyeremukhin, Izakson and many other TsAGI helicopter engineers and virtually halted further work through fear of accusation of sabotage.

After much calculation Bratukhin dared 1938 to begin alterations and in spring 1938 aircraft emerged as **11-EA PV** (*Propulsivnyi Variant*). Main rotor hub fitted with improved blades entirely dural with better profile. Auxiliary propellers replaced by pairs of anti-torque rotors from 5-EA mounted at tips of outriggers of welded steel tube, increasing distance between thrust axes from 8,0 to 11,0 m. Removal of wing improved vertical performance, and smaller screws at greater distance from fuselage reduced power loss in countering torque. Idea of making convertible helicopter/autogyro abandoned. PV ready late 1939 and in Chyeremukhin's absence D.I. Savelyev took over flight test, making tethered flights early 1940 and free flights from October. Under test director V.P. Lapisov reconstructed machine demonstrated excellent lifting power and good control, but ancient engine no longer ran well (no spares for many years) and programme halted early 1941 for new Soviet engine. Never flew again.

DIMENSIONS Main-rotor diams (large blades) 15,4 m (50 ft 6⅓ in), (small blades) 9,2 m (30 ft 2¼ in); span of wing 10,7 m (35 ft 1¼ in); length (ignoring rotor) 8,3 m (27 ft 2¾ in); height 3530 mm (11 ft 7 in).

ENGINE One 630 hp Curtiss Conqueror.

WEIGHTS Empty, not known; loaded 2,6 t (5732 lb), (PV) 2250 kg (4960 lb).

PERFORMANCE PV reached 60 km/h (37 mph) at 50 m.

Autogyros

2-EA Based on tandem-seat Cierva C.19 Mk III, built at TsAGI OOK under direction of Izakson to design of I.P. Bratukhin and V.A. Kuznetsov and completed 1931. First Soviet autogyro for methodical research and development. Fuselage and twin-fin tail welded mild-steel tube with fabric, wing wood and rotor-

blade spars and pylon struts welded KhMA. No mechanical drive to rotor. Research complete 1933 and 2-EA assigned to *Maksim Gorkii* propaganda squadron.
DIMENSIONS Rotor diam 12,0 m (39 ft 4½ in); span 6,7 m (22 ft 0 in); length 6,5 m (21 ft 3⅞ in).
ENGINE One 225 hp GR Titan (Bristol licence).
WEIGHTS Empty 765 kg (1687 lb); fuel 90 kg; loaded 1032 kg (2275 lb).
PERFORMANCE Max speed 160 km/h (99 mph); min speed 58 km/h (36 mph); climb to 3 km, 20 min; ceiling 4,2 km; endurance 1 h; take-off 60 m; landing 0–6 m.

A-4 Designation from *Avtozhir* (autogyro); decree by NII VVS 1932 for all-Soviet autogyro, and preparations for production organized forthwith for use as military trainer and observation machine. Design led by N.K. Skrzhinskii using known Cierva technology, regarded as minimal risk. Structure similar to 2-EA but single fin, more power, dual controls. First flight 6 November 1932; second flight three days later resulted in unexplained rotor vibration and loss of lift, with heavy impact on ground despite maximum power. Production had begun and frantic research with different rotors eventually yielded satisfactory machine, passing NII tests late 1933. Ten delivered 1934 (possibly a few more later) and served as trainers and in field manoeuvres.
DIMENSIONS Rotor diam 13,0 m (42 ft 8 in); span, as 2-EA; length 7,2 m (23 ft 7½ in).
ENGINE One 300 hp M-26.
WEIGHTS Empty 1065 kg (2348 lb); fuel/oil 95 + 20 kg; loaded 1365 kg (3009 lb).
PERFORMANCE Max speed 176 km/h (109 mph); min speed 50 km/h (31 mph); climb to 3 km, 21 min; ceiling 4,1 km; endurance 1·3 h; range 185 km (115 miles); time 360° turn 15 s; take-off 70–100 m; landing 3–10 m.

A-6 Light autogyro designed at OOK by Kuznetsov. First rotary-wing machine with folding blades, and also folding wings. Construction as before except balloon tyres instead of shock struts. Flown Ts.A. Korsinshchikov early 1933 and from start showed outstandingly good flying qualities, far better than A-4 on which all official attention was polarized. Following various research programmes in winter 1933, one of which was testing V (butterfly) tail incorrectly ascribed by Shavrov to A-8, A-6 led to A-8 and A-13.
DIMENSIONS Main-rotor diam 11,0 m (36 ft 1 in); span, not known but wing area 5,9 m² (63·5 ft²); length 6,3 m (20 ft 8 in); height 3,2 m.
ENGINE One 100 hp M-11.
WEIGHTS Empty 562 kg (1239 lb); fuel/oil 67 kg; loaded 815 kg (1797 lb).
PERFORMANCE Max speed 142 km/h (88 mph); min speed 53 km/h (33 mph); ceiling 2 km; endurance 2·5 h; take-off 50 m; landing 0 m.

A-8 First flown 29 June 1934, this was virtually an A-6 with two major alterations: wings had 5° dihedral instead of upturned tips, and as well as ailerons direct rotor control of roll was provided, even during autorotation (and found to be vastly superior to ailerons except at max speed). Other changes included auxiliary fins on tailplane and first air/oil shock struts in Soviet Union.
DIMENSIONS As A-6 except wing area 5,8 m² (62 ft²).
ENGINE One 100 hp M-11.
WEIGHTS Empty 595 kg (1312 lb); fuel/oil 67 kg; loaded 837 kg (1845 lb).
PERFORMANCE As A-6 except min speed only 48 km/h (30 mph) and ceiling 2560 m.

A-7 First of new TsAGI family developed by 3rd Brigade under Kamov from 1931 to meet NII VVS demand for powerful autogyro for front-line duties such as artillery spotting, recon and liaison. Originally designated **7-EA**, broke new ground in many areas. Three-blade rigid rotor with clutch for spin-up to 195 rpm (max in flight 200) for jump start (before achieved by Cierva). Blade spar KhGSA tube, ribs and stringers wood, skin ply over leading portion and *Enerzh-6* stainless sheet to rear. Fuselage welded KhMA steel tube with dural skin, with integral fin. Tail dural with fabric covering, including auxiliary fins below tailplane. Wing wooden, with ply skin. Tricycle landing gear, one of first in world, with steerable nosewheel (believed world first) and spats on all wheels. Townend ring on engine, metal propeller. Slotted elevator and special protection against overturning in gusty conditions or because of short wheelbase on rough ground. Flown by Korsinshchikov 20 September 1934, but prolonged development needed – interrupted by sensational appearance at Tushino August 1935 – until released for NII tests December 1935. Passed NII tests by A.A. Ivanovskii 1936 and cleared with small changes for use as observation and spotting platform. Same prototype shipped to Greenland 1938 to help in rescue of Papanin expedition, but not needed. Improved **A-7bis** of 1936 with modified rotor pylon and other changes led to **A-7-Za** of which five built 1940 (see Kamov) and used by VVS. Lighter airframe, improved fuselage, no spats, synchronized PV-1 (later ShKAS) and twin PV-1 in rear cockpit. Active career included participation in 1938–1940 Tian-Shan expedition and sporadic reconnaissance missions during the Second World War.
DIMENSIONS Rotor diam 15,2 m (49 ft 10½ in); span 10,4 m (34 ft 1½ in); wing area 14,7 m²; length not known.
ENGINE One 480 hp M-22.
WEIGHTS Empty (7) 1300 kg, (bis) 1474 kg, (Za) 1225 kg (2701 lb); fuel/oil (7) 330 kg; loaded (7) 2056 kg, (bis) 2224 kg, (Za, max) 2300 kg (5071 lb).
PERFORMANCE Max speed (7) 210 km/h, (bis) 194 km/h, (Za) 221 km/h (137 mph); min speed 53 km/h; ceiling 4,7 km (15,400 ft); climb to 3 km (3 models) 16/22/19 min; endurance 4/4/2½ h; range 600/600/400 km; take-off 60/75/75 m; landing 18/20/18 m.

A-12 OOK 6th Brigade under Skrzhinskii designed A-10 six-seat transport autogyro with M-22 in 1934 but dropped this in favour of high-speed wingless machine with fully controllable rotor. Design in parallel with small A-14 which flew first and assisted perfection of A-12 wingless autogyro. Direct-control rotor derived from A-7, with similar engine drive before take-off. Roll control by rotor only, tail with central rudder (extension of fuselage) and two Scheibe fins on strut-braced tailplane with elevators. Shavrov loosely describes fuselage and engine as I-16 (fighter); in fact steel-tube with fabric, and engine cowl with gills. Two-position Hamilton propeller, single-seat cockpit, very strong main gears with oleo struts and wide-track spatted wheels with toe brakes. Cautious taxiing and hops 10 May 1936 by A.P. Chyernavskii, eventually 17 h 55 min in 43 flights until rotor blade came off 23 May 1937 killing I. Koz'yrev. Cause never found but ascribed fatigue; almost halted autogyro work.
DIMENSIONS Rotor diam 14,0 m (45 ft 11⅛ in); length 6,3 m (20 ft 8 in).
ENGINE One 670 hp Wright Cyclone (later believed M-25).
WEIGHTS Empty 1343 kg (2961 lb); fuel/oil 165 + 17 kg; loaded 1687 kg (3719 lb).
PERFORMANCE Max speed 245 km/h (152 mph); min speed 52 km/h (32 mph); ceiling 5570 m (18,275 ft); endurance 1½ h; take-off 25 m; landing 5–10 m.

A-13 Two-seat liaison machine developed from A-6 and A-8. Direct-control inclined rotor with folding blades, folding dihedralled wings and twin-finned tail, internal engine starter and clutch-in drive for rotor before take-off. First flown on skis March 1936; (Shavrov) successful in factory tests, (Něměcek) it was a failure and scrapped.
DIMENSIONS Rotor diam 11,5 m (37 ft 8¾ in); span not known but area 5,6 m² (60 ft²).
ENGINE One 100 hp M-11.
WEIGHTS Empty 540 kg (1190 lb); fuel/oil 50 kg; loaded 802 kg (1768 lb).
PERFORMANCE Max speed 151 km/h (94 mph); min speed 45 km/h (28 mph); ceiling 3 km; endurance 2 h; range 250 km; take-off 40 m; landing 0 m.

A-14 Final 2nd Brigade (Kuznetsov) autogyro to be flown, derived from A-6 and A-8 without wings and first to be flown in Soviet Union. Trouble-free flight 17 September 1935 and subsequently major research tool.
DIMENSIONS Rotor diam 11,0 m (36 ft 1 in); length 6,3 m (20 ft 8 in).
ENGINE One 100 hp M-11.
WEIGHTS Empty 576 kg (1270 lb); fuel/oil 67 kg; loaded 815 kg (1797 lb).
PERFORMANCE Max speed 167 km/h (104 mph); min speed 45 km/h (28 mph); endurance 2½ h; take-off 50 m; landing 0 m.

A-15 Intended as fastest autogyro of day, two-seat wingless machine using A-12 and A-14 technology and with usual welded KhMA structure, Scheibe fins on braced tailplane with elevators and direct-control rotor. Main gears with vertical shock struts carried on triangulated outriggers each side of fuselage. Pilot with synchronized ShKAS and observer with twin ShKAS and AFA-13 reconnaissance camera. Chief designer M.L. Mil, construction manager A.A. Kuznetsov. Completed April 1937 and taxi tests begun by Chyernavskii and Ivanov, but A-12 crash caused further work to be halted. No reason to doubt airworthiness of A-15 but effectively terminated Soviet autogyro development. Autogyros picked up again at Kharkov, Kuibyshyev and Riga 30 years later, making little use of TsAGI accomplishments.
DIMENSIONS Rotor diam 18,0 m (59 ft 0⅝ in); length 8,6 m (28 ft 2½ in); height 4,1 m (13 ft 5½ in).
ENGINE One 730 hp M-25V.
WEIGHTS Empty 1695 kg (3737 lb); fuel/oil 385 + 40 kg; loaded 2560 kg (5644 lb).
PERFORMANCE Est max speed 260 km/h (162 mph); min speed 50 km/h; ceiling 6,4 km (21,000 ft); take-off 35–60 m; landing 0 m.

Tsybin

Pavel Vladimirovich Tsybin was important engineer working at NII GVF and at LII in period 1940–1960. Collaborated with Kolyesnikov on KTs-20 assault glider 1940, subsequently designing following types.

Ts-25 Assault glider built to meet VVS specification for Aviation of Airborne Troops (AVDV) issued early 1944 calling for 2,5-t payload. No direct rival known. Simple high-wing transport of wooden construction with wing tapered from root and braced by steel-tube strut at main spar. Slotted flaps and ailerons carried on brackets beneath wing. Except for full-section fabric-covered nose, manually hinged to right, entire fuselage and fin ply-skinned with four circular windows each side and door on right. Side-by-side cockpit for two pilots above unobstructed hold, access by internal steps. Tricycle landing gear, jettisoned on combat mission for landing on three skids. Original design load was anti-tank gun (57-mm M-1943) plus Jeep.

Produced in small series from 1945; some used by AVDV for manoeuvres, at least one with 25 removable passenger seats tested as civil mixed-traffic glider on routes between Moscow, Novosibirsk, Gorkii and Kuybishyev, and in 1952 two handed to Czech air force (where designated NK-25).

DIMENSIONS Span 24,38 m (79 ft 11 7/8 in); length 16,15 m (52 ft 11 4/5 in); wing area 75,0 m^2 (807 ft^2).

WEIGHTS Empty 1787 kg (3940 lb); loaded 4,2 t (9259 lb).

PERFORMANCE Max tow speed 230 km/h (143 mph); landing speed 90 km/h (56 mph).

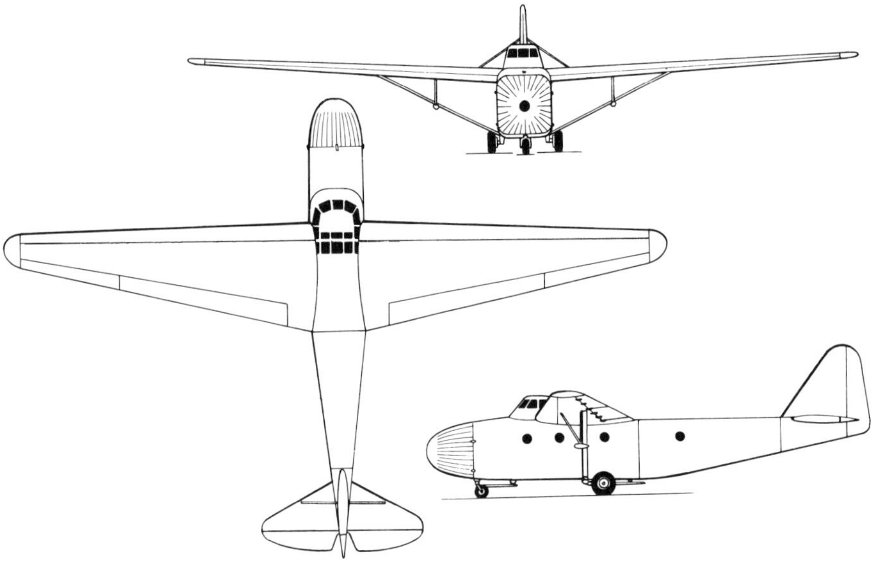

Ts-25

Ts-25 (NK-25)

LL-2

Ts-25M Powered version of Ts-25, believe single aircraft converted from production glider 1946. Prototype used for NII trials but no production.

DIMENSIONS As Ts-25.

ENGINES Two 165 hp M-11FR-1.

WEIGHTS Not known but empty about 2350 kg (5181 lb); loaded probably 4,5 t (9921 lb).

PERFORMANCE No data.

LL, EP In 1945 LII responded to need to research new wing shapes by commissioning series of *Letayushchye Laboratoriya* (flying laboratory) or *Eksperimentalnyi Planer* (experimental glider) aircraft designed by Tsybin and built 1946. **LL-1**, EP No 1, also called Ts-1, had 5% straight wing; **LL-2**, EP No 3, had wing swept forward 30°; **LL-3** was to have various wings including VG 0-30° and oblique wing pivoted at centre. All wings 10 m^2 area, attached together with tailplane by transducers measuring forces, moments, vibration and other factors, and with left surfaces tufted for photography and right surfaces covered with static pressure points connected to fuselage instrumentation. All three fuselages similar, wood monocoques of almost perfect streamline form with unpressurized pilot cockpit near nose. Wings mounted at mid-position with conventional ailerons and flaps, LL-1 wing wooden and LL-2 duralumin. Swept tail with tailplane half-way up fin. Provision for water ballast tanks at CG and for eventual fitting of solid-propellant rocket giving 1,5-t thrust for 8 to 10 s with nozzle at extreme tail. LL-3 never completed, but LL-1 and LL-2 made over 100 flights 1947–1948 in hands of Hero of Soviet Union Ahmet-Khan Sultan, S.N. Anokhin and N.S. Rybko. Flights made under tow (usually Pe-2), taking off on jettisonable trolley, casting off at about 8 km and making straight steep dive before jettisoning ballast and landing on skid.

DIMENSIONS Span (LL-1) 7,1 m (23 ft 3½ in); length about 8 m (26 ft).

WEIGHTS (typical) Empty 1 t (2200 lb); loaded 2 t (4400 lb).

PERFORMANCE (LL-1) 1050 km/h (652 mph, M 0·87) in 45° dive; (LL-2) 1150 km/h (715 mph, M 0·95); landing speed 120 km/h (75 mph).

NM-1 Major VVS plan for an uninterceptable RSR (*Reaktivnyi Samolyet Razvyedchik*, jet reconnaissance aircraft) in 1955–1958, with design speed of 3000 km/h at 30 km altitude, had to be underpinned by flying scale model of proposed configuration as well as testing of proposed tip turbojet/ramjet combination. Aerodynamic model was assigned to Tsybin as extension of

LL programme. Designation from *Nauchnaya Model*, scientific model. Single example built differed from RSR and in some ways more nearly resembled Myasishchyev M-50. Circular-section fuselage said to be welded steel tube frame with dural and ply skin, trapezoidal wing (not unlike that of LL-1 but lower aspect ratio) dural, thicker than RSR's 2·5% trapezoidal profile, and propulsion by plain tip-mounted turbojets. Take-off from central jettisonable trolley and retractable tailwheel, landing on large central skid, tailwheel and retractable outrigger wheels under engine nacelles. NM-1 completed late 1957 and flown by A-K Sultan as glider, towed by Pe-2, and subsequently by Anokhin. Dangerous at low speed and high angle of attack, and eventually RSR idea abandoned through propulsion difficulties and inability to find safe configuration. NM-1 made 11 flights, all except first under power, but scrapped 1960.

DIMENSIONS Span 10,3 m (33 ft 9½ in); length 26,6 m (87 ft 3¼ in).
ENGINES Two 2,2-t (4850-lb) AM-5.
WEIGHTS No data.
PERFORMANCE Design Mach number 2·8 in dive; highest speed reached 490 km/h (304 mph).

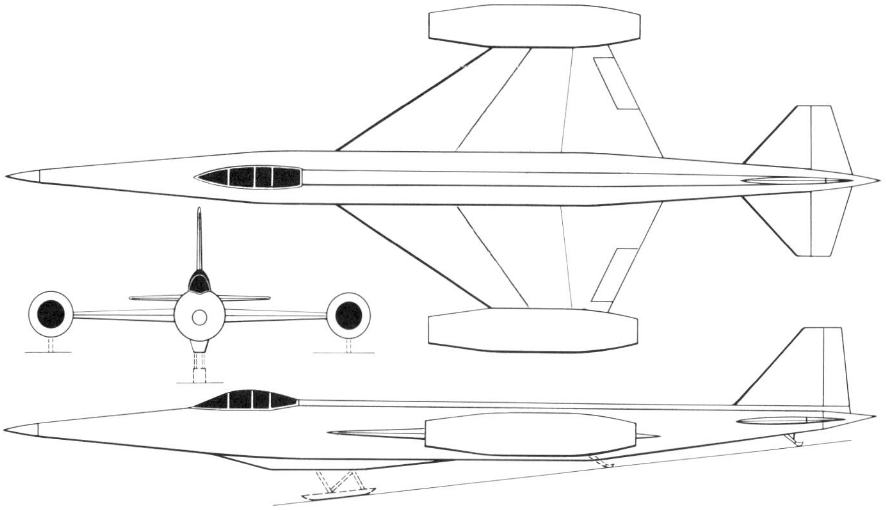

NM-1

Tupolev

Andrei Nikolayevich Tupolev was responsible for more types of diverse aircraft than any other designer in history. From early stage his seniority put him more in position of administrator than designer, many of aircraft described below being created under Tupolev direction by teams led by Sukhoi, Petlyakov, Arkhangyelskii and Myasishchyev. As whole, however, combined ANT-Tu family has no parallel.

A.N. Tupolev

A.N. Tupolev born 10 September 1888 at Pustomazov, near Kalinin, son of lawyer exiled for revolutionary activities. Mech engineering MVTU under Zhukovskii 1908, arrested 1911 for revolutionary activities but not exiled and returned MVTU 1914. Engineer at Duks factory 1915, remained there in Revolution and 1918 co-founder with Zhukovskii of TsAGI. With I.I. Sidorin chief technical member of 1920 NTK VVF (state scientific commission on aircraft materials), member of KOMTA (which see) and founder and director of TsAGI AGO (*Aviatsii i Gidrodinamiki Otdel*, aviation and hydrodynamics group) supervising various aero and sea designs including aerosleighs and hydroplanes which to this day continue to be major Tu products. Head of 1922 TsAGI state committee on metal aircraft construction (other members included Sidorin, A.I. Putilov and V.M. Petlyakov). Strong Junkers influence in initial metal aircraft by Tupolev (1923–1924) and AGOS (aero, hydro and experimental construction) formed by Tupolev 1925 as principal TsAGI design bureau. Appointed additionally 1931 chief engineer of GUAP, but arrested 1936 in strategic move to group major design strength in 'special prisons' as done earlier with Polikarpov and others; ridiculous charge was that he had passed design of Bf 110 to Germans. Lubyanka and Butyrkii prisons followed by TsKB-39 (OGPU, later NKVD, special prison named for Menzhinskii, chief of OGPU) where led KB-103 team to build Aircraft 103, later Tu-2, gaining freedom and first Stalin Prize 1943. Managed Soviet copy of B-29 from 1944 using derived technology in long and important succession of military and civil piston, turboprop and jet aircraft. Followed Boeing 7-7 sequence in assigning OKB numbers ending in 4 to civil transports, resulting in out-of-sequence later types. Andrei Tupolev died 23 December 1972; OKB continues to specialize in large aircraft, with no known General Constructor but with chief designer for each programme, that for Tu-144 having been founder's son Dr Alexei Andrievich Tupolev. Chief designer subsonic transports Dmitrii Markov, deputy OKB head Andrei Kandolov.

ANT-1 Perfection of Kolchug duralumin-type alloy in early 1922 led to pre-production fabrication of sheet and rolled sections such as angles, top-hats and Z in standard thicknesses and section sizes. To put specimens to use in actual airframe Tupolev himself designed small single-seater with minimum-risk structure using mainly

ANT-1

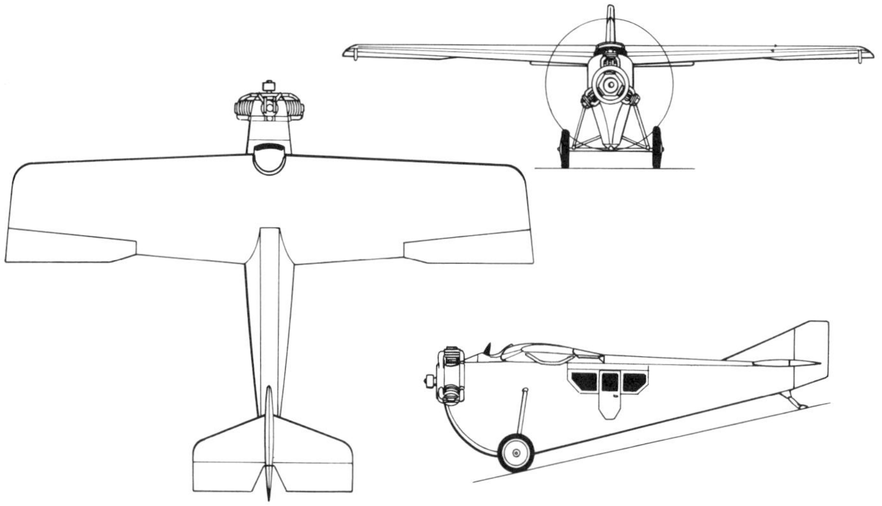

ANT-2

wood but with wing ribs and tail ribs (some reports suggest whole tail) of Kolchug sheet, and with Kolchug sections used for frame of ailerons and some other parts. Fabric covering, generally very simple though with differentially geared ailerons. Designed August–September 1922, first flight October 1923. Successfully tested by Ye.I. Pogosskii and N.I. Petrov; made many flights but not preserved.
DIMENSIONS Span (Shavrov, Simakov) 7,2 m (23 ft 7½ in), (Něměcek) 10,94 m (35 ft 10¾ in); length 5,4 m (17 ft 8⅝ in), (Něměcek) 5,98 m; wing area 10,0 m² (108 ft²), (Něměcek) 15 m² (161 ft²).
ENGINE One 35 hp six-cylinder Anzani radial.
WEIGHTS Empty 229 kg (505 lb), (Něměcek) 180 kg; fuel/oil 24 + 9 kg; loaded 360 kg (794 lb), (Nemecek) 267 kg.
PERFORMANCE Max speed (Shavrov) 125 km/h (78 mph), (Simakov) 135 km/h (84 mph), (Nowarra) 60/70 mph; practical ceiling 400 m, (Něměcek) 2 km; endurance 4 h; landing speed 70 km/h.

ANT-2 Success of ANT-1 prompted Tupolev to design this light transport with all-Kolchug airframe, first all-metal aircraft in Soviet Union. Design reminiscent of Junkers K 16 and skinned with same form of corrugated sheet (8 mm height, 40 mm pitch) in same gauges. Two-spar cantilever high wing with 13 truss ribs each side mounted on deep pot-bellied fuselage with almost flat sides coming together on lower centreline to give near-triangular section. Open pilot cockpit at leading edge, cabin with door on left and two seats facing each other. Main gears with wheels or skis, rubber springing inside fuselage (neater than K 16) and Kolchug tube skids under wingtips. Control surfaces corrugated skin, ailerons/elevators with push-rods. Like ANT-1, result of detailed stressing throughout primary structure; workers included Putilov, Petlyakov, both Pogosskii brothers, Nekrasov, Kondorskii and Zimin. First flown by N.I. Petrov 26 May 1924. Completely successful, apart from poor weathercock stability rectified by increasing height of vertical tail. Valued research tool in early AGOS programmes but too limited a transport for production. Preserved at Monino.
DIMENSIONS Span 10,0 m (32 ft 9¾ in); length 7,5 m (24 ft 7¼ in); wing area 17,5 m² (188 ft²).
ENGINE One 100 hp Bristol Lucifer.
WEIGHTS Empty 523 kg (1153 lb); fuel/oil 55 + 12 kg; loaded 836 kg (1843 lb).
PERFORMANCE Max speed 170 km/h (105·6 mph) at SL, 155 at 3 km; climb, 8·5 min to 1 km, 21·5 to 2, 48 to 3; service ceiling 3,3 km (10,-800 ft); range 425 km (264 miles), (Něměcek) 560 km; endurance 2·5 h, not reconciled with range; take-off 290 m/8 s; landing 150 m/6 s/78 km/h.

ANT-3, R-3 Proof of Kolchug construction having been gained with ANT-2, VVF took important decision July 1924 to adopt this construction for major military aircraft. AGOS (Tupolev personally) charged with building single-engined reconnaissance aircraft and large twin-engined bomber in all-Kolchug structure. Former authorized as R-3 forthwith, with AGOS designation ANT-3. Conventional single-bay biplane with Liberty engine (later M-5) but after studying Shishmaryev R-III Tupolev put upper wing very close to fuselage. Deep fuselage with same near-triangular section as ANT-2, with depth almost sufficient to fill gap between wings. Sesquiplane layout with 24,5 m² upper wing with two spars and 12,5 m² lower wing with single spar. Y-type interplane struts of Kolchug sheet wrapped to streamline form linking all spars. Various forms of Kolchug used for primary structure, entire skin (even control surfaces, ailerons upper wings only) being 40 × 8 or 20 × 5 mm corrugated sheet, tail control surfaces having large horn balances. Same control system as ANT-2, cables to rudder only.

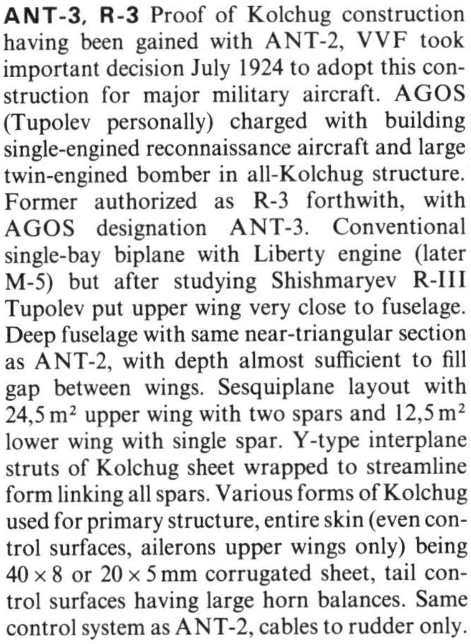

ANT-3 Proletarii

Upper wing on two Kolchug fairings linking spars to fuselage frames, widely spaced lift wires with vee anti-lift wires joined at foot of interplane strut each side. Pyramid-type main gears with tall main strut incorporating rubber shock-absorbers in large faired section. First aircraft completed as passenger machine with rear cockpit having forward-facing seat and windscreen for passenger or mechanic. Liberty engine cooled by two Lamblin radiators and driving Chauvière laminated-wood propeller. Registered RR-SOV and bearing slogan *Aviakhim SSSR Proletarii*. Rolled out at NOA (scientific experimental aerodrome) July 1925 and flown by V.N. Filippov early August. Excellent aircraft, factory tests complete October, and in December (before NII tests) decision for series production at GAZ-5 of ANT-3 aircraft both for propaganda tours and as military R-3. GosNII tests by M.M. Gromov and V.S. Vakhmistrov April 1926. First ANT-3 prepared for European tour and on Gromov's advice re-engined with Napier Lion for better performance with more fuel. With mechanic Ye.V. Radzevich left Moscow 30 August 1926 and flew Königsberg/Berlin/Paris/Rome/Vienna/Prague/Warsaw/Moscowin 34 h 15 min (7150 km) returning 2 September. First Soviet aircraft seen in outside world. Napier aircraft (**R-3NL**) superb in all respects and 30 already ordered for VVF, but engine expensive and for various reasons replaced in first production series by Liberty (about 12 aircraft) and M-5 (18). Great difficulty in issuing drawings and training workforce, and first production aircraft eventually flown GAZ-5 June 1927. This was civil ANT-3, prepared for even longer propaganda flight, registered RR-INT and inscribed *Osoaviakhim SSSR Nash Otvyet* (our answer). Flown by S.A. Shestakov with mechanic D.V. Fufayev Moscow / Sarapul / Omsk / Novosibirsk / Krasnoyarsk / Irkutsk / Chita / Blagoveshchyensk / Spassk / Nan Yang / Okayama / Tokyo in almost constant bad weather about 22 000 km (described as 20 000 km in Soviet accounts) in 153 h flown between 20 August and 1 September 1927. Aircraft then flew back. M-5 outdated engine, and 1926 deal with France for some 100 Lorraine-Dietrich engines resulted in last 79 military R-3 having this engine, known thus as **R-3LD**. Like most preceding Liberty and M-5 aircraft, flat frontal radiator, in this case almost circular instead of rectangular and with prop shaft near bottom. Minor airframe modifications and almost all armed with synchronized Vickers (later PV), twin movable Lewis or DA on Scarff ring in observer cockpit, ten underwing racks for light bombs and hand-held camera. A.I. Putilov schemed *Shturmovik* (attack) version with 400 kg armour protecting engine and cockpits, not built. One aircraft converted on line at end of run March 1929 with BMW VI, even better aircraft but no reserve strength in structure and so no production. One series R-3 converted as **PS-3** transport and used by Aeroflot in Yakutsk directorate.
DIMENSIONS Span 13,02 m (42 ft 8⅝ in); length (NL, M-5) 9,42 m (30 ft 10⅞ in), (LD, 9885 mm (32 ft 5⅛ in); wing area (see text) 37 m² (398 ft²).
ENGINE (Prototype) one 400 hp Liberty, then 450 hp Napier Lion, (production) Liberty or M-5, finally 450 hp Lorraine-Dietrich, one aircraft 730 hp BMW VIz.
WEIGHTS Empty (Liberty) 1335 kg, (Lion) 1390 kg, (M-5 series) 1377 kg (3036 lb), (LD)

1340 kg (2954 lb); fuel/oil, 343+34 kg, then (Lion and M-5) 387, (L D) 322+30 kg; loaded (Liberty) 2085 kg, (Lion) 2144 (2400 max), (M-5) 2128 (4691 lb), (LD) 2090 (4608 lb).

PERFORMANCE Max speed (Liberty) 207 km/h, (Lion) 226 km/h, (M-5) 194 km/h (120·5 mph), (LD) 204 km/h (127 mph), (BMW) 229; climb to 1 km (Lib) 4·7 min, (Lion) 3·5, (M-5) 3·9, (LD) 4·2; service ceiling (LD, typical) 4920 m (16,-140 ft); range (L D) 880 km (550 miles); 360° turn (NL, LD) 21 s; TO (M-5) 200 m/15 s, (NL) 160m/10 s; landing 140–180 m/11–14 s/85 km/h (53 mph).

ANT-4, TB-1 Result of July 1924 VVF demand for all-Kolchug heavy aircraft, this was one of most significant aircraft of its day and especially for Soviet Union. First large ANT, established basis for all subsequent large all-metal monoplanes up to ANT-42. Drew heavily upon Junkers structure, and German company began proceedings 1926 against TsAGI and Tupolev personally on grounds of infringing patents covering Junkers metal wing construction (action not successful). Claimed to be first large twin-engined all-metal monoplane bomber in world. Assigned chiefly to new AGOS brigade under Petlyakov, designed at old TsAGI headquarters and prototype construction begun 11 November 1924 in large workshop on second (UK = first) floor in knowledge walls would have to be demolished to get aircraft out. Completed 11 August 1925 in seven major portions, two months needed to get parts out of building, take to Moscow Central Aerodrome and assemble. Unpainted, two Napier Lion engines with British propellers, large Junkers ski landing gear with trolley under rear ski for ground manoeuvres, removed before take-off. Successful 7-min flight by A.I. Tomashyevskii 26 November 1925. Skis heavy and weak, and no further flight possible until redesigned; then 35-min flight 15 February 1926 followed by first properly planned GosNII state tests 26 March onwards with Tomashyevskii at Central Aerodrome and N.N. Morozov at Ostekhburo. Tomashyevskii made 25 test flights 11 June to 2 July 1926 (always with second pilot or mechanic) expressing opinion '1st-class'; but as yet no test of solo handling, night flying, nav, photo, radio or armament. Decision to build in series for many duties, primarily as VVF heavy bomber, using cheaper engine than Lion and if possible Lorraine-Dietrich as in R-3. Only possible production base Fili works, where Junkers operation closing down and 40 skilled light-alloy workers available. April 1927 NTK UVVS decision to use BMW VI engine, subsequently substituting M-17.

Classic wing used with improvements and changes of scale in many subsequent ANTs. Profile Tupolev A^0 (Junkers/TsAGI) with ruling t/c 20%. Structurally 13,5-m centre section with five spars and 18 ribs, removable leading/trailing edges; removable 6825 m outer panels with 10 ribs each, held by new-type joints not copied from Junkers coupling nuts but using tapered conical bolts fitting in reamed holes. (Note, joint near aileron, not near engines, and span was increased by large projecting ailerons.) Spars Kolchug trusses riveted from tube and deep channel sections, booms being elliptical tubes 72,6 × 65,6 mm at root tapering to 30 × 25 mm at tip, all joints by four rows of five rivets; 2-mm sheet gusset at each joint between diag spar-web tubes and main booms. All ribs Kolchug trusses, A-section ribs being full wing profile with corrugated 40 × 8-mm skins (basic sheet thickness 0,33 mm but narrow walkway inboard of 0,8 mm) laid in strips between them, L-section ribs lying beneath skin with closed riveted joints. On prototype, extra skin stiffening by straps with closed riveted joints. On prototype, extra skin stiffening by straps of 1,5-mm thickness and 100 or 150-mm wide arranged under skin at 45° (not used in later examples). Fuselage built up mainly of A-section upper longerons and 21 A-section frames, tubular lower longerons and sternframe, with 0,3 mm (40 × 8 mm) corrugated skin using

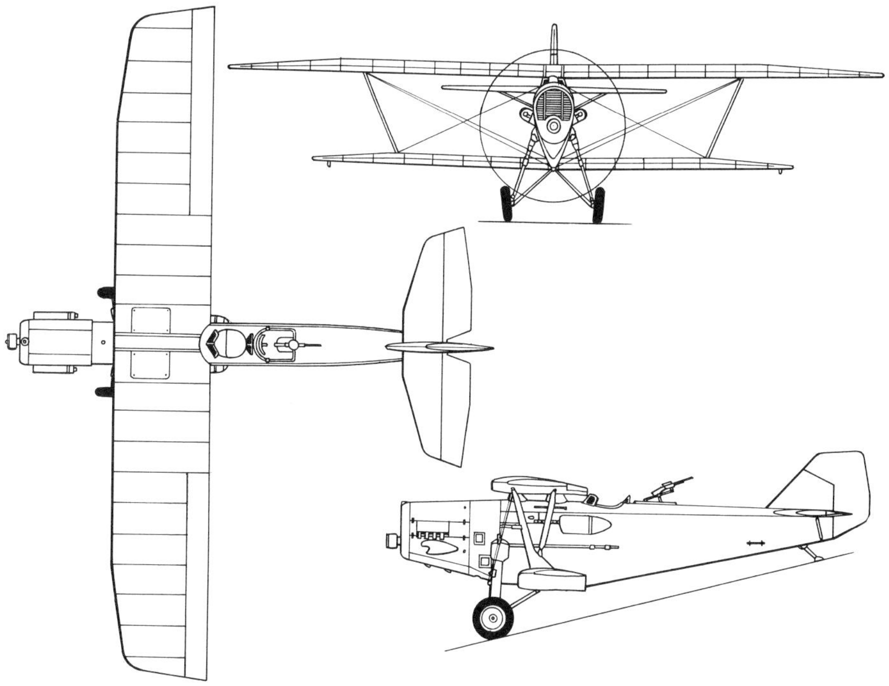

ANT-3, R-3

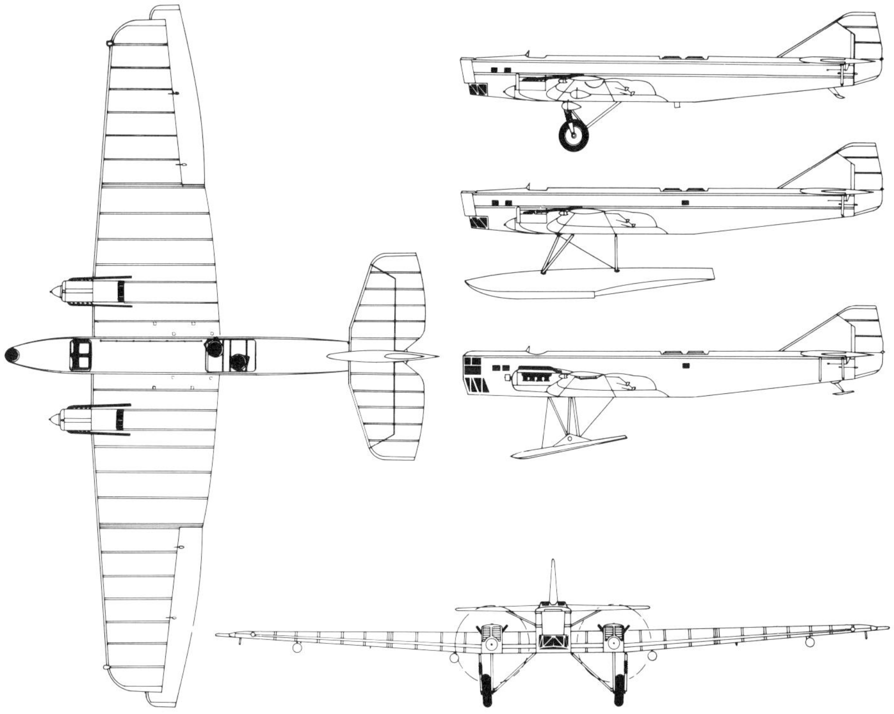

ANT-4, TB-1; middle side view, TB-1P; lower, ANT-4 prototype

open riveting. Structurally three parts, F-1 (nose), F-2 (integral with wing, from first to fifth spars), F-3 (aft of fifth spar). Trapezoidal cross-section with sloping sides as in previous ANTs but this time with width at bottom. All flight-control surfaces with Kolchug tube structure (plus sheet webs in tailplane) and corrug skin (20 × 5 mm) with large horn balances which in aileron projected beyond wingtip. Main gear struts imported Ni-Cr steel tubes (130 kg/mm²) with machined ends and rubber shock-absorption, wire wheels with 1250 × 250 mm tyres, no brakes. Sukhoi did steel-shod tailskid. Galvanized-iron fuel tanks in wings, initially 2360 lit (519 gal); CG at 34·1/34·3% MAC. Lion engines on welded steel-tube frames, each with twin Lamblin radiators under wings, short exhaust pipe from each cylinder. Fuselage equipped for side-by-side pilots with dual control by push/pull rods to ailerons and tailplane, cables to rudder. Glazed nose for nav, cockpit behind wing for observer. Tests soon resulted in additional tankage, Tomashyevskii making 12-h flight 10 July 26 and landing with 1075 kg load (does not mean residual fuel). Overload test 1928 (possibly on *dubler-etalon*) took off at 8790 kg with 3850-kg disposable load and demonstrated (Moscow/Voronezh/Moscow) tactical radius 800 km, but this was exceptional.

Second aircraft *dubler-etalon* (doubler standard) served as prototype of TB-1 bomber, completed February 1928 at TsAGI and taken in pieces to Central Aerodrome where ready for test July. Flown by M.M. Gromov, S.A. Danilin and mechanic Kravtsov. State tests 15 August 1928 to 26 March 1929. Powered by BMW VI (7·3z) engines of 500/730 hp, windmill elec generator on each inboard LE 0,7 m from root, new nose with glazed lower part and longer forward-sloping upper cockpit for gunner. Entry via ventral hatch between Nos 1–2 spars, ladder carried on board. Crew five, including three dorsal gunners each with Lewis. Provision for 730-kg bombload, or SBR-8 bomb installation or containers of small bombs in fuselage centre section F-2, plus complete radio and camera installations. Span reduced by clipping aileron horn balances, surprising because rudder horn increased and TB-1 always notorious for exhausting control forces, not easy to perform manoeuvres solo. TE of ailerons continued to curve behind TE of wing. Third aircraft, *dubler* TB-1 (**ANT-4bis**), first built at GAZ-22, former Junkers factory at Fili, subsequently centre for large ANT aircraft. Completed July 1929, BMW VI engines in standardized installations with almost rectangular frontal radiators, crew of five (two pilots, engineer/gunner, nav/bomb, nose gunner and second dorsal gunner) often increased to six with full-time engineer, internal provision for bombload 1 t, armament three pairs DA on Scarff rings. GosNII state tests 1 August/19 October 1929 and after fitting M-17 engines on operational trials winter 1929–1930 flown by Gromov, P.M. Stefanovskii and A.B. Yumashyev. Series production under way mid-1929 and first true production machine completed as unarmed civil propaganda aircraft URSS-300 named *Strana Sovyetov* (Land of Soviets) for flight eastwards to New York. Petlyakov in charge of land sectors, R.L. Bartini for water sectors including design and manufacture of floats and conversion to/from wheels. Bartini used JuG-1 floats lengthened 0,4 m to handle

TB-1 converted to G-1 with container (military)

increased weight; this spurred TsAGI to design better float. Crew: S.A. Shestakov and F.Ye. Bolotov (pilots), B.V. Sterligov (nav), D.V. Fufayev (eng). Left Moscow 8 August but badly damaged forced landing north of Chita. Crew made way back to Moscow, organized second aircraft, same markings, and left in this 23 August 1929. Despite incessant engine trouble completed flight via Ormsk/Novosibirsk/Krasnoyarsk / Chita / Khabarovsk (5–12 Sept, floats fitted) / Petropavlovsk / Attu / Seward / Sitka (emergency landing and engine change south of Sitka)/Seattle (13–18 October wheels fitted)/San Francisco/Salt Lake City/Chicago/Detroit/New York (1 Nov). Total 21 242 km in 137 h flying (155 km/h, 96 mph).

Production TB-1 delivered 1929–August 1932, total 218 including 66 TB-1P (see later). Standard VVS bomber and used extensively for survey, airborne forces research and numerous experiments. October 1933 trials by V.I. Dudakov with six a.t.o. rockets, two under and one above inner wing on each side, total weight 469 kg (later jettisonable), take-off time reduced to 'several seconds' (from typical 15), pilot N.P. Blagin. First major parent aircraft in *Zvyeno* trials (see Vakhmistrov). In 1933–1935 military engineer A.K. Zapanovannyi and pilot I. Belozerov completed major trials programme inflight refuelling, piping fuel R-5 to TB-1, TB-1 to TB-1, and finally TB-1 to I-15 and I-16 simultaneously. P.I. Grokhovskii (which see) used TB-1 for initial VVS trials into supply dropping by parachute. From 1935–1939 major research programme of remote radio control of TB-1, initially with preset bang/bang commands and finally with true analog remote piloting, claimed world first. Much used in Arctic, wheels/skis/floats; Aviaarktika aircraft large vee windshield for flight deck and raised fairing downstream; 5 March 1934 TB-1 flown by A.V. Lyapidyevskii was first to succeed in landing on ice to rescue crew of *Chelyuskin*. February 1937 F.B. Farikh flew civil N-120 Moscow/Sverdlovsk/Irkutsk/Anadyr/Cape Wellen/Arkhangel/Moscow (with many intermediate stops) in air temp −40° to −70°C.

TB-1P standard seaplane. Conference 15 January 1926 on floats and skis for TB-1, floats postponed two years and Junkers used as expedient. October 1928 UVVS bought floats from Short Brothers, dural with steel joints and brazier (lens)-head rivets, neatly made. Copied at TsAGI as Project Zh, final production form fuller nose, modified rivet (snap-head) and joints sealed by red-lead tape. Zh float 10,66 m long, 1,15 m wide and high, vol 7,25 m³, weight with joints 299 kg, whole float gear with struts 816 kg. From 1932 series floats, over 100 pairs, most used on 66 TB-1P of which 60 were MA torpedo droppers carrying weapon under fuselage. Skis studied by 15 January 1926 meeting because those used for first ANT-4 inadequate. Five sets made by TsAGI, GAZ-8, GAZ-25 and N.R. Lobanov; TsAGI (dural) good but costly, and final choice was streamlined wooden form with cable bracing, 3700 × 900 mm, wt of pair 230 kg, 200 pairs made and used in winter by TB-1. On expiry of VVS life about 90 aircraft stripped for use as freighters by Aeroflot, designation **G-1** (*Gruzovoi* 1, cargo 1). Most tired airframes, many repairs, in some cases several hundred kg heavier than when new but removal of armament compensated. Many carried large ventral cargo container. Served nine years (1936–1945) on such duties as carrying sulphur from Ashkhabad mines. Airframe time average 4800 h when scrapped, no in-flight breakage.

DIMENSIONS Span (first) 29,6 m (rest) 28,7 m (94 ft 1$\frac{15}{16}$ in); length (first) 17,3 m, (rest) 18,00 or 18,01 m (59 ft 0$\frac{2}{3}$ in), (TB-1P) 18,9 m (62 ft 0 in); wing area (first) 121,5 m², (rest) 120,0 m² (1292 ft²).

ENGINES (1) two 450 hp Napier Lion, (2) 500/730 hp BMW VI 7·3z, (series) 680 hp BMW VI or M-17.

WEIGHTS Empty (1) 4014 kg, (series) 4520 kg (9965 lb), (*Strana S*) 4630 kg, (TB-1P) 5016 kg (11,058 lb), (G-1) 4500 kg; fuel/oil (series) 1500 + 110 kg, (*Strana S*) 2350 + 155, (TB-1P) 884; loaded (1) 6.2 t, (series) 6810 kg (15,013 lb), (*Strana S*) 7928, (TB-1P, G-1) 7,5 t (16,535 lb).

PERFORMANCE Max speed (1) 196 km/h, (series) 178 km/h (111 mph), (*Strana S*) 207 km/h, (1P) 186 km/h; cruise 156 km/h (97 mph); time to 1 km (typical) 5·5 min, (1P) 7·1, (G-1) 9·5; service ceiling (1) 4163 m, (series) 4830 m (15,850 ft), (1P) 3620, (G-1) 2850; endurance typically 6 h, LR tanks 12 h; range (series, M-17) 575 km (357 miles) with max bombload, 1000 km no bombs, (G-1) 950; time 360° turn (1) 47 s, (series) 26 s, (1P) 40 s; take-off (typical) 260 m/17 s, (1P) 660 m/26 s, (G-1) 18 s; landing (typical) 170 m/15 s/85 km/h (53 mph), (1P) 150 m/12 s/90 km/h.

ANT-5, I-4 Kolchug airframe (henceforth called dural) also spurred demand for fighter for comparison with trad structures. As part of 1925 decree calling for speedy elimination of foreign combat types, meeting 21 September 1925 decided to issue order for dural fighter to TsAGI. Assigned to P.O. Sukhoi as first major design under Tupolev supervision. Bold decision to build sesquiplane, almost parasol monoplane. Upper wing RAF profile t/c 16% max at outer extremity of parallel centre section and 12% on centreline and at tips, area 19,8 m²; small lower wing $4 m^2$. Upper wing three spars, made left/right joined on centreline, typical truss structure with ten A-profile ribs in each half-wing with 40 × 8 mm corrugated skin in strips between them held by closed rivets to spars and intermediate L-section small internal ribs. Single spar lower wing with four A-section ribs and three intermediate inner ribs each side, vee-type interplane diagonal bracing strut linking first outboard A-rib of lower wing to fifth of upper. Rest of airframe typical ANT dural structure, imported engine on welded steel-tube mounts with smooth dural cowl continuing profile of large rounded spinner and leaving cylinders exposed, with two short exhaust pipes from each cylinder. Fine-pitch (20 × 5 mm) skin on tail, unbalanced ailerons upper wings only. Two synchronized PV in top of fuselage. First ANT-5 completed July 1927, and after factory tests transferred to NII VVS September: M.M. Gromov, A.F. Anisimov, A.B. Yumashyev and I.F. Kozlov opinion 'no better fighter in world'. Production decision December 1927, designation I-4 (though I-3 not then built). I-4 *dubler* flown with more powerful Jupiter VI August 1928. First production I-4 completed 15 October 1928; heavier, and poorer performance, but still considered competitive. Production slowly built up but 242 built in one year (1932) at GAZ-22 and total at termination January 1934 was 369, not including two prototypes. Numerous modifications. From start of production, larger vertical tail with horn-balanced rudder, larger square-tipped horizontal tail, helmeted cowls on engine with front exhaust collector ring inside crankcase fairing, more pointed spinner, wire-spoked wheels left unskinned and improved tank/gun arrangement. **I-4Z** (*Zvyeno*, see Vakhmistrov) conversion of three 1930 aircraft with very small (0,5 m each side) lower wings and attachment points on main-gear axle (left/right) and on ventral centreline under cockpit. Flown from TB-1 and TB-3 with both wheel and ski gear. I-4 with four guns, two in upper wing, tested on ground only. Many fitted with four 50-kg bomb racks. **I-4bis** major rebuild completed mid-1931 (at least two aircraft). Lower wing removed completely, struts attached to fuselage, upper wing rebuilt with pilot-controlled slats over outer 44·5% span, radically different engine installation with combination of long helmets with Townend ring, pointed spinner and Bristol type front exhaust ring. Faster, better stability but poorer manoeuvrability; and decision to make future slats automatic. **I-4P** flown with AGOS floats August 1931; no attempt at test programme because seaplane fighter thought useless. December 1931 one I-4 tested GDL/Kurchyevskii DRP and APK in 76-mm calibre; one gun in each wing 1 m in from strut rib and thus well beyond propeller disc, later mounted under outer wing midway between strut rib and tip. One cannon exploded during ground testing, but I-4 (no subdesignation known) important research platform for these guns. Another I-4 used 1935 for rocket a.t.o. trials, at first with two 5-kg gunpowder motors each giving 250-kg for 2 s, and finally with triple unit each side of fuselage at TE of lower wing giving 500 kg (1000 kg for aircraft) for 2,5 s; each motor 110 mm diam by 600 mm long. I-4 remained in VVS service in fighter regts 1928–1937, remarkable record.

DIMENSIONS Span 11,4 m (37 ft 4¾ in), (lower wing 5,7 m); length 7,28 m (23 ft 10⅔ in); wing

ANT-5 prototype

I-4bis

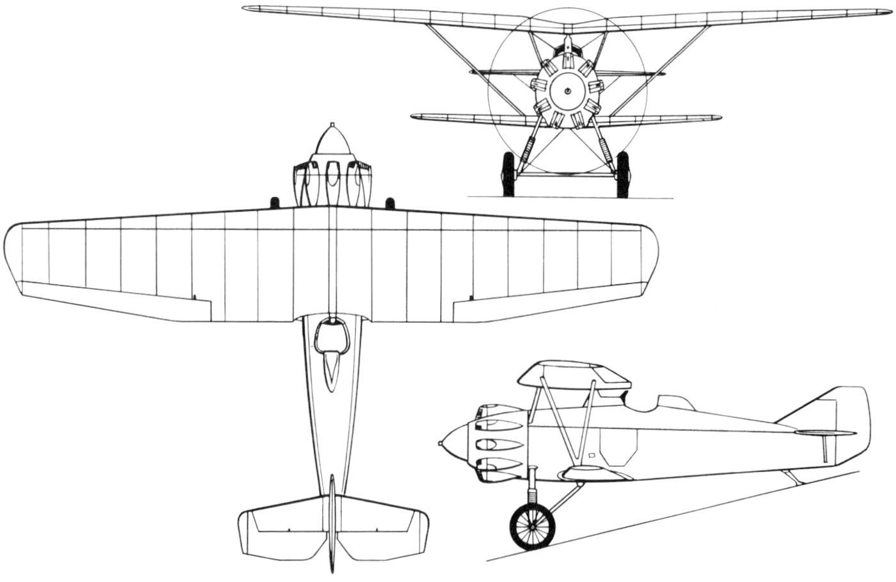

ANT-5, production I-4

ANT-6 prototype, probably December 1930

area 23,8 m² (256 ft²), (bis) 19,8 m².
ENGINE One Bristol Jupiter, (1) 420 hp GR9B (Jupiter IV, French-built), (2) 480 hp Jupiter VI, (series) 480 hp M-22.
WEIGHTS Empty (1) 921 kg, (series) 978 kg (2156 lb), (bis) 973 kg; fuel/oil 236 + 25 kg; loaded (1) 1343 kg, (series) 1430 kg (3153 lb), (bis) 1385 kg.
PERFORMANCE Max speed (1) 246 km/h at SL, 250 at 3,5 km, (series) 220 at SL, 231 (144 mph) at 5 km, (bis) 268 at SL (167 mph); climb to 1 km (typical) 1·8 min; service ceiling (1) 8,2 km, (series) 7 km (23,000 ft), (bis) 7 km; range 840 km (522 miles); time 360° turn (1) 11 s, (series) 13 s; take-off (series) 90 m/7 s; landing 210 m/19 s/ 95 km/h.

ANT-6, TB-3, G-2 This heavy bomber was first Soviet aircraft to be ahead of rest of world, and one of greatest achievements in aviation history. Though only direct extrapolation of ANT-4, it was not only largest landplane in world but established configuration universal for large aircraft in Second World War and to end of piston era, and also provided foundation for even larger ANT successors. Unlike other giants of day (Inflexible, Do X) design was sensibly planned to meet operational requirement and was highly competitive aerodynamically, structurally and in detail engineering. Sustained immense production programme which not only for first time demonstrated large national GAZ capability but also national ability to update sound basic design by sustained effort over long period. It furnished the Soviet Union with greater strategic airpower than any other nation in 1930s, but execution of VVS leaders who believed in such airpower – eg, Marshal Tukhachyevskii, Gen Alksnis – resulted in truncated programme for successor (Pe-8) and decay in VVS strategic capability at most vital time. In 1941 Allies tended to compare TB-3 with their own Second World War bombers; its design contemporaries were Curtiss B-2, Keystone B-6, HP Hinaidi and Heyford, showing true magnitude of AGOS achievement.

Genesis in 1925 discussions between Ostekhburo and TsAGI on natural next step beyond TB-1: 2000 hp heavy bomber in landplane and floatplane versions. Engineering planning under Tupolev began in May 1926 as **ANT-6**, assigned to Petlyakov brigade. VVS requirement kept changing and not settled until December 1929. By this time Tupolev had also designed large ANT-14 transport, with wing, vertical tail, fuel system and landing gear having considerable commonality. Bomber could not have ANT-14's five engines and more powerful engine sought, choice falling on Curtiss V-12 subsequently used in many other Soviet aircraft but never licensed. Long delay from 1925 partly due to lack of factory capacity which had delayed TB-1; VVS wished to operate TB-1 before accepting much larger successor. By 1929 pressure for floatplane version faded, and first detail tunnel model tested 3 December 1929, followed by successful full-scale mock-up review 21 March 1930. Prototype construction at GAZ-22 very rapid, and excellent handbuilt ANT-6 fully assembled at Central Aerodrome 31 October 1930.

Wing of Tupolev A⁰ profile as in ANT-4, t/c 20% root and 10% tip, chord 8,0 m root and 2,95 m tip. Structurally, centre section (7 m) and outer wings each made in four easily unbolted parts of 4-m span for rail transport, two of joints in line with engines. Centre section integral with F-2 fuselage section as in ANT-4, leading and trailing edges removable to give chord 4 m for easy transport. Outer panels forward leading edge and whole trailing section removable. Four spars tip to tip, each dural truss using riveted elliptical tubes up to 100 × 90 mm section with tapering booms and cone-bolts at steel joints. Truss ribs at 1,8-m spacing, 12 in each outer plane with 3-mm sheet gusset at all joints. A-section ribs to full wing profile with wing shape maintained by light stringers between spars each a trihedral girder formed from three strips with lightening holes riveted together. Skin larger corrugations than previously, 50 × 13 mm, thickness 0,3 or 0,33; 0,5 mm over upper surface of centre section (boots allowed, elsewhere soft shoes) and walkways near engines between spars 1 and 2 skinned with 0,8-mm. Leading edge each side of each engine hinged and containing folding ladder, eight in all. Fuselage scaled-up ANT-4 with modest increase in section and most of length true rectangular section with severe outlines softened by curved top decking. Structurally a scale of ANT-4 but with six of A-section frames formed into bulkheads with 1,5-m doors separating cabins for nav/bomb in glazed nose from open side-by-side cockpit and engineer and radio/gunner cabins to rear. Prototype provision for three dorsal Scarff rings as in TB-1, no guns fitted nor bombing equipment. Flight-control surfaces with 25 × 8 mm corrugated skins, elevator with rigid (push/pull) system hinged to tailplane with 14° incidence adjustment by screwjack from cockpit, rudder with cable control and multiple-bungee tension device released by pilot to offset rudder following major asymmetric loss of power, ailerons with horn balances overhanging wingtips and cable circuits with two reduction gears and tension-compensators to give positive control with reduced pilot effort. Engines driving Curtiss aluminium propellers and mounted on welded M1 mild-steel trusses with three-point attachment (bolts to welded lugs, no vibration isolation) to front spar. Underslung water radiators at 45°, shutters at duct inlet. Inflight access to engines via wing is oft-quoted error. Four 1950-lit fuel tanks each divided into three compartments of dural sheet with special pan-head rivet and washer joints sealed by shellac-coated paper gaskets (tanks lasted life of aircraft).

Unpainted prototype mounted on special wooden skis basically scaled from ANT-4 type though more streamlined. Operationally basic aircraft with seats for five, including three/four engineers. First flight by M.M. Gromov 22 December 1930, hair-raising take-off in which power rapidly lost and right wing only just missed hangar in unscheduled turn near stall. Power then came on again: transpired elevator loads had built up during run until both hands needed on wheel, while vibration caused throttle levers to close! After frantic signals by Gromov, mechanic kept holding levers. Flawless first flight in other respects, and 20 February 1931 NII VVS recommendation for series construction as **TB-3**, but with M-17 engine. First ANT-6 returned to AGOS for change of engines and rectification of various deficiencies. Elevator load removed by changed CG and surface trim, final CG at 30·2% empty and 30·8 full load. Aileron horns removed (span reduced), tailplane span increased, balancing slots on ailerons and rudders, tailskid redesigned as scale of Sukhoi's ANT-4 type. New engine installation with better cowled radiator and 3,5-m TsAGI wooden two-blade propellers. Skis replaced by large (2000 × 450 mm) wheels supplied by The Palmer Tyre Ltd; these (also used at first on ANT-14) found to be weak and TsAGI designed gear with tandem 1350 × 300 mm wire wheels in welded steel-tube bogie frame on main leg with 12 rubber-plate shock-absorbers with V-type lateral braces.

GAZ-39 ('10th anniversary of October') studied drawings from July 1930; and by late 1932 three GAZ had reached combined output claimed to be three TB-3 every two days. Production began late 1931, prior to second rollout of prototype brought up to production standard on 4 January 1932. Flown A.B. Yumashyev and leading engineer I.P. Petrov and pronounced ready for service duty. In addition to listed improvements fitted with armament. External racks of girder type under centre section and fuselage for 2-t (4410 lb) bombload in Der-9, 13, 15 or 16 containers, Sbr-9 electromechanical release gear (weight with racks 437 kg) and 349 kg other military gear. Tur-6 (Scarff-derived) ring mount in nose with twin DA; two Tur-5 rolling-type rings at diag-opposite corners of large cockpit aft of wings each with twin DA; two B-6 turrets extended/retracted under wing near outer engines between spars 2 and 3 with handcrank traverse and hand-aimed DA. Total ammunition: 100 drums of 63 rounds. MF/HF radio with aerial wire strung between fuselage masts, tandem windmill DC generators on top of fuselage.

Modification continued even before first production aircraft complete. September 1931 imported KhMA steel in engine mount and wing joints replaced by local KhNZA, but main-gear half-axles continued to be imported. Major snag with early production TB-3 was weight escalation. Part of this due to extra combat gear, plus brackets, partitions, steps and seats not in prototype; part to plus-tolerances on all raw materials; part to rough hand-welds and poor workmanship, excessive weight of main bogies and excess wire-gauge in elec systems; part even to mass of thick and sloppily applied exterior paint. Elimination of imported steel had also required greater material mass, and various added systems could have been lighter with proper design from outset. TsAGI put major effort on reducing weight, and suggestions at GAZ level were rewarded at 100 rubles per kg saved in production. B-6 turrets were removed with second production block and main gears, elec cables, tanks, bombing system and fuselage lightened. Individual aircraft at first (October 1932) varied by 'tens or even hundreds of kg' and in some cases suffered vibration or structural cracks because of weight-reduction programme, but no inflight breakup and by mid-1933 stabilized at about 10,97 t empty without armament or detachable equipment.

Single TB-3 *Zadrayennyi* (battened down) modified 1933 with armament removed, all apertures and turrets faired, no aerials or other protrusions and long spats on bogies. Speed and thus range improved by only 4·5%, greater gain of 5·5% resulting from smooth fabric skin over wing from LE to rear spar on upper surface, tested on one aircraft 1 January/11 February 1935. **TB-3/M-17** remained in service to 1939, many later going to Aeroflot (see G-2). During 1933 painstaking small improvements cleared overload weight to 19,5 t and by refinements to carburation and ignition improved range without bombs to 3120 km. In 1934 introduction of stronger D6 and D16 to wing structure enabled tips to be extended, improving field length and ceiling. Engine-out handling improved by replacing bungee bias by rudder servo, and tail design refined in shape. Aileron gearing improved and from mid-1933 production launched of improved skis tested previous winter with fine aerodynamic shape, size 5540 × 1460 mm (tail 1000 × 450 mm) with springing by ten 16-mm bungees in front and four behind.

In 1931 discussion of M-34 engine led to prototype flying with M-34 in February 1933 and to NII trials with two series aircraft October 1933. After building about 400 TB-3/M-17F production switched to **TB-3/M-34** late 1933, 'several tens' of this model. Visually distinguished by new radiator installation in neat duct further back under wing, with integral oil cooler, and gondola for bomb-aimer. Main 1933 advance was flight of series TB-3 with M-34R with reduction gear driving 4,15-m propeller. NII tests completed 16 October 1933, approved for production February 1934. **TB-3/M-34R** introduced tail gun position, small curved cutout at base of rudder but initially without changing rear-fuselage shape and without communication with rest of crew. In production this position (twin DA) was refined and neatly faired in, intercom added and catwalk through rear fuselage. Main gears redesigned with oleo-pneumatic shock struts and hydraulic brakes on rear wheels; tailskid replaced by castoring wheel. In 1935 new main gears with single wheels 2000 × 450 mm, hydraulic brakes, often retrofitted to M-17 aircraft. Further improvements in 1935 TB-3/M/-34R included TsAGI-assisted fairings on nacelles, wing roots, fin and tailplane and fairings on main-gear legs (latter often removed). Both windmill generators made retractable. One modified aircraft set record flight 18·5 h. In 1933–1934 nine special **TB-3/M-34RD** built for overseas goodwill visits to Paris, Warsaw, Rome, Vienna and Prague. Extra tanks, refined cowlings, turrets faired over and bogie main gears with disc wheels with brakes on all four. In addition several (believed six) aircraft with single main wheels and three-blade metal propellers, demonstrating substantial performance gain. In 1935 major test programme August–October of **TB-3/AM-34RN** with startling improvement in speed at alt and in ceiling. Inner engines four-blade wooden propellers, outers two-blade. Built with tandem gear, 2-m wheels substituted. New armament with Tur-8 (single ShKAS) in nose, dorsal, ventral (new rear-firing hatch) and tail; 2-t bomb-

TB-3/M-34RD

load using containers Der-19 or -20 or KD-2, release gear Sbr-9 and Esbr-2, bombsight SPB-2, OPB-1 and KB-5.

Final production **TB-3/AM-34FRN** and FRNV, tested by Yumashyev 11 September 1936 and set national records, eg, 8116 m with 5-t load, followed later by 8980 m with no load, 6605 with 10-t load and 2700 m with 12-t. Extra tanks in outer wings, improved main gears with more powerful brakes (2-m wheels), Flettner tab on rudder, redesigned nose with enclosed turret, improved wing fairings, three-blade metal propellers, smaller radiators in improved ducts. Though immensely improved in performance and handling, basic design becoming dated and production terminated early 1937 at 818 aircraft. FRN/FRNV in last 90 except for single example, **TB-3D** (*Dieselnyi*) with Charomskii AN-1 engines, flown late 1935. To assist onset of SB (ANT-40) production, TB-3 manufacture halted autumn 1934 to spring 1935, and from 33 onwards rate of output slowed. Few early aircraft brought up to later standards, and more than 170 TB-3/M-17F converted 1939–1941 to civil G-2 standard (no G-2 built as such). More than 80 similar (often same) aircraft previously converted as bomber/transports, usually with armament removed, for glider towing, paratroop dropping and trials with heavy slung loads including light armoured vehicles. Among remarkable achievements of military G-2 were successful para-drops of Grokhovskii (which see) supply containers weighing 2,5 t, T-27 armoured car (1,7 t) and airborne assault of 1200 paratroops 170 km behind front in 1936 manoeuvres. In 1937–1938 A.N. Tyagunin flew G-2 one metre above water on several occasions as 4-t T-37 amphibious tank was set free without parachute, on final test with crew inside. Like G-1 all G-2s had over 2000 h and were tired and much-repaired but after conversion, with side and ventral doors, strong cargo floor with lashing points and complete structural audit they gave vital service throughout the Second World War. Final G-2 conversions had AM-34RN engines and at 22 t could carry over 7 t cargo.

TB-3/AM-34FRN

ANT-6A

ANT-6As

Final variants were TB-3/AM-34RN modified on production line for use by *Aviaarktika* as chief aircraft supporting first permanent Soviet bases in Arctic. Five **ANT-6A**, also called **ANT-6/M-34R**, registered N-166 and N-169/-172, modified with completely enclosed fuselage and flight deck, exhaust and combustion cabin heaters, limited (carb-air) de-icing, new nose packed with instrumentation, extra radio and navaids, quick-conversion wheel/ski main and tail gear, 14,0-m braking parachute, extensive emergency and survival eqpt and red-painted upper surfaces, assigned to Dr Otto Schmidt's expedition which finally left Central Aerodrome 21 April 1937. Much heavier than other ANT-6s, packed with cargo and up to 22 men aboard, flagship N-170 made seven abortive take-off runs in flat calm and soft snow before getting away. On 21 May M.V. Vodopyanov radioed from N-170 he had landed on ice 20 km from North Pole and set up radio beacon. This was start of air conquest of Soviet Arctic, story without parallel; N-169 was still at work in May 1941 and three *Arktika* aircraft were active in 1944. Sadly, no ANT-6 preserved.

DIMENSIONS Span (1) 40,5 m, (series M-17) 39,5 m (129 ft 7½ in), (series, 1934 on) 41,8 m

(137 ft 1⅜ in); length (1,2,3) 24,2 m, (series) 24,4 m (80 ft 0⅝ in), (1935, M-34RN on) 25,1 m (82 ft 4¼ in); wing area (1) 231 m², (1932–1933) 230 m² (2476 ft²), (1934 on) 234,5 m² (2524 ft²).
ENGINES (1) four 600 hp Curtiss V-1760 Conqueror, (2,3) 730 hp BMW VI, (1932–1934) 715 hp M-17F, (1934) 830 hp M-34 or M-34R, (1935) 970 hp AM-34RN or 900 hp FRN, (some late aircraft) 1200 hp AM-34FRNV.
WEIGHTS Empty (1) 9375 kg, (2) 10,08 t, (first series, GAZ-39) 11 207 kg (24,707 lb), (standard M-17F) 10 967 kg (24,178 lb), (M-34) 12,7 t (27,998 lb), (M-34R) 13 230 kg (29,167 lb), (G-2, M-17F) 11 179 kg, (G-2, M-34RN) 13 417 kg, (ANT-6A) 12,5 t; fuel/oil (1) 2610 kg, (1934, M-34R) 2020 + 300, (RN) 2460 + 360, (G-2, M-17F, probably same as M-17F TB-3) 1600 + 160, (ANT-6A) 7280 + 550; loaded (1) 16 042 kg, (2) 16 387 kg, (M-17F standard) 17,2 t (37,919 lb), (M-34) 18,1 t, (M-34R) 18,6 t, (RN) 18 877 kg (41,616 lb), (G-2, M-17F) 17 t, (G-2, RN) 22 t (48,500 lb), (ANT-6A) 24,05 t (53,020 lb).
PERFORMANCE Max speed (1) 226 km/h at SL, (2) 213 km/h, (TB-3, M-17F) 197 km/h at SL (122 mph), 177 at 3 km, (M-34) 207 km/h at SL (129 mph), (RN) 245 km/h at SL, 288 km/h (179 mph) at 4 km, (FRN) 300 km/h (186 mph) at 5 km, (G-2, M-17F) 198 km/h at SL, (G-2, RN) 280 km/h at 3 km, (ANT-6A) 240 km/h at SL, 275 km/h (171 mph) at 3 km; time to 1 km, (TB-3, M-17F) 9·2 min, (M-34) 7, (R) 4·1, (G-2, M-17F) 24·0, (G-2, RN) 8·0, (ANT-6A) 8·8; service ceiling (1) 5,1 km, (TB-3, M-17F) 3,8 km (12,470 ft), (R) 4,5 km, (RN) 7740 m (25,400 ft); (FRN) 8 km (26,250 ft), (G-2, M-17F) 2,2 km (7200 ft); range (M-17F) 1350 km (840 miles), (M-34, typical) 1000 km (620 miles), (ANT-6A) 2500 km (1550 miles); time 360° circle (1) 54 s, (TB-3, typical) 36–40 s; take-off (1) 200 m/18 s, (M-17F) 300 m/28 s, (RN) 400 m/26 s, (G-2) often 625 m/40 s; landing (1) 150 m/13 s/106 km/h, (M-17F) 330 m/110 km/h; (M-34) 270–330 m/22 s/122–129 km/h (80 mph); (ANT-6A) over 400 m/159 km/h.

ANT-7 (R-6 transferred to Aviaarktika)

ANT-7, R-6, PS-7 TsAGI and GosNII proliferated dural twin-engined aircraft in second half of 1920s, as far as possible using common or broadly similar parts. Discussion in 1924 had ranged over several possibilities, one being modern monoplane with two 500 hp engines expected to be as fast as fighter with one similar engine. Such machine seen as long-range escort, 'cruiser' fighter (able to penetrate deep into hostile airspace by itself), bomber, recon aircraft and torpedo carrier. Tupolev made proposal summer 1925 for scaled-down TB-1 using same engines. Design started October 1926 at low priority; VVS finally issued requirement for 'air fighting aircraft' 8 January 1928. AGOS wished engines to be Hispano-Suiza V-12 or Jupiter, but design conference early 1928 agreed BMW VI (licensed as M-17) and that, because of TB-1 experience, only one prototype need be built and that production planning be implemented forthwith. Prototype ANT-7 flown by M.M. Gromov 11 September 1929.

Wing 80 m² compared with 120 for TB-1; A-section rib at end of centre section identical in both but no other common part. Centre section reduced span and rectangular in plan; outer panels t/c 18 to 14%, four spars throughout, eight A-section ribs in each panel. Ailerons constant chord, not projecting behind TE of wing and extending over entire span of outer panel. Improved low-friction control circuit, ball-bearing bell-cranks, small balance horn projecting beyond wingtip. Fuselage smaller than TB-1 and esp reduced cross-section, pure rectangle with round top decking, cockpit for two pilots side-by-side (in practice one often mechanic, ie, flight engineer, who assisted harsh manoeuvres as in TB-1 and TB-3), nose and dorsal cockpits for gunners or other crew members; unlike TB-1 not easy to crawl from one cockpit to another and in most ANT-7s impossible. Provision in prototype for fourth crew-member to use sliding turret (derived from B-6 of TB-3) in underside of centre fuselage. Simple pyramid main gears with rubber springing, no brakes but tailskid. Horizontal tail actually fractionally greater span than ANT-4 but much smaller chord; tailplane adjustable from cockpit ±5° and all tail skins finer (20 × 5) corrugations than standard 40 × 8 used elsewhere. Honeycomb water radiators cranked in and out from underside of centre section by pilot. Engines on French AM type steel tube mountings, rigid dural pipe fuel system, exhausts gathered into pipe across wing. Prototype tail modified, and in early 1930 given planned armament of twin DA in nose Tur-6, twin DA in dorsal Tur-5 and single DA in ventral 'dustbin'; up to 500 kg external bombs including 406-mm torpedo, Der-7 small-bomb containers and other options; Sbr-8 release system.

NII state tests were begun May 1930, no factory tests having been made. GAZ-22 already tooled up and production of basic multi-role recon aircraft began as R-6 mid-1930. Production aircraft had several changes, most noticeable being installation of radiators in fixed 45° inclination in duct under engine, now M-17F. Remarkably, not until final state testing of first production R-6, 5 October 1931, was it decided buffeting of tail unacceptable. Cure accepted was to rivet fixed flap at 29° angle right across centre-section TE, reducing speeds 7–8 km/h. Smooth flight ensued and R-6 production went ahead, terminating at 45th aircraft late 1932. Whole programme transferred to GAZ-31 and R-6 then built at much higher rate there with wheel, ski and Zh-type float gear. Total programme closed June 1934 at 435 in several versions. **KR-6** (*Kreiser Razvyedchik*, cruiser reconnaissance) carried no bombs and had crew two/three, with dustbin removed, wing-root fillets, considerably greater fuel (tanks in outer wing as well as centre section) air/oil oleo legs, S.S. L'vov exptl wheel brakes and Zapp flaps copied from Northrop. **MR-6**, also designated **KR-6P**, was floatplane assembled at Taganrog, with remarkably little reduction in speed despite marked increase in weight. Several basic R-6 used in research and test programmes including use as engine testbed, cooling-radiator research (eg, ducted radiators in wings, mainly by Myas-

ANT-6/AM-34FRNV (Aviaarktika *variant*)

ishchyev's team, anti-vibration flaps being then removed), glider towing, armament trials (virtually every Soviet aircraft gun and RS projectile) and mapping/survey with two or even three large cameras.

Obsolescent even at end of production run, and by 1935 transferred mainly to advanced training (until 1938) and as utility transport, often with structural modifications to allow carriage of engines and other large loads (until late 1944). From 1935 at least 220 transferred to GVF, serving in all Aeroflot directorates, with Glavsevmorput and in almost all major Arctic expeditions. Basic civil transport designated **PS-7** or **P-6** (*Passazhirskii*). Almost all were down on performance due to age and local repairs, but lightened by removal of armament; normal PS-7 was little modified, original cockpit floors being used for up to 700 kg cargo loaded through gunner cockpits. One example, **R-6 Limuzin,** rebuilt in RVZ workshop with enlarged and enclosed centre fuselage seating nine passengers, flown July 1933; crashed (no fault of aircraft) 5 September 1933 on Moscow–Crimea flight killing P.I. Baranov, A.Z. Goltsman and others. Many civil machines were seaplanes, designation **MP-6,** with Zh-type floats, 22–31 km/h slower than military seaplanes and at first riddled with snags, three crashing on test. P.G. Golovin surveyed North Pole in R-6 prior to landing of 1937 expedition led by I.D. Papanin (subsequently rescued nine months later, 1560 km away on ice-floe, by ship-based U-2).

DIMENSIONS Span 23,2 m (76 ft 1$\frac{1}{3}$ in); length (1) 14,7 m, (R-6 and most land variants) 15,06 m (49 ft 4$\frac{15}{16}$ in), (seaplanes) 15,71 m (51 ft 6$\frac{1}{2}$ in); wing area 80,0 m² (861 ft²).

ENGINES (prototype and *Limuzin*) two 730 hp BMW VI, (R-6) 715hp M-17F, (KR and civil) 680hp M-17.

WEIGHTS Empty (prototype) 3790 kg, (R-6) 3856 kg (8500 lb), (MR) 4640 kg (10,229 lb), (KR) 3870 kg (8532 lb), (PS) 3520 kg (7760 lb), (MP) 4457 kg (9826 lb); fuel/oil (R) 1385 kg, (*Limuzin*) 1300 + 120, (KR) 2200 + 200; loaded (prototype) 5173 kg, (R) 6472 kg (14,268 lb), (MR) 7,5 t (16,535 lb), (KR) 5992 kg (13,209 lb), (PS) 6250 kg (13,779 lb), (MP) 6750 kg (14,881 lb).

PERFORMANCE Max speed (prototype) 222 km/h at SL, (R) 230 km/h (143 mph) at SL, 216 at 3 km, (*Limuzin*) 248 at SL, (MR) 234 at SL, (KR) 226 at SL, (MP) 211 at SL; climb to 2 km (prototype) 7·1 min, (KR) 13·0, (MP) 34; service ceiling (R) 5620 m (18,440 ft), (MR) 3850, (KR) 5120, (MP) 3360; range (pro) 1780 km, (R) 800 km (500 miles), (MR) 492 km, (KR) 1480 km, (MP) 700km; take-off (R) 160 m/11 s, (MR) 600 m/35 s; landing (R) 250 m/24 s/110 km/h.

ANT-8, MDR-2 This flying boat was yet another spin-off all-metal twin decided upon in 1925 but AGOS design staff could not tackle everything at once and landplanes had priority. Eventually design went ahead, under direction of one of Pogosskii brothers (Ivan Ivanovich, head of KOSOS marine aircraft brigade). Wing based on that of ANT-7 and almost identical to ANT-9; horizontal tail almost identical to ANT-7 (not -9). Mock-up review 26 July 1930; prototype completed 1 December 1930 and flown 30 January 1931.

Tupolev regarded ANT-8 as research tool; in-house designation not **MDR-2** (marine long-range recon) but **MER** (marine exptl recon). AGOS had little experience of marine aircraft and adopted ultra-conservative approach to prove hull design with minimal risk. Hull all-dural, deep and fairly narrow. Strong planing bottom and rigid upper hull with 27 main and 15 intermediate frames, heavy upper longerons, double chine stringers, twin keel from 3-mm sheet with 25 transverse watertight bulkheads 3 or 4-mm sheet. Planing bottom with central keel and two parallel auxiliary keels as pioneered by German Romar, finally curving down at chines; heavily riveted front step of 2,5-mm plate, second step 2,5-m aft of wing TE and planing bottom continued to tail. Hull mass 1395 kg, 42 kg/m³ (25 being a common value). Stabilizing floats close to hull and took part of weight at rest; deep draft and nose-up angle on paired steel-tube N-struts with lateral brace. Exceptionally seaworthy, could safely operate in higher waves than any known contemporary aircraft. Engines on high paired N-struts with V lateral brace, pusher installation chosen to keep propellers remote from waves. Tanks in centre section, frontal radiators as TB-1 and same propellers. Wing similar to ANT-7 but shorter ailerons; same horizontal tail but braced by two (not parallel) struts each side without variable incidence near top of new-design vertical tail. Skins 40 × 8 mm corrugations on wing, 20 × 5 mm on tail. Floats smooth skin, and hull smooth but stiffened by four semicircular-section (40-mm rad) external stringers each side. Enclosed cockpit two pilots; Tur-6 bow cockpit with twin DA, Tur-5 retractable aft of wing with twin DA, bombs under wing roots, two 250 kg on DER-13 gear or four FAB-100 on DER-7.

Factory tests completed inside a week in 3 h 47 min flying. NII testing 15 February to 17 March 1931 by S.T. Rybalchuk; generally satisfactory but required enlarged floats and rudder. Further NII tests 8 October to 14 November 1931 by Gromov, Bukholts and N.G. Kastanayev; empty weight had grown and despite increase in gross weight 6665 to 6920 kg disposable

MP-6

ANT-9 prototype at Rome

load 2360 fell short of design figure 2,6 t. Take-off and landing judged fast (by ancient flying-boat standards) and general conclusion was MDR-2 would soon be obsolete. Newer types were in prospect (MDR-3) and so MDR-2 was rejected; this proved major error, as it was sound and seaworthy and could have served long periods while successors were failures. **MRT-1** was proposal for civil regional transport, turned down for same reason of supposed obsolescence plus prospect of ANT-11.

DIMENSIONS Span 23,7 m (77 ft 9 in); length 17,03 m (55 ft 10½ in); wing area 84 m² (904 ft²).

ENGINES Two 680 hp BMW VI.

WEIGHTS Empty 4560 kg (10,053 lb); fuel/oil 1100 + 90 kg; loaded 6920 kg (15,256 lb).

PERFORMANCE Max speed 203 km/h (126 mph) at SL; cruise 166 km/h (103 mph); time to 1 km, 7 min; service ceiling 3350 m (11,000 ft); range 1062 km (660 miles); endurance 5 h; time 360° turn, 34 s; take-off 29 s; landing 15 s/115 km/h.

ANT-9, PS-9 Though Kalinin provided indigenous light transports, lack of Soviet airliner for trunk routes caused question to be raised mid-1927, and Tupolev called to Kremlin discussion 8 October 1927. Order from GVF for large passenger aircraft, initially for Deruluft international services, placed December 1927. Mock-up review October 1928, prototype begun forthwith and ANT-9 planned for major production in first Five-Year Plan. Prototype URSS-309 *Krylya Sovyetov* (Soviet Wings) rushed to completion in time for May Day 1929; parts assembled in Red Square 28 April. First flight believed 7 May; NII GVF trials from late May. Gromov, Mikheyev and Spirin flew Moscow/Odessa/Sevastopol/Odessa/Kiev/Moscow 6–12 June. Gromov with eight passengers then flew Moscow/Travemünde/Berlin/Paris/Rome/Marseilles/London/Paris/Berlin/Warsaw/Moscow 9037 km in 53 h between 10 July and 8 August 1929. Basic aircraft satisfactory, but production had to use engine other than imported Titan, and M-26 selected.

Wing based on ANT-7, outer panels identical but centre-section 0,25-m greater span (one rib) on each side. Fuselage and tail new but typical AGOS dural construction. Main cabin of constant rectangular section with five strong built-up frames forming vert boundaries to four Celluloid windows each side. Nine passenger seats (5 right, 4 left), door aft on left side. Enclosed cockpit for two pilots ahead of high wing, access up two steps through cabin front bulkhead. Wing reduced cabin height but interior described as roomy. Bulkheads and frames aft of cabin cross-braced. Main gears with vertical shock struts pin-jointed to lower boom of front spar, multiple rubber shock-absorbers, V lateral braces to fuselage of streamline-section dural sheet. Wire wheels 1100 × 250 mm or ANT-7 type skis. Horizontal tail much broader chord than ANT-8 or -7, tailplane derived from TB-1 but reduced span, ±5° incidence, large horns on all control surfaces. Five-cylinder Bristol (GR-built) radials completely uncowled, two-blade wooden propellers with spinners, 972 lit fuel in two centre-section tanks.

Prototype pleasant to fly, good ratio payload to empty weight, stable hands-off, could maintain 1200 m with nose engine shut down, 200 m with either wing engine shut down. Testing completed September 30. To avoid imported engine M-26 selected for production, uncowled except for cylinder baffles and driving Soviet aluminium AMTs two-blade propellers. Engine badly down on power and unreliable, and because of varied faults production of engine halted soon after first production ANT-9 flew early 1931. Series aircraft equipped with radio, nav lights, landing light recessed inside left LE, windmill generator above fuselage. Four wing tanks instead of two. Usually toilet and small baggage hold at rear of cabin. Mid-1931 decision to fit imported US engine with Townend-ring cowl and ground-adjustable Hamilton three-blade dural propeller, slightly reduced fuel, major alteration to tail area esp increased height of rudder, retrofitted on most aircraft already built. About 12 aircraft built with three engines, all eventually receiving US engine. For main series no Russian engine appeared suitable, and decision was major redesign to convert to twin, with M-17 engine in installation almost identical to ANT-7. This version designated PS-9 in GVF service (AGOS designation believed ANT-9bis), economics penalized by heavier re-stressed centre section, most of cut in disposable load being reduced fuel though range claimed unaltered. This was main production version, about 70 of this type delivered 1932–1933 (thus, about 83 in all). Three-engined ANT-9 saw small-scale use, two supplied 1933 to Deruluft having modest increase in cruising speed from

PS-9

Military ANT-9 (possibly designated G-3)

fabric covering over corrugated wing. Military bomber/transport with two gun turrets and six-stretcher ambulance versions not developed, but several (believed all three-engined) served with VVS as staff transports and in paratroop exercises. Basic PS-9 established high reputation. One paid for by *Krokodil* (satirical magazine) for *Maksim Gorkii* propaganda squadron had spatted main wheels with painted claws and long plywood nose with painted crocodile teeth, mods designed by V.B. Shavrov. Another, L-183, logged 5205 h by 1942, outstanding for 1930 transport. At least one survived until 1945.

DIMENSIONS Span (prototype, M-26) 23,71 m, (series) 23,8 m (78 ft 10 in); length (prototype, M-26) 17,00 m, (J6) 16,65 m (54 ft 7½ in), (PS-9) 17,01 m (55 ft 9¾ in) over pitot; wing area 84,0 m² (904 ft²).

ENGINES (prototype) three 230hp GR Titan, (first series) three 300 hp (actually about 240) M-26, refitted with 300 hp Wright J6 Whirlwind; (PS-9) two 680 hp M-17.

WEIGHTS Empty (prototype) 3353 kg, (M-26) 3950, (J6) 3680 (8113 lb), (PS-9) 4400 (9700 lb); fuel/oil (prototype) 700 kg, (M-26) 1130, (J6) 920 + 80, (PS) 720 + 70; loaded (prototype) 5043 kg, (M-26) 6 t, (J6) 5690 (12,544 lb), (PS) 6,2 t (13,668 lb).

PERFORMANCE Max speed (prototype) 209 km/h, (M-26) 185, (J6) 205 (127 mph), (PS) 215 (134 mph); cruise (J6) 170 (105·6 mph), (PS) 180 (112 mph); time to 1 km, (J6) 8·5 min, (PS) 6; service ceiling (prototype) 3810 m, (M) 3400, (J) 4500 (14,760 ft), (PS) 5100 (16,730 ft); range (prototype, M) 1000 km, (J, PS) 700 (435 miles); take-off (J) 170 m/16 s; landing (J) 150 m/18 s/93 km/h.

ANT-10, R-7 Original R-3 having failed to supplant R-1 as mass-produced VVS recon aircraft, emergence of R-5 triggered AGOS to design rival using dural construction. ANT-10 based on ANT-3 but fuselage of improved form with smaller frontal area, much larger wings (upper wing scaled up from ANT-5) with large gap between fuselage and upper wing, fuel tanks in upper wing (583 lit, much more than standard R-3), newer and more powerful engine (installation almost identical to TB-1 except for exhaust pipes on each side of fuselage), raised observer seat for better all-round view, nav lights and radio with battery charged by windmill generator on upper centre-section, two synchronized PV-1 (only one in R-3) and bomb load (believed 500 kg) under fuselage. Project launched July 1928, construction decision with VVS designation R-7 on 28 March 1929, aircraft on factory test 30 January 1930. Satisfactory but performance surprisingly poor considering slightly smaller and lighter than R-5. NII tests March, returned to AGOS for installation of military equipment and rectification of faults. NII-tested again, late 1930, but decided no advantage over R-5.

DIMENSIONS Span 15;2 m (49 ft 10½ in); length 10,9 m (35 ft 9⅛ in); wing area 49,0 m² (527 ft²).

ENGINE One 680 hp BMW VI.

WEIGHTS Empty 1720 kg (3792 lb); fuel/oil 450 kg; loaded 2920 kg (6437 lb).

PERFORMANCE Max speed 235 km/h (146 mph) at SL; cruise 184 km/h (114 mph); time to 1 km 3·1 min; service ceiling 5560 m (18,240 ft); range 1100 km (685 miles); endurance 5 h; time 360° turn, 25 s; take-off 150 m/10 s; landing 300 m/22 s/90 km/h.

ANT-11 Tupolev held discussion with GVF and Glavsevmorput early 1929 on requirement for large civil transport flying boat, much more capable than ANT-8; same size aircraft also required for military MK (see ANT-22). ANT-11 project launched with scaled-up hull with same skin (smooth but with external bead stiffeners) and four M-17F or M-22 on pylons above wing (believed four separate tractor nacelles). Never built, but calculations and hull design greatly assisted ANT-22.

ANT-12, I-5 As part of first Five-Year Plan Tupolev was assigned task of designing new single-seat fighter by Aviatrust, acting as agency of government. Programme launched at meeting 22 June 1928, stipulated engine being geared Jupiter VI for which Aviatrust was completing licence-negotiation. Conventional biplane, not all-dural but mixed construction, corrugated-skin wings but wood semi-monocoque fuselage, two synch PV. Service designation I-5, same timing as rival Polikarpov (later TsKB) I-6. Prototype timed to fly September 1929, but AGOS overloaded with all-dural large aircraft and received permission to drop ANT-12; service designation transferred to new design VT-11 by Polikarpov.

ANT-13, I-8 Another of projects overloading AGOS in late 1920s was this small biplane fighter, conceived as exercise in using new steels studied by Tupolev on 1928 visit to Krupps and other German companies. Three Ni-Cr stainless and two Cr-Mo (chrome/molybdenum) high-strength steels promising, and Tupolev had specimens in suitcase on return. TsAGI and VIAM tests supported calculations for ANT-13 using Cr-Mo steel for welded truss fuselage, stainless for small and simple spars of wings, rest being dural with fabric covering. Extremely small, no bracing wires, aiming at very high performance with imported Curtiss engine. Received service designation I-8 and popularly called *Zhokei* (Jockey) after contemporary Vickers fighter. CG at 22–23%, all flight controls by cable, direct-drive engine to metal propeller, spatted wheels, two synch PV-1. In early 1939 AGOS management decided no possibility of continuing without dropping other programmes; but on initiative of engineer V.M. Rodionov decision privately to develop further and complete prototype; every worker donated 70 h and sponsorship freely given by UVVS in competition with OSS. Need formally affirmed 30 December 1929, mock-up review 30 January 1930, design acceptance 6 April 1930 and completed October, flown Gromov 28 October. First time 300 km/h exceeded in Soviet Union, but decision not to license engine and existence of I-5 as major programme influenced adverse production decision—though handling unquestionably good.

DIMENSIONS Span 9,0 m (29 ft 6⅓ in); length, not recorded; wing area about 20 m² (215 ft²).

ENGINE One 700 hp Curtiss Conqueror V-1570.

WEIGHTS Empty 960 kg (2116 lb); loaded 1424 kg (3139 lb).

PERFORMANCE Max speed 303 km/h at SL, 310 (193 mph) at 3 km; time to 1 km, 1·0 min, to 5 km 6 min; service ceiling 8,5 km (27,890 ft); range 440 km (273 miles), 1·8 h; landing speed 118 km/h (73 mph).

ANT-14 This large passenger airliner was result of Tupolev's enthusiasm, coupled with fact AGOS had capability to build it, rather than having place in Five-Year Plan or order from GVF. Funding difficult to establish, but in fact costs remarkably low because major sections of wing, vertical tail and landing gear already designed for ANT-6. Completely new fuselage, most capacious of any landplane of era, usual all-dural structure with skin mainly 40 × 8 mm corrugated, detail structure same as ANT-9 but much larger square cross-section (3,2 × 3,2 m externally) seating passengers 2 × 2 instead of 1 × 1; truss frames, cross-braced behind cabin, seven windows each side, door aft on left. Wing as ANT-6 except centre-section 0,8-m greater span (wider fuselage) and straight taper on TE root to mid-span each aileron. No horn balances on ailerons. Four tanks in wing and one in nose, total capacity smaller than any ANT-6 except

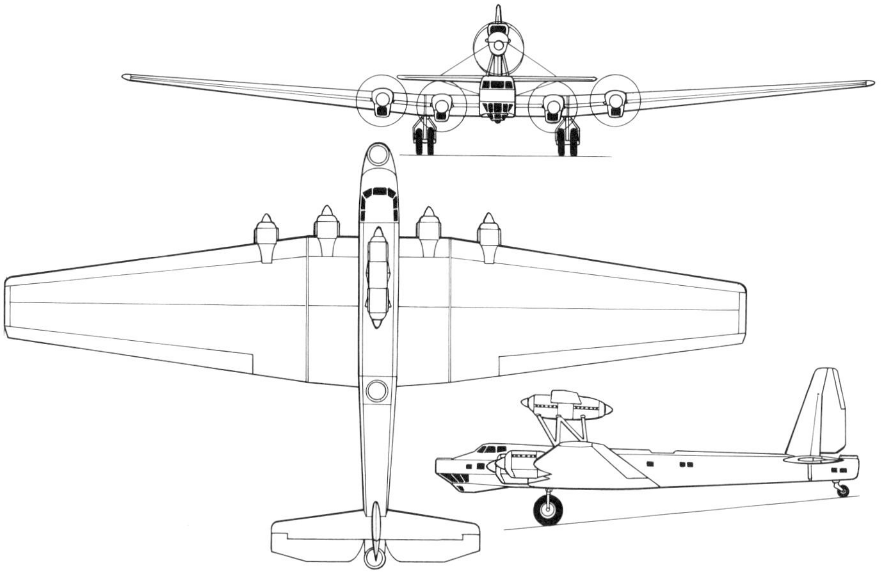
ANT-16, TB-4

M-17F G-2. Imported engines (later licensed), direct drive 3,2-m two-blade wooden propellers, Bristol front exhaust collector ring. Nose engine uncowled, wing engines with unusual Townend rings with helmets. Two oil coolers in leading edge 1 m away on each side of each engine, four folding ladders in hinged LE sections between engines also serving as maintenance platforms. One of very few five-engined aircraft. Completed with large but thin (2000 × 450 mm) main wheels, with primitive brakes, all by Palmer Tyre, plus tailskid on steel-tube frame off aft face of stern frame under cut-away rudder. Bracing of horizontal tail (much smaller than ANT-6) arranged to allow ±5° variable incidence. At last moment AGOS built large dorsal observation blister above fuselage between wing spars 2 and 3; eight rows of 2 × 2 passenger seats.

Aircraft initially registered L1001, built rapidly and flown by Gromov 14 August 1931. Virtually nothing wrong apart from structural failure of main wheels, quickly replaced by TB-3 type locally designed tandem bogies with steel-tube frames carrying 1350 × 300 mm wheels. Extra row of seats installed, giving 36 passengers and crew of five (at least four were flight crew ahead of cabin). No quarrel with aircraft except far too large for any Aeroflot route. Languished for over a year, doing little flying but having various modifications including removal of ring cowls from wing engines, improved exhaust system fitted, dural ground-adjustable propellers, tailwheel and elec system. In 1932 sponsored by newspaper *Pravda* and named thus; assigned to *Maksim Gorkii* propaganda squadron as flagship and intensively used in joyrides over Moscow as well as fund-raising sorties, twice to Kharkov and once to Leningrad, to collect money for ANT-20. Retired 1941 after carrying 40,000 passengers (then record) without accident. Fuselage served during Second World War as cinema in Moscow Central Park of Culture.

DIMENSIONS Span 40,4 m (132 ft 6½ in); length 26 485 m (86 ft 10¾ in); wing area 240 m² (2583 ft²).

ENGINES Five 480 hp Gnome-Rhône GR9-AKX (Jupiter license).

WEIGHTS Empty (as built) 10 828 kg (23,871 lb); fuel/oil 1990 + 166 kg; loaded 17 530 kg (38,646 lb).

PERFORMANCE Max speed 236 km/h (147 mph) at SL; cruise 195 km/h (121 mph); time to 1 km, 4·9 min; service ceiling 4220 m (13,850 ft); range 900 km (560 miles) (Shavrov 150 km is error); take-off 250 m/18 s; landing 220 m/14 s/105 km/h.

ANT-15 Unbuilt design for all-dural two-seat biplane fighter with M-34 engine, intended to have smooth wing skins.

ANT-16, TB-4 This enormous bomber was seemingly natural successor to TB-3, launched by Tupolev as AGOS project March 1930 with approval but no actual order from VVS. Subsequently Tupolev did obtain financial cover for single prototype, service designation TB-4, but no intention of order for bomber use until experience gained with TB-3. Same layout but scaled up 35% linear and almost 100% area and weight. Engine power, however, only 50% greater than TB-3/M-34 and even in design stage Tupolev had agonizing second thoughts over two tandem pairs of extra engines, one each side, instead of one pair on centreline. Eventually Tupolev chose to concentrate on load-carrying rather than performance. Thus wing built with 10,5-m centre section with t/c 16·6% root and 17·5% at steel structural joint to 21,75-m outer panel, where t/c tapered to 14% approx at tip. Except for direct short exhaust pipes from each cyl, engine installations similar to original M-17 with slanting water radiators directly below, exit under wing LE, two-blade wooden propellers. Extra pair on high steel/dural struts above frames 2 and 4 of F-2 fuselage section, water circuits between engines cooled by two radiators in dorsal box. Usual oval-section riveted-aluminium fuel tanks in wings, hinged LE sections with access ladders and thick (0,8-mm) sheet walkways above wing near engines; in addition novel feature of inflight access via crawlway between LE and front spar, and access via steps inside large pylon fairing to tandem centreline engines also considered but not pursued because of difficulty of stressing cowlings for opening. Fuselage equipped for ten of crew of 12, others being in underwing turrets (not fitted to prototype). Improved nose with large glazed underside and same ventral gondola for bomb-aimer as late models of TB-3. Large pilot cockpit with open roof but all-round windshield with glass windows. Main structure scaled from TB-3 but with five half-round external stiffening beads each side as introduced in ANT-8. Largest new design task was internal bomb bay, by far biggest ever attempted, housing 4 t of max 10 t (standard overloads 40 FAB-250 or 20 FAB-500). Bay comprised front section, by K.P. Svneshnikov's AGOS brigade and rear section by V.M. Myasishchyev's. Each bay 1,8-m wide and high and 2,5-m long, with powered doors, front between spars 1–2 and rear between spars 2–3, with sloping bracing walls and total five strong transverse frames. Rest of bombload (if any) hung on external beams under centre section and inboard outer wings. No details of defensive armament beyond total two hand-aimed 20-mm and ten DA. Cannon possibly in nose and tail positions and most 7,62-mm in pairs. Slender ailerons occupying most of trailing edge of outer panels, no horns; small horns on elevators, not projecting beyond tailplane (latter single strut on underside, not known if var-inc); rudder without balance but servo on TE. Large main gears each with twin Soviet-built 2000 ×

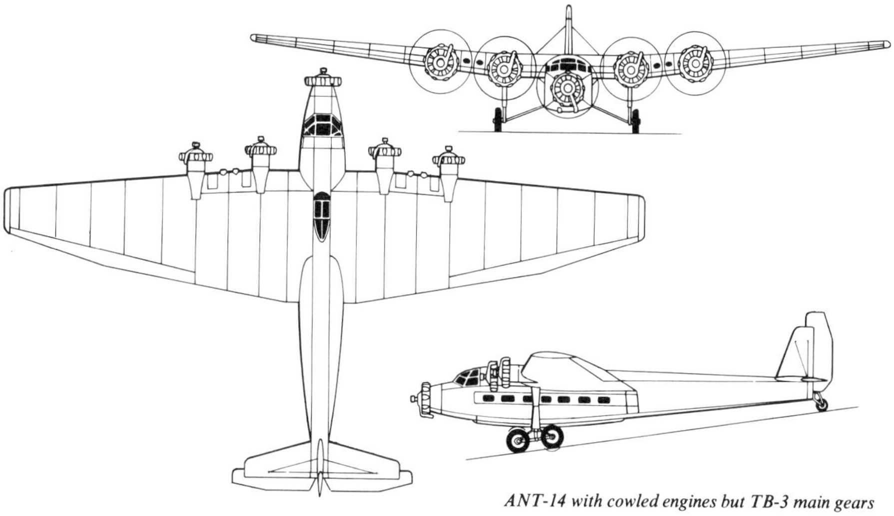
ANT-14 with cowled engines but TB-3 main gears

450 mm wheels side-by-side in welded KhMA tube frame incorporating large fairings over rubber-disc shock-absorbers, track 10,645 m. Castoring tailwheel.

First flight M.M. Gromov 3 July 1933. Unimpressive performance, and control forces, especially aileron, so high that only just possible with both pilots exerting full effort. Ailerons divided inner/outer to avoid pivots jamming and surface balance greatly increased; on second flight almost no effort needed and lack of 'feel'. On third flight aircraft reasonable to fly but performance still disappointing. Gromov suggested propellers blowing against wing 2-m thick were ineffective; Tupolev re-studied efficiency of tandem upper propellers. TB-4 subjected to full test programme by NII pilots Stefanovskii, Ryazanov, Nyukhtikov, but take-off, climb, altitude and manoeuvrability unacceptable. At normal gross could not equal 1934 TB-3 for range/bombload. Best achieved (at 37 t) was 8 t (17,637 lb) bombload over 940 km. Tupolev proposed fitting M-35 engines, never carried out. This aircraft was black mark in wasting money, but possibly essential stepping stone towards ANT-20. Largest landplane of day, never announced publicly; used in film *Bolshoi Krylya* (Big Wings) 1935 in which simulated crash, scrapped 1936.

DIMENSIONS Span 54,0 m (177 ft 2 in); length 32,0 m (105 ft 0 in); wing area 422 m² (4542 ft²).
ENGINES Six 830 hp M-34 (not M-34R as often reported).
WEIGHTS Empty 21,4 t (47,178 lb); fuel/oil 4950 kg; loaded 33,28 t (73,369 lb), (overload) 37 t (81,570 lb).
PERFORMANCE Max speed 200 km/h (124 mph) at SL, 188 (117) at 5 km; cruise 159 km/h (99 mph); time to 1 km, 12·4 min; service ceiling 2750 m (9000 ft) at normal gross; range 1000 km (620 miles); range at 37 t with 2 t bombs, 2000 km (1240 miles); take-off 800 m/36 s; landing 400 m/105 km/h.

ANT-17, TShB Another of casualties of need to concentrate on one or two vital large aircraft programmes, (especially TB-3), this armoured *Shturmovik* was on drawing board 1930 and construction of at least one prototype started. Subject of direct VVS order, and cast in same mould as French *multiplaces de combat* (multi-seat fighters) of same era but with important addition of extensive armour and relatively heavy bombload. All-metal sesquiplane, believed corrugated dural, with some kinship in wings to ANT-5 and in tail to AGOS large aircraft. Two water-cooled engines mounted direct on lower wing in streamlined nacelles, honeycomb matrix radiators extended on sliding mounts under engines, long exhaust pipes, two-blade wooden propellers. Rather bluff fuselage filling space between wings housing pilot in open cockpit ahead of upper leading edge, front gunner with twin DA, rear gunner/radio with twin DA and probably fourth crew-member to navigate and load large guns. DPK and other large recoilless cannon rejected in favour of two conventional guns of 37 or 45-mm calibre in fuselage firing obliquely down below nose, backed up by reported four fixed (presumably inclined) machine guns. Bombload up to 600 kg, believed all external. Exceptional armour protection of engines and crew, total mass 1 t of which 300 kg to be stressed as part of airframe. Project dropped winter 1931–1932. All data except engines are estimates.

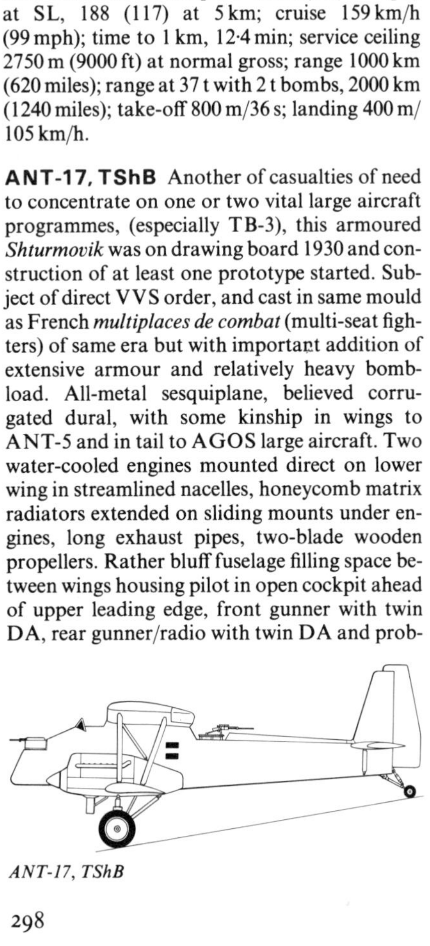

ANT-17, TShB

ANT-20 with R-5 escort

DIMENSIONS Span 18,5 m; length 11,7 m; wing area 57 m².
ENGINES Two 830 hp M-34F.
WEIGHTS Empty 3600 kg; loaded 5700 kg.
PERFORMANCE Max speed 255 km/h (158 mph).

ANT-18 Not one drawing or model appears to survive of this even larger armoured *Shturmovik*, parallel project to ANT-17, which was more powerful derivative of ANT-7 monoplane. Fuselage closely akin to ANT-17 and same crew, but different armament (DPK + 4 PV firing ahead, two pairs movable DA, 1-t bombs) and armour; and same engine installations but on large monoplane wing almost same as ANT-7. Active project 1930 but prototype construction not believed started and no service designation known. Data are estimates.

DIMENSIONS Span 23,2 m; length 13,0 m; wing area 80,0 m².
ENGINES Two 830 hp M-34F.
WEIGHTS Empty 4400 kg; loaded 7 t.
PERFORMANCE Max speed 275 km/h (171 mph).

ANT-19 Unknown.

ANT-20, MG Initials are those of Maksim Gorkii, famed Soviet writer, whose career began 25 September 1892, date celebrated annually in Soviet Union. For 1932—40th anniversary—president of Yurgaz (M.Ye. Koltsov) launched nationwide appeal for funds to build colossal aircraft to serve as flagship of newly formed *Maksim Gorkii Agiteskadril* (propaganda squadron). Gigantic project started, up to 6 million rubles (then £2m, US$8m) raised, and formidable 'technical Soviet' formed with representatives from some 100 institutions to assist design. Despite this Tupolev, inevitably chosen as chief designer, still managed to accomplish the task—and quickly. AGOS assigned formal contract July 1933, but by that time design already almost complete and manufacture of details in hand. In mid-31 AGOS had drawn passenger version of ANT-16 with four AM-35R, extended span and various refinements and given bureau number ANT-20. This formed basis for MG, number being retained, though in absence of AM-35R two extra wing engines added. Though direct extrapolation of known structure, ANT-20 was fantastic technical achievement, by far largest aircraft in world and, unlike Do X (only serious rival), thoroughly efficient aircraft tailored to particular task which it performed to complete satisfaction. Unlike original TB-4, pleasant and not exhausting to fly; and soundness of design shown by long and intensive service of structurally similar ANT-20bis.

AGOS team leaders under Tupolev: Petlyakov and Arkhangyelskii; B.M. Kondorskii (general design), V.N. Belyaev (chief stressman), B.A. Saukke (chief engineer), Ye.I. Pogosskii, A.A. Yengibaryan (equipment/fittings) and N.S. Nekrasov. Structural basis ANT-16 but scaled up and refined. Wing profile TsAGI-6, t/c 20% root tapering to 10% tip, aspect ratio 8·2 (remarkable for 50 years ago). Traditional structures of three spars and built-up ribs retained, but because of great length of all members plain tube replaced by complex (usually closed-tube) sections riveted from wrapped sheet. Typical spar booms were 6-mm sheet wrapped into 160-mm diam or ellipse 160 × 190 mm. As usual, A-type ribs projecting just outside wing profile, skin 0,3 to 0,8 mm thick with 50 × 16 mm corrugations in strips between them. Centre section 10,645 m span, straight LE, same TE taper as outer panels, chord at outer joint 11,0 m exactly, two A-ribs each side of fuselage. Outer panels each 26,18 m span, tapering to 3,2 m chord at start of screwed-on semicircular tip, ten A-type ribs each side with skin stiffened by underlying L-section ribs and spanwise stringers. Ailerons divided into four sections each side to avoid TB-4 trouble of hinge-binding with wing-flexure, total 31,3 m². Tailplane symmetric section, 18,3-m span, 40 × 8 skin, two pairs bracing wires each side above and below but still capable of inflight adjustment ±5° with new addition of elec drive as well as manual. Static balance on rudder, servo rudder with elec positioning for trim, manual actuation to drive main surface. Dual flight controls almost entirely by steel cables with auto-tensioners to allow airframe flexure and gearing for ailerons. Main gears based on TB-4 but stronger KhMA struts with air/oil oleo strut resting at top in ball/socket and forked trunnion under front spar, similar large forked yoke rear brace pivoted to third spar and single lateral strut to front spar at fuselage root. Specially made 2000 × 450 mm wheels with four-shoe pneu brakes in side-by-side pairs. Tupolev proposed deep trousers over whole gear as in ANT-26 but accepted scheme was large aluminium spats stiffened by three exterior beads, removed after rollout but before first flight. Tailwheel 900 × 200 mm on KhMA castoring sprung leg.

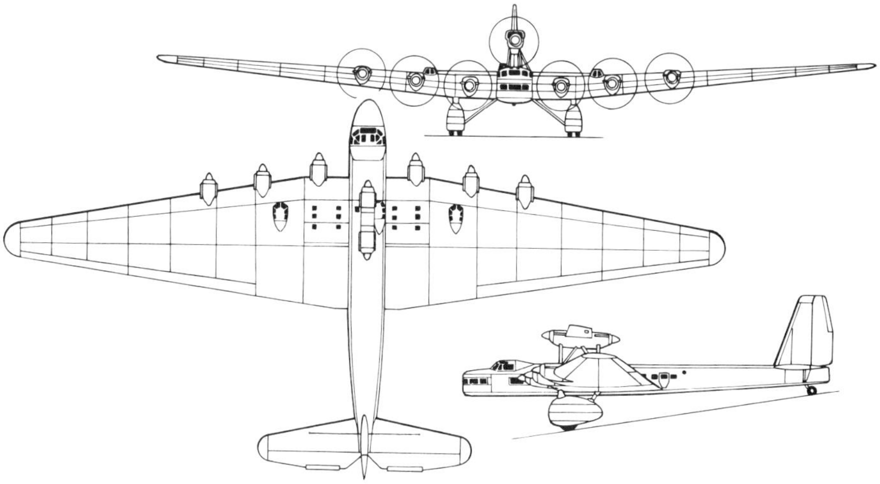

ANT-20 (with spats)

Tupolev disliked pylon tandem engines but could not achieve required power with six wing engines. Wing engines cantilevered far ahead of front spar on welded KhGSA trusses driving 4 m two-blade wooden propellers, water cooling radiators in short ducts under LE some resemblance TB-3/M-34. Upper centreline engine struts and cowls different from TB-4; Tupolev considered large dural pylon with ladder access in flight but accepted conventional arrangement with four pairs triangulated struts, single large ducted radiator above. Fuselage typical AGOS dural box 32,5 m long, 3,5 m wide and 2,5 m high but with flight deck projecting above at upper level. Structurally five parts, joined by steel eye/lug bolted joints at four longerons: F-1 nose saloon, four twin and three single glass windows, two seats in front, two pairs behind, with separate nav cabin to rear; F-1bis plywood roofed cockpit for two pilots, lower cabin for four pairs passengers, rear radio operator; F-2 between spars telephone (intercom) exchange with 16 lines, secretaries, toilet; F-3 buffet-bar, storeroom, film projector and photo library and processing lab, radio racks; F-4, cross-braced structure, unused. Inner wings offered spaces between spars and ribs roughly 2-m cube each, used for payload throughout. Usable floor area 109 m² (varied with mission). Normally four 2/3-berth sleeper cabins in centre-section on each side, small windows in roof and (three each side) in floor. Normal accomodation eight crew and 72 passengers, entry via large section of underside of F-2 hinged down from rear with integral stairs (when new, +red carpet). Roomy, access front/

ANT-20 under construction (note right engineer cockpit)

rear on centreline and into wing between spars 1/2 and 2/3 on each side. Wing compartments housed 30 hp APU/generator and central electric station, audio/recording station with 'voice from sky' loudspeakers, four radio transmit/receive stations, printing press, pharmacy, laundry, leaflet dispenser and pneumatic-post tube centre. Outboard of centre section was cockpit between spars 1/2 each side for flight engineer with blister canopy above wing upper surface. Outboard of centre section all fuel in 28 riveted aluminium cylindrical tanks in groups of 8, 4 and 2 each side, total 9400 lit (2067 gal). All engines started by compressed-air system.

Construction occupied only nine months, and parts left GAZ-22 3 April 1934 by road for assembly Moscow Central Aerodrome. Registration L-759 applied. Accepted by special committee 24 April, flown 35 min by M.M. Gromov 17 June 1934. Second flight 19 June over Red Square during meeting of Chelyuskin expedition. After factory tests and installation of autopilot (first in USSR) and array of electric-light bulbs on underside of wings for displaying slogans (believed later removed), joined *Agiteskadril* as flagship 18 August 1934. Established excellent record of serviceability and impressed all with size and majesty. Engines flight idling for air/ground broadcasting, established routine of two types of mission with crew eight (payload of passengers, mostly rewarded for public service) or crew 20 (using all on-board propaganda gear). Often escorted by small aircraft, I-5 or I-16, to show size; 18 May 1935 escort N.P. Blagin in I-5 attempted unauthorized loop around MG wing and hit wing squarely from below. Aircraft crashed locked together killing Blagin, TsAGI pilot I.S. Zhurov, squadron pilot I.V. Mikheyev, ten crew and 33 passengers.

DIMENSIONS Span 63,0 m (206 ft $8\frac{1}{3}$ in); length (ground) 32,9 m (107 ft $11\frac{1}{4}$ in), (flight attitude) 32,476 m (106 ft $6\frac{3}{4}$ in); height (on ground, over front centreline prop) 10,6 m, (flight, over fin) 11,253 m; wing area 486 m² (5231 ft²).

ENGINES Eight 900 hp M-34FRN.

WEIGHTS Empty 28,5 t (62,831 lb) (airframe 17,85, power installation 10,65); fuel/oil 7150 kg; loaded 42 t (92,593 lb).

PERFORMANCE Max speed 220 km/h (137 mph) at SL, about 250 km/h (155 mph) at 5 km; service ceiling 4,5 km (14,760 ft); range 1200 km (750 miles); take-off/landing, both 400 m; landing speed 100 km/h (62 mph).

ANT-20bis, PS-124 Also known as MG bis and (from its civil registration) L-760, this was planned as first of several replacements for lost *Maksim Gorkii*. Fantastic emotion swept nation in aftermath of crash and 35 million rubles quickly collected to build whole fleet of giants. Authorization received to build mighty squadron of 16 MGs, first repeating name of lost L-759, others named for party leaders and revolutionaries. Intended these aircraft should be *dubler* ANT-20s, but several factors transpired to change plan. More powerful engines made it possible to dispense with tandem pair on centreline. Structural refinement was accompanied by various changes to systems, and 1936 arrest of Tupolev at start of work caused upheaval and delay. Programme assigned to different GAZ outside Moscow where project placed under deputy director Boris Andreyevich Saukke, who had been on original AGOS ANT-20 team. Industry had no chance of building 16 giants, but work began on first, L-760, early 1938. By this time feelings had changed; *Agiteskadril* was running down, and certainly did not want another MG. Decision to redesign as straightforward civil airliner, and no attempt made to build any further examples. Apart from using just six more-powerful engines, with three-blade 3,5-m constant-speed propellers, radiator ducts with inlet shutters and proper aerodynamic profile and exhaust stacks inside cowls terminating in single small pipe projecting above LE, ANT-20bis differed significantly in airframe (appreciably heavier), fuel system and many other parts. Nose lengthened, with landing light (in MG in LE between engines 2/3 and 4/5), larger nose cabin with nine wide windows extending to front of cockpit, improved cockpit with only four large glass windows and better roof profile, all crew grouped amidships, vertical tail of reduced height but increased chord, two pairs dural bracing struts each side for tailplane (probably fixed-incidence), spats on main gears retained. ANT-20bis test-flown by Gromov and E.I. Schwarz late 1939; after NII tests passed to Aeroflot with designation PS-124, accomodation for 64 day passengers in fuselage and centre section, with crew of nine. Put to work on route Moscow-

ANT-20 after upper surfaces painted red and re-registered I-20

ANT-20bis, PS-124

Mineralnye Vody. Re-engined December 1940, then after invasion assigned to heavy utility transport in rear areas. Damaged beyond repair in heavy landing 14 December 1942 after flying 272 h total-time. Last corrugated-skin aircraft in USSR.

DIMENSIONS Span 63,0 m (206 ft 8⅓ in); length 34,1 m (111 ft 10½ in); height (over fin, on ground) 7,7 m; wing area 486 m² (5231 ft²).

ENGINES (as built) six 1200 hp AM-34FRNV, (1941) 1200 hp AM-35.

WEIGHTS Empty 31,3 t (68,783 lb); fuel/oil 5830 + 370 kg; loaded 44 t (97,000 lb), in wartime usually operated at 45 t (99,206 lb).

PERFORMANCE Max speed 235 km/h (146 mph) at SL, 275 km/h (171 mph) at 3,5 km; cruise at 3,5 km 242 km/h (150 mph); service ceiling 5,5 km (18,000 ft); range (Shavrov) 1300 km (800 miles); take-off 500 m/26 s; landing 500 m/32 s/100 km/h.

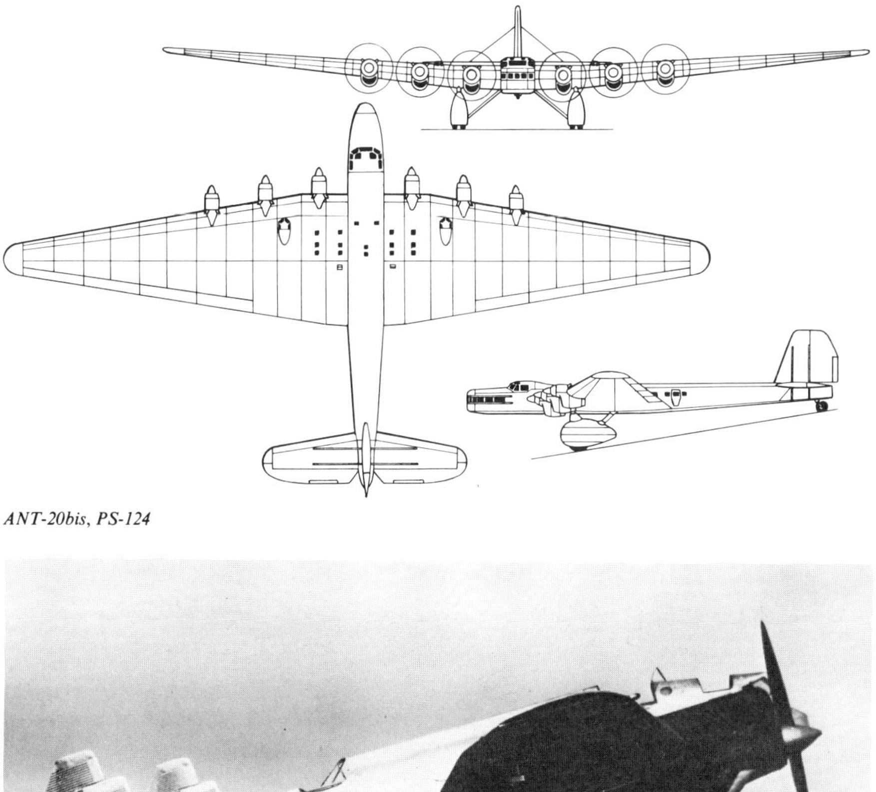

ANT-20bis, PS-124

ANT-21, MI-3 Launched by VVS prototype order 18 January 1932, this multi-seat fighter, broadly successor to KR-6, was important in effecting transition from corrugated to smooth skin. Assigned to Arkhangyelskii's brigade, design used actual parts of KR-6 in wing (including spar booms) but with reduced t/c and span, bending moments coming out unchanged. Fuselage completely new, dural stressed-skin semi-monocoque with oval section, part flush-riveting, large wing root fillets. Engine installations almost exactly as KR-6 but with ducts for slanting ventral radiators continued to rear to provide compartments for retracted main gears, first in KB. Single KhMA air/oil shock strut with two welded diagonal side braces at top and fork at bottom for 1000 × 250 mm wheel retracting to rear by single hyd jack acting on rear breaker strut. Four wing tanks, capacities unknown. Twin-finned tail with corrug (believed 25 × 10 mm) skin, elevators with tabs and internal mass-balance on fixed-incidence tailplane, rudders with large horns at top. Single pilot in

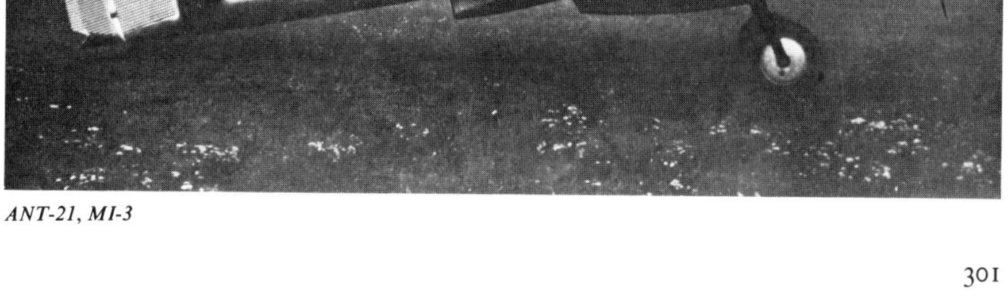

ANT-21, MI-3

open cockpit high above LE with two fixed PV-1 in nose, front gunner in KR-6 type nose with twin hand-aimed PV or DA and similar pair in rear dorsal position (believed Tur-6B); aircraft also built with lower rear position under wing TE for one DA manned by fourth crew-member, not known if gun fitted. This deep centre fuselage intended house 600-kg bomb-load, never equipped for this.

Prototype completed as MI-3 (*Mnogomestnyi Istrebitel*, multi-seat fighter), flown Gromov 1 August 1933 without problems. Popularly called *Mitrich*, liked by TsAGI pilots until 14 September 1933 when I.F. Kozlov made gentle dive to see how far beyond 350 km/h possible. Violent rudder flutter broke upper hinge of one rudder which then went hard-over and rotated aircraft 180° in yaw. This rudder separated but says much for strength of MI-3 that pilot made normal landing. Aircraft replaced by **ANT-21bis, MI-3D** (*dubler*). Completely redesigned fuselage and tail with enclosed nose for gunner with five main windows, two lower front windows and one 20-mm (or UBS) in pivoted socket; fighter-type cockpit with sliding canopy and optical sight for fixed guns (no details); long 'greenhouse' with folding rear section for dorsal gunner (probably UBS or twin DA); ventral tunnel and lower rear gun position removed. New tail with smooth dural skin, tailplane braced fairly high on single fin, mass-balanced rudder without horn and with Flettner tab. Many other changes including ailerons increased area; but report (Něměcek) that AM-34RN engines fitted not found in any Soviet literature; label on model states M-17B. Further comment that wings had fabric overlayer to reduce drag not borne out by good photos of both aircraft. Mi-3D completed April 1934 and put through NII testing July-December. Failed because of organic defects; in any case no longer really competitive. Main significance was as stepping-stone to SB.

DIMENSIONS Span 20,76 m (68 ft 1⅓ in); length (both) 12,3 m (40 ft 4¼ in); wing area 55,1 m² (593 ft²).
ENGINES Two 680 hp M-17B.
WEIGHTS Empty (3) 3,8 t (8377 lb); loaded 5260 kg (11,596 lb).
PERFORMANCE (3) Max speed 351 km/h (218 mph) at SL, 356 (221) at 3 km; service ceiling 7885 m (25,870 ft); range (Něměcek only) 1200 km; no other reliable data.

ANT-21bis, MI-3D

MI-3D after modifications (tail struts, nose probe)

ANT-22, MK-1 Believed still largest marine aircraft flown in the Soviet Union, this twin-hull flying boat is supposed to have been influenced by Savoia-Marchetti designs but Tupolev said he adopted configuration for several logical reasons, one being to avoid problems of single gigantic hull. Designation from *Morskoi Kreiser* (sea cruiser), long-range aircraft for ocean recon and bombing; Tupolev also schemed civil transport. Preceded by unbuilt ANT-11 and by 1930 project by TsKB (Bartini), which were too large for various civil requirements but too small for continually upgraded military demand. Project grew out of ANT-11 and single prototype funded December 1931; completed August 1934.

All-metal flying boat with trad AGOS wing but smooth hulls derived from ANT-8 and ANT-11. Wing broadly similar to TB-3 and TB-4, roughly midway between in size, TsAGI-6 profile, root t/c 20%, built as 16-m centre section of constant profile and 17,5-m tapering outer panels. Four spars, closed booms in centre section 125 × 113 mm, drawings show no A-profile ribs in centre section but ten in each outer wing dividing corrugated skin (size/gauge not known) into 11 chordwise panels. Dural hulls 15,0-m apart on centrelines built as broad two-step planing bottoms (3,5 and 4,5-mm sheet at steps) with multiple keels and bulkheads and large hatches for inspection, superimposed by narrow upper portions with usable interior, relatively simple and light construction and smooth Alclad skin stiffened by two sets (front and rear, at different levels) of external half-round bead siffeners. Smooth-skinned tail on each hull with high-aspect-ratio upper 19,0-m tailplane projecting beyond fin on each side braced by wires and central inverted vee struts to narrow lower tailplane joining hulls and required because of short moment arm (only 2·2 MAC). Hulls interchangeable, each with nose, dorsal and tail turret, extremities each twin ShKAS and mid turret behind wing TE with Oerlikon 20-mm. Bombload up to 6-t (13,120 lb) hung under centre section, wide variety of poss loads. Flight crew reported eight; if correct three gunners must also have acted as nav, radio, engineer. Side-by-side pilots in cockpit in small nacelle ahead of LE on centreline, emergency access via LE to hulls. Engines in tandem nacelles basically similar to TB-4 but larger radiator ducts on top between engines and, for CG reasons, engines on struts raked as far forward as poss. Same type 4-m propeller as ANT-20. Same 30-hp APU and generator set as ANT-20, compressed-air starting, full electrics, intercom and four radios.

Factory test began 8 August 1934, no particular problem but prolonged until May 1935. Outstanding on water, handling in air good though poor climb and ceiling. On paper, great capacity for overload, but when burdened with full military equipment performance sank to unacceptable level. NII tests 27 July–15 August 1935 showed following figures with 6-t bombload: max speed 205 km/h; time to 1 km, 18 min; service ceiling 2250 m. These figures were at only 33,56 t, 9,44 t below max overload. VVS appreciated ability to operate in wind 12 m/s with waves to 1,5-m, but no production. Last two missions were world record 8 December 1936 by T. V. Rybenko and D.N. Ilinskii; first carried 10,04-t useful load to 1942 m; second lifted 13-t load (just).

DIMENSIONS Span 51,0 m (167 ft 3⅞ in); length 24,1 m (79 ft 0¾ in); wing area 304,5 m² (3278 ft²).
ENGINES Six 830 hp M-34R.
WEIGHTS Empty 21 663 kg (47,758 lb); fuel/oil 5,1 t; loaded (normal) 29 450 kg (64,925 lb), (overload) 33 560 kg (73,986 lb).
PERFORMANCE (normal gross) Max speed 233 km/h (145 mph) at SL; cruise 180 km/h (112 mph); time to 1 km, 10·3 min; service ceiling 3,5 km (11,480 ft); endurance 7 h; range 1350 km (840 miles) (at 4,36 kg fuel/oil per km ultimate range at overload wt was 4700 km, never approached in practice); time 360° turn, 85 s; take-off/landing both 600 m; alighting speed 110 km/h.

ANT-23, I-12 This unconventional fighter was brain-child of Viktor Nikolayevich Chernyshov, brigade leader at AGOS TsAGI. According to Něměcek and Western accounts his objective was to use Kurchyevskii recoilless gun tubes as structural parts of airframe; some West-

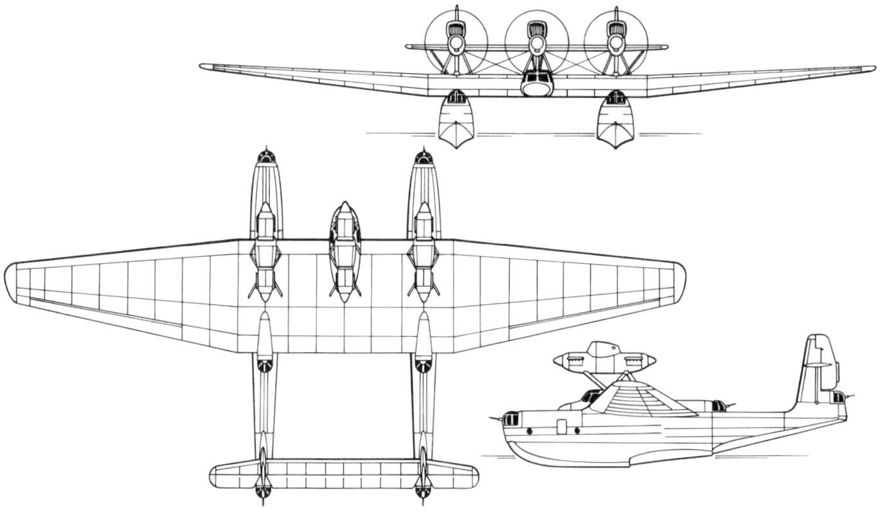

ANT-22, MK-1

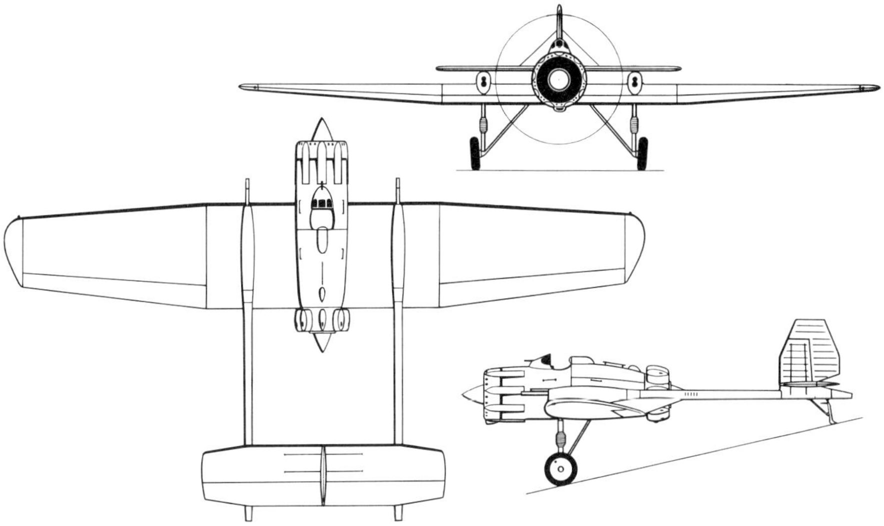

ANT-23, I-12

ern accounts go so far as to say this twin-tail-boom aircraft used gun barrels as tailbooms. It was not quite like that; he adopted twin-boom layout to get two engines in frontal area of one, and used tubes for tailbooms in order to carry gas from rear nozzles of cannon. More curiously, non-Soviet accounts give weapons as APK-100 (see Armament section) while Soviet documents all state they were quite small APK-4, and in description in Zhukovskii museum it is made clear larger guns were thought to pose gas-discharge problems and pressure shock in tail booms. Guns did not bear structural loads.

All-metal airframe with smooth stressed-skin covering. Wing unlike other AGOS designs, TsAGI 18% profile, rectangular 5,4 m centre section, tapered outer panels with slotted ailerons along entire TE. Two spars and 1,2 m-spaced ribs all built up from dural tube and rolled sections, skin in chordal strips with external rolled L-flange stiffener every 150 mm, every eighth strip being riveted to rib below, thickness 0,8 or 1,0 mm. Similar structure in tail, fin on centreline braced by two struts each side to two-spar tailplane. Raw material for tail booms unbelievably described, even in Soviet accounts, as 'water pipes', machined internally and externally to 170 mm diam with wall thickness varying 1 to 3 mm. Each boom made in three parts, each about 1,5 m long, joined by threaded ends. Front of each boom fastened to both spars and 76 mm APK-4 inserted with surrounding airspace and with much of barrel protruding at front. Light dural fairing bulge over wing to improve aerodynamic form of front of boom, tail controls by push/pull rods located in external guides above booms. Rubber-sprung main gears, tall to allow clearance for rear propeller, tailskid under each boom. Engines on welded KhMA mounts forming ends of similarly made truss fuselage with light dural covering. Front engine with helmeted Townend ring as in I-4bis, rear engine reverse helmets, 2,8 m wooden two-blade propellers with spinners and Bristol gas starting system. Riveted AMTs fuel tanks between each engine and pilot in open cockpit with Aldis sight.

ANT-23 sponsored by VVS with designation I-12, prototype completed at end 1931 and unofficially named *Baumanskii Komsomolyets* after famed revolutionary who until death 1905 worked near TsAGI site. One flight 1931 and 32 in 1932. Still on factory test 1933 but rarely flown; performance disappointing (Shavrov cites long main gears, externally stiffened wing skins and draggy engines) but worst feature judged to be great difficulty of pilot escape in air because of revolving rear prop. Second aircraft, **ANT-23bis**, under construction 1932 with unknown improvements, never completed. No foundation found in Soviet literature for common Western story that aircraft made forced landing after cannon exploded in air, severely damaging controls, I.F. Kozlov unable to escape.

DIMENSIONS Span 15,6 m (51 ft $2\frac{1}{8}$ in), ANT-23bis reported East Germany 14,0 m); length 9,5 m (31 ft 2 in); wing area 30,0 m^2 (323 ft^2).

ENGINES Two GR9AK (licensed 525 hp Jupiter VI).

WEIGHTS Empty, not known; loaded 2400 kg (5291 lb).

PERFORMANCE Max speed 300 km/h (186 mph) at SL, 280 km/h (174 mph) at 5 km; no other data.

ANT-24 Little information on record about this twin-engined heavy fighter which came between MI-3D and ANT-29. One prototype authorized November 1932, no evidence construction started. No data.

ANT-25, RD World records were always important to Soviet Union. By 1931 national capability had matured and several important records appeared within grasp, if only for reason existing FAI records had been gained by modified existing machines rather than by 'clean sheet of paper' designs. TsAGI informal discussion 20 May 1931 ranged over speed, range and alt; decision to go for range. Tupolev did quick calcs showing ease with which French figure could be beaten by purpose-designed monoplane with greater aspcct ratio and rctrac gcar. Series of meetings at Revolutionary War Council established special commission to build aircraft to Tupolev design and organise flight. Meeting 7 December 1931 agreed to aim at 13,000 km using ANT-25, official designation RD (*Rekord Dal'nost*, record distance), flight set for summer 1932; major task to provide improved equipment, train crew(s) and build paved runway. From start funding had one eye on importance of long range to future bombers. Further executive committee formed under K.Ye. Voroshilov to manage programme, including M-34 engine by Mikulin KB and building of runway. Design of RD often ascribed to Sukhoi but Tupolev adamant all his brigades played important role and refused to credit any one individually. Work took much longer than anticipated: design finished July 1932 but first RD not complete until 11 months later, and then only with direct-drive M-34. August 1932 work began on **RD** *Dubler* (double) with geared M-34R. Original direct-drive RD flown by M.M. Gromov 22 June 1933; RD *dubler* flown by Gromov 10 September 1933.

Design based on remarkable cantilever wing with aspect ratio 13·1. Modified TsAGI-6 profile, t/c 20% root, 19·2% half semi-span, 18·5% tip. Remarkably, traditional corrugated structure adopted, with 3,75-m centre section and two 15,125-m outer panels, latter with 5° dihedral. Two main spars, plus auxiliary rear spar, all with usual elliptical-tube booms but this time KhMA heat-treated to 140 kg/mm^2, with truss web members and joint gussets all D6. Built-up truss ribs, 18 of A-type each side of fuselage projecting above wing profile with intermediate internal ribs; 40 × 8 mm skin riveted between each pair of A-ribs. Ailerons divided into four sections each side with slotted nose, inset hinges giving 100% mass balance and with servo drive tab on section 2 (numbered root to tip) on each side, sections 1 and 2 slightly greater chord. Oval-section fuselage in two parts, front integral with centre-section of wing, with strong truss internal structure and welded KhMA engine mount, lighter rear monocoque with L-section frames and stringers, smooth skin throughout but not flush-riveted, thickness 0,8 or 1,0 mm. Tail all-dural with corrugated skins, fixed tailplane with seven A-type ribs each side, elevators with 100% balance by recessed hinges, rudder part-balanced by recessed hinges on welded KhMA pyramids and part by small horn at top. Main gears with single air/oil shock strut of KhMA with twin side braces all hinged to front spar, rear bracing strut normally located at base of rear spar but on retraction pulled by elec motor and cable system along channel tracks almost to TE of wing, gear folding to rear; two 900 × 200 mm tyres on each leg, half-projecting from wing ahead of box fairing (high drag, especially on take-off). Balloon tyre on tailwheel on fixed leg, half-projecting from fairing. Simple engine installation, large 4,5-m two-blade wooden propeller, water radiator cranked by pilot in vertical slides to extend beneath rear of cowling. Fuel relieved wing bending by being distributed in small tanks right across span between two main spars; centreline and inboard fuel used first to reduce wing loads. (Significant that, at time when fatigue ignored elsewhere, wing design factor was given as 3·0 to 4·8 depending on number of flying hours.) Fully enclosed accommodation, with tandem sliding or hinged canopies, for crew of three: pilot, radio/nav and engineer. Extremely comprehensive equipment including first Soviet gyro-compass, electro station generating 500 W at 12 V, various MF and HF radios including collapsible mast for emergency use after forced landing, sextant in hinged roof station and retractable ventral periscope.

Original RD was flown with M-34 with direct drive and compression ratio of 6, giving 750 hp. Though it showed good flying qualities it was soon clear max endurance could not exceed 48 h, putting any world record out of reach. This aircraft ceased to be of much interest, though it later flew with M-34 of compression ratio 7, giving 874 hp, and reaching 212 km/h. All hopes were focussed on **RD dubler** with geared M-34R engine. This was immediately distinguished by different nose with higher thrust-line and improved profile. Less obvious was vertical tail of increased chord, with servo-tab rudder. Original *dubler* engine had compression ratio 6·8 giving 900 hp driving two-blade prop. In February 1934 engine of 6·6 c.r. was substituted, and later a 4,5 m propeller with three ground-adjustable light-alloy blades. This enabled full 6,1 t fuel load to be uplifted, though actual load never exceeded 5 t at this stage, giving 66-h endurance. Range still well short of design figure, though better than existing record, and Tupolev recognized a basic problem was corrugated skin. TsAGI had established, for example, that airflow was seldom aligned with corrugations, and penalties much greater than previously believed. Entire wing and tail was thereupon covered with fabric, wrapped carefully around leading edges and sewn through many small holes with curved needles and tautened with dope. Propeller blades polished, fillet doped and sealed and attention paid to various other aerodynamically poor areas. Result was dramatic; drag at cruise was reduced by 36% and take-off weight increased. In mid-1934 engine installation completely redesigned, with engine moved back 0,4 m and different radiator mounted in duct beneath engine with pilot-controlled entry shutters and variable flap at exit. Cowling sealed to reduce drag and exhaust stacks ducted to narrow fishtails near pilot canopy with surrounding ram-air pipe on each side providing heating for all three cockpits (some accounts state gas itself entered cockpits!). Completely new vertical tail with increased height and rounded profile. Most of these changes effected by mid-1934 when special paved runway at Shchyelkovo, with deliberate slope, was finished. Chosen crew, M.M. Gromov, A.I. Filin, I.T. Spirin, twice attempted max number circuits of triangle Moscow/Tula/Ryazan or Moscow/Ryazan/Kharkov only to be thwarted by engine trouble; 30 June 1934 reached 4465 km in 27 h 21 min and three weeks later 6559 km in 39 h 1 min. On 10 September 1934 same crew orbited this triangle 75 h 2 min covering 12,411 km, a new closed-circuit (even if multi-lap) record. Plan then made for what had always been main objective: over North Pole to USA. In midst of preparations Gromov fell ill, and new crews organised under Levanevskii and Chkalov. In August 1935 Levanevskii's crew

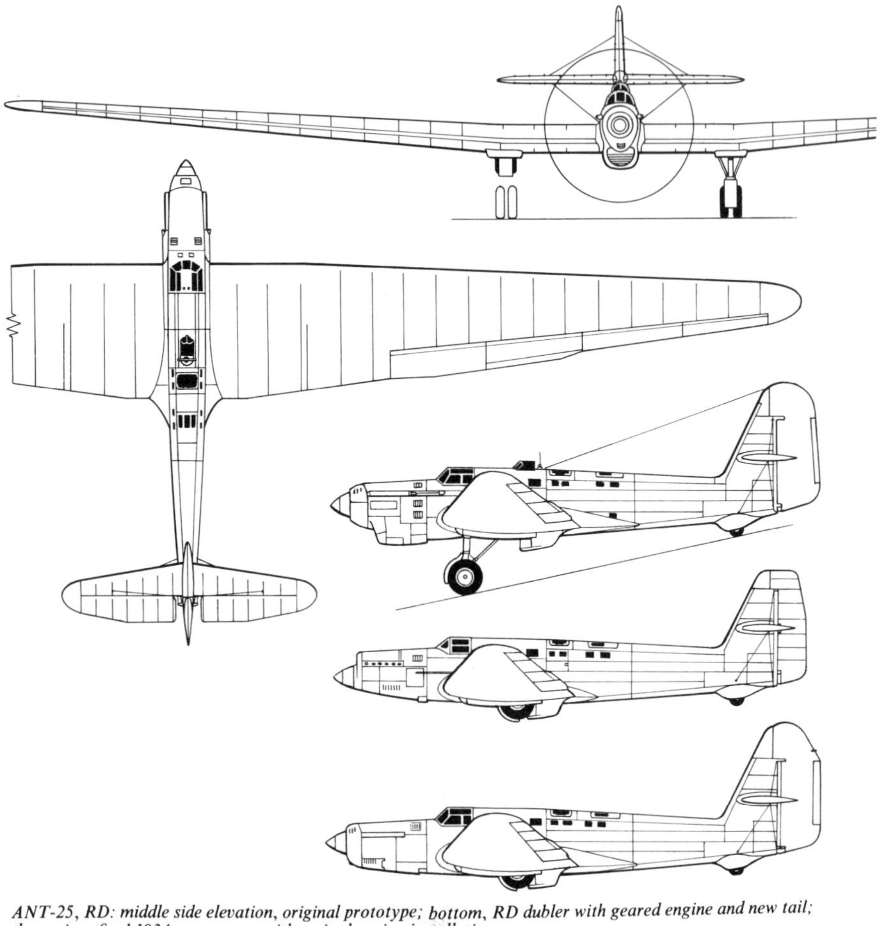

ANT-25, RD: middle side elevation, original prototype; bottom, RD dubler with geared engine and new tail; three-view, final 1934 appearance with revised engine installation

RD at Udd, 23 July 1936

flew towards Pole but suffered engine problems and struggled back to Leningrad. Decision to do Arctic testing: V.P. Chkalov, G.F. Baidukov and A.V. Belyakov detailed to use aircraft now painted with red wings and tailplane, with registration NO25-1, leaving Moscow after midnight 20 July 1936 and flying Franz-Josef Land, Severnaya Zemlya, Petropavlosk Kamchatskii towards Nikolayevsk but had to land on island Udd (since named Chkalov), 9374 km in 56 h 20 min. Using experience, same crew took off for USA 18 June 1937; despite prolonged mechanical and weather adversities just managed to cross US frontier landing Portland (Washington, not Oregon) 9130 km in 63 h 25 min (FAI recognized great-circle 8504 km). Final and greatest RD flight was by M.M. Gromov, A.B. Yumashyev and S.A. Danilin, leaving Moscow 12 July 1937 with record 6230 kg fuel and oil; easy flight, no bad weather, landed San Jacinto, Calif, 11,500 km (10 148 gt circle) in 62 h 17 min, with 1500 kg unused fuel.

In winter 1933–1934 VVS ordered 50 slightly modified ANT-25 for use as long-range research and military crew training aircraft. Total order not completed, but 20 were built by spring 1936 including at least 14 with smooth skins on wings and tail and used for many research programmes including manufacturing techniques (including flush riveting and welding), engines (including Jumo 207 and, as **RDD**, RD *Dieselnyi*, Charomskii AN-1) and military equipment. Strangely, none made attempt on distance record nor on absolute altitude, for which RD would have been exceptional contender with different propulsion. Four military RDs were, however, rebuilt as BOK-1, BOK-7, BOK-11 and BOK-15.

DIMENSIONS Span 34,0 m (111 ft $6\frac{9}{16}$ in); length (1st) 13,4 m (43 ft $11\frac{1}{2}$ in), (dubler) 13,08 m (42 ft 11 in); wing area 87,1 m² (937·5 ft²).

ENGINE (1st) one 750 or 874 hp M-34, (dub) 900, later 950, hp M-34R; (mil RD) see text.

WEIGHTS Empty (1) 3,7 t (8157 lb), (d, as built) 3784 kg, (d, 1936) 4,2 t (9259 lb); fuel (1936) 5880 + 350 kg; loaded (1) 8 t (17,637 lb), (d, 1933) 10 t, (d, 1936) 11,5 t (25,353 lb).

PERFORMANCE Max speed (874 hp) 212 km/h at SL, (d, 1933) 244 km/h, (d, 1936) 246 km/h (153 mph) at SL; service ceiling (d, full load) 2,1 km, (light) 7850 m (25,750 ft); endurance/range (1) 48 h/7200 km, (d, 1933) 66 h/10 800 km, (1936) 80 h/13 020 km (8090 miles); take-off (1) 1 km, (1936) 1,5 km.

ANT-26, TB-6 In 1929 most of AGOS projects of 1925 had either flown or completed preliminary design stage, and with considerable growth of organization (450 engineers) Tupolev was not backward in launching new projects. Despite inexorable square/cube law he believed his teams could extrapolate same basic monoplane structure up to eventual span 200 m, with gross weight 150 t. As next two stages AGOS was authorized to proceed to 54 m/33 t TB-4 and 63 m/42 t MG; Tupolev schemed bomber version of MG and at same time, early 1932, put small team to do further engineering calculation on 1929 project for further stage sized to 95-m/70-t. This received project number ANT-26 and was funded by VVS as TB-6. Meanwhile **ANT-20V** (*Voennyi*, war) was designed in some detail but never funded; would have had 2-t bombload (possible misprint for 12 or 20) and Tur-5, Tur-6, sliding dustbin and ball turrets for two Oerlikon 20-mm and 12 DA (later ShKAS). This was officially terminated January 1933 and it may have been at same time TB-6 was permitted to go ahead. Three years were spent in stressing structure, testing models in tunnels and in enormous task of basic engineering design. ANT-28 was projected as transport variant.

ANT-26 was by far largest aircraft in world, and Tupolev was most anxious it should not be obsolescent when it appeared. Though underlying structure was trad diagonally-braced truss spars and ribs, all skins were smooth and there were no A-profile ribs to break contour of wing surfaces. Greatest problem was inevitable thickness of wing, which (as discovered with TB-4) could seriously reduce propulsive efficiency of propellers ahead of LE. TsAGI studied five propulsion configurations and several wing forms before deciding on modified TsAGI-6 profile (about 20% ruling t/c) with eight engines on LE and two tandem pairs above. It would have been possible to put all 12 on LE but this would have involved problems in resolving thrust outboard and appeared to offer poorer propulsive efficiency despite reduced performance of rear tandem propellers working in slipstream. More important, Tupolev hoped later to use engines of 1300/1500 hp and eliminate pylon-mounted tandem units, as with ANT-20bis. Structurally wing was to have four main spars with 140 kg/mm² KhGSA booms, built as centre section and tapering outer panels with dihedral. Fuselage oval section at front changing to rectangular with rounded corners approx same size as MG but rather longer. Fixed tailplane on slightly raised platform on rear fuselage carrying large centreline and two smaller aux fins all braced by single inclined strut each side. Main landing gears with four-wheel bogies in tandem pairs (tyre size not known but smaller than MG) on single shock struts raised vertically into large fairings beneath wing at extremity of centre section. No crew in wing, and volume so large tanks for max fuel occupied only small proportion of space between front two spars. Normal crew 12, defensive armament one 37 mm (probably in tail turret), four 20 mm and four pairs ShKAS (two 20 mm probably in large turrets at rear of outer nacelles); bombload up to 20 t, normally 4 t for 2500 km. Most Soviet observers doubt that construction of TB-6 prototype ever started, though TsAGI built and flew (test-pilot B. N. Kudrin) a scale model tandem-seat glider of some 20 m span which may have been ANT-30. By late 1935 little was unknown about TB-6 but poor performance of TB-4, vulnerability of such large but relatively slow bombers and number of faster, more agile twin-engine bombers of SB-2 type purchased for same money resulted in 1936 decision to discontinue project. Supposed waste on giant bomber and ANT-28 transport may have played part in framed charges against Tupolev in 1936.

DIMEMSIONS Span 95,0 m (311 ft $8\frac{1}{8}$ in); length 39,0 m (127 ft $11\frac{1}{2}$ in); wing area about 800 m² (8600 ft²).

ENGINES Twelve 900 hp M-34FRN.

WEIGHTS Empty about 50 t (110,000 lb); loaded 70 t (154,000 lb), (max) 76 t (167,500 lb).

PERFORMANCE Max speed est 300 km/h (186 mph); range with 20 t bombload 1000 km, with 4 t about 2500 km.

ANT-27, MDR-4, MTB-1 Abysmal performance of MDR-3 (see under Chyetverikov) caused grave concern to MA and industry; lacking confidence in designer to produce solutions, whole programme (without Chyetverikov's participation) was transferred to KOSOS TsAGI at end 1932. Tupolev and leader of KOSOS marine aircraft brigade, I. I. Pogosskii, redesigned MDR-3 leaving nothing but basic hull structure. Wing was completely new, though derived from previous AGOS wings, with considerably greater span and area though tapering from root with unchanged root chord. Centre section with A-profile ribs, 40 × 8 mm corrugated skin; outer panels fabric covered (new to TsAGI brigades). New propulsion group comprising three more powerful water-cooled engines (in place of two tandem pairs), centre engine being pusher, all with circular radiator on front of nacelle and with geared drive to 4 m wooden two-blade props. Hull stiffened with AGOS (Pogosskii) style half-round external stiffeners, four each side. New single-fin tail with high braced tailplane and rear turret closely

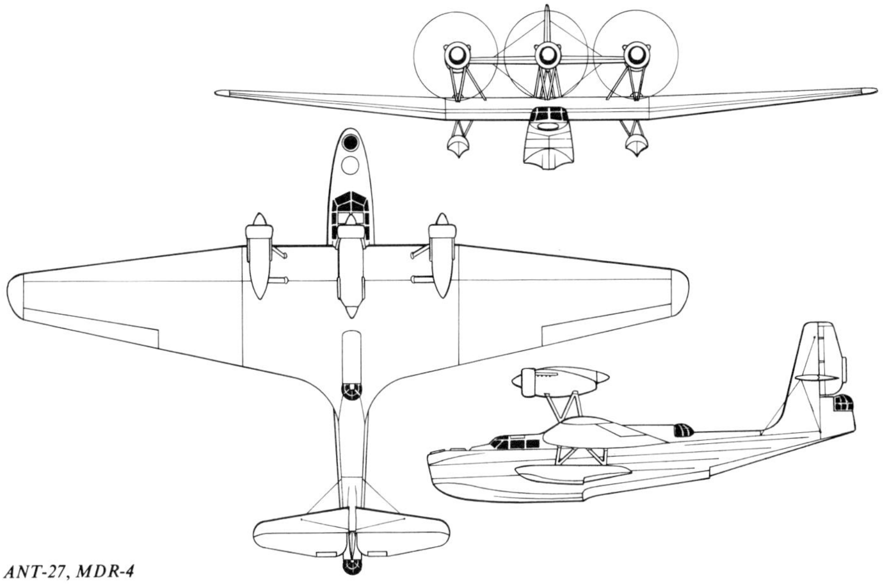

ANT-27, MDR-4

similar to MK-1. Armament (not seen in photos) 20 mm Oerlikon in Tur-9 dorsal turret, twin ShKAS in nose cockpit and same in tail turret (second nose cockpit believed not used for guns); bombload not known but at least 500 kg. Single aircraft completed Taganrog and tested March 1934. In course of factory tests 15 April crashed (Něměcek, on take-off) killing Pogosskii.

Urgent need for good large flying boat resulted in almost immediate order for second aircraft. This incorporated various changes, designation **ANT-27bis**, MTB-1 (*Morskoi Torpedonosyets-Bombardirovshchik*, sea torpedo-bomber). Basically similar but with much greater fuel capacity, many refinements (probably deicing, night and all-weather capability but no details) and hardpoints under inner centre section for two torpedoes or up to 2 t bombs with reduced fuel. Owing to sharp need for such aircraft MA decided to adopt MTB-1 prior to start of flight tests, and preparations made (not at Taganrog) for series production. First aircraft began factory testing May 1935; on 23 September 1935, prior to handing over at factory, suffered second fatal crash caused by separation of fabric from wing. Despite this, after urgent board of enquiry, decision to continue production, five MTB-1 being delivered 1936 and ten 1937 at which point production terminated. Despite sorry history and poor performance, service life satisfactory, used as ocean reconnaissance as well as torpedo-bombing, until 1942. Shavrov reports project for passenger version, ANT-29; this number was assigned to different aircraft.

DIMENSIONS Span 39,4 m (129 ft 3¼ in); length 21,9 m (71 ft 10¼ in); wing area 177,5 m² (1911 ft²).

ENGINES Three 830 hp M-34R.

WEIGHTS Empty (4) 10,5 t (23,148 lb), (1) 10,521 kg (23,194 lb); fuel/oil (4) 2450 + 196 kg, (1) 3746 + 370; loaded (4) 14,660 kg (32,319 lb), (1) 16,250 kg (35,825 lb).

PERFORMANCE Max speed (4) 232 km/h (144 mph) at SL, 211 at 3 km, (1) 225 at SL (140 mph), 200 at 3 km; climb to 1 km (4) 4·6 min, (1) 5·4; service ceiling (4) 5450 m (17,880 ft), (1) 4470 m (14,665 ft); endurance (4) 7 h, (1) 11 h; range (4) 1230 km (often reported as 2130), (1) 2000 km; time 360° circle (4) 30 s, (1) 35 s; take-off (4) 30 s; alighting speed (4) 100 km/h, (1) 105.

ANT-28 Transport version of the ANT-26 bomber, this enormous aircraft used a basically similar airframe but was quite different in detail. Major differences included long MG-like nose with row of large windows, two rows of five cabins on each side of fuselage inside wing, each providing accommodation at two levels, large single-finned tail, plain fixed landing gear and four integral stairways for access on ground. No provision for heavy or bulky freight except as underslung external load. In project stage 1933, so far as known purely military though no known defensive armament. Little published, but Tupolev said (about 1965) Petlyakov led design team and both he and Tupolev felt strongly ANT-28 should have been built, in contrast to TB-6 whose termination was generally considered wise. He said, from memory, max number of troops or other passengers about 250.

DIMENSIONS Span 95,0 m (311 ft 8⅛ in); length 40,0 m (131 ft 3 in); wing area about 800 m².

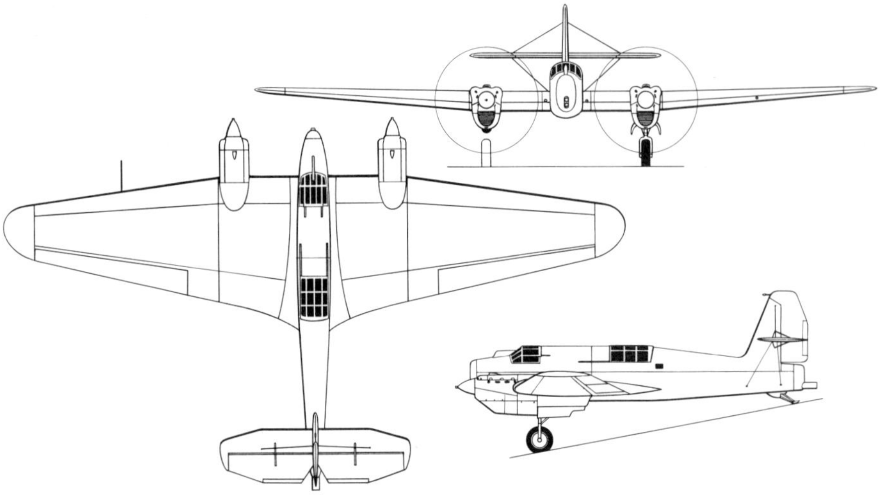

ANT-29, DIP

DIP with two DRP guns

ENGINES Twelve 900 hp M-34FRN.

WEIGHTS Empty about 47 t (103,600 lb); loaded 76 t (167,550 lb).

PERFORMANCE Max speed est 290 km/h (180 mph); range with 25 t payload 3600 km (2250 miles).

ANT-29, DIP A natural successor to MI-3D and immediate ancestor of SB family, this twin-engined fighter was first AGOS monoplane with smooth metal skinned surfaces throughout. Western reports and drawings curiously garbled, and even Soviet artwork leaves much to be desired, Shavrov's three-view having inaccurate front view to different scale from plan and with accompanying metre scale wrongly numbered. ANT-29 was funded by VVS September 1932 as more modern and faster twin-engined fighter than ANT-21 series, and several novel features, especially armament, were schemed for it. In particular it was planned as first fighter with internal fuselage installation of a Kurchyevskii recoilless cannon. Wing incorporated numerous new features. Profile not known but t/c measured off large drawing as only 13% at root and less at tip, two strongly made girder spars widely spaced at 16·6% and 66·6% root chord, wing divided spanwise into small root stubs and carry-through members integral with fuselage, 3 m centre section on each side (with dihedral, not shown in published drawings) and 5,9 m outer wings, smooth dural skin mainly 1 mm with flush riveting (believed new to bureau) ahead of front spar. Balanced ailerons in two sections each side, no tabs, centre section with split flaps (new to bureau). Slab-sided fuselage with wing in low/mid position, pilot above leading edge with hinged and folding canopy, radio/gunner aft of TE with canopy pivoting forwards. Single fin carrying fixed-incidence tailplane well above fuselage with bracing strut each side, aerodynamically and mass-balanced elevators, rudder with upper horn and forward-projecting mass balance and TE tab. Main gears with 900 × 280 mm tyres in forks in single oleo struts electrically retracted to rear into rear of each nacelle with bay closed by twin doors allowing part of each tyre to protrude; fixed tailskid. Engines neatly cowled with integral radiator on underside in duct with pilot-controlled shutters at inlet. Chauvière 350-series 3,5 m three-blade dural v-p propellers, new to bureau; fuel in four metal tanks behind front spar. Planned armament one four-inch (101·6-mm) DRP in fuselage, with rounds loaded by rear crew-member; one contemporary drawing clearly shows this, but others show two such guns closely superimposed on left side of fuselage, confirmed by photo. Gun length about 4 m, exhaust blast discharged through one (two?) large steel tube projecting from tail-end of fuselage. In addition one 20 mm Hispano between cylinder banks of each engine firing through prop hubs, and provision for synchronized gun mounted externally above each engine for aiming assistance; photo appears to show different installations on left and right engines. All aimed by pilot with unusual optical sight in form of tube faired into blade on centreline ahead of windscreen (all guns were horizontal). Rear crew member had hand-aimed gun, shown as single weapon (probably ShKAS) in contemporary drawings. No bombload.

Priority on SB and other types delayed flight until well after start of SB flight-test. Single prototype DIP (*Dvukhmyestnyi Istrebitel Pushyechnyi*, two-seat cannon fighter) ready for flight at TsAGI airfield February 1935 but final inspection revealed several defects, and in particular control surfaces were returned to be reskinned. Eventually whole aircraft returned to ZOK for complete inspection and rectification of faults, and did not fly until end of year. Though in some respects outstanding, aircraft riddled with troubles (eg, longitudinal instability). Completely failed NII testing about May 1936. This was really end not only of this series of heavy fighters but also of recoilless cannon, final attempt being ANT-46.

DIMENSIONS Span 19,19 m (62 ft $11\frac{1}{2}$ in); length (excl gun and pipe) 13,2 m (43 ft $3\frac{3}{4}$ in); wing area (Shavrov) 55·1 m^2, (calc from TsAGI drawings) 53,1 m^2 (572 ft^2).
ENGINES Two 760 hp Hispano-Suiza 12Ybrs.
WEIGHTS Empty 3,9 t (8598 lb); fuel/oil 720 + 80 kg; loaded 5,3 t (11,684 lb).
PERFORMANCE Max speed 320 km/h at SL, 352 (219 mph) at 4 km; no other reliable data but endurance est 10 h max.

ANT-30 Unknown; possibly used for civil passenger variant of ANT-22, 27 or 28, or small-scale glider for ANT-26 research.

ANT-31, I-14 Designed by Sukhoi's brigade at KOSOS TsAGI from early 1932 this neat fighter was in many respects most modern in world. First in Soviet Union with retractable landing gear, braked wheels, long-chord NACA cowl, smooth stressed skin on fuselage and integral fin, enclosed cockpit and outstanding armament. Negative feature was retention of corrugated skin on wings and horizontal tail. Wing of NACA 16% profile, two spars of KhGSA tube booms and riveted KhMA truss webs, ribs riveted from rolled sections, skin 1,0 and 0,8-mm, corrugation details unknown. Long-span slotted ailerons, no flaps, wing made as horizontal centre section and outer panels with considerable dihedral. Stumpy fuselage with modern structure of L and top-hat frames, L stringers and flush-riveted skin 0,8-mm throughout. Integral fin of remarkable height and small chord carrying braced horizontal tail (apparently 25 × 5 mm corrugation) well above fuselage. Large fuel tank on CG above wing, cockpit behind trailing edge with glazed enclosure having roof hinged upwards at rear. Imported engine in locally designed installation with Bristol front collector ring around crankcase, large NACA cowl extending behind LE and direct drive to two-blade wooden propeller. Wide-track main gears with single oleo struts, inward and rear bracing struts, and retraction inwards by cockpit handwheel and cables. Normal armament one synch PV-1 upper right fuselage, two APK-37 under outer wings outboard of prop disc and discharging at rear well below tips of horizontal tail. Alternative (believed never installed), two ShVAK under wings, two PV-1 above fuselage and four D-1 bomb containers. Sight faired into dorsal blade as in ANT-29.

ANT-31 first prototype

Completed by ZOK TsAGI and flown by K.A. Popov May 1933. Generally good performance despite having to fly with fixed skis (late thaw) and most handling excellent, but (Shavrov) some aspects of control difficult and only a touch of control needed for manoeuvres, recovery from spin in $1\frac{1}{2}$ turns, (Něměcek) in tight turn tailplane in wake of wing and ineffective.

Decision to build second aircraft, **ANT-31bis**, **I-14bis** (said, not in USSR, to be also called I-142), with more powerful engine and

ANT-31bis, I-14bis

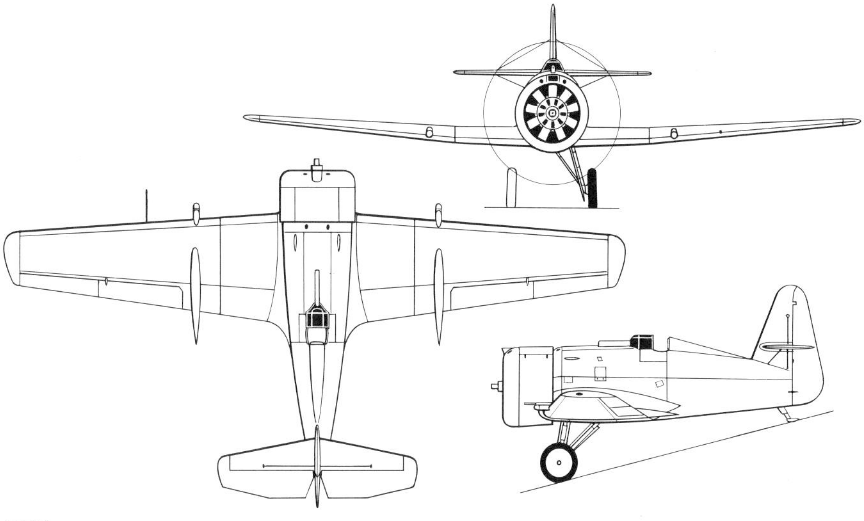

I-14bis

many changes. Redesigned wing and horizontal tail with different aerodynamic form and smooth stressed skin, new narrow-track landing gear retracting outwards, new narrow cockpit without canopy (bewailed by Shavrov as retrograde, but insisted upon by pilots), intended two APK-37 (not installed at rollout). Completed March 1934 and on factory and NII test to October. NII testing favourable and measured figures outstanding, but problems with spinning and with gear retraction mechanism. Pilots also had trouble with narrow track; original gear much better. Despite this, production order placed with more powerful licensed engine, revised armament two APK-11 and two ShKAS, modified horizontal tail to improve stability in sustained turn and other changes. Order for 55 I-14bis placed, possibly as safeguard against problem with I-16, but only 18 completed and delivered, last December 1936, because of I-16's success.

DIMENSIONS Span 11,2 m (36 ft 9 in); length (both) 6,1 m (20 ft 0 in); wing area (14) 16,8 m² (181 ft²), (bis) 17,0 m² (183 ft²).

ENGINE (14) One 580 hp Bristol Mercury VIS2 (not VS), (bis) 712 hp Wright Cyclone SGR-1820-F2, (production) 730 hp M-25A.

WEIGHTS Empty (14) about 1088 kg, (bis) 1169 kg, (production) 1170 kg (2579 lb); fuel/oil (production) 200 kg; loaded (14) 1455 kg, (bis) 1524 kg, (production) 1540 kg (3395 lb).

PERFORMANCE Max speed (14) 316 km/h at SL, 384 at 5 km, (bis) 323 at SL, 414 at 3 km, (production) 375 (233 mph) at SL, 449 (279 mph) at 3400 m; time to 1 km, not recorded, to 5 km (14) 8·2 min, (bis) 9·6, (production) 6·5; service ceiling (14) 9,4 km, (bis) 7,2, (production) 9430 m (30,940 ft); range, no data; time 360° circle 16·5/14/14 s; take-off (14) 120 m, (production) 230 m; landing (14) 260 m, (production) 320 m/129 km/h.

ANT-32 Projected single-seat fighter in KOSOS 1934 programme, monoplane with conventional cannon armament (possibly *moteur-canon*), not built.

ANT-33 No information.

ANT-34 Projected development of ANT-29 with conventional cannon armament in fuselage, two seats, two Wright Cyclone F2 engines, smooth skin throughout, not built.

ANT-35, PS-35 Success of vitally important SB family led not only to civil variants but also to purpose-designed civil airliner using similar parts. Earlier ANT type number suggests prior project deferred until SB in production; certainly little work done until 1934 Aviavnito competition for two sizes of civil airliner, with latest tech features. Tupolev then assigned Arkhangyelskii's brigade to produce an entry using ANT-35 type number. Curiously Shavrov makes no attempt to describe this aircraft, merely stating it used 'wings, tail, landing gear and row of other details without alteration' from SB. This was not so: airframe differed throughout, though main gears were similar. Wing of typical KOSOS light-alloy construction with horizontal centre section extending to outer edges of nacelles and outer panels with 7° dihedral; straight taper from root on TE, two main and two secondary spars with riveted truss construction, ribs part pressed from sheet, skin 0,6/1,0 mm on c/s, 0,5/0,6 mm outer wings, riveting around LE to front spar being flush. Split flaps, three sections each side (two c/s, one outer wing) hydraulically driven to 60°. Modern tail unit of mainly pressed-sheet construction with flush riveted 0,5-mm skin on LE. Control surfaces with deeply inset hinges and with small horn balance on rudder, smooth LE skin but 20 × 5 mm corrugated skin aft of spar. Trim tabs throughout, dual pilot control with electric autopilot. Main gears welded KhMA fork for 1000 × 300 mm tyre, pneumatic brakes and hydraulic retraction rearwards into bay with twin doors leaving part tyre protruding. Fixed balloon tailwheel. French engines in NACA long-chord cowls with rear adjustable gills driving three-blade 3,2-m ground-adjustable dural props. Fuselage semi-monocoque of relatively small (1,5 × 2 m) section, five windows with adjacent seat each side, door rear on left with rear toilet and baggage, each passenger having individual hot-air outlet (exhaust heat-exchange system), light and ventilator. Payload 840 kg.

Construction of prototype NO35 swift and (Shavrov) totally free from complication. First flight M.M. Gromov 20 August 1936; on factory test showed good qualities, flew Moscow/Leningrad/Moscow (1266 km in 3 h 38 min) 15 September, and in November/December flew to Paris and back for static display at Salon de l'Aéronautique. Judged easily best of Aviavnito twin-engined submissions, but cabin ceiling too low (1,68 m max on centreline) and serious obstruction by spars passing through fuselage at backs of 2nd and 3rd seat rows. Second aircraft therefore built, **ANT-35bis** with longer and deeper fuselage offering centreline interior height 1,83 m (6 ft) and with raised floor giving underfloor baggage space (as well as larger compartment at rear) and only slight ridges at spar booms. Engines changed for M-62 (Cyclone) driving VISh-2 (licensed Hamilton) propellers, D/F loop aerial for HF radio above cockpit roof, pilot/passenger emergency hatch in roof, increased fuel capacity 990 lit in centre section, carb-air inlet in upper lip of cowl. Accepted by Aeroflot and assigned service designation PS-35 (*Passazhirskii Samolyet*); series production of 11 aircraft 1937–1939. Used on Moscow to Riga/Stockholm, Prague, Leningrad, Lvov, Simfero-

PS-35 after forced landing

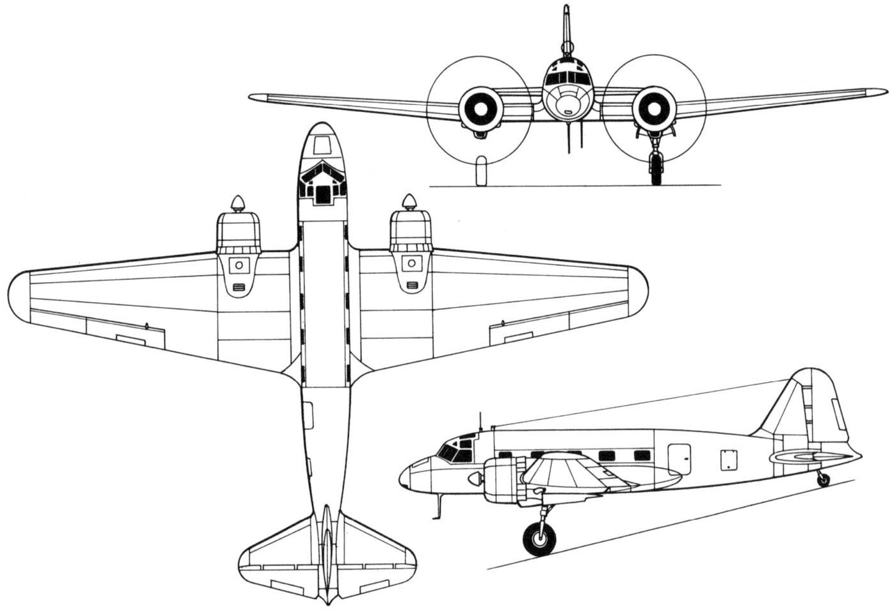

ANT-35, PS-35

pol and Odessa to June 1941. Never seen on skis but in winter spinners removed and perforated baffle added at front of engine. Engine installation identical to Li-2; speed higher but much less payload. Several continued to fly in rear areas during Second World War.

DIMENSIONS Span 20,8 m (68 ft 2⅞ in); length (ANT) 14,95 m (49 ft 0⅝ in), (PS) 15,4 m (50 ft 6¼ in); wing area 57,8 m² (622 ft²).

ENGINES (ANT) two 800 hp GR 14K, later M-85, (PS) two 1000 hp M-62IR.

WEIGHTS Empty (ANT) 4710 kg (10,384 lb), (PS) 5012 kg (11,049 lb); fuel/oil (A) 690 kg, (P) 710+90; loaded (A) 6620 kg (14,594 lb), (P) 7 t (15,432 lb).

PERFORMANCE Max speed (A) 350 km/h at SL, 376 km/h (234 mph) at 4 km, (P) 350 at SL, 372 (231 mph) at 1,5 km; time to height (P) 6·1 min to 3 km, 13 to 5; service ceiling (A) 8,5 km, (P) 7,2 (23,620 ft); range with 10 pax (A) 920 km, (P) 1640 km (1020 miles); take-off (P) 225 m/10 s; landing 300 m/19 s/105 km/h (65 mph).

ANT-36, RD-VV, DB-1 In January 1933 KOSOS was instructed to begin work on military ANT-25 designated RD-VV (*Voyennyi Variant*). In most respects identical to final ANT-25 except for mid-fuselage rebuilt to incorporate bomb bay with four FAB-100 hung nose-up in compartments between wing spars 1 and 2 with spring-loaded lower doors opened by bombs on release. Above this bay, observer/gunner cockpit with DA (one drawing shows twin DA). Development assigned N. A. Fomin under supervision of Sukhoi, but by 1934 VVS had decided such slow and near-defenceless aircraft would not be effective, and prototype RD-VV never completed. Parts were used in manufacture of first DB-2 (ANT-37).

ANT-37, DB-2 Recognizing futility of trying to make effective bomber from RD, Sukhoi's brigade assigned December 1934 to creating new long-range twin-engined bomber using whatever RD parts were suitable. Believed to be Sukhoi's idea; much larger project than ANT-36 and whole Sukhoi brigade assigned, with direct Tupolev supervision. Sukhoi retained basic wing structure but completely altered rib peripheries to accept dural stressed skin, without corrugations, flush-riveted around LE as far as front spar. Span slightly reduced, ailerons increased in chord (projecting behind wing TE throughout instead of only two inner sections as on RD) and number of sections reduced to three. Almost entirely new fuselage, stressed-skin semi-monocoque, with accommodation for nose gunner in glazed turret filling whole depth of nose, pilot in enclosed cockpit with rearward-sliding hood above LE and mid-upper radio/gunner with retrac turret. Planned armament 20 mm in nose, twin ShKAS in dorsal turret, not fitted. Engines mounted on steel-tube frames at extremities of centre section in long-chord NACA cowls with rear cooling gills, carb-air inlets at bottom lip of cowl, 3,25 m two-blade wooden fixed-pitch props. Bomb bay in fuselage between wing spars increased to carry four FAB-250 or other loads totalling 1 t with powered doors. Tail based on ANT-25 but greater chord and reduced height, smooth skin and horizontal tail only just above fuselage. Landing gear with twin doors closing over legs, twin-wheel units being housed as before upstream of fixed rear fairing. Simple fixed tailwheel.

Prototype ANT-37, service designation DB-2 (*Dal'nii Bombardirovshchik*, long-range bomber), first flown 16 June 1935. Generally satisfactory but onset of tail buffet as speed increased and 20 July 1935 in shallow dive violent vertical oscillation of horizontal tail caused total structural failure of rear fuselage; pilot K.K. Popov and leading engineer M.M. Yegorov escaped by parachute but electrical engineer on board killed. Major research programme begun into flight control surfaces and systems, aerodynamic buffet and induced flutter, published in *Tekhnika Vozdushnogo Flota* (air fleet engineering) in late 1935. Sukhoi quickly completed *dubler*, **DB-2D**, with many modifications including improved wing/body fairing, strengthened rear fuselage and completely redesigned tail with defects corrected, with insignificant weight penalty. Three-blade Hamilton (VISh-2) propellers, carb-air inlets moved back to cowl gills, modified tankage. Tested February 1936 and in NII trials 20 August 1936 demonstrated 1-t bombload carried Moscow/Omsk/Moscow 4995 km at 213 km/h average. After evaluation against Ilyushin possibilities ANT-37 ordered into production as DB-2, but order switched to TsKB-30 (became DB-3) on personal insistence of Stalin.

On direct government order KOSOS also built third aircraft, **ANT-37bis (DB-2B)** as unarmed long-range research and record-breaking machine; Tupolev said he remonstrated, pointing out no chance of exceeding RD figure for range, or any height or speed records, but order remained. Sukhoi refined airframe in further small details, with hemispherical glazed nose with curved panes of moulded Plexiglas, flush rear cockpit and retractable tailwheel. Fully equipped nav station in nose and radio station in rear cockpit. Fully retractable landing gears with bays closed by doors with no part of tyre projecting, fully retractable tailwheel, electrical operation by pushbuttons, first in Soviet Union. Considerably greater fuel capacity in 12 wing tanks, matched by greater engine power; engine installations as DB-2 dubler except addition of spinners. Rapid production of three DB-2B, a fourth with even greater outer-wing tankage not being completed. First aircraft flown February 1936 and named *Rodina* (motherland). After long wait same aircraft set world women's long-distance record 24/25 September 1938 in hands of V.S. Grizodubov, P.D. Osipenko and M.M. Raskov, flying Moscow 5908 km to wheels-up landing in flooded valley of Amur near Kerbi in 26 h 29 min. Subsequently long career with Aeroflot and, during Second World War, at Moscow factory as research and trials aircraft.

DIMENSIONS Span 31,0 m (101 ft 8½ in); length (both, approx) 15,0 m (49 ft 2½ in) (published drawings are inaccurate, showing length 12,5–12,8 m); wing area 84,9 m² (914 ft²).

ENGINES (2) Two 800 hp GR K14, (2D) 800 hp M-85, (bis) 950 hp M-86.

WEIGHTS Empty (2) 5,8 t (12,787 lb), (bis) 5855 kg (12,908 lb); fuel/oil (2) 4050+380, (bis) 5525+430 kg; loaded (2) normal 9450 kg (20,833 lb), overload 11,5 t (25,353 lb), (bis) 12,5 t (27,557 lb).

PERFORMANCE Max speed (2, normal weight) 301 km/h at SL, 342 (213 mph) at 4 km, (bis) 300 at SL, 340 (211 mph) at 4,2 km; endurance (bis) 30 h; range (2) 5000 km, (bis) 7300 km (4550 miles); take-off (bis, full load) 1 km.

ANT-38 Projected high-speed bomber of 1934, believed to be standard bomber version of ANT-41 torpedo carrier.

ANT-39 Not known.

ANT-40, SB/SB-2/SB-3, PS-40/-41, MMN Numerically most important bomber in world in late 1930s, this family was first modern stressed-skin aircraft produced in quantity in the Soviet Union and probably most formidable bomber of mid-1930 era. Many versions saw extensive action in Spain, Far East, Mongolia, Finland and against invaders during Second World War, as well as various GVF duties in

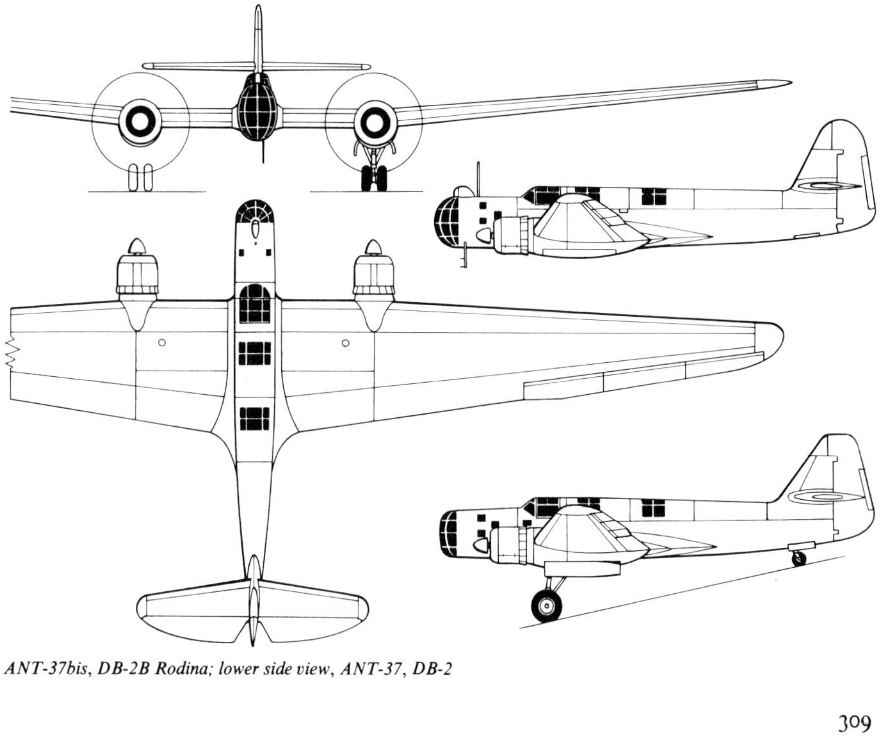

ANT-37bis, DB-2B Rodina; lower side view, ANT-37, DB-2

civil variants, as trainers and in many secondary roles. Closely related variants SB-RK, RK and KR described earlier, see Arkhangyelskii Ar-2.

Predictably, plenty of room for confusion. Soviet accounts (not only Shavrov) give April 1934 as first flight, ignore designation SB-1, state fuel capacity 1670 lit (1200 kg) but give mass as 530 kg, give designation ANT-40 for first water-cooled (Hispano) aircraft and length of first (Wright-engined) prototype as 10,48 m. None of this tallies with Western accounts, which are largely erroneous, and following is best compromise.

VVS requirement for SB (*Skorostnoi Bombardirovshchik*, fast bomber) issued by NII October 1933 and KOSOS immediately took up challenge, basing **ANT-40** submissions on ANT-29 and other existing designs. Assigned by Tupolev to Arkhangyelskii brigade, work beginning January 1934. Clean stressed-skin aircraft with smooth skin, wing raised to provide room for internal bomb bay, otherwise similar to ANT-29 wing but of simpler construction. Centre section 5 m wide tapered on TE only, no dihedral on upper surface, outer wings 5° dihedral, TsAGI-6mod profile t/c 16% tapering to 12,5 at tip. Two spars throughout with 30-KhGSA tube lower booms, other members wrapped sheet and L-section diag bracing. Ribs riveted truss construction with U (top hat) periphery and tubular/diag bracing, ruling spacing 200/250 mm. Centre-section skin 0,6/1,0 mm, outer wings 0,5/0,6 mm, flush-riveted throughout. Stumpy fuselage, modern structure with U-section frames and stringers, main frames (eg, at spars/bomb bay) pressed from sheet (no closed tubes or complex sections). Skin applied mainly in long strips arranged axially, ruling gauge 0,5 mm flush-riveted. Broken into three sections, F-1 for nav/bomb with glazed noze (Celluloid panels) with vertical slit for ShKAS; F-2 with integral wing centre-section set at +2° and including enclosed pilot cockpit and bomb bay; F-3 with radio/gunner able to aim guns through upper aperture covered by hood sliding forwards and lower hatch slid forwards internally. Welded KhMA landing gear forks with 950 × 250 mm tyres, single oleo legs with side braces pulled to rear by hydraulic jack (unusual for KB) acting on midpoint of rear breaker strut, much of tyre exposed at open end of nacelle but doors closed over legs. Wright Cyclone engines in short NACA cowls without gills, centrelines 4,8 m apart, 3,2-m Hamilton three-blade bracket-type props. Flight controls mainly push/pull rods, unbalanced ailerons and rudder, tailplane fixed incidence (0°), trimmers on rudder and right aileron. Four sections split flap, hydraulic drive to max 60°.

This aircraft, service designation SB (no suffix), first flown 25 April 1934 and factory tested after fitting M-87 engines from 29 June 1934, by K.K. Popov and I.S. Zhurov, until 29 September when damaged in landing accident. Rebuilt with much longer fuselage and more tapered outer wings of same span but area reduced from 47,6 to 46,3 m². Repeated factory testing 5 February 1935 to July 1935, but not submitted to NII test because of superior performance of ANT-40. Subsequently used as hack to develop retractable skis.

ANT-40 was first with water-cooled Hispano-Suiza engines, fitted for comparative purposes. Wing same 19 m span but much greater chord giving area 51,92 m²; taller vertical

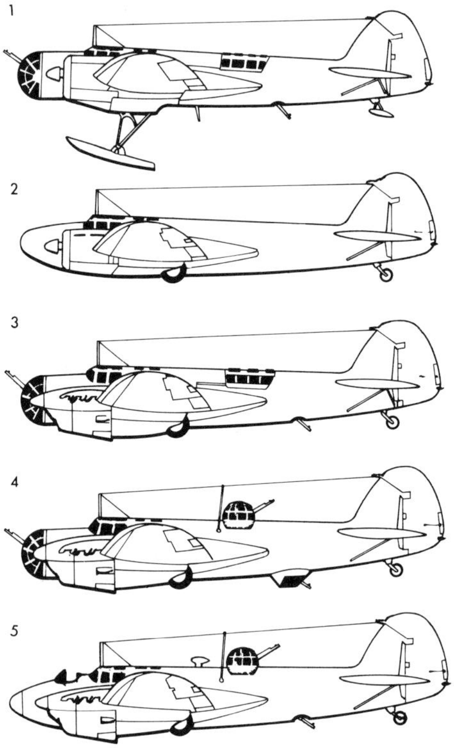

ANT-40 variants: 1, SB-2 with skis; 2, PS-40; 3, SB-2/M-103; 4, SB-3; 5, USB (without A-7 towing provisions)

tail and horn-balanced rudder, ailerons with partial balance (both aerodynamic and mass). First flown 7 October 1934 and after encouraging factory tests completed NII test programme February/July 1935. Direct frontal radiators, twin exhaust pipes to open rear of nacelle above wing, two-blade 3,3 m metal props, wire-braced tailplane, fixed tailwheel, landing light in left LE, tabs on both elevators and both ailerons. Twin ShKAS in nose, one or pair in upper rear and one in lower rear, total 4420 rounds; bombload four FAB-100 (overload, six) hung nose-up, various other loads possible. Production planned at two factories (believed GAZ-6 and GAZ-22) from mid-1934 and series aircraft designated SB-2 began to appear end 1935. These incorporated changes, some of which (those asterisked) were introduced with last prototype, ANT-40$_2$, on factory test September 1935 to February 1936. Also designated **SB-2 IS** (believed for *Izmeneniya Samolyet*, altered aircraft), introduced licesed M-100 engines mounted 100 mm further forward, LE of outer wings swept back at 9° instead of 4·5°, larger tail surfaces, elevators with inset hinges and 50/80% mass-balance, powered MV-2 or MV-3 dorsal turret with twin ShKAS, and bomb bay able to take six FAB-100 vertically or two FAB-250 Horizontally. Later ANT-40 used for armament trials including various arrangements of RS-132 rockets under outer wings and battery of four 20 mm Sh VAK under fuselage with 520 rounds.

Most important mods introduced at start of production were increase in dimensions and final rectification of defects. Span and length significantly extended but with curiously small change empty weight; wing area jumped to 56,7 m² to permit future weight growth and avoid inability to use existing fields (stipulated in 1933 requirement). Flush riveting abandoned (problems) except for LE of wing and tail. Landing gears strengthened and improved mechanically, and aircraft cleared for use with fixed skis (main 2800 × 820 mm, tail 800 × 320 mm); single SB-2 flown with retractable skis previously proved with SB prototype. Production as well as development assigned to Arkhangyelskii, ceaseless struggle to keep weight down and never did achieve desired nose angles of gunfire and vision nor escape for nav from nose in wheels-up landing. Series aircraft cleared for operation from hard surface at 6,5 t which at 0,525/0,625 kg fuel per km equated to 2150 km. During manufacture of first blocks 1936 engine changed to M-100A, distinguished by wider (near-circular) cowl with improved front radiator fitted with pilot/thermostat venetian blinds and ventral air exit; prop changed from VISh two-position bracket-type to VISh-2 fully variable, adding 1 km to ceiling, no change in speed. Outstanding well-recorded performance in Spanish war, acquired popular name *Katyushka*. One 1937 aircraft completed as dual trainer, similar to later USB.

From late 1936 one series aircraft modified as civil transport, prolonged test and in 1938 appreciable number completed in this form and delivered to Aeroflot with designation PS-40

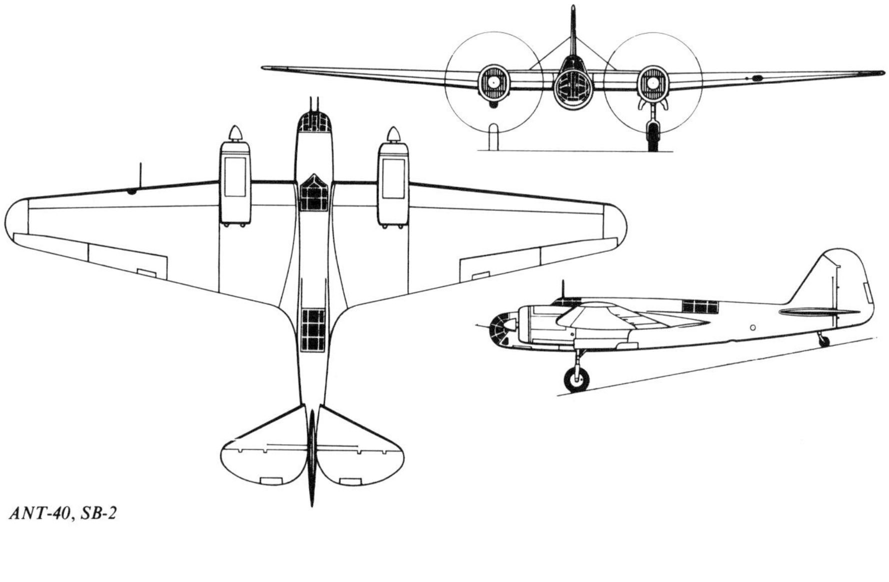

ANT-40, SB-2

(*Passazhirskii Samolyet*). Despite designation, used almost exclusively for freight, three removable aluminium boxes total 2,58 m^3 (author suggests this was volume of each box), with closure net at top, cleared to 6,4 t and often on fixed skis. Single PS-40 with training cockpit in nose tested 11/16 March 1938. First license agreement for Soviet aircraft with Czech government March 1937 for SB-2 with Czech equipment and Avia-built HS12Ydrs engines, designation **B-71**; 53 assembled GAZ-6 and intended 161 by Avia/Letov/Aero but none complete by Nazi occupation and only 66 by Avia plus 45 by Aero for Luftwaffe. In contrast Soviet output by 1938 was 13 per day.

Development of improved Klimov engines led late 1935 to **SB-2bis**, first flown October 1936 using SB airframe and subsequently refined. Main change M-103 engine in improved cowl with radiator of different shape in ventral tunnel requiring deeper cowl and nacelle which still did not enclose wheel. External exhaust pipes discharging above wing, VISh-22 constant-speed props mounted (longer engine) further forward, two extra wing tanks, often elec starters though Hucks dogs retained. Restressed airframe for greater weights, provision for underwing Der-19 bomb pods, 280 lit long-range tanks or RS-82/132 rockets (rarely seen in photos), and from early in production improved elec system and radio-gunner given MV-2 turret. Later 1938 lower rear position redesigned as permanent ventral gondola with glazed windows, still operated by dorsal radio/gunner. First M-103 aircraft set alt 12 695 m (no FAI instruments) 1 November 1936; series SB-2bis (believed first) set homologated 12 246,5 m with 1 t payload 2 September 1937, pilot M.Yu. Alekseyev.

SB-2 captured June 1941

B-71 in Luftwaffe service

SB-2bis captured by Finland

In late 1937 sale of over 200 SB-2 (some ex-VVS) to China used up last of original stocks, deliveries with original armament and equipment and Russian instruments and instructions. Persistent Western accounts of SB-3 with M-103A engines not found in Soviet records. Original SB-3 was production trainer, also called **USB** but not SB-2UT. Unchanged basic airframe, M-103 engines, instructor in open nose cockpit from which head poked by raising seat only when dire emergency. At least 550 built new or converted, standard tug for trains of A-7 sailplanes and for transport gliders during the Second World War, widely used to support partisans. **SB-3bis** tested by Stefanovskii and Lipkin 1938 but rejected, improved cowling with inlet further back and changed arrangement of water and oil cooling matrices. Retractable skis not normally fitted to bombers but 1939 civil transport **PS-41**, also called **SB-3G** and **PS-40bis**, cleared to 7 t with M-103U engines and strengthened wheel gear or tandem-leg ski gears folding to rear with same mechanism as for wheels; skis as before except main pair wider (910 mm). **PS-41bis** similar but with underwing points plumbed for long-range tanks, 270-kg capacity each (litres not stated).

Production completed about January 1941 at approx 6656 aircraft. This included several non-standard versions. MMN (*Modifikatsya Men'she Nesushchye*, modified smaller lifting surface) was unsuccessful 1939 attempt to gain speed at expense of all else: M-105 engines, streamlined nose, small wings, only three ShKAS but bombload 1 t. Not easy to handle and fast landing, helped to develop engine installation of SB-RK (see Arkhangyelskii Ar-2) and then passed to Aeroflot where used as trials aircraft nicknamed *Shchuka* (pike). Another SB-2bis (no designation known) rebuilt by I.P. Tolstykh at TsAGI 1940 for research into tricycle landing gears (used previously in KhAI-4 and SAM-13). Fixed gear, both wheels and skis, with instrumentation and ventral camera installation to study aircraft behaviour, shimmy and other problems; pilot Gallai liked it and good results. Passed to LII NKAP 1941.

DIMENSIONS Span (ANT-40, 40_1, 40_2) 19,0 m (62 ft 4 in), (rest) 20,33 m (66 ft 8½ in); length (40) 10,48 m, (40_1) 12,15 m, (40_2, PS-41, SB-3bis) 12,27 m (40 ft 3 in), (SB-2, 2bis, PS-40) 12,57 m (41 ft 2¾ in), (SB-3) 12,88 m (42 ft 3 in); wing area (40) 47,6 m^2, later 46,3, (40_1) 51,92 m^2, (40^2) 51,95 m^2, (rest) 56,7 m^2 (610 ft^2).

ENGINES (SB) Two 730 hp Cyclone SGR-1820-FF2, later 730 hp M-87, (40_1, 40_2) 760 hp

HS12Ybrs, (SB-2) 750 hp M-100, later (and all PS-40) 860 hp M-100A, (2bis, 3, 3bis) 960 hp M-103, (PS-41) 960 hp M-103U.
WEIGHTS Empty (40) 3210 kg, (40_1) 3464 kg, (40_2) 3900 kg, (SB-2) 4060 kg (8951 lb), (PS-40) 4138 kg, (2bis) 4768 kg (10,511 lb), (3) 4680 kg, (PS-41) 4380 kg, (41bis) 4810 kg; fuel/oil (prototypes) 530 + 60 kg, (SB-2, 2bis) 1200 kg, (PS-41) 1200 + 100, (41bis) 1730; loaded (40) 4828 kg, (40_1) 5000 kg, (40_2) 5468 kg, (SB-2) 5628 kg (12,407 lb), (PS-40) 5706 kg, (2bis) 6380/7880 kg overload (17,372 lb), (3) 6050 kg, (3bis) 6186 kg, (PS-41) 7 t.
PERFORMANCE Max speed (40) 403 km/h, (40_1) given as 351 km/h, certainly error, (40_2) 418 km/h at 5,3 km, (SB-2) 326 at SL, 393 (244 mph) at 5,2 km, (PS-40) wheels 372 SL, 423 at 4 km, skis 308 SL, 341 at 3,4 km, (2bis) 375 SL, 450 (280 mph) at 4,1 km, (2bis overload) 353/414, (3) 375/450, (3bis) 400/486 (302 mph), (PS-41) 372/428; climb to 1 km (SB-2) 2·8 min, (2bis) 1·8, (PS-41) 2·1 min; service ceiling (40_2) 9560 m, (SB-2) 9 km (29,530 ft), (2bis overload) 7,8 km, (3bis) 9,6, (PS-41) 7750/9400 m; range (40_2) 580 km, (SB-2) 1250 km (777 miles), (2bis overload) 2300 km, (PS-41) 1130 or (overload) 1940 km; time 360° circle (2, 2bis) 21/28 s, radius 280 m; take-off (2) 300 m/16 s, (2bis overload) 455 m/21 s, (PS-41 overload) given as 600 m/32 s; landing (most) 300 m/32 s/122 km/h, (2bis overload) 475 m, (PS-41, min) 220 m/12 s.

ANT-41, T-1 This torpedo bomber was related to SB family but heavier and more powerful. Project launched with order for two prototypes March 1934, assigned to KOSOS exptl aircraft bureau led by V.M. Myasishchyev and first aircraft completed June 1936. Two-spar wing derived from existing TsAGI designs but increased chord and area, ailerons in two sections, large split flaps. Fuselage based on ANT-40 but stronger construction especially along internal weapon bay where main frames heavy box section. Many other frames of closed profile, stringers L and box profiles, all exterior skin flush-riveted. Vertical tail as SB, broad horizontal tail with straight sharp taper. Engines in well-streamlined cowlings driving large (4,0 m) three-blade propellers, water radiators in wing, two per engine, fed by duct from LE inlets and with aft-facing exit apertures in upper surface behind rear spar. Crew of three as in SB, main gears as SB but tailwheel retractable, large fuel capacity between wing spars, bombload two FAB-500 or two small 406 mm torpedoes side-by-side, overload two 980 kg torpedoes.

First flight June 1936 by A.P. Chernavskii and two crew, better all-round performance than SB and good handling, every expectation of very successful aircraft. On 14th flight T-1 suddenly broke up in air; crew escaped. Cause traced to inadequate aileron mass-balance (80 instead of 105%) resulting in flutter violent enough to cause failure of wing. Plans for T-1 production immediately stopped; later manufacture of second aircraft, ANT-41bis, also discontinued.
DIMENSIONS Span 25,73 m (84 ft 5 in); length 13,8 m (45 ft 3⅓ in); wing area 88,94 m² (957 ft²).
ENGINES Two 1275 hp M-34FRN.
WEIGHTS Empty 5846 kg (12,888 lb); fuel/oil 1900 + 150 kg; loaded 8925 kg (19,676 lb).
PERFORMANCE Max speed 435 km/h (270 mph) at SL, greater at height; service ceiling 9,5 km (31,170 ft); range (Shavrov) 4200 km (this seems error, might be 2400); take-off 370 m; no other data.

ANT-42, Pe-8 Described under Petlyakov as Pe-8.

ANT-43 Not to be confused with PS-43 (no PS number was assigned), this KOSOS high-speed transport was designed 1936. Clean low-wing monoplane with flush-riveted skin, 800 hp GR14Krsd engine, seven seats (this is believed to include pilot), construction described as similar to I-14 (suggesting Sukhoi's brigade), main gears retracting inwards. Radical manufacturing method, commonly used other countries, of photographing from templates direct to metal sheet. Master templates only reference, no conventional drawings. After much argument TsAGI (afraid of reprisals after any trouble) refused to permit ANT-43 to go to flight test. No data.

ANT-44, MTB-2 Also called **TsAGI-44**, this was one of TsAGI programmes directly under Tupolev supervision, until his arrest. Launched early 1935 to meet NII VVS (MA) need for large ocean-going reconnaissance/bombing flying boat or amphibian, more modern design than previous AGOS and KOSOS marine aircraft and in 1935 one of first in world to have four engines on LE of wing mounted direct to hull. Wing TsAGI-6mod profile, 15% t/c over constant-profile with centre section dihedral, outer wings evenly tapered with upper surface horizontal. Two main spars, tubular truss structure but some outer ribs pressed from sheet; two-section balanced ailerons, slotted flaps on centre section and inboard outer panels. Deep but well-profiled hull, tested in TsAGI towing tank, broad V-section planing bottom with main step at 90° and rear bottom tapering to aft knife-edge, narrower upper hull accommodating crew 7/8. Single fin carrying braced fixed-incidence tailplane, all control surfaces mass balance and tabs. First aircraft with French engines, KOSOS installations, wing LE hinged down each side to form work platforms, fuel between spars of wing, fixed underwing floats, provision for beaching chassis, armament three ShKAS in nose and tail turrets and sliding roof over rear dorsal cockpit (unusual change in level along top of rear hull); 2,5 t load of bombs, mines or other dropped stores carried under centre section.

First aircraft completed Sevastopol and test flown by T.V. Ryabenko and Il'inskii 19 April 1937; successful factory testing followed by NII

ANT-44D

tests late 1937. Second aircraft **ANT-44bis, ANT-44D**, built as amphibian with large single-wheel main gears pulled up (not retracted) for water operations by hydraulic jack acting on hinge of main oleo leg; castoring tailwheel aft of stern knife-edge. ANT-44D also had more powerful Russian-built engines, VISh-3 propellers of 3,5 m diameter, and MV-series dorsal turret in place of sliding hatch, larger vertical tail with rudder inset hinges but no horn balance, similar change to elevators. First flight Ryabenko 7 June 1938; subsequently TsAGI tests from Moscow reservoir and NII tests Sevastopol. No real deficiencies but decision not to build in series and

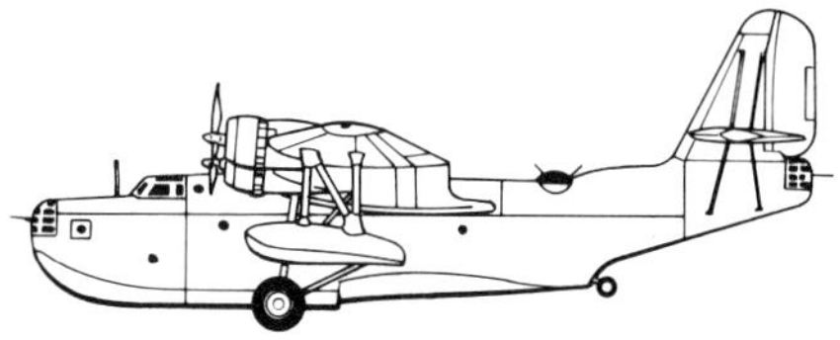

ANT-44D

all development ceased Jan 1940. Later I.M. Sukhomlin set five amphibian class records: 17 June 1940, 1-t load to 7134 m; 19 June two flights, 6284 m with 2 t and 5219 m with 5 t; 28 September, with underwing floats jettisoned, 1000-km circuit (Kerch/Kherson/Taganrog) with 1 t payload, 277,45 km/h; 7 October, same circuit with 2 t at 241,9 km/h. During the Second World War both aircraft flew transport and other missions, often in command of Sukhomlin, 1941-1943 in Black Sea area. Western report that ANT-44 was brought up to ANT-44D standard not easy to confirm, though some evidence defensive armament increased after 1941.
DIMENSIONS Span 36,45 m (119 ft 7 in); length 22,42 m (73 ft 6¾ in); wing area 144,7 m^2 (1558 ft^2).
ENGINES (44) four 810 hp GR14Krsd; (44D) 950 hp M-87.
WEIGHTS Empty (44) 12 t, (44D) 13 t (28,660 lb); loaded (44) 18,5 t, 21,5 overload (47,400 lb), (44D) 19 t (41,887) lb).
PERFORMANCE Max speed (44) 330 km/h at SL, (D) 355 (221 mph) at SL, more at height; time to 1 km, (44) 3·5 min, (D) 3 min; service ceiling (44) 6,6 km (21,650 ft), (D) 7,1 (23,300 ft); range (44) 4500 km (2796 miles); endurance (44) 16 h, (D) 14 h; alighting speed (44) 125 km/h, (D) 130.

ANT-45 Unbuilt KOSOS design for 1936 low-wing two-seat fighter (Western report aircraft was based on Vultee V-11 is incorrect).

ANT-46, DI-8 Another heavy fighter in same family as ANT-29 and SB series, ANT-46 was ordered as single prototype December 1934 with VVS designation DI-8 (*Dvukhmestnyi Istrebitel*, two-seat fighter). Assigned to Arkhangyelskii on condition it did not interfere with SB, but troublefree development and first flight 9 August 1935. Project thus ran only weeks behind ANT-29 (DIP) but later and better aircraft with higher performance. Airframe remarkably similar to regular SB-2, with essentially same span and similar area. Even slimmer fuselage with pilot at LE in fighter-like cockpit, radio operator with twin ShKAS at TE, main armament two APK-100 buried in outer wings between ailerons and flaps outboard of prop discs, four ShKAS in nose with 2000 rounds. So far as known, successful factory test programme, completed June 1936, but Tupolev's arrest and termination of Kurchyevskii KB made it impossible to continue, and DI-8 never submitted for NII testing.
DIMENSIONS Span 20,3 m (66 ft 7¼ in); length 12,3 m (40 ft 4¼ in); wing area 55,7 m^2 (600 ft^2).
ENGINES Two 800 hp GR14Krsd.
WEIGHTS Empty 3487 kg (7687 lb); loaded 5280 kg (11,640 lb).
PERFORMANCE Max speed 357 km/h at SL, 400 (249 mph) at 4 km; time to 3 km, 7·6 min; service ceiling 8080 m (17,800 ft); range 1780 km (1100 miles); landing speed 117 km/h.

ANT-47 Unbuilt fighter project of 1937, design in Tupolev's absence.

ANT-48 Unbuilt high-speed bomber project of 1936.

ANT-49 Unbuilt project for reconnaissance version of SB-2 1936, M-100A engines, three cameras in heated bay in place of original bomb bay, augmented fuel tankage.

ANT-50 High-speed passenger transport project 1937, said to be based on ANT-35, two M-34 engines, not built.

ANT-51 Single-engined tac-recon and attack aircraft begun 1936 in Sukhoi's brigade under Tupolev supervision; after latter's arrest managed by chief engineer GUAP (position from which Tupolev dismissed) and prototype built at KOZOK 1937. One of designs in Ivanov programme, modern Sukhoi dural stressed-skin construction, flush exterior riveting. Tandem-seat cockpits with long greenhouse canopy, main gears fixed and spatted, fixed tailwheel, four ShKAS in outer wings, single ShKAS in rear cockpit, internal bay for 300-kg bombload. First flight M.M. Gromov 25 August 1937, fair performance and handling but needed retrac gear and more power; and KOZOK instructed to economize on light alloy. Sukhoi developed two further prototypes under Ivanov programme, both flown 1939, with later engine, three-blade prop of greater diameter, main gears fully retracting inwards into wing, wooden monocoque fuselage and more eqpt. NII tests 1939, led to BB-1 and Su-2 described under Sukhoi.
DIMENSIONS (all) Span 14,3 m (46 ft 11 in); length (1937) 9,92 m, (1939) 10,25 m (33 ft 7½ in); wing area 29,0 m^2 (312 ft^2).
ENGINE (1937) One 820 hp M-62, (1939) 950 hp M-87A, later 950 hp M-87B.
WEIGHTS Empty (1937) 2604 kg, (1939) 2816 kg (6208 lb); fuel/oil (1939) 550 kg; loaded (1937) 3937 kg (8679 lb), (1939) 4030/4080 kg (8995 lb).
PERFORMANCE Max speed (1937) 360 km/h at SL, 403 (250 mph) at 4,7 km, (1939) 375 at SL, 470 (292 mph) at 4 km; time to 5 km (1937) 16·6 min, (1939) 11·5; service ceiling (1937) 7440 m, (1939) 8800 (28,900 ft); range (1937) 1200 km, (1939) 1160 (720 miles); take-off (1937) 380 m/20 s; landing 240 m/16 s/120 km/h.

ANT-52 No information.

ANT-53 Unbuilt 1936 project in Petlyakov brigade for high-alt long-range bomber and strategic reconnaissance aircraft with four M-34FRNV engines, possibly intended for pressure cabin.

ANT-54 to **ANT-56** One of these was assigned to SRB (*Skorostnoi Razvyedchik Bombardirovshchik*) described under A.P. Golubkov; Shavrov says research difficult.

ANT-57, DPB Evidence suggests this number assigned to one of Tupolev's own projects drawn whilst in prison 1937; long-range high-altitude dive bomber with four M-105.

ANT-58, Aeroplane 103, FB, Tu-58 This important prototype led to Tu-2, programme exceptional for scope and complexity even for Soviet Union. Main technical description appears under ANT-61, basic production Tu-2S; post-war variants also described separately but all consecutive and as far as possible in chronological sequence even where this disarranges ANT number sequence.

When Tupolev was arrested about October 1936 much time wasted because plans for use of such design leaders had not been worked out; about 18 months spent in Lubyanka and Butyrkii prisons, occupying cell with his wife and drawing board. Vague command to design aircraft to beat Ju 88, and proceeded to scheme ANT-58 (number by chance same as cell at Butyrkii). No proper organization until 1938 when detained lead designers were formed into OTBs (*Osoboye Tekhnichyeskii Buro*, personal technical bureau) numbered from 100, Tupolev being No 103. Aircraft thus called **Samolyet 103**; later led to ANT numbers 58-69 inclusive and Tu numbers 1 to 10. Design based for horizontal and dive bombing but also later adapted to torpedo, reconnaissance, air-combat, LR interception, *Shturmovik*, transport and training roles. Clean mid-wing monoplane with large bomb bay beneath wing, twin-finned tail and crew of three: pilot ahead of wing in large fully glazed cockpit with hinged side and roof, reflector sight for two ShVAK in wing roots firing ahead, nav/bomb facing forward with small chart table behind pilot and alternative prone bomb position in glazed nose, radio/gunner in

ANT-46, DI-8

ANT-58, 103

ANT-58, 103

remote rear cockpit with twin ShKAS above and below, latter aimed via periscope after sliding forward hatch in floor, with additional observation porthole each side and glazed lower area to rear of bomb bay. Engines underslung with long nacelles completely housing retracted main gears, radiators in ducts under engines, oil coolers in separate external ducts on side of nacelle, 3,4 m VISh-61T three-blade c/s props, fuel in self-sealing wing tanks. Max bombload 3-t, twin bomb doors. Electrical slatted divebrakes under outer wings. Design approved and prototype construction authorized 1 March 1940. Authority also for second aircraft with fourth crew member, built as ANT-59. Original Aircraft 103 built rapidly by OKB-103 experimental manufacturing dept led by R. L. Bartini and S.P. Korolev. Complete except for engines 3 October 1940; engine non-delivery and snags delayed first flight until 29 January 1941, pilot M.A. Nyukhtikov (often said in West to be M.P. Vasyakin) with leading engineer V.A. Miruts. Outstanding aircraft, assigned service tag FB (*Frontovoi Bombardirovshchik*, frontal bomber) and also called Tu-58. Factory test at GAZ-156 complete 28 April 1941, CG demo 25·6/30·6%, still lacking much equipment and both sets rear guns not fully developed. NII tests June 1941; later (date not known) lost when back at KB (evacuated to GAZ-166) following fire in right engine, Nyukhtikov escaping but engineer A. Akopyan killed when parachute caught on tail.

DIMENSIONS Span 18,7 m (61 ft 4¼ in); length 13,2 m (43 ft 3½ in); wing area 48,4 m^2 (521 ft^2).

ENGINES Two 1400 hp AM-37.

WEIGHTS Empty 7626 kg (16,812 lb); fuel/oil 2147 kg; loaded 9950 kg normal, 10 992 kg (24,233 lb) max.

PERFORMANCE Max speed 482 km/h at SL, 635 (395 mph) at 8 km; time to 5 km 8·6 min; service ceiling 10,6 km (34,780 ft); range (Shavrov, doubted by author) 2500 km (1550 miles); take-off 440 m; landing 730 m/155 km/h.

ANT-59, 103U Second prototype with redesigned longer fuselage providing for fourth crew-member to fire single ShKAS from lower rear hatch; raised canopy over pilot and nav and latter seated facing aft with twin ShKAS augmenting rear dorsal pair; ten RS rockets under outer wings. Taller fins/rudders, oil coolers in wings with LE inlets, 3,8 m VISh-61P (later VISh-61Ye) props all with 150 mm cooling-air hole in spinner. Remarkable CG range 16·3/32·25%. First flight 18 May 1941 by Nyukhtikov and Miruts; NII testing complete autumn, and strong recommendation immediate series production, agreed September 1941. Great problem with evacuation of OKB and abandonment of snag-ridden AM-37; after studying AM-39F decision to fit M-82 (ASh-82), task needing 1500 new drawings, done under pressure during evacuation and Aircraft 103U flew again 1 November 1941 with M-82 engines driving AV-5-167 props (same 3,8 m) and other minor changes such as longer nacelles. Speed reduced at height but increased at low level, and floatless (injection) carbs greatly improved negative-g behaviour.

DIMENSIONS Span 18,8 m (61 ft 8¼ in); length 13,8 m (45 ft 3⅓ in); wing area 48,52 m^2 (522 ft^2).

ENGINES As 103, then two 1480 hp M-82.

WEIGHTS (AM-37) empty 7823 kg (17,246 lb); fuel/oil 2456 kg; loaded 10 435 normal, 11 477 kg (25,302 lb) max.

PERFORMANCE (AM-37) max speed 409 SL, 610 (379 mph) 7,8 km, (M-82, 484 SL, 530 at 3,2 km); time to 5 km 9·5 min; service ceiling 10,5 km; range 1900 km (1180 miles); take-off 435 m; landing 765 m/155 km/h.

ANT-60, 103V Production prototype with effort made throughout to reduce number of parts and man-hours, and planned for mass-production with greater emphasis than ever before on accurate tooling, control desks, bench-made wiring looms and pipe-runs, and widest range of subcontracted accessories. Two main assembly lines established at GAZ-166 and (later) 156, and major parts made at many others. Aircraft 103V very similar to re-engined 103U except in minor details of eqpt and in using saw-tooth profile corrugated sheet in wings instead of rectangular parallel-face corrugations, with saving in mass. Aircraft built 1 August to 13 November

ANT-59, 103U

103U re-engined with M-82

ANT-60, 103V

1941, flown by M.P. Vasyakin 15 December and after some rectification of engine faults completed NII testing 22 August 1942. After further testing and rectification began VVS service as instructor trainer, designation **103VS**.
DIMENSIONS As before except length 13,71 m (44 ft 11¾ in).
ENGINES Two 1480 hp ASh-82.
WEIGHTS Empty 7335 kg (16,171 lb); fuel/oil 2411 kg; loaded 10 343 kg normal, 11 773 kg (25,955 lb) max.
PERFORMANCE Max speed 460 SL, 528 km/h (328 mph) at 3,8 km; time to 5 km 10 min; service ceiling 9 km (29,530 ft); range 2000 km (1242 miles); take-off 516 m; landing 640 m/152 km/h.

ANT-61, 103S This aircraft, No 100308, was regarded as first series example. Important changes in equipment including substitution of single UBT for ShKAS at all three movable gun positions and elimination of underwing dive brakes. Vertical tail surfaces redesigned with further slight increase in height and more pointed top. More powerful model of ASh-82, further simplified systems and lower rear gunner given three small portholes each side. NII test 13 September to 28 October 1942, by which time full production beginning at GAZ-166, only to be halted April 1943 because of supposed urgent need for Yak-7, subsequently built there; Western accounts claim Tupolev aircraft almost rejected as too complex, giving this as reason for switching Omsk plant to fighters, but such decisions were taken more than a year earlier (when ANT-60 simplified) and by 1943 at least 12 major factories were engaged in programme with two (possibly three) assembly lines. About 2 November 1942 Aircraft 100308 and next two to be completed were sent to Kalinin front to join 3-Yu VA (3rd Air Army) commanded by M.M. Gromov for combat trials. Outstanding success.
DIMENSIONS As 103U, ie, length 13,8 m.
ENGINES Two 1700 hp ASh-82NV.
WEIGHTS Empty about 7,4 t; loaded 10 538 normal, 11 768 kg (25,944 lb) max.
PERFORMANCE Max speed 521 km/h (324 mph) at 3,2 km; time to 5 km, 5·2 min; service ceiling 9 km; range 2020 km (1255 miles); take-off 450 m; landing 545 m/152 km/h.

ANT-61, Tu-2S First true production aircraft was No 100716, with direct-injection engines and AV-5-167A propellers, and rocket rails removed. Other small changes included simpler nose glazing, longer detachable wingtips (Shavrov states tips cut off, misleading), further revision of electric, hydraulic and fuel systems, and refined armour. Aircraft designated **Tu-2** early 1943 and Tupolev and team released from

ANT-61, 103S

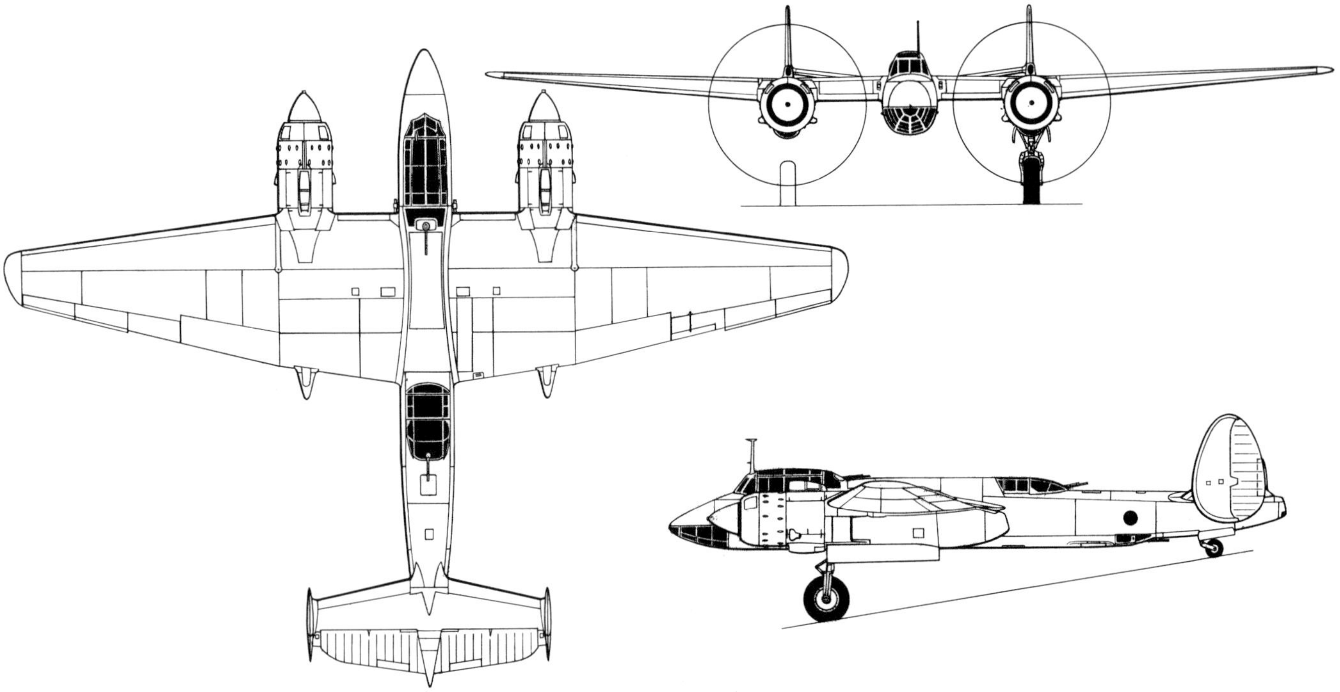

ANT-61, Tu-2S (late series)

Tu-2S (possibly first series aircraft)

detention 15 April 1943 and allowed to return to own GAZ where series production (seriously delayed by previous absence of design team) was organized by Tupolev himself, who was awarded Stalin Prize summer 1943. Aircraft 100716 completed August 1943, first flight 16 August and completed factory test at GAZ-156 and NII test 16 December 1943. About 15 months wasted by terminating production at Omsk and prolonged tinkering long after Tu-2 was fit for service; as it was, large numbers did not reach front-line units until well into 1944.

Aerodynamically outstanding, particular attention to low drag with stiff sandwich wing skins, flush riveting on all external surfaces and painstaking attention to detail on original Aircraft 103, as witness speed higher than any Soviet fighter then in service. Wing TsAGI-40 profile 13·75% root, 9·9% tip, MAC 2885 mm, main structural box formed by LE web at 6·3% chord and single main spar at 35·4% joined by double skins with inner corrugated layer (corrugations spanwise) with thickness 1,5 mm upper and 1,0 mm lower surface. Horizontal centre section tapered only on TE, span 6,56 m, joined by 19 bolts each side to 6,15 m outer panels with taper and 5° dihedral. Third light rear spar at 77% to carry Schrenk-type split flaps on piano hinges, set 15° take-off and 45° for landing. Three-section balanced Frise ailerons with tabbed No 1 section and Nos 2 and 3 increased chord (projecting aft of TE on most series aircraft). Ruling structural material D16-T except for 30KhGSA at landing gear and engine mounts. Fuselage semi-monocoque with 44 ring frames pressed from sheet and four strong but open-section longerons, some L and top-hat frames and stringers but stringers later almost eliminated from mid-fuselage, skin 1,5 mm, thinner at ends (in first two production blocks of 500 each, forward fuselage redesigned in glued *shpon*, with some steel reinforcement). High fixed tailplane with 8° dihedral with inset hinges carrying balanced tabbed elevators and rudders with tabs or ground-adjustable TE strips (in first two production blocks fins often wood with bakelite-ply skins; by 1944 D16-T returned with simple pressed ribs and 0,8 mm skin). Engines on KhGSA welded tube mounts in tight cowls with rear exhausts grouped in cluster each side (various arrangements), carb-air in at top, oil cooler in duct at bottom. Fuel in four inner and four outer tanks between spars, self-sealing and with NG (neutral gas) protection, total 2800 lit (616 gal). One (sometimes two) landing light hinged down below each outer wing. Hydraulic pump on both engines serving landing gear, flaps, bomb doors and wheel brakes (in some aircraft landing gear pneu). Main gears 1142 × 432 mm on forks on single struts retracting to rear; tailwheel 470 × 210 mm also retracting fully to rear, in all cases with twin doors. Access to nose via glazed ventral hatch. Pilot in armoured seat with canopy folding up at roof and down at sides, reflector sight for twin ShVAK in wing roots (usually 100 rounds each), ram's horn flight control by push/pull rods with provision for dual. Nav/bomb with aft-firing UBT with 200 or 250 rounds and prone nose position with stabilized sight for level bombing. Radio op at upper rear with tip-up seat and UBT with 250 rounds. Lower rear gunner with UBT with 250 rounds sighted by ventral periscope. Bombload up to 4 t, all internal in bay with twin hydraulically driven doors, max weapon size FAB-1000.

During course of production, chiefly postwar, series Tu-2 grew in structure mass and equipment until by 1947 empty weight had risen by roughly 1 t, from 7,4 to 8,4 t. Engines did not change but installation varied through numerous mods affecting cowl panels (reduced diameter, with 28 small blisters for valve gear), exhaust (short pipes no longer visible), cooling-air outlet (in sides of nacelle, contoured to give positive thrust at high power), carb-air (inlets reprofiled and lengthened, with filter and anticing provision) and oil cooler (better radiator in reprofiled duct). Most late batches returned to single porthole each side (larger than in proto-

types) for lower rear gunner. There were also variations in wheel size; no Tu-2 seen on skis. Total wartime production given in Western accounts as 1111, fraction of what was possible with properly managed programme; post-war output until 1948 up to 2527 (excluding variants), Soviet accounts state 'about 3000'.
DIMENSIONS Span 18,86 m (61 ft 10½ in); length 13,8 m (45 ft 3¼ in); wing area 48,8 m^2 (525 ft^2).
ENGINES Two 1850 hp ASh-82FN.
WEIGHTS Empty (1943) 7474 kg (16,477 lb), (1948) 8404 kg (18,527 lb); fuel/oil 2016+ 300 kg; loaded (1943) 10 360/11 360 (max 25,044 lb), (1948) 11 450 kg (25,243 lb).
PERFORMANCE Max speed (1943) 482 km/h at SL (300 mph), 547 km/h (340 mph) at 5,4 km, (1948) 550 (342 mph) at 5,7 km; time to 5 km (1943) 9·5 min, (1948) 10·8; service ceiling (1943) 9,5 km (31,170 ft), (1948) 9 km (29,530 ft); range (1943) 2100 km (1300 miles), (1948) 2180; take-off (1943) 485 m, (1948) 540; landing (1943) 675 m/ 158 km/h, (1948) 500 m.

Tu-2M Believed designation for series aircraft modified 1943 with ASh-83 engines driving AV-5V props with four broad hollow-steel blades.
DIMENSIONS As Tu-2.
ENGINES Two 1900 hp ASh-83.
WEIGHTS Loaded 10 585/11 575 kg (max 25,518 lb).
PERFORMANCE Max speed 605 km/h (376 mph) at 8,8 km; time to 5 km, 8.5 min; service ceiling 10,4 km (34,120 ft); range 1950 km; take-off 480 m.

ANT-62, Tu-2D From 1941 Tupolev had schemed **103D** long-range bomber version with longer outer wings and revised forward fuselage for dual pilots. In 1944 time could be spared to build this, and Aircraft 100714 completed as long-range bomber with extended outer wings containing four additional fuel tanks; new pilot cockpit seating two pilots side-by-side, second pilot on right; nav moved to nose in enlarged compartment resulting in nose 0,6-m longer and appreciably wider, with extensive side glazing; tail extended in span (5,4 to 5,7 m) and height. Rest of aircraft and armament unchanged. Completed June 1944 and NII tested until 1 March 1945. Basis for several later versions.

ANT-62, Tu-2D

Tu-2D nose

DIMENSIONS Span 22,06 m (72 ft 4½ in); length 14,42 m (47 ft 3¾ in); wing area 59,05 m^2 (636 ft^2).
WEIGHTS Empty 8316 kg (18,333 lb); loaded 12 290/13 340 kg (max 29,409 lb).
PERFORMANCE Max speed 465 km/h at SL (289 mph), 531 km/h (330 mph) at 5,6 km; time to 5 km, 11·8 min; service ceiling 9,9 km; range 2790 km (1734 miles); take-off 480 m; landing 610 m/149 km/h.

Tu-2M

104, Tu-2/104 Like Pe-2, attempts were made to turn Tu-2 into bomber-destroying interceptor, in this case with radar. Redesigned nose housing large radar and gunsight system (team led by A.L. Mints) with two VYa-23 in underside of forward fuselage. Normal crew 2. First flight 18 July 1944 (A.D. Perelyet, with leading engineer L.L. Kerber). Radar operative 1945, first such trials with fighter in the Soviet Union.

ANT-63, Tu-2SDB Two aircraft modified in 1943–1944:

No 1, **SDB** (*Skorostnoi Dnyevnoi Bombardirovshchik*, fast day bomber), originally an early Type 103 rebuilt with modified airframe, more powerful liquid-cooled engines driving 3,6 m AV-5LV-22A three-blade props, dive brakes removed, fuselage rearranged for crew of two (pilot and nav/bomb), all guns removed except wing-root ShVAK, bombs as before and most of details as Tu-2S. First flight 21 May 1944 (A.D. Perelyet) and joint GAZ/NII tests 5 June to 6 July.

No 2, **SDB-2**, with AM-39F engines (same props), totally new main gears with single oleo legs of increased length passing straight down to inner end of axle, larger tailwheel tyre (480 × 200 mm), hydraulic system with all tubing dural instead of steel, same 5,7 m horizontal tail as Tu-2D, crew 3 (as No 1 but radio/gunner at rear) in armoured cockpits, rear guns ShKAS, extra fuel in wing. First flight 14 October 1944; combined test programme by M.A. Nyukhtikov and leading engineer V.A. Shubralov complete 30

ANT-63, Tu-2SDB

June 1945. Neither SDB had adequate nav vision, but No 2 was judged superior aircraft and would have gone into production had it not been for Type 68 (Tu-10).
DIMENSIONS As Tu-2 except length (1) 13,2 m (43 ft 3½ in), (2) 13,6 m (44 ft 7½ in).
ENGINES (1) two 1870 hp AM-39, (2) 1870 hp AM-39F.
WEIGHTS Empty (1) not known, (2) 8280 kg (18,254 lb); loaded (1) 10 100/11 850 kg (max 26,124 lb), (2) 10 925/11 850 kg (same).
PERFORMANCE Max speed (1) 645 km/h (401 mph) at 6,6 km, (2) 547 at SL, 640 (398 mph) at 6,8 km; time to 5 km (1) 7·45 min, (2) 8·7; service ceiling (both) 10,1 km (33,140 ft); range (1) 1830 km (1137 miles), (2) given by Shavrov 1530, should be 2530 (1570 miles); take-off (1) 470 m, (2) 535; landing (1) 550 m, (2) 650 m/156 km/h.

Tu-2 Paravan Two production aircraft modified for trials with deflectors for barrage-balloon cables. Steel deflector cable attached to tip of 6 m dural monocoque cone cantilevered ahead of aircraft nose and extending 13,5 m each side to cable cutter at tip of wing. First aircraft on test September 1944 with 150 kg ballast in tail and most combat equipment removed.
DIMENSIONS Length 19,8 m (64 ft 11½ in).
WEIGHT Empty 9150 kg (20,172 lb); loaded about 11 t.
PERFORMANCE Max speed 537 km/h (334 mph) at 5450 m; time to 5 km, 11 min; service ceiling 9150 m (30,000 ft).

Tu-2 No 18/11 No details available of this production aircraft completed 1944 with various changes to exterior finish and equipment. Flight characteristics almost unchanged. Comprehensive data suggest one change may have been high-lift flaps.
DIMENSIONS, ENGINES As Tu-2.
WEIGHT Loaded 10 500/11 520 kg.
PERFORMANCE Not greatly different from regular Tu-2 except take-off 425 m; landing 510 m.

Tu-2Sh Several production aircraft completed 1944–1946 as armoured *Shturmoviks*, with increased protection and different armament. Tu-2Sh stemmed from proposal by A. V. Nadashkevich, head of OKB's armament section, for use against infantry. Original 1944 aircraft had PPSh automatic grenade dispensing system, modernized version of that for 300 grenades installed by Nadashkevich in TsKB TSh-1 in 1931. A later (1946) Tu-2Sh was heavily armed two-seater with upper rear UBT, twin ShVAK in wing roots (report says 'sides of fuselage' suggesting guns relocated) and nose occupied by two NS-45 and two NS-37. Data for this machine.
DIMENSIONS, ENGINES As Tu-2.
WEIGHTS Not known.
PERFORMANCE Max speed 575 km/h (357 mph) at 5,8 km; time to 5 km, 9·0 min; service ceiling 10 065 m (33,022 ft); range 2500 km (1553 miles); landing speed 160 km/h (99 mph).

Tu-2K At least two production aircraft modified 1944 and 1945 for ejection-seat trials; designation from *Katapult*.

Tu-2G Designation probably from *Gruzovoi*, freight; several production aircraft modified 1944–1950 for carrying cargo internally and externally and especially for parachuting of bulky

Tu-2N

Tu-2 Paravan

Tu-2G with GAZ-67b scout car

loads, well-known 1949 example of latter being GAZ-67b scout car (378 km/h, 6 km service ceiling). This particular aircraft one of several Tu-2s known with 3,6 m AV-5V prop hubs with four experimental hollow steel paddle blades with square tips.

Tu-2N Single production aircraft fitted early 1947 with R-R Nene 1 in large pod under forward fuselage, to assist performance measurement of engine for TsIAM and support projected Tu-22 and Type 77.

ANT-68, Tu-10 Production aircraft completed early 1945 with liquid-cooled engines (AM-39FNV) driving 3,8-m AV-5LV-22A three-blade props, crew of four, 4 t bombload, strengthened main gears and outer-wing dihedral reduced 1·5°. First flight by A.D. Perelyet 19 May 1945, outstanding performance; factory test by F.F. Opadchii to 7 July, NII tests to 30 July. Damaged and in course of repair refitted with AM-42 engines with four-blade 3,8 m AV-5LV-166B props and other small changes. Intended to fly with AM-40 engines with same props, not fitted. Erroneously designated Tu-4 when built in small production series, believed 50, 1946–1947.

DIMENSIONS As Tu-2.

ENGINES Two 1850 hp AM-39FN-2 (data for this), later 2000 hp AM-42.

WEIGHTS Empty 8870 kg (19,555 lb); loaded 11 650/12 735 kg (max 28,075 lb).

PERFORMANCE Max speed 520 at SL, 641 km/h (398 mph) at 8,6 km, (with 4 t bombload 635 at 7,1 km); time to 5 km 10·0 min; service ceiling (4 t bombload) 9,8 km, (2 t) 10,45, (one engine) 7 km; range 1740 km (1080 miles); take-off 525 m; landing speed 190 km/h (118 mph).

Tu-2T A torpedo-carrying Tu-2 had been in original scheme for Aircraft 103, but not realized until design effort could be spared 1944. Tu-2T (*Torpedonosyets*, torp-carrier) stemmed from two prototypes taken off 1944 production line. First, **NT** (*Nizkii*, low), few changes apart from addition of TD-44 pylon and Der-4-44-U safety system under each wing root for 45-36-AN air torpedo, with TsAGI tail controls. Combined factory/NII tests February/March 1945, good results (data for this aircraft). Second Tu-2T had supplementary fuel tanks (1020 lit, 224 gal) in sealed bomb bay, strengthened landing gear and other changes. First flight by Opadchii and V.P. Marunov 2 August 1946; remarkable ability to fly 3800 km; speed with two torpedoes 490 km/h, or just over 500 with one. Also flown with three 800 kg torpedoes, but not cleared as normal load. Described as first purpose-built torpedo aircraft in Soviet Union (not true, R-5T) and built in series 1947 for AV-MF, serving in all three main fleet theatres until mid-1950s.

DIMENSIONS, ENGINES As Tu-2.

WEIGHTS (No 1, loaded) 11 423/12 389 kg (max 27,313 lb).

PERFORMANCE Max speed 505 km/h (314 mph) with one torp, 493 with two; service ceiling 7,5 km (24,600 ft); range 2075 km (1289 miles); take-off 580 m; landing 480 m/159 km/h.

UTB Almost different enough to be described separately, this crew trainer was genuinely needed by VVS but was scorned by Tupolev; he (according to accounts of others) could not be bothered with it, as beneath his dignity, and it was left to Sukhoi's now independent OKB to pick it up in 1946. Often, but not always, called **UTB-2** (UTB, *Uchyebno-Trenirovochnyi Bombardirovshchik*, training bomber), this used simplified Tu-2 airframe restressed to lower factors, low-powered engines in short cowls with VISh-111V two-blade v-p metal props, large flight deck with full roof glazing and room for one or two pilot seats at front, with dual control, and one or two nav seats at rear, with new access tunnel through where bomb bay had been to rear rad/gunner cockpit with VUB-68 mount for UBT and 60 rounds. External belly racks for four FAB-50 or FAB-100 bombs aimed by trainee bomb/nav through glazed nose. Main tyres 900 × 300 mm, tail 440 × 210 mm. No lower rear position. Totally different fuel and accessory systems, ailerons, flaps and many other parts. First flight summer 1946; production UBT-2 (at least 500, about 100 for Poland) delivered 1947.

DIMENSIONS Span 18,86 (as Tu-2); length 13,985 m (45 ft $10\frac{1}{2}$ in); wing area 48,8 m^2 (as Tu-2).

Tu-2Sh

ANT-68, Tu-10

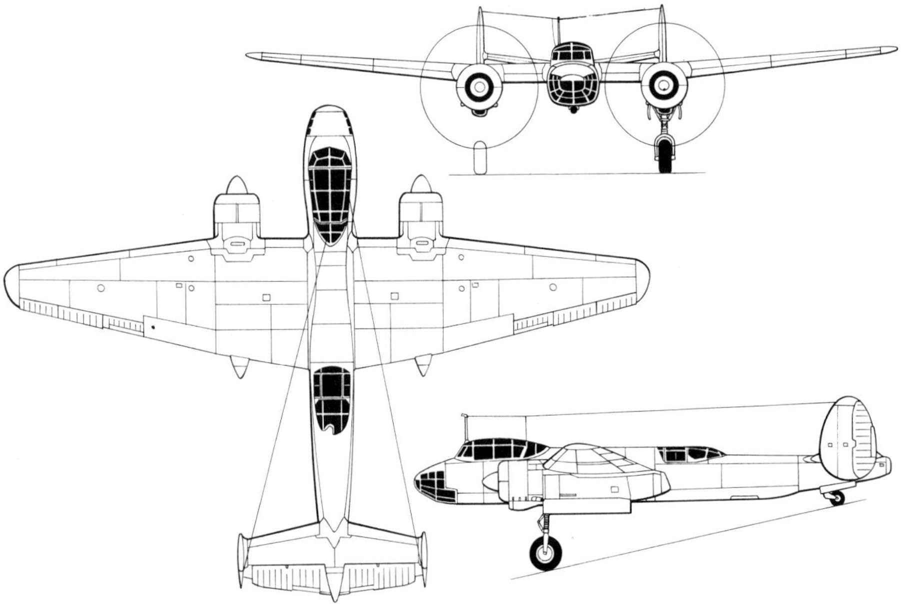

Sukhoi UTB

ENGINES Two 700 hp ASh-21.
WEIGHTS Empty 5020 kg (11,067 lb); loaded 6550 kg (14,440 lb).
PERFORMANCE Max speed 380 km/h (236 mph) at 1,9 km; time to 3 km, 8 min; service ceiling 6 km (20,000 ft); range 950 km (590 miles); take-off 460 m; landing 345 m/125 km/h.

ANT-67 Another of big-span dual-pilot family, this long-range test-bed was flown with Charomskii diesels on 12 February 1946 (pilot A.D. Perelyet). Fine-looking five-seat aircraft with fully cowled engines with single exhaust stacks, AV-5L three-blade props and 1260 mm main tyres causing slight bulges in doors. Ailerous of extended chord resulted in slightly greater wing area. Exceptional range, but deep flaws in engine (incorrectly reported in West as ACh-30) caused termination in 1947.
DIMENSIONS Span 22,06 m (72 ft 4½ in); length 14,42 m (47 ft 3¾ in); wing area 59,12 m^2 (636 ft^2).
ENGINES Two 1900 hp ACh-39BF.
WEIGHTS Empty 8323 kg (18,349 lb); loaded 13 626/15 215 kg (max 33,543 lb).
PERFORMANCE Max speed 509 km/h (316 mph) at 6,2 km; time to 5 km, 13·0 min; service ceiling 8850 m (29,000 ft); range 5000 km (3100 miles); take-off 530 m; landing 700 m.

ANT-62T No Tu-2 type number known for this torpedo version of long-span ANT-62, first flown 2 January 1947. Same main legs as second prototype Tu-2T but 1260 mm tyres with bulged doors; crew accommodation as ANT-62. Data as ANT-62 except max speed with two 45-36-AN torpedoes, 13,5 t weight, 501 km/h (311 mph) at unstated height, range given (Shavrov and others) as 3800 km (2360 miles), showing bomb-bay fuel.

ANT-63P, Tu-1 Three-seat long-range escort fighter and interceptor, intended eventually to carry radar. Basically a modified Tu-10 (68) with AM-43V engines driving four-blade AV-9K-22A props, no lower rear crew position, main cockpit with pilot on centreline and nav/radar observer at rear facing forward. Armament two NS-45 in lower part of nose, two NS-23 in wing roots and twin UBT, bombload 1 t. Nose above large guns configured for PNB-1 'Gneiss-7' radar, based on German FuG 220 with tail-warning aerial. Factory test 30 December 1946 to 3 October 1947; one of highest performances of family but no production.
DIMENSIONS As Tu-2 except length (excl guns) 13,6 m (44 ft 7⅓ in); with guns 13,72.
ENGINES Two 1950 hp AM-43V.
WEIGHTS Empty 9460 kg (20,855 lb), heaviest of family; loaded 12 755/14 460 kg (max 31,878 lb).
PERFORMANCE Max speed 479 km/h (298 mph) at SL, 641 km/h (398 mph) at 8,6 km; time to 5 km, 11·6 min; service ceiling 11 km (36,090 ft), with No 65 (Tu-2DB) highest of family; range 2250 km (1400 miles); take-off 605 m; landing 560 m.

Tu-2R, Tu-2F, Tu-6 Several factory and field conversions of Tu-2 bombers as reconnaissance aircraft made from 1943, with three/four cameras with individual ventral doors, but not until 1946 did purpose-designed variants appear: Tu-2R (*Razvyedchik*) with standard airframe and **ANT-64**, Tu-2F (*Fotorazvyedchik*) with long-span wing for high-alt operation, and new forward fuselage with nav station in nose. It was expected Tu-2R would be built in series, with service designation Tu-6 assigned. Four-seat aircraft with long-range tanks and provision for three or four reconnaissance cameras (usually AFA-33, AFA-3c/50 and AFA-33/50 or 33/100) all in former bomb bay and causing ventral bulge. First flown October 1946, NII testing successfully completed 9 April 1947. First purpose-designed reconnaissance aircraft in Soviet Union (doubtful claim) but no production, largely because piston-engined. Later fitted with large mapping radar in place of glazed nose. Data for this aircraft.

ANT-67

ANT-63P, Tu-1

Tu-2R field conversion (note belly camera doors)

DIMENSIONS, ENGINES As Tu-2.
WEIGHTS Empty 8205 kg (18,089 lb); loaded 10 585/12 800 kg (max 28,219 lb).
PERFORMANCE Max speed 509 km/h (316 mph) at SL, 545 km/h (339 mph) at 5,5 km; time to 5 km, 10·3 min; service ceiling 9050 m (29,700 ft); range 2780 km (1727 miles); no other data.

RShR, Tu-2RShR This 1946 prototype was dedicated anti-armour aircraft with 57-mm RShR gun mounted on lower centreline of nose, with barrel and muzzle brake projecting only about 0,5 m. Basic aircraft very like Tu-2Sh with crew of two: pilot and nav/radio operator who reloaded gun breech in bomb bay. Main legs inclined to place wheels 125 mm further forward. NII tests completed 28 February 1947; no production. Data as Tu-2.

ANT-65, Tu-2DB Penultimate DB (*Dalnii Bombardirovshchik*, long-range bomber) variant, this was based on long-span wing and twin-pilot cockpit, with bombload and weapons as Tu-2 but advanced liquid-cooled engines supercharged by TK-1B (TK-300) exhaust turbos, driven by exhaust from right-hand bank of cylinders on each engine (left bank had plain ejector exhausts). AV-5LV-188B three-blade props with mechanical control, 3,8-m diameter. Main wheels 125 mm further forward as in Tu-2RShR. Crew of five. First flight by Opadchii 1 July 1946. Exceptional performance considering high gross weight, but Tupolev more interested in Tu-4 and did not submit for NII test, especially as engine defective and cancelled.
DIMENSIONS Span 22,06 m (72 ft 4½ in); length 14,42 m (47 ft 3¾ in); wing area 59,12 m² (636 ft²).
ENGINES Two 2200 hp AM-44TK.

Tu-6 (note rear end of camera bulge)

ANT-65, Tu-2DB (showing turbos)

ANT-65, Tu-2DB (plain ejector exhausts)

ANT-69, Tu-8

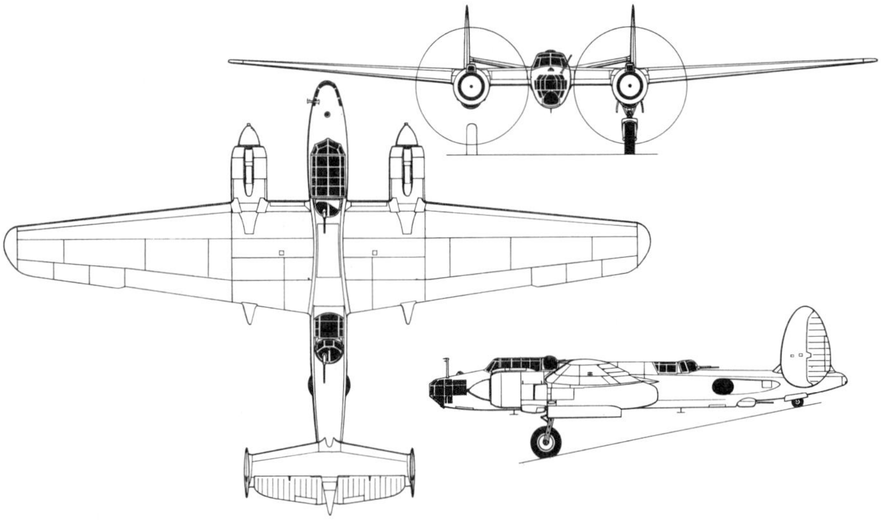

ANT-69, Tu-8

WEIGHTS Empty 9696 kg (21,177 lb), highest of family; loaded 13 450/16 450 kg (36,265 lb).
PERFORMANCE Max speed 578 km/h (359 mph) at about 7 km; service ceiling 11 km (36,090 ft); range 2570 km (1600 miles).

ANT-69, Tu-8 Last of basic line, this DB (long-range bomber) was heaviest variant and a most refined and impressive aircraft, but it arrived into OKB dominated by Tu-4 and a world turning swiftly to jets. Airframe based on ANT-62 (Tu-2D) but with further increase in chord to give greatest area of series. Main wheels 125 mm further forward as in RShR, larger tyres to match gross weight (main 1170 × 435 mm, tail 580 × 240 mm). Five seats, completely revised defensive armament with B-20 on right side of fuselage fired by pilot, B-20 with 190 rounds fired from rear of main cockpit by nav/bomb or, usually, second pilot on swivel seat, third B-20 with 250 rounds in MV-11 dorsal turret and fourth/fifth B-20 in pair in ventral turret (type unknown) aimed by fifth crew-member via remote sight/control system using diagonal beam portholes upstream of recessed sides of rear fuselage. Fuel capacity as ANT-62, bombload increased to 4,5-t max. First flown December 1946 and tested with great success until 20 April 1948 when abandoned. **Tu-8B** (AM-42) and **Tu-8S** (ACh-39BF) never tested.
DIMENSIONS Similar to ANT-65.
ENGINES Two 1850 hp ASh-82FN.
WEIGHTS Empty not known; loaded 14 250/16 750 kg (max 36,927 lb), highest of family.
PERFORMANCE Max speed 515 km/h (320 mph) at 5,7 km; time to 5 km, 17 min (longest of whole series); service ceiling 7650 m (25,000 ft); range 3645/4100 km (max 2550 miles).

Project 64 Despite pressure from OKBs and existence of good long-range twin-engined bombers (eg, by Ilyushin and Myasishchyev, and to lesser degree long-span Tu-2s) Soviet strategic bombers were accorded low priority during the Second World War and fell behind those of Allies, especially the B-29. Stalin made at least

Tu-4

three formal requests to US for lend-lease B-29s, without success. By mid-1944 decision taken to base future strategic aircraft on B-29 and continued attempts by clandestine methods to obtain full details and if possible pattern aircraft. Meanwhile, at high priority, Tupolev OKB instructed to design near-copy, using existing Soviet engine. Project 64 (not ANT-64) launched early 1945. Appearance similar to B-29, aspect ratio about 12, NACA-2330 profile, liquid-cooled engines with twin turbochargers and four-blade props, pressurized forward fuselage for six: two pilots, nav/bomb, engineer, RLS (radar) and gunner; rear pressurized tail turret for seventh crew-member; three turrets each with twin B-20, internal bay for normal 5 t bombload; fuel and range much less than B-29, flaps and tricycle gear hydraulic. Continued as insurance until early 1946 when, after extensive tunnel-testing and release of many drawings, Aircraft 64 halted in favour of direct copy of US aircraft as Tu-4.

DIMENSIONS Span 42,8 m (140 ft 5 in); length 29,0 m (95 ft $1\frac{3}{4}$ in); wing area 152 m² (1636 ft²).

ENGINES Four 2200 hp AM-44TK.

WEIGHTS Loaded 36 t (79,365 lb), much less than B-29.

PERFORMANCE Max speed 600 km/h (373 mph) at 6 km; range with 5 t bombload 3000 km (1864 miles).

Tu-4 Project 64 always regarded as insurance against failure to obtain specimen of B-29 or particular insuperable difficulty in making copy of US aircraft. Had no B-29 been acquired it would certainly have continued, but direct copy saved so much time and cost that plans to do this were put in hand even before any B-29 was in Soviet hands. In particular, Shvetsov KB began even late 1943 to prepare plans of GE turbocharger and Wright R-3350 engine. Vital assistance from 'capture' (they were property of an ally) of three operational B-29s: 29 July 1944, B-29-5-BW 42-6256; 20 August 1944, B-29A-1-BN 42-93829; 21 November 1944, B-29-5-BW 42-6358. Task of dismantling and analysis without precedent: Tupolev said over 105,000 items were checked for material specification, function, manufacturing processes, tolerances and fits, and translated into Soviet equivalents with drawings by over 1000 draughtsmen. Many parts and sub-systems new to Soviet experience; others (pressurization system, turbo and armament control) totally different from established Soviet practice. Full-scale programme begun first week 1945 at highest priority to create copy for DA with designation Tu-4; no known OKB number. Pre-production batch of 20 ordered (almost certainly GAZ-125), and preparations for series manufacture at two other plants both east of Urals.

Tu-4

In fact, few parts of Tu-4 emerged identical to US counterpart, even primary structure being slightly different materials, mainly D16-T, in metric gauges generally fractionally thicker (airframe of first aircraft 15 196 kg) and with many compromises in piping and cables. Wing profile RAF-34 20%/10%, several structural changes and much trouble over 75-micron interference fit of main wing bolts, integral tanks and stress-relief and accurate machining of thick wing-box skins in newly formulated D16-ABTN. Eventually integral tankage abandoned in favour of 22 flexible cells, reducing capacity. Tyres 1450 × 520 mm (main) and 950 × 350 mm (nose) with modified brakes and steering (agents unsuccessfully tried to buy spare wheels, tyres and brakes on US market 1946, US still disbelieving rumours of attempt to copy B-29). Many engineering changes in engine, TK-19 turbo and 5056-mm V3-A3 or V3V-A5 props. Pressurized tunnel linking forward/mid cabins omitted. Two bomb bays redesigned in detail to carry 6-t (8-t max) various Soviet bombs. Totally redesigned defensive armament with major changes to control system and assignment of control to sighting stations: initially five pairs of UBT, mid-1949 five pairs B-20E and finally (about 1951) five pairs NS-23 in first major advance over US aircraft (this defensive system basic for that of future turboprop and jet bombers).

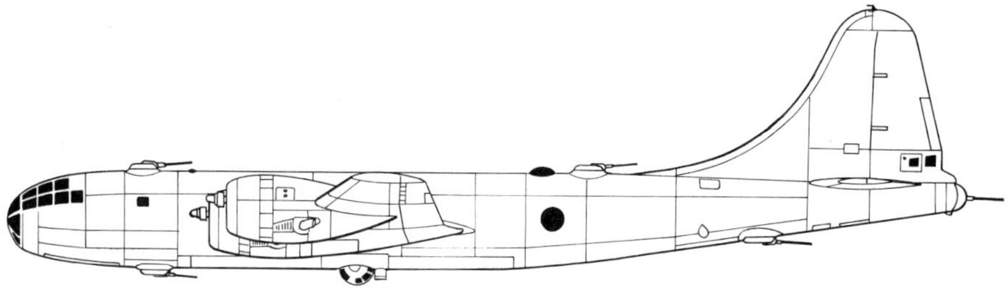

Tu-4 (1951 series)

First three aircraft assigned respectively to N.S. Rybko, M.L. Gallai and A.G. Vasilchyenko. First successfully flown (7½ months after Tu-70) 3 July 1947. Severe and prolonged problems with almost all systems, especially props, turbos and armament, in engine cooling (fires), and in fabricating high-quality blown Plexiglas giving distortion-free vision for pilots and gunners. About two years elapsed before 20th aircraft flew, but by that time fairly mature aircraft and 300 in service by 1950, over 120 completed by 1949 but not cleared for test. As far as known no bombing radar installed before mid-1950s but *Cobalt* radar gunsight system operational in single Tu-4 by 1952 with separate operator at rear of mid-fuselage compartment. Not fitted to rest of DA force.

Total number built about 400. From 1952 used for several trials and research programmes. **Tu-4LL** (flying lab) designation of three aircraft greatly modified 1953 to flight-test NK-12 turboprop, five times power of ASh-73 and with prop restricted to 1½ times existing diameter. Big experimental engines installed in No 3 (right inner) position. Programme under chief engineer D.I. Kantor and chief test pilot M.A. Nyukhtikov. Programme completed 1954 but not before A.D. Perelyet had been killed in first aircraft (believed hit by disintegrating prop though there are other stories). **Tu-4T** single assault transport built 1954 with provision for 28 paratroops; believed unpressurized. Another converted for 52 normal day passengers (troops) without parachuting provision. At least 12 converted 1952–1955 as air refuelling tankers, various methods, and others as engine and radar testbeds.

DIMENSIONS Span 43,05 or 43,08 m (141 ft 4 in); length 30,18 or 30,19 m (99 ft 0⅜ in); wing area 161,7 m² (1740 ft²).
ENGINES Four 2400 hp ASh-73TK.
WEIGHTS Empty (25th aircraft) 35 270 kg (77,756 lb); fuel/oil 13 480 + 800 kg; loaded 47 600/54 500 kg (max 120,150 lb); overload 66 t (145,500 lb).
PERFORMANCE Max speed 420 at SL, 558 km/h (347 mph) at 10 km; time to 5 km, 18·2 min; service ceiling 11,2 km (36,750 ft); range 5100 km (3170 miles) with 6 FAB-1000 bombs; take-off 960/2210 m; landing 1070/1750 m (latter at max 48 t)/172 km/h.

Tu-70 Passenger airliner derived from B-29 in parallel with Tu-4 bomber. Despite Aeroflot having in 1945 issued vague requirement for such aircraft, it was in fact pure initiative of Tupolev OKB, and funding gained from GVF with reluctance, especially as money previously voted for prototype Il-18*. Much simpler task than Tu-4 because in absence of eager customer OKB could take its own decisions and adopt cost-cutting methods. Even more direct copy of B-29 than Tu-4 and incorporated landing gears (and tail bumper), fin/rudder and other parts removed from B-29s. Engines may have been American, though always given as ASh-73TK in Soviet accounts. OKB designed new fuselage with circular section but diam increased from 2,9 to 3,5 m. Forward floor including flight deck, then one step up across wing box and two steps down to rear floor at slightly lower level. Galley at wing box with cooker and refrigerator and two roof portholes each side. Main cabins with long rectangular windows, rear cabin with portholes. Designed in *Luxe* version with 48 seats and crew eight, later refurnished for 72 passengers and crew six. Designed to be pressurized but system not originally operative. Glazed nose for nav, D/F loop acorn below forward fuselage, airframe deicing not fitted at first flight (poss later). Span increased by larger fuselage and more rounded wingtips. Flown by F.F. Opadchii 27 November 1946 when first Tu-4 still in early erection stage. Never was a civil aircraft, and following NII testing retained by VVS as occasional staff transport.

DIMENSIONS Span 43,83 m (143 ft 9⅝ in) (Western report, 44,25 = 145 ft 2⅛ in); length 35,61 m (116 ft 10 in); wing area 162,7 m² (1751 ft²), (Western account 166,1 = 1788).
ENGINES Four 2400 hp ASh-73TK.
WEIGHTS Empty 33 979 kg (74,910 lb); loaded 51,4 t (113,316 lb).
PERFORMANCE Max speed 563 km/h (350 mph) at 8 km; service ceiling (33,500 ft); range 4900 km (3,050 miles).

Tu-75 According to Western accounts this further transport derivative of B-29 was built 1950 to meet military requirement. Probably also used actual B-29 hardware because initially funded by OKB, though bore VVS markings when flown. Intended to have large rear door forming loading ramp for vehicles and openable in flight for paradropping troops or heavy loads. William Green insists sole Tu-75 did not have this fitted (Shavrov says it did) but instead had ventral loading hatches, openable in flight, at front and rear. No armament but usual nav glazed nose and B-29 type tail compartment, presumably for observation of air-drops. Fuselage apparently identical structurally to Tu-70, but fitted internally for carriage of 10-t (22,046 lb) military freight or with tip-up wall seats for 100 troops or paratroops. Fitted from start with airframe deicing; not known if pressurized. Flown by V.P. Marunov summer 1950. No record of NII testing, though Tu-75 used for several flights with actual military loads. Intended production Tu-75 would have had defensive armament, believed three pairs UBT, in rear turret and upper forward and lower rear remote-con-

Tu-70

trol turrets sighted from dorsal blister behind forward turret and side blisters at extreme rear of pressure cabin ahead of tail.
DIMENSIONS As Tu-70.
ENGINES As Tu-70.
WEIGHTS Empty, not known; fuel/oil 20 500 + 900 kg; loaded 56,6 t (124,780 lb).
PERFORMANCE No reliable data.

Tu-80 Having obtained design of B-29 it was natural immediately to study ways of improving it. Myasishchyev did major redesign (DVB-202); Tupolev followed path of logical small steps. After studying several alternatives, first step, OKB number Tu-80, was relatively minor. Range was increased by redesigning wings with integral tanks, as in B-29 but using different materials, giving 15% more fuel in only slightly greater span. Section unchanged but wing structurally re-planned with longer centre section and slightly shorter outer panels with dihedral reduced to 0°, integral tankage throughout. New engines, installations redesigned with higher thrustlines, circular cowlings, separate ventral oil-cooler ducts and aerodynamics similar to US R-4360 in B-50. Redesigned forward fuselage establishing arrangement for crew repeated in Tupolev bombers for almost 20 years, with glazed nose for front gunner and nav/bomb, separate cockpit for two pilots with conventional windscreens (pilots had difficulty with internal reflections and optical distortion in early Tu-4s) and radar/nav seated behind facing to rear with large mapping/bombing radar in pressurized underfloor compartment. Communication tunnel restored to rear-fuselage compartment with several changes including lateral observation windows upstream of recesses in fuselage sides as in ANT-69 (Tu-8). Extra nose length balanced by enlarged vertical tail with no structural part common to Tu-4. Modified gun turrets, twin NS-23 throughout, upper front turret retractable, rear turret inclined main window, and all offering minimal drag (these were not fitted to Tu-80 at roll-out and no photographs are known showing armament fitted). Tupolev said much later he attempted to make airframe lighter, but did not have much success.

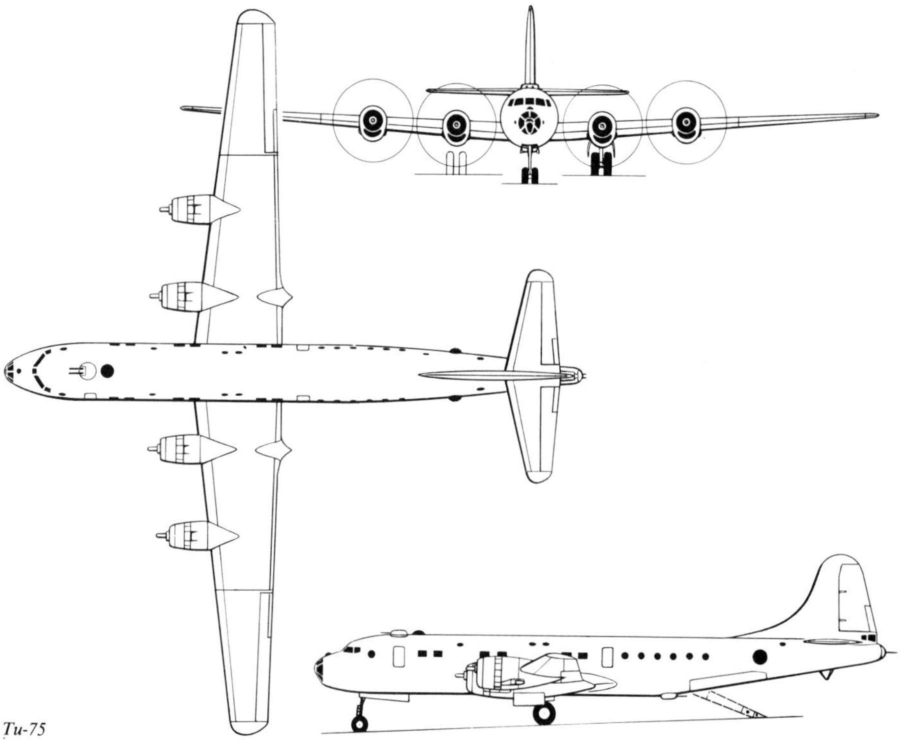
Tu-75

Tu-80

Tu-80

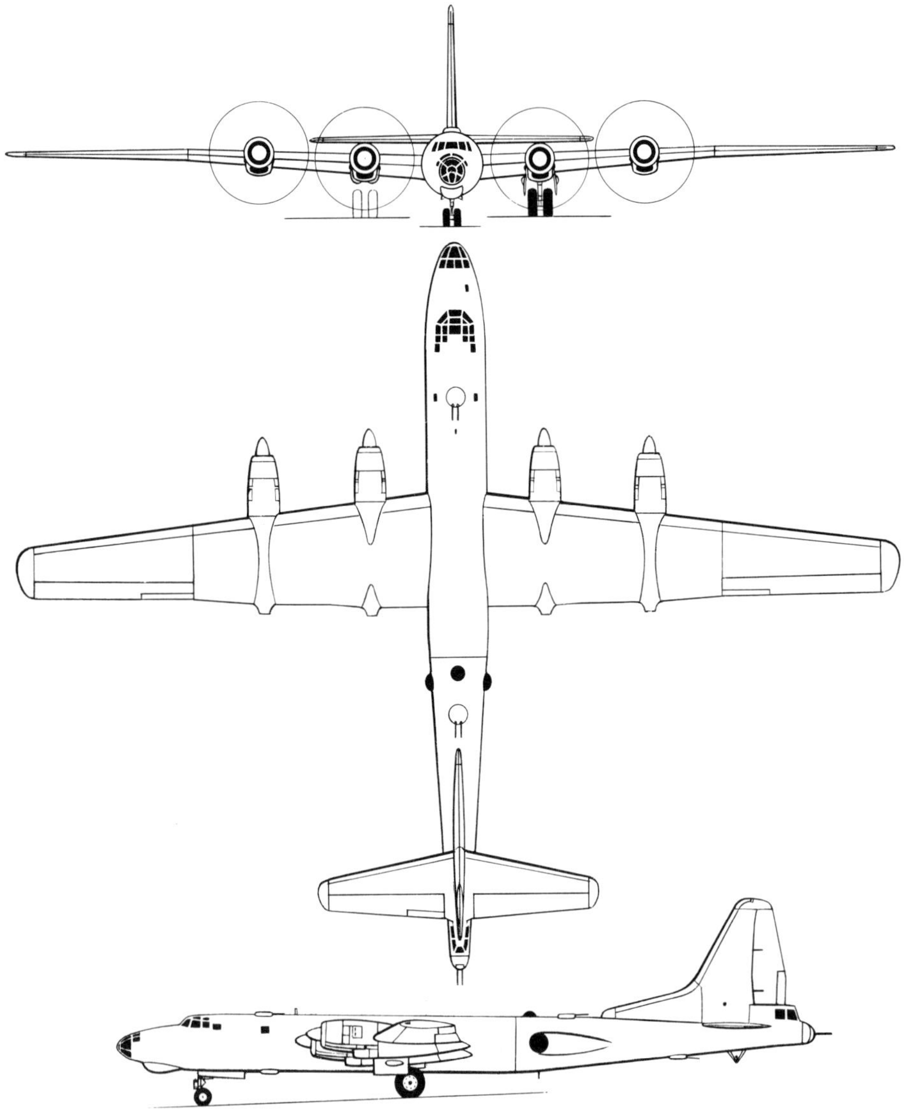

Tu-80

Common report (Czech and UK) that Tu-80 had 'lighter spars' is erroneous; weight of wing was actually greater. First flight November 1949. Completed factory test but NII testing not attempted because of imminence of much more important Tu-85.

DIMENSIONS Span 44,30 m (145 ft 4 in); length 36,60 m (120 ft 1 in); wing area 172 m² (1851 ft²).

ENGINES Four 2400 hp ASh-73FN.

WEIGHTS Empty, not recorded; fuel/oil 24 000 + 920 kg (Shavrov's 4000 is misprint); loaded 53 420/60 600 kg (max 133,598 lb), overload cleared to unknown higher weight.

PERFORMANCE Max speed (Shavrov) given as 650 km/h (404 mph) at 10 km; despite better fineness ratio and lower-drag nacelles seems optimistic. No other data.

Tu-85 To meet 1948 VVS requirement for truly intercontinental bomber, able to match B-36, OKB produced ultimate extrapolation of Tu-4 with much more powerful engines and almost doubled fuel capacity (note: Shavrov's fuel figures for Tu-4 and Tu-80 are nonsense). Entire Tu-85 design was within known technology, except for use of dramatically larger sheet members in heavier gauges than any previously made in the Soviet Union. Great success achieved with lightweight wing construction, with fewer ribs than in Tu-80 despite much greater span. Few wing parts common to Tu-80, though same profile and t/c. Rectangular centre section with dihedral starting at break, skin thickness up to 10 mm between spars with first Soviet use of machined skin (though not to form integral stiffening webs but to reduce thickness between spars and ribs). Extensive use of precision-fit countersunk bolts instead of rivets. Fuselage almost identical to Tu-80 except for insertion of extra bays (14 additional frames, six ahead of wing and eight aft) to provide increased bomb-bay capacity for max 20 t bombload (44,090 lb) in front and rear compartments, and longer rear pressure cabin with bunks for one complete crew. Thus total crew 16, eight on duty (as Tu-80) and eight resting. Communication tunnel lengthened to 14 m. Defensive armament as Tu-80: ten NS-23 with same remote sighting stations. Choice of two completely new engines, and OKB given order for three airframes, one for static test, one for flight test with ASh-2 and one for flight test with VD-4K. Both flight aircraft believed to have flown with VD-4K, in beautifully designed installations with cooling air entering at front and engine air supply to two-stage supercharger system via large dorsal inlet. Cooling air and exhaust ducted through wing and expelled from common ejector nozzle at trailing edge as in Republic XF-12. Reversing props with four solid-dural blades 4,5 m diameter. New twin-wheel landing gears designed in OKB as scale of B-29 units with advanced materials and 9-ply tyres to handle doubled aircraft weight. Redesigned tail surfaces with less taper and blunter tips; all flight controls manual and flaps/gear/bay doors remaining electric.

Though Tupolev accepted slight reduction in wing aspect ratio (11·4 instead of 11·5) he regarded Tu-85 as structurally his greatest achievement, having regard to its timescale. Though smaller than ANT-20 and much smaller than TB-6 it was much heavier and more powerful and its fuel capacity of 61 200 lit was greater than for any other piston-engined aircraft except B-36. Prototype construction amazingly rapid, and within two years of specification first Tu-85 was in air in January 1950. Believed both aircraft completed (Něměcek states 'several') but photos

Tu-85

known of one only. Possibly over-hasty decision to terminate in view of jet and turboprop possibilities; it was to be 1956 before Tu-4 was to be replaced by aircraft offering similar range to Tu-85.

DIMENSIONS Span 55,94 m (183 ft 6¼ in); length 39,31 m (128 ft 11¾ in); wing area 273,6 m² (2945 ft²).

ENGINES Four 4300 hp VD-4K.

WEIGHTS Empty 55,4 t (122,134 lb); fuel/oil 44 t (97,000 lb); loaded 75 t normal, 107 max (235,891 lb).

PERFORMANCE Max speed 563 km/h at SL (350 mph), 665 km/h (413 mph) at 10 km; service ceiling 13 km (42,650 ft); range (max) 13 000 km (8000 miles), 12 000 (7450 miles) with 5-t bombload; take-off 1640 m; landing 1500 m/185 km/h (115 mph).

Tu-4TVD Cancellation of Tu-85 made it clear nothing would replace Tu-4 until later in 1950s, and OKB as private venture made proposals for Tu-4 re-engined with turboprops (TVD, *Turbovintnovoi Dvigatel*, turboprop). Choice of two possible engines, both robust single-shaft axials: VK-2 and NK-4. Competitive battle between these engines described in Engines section. Tupolev schemed Tu-4 with both engines, NK-4 installation having curiously high thrust-lines. Appreciable gain in performance but reduction in range despite various measures to increase fuel capacity. Neither aircraft built, though several Tu-4s assisted flight development of these and many other engines.

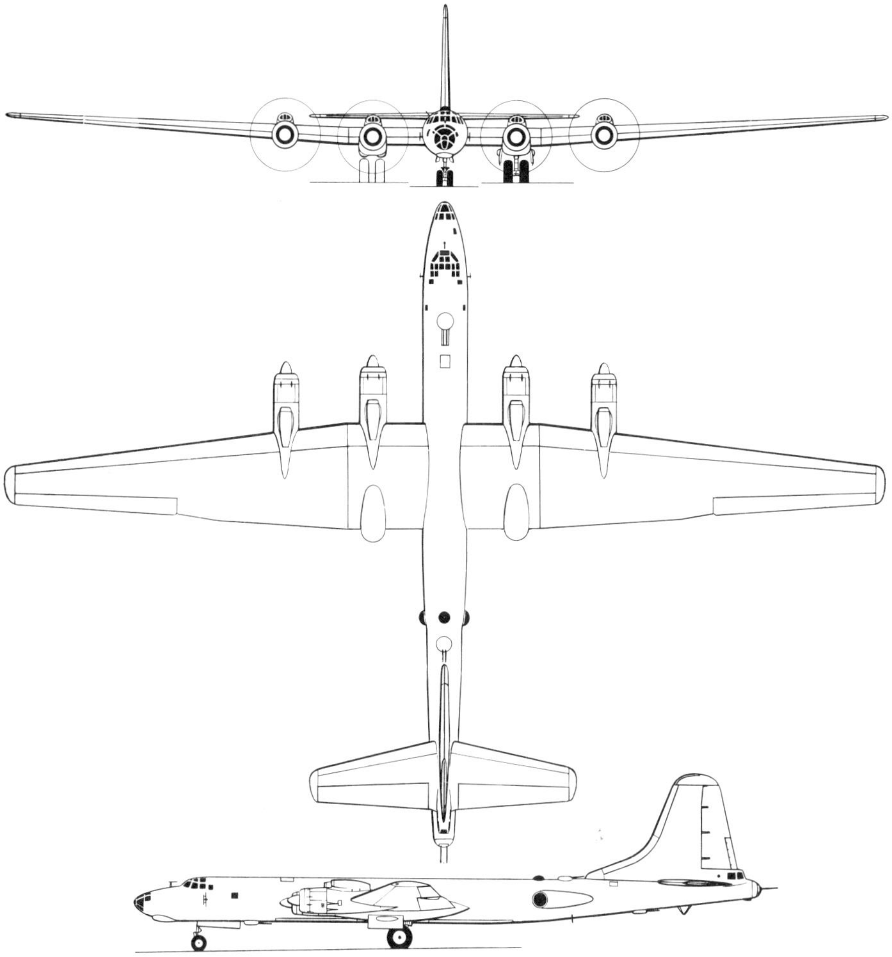

Tu-85

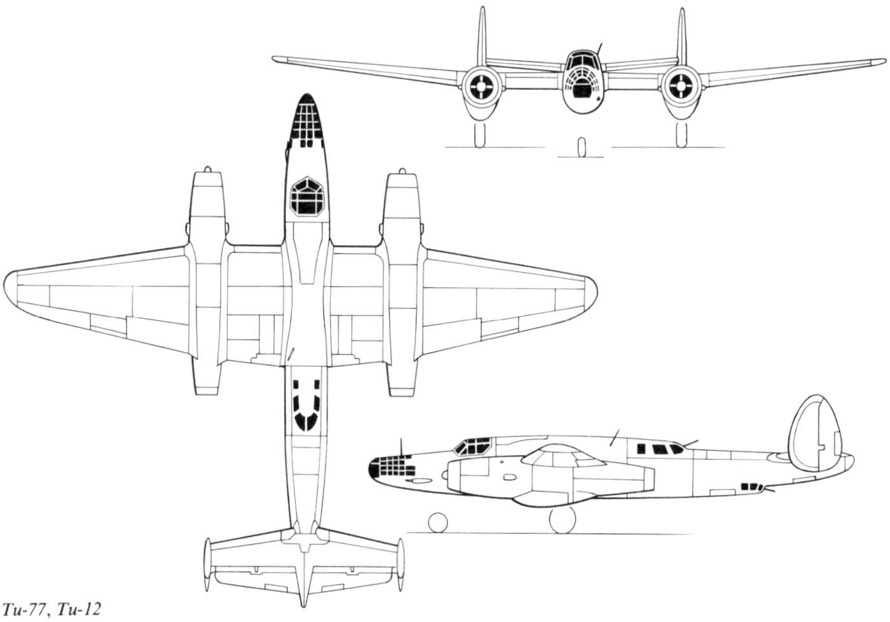

Tu-77, Tu-12

Tu-22* Unbuilt project for Tu-2 with ASh-82FN engines plus RD-45 or Nene I jet in rear fuselage, with dorsal inlet duct curving down under swept horizontal tail. Several objections, one being excessive wing-loading.

Tu-2/Nene Imported Rolls-Royce Nene was quickly introduced to Tupolev OKB since Tu-2 was its first installation in Soviet Union (two aircraft, February 1947, pod under fuselage). Even before acquisition of Nene engines, one series Tu-2 had been earmarked for conversion to actual propulsion by these engines, and by May 1947 it was completed with two Nenes, long wing nacelles, tailwheel gear retained. No objective beyond gaining experience with engine and measuring performance. Believed to have taken part in Aviation Day 3 August 1947 together with Tu-12 and Il-20. Led to Tu-12, Type 77. Dimensions as Tu-2; no other data.

Tu-12, Tu-77 Unlike converted Tu-2 this was properly designed jet bomber to meet VVS requirement, though still using Tu-2 as basis. Project started mid-1946 prior to acquisition of Nene, and at outset expected to use Soviet copy (see Engines section). Most of Tu-2 wing retained but restressed with heavier-gauge materials for greater weight and higher IAS, with two extra tanks at wingtips. Tail likewise strengthened. Fuselage generally retained but increased in depth 0,5 m to provide for additional fuel and equipment and with redesigned nose with greater length and complete glazing (not same as long-nosed Tu-2 variants). No pressurization. Engines mounted further apart than in Tu-2: 5,2 m for centrelines, track and span of tail unit (fin centrelines). Moving engines out increased apparent size of centre section but in fact wing size overall unchanged. Long (6,2 m) nacelles fully underslung and designed by OKB unlike those of Il-28 and with short main gears with large wheels rotating 90° on single legs to lie flat in wide bulge in underside of nacelle, leg retracting forwards. Single nosewheel retracting to rear, all bays having twin doors. New pilot cockpit on centreline with deep hinged side windows and glazed roof but no rear vision. One fixed NR-23 on left side of nose, two rear gunners each with UBT, bomb bay for up to 3 t bombload. First Type 77 built at Tu-2 production plant and flown by A.D. Perelyet 27 June

Tu-73

1947. Two flew in 3 August 1947 show at Tushino. First Soviet jet bomber, several quickly built (all by September 1947) but regarded as strictly interim and precursor to later designs.

DIMENSIONS Span 18,86 m (61 ft 10½ in); length 16,45 m (53 ft 11⅔ in); wing area 48,8 m² (525 ft²).

ENGINES Two 2270 kg R-R Nene I.

WEIGHTS Empty 8993 kg (19,826 lb); fuel (max) 6727 kg; loaded 14,7 t; with 4080 kg fuel, max 15 720 kg (34,656 lb).

PERFORMANCE Max speed 778 at SL, 783 km/h (487 mph) at 5 km; service ceiling 11 370 m (37,300 ft); range 2200 km (1367 miles); take-off 1030 m; landing 885 m/163 km/h.

Tu-72, Tu-73, Tu-78 Unlike Type 77 these designs were undertaken to meet later VVS requirement for jet bomber for major deployment, document issued not later than September 1946. Called for 3 t bombload, defensive armament of 23 mm guns, fixed nose guns and speed over 800 km/h for greatest combat radius attainable. Responses from Ilyushin and Tupolev; latter assigned project as **Type 72** to Arkhangyelskii, who adopted many major items from existing Tu types including rear sight station and remote-directed turrets. Otherwise clean sheet of paper design, larger than Type 77 and, to meet requirement, fully pressurized. Straight wing of 12% TsAGI SR-5S profile made as rectangular horiz centre section and tapered outer panels with 5° dihedral, simple structural box with plate spars and machined skins forming integral tankage. Basically circular-section fuselage with pressurized nose for nav/bomb and tandem cockpit for pilot and radio/gunner seated back-to-back. No access to pressurized rear compartment for gunner sighting through large left/right recessed windows as in Tu-69, Tu-80, Tu-85. Two electrically controlled turrets, upper forward and lower rear, each with twin B-20; two NR-23 firing ahead aimed by pilot. Engines mounted centrally on wing with spar booms in form of encircling banjo rings, engine/nacelle centreline apparently at about +3° incidence. Single-wheel tricycle landing gear with nose unit retracting to rear under pressure floor and main gears hinged to wing immediately inboard of nacelles and retracting inwards with large bay door hinged next to fuselage. Fixed tailplane with 40° sweep mounted half-way up fin. Additional fuel cells above fuselage weapon bay approx same cross-section as Tu-2 but greater length and capacity.

Tu-73

Tu-78

Tu-78

Tu-81

According to Něměcek Tu-72 designed for MA (naval aviation) and flown by Opadchii September 1947; this not confirmed by Soviet sources which state aircraft was rival to Il-28 for VVS order, and was in fact never built. This was because performance figures appeared to show that two Nene engines inadequate thrust for requirement (Western reports claim Arkhangyelskii worried about reliability of engines; not mentioned in Soviet reports where reliability of Nene and Derwent is stressed as goal at which native engine designers should aim). Arkhangyelskii's answer was to add smaller third engine in tail, fed by S-duct with inlet at front of dorsal fin with retractable fairing to close duct off in cruise with tail engine inoperative (two Nenes adequate for cruise). Dimensions slightly increased and main engines repositioned in underslung nacelles extending well ahead of wing to balance added mass at tail. By start 1947 decision to redesign main gears to fold into underside of nacelle with geometry similar to Type 77 but larger wheel and stronger leg. About March 1947 OKB still tinkering with design, assigned number Tu-73, when Stalin gave order (and to Ilyushin) to start building prototype immediately. Tu-73 flown by F.F. Opadchii 29 December 1947, well ahead of Il-28 (Něměcek, flown by Nyukhtikov 29 October 1947, conflicts with Soviet accounts). Good performance, no major snags, record flight time in first month (38 h, not previously equalled in OKB, possibly not in the Soviet Union). Swift development of second prototype as reconnaissance version (no details of sensors but probably as Type 79 and Tu-81R) with designations **Type 73R** and **Tu-74**. This not built and actual second aircraft, Tu-78, differed in nose glazing and vertical tail and also in having Soviet-built engines.

OKB's greater resources compared with Ilyushin enabled progress to be swifter, and Tu-78 was well into flight test programme, begun 17 April 1948, before first Il-28 flew in July. All Tupolev models were larger than Ilyushin and had larger bombload and greater range; in case of unbuilt reconnaissance versions, including projected **Tu-78R**, difference in range was near 2:1. Nevertheless the Ilyushin was cheaper and more agile, and in late 1948 Marshal Vershinin ordered direct competitive evaluation of Tu-78 and Il-28 by three regular VVS crews. All picked the Ilyushin, and only future for Tupolev series lay with MA, which in fact preferred the design offering greater range and bombload and was less concerned about manœuvrability. Tu-78 was last of original trimotor family which represented loss in man-hours and time caused mainly by Klimov's inability to predict thrust-growth possible from Nene engine.

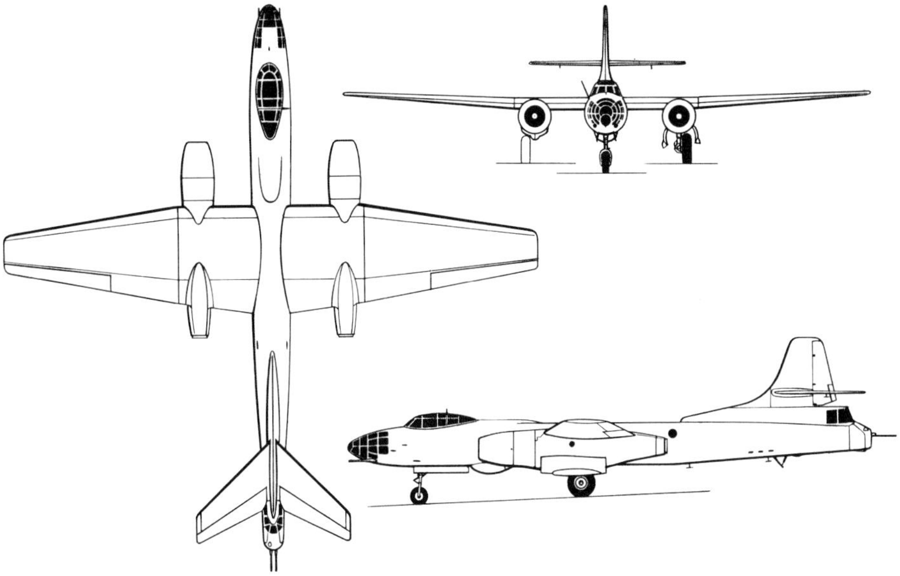

Tu-14

DIMENSIONS Span (72) 19,7 m (not built), (73, 78) 21,71 m (71 ft 2¾ in); length (72) 19,05 m, (73, 78) 20,32 m (66 ft 8 in); wing area (72) not recorded, (73, 78) 67,36 m² (725 ft²).

ENGINES (72) two R-R Nene I, (73) two 2270 kg Nene I, one 1590 kg Derwent, (78) two RD-45, one RD-500, same ratings.

WEIGHTS Empty (72) not recorded, (73) 14 340 kg (31,614 lb), (78) (Shavrov) 14 340, (others) 14 290; loaded (72) no accurate est, (73) 21,1 t normal, 24,2 max (53,351 lb), (78) 21 110 kg normal (46,539 lb).

PERFORMANCE Max speed (72 est) 820 km/h at 5 km, (73) 840 km/h at SL, 872 km/h (542 mph) at 5 km, (78) 875 km/h (544 mph) at 5 km; time to 5 km (78) 9,1 min; service ceiling (73, 78) 11,5 km (37,730 ft) (these poor climb/ceiling figs not comprehended); range (72 est) 3000 km, (73) 2810 (1746 miles), (78) 2800 (1740); take-off (73) 740 m; landing (73) 1170 m/173 km/h.

Tu-14, Tu-79, Tu-81, Tu-89 Well before competitive fly-off against Il-28 Arkhangyelskii had learned from Klimov of greater thrust possible from VK-1. Decision taken summer 1948 to revert to twin-engined aircraft with reduced basic weight and increased fuel; MA had never liked third engine and OKB had never established best cruise technique with two or with three engines. First of new series Tu-79 with few changes except removal of tail engine, rearward shift in installation of main engines to balance loss of tail mass, increase in fuselage fuel (small, no data) and increase in defensive armament to six NR-23 (two pairs in turrets and two fixed in lower part of nose fired by pilot). Not known if this aircraft was built; no record of flight test.

Further study showed possibly better answer was to fit tail turret similar to Tu-80/Tu-85) with radio racking at tail and remove other movable guns, reducing crew to three. Shift in CG enabled existing nacelles and engine installation to be retained and substantially reduced basic weight (though empty weight naturally grew by at least 1 t as result of combat equipment). Result was Tu-81, first flown 1949 (no date published). Following NII trials accepted June 1949 for MA service as Tu-14 and series of about 500 ordered, possibly from GAZ-125. First Tu-14s complete before end 1949. Popular and successful aircraft though at maximum weight marginal on one engine. Bombload 3 t (6614 lb) including FAB-3000; armament two fixed and two rear-turret NR-23. Operative ILS, radar altimeter and PSB-N nav/bomb radar. All flight controls manual, spring tab on rudder, fixed tailplane. OKB designed and tested two further variants, **Tu-81R (Tu-14R)** reconnaissance with fuel and cameras in place of bombs (AFA 33-20, 33-50/75 and 33-100 cameras and drift sight) and Tu-89 **(Tu-14T)** with bomb bay for two 45-36-A torpedoes. Believed most, possibly all, production Tu-14s were of 14T type though all aircraft with weapon bay had capability for conventional bombing. No evidence Tu-14R produced in series. For unstated reasons production suddenly terminated, long before completion. GAZ-125 may have been needed for Tu-16. Only relatively small number (at a guess 100) put into MA operational use, but these enjoyed at least a decade of service 1951-1961.

DIMENSIONS Span 21,686 m (71 ft 1¾ in); length (81) 21,945 m (72 ft 0 in), (89T) 21,69 m (71 ft 2 in); wing area 67,36 m² (725 ft²).
ENGINES Two 2700 kg VK-1.
WEIGHTS Empty (81) 14,43 t (31,812 lb), (89) 14,49 t; fuel (89) 8,7 t; loaded (81) 21 t normal, 24,6 (54,233 lb) max, (89) 21 t normal, 25,35 (55,886 lb) max.
PERFORMANCE Max speed (81) 800 at SL, 861 km/h (535 mph) at 5 km, (89, poss with external torps) 774 at SL, 845 km/h (525 mph) at 5 km; time to 5 km (both) 9·5 min; service ceiling (81) 11,5 km (37,730 ft), (89) 11,2; range (both) 3010 km (1870 miles); take-off (81) 1250 m, (89) 1200; landing (81) 1120 m/175 km/h, (89) 1100/176.

Tu-82 In parallel with straight-wing bombers leading to Tu-14 OKB designed smaller aircraft with same propulsion but swept wings. Tu-82 often called experimental but in fact intended as frontal (tactical) bomber, and prototype (flown A.D. Perelyet February 1949) carried full armament. Two-spar wing similar in profile and detail structure to Tu-81 but smaller and with ¼-chord sweep 34°18′. Fuselage about 4 m shorter than straight-wing series and based on that of Type 72, crew three. Two aircraft in this family built: Type 82 with armament believed to comprise upper forward and lower rear turrets aimed by radio/gunner back-to-back with pilot and Type 83 with twin NR-23 in tail turret. Both had two NR-23 (one Soviet report, B-20) firing ahead. Bombload up to 2 t normal in internal bay. Swept tail, 40° on LE throughout, underslung engine nacelles and main gears similar to Type 78, nose gear longer because of sharp positive ground angle needed by new wing. Type 82 had at least two small fences, outboard of nacelles. No information on flaps, flight controls believed manual. This aircraft, in tradition of Tu-2, was considerable success, and though it had first swept wing by OKB (and was first swept bomber in Europe) had low structure weight. Type 83 intended as production prototype, but despite good NII trials early 1950 decision not to build in series because of large numbers of Il-28. Tupolev argued straight-wing Ilyushin was interim, but had no success. As the 1940s ended, Tupolev dropped tactical aircraft to concentrate on large strategic bombers and airliners.

DIMENSIONS Span 17,81 m (58 ft 5⅛ in); length 17,57 m (57 ft 7¾ in) (Němĕcek 18,6 m, Alexander 19,925 m); wing area 45,0 m² (484 ft²).
ENGINES Two 2700 kg VK-1.
WEIGHTS Empty 9526 kg (21,000 lb); loaded 13,5 t normal, 18,34 (40,432 lb) max.
PERFORMANCE Max speed 870 at SL, 934 km/h (580 mph) at 4 km; service ceiling 11,4 km (37,400 ft); range 2395 km (1488 miles); take-off 1100 m; landing 550 m/200 km/h.

Tu-86 Unbuilt 1950 project for swept-wing bomber with fuselage based on stretched Tu-14 and wing scaled up from Type 82 to span of 25,5 m; engines two TR-3 or AM-02.

Tu-16, Tu-88, N Use of letter N to designate this programme unusual by OKB and may have indicated exceptionally tight security at start; also unsubstantiated report another designation was TsAGI-288. Development by Mikulin KB of large AM-3 (RD-3) turbojet opened way to really capable long-range bombers, far larger than any previous Soviet jet aircraft. Type 86 accordingly dropped and OKB given order summer 1950 for three prototype Tu-88 (one probably static test specimen) in competition with smaller Il-46; at same time even larger bombers launched for DA's intercontinental missions (Tu-95 and M-4, latter using four AM-3 engines). Tu-88 fuselage natural extrapolation of previous practice with few innovations, but wing was not only much larger than any previous Soviet swept wing but also introduced new light-alloy (equivalent to DTD.683) and main skins even thicker than Tu-85. Landing gears also innovation, first bogie in Soviet Union and established OKB trademark in folding into pods on wing trailing edge.

Wing of 12·5% t/c at root, 7·2% tip, SR-5S profile, LE sweep 42° from root to structural break 6,5 m from centreline, 35° thence to tip, −5° anhedral at rest (around −1° in flight), main box with machined skins forming integral tankage unbroken by landing gear, fixed LE with hot bleed-air anticing (exhausted from slits at tip), TE with slight change in sweep at main-

Tu-14T (revised rudder and turret)

Tu-14

Tu-16 Badger-A refuelling trial

gear pods, two upper-surface fences each side (usually 200 mm deep and extending to LE but geometry varies) at structural break and at flap/aileron junction. Two sections of TsAGI area-increasing flap on each wing running on steel tracks and driven by ballscrews with duplex elec actuators, max 35°. One-piece balanced slotted ailerons, manual drive via geared tabs. Tail almost a scale of Tu-82 with 40° sweep on fin, 45° on tailplane (fixed incidence part-way up fin), tabbed elevators but rudder with trim tab only and hydraulic boost. Oval-section semi-monocoque fuselage structurally divided into four sections with F-2 (centre portion) built around two strong frames in 30-KhGSA with side lobes encircling engines with bolted detachable lower arcs for engine-change. These engine rings centred on fuselage equator, but wing attached high on outer periphery mainly to assist access to engines via large hinged lower doors. Both frames mate with main wing spars but only rear frame carries front of engine, front frame encircling duct. In Tu-88 prototype engines had axial ducts but this was later modified to give favourable (Küchemann) pressure distribution and a few small changes made 1954 to conform more nearly with area rule, result being curved ducts, reduced fuselage tankage and engines canted outward which also minimizes engine-out asymmetry (no problem on this aircraft). Nose magnesium-alloy framed, skin normally 3 mm. Pressurized (max 0,5 kg/cm^2) forward fuselage with nav/bomb in glazed nose, two pilots side-by-side and radar/gunner at rear with upper sighting dome; pressurized tail crew compartment (in prototype only, linked by access tunnel) with two gunners, one sighting through left/right blisters, one in tail turret. All rear guns remotely controlled, system almost identical to previous eg, Tu-85: twin NR-23 in tail, lower rear (side sight stations) and recessed upper forward (dorsal dome); single NR-23 with barrel projecting on right of nose fired by pilots. Single weapon bay about 6,5 m long with elec driven retracting doors, max bombload 9 t (19,841 lb). Fuel in fuselage cells and integral wings, total 44 900 lit (9877 gal) with advanced capacitance contents instrumentation and flow-proportioner and inert-gas protection system. Bogie main landing gears, track 9775 mm, tyre size/pressure not reliably known, multi-disc anti-skid brakes, electrical retraction rearwards with bogies somersaulting to lie inverted in trailing-edge box fairings with twin doors. Steerable twin-wheel nose gear also retracting to rear. Main entry door with integral steps ahead of nose gear. Electric engine-starting, raw AC thermal deicing of tail and pilot windshields, hot bleed-air engine inlets.

Tu-88 flown with AM-3A engines first quarter 1952, pilot reported as N.S. Rybko. Predictably outstanding aircraft and contest with Il-46 a walkover. Second aircraft flown later 1952 with 3M engines (VVS designation RD-3M) and various changes including slightly increased span, improved autopilot, *Argon* nav/bomb radar in undernose blister with main circuits in pressurized fuselage (radome unpressurized) and comprehensive avionics including Bee Hind tail-warning radar, HF rail aerial, SRO-2 IFF above nose and remote-control chaff/flare dispenser. Selected late 1952 for service with DA and AVMF as Tu-16, major production programme involving several GAZ though believed one assembly line (not Vnukovo, poss Kharkov or Kazan). Tu-88 and eight Tu-16s took part in May Day parade 1954 and believed entered service late same year; 54 flew in Aviation Day parade 1955. Production continued to about 1959, total about 2000 not including Chinese-built version (see later). Proved to be a versatile and fatigue-free aircraft, roughly 1000 in Soviet Union still flying on many duties with typical flight-times in excess of 6000 h. Following variants are mainly rebuilds; NATO code-names are used as true designations not yet known:

Badger-A Basic bomber with crew, bombload and equipment as described. Most Tu-16s believed built in this form. Same designation applied to flight-refuelling tanker conversion with bomb-bay tanks and hose trailed from right wingtip to reception receptacle on left tip. Supplied to Iraq, and also to China where put into production in incredible unlicensed copying job rivalling Tupolev copy of B-29 (Chinese designation **H-6**, over 100 in use, mainly in anti-flash

Tu-16 Badger-B (Indonesia)

Tu-16 Badger-C

white, used for several free-fall nuclear tests and supplied to Pakistan).

Badger-B Initial anti-ship variant with underwing pylons for AS-1 Kennel ASMs guided by *Komet III* I-band radar; introduced A322Z doppler, RV-10 or RV-17 radar alt and SRZ-2 interrogator. Supplied to Indonesia, with missiles. Rebuilt as Badger-G.

Badger-C Second anti-ship variant with bomb bay reconstructed to carry single AS-2 Kipper recessed on centreline; nose redesigned for large radars including Puff Ball missile acquisition system and A-329Z missile guidance, no nose compartment or visual bomb capability. Nose gun removed.

Badger-D Maritime reconnaissance/Elint variant, row of three passive receiver blisters on ventral centreline, comprehensive multi-sensor reconnaissance capability, nose similar to C but no ASM link and no offensive capability.

Badger-E Rebuild of A for basic optical reconnaissance with bomb bay used for various large camera pallets and extra fuel; original nose retained.

Badger-F Similar to E but with wing pylons carrying Elint pods, believed passive multi-band receivers; normally operated in company with a D or E.

Badger-G Advanced anti-ship or stand-off missile platform with wing pylons for AS-5 Kelt or AS-6 Kingfish; nose as A but Short Horn nav/bomb radar and various other avionics not on A. With simpler avionics supplied to Egypt, with AS-5 (fired against Israel 1973).

Badger-H Dedicated EW platform with nose superficially as A but bomb bay exchanged for multi-waveband receiving and analysis, jamming and payload dispensing capability, including chaff, jammer and flare payloads from ventral chute and ejector tubes.

Badger-J Alternative dedicated EW platform with dispensing systems replaced by enhanced receive/analysis/jamming installation which includes large ventral canoe aerial(s).

Badger-K Long-range Elint variant, highest internal fuel capacity and various receivers and analysers with aerials on underside.

Most of these versions have wing pylons plumbed for external tanks and left wingtip arranged to catch and engage with FR hose. Most also retain original defensive armament. Electronics in most versions on Elint missions are tailored to NATO ship systems rather than air to ground emitters.

Tu-104G Demilitarized GVF aircraft (numbers between L-5402 and 5411) used for crew training and route-proving prior to introduction Tu-104 by Aeroflot; nickname *Krasnyi Shapochka*, Little red riding hood.

DIMENSIONS Span (88) 35,5 m (109 ft 11 in), (prod) 32,93 m (108 ft 0½ in); length (except C, D) 34,8 m (114 ft 2 in), (C, D) 36,6 m (120 ft 1 in); wing area 164,65 m^2 (1772 ft^2).

ENGINES (88) two 8750 kg AM-3A, (all subsequent) 9500 kg RD-3M.

WEIGHTS Empty (88) 37,2 t (82,011 lb), (typical production) 40,3 t (88,845 lb); fuel (normal internal) 36,6 t; loaded (88) 72 t, (all production) 75,8 t max (167,108 lb).

PERFORMANCE Max speed (88) 992 km/h at 6 km, (A) 1050 km/h (652 mph) at 6 km, (typical late conversion) 960 km/h (597 mph); service ceiling (88) 12,8 km, (A) 15 km (49,200 ft), (modern, max wt) 13 km (42,650 ft); range (88) 5760 km, (A) 7800 km (4850 miles), (max weapon load) 4800 km (3000 miles), (typical modern, max internal but no ext fuel) 7300 km (4540 miles); take-off (A) 1250 m; landing (A) 1100 m/225 km/h (140 mph).

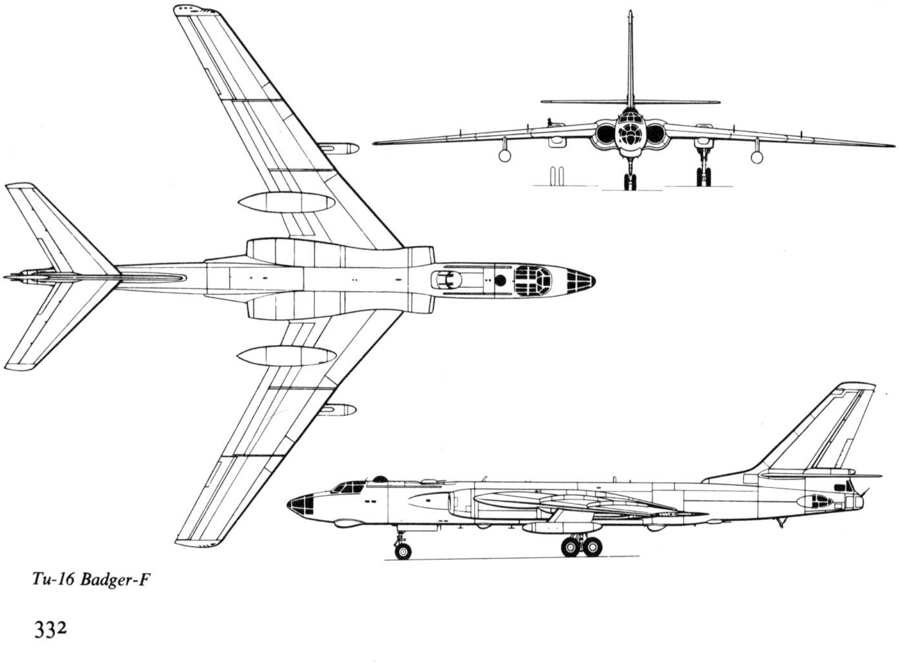

Tu-16 Badger-F

Tu-20, Tu-95, Tu-142 Termination of Tu-85 was calculated risk based on premise than either M-4 or Tu-95 would enter DA service as intercontinental bomber with swept wing and much higher over-target speed and height. Tu-95 programme resulted from 1950 planning meeting and spring 1952 final agreement on design, handled by Arkhangyelskii, and mock-up review. Whole project rested on NK-12 engine and AV-60 series propeller, both totally new in technology and posing considerable risk. By contrast, airframe almost entirely within OKB experience, fuselage being that of Tu-85 with slight stretch and other minor changes including increased cabin dP and thicker skins. Tail designed in parallel with Tu-88 and closely similar. Wing a major structural challenge though again able to draw on aerodynamics and structure of Type 88. Objective was bomber even larger than Type 85, 75% heavier and three times as powerful. In general programme a startling success, resulting in one of the world's largest and longest-lived military aircraft with unique turboprop propulsion to Mach numbers near 0·8.

Wing SR-5S profile, 12·5% root tapering to unknown lower t/c at tip, three spars root to tip plus fourth from root to structural break (90° to rear spar) inboard of outer engines, with further primary joint at flap/aileron junction (again 90° to rear spar). LE sweep 37° to first break, 35° outboard; TE straight (unlike Tu-114). Three 200 mm fences similar to Tu-88 from near LE to TE on each wing, inboard fence in gap between prop wakes and middle fence between flaps and ailerons; area-increasing flaps (described in West as Fowler type, but geometry differs) with duplicated electric ballscrew drives; tabbed three-section ailerons with hydraulic boost but not fully powered; single hyd spoiler ahead of inboard end of aileron used at all speeds. Fuselage of same circular section as B-29 and similar three-compartment crew accommodation with tunnel linking front and rear cabins. Original defensive armament ten NR-23 in two dorsal, two ventral and tail turrets, with dorsal sighting dome at rear of forward compartment and lateral sight stations for ventral guns as in Tu-16; at early stage front upper and lower turrets eliminated leaving six guns only, no fixed nose gun. Internal weapon bays of equal size each designed for free-fall thermo-nuclear bomb but able to take max load of 10 t conventional bombs. Original crew probably eight, no attempt at accommodation for spare crew because Tu-95 missions flyable in shorter time than 85. Swept tail scaled from Tu-88 with fixed 45° tailplane part-way up fin; all control surfaces said to be hydraulically boosted (not powered). Bogie main gears with 1500 × 400 mm tyres and anti-skid brakes, whole unit cushions shocks by oleo compression whilst swinging up to rear; duplicated elec retraction to rear, bogie somersaulting to lie inverted in large faired compartments forming extensions of inboard nacelles, track 14,00 m. Tall steerable

Tu-20 Bear-A with both rear turrets removed and FR probe added

twin-wheel nose gear, single strut with side braces, elec retractable to rear into unpressurized compartment. Braking parachutes (2) in rear-fuselage compartment. Engines cantilevered far ahead of wing on four 30KhGSA struts attached to rear of main inlet casing; constant-speed 8300 rpm operation driving 5,6-m AV-60N eight-blade reversing propellers (two four-blade units, each with solid dural elec de-iced blades) at 750 rpm with tip Mach cleared to 1·08. Electric (later electronic) control system schedules fuel flow to power demand and in cruise and high-speed flight blade pitch is amazingly coarse, often appearing almost feathered. Bifurcated jetpipes. Oil radiators in ducts under each engine. Heat exchangers for wing LE anticing, bleed air for inlets, tail thermally de-iced, believed by combustion heater(s) and not by alleged electric means. Fuel in wing box tanks, including integral, original max capacity 72 980 lit (16,053 gal), subsequently greatly increased.

First flight of **Type 95** delayed by engines and missed 1954 May Day, being accomplished about four months later, pilot/date unknown. A promising start, apart from severe problems with engine and propellers (though test-pilot Perelyet was not killed in Tu-20 or Tu-114 but in Tu-4LL as explained earlier). Tupolev said later no aircraft lost in factory or NII test programme; believed ten were used (seven flew Aviation Day 1955), with DA service starting early 1956, with engine power/rpm restricted, allotted service designation Tu-20. While Pentagon over-reacted to M-4 it undervalued Tu-20, and did not expect ensuing variety of subtypes and duties over 30-year period. No details of GAZ or timing of production but Western consensus is 300 total, originally completed 1961. Most or all built as original bomber, but many rebuilds by industry and VVS modification centres to following known versions, identified by NATO names:

Bear-A Original bomber, differed from prototype in removal of rear dorsal turret, addition of spoilers for greater roll-rate, retractable twin wheels instead of tailskid, mission avionics including A321 ADF, A322Z doppler, Bee Hind tail warning, A325Z/321B Tacan/DME, Short Horn nav/bomb radar, variable-incidence tailplane driven by irreversible ballscrew for trimming purposes. SALT estimate 1979 total 113 of this and B version (without ASM) still in DA service.

Bear-B Designation applied to 15 aircraft seen Aviation Day 1961 with large ASM (so-called AS-3 Kangaroo) recessed in modified weapon

Tu-104G, Tu-16G (Tu-16 in background)

Tu-20 Bear-D

bay, with retractable nose fairing, and large nose radar (Crown Drum, low end of I-band) for high-definition surface search and A336Z missile guidance. No nose station for navigation nor visual bomb capability. Some of this series had additional rear dorsal twin-23mm turret, now usually removed, and from 1962 FR probes appeared on upper centreline of nose with external pipe fairing along right side of fuselage. AS-3 continues in service, but some B models appeared about 1970 with supersonic AS-4 Kitchen ASM in further reconstructed recess with fairing doors. B-variants in strategic-reconnaissance role have blister on right of rear fuselage and are believed assigned to AV-MF.

Bear-C First seen 1964, retained MR equipment but added dedicated reconnaissance/Elint, similar to B but with no weapons capability; large nose radar retained, together with FR probe and three turrets, but bomb/ASM capability traded for about 19 000 lit extra fuel and various EW items including ventral blister radomes (including same as Badger-H) and blister on both sides at rear.

Bear-D First seen 1967, various slightly different rebuilds of Bear-A for AV-MF multi-sensor reconnaissance; Mushroom I-band chin radar, major Big Bulge I-band belly radar, blister both sides at rear, slim pods on tips of tailplane (not anti-flutter masses, may house front/rear aerials for Sirena 3 warning system), lengthened FR probe, larger tail-warning/fire-control radar (believed Box Tail) and numerous other new aerials and unknown excrescences. Twin outlets in top of fuselage to rear of forward crew compartment may be exhaust for added electricity generating plant. One important task of D is target detection and data transmission by secure A346Z J-band digital link to SSM-armed warships, with ability to provide inflight course-correction and target update to missiles in flight. Since 1978 D-variant seen with tail turret replaced by long tail fairing housing electronics and with at least four aerials visible, identical to tail fairing of Tu-126.

Bear-E AV-MF rebuild of A for multi-sensor maritime reconnaissance, with aft bomb bay occupied by fuel and six/seven optical cameras in large detachable pallet conforming with fuselage curvature and also housing other sensors (almost certainly including IR linescan and SLAR). Usually two blister radomes under forward weapon bay. Retains guns, FR probe, rear-fuselage blisters and nose nav station but no radar except small nose mapping set.

All these variants are believed to have stemmed from original run of about 300 aircraft, completed early 1960s. Majority (SALT-2 est

Tu-20 Bear-D

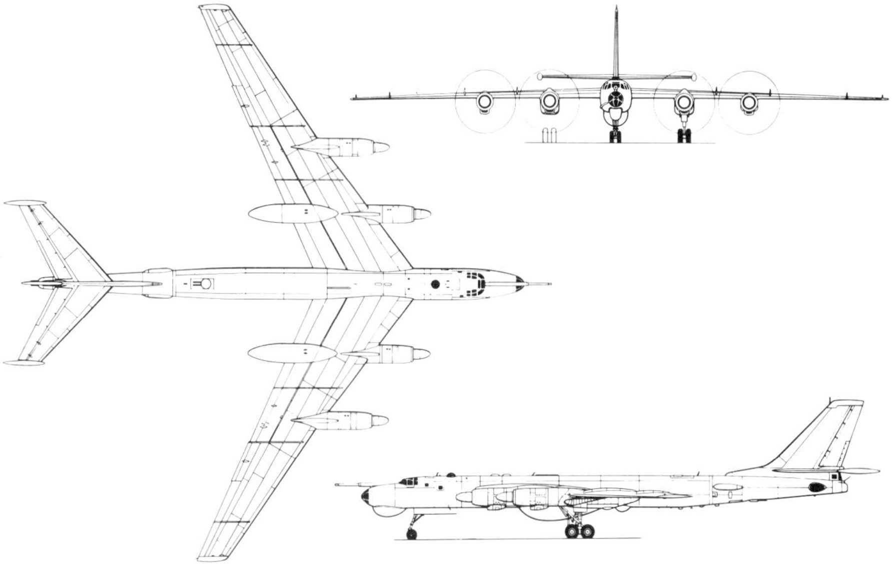
Tu-20 Bear-D

113 aircraft) retained by DA, with offensive capability but added EW sensors and ECM, mainly still called Bear-A and B. Remainder of original aircraft still flying operated by AV-MF as C to E. In early 1960s question arose of continuing production, resulting eventually in Tu-142, next entry.

DIMENSIONS Span (actual) 51,1 m (167 ft 7¾ in), (Alexander) 50 m, (Green, *Jane's* and others) 48,5 m (159 ft 1½ in); length (Něměcek) 49,5 m (162 ft 4¾ in), (Western accounts) 47,5 m (155 ft 10 in) excl FR probe; height 12,12 m; wing area (actual) 310,5 m^2 (3342 ft^2), (erroneous Western) 292,6 m^2 (3150 ft^2).

ENGINES (95 No 1) four 12,000 ehp NK-12 derated to 9750 shp, (1956 production) full-rated NK-12, (from about 1958) 14,795 ehp NK-12M.

WEIGHTS Empty (A, author est) 86 t (190,000 lb); Fuel (A) 58,5 t, (C) 73,6 t; loaded (max) (A) 154,2 t (340,000 lb), (C) about 169 t (372,575 lb).

PERFORMANCE Max speed (A, Něměcek) 950 km/h (590 mph), (later models, typical, Green) 853 (530) at 9 km, (*Jane's*) 805 (500) at 12,5 km; typical cruise (not loiter) 708 (440) at 11 km; time to 5 km (author est at max wt) 13 min; service ceiling (Něměcek) 14 km (46,000 ft), (Green) 13,5; range (A, Něměcek) 17 500 km (10,900 miles), (A, with 11,34 t bombs, DoD est) 12 550 (7800); take-off (author, 169 t) 2450 m; landing (author) 1400/210 km/h.

Tu-142 This designation has been attributed to all AV-MF Bear aircraft; author's belief it applies only to new-build aircraft planned 1960s and coming off production line from late in decade. Possibly some are rebuilds, but most appear to be new and entering service at rate of about 12 per year and normally replacing older aircraft or attrition. NATO designation Bear-F, first positively identified 1973. Completely new aircraft planned from start for long-range ASW (anti-submarine warfare) missions. Increased fuselage length, restressed wing possibly almost same as Tu-126 but without wide-chord flaps. Fuselage stretched mainly ahead of wing, and structurally redesigned with entire rear area pressurized and devoted to sonobuoy stowage and dispensing (includes retro-launcher), crew rest accommodation and galley, side fairings and turrets removed, leaving tail turret as sole defensive armament. Unknown belly I/J-band radar, smaller than Big Bulge, plus (optional) chin radar smaller than Mushroom. Considerably further increased fuel capacity, restressed landing gear with larger tyres (and probably increased-capacity brakes) resulting in larger main-gear boxes with longer fairings (some reports deny these house larger wheels) and bulged nose-gear doors. Tip pods on tailplane, in some aircraft large pod pointing to rear from top of fin, observation blisters each side at rear of forward compartment, dorsal sight station probably removed, little Elint or ECM compared with Bear-C, D, E. About 45 in use 1982 and believed continuing in low-rate production with no known successor.

DIMENSIONS span 51,1 m (167 ft 7¾ in); length (excluding probe) 49,5 m (162 ft 4¾ in); wing area, probably 310,5 m^2.

ENGINES Four NK-12M, or MA.

WEIGHTS Empty (author est) 90 t; loaded (*Jane's*) 188 t (414,462 lb).

Tu-142 Bear-F (weapon-bay doors open)

PERFORMANCE Generally inferior to Tu-95 variants except range about 30% greater with any given warload.

Tu-91 This turboprop attack prototype was among new aircraft shown to Western delegation at Kubinka June 1956; remarkably not one of delegation produced a published sketch, and only attempts so far seen in West are not only totally dissimilar but obviously a parody of true shape. Despite similarity to British GR.17 ASW (anti-submarine) aircraft main purpose always said to be *Shturmovik*, and thus rival to Il-40, though configuration unsuitable for armour and low vulnerability to ground fire. Basic features included all-metal stressed-skin construction, low unswept wing, twin four-blade props (believed single contraprop driven by one engine), engine inlet to rear of nose gear, engine near c.g. driving through long extension shafts, twin jetpipes in sides of rear fuselage, side-by-side crew of two close behind prop, and external carriage of all weapons. Reported remote-control gun (said to be ShKAS, unlikely,) in extreme tail. Ordnance said to include up to 3 t (6614 lb) bombs, mines or torpedoes, or rockets to RS-182 size or pod with two NS-23 guns, under centreline and four wing stations. (Němeček has sketched torpedo version with all-glazed tandem cockpits, internal weapon bay and retractable tailwheel.)

OKB had no experience of such aircraft, and reading between lines Tupolev would have had no interest had it not been for availability of P.O. Sukhoi in 1950. This enabled brigade to be assigned to project under extremely experienced attack designer. Similarly to Il-20 obvious, though Tu-91 considerably larger and more powerful. After Sukhoi's OKB reinstated 1953 this project remained with Tu and was reportedly assigned to V.A. Chizhyevskii (see BOK). Prototype probably flew about 1955, having waited for engine for at least a year (first flight said to be by K. Zyuzin). Popular names *Tarzan*, *Bychok* (bull calf). Said to have been pleasant to fly over speed range 280/710 km/h with excellent all-round performance, but terminated by Khrushchyev's decision to halt all *Shturmovik* aircraft in 1957.

DIMENSIONS Span 17,17 m (56 ft 4 in); length 16,35 m (53 ft 7¾ in); wing area unknown.
ENGINE One 6000 shp NK-6.
WEIGHTS Loaded said to be 14 t (30,865 lb).
PERFORMANCE Max speed 710 km/h (441 mph); cruise 650 (404); service ceiling 8 km (26,250 ft); range 2400 km (1500 miles).

Tu-98 Another prototype shown to Western delegation June 1956, this large high-subsonic (marginally transonic) attack-bomber is even less known than Tu-91. For several years ascribed to Yakovlev (called 'Yak-42' in West) and to Ilyushin, and even today no design details apart from persistent report engines were AL-7F. Data are estimates, and following is best consensus of main features. Designed to use well-tried bomber crew compartment and bomb bay attached to different aircraft with transonic performance. Advanced wing of thick-skinned construction, able to bear bending moments of high-speed flight with all aircraft mass on centreline, thinner than Tu-88 and more sharply swept (LE about 60° inboard, 55° outboard) with one fence each side. Circular 2,9-m diam forward fuselage similar to Tu-88 but with nav/bomb station extended to form glazed cone of not more than 14° semi-angle; slightly bulged chin radar, total crew probably three, possibly four (reported 7 is nonsense). Twin afterburning engines in widened and area-ruled rear fuselage fed via very long ducts above wing with semicircular inlets (believed plain, without centrebody or obvious variable geometry, but sharp-lipped) close to cockpit. Similar installation used again in Tu-28 series, which also had derived wing. Large fuel capacity between ducts, aft of main-gear bays, and probably in wet wings and fin. Tricycle landing gears retracting into fuselage, no details but nose gear aft of radar and main units probably first use of same bogie as Tu-28. Large highly swept vertical tail, slab tailplanes low on fuselage, outboard ailerons, all flight controls probably fully powered (new to OKB). Weapon bay similar to previous B-29 derived bombers but shallow because of presence of wing box. Bombload probably 6-t (13,230 lb) maximum. Remote-directed tail cannon (omitted from oft-pictured Western recognition model) with Bee Hind or similar radar; pod at tip of fin and probably braking parachute box under fuselage (often said to be in large pod above rear fuselage below rudder but this must house gun-direction radar). Persistent report of inbuilt rockets at rear, usually said to number six and to be for both a.t.o. (assisted take-off) and supersonic boost at high alt, no known evidence and questionable.

Tu-98 had flown prior to June 1956 presentation to West (Němeček, flew 1955) and probably competed with Il-54 and possibly much smaller Yak-26. Difficult to sift sense from mass of garbled misinformation on Tu-98 (such as reports of carrying AAMs as interceptor, using rockets for dash interception) but there is no doubt this was serious and apparently successful transonic bomber, though not remotely in class of B-58. According to Green, more experimental than combat aircraft, but only reason for termination probably doubtful advantage of a little more speed than Tu-16, at cost of much higher fuel consumption, plus hugely expensive ICBM programme. This was a time when, in the Soviet Union as much as America, missiles were judged to be making bombers of limited interest.

DIMENSIONS Span about 20 m (65/66 ft); length about 31 m (102 ft); wing area, not published but about 82 m² (883 ft²).
ENGINES Believed two 10 t (22,046 lb) AL-7F.
WEIGHTS Est loaded 54 t (119,000 lb).
PERFORMANCE Max speed said to be 1238 km/h (769 mph, M 1·17) at 12 km; max dry thrust 1060 km/h (659 mph) at 6 km; range probably about 3000 km (all at height, with bombload, dry thrust) (3500 miles seen in Western accounts is optimistic).

Tu-104 No large modern passenger aircraft has been produced as cheaply or effortlessly as this re-fuselaged derivative of Tu-88 (Tu-16) bomber. Tupolev said later he had shown drawing to Stalin and gained latter's approval a few weeks before his death in February 1953. In retrospect a fairly obvious derived aircraft, but OKB fortunate in receiving GVF go-ahead and funding by autumn 1953 (in Britain Avro Atlantic and H.P.97 never left the drawing board). Main design task was new fuselage and uprated environmental system handling more than three times pressurized volume. Minor changes design of new wing centre section between engines, absent in Tu-88, longer nose gear and bag-type wing tankage. Resulting aircraft had no appeal to Western operators, despite initial selling price £425,000, because by any normal DOC formula relatively uneconomic. But in Soviet context Tu-104 wrought transformation of all long-distance routes with much greater carrying capacity than existing eqpt (Il-12 or Il-14 usually with 18/21 seats) and 2½ times speed. Typical example, flight time Moscow/Irkutsk fell on introduction of Tu-104 from 13 h 50 min to 5 h 30 min. Restored OKB to position of pre-eminence in GVF passenger aircraft sustained for next 25 years.

Wing closely similar to Tu-88 in early variants, except for new wide centre section with three heavy plate spars with KhGSA booms tying banjos encircling engines. Latter in almost straight ducts with circular inlet well outboard of fuselage, unlike Tu-88, and requiring no boundary-layer bleed. Rest of wing apparently unchanged. Fuselage diameter increased from 2,9 to 3,4 m, pressurized at original 0,5 km/cm²

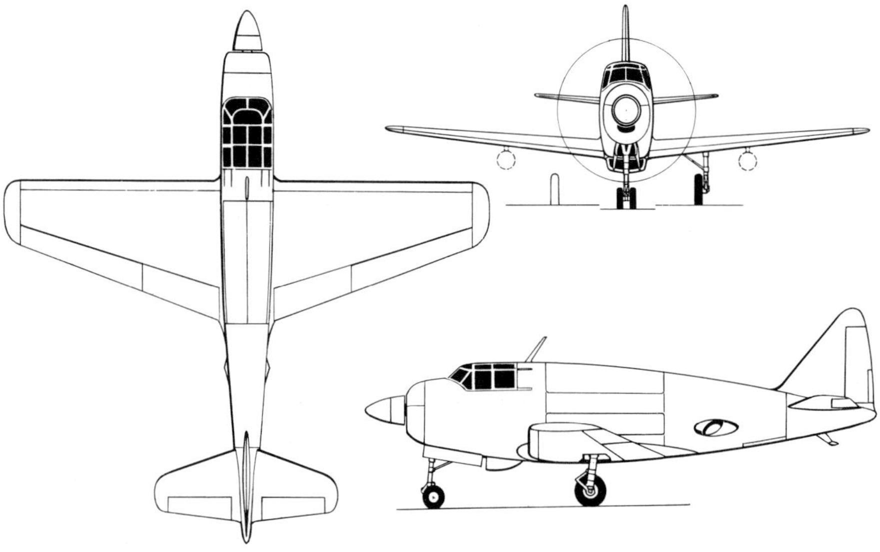

Tu-91

Tu-104 prototype

level from nose to bulkhead at LE of tailplane, with normally closed pressure bulkhead (flat) at Frame 11 between flight deck and 142,3 m³ main cabin. Flight deck similar to Tu-88 though military equipment deleted, different nose glazing, smaller mapping radar in chin location and with provision for flight crew three (two pilots, nav) to five (add radio, eng). Main passenger cabin 16,11 m long, 3,2 wide and 1,95 high. Divided into small forward section with four circular windows each side and large rear section by inconvenient raised floor over wing centre section. In prototype and early aircraft raised area used for galley, with three roof windows left of centreline and two right-side windows higher than remainder. Main rear cabin with seven windows each side; toilets each side at rear and another forward on right; total of seven windows removable inwards as emergency exits. Except in prototype, six small underfloor baggage/cargo holds with plug doors on ventral centreline. Rest of aircraft generally as Tu-88, though tailplane (curiously shown with reduced sweep in most Western three-views, and in Simakov's book with span given as 15,1 m compared with 11,75 for Tu-88) lowered to upper part of fuselage and elevators separated from roots by fixed inboard sections. Nose gear moved much further forward and lengthened to reach higher fuselage.

Prototype L-5400 flown by Yu.I. Alasheyev 17 June 1955 and according to Něměcek took part in Aviation Day at Tushino (author believes confusion with a Tu-104G, ie, civil Tu-16, probably L-5402). Flight development successful, and production Tu-104 established as 50-seater. Two small compartments ahead of spars with 6 and 8 seats and tables, then 8-seat cabin aft of spars and rear cabin for 28 in forward-facing pairs each side of aisle. Interior judged quaintly Victorian by Western observers. Heavy brass-finish baggage racks along sides with numerous hooked-on coat hangers, emergency oxygen at knee level along walls, Plexiglas windows in non-structural dividing bulkhead partitions, tables mahogany and antimacassars lace. Fuel capacity 33 150 lit (7292 gal), derated engines with elec starting, operating pressurization and anti-icing. Avionics included British VOR and ILS. Crew training under A.K. Starikov started with Tu-104G (demilitarized Tu-16) summer 1955 and continued with NII trials of L-5400 October 1955. Aircraft passed all test programmes winter 1955–1956 and L-5400 flew to London Heathrow 22 March 1956 causing intense interest. Reason for flight was to bring head of KGB to discuss visit of Soviet leaders following month when 5400 returned to London accompanied by first two series machines, 5412 and 1413. Line service begun to Irkutsk 15 September 1956, followed by Prague 12 October. Subsequently Tu-104 variants used by every Aeroflot directorate and leading Soviet passenger aircraft until mid-1960s.

Robust engine enabled TBO to rise slowly from 300 to 2000 h, and to be fully rated for civil purposes as AM-3M, in turn enabling OKB to increase gross weight. Resulting **Tu-104A,** flown winter 1956–1957, believed to be L-5421, increased seating to 70: forward cabin with four rows 2+2 and rear cabin with aft-facing 2+2 and ten rows forward-facing 3+2, generally modernized furnishings, small changes elsewhere. Public showing Vnukovo 10 July 1957, set three class records later: 6 September 1957, 11 221 m with 20 t load; 11 September 1957, 847,498 km/h over 2000-km circuit with 2-t load; 24 September 1957, 970,821 km/h over 1000-km circuit with 10-t load. Replaced Tu-104 on production line at Kharkov at about 11th aircraft and large number built.

Fully rated engine enabled OKB, in this programme under Tupolev's personal direction, to increase payload further. By 1958 first Tu-104 (L-42399) introduced 1210 mm (3 ft 11½ in) stretch, new fuselage also used in Tu-110 described later, dP increased to 0,57 kg/cm², AM-3M-500 engine, three windows above wing on each side (none in roof) at slightly higher level, revised underfloor holds with greater capacity (lowered hold floors and raised passenger floor) and more sensible doors on right side, considerably increased flap and wing chord to maintain field length despite greater weight, and normal interior for 100 passengers, seated 3+2, in cabins seating 30 (front), 15 (over wing, galley being aft of flight deck) and 55 (rear cabin). Entered service with GVF designation **Tu-104B** on Moscow/Leningrad 15 April 1959 and large number subsequently built, production being completed 1960 at about 200 of all variants. Tu-104B records: 1 August 1959, 1015,86 km/h over 2000-km circuit with 15 t load; 4 August 1959, 12 799 m with 25 t payload, both far in advance of Tu-104A.

Tu-104V designation applied by Aeroflot to Tu-104A series aircraft modified internally to

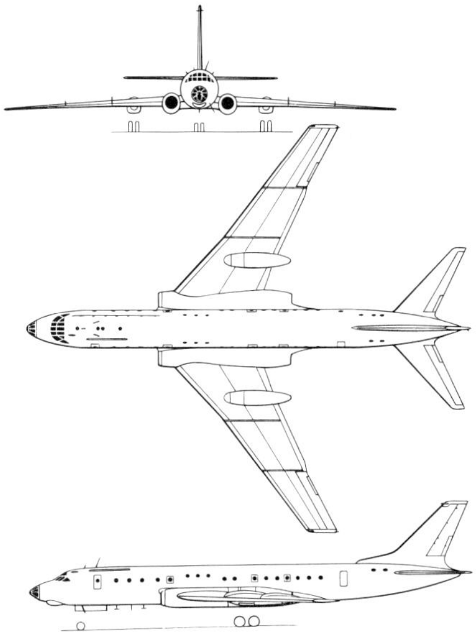

Tu-104B

design by GVF engineer Kh. Izmiryan to carry 100 passengers (cabin for 25, 15 and 60) by re-arranging toilets and wardrobes. **Tu-104D** designation of similar in-service mod raising accommodation to 85 only, later also increased to 100, but with 3M-500 engines. **Tu-104Ye** (104E) designation of aircraft, believed early 104B (poss first to have 3M engines) used 2 April 1960 to set 2000 km circuit record with 15 t load at 959,94 km/h. Most B refurnished in GVF shops for 104 or 115 pax from 1967. Only foreign customer CSA, five plus a replacement supplied from November 1957, basically 104A with 81 seats (author was on two press trips with CSA, several guests complained of eardrum trouble but aircraft appeared simple, tough and well-liked though heavy aileron at high IAS and rather noisy at rear). Small number used by VVS for staff transport and cosmonaut training in weightless flight. In 1964 first line aircraft, 5412 (re-registered 42318) intensively flown as structural fleet leader, in 1967 transferred to tank testing. By 1981 this type withdrawn from line duty after circa 80 million passengers carried nearly 20b t-km with reliability and safety better than any other Soviet aircraft. One or more used by Gidrometsovcentr as met platform with weather radar (pointed nose) and wing pylons for cloud-seeding rockets. In retrospect, GVF needs might have been better served by straight-wing aircraft with shorter field length, though costly improvement of over 80 airfields demanded by Tu-104 would have had to happen eventually.

DIMENSIONS Span 34,54 m (113 ft 3¾ in) (incorrectly given by Simakov book as 32,93); length (104, A, V) 38,85 m (127 ft 5½ in), (B, D) 40,05 m (131 ft 4¾ in); wing area (104, A) 174,4 m² (1877 ft²), (B, D) 183,5 m² (1975 ft²).

ENGINES (L-5400) two 6750-kg AM-3 derated, (104) first year as 5400, later as 104A, (A) 8,7-t AM-3M, (B) first few as A, most 9,7 t AM-3M-500, (V) as A, (D) AM-3M-500.

WEIGHTS Empty (5400) 39,51 t, (104) 41,6, (B) 42,5 (93,695 lb); max fuel (believed all) 26,5 t; max take-off (5400) 71 t, (104) 76 t (167,550 lb), (B) invariably given as same (76 t) despite greater payload, power and wing area.

PERFORMANCE Max speed (all) 950 km/h (590 mph) at 10 km; cruise (B) typically M 0·72, about 770 km/h (478 mph) at 10 km (Aeroflot claim 800/850, never known in line use); service ceiling about 11,5 km (37,730 ft); range with max payload against 50 km/h wind with 1 h reserve, (104) 2650 km with 5,2 t (1647 miles, 11,464 lb), (A) same with 9 t (19,841 lb), (B) 2100 km with 12 t (1305 miles, 26,455 lb); take-off (all, MTO) 2200 m (7220 ft); landing (all, 61 t) 1850 m (6070 ft)/240 km/h.

Tu-110 In parallel with Tu-104 OKB assigned brigade under Markov (initials given as G.C. but in fact Dmitri Markov, present chief constructor Tu-154) to prepare four-engined variant expected to become standard production version. Major redesign incorporating new fuselage and extended-chord wing already described under Tu-107 (Tu-104B). Engines installed as D.H. Comet with inboard wing (greater span than 104) spars pierced for engines and jetpipes slightly underslung, with banjo forgings in KhGSA joining spar booms round engines, lower sections removable for engine change downwards. Said to reduce structure weight in comparison with fuselage-hung 104 engines but main result was greater wing area. No change in vertical tail. Prototype finally emerged according to plan except retention of mid-cabin roof windows instead of left side. Objective was increased safety (and thus wider sales appeal), greater range and, secondary consideration, better economics. Flown spring 1957 (date unknown); rejected by GVF despite report of superior handling and field length, probably because 104 adequately doing job. Prototype assigned to VVS but with apparent civil number 5600 and in 100-seat (30/15/55) configuration exhibited 10 July 1957. Believed this aircraft only; possibly later rebuilt as 104Ye.

DIMENSIONS As 104 except span (Něměcek) 37,5, (Stroud) 36,94, (Alexander) 37,94 (124 ft 5¾ in); wing area not published but about 200 m².

ENGINES Four 5,5 t (12,125 lb) AL-5.

WEIGHTS Empty not known but about 43 t; max about 79 t (Něměcek gives 79,3, 174,824 lb).

PERFORMANCE Max speed said to be 1000 km/h (621 mph) at 11 km; cruise probably faster than 104B, invariably given as 800/900 km/h; initial climb (3-eng, landing) 5/6 m/s (984/1181 ft/min); service ceiling 12 km; range at 800 km/h with max (12 t) payload, 1 h reserve (no mention of headwind) 3300 km (2050 miles) (Alexander gives this for 900 km/h, at variance with Aviaexport); max fuel 5000 km; take-off 1,6 km; landing claimed 1200 m.

Tu-114D, Tu-116 As parallel project to support Tu-114 passenger aircraft OKB assigned Arkhangyelskii to build direct civil variant of Tu-95 (Tu-20). This was relatively simple, and Tu-116 first flew late 1956, about a year before prototype 114. As far as can be seen from walk-around, few changes compared with VVS aircraft. Forward crew compartment virtually unaltered though smaller mapping-only radar (presumed same as Tu-104) and duplicated VOR/ILS. Weapon bay skinned over and said used for fuel (author disbelieves reported weight, see data). Rear fuselage furnished for payload, 24/30 passengers in 2+2 seats, galley, two toilets, or various cargo provisions (details not known but well aft of CG). Rear pressurized compartment and turret replaced by tailcone, twin braking parachutes; wing, flaps and tail as bomber. Probably access tunnel linking front and main cabins, separate ventral door with stairway from ground to rear cabin with emergency side door (believed later used as normal when GVF had tall enough airfield steps). Purpose of Tu-116 to prove propulsion system in civil operation, prove routes and airfields (latter had virtually no means of handling aircraft in 1957) and if possible set records and gain publicity. First aircraft completed NII GVF testing early 1958; three examples known, civil No 76462 (believed to have been first) and military 7801, 7802. No 76462 accepted by Aeroflot and designated Tu-114D (*Dalnyi*, long-range), though more accurate title would have been Tu-20G. First major flight to be revealed Moscow/Irkutsk/Moscow April 1958, but biggest publicity task was series of three zig-zag tours of the Soviet Union later in 1958 with 24 officials and journalists covering 34 400 km (landings at Vladivostok, Tashkent, Minsk for night stops) in 48 h 30 min. Surprisingly, 76462 never used for round-world or any other overseas flight, except short trip to Prague. Must assume

Tu-114 series aircraft

Tu-110

Tu-114D

similarity to Tu-20 regarded as security risk. Report of 76462 flying 'urgent long-haul missions' for Aeroflot but in fact no evidence ever in line service. Two military Tu-116 still in use late 1970s, unknown duties and no known overseas missions.

DIMENSIONS Presumed as Tu-95 (Tu-20).

ENGINES Originally four NK-12M; later possibly NK-12MV.

WEIGHTS No data apart from reported Max take-off weight 121 926 kg (268,796 lb), about 40 t below expected figure.

PERFORMANCE No data but should have been faster and longer-ranged than Tu-20 or Tu-114.

Tu-114 Like Tu-104 this transport derived from Tu-95 was logical development, main problem being sheer size and weight of aircraft for which GVF runways in mid-1950s totally unprepared, and inability of routes to fill 220 seats. Like Tu-95 and Tu-116 assigned to Arkhangyelskii, said to be to fulfil GVF 1953 requirement. Though completely civil programme, widely publicized by Soviet Union, amazing difficulty in discovering true facts. First flight incorrectly reported 1955, and said to have completed factory tests 1956. Basic design figure, diam of fuselage, seems never to have been published, and existing drawings clearly inaccurate. Recent Soviet and Czech articles give span 54,00 m, length 47,20 m and wing area 283,7 m², all wildly different from accepted figures and in some cases clearly nonsense (it means length much less than original bomber and wing area much less despite transport's increased chord!).

Turning existing Tu-95 into passenger transport almost same task as done by Tupolev himself with Tu-88/104. Bomber already had a wing centre section but despite moving wing from mid to low position this had to be extended, slightly increasing span, though structure outboard of fuselage virtually unchanged, except major increase in chord of secondary upper-surface and underlying flap at TE. Same thing done by OKB several times previously, most recently with Tu-104B. Flaps often called Fowler but differ in having only small overlying portion of fixed upper surface and resemble track-mounted plain flaps. Operation several times (most recently Němček 1981) reported hydraulic, major break with all B-29 successors. Horizontal tail lowered to fuselage, trimming by variable-incidence tailplane, all flight controls hyd boosted. Main landing gear as Tu-95, nose gear set new record height, twin left/right inclined 30KhGSA struts meeting at steerable lower twin-wheel unit, single rear strut pulling unit up rearwards into unpressurized box. Enormous fuselage with circular section about 4 m diameter (cabin interior width 3920 mm), fully pressurized 0,59 kg/cm² back to pressure bulkhead aft of LE of tailplane. Passenger floor almost exactly on horizontal diameter, leaving underfloor depth sufficient for galleys and walk-in service compartments as well as front (24 m³) and rear (46 m³) cargo holds (holds, total 70 m³, much smaller than could have been, and smaller than in stretched DC-8). Efficient environmental system provides fresh air via large ram inlet under fuselage and using part engine bleed air, but details unknown (NK-12 strange engine with variable pressure ratio at constant rpm and in high-altitude cruise may have supplied sufficient air for cabin and wing LE deicing). LE thermal protection probably by heat exchangers in twin jetpipes. Tailplane, props and windshields raw AC, fin rubber boot. Heavy plate around lower fuselage in plane of props, reported as protection against ice but author's view steel plate armour against blade (this was major hazard in early NK-12 testing, but service record in Tu-20 and Tu-114 was exemplary).

Prototype L5611 first flown 3 November 1957, immediately before 40th anniversary of Revolution, and named *Rossiya* (Russia). Technically already well-developed, and no significant visible engineering change prior to completion of GVF NII testing late 1959 (after display in static park at 1959 Paris Salon) but severe operating problems with GVF airfields and equipment, and line service did not begin until 24 April 1961 (Moscow/Khabarovsk, 6800 km in 8 h 15 min schedule). Wide range of interior layouts for upper deck, though all aircraft with same window and door arrangement. Normal crew nav (nose), two pilots, eng, rad, two in underfloor galley and three or more cabin crew. High-density 220-seat interior first in world with seats 4+4; more common arrangements were 170 seats (main cabins for 42, 48 and 54) or 145, or only 120 on longest routes, in each case with four small compartments just behind wing with two divans each or six seats and folding bunk. Most configurations provided middle cabin, and possibly seats elsewhere, with tables in restaurant style. While GVF preparing for Tu-114, test crew under I.M. Sukhomlin established many records including: 24 March 1960, 1000 km circuit with 25 t payload, 871,38 km/h; 1 April, 2000 km circuit with 25 t, 857,277 km/h; 9 April, 5000 km circuit with 25 t, 877,212 km/h; 21 April, 10 000 km circuit (Moscow/Sverdlovsk/Sevastopol/Moscow) with 10 t, 737,-352 km/h; 12 July 1961, height 12 073 m with 30 t payload. Another notable flight non-stop Moscow/New York with N. Khrushchyev (then prime minister) 15 September 1959. By 1962 overseas routes being explored, longest (with two shift crews and 80 passengers) being to Havana, with outbound refuel at Murmansk, return being non-stop 10 900 km. Total production put at about 30, of which 25 identified in Aeroflot line service on routes to Delhi, Montreal, Tokyo (in partnership with Japan Air Lines whose insignia was carried), Paris and Conakry/Accra. By 1971 fleet had carried 3 million passengers 130 million-km, but since replaced by Il-62, process complete in 1975. In its day world's largest and heaviest airliner and still largest propeller aircraft ever in regular use (B-36 greater span but much smaller body and less than one-quarter as powerful).

DIMENSIONS (accepted) span 51,1 m (167 ft 7¾ in); length 54,1 m (177 ft 6 in); height 16,05 m; wing area 311,1 m² (3348 ft²).

ENGINES (5611) NK-12 derated to 9000 ehp, (1958) NK-12M rated at 12,000 ehp; (1962) 15,000 ehp NK-12MK.

WEIGHTS Empty (typical) 91 t (200,600 lb); fuel 60,8 t; loaded (normal) 164 t (361,552 lb), (max) 175 t (385,800 lb), also given as 171 t.

PERFORMANCE Max speed 870 km/h (541 mph) at 8 km; cruise 770 km/h (478 mph) at 9 km; service ceiling 12 km; range (171 t, 15 t load, 1 h reserve) 8950 km (5561 miles), (171 t, 30 t load, 1 h reserve) 6200 km (3853 miles); take-off (175 t) 2700 m, (171 t) 2500; landing (128 t, MLW) 1550 m/205 km/h.

Tu-28, Tu-102, Tu-128 This family of large supersonic aircraft was chief result of Tu-98 of mid-1950s. Original Tu-102 design of 1957 was multi-role fighter-reconnaissance aircraft, using almost identical fuselage (except for nose) and with bogie main gears retracting into wing TE fairings. Original design believed funded as rival to La-250, but missions were broadened. Powerful nose radar for air/air use, with two underwing AAMs, and large ventral mapping and air-surveillance radar, possibly combined with other sensors, seen on two prototypes displayed at Aviation Day 1961. Compared with Tu-98, nav relocated in rear tandem cockpit, vertical tail smaller (cut off at Mach angle) and two canted ventral fins at rear. This impressive type caused as much confusion as Tu-98, and at first likewise believed to be Yak design. Tu-102 was to have entered VVS service as Tu-28 (even, non-fighter, designation) but never adopted and instead used as basis of pure long-range interceptor Tu-128, which did enter production as **Tu-28P**. Tu-128 revealed Aviation Day 1967 when 12 flew over at high speed. Seen to be without ventral fairing or rear ventral fins, but carrying four AAMs. Eventually recognized as world's largest all-weather interceptor, meeting 1962 requirement more severe than that of La-250 though drawn up after cancellation of B-70.

Tu-102, Tu-28

Wing typical Tupolev with main box bounded by straight spars at 5% and 40% and forming limited integral tankage; believed OKB's first production aircraft with machined-plank integrally stiffened skins. LE sweep 56° inboard, 50° outboard, single fence wrapped round LE and extending back to front of aileron near inboard end. On original wing fully powered ailerons extended close to tips and had outer sections of extended chord; production aileron stops short of tip (wing span unchanged) and TE straight except for about 10 mm greater chord on aileron tab at inboard end. Not seen in photos but author guesses roll augmented by spoilers. Hydraulic Fowler flaps outboard of pods and on inboard wing with TE 90° to fuselage. Fixed LE, and no airbrakes visible (except for possible spoilers). Long fuselage with obvious area ruling, long inlet ducts from apparent fixed semicircular inlets identical to Tu-98 splayed out far from wall of fuselage, two square suck-in aux doors in duct above wing. Engines not positively identified but Tu-128 prototypes probably had AL-7F; guesstimated thrust per unit for production aircraft varies from 19,180 lb to 27,000 lb in common Western accounts. At least 11 000 lit fuel in four-plus tanks in fuselage, total internal capacity about 25 000 lit (5500 gal), external tanks normally unnecessary, but author assured can be carried; no FR probe seen to date. Powered slab tailplanes with geared elevators in mid position, fractionally higher than wing, relatively modest vertical tail with dorsal fin extending from ram inlet to cool afterburner surrounding structure. Bulky, powerful I-band radar (NATO name Big Nose) giving 100-km lock-on against large aircraft and with secondary illumination (CW) function for radar-guided AAMs. Latter carried in two pairs, two AA-5 Ash with IR homing and two with semi-active radar homing; in most situations one of each fired against single target. Pilot cockpit with acute vee windshield and rear-hinged clamshell hood, nav with similar hood mainly aluminium with two windows each side, suggesting radar display poor in bright sunlight. Crew board via large wheeled platform with 11-rung ladder. Bogie main gears trail with front wheels lower than rear, like all other OKB's bogies, folding to rear into large TE boxes complying with area ruling and since 1965 also housing other equipment (tail-warning or dispensers). With this aircraft retraction almost certainly hydraulic. Steerable twin-wheel nose gear folds to rear (shown retracting forwards in most Western drawings). External HF rail aerial along right flank of forward fuselage, bleed-air LE anticing (tail system unknown), no obvious provision for tail bumper, but braking parachute in ventral box and anti-skid brakes.

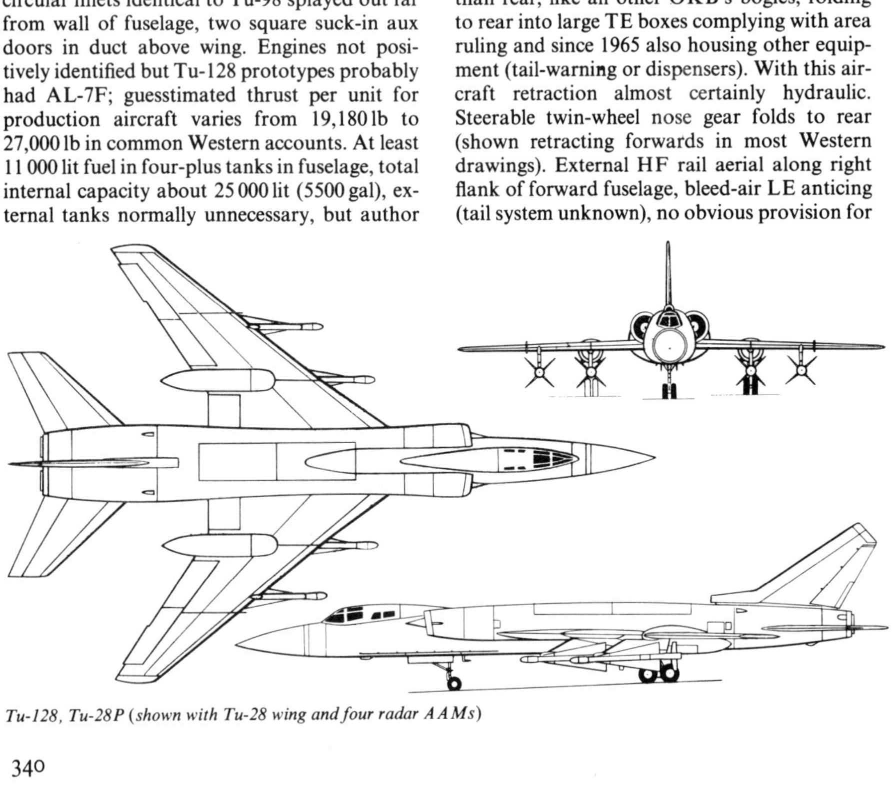

Tu-128, Tu-28P (shown with Tu-28 wing and four radar AAMs)

Production interceptor first flown about 1966 and accepted into VVS PVO service as Tu-28P about 1968. Primary task always believed in West to be early interception of strategic bombers carrying stand-off or cruise missiles as far as possible from their objectives. Operated in conjunction with Tu-126 (later Il-76 Awacs) direction aircraft. Total est 1971 (DoD) at 126 aircraft, since revised slightly upward but never thought to number more than 200. Since 1975 obvious need to update avionics and provide complete look-down/snap-down and snap-up capability, and no reason to doubt this is being done despite various rumours of replacement by interceptor version of Tu-22. Data are estimates.

DIMENSIONS Span 18·1 m (59 ft 11¾ in); length (Green) 27,2 m (89 ft 3 in); wing area (author) 80 m² (860 ft²).

ENGINES (102) two 10 t AL-7F, (128) two 11,2 t AL-21F.

WEIGHTS (est) Empty (128) 24·5 t (54,000 lb); internal fuel 13 t; loaded 40 t (88,000 lb); poss cleared to higher weights with external fuel.

PERFORMANCE Max speed 1850 km/h (1,150 mph, M 1·74) at 11 km; service ceiling 20 km (65,600 ft); loiter endurance 6 h; range 5000 km (3100 miles); field length 200 m.

Tu-22, Tu-105, Yu This striking large supersonic aircraft was revealed at Aviation Day 1961 when ten flew over to cause alarm to Western observers but not confusion: no OKB could have built it but Tupolev. Original design about 1955, considered probably Myasishchyev, to fly missions of Tu-16 but with sharply increased ability to penetrate sophisticated defences. Marked kinship, aerodynamic and structural, with smaller Tu-98 and 102 families, but unusual mounting of twin engines in short optimized nacelles above rear fuselage with vertical tail carried above. Not in class of B-58 but formidable in European or regional context; and difficulty of assessment shown by fact Western range estimates extend from 6500 km (Sweetman and author) through 4815 (Alexander) to 2250 (*Jane's*).

Wing modified TsAGI SR-5S profile, t/c unknown but about 9%/7%, LE sweep 70° at root, 50° to fence and 45° thence to tip; small tip pods contain avionics and pitot heads (vary slightly, especially left wing). Structure of wing similar to Tu-98/102 with spars at 10% and about 60% outboard, rear spar bifurcating at structural break (90° to LE) at main gears to give three spars inboard. Integral-tank wing box with machined skins, fixed LE, single fence as in 98/102 wrapped round LE and extending aft to aileron/flap junction. Fully powered ailerons (structurally inboard/outboard sections moving as one) and hydraulically driven large-chord flaps, said to be Fowler type but in fact tracked plain flaps with no fixed wing above (hence cannot increase area) driven to 30° outboard of pods and 50° inboard for landing, depressed about 15°/25° on normal take-off. No spoiler/airbrake, but twin braking parachutes (seldom seen) in box under rear fuselage. Fuselage circular-section variable diam nose/tail to conform to area ruling, wing low/mid position above weapon bay. Forward section pressurized for normal crew of three in tandem all entering via ventral hatches hinged down from rear but needing

Tu-22 Blinder-B on take-off, missile bay doors replaced

short ground ladders or platforms. Front compartment immediately aft of main radar and pressure bulkhead has two large rectangular windows low on each side and smaller side window further back on right, but no capability for visual bombing; ventral blister extends aft to nose gear (incorporating entrance doors) with TFR or other forward-looking sensor at front. Pilot on centreline has heavily framed metal canopy with vee windscreens; commonly said to have upward-ejection seat but no roof hatch and similar ventral door as other crew. Third crewmember faces forwards on centreline with rectangular window each side and again has central hatch. Front and rear crew cover duties of nav, radar, missile guidance and systems, and backseater also manages rear defence by single gun (often called NS-23 but almost certainly NR-23) directed by Fan-Tail radar and with believed ability to fire normal types ammunition or quickly switch to chaff. Entire mid-fuselage available for fuel, total body/wing fuel about 45 000 lit/36 t (9900 gal/79,400 lb). Dorsal spine from cockpit to fin, lower part of which merges into left/right engine nacelles, engines being hung each side of fin spars; normal access to underside of engine by opening large hinged lower mid-section of cowl. Slab tailplanes mounted low on rear fuselage, tips cropped at Mach angle (M 1·5). All flight controls fully powered, rudder and both ailerons tabbed. Typical OKB landing gear, all units retracting to rear (prob hyd) with bogies trailing front-wheels down and overturning to lie inverted in wing TE fairings; main tyres about 125 × 305 mm with multi-disc anti-skid brakes. Large retractable tailskid at tailplane frame. No known provision for a.t.o. rockets.

First flight, said to be by Alasheyev, probably 1959. Programme based at Kazan. Production engine not ready, and prototype, with OKB title Aircraft Yu, could even have had AM-3Ms (barrel-like cowlings). At 1961 display nine, called Blinder-A by NATO, represented basic aircraft with normal weapon bay with double-hinge left/right doors for free-fall bombs (max about 10 t) and Short Horn nav/bomb radar in nose with radome forming lower half of 15° semi-angle nosecone. In recon configuration apparent large linescan or SLAR between this radar and crew compartment, and several pre-production Yu aircraft had no front windows and different ventral blister. Production engine resulted in projecting variable nozzle, without previous upper lip of airframe, and at least four small ram inlets on cowl; afterburner always used for take-off/supersonic dash, but range based on 95% dry operation. Tenth aircraft in 1961 show, called Blinder-B, first of missile-carrying variants with AS-4 Kitchen ASM recessed in weapon bay with doors cut away to fit missile, Down Beat nose radar with larger scanner in wide radome, attachment for FR probe above nose with plumbing internal, strike cameras and payload (chaff/flares/jammers) dispensers in landing-gear pods, comprehensive ILS/VOR/SRO-2D/Sirena-3/A-325Z avionics and other changes. Variation in wingtip pods as mentioned. These were main production versions, believed originally to number 200. Chief operator DA, and some 140 judged still in service 1982 as well as a few still with Iraq (used in action against Kurds) and about 17 with Libya (at least one bombed Tanzania in support of Uganda). A dedicated reconnaissance variant, Blinder-C, has no weapon bay and lower fuselage packed with sensors and EW equipment including six/seven large optical cameras, SLAR, linescan and apparent variety of Elint and ECM installations; about 60 built, most remaining in AV-MF service for maritime missions. Training variant, Blinder-D, first seen 1968 with instructor cockpit above and behind pupil pilot in place of normal backseater, assumed designation **Tu-22U**. Also in 1968 first recognition of new engine with improved nacelle having smaller inlet with translating inlet lip moved forward at take-off to admit extra air around periphery, modified doors and cooling inlets and new convergent/divergent nozzle with longer petals similar in

Tu-22 Blinder-D (Tu-22U?)

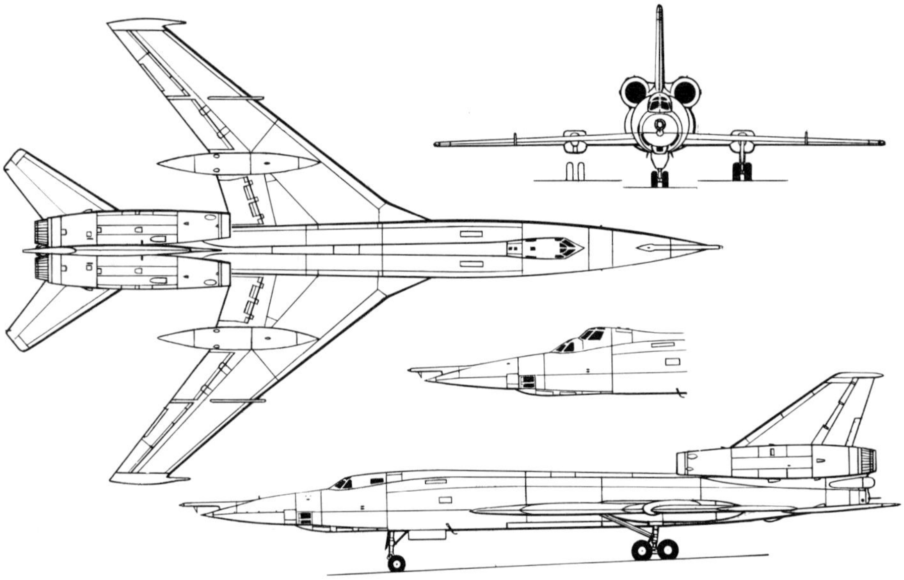

Tu-22 Blinder-A (inset, nose of Blinder-D)

Tu-124

shape to US J79 giving optimized variation in area and improved dash speed/range.

Importance of Tu-22 diminished at start by concentration on strategic missiles and since mid-1970s by Su-24 extending capability of Frontal Aviation; at same time, Western dismissal of this aircraft not justified and most range estimates must divide true figure by 2. Aircraft needs long strong runway and report of rough-ground operation refers to one-time trial programme. Author believes 14+ rebuilt as Tu-22M. No confirmation of persistent report of interceptor version for PVO. Data estimated.

DIMENSIONS Span 28,0 m (91 ft 10 in); length (no probe) 40,53 m (132 ft 11⅔ in); wing area 155 m² (1650 ft²).

ENGINES At least two different types of afterburning turbojet, initially possibly based on AM-3 (RD-3) and since mid-1960s a new engine, almost certainly Koliesov VD-7 or 7F, rated at about 14 t (30,900 lb).

WEIGHTS Empty about 40 t (88,000 lb); fuel 36 t; max about 85 t (187,500 lb).

PERFORMANCE Max speed 1600 km/h (995 mph, M 1·5) at 11 km; about 890 km/h (550 mph) at SL; service ceiling 14 km dry, 18 km (59,000 ft) with afterburner; range without FR (ferry) 6500 km (4040 miles), (max weapons) 5500 km (3420 miles); tac radius including 400 km supersonic dash 2800 km (1750 miles); take-off 2500 m; landing 1600 m/250 km/h.

Tu-124 Though almost indistinguishable at a distance from Tu-104 this short-haul airliner is totally new design and much smaller. Designed (believed by brigade under Markov) to meet 1957 GVF specification for modern transport to replace Il-14 on routes shorter than 1800 km from small airports. Sensible decision taken to adhere to Tu-104 layout exactly but scaled down (25% linear, 50% weight) and powered by new turbofans designed for this aircraft, first Soviet engine planned for civil application. Result was attractive, with short but robust landing gear holding body at same height as Il-14, ability to use 1800 m unpaved airstrip, and no major shortcoming. Marked complete break from B-29 technology and on entry to service was first turbofan short-haul transport in world.

Wing aerodynamically scaled from Tu-104 with similar slight kink in LE, 35° sweep at LE outboard, but increased t/c inboard and totally redesigned movable surfaces; sharp kink at landing-gear pods, 90° to fuselage inboard and straight sweep outboard, hydraulic double-slotted flaps (large chord inboard of pods), manual spring-tabbed ailerons and spoilers ahead of outer flaps driven asymmetrically to 52° in air to assist roll and flicked open on touchdown as lift-dumpers; large hydraulic airbrake under fuselage driven to 40° and normally open on approach. Twin upper-surface fences each side, fixed LE, about 3° anhedral on ground, retracted flaps increased wing chord but much less than on Tu-104. Manual elevators and rudder, again with spring tabs, and tailplane with elec irreversible trim. Wing anticing by bleed air as in Tu-104, but fin and tailplane electrothermal, using raw AC in glassfibre elements beneath skin. Fuselage circular section, same 2,9 m diam as B-29 and jet bombers, pressurized to dP 0,57 km/cm² by system energized by engine bleed, all doors plug-type. Short landing gears with hyd retraction to rear, main tyres 865 ×

280 mm (6,5 kg/cm²), bogie stowed inverted, nose tyres 660 × 200 mm (same), anti-skid multi-disc brakes, optional mudguards on nose gear, emergency braking parachute. Normal fuel capacity 13 500 lit (2970 gal) in integral centre-section and outer-wing tanks and 4 flex cells in inboard wings, pressure-fuelling under each wing. Engines in straight-through nacelles with top level with wing upper surface and jetpipe inclined downward. Each engine carries DC starter/generator; emergency ram-air turbine in each wing for immediate purpose of driving tank booster pumps. Minimum flight crew two pilots and nav in glazed nose; optional seat for radio operator or second nav. Usual GVF mapping radar and all expected avionics, retrac landing lights each side of nose, towing point on nose leg after steering disconnected.

Prototype Tu-124, L-45000, flown unknown date June 1960. Generally troublefree development and aircraft popular with pilots and ground crew. Numerous proving flights 1962 and basic aircraft entered service Moscow/Tallinn 2 October 1962. Equipped as 44-seater, with all seating 2 + 2, forward cabin 12, small raised mid-cabin over wing eight seats and rear cabin 24; insufficient underfloor depth for holds, cargo and baggage accomodated on main floor on right side behind flight deck and at extreme rear. Furnishing more modern than Tu-104 fleet with fluorescent lights and synthetic fabrics in cream, pale green or grey. Toilet and coat space aft and galley forward on left. Production replaced Tu-104 at Kharkov and main run was of **Tu-124V** with minor changes and 56-seat interior arranged 12/12/32. Surprising that no other air-

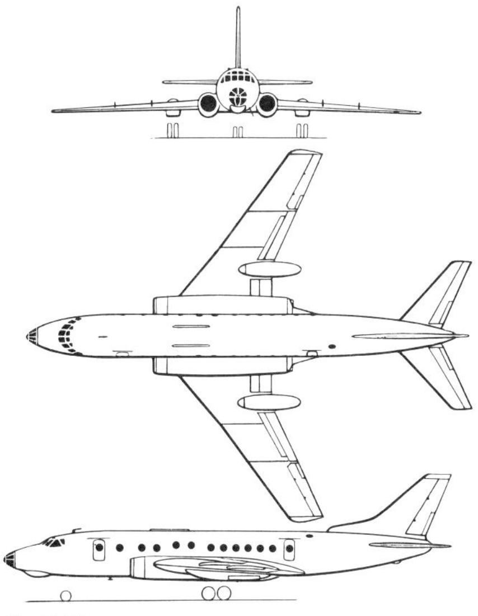

Tu-124V

line (except three for CSA and two for Interflug) bought this cheap ($1·45m in 1965) and reliable aircraft which would probably have been internationally certificated had it been submitted. Gained excellent reputation with virtually all Aeroflot directorates, published DOC being 22 US cents per short-ton mile. One successfully ditched in Neva (Leningrad) without passenger injury and re-entered service. Total production about 100, including small number of **Tu-124K** and **K2.** Strange that Něměcek describes K as mixed pax/cargo with 36 seats and rest of 6 t

Tu-124V in GVF repair factory, Minsk (radome removed)

payload made up of freight and K2 as all-cargo variant with large door and reinforced floor. In all Western accounts K is said to be de luxe 36-seat model (detailed descriptions of furnishing published) and K2 described as 22-seat VIP aircraft, used by Indian air force (three bought 1966, still used). Interflug passed their aircraft on to LSK (air force of DDR) and only other customer was Iraqi air force.

DIMENSIONS Span 25,55 m (83 ft 9⅞ in); length 30,58 m (100 ft 4 in); wing area 119,3 m² (1284 ft²).

ENGINES Two 5,4 t D-20P.

WEIGHTS Empty 22,5/22,8 t (50,485 lb); fuel 10,8 t; loaded (normal) 36,5 t (80,467 lb), (max) 38 t (83,774 lb).

PERFORMANCE Max speed 970 km/h (603 mph) at 8 km; cruise 800 km/h (497 mph) at 10 km; service ceiling 11,7 km (38,400 ft); range (max 6 t payload) 1220 km (758 miles), (max fuel and 3 t payload) 2100 km (1305 miles); take-off (36 t) 1300 m; landing (32 t) 930 m/200 km/h.

Tu-126 First revealed to West in documentary propaganda film of 1968, this huge Awacs (airborne warning and control system) type aircraft is derived from Tu-114; author believes all were rebuilt ex-Aeroflot aircraft. Timing is correct, and if Tu-20 is any guide there is no serious airframe life problem.

Though there are important changes to basic Tu-114, Tu-126 centres around its surveillance radar, result of at least a decade of development. Called Flat Jack by NATO, aerial is a rotating 'saucer' of about 11 m (36 ft) diameter, mounted above rear fuselage on single long-chord unbraced pylon. Ample room in fuselage for power generation system (gas-turbine driven in rear fuselage), large racking bays for radar and signal processors giving azimuth split and constant false-alarm rate, advanced IFF and digital data-link to ground and almost certainly to friendly aircraft. Entire fuselage remains pressurized, with large data-processing installation and operator consoles providing human interfaces. Few details of radar publicly guessed, though electronic scanning is certain; initial radar probably not pulse-doppler, leading to US assessment it was of limited effectiveness over water and ineffective over land. This appears foolish judgement; Soviets do not produce such useless defence hardware. Extent to which overland downlook technology incorporated at start unknown, but designers could hardly have ignored flood of information emanating from the USA. Visible airframe modifications include nose FR probe, large fairing above forward fuselage, three substantial dielectric blisters on rear fuselage (two ventral centreline, one left side) with some resemblance to those on EW/Elint variants of Tu-16 and Tu-95 Tu-142, large ventral fin with three aerials, liquid drains and tandem bumper wheels, large extension to rear fuselage with cooling inlet and various small aerials identical to that seen on Bear-D since 1978, and Bear-type streamlined pods on tips of tailplane. Modifications to main-gear pods which may contain avionics or other eqpt. Flight crew probably four and mission crew about ten.

First flight probably 1967 or 1968. System fully operational 1971 when one detached to Indian AF to serve in war against Pakistan. Though less than ideal in having propeller vibration, relatively high interior noise-level and radar interference from large propellers, Tu-126 certainly cost/effective way of getting small number (est 12) of large long-endurance Awacs platforms into service. All probably delivered 1972 and undoubtedly since subjected to considerable electronic improvement. Due to be supplemented and eventually replaced by Mainstay variant of Il-76.

DIMENSIONS As Tu-114 except length 55,2 m (181 ft 1 in), (with FR probe) 57,3 m (188 ft 0 in).

ENGINES Four 15,000 ehp NK-12MK.

WEIGHTS Empty about 105 t (231,500 lb); fuel, probably 65 t; loaded 170–175 t (386,000 lb).

PERFORMANCE Max speed (*Jane's*) 850 km/h (528 mph) at height; operating speed about 520 km/h (323 mph); service ceiling about 11 km (36,000 ft); endurance 25 h; range without FR about 12 550 km (7800 miles).

Tu-134 Though Tu-124 was excellent short-haul jet its outdated layout inherited from Tu-104 resulted in high structure weight, reduced engine efficiency, impaired wing/flap geometry and high interior noise and vibration. Fashionable rear-engined T-tail configuration solved most of these problems, though doing little for structure weight, and about 1962, as Tu-124 entering service, GVF agreed with OKB to fund Tu-124 derivative with this configuration. Designation **Tu-124A**, assigned to brigade under Leonid Selyakov with Arkhangyelskii (far senior in age and experience) as deputy.

Wing differs from 124 in having increased-span centre section (without engine installations) and outer-wing panels, two-section ailerons with spring and trim tabs, increased-travel flaps, all sections coming down together to 20° for take-off, 38° for landing, and slightly less static anhedral (1° 30′). Fuselage same diam but 1,6 m longer and with wing box at last accommodated under level floor throughout giving constant 1,96 m headroom along aisle. New engines derived from those of 124 but with greater power and efficiency, hung on short stubs on two frames at rear of fuselage within pressurized portion. Considerably larger vertical tail carrying variable-incidence trimming tailplane and manual geared-tab elevators. Airframe anti-icing as 124: bleed for engines, wing and fin, electric for tailplane. Three fuel tanks (believed all integral) in each wing, system capacity 16 500 lit (3629 gal) with pressure coupling at right LE. Landing gears as 124 but strengthened, and main tyres enlarged to 930 × 305 mm and pressure reduced to 6 kg/cm² (85 lb/in²) for poor surfaces, increased-capacity brakes, no braking parachute or thrust reversers.

This basic prototype outline accepted by GVF August 1962, by which time two aircraft on 124 production line (45075, 45076) had been set aside for completion as 124A. First flight probably 1963, though some observers claim earlier (Něměcek, autumn 1962; Green, late 1962). No announcement, but designation changed to **Tu-134** and aircraft unveiled on 100th test flight 29 September 1964. By this time several other 134s had flown, but like many modern Soviet civil transports development was protracted and despite use of large number of production aircraft no passenger service flown until September 1967 (Moscow/Stockholm), after several aircraft had flown unscheduled domestic cargo services. Attractive aircraft, improvement on Tu-124 and contrary to original idea a different and more capable vehicle. Original Tu-134 flight crew two pilots plus nav, one cabin crew, 64 passengers 2 + 2 (16 first class in forward cabin, 20 tourist mid and 28 tourist rear). No underfloor holds, cargo/baggage being as before at extreme rear and behind flight deck, moved to left side with galley on right. Seating soon increased to 72, with 44 in front cabin and 28 in rear. In 1967 main electrical power system settled as frequency-wild AC from inverters, and in 1969 engines fitted with constant-speed drives (English Electric) to alternators, first in Soviet line service. Later same year reversers of twin-clamshell target type introduced, engine designated Series II. Final absentee, APU, introduced 1970 for main-engine start (electric), and ground electric power and air-conditioning.

By this time production at Kharkov had switched to **Tu-134A**, first flown prior to 1970. Designation thought to apply to APU-fit but in fact numerous mods including fuselage lengthened by 2,7 m (at first announced as 2,8), further strengthened landing gear with same wheels/brakes/tyres as Il-18 (but tyre pressure held at original level), Srs II engine standard, locally strengthened wing, VHF probe forming

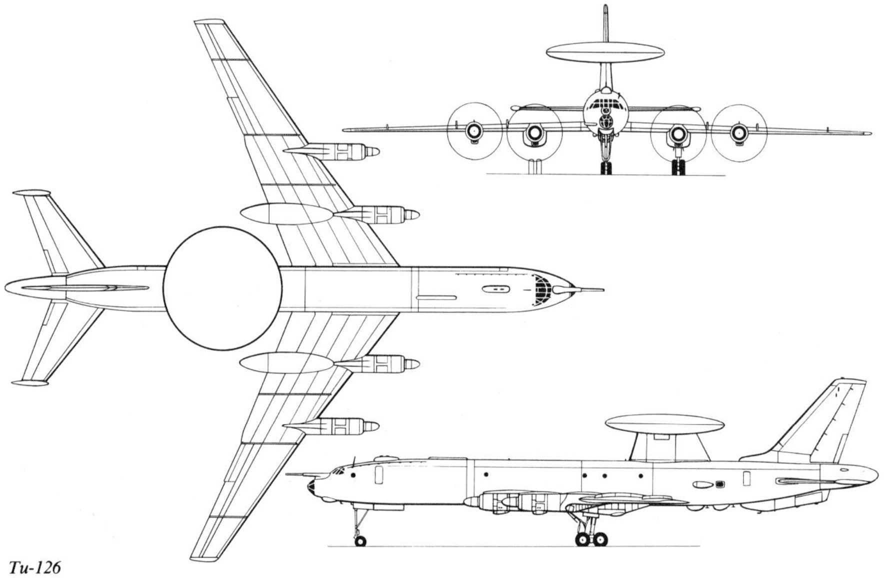

Tu-126

Tu-134 (Malev, Hungary)

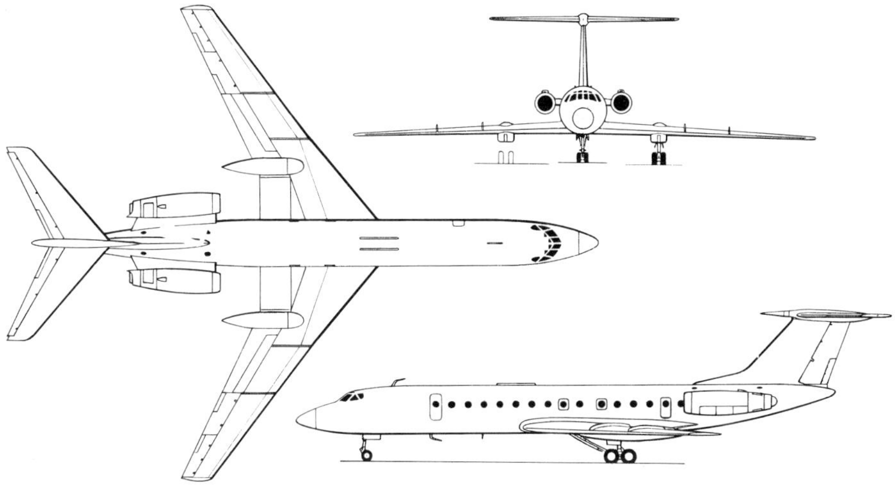

Tu-134A

long pointed nose to tail/fin bullet, and improved avionics (Arkhangyelskii claimed Cat III landing but certainly not certificated for this). All known subsequent airline deliveries with 28-seat rear cabin; front cabin various (inc 12 first-class) up to total capacity 84, all 2+2, high-density reducing baggage space, normally 4,0 or 6,0 m^3 forward and 8,5 aft. First Soviet transport to sell to several foreign airlines, including CSA, Interflug, Malev, Balkan Bulgarian, LOT and Aviogenex. Third Aviogenex (1971) was first to do away with visual nav station in nose and replace it by chin-radar. Aeroflot said over 90 delivered in one 12-month period 1971–1972 and total built about 300, including at least 56 for export. **Tu-134A3**, lightweight seats increase max to 96 giving much better seat-mile costs; D-30 Series III engines unstated higher thrust. **Tu-134B** has no navigator but forward-facing cockpit retains engineer at side panel; spoilers usable for direct lift control. Production ended late 1970s.

DIMENSIONS Span 29,0 m (95 ft 1¾ in); length (134) 34,35 m (112 ft 8⅓ in), (A) 37,05 m (121 ft 6¾ in); wing area 127,3 m^2 (1370 ft^2).

ENGINES (134) two 6,8 t D-30, (A) D-30 Srs II, same rating; (A3) Srs III, higher rating.

WEIGHTS Empty (OWE) (134) 27,5 t (60,626 lb), (A) 29,05 t (64,045 lb); fuel 14,4 t; loaded max take-off, (134) 44,5 t (98,104 lb), (A) 47 t (103,600 lb).

PERFORMANCE Max cruise (134) 900 km/h (559 mph), (A) 885 (550) at 42 t at 8,5/10 km; normal cruise 750 km/h (466 mph) at 11 km; service ceiling after (max take-off) 11,9 km (39,050 ft); range (134, max 7 t payload, 1 h reserve) 2400 km (1490 miles), 134A with max 8,2 t payload at 800 km/h at 11 km, no reserve stated) 1890 km (1174 miles); take-off field length (BCAR) (134) 2180 m, (A) 2400 m; landing (MLW field length) (134) 2050 m, (A) 2200 m; landing run with reversers (A) 780 m.

Tu-144 Possibly most impressive civil aircraft in history, this striking SST was first in world to fly and was expected to lead to early use of at least 75 to transform travel times throughout world's largest country. Instead Tu-144 designation has identified succession of completely redesigned aircraft. Only now, after billions of

Tu-134A (Aviogenex, Jugoslavia)

rubles have been spent, is a third-generation Tu-144 likely to enter sustained passenger service.

Original GVF requirement dated 1963, based on premise Aeroflot already then saved average 24·9 h journey-time per passenger and with widespread use of SST this could rise to over 36h. Programme cost expected to be three times as great as estimate for Il-62 (previous highest) but immediate decision to undertake largest-ever research programme at TsAGI, TsIAM and elsewhere to underpin slender-delta aircraft made mainly of light alloy to cruise at Mach 2·35 for 6500 km with 121 passengers. Design authorized at OKB under personal supervision of A.N. Tupolev but with his son Alexei Andreyevich named as chief designer and Yu.N. Kashtanov chief engineer. Propulsion assigned N.D. Kuznetsov. Two flight prototypes and static/fatigue specimen ordered early 1964, and project disclosed with model at Paris Salon 1965. Gross weight then 130 t (286,600 lb). Problems much greater than anticipated and translating concept into engineering drawings many times greater than any previous Soviet aircraft. Mikoyan charged with building Analog-144 to fly wing scaled down to fit MiG-21, but this severely delayed by inability to settle details of wing and elevons. Throughout 1964–1966 arguments raged on omission of tailplane; despite increasing tunnel evidence on c.p. movement and need for take-off/landing flaps, decision finally taken to adopt same tailless configuration as Concorde. Many other details closely similar to Anglo/French SST, but TsAGI decided 9·9% drag saved in cruise by grouping engines in box at rear and achieving favourable pressure distribution under wing. Author corresponded with A.N. Tupolev on this point, arguing such result possible only with down-turned wingtips (Alfred Eggers, NASA), but was assured 'favourable interaction of normally disadvantageous shock-waves' would give desired result, even though at this time wing substantially horizontal throughout. Only one aircraft seen by UK delegation to Zhukovskii factory 1967 but told two other airframes well advanced and first flight early 1968. First flight article, 68001, made maiden flight 31 December 1968, accompanied by Analog-144; crew Edward Elyan, copilot Mikhail Kozlov, flight-test director V.N. Benderov and engineer Yu. Seliverstov (picture, page 11).

First prototype slightly larger than Concorde, with LE more clearly swept at two angles (about 76° and 57°) and whole surface in one plane except for modest conical camber on inboard LE. T/c not published but A.N. Tupolev 'We had to think in terms of 2·5%'. Rectilinear structure of multiple spars attached to ten fuselage frames, mainly machined forgings, with skins chemically-milled. Ruling material VAD-23 aluminium alloy with titanium LE and titanium or steel in region of engines, landing-gear rib and other highly stressed or hot areas. Trailing edge on each side formed by four approx-square elevons each driven by two power units faired into underside of wing. Three separate hydraulic systems (assumed regular 210 kg/cm² but said to use new-spec fluid) with majority-vote feature to give quad reliability. Failure of one system or one actuator is normally confined to one elevon on each wing, unstated provision against hard-over runaway demand. This was first civil fully powered aircraft in the Soviet Union, prolonged research at TsAGI and at O.K. Antonov OKB where prototype wings actually built. Likewise rudder divided into upper half with two power units on right side and lower half with two power units on left, each power unit in different system. Fuselage of basically circular section (often incorrectly drawn with almost flat underside)

Tu-144 low-speed tunnel test, 1966

Tu-144 first landing, accompanied by Analog-144

about 3,4 m diam, with forged frames and thick chemically-milled skin, integrally stiffened with crack-stoppers along row of small rectangular windows, 25 each side, excellent exterior finish. Underside rear fuselage titanium/steel. Interior width 3,05 m (120 in), height along aisle 2,16 m (85 in) over passenger section 26,5 m (87 ft) long, 120 seats (max 126) mainly 3 + 2, all baggage/cargo on same deck front and rear, loading said to be via ventral doors (not on 68001) or by mechanical conveyors over wing, two main doors each side 1680 × 762 mm (66 × 30 in), small Class 2 emergency door each side at rear. Flight crew 3, pilots side-by-side with nosecone drooping 12° for take-off/landing. Engines in pairs, originally to have been in one box of four with rectangular secondary nozzles XB-70 style but modified 1976 with four distinct circular cowls fed by two paired ducts with wide centreline gap for nose gear. Nacelles sacrificed lightness for aerodynamic advantage of shape and position, with extremely long ducts from plain fixed-geom inlets giving good airflow at engines and overall length 23 m (75 ft), structure titanium except for light-alloy access doors around engines upstream of turbines. No reversers. Remarkable main landing gear with 12-wheel bogie (4 tyres on each of three fixed axles) retracting forwards, unusual for OKB, bogie rotating 180° to lie inverted in wing; despite 13 kg/cm² (185 lb/in²) tyres of minimum size, long fairings necessary in wing upper surface and bay doors in line with each wheel. Tall nose gear almost identical with Tu-114 retracts rearwards into large ventral fairing beneath pressurized fuselage and between engine ducts. Brakes on all 26 wheels, main gears having quad steel-plate brakes each side of beam on each axle. Braking parachute in rear fuselage. Fuel in integral tanks in outer wing, LE inboard and bottom of fuselage, with trim tanks nose/tail, announced capacity 87500 lit (19,247 gal, 70 t). Pipes to tail trim tank external on 68001 confirming late modification.

First flight was frantic effort to beat announced deadline on last day of year, but 30-minute trip with gear down said to be satisfactory. Contrary to prevalent story engine had not only run over 1800 h at that date but had flown extensively (over 40 h) on testbed (believed Tu-16 with engine on ventral centreline). Early flying devoted not only to performance/handing but also to getting duplicated environmental systems working, installing variable inlets and control system, inertial/doppler nav and autopilot (said to be tied by computer of analog type, basically an error by OKB). All four test crew with upward ejection seats. Mach 1 exceeded 5 June 1969, Mach 2 on 26 May 1970, later reached 2·4. Publicly unveiled Sheremetyevo 21 May 1970, MAP Deputy said 'aircraft already in series production' at Voronezh, but no announcement made of second prototype flight (possibly 1971, believed No 68002) and next aircraft seen was pre-production 77101, flown spring 1973. This was virtually a different design, with dramatic aerodynamic, structural and systems changes. New fuselage with length increased by 6,3 m (20 ft 8 in), greatly modified structure and materials, 34 windows each side and Class 1 exit at rear each side. New wing with span increased 1,15 m (4 ft) and completely different aerodynamics and structure with considerable camber across entire chord root to tip and marked downward curvature at TE, skins integrally stiffened by machining from slab and completed panels then attached by welding instead of riveting. Much more extensive honeycomb structure, most movable surfaces titanium alloy (extensive use Ti/4V and similar). Redesigned engine nacelles resembling Concorde with oblique rectangular inlets separated by deep central splitter, electrically de-iced inlets, variable upper/lower profile (not fully developed spring 1973) and four improved variable nozzles separated by width of fuselage and extending aft of wing TE. Redesigned landing gears. Main gear with eight-wheel bogies (four tyres on each of two axles), tyres 950 × 400 mm, attached to forged frames in engine nacelles and retracting forwards between each pair of engine ducts; during retraction bogie first rotates 90° inwards about axis parallel with fuselage to lie upright in narrow thermally insulated and cooled bay between ducts. Nose gear moved forwards 9,6 m (31 ft 6 in) and of necessity made even longer; redesigned to retract forwards into unpressurized underfloor box within fuselage. All legs ultra-high-strength steel, nose gear carrying six (previously four) landing/taxi lights. Major aerodynamic improvement by addition of retractable canards of 6,1 m (20 ft) span to top of fuselage just aft of flight deck. Each surface almost rectangular, with double LE slat and double-slotted TE flap, swinging open forwards to zero sweep but sharp anhedral; this powerful lift at nose enables elevons to deflect down instead of up to give greatly improved lift overall at low speeds, improve low-speed handling and agility and reduce field length. Previously, without canards, 68001 had flown at 21·2° AOA. Ejection seats replaced by massive hydraulically opened entry door on left of nose. Nosecone redesigned like Concorde with greater glazed area. Fuel capacity increased to 118 750 lit (26,121 gal) with greater capability for rapid transfer nose-tail (Elyan said at this time transfer aft at M 0·7 and back when decelerating thru 1·5; he confirmed afterburner not used in cruise, despite Western reports).

Eight production aircraft seen at Voronezh during French visit December 1972; second aircraft, 77102 flew at 1973 Paris Salon and suffered inflight breakup during unplanned violent pitch

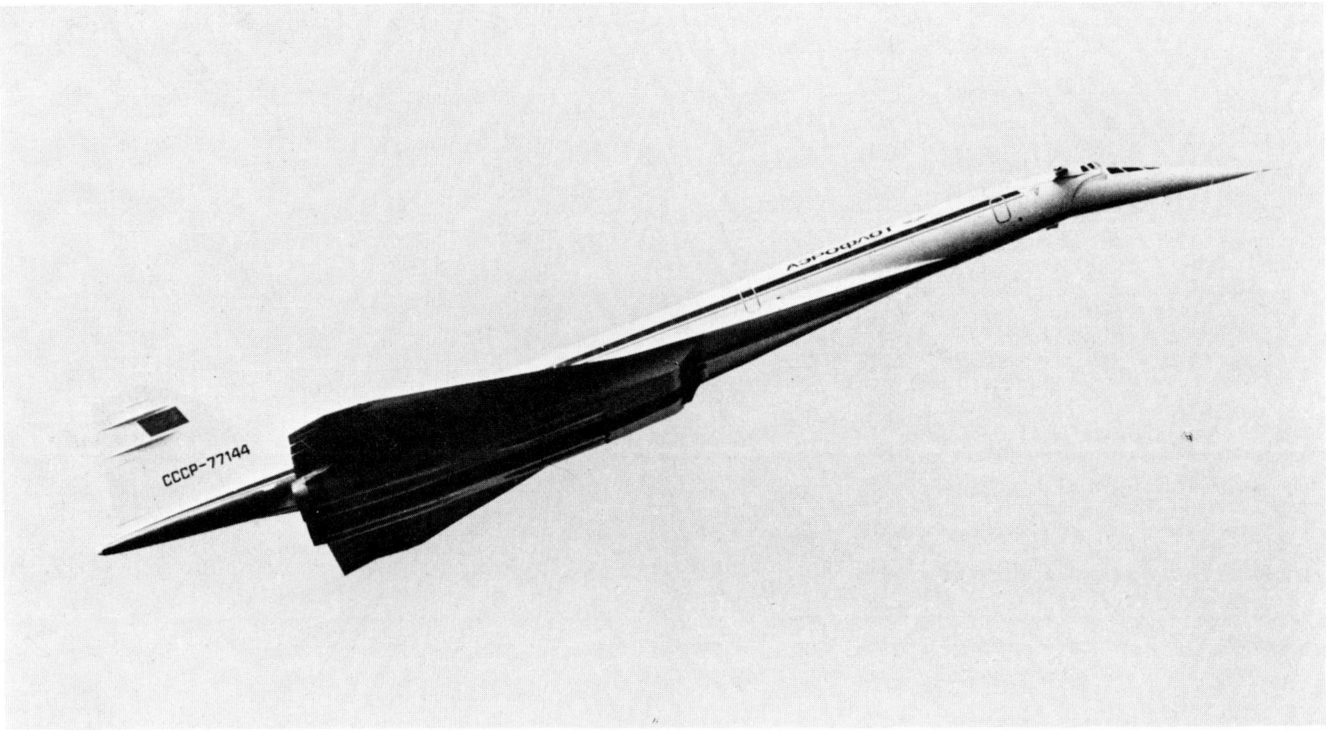

Tu-144, possibly first series aircraft

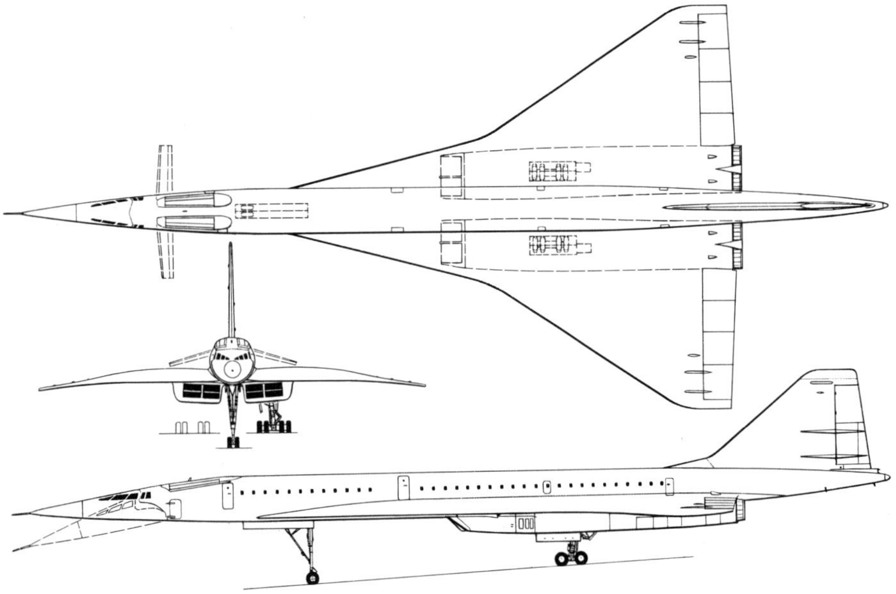

Tu-144 series aircraft

manoeuvre 3 June 1973, killing Kozlov and Benderov among others, report never published. No apparent major modification needed and No 77106 began proving flights Moscow/Alma Ata with cargo 26 December 1975, flying 3260 km sector regularly in under 2 h block time (77106 retired to Monino 1980). Normal passenger accomodation 140: 11 in first-class front cabin seated 2 + 1, 30 in mid cabin 2 + 3 and 75 in rear cabin 2 + 3, final 24 seated 2 + 2. Rear baggage/cargo accessed via door at TE on right. From 22 February 1977 series of 50 proving flights Moscow/Khabarovsk. At last, about five years behind planned schedule, passenger service began Moscow/Alma Ata 1 November 1977; five of next six flights cancelled but 102 revenue flights made when service suddenly terminated 1 June 1978 following fatal accident to another Tu-144 not in airline service. By that time 13 aircraft flown, presumably ten being production machines.

From 1970 reports emerged about Koliesov engines with variable (turbofan/turboramjet) operating cycle. In 1973 it was said thrust reversers would be fitted, and in 1979 **Tu-144D** was announced incorporating new engines and many other significant changes. First announced flight by Tu-144D took place 23 June 1979 when one flew Moscow/Khabarovsk 6185 km in 3 h 21 min with A.A. Tupolev on board. MGVF Deputy said at this time 144D was '50% more economical in operation' and was 'ready for series production'. Comment also made new engines could 'meet international requirements for noise emission'. As book went to press no hard fact known about 144D but every indication it is a further major advance, but perhaps not so different that existing 144s cannot be rebuilt. Late 1981 detailed GVF plan for 1982–1985 made no mention of Tu-144, and major account of Kuznetsov's career conspicuously omitted reference to NK-144 engine. Author informed April 1982 regular cargo service Moscow–Tashkent.

DIMENSIONS Span (prototype) 27,65 m (90 ft $8\frac{1}{2}$ in), (production) 28,80 m (94 ft $5\frac{7}{8}$ in); length (prototype) 59,40 m (194 ft $10\frac{1}{2}$ in), (production) 65,7 m (215 ft $6\frac{2}{3}$ in); wing area (prototype) 421 m², (production) 438 (4715 ft²).

ENGINES Four NK-144 afterburning turbofans rated with full afterburner at (prototype) 17,5 t (38,580 lb), (production) 20 t (44,090 lb); (144D) believed Koliesov variable-cycle.

WEIGHTS Empty (prototype) about 79 t, (production) 85 t (187,390 lb); max fuel (prototype) 70 t, (production) 95 t; (prototype) design 130 t, actual 150 (330,700 lb), (production) 180 t (396,830 lb), (144D) about 190 t.

PERFORMANCE Max speed (all), also max cruise, 2500 km/h (1550 mph, M 2·35); normal cruise 2100 km/h (1305 mph, M 1·98) whilst drifting up from 16 to 18 km (max 59,000 ft); max climb from max take-off (production) 50 m/s (9843 ft/min); range (prototype) no meaningful figure but far short of 6500 km objective (est generally around 3200 km), (production) 6500 km with 140 pax (4300 miles), (144D) 7000 km (4350 miles) with max payload; take-off (prototype) 2300 m, (production) 1980 m; landing (prototype) 1490 m/305 km/h, (produc-

Tu-154 production at Kuibyshyev, 1972

tion) only known fig is *Jane's* 2,6 km, curiously high for only 280 km/h (174 mph).

Tu-154 Large trijet closely similar to stretched 727 in capability but with larger airframe and much larger and more powerful engines because of demanded ability to use short unpaved airports. Designed initially by team led by S.M. Yeger but about 1970 Dmitri Markov appointed project chief designer. Major GVF requirement, about 1964, for jet to replace Tu-104, Il-18 and An-10 offering dramatic advance in fleet mean cruise speeds without requiring significant airfield improvement. Range specified was severe, stages to 6000 km though with reduced payload.

Configuration essentially scaled-up Tu-134 with three engines and triplexed hydraulic and flight-control systems. Wing profile unknown, sweep 40° to structural break (90° to rear spar) at main gear, 38° to tip, 35° mean at 25% chord, dihedral 0° (not +3° as often reported), incidence +2·5° decreasing outboard. Exceptional high-lift provisions including OKB's first use of slats: hydraulic slat in five sections on outer 80% of each wing, hydraulic triple-slotted flaps (close similarity to 727 geometry) inboard and outboard of pods, fully powered ailerons extending from fence to tip, four section hyd spoiler above each wing, outermost differential for low-IAS roll, mid two sections symmetric airbrakes and innermost (inboard of pods) airbrake and also lift dumper. Tail almost exact scale of 134 though tailplane sweep increased to 45° (40° at 25%) and flight-surfaces honeycomb skins and fully powered by triplexed system without manual reversion, tailplane becoming primary control as well as trimming surface. Large fuselage with circular section 3,8 m (149·6 in) diameter, almost same as Tu-114 (except for Trident all major Western jetliners by this time no longer used circle) with straightforward fail-safe structure and level floor unobstructed by wing box. Max dP 0,63 kg/cm² (9 lb/in²). Basic interior width (*Jane's*) 3,5 m, (*Flight*) 130 in (3,30 m); usable length 27,45 m (90 ft), rectangular windows in crack-stop panels, two doors ahead of wing on left, two service doors opposite, all 1650 × 762 mm (65 × 30 in) opening outward. Unlike 124 and 134 underfloor cargo/baggage holds, two forward of wing total 38 m^3 and small unpressurized compartment aft. Main gears with six-wheel bogies (left/right wheel on each of three fixed axles) with 930 × 305 mm tyres at 8 kg/cm^2 (114 lb/in^2) retracting hydraulically rearwards to stow bogie inverted in wing pod. Steerable nose unit, 800 × 225 mm tyres, retracting backwards. Side engines hung on rear fuselage with R-R (Greatrex) type reversers, centre engine fed via S-duct, no reverser. Two integral tanks each wing, service tank in centre section, total 41 140 lit (9050 gal); optional four c-s flex cells raising total to 46 825. Airframe de-icing by bleed air except elec heating of slats and windscreens. Main elec power from CSD alternators, avionics include moving-map GPI, VOR/DME, 3-channel autopilot with hybrid flight-control computer and initial clearance to Cat II ILS. Two pilots and engineer, plus jump seats for nav or supernumeraries. Passenger accommodation for 128 to 167 with bulk seating 3 + 3.

Prototype 85000 flown by N. Goryanov 4 October 1968, static display at 1969 Paris Salon with vaguely reported engine mods, and 85006 used for Press flight August 1970. Production at Kuibyshyev authorized 1971 after NII testing six development aircraft and first production machine (believed 85701) delivered Aeroflot August 1970. Increasing number used for internal cargo flights winter 1970–1971 and scheduled cargo from July 1971. First passenger services (irregular) to Tbilisi July 1971; scheduled passenger from 9 February 1972 to Mineralnye Vody via Simferopol; international service 1 August 1972 to Prague. Prolonged efforts to develop Tu-154 as modern aircraft with 30,000 h airframe life (modest by Western standards), Cat III landing and no piloting problems, but many difficulties and objectives hard to attain. Delivery 1974 of **Tu-154A**, line service from 1975, more powerful engine, centre-section tank 8250 lit (6,6 t) contents transferable to main system only on ground, auto connect flaps/tailplane to maintain trim (pilot over-ride if + 3° tailplane movement demanded), two emergency exits at rear, improved systems and augmented avionics.

Production, said to be moved to different factory, switched 1977 to **Tu-154B**; no clear explanation of differences but main change appears to be improved roll-control from extended-span spoilers and shorter ailerons; other changes include additional flap/tailplane link, incorporation of centre-section tank in fuel system, improved interior arrangement with rearward extension of usable space (not clear if pressure-bulkhead moved) for three extra toilets at rear, with final arrangement two doors at front and four emergency-exit doors and four windows for typical seating 62 front cabin and 98 rear (max 169 but reports of 180, not seen in practice), new nose radar and trials 1977 of Thomson-CSF/SFIM (French) NKP-154T landing aid with chin TV blister and four Petetron CRT displays to assist Cat II ILS (Cat III not mentioned). Persistent rumours of all-cargo and VIP versions. Production of all variants about 400 and continuing 1982; customers include Balkan Bulgarian, Malev, Tarom, CAAK and Egyptair (aircraft returned following accident). **Tu-164** previously called Tu-154M, improved re-engined version first reported late 1981; Soloviev D-30KP engines (as in Il-76), more fuel, large freight door, range with 154 passengers 4800 km (2983 miles).

DIMENSIONS Span 37,55 m (123 ft 2¼ in); length 47,90 m (157 ft 1⅞ in); wing area 201,45 m^2 (2168 ft^2).

ENGINES (154) three 9,5 t (20,950 lb) NK-8-2, (A, B) 10,5 t (23,148 lb) NK-8-2U.

WEIGHTS Empty (154) 43,5 t (95,900 lb), (A, B) 50,775 t (111,938 lb); fuel (154) 33,15 t, (A, B) 39,7; max take-off (154) 90 t (198,416 lb), (A) 94 t (207,231 lb), (B) 96 t (211,640 lb).

PERFORMANCE Max speed 575 km/h IAS or M 0·9; normal cruise 900 km/h (560 mph) at 11/12 km; LR cruise 850 km/h; range at 11 km, no reserves (154, max payload 20 t, 158 pax + 5 t cargo) 3800 km (2361 miles), (154B, max payload 18 t) 2750 km (1708 miles) (Aviaexport do not explain how more efficient B, with greater fuel capacity, has shorter range with lower payload); take-off (154) 1140 m; balanced field length (154) 2100 m, (B) 2200.

Tu-22M, Tu-26 Fundamental drawback to Tu-22 was poor cruise efficiency with wing tailored to supersonic flight, combined with relatively long field length for same reason. As with smaller Sukhoi attack types, answer was variable geometry. From Tu-22 was developed new generation of swing-wing bombers of vastly greater capability, first seen in US reconnaissance pictures 1969 and assigned NATO name Backfire. Believed to be designated Tu-26, but called Tu-22M by USSR in SALT-2 documents. Author's belief is that Tu-22M was swing-wing Tu-22 seen 1969 and subsequently built in modest numbers. Designation publicly applied by Russians to second-generation aircraft having little kinship with Tu-22 beyond OKB likeness, size, and main fuselage/glove.

Original aircraft, called Backfire-A, believed to have OKB designation **Tu-136** and incorporated most parts of Tu-22. Modification of Tu-22 with variable-sweep wing was obvious first step, taken about 1966 with relatively small risk following extensive TsAGI tunnel research. At least two prototypes built at Kazan, undoubtedly Tu-22s rebuilt and in author's view retaining fuselage, inboard wing, landing gear and vertical tail. New horiz tail and outer wing panels with synch hydraulic drive 20° to 55°. By 1973 said to have been 12 development aircraft, probably all ex-Tu-22 airframes, and said later to have equipped a VVS operational unit. An important stepping stone to main production aircraft but probably never intended for sustained service and no point in guessing at data.

Backfire-B, possibly Tu-26 in VVS service and with unknown OKB number around 150, new aircraft retaining only basic structure of inboard wing (restressed and many changes), most of fuselage barrel and vertical tail. In conformity with TsAGI variable-geometry shape pivots are far outboard and only about half area of wing is variable. Centre section passes through fuselage

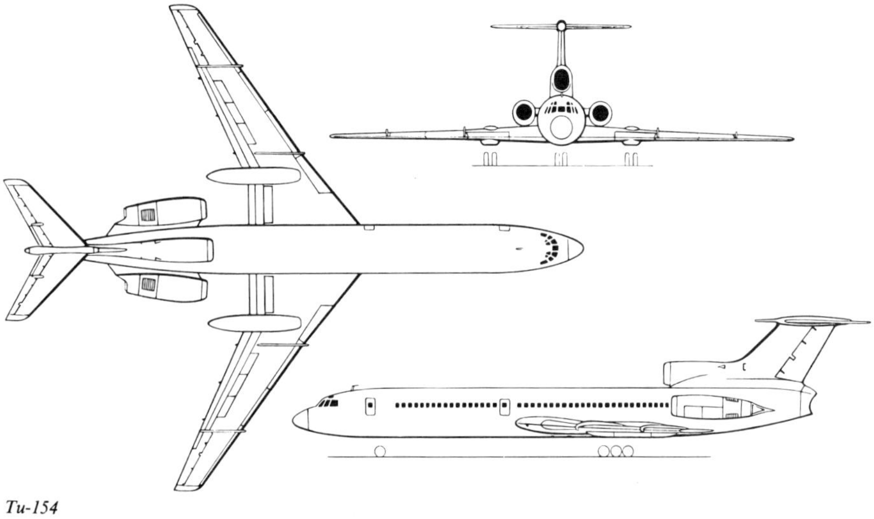

Tu-154

Tu-154B

Tu-22M Backfire-B with external multiple-store carriers

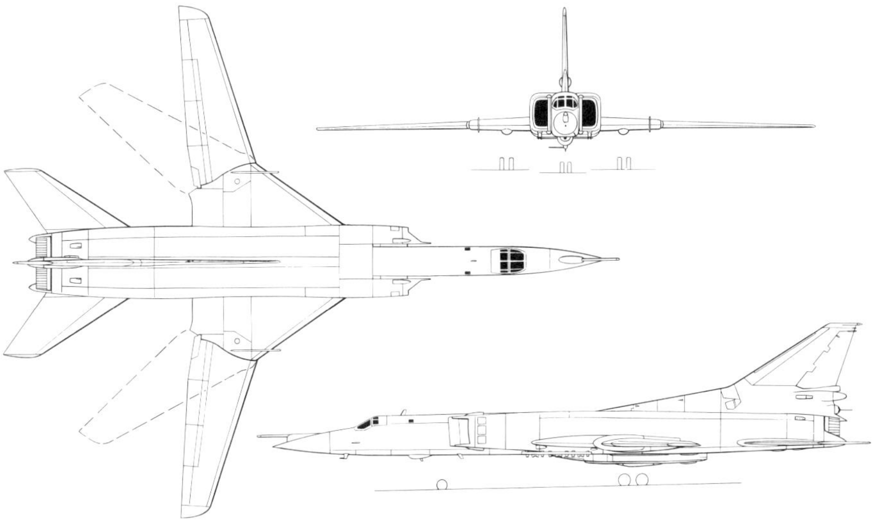

Tu-22M Backfire-B with AS-4 Kitchen

above bomb bay and has no movable surfaces apart from large-chord plain flaps, root t/c about 5%, whole box forms integral tankage back to main-leg bay. Outer panel exact TsAGI form as in Su-24 and other designs and close similarity to US B-1: trailing edge double-slotted flaps in four sections (outer section often said to be aileron) with duplex drives modulated according to sweep and normally used only for take-off and landing, LE full-span powered slat, roll control by long-span (believed three-section) spoilers also serving (not all sections) as air-brakes and lift dumpers. Fence just inboard of pivot extending around LE and back to edge of centre section at 50% chord. Static dihedral 0°, photos show much flexure even at landing. Sweep 20°/55°, believed fully variable. No evidence of outerwing pylons. Fuselage not circular but narrow oval (new to OKB) with long supersonic nose radome and FR probe on centreline above, crew compartments for pilots side-by-side and two nav/systems operators behind with side windows, none ejecting downward. By mid-length fuselage totally merged into large box-like downstream structure with long inlet ducts curving above wing and inwards to afterburning fan engines close together at tail. Large sharp-lipped inlets almost vertical but sharply inclined back (oblique shock appropriate to about Mach 2) with boundary-layer ejector ducts above and below and three square auxiliary suck-in doors each outer wall. Speculation (Green) engines have reversers. Large fuel capacity aft of pressure bulkhead and between ducts, outboard on rear fuselage and in vertical tail, possibly also beneath duct and wing on each side. Main landing gear bogies each with three pairs wheels in tandem pivoting inwards to occupy long but narrow bay under centre-section spars, leg being covered by door attached to leg which may even be joined to large curved door over bogie bay (fuselage-hung door has problem clearing ASM wings). Nose gear retracts backwards. Vertical tail derived from Tu-22 but raised on large dorsal fin extended at rear into Fan Tail radar and twin-23 tail guns above pen-nib fairing between nozzles. Tail guns may be used to dispense chaff. Slab tailplanes, poss tailerons (speculation) mounted on powered spigots low on fuselage, appreciably larger area than Tu-22. Probable extensive honeycomb construction, especially in control surfaces. Rear fuselage underside recessed between engines, large door could be airbrake (has apparent actuator fairing) and parachute bay door. Apparently left/right retractable tail-bumpers. Extensive avionics including comprehensive integral ECM, front and rear ventral blisters, main radar called Down Beat, various recognized (Sirena 3, SRO-2IFF etc) antennae but nothing on tips of wings or tailplane. Internal weapon bay assumed but not known to author. AV-MF aircraft carry recessed AS-4 Kitchen ASM or two AS-6 Kingfish ASMs (major armament), borne under large pylons below inboard (fixed) portion of wing. Present series may have traded AS-4 option for extra internal fuel and avionics. Triple tandem rack under each inlet duct available for numerous other stores. Assumed nominal weapon load (*Jane's*) 9435 kg (20,800 lb) but with reduced fuel has lifting ability several times as great. These large tandem weapon racks, standing well away below airframe, pose high drag even when empty and for long mission of strategic nature would either not be used or would carry decoys, cruise missiles and other payloads and jettisoned before or after primary weapon-release.

Sensation caused by this aircraft in West as great as by Bounder and Bear more than 20 years previously. In SALT-2 negotiations Soviet position was consistently maintained that Backfire-B is tactical weapon, and thus not subject to provisions of treaty and numbers not included in count of Soviet strategic platforms. Childish episode ensued in which Soviet negotiators even stated aircraft had no FR capability and removed probes; after signature of treaty, probes replaced. Main US concern was ability to attack continental US, and with limited weapon load, such as cruise missile, Backfire-B could fly from bases in Soviet Union to target

Tu-22M Backfire-B, clean configuration

almost anywhere in USA except extreme south and return (hi-hi-hi, with one FR engagement over Arctic). Following data, estimated from consensus of published Western assessments, clearly indicates potential of this aircraft. Though not intended as long-endurance platform in same class as Bear (Tu-142 especially) early Backfire was watched on Western radar for 10 h following FR engagement during development flying. Several small differences noted in production aircraft (eg, hemispherical or streamlined Fan Tail radome) and latest cruise missile(s) not yet seen in West though carried on many development flights by these aircraft. Production at Kazan said to have been increased 1978–1980 with significant expansion of factory, and monthly rate now 3·5 instead of 2·5. Total in service late 1981 put at 180 (75 with AV-MF) and expected to exceed 300 by end 1983. New version with revised ramp intakes (à la MiG-25) revealed 1983; dubbed Backfire-C by NATO. DA strategic squadrons in purely offensive role and others with AV-MF in multi-sensor EW, reconnaissance and, particularly, anti-ship missions throughout northern hemisphere.

DIMENSIONS Span (20°) 34,45 m (113 ft 0 in), (55°) 26,21 m (86 ft); length (incl probe) 42,0 m (137 ft 10 in); wing area (20°) 170 m² (1830 ft²).

ENGINES Two afterburning turbofans, almost certainly similar to NK-144 (poss afterburning rating slightly higher than civil 20 t, 44,090 lb).

WEIGHTS Empty about 54 t (119,000 lb); max fuel about 57 t (internal); max loaded about 122 t (269,000 lb).

PERFORMANCE Max speed (clean, 11 km and above) 2130 km/h (1322 mph, M 2), sustained dash speed 1915 km/h (1190 mph, M 1·8); cruise, M 0·8 hi down to M 0·65 at low alt; combat radius with typical weapon load (DoD estimate, hi-lo-hi, with 320 km dash and another 320 km at SL) 5500 km (3420 miles); ferry range about 12 000 km (7500 miles); field length about 2500 m.

Tu Ram-P, Blackjack Rumours of new long-range bombers, later than Backfire, gave way on 25 November 1981 to first known satellite photos of such aircraft parked at Ramenskoye next to two Tu-144s. New bomber, called Ram-P by US DoD, is similar to Rockwell B-1 in configuration, but larger. Size suggests completely fresh design, not based on Tu-22M (or Tu-144), though certain aspects (including propulsion) probably owe much to Tu-144D.

Unlike Tu-22M new bomber has fully-pivoted wing, with no fixed centre-section other than minimal glove of large root chord, swept up to 75°, leaving pivots close to fuselage. Outer wings have high aspect-ratio (greater than Tu-22M) and aerodynamically this aircraft looks unequalled for combination of high-Mach dash and long range at Mach 0·9. Feature of greatest interest, not resolvable from electronically transmitted satellite vidicon printout, is number and location of engines. At first glance there appear to be four at wing roots. Number of engines may be three, centreline having ventral inlet. Alternative configuration is that all engines have grouped ventral inlets aft under belly. Crew in pressurized compartment behind avionic-filled nose. Single large fin, with dorsal spine, carrying swept tailplane half-way up.

Picture published in *Aviation Week* for 14 December 1981, with comment 'aircraft with similar tail section was seen at Ramenskoye in 1979'. Data are guesstimates, dash speed and range being DoD figures

DIMENSIONS Span (min sweep) 53 m (174 ft), (max sweep) 29 m (95 ft); length overall 57·5 m (188 ft 8 in); wing area 232 m² (2500 ft²).

ENGINES Three of four augmented turbofans, probably related to Koliesov variable-cycle engines of Tu-144D.

WEIGHTS Empty 65 t (143,000 lb); max loaded 180 t (397,000 lb).

PERFORMANCE Maximum speed (hi-alt dash) 2450 km/h (1520 mph, Mach 2·3), (SL) subsonic; range on internal fuel (no air-refuelling top-up) with max weapons, 13 500 km (8390 miles).

Tyrov

This is best English spelling of name, but Russian rendering Tairov (which English person would pronounce differently) leads to aircraft designations Ta. Vsyevolod Konstantinovich Tyrov was lecturer at MAI circa 1930–1934, and in 1934–1935 first deputy in Polikarpov OKB. Late 1935 helped form OKO at Kiev and became chief constructor. OKO managed several major projects until Tyrov was killed flying Moscow/Kuibyshyev December 1941.

OKO-1 Straightforward passenger transport funded in part by Ukrainian regional government. Clean low-wing monoplane with trousered landing gear. All-wood construction except for dural control surfaces with fabric covering and dural skin on underside of split flaps. Two-spar wing made in one piece, with two metal fuel tanks inboard, ply skin. Monocoque fuselage basically circular section, enclosed cockpit for two pilots side-by-side, main cabin with three seats each side or 550 kg cargo. Engine in long-chord metal cowl with louvred front baffle plate (poss based on I-16) and driving Hamilton-type two-blade VISh-6 propeller. Split flaps elec drive, pneu wheel brakes, trimmers on all tail control surfaces, lighting and instruments for blind or night flying, cabin heated and sound-proofed (lagged with Viamiz material), full GVF service eqpt. First flight October 1937 and testing completed June 1938. Performance regarded as outstanding; no reason known for failure to win order.

DIMENSIONS Span 15,4 m (50 ft 6¼ in); length 11,6 m (38 ft 0¾ in); wing area 35,1 m² (378 ft²).

ENGINE One 730 hp M-25A.

WEIGHTS Empty 2370 kg (5225 lb); fuel/oil 364 + 42 kg; loaded 3,5 t (7716 lb).

PERFORMANCE Max speed 305 km/h at SL, 347 (216 mph) at 2,6 km; time to 1 km, 3 min; service ceiling 6740 m (22,100 ft); range 1700 km (1060 miles) with full payload, 2300 km max fuel; take-off 420 m/20 s; landing 430 m/22 s/95 km/h.

OKO-4 Small single-seat sesquiplane fighter/attack (Shavrov: *Shturmovik*, implying armoured) aircraft powered by M-88. Armament two BS plus 100 kg bomb. Prototype built from mid-1938 but when completed following year clearly unsuccessful and removed from factory programme without being flown.

Ta-1, OKO-6 This twin-engined escort fighter was built to meet VVS requirement of early 1938 in parallel with several other similar aircraft. Though large project for OKO, **No 6** was carried through rapidly and successfully, and aircraft had potential for combining exceptional speed and firepower, though of course with basic lack of agility of relatively large fighter. Single-seat mid-wing, mixed construction. Wing with two spars each 30KhGSA T-section booms and D1 plate webs, rubber-pressed D1 sheet ribs, flush-riveted D1 skin except LE skinned with thick Elektron, TsAGI flaps. Slim fuselage semi-monocoque, mainly D1 but with all-wooden tail section. Conventional single-finned tail with stressed-skin fin/tailplane and fabric-covered control surfaces with trimmers. Engines in close Elektron cowls, direct drive to VISh-23 propellers yet (puzzling) engines handed to eliminate torque, left engine having RH rotation (must be inserted gearwheels with 1:1 ratio in right engine). Fully retracting landing gear all units folding to rear into compartments with twin doors, main gears twin oleo struts and retractable actuator working on hinge at mid-point of rear bracing strut. Heavy armament of four ShVAK-20 in underside of forward fuselage, two BS in top of nose ahead of cockpit. Compact cockpit with sliding canopy, bullet-proof front windscreen and armour ahead and behind. First flight 31 December 1939 by Yu.K. Stankevich. Tested by LII until summer 1940 when con-rod broke. Directional stability unsatisfactory and second prototype, **OKO-6bis**, built with tailplane of increased span with added tip fins. Later original vertical tail removed and replaced by larger twin fins and rudders. More powerful engines with reduction gears, both LH rotation. Outer wings modified with tips moved forward to balance heavier engines. Winter 1940–1941 original aircraft designated Ta-1 and second **Ta-3.** Second aircraft flown end October 1940, excellent performance but according to Shavrov destroyed February 1941 when A.I. Yemelyanov lost control following another con-rod breakage. Another Soviet account gives armament of OKO-6bis as reduced to four ShVAK and two ShKAS and makes no comment on loss of this aircraft; moreover, it states Ta-3 was yet a further development with M-89 engines, increased-area outer wings and improved armament, flown May 1941 by Stankevich. Armament given as one 37 mm gun (type unstated) and two ShVAK. This is clearly aircraft described by Shavrov and Monino as third prototype, **Ta-3a,** first flown end May 1941 until interrupted by war evacuation September 1941. Alternative history introduces a **Ta-3bis** of 1942 with increased dimensions (Němĕcek thinks this is same as 3a), weight 6626 kg and range 2065 km. This aircraft said to have flown, and given great satisfaction, but called for more powerful engine such as M-82. Strange, because according to Shavrov all work ceased upon Tyrov's death.

DIMENSIONS Span 12,66 m (41 ft 6⅓ in); length 9,83 m (32 ft 3 in); wing area not recorded. Height 3,76 m (12 ft 4 in).

ENGINES (OKO-6) two 1000 hp M-88, (6bis) (Shavrov) 1100 hp M-88A, (Němĕcek, Ponomaryev) 1100 hp M-88R, (Ta-3, Ponomaryev) 1150 hp M-89.

WEIGHTS Empty, not recorded; loaded (6) 6 t (13,228 lb).

PERFORMANCE Max speed (6) 488 km/h at SL, 567 (352 mph) at 7,5 km, (6bis) 477 at SL, 595 (370 mph) at 7,2 km, (Ta-3) 460 at SL, 580 (360 mph) at 7,1 km; time to 5 km (6) 5·5 min, (bis) 6·3 min; service ceiling (3) 11,1 km (36,400 ft); range (3) 1060 km (660 miles).

OKO-7 Tyrov's last known design, heavy high-speed fighter to 1940 VVS requirement, two M-90 or AM-37, three ShVAK and two ShKAS.

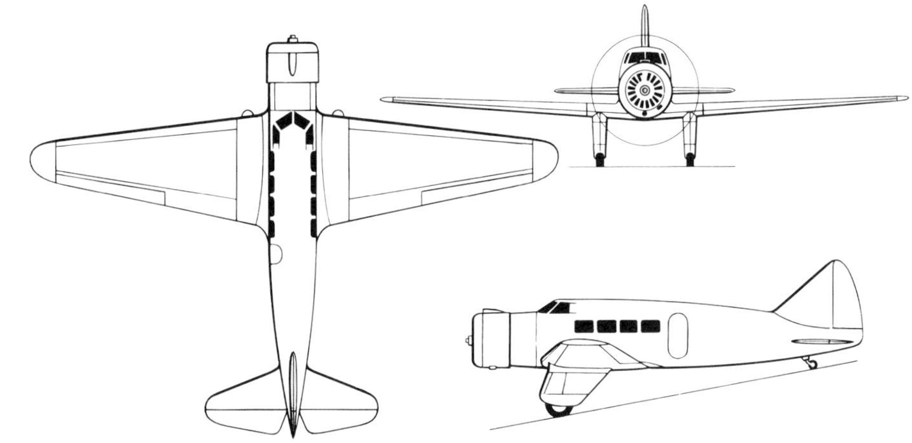

OKO-1

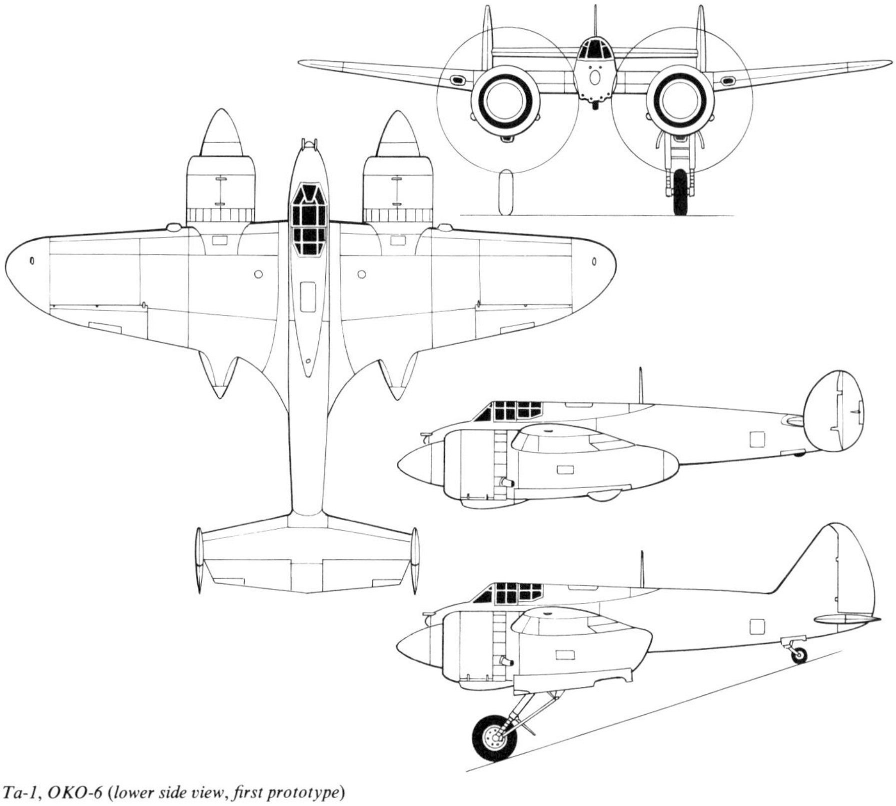

Ta-1, OKO-6 (lower side view, first prototype)

Vakhmistrov

Vladimir Sergeyevich Vakhmistrov was a senior LII research engineer. One of his projects of 1930 was development of glider for use as air/air gunnery target, and he eventually perfected method of carrying it on upper wing of R-1 and releasing in flight. This suggested one of first 'parasite' schemes: fighters carried by bombers far over hostile territory and if necessary released for their protection, thereafter hooking back on. Vakhmistrov did preliminary calculations and then obtained VVS approval for flight test. First combination, called *Zvyeno* (link) 1 or **Z-1**, chosen to be TB-1 carrying I-4 above each wing. TsAGI study and tunnel tests followed. Aircraft modified (see I-4, ANT-5) for purpose. Each fighter positioned behind wing of bomber and hauled up wooden ramp by ropes from towing crew from front. Secured by hold-down link on maingear axle and rear fixture on tripod attached to bomber wing holding fighter beneath cockpit. First flight Monino 3 December 1931, fighters flown by V. Chkalov and A.F. Anisimov, bomber by A.I. Zalevskii and A.R. Sharapov with Vakhmistrov as observer. (Group photo said to show team includes Vladimir Morozov, described by Němĕcek as inventor's assistant, in flying clothing, but not Sharapov.) Take-off with fighter engines full power. Co-pilot, presumably Sharapov, detailed to release fighters; improperly briefed and released Chkalov's axle without waiting for fighter pilot's signal he had released rear attachment: I-4 reared up but Chkalov was quick enough to release rear hold-down before disaster. Release of other I-4 some seconds later according to plan. Original plan had been to let both go together, and this incident showed TB-1 rock-steady with fighter on one wing only. Many further Z-1 tests, including (Něměcek only) simulated I-4 bombing attack on Kiev after release.

Next combination, **Z-Ia,** comprised TB-1 with two I-5. This was first flown September 1933 by pilots I.F. Grozd and V.K. Kokkinaki, with TB-1 flown by P.M. Stefanovskii. Testing then progressed to much larger TB-3, starting with Zvyeno **Z-2** comprising TB-3 carrying I-5 on each wing and a third above fuselage. Flown August 1934 by Zalevskii (TB-3), Suzi, S.P. Suprun and T.T. Alt'nov. **Z-3** would have hung I-Z fighter under each wing of TB-3. Story circulates in West that when this was tested (no date given) Grozd and Korotkov flew fighters and latter made various mistakes, slammed against wing and fell away only on TB-3 touch-down, Korotkov being killed. Russians deny this but admit Z-3 never successful. **Z-4** unknown. **Z-5** first attempt at hooking back on; combination chosen to be single I-Z with large suspension structure of steel tubes with curved top guide terminating at rear in sprung hook releasable by wire to cockpit (exact copy of F9C Sparrowhawk). TB-3 had large steel-tube trapeze under fuselage, folded up for take-off and landing. Prolonged tests with TB-3 flown by Stefanovskii and I-Z by V.A. Stepanchenok, latter practising

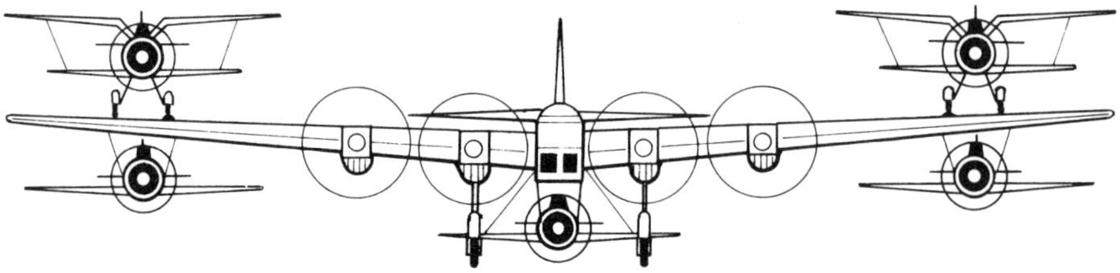

Zvyeno Aviamatka *with two I-15, two I-16 and I-Z.* Aviamatka *scheme (after Shavrov)*

by breaking strings holding rows of coloured flags one by one. Final hook-on successfully accomplished 23 March 1935, first under-fuselage hook-on in world. Final combination of original series **Z-6** was TB-3 with I-16 under each wing, suspended between two large V-strut links of aluminium streamline tubing picking up sliding horiz spigots above main spar. First flight August 1935 (exact date not known), TB-3/AM-34 flown by Stefanovskii, fighters by K.K. Budakov and Nikashin (Western account: Suprun and Eyseyev).

Culmination of concept was grotesque *Aviamatka* (mother aircraft) in which in November 1935 TB-3/AM-34 took off carrying two I-5 above wings, two I-16 below wings and with under-fuselage trapeze. While flying over Monino trapeze was lowered and Stepanchenok hooked on in I-Z, making combination of six aircraft of four types. After several passes all fighters released simultaneously. By this time Vakhmistrov had scheme for specially designed ultra-fast fighters (see I-Ze entry) carried in large number (6 or 8) under/over large tailless bomber (full-scale derivative of Kalinin VS-2). When purges began this withered through elimination of its supporters, but Vakhmistrov did manage to fly one final combination. SPB, described under I-16, replaced I-16 underwing fighters by slightly modified I-16s carrying two FAB-250 bombs each. First flown July 1937, TB-3/AM-34RN flown by Stefanovskii, dive bombers by A.S. Nikolayev and I.A. Taborovskii; photo shows flattened tyres of bomber, and small speed margin made control difficult.

Unexpectedly, Vakhmistrov managed to fly one more combination; **Z-7** with I-16 under each wing and third latched on fuselage trapeze in air was tested November 1939, pilots Stefanovskii, Suprun and Nyukhtikov, though severe difficulty. Final outcome of all *Zvyeno* experiments was decision early 1940 to form combat unit with SPB. Equipped with six modified TB-3/AM-34RN and 12 SPB, based Yevpatoriya. Made one famous combat mission 25 August 1941 against Danube bridge at Chyernovod, Romania (main rail link to Constanta). This bridge was destroyed. Other missions, from Crimean bases, but no details. Strange reference in Shavrov states this system 'tested 25 May 1943'.

I-Z, I-Ze Project for simple fighter drawn by Vakhmistrov 1934–1935: low-wing monoplane with 850 hp GRKrs engine, 1910 kg but only 7,75 m span and 10 m² wing, speed 518 km/h. No landing gear except centreline skid. Prototype started but discontinued 1936 at start of purges.

Z-7 (SPB carried by TB-3/AM-34RN) before combat mission

Yakovlev

A.S. Yakovlev

AIR-1 at academy

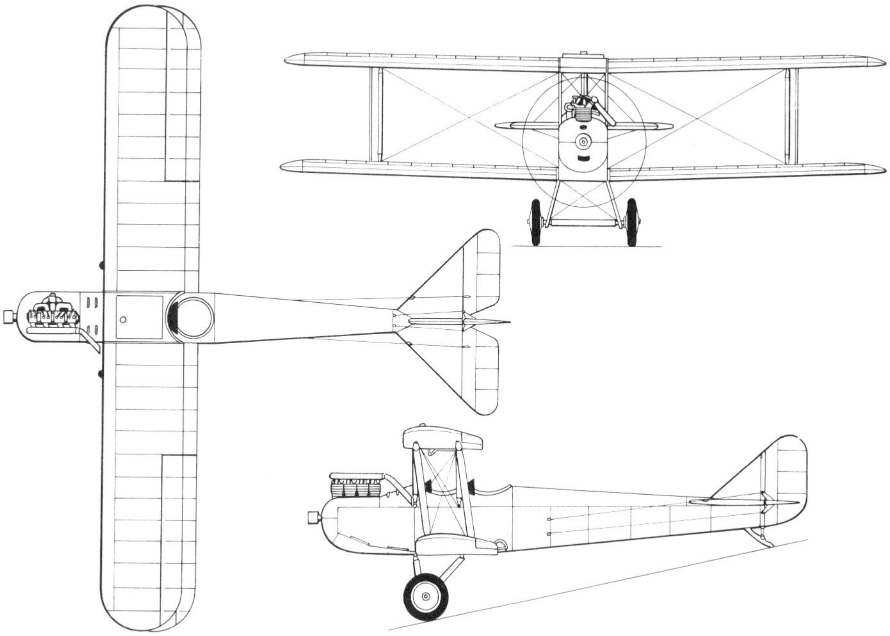

AIR-1

Aleksandr Sergeyevich Yakovlev rose from humble start to become top Russian fighter designer during the Second World War and deputy aviation minister. His OKB has produced exceptional diversity of aircraft, though he personally liked small sporting types. Most exceptionally for his generation he was never imprisoned. For many years he has been chief father-figure invited to sit in at all top decision-making, especially concerning aircraft design.

Born 19 March 1906 to prosperous family (father worked for Nobel Oil in Moscow). Teenage aviation enthusiast, managed via K.K. Artseulov to be appointed helper to V. Anoshchyenko building glider for Koktebel meeting 1923. Following year, with technical help from Ilyushin, built his own glider, successful, but lacked army service necessary to enter VVS. With Ilyushin's help got job March 24 as menial labourer at VVA workshops, and gradually learned workshop processes, aircraft design and entire technology from strictly practical shop-floor basis. In 1926 with help from V.V. Pyshnov designed powered aeroplane, VVA-3; excellent design and not only set world class record but gained entry for Yakovlev to VVA 1927. Other designs followed, designated AIR for A.I. Rykov, then Lenin's successor as Chairman of Council of People's Commissars. Graduated 1931 and joined Polikarpov KB not as designer but as engineering supervisor, giving freedom to create own sporting prototypes with distinctive red/white colour scheme. This frowned on, and when AIR-7 lost aileron in flight Yakovlev expelled from plant. After much lobbying awarded derelict bed factory on Moscow Leningradskii Prospekt, gathered own team and July 1934 set up OKB which is still on same site with Yak museum. Rykov victim of purge 1937, Yakovlev changed to Ya designations. Amongst many lightplanes, powerful Ya-22 put him on military and political map, showered with honours. On 1 January 1940 first Yak-1 (then called I-26) rolled out, first of 37,000 derived Yak fighters outnumbering all other fighters of the Second World War. On 9 January 1940 appointed Deputy Commissar of Aviation Industry and head of Dept of Experimental Aircraft Construction and Research, throughout war spending morning at OKB and rest of day to about 2 am at NKAP. Organized industry evacuation from Moscow area September/October 1941. Helicopter dept 1944 (Western accounts) or 1946 (Soviet histories), terminated 1960. Post-war great variety of fighters, trainers, assault gliders, night interceptors and derived tactical aircraft, aerobatic mounts, large jetliners and jet VTOLs. Still titular head OKB, deputy is son Sergei Aleksandrovich.

AIR-1, VVA-3 Success with gliders naturally led to wish to design aeroplane, conceived as 18 hp *Aviette* (ultralight). Discussed with senior VVA students, especially Pyshnov and Ilyushin. Former stressed two-seat dual trainer with more powerful engine would be more useful, and offered essential technical help. A year from late summer 1925 on design and drawings, approved Osoaviakhim 26 August 1926 and funds allotted (some added by Pioneers youth movement) and aircraft built in VVA lab by designer and his friends 5 to 11 pm daily. Generally positive attitude by VVA, but some jealousy (Yak a mere manual worker) and one final-year student sent report of faulty detail design, causing ban on work and prolonged interrogations of designer until Pyshnov bravely submitted personal guarantee of VVA-3 airworthiness. Completed on wire wheels 1 May 1927; after fitting skis flown by Yak's squadron commander, Yuri I. Piontkovskii, 12 May 1927.

Single-bay tandem dual biplane, constant-section (Göttingen 387) wings with two wood box spars and 13 ribs in each of four identical wings, ply LE, fabric elsewhere, upper/lower ailerons again ply LE and fabric with aluminium-tube tie-rod links, upper centre-section same width as fuselage with galvanized iron tank 65-lit of deeper aerofoil section inserted. Wooden frame fuselage with wire-braced trusses, fabric except for aluminium front cowl (engine cylinders exposed) and ply skin to rear of front cockpit and ply decking back to tail. Wooden tail, ply-skinned except fabric aft of spar on movable surfs. Control wires emerged from fuselage behind rear cockpit, rudder wires needing slots cut in tailplane LE. Bungee-sprung landing gear and tailskid. Many aluminium details (eg, top of fuselage above tailplane LE), padded leather edges to cockpit cut-outs, aluminium celluloid windscreens. Ply skin varnished, rest doped white with red trim (eg, fin, prop and most of each aileron). Wire wheels later given thin aluminium discs. Simple and positive to fly. With Osoaviakhim permission, long-range flight began 12 June 1927, Moscow-Kharkov/Sevastopol. Long-range tank then put in passenger seat (in place of designer, who returned by train) and faired over. Piontkovskii returned non-stop 1240 km in 15 h 30 min, world class record. By this time called AIR-1, and civil registration R-RAIR, all to please commissar Rykov. Autumn 1927 took part in Odessa Mil District manoeuvres. Preserved at OKB.

DIMENSIONS Span 8,85 m (29 ft 0¼ in); length 6,99 m (22 ft 11⅛ in); wing area 18,7 m^2 (201 ft^2).

ENGINE One 60 hp ADC Cirrus.

WEIGHTS Empty 335 kg (739 lb); fuel/oil (normal) 50 kg; loaded 535 kg (1179 lb).

PERFORMANCE Max speed 140 km/h (87 mph) (recent account by Zasypkin, 150 km/h); cruise 120 km/h; time to 1 km, 8 min (3 km, 35); service ceiling 3850 m (12,630 ft); range (normal) 500 km (311 miles); take-off 80 m/8 s; landing 60 m/6 s/60 km/h.

AIR-2 In 1928 Yakovlev tinkered with AIR-1 design and assisted by awards for long-range record built second aircraft called *Pioner* (pioneer). Eventually six built in four versions, but historical record confused. Shavrov, first flew 1928 with M-23 and enclosed cockpit, later (1929) with Walter and Siemens (land and seaplane). Recent account by Yu. Zasypkin more plausible, and used as basis here. First AIR-2 flew with Cirrus but in better aluminium-sheet cowl. Larger fuel tank, cabane braced by diagonal forward struts, slightly modified wings with full-span ailerons on lower planes only, rounded LE on tailplane, rudder cables internal emerging close beside fin. Flown late 1928. No mention by Zasypkin or Kondratyev of Walter engine, though Shavrov provides full spec (given in data). By late 1929 second aircraft, **AIR-2s** (or **AIR-2S**), built with Siemens engine and several other changes, and with twin floats designed by V.B. Shavrov on struts of wire-braced mild-steel tube with al fairings. Red trim, with red/silver striped vertical tail which became Yak trademark. AIR-2s taken to Gorkii Park and flown 18 May 1931 from Moscow River by B.L. Bukholts and Shavrov. Later flown by Piontkovskii, Yakovlev and others with complete success; Bukholts flew it under Old Crimea Bridge on Moscow River. Two similar aircraft built with interchangeable float/wheel gear, latter having bracing strut not behind but in front, pinned to bottom of engine-mount structure and with foot-step to assist work on top cylinder of engine. Final one (maybe two) aircraft had enclosed cockpits with side-folding individual Celluloid hoods, slats on upper wing (set at increased incidence) and powerful slotted ailerons on lower wing. Three-cylinder Soviet engine with aluminium-sheet front cowl, simple electric light system for night flying. First flown July 1931; instant response to controls during spin recovery but hoods resonated with engine vibration.

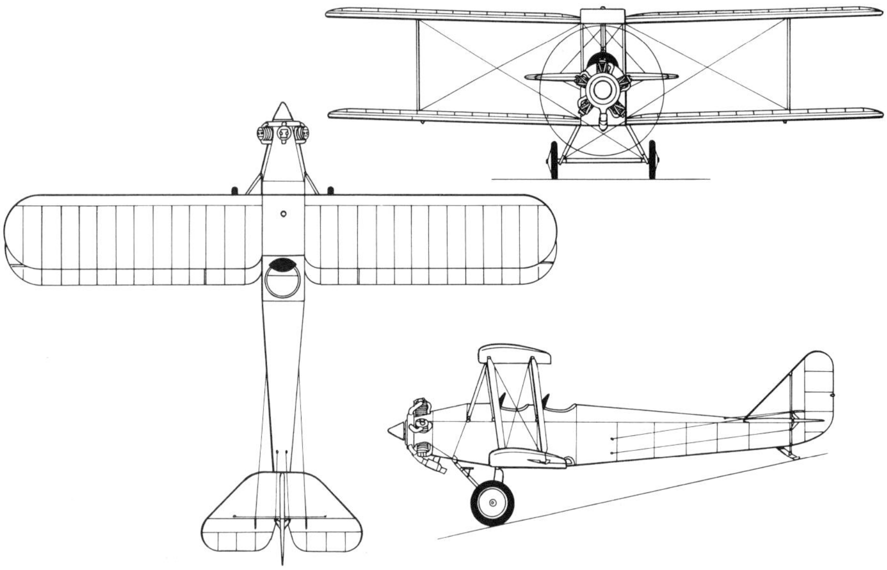

AIR-2

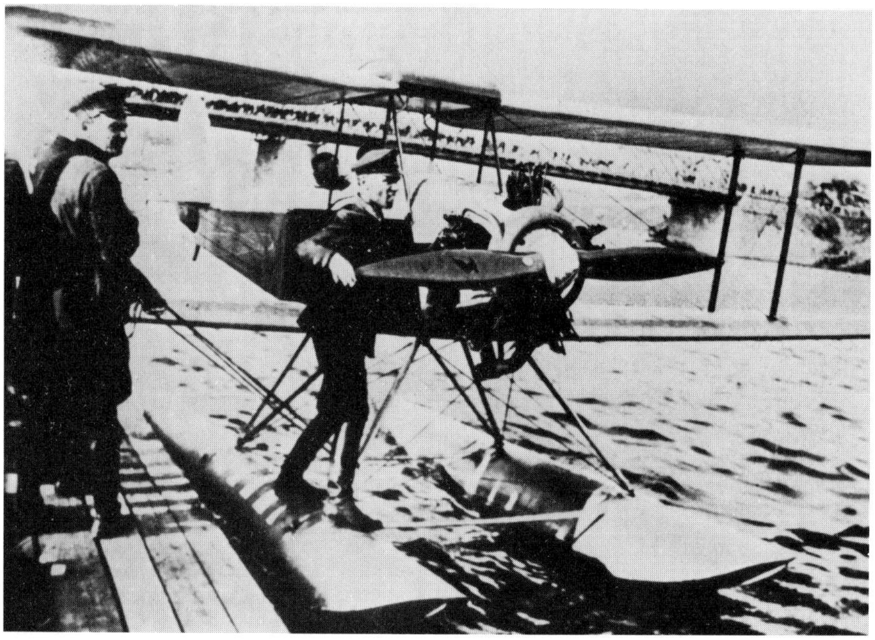

AIR-2S (Yakovlev standing on float)

DIMENSIONS Span 8,9 m (29 ft 2½ in); length 7,0 m (22 ft 11½ in), (2s seaplane) 7,7 m (25 ft 3 in); wing area 18,7 m^2 (201 ft^2).

ENGINE One 60 hp Cirrus, 85 hp Siemens Sh 11 or 65 hp M-23; also said to have flown 1929 with 60 hp Walter NZ-60.

WEIGHTS Empty (Siemens 2s) about 470 kg, (land) 420 kg (926 lb), (M-23) 403 kg (888 lb); fuel/oil 72+11 kg; loaded (2s) about 710 kg (1565 lb), (land) 660 kg (1455 lb), (M-23) 646 kg (1424 lb).

PERFORMANCE Max speed (2s) 140 km/h (87 mph), (land) 150 km/h (93 mph), (M-23) 141 km/h; time to 1 km (M-23) 8·7 min (46 min to 3 km); service ceiling (M-23) 3534 m (11,594 ft); range (M-23) 540 km (336 miles); take-off (M-23) 80 m/7 s; landing 140 m/9 s/60 km/h.

AIR-3 Designer's glider experience used in this parasol monoplane, again using almost same fuselage and tail as AIR-2. Wing again Göttingen 387 section, rectangular centre section of constant profile and tapered outer panels, dihedral 0° on upper surface. Two box spars with spruce booms basically 60 × 40 mm, twin webs 2 mm ply (3 mm at outer-panel joint), rib trusses glued and pinned from 6 × 6 with 1 mm ply. Neat ply skin from front spar on underside to rear spar above, giving better aerodynamic efficiency. Three metal fuel tanks, total 176-lit, recessed flush with aerofoil in centre section between spars. Centre section on same cabane struts as AIR-2; main wing struts parallel each side from bottom of fuselage to spars ½-way between last two ribs of c-s, wrapped mild-steel sheet with streamline section 64 × 32 mm. Fuselage as before, longerons 27 × 27 mm mid-section, 20 × 20 mm at tail. Engine on welded steel-tube mount, designed for Czech Walter but provision for M-23 and fitted later. Al-sheet nose, oil tank in front of front instrument panel. Landing gear as AIR-1 but stronger with steel tubes (most 27 mm OD by 1,5 mm) faired by wood, axle 44 OD × 1,5 mm.

Built at GAZ-39 from April 29, completed end June and tested for VVA by A.I. Filin, later with Piontkovskii, D.A. Koshits and A.B. Yumashyev. Later based at October Field, painted red fuselage with SSSR-310 white on left and *Pionerskaya Pravda* (young communist paper) on right. From 26 August 1929 used for intensive trials between Moscow and Mineralnye Vody, 1750/1830 km, non-stop, usually flown by Filin and (Yakovlev's books) Kovalkov, (recent histories) A.F. Korolkov, best time 10 h 23 min on 6 September, flew 12 000 km in three months. In 1938 made 'invisible', see Kozlov E1.

DIMENSIONS Span (Shavrov) 11,0 m (36 ft 1 in), (Simakov) 11,2, (scaled from OKB drawing) 11,10; length 7,1 m (23 ft 3½ in); wing area 16,5 m² (178 ft²).

ENGINE Originally one Walter NZ-60 rated 60 hp (Zasypkin 80 hp is puzzling, as is Němĕcek 85 hp Siemens); by February 1931 had 65 hp M-23.

WEIGHTS Empty 392 kg (864 lb); fuel/oil 176 + 20 kg; loaded 762 kg (1680 lb).

PERFORMANCE Max speed 146 km/h (91 mph) though with favourable wind averaged 166,8 on best trip, see above; time to 1 km, 6 min (34 min to 3,2); service ceiling 4,2 km (13,780 ft); range 1835 km (1140 miles); take-off 60 m; landing 66 km/h (41 mph).

AIR-4 Essentially AIR-3 with new main landing gear, divided (pyramid) type with rubber-sprung shock strut from wheels to pin-joint linking front main wing strut to V-struts attached to fuselage. Cabane struts sloped to pick up wing further outboard, fuel capacity 110 lit, more comfortable cockpits with complete dual insts, other detail changes. Two built at GAZ-39, SSSR-311 and 312 (both striped tail, red fuselage with black-lined silver side panel), tested September 1930. Following month respectively crewed by S.K. Ogorodnikov/Ya.Ya. Piontkovskii and Yu.I. Piontkovskii/B.N. Podlesnyi on long met flights on two different circuit patterns between Moscow and Sevastopol.

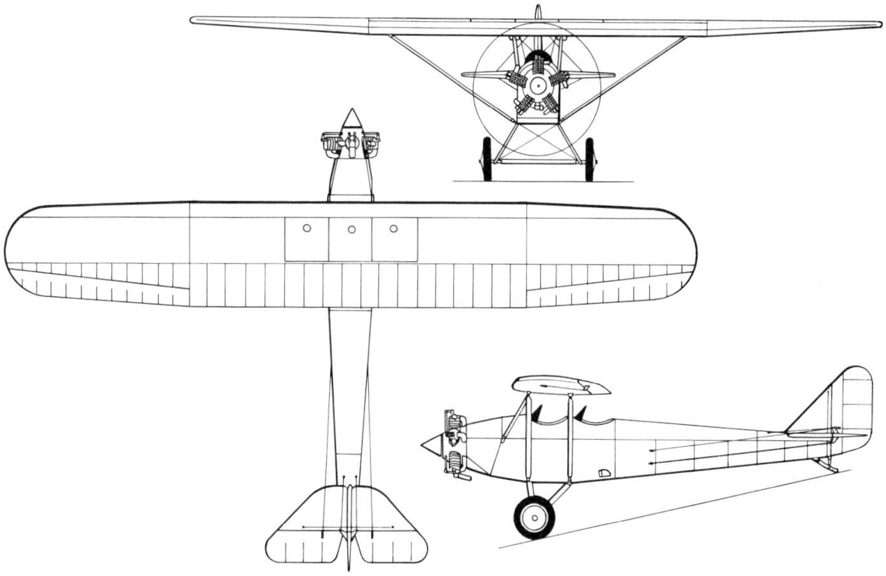

AIR-3

Late 1930 re-engined with M-23. Early 1933 selected by NII GVF and TsAGI as vehicle for major attack on achieving maximum lift coefficient. First AIR-4, still with Walter engine, fitted with new wing by B.N. Zalivatskii and L.M. Shekhter. Work apparently done at NII; aircraft redesigned **E-31** and given this registration. Wing similar structure and profile but made in one piece to square tips beyond which were then-novel ailerons forming complete rounded tips, pivoted about steel-tube aileron spar 25% chord held in last three ribs of wing, movement ±15° (Zasypkin), +30°/−60° (works drawing), long tube ahead of aileron root with streamlined lead weight on tip. Entire trailing edge of fixed wing occupied by four sections large Schrenk flap driven by worm gear from cockpit. Span/area of wing increased by ailerons, but flaps produced mainly high drag at full deflection 60°. Alternative designation of E-31 was *Mekhanizirovannyi Krylo*, mechanized wing. Flown about July 1933, outstanding results; C_L-max not recorded but lowest min-flight and landing speeds then known for conventional aeroplane with modest penalties in other performance.

AIR-3 (pilots Filin and possibly Koshits)

DIMENSIONS Span (4) 11,1 m (36 ft 5 in), (E) 12,55 m (41 ft 2⅛ in); wing area (4) 16,5 m² (178 ft²); (E) 18,05 m² (194 ft²).

ENGINE One 60 hp Walter NZ-60, (second, 1930) 65 hp M-23.

WEIGHTS Empty (4) 395 kg (871 lb), (E) 440 kg (970 lb); fuel/oil 65 kg; loaded (4) 630 kg (1389 lb), (E) 670 kg (1477 lb).

PERFORMANCE Max speed (4) 150 km/h (93 mph), (E) 145 km/h (90 mph); time to 1 km (4) 6 min (30 min to 3); service ceiling (4) 4 km, (E) still climbing at 5,2; range (4) 500 km (310 miles), (E) 450 km; take-off (4) no data, (E) about 50 m/5 s; landing (4) 100 m/10 s/66 km/h, (E) 40 m/4 s/34 km/h (21 mph) (Zasypkin and Kondratyev both claim E-31 flown at 35 km/h and could land at 30 TAS).

AIR-5 Logical next stage beyond original AIR-4, this light transport incorporated designer's lately acquired knowledge of welded-steel tube structures. Enclosed cabin fuselage made of welded MS (mild-steel) tube using designer's own accurate jigging. D1 dural skin over engine crankcase and back to cabin, fabric to rear. Two-spar wooden wing with ply skin to front spar, fabric elsewhere. Ailerons Frise type with large slots, wood/fabric but ply skin around LE to spar. Tail D1 dural and fabric, tailplane with pilot-adjusted incidence and asymmetric duo-convex section. Pyramid-type divided landing gear with welded steel tubes and rubber-sprung shock strut. Main wing struts riveted MS streamline section with added vertical braces from struts to spars. Comfortably furnished cabin with 4 to 5 total seats, single pilot, door each side. Single AIR-5 built 1931, red fuselage, striped tail, registered No 38. Excellent aircraft but no available production engine (proposal to license Whirlwind as M-48 never implemented).

DIMENSIONS Span 12,8 m (42 ft 0 in); length 8,0 m (26 ft 3 in); wing area 23,0 m² (248 ft²).

ENGINE One 200 hp Wright Whirlwind J-4.
WEIGHTS Empty (Shavrov) 812 kg (1790 lb), Něměcek) 670; fuel/oil (Shavorv) 200 + 20; loaded (Shavrov) 1390 kg (3064 lb), (Něměcek) 912 kg.
PERFORMANCE Max speed 193 km/h (120 mph); cruise 159; time to 1 km 6·5 min (27 min to 3); service ceiling 4275 m (14,000 ft); range 1000 km (620 miles); take-off 100 m; landing 100 m/75 km/h.

AIR-6 Yakovlev next designed similar small transport to reduced scale matched to readily available 100 hp engine. Resulting AIR-6 identical in detail design to AIR-5, probably overstrength as same sections and detail fittings, but scaled down with two wing tanks of 75 lit each and fuselage tailored to two (max three) seats. Prototype two seats in tandem, door each side, painted as AIR-5. Ideal for GVF purposes and factory (one report, GAZ-56) completed 468 between 1934–1936 including 20 ambulance variant (possibly designated **AIR-6S**) with larger triangular door on left and provision for attaching standard GVF stretcher and with seat for medic. At least one aircraft with spats and Townend-ring cowl, first in world formally called Executive Aircraft; at least one used by GVF central direction committee. Flight of (believed three) AIR-6 flew Moscow/Irkutsk/Moscow in stages 1934. In 1933 one fitted twin floats designed by V.B. Shavrov (not quite same as AIR-2 floats, larger and difficult to make with frames of curved glued pine sections 4 × 12 mm). Eventually several float examples, not all identical but all called **AIR-6A.** Rather sluggish (floats weighed 120 kg, compared with 35 kg for land gear) but one set class record 583 km in 6 h 5 min and 23 May 1937 Ya. B. Piss'menyi flew one with extra tanks Kiev/Batum 1297 km non-stop 10 h 25 min.
DIMENSIONS Span (Shavrov) 12,0 m (works drawing) 11 905 mm, (Něměcek) 12,07 m for both 6 and 6A (39 ft 7¼ in); length (6) (Shavrov, Něměcek) 8,0 m, (works drawing) 7880 mm (25 ft 10¼ in), (Simakov, error) 7100 mm, (6A) (Shavrov) 8,5 m, (Něměcek) 8,55 (28 ft 6⅛ in); wing area 19,8 m² (213 ft²).
ENGINE One 100 hp M-11.
WEIGHTS Empty (prototype) 584 kg (1287 lb), (production) 610 (1345 lb), (6S) 620, (6A) (Shavrov) 668 (1473 lb), (Něměcek, doubtful) 610; fuel/oil (normal) 110 + 12 kg; loaded (prototype) 843 kg, (production) 900 kg (1984 lb), (6S) 1000 (2205), (6A) (Shavrov) 958 (2112 lb), (Něměcek) 900 kg.
PERFORMANCE Max speed (prototype) 166 km/h), (production) 162 (101 mph), (Něměcek) 169, (6S) 156, (6A) 150 (93 mph), (Něměcek) 162; time to 1 km (production) 6·6 min (29·3 to 3 km); service ceiling (production) 4 km, (6S, 6A) about 3 km; range (all land) 650 km (400 miles), (Něměcek, doubtful) 850, (6A, normal tanks) 600, (Něměcek, doubtful) 1000; take-off (prototype) 70 m/7 s, (production) 90 m/9 s, (6A) 10 s; landing 120 m/13 s, (6S) 165/15, (6A) 150/12, all with speed 68/70 km/h.

AIR-7 Main occupation of GAZ-39 design office was I-5 fighter, and Yakovlev became obsessed with belief he could design much faster aircraft using same engine. Winter 1931–1932 spent in project study which settled on tandem-seat sporting machine with braced low wing. Wing 8% Göttingen 436 profile, wood structure with two spars bolted to centre section integral with fuselage, ribs glued/pinned from pine sections and ply, ply skin over LE, fabric aft of front spar. Fuselage rectilinear truss of welded mild-steel tube built up with wood/D1 secondary structure to more rounded shape, dural panels to front of cockpit, fabric thence to tail. Main fuselage bay ahead of cockpit welded to centre-section spars, span 2,3 m between outer bolt-holes carrying wings and main landing gear, with two parallel struts (steel tube of streamline section) from tips of c-s spars to upper longerons of fuselage. Main gears mainly steel tube with rear V-struts providing pivot for horizontal fork locating wheel (710 × 135 mm tyre) fore/aft and vertical fork and single leg forming shock strut with 12 rubber and 13 steel interleaved washers. Surrounding trouser fairing aluminium, wire bracing streamline profile 18 × 4 mm. Tail and ailerons D1 and fabric, fin offset 1·5° to counter torque, slotted ailerons in inner/outer sections. Engine in Townend-ring cowl driving 2700 mm prop with two polished dural blades. Oil tank top of first fuselage bay, oil cooler between bottom cylinders, two fuel tanks in second fuselage bay, total 400 lit. Tandem cockpits, passenger in rear with three flight instruments, folding celluloid hoods, pitot tube under outer right wing, venturi for gyro turn/slip (Kollsman).

Basically simple aircraft, construction started April 1932 and though unpopular with designer's employers caused intense interest among Chkalov and other VVS test pilots. Completed November 1932 in usual red/silver livery, no registration. First flight 19 November 1932 by Yu.I. Piontkovskii with 80 kg ballast on rear seat. Exceeded designer's estimate of 320 km/h and fastest aircraft in country. In 1933 flown by many pilots with generally glowing opinions, 25 September 1933 flown by Piontkovskii to national speed record of 332 km/h, engine overspeed 80 rpm. Many suggestions for AIR-7 to be produced in series as fighter or as transport for newspaper matrices to other cities. Early 1934 special show for VVS officers and other VIPs, with L. Malinovskii, Osoaviakhim deputy chairman passenger. Bad weather, aileron came off at high speed at low level, Piontkovskii made

AIR-7

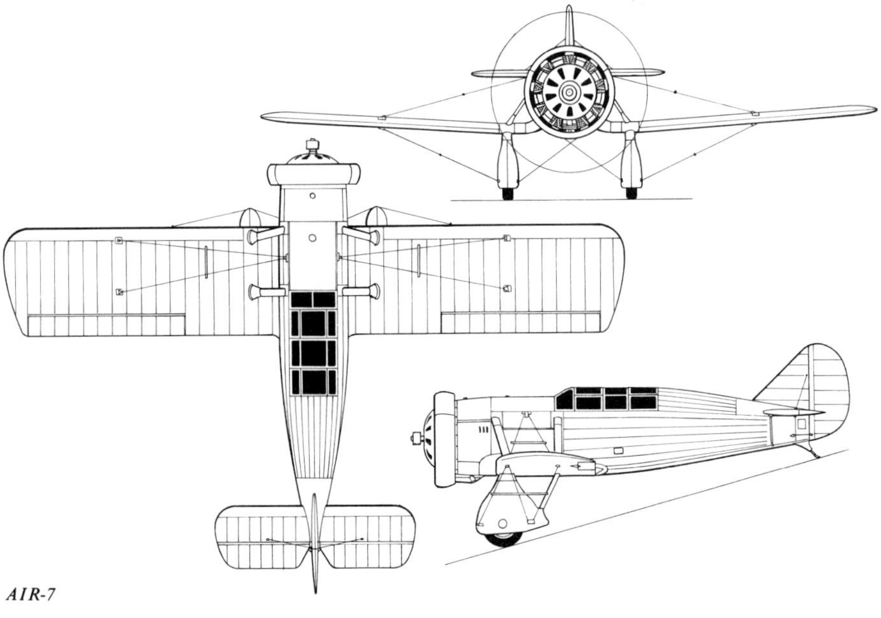

AIR-7

masterly forced landing in railway yard. Discovered design error; Shavrov states failure due to flutter. Commission (which heard no evidence from Yakovlev) concluded 'to forbid Yakovlev to carry on with design work and to notify government he is unworthy to receive award' (he had been recommended for decoration). History now rewritten, and 1981 account makes no mention of forced landing and states Yak and Piontkovskii received Order of Red Star! Yak and associates eventually evicted from GAZ-39 and forbidden to build any more aircraft.

After great difficulties Yak's party membership enabled him to win limited support from Ya. E. Rudzutak, chairman of party central control commission, who sampled 'executive' AIR-6 and eventually got NKAP to offer \ k old bed factory on Leningradskii Prospekt, near Moscow Central Aerodrome. This was converted to aircraft production autumn 1934 and home of OKB-115 ever since.

DIMENSIONS Span 11,0 m (36 ft 1 in); length 7,8 m (25 ft 7 in); wing area 19,4 m² (209 ft²).

ENGINE One 480 hp M-22.

WEIGHTS Empty (Shavrov) about 690 kg (1521 lb), (Něměcek, Zasypkin) 1000 (true figure must be about 900 kg); fuel/oil 300 kg; loaded 1400 kg (3086 lb).

PERFORMANCE Max speed 332 km/h (206 mph); time to 1 km 3·6 min (12 to 3); service ceiling (Něměcek) 5,8 km (19,000 ft); range 1300 km (808 miles); landing 150 m/110 km/h.

AIR-8 Single AIR-4 type aircraft built at GAZ-39 mid-1934 with small modifications requested by VVS. Wing increased area but same span, not explained. Main landing gears with low-pressure balloon tyres and modified shock-strut extending up to wing, presumably for rough-field or snow operation. First flown with M-23 but incurable vibration resulted in substitution of 60 hp Walter and finally 85 hp Siemens (data for this). Passed NII GVF testing 1934 but never put to use.

DIMENSIONS As AIR-4 but wing area 18,0 m² (194 ft²).

ENGINE One 85 hp Siemens Sh 11.

WEIGHTS Empty 430 kg (948 lb); fuel/oil 85 kg; loaded 675 kg (1488 lb).

PERFORMANCE Max speed 150 km/h (93 mph) landing 65 km/h. No other data.

AIR-9 One of least-known Soviet aircraft, this simple sports machine was first in series of Yak low-wing sporting and training aircraft made in vast quantities to present day. Designed 1933 as contender in Aviavnito contest for tandem cabin tourer/trainer powered by M-11. Structurally similar to AIR-7: welded mild-steel tube fuselage with light secondary fairing structure, wooden two-spar wing with ply skin over upper surface and on underside back to front spar, dural tail with fabric, fabric-skinned fuselage and fabric rest of wing except dural/ply flaps, latter innovation for Yak. Tandem cockpits with dual control and folding Celluloid hoods. Wire-braced spatted main wheels on single rubber shock struts. Engine in helmeted cowl, prop with spinner. Contest laid stress on safe flight, hence auto slats over 60% span. Yak began prototype at GAZ-39 but soon evicted. Construction continued in wooden hut, then no progress possible until OKB established July 1934. Two eventually completed April and October 1935, first, AIR-9, with inverse-slope windscreen and second (**9bis**, sometimes called **9A**) with normal windscreen and Townend-ring cowl. Second (9bis) used by Irina Vishnyevskii and Yekaterina Mednikova 3 May 1937 for women's class record climb to 6518 m.

DIMENSIONS Span 10,2 m (33 ft 5⅝ in); length 6,9 m (22 ft 7⅝ in); wing area 15,5 m² (167 ft²).

ENGINE One 100 hp M-11.

WEIGHTS Empty (9) 530 kg, (bis) 525 (1157 lb); fuel/oil 100 + 12 kg; loaded (9) 799 kg, (bis) 797 kg (1757 lb).

PERFORMANCE Max speed 215 km/h (134 mph); cruise 187; time to 1 km 4·5 min (18 to 3); service ceiling (Shavrov) 5,7 km (18,700 ft), (Něměcek) 6578 m for both (21,580 ft); time 360° circle 9 s; range 750 km (466 miles); take-off 90 m/9 s; landing, 65 km/h (40 mph).

AIR-10 Derived from AIR-9 but with open cockpits, built to VVS standards with mods to fit it to tough life as primary and intermediate pilot trainer. Airframe closely similar to AIR-9 except locally strengthened to give design factor increased from 8 to 10, with wire bracing removed except strut fin/tailplane. No Townend ring or spinner, tandem cockpits with mil eqpt and frameless Plexiglas windshields, no slats but flaps retained and trimmers added to meet VVS requirement. Single aircraft in OKB red/silver livery, took part in prolonged U-2 replacement contest 1935–1936 and won 500 km trial (Piontkovskii/Demeshkyevich). No production but development continued via Ya-20. Later (May 1937) tested on floats from AIR-6.

DIMENSIONS Span 10,2 m (33 ft 5⅝ in); length 6,8 m (22 ft 3¾ in), (on floats) 7,3 m (23 ft 11½ in); wing area 15,5 m² (167 ft²).

ENGINE One 100 hp M-11.

WEIGHTS Empty 516 kg (1138 lb), (floats) 570; fuel/oil 100 + 12 kg; loaded 788 kg (1737 lb).

PERFORMANCE Max speed 217 km/h (135 mph), (Něměcek, 200, error), (floats) 199 km/h (124 mph); time to 1 km 4·4 min (16 to 3); service ceiling 5,7 km (18,700 ft); range 750 km (466 miles), (floats) 700; time 360° circle 9 s; take-off 100 m/10 s; landing 120 m/15 s/70 km/h.

AIR-11 Using almost same airframe as immediate predecessors, this neat cabin aircraft still looks modern today. Designed first quarter 1936, intended as three-seat tourer or single-seat mailplane with 200-kg mail load. Wider than predecessors with room for two seats side-by-side at front, third at rear. Fitted with flaps but no slats. Tailplane braced below only. Full blind-flying panel, even shelf for radio (not installed), exceptional soundproofing, exhaust-muff heating. Completed late November 1936, successful GOS NII testing. Later won Sevastopol/Moscow contest, then after much pleading given to S.V. Ilyushin as his personal mount commuting from OKB to GAZ at Voronezh. About a year later Ilyushin scarred across face for life in night forced landing; mechanic had forgotten to replenish Gipsy's oil.

DIMENSIONS Span 10,2 m (33 ft 5⅝ in); length 7,1 m (23 ft 3½ in); wing area 15,5 m² (167 ft²).

ENGINE One 130 hp D.H. Gipsy Major I.

WEIGHTS Empty about 570 kg; loaded 860 kg (1896 lb).

PERFORMANCE Max speed 206 km/h (128 mph); cruise 187 (116); time to 1 km 5·2 min; service ceiling 4480 m (14,700 ft); range 720 km (447 miles); take-off 200 m; landing 140 m/92 km/h (57 mph).

AIR-12 Though yet another in same family, this 1936 one-off racer incorporated several unusual features, most notable being fully retractable main landing gear. Structure as before though aluminium trunnions in wing to take main gears with vertical rubber-disc shock struts and pinned rear braces, retracting inwards under cable from cockpit crank-handle. Wing of increased span with straight TE and all taper on LE (even then CG not quite far enough aft with heavy pilot). Aluminium skin over nose as usual, no attempt to fair cylinder heads. Pilot in open cockpit well aft of wing with narrow Plexiglas windshield extending over 1 m ahead of pilot's face and left cockpit wall hinging down for access. Large fuselage bay above wing either for passenger, with transparent roof, or aux fuel tank for long-range flight. Though intended for competitive sport, use of regular M-11 ensured mundane performance. First flight about end-August 1936 and on factory test by Piontkovskii solo with aux tank flew Moscow/Kharkov/Sevastopol/Kharkov about 2000 km in 10 h 45 min flying time on 21 September. Later fitted with M-11Ye and gained women's class record 24 October 1937 with Moscow/Aktyubinsk (1444 km straight-line) flown by V.S. Grizodubov and M.M. Raskova.

DIMENSIONS Span 12,0 m (39 ft 4½ in); length 8,03 m (26 ft 4¼ in); wing area 17,0 m² (183 ft²).

ENGINE One 100 hp M-11, in 1937 one 150 hp M-11Ye.

WEIGHTS Empty 550 kg (1212 lb); loaded probably about 960 kg. No other data.

PERFORMANCE Max speed 218 km/h (135·5 mph); no other data.

AIR-13 Not recorded.

AIR-14, UT-1 First of Yak's smash hits, this followed exactly same aerodynamics and structural principles but was scaled down to single-seat size and stressed to factor of 10 for unlimited aerobatics. It began as another of designer's fun aircraft, but with his political disgrace in distant past it was accepted by VVS as standard advanced trainer for fighter pilots.

Fuselage truss welded MS tube braced with piano wire tightened by turnbuckles. Engine on separate welded frame attached at front by four bolted fittings. Wooden one-piece wing with front and rear spars at 13·5 and 56% chord with sharp taper mainly on TE. Ply skin except aft of rear spar inboard of ailerons (no flaps). Unbalanced control surfaces of D1 with fabric aft of D1 LE, ailerons hung on three brackets below wing with large slots in neutral position. Usual braced fork-fittings for main wheels with 500 × 125 mm tyres and rubber-disc shock absorbers, faired inside large aluminium spat and leg trouser moving vertically with wheel. Steel-leaf sprung tailskid. Cylinders uncowled, top three with short exhausts and two bottom cylinders discharged via carb-air heater duct. Two metal fuel tanks ahead of cockpit. Venturi for gyro turn/slip.

Recent account by today's deputy general constructor S. Yakovlev states first flight 1935; previous histories agreed following year. OKB still has prototype in usual livery, silver replaced by white for first time. Piontkovskii did 300 landings in one day and 1000 over next several days; state tests completed 29 March 1936. Not simple to fly and need for care and precision likened to I-16 and sparked off VVS interest, formally ex-

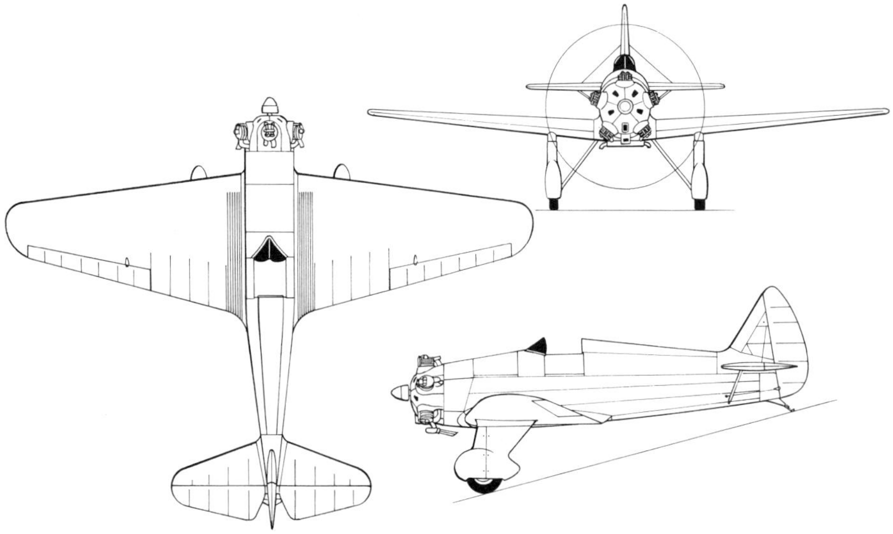

AIR-14, UT-1

UT-1 preserved at OKB

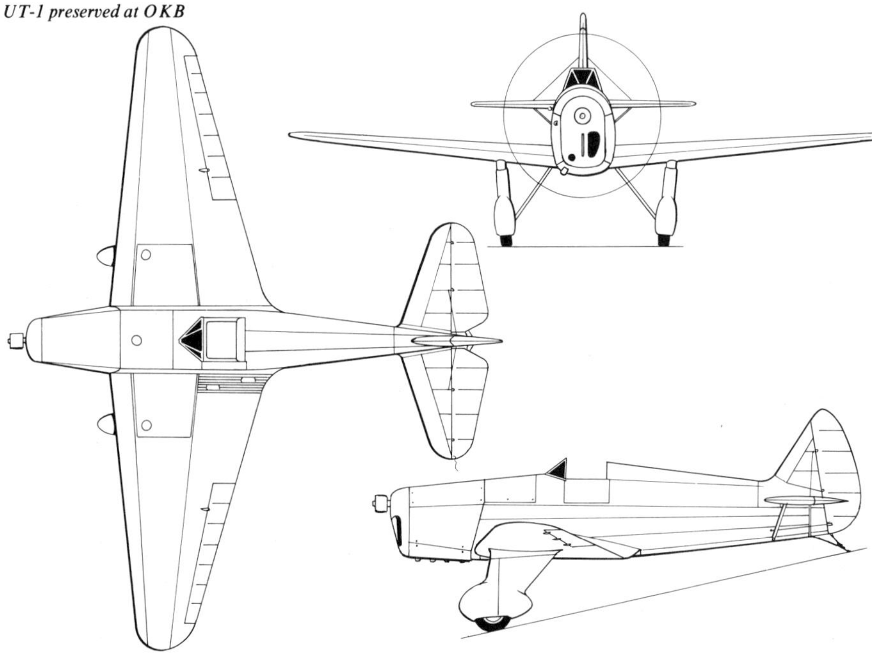

AIR-14 with MV-4 engine

pressed April 1936. Test programme repeated with M-11G and various fuel and control system changes, finally agreed VVS spec August and production authorized following month at two plants, service designation **UT-1.** Various snags and OKB called in to overcome failure to weld accurate fuselages, leading to today's universal method in which OKB production team automatically take up residence at GAZ. Eventually run of 1241 produced by early 1940. Standard advanced fighter trainer and also used for liaison and as hack by senior officers, examination mount for instructors, aerobatic display and sporting aircraft. Almost all had M-11Ye engine, some spade-grip stick.

In 1936–1938 eight class or point/point records including speed, distance and height. In 1937 flown on twin floats, OKB no record of separate designation but Něměcek states called **UT-1V.** This gained 100-km class record at 218 km/h Piontkovskii 2 October 1937, record distance 1174 km (straight-line) Moscow/Ufa by D.N. Fedoseyev 21 December 1937 and women's 100-km at 197,27 km/h by Ye. Mednikova 23 September 1938. In 1939 most modified for sustained inverted flight, trousers/spats removed, some for towing small gliders, at least one enclosed cockpit. In the Second World War many OKB, VVS or unauthorized mods. In 1941 L.I. Sutugin fitted oleo legs, M-12 engine and synchronized gun. A.I. Volkov designed complete installation of two ShKAS with 200 rounds each faired into landing gear. K.A. Moskatov installed two synch ShKAS and underwing RS-82 (believed one each side). Many other armament schemes, numerous such aircraft saw action 1942. OKB has flyable example with twin synch ShKAS and post-war panel with newer insts, another with VVS-profile wing (unsuccessful because increased landing speed), modified landing gear, props and other changes. At least one had engine moved 0,28 m forward; another had MV-4 engine leading to Ya-18.

DIMENSIONS Span 7,30 m (23 ft 11⅓ in); length (Shavrov) 5,78, (most other accounts) 5,75 m (18 ft 10⅓ in), (V) 6,4 m (21 ft 0 in); wing area (Shavrov) 8,3 m², (other accounts) 9,7 m² (104 ft²).

ENGINE (prototype) one 100 hp M-11, (later) 115 hp M-11G, (most) 150 hp M-11Ye.

WEIGHTS Empty (1936) 419 kg, (M-11G) 434 kg, (Ye) 429 kg (946 lb), (V) 505 kg (1102 lb); fuel/oil 79 kg; loaded (prototype) 587 kg, (G) 596/618 kg, (Ye) 598 kg (1318 lb), (V) 673 kg (1484 lb).

PERFORMANCE Max speed (prototype) 249 km/h, (G) 240, (Ye) 257 (160 mph), (V) 218 (135 mph); time to 3 km (G) 12 min, (Ye) 8·7; service ceiling (prototype) 5840 m, (G) 5 km, (Ye) 7120 m (23,360 ft); time 360° circle (prototype) 9 s; range (Němĕcek, G or Ye) 520 km (323 miles); take-off (prototype) 230 m, (Ye) 90 m; landing (prototype) 150 m, (G) 190/90 km/h, (Ye) 140/85 (slower and shorter landing with more powerful engine not explained).

AIR-15 One of aircraft actually built for which few details can be found. Almost certainly derivative of AIR-14, built for racing 1936 with experimental wing to formula (profile) of F.G. Glass (so-called zero-moment section). No details of flight results but passed to TsAGI for research.

AIR-16 Another aircraft completed but almost lost without trace. Superficially similar to AIR-

11, with four-seat enclosed cabin, but much more powerful engine. Shavrov states finished AIR-16 was on Central Airfield 1937 but never released for flight. OKB has drawing showing retractable gear, uncertain if this was fitted.
DIMENSIONS Presumed as AIR-11.
ENGINE One 220 hp Renault MV-6.
WEIGHTS, performance No data.

AIR-17, UT-3, No 17 This twin-engined machine was complete break with small sporting types and also believed first to be completed after purge of A.I. Rykov and Yak's decision to abandon AIR designations. Designed early 1937 as trainer for pilots of large civil and military aircraft with added capability of training other members of crew if necessary. Structure similar to previous designs. Fuselage welded MS tube with D1 and ply secondary structure (fairings and floors) and fabric covering, wooden one-piece two-spar wing but this time Clark YHC section, D1/fabric control surfaces and hydraulic system driving Schrenk flaps and rearwards-retracting single-leg main gears copied from SB. Prototype built as military crew trainer with pilot above LE with folding canopy, glazed nose for nav/bomb with small table and ShKAS in pivoted nose mount, and rear radio/gunner with ShKAS. Něměcek states a fixed gun and bomb bay, but not shown on contemporary display model and OKB record shows four FAB-50 carried externally. First machine with French engines driving electrically-controlled Ratier props, painted OKB livery and flown on retractable skis 31 December 1937. Successful factory and NII VVS testing led to decision to produce in series with designation **UT-3** (UT-2 was already on order). Two GAZ instructed to prepare for manufacture, but indecision over engines, props and crew arrangement delayed issue of drawings. French prop never licensed, and fourth Ya-17 had Gipsy Six engines and D.H. fixed-pitch props. Eventually locally produced AV-3 prop available, but decision then taken to ignore nav/bomb/gunnery training and concentrate on pilot. Several further examples delivered to VVS 1941 with pupil and instructor in tandem dual pilot cockpits with glazed roof canopies sliding on rails. These introduced new main gears with single leg on inner end of axle and no fork fitting. They still had Renault engines and for this and other reasons VVS lost interest and terminated programme. One GAZ had already produced some series machines; according to Shavrov about 30 completed of which 20 delivered. VVS never did use any light twin for crew-training. Ya-19 was civil transport variant.
DIMENSIONS Span 15,02 m (49 ft 3¼ in); length believed 11,1 m (36 ft 5 in); wing area 33,42 m² (360 ft²).
ENGINES Two 220 hp MV-6, (4th prototype) 205 hp D.H. Gipsy Six II.
WEIGHTS No data except max loaded (Shavrov) 2742 kg (6045 lb), (Něměcek) 3108 (6852).
PERFORMANCE Max speed 273 km/h (170 mph); time to 1 km 4·4 min; service ceiling 6,1 km (20,000 ft), (Něměcek) 5 km; range, no Soviet data but Něměcek 1000 km (620 miles).

Ya-18 This trim racer stemmed from UT-1 re-engined with MV-4 in 1937 and was built on OKB account as another of designer's sporting aircraft. Main differences were tightly enclosed cockpit and retractable landing gear. Cockpit featured transparent skin around sides, left side folding down in usual manner, and narrow windshield and hood tailored to pilot's head, hood sliding to rear. Landing gear almost identical to AIR-12. Other major change was fuel in left/right wing tanks between spars outboard of fuselage. Single aircraft with usual striped rudder but otherwise white. OKB has record of Piontkovskii's enthusiastic report but no data except 300 km/h attained. Same aircraft later flown on UT-1 floats.
DIMENSIONS Span 7,3 m (23 ft 11⅓ in); length 6,03 m (19 ft 9⅓ in); wing area 9,7 m² (104 ft²).
ENGINE One 140 hp MV-4.
PERFORMANCE 300 km/h attained (186 mph). No other data.

Ya-19, No 19 One of OKB projects in immediate post-AIR period when, pending general adoption of Ya designations, many aircraft were simply known by No. First of these was No 17, better known as UT-3, and No 19 was its civil transport derivative. Though drawings based on those of UT-3, many significant changes, notably first use of stainless steel in primary structure by OKB. Well-streamlined oval-section fuselage built around primary truss of welded 30KhGSA tube with piano-wire bracing. Skin dural flush-riveted over nose, ply to rear of cabin and fabric from there to tail. Wing identical to UT-3 except no bomb racks, same slotted ailerons and Schrenk flaps. Main gears as for pre-production UT-3 with SB type geometry and fork fitting for wheel with tyre 650 × 250 mm. Comfortable cockpit with full glazing, usually

Ya-19

Ya-18

single pilot only. Main cabin with five passenger seats, or three stretchers and attendant seat, or (drawings prepared) reconnaissance/survey cameras, cargo and other duties. Prototype flown late 1938 and factory tested in white/striped-rudder livery on wheels and skis. Passed GOS NII tests spring 1939 (pilots G.A. Muratov, E.I. Schwartz); at aft CG (31·3/32·5%) fin considered too small and rudder large, but overall excellent transport and strong wish to build in series. In prevailing atmosphere this not possible; no aircraft in this category until wartime Yak-6.

DIMENSIONS Span 15,02 m (49 ft 3⅓ in); length not known but about 11 m (36 ft); wing area 33,42 m² (360 ft²).

ENGINES Two 220hp MV-6.

WEIGHTS Empty 2134 kg (4705 lb); fuel/oil 250 + 28 kg; loaded 2950 kg (6503 lb).

PERFORMANCE Max speed 256 km/h (159 mph); cruise 239 (149); time to 1 km 5·3 min; service ceiling 5,6 km (18,370 ft); range 870 km (540 miles); take-off 410 m/17 s; landing 365 m/90 km/h.

Ya-20 (pre-war civil)

Ya-20, UT-2 Most important of Yak's pre-war programmes, though still little known in world at large, this was standard Soviet primary pilot trainer throughout the Second World War. Set national record for low price, and basic design for many subsequent training and sporting aircraft.

Original Renault-engined prototype **No 20** in usual white livery with striped tail and bearing number 3 flown unknown date 1937. Complete break with past in all-wood airframe, using MS or D1 only for simple pressings and sheet laminates at major joints. Fuselage spruce/pine built up on wire-braced truss integral with engine mounts. Main frame at front of each tandem cockpit integral with 2,24 m centre section spars. Ply top decking, fabric elsewhere. Outer wing panels, Göttingen 387 section, 5° dihedral on LE from straight c/s with joints at two spars reinforced by three MS plate laminates bolted each side of spar booms to give ultimate load factor 10 (common to all variants); ply ribs, multiple stringers and ply skin. Slotted ailerons with fabric covering over ply nose, mounted on brackets beneath lower surface and driven via rods/bellcranks. Entire tail D1 (only metal structure) with fabric covering wrapped over flush-riveted D1 on all LE including large horn on rudder, cable actuation. Usual welded MS landing gear with fork fittings on rear bracing strut and main leg with stack of 16 rubber shock-absorbers; tyre 500 × 125 mm, surrounded by large spat/leg-trouser of aluminium in front/rear sections. Tailskid multi-leaf steel spring, each laminate 50 × 5 mm. Engine in aluminium cowl driving 1,96 m wooden propeller. Welded 90 lit fuel tank in each side of c-s between spars outboard of fuselage; welded oil drum ahead of front instrument panel. Open cockpits with padded leather edges and folding sidewall on left. Comfortable padded seats on aluminium-tube basis made at OKB. Baggage hatch in decking behind rear seat.

Second aircraft made to same standard with M-11Ye and only 76 lit fuel. Both showed outstanding qualities, and September 1937 decision to develop as standard VVS primary trainer, designation UT-2. As MV-4 not produced in Soviet Union choice fell on radial engine and

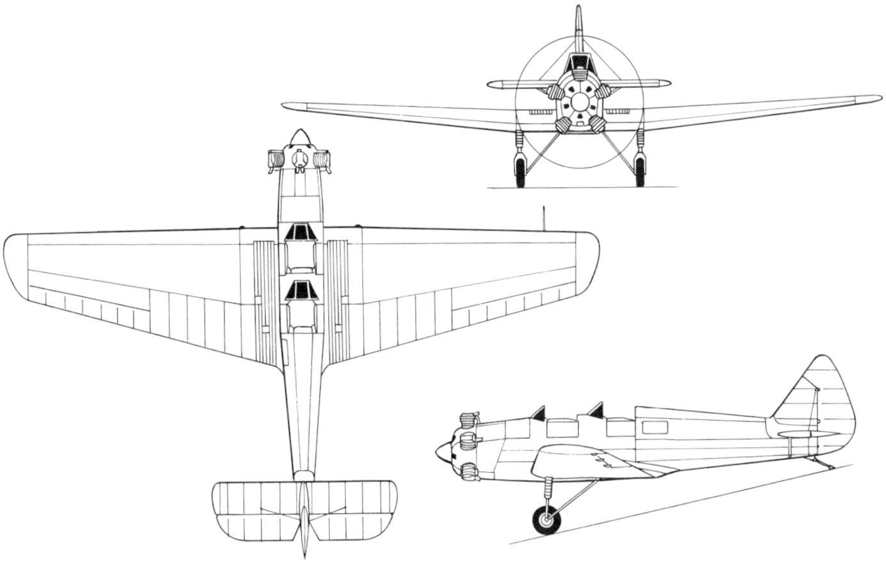

UT-2 (original wing plan)

further examples produced with many small mods including bucket seats for VVS pilot parachute, compass, gyro turn/slip and enlarged fuel tanks total 200 lit for 7 h endurance. Despite 102 kg extra fuel performance still adequate and decision late 1937 to put into production with no further changes at five GAZ. Original Renault aircraft by this time flying on AIR-6 modified floats, with aluminium-faired MS-tube struts (similar floats later tested on M-11Ye aircraft and put on a few series machines). Series aircraft from October 1938, trouble free except for major OKB investigation of flat spins (previously avoided in USSR), mainly by test-pilot V.L. Rastorguev, which led to modification of aileron/elevator control and setting of tailplane. By 1939 series engine switched to less-powerful M-11, and by 1941 various changes in materials combined with changed wing geometry with increased sweepback and 7° dihedral to give designation **UT-2M**. Modified wing associated with sharply reduced fuel capacity (88 lit total) better matched to less-powerful engine. Further spin testing led to reduction of aileron area, series UT-2M receiving lavish praise. From 1940 landing gear fairings almost always omitted; alternative skis standard. After June 1941 large numbers given various field mods including fixed guns, bombs and glider tow-hooks; no known OKB participation but four FAB-50 a common close-support bombload.

Many further wartime changes included aircraft modified at front-line in 1942 by K.A. Moskatov with aileron/elevator trimmers and enclosed cockpits with strong welded-steel crash arches; tested with two ShKAS and underwing RS. OKB took up and introduced further improvements using series aircraft 23 and 24 (retained for development). Former also tested with MV-6 engine as **UT-23** but no series MV-6 engines. Important mod was **UT-2MV** of 1943 in which basic UT-2M was modified over period of several months first with enclosed cockpits with sliding hoods, later with helmeted engine cowl, pneumatic-operated split flaps (50°), tailwheel and modified main gears with oleo shock struts (on first aircraft, with spats). This was refined by 1944 into Yak-18. Original UT-2, UT-2M remained in production until 1944 (some reports, doubted by OKB, until 1946), total given as 7243 excluding development prototypes. Used at all pilot schools until 1948, graduated well over 100,000 pilots. Many post-war to aero clubs.

DIMENSIONS Span (prototype) 10,18 m (33 ft 4¾ in), (production) 10,2 m (33 ft 5½ in); length (No 20) 7,3 m, (M-11Ye) 7,11, (production) 7,0 m (22 ft 11¾ in), (floats) 7,65; wing area 17,12 m² (184 ft²).

ENGINE (No 20) one 140 hp MV-4, (2nd and pre-production) 150 hp M-11Ye, (production from 1939) 100 hp M-11, (MV) 115 hp M-11D.

WEIGHTS Empty (No 20) 572 kg, (M-11Ye) 574, (initial production, M-11Ye) 578, (standard 1939) 616 (1358 lb), (floats) 677, (MV) 792; fuel/oil (No 20) 156 kg, (M-11Ye) 60, (production, 1938) 162, (1939, M-11) 64, (1940 on) 146; loaded (No 20) 893 kg, (Ye) 804 kg, (production 1938) 916 kg (2019 lb), (M-11) 856 kg (1887 lb), (floats) 1003 kg, (1940 on) 938 kg (2068 lb), (MV) 1150 kg.

PERFORMANCE Max speed (No 20) 240 km/h, (Ye) 230, (1938 production) 215 (134 mph), (floats) 210, (39) 210 (130·5 mph), (MV, at SL) 177; time to 1 km (No 20) 4 min, (Ye) 3·5, (production 1939) 4·8, (1940) 5·8, (MV) 8; service ceiling (No 20) 6,1 km, (Ye) 6,5, (floats) 3267 m, (1939 production) 3,5 (11,500 ft), (1940) 3,1 (10,200 ft), (MV) 3,35; range (No 20) 1200 km (not 830), (Ye) 450, (1938 production) 1000 (620 miles), (1939) 500 (310), (1940) 1130 (700), (MV) 925; time 360° circle 14 s (floats 16); take-off (1939) 200 m/13 s; landing (1939) 235 m/16 s/90 km/h (earlier 85 km/h; 1940 on, 95).

Ya-21, No 21 Inspired by Mew Gull (he said) Yak built racing aircraft winter 1938–1939 with six-cylinder Renault and airframe much modified from Ya-18. Curiously he did not use latter's retractable landing gear. Göttingen 387 wing slightly strengthened and fitted with D1 dural Schrenk flaps manually driven by worm gear to 55°. Welded MS fuselage greatly modified with long engine mounts, welded 170-lit fuel drum extending down between spars, and cockpit behind TE of wing. Canopy almost identical to AIR-18. D1/fabric tail with D1 LE skin; elevator push-rods (unusual for OKB). D1/aluminium sheet cowl with carb-air inlet on right and six ventral exhaust stacks, two-blade v-p metal propeller, 2120 mm diam (not Ratier). Main tyres 500 × 125 mm, rubber shock struts, no brakes. Flown in OKB livery about April 1939, much of construction and testing being by A.S. Yakovlev. Believed No 21 served as his personal aircraft during the Second World War. Shavrov states modified 1940 and redesignated **No 25 (Ya-25)** but no details known. Data for original form.

DIMENSIONS Span 7,3 m (23 ft 11⅓ in); length 6,4 m (21 ft 0 in); wing area 9,7 m² (104 ft²).

ENGINE One 220 hp MV-6.

WEIGHTS Empty 610 kg (1345 lb); fuel/oil 125 + 15 kg; loaded 830 kg (1830 lb).

PERFORMANCE Max speed 322 km/h (200 mph), (Shavrov states 290); initial climb 6 m/s (thus 1 km in 2·75 min); service ceiling 9,1 km (30,000 ft, optimistic without oxygen); range 715 km (444 miles); take-off 150 m; landing 190 m/85 km/h.

Ya-22, BB-22, Yak-2 In May 1938 Yakovlev was invited to build high-speed combat aircraft for VVS and accepted with enthusiasm despite lack of experience. From start design was low-wing monoplane of mixed construction with two M-100 series engines, first prototype having fairings for two ShVAK under fuselage (guns not fitted) and intended chiefly as fighter. Like many Yak aircraft an excellent performer subsequently built in considerable numbers in several variants; full story not previously told (BB-22 often thought same as Yak-4).

Wing of Göttingen 387 profile modified with flat underside, made as centre section integral with fuselage mid-section, wholly wood construction, usual two box spars with ply ribs glued and pinned and stressed for factor of 8 (in this context means 8 g ultimate strength). Dihedral 6° from roots. Ply skin throughout, graded thickness. Schrenk flaps of D1 structure inboard/outboard of nacelles, hyd drive to 55°. Ailerons of D1 with fabric covering over D1 LE skin, hung on hinges below wing in usual way. Fixed tail surfaces D1 with stressed skin, movable surfaces as ailerons but with trimmers. Main mid-portion of fuselage wood with ply skin, integral with c/s of wing. Nose D1 with stressed skin flush-riveted. Rear fuselage welded 30KhGSA tube with wood upper decking and fabric covering. Landing gear strengthened version of Ya-17 with welded MS fork to single wheels with 550 × 250 mm tyres, hydraulic retraction rearwards into nacelles with twin doors enclosing bay completely. Fully retractable tailwheel. Fuel in four wing tanks between spars and two large tanks in mid fuselage, total 1232 lit. Pilot ahead of LE with remarkably broad cockpit enclosed by sliding hood, nav aft of TE with hinged hood. Wing stressed for bombs hung under spars, four FAB-100 on drawings but no racks fitted. M-103 engines neatly cowled with carb-air inlets on underside, oil-cooler ram inlets on outer sides, glycol radiators inside rear of nacelle behind wheel bay with vertical slit inlet each side and adjustable vertical exit doors aft of TE. VISh-22 three-blade c/s 3,1 m props.

First **No 22** in OKB red livery flown by Piontkovskii early 1939 (one report, 22 February). Outstanding aircraft, fastest in Soviet Union. Handling generally good and rather precipitate Stalin command 15 March 1939 to put into immediate production at two GAZ with mission short-range bomber (*Blizhnii Bombardirovshchik*, hence designation **BB-22**. Yakovlev had already organized special group called KB-70 to speed production by photocopying over 3300 drawings. Personally called to Kremlin 27 April 1939 and interrogated; then awarded Order of Lenin, ZIS car and 100,000 rubles. But getting BB-22 into production was major task, complicated by 100 + engineering change orders which included redesign of centre fuselage so that navigator was seated directly behind pilot with large glazed area over both cockpits, elimination of fuselage tankage and addition of internal bay for various bombloads up to 400 kg (Kondratyev states max 600 kg). Light defensive armament two ShKAS, one fixed in nose and one aimed by nav from opened cockpit. Two extra wing tanks but not bringing capacity up to original value (about 720 lit only). First production BB-22 completed 31 December 1939 and flown on retractable skis 20 February 1940. OKB simultaneously built two further prototypes of derivatives for different missions, both with regular VVS livery. **R-12** (*Razvyedchik*, reconnaissance) had three AFA-33 cameras managed by nav, and weapon bay converted to dispense flash cartridges. **I-29 (BB-22IS)** long-range escort fighter with restored fuselage tank and two ShVAK under fuselage. Both tested 1940–1941

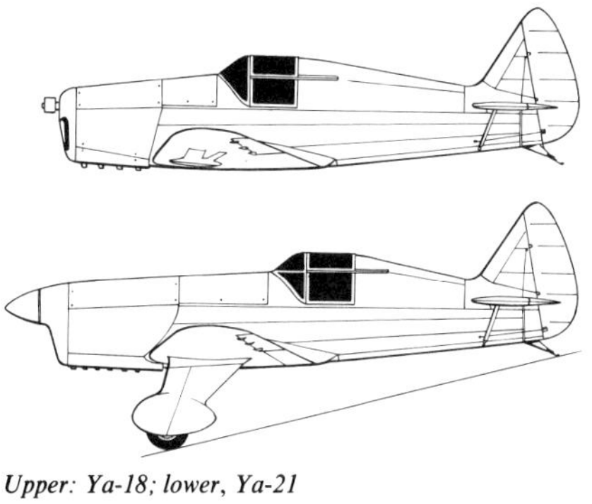

Upper: Ya-18; lower, Ya-21

Ya-22

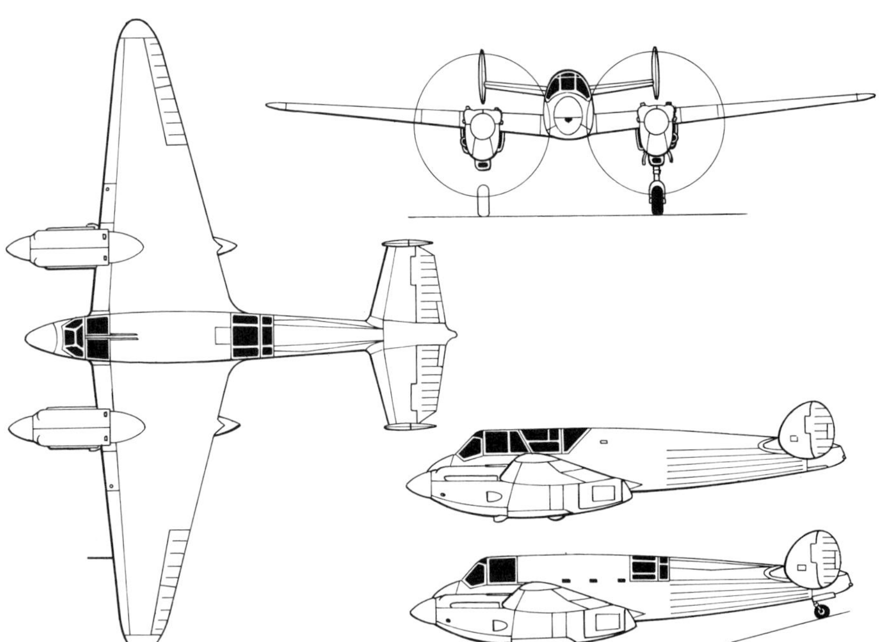

Ya-22; upper side view, production Yak-2

with bomber but only latter produced in series, designated Yak-2 from 1941. Total with Yak-4 about 600, majority being Yak-4.

DIMENSIONS Span 14,0 m (45 ft 11⅛ in); length (all) 10,18 m (33 ft 4¾ in); wing area 29,4 m² (316·5 ft²).

ENGINES Two 960 hp M-103.

WEIGHTS Empty (series BB) 3863 kg (8516 lb); fuel/oil 500 + 56 kg; loaded 5023 kg (11,074 lb).

PERFORMANCE Max speed (Ya-22) 399 at SL, 567 km/h (352 mph) at 5 km, (series) 530 km/h (329 mph); time to 7 km (Ya) 8 min 42 s; service ceiling (Ya) 11,8 km (38,700 ft), (series) 8,8 (28,870 ft); range (Ya) 1050 km (652 miles), (s) 800 (497); take-off (Ya) 220 m/6·5 s; landing speed (Ya) 150 km/h.

Yak-4 This designation was originally applied to series Yak-2 with M-105 engine but during 1940 progressive changes turned Yak-4 into substantially different aircraft. Fuselage again redesigned with cockpits even closer under different glazed canopy extended down beside pilot to give good view obliquely down inboard of engines and with lower rear fuselage of smaller cross-section to improve nav's field of fire. According to data reduced in length, but not shown in drawings except at extreme tail. New main landing gear with twin narrower wheels of larger diam (tyres 700 × 150 mm) on single oleo leg with large part of wheels protruding through closed bay doors. OKB received some of first pre-production batch of M-105 engines shipped by Klimov, installed in different cowls with small dural panels held on dural fixed structure by Dzus fasteners. Ducted oil coolers beneath engines but rear-nacelle main radiators retained. Radio installed with aerial mast above right engine nacelle. Modified weapons bay, and reported racks for external bombs (four FAB-100) but latter not found in Soviet reports. Improved armour and tank protection (all fuel in wings).

Yak-4 succeeded Yak-2 in production late 1940, accounted for most of 600 aircraft delivered. Not widely used because in front-line conditions airframe quickly became tired and affected flight characteristics. Shavrov comments that structure broke logic of airframe development and crews lost confidence, possibly implying structural failures. Western reports that most Yak-4s soon used as transports denied by OKB, but clear that great promise of this aircraft not realized and Stalin was once again foolishly captivated by high performance. Little reliable data.

DIMENSIONS Span 14,0 m (45 ft 11⅛ in); length 9,34 m (30 ft 7¾ in) (this appears to be length of fuselage); wing area 29,7 m² (319·7 ft²), (Němeček 32 m², 344 ft², may be gross figure).

ENGINES Two 1050 hp M-105.

WEIGHTS Only data loaded 5,2 t (11,464 lb).

PERFORMANCE Max speed 545 km/h (339 mph) at 5 km; time to 1 km, 1·1 min; service ceiling 9,5 km (31,170 ft); range (OKB figure) 1200 km (746 miles).

Ya-26, I-26 Yakovlev's chief ambition was to build a small, high-speed fighter. As soon as design effort on No 22 was tailing off he obtained NKAP authority to begin design of 'frontal' fighter; this was in November 1938, not subsequent to January 1939 Kremlin meeting of OKB heads. Yak already on good terms with Klimov and planned **No 26**, or Ya-26, around M-106 of 1350 hp. From outset determined to keep aircraft small and put all armament in fuselage. Studied stressed-skin structures, and saw Bf 109 and Spitfire, but adhered to OKB traditional mixed construction, which was known quantity, did not impose severe penalties, was easy to repair and used materials not in short supply.

One-piece wing Clark-YH profile, t/c 14% root and 10% tip, dihedral 5°30′ from root, incidence 0°30′. All-wood structure with usual pair of widely spaced box spars, ply/pine strip ribs with cut-outs and birch-ply skin with varnished fabric overlayer. Schrenk flaps (not following TE of wing but at 90° to fuselage, following hinge line along kinked rear spar) driven by single pneu ram to 50°, wholly D1 construction. Ailerons D1 with fabric covering, Frise type with slots and hinged behind rear spar (not to brackets below wing). Fuselage built around truss of welded 30KhGSA with diagonal (Warren) bracing, oval section ahead of instrument panel achieved by D1 secondary structure carrying Dzus-fastened D1 cowl and access panels. Aft of cockpit plywood formers above and below carried light pine laths with thin birch-ply upper decking and overall covering of fabric. Tail D1 with fabric covering, tailplane symmetric, fixed, span 3,4 m, tail control surfaces driven by cables (ailerons by push-rods) on plain hinges, elevators with simple extended mid-section LE for balance, all surfaces with trim tabs. Main landing gear with air/oil shock struts and single curved fitting holding inboard end of axle, tyres 650 × 200 mm, pneumatic retraction inwards

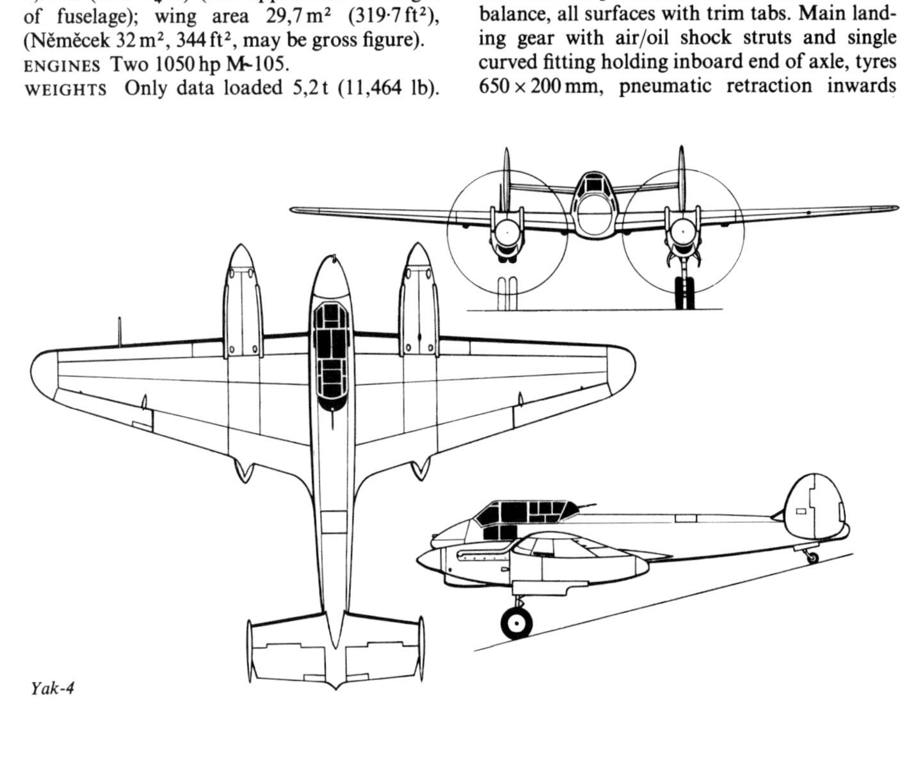

Yak-4

Ya-26 (second aircraft)

ahead of spar, track 3,25 m. Fully retractable tailwheel 300 × 120 mm with two doors. Engine, second-best choice of M-105P because 106 not available, mounted direct on forward fuselage tubes without vibration dampers, with glycol radiator and oil cooler in controllable duct under wing TE, carb-air inlet under wing LE, plain exhaust stubs. Three-blade 3,0 m (139 kg) VISh-61 prop with manually variable pitch. Four flexible fuel cells between wing spars outboard of fuselage, inners 130-lit and outers 74. Cockpit with bucket seat above rear spar, fully glazed Plexiglas windscreen (unarmoured), sliding hood (spring-latch either open or closed) and fixed Plexiglas rear section; small 8-mm armour plate behind pilot's head. Planned armament one ShVAK mounted on engine firing through spinner (120 rounds) and two ShKAS in top decking (500 rounds each). Alternative to ShVAK, one UBS with 250 rounds. PBP-1a reflector sight, RSI-3 radio with mast behind cockpit (not on prototype).

Prototype Ya-26 NKAP designation I-26 completed 1 January 1940 in OKB red livery, dubbed *Krasavits* (beauty). Flown without armament or radio by Yu.I. Piontkovskii 13 January 1940. Generally excellent, no problem with wheeled gear on ice/snow, GAZ testing yielded 586 km/h but because of manufacturing defect crashed 27 April, killing Piontkovskii. By this time complete confidence, no need for modification apart from various planned changes, and even at time of crash decision taken to produce in large series at two GAZ, one being No 115 adjacent to OKB. Second prototype flown by P.Ya. Fedrovi late April 1940, 42 engineering changes including relocation of oil cooler to separate duct under engine, carb-air duct divided and taken to inlets at wing-root LE, ejector exhausts, increased fin chord, fixed tailwheel and modified canopy and rear upper decking (previously narrow behind canopy, subsequently rounded to full width of fuselage). Flew in Tushino May Day parade, NII testing by P.M. Stefanovskii begun 10 June 1940 and completed with several pre-production aircraft November. Designation changed to Yak-1 December.

DIMENSIONS Span 10,0 m (32 ft 9⅔ in); length 8,50 m (27 ft 10⅔ in); wing area 17,15 m² (184·6 ft²).

ENGINE One 1050 hp M-105P.

WEIGHTS Empty 2206 kg (4863 lb); fuel/oil 305 kg; loaded 2701 kg (5955 lb).

PERFORMANCE Max speed (1) 490 at SL (304), 586 km/h (364 mph) at 3 km, (2) 579 at 3 km; time to 5 km (1) 4·9 min; service ceiling 10,2 km (33,465 ft); range 700 km (435 miles); time 360° circle 24 s; take-off 300 m; landing 540 m/130 km/h (81 mph).

Yak-1 Urgent need to modernize VVS fighter regiments over-rode recognition that in 1940 Yak-1 was immature, and completion of 64 by year-end was judged more important than their shortcomings. Among latter were poor firepower, modest power/weight ratio, unreliability of gear/flaps, difficulty of manually sliding hood, severe vibration from engine causing fatigue failures of pipes, and various snags with armament. OKB-115 began diverse development programme which within weeks in late 1940 had resulted in designs for lightweight Yak-1M, high-altitude Ya-28, all-metal Ya-30 and Ya-27 trainer, all dealt with separately here. Main production built up on massive scale at GAZ-115 and, after evacuation, at GAZ-153 and 286. Though Yakovlev confirmed only one set of OKB drawings originally issued, and copied for each plant, numerous local changes crept in and, with extensive hand-work, eventually there were countless small differences even between successive aircraft. Data are for standard aircraft; very few Yak-1s had PF engine, though from October 1941 usual engine was PA, driving slightly modified VISh-61P prop with hole in spinner for ShVAK or UBS. Three main armament schemes, all built in series: ShVAK plus two ShKAS (all aircraft prior to mid-1941); ShVAK plus one UBS (left side); two UBS, one through prop. On almost all from mid-1941 provision for two FAB-100 or six RS-82 under wings.

Great confusion still exists over sub-types and even dimensions. Many Western writers still believe Yak-1M had short-span wing and cut-down rear fuselage. What is still not clear is whether more pointed wing, fitted to numerous Yak-1, 1B and M, from early 1942, did have

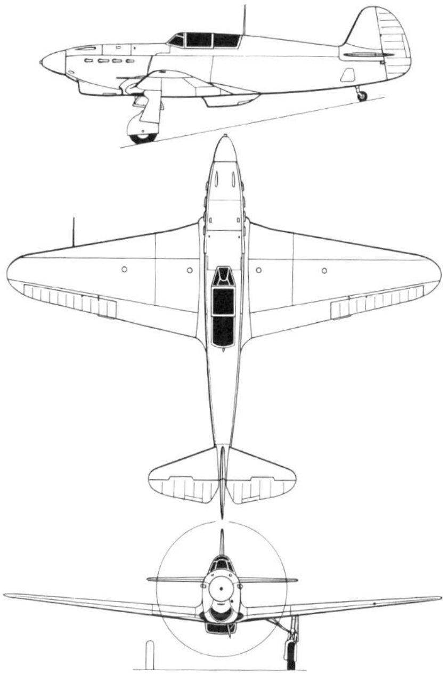

Yak-1

Yak-1

increased span of 10,25 m, 33 ft 7½ in, same as Yak-7. Soviet opinion is unanimous span never varied from 10,0; author does not share this view which, if true, would mean reduced wing area and total redesign of wing from root (because LE/TE remained straight). Figure 10,25 thus appears in data, but still subject for argument.

Among superficially obvious mods introduced to production (not necessarily all production) from late 1941 were more efficient carb-air inlets, altered main-leg fairing plates and replacement of Plexiglas top decking aft of cockpit by plywood with curved Plexiglas window each side. Rear view imperfect and various studies at OKB with mock-up to improve; answer found by front-line IAP (CO Maj F.I. Shinkarenko) which boldly removed wooden secondary structure above fuselage truss and rebuilt it at reduced height allowing for moulded Plexiglas rear canopy giving excellent (if slightly distorted) all-round view – though pilot handicapped by rigid shoulder harness which prevented body rotation. Modified aircraft designated **Yak-1B**; after NII tests July 1942 accepted by OKB and VVS as standard and Yak-1B was standard production type from first week 1943. Similar canopy and rear fuselage on Yak-1M and subsequent variants Yak-9 and Yak-3.

Much more difficult development was programme of weight-reduction undertaken from October 1940 (lead engineer K.V. Sinelshchikov) under designation **Yak-1M**. More than 450 mods drawn 1941–1943 and most incorporated to production. OKB confirm Shavrov, Simakov and other historians who claim final Yak-1M loaded weight brought down from around 2850 kg to 2655–2660 despite extra weight of PF engine and constant-speed VISh-105SV prop. Original 1M had ShVAK and BS, *dubler* (second copy) two UBS, fuel capacity actually slightly increased, retractable tailwheel and latest standard tank protection and armour. Much better close-combat aircraft (note speeds at SL and height) and 360° time cut from 19 to 17 s. Production Yak-1M from GAZ-286 from late 1942 but did not replace Yak-1 entirely. Yak-1M was basis of Yak-3.

Production of Yak-1B and Yak-1M tailed off early summer 1943. Accepted total, excluding prototypes and development aircraft, 8721.

DIMENSIONS Span (most) 10,0 m (32 ft 9⅔ in), (pointed wing, not confirmed by USSR) 10,25 m (33 ft 7½ in); length 8,48 m (27 ft 9⅞ in) (usually given in West as 8,47, not found in Soviet writings); wing area (normal) 17,15 m² (184·6 ft²), (pointed) official figure also 17,15.

ENGINE Usually 1050 hp M-105P, (October 1941) 1100 hp M-105PA, (Yak-1M) 1180 hp VK-105PF.

WEIGHTS Empty (1940) 2347 kg (5174 lb), (1942) 2443 (5386), (1M) 2199 (4848); fuel/oil (normal) 310 kg; loaded (1940) 2847 kg (6276 lb), (1942) 2906 (6407), (1M) 2660 (5864).

PERFORMANCE Max speed at SL (1940) 540 km/h (336 mph), (1942) 518 (322), (1M) 570 (354); at height (1940) 600 (373) at 3 km, (1942) 585 (364) at 3,8 km, (1M) 650 (404) at 4,5; time to 5 km (1940) 5·4 min, (1942) 6·5, (1M) 4·1; service ceiling (1940) 10 km (32,800 ft), (1M) 10,8 (35,450); time 360° (1940) 19 s, (1942) about 20 s, (1M) 17 s; range (1940) 700 km (435 miles), (1942) 685 km (426), (1M) 900 (559); take-off (1940) 340 m, (1942) 420, (1M) 260; landing (1940–1942) 540/135 km/h, (1M) 400/126.

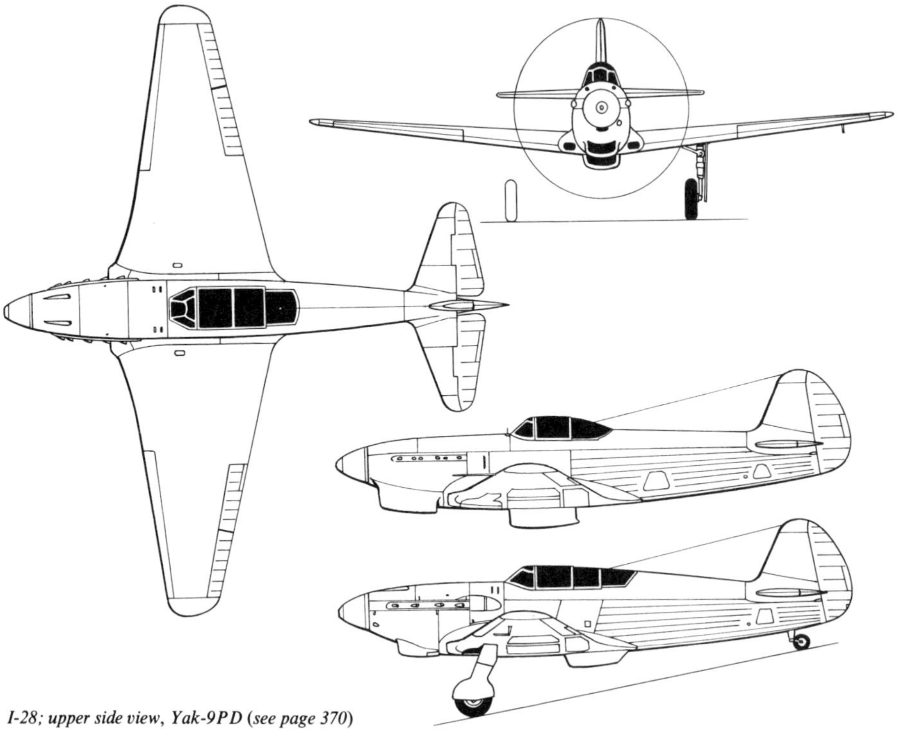

I-28; upper side view, Yak-9PD (see page 370)

Yak-1 experimentals Several Yak-1 variants built for research and never intended for production or, after testing, were not accepted as series types. Chronologically first were the No 28 **(Ya-28, I-28)** series of high-altitude fighters. Single seat but long glazed rear deck, one ShVAK + two ShKAS, new wing built of wood with modified structure, reduced span and outboard automatic slats. PF engine in revised installation with Dollezhal two-stage supercharger. With this engine achieved 650 km/h at 8,5 km and in June 1942 modified I-28 reached 12 890 m (42,290 ft) and 665 km/h at 10 km. No data on propeller or on number built. Two further Ya-28, designated **Yak-5**, had same wing with ply skin (Shavrov) implying that others had metal skin (denied by OKB).

Metal wing was main feature of **I-30** (No 30, Ya-30), first flown by Fedrovi· autumn 1941; confusingly, in view of later fighter with same designation, this received VVS designation Yak-3 though it never went into production. It repeated new wing plan of Ya-28 but with centre section having 0° dihedral on underside (−6° on upper surface at thickest point) and + 5° 30′ on outer panels, but reduced span and area. Wholly D1 construction with plate spars, machined T and L booms and pressed sheet ribs. Automatic slats almost full span of outer panels; fabric-covered ailerons with inset trim tab on left. Fuselage basically as original No 26 but detachable D1 panels extended to rear of cockpit (canopy 1940 style). Exceptionally heavy armament of two ShKAS in top of cowl and three 20-mm ShVAK (one on centreline, others inboard in outer wings) each with 100 rounds. Engine fitted with Dollezhal E-100 gear-driven supercharger. This I-30 had coolant radiator further forward than in any other wartime Yak fighter; another unusual feature was absence of radio mast, wire entering fuselage at fairlead in top decking behind cockpit. Second I-30 had even heavier armament of three ShVAK and four ShKAS, latter in left/right pairs above engine. Distinguished by absence of oil cooler under engine, combined with coolant radiator in duct restored to usual location under TE. Other features of second aircraft were retrac tailwheel, radio mast with twin HF wires and pitot on left LE (first I-30 pitot on mounting below tip of left wing). Impressive aircraft but after prolonged testing decided great increase in weight, part being extra fuel made possible by metal wing, depressed combat performance and manoeuvrability too much. OKB received notice to standardize on one cannon and two UBS, continuing with established fighters of mixed construction.

Final known variant, believed to be No 33 **(Ya-33)**, fitted with 1350 hp VK-106 engine as originally planned in 1939. According to Shavrov, built in small series, with armament one MP-20 and one UBS. Engine immature and abandoned mid-1943; date of this Yak variant winter 1942–1943.

DIMENSIONS Span, as Yak-1 except I-28 and I-30 9,74 m (31 ft 11½ in); length, as Yak-1 except I-30, Ya-33, 8,50 m (27 ft 10¾ in); wing area, as Yak-1 except I-30 (measured with planimeter from drawing) 17,05 m².

ENGINE See text.

WEIGHTS (I-28, Yak-5) loaded 2990 kg (6,592 lb); (I-30) empty 2550 kg (5,622 lb); fuel/oil 383 kg; loaded 3130 kg (6900 lb); (I-33) loaded 2,9 t (6393 lb).

PERFORMANCE Max speed (I-28) 650 km/h (404 mph) at 8,5 km, (another I-28) 665 (413) at 10 km; (I-30) 490 (304) at SL, 584 (363) at 4,75 km; (I-33) 535 (332) at SL, 610 (379) at 3,6 km; time to 5 km, (I-28) 4·0 min, (I-30) 7·0, (I-33) 5·2; service ceiling (I-28) 12 km (39,400 ft), (I-30) 9,9 (32,500), (I-33) no data; range (I-28) no data, (I-30) 900 km (559 miles), (I-33) no data; take-off (I-28) 240 m, ((I-30) 570 m, (I-33) no data; landing (I-28) 390 m, (I-30) 700 m/145 km/h, (I-33) no data.

Yak-7, Ya-27, UTI-26 Yakovlev planned tandem two-seat variant of Ya-26 almost in parallel, Ya-27 being in fact fifth aircraft built and flown by Fedrovi before 4 July 1940. (Ponomaryev, Hornat say 'spring 1940'). Tandem cockpits with dual control, but intended not only for pilot conversion to I-26 but also as liaison and transport aircraft especially to assist in regimental mobility. Structure based on No 26 but in some respects simplified, general rule being fewer separate parts. Designed to same factor but appreciably lighter aircraft despite extended (more pointed) wingtips and second seat added behind original. Removal of most armament, just one ShKAS left on left side of cowl, accentuated rearwards shift of CG which was countered by removal of armour and radio and repositioning of main coolant radiator further forward under wing. Outstanding handling, much better at low speeds than Yak-1 and generally easier to fly accurately. Early decision in principle (before end-1940) to build in large series as Yak-7.

Yak-1 (GAZ-286 early 1942, retractable skis, curved rear windows, no radio)

Limited production began spring 1941 at GAZ-115 but NII testing by Stefanovskii and Suprun threw up suggestion of building single-seat version as fighter. First experimental single-seater, still just called Yak-7, flown early June 1941 and with 105P engine, VISh-61P prop and armament of one ShVAK and two UBS (heavier than Yak-1) achieved 613 km/h (height

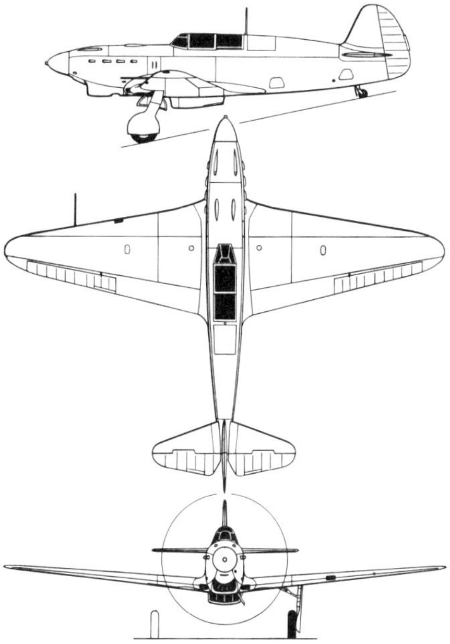

Yak-7B

unstated). In July decision to designate fighter **7A** and tandem-seater **7V** (from *Vyvoznoi*, a conveyance). With utmost urgency GAZ-292 assigned entirely to manufacture of both variants, and built up output rapidly enough to win plant Order of Lenin July 1942. By late 1941 fighter 7A had been replaced in production by **7B** with span restored to original value and relatively comprehensive equipment including: standard armament one ShVAK (from late 1942, MP-20) with 130 rounds, two UBS with 300 rounds, two FAB-100 or six RS-82; RSI-4 radio, RPK-10 radio compass, full blind-flying panel, nav lights, landing light (left LE, also on some late Yak-1s) and landing-gear position lights. Other changes in 7B included simpler main gears with straight shock strut going to outer end of axle and one-piece leg door, improved cockpit sealing, jettisonable hood (also on about half final batches of Yak-1), simpler carb-air inlets flush with wing-root fairing, improved ventilation (especially of gun gases) around engine by small inlets behind spinner and twin side louvres ahead of firewall, and provision behind cockpit (where instructor sat in 7V) for cargo, ground crew or 100-lit auxiliary tank. This increased weight to 3040 kg, reducing performance and agility even with PF engine and VISh-105SV prop, but still adequate and a much tougher and better aircraft in front line than Yak-1 (or, said Suprun, any other available fighter).

Production of Yak-7 continued until first quarter 1943. As far as possible B and V were made identical, but weight of evidence is that V continued to use long-span wing, which had same area as original because of pointed tips. OKB and various field organizations designed retractable skis for Yak-7 but these seldom seen. In contrast, significant proportion of 7V were built with simple fixed main gears (essentially regular gear with mechanism and fairings removed, and with bay skinned over) with interchangeable wheels/skis. Most of these did not go to schools but were used as transport/liaison aircraft. All had provision for dual control, but rear (instructor) cockpit stick easily unclipped and seat removed. Total deliveries of series versions 6399, of which about 5000 were 7B. Experimental versions are described separately.

DIMENSIONS Span (UTI-26, Yak-7, 7V) 10,25 m (33 ft 7½ in), (7B) 10,0 m (32 ft 9⅔ in); length (all series variants) 8475 mm (27 ft 9⅔ in); wing area (both spans) 17,15 m^2 (184·6 ft^2).

ENGINE (UTI, 7, 7A) one 1050 hp VK-105P, (7B) 1180 or 1240 hp VK-105PF, (7V) P or, more often, PF.

WEIGHTS Empty (UTI) 2464 kg (5432 lb), (7,A) 2518 (5551), (7B) 2480 (5467), (7V) 2330 (5137); fuel/oil (usual) 305 + 35 kg; loaded (UTI) 2750 kg (6063 lb), (7,A) 2895 (6382), (B) 3040 (6702), (V) 3050 (6724).

PERFORMANCE Max speed (UTI) 500 km/h (311 mph) at SL, 586 (364) at 4,6 km, (7,A) 540 at SL, 593 (368) at 3 km, (B) 514 at SL, 570 (354) at 3,6 km, (V) 605 (376) at 4,2, (V, fixed gear) 502 (312) at 4,2; time to 5 km (UTI) 5·5 min, (7,A) 6·1, (B) 5·8, (V) 6·0; service ceiling (UTI) 10,7 km, (7,A) 10, (B) 9,9 (32,480 ft), (V) 9,9;

Yak-7V (fixed landing gear, canopy to both cockpits)

range (A, B) 820 km (510 miles); time 360° circle (UTI) 22 s, (others) 19 s; take-off (UTI) 340 m, (B) 430 m; landing (UTI) 750 m/125 km/h, (B) 620 m/145 km/h.

Yak-7 experimentals As with other Yaks several Yak-7 were built with metal-spar wings and at least one with all-metal wing. First of this series had wing designed after meeting with Polikarpov on I-185 in 1941 and drew on that OKB's experience. According to OKB span 10,0 m, despite some reports (eg, Jiří Bašný) 9,74. Both spars machined D1 webs and T or L booms of 30KhGSA; rest of structure wood, with ply/fabric covering. Test wing made January 1942 and several wings followed, averaging 481 kg compared with 560 for all-wood wing. Except for first all took advantage of greater internal volume to increase fuel tankage to 665 lit, leading to designation **Yak-7D** (*Dalnost*). By late 1942 several further pre-production aircraft built with Yak-1B type canopy and designation **Yak-7DI** (*Dalnii Istrebitel*, long-range fighter) with one ShVAK and one UBS and range over 1000 km. These became first Yak-9, where data appear.

In conformity with policy of providing alternative engine sources one Yak-7 earmarked for conversion to M-82 engine first half 1941. Major rebuild but no designation known except **Yak-7M-82**. New short-span wing closely similar in plan to I-30 but wooden structure and no separate centre section; same plan form later adopted with metal spars for Yak-9. Like I-30 heavy armament with 20 mm ShVAK in each wing immediately outboard of main gears; also one UBS on left side of fuselage just above wing firing through blast channel in cowl. Largely redesigned fuselage with new steel main truss of much greater width at front, built up to circular section matching engine and accommodating extra fuel tank more than making up for loss of wing fuel caused by cannon. Shvetsov KB assisted with engine installation with complete regulation of airflow, oil cooler in duct between wheel bays and (according to latest Soviet drawing) all exhausts grouped into single pipe each side. Canopy and rear fuselage as Yak-1B, fixed tailwheel, landing light between left cannon and slat. First flight by Fedrovi 28 February 1942; testing dragged on for succession of reasons, and success of La-5 gradually caused loss of interest.

Mid-war (early 1943) production Yak-7B was completed with Shchyerbakov GK (pressure cabin) and extensively flown with complete success; no point in series production in view of modest flight performance but useful data. **Yak-7T** designation covered at least two 7B modified with heavy anti-armour guns, one having NS-37 and another poss (not confirmed) having NS-45. These installations of early 1943 preceded and assisted Yak-9T. **Yak-7K** (*Kuryeskii* or *Kur'yer*, courier) was 1944 VIP transport with comfortable passenger cockpit at rear delivered to VVS order; several 7K field conversions.

Yak-7PVRD was one (poss two) series 7V modified at MAI 1944 as instrumented testbed for DM-4C ramjet, one of latter being mounted on short pylon beneath each wing with reduced-span aileron and flap. Few changes to fuel system, ramjets burned regular 100-octane; start/ignition and throttle controls in front cockpit but test controls and instruments, and ciné camera, in rear cockpit. Max speed increase said to be 90 km/h. Another Yak-7B fitted late 1944 with Glushko ZhRD (rocket), flown 1945 by V.L. Rastorguev but not as extensively as Yak-3R and La-7R. Data are for Yak-7/M-82.

DIMENSIONS Span 9,74 m (31 ft 11½ in); length 8,17 m (26 ft 9⅔ in); wing area 17,15 m^2 (measured from drawing, 17,05 m^2, 183·5 ft^2).
ENGINE One 1330/1700 hp M-82.
WEIGHTS Empty 2555 kg (5633 lb); fuel/oil 480 + 48 kg; loaded 3230 kg (7121 lb).
PERFORMANCE Max speed 515 km/h (320 mph) at SL, 571 (355) at 2650 m; time to 5 km, 5·5 min; service ceiling 10,4 km (34,100 ft); range 960 km (600 miles); time 360° circle 18 s.

Yak-9 Partly by chance Yak fighter family in 1940–1941 split into two basic series, one (1M leading to 3) ultralight for close combat, and another (7DI leading to 9) introducing metal construction to wing to increase capacity for fuel for greater range. Though always short on firepower by most standards, Yak-9 soon became by far most important fighter on all Soviet fronts, by 1944 outnumbering all others combined and remaining in production after the war.

Original Yak-9 entered production mid-1942 as refined derivative of Yak-7DI. External changes included slightly larger rudder with more vertical hinge axis, improved profiles to oil and coolant radiator ducts, and standardization on simple TE trim tabs on ailerons, bent by pliers. Wing span 10,0 m as before but metal spars. Front spar two flanged girders back-to-back, rear single, all with D1 plate webs and 30KhGSA flanged booms. Section modified Clark-YH, 16% at root. Total 38 ribs, wood except D1 between spars at four (main gear/root) locations; wooden stringers and ply skin of 8, 4 and 3 mm thickness overlain with doped varnished fabric. Nitrocellulose dope caused trouble in spring 1943 with first fabric and then ply peeling off Siberian wings (story of designer carpeted by Stalin) and in recent histories, including by Yak himself, put down to water-porosity of imported dope. Ailerons fully balanced with inset hinges, D1 with fabric over D1 LE. Split (Schrenk modified) flaps all D1 structure (different from Yak-1, Yak-7) with pneumatic actuation to 55°. Main gears as 7DI, tyres 650 × 220 mm, pneumatic retraction and drum brakes. Fully retractable tailwheel with 300 × 125 mm tyre. Fuselage truss 30KhGSA with D1 secondary formers carrying D1 cowl and access panels ahead of cabin, ply sides to mid fuselage and wood formers and stringers aft with ply top skin and fabric overall. Tail mainly wood fixed surfaces, D1/fabric movable with inset hinges, mass balance and (elevators) mid-span aerodynamic balance. Initial engine VK-105PF or PF-1 with 3,0 m VISh-61P (139 kg) prop, compressed-air starting, exhaust usual 1-2-2-1 stubs. Fuel 480 lit (105·6 gal) in four protected rubber/fabric tanks between spars, later with mid-fuselage tank added. Oil 48 kg behind engine. Main radiator 0,19 m^2 under wing as in Yak-7DI, oil cooler 0,07 m^2 in duct under engine. Usual armament one ShVAK or MP-20 with 120 rounds and one UBS with 200 rounds (in some Yak-9 two UBS with 150 each). Structural provision for two FAB-100 or six RS-82 under wings, seldom used. Normal equipment full blind-flying panel, RSI-6 transmitter and RSI-4 receiver with vertical mast behind canopy and one/two wires to fin, GS-10-350 or GS-650 DC generator and engine-driven air compressor. Gun cocking electro-pneumatic.

First series Yak-9s came off line at GAZ-292 about October 1942, soon followed by GAZ-153 and GAZ-286; except for specialized Yak-3 and experimental aircraft Yak-9 was by spring 1943 only Yak fighter. In action at Stalingrad late November 1942 and over whole front by February 1943. By latter month most factories had switched to new wing with D1 ribs throughout, reduced span and blunt tip (same area). By April 1943 usual engine was PF-3 driving VISh-105S or VISh-105SV prop. More than 15 OKB or field variations in armament followed including three ShVAK or MP-20 (two in wings) and every available heavier-calibre gun including NS-37, OKB-16-37, 11P-37, NS-45, T-111P, VYa-23 and MP-23. Most armament schemes did not change designation though there are numerous Soviet references to standard model with two UBS being designated **Yak-9M** (*Modifikatsirovannyi*), designation also applied to post-war Polish dual trainer variant.

First major production variant May 1943 was **9D** (*Dalnostnyi*, long-distance) with two extra unprotected tanks between spars in outer wings increasing capacity to 670 lit, plus optional supplementary tank under cockpit giving total

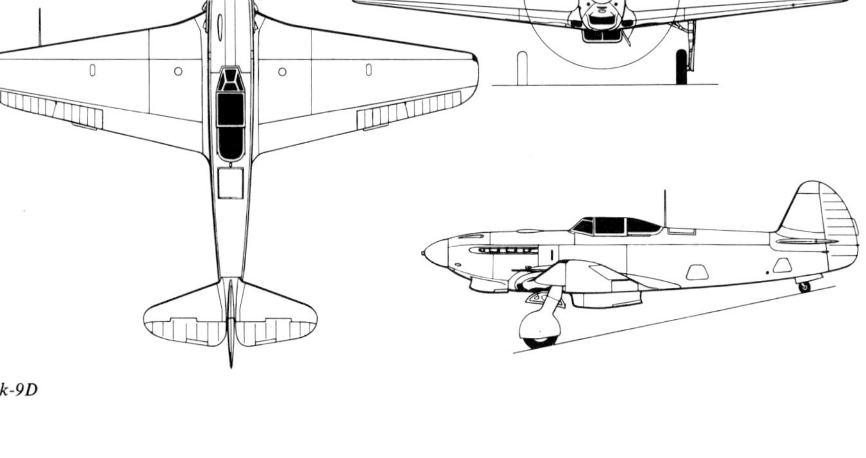

Yak-9D

880 lit. Larger mod resulted in **Yak-9T** (*Tankovyi*) with armament designed for attacking armour. First 9T on test December 1942 with 11P-37 gun firing through prop with 30 rounds and two UBS with 110 each. All these big-gun aircraft had cockpit and firewall moved back 400 mm to preserve CG and allow for length of gun. Barrel projected from spinner (included in length in data). Most had wing racks for boxes of PTAB-2,5 bomblets. Other aircraft with this designation had one MP-20 with AP ammo and one or two UBS, one VYa-23 and one UBS, or one MP-23-VV and one UBS. Fuel capacity reduced to 360 lit. Closely related variant, also 1943, was **Yak-9K** (*Krupnokalibernyi*, heavy calibre) or Yak-9-45, with OKB-16-45 with 15 rounds; all T and K were built in small numbers and proved successful against PzKW VI tank and also with HE rounds as destroyers of bombers. One K tested with OKB-16-57 gun was not so successful; even with 45 mm recoil of each shot was frightening.

Yak-9B another short-run variant and heaviest of all wartime Yak fighters. Designation from *Bombardirovshchik*, provided with internal bomb bay behind cockpit carrying four FAB-100 at 80° nose-up inclination, alternatively up to 128 PTAB-1,5 or 2,5. Usual armament one ShVAK and one UBS, but some had only UBS (through prop); first tested March 1943 and generally successful when well flown (Yak was averse to any external bombs or drop tanks). **Yak-9MPVO**, also called **Yak-9PVO** (designation from MPVO defence organization), built in small numbers for night interception with FS-55 searchlight/landing light in left leading edge and RPK-10 radio compass in rear fuselage, often under transparent dorsal hatch.

Second-generation Yak-9 was developed mid-1943 as **Yak-9U** (*Uluchshyennyi*, improved), replacing original in production autumn 1944. First 9U flown December 1943 with original engine (but an experimental version had VK-107U listed) and differed mainly in thorough revision of airframe to reduce drag. Apart from improvement to canopy, rear fairing and upper rear fuselage, major changes included fuselage ply skin 3 mm instead of 2, modified wing with D1 ribs and rounded tip of greater span and area, relocation of wing 100 mm further forward (on aircraft with VK-107 engine), and complete redesign of cooling systems. Main radiator enlarged to 0,24 m² in internally profiled duct moved back aft of wing to preserve CG and reduce drag. Two new enlarged oval inlets in wing root LE, that on left serving new-matrix oil cooler inside fuselage between spars exhausting via flat nozzle (giving propulsive thrust) under wing just on left of main-radiator inlet, and right inlet serving carburettor. Engine exhausts row of six equal ejector pipes each side. Basic four-tank fuel system increased in capacity from 318 to 355 kg and oil from 26 to 35; even with original engine conferred a substantial gain in all-round performance when entered service about June 1944. VK-107A at last cleared for production late August 1944 and fitted to 9U (no change in designation) from late autumn driving 3,1 m VISh-107LO prop; usual armament one MP-20 with 120 rounds and two UBS with 170 each. Apart from modest firepower an outstanding fighter. A variant, **Yak-9P** (*Pushyechnyi*, cannon), replaced UBS by one (or, according to recent accounts, two) synchronized ShVAK or MP-20, giving up to three cannon in fuselage to keep abreast of rival La. Shavrov reports this variant had extended-span wing, and offers what appear to be nonsensical figures (not repeated in data here) for record climb (3·6 min to 5 km) and altitude (11,9 km) for variant despite use of VK-105 engine and gross wt 3170 kg, appreciably heavier than normal 9U.

Third series variant of 9U was **Yak-9R** (*Razvyedchik*), also sometimes called **9F** (*Fotorazvyedchik*) or even **UF** for tactical-reconnaissance and survey. Small series delivered 1944 and in various Warsaw Pact forces in 1950s.

Final wartime production introduced modified airframe with D1 flush-riveted stressed skin throughout, retaining steel fuselage truss. This

Yak-9DD at Bari, Italy

Yak-9U (post war, Polish)

Yak-9K (45mm gun in 9U airframe, no production)

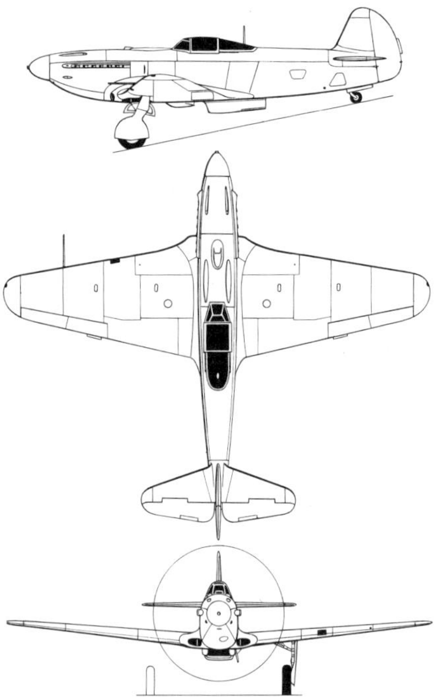

Yak-9U

followed prolonged structural research and could have led to further major improvement in fuel capacity, but Yak lost interest in piston fighters by 1945. Not mentioned by Shavrov, metal-skinned two-seat **Yak-9UT** (designation *Uchyebno-Trenirovochnyi*, trainer) came into production early 1945, few built. Last few **Yak-9UV** (*Uchyebno Vyvoznoi*, training conveyance) were also metal-skinned, but most UV were merely tandem (usually not dual) variant of U, normally with 105PF-2 engine and original wood/fabric skin.

Production of Yak-9 ceased late August 1945 at recorded 16,769, of which over 3900 were of U and derived versions. Post-war there were many local mods and national (eg, Polish, Bulgarian) versions. A common mod was to fit RPK-10 radio compass as in wartime MPVO, Western (not Soviet) writers calling this Yak-9P (from *Perekhvatchik*, interceptor); not a Soviet designation and not known by OKB.

DIMENSIONS Span (early) 10,0 m, (production 1942–1944) 9,74 m (31 ft 11½ in), (9U and variants) 9,77 m (32 ft 0⅝ in), (P) 10,35 m (33 ft 11½ in); length (7DI) 8,55 m, (9) 8,50 m (27 ft 10⅝ in), (9T) 8,52/8,65, (K) 8,87 m (29 ft 1¼ in), (U and variants) 8,55 (28 ft 0⅝ in), (P) 8,71; wing area (most) 17,15 m² (184·6 ft²), (U and variants) 17,25 (185·7), (P) 17,3 (186·2).

ENGINE (early) one 1180 hp VK-105PF, (1943) 1240 hp PF-2 or PF-3, (U and variants from September 1944) 1650 hp VK-107A.

WEIGHTS Empty (7DI) 2360 kg, (early 9) 2200 kg (4850 lb), (9D) 2770 kg (6107 lb), (DD) 2801 kg (6175 lb), (T) 2750 kg (6063 lb), (U) 2575 kg (5677 lb), (P) 2280 kg (5026 lb); fuel/oil (9) 326 + 48 kg, (D) 590 + 48, (DD) 630 + 56, (T) 260 + 26, (U) 355 + 35; loaded (DI) 3035 kg, (9) 2875 kg (6338 lb), (D) 3115 kg (6867 lb), (DD) 3300 kg (7275 lb), (B) 3460 kg (7628 lb), (T) 3060 kg (6746 lb), (U, 105PF) 2900 kg (6393 lb), (U, 107A) 3098 kg (6830 lb), (P) 3170 kg (6989 lb).

PERFORMANCE Max speed (I) 505 km/h at SL, 560 (348 mph) at 4 km, (9) 533 (331) at SL, 597 (371) at 4 km, (D) 540 (336) at SL, 600 (373) at 3 km, (T) 532 (330·5) at SL, 593 (368) at 3 km, (K) 516 (321) at SL, 573 (356) at 4 km, (U, 105PF) 558 (347) at SL, 620 (385) at 4 km, (U, 107A) 610 (379) at SL, 698 (434) at 5 km, (P) 668 (415) at 5 km; time to 5 km (DI) 6·1 min, (9) 4·9, (9, 42) 5·5, (D) 6·1, (K) 5·7, (U, 105PF) 4·8, (U, 107A) 3·8, (P) 3·6; service ceiling (DI, 9, D, T) 10 km (32,800 ft), (B) 8850, (K) 9,0, (U, 105PF) 10,4, (U, 107A) 11,9 (39,000), (P) 12,2; range (DI) 1000 km, (9) 800 (500), (D) 1330 (826), (DD) max on test 2300 (1429), (T) 780 (485), (K) 595 (370), (U) 870 (540); time 360° (typical) 18 s; take-off (typical) 370 m, (B) 1335, (U) 380; landing (typical) 550/135 km/h, (T, K) 450/140, (U) 535/140.

Yak-9 experimentals Impossible to cover all field and even OKB variants but no Yak-9 known with ramjets, rocket or pressure cabin. Skis rare, and planned twin-float version not built. One of first significant variants was 9/106 flown October 1942 with M-106 engine with single-stage supercharger (take-off rating 1350 hp) and used to help Klimov engine KB until engine abandoned. **Yak-9M** is used in some accounts to describe versions other than that generally accepted for production series. **Yak-9K** said by OKB and Shavrov to be experimental bomber very similar to Yak-9B; said by Bašný, Green and others to be lightweight (*Lyegkii*) high-altitude version with M-105RD (author believes error for PD) with two-stage supercharger and only one UBS and one ShKAS and 365 lit fuel, poor performance.

More important high-altitude prototype was **Yak-9PD**, which picked up in late 1942 where Yak No 28 (see Yak-1 experimentals) left off. Designation from VK-105PD engine with Dollezhal two-stage gear-driven supercharger and high-altitude ignition and other changed features. Unlike I-28, Yak-9PD had Yak-9 airframe (with late-model 9,77 m wing instead of short-span wing with slats, curious choice for this model). Distinguished by extremely deep rad and oil cooler ducts, modified cowl profile and no guns above, just one 20 mm (ShVAK, then MP) (Shavrov says one UBS). Flown on factory test by I. Shuneiko from spring 1943; in July assigned to intercept high-flying German reconnaissance aircraft in Moscow area, flown by Guards Lt L. Samokhvalov with fair results even at high angle of attack near ceiling. Believed several PD built and tuned to reach 14,5 km (47,570 ft) later in 1943.

Another 1943 entrée was the **Yak-9U/107U**, fitted with a Klimov experimental engine rated at 1875 hp and driving special VISh-107 prop with broader than usual blades. Problems with weight and CG position, overheating of cockpit and peeling of wing skin at high speed. Engine not reliable enough. **Yak-9R** (*Razvyedchik*) and **9F** (*Foto*) designations also applied to experimental reconnaissance variants and small-run production types, some having large oblique camera behind cockpit. **Yak-9 Kur'yer** (*Courier*) was sleek unarmed liaison aircraft modified from original series production; at least two built and flown with pilot/cargo, pilot/passenger, pilot/two passengers.

DIMENSIONS Except PD, above were all as Yak-9 with 9,74 m wing; Kur'yer had fuselage of original length.

ENGINE See text.

WEIGHTS Loaded (PD) 2745 kg (6052 lb), (9U/107U) 3400 kg (7496 lb).

PERFORMANCE Max speed (PD) 690 km/h (429 mph) at 9 km, (U/107U) 720 (447) at 5 km; service ceiling (PD) about 14 km, (107U) given by Shavrov as only 8 km, surely error?

Yak-3 Possibly the most agile monoplane of the Second World War, this short-range dogfighter resulted from late-1941 VVS requirement for best fighter for close combat at low/medium heights over the battlefront. No OKB numbers known; like Yak-9 these never published but in range 31 to about 45. Project started late 1941, objective being smallest, lightest and lowest-drag aircraft to use M-107 engine and carry armament of one ShVAK and one UBS. Konstantin Sinelshchikov managed this programme as well as light-Yak (Yak-1M) but in 1942 priority was on quantity; next-generation fighter, already assigned Yak-3 designation (which had been used already for I-30), was shelved for over a year. This was unfortunate, as M-107 was delayed even longer and M-105 could not achieve desired ratio of power to weight. Yak-3 held in abeyance until restarted under O.K. Antonov August 1943. Thus La-5 remained sole Soviet air-superiority aircraft with high power/weight ratio until Yak-3 became available in mid-1944 (a year later than said in many Western histories).

At outset of Yak-3 work in October 1941 decision had been taken to use smaller wing, of 9,2 m span, 14,85 m² area and 14% thick on centreline chord of 1,8 m, aileron and flap areas being 1,0 and 2,6 m². Wing of this design completed early 1942 but believed not flown until late in year, on modified Yak-1M. This aircraft had cut-down rear fuselage and rear-view can-

Yak-9U captured in Korea

opy of Yak-1B, fully retractable tailwheel, new streamlined radiator installation with long duct aft of wing, more streamlined oil cooler installation under engine and low-drag frameless windscreen. Designation of this aircraft not known, nor that of propeller with three broad blades with root cuffs. Tested by S.N. Anokhin late 1942, later also by Yumashyev, with results beyond expectation. Further refinement actually increased empty weight slightly but continued to reduce drag, chief alteration being replacement of oil cooler by twin parallel oil radiators inside wing between spars inboard of root, served by symmetric enlarged wing-root inlets and discharging via ejectors under centre-section lower skin. Inboard end of each wing-root inlet continued as before to feed supercharger. Main gears had leg fork on inner side of wheel, unlike Yak-7 and Yak-9. Wheel-well doors added hinged near centreline, wing and tailplane roots further improved in profile, radio mast eliminated and engine given six equi-spaced ejector exhausts each side. VK-105PF-2 was rather more powerful than PF used in Yak-1M and 7B, but substantially below power of VK-107 or engines of German fighters. Even more sparsely equipped than other Yaks, with single HF channel, no cockpit trimmers or landing-gear indicators, no heating, and fuel gauges on wing tanks themselves.

Soviet records on development of Yak-3 are sparse, but first prototype listed as Yak-3 flew in 1943, Western accounts incorrectly saying early in year. Common Western statement that flight trials complete by April 1943 cannot be true; first Yak-3 was not received for NII testing until 3 March 1944, and aircraft not cleared for production until June. First unit was 91st Regt equipped 16 July 1944. One reason for further delay was catastrophic failure of left wing during

Yak-3

snap roll, causing Sergei Anokhin to lose eye and suffer other injuries; but according to Yak, Anokhin 'went up and *deliberately* [author's italics] destroyed the plane in the air, providing valuable data ...' After long recuperation he returned to OKB in jet era as chief test pilot.

Once cleared for production – tragically, about two years later than could have been achieved – Yak-3 was built with remarkable speed by GAZ-286, GAZ-115 and GAZ-124, the latter a reopened facility in Moscow area. Deliveries 21 in July 1944 but reached over 100 in August and by termination at end May 1945 had reached an official total of 4848. This brought final total of wartime Yak single-engined fighters, exclusive of experimental models, to 36,737. Yak-3 was outstanding in ease and precision of control, rate of roll, turning circle (see data) and manoeuvres in vertical plane. Vital fact, heavily stressed by Soviet historians, is that it outmanoeuvred Bf 109G and Fw 190A, especially at heights below 6 km (20,000 ft). French Normandie-Niémen regt unanimously selected it in preference to any other Allied fighter in late summer 1944 (unit returned with 42 aircraft to France in 1945). Extensive combat history of Yak-3's brief operational life is full of remarkable ascendancy over a depleted Luftwaffe.

Throughout 1943 Klimov worked to release VK-107A but this did not fly in a Yak-3 until 1944. Though small number of series aircraft were produced with this engine it is dealt with as experimental version. Several VK-107A-powered Yak-3s were used for test programmes in 1944–1945, at least one having two B-20 guns above engine, but this armament remained experimental. Improved wing with 30KhGSA spar booms and D1 webs and ribs, but ply/fabric skin, introduced late 1944 to some aircraft (possibly one GAZ only); no designation known. Other Yak-3s are covered in experimental variants which follow.

DIMENSIONS Span 9,20 m (30 ft 2¼ in); length 8,49 m (27 ft 10¼ in); wing area 14,85 m² (160 ft²).

ENGINE One 1240/1300 hp VK-105PF-2.

WEIGHTS Empty (typical) 2105 kg (4641 lb); fuel/oil 275 + 30 kg; loaded 2660 kg (5864 lb).

PERFORMANCE Max speed 570 (354 mph) at SL, 660 km/h (410 mph) at 3,2 km, 651 km/h (405 mph) at 4 km; initial climb 19,3 m/s (3800 ft/min); time to 5 km, 4·1 min; service ceiling 11,8 km (38,715 ft); range 710 km (440 miles); time for 360° circle 18·7 s; take-off 290 m; landing 480 m/144 km/h (89·5 mph).

Yak-3 experimentals By far most important were numerous (around 50) aircraft fitted with VK-107A engine from about August 1944 on-

Modified Yak-1M used as Yak-3 development aircraft

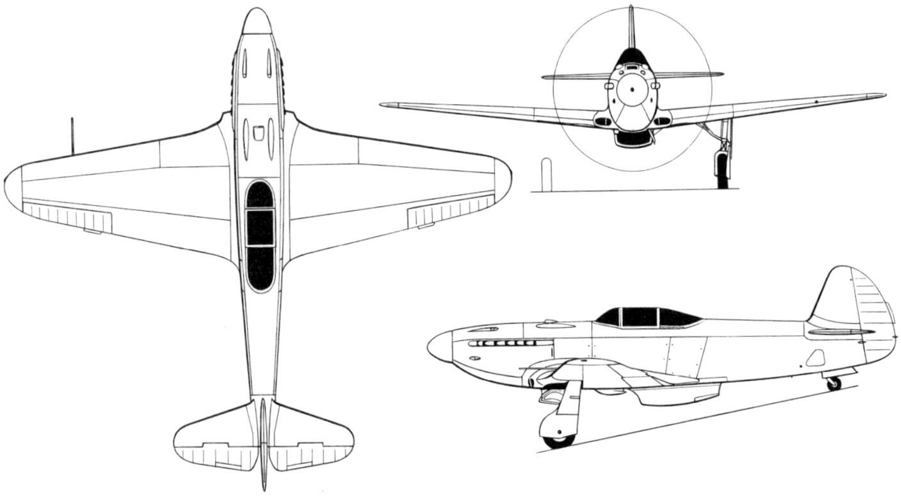

Yak-3/VK-107A

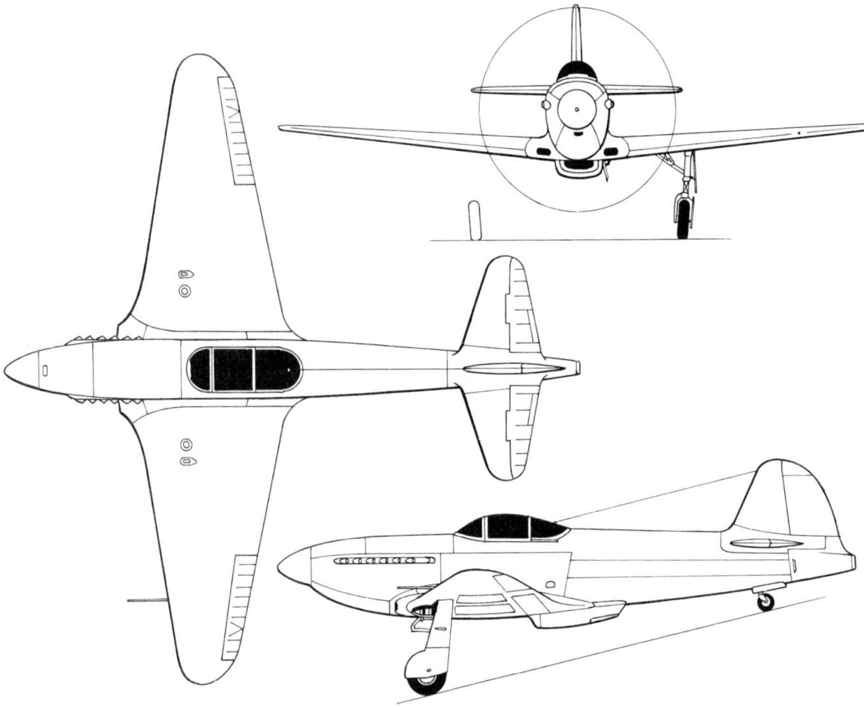

Yak-3RD

wards. This engine was still unreliable (Shavrov ascribes trouble to excessive boost pressure) and never cleared for full production in this installation. Yak-3 with this engine was fractionally longer, had cockpit moved 320 mm aft to preserve CG, radiator increased in size to 0,26 m² in deeper duct and, usually, propeller with broader blades. Several aircraft with this engine featured redesigned airframe with all light-alloy stressed-skin covering (though retaining original steel-tube fuselage truss). Another Yak-3 was fastest of all piston-engined Yak fighters, with VK-108 engine. Designated variously Yak-3/VK-108 and **Yak-3B/108**, it was designed from 1 August 1944, completed 7 October and flown by V.L. Rastorguev 19 December. Armament one NS-23 with 60 rounds, but any of the other schemes could have been installed. With this gun fitted, climb to 5 km in 3·5 min was exceptional for a piston-engined fighter. Speed given in data reached 21 December 1944.

Yak-3T (*Tankovyi*, as in Yak-9T) was anti-tank aircraft with 37 mm N-37 and two synchronized B-20S. One Yak-3T had 57 mm (OKB-16-57) installed; this made just one flight, by A.B. Yumashyev.

Yak-3P (*Pushyechnyi*, cannon) had heavier air-combat armament of three B-20 (two in wings) and two UBS; this was considered most formidable air-combat fighter of the war by VVS historians. **Yak-3R** or **Yak-3RD** was single Yak-3 off production line (one of first) set aside in May 1944 for rocket installation. Glushko RD-1 (KhZ) installed in modified tail end of fuselage projecting behind cut-away rudder, with acid-kerosene tanks under and behind cockpit, kerosene on left. Flight test by Rastorguev showed performance beyond design limits of aircraft (speed 801 km/h while in shallow climb) but numerous problems. On second flight kerosene tank burst. On third, 16 August 1944, rocket system exploded in flight; Rastorguev, who hated this aircraft, was killed. (As same pilot flew VK-108 Yak-3 in December 1944 there is error here; author suggests Yak-3R blew up 16 August 1945?)

Though aerodynamics were matched to low/medium heights, Yak-3 was so good attempts were made to develop high-altitude variants. OKB has record of **Yak-3V** with span extended beyond that of other fighters (11 m); no record of prototype being built. **Yak-3PD** was high-altitude one-off powered by experimental VK-106; described as fighter-interceptor, may have had pressure cabin, armament not recorded but flew 1944. Found only in Western accounts, **Yak-3TK** said to have turbocharged engine; not seen in photos and aircraft pictured in West as being TK is in fact VK-108 prototype. (Turbocharged aircraft would not have normal stub exhausts.)

Perhaps most attractive and successful experimental variant was **Yak-3U** (*Uluchshyennyi*, improved), built over relatively long period 1944–1945 and one of best installations of ASh-82FN radial engine. OKB almost started from scratch, whilst using basic wing and fuselage truss of series aircraft, and many fundamental dimensions differed. Truss was wider, to match broader engine, and fuselage was all-metal stressed skin (though of course different from other stressed-skin Yak-3s). Wing retained basically wooden structure but span increased 100 mm each tip. Oil coolers remained hidden in centre section, but ejector outlets made flush with underskin; supercharger inlets at inner end of wing-root inlets as before. Whole installation and fuselage sealed, with exhausts grouped at sides inside variable cooling-air exit flap. Twin B-20 guns above (one report states NS-23). Cockpit not pressurized and radio mast added. Such was care taken that, despite massive engine, empty weight about 200 kg less than series machine. First flight 12 May 1945 by Fedrovi who handled entire programme of several tens of flights. Best combat manoeuvrability of any known fighter and considerably faster than series Yak-3 at all heights, but regarded in 1945 as obsolescent in concept.

Final variant was **Yak-3UTI** intermediate trainer with low-powered ASh-21 engine and tandem cockpits. This is described under Yak-11.

DIMENSIONS Span 9,2 m as Yak-3 except (Yak-3U) 9,4 m (30 ft 10 in); length 8,48 m as Yak-3 except (VK-108) 8,50 (27 ft 10¾ in), (3U) 8,36 (27 ft 5⅛ in); wing area, 14,85 as Yak-3 except Yak-3U slightly greater (figure not recorded).

ENGINE See text.

WEIGHTS Empty, not known; fuel/oil (most) 275 + 30 kg, (107A, 108A) 350 + 35, (RD) 200 + 25 plus unknown acid/kerosene; loaded (107A) 2984 kg (6578 lb), (106) 2935 kg (6470 lb), (108) 2830 kg (6239 lb), (3RD) 2915 kg (6426 lb), (3U) 2790 kg (6151 lb).

PERFORMANCE Max speed at SL (107A) 610 km/h (379 mph), (106) not known, (108) 625 (388), (RD) not applicable, (3U) 620 (385); max speed at height (107A) 720 (447) at 6 km, (106) not known, (108) 745 (463) at 6 km, (RD) 801 (498) (Western accounts, 820, 509·5) at 7,8; (3U) 710 (441) at 6,1 km; time to 5 km (107A) 3·9 min, (108) 3·5, (RD) est 3·5, (3U) 3·8; service ceiling

(107A) 11,8 km (38,700 ft), (106) 12,0, (108) 12,2, (RD) est 15, (3U) 11,5 (Něměcek, 11,0); range (107A) 1600 km (994 miles), (RD) about 500 (311), (3U) 710 (441); time 360° circle (107A) 18 s, (3U) 17 s; landing (107A) 500 m/145 km/h, (3U) 400 m/136 km/h.

Yak-5, UT-2L has been described in section on UT-2 as major redesign of late 1943 to bring trainer closer in technique and equipment to fighters by adding flaps, brakes and enclosed cockpit. At same time OKB took it upon itself to go one step further and designed (Yak himself led team) single-seat advanced trainer with retractable landing gear and gun. By this time Yak no longer published original OKB numbers and assigned new series carrying on from VVS designations for wartime fighters, so single-seater became Yak-5 (it was also assigned one of earlier OKB numbers, probably in 50s); Yakovlev used all available numbers, even, as here, assigning odd numbers to aircraft other than fighters. Airframe almost identical to UT-2L apart from elimination of front cockpit; remaining cockpit in same place as instructor in UT-2L. This left room for considerable fuel, but not utilized; tankage was minimal, just 43 lit in centre section on each side with usual wing-mounted gauges. Radio fitted, same RSI-4/-6 as fighters with wire but no mast. Same manual landing flap under centre section as UT-2L. Main gears with air/oil shock struts attached to inner ends of axles carrying braked wheels with 500 × 125 mm tyres, manually (later pneumatically) retracted backwards leaving wheels part-exposed. PBP reflector sight for single ShKAS on left of top decking with muzzle near left of helmet for top cylinder. Engine installation as UT-2L but driving VISh-237 variable-pitch prop. Castoring tailwheel 200 × 80 mm.

Yak-5 began flight test September 1944 and showed outstanding handling. Could fly rings round any UT-2, and reason for landing speed higher than UT-2L (47 mph, 75 km/h) not understood. Unfortunately Yak-5 suffered primary structural failure during barrel roll, attributed to poor quality wood. In any case VVS decided next generation of trainers should be of basically metal construction.

DIMENSIONS Span 10,5 m (34 ft 5⅓ in); length 7,32 m (24 ft 2 in); wing area not known but about 16,9 m² (182 ft²).

ENGINE One 115 hp M-11D (often reported as 145 hp).

WEIGHTS Empty 770 kg (1698 lb); fuel/oil 62 + 8 kg; loaded 940 kg (2072 lb).

PERFORMANCE Max speed 250 km/h (155 mph) at SL; no data on climb or ceiling; range 450 km (280 miles); landing speed 85 km/h (53 mph).

Yak-6 in front line. Hucks starter at extreme left

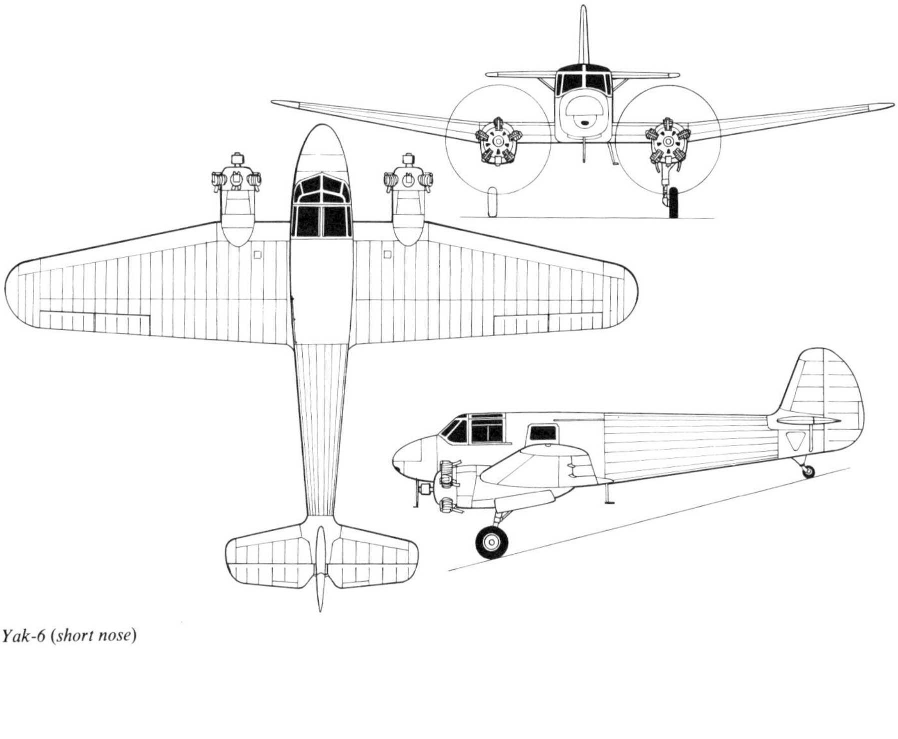

Yak-6 (short nose)

Yak-6, NBB This aircraft was designed by Yak himself in second half 1941 as simple utility aircraft, making minimal demands on constructors or users, to serve as NBB (*Nochnoi Blizhnii Bombardirovshchik*, night short-range bomber) and multi-role transport, an improved successor to Po-2. Hoped to carry 1 t bombs using two 190 hp M-12 engines but unavailability of these resulted in fall back on lower-power M-11F. Despite this, simplicity of aircraft resulted in production decision.

Basic structure wood with some fabric covering. Wing of Clark-YH section, max t/c (at outer end centre section) 16·8%. Centre section tapered on TE only, dihedral 0°; outer panels fully tapered, dihedral 8°. Two box spars, ply ribs, ply skin over LE back to front spar, fabric elsewhere. Slotted wood/fabric ailerons each hung on three brackets well below surface, driven by bellcranks and levers pivoted to top of aileron spar. Single dural flap across centre section, perforated Schrenk type, manually actuated by transverse rods and pivoted links driven from cockpit handwheel. Fuselage a rounded box with four longerons. Wing had light stringers (10 forward of wing TE, 22 aft) and 10 transverse frames, with glued *shpon* nose, ply skin forming semi-monocoque ahead of TE and fabric aft. Tail wood/fabric with ply skin LE to front spar, tailplane with variable incidence on prototype only, pilot-actuated trimmers on rudder and elevators. Welded steel-tube nacelle trusses with dural skin extended forward to enclose crankcase and form small baffles round cylinder barrels; installation made from same drawings as UT-2 with same carb-air heating by two lower cylinder exhausts. Drum oil tank in nacelle, 195 lit (42·9 gal) dural fuel tank in each side of centre section between spars. Two-blade fixed-pitch 2,2 m wooden props. Prototype built with main landing gears each with single air/oil shock strut with pinned side braces, welded to inner end of axle carrying pneu-braked wheel with 600 × 180 mm tyre, retracted to rear by crank-arm to sliding trunnion driven by cables to handwheel in cockpit. Sprung castoring tailwheel, 255 × 110 mm.

Prototype completed as NBB with enclosed cockpit for two with dual pedals and control-column fittings but spectacles yoke not fitted on right side. Rear cabin with roof hatch (left/right halves folding inwards) and pintle for ShKAS with satchels for eight ammo drums on walls. Five racks under centre section for FAB-100 or Der containers from 50 to 250 kg, max total load 500 kg (1102 lb). Windmill generator on right side of fuselage, 12A-30 battery, RSI-3/4 radio and D/F loop under nose. First flight about June

1942, completed NII tests September 1942 and cleared for production with modifications including improved outer panels, reduced dihedral, wing-root fillets, larger ailerons, main cabin equipped for transport with seats for four passengers (door on left) or 500 kg (1102 lb) cargo load (loaded through large hatch on right). Except for first few, production Yak-6 had simple fixed main gear with bay sealed by detachable dural doors. Though of low performance, about 1000 built and used with great effect in front line, both as transport and as close-support and night attack aircraft with various arrangements of pilot-aimed bombs and up to ten RS-82 rockets under outer wings. Said to have acquired popular name *Dyerevyannyi Duglas* (wooden Douglas, ie, small partner of Li-2). Standard utility transport of VVS regiments 1944–1950. Known with glider hook, skis, photo-survey gear and ambulance conversion; not seen on floats.

At least one VVS Yak-6 known as **Yak-6 Modifikatsirovannyi** (not as Yak-6M) with TsAGI-managed aerodynamic improvements including original angle of dihedral, different outer wings with all taper on LE and more pointed tip, retractable main gears, fully cowled engines with helmets over cylinders, VISh-327 props with spinners, pitot head projecting ahead of nose instead of on strut beneath nose, variable-incidence tailplane and increased fuel/oil tankage.

DIMENSIONS Span 14,0 m (45 ft 11⅛ in); length 10,35 m (33 ft 11½ in); wing area 29,6 m² (319 ft²).

ENGINES Two 140 hp M-11F.

WEIGHTS Empty (NBB) 1368 kg (3016 lb), (6) 1415/1433 kg (max 3159 lb); fuel/oil (NBB) 250 + 28 kg, (6) 304; loaded (NBB) 2350 kg (5181 lb), (6) 2,3 t (first batch) or 2,5 t (most) (5511 lb).

PERFORMANCE Max speed (retractable gear) 230 km/h (143 mph), (fixed) (Shavrov) 183 km/h (114 mph), (Malinovskii) 211 (131); time to 1 km (NBB) 9·5 min, (6) 7·5; service ceiling (6) 3380 m (11,090 ft); endurance (Shavrov) 4 h, (Malinovskii) 6 h 40 min; range (Shavrov) 580 km (360 miles), (Malinovskii) 1140; take-off (Shavrov) 280 m, (Malinovskii) 255; landing (Shavrov) 265 m/93 km/h (58 mph), (Malinovskii) 115 m.

Yak-8 Still expecting M-12 engine to become available, small team under Antonov developed Yak-6 *Modifikatsirovannyi* into this larger aircraft in late 1943, prototype flying in VVS markings early 1944. Basic design similar and wing believed identical to predecessor. Fuselage considerably larger, because Yak-8 was dedicated transport, with no secondary roles. Max body width remained 1240 mm but external depth of fuselage increased from 1500 to 1760 mm, giving much better headroom internally, and length increased. From nose to wing TE structure strengthened with main frames built-up boxes 80 mm deep, with 2 mm ply skin throughout. Extreme nose and entire rear fuselage identical to Yak-6 Mod. Tail construction unchanged but surfaces enlarged with greater height/span and almost straight edges. Engine installations and main gears same as Yak-6 Mod, though engine slightly more powerful. Engines drove air compressor, hydraulic pump and generator, gear retraction being hydraulic. Assumed flap likewise. Brakes remained pneumatic. Tailwheel smaller, tyre 220 × 110 mm. Tankage same as Yak-6 Mod (greater than series Yak-6). Cockpit as Yak-6 Mod, main cabin with seats for six passengers with three Yak-6 size windows each side.

With end of war in sight VVS declined to adopt Yak-8 and all expectation rested on large order from GVF. Flight test programme was satisfactory but no order placed. Něměcek and others blame poor performance; OKB state this was not so, and sole reason was general belief future lay with all-metal aircraft.

DIMENSIONS Span 14,8 m (48 ft 6⅔ in); length 11,35 m (37 ft 2⅞ in); wing area 30,0 m² (323 ft²).

ENGINES Two 145 hp M-11FM (M-11M).

WEIGHTS Empty 1750 kg (3850 lb); fuel/oil 340 kg; loaded 2,7 t (5952 lb).

PERFORMANCE Max speed 248 km/h (154 mph) at SL; cruise 190 (118); time to 1 km, 6·4 min; service ceiling 3 km (9850 ft); range 730 km (454 miles); endurance 4·5 h; take-off 410 m; landing 260 m/100 km/h (62 mph).

Yak-10 (Yak-14*) Designed originally by Yak himself in 1944, this simple four-seater, originally designated Yak-14, flew in VVS markings and thus had military sponsorship. So did Yak-13 (originally called Yak-12) designed at same time, and according to V. Kondratyev these aircraft were designed specifically to facilitate direct comparison between strut-braced high-wing machine with fixed gear and cantilever low-wing aircraft with retractable gear. Shavrov goes so far as to claim Yak-10 was intended as civil transport; other writers have incorrectly called this aircraft early Yak-12.

Yak-14* was almost direct extrapolation of AIR-6, and like earlier type was of very mixed construction. Four-seat cabin fuselage built around welded truss of mild-steel tube with D1 sheet over nose, door and rear hatch, fabric elsewhere. Wing of 11% Clark-YH profile, wooden two-spar structure with ply LE and fabric elsewhere, braced by vee-struts. Tail and all control surfaces D1/fabric. Rubber-sprung main gears with neat faired legs and spats over 500 × 150 mm wheels with brakes; tailwheel 200 × 80 mm. No slats, flaps or tabs; essence of concept was simplicity for easy handling, low cost and good reliability. Yak-14* flew late 1944 and immediately showed bad qualities. Considerable tinkering with several aircraft (believed all military) ensued, designation being changed to Yak-10 early 1945. Eventually passed NII tests June 1945. Uninspired design, but 40 built and used in several versions, without spats and with improved engine installation and VISh-327 propeller. **Yak-10V** (*Vyvoznoi*, carrier) had dual control; **Yak-10S** (*Sanitarnyi*) had long hatch for loading stretcher on left side; **Yak-10G** (*Gidro*) had two AIR-6 type floats and, though it passed factory tests on completion in 1946, its performance was unacceptable. One 1946 series machine had M-11FR of 160 hp and specially designed skis (main 1930 × 340 mm, tail 460 × 120 mm; data appear under (L) for *Lyizhi*, skis. Yak-10 did not form basis of later Yak-12.

DIMENSIONS Span 12,0 m (39 ft 4½ in); length 8,45 m (27 ft 8⅔ in) (Ponomaryev, 8,9); wing area 22,0 m² (237 ft²).

ENGINES (most) one 145 hp M-11FM, (L) 160 hp M-11FR.

WEIGHTS Empty (prototype) 792 kg, (production) 822 kg (1812 lb), (L) 812 kg; fuel/oil 94 + 14 kg; loaded (prototype) 1150 kg, (production, L) both 1170 kg (2579 lb).

PERFORMANCE Max speed (prototype, production) 200 km/h (124 mph), (L) 195 (121); initial climb (production) 3,6 m/s (709 ft/min); time to 1 km (prototype) 5·5 min, (production) 6·2, (L) 9·5; service ceiling (prototype) 3,4 km, (production) 3,2 (10,500 ft), (L) 2550 m; range 365 km (227 miles), (L) 350; take-off (prototype) 260 m, (production) 285, (L) 350; landing (production) 360 m/80 km/h.

Yak-11 OKB discussed advanced fighter/trainer variant of Yak-3 with VVS mid-1944 and design went ahead at once; though low priority, OKB grown so large plenty of spare design capacity. Prototype Yak-3UTI (Yak-UTI) flown 1945. Many parts common to Yak-3 (wing span as Yak-3U, 9,4 m) and designed to exceptional factor 15·4; first installation of ASh-21 engine and VISh-111V-20 prop, and fitted with UBS and 100 rounds plus wing racks for two FAB-100 or other loads. No evidence of major shortcoming but no production. Used as basis for slightly refined aircraft designated Yak-11 first flown 1946; precise differences and first-flight date not known but evidence Yak-3UTI had short-chord cowl. Yak-11 no longer used identical Yak-3 parts, though differences generally small. Fuselage modified shape with welded 30KhGSA truss, ply covered forward and fabric aft, on wood stringers with ply top decking. Tandem cockpits (neither in original position) each with sliding canopy in long glasshouse. Well-equipped cockpits; pilot's notes key 53 items (Yak-3, 38 items). All-metal two-spar wing with Clark-YH profile, 5° dihedral from root, D1 flush-riveted skin 2 mm over LE to front spar, 1 mm elsewhere. Tail, ailerons and control surfaces D1 with fabric. Neat engine installation on rubber anti-vibration mounts in

*Yak-10, Yak-14**

Yak-11 (UK air-show paint scheme)

long-chord cowl faired into fuselage with exhaust collector ring discharging below; side exits for cooling air with adjustable flaps. VISh-111V-20, two blades, constant-speed, 3 m diameter, large spinner. Oil tank 38 lit with dorsal vent, cooler in wing served by ram inlet left wing root, exit chute in undersurface. Split flaps mistakenly called Frise; visually similar to basic Schrenk of Yak fighters, two positions 0° and 40° (landing position sometimes 43°). Main landing gear with 600 × 180 mm tyres retracting inwards ahead of front spar; tailwheel with 255 × 110 mm tyre retracting aft with two doors. All these services, flaps, gear, brakes and cooling-air flaps actuated from pneumatic system with main and emergency bottles charged by engine-driven piston compressor. Fuel in 173 lit protected tank in each wing feeding small 13,5 lit tank behind engine. UBS on left of decking firing through cowl lip, 100 rounds; same variety of underwing loads up to 100 kg each side; provision for various role fits including PAU-22 combat ciné camera in fairing above windscreen.

NII testing completed October 1946, generally excellent aircraft though really agile only in roll; soon cleared for production with deliveries from mid-1947. Series aircraft slightly heavier with extra equipment, RSIU-3M/-4M radio with mast behind rear cockpit, fixed tailwheel, often ShKAS instead of UBS and landing light in left LE. Total given as 3859 of basic series Yak-11 plus 707 under license from October 1953 by LET at Kunowice, Czechoslovakia, as C-11 (originally Le-10), all with ShKAS. In early 1950s Yak OKB produced modified variant **Yak-11U** with nosewheel for training jet-fighter pilots. Castoring nosewheel retracted pneumatically to rear with two doors. Various other changes and, like series aircraft by this time, no spinner. RSI-6 radio, improved 2-SV ciné camera and, like some series machines, glider tow hook. According to Shavrov, Yak-11U replaced Yak-11 in service after latter had been in use 11 years, ie, in 1958. Western accounts do not mention Yak-11U and state that only one nosewheel Yak-11 was built, a C-11U in Czechoslovakia. This is certainly incorrect as OKB has photos showing several VVS Yak-11Us, but number built may have been small. Series Yak-11s gained numerous C-1d class records in 1951–1954, one of best being 100 km circuit at 479,97 km/h. Widely used by all Warsaw Pact and some Arab countries, Albania, China, Afghanistan and Vietnam, as well as by Dosaaf clubs.

DIMENSIONS Span 9,40 m (30 ft 10 in); length 8,50 m (27 ft 10⅔ in); wing area 15,4 m² (166 ft²).
ENGINE One 570 hp ASh-21.
WEIGHTS Empty (3UTI) 1740 kg, (11) 1900 kg (4189 lb), (11U) 2066 kg (4555 lb); fuel/oil (3UTI) not known, (11, 11U) 230 + 24 kg; loaded (3UTI) 2250 kg (4960 lb), (11) 2440 kg (5379 lb), (11U) 2515 kg (5545 lb).
PERFORMANCE Max speed (3UTI) 434 km/h at SL, 478 (297 mph) at 2,5 km, (11) 424 (263) at SL, 465 (289) at 2,5 km, (11U) 414 at SL, 460 at 2250 m; climb, no data; service ceiling (3UTI) 7,3 km, (11) 7950 m (Shavrov), 7,1 km (23,295 ft) (most other sources), (11U) 7,2 km (Shavrov); endurance (Shavrov) 4·5 h, (others) 4,3 h; range (11, Shavrov) 1250 km, (others) 1280 or 1290 (800 miles); take-off (11, Shavrov) 395 m, (others) 500; landing (11, Shavrov) 500 m/89 km/h (this is error; 3UTI speed 130 and typical 11 figure 127), (DDR, Peter Stache) take-off 500 m landing 400 m.

Yak-12** In early 1947 Yak decided to build a better high-wing utility cabin machine to replace Yak-10, and resulting Yak-12 (no relation to previous Yak-12) flew same year. Totally new design, but traditional mixed construction. Wing Clark-YH rectangle with two spars, wood construction, ply skin over LE as far back as front spar, glued fabric over whole wing. Dihedral 3° 30′, braced by drawn D1 V-struts pinned to both spars and meeting at bottom of fuselage. Triangle of sub-struts bracing mid-points of main struts together and to front spar of wing. Fixed D1 slats along entire LE, D1/fabric slotted ailerons with inset hinges at mid-depth (unusual for OKB) and plain manual flaps inboard. Fuselage completely reprofiled compared with Yak-10, basis welded truss of KhNZA tube with some secondary wood formers and stringers and fabric covering. Tail entirely D1/fabric with wire bracing. Fuel in two 100 lit aluminium tanks between spars just outboard of fuselage. Engine installation same as Yak-18 with helmeted cylinders and fixed-pitch aluminium prop. Improved low-drag main gears with pin-jointed legs sprung by rubber in fuselage attached to axles by steel tapes, low-pressure tyres 600 × 180 mm. Fixed tailwheel 200 × 110 mm. Standard ski installation provided, believed interchangeable with Yak-18. Side-by-side bucket seats with flight controls on left, cable operation except push/pull in wings. Normal missions liaison and artillery spotting (*korrektirovshchik*) with RSIU-6 radio. Small number built, believed all for VVS, and a few with third seat at rear.

Yak-12S (*Sanitarnyi*, ambulance) flown 1948 with mounting for single standard stretcher loaded through large triangular hatch in left side. Standard agreed late 1948 with seat for attendant and stowage for 22 kg medical kit. Replaced U-2S progressively. Second 1948 version **Yak-12SKh** (agricultural) equipped with glassfibre or metal tank for chemical dispensed through aluminium-sheet fabricated spreader below fuselage in almost same installation as Po-2AP. Several different variations but built only in small numbers because underpowered. From start Yak had suffered from absence of M-12 engine and waited for forthcoming AI-14. Last of original M-11FR series was single **Yak-12GR** (*Gidro*) with AIR-6 type twin floats. In this case lack of power made performance marginal.

AI-14R engine flight tested in Yak-12 June 1950. In late 1951 resulted in production **Yak-12R**. New engine of almost doubled power in long-chord cowl with collector ring to ventral exhaust outlet, radial shutters (usually 28) to regulate airflow, side cooling-air exits, two-blade 2,75 m VISh-530D-11 bracket-type two-pitch prop. Redesigned wing with greater span and area, entirely D1 structure and flush-riveted D1

Yak-12S used as AI-14R engine testbed

over LE, fabric elsewhere. Similar D1 skin for top of fuselage and much of area previously ply-skinned, including all-D1 stretcher hatch. Smaller fuel tanks but surprisingly little difference in range. Larger wing was one of several changes to enable 12R to use smallest and most confined fields and clearings. Special dozer blade (*soshnik*, spade) smoothed surface and reduced take-off run by up to 50 m. First mass-produced variant (at least 1000) initially for VVS as two-seat liaison, with occasional third seat, and from 1953-1954 in several related civil transport forms for GVF with normal upholstered seats and in some models provision for small cargo load or stretcher.

In 1955 OKB produced **Yak-12M** with better overall distribution of masses and areas, balancing heavier engine by longer rear fuselage and enlarged tail, vertical tail area increased 41% and horizontal 36% with two bracing struts. For first time a true four-seater, with substantial increase in allowable weights. Produced in ag and ambulance models, former with alleged 2 h spray/dust between reloads; another model December 1955 configured for sport parachuting, with door on right equipped with running-board.

Final production variant, of 1957, was **Yak-12A** with new wing and many other improvements. Wing of Cessna profile/plan, left/right wings each one piece but with discontinuity at 55% semi-span. Inboard untapered, two spars widely separated at root but meeting at 34% chord at discontinuity; outboard single spar at 34% chord with taper on TE. Manual plain flaps on inboard section, slotted ailerons outboard. All D1 structure with riveted D1 over LE and back to rear spar inboard and single spar outboard; fabric to rear. Ailerons/flaps D1 over LE, fabric to rear. Wing braced by single pin-jointed aerofoil-profile strut meeting Y-junction of spars, with secondary sub-strut joining mid-length of strut to wing. Fixed slats replaced by retractable slats on outboard section only. Vertical tail as 12R but new horizontal tail with bracing (wire) above and below, D1 skin back to front spar and improved controls and tabs. Larger fuel tanks in tapering space between wing spars. Landing light in left LE. Completely revised cabin interior with US-style panel, wheel instead of stick, and even more comfortable seats for pilot (left) and passenger in front and two-seat divan at rear. Despite much-increased weight, considerably faster and longer-range. Over 1000 built, mainly GVF local service with greatly improved economics.

Only known experimental version is **Yak-12B** STOL model with 300 hp AI-14RF and rectangular lower wing of 10 m span with full-span slotted flap (four flaps in all, pneu actuation) and single interplane struts. Several versions widely exported, military and civil. Yak-12, Yak-12R and Yak-12M licence-built in Poland by WSK-Swidnik, later developed into PZL-101 Gawron. Also basis for several Chinese aircraft in this class.

DIMENSIONS Span (12, S) 12,0 m (39 ft 4½ in), (R, M, A) 12,6 m (41 ft 4 in); length (12, S) 8,36 m (27 ft 5⅛ in), (R) 8,49 m (27 ft 10¼ in), (M, A) 9,0 m (29 ft 6¼ in); wing area (12) 21,6 m² (232·5 ft²), (S) 22,0 m² (237 ft²), (R, M) 23,8 m² (265 ft²), (A) 22,66 m² (244 ft²).

ENGINE (12,S) one 160 hp M-11FR, (others) one 260 hp AI-14R.

WEIGHTS Empty (12) 830 kg (1830 lb), (S) 852 kg (1878 lb), (R) 912 kg (2011 lb), (M) 1026 kg (2262 lb), (A) 1059 kg (2335 lb); fuel/oil (12/S) 145 + 14 kg, (R,M) 135, (A) 165; loaded (12) 1185 kg (2612 lb), (S) 1232 kg (2716 lb), (R) 1172 kg (2584 lb), (M) 1450 kg (3197 lb), (A) 1588 kg (3501 lb).

PERFORMANCE Max speed at SL (12) 169 km/h (105 mph), (S) 172 (107), (R) 184 (114), (M) 182 (113), (A) 220 (143); cruise (except A) about 150 (93), (A) 190 (118); time to 1 km (typical) 8 min; service ceiling (12) 3 km, (R) 5,8, (M) 4160 m, (A) 4550 (Shavrov, 4 km); range (12) 810 km, (S) 620, (R) 550, (M) 765, (A) 1070 (665 miles); endurance (12, S) 4 h, (R, M) 3 h, (A) (Shavrov) 3·5 h, (Taradeyev) 7 h; take-off (12) 130 m, (R, Shavrov) 52, (M) 126, (A) 153; landing (12) 110 m/67 km/h, (S) 100/68, (R) 81/66, (M) 90/82, (A) 131/90.

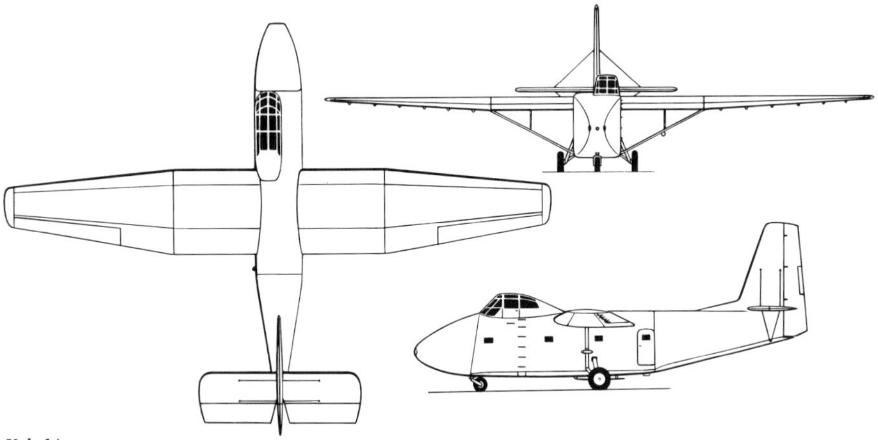

Yak-14

Yak-14 (Czech NK-14)

Yak-13 First flown November 1944, this neat low-wing cabin aircraft was designed to afford direct comparison with braced high-wing Yak-10. Original designation, **Yak-12** (unrelated to later aircraft just described). Yak-10 and Yak-13 had as nearly as possible same engine installation, cabin, rear fuselage and tail, though Yak-13 fuselage was shallower. Apart from welded-tube fuselage truss construction virtually all-wood, with fabric covering. New wing designed for this machine, with horizontal but tapered centre section (Clark-YH, 15%) with ply covering, and tapering outer panels to 9% tip, two spars throughout, ply skin as far back as front spar. Ailerons and tail D1/fabric. All-D1 split landing flap under centre section, manually driven to 40°. Main gears with neat single shock struts to outer ends of axles for 500 × 150 mm braked wheels, manual cable/winch retraction inwards ahead of front spar. Castoring tailwheel 200 × 80 mm. Fuel in two 75 lit tanks in centre section; engine helmeted with short ventral stub exhaust, VISh-327 prop. Comfortable cabin with fully glazed canopy (sliding, later left/right halves hinged upwards at centreline of roof). Four seats, but (Shavrov) for practical purposes a three-seater. Aerobatic, fitted booster coil and starter but no instrumentation for night flying or a radio. Completed NII trials 1945; much better performance than Yak-10 but latter formula, after fresh start as Yak-12**, offered greater promise for VVS/GVF purposes. Next streamlined four-seater Yak-18T of 1966.

DIMENSIONS Span 11,5 m (37 ft 8¾ in); length 8,45 m (27 ft 8¾ in); wing area not recorded but drawings suggest 18,8 m² (202 ft²).

ENGINE One 145 hp M-11FM (M-11M).

WEIGHTS Empty 868 kg (1,914 lb); fuel/oil 108 + 14 kg; loaded 1230 (2,712).

PERFORMANCE Max speed at SL 250 km/h (155 mph); initial climb 4,2 m/s (827 ft/min); time to 1 km, 4·3 min; service ceiling 4 km; range (Shavrov) 660 km, (Kondratyev) 815 (506 miles); take-off 330 m; landing 375 m/89 km/h.

Yak-14 This designation was used originally for Yak-10. Used again for OKB submission to meet the final *desant* (assault) glider specification issued mid-1947. Called for 3,5 t payload and made other important demands to meet A-VDV needs, with some interest by GVF which was still studying civil cargo gliders and glider trains. Ilyushin assigned metal glider (Il-32), Yak a wooden one. Yak-14 designed second half 1947, neat and straightforward. Hold cross-section 2 × 2 m (79 × 79 in) with max values ahead of wing 2,3 × 2,25 m; usable length 8 m (26 ft 3 in). Entirely wood structure with steel fittings. Nose hinged to open vertically (gas bottle or hand pump with stand-by winch/cable) for full-section access including small vehicles and artillery. Fabric-covered rear fuselage, detached for unloading on combat mission. Two-spar high wing, rectangular centre section and tapered outer panels with strong ribs at interconnection incorporating anchor for bracing strut (believed drawn or wrapped-MS). Full-span slotted flaps driven by gas bottles with manual (80:1 ratio) crank emergency, outer sections carrying inserted slotted ailerons. Wire-braced tail with rudder trimmer. Steel-tube steps up fuselage exterior to flight deck mounted above left side of fuselage seating two pilots side-by-side with optional third jump seat at rear. Door on left of cockpit, all-round glazing, no known armament apart from infantry weapons but at least one glider with radio. Canvas seats for 35 troops, normal door at rear on left. Tricycle landing gear jettisoned on combat mission with skid landing. Satisfactory NII tests 1948, immediate production and reported 413 gliders built. According to Němeček, one with mixed construction. Limited use in manoeuvres, in September 1955 three supplied to Czech air force, designated NK-14.

DIMENSIONS Span 26,17 m (85 ft 10⅓ in); length 18,44 m (60 ft 6 in); wing area not known.

WEIGHTS Empty 3095 kg (6823 lb); loaded 6750 (14 881).

PERFORMANCE Tow speed 300 km/h (186 mph); sink after release (no flap) − 2,6 m/s; landing 380 m/93 km/h.

Yak-15

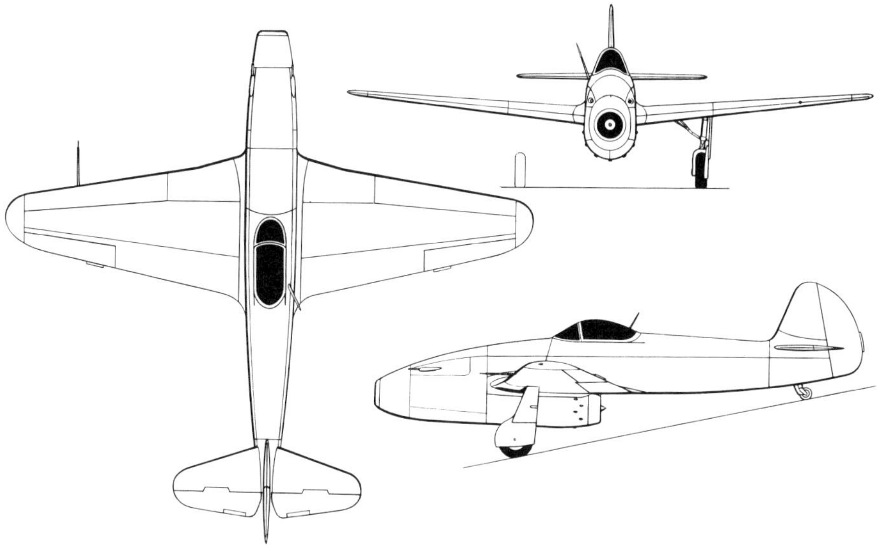
Yak-15

Yak-15 First jet (as distinct from rocket) aircraft completed in Soviet Union, this simple fighter was jet derivative of Yak-3, sole example apart from Swedish J21R of successful production jet fighter based on piston-engined design. This was possible because at late-February 1945 Kremlin meeting Stalin had instructed Yak to build jet fighter using single German engine, matching size of existing piston fighters (La had same instruction but made fresh start with La-150). Yak explained his intentions in a positive way, not suggesting that compromised result would be second-rate, and gaining support from promise of fast timing; in prevailing mood, even inferior jet fighter in numbers would have been preferred to better one later. Crash programme headed by Ye. Adler and Leon Shekhter, basic 3-view layout complete in three days and first drawing issued late May.

Existing Yak-3 production drawings retained for most of tail, wing and landing gear, and much of centre and rear fuselage also retained apart from using metal skin as Yak-3U. New forward fuselage of chiefly D1 construction though with steel firewall at front spar and welded-steel-tube fuselage truss extended forward to two main frames carrying engine. Latter based on Jumo 004B, though in this particular RD-10 form rearranged with accessories on top to suit unusual installation. Axis of engine inclined slightly nose-up, with rear half under wing and nozzle as close as possible under TE to minimise base drag. This required that D1 front spar be arched over engine; both spars also slightly strengthened by using thicker material for booms. Skin of forward fuselage all D1, almost all detachable for access to engine, accessories and armament. Design armament one ShVAK and two UBS, changed during prototype construction to two B-20 and finally to two NS-23 giving heavier firepower for reduced weight. This enabled larger fuel tank to be accommodated in rear fuselage, but in fact only part of available 780 lit capacity of four wing tanks, nose tank and rear-fuselage tank was used, normal limit being only 310 lit (68 gal), on grounds of weight. Features included heavier sheet skin on underside of fuselage downstream of jet nozzle, D1 skin on lower half of rudder, tailwheel with bulged protective fairing when extended from twin-door retraction bay, blown acrylic canopy sliding aft on rails, frameless (not bulletproof) windscreen, gyro gunsight and HF

Yak-15 preserved at OKB, note canopy and mast

radio with wire from fin to short mast beside canopy.

Prototype Yak-15 hand-built with utmost urgency, incorporating successive modifications resulting from tunnel testing or to clear mechanical problem caused by absence of engineering mock-up. First engine installed believed to be modified Jumo 004B, though always described as RD-10 in Soviet literature. Taken to airfield, believed Zhukovskaya but possibly Khodinka, first week October 1945. Ground running, taxiing and, according to Yak, 'short flights' (ie, hops just above runway). Could have flown six months ahead of all other Soviet jet aircraft, but decision taken to carry out careful investigation of effect of varying thrust on trim, on jet flow at high angles of attack and similar problems in tunnel (almost certainly TsAGI T-101 tunnel at Zhukovskaya). Yak has described spectacle of prototype at full power in this tunnel, with forces, moments and temperature of underskin being measured. Latter replaced by KhGSA sheet. Programme completed before end of year, but NII did not immediately grant clearance for flight – partly because of prolonged heating troubles with tailwheel, eventually made wholly of metal – and also because Chkalovskaya runway was under water from thawing snow and fresh rain. Not until 24 April 1946 were both MiG-9 and Yak-15 ready (author suspects this was political, and that Yak could have flown months earlier). Toss of coin put MiG in air first. Then Yak-15 made completely successful flight in hands of Mikhail I. Ivanov. Both prototypes made public debut at Tushino Aviation Day 18 August 1946. Stalin then decreed that 12 of each should participate in October parade, 80 days hence! Yak himself was sent, with Deputy Minister A. Kuznetsov, to chosen GAZ with instructions not to leave until 12th aircraft despatched. Task completed using inefficient hand-building, initially with no production jigging. First pre-series Yak-15 crated and sent by rail 20 September, next on 5 October and last of required dozen on 21 October. (Tushino fly-past was cancelled by fog.)

First of these pre-series aircraft flew 5 October and began NII testing immediately. NII programme under P.M. Stefanovskii free from serious trouble, apart from low endurance. Full aerobatic routine successfully explored. With two NS-23 with 60 rounds each at weights around 2,6 t, lightest jet fighter in history. Same GAZ that built pre-series, almost certainly No 153, assigned full production of batch believed to be 280 (often thought to be 400 in West). **Yak-21** was designation of single tandem-seat dual-control trainer built by modification of a pre-series aircraft late 1947; streamlined canopy, painted dark green with number '101' on nose. At least one example was also built of **Yak-15U** (probably *Uluchshyennyi*, improved) with nose-wheel landing gear. This necessitated redesigned wing with different main legs (see Yak-17) pivoted to front face of rear spar and retracted gear replacing original inboard tank. Full fuel still available from using front-rear fuselage tanks (usually empty on weight grounds), but, like original machine, Yak-15U was still only a stop-gap. Yak explained that his objective had been to conquer pervading feeling that jet fighters were difficult and dangerous, mastered only by supermen, by making Yak-15 as much like a Yak-3 to fly as possible.

DIMENSIONS Span 9,2 m (30 ft 2¼ in); length 8,78 m (28 ft 9¾ in); wing area 14,85 m^2 (160 ft^2).
ENGINE One 900 kg thrust RD-10.
WEIGHTS Empty 2350 kg (5181 lb); fuel/oil (theoretical) 580 kg (1279), (practical) 223 (492); loaded 2635 (5809).
PERFORMANCE Max speed, 700 km/h (435 mph) at SL, (Shavrov) 805 (500) at 5 km, (other accounts) 786 (488) or 765 (476); climb (Shavrov) to 5 km in 4·8 min, to 10 km in 13·8; service ceiling 13 350 m (43,800 ft); range (Shavrov) 510 km (317 miles) (others have suggested 740 km), but limited in practice to 350 km (217 miles) except for economy cruise; time 360° circle 26 s; take-off 600 m; landing 530 m/135 km/h (84 mph).

Yak-16 Rejection of Yak-8 left Yak in no doubt GVF needed rather larger passenger transport of modern design with all-metal construction, to partner Li-2 and Il-12 on lower-traffic routes. Yak-16 was designed by largely new stressed-skin engineering team and built under direction of former flying-boat designer P.D. Samsonov. Simple airframe with Clark-YH wing, two spars, horizontal centre section and tapered outer panels with dihedral, oval-section fuselage and clean unbraced tail. Slotted ailerons, rudder and elevators fabric-covered, all with tabs. All-D1 split flaps on centre section and outer panels with pneumatic actuation to 40°. Main gears with single oleo legs to inner ends of axles for wheels with 900 × 300 mm tyres, retracting forwards to leave wheel part-exposed, brakes and retraction pneumatic. Castoring fixed tailwheel 470 × 210 mm. Four wing tanks total 1800 lit (396 gal); two 35 lit oil tanks. Engines in neat cowls with gills and ventral exhausts, oil coolers in wing inboard of nacelle with LE inlet, VISh-111Va two-blade constant-speed props with large spinners. Flight deck for pilot (room for seat on right side, not fitted) and radio operator with astro dome behind; main cabin normally five passenger seats each side, each with rectangular window; door aft on left. Small toilet and 100 kg baggage or freight compartment at rear. Riveting round-head throughout. Single prototype extensively tested from June 1947, but GVF showed no interest. Registration I985; Shavrov's 'I975' is erroneous retouch. Second aircraft, L4590, may later have been tested by VVS with number 464 on fuselage. OKB believe only two built. Aroused little interest and Yak-16 became first Soviet aircraft to make major foreign sales effort, appearing at European shows and trade fairs and even completing sales tour of South America. Shavrov states VVS version had gun turret behind flight deck; this not known at OKB and possibly not built.

DIMENSIONS Span 21,5 m (70 ft 6½ in) (Něměcek 20 m, *Jane's* 17); length 15,60 m (51 ft 2⅛ in) (Něměcek 14,5, *Jane's* 11); wing area 56,2 m^2 (605 ft^2).
ENGINES Two 570 hp ASh-21.
WEIGHTS Empty 4465 kg (9843 lb); fuel/oil 480 + 45 kg; loaded 6050 kg (13,338 lb).
PERFORMANCE Max speed 350 km/h (217 mph) at SL, fractionally more at 2–3 km; cruise 300 (186); time to 1 km, 2·3 min; service ceiling 7,7 km (25,260 ft); range 800 km (500 miles); take-off (Aviaexport claim) 260 m; landing 550 m/106 km/h.

Yak-17 This was a logical modest next step beyond Yak-15, retaining mixed construction yet with far more detail redesign than immediately apparent. Obvious advantage of nose-wheel landing gear, tested on Yak-15U, led to more extensive redesign to achieve optimum fighter with underslung RD-10. Accommodation of retracted nose gear had proved impossible in 15U, and presence of low-slung engine still posed insuperable problem. In Yak-17 nose gear continued to be largely external, with 700 × 190 mm wheel on levered-suspension oleo strut carrying large fairing forming front half of ventral bulge over unit when retracted. Partly because of extra side area of this fairing vertical tail was redesigned with new stressed-skin fin of considerably greater height. Mixed-construction airframe carefully restressed for increased weights and airspeeds, design factor 12, main strengthening in wing spars, inboard ribs and fuselage truss. D1 split flaps and landing gears pneumatic, main legs being same levered-suspension forgings as on 15U and pulled inwards by Y-type breaker strut to lie between spars, with D1 bay door hinged at wing root. Reduction in wing tankage now countered by adding 300 lit jettisonable external tanks under wing-tips, requiring only local structural revision but restricting aerobatic capability when attached. Increased weight matched by more powerful engine fed by slightly enlarged inlet duct; Western statement nose was cut back not borne out by identical overall length of Yak-15 and Yak-17 and fact that whole duct was enlarged (from 525 to 555 mm).

Prototype Yak-17 flew early 1947 and completed NII testing in time for part of original (500 or 1000?) order for Yak-15 to be completed

Yak-17

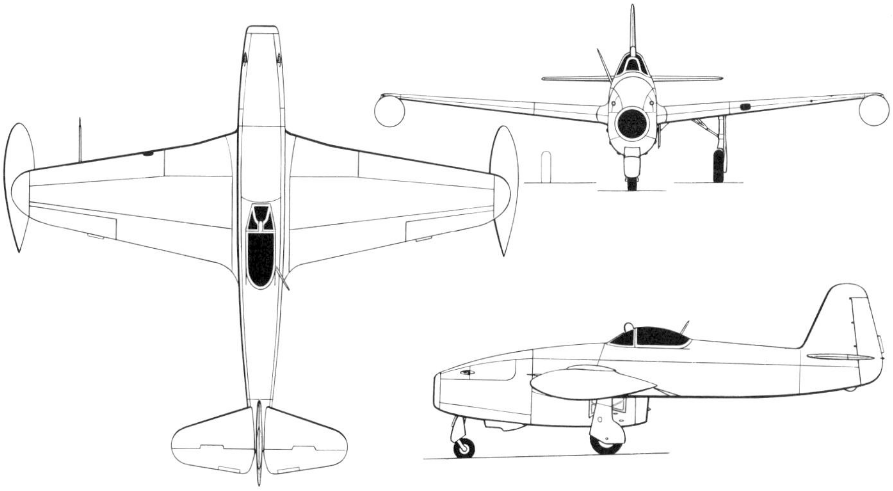

Yak-17

Yak-17UTI

as Yak-17s. Armament remained two NS-23 with 60 rounds, no underwing weapons. Production aircraft had flat bullet-proof windscreen, landing light (left or right LE), rear-view mirror (above windshield if fitted) and ciné camera (above windshield or in left LE). Example at Monino has non-standard angular canopy with large Yak-11 type camera above. Offered to Warsaw Pact air forces but believed no takers, despite Czech designation S-100 and example in Prague-Kbely museum (single examples presented Czech and Polish AFs). Total production believed 430, completed late 1948.

Not known whether this total includes output of **Yak-17UTI** trainer (several Western accounts claim it does). Shavrov states 'UTI landing gear tailwheel type supplied with steel rim instead of pneumatic'. This not understood; all UTIs known were fitted with same nosewheel gear as Yak-17 fighter, though nose gear lacked fixed fairing. This change was welcomed by pilots, who – once they had overcome basic fear of jet – complained about poor forward view with tailwheel and applauded Yak-15U and Yak-17. Even so, instructor in rear cockpit of 17UTI did not have much forward view, in those days staggered tandem cockpits had not been thought of.

Instrumentation identical in both cockpits, and rest of aircraft almost exactly as Yak-17. Rear seat approx same position as in single-seater but canopy quite different with flat front windscreen set at more upright angle, two sliding hoods and fixed Plexiglas rear fairing with RSI-6 radio mast. Prototype UTI flown mid-1947 with gyro sight and single fixed UBS, but production trainer unarmed. Not fitted with tip tanks and limited flight endurance caused problems in planning training sorties. As only jet trainer available, sold in small numbers to China. Possibly used by Polish air force; certainly one civil example (SP-GLM) used by IL (Aviation Institute) at Warsaw-Okecie 1956–1966 approx.

DIMENSIONS Span 9,2 m (30 ft 2¼ in); length (both) 8,78 m (28 ft 9⅔ in); wing area 14,85 m² (160 ft²).

ENGINE One 1 t thrust RD-10A.

WEIGHTS Empty (17) 2430 kg (5357 lb), (UTI) not known but closely similar; fuel/oil (17) 360 internal, 433 kg external; loaded (17) 2890 kg (6371 lb), or with external fuel 3323 (7326), (UTI) 2925 (6448).

PERFORMANCE Max speed (17) 720 km/h SL to 2,5 km, 751 (467 mph) at 6 km; time to 5 km (both) 5·8 min; service ceiling (17) 12 750 m (41,830 ft), (UTI) 12 km (39,370 ft); range (17) 717 km (446 miles) with tip tanks, (UTI) 300 km (186 miles); take-off (UTI) 640 m; landing (both) 700 m/152 km/h.

Yak-18 Descended from UT-2 this family has grown to encompass many single-seat aerobatic aircraft as well as totally redesigned four-seat cabin machine, in addition to tandem trainers standard throughout WP air forces since the Second World War. Origin was UT-2MV of 1943, from which OKB developed more powerful tandem trainer with retractable main gear (as pupil-pilot exercise, not to improve performance) and part metal skinning over fuselage and wings. This prototype, Yak-18, flown unknown date late 1945.

Wing Clark-YH, 14·5% at root and 9·3 at tip, rectangular centre section with 0° dihedral, tapered outer panels with 6° 30′ dihedral, two-spar D1 construction with pressed ribs and riveted D1 skin over LE back to front spar, fabric remainder. D1/fabric slotted ailerons, split flap over centre section with manual operation to 55° for landing. Fuselage welded-MS tube truss with wood formers and stringers, D1 panels (many detachable) from nose to rear cockpit, fabric aft. Tail D1/fabric, wire-braced. Tandem cockpits with bucket seats (padded seats for civilian pilots with back-type parachute) and dual controls. First prototype with fixed landing gear with single side-braced oleo struts carrying braked 500 × 150 mm wheels. All subsequent aircraft with legs folding rearwards mechanically, with pilot/cable operation, legs lying externally beneath wing and half wheel exposed. Fixed cas-

Yak-18 (North Korea) with tailplane braced above and below

Yak-18s

toring tailwheel. Engine on steel-tube mounts, initially without rubber vibration absorbers fitted later, with pressed D1 helmeted cowl and driving VISh-327 prop. Two 65 lit aluminium tanks in centre section, drum-type oil tank behind engine. No armament, initially no radio.

Prolonged factory and NII testing completed late 1947, and series production authorized with HF radio (usually RSIU-3M/-4M), blind-flying instruments, engine-driven generator, nav lights, cockpit lighting and, later in production, V-501 prop. Replaced UT-2 and Po-2 in all military and civilian training units and Dosaaf clubs with clearance for unrestricted aerobatics including flick manoeuvres. Engine cowl improved early 1950s, spinner usually omitted, ARK-5 radio compass installed and pneumatic system added with engine/compressor-charged bottle to operate landing gear retraction and wheelbrakes, flap remaining manual. Civil pilots gained eight FAI class records including 100 km circuit at 262,771 km/h (16 September 1949), 2000 km circuit (in two flights) at 209,664 km/h (16 September 1949), non-stop flight of 2004,62 km (25 September 1954) and height of 6311 m (18 June 1954). Aircraft widely accepted and exported outside Warsaw Pact, including barter with Austria for steel sheet.

Yak-18U (*Uluchshyennyi*, improved) flown 1954, entered production 1955 though not replacing original model. Tricycle landing gear with different main units hinged to rear spar with legs on inside of wheels, retracting forwards with upper part of wheel in small recess in wing ahead of front spar. Nose gear with long single steel-tube leg pivoted to bottom of engine mount frame, on front of lengthened forward fuselage, with rear breaker strut pulled up to fold unit to rear with half wheel (400 × 130 mm) exposed. As in Yak-18, provision for belly landing on retracted gear with no damage except to prop, and bottom of cowl. Tailwheel replaced by fixed bumper, dihedral of outer wings increased to 7° 20′, landing light(s) in left LE, cowl further improved with large open inner front to improve cooling in climb (or in glider towing which was task of many aircraft with modified lower rudder and hook), welded-tube access step added on left at TE of wing. Performance, hardly sprightly in Yak-18, deteriorated with greater weight.

Yak-20** rectified problem with much more powerful AI-14R as used in Yak-12 since 1950. New engine in smooth long-chord cowl with oblique trailing edge, made in detachable or hinged upper/lower halves. Rear collector ring with twin ventral exhaust pipes, front of cowl open but fitted with 28 pilot-controlled radial shutters to regulate cooling airflow. V-530-D35 controllable (counterweight-type) 2,3 m prop, oil cooler in duct in right wing root. Airframe locally strengthened, span slightly increased, tail redesigned similar to Yak-12A, fuel tanks enlarged to 65 lit each, pneumatic system (0,49 MPa on all subsequent models) extended with main/emergency and actuator added to drive flaps via push/pull spanwise rods, canopy made deeper to increase pilot headroom, avionics greatly improved with HF/VHF radio, telephone-type intercom in place of Gosport tube, improved blind-flying instruments, marker receiver, radio compass and better nav lights. NII tested spring 1957 and cleared for production same year, replacing all previous variants at Arsen'yev plant (East Siberia) where Yak general-aviation types by this time centred. In production redesignated **Yak-18A**.

Belated recognition of importance of international aerobatic contest (then Lockheed, UK, Trophy) prompted development of dedicated aerobatic single-seat variant. Competitions 1955-1959 missed whilst exploring front and rear

Yak-18A

positions of single-seat cockpit and numerous other argued features. In early 1959 several production aircraft built as **Yak-18P** (*Pilotazhnyii*) in two forms. All had longer-span ailerons and modified fuel system permitting 5 minutes inverted flight at any power setting. Most promising machine had front cockpit retained and rear cockpit eliminated, and neater main gears retracting inwards to lie wholly within wing between spars. An alternative scheme, also tested, eliminated front cockpit and retained rear, this being a converted Yak-18A and retaining original landing gear. B.N. Vasyakin gained 5th place in 1960 championships at Bratislava with rear-cockpit Yak-18P. In 62 championships at Budapest four front-cockpit machines participated, gaining 2nd (Lochikov), 7th, 9th and 10th places. In 1964 at Bilbao slightly modified Yak-18Ps with fin/rudder of increased chord and stressed to $+9\,g/-6\,g$ gained 4th, 5th, 6th, 7th places, and women gained 1st, 2nd, 3rd, 4th. Aerobatic development continued with **Yak-18PM** of 1965, with more powerful AI-14RF driving V-530D-25 prop, rear cockpit moved 120 mm further back than original rear cockpit, dihedral reduced from 7° 20′ to 2°, flap replaced by instant-action 3 m² airbrake under belly, and various minor changes. Result was great improvement in performance (eg, see climb data) and CG moved from 20 to 26% chord giving near-unstable agility. Yak-18PM decisively won 66 championships at Moscow Tushino. At Hullavington (UK) in 1970 joined by single **Yak-18PS**, similar to PM but with tail-wheel gear using rearward-retracting main legs pivoted to front spar as in original Yak-18, legs passing outside wheels, and other changes including oil cooler in duct under nose. Aerobatic series continued with Yak-50, Yak-52, Yak-53, and Yak-55 described in following entries.

Last variant, **Yak-18T**, was completely different aircraft, first announced by OKB as work of son Sergei Yakovlev, though designer later named as Yuri Yankyevich. Planned late 1964 for GVF in five variants: primary trainer, advanced trainer (instrument flight and all-weather radio), transport for three passengers and baggage, mail/cargo for 250 kg, and ambulance with one stretcher and attendant. Totally new and much larger fuselage, rounded box semi-monocoque wholly of stressed-skin without welded-tube truss (rear fuselage spot-welded). Two-spar wing with stressed-skin centre section extended in span from 2500 to 2706 mm, still 14·5% Clark-YH, outer panels basically as Yak-18A with 7° 20′ dihedral, slotted ailerons and pneumatic split flap. AI-14RF in prototype as in Yak-18PM but new broad oil cooler in duct in right inboard wing, and fuel tanks enlarged to 104 lit size and repositioned between spars in outer wings outboard of main gears. Improved pneumatically retracted landing gear with smoother differential brakes, tyres 500 × 150 mm; 400 × 130 mm nose gear almost completely housed in fuselage when retracted. Comfortable and well-equipped cabin with large door both sides; roof window only at extreme front. Normally side-by-side dual controls with lateral control by wheels. Removable divan for two at rear as alternative to cargo, plus large rear baggage compartment accessed via door on left also used to load stretcher. Comprehensive avionics fit including VHF/UHF and intercom, ILS, VOR/DME, radio altimeter and flight recorder.

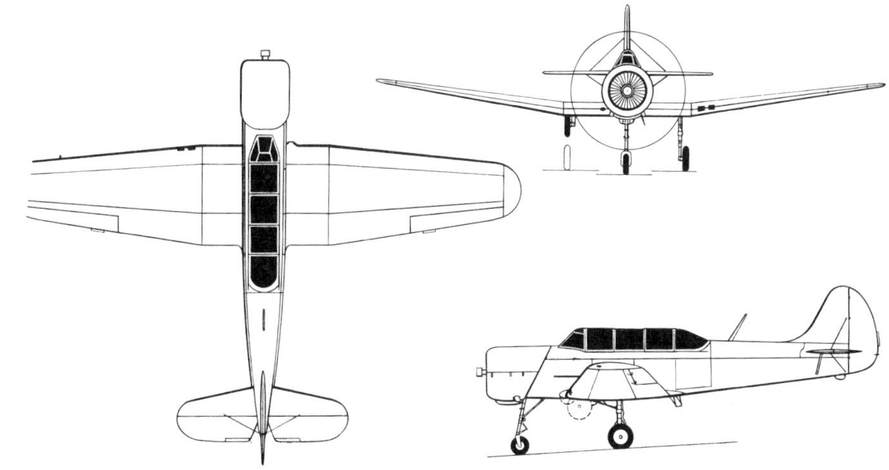

Yak-18A

Yak-18P

Yak-18PM

Capable electrical system includes starter and full night equipment with rotating beacon. Prototype in white OKB livery, unregistered, shown at Paris 1967; two tested in 450 flights 1968–1969 at Sasov by G.A. Taran leading to numerous mods, chief being installation of new Vedeneyev engine driving V-530TA-D35 prop. Prolonged further trials by pre-production aircraft culminated in intensive testing throughout 1973 of four series machines from plant at Smolyensk. Whole 1974 intake (100 pupils) at Sasov trained on Yak-18T and by 1981 over 1000 in use including first ambulance, Aeroflot line-service and liaison examples, with skis cleared and floats on test. Various military, fire patrol and photo versions planned.

Production of original Yak-18 variants terminated end-1967 with 6760 produced. Including Yak-18T total will probably soon exceed 8000.

DIMENSIONS Span (18,U) 10,3 m (33 ft 9½ in), (A,P,PM,PS) 10,6 (34 ft 9¼ in), (T) 11,16 (36 ft 7¼ in); length (18) 8,07 (26 ft 5¾ in), (U) 8,53 (27 ft 11¾ in), (A,P,PM,PS,T) 8,35 (27 ft 4¾ in); wing area (18,U) 17,00 m² (183 ft²), (A,P) 17,80 (191·6), (PM,PS) 17,9 (192·7), (T) 18,75 (201·8).

ENGINE (18,U) one 160 hp M-11FR, (A,P) 260 hp AI-14R, (PM, PS) 300 hp AI-14RF, (T) 360 hp M-14P.

WEIGHTS Empty (18) 816 kg (1799 lb), (U) 970 (2138), (A) 1025 (2260), (P) 818 (1803), (PM) 825 (1819), (T) 1200 (2646); fuel/oil (18) max 112 kg, (U,A) 94 + 14, (P,PM,PS) 50, (T) 150 + 25; loaded (18) 1120 (2469), (U) 1300 (2866), (A) 1316 (2901), (P) 1065 (2348), (PM) 1100 (2425), (T) 1650 (3637).

PERFORMANCE Max speed (18) 248 km/h (154 mph), (U) 146, (A) 260 (162), (P) 275 (171), (PM) 315 (196), (T) 295 (183); cruise (18) 195, (U) 186, (A) 224, (P) 256, (PM) 282, (T) 250; initial climb (18) 3,5 m/s, (U) 2,4, (A) 5,4, (P) 8,6, (PM) 10,0, (T) 5,0; service ceiling (18) 4 km (13,123 ft), (U) 3,4, (A) 5,06, (P) 6,5, (PM) 7,0, (T) 5,5; range (18) 1050 km (652 miles), (U) 780, (A) 750, (P) 420, (PM, PS) 400, (T) max fuel, 900 (560); take-off (18) 205 m, (U) 295, (A) 215, (P, PM) 140, (T) 400; landing (18) 270/89 km/h, (U) not known, (A) 250, (P, PM) 130, (T) 500/100.

Yak-50

Yak-50, Yak-52** Continuing Yak-18 family development, led by Sergei Yakovlev and Yu. Yankyevich, resulted in new aircraft for 1976 world aerobatic championships at Kiev which repeated Yak-50 designation previously used for fighter (aircraft described here because of ancestry). Based on tailwheel, aft-cockpit Yak-18PS but new airframe. Left/right wings (based on Yak-20* of 26 years earlier) simple straight-tapered panels attached to fuselage, Clark-YH, 14·5/9%, dihedral 2°, D1 stressed-skin structure with main spar at 37·5% and auxiliary spars inboard at LE and TE to carry movable surfaces, five L-section stringers above and five below, 15 pressed ribs each wing, riveted skin. Fabric-covered slotted ailerons each mounted on two forged brackets from below, push-rod actuation, ground-adjustable tabs, D1 split flaps inboard operated by links from push/pull rods to pneumatic rams in fuselage. All-D1 stressed-skin semi-monocoque fuselage (no steel-tube truss) with fabric covering aft of cockpit. D1 stressed skin fin and tailplane, fabric-covered rudder with ground-adjustable tab and elevators

Yak-18T

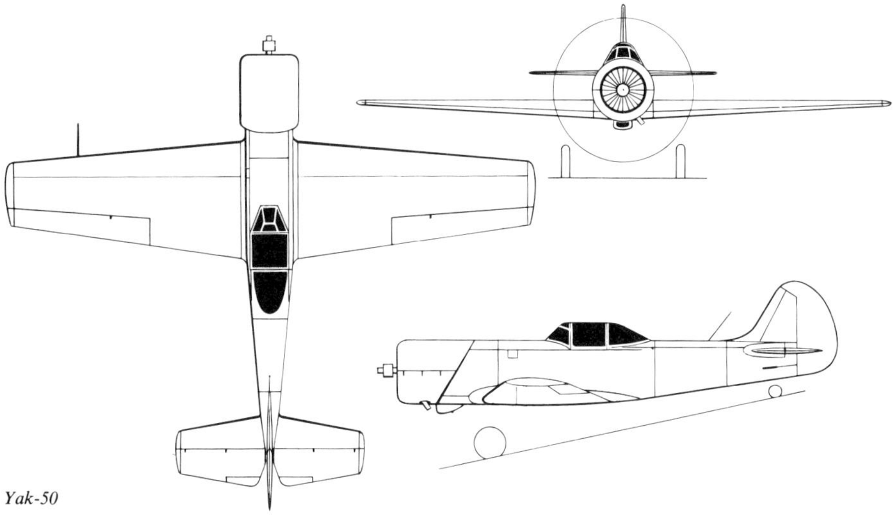

Yak-50

with pilot-controlled tabs. Engine installation generally as Yak-18T but prototype fitted with large spinner on V-530TA-D35 prop of 2,4 m diameter (not 2,0 as often reported), fuel in single 55 lit tank in forward fuselage, and oil cooler in short duct under nose behind cowling. Prototype also fitted with teardrop canopy and fixed, spatted main gears with 500 × 150 mm tyres; fixed 200 × 80 mm tailwheel. Standard vhf radio with whip aerial ahead of fin, 27-V battery behind seat. Prototype completed at Progress Works, Arsen'yev, and tested by Anatoli Sergeyev mid-1975, cleared to unrestricted +9/−6 g manoeuvres. Aircraft 02 built with Yak-18PS type main gear folding to rear with wheels part-exposed, Yak-18PS canopy with fixed rear portion, and spinner omitted. This became series type, six of which swept board in 1976 world championships. Substantial number built for Dosaaf and used throughout Warsaw Pact. Three-bladed Hoffman prop fitted 1982.

Yak-52 is primary trainer variant. Based on on stressed-skin airframe of Yak-50 but important differences. Tandem cockpits (rear seat in unchanged position) with usual pair of sliding canopies, front (pupil) with some additional instruments but instructor with all light and other electric switches. Tricycle landing gear with single oleo legs, main tyres 500 × 150 mm, nose 400 × 150 mm, all retracted by pneumatic rams but entire gear remaining exposed outside aircraft and designed for inadvertent gear-up landing. Fuel in two 65 lit tanks in wing roots ahead of spar feeding small (5,5 lit) inverted-flight fuselage tank. Oil cooler in broad duct under root of right wing behind spar with controllable exit flap. Electric battery in left wing. Designed by Komsomol members under OKB guidance at Arsen'yev and prototype in OKB livery built in 12 months 1978–1979. Demonstrated Tushino 8 May 1979 and completed NII testing same year. Production assigned to IRAvB, Bacau, Romania, with plan to deliver 2000 at 36 per month, low rate production from mid-1980.

DIMENSIONS Span 9,5 m (31 ft 2 in); length 7676 mm (25 ft 2¼ in); wing area 15,0 m^2 (161·45 ft^2).

ENGINE One 360 hp M-14P.

WEIGHTS Empty (50) 765 kg (1686·5 lb), (52) 1 t (2205); fuel/oil (50) 40 + 14 kg, (52) 180 + 25; loaded (50) 900 (1984), (52) 1290 (2844).

PERFORMANCE Max speed (50) 320 km/h (199 mph), (52) 285 (177); limit in dive 470 (292); initial climb (50) 16 m/s (3150 ft/min), (52) 10 (1970) (given as 7,5 in recent account by Kondratyev); service ceiling (50) 5,5 km, (52) 6,0; range (50) not published, but 495 km with 120 lit auxiliary tank, (52) 500 km; take-off (50) 200 m, (52) 160; landing (50) 250/110 km/h, (52) 260/110.

Yak-53 This single-seat aerobatic-championship aircraft is a modified Yak-52, but appears to have been produced at the Yak OKB rather than in Romania. Can alternatively be regarded as Yak-50 with Yak-52 landing gear, retaining feature of leaving retracted wheels exposed. Simplified flight controls without spring bias, all avionics removed except VHF com.

DIMENSIONS As Yak-52.

WEIGHTS Empty 900 kg (1984 lb), loaded 1060 kg (2337 lb).

PERFORMANCE As Yak-52 except max speed 300 km/h (186 mph), max climb 900 m (2953 ft/min), take-off 150 m (493 ft), stalling speed 115 km/h (71·5 mph).

Yak-55 Made surprise debut at Spitzerberg, Austria, in World Aerobatic Championships during 1982. Marked departure from preceding Yak aerobatic series, only common feature being M-14P radial. Flown into 16th place at Spitzerberg by bureau test-pilot M. Molchaniuk. Construction all-metal, with mid-mounted cantilever wing of thick section and low aspect ratio; incidence and dihedral nil. Control surfaces horn-balanced, tailwheel steerable, spring-leaf landing gear, and bubble canopy. Structure stressed to ±9 g.

DIMENSIONS Span 8,20 m (26 ft 10¾ in); length 7,48 m (24 ft 6½ in); wing area 14,30 m^2 (153·9 ft^2).

ENGINE One 360 hp M-14P.

WEIGHTS Max take-off 840 kg (1852 lb).

PERFORMANCE Max speed 320 km/h (199 mph), initial climb 960 m/s (3150 ft/min), take-off 150 m (492 ft), landing 200 m (656 ft).

Yak-55

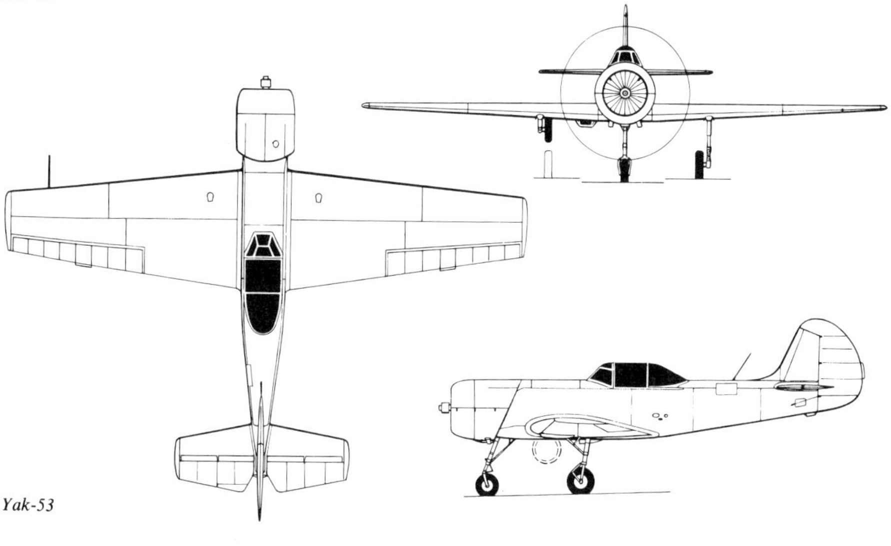

Yak-53

Yak-19 First stressed-skin aircraft designed as such from outset by OKB, this uninspired jet fighter was completely fresh design tailored to more powerful version of RD-10. Midmounted wing, TsAGI S-1-12 laminar section 12% thick at root, tapering to KV-3-12 (still 12%) near tip, equal taper (taper ratio 2·5, aspect ratio 5·6), dihedral 3·5°. Two spars, pressed ribs, skin 1,2/1,8 mm, flush-riveted (first time at OKB). Frise ailerons, manual, metal-skinned; TsAGI split flaps, hydraulic. Barrel fuselage with nose inlet to left/right ducts past unpressurized cockpit and over wing spars to engine in rear fuselage with reheat nozzle at extreme tail (new to USSR); flush-riveted skin 0,8/1,8 mm. Rear fuselage detachable, with engine, latter then withdrawn forwards. Fixed tailplane mounted half-way up tall fin, rudder/elevators manual, metal-skinned and divided into upper/lower and left/right sections with fixed cruciform at centre (no bullet). Tricycle landing gear with levered-suspension main legs and 570 × 135 mm tyres, brakes and retraction pneumatic with leg housed in wing between spars and wheel in fuselage. Nose gear 375 × 135 mm, castoring, levered suspension, pneumatic retraction forwards with twin doors to narrow compartment between ducts. Primitive ejection seat, flat bulletproof windscreen, sliding canopy. Total 815 lit fuel in two fuselage tanks, plus 11 lit petrol for two-stroke starter engine and 14 kg oil. Intended 200 lit tip tanks not installed. Electrically-driven pump supplying supplementary fuel to crude afterburner; no details of nozzle. Original armament two Sh-Z 23 mm cannon (unknown to author) with 150 rounds. Believed first aircraft assigned to Anokhin after his recovery from Yak-3 break-up; first flown early 1947 and factory testing completed 21 August 1947; not submitted for NII testing as engine outdated. OKB has no knowledge of versions with Derwent or RD-500 engine despite persistent Western reports.

DIMENSIONS Span 8,70 m (28 ft 6½ in); length 8,11 m (26 ft 7¾ in); wing area 13,5 m² (145 ft²).
ENGINE One 1100 kg (reheat) RD-10F.
WEIGHTS Empty 2192 kg (4832 lb); fuel/oil 658 + 14 kg; loaded 3 t (6614 lb) or 3350 (7385) with tip tanks, never fitted.
PERFORMANCE Max speed with reheat 875 km/h at SL and at 10 km, 904 (562 mph) at 5 km, normal cold thrust 760 at SL, 818 at 5 km and 788 at 10 km; initial climb (reheat) 25,8 m/s (5080 ft/min), (cold thrust) 16,4 (3228); time to 5 and 10 km (cold) 3·9 and 10·5 min; service ceiling 15 km (49,200 ft); range (Shavrov) 1000 km (OKB, 700; 1000 with tip tanks); take-off 550 m; landing 520 m/180 km/h (112 mph).

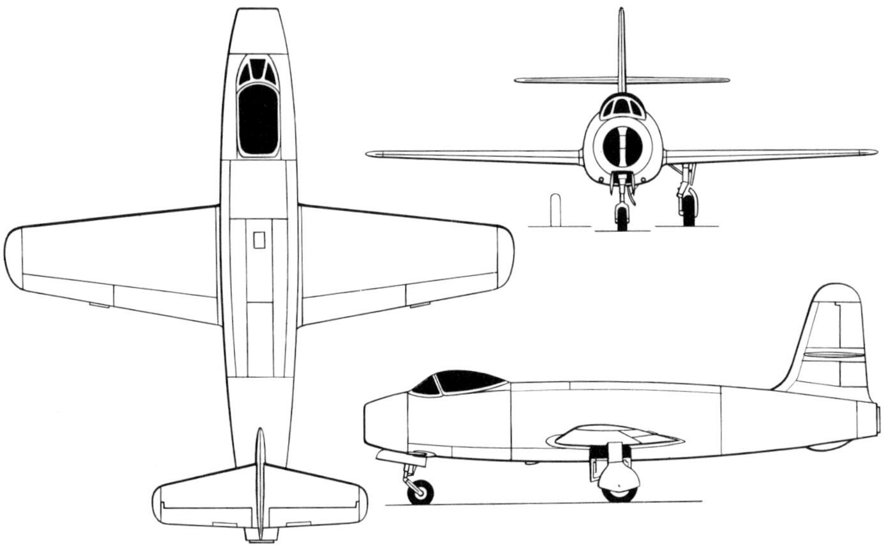

Yak-19

Yak-20* Little published about this simple side-by-side trainer and sporting aircraft designed in three months summer 1950 and test-flown at end of year (believed one of first aircraft projects at Arsen'yev, but this may not be so). Smaller and much lighter than Yak-18, and costing half as much to buy and operate, Yak-20 ought to have found wide market. Fuselage retained welded steel tube truss with secondary wood stringers and fabric covering, with width for two pilots side-by-side. New simple single-spar wing, Clark-YH 14·5/9% thick, D1 construction with riveted skin over LE to front spar, fabric to rear. Slotted Frise ailerons worked by push-rods, 17° down and 20° up, slotted flaps inboard set by pilot linkage to 18° for take-off and 32° for landing. New Ivchyenko engine on rubber mounts at front of tubular truss, D1 cowl in hinged upper/lower halves, 2 m V-515 controllable-pitch (counterweight type) prop. Fuel in two 35 lit tanks in wing roots ahead of spar. Tail D1/fabric but with D1 skin over fin LE. Simple main gears with 500 × 150 mm wheels on welded V-type legs (joined by fairing) hinged to deflect outwards, inner bracing strut having wrapped rubber shock-absorber bungee on transverse fuselage member. Tailwheel 200 × 80 mm sprung by loop of rubber. Sliding canopy moulded in left/right halves in D1 frame, dual stick-type controls, venturis ventral (large) and on right side, no radio. Prototype painted in VVS insignia, tested by Anokhin and Georgii Shiyanov and from 1 January 1951 flown by numerous Dosaaf members. Proved capable of performing all required aerobatics with two pilots, apparently no major shortcoming. Kondratyev reports decision urgently to place massive order for Dosaaf, without explaining why no series aircraft built.

DIMENSIONS Span 9,56 m (31 ft 4⅜ in); length 7,06 m (23 ft 2 in); wing area 15,0 m² (161·5 ft²).
ENGINE One 80 hp AI-10.
WEIGHTS Empty 470 kg (1,036 lb); fuel/oil 50 + 10 kg; loaded 700 (1543).
PERFORMANCE Max speed at SL 160 km/h (99 mph); cruise 142 (88); climb, not known; service ceiling 3 km (9850 ft); range 400 km (249 miles); take-off 295 m; landing 180/60 km/h.

Yak-21 Dual tandem Yak-15, described in that entry.

Yak-22 Not known, possibly **Yak EG**.

Yak-23 Yak-19 had from start been considered interim fighter, and OKB half-expected it would remain prototype (though it was a fighter, not as sometimes reported a research aircraft). Yak-23 was derived aircraft using much better British-based centrifugal engine. Important difference was return to *redan* (stepped) layout, with engine in nose and nozzle under TE. Design to meet October 1946 demand for next-generation fighter able to use existing airfields and facilities and not incorporating swept aerodynamic surfaces. Extraordinarily quick design possible because same drawings used for wing (with tip tanks) and landing gear as Yak-19.

New fuselage of stressed-skin construction identical in material, frames, stringers and technique to Yak-19, without welded tube truss. Engine in sealed plenum chamber ahead of front spar (latter arched over jetpipe) with entire nose

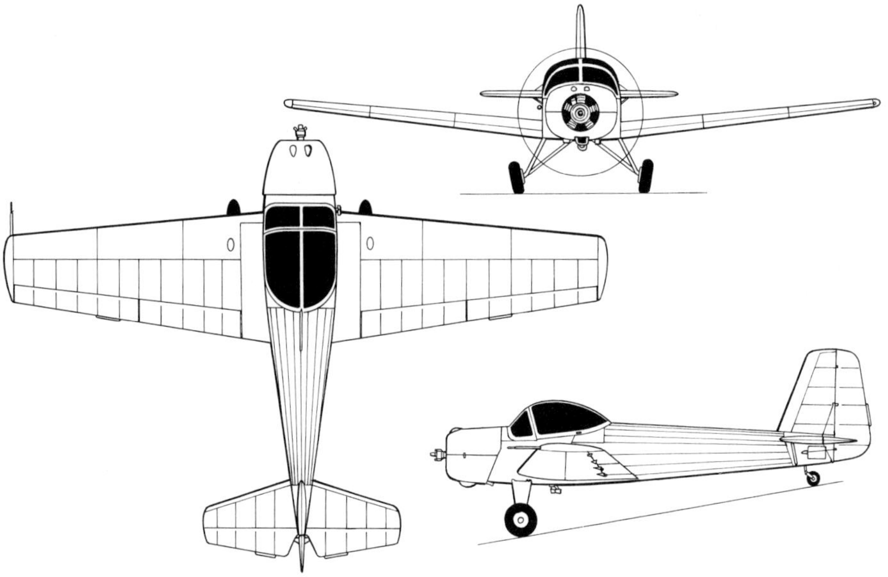

Yak-20

section ahead of diagonal frame removable for access or for engine-change. Internal fuel 920 lit in protected tanks immediately ahead of and behind unpressurized cockpit; tip tanks each 200 lit (44 gal). Improved ejection seat, but still simple and driven by single cordite charge. Sliding teardrop canopy, 57 mm bulletproof windscreen and 8 mm back armour. RSIU-6 hf radio with mast and wires. Push/pull rods to tabbed elevators on tailplane fixed at 0·5° part-way up fin; rudder with ground-adjustable tab driven by cables. Tail all stressed skin, horizontal tail reduced from 3 m^2 in Yak-19 to 2,96 m^2 and vertical from 2,03 to 1,64. Shavrov gives armament as 'two Type 150P 23 mm *and* two NR-23K'; appears error and 150P not known to author. Accepted armament, two NS-23 *or* NR-23 each with 90 rounds.

Prototype flown mid (believed 17 June) 1947 by Ivanov; Anokhin, not yet fully back in harness, also flew it. Successful and attractive aircraft, no problem with jet noise or heating on rear fuselage and only visible mods were to reduce height of rudder, add 5° dihedral to tailplane and tinker with landing gear and nozzle fairing. Combat camera and landing light added in inlet bifurcation above nosewheel bay, tip-tank attachments modified to accept alternative 60 kg bombs and radio added. Factory testing completed 12 September 1947 and following good NII report cleared for production early 1948. Intended batch (1000 or 500?) curtailed at 310 because of success of more potent MiG-15. Series Yak-23 had NR-23 guns, RPKO-10M homer/radio compass and slightly larger stainless skin on underside at rear. Service with VVS brief, but popular with Warsaw Pact air forces (Czech designation S-101). Could outclimb MiG-15, and Polish civil-registered Yak-23 set record 21 November 1957 by reaching 3 km in 119 s and 6 km in 197 s.

OKB built one **Yak-23UTI** in first half 1949, tested by G.S. Klimushkin. Rear cockpit retained but given different bulged canopy with fixed rear portion. Forward cockpit for pupil severely reduced fuselage tankage (660 lit total) and had additional combat camera above windscreen. Height of vertical tail increased. Armament, one UB on left side of nose. Prototype unpainted, nose number 50. Shavrov comments could use poor dirt airfields with bad approaches, though in such regard identical to fighter. He also reports series production, not confirmed by other accounts and explicitely denied by some. In addition, one series Yak-23 was rebuilt by CTIA, Romania, as tandem dual trainer with extra cockpit added behind first. This must have been constricted, and demanded ballast in lieu of instructor; it left forward tank and eliminated rear-fuselage tank. New steeper windscreen and tandem canopies both hinged to right. No designation known for this machine which flew in 1956.

DIMENSIONS Span 8,37 m (28 ft 7$\frac{3}{4}$ in); length (Shavrov) 8,12 m (26 ft 7$\frac{2}{3}$ in), (Něměcek, Janecka) 8,16, (Butowski) 8,11; wing area (most accounts) 13,5 m^2 (145 ft^2), (Janecka, Alexander) 13,6.

ENGINE One 1590 kg thrust RD-500.

WEIGHTS Empty (prototype) 1980 kg, (production) 2 t (4410 lb), (UTI) 2220 (4894); fuel/oil 760 kg (1085 kg with tip tanks) + 12, (UTI) 530 (850 with tip tanks) + 12; loaded (production) 3036 kg (6693 lb) or 3384 (7460) with tip tanks, (UTI) 2950 (6504) or 3300 (7275) with tip tanks.

PERFORMANCE Max speed (Shavrov, production) 923 km/h (574 mph) at SL, 868 (539) at 5 km, (Janecka) 913/975 depending on height; initial climb 47 m/s; time to 5 km and 10 km (production) 2·3 and 6·2 min; service ceiling (production) 14,8 km (48,600 ft), (UTI) 14 km; range (production, Shavrov) 755 km (469 miles) internal fuel, 1030 (640) with tip tanks, (Janecka) 920/1200 (572/746), (UTI) Shavrov gives impossible 1280 but max endurance 1·7 h; take-off 440 m (UTI, 400); landing 485 (UTI, 500)/157 km/h (97·6 mph), (several accounts give 152 km/h landing speed).

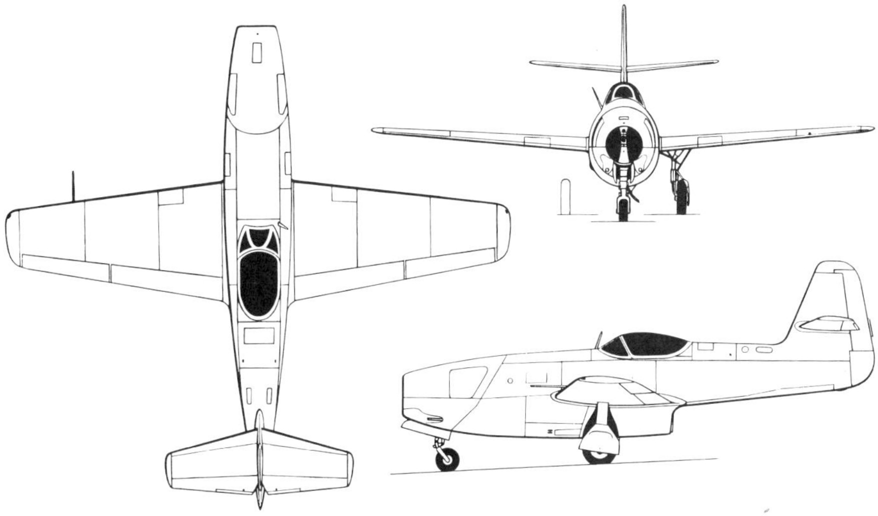

Yak-23

Yak-23 (object above wing root is ladder)

Yak EG OKB formed helicopter group in 1944 (according to Shavrov and some other accounts 1946, but this must be incorrect) and assigned design management to Igor A. Yerlikh. Adopted coaxial configuration with pair of two-blade rotors with max vertical separation. Maximum help from TsAGI, and OKB engineers also visited Breguet which had flown Dorand coaxial machine before war and was completing prototype G-11E. No direct liaison with Kamov but GUAP provided funds and oversaw both teams, which (except for pilot controls) did come to similar conclusions. Rejecting TE outrigger tabs considered at start, rotor fully articulated with friction dampers and controlled by modern cyclic/collective levers acting via oil dashpots on swash-plates, with yaw control by pedals giving differential collective to upper/lower rotors. Blades built up laminated hardwood and pine with ply covering overlain by glued fabric. Simple fuselage based on welded steel truss with D1 sheet from nose to rear of engine compartment, fabric at tail. Two seats side-by-side in nose (not known if dual control) with door each side. Radial engine in normal attitude with forward drive via cooling fan and centrifugal clutch to bevel box and rotor shafts, with hydraulic coupling and additional oil-depressed spring which on failure of drive forced blades into autorotative pitch. Tricycle landing gear with vertical oleo struts; ground resonance avoided by pure chance. Completed early 1947 with long fabric-covered rear fuselage carrying twin-finned tail and tailskid. Tested by V.V. Tezavrovskii who made 40 tethered hovers followed by 75 flights

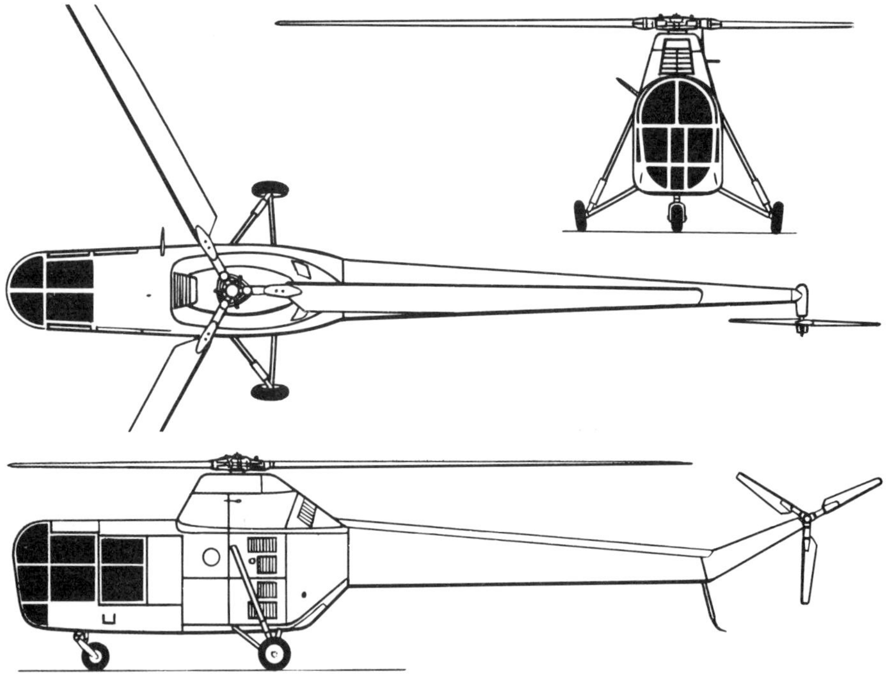

Yak-100

for total airborne time of 20 h. EG (*Eksperimentalnyi Gelikopter*) flew, but CG too far aft and tail removed; oil tank moved from engine compartment to rear cockpit bulkhead, skid removed and rear fuselage re-faired. Normal rotor rpm 233, severe vibration, and though positive control never lost, stick force and phugoid instability worsened beyond 30 km/h forward speed, severely limiting practical value of EG. After prolonged investigation Yak decided to leave this configuration to Kamov.

DIMENSIONS Diameter of rotors 10,0 m (32 ft 9⅔ in); length of fuselage 6,35 m (21 ft 5 in).

ENGINE One 140 hp M-11FR-1.

WEIGHTS Empty 878 kg (1936 lb); fuel/oil, not known but not able to carry fuel plus two crew; loaded 1020 kg (2249 lb).

PERFORMANCE Max speed (Shavrov) 70 km/h, but did not exceed 60 km/h and at this speed stick force so great as to be impractical; ceiling given as 250 m hover and 2,5 km in forward flight, but in fact greatest height actually reached was 180 m; range, in theory 235 km claimed, but again in practice much shorter.

Yak-100 This helicopter looked like exact copy of S-51, though Yak insisted OKB team, under Yerlikh, merely reached similar design conclusions. Complete reversal of original scheme, this single-rotor machine did retain similar dynamic parts, drive and hub mechanism with damped flapping, feathering and drag hinges and hydraulic-dashpot control via swashplate. Three main blades of hardwood and pine as before, with ply skin and glued fabric overall. Root of each blade in upper/lower halves of bolted D1, steel hub. Main change in engine installation was to copy S-51 vertical engine mount with several changes needed to enable engine to run in this attitude. Cooling fan, clutch/freewheel and reduction gear and angle box for tail rotor were more Sikorsky than scaled-up EG, though pilot controls and control system retained OKB belief in spring and oil vibration dampers (this time with pilot adjustment) and in spring-loaded actuation of pitch into autorotation following loss of drive torque. Pedal control of tail-rotor pitch. Airframe based on welded steel-tube frame carrying landing gear, seats, rotor hub and engine. Skin riveted D1, and cranked tail-boom D1 monocoque. Basic design completed late 1947 as tandem trainer or as transport with single pilot in front and two-seat divan or other payload behind. Two prototypes built, first with VVS funds and bearing VVS insignia. Began factory test November 1948, initially suffered from severe vibration and apparent blade flutter. Blades given ground-adjustable TE tabs and eventually modified with CG further aft, behind flexural axis. These blades first fitted to No 2 Yak-100, which began test July 1949. Factory test complete June 1950 and NII tests successfully accomplished later same year, but Mi-1 already adopted and Yak-100 lost by being later.

DIMENSIONS Diameter of main rotor 14,5 m (47 ft 6⅞ in); length of fuselage 13,9 m (45 ft 7¼ in); tail rotor 2,6 m (102·36 in).

ENGINE One 420 hp AI-26GRFL.

WEIGHTS Empty 1805 kg (3979 lb); fuel/oil 80 + 14 kg; loaded 2180 (4806).

PERFORMANCE Max speed claimed 170 km/h (106 mph); ceiling (hover) 2720 m, (forward-flight) 5250 m (17,200 ft); range, claimed 325 km (202 miles).

Yak-24 This large and powerful transport helicopter was created under pressure in response to direct order of Stalin at Kremlin meeting autumn 1951 (in his first autobiography Yak gave date of this meeting as 'end of summer 1952'). Instruction was for Mil to build single-engine machine with 1200 kg military load, Yak a machine with twice this load, prototypes to be ready in a year. Mil had already prepared suitable design, and Yak gained permission to use essentially same main rotor and drive from similar engine, merely doubling up to use two engine/rotor systems at ends of boxcar fuselage. Yak awed at size of task and short timescale, assembled large team including Yerlikh, veteran helicopter man N. Skrzhinskii, P.D. Samsonov (famed flying-boat designer who had long managed Yak prototype dept), L. Shekhter, L.S. Vil'dgrub and many other well-known engineers. Plan was to build four Yak-24, already called **LV** (*Letayushchaya Vagon*, flying wagon), two for static and resonance test and two for flight. Promised 'unlimited support' in crash programme, Yak-24 used full resources of TsIAM, TsAGI, VIAM and other labs.

Basic engine/rotor design described under Mi-4. Fuselage functional container based on welded KhGSA truss with minimal secondary stringer/fairing formers of D1 or wood. Unstressed D1 sheet covering over front and rear engine bays and large fin, fabric elsewhere. Aluminium plank cargo floor with full-section access via rear ramp/door; passenger door forward on left side. Rear rotor mounted on top of vertical fin (TE curved to right to give side-thrust to left in flight) with drive from engine installed in normal horizontal attitude at base of fin, with open cooling-air inlets each side of fin and clear-

EG

Yak-24 (late series)

ance under engine for vehicles and other cargo on ramp. High-speed connecting shaft to front rotor, mirror-image with rotation anti-clockwise seen from above, driven by engine at 60° angle between cockpit and cabin. Nose cockpit for two pilots, radio-operator and engineer, entirely glazed with aft-sliding door each side and sliding door(s) at rear giving restricted access past engine to main compartment. Latter measured 2 × 2 × 10 m (78¾ in square by 32 ft 9⅔ in long) with intended accommodation for up to 40 troops on canvas wall seats or light vehicles or 4 t (8,818 lb) cargo, with crane operation using central hook on underside of fuselage. Four similar levered-suspension landing gears, each normally castoring ±30°, on rigid welded steel-tube outriggers. No details on fuel tanks.

While numerous establishments tested complete engine/rotor rigs, blade fatigue and truss structure of fuselage, first flight article readied spring 1952 and began 300 hr endurance test with wheels tied down. Vibration in evidence from start, and usually severe. With greater experience OKB might have recognized a fundamental N_1 main-rotor mode and altered critical dimension. As it was, at 178th hour, rear engine tore free from fatigued mounts, machine being destroyed by fire. Second flight article, ie, 4th airframe, finally began tethered flight piloted by Sergei Brovtsyev and Yegor Milyutchyev – who proved to be excellent team – on 3 July 1952. Hops at partial power were followed by full-power flights, when vibration reared its head dangerously. Five months by every available expert found no cure; then Yak claims he personally ordered 0,5 m (19·7 in) cut off each main-rotor blade. This effected immediate great improvement. No 4 aircraft delivered for NII test October 1953, but destroyed when tethers snapped during ground running. OKB delivered

Yak-24 (early series)

improved aircraft with numerous mods including modified tail with no fins but braced tailplanes with dihedral 45°. This finally passed NII April 1955 and production began at GAZ in Leningrad. First four pre-series Yak-24 (visibly not all identical) flew at Aviation Day at Tushino, August 1955. Series version had strengthened floor with tracks for vehicles, tie-down rings, attachments for pillars carrying 18 stretchers, full radio and night equipment and facilities for field servicing. Normal max load 20 armed troops or 3 t (6614 lb). Probably about 100 built, most with tailplane dihedral only 20° and with fixed endplate fins canted 3°30′ to give side-thrust to left. On 17 December 1955 Milyutchyev took payload 2 t to 5082 m and Tinyakov lifted 4 t to 2902 m.

OKB produced several improved versions but none believed to have been built in series. **Yak-24U** (*Uluchshyennyi*, improved) flew December 1957 with numerous mods resulting from prolonged research. Rotor blade length unchanged but diameter restored by adding long tubular tie at root. Side-thrust at tail reduced by canting axes of rotors 2°30′ (front to right, rear to left), so curved rear of fin removed. Fuselage frame strengthened, metal skinned throughout and cabin increased in width 0,4 m (15¾ in). Flight-control system fitted with two-axis autostab and autopilot of limited authority, developed within OKB. External slung load attached to winch in roof of cabin with large door in floor. Rear landing gear oleos changed in rate to eliminate last vestiges of ground resonance, and other minor changes including revised fuel system. In production (believed at Urals GAZ) from early 1959, though number believed small. This variant could at last lift 40 troops or 3,5 t (7716 lb) and at least some production machines had tailplane dihedral 0°.

At least one example built by 1960 of **Yak-24A** (designation from *Aerolinyi*, airline) similar to late Yak-24U with horizontal tailplane and latest avionics but with comfortable civil interior for 30 passengers seated 2+1. Continuous glazing down sides of fuselage (like airliners of 1920s), compartment for 300 kg baggage and fold-down steps at door; rear freight door eliminated. Appeared in Aeroflot markings though apparently without civil registration, and never seen in service. A further example built by 1960 of VIP model, **Yak-24K** (believed from *Kupé*, coupé or compartment). Fuselage shorter, electrically extended airstairs and luxurious accommodation for (usually) nine passengers with four large windows each side. Curiously this machine had 20° tailplane dihedral. Final known variant, believed never built, was **Yak-24P** (believed *Passazhirskii*). Models and brochures showed this to be powered by two turboshaft engines (said to be Ivchyenko) both mounted above main cabin with inlets facing each other. This not only almost doubled power but enabled full length of interior to be put to use, with 30 passengers (again seated 2+1) and rear toilet and baggage compartments. Seven large and two small windows each side.

Yak-24 posed immense problems, and though it took much longer than Stalin's year, development was eventually completed to point at which this Flying Wagon could be put into military service. It was used for various purposes including crane role and for special photo missions, but remained a slow and rather unpopular machine. Had OKB persevered it might have produced more satisfactory machines with turbine engines, but it was glad to leave helicopter field to others.

DIMENSIONS Diameter of four-blade main rotors, (prototype, 24U, A, K and P) 21,0 m (68 ft 10¾ in), (production 24) 20,0 m (65 ft 7⅓ in); length of fuselage (most) 21,3 or 21,34 m (70 ft 0⅛ in), (A) 22,1 m, (K) not known but about 19 m.

ENGINES Two 1700 hp ASh-82V.

WEIGHTS Empty (pre-production) 10 607 kg (23,384 lb), (U) 11 t (24,250 lb); fuel/oil, not known; loaded (24) 14,24 or 14,27 t (31,459 lb), (U) 15,83 (34,899), (A) 16,0 (35,273), (P) 18 (39,683).

PERFORMANCE Max speed (24, U, A, K) 175 km/h (109 mph), (P) 210 (130·5); cruise 156 (97); ceiling (hover) (24) 2 km, (U) 1,5, (forward flight) (24) 4,2, (U) 2,7; range (24) 265 km (165 miles), (U) 255 (158), (A) 200 (124); take-off and/landing, within 50 m (164 ft).

*Yak-25**

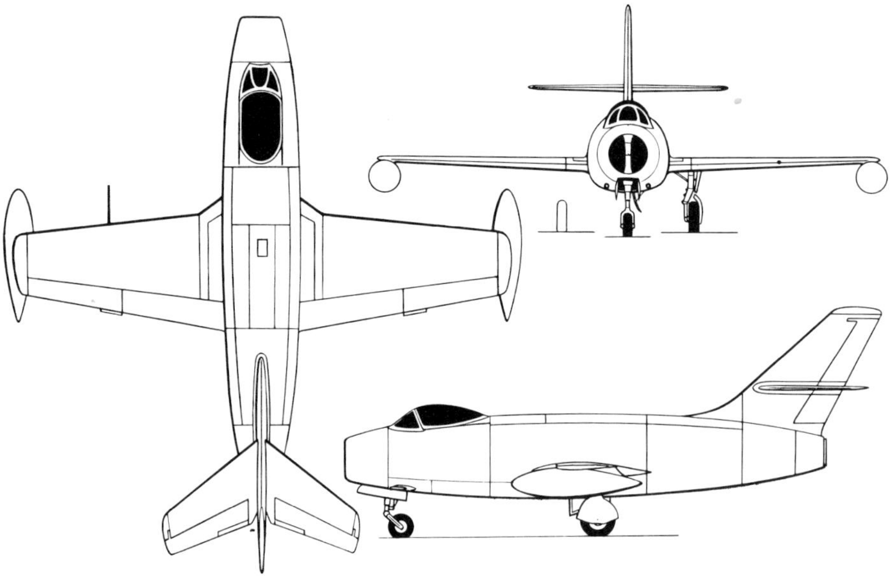

*Yak-25**

Yak-25* First aircraft to bear this designation was small further step beyond Yak-19 and based on similar airframe though with swept tail. Wing similar family to Yak-19 and Yak-23 though improved all-metal construction and with later high-speed 'laminar' section, S-9S-9 at root tapering to KV-4-9 at tip, 9% thickness throughout, with aspect ratio 5·64 and taper ratio 2·5. OKB's first wing with welded 30KhGSA T-booms on two main spars and V-95 webs, tip to tip. Short centre section with auxiliary spar carrying landing gear (again similar to Yak-19 and Yak-23). Fuselage based on Yak-19 but longer and with plenum chamber amidships for centrifugal engine of greater diameter (though frontal area actually less than either Yak-19 or Yak-23). OKB's first pressurized-cockpit jet, with aft-sliding canopy and 57 mm bulletproof windscreen. Cordite ejection seat with leg restraints and 8 mm back armour. Internal fuel capacity 875 lit (192·5 gal). Swept tail with fixed tailplane swept at 35° (often said to be 45°) on LE, 3 m² area, mounted 1 m above fuselage on vertical fin said by Shavrov to be swept at 45° angle but shown on drawings as 40° on LE. Total vertical tail area 2,12 m². Complete rear fuselage and tail removed for engine access. Hydraulic system in place of many power functions previously pneumatic, and hydraulic boosted flight controls (certainly ailerons). New feature in powered speed brakes in place of lower section of rudder, opened automatically by pitot/static system to restrict airspeed to safe level. Armament three NR-23 each with 75 rounds. Same 200 lit (44 gal) tip tanks as Yak-23; Western report giving drop-tank capacity as 162,5 lit (35¾ gal) cannot be confirmed from any Soviet source. First of two prototypes (number 15) began flight-test programme under Anokhin 31 October 1947. Great improvement on any previous Yak fighter and demonstrated excellent manoeuvrability with rapid roll and performance seldom attained by any straight-wing aircraft. Unfortunately factory test continued to 3 July 1948, by which time higher performance of MiG-15 was evident. OKB never again recovered its former ascendancy in fighters.

DIMENSIONS Span 8,8 m (28 ft 10½ in); length 8,66 m (28 ft 5 in); wing area 14,0 m² (150·7 ft²).

ENGINE One 1590 kg thrust RD-500.

WEIGHTS Empty 2285 kg (5037·5 lb); fuel/oil 700, 1025 kg with tip tanks; loaded 3185, with tip tanks filled 3535 (7793).

PERFORMANCE Max speed 982 km/h (610 mph) at SL, 953 (592) at 5 km; time to climb to 5 and 10 km, 2·5 and 6·3 min; service ceiling 14 km (45,932 ft); range 1100 km, or 1600 (994 miles) with tip tanks; take-off 510 m; landing 825 m/175 km/h.

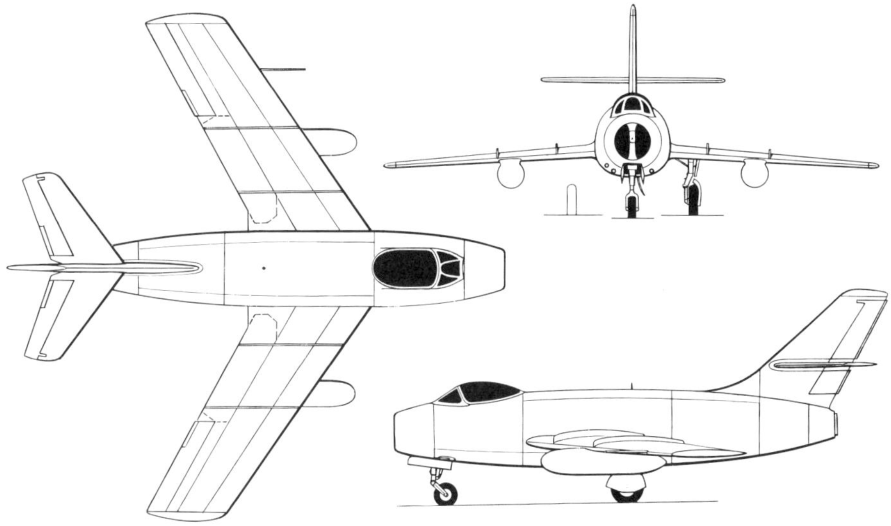

*Yak-30**

Yak-30* First aircraft to carry this designation, which curiously is even and thus not normally assigned to a fighter, was OKB's answer to March 1946 requirement for Mach 0·9 interceptor for use from existing unpaved airfields. Design based upon Yak-25 but with entirely new swept wing mounted in mid position, in turn calling for different main landing gear. Wing of basically TsAGI S-9S series but swept 35° at LE, with dihedral −2°; aspect ratio 5, taper ratio only 1·5. Two spars throughout with 30KhGSA booms and V-95 webs, skin flush-riveted D16 of ruling thickness 2 mm. Boosted tabbed ailerons, TsAGI slotted split flaps and four full-chord fences; TE kinked to short unswept inboard portion. Fuselage basically same as Yak-25 but longer, though internal fuel unchanged. Identical cockpit, canopy and seat as Yak-25 and same armament of three NR-23 with 225 total rounds. Split speed brake at tail retained, though no longer any Mach limitation. Fuselage slightly greater cross-section as perfect circle (1,36 m) instead of oval 1,36 wide and 1,34 high. Fin essentially as Yak-25 but tailplane slightly enlarged to 3,05 m², still 35° (not 45°). Drop tanks slightly modified to fit as slippers under wing at mid-span, same 200 lit capacity. First prototype (number 42) flown by Anokhin 4 September 1948, too late to rival MiG-15. Second Yak-30, number 54, had various minor changes, most obvious being revised maingear doors forming large section of fuselage skin. Mach 0·935 often demonstrated and handling generally good, but out-classed by MiG-15. Factory testing concluded 16 December 1948 without submission to NII. Anokhin noted unsuccessful wing profile and dissatisfaction with aileron balance.

DIMENSIONS Span 8,65 m (28 ft 4½ in); length 8964 mm (29 ft 5 in); wing area 15 m² (161·5 ft²).
ENGINE One 1590 kg thrust RD-500.
WEIGHTS Empty 2415 kg (5324 lb); fuel/oil 700/1000 kg; loaded 3305 (7286), or with drop tanks 3630 (8003).
PERFORMANCE Max speed 1060 km/h (659 mph) at SL, 1025 (637) at 5 km; time to climb to 5 and 10 km, 2·6 and 6·6 min; service ceiling 15 km (49,200 ft); range 1000 km (621 miles), or 1500 (932) with drop tanks; take-off 510 m; landing 610 m/188 km/h.

Yak-50* First aircraft to carry this designation (second, aerobatic machine of 1975, described previously), which again had a non-fighter even number, was dramatic attempt to equal performance of MiG OKB by using same VK-1 engine and increasing sweep throughout. Described as light fighter/interceptor, and intended to meet requirement for single-seat all-weather aircraft, but real value was in providing basis of later Yak-25**. Wing of unknown section (believed SR-9 series) with constant chord and generally unvarying profile outboard of short centre section with TE at 90°. Ruling sweep angle 45° throughout, dihedral −5°, skin stretch-formed and 3 mm thick between spars, three fences each side (outers only as far as aileron LE), aspect ratio 4. Fuselage enlarged to 1,4 m diameter and lengthened to 9465 mm (excluding tail). Dummy radome at top of inlet in nose, ducts enlarged to handle mass flow increased from 29 to 45 kg/s, pressurized cockpit redesigned with lower-drag canopy, wing in true mid-position, rear fuselage and tail detachable

*Yak-50**

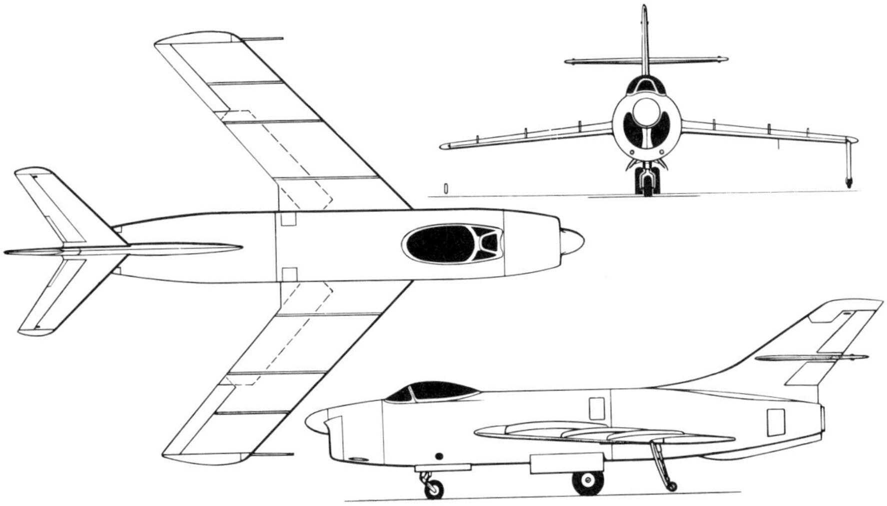

*Yak-50**

DIMENSIONS Span 8010 mm (26 ft 3⅓ in); length 11 185 mm (36 ft 8⅓ in); wing area 16,0 m² (172 ft²).

ENGINE One 2700 kg thrust VK-1.

WEIGHTS Empty 3085 kg (6901 lb); fuel/oil 850 + 10 kg; loaded (½ fuel) 3650, (max fuel) 4100 (9039).

PERFORMANCE Max speed, 1170 km/h (727 mph) at SL, 1135 (705) at 5 km, 1065 (662) at 10 km, M-max 1·03; initial climb 68 m/s (13,390 ft/min); time to 5/10/15 km, 1·5, 3·5 and 7 min; service ceiling 16,6 km (54,462 ft); range 1100 km (684 miles); take-off 587 m; landing 965 m/200 km/h (124 mph).

for engine access. Sweep of vertical tail increased to 45°, increased in area to 3,0 m², horizontal tail at last swept 45° and reduced in size to 2,86 m², tailplane still fixed. Top of fin dielectric aerial, rudder in upper/lower parts, airbrakes relocated on sides of rear fuselage, ventral strake/fin of 0,344 m² added to increase high-Mach yaw stability. Completely new area-increasing tracked flaps of basically Fowler type moving parallel to fuselage (unlike Yak-30). Considerably greater fuselage fuel, 1065 lit (234 gal). Completely new tandem (*velosipedno tipa*, bicycle type) landing gears, rear twin 600 × 150 mm wheels taking 85% of total weight. New nose gear retracting to rear, plus outrigger tip-protection gears with extremely small solid-tyred wheels retracting to rear housed in fixed tip fairings downstream of large pitot heads. Armament reduced to two NR-23 each with 80 rounds. Believed braking parachute added to prototype (only one aircraft known, number 35). Flight test programme by Anokhin opened 15 July 1949. Soon proved to have tremendous performance; few fighters of era could equal speed and climb, and manoeuvrability also outstanding with rate of roll better than MiG-15 and tighter turning circle. VVS interest focused on low gross weight, well below MiG-15 and conferring great high-altitude performance and good handling despite wing area 16 compared with 22,6 m². In general Yak-50 outperformed predicted figures for new MiG SI, later called MiG-17, which was to fly a year later. Yak almost made it with this fighter, but ultimately giant established programme with existing MiG-15 proved unshakeable. (Not even MiG-17 could alter it for another 2½ years). Eventually factory test programme was halted 30 May 1950. Only real fault was poor directional stability at high speed on ground (identical snags hit Hawker P.1127 decade later) and Anokhin said uncontrollable on wet surface. Flying continued in support of Yak-25, mainly to perfect landing gear.

Yak-1000 Another inexplicable OKB number, this was assigned to a remarkable experimental fighter designed 1949 to explore configuration for supersonic interceptor. Again *velosipedno* landing gear was adopted, because at this time problems with Yak-50 were not yet manifest. Configuration faintly like Douglas D-558-I Skystreak, with long barrel-like fuselage of mini-

Yak-1000

mum cross-section tailored to slim axial engine of highest possible thrust. Pressurized cockpit near nose with rudder pedals right in bifurcation of duct, pilot being in semi-reclining posture in modified ejection seat to reduce frontal area. Low-drag canopy without any fighter attributes such as flat bulletproof windscreen. Air ducts passed only above three spars of wing inside fuselage (fuel and gear below). Engine installed immediately aft of rearmost spar with short jet-pipe in removable rear fuselage and tail unit. Wing of low aspect ratio and sharp taper, entire surface aft of rear spar hinged to form slotted flap (geometry unknown) incorporating powered aileron. Landing-gear units apparently same as Yak-50, but outriggers moved inboard to point at which chord of wing equalled length of leg. Low aspect ratio tail with fixed tailplane carried well aft on fin so that powered elevators were downstream of rudder. Airbrakes on sides

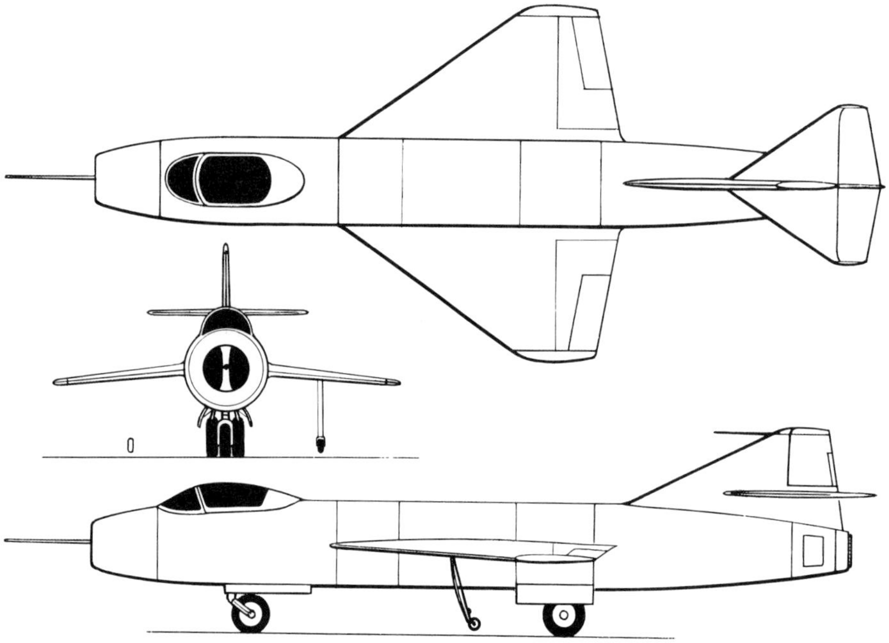

Yak-1000

of rear fuselage, braking parachute unknown location. Limited fuel capacity ahead of and behind main-gear bay; space for two cannon in lower part of nose, not installed. Lyul'ka once gave impression this aircraft flew, but in fact taxi tests (believed by Anokhin) in 1951 showed such dangerous instability whole programme eventually abandoned. Yak-1000 certainly severely damaged in these pre-flight tests and may well have overturned. Only known example, No 34, returned to OKB for repair but this not carried out. Curious Western story gives design speed as 1150 km/h, slower than much larger and less-powerful Yak-50; actual figure was 1750 km/h, M 1·65, or 2000 (M 1·88) with planned afterburner.

DIMENSIONS Span 4,52 m (14 ft 10 in); length, excl instrument boom, 11,69 m (38 ft 4$\frac{1}{8}$ in).
ENGINE One 5000 kg thrust AL-5.
No other data.

Yak-200

Yak-200 Yet another strange designation (actual OKB number must have been in region of 65), this military crew-trainer flown in 1953 is one of least-known Soviet aircraft. Almost all available information is contained in single photo, which most unusually is air-to-air. This shows apparent kinship of engines, nacelles, main landing gear and possibly wings and tail to Yak-16 transport. Commonly described as all-metal, but this difficult to substantiate. Also described as four-seat, but again this could be mistaken and three might be correct. All that can be deduced with certainty is that fuselage was designed for dual side-by-side pilot training in wide cockpit with framed sliding canopy, and long nose provided station for visual bomb aiming and for separate navigator at table illuminated by four roof windows. Nose access via door on right side. Light bombload in internal bay under mid-mounted wing. Latter had centre-section and dihedralled outer panels not identical to Yak-16. Tail cropped at top and horizontal tail with dihedral. Engines driving props without spinners and neatly cowled on long nacelles projecting well aft of TE. Tricycle landing gear with nose unit retracting to rear, main units forwards, all wheels projecting when retracted. Fuel in wing inboard of nacelles; pitot on right wing (on long strut under nose on Yak-16); VHF whip aerial ahead of fin. No radar, astrodome or movable guns. Only known photo shows individual aircraft number 52 and VVS markings.

DIMENSIONS Not known; one report of span/length 17 and 11 m unconfirmed.
ENGINES Two 570/730 hp ASh-21.
No other data.

Yak-25** Unlike La, Yak produced a jet fighter to support a major programme through 1950s, and by exceptional sustained development through 1960s also. Originally planned to meet requirement for capable all-weather and night interceptor (Kremlin request, 18 November 1951), which was also tendered for by La-200 and MiG I-320, Yak-25 appeared dramatically bold and new design when first seen. In fact it was direct scale of Yak-50, with two engines on wings to leave nose free for enormous radar. OKB number, probably in region of 60, never published; **Yak-25**, previously used for single-jet fighter, was VVS designation allocated after type had been accepted.

Adoption of Yak-50 configuration, modified for two engines, proved great success and solved all problems except continuing thorny one of stability and control on ground. By this time OKB completely switched to all-metal stressed-skin structures, and with Yak-25 adopted tapered plate (up to 4 mm at root) between parallel spars of 45° wing, which retained SR-9 series profile, constant chord outboard of short inboard section (integral, not structurally separate) with 90° TE, progressive taper in thickness to give 6·1% thickness at tip (inboard of gear pods) and anhedral reduced from −5° to constant −3°. New slim axial engines carried on welded 30KhGSA frames ahead of wing box and closely underslung in low-drag nacelles just projecting behind TE. Small ram inlet in intake

*Yak-25*** (series, before delivery)*

lip and large oil-cooler scoop on top of cowl. Sides and accessories of engine accessed by large left/right hinged cowl panels with Camloc-type fasteners. Nacelles found to obviate need for inboard fences, but full-chord fence at inner end of aileron and another fence at mid-span of aileron, not extended across latter. Ailerons believed to be manual, with spring tabs. Hydraulic split flaps inboard (constant-chord) and outboard of nacelles. Large fuselage of circular section. Entire nose dielectric radome, possibly largest such moulding in Europe in early 1950s (equalled in volume only by APS-20 AEW radar), probably caused severe problems with erosion by rain and hail. Heavy and bulky radar, not based on any particular Western set, operating in I-band at 9·3/9·4 GHz (same signal as interceptor MiG-19) with three different scan modes for different tasks, all distinguished by high PRFs (pulse-recurrence frequency). NATO name Scan Three in consequence. Installed mass 493 kg (1087 lb) including power supply, cabling and tail-warning set with small scanner in tailcone. Pilot and radar-navigator in tandem ejection seats of greatly improved type with face-blinds, calf garters and additional handle on seat-pan. Strongly framed 57 mm thick windscreen, large canopy sliding 2,2 m to rear, cockpit pressurized and heated, rear bulkhead adjacent to front spar of carry-through wing structure. Tail exact scale of Yak-50 but with more pronounced kink at LE of dorsal fin faired into spine along fuselage to cockpit. Airbrakes on sides of rear fuselage. Landing gear almost exact scale of Yak-50 but with main unit retracting forwards and steerable nose gear carrying forward door at front of levered-suspension leg. Tip outrigger gears on single struts with fairings which in retracted position form underside of tip pods also carrying pitot heads. Armament two N-37, each with 56 rounds, with barrels in fairings beneath fuselage between nose and main landing gears. No reliable evidence found for Western report of box of 55 mm rockets. said to be mounted between guns and extended prior to firing; such armament not on squadron aircraft.

OKB built succession of static-test, system-test and prototype aircraft, first believed to fly 1953. Yak has written of Kremlin meeting in 1952 at which he managed to persuade Stalin Yak-25 was better than La-200B despite Beria's preference for latter, and in such a way that he implies flight-test results were already in; and Něměcek even claims Yak-25s (plural) took part in Tushino parade in 1952. Correct history has not been disclosed (neither have data, see later), but Yak-25 was in production by late 1954 and five examples, plus prototypes of two developments, certainly participated in Tushino parade August 1955. Few details are known of engineering changes during development but production aircraft had airbrakes close behind wing, much further forward than on previous Yak fighters, forward door of main as well as nose gear hinged to leg, and ventral fin with protective skid. Except for first few aircraft most Yak-25 were powered by improved RD-9 (former AM-5) giving enhanced performance; no evidence this was accompanied by designation Yak-25F. Total series possibly no more than 1000, completed about 1958. Standard in PVO regiments well into 1960s, though by that time obsolescent in performance and technology. Even at entry to service in 1956 curve-of-pursuit attack with guns was considered passé, and Yak-25 performance was inadequate.

Yak-25 Flashlight-B

Yak-27R

Even today it is difficult to determine correct data for this familiar and widely used aircraft. Official figures are clear enough but are irreconcilable with common sense. To fly mission with RD-9 engines fuel must have been close to 6,4 t (this was max fuel for rival La-200B). Empty weight cannot have been significantly less than 9 t (La-200B was 8,8). Thus gross weight must have been about 15 t, in turn demanding wing area not far short of 40 m² (this was precisely wing area of La). Yet official figures, to this day published in the Soviet Union, give gross weight as 'over 9 t' matched to wing area 28,94 m². Mgr Piotr Butowski even gives max weight as 9220 kg, suggesting precision that flies in face of fact. Further difficulty arises from common qualification 'with supplementary tanks' to quoted 3000 km range. No such tanks are known on Yak-25, and mass 6,4 t is for basic internal fuel. Supplementary tanks for 3000 km would make aircraft even heavier. Derived versions are described separately.

DIMENSIONS Span (official) 11,0 m (36 ft 1 in), (Němĕcek) 12,34 (40 ft 5$\frac{7}{8}$ in); length (official) 15 665 mm (51 ft 4$\frac{3}{4}$ in), (Němĕcek) 16,65 (54 ft 7$\frac{1}{2}$ in); wing area (official) 28,94 m² (311·5 ft²), (Němĕcek) 37,12 (399·6), (author's est, net) 33,5 (360 ft²).

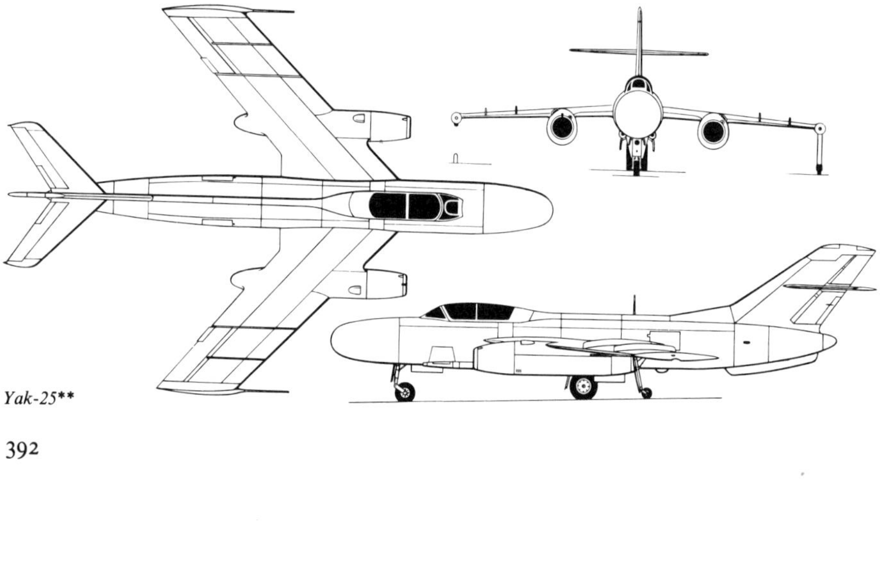
*Yak-25***

ENGINES (prototype and initial production) two 2200 kg AM-5, (main production) two 2600 kg RD-9.
WEIGHTS Empty (official) not given but could not exceed 5 t, (Němeček) 9850 (21,715 lb), (author's est) 8 t (17,640); fuel, not given but must be in region of 6/6,4 t; loaded (official) just over 9 t (19,840 lb), (Němeček) 16 t (35,273), (author's est) normal 10,5 t (23,148), max 14 t (30,865).
PERFORMANCE Max speed (official) 1090 km/h (677 mph) at 5 km; climb, no data but unimpressive; service ceiling (official) 13,9 km (45,600 ft); range (official) 3000 km (1865 miles).

Yak-25 developments This title is necessary because basic Yak-25 as described previously was used as starting point for numerous derived aircraft Such development began not later than early 1953 and encompassed variants for different missions, afterburning engines, different engine types and aerodynamic crutches to push up M-max. To prevent confusion NATO codenames will be used, with comment on possible true designations.

First two developments disclosed participated as single prototypes at 1955 Aviation Day at Tushino. Name Flashlight-B allocated to fighter/reconnaissance prototype with second crewmember moved from behind pilot to glazed nose. Flashlight-C assigned to improved night fighter. (Original Yak-25 hence called Flashlight-A.) Both new prototypes had afterburning engines in noticeably longer nacelles, wing LE extended forwards about 585 mm at LE, from point well inboard of nacelles, giving LE sweep at root increased from 45° to 62°; LE kink, in line with that already at TE, reduced root t/c to about 7% and significantly increased max operating Mach, to about 0·95, attained with afterburner. Consensus appears to agree these aircraft were respectively **Yak-25R** (*Razvyedchik*, reconnaissance) and **Yak-27P** (*Perekhvatchik*, interceptor). Former introduced a heavily framed pointed glazed nose carrying a remarkably large pointed instrumentation boom which was probably fitted to prototype only (both wingtip pitots were retained). Small mapping radar carried under floor immediately ahead of nose gear. Single NR-23 said to be mounted on right side of forward fuselage, aimed by pilot. Fighter variant introduced pointed radome, greatly reducing drag at full power. Over next two years these and related prototypes introduced enlarged outer wing giving better high-Mach performance at height, especially when pulling g. New wing had extended span by adding extra tip outboard of outrigger gears (now in streamlined underwing blisters) with large chord equal to that of extended outer leading edge which also introduced slight droop. Original fences replaced by single fence at dogtooth (discontinuity at inboard end of extended chord) extending around LE and back over upper surface to terminate at rear spar in line with inboard end of aileron. Called Flashlight-D, glazed-nose aircraft with new wing is called **Yak-27** (no suffix) by Butowski, though he gives original span. Green calls it **Yak-27R** and assigns code-name Mangrove. *Jane's* agreed after originally stating Mangrove to be trainer version of Flashlight, while Alexander states Mangrove is Yak-28 (not yet described). Butowski introduces designation **Yak-26** for dedicated bomber with internal weapon bay (short but full cross-section of body under wing). Green ascribes Yak-26 designation to high-altitude reconnaissance aircraft called Mandrake by NATO and **Yak-25RD** by most Western observers. RD not explained; could be *Rekord Dalnost* (record distance) but though Green speculates on this variant having a wet (ie, integral-tank) wing, weight considerations make this unlikely. Completely new shoulder-high wing with zero sweep confers outstanding high-altitude cruise performance, though at modest speeds. Only one good photo known of Mandrake with single-seat cockpit, large streamlined wingtip pods and blunt nose similar to Yak-25 though not necessarily dielectric. This

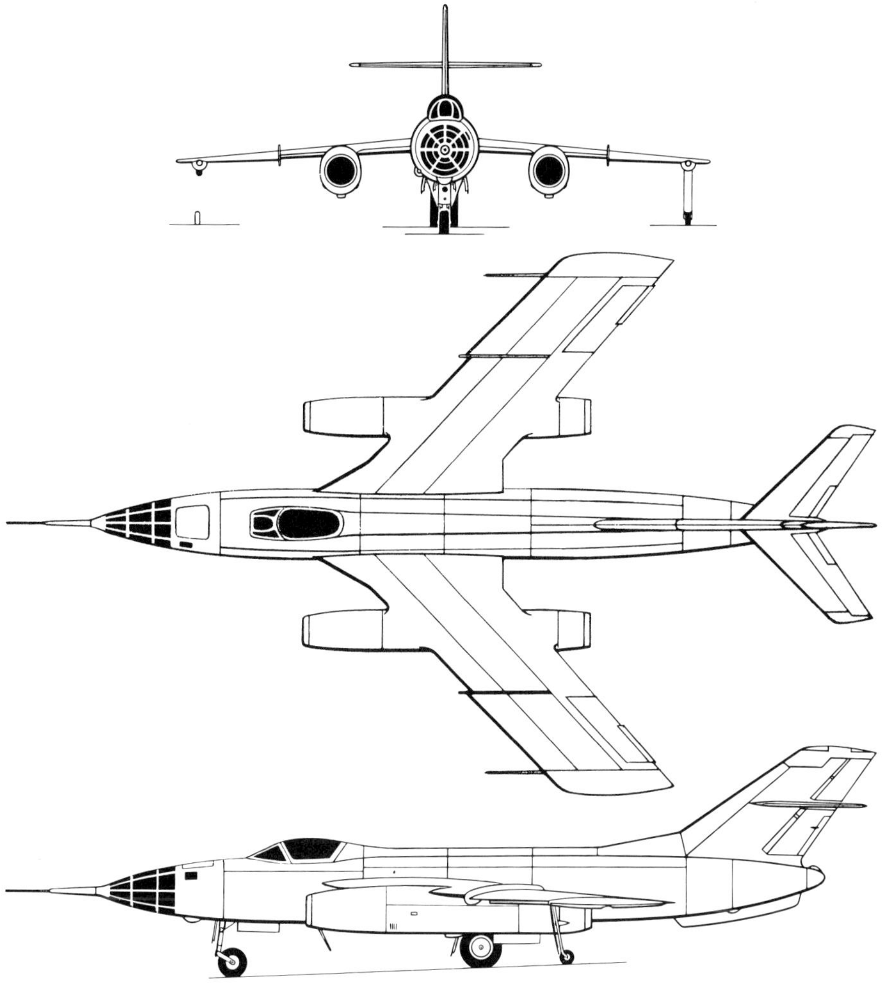
Yak-25R (possibly Yak-27R)

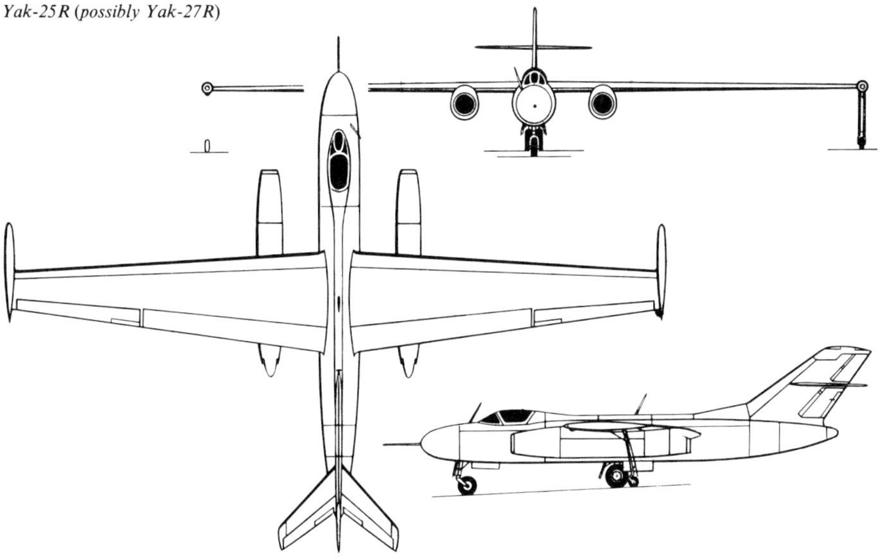
Yak-25RD (or Yak-26) Mandrake

aircraft was painted with contrasting stripes on wing, fuselage, nacelles and tail, with individual number (984) not on nose but at rear. Vertical tail greatly increased in chord but underfin keel removed. Dorsal aerial amidships changed to VHF whip, and additional inclined rigid mast added on right ahead of windscreen. In service by 1959 and several made overflights of China, India, Pakistan and other countries. No point in speculating on sensors but substantial number of such aircraft believed produced by conversion of Yak-25 withdrawn from PVO. One variant, called **RV** (*Rekord Vysota*, record height), set records over Bykovo piloted by V. Smirnov: 1-t load to 20,456 m (67,113 ft), and 2 t to 20,174 (66,188). This had 4 t R-37V engines, also stated by *Jane's* to be standard in final multi-role tactical-reconnaissance aircraft called Flashlight-D by NATO, as noted above, and generally believed only member of entire family to have been built in series from new other than original Yak-25 and later Yak-28. Deliveries to FA and other units about autumn 1959. Nav/bomb believed to have ejection seat fired through hatch in roof of nose. Armament one gun, said to be NR-30, on right side of nose. Different fits of cameras and other mission equipment seen in development aircraft, and could carry bombs internally. No evidence of underwing pylons. Radars said to be Short Horn for nav/mapping and Bee Hind tail warning; latter unlikely.

Landing gear did not visually alter in all these Yak-25 derived aircraft. Contrary to experience with Harrier it was not found necessary to restrict roll-freedom on ground, and when parked one outrigger was invariably clear of ground. Nose gear believed castoring, not steerable. Some later aircraft, notably Flashlight-D, introduced modified tail with one-piece rudder and cut-outs in TE of elevators. Rebuilds of original Yak-25 included not only Mandrake but also variety of EW platforms, target tugs and radio-controlled target aircraft. Many were still in use in such roles in late 1970s. Data are estimates.

DIMENSIONS Span (most) 12,95 m (42 ft 6 in), (Mandrake) 21,5 m (70 ft 6½ in); length (most) 16,8 m (55 ft 1⅓ in), (Mandrake, includes nose probe) 15,9 m (52 ft 2 in); wing area (early) as Yak-25, (most) 36 m² (387·5 ft²), (Mandrake) 44,7 m² (481 ft²).

Yak-28 Brewer-A

Testbed for Yak-28 landing gear

ENGINES (most) two 3275 kg thrust RD-9B or RD-9F afterburning turbojets, (Mandrake) two 2600 kg RD-9 or 4 t R-37V turbojets.

WEIGHTS Empty, in range 7,8/8,5 t; max loaded (most) 10,5/11,8 t, (Mandrake) 14 t for long-range mission?

PERFORMANCE Max speed (except Mandrake) 1100 km/h (684 mph) at 11 km, (Mandrake) 750 km/h with RD-9 or 825 km/h with R-37V; service ceiling (most) 15,25 km (50,000 ft), (Mandrake) 19 km with RD-9, 20,5 km with R-37V; range (at height, most) 1800 km (1120 miles), (Mandrake, either engine) 4000 km (2490 miles); take-off (typical) 950 m with after-burner; landing (most) 1,2 km/195 km/h, (Mandrake) about 600 m/140.

Yak-25, icing trials for Yak-28 extended inlet

Yak-28 Though developed from Yak-25/26/27 series this important family of tactical aircraft, with even-number (non-fighter) designation, shared few common parts and were almost new designs. Fundamental new features were shoulder (mid-high) wing, much more powerful engine, and long-wheelbase bicycle landing gear with weight shared almost equally by front/rear twin-wheel units. Original wing retained, though with heavier skin gauges and machined panels between spars. Everything done to increase chord, giving t/c roughly 5·5% at root and tip and below 7% everywhere. LE inboard of engines swept at constant 60° and TE unswept, giving increased area and chord with unchanged wing depth. TE flaps now of plain slotted type, broad rectangles without tracks; axial fence on upper surface from LE upstream of flap at mid-span of latter. Other fences removed, though dogtooth and extended/drooped outer LE retained. Slotted flap outboard of engines of greater span and area. Reduced-span powered ailerons, original TE tabs now extending full span of surface. Fuselage as previous generation though lengthened and greatly stiffened for increased weight, airspeed and sagging between widely spaced landing gears. Nose gear hydraulically steerable, twin wheels with brakes and 750 x 200 mm tyres, retracting forwards into bay with tandem pairs of doors. Rear unit, wheelbase approx 9,5 m, twin tyres (approx 900 x 200 mm), similar disc brakes, retracted rearwards on short leg into bay with two doors. This gear's share of weight reduced from 85 to below 60% and as far aft as possible to provide max length of weapon bay equally disposed fore/aft of CG Outrigger gears unchanged, though differences introduced with sub-types. Weapon bay probably dictated increased height of wing, providing room for particular nuclear weapon of diameter too great to fit under original wing spars. Larger but shorter afterburning engines in nacelles of flat-sided oval cross-section with prominent inlet centrebodies and with engine's variable-nozzle petals visible downstream of nacelle. Underwing pylon immediately outboard of dogtooth plumbed for pointed slipper-type drop tank of about 1000 lit (220 gal). Tail broadly as before but vertical surfaces enlarged, rudder a single powered surface and horizontal tail swept at sharper 50° angle and redesigned as powered tailplane with camber-increasing elevators with cut-outs for rudder movement (not shown in previously published 3-views). Increased tailplane/elevator power needed to rotate about rear main gear on take-off.

OKB developed family with at least 20 aircraft in 1960–1963, several being revealed in 1961 Aviation Day where NATO code name was initially Firebar, then Brassard and finally Brewer, Firebar being restored for interceptor variant. Original models were two tactical/reconnaissance types, one bomber, one interceptor and a trainer. Soviet designations are believed to be known and are repeated here, though some may be incorrect despite their having appeared in Soviet magazines. Original variant with glazed nose, Brewer-A, believed to be original Yak-28 and not to have been intended for production. Pilot in single-seat centreline cockpit with sliding canopy, flat bulletproof windscreen and sight for gun (believed NR-30) on right side of nose. Nav/bomb in nose compartment as in previous glazed-nose models, rear fuselage weapon bay, provision for underwing tanks (not often seen on these aircraft) and outrigger gears folding into fairings downstream of pointed cones as on Yak-26/27. Tail-warning as in earlier tactical aircraft. Prominent stiffening strakes along each side of weapon bay, and in some aircraft bay itself is bulged or forms projecting rectangular box.

Yak-28L Brewer-B

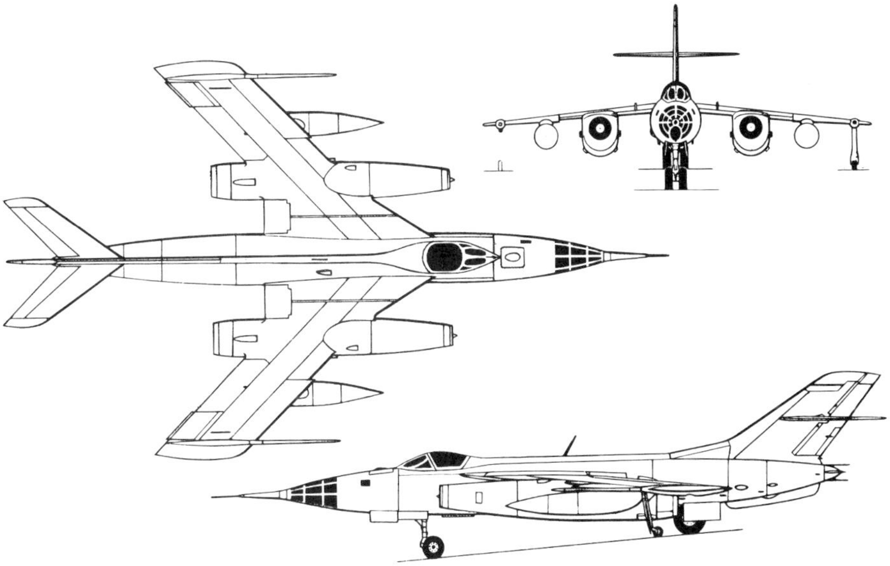

Yak-28I Brewer-C

Yak-281 Brewer-B, believed to be sole tactical-bomber production version, similar to Yak-28 but with Short Horn radar aft of nose gear and full mission equipment including Swift Rods ILS with projecting dipole aerials downstream of tailcone. Seen at 1961 parade, in service before spring 1963. Max internal bombload commonly but unofficially given as 2 t (4409 lb); report of external stores pylon (for UV-16 or 32-57 pods) inboard of engines but no evidence seen by author.

Yak-281 (meaning unknown), Brewer-C, replaced Yak-28L in production about 1963. Developed in parallel with 28P interceptor and like that aircraft introduced three major new features: longer fuselage, longer engine inlet ducts and longer wingtip probes. Fuselage extended 0,78 m ahead of wings, giving larger nav/bomb compartment; radar and nose gear likewise moved forward but pilot cockpit unchanged location. Engines fed by ducts extended forward 0,78 m to circular inlet with only extreme tip of centrebody projecting. Mass flow and engine type unchanged. Thermal inlet anticing. Probes projecting ahead of outrigger gears exactly doubled in length and reported to be (stated as fact by *Jane's*) filled with lead to counter flutter and torsional flexure of outer wing under g.

Yak-28P, Firebar, all-weather interceptor variant, developed to replace Yak-25 from 1962. Built in two series, original 28P having short nacelles, short tip probes and short nose radome, and later model having all three lengthened. Usual fighter crew accommodation in tandem with long aft-sliding canopy. Normal radar Skip Spin (*Uragan* 5B) 100 kW set developed from Yak-25 radar to work in J-band and provide search/track to 60 km and at shorter ranges tracking input to Anab and Atoll AAMs and target-illumination for radar-homing version of Anab. Normal armament two Anab, one IR and one radar; often seen with two Atoll or Advanced Atoll on smaller pylons further outboard. No guns, and weapon bay occupied by fuel. Fitted with SRO-2 IFF, Swift Rods ILS and all-round radar warning (unknown, not a Sirena series). In PVO service about winter 1963–1964 and replaced from 1967 by 28P with long radome giving lower supersonic drag and reduced erosion, long inlet nacelles (also fitted to earlier production 28Ps) and long lead-filled

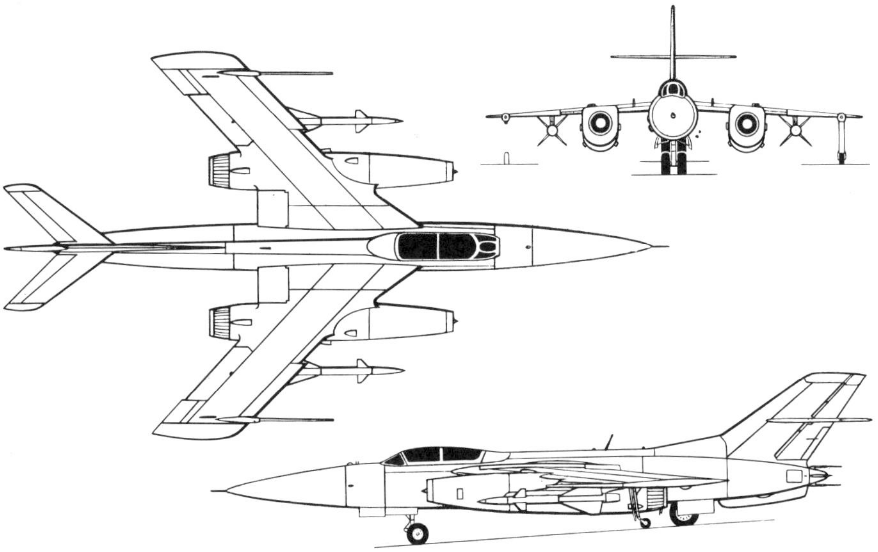

Yak-28P

tip probes. Recent Soviet and Polish drawings suggest 28P has larger vertical tail than other variants; author has no photographic evidence.

Yak-28U, Maestro, tandem dual-control pilot trainer. No radar, plain metal nose with usual long instrument boom and retrac landing lights under, short nacelles, short tip probes, weapon bay usually occupied by fuel (but in some aircraft apparently carrying reconnaissance pack), no gun, not seen by author with underwing pylons. Rear (instructor) cockpit as on tactical reconnaissance aircraft, added front pupil cockpit with separate hood hinged to right. 28U may be all rebuilds of early Yak-28 and Yak-28L.

Yak-28R, Brewer-D, multi-sensor reconnaissance aircraft not seen before 1969. May have been a rebuild, but glazed nose has fewer but larger glass panes, rear edge being oblique instead of vertical. Only known with long fuselage, inlets and tip probes. Short Horn may be replaced by different radar with radome slightly different profile. Former weapon bay may be occupied by any of at least three sensor groups including camera pallet, SLAR (side-looking airborne radar) and recessed major container for unknown sensors almost certainly including IR linescan. Nine extra electronics aerials in four groups on fuselage but Swift Rods ILS omitted. Normally flies with drop tanks.

Final known variant, Brewer-E (true designation unknown but could be **Yak-28E**), was first known Soviet EW (electronic-warfare) platform. First seen 1970, probably all rebuilds of tactical reconnaissance aircraft, long fuselage, inlets and tip probes, single pilot cockpit and forward compartment for ECM operator. Weapon bay filled with active jammers; may have extra AC generation capability in fuselage or larger engine alternators. No glazing in nose apart from small window each side; behind nose boom are azimuth/elevation ECM blisters, behind which is a large ring of six dielectric panels for forward-hemisphere emissions. Main jammer power radiated from drum container carried semi-recessed under belly, but fuselage has numerous other emitter and passive receiver aerials which vary slightly. According to *Jane's*, carries rocket pods outboard of drop tanks. These are most likely to fire dispensed payloads, not for ground attack. Brewer-E was designed to accompany FA attack aircraft on missions against sophisticated defences, or to precede an attack by seeding airspace and partly neutralizing the enemy. This is understood to be sole survivor of all twin-jet Yak aircraft of 25/26/27/28 families whose active service life is continuing into 1980s. At least 1500 of earlier models exist and some are probably being rebuilt as Brewer-E or converted as targets or trials platforms. Data are estimates.

DIMENSIONS Span 12,95 m (42 ft 6 in); length (original short-body variants) 21,5 m (70 ft 6½ in), (all long-body) 22,3 m (73 ft 2 in), (28P original) 21,7 (71 ft 2¼ in), (28P current) 23,0

Yak-28P (almost certainly OKB development aircraft)

Yak-28U

(75 ft 5½ in); wing area 37,6 m² (405 ft²).
ENGINES Two 4,6/6,2 t (10,140/13,670 lb) thrust R-11F afterburning turbojets.
WEIGHTS Empty, in range 9,0/10,5 t; fuel, max about 8,5 t; max loaded (U) about 15,3 t, (others) about 19 t (41,900 lb), (28P max) 19,9 t (44,-000 lb).
PERFORMANCE Maxspeed (all) about 1180 km/h (733 mph, M 1·11) at 10 km (Butowski suggests 1500, M 1·41); initial climb (Green and other Western writers) 142 m/s (28,000 ft/min); service ceiling (Soviet figure) 16 km, (common Western est) 16,764 km (55,000 ft); range, varies with type but Western est with bomb-bay or underwing tanks is 1600 km max (1000 miles); (Yak-28P combat radius, all-hi, DoD est) 900 km (560 miles); take-off, about 1 km; landing about 1200 m/240 km/h.

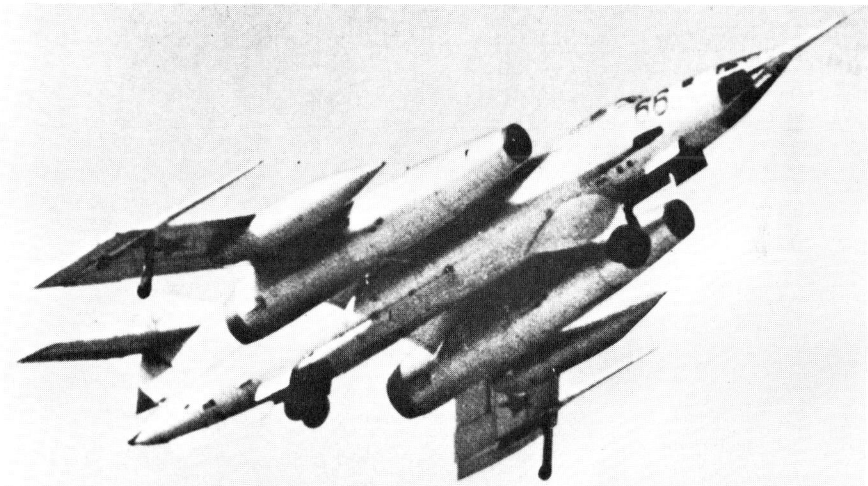

Yak-28R Brewer-D

Yak-30, Yak-32** Though unclassified and exhibited publicly, these jet trainers have never been described except in general terms; as they were not adopted, Soviet interest is minimal. Yak-30, OKB number **Yak-104**, also called **No 104**, built 1959 to meet VVS requirement for efficient jet trainer, designed for job and not modified from fighter. Stress laid on low cost, reliability, long life. Tumanskii KB charged with producing new small turbojet; Yak team, members unknown, adopted all-metal stressed-skin construction with tandem ejection seats. Wing SR-9S series, two spars, pressed ribs, flush-riveted skin, pneumatic split flaps, manual ailerons with spring tabs, pitot on left LE. Well-streamlined fuselage with long nose with landing/taxi light, upper half nose hinged up for access. Tandem unpressurized cockpits (no radio), rear instructor seat slighter higher than pupil but cill of single aft-sliding canopy horizontal, dorsal spine to swept vertical tail carrying unswept fixed tailplane and spring-tab elevators with cut-outs for rudder. Engine in bottom of fuselage aft of rear spar of low-mounted wing fed by shallow root inlets. Complete left/right cowls hinged and removable to expose engine; no jetpipe. Fuel in 600 lit (132 gal) tank above wing in fuselage. Nosewheel landing gear, all three units single levered-suspension legs, tyre sizes not known to author, retraction inwards (main) between spars or forwards into nose. Nose gear said to be steerable but appearance suggests otherwise. Provision for armament in specification but none fitted. Yak-104 won over contenders from at least one other OKB and six prototypes or static-test aircraft built 1960–1961, VVS designation Yak-30. Competed against Polish TS-11

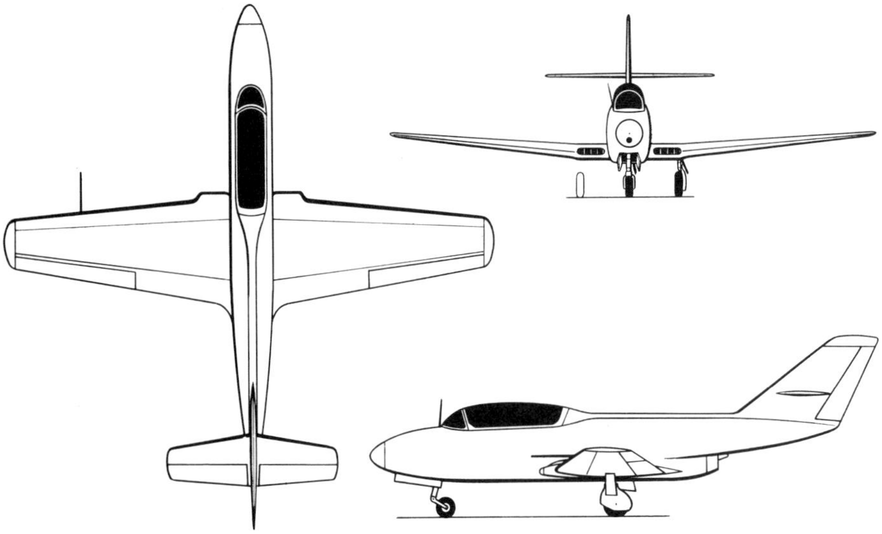

*Yak-30***

and Czech L 29 in Moscow August 1961; L 29 adopted. Immediately after choice, one Yak-30 set 15/25 km speed record 767,31 km/h, engine called 'TRD Mk 29, 850 kg'. Three days later, 25 September 1961, another set C-1d class record altitude 16128 m with 'TRD Mk 29,1050 kg'.

Yak-32 was single-seat sporting derivative, rear cockpit deleted but no change in fuel capacity and believed no other significant difference. Two built in parallel with Yak-30, funded by Dosaaf and both gave aerobatic display 1961 Aviation Day. Height (C-1d class record) 14283 m set 22 February 1961; data included above-average weight (2137 kg) and below-normal thrust (800 kg). In 1965 Yak-32 set 15/25 km speed 775 km/h. Yak-30 No 90 and Yak-32 No 70 parked on field at 1966 World Aerobatic Championships.

DIMENSIONS Span 9,38 m (30 ft 9¼ in); length 10,14 m (33 ft 3¼ in); wing area 14,3 m² (154 ft²).

ENGINE One 900 kg RU-19.

WEIGHTS Empty (30) 1555 kg (3428 lb), (32) 1435 (3164); fuel/oil 480 + 20 kg; loaded (30) 2250 (4960), (32) 1930 (4255).

PERFORMANCE Max speed (30) 660 km/h (410 mph) at low level, (32) 700 (435); record speeds are not explained, especially as thrusts given were if anything below normal; initial climb (30) 18 m/s (3540 ft/min); service ceiling (30, official figure) 11,5 km (37,730 ft), but see record climb figs; range (30) 965 km (600 miles), (32) endurance given 2¾ h but must be at slow econ cruise and range unlikely to differ; take-off 425 m; landing 450/140 km/h.

Yak-36 OKB selected about 1962 to build first known Soviet jet-VTOL aircraft. Prof Matveyev and A.N. Rafaelyants, and possibly others from Turbolyet team, transferred to OKB, and NII funding for aircraft and series of jet-lift engines. Decision not to fit so-called composite scheme of cruise plus lift jets, but to use lift/cruise engine(s) with vectored thrust in small single-seat airframe designed for high-subsonic performance. Numerous (believed about 12) Yak-36 built, two displayed Aviation Day 1967 (No 37 flying, No 38 static). Details not disclosed and following is deduced or speculative.

All-metal stressed-skin, mid-mounted wing, powerplant in lower forward fuselage with nozzles below wing roots, cockpit at upper level, many features (tail, landing gear) reminiscent of Yak-25. Wing apparently SR-9S profile, 40° cropped delta with −5° or −6° anhedral and fixed LE, TE occupied by tabbed ailerons and area-increasing slotted flaps. Large plain nose inlet immediately bifurcated into left/right ducts universally assumed to lead to two small turbojet or turbofan engines occupying lower part of forward fuselage. Prominent bulges at assumed engine locations with geometry suggesting engine of R-11 size on each side, with all efflux discharged through lateral rotary cascade deflector identical in geometry with Rolls-type patented 1961. Left/right nozzles driven in unison aft for thrust and down through at least 90°; not seen at Domodyedovo in forwards braking position but assumed capable. Reaction control jets in wingtip pods, at tail and on long pipe ahead of nose; apparently no provision for eliminating

Yak-32

uncontrollable roll-couple on single-engine failure. Pilot in ejection seat in pressurized cockpit with thin moulded windscreen and sideways-hinged canopy. Tail based on Yak-25/28 but smaller (tailplane span 3500 mm instead of 4500) and tailplane mounted higher up fin. Tailplane believed fixed; other surfaces almost certainly powered. Fuel tank behind cockpit, dorsal spine linking cockpit to fin. Landing gear of *velosipedno* type similar to Yak-50 but with nose unit and outriggers all retracting forwards and main unit to rear. Nose gear retracts to occupy front of inlet bifurcation with twin doors hinged to large left/right flap hinged down from rear to improve pressure/flow under fuselage and minimize reingestion of hot gas. Edges of these doors carry angle strakes. Further strakes on each side of centre fuselage, between which is second (smaller) rear-hinged door lowered in jet-lift mode. Double-hinged door ahead of twin-wheel main gear believed to act as hot-gas deflector, bay/leg door and airbrake. Large left/right canted ventral strakes on rear fuselage. Outriggers fold forward into oval-section tip fairings extended far ahead of LE; large freedom in roll, outrigger often 15 cm off ground when parked.

Large and prolonged flight programme both in OKB and NII, lead pilot believed OKB's V.G. Mukhin. Trapeze structure under tail too frail for tail bumper and surmised as telemetry aerial. Aircraft No 38 carried UV-16-57 rocket pods on wing pylons, and one Yak-36 said to have had internal gun. One aircraft did prolonged autostab trials (No 37 flew manually at Domodyedovo in 1967) and another completed deck programme aboard ASW cruiser *Moskva*. No photo known since 1967. Data are estimates.

DIMENSIONS Span (scaled from *Monografie* 3-view) 7875 mm (25 ft 10 in), (*Jane's*) 8,25 m (27 ft 0 in); length overall (*Monografie*) 16,05 m (52 ft $7\frac{7}{8}$ in), (*Jane's*) 17,5 m (57 ft 5 in); fuselage excl nose probe (*Jane's*) 12,5 (41); wing area (net, scaled from *Monografie*) 14,85 m^2 (160 ft^2).

ENGINE(S) Probably two modified R-11, about 4 t thrust each, or R-13, about 5 t each.

WEIGHTS Empty in region of 6 t (13,200 lb); loaded unlikely to exceed 7,5 t (16,500 lb).

PERFORMANCE Max speed probably at least 900 km/h (559 mph); capable of rolling STO but normally seen in VTO mode; modest range/endurance and poor at high alt.

Yak-36MP Despite designation this AV-MF operational type is fresh design, bearing only distant kinship with V/STOL research Yak-36. Meaning not known but M probably *Morskoi* (sea, marine); P conceivably *Perekhvatchik* (interceptor), and one mission known to be to destroy large maritime aircraft such as P-3 Orion, S-3 Viking, Nimrod and Atlantic. NII requirement dated about 1970, following completion of early Yak-36 programmes. Never seen on ASW cruisers *Moskva*, *Leningrad*, and timed to be in service only on completion of *Kiev*, first of much larger multi-role ships since joined by *Minsk*, *Novorossisk* and one as yet (1983) incomplete. *Kiev* shakedown cruise summer 1976, so first flight of Yak-36MP probably not later than 1974. Other design missions include surface attack, but lack of STO capability restricts payload.

Wing believed same as Yak-36, SR-9S profile, 40° LE, anhedral 5°, fixed LE but TE differs in having powered wing-fold at inner end of untabbed aileron and small area-increasing slotted flaps not occupying whole inboard TE. New fuselage, tail and landing gear, and because of addition of lift jets and much greater fuel capacity entire fuselage arrangement re-thought, with pilot in nose, lateral inlet ducts and fuel distributed among several tanks. Most observers agree there is one main lift/cruise engine, often said (because of sooty efflux) to be based on AL-21. Author finds equal grounds for suggesting two smaller engines, R-13 fitting nicely and matching both inlet duct and nozzle, and avoiding problem of either arching spars over engine or using heavy forged rings. A further point is that R-13 or similar-size engine might be changed with aircraft standing on wheels, difficult with single large engine unless removed upwards or to rear. Plain fixed-geometry inlets with probable thermal anticing and (usually) six suck-in auxiliary doors on outer side for use at low ram pressures. Nozzles unrelated to Yak-36 and similar to those of original British RB.193: 90° pipe elbow rotating 100° on hot-gas seal and in VTO mode at 100° position to provide forward thrust equal to horizontal component of thrust from lift engines. Latter, ascribed in West to Koliesov, probably same as fitted to STOL versions of MiG-21 and Su-15 etc. Two engines in tandem inclined at about 10° with hinged upper door (sprung flaps reduce drag in jet-lift mode) and left/right ventral doors. No known provision for vectoring lift jets but they almost certainly provide part or all of bleed air for control nozzles of remarkably small and neat design above/below wingtips and at extreme tail. How these nozzles operate speculative, but can

Yak-36

Yak-36

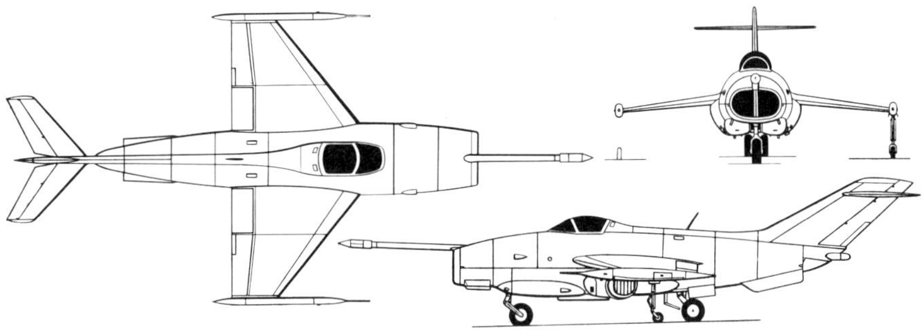

Yak-36

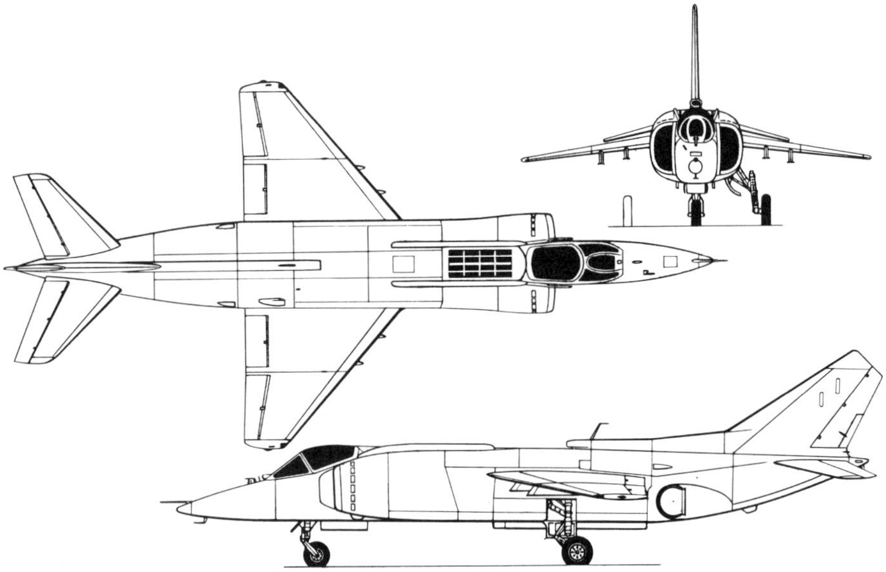

Yak-36MP Forger-A

impart pitch, yaw and roll with great precision under control of high-authority autostab system without which aircraft cannot fly. Ram-air, possibly for cooling but certainly for q-feel, at front of dorsal spine leading to tail unrelated to previous OKB designs. Fin cropped at angle for Mach 1·25, UHF/VHF tip and side flush aerials (probably VOR type) with small powered tabbed rudder. Fixed slightly swept tailplane with about 15° anhedral, elevators (probably powered) with inset hinges and no tabs. Pressurized cockpit with flat bulletproof windscreen, canopy hinged to right, advanced ejection seat and HUD. Nose IR sensor and radar-ranging sight, no radar or laser carried internally. Twin pitots above nose, Swift Rods ILS under nose and/or on dorsal spine, UHF/Tacan aerial ahead of windscreen sometimes replaced by SRO-2M (Odd Rods) IFF which is usually installed under tail. Neat levered-suspension conventional nosewheel landing gear, nose unit with fork trunnion and retracting to rear and main gears folding forward into flanks of mid-fuselage. High-pressure tyres, main about 570 × 170 mm, nose about 500 × 170 mm. Fixed rear

Yak-36MP Forger-B (aircraft '04') with Forger-As aboard Kiev

tail bumper. Constant-section straight ventral strakes along belly from LE to nozzles immediately inboard of main-gear doors, no other cushion-augmentation device.

This neat aircraft was developed in first half 1970s, with parallel tandem dual **(36MU?)** version, probably used only as conversion trainer, with extended forward and rear fuselage. Extra (pupil) cockpit in nose displaces ranging radar, SRO-2M and other avionics, and has seat at lower level under long side-hinged canopy. No wing pylons, whereas single-seat 36MP normally has four close-spaced deep pylons under inboard fixed wing. Carries Aphid/Atoll AAM, UV-16-57 pod, GSh-23 gun pod, ECM pod, various reconnaissance pods, 600 lit (132 gal) drop tank or bombs to normal max 2 t (4409 lb). All evidence points to auto guidance from ship linked to flight autostab/autopilot in VTO and conventional slow (finally vertical) landing, with exactly repeatable precision. STO never seen and assumed impossible, thus no heavy weapon load nor Viffing. Radar-tracked beyond Mach 1 on level, but inlets confirm disinterest in supersonic performance. Aircraft seen at sea with *Kiev*, *Minsk* differ in detail, even in 1981, and AV-MF appears still to be exploring techniques. Yak-36MP now has dorsal strakes over the intake for lift engines, either side of door, to reduce reingestion of hot gas during hover. Yak OKB has probably flown fundamentally improved successor.

DIMENSIONS Span (author) 7,6 m (25 ft), (*Jane's*) 7,0 m (23 ft); length (single-seat) 15,0 m (49 ft 3 in), (two-seat) 17,66 m (58 ft); wing area (Green) 15,8 m (170 ft²).

ENGINES Two (author) lift/cruise turbojets, probably derived from R-13 and each rated at about 5 t (11,000 lb) thrust, (most observers) one lift/cruise engine such as variant of AL-21 rated at 8 t (17,640 lb); two lift jets each rated at (Green and many others) 3630 kg (8000 lb), (*Jane's*) 2540 kg (5600 lb).

WEIGHTS Empty, in region of 7,7 t (17,000 lb); internal fuel, about 2,2 t; max loaded, about 12 t (26,500 lb).

PERFORMANCE Max speed (clean, at height) about 1400 km/h (870 mph, M 1·3); initial climb (*Jane's*) 75 m/s (14,750 ft/min); service ceiling (*Jane's*) 12 km (39,400 ft); mission radius (Green) about 240 km with attack stores, all lo, no tanks, about 370 km with attack stores, no tanks, all at height, and at least 560 km in reconnaissance role with two tanks and pods; ferry range, about 2000 km (1240 miles); VTOL.

Yak-36MP over wake of Kiev

Yak-40

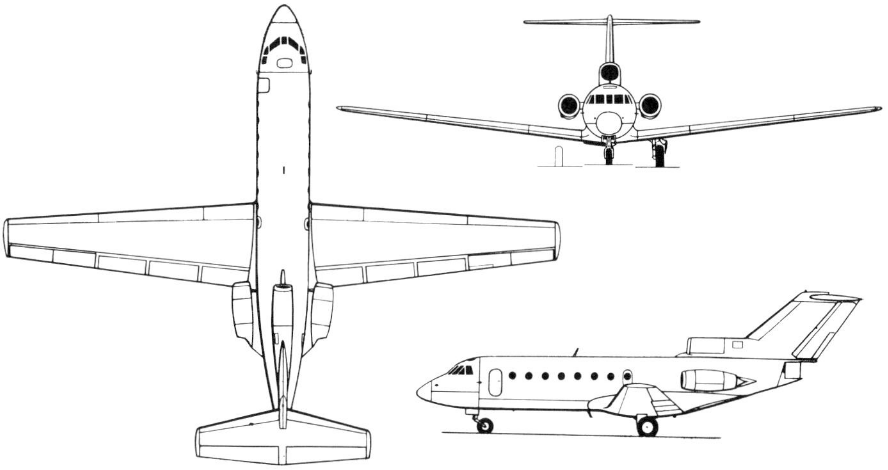

Yak-40

Yak-40 Agreed autumn 1964 as replacement for all major short-haul GVF (Li-2, Il-12 and Il-14 and to small extent An-2), Yak himself being instrumental in securing adoption of STOL jet, then a new concept. Required new engine from Ivchyenko, sized also for trainer and executive aircraft and with two giving sufficient cruise thrust, third for take-off boost (plan dropped during flight test in favour of all three being used in cruise). Yak led team, with Adler chief engineer and son Sergei chief project engineer; OKB number believed 165. Careful compromise between demand for economy and STOL performance (Class 5 grass fields 700 m max), all-round modernity for long service life and export success, need to meet international certification including 30,000 h airframe life, reliability and independence of ground support.

Three engines resulted in rear-engine T-tail layout with low wing unusual in aspect ratio 8·93 and 0° sweep. Section SR-9 series, 15/10%, dihedral 6° (later reduced, as noted) structurally in left/right halves joined on centreline with straight main spar tip-to-tip, auxiliary front/rear spars, chemically-milled skins, assembly by spot-weld/bonding/riveting with bolts and steel forgings at main joints (eg, centreline). Manual ailerons, tab on right only, split inner/outer halves for wing flexure. Plain flaps split into three each side for flexure, hydraulic drive to 15° take-off, 35° landing. Spoiler/dumpers omitted at late stage. Fuselage circular section 2,4 m diameter, again D1 structure assembled by spot-

Yak-40 production at Saratov

welding/bonding/riveting and with one-level floor of low-density foam sandwich. Fin sweep often given as 52° at ¼-chord but in fact 50° at LE; large fixed bullet at top upstream of hinge for electrohydraulic trimming tailplane, unswept, 13,03 m² with manual elevators, one-piece manual tabbed rudder. Levered-suspension nitrogen-oleo landing gear, main 1120 × 450 mm max 393 kPa (circa 57 lb/sq in), nose 720 × 310 mm, steerable. Nose unit forwards, main inwards with no doors, hydraulic brakes and retraction. Bogies omitted at late stage, though initially offered as alternative standard. Engines 1 and 3 hung on rear frames and 2 inside tail of fuselage fed by S-duct with APU above it to provide air for engine start and limited cabin heat on ground. Bleed-air LE heating of wings and tail, electrically heated windscreen. Cabin dP 29 kPa (c4¼ lb/sq in). Hydraulic system 15,2 MPa (c2200 lb/sq in). Fuel 3800 lit (835·9 gal) in integral tanks forward of main spar. Flight deck for two-crew, autopilot, Grosa-40 weather radar, ILS for 500/50 m (later Cat 2). Three DC generators, Ni/Cd batteries. Cabin length 6,7 m normally seating 24 (2+1) aligned with eight circular windows each side, hydraulic rear ventral airstair and service door forward on left.

First of five prototypes, No 1966, flown 21 October 1966. Rapid flight-test and NII clearance 1968 for series at GAZ-292 Saratov. Dihedral reduced to 5°30′; fin/tailplane bullet removed; main gears strengthened for increased gross weight; fuel capacity increased to 3900 lit (858 gal) (intention to use wet fin but extra fuel finally put in outer wings, as far as inboard end aileron); clamshell reverser added to No 2 engine; Nos 1 and 3 engine pylons and cowl nozzles redesigned; titanium and steel structure introduced round engines, and control rods protected; avionics improved and Collins export **Yak-40EC** variant offered. Aeroflot passenger service 30 September 1968, delivery eight per month to just over 800 completed summer 1976. Modest export success and many license negotiations reached advanced stage, TFE731-powered **ICX LC-3** assembled in 1981 at Wheatfield NY using Saratov-kits but project halted by poor sales. Stretched **Yak-40M** not built, but standard aircraft could seat 27 (2+1) or 32 (2+2, seven rows right, nine left), max payload 2720 kg (6000 lb). Numerous executive, military, mixed or all-cargo (large door on left) and special-purpose variants including air-data lab and TV-equipped particle counter aircraft. **Yak-40B** (VVS) and **40V** (export) announced with AI-25T with aircooled blades, but in fact exported civil aircraft all had standard engine.

DIMENSIONS Span 25,0 m (82 ft 0¼ in); length 20,36 m (66 ft 9½ in); wing area 70 m² (753·5 ft²).

ENGINES Three 1,5 t (3307 lb) AI-25, (40B) 1,75 t (3858 lb) AI-25T.

WEIGHTS Empty (early) 9 t (19,685 lb), (series) 9,4 (20,725); fuel 4 t (8818 lb) max; loaded (early) 13,75 (30,313), (series) 16,2 (35,714).

PERFORMANCE Max speed 600 km/h (373 mph) at SL; max cruise 550 (342) at 7 km; initial climb 8 m/s (1575 ft/min); service ceiling, 8 km (same as max cruise height); range (initial, at 550 km/h) 600 km (373 miles), (series, max payload, 470 km/h at 8 km) 1800 km (1118 miles); take-off (initial) 550 m, (series) 700 m (2297 ft); landing 500, 320 (1050) with reverser/110 km/h.

Yak-42 This much-enlarged successor to Yak-40 has proved OKB's longest development task, demonstrating Soviet Union's surprisingly long timescales with modern civil aircraft. Yak accepted job about 1972 as potentially largest-ever GVF programme, for standard regional transport; planned 2000 to be bought, replacing not only Tu-134 and other jets but even An-2 in areas where traffic has risen and longer runways built. First HBPR (high bypass ratio) turbofan in country ordered from Lotarev for this aircraft, design generally being scaled-up Yak-40 but with some sweep and reliance on high-lift devices for field length of 1,8 km (compared with 0,7 for predecessor). Model and mock-up revealed June 1973.

Wing believed SR-9 series, section details not known but t/c about 8·5/6·5%, dihedral 0°; despite much tunnel testing unique decision to fly two sweep angles, first 11° and subsequently 25° (later changed to 23°). Structurally 13,05 m centre section with 90° TE, and left/right outer wings, all with chemically-milled skins on two-spar torsion box with secondary leading/trailing structure including honeycomb. Wing movables subject to prolonged change and research. Ailerons eventually fully powered, and after flight test changed in design and split into inner/outer halves in separate circuits. Hydraulic LE slats extensively tunnel tested and believed flown on first Yak-42 (OKB number not known) but omitted about 1976. Final standard of flap area-increasing tracked slotted type (near Fowler) in two sections each side, hydraulic drive to unknown angle (28° at one stage). Three flight/ground, roll/airbrake spoilers ahead of outer flaps, lift dumpers inboard. Circular fuselage,

Yak-42 pre-series (twin-wheel gears)

3,8 m (149·6 in) diam, dP 48·9 kPa (7·16 lb/sq in), with engines hung exactly as Yak-40, APU above S-duct with exhaust on right. Rear fuselage and tail reshaped about 1974 to become higher and less-swept. Acorn bullet survived in this aircraft, powered tailplane primary surface $+4°/-8°$ with tabbed elevators, tabbed one-piece powered rudder. Landing gear with nitrogen oleos, main 1300 × 480 mm twin wheels retracting inward with doors over legs only; hydraulic brakes and retraction. Nose unit, twin wheels, steerable, 930 × 305 mm, hydraulic retraction forwards with auto-brake to arrest wheelspin (not used on landing). No reversers or parachute, complete reliance on lift dumpers and multi-disc main brakes. Fuel eventually settled (1976–1980) at 15 795 lit (3474·4 gal) in main wing box integral cells; in 1981 slightly increased. Bleed-air used for LE wing/tail de-icing and environmental systems, probably same for inlets, electrically heated windscreens. Two-crew flight deck with third jump seat. SAU-42 flight control linked with autopilot and area-nav system, weather radar, ILS working towards Cat 3 (appreciable US/UK/France contribution includes both technology and hardware).

First prototype, No 1974, flown 7 March 1975. Wing swept 11°, heavy hydraulically-powered crew door forward on left serving as escape door at all IAS; main hydraulically-powered ventral airstair at rear. Apart from test gear, equipped as 100-seater (basically 3+3) with large carry-on baggage/coat compartments front and rear. Second aircraft, No 1975, with many changes including longer fuselage with 19 instead of 17 windows each side, 120 seats and no carry-on baggage (though two coat areas). Two shallow underfloor holds, forward for six 2,2 m³ bins and rear for three bins, total vol

Yak-42 series aircraft at Krasnodar, 1981

26,2 m³ (924·5 ft³), all loaded through door ahead of wing on right and positioned by chain conveyor. Third aircraft, No 1976 (later in line-service as 42303) with de-iced tail, improved main-gear fairings and emergency exits (two each side) moved forward closer to LE. Max payload 14,5 t (32,000 lb). Decision on 23° swept wing taken about 1976, max weight increased 1981 as data, and main gears given 4-wheel bogies (tyre size unknown). As entry written (1982) latest news is inclusion in list of new types to be introduced by Aeroflot 1981–1985 period. Stretched 140-seat version expected 1982–1983.

DIMENSIONS Span (11°) 35,0 m (114 ft 10 in), (23°) 34,2 (112 ft 2½ in); length overall (1st) 35,0 m (114 ft 10 in), (subsequent) 36,38 m (119 ft 4¼ in); wing area (all) 150,0 m² (1615 ft²).

ENGINES Three D-36 each rated (1st) 6320 kg (13,933 lb), (subsequent) 6350 (14,330).

WEIGHTS Empty (not 1st a/c) 28,96 t (63,845 lb); fuel 12,65 t (27,888 lb); loaded (1st) 50 t (110,230 lb), (2nd) 52 (114,640), (1981) 53,5 (117,945).

PERFORMANCE Max speed (VNE) not published; max cruise 870 km/h (540 mph) at 7,6 km; normal cruise 810 km/h (437 kt, 504 mph) at 7,6 km; climb/ceiling, no data; range (max payload, 770 km/h, 9 km) 900 km (559 miles), (10,5 t payload, 770, 9 km) 2000 km (1243 miles), (6,5 t, 770, 9 km) 3000 km (1864 miles); take-off field length (ISA, SL) 1,5 km (4920 ft), (ISA + 20) 1,9 (6230); landing field length (ISA, SL) 1,8 (5900)/180.

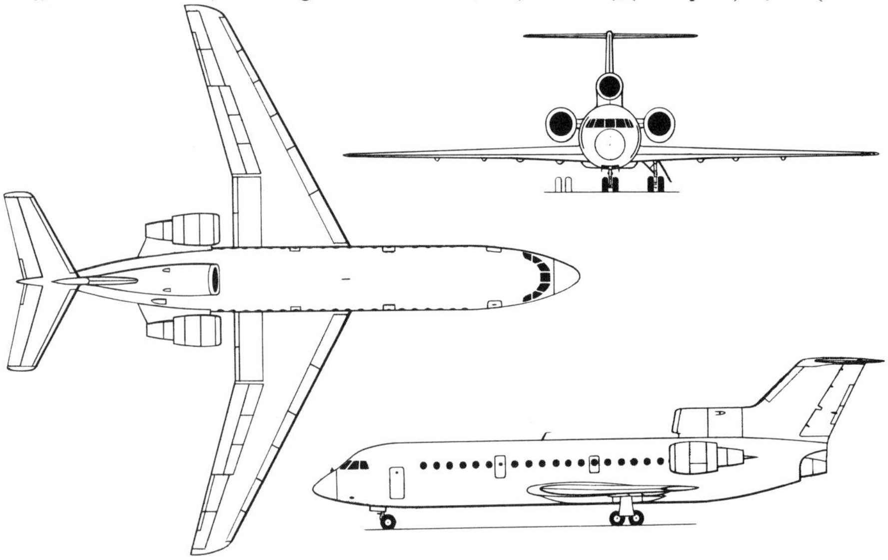

Yak-42 series aircraft (original top of fin)

Yatsyenko

Vladimir Panfilovich Yatsyenko (1892–1970) was worker in pre-1917 aero factory, qualified as engineer 1924, on drawing board at TsKB on foundation as member of Polikarpov's stressing team, rose to replace S. A. Kochyerigin in managing release of DI-6 through NII tests and entire produc-

Yak-42 production at Smolyensk with final top of fin. Note Yak-18T line

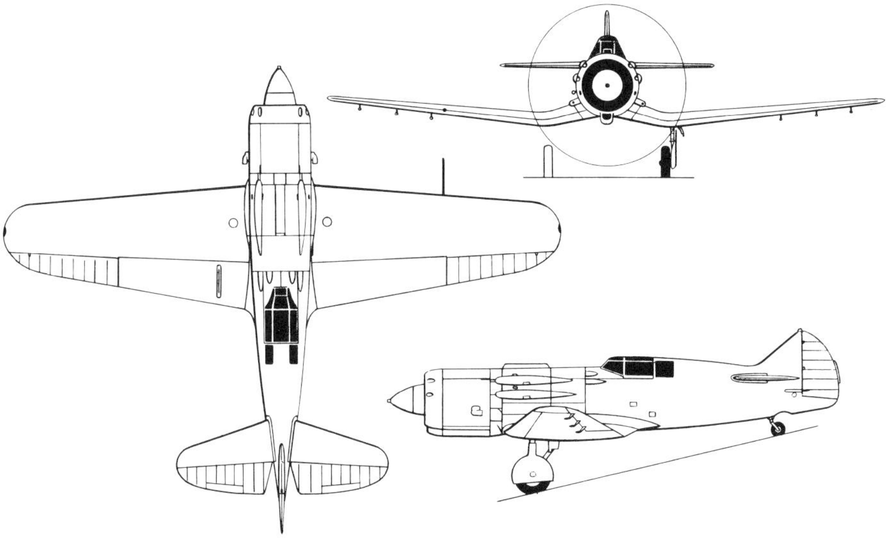

I-28

tionprogramme. FollowingclosureofhisKBJanuary 1941 assigned to Il-2 production; after evacuation worked for Ilyushin and Mikoyan, retiring on pension 1966.

I-28 While still in charge of DI-6 production Yatsyenko completed project design of new fighter and submitted to NII VVS. August 1938 design accepted as I-28, and before 1 October 1938 personally assigned to build two prototypes of **I-287** (7th mod). Planned engine M-90 not available and M-87 adopted with only slight changes from Il-4 programme, driving slightly modified Il-4 prop, 3 m VISh-23Ye. Wing of inverted-gull form to reduce landing-leg length, two spars of wooden box construction, simple ply ribs, ply skin built up from glued *shpon* with thickness 12 mm at root and 4 mm at tip, polished to mirror finish. Balanced push-rod ailerons 40% semi-span Dl/fabric. All-Dl Schrenk flaps with pneumatic actuation to 45°. Forward fuselage simple welded KhMA steel tube frame carrying engine, guns and tank; rear *shpon* semi-monocoque, all with mirror finish. Long (record says NACA-type) constant-diameter Dl engine cowl covering accessories, oil tank, part fuel tank, and gun barrels. Ventral oil cooler, unusual lateral exhausts (two pipes, 7 cylinders each) projecting through sides of cowl, large spinner. Wooden fixed tail integral with fuselage, Dl/fabric control surfaces with inset hinges (unlike triple mass balances on ailerons) and tab on each elevator, push-rod actuation. Main gears with rear-braced oleo legs, 600 × 170 mm tyres, pneumatic brakes and pneumatic inwards retraction, doors on legs but not on wheel bay. Retractable tailwheel. Cockpit well aft of wings, with rear-sliding hood. Armament two ShVAK-20 with 300 rounds and two ShKAS with 1700.

Aircraft completed day before due date of 1 May 1939, though 30 April not necessarily first flight. DI-6 production GAZ pilots almost certainly spent a day or two in ground running and taxi tests. Factory testing completed 'late spring' and I-28 flown to NII test programme by Stefanovskii 10 June 1939, task shared with Kub'shkin. Near end of NII tests Stefanovskii made terminal-velocity dive and at about 8 km level at 725 km/h aircraft broke up. Later found steel casting in tail fractured, but Soviet accounts claim tail struck by disintegrating engine cowl. Stefanovskii flung out and descended by parachute. Second aircraft completed with more powerful engine, open cockpit and armament of one ShVAK and two UBS, plus four RS-82 or FAB-100 (overload). By this time GAZ had order for 30 series I-28 and for prototype **I-28Sh** attack version, gross weight 2911 kg. Second prototype was flown (Něměcek, August 1939) and five production fighters completed, but programme terminated February 1940. One series I-28 completed taxi tests. GAZ assigned to Yak-1.

DIMENSIONS Span (Ponomaryev) 10,4 m (34 ft 1⅓ in), (Shavrov, believed incorrect) 9,6 m (31 ft 6 in); length 8,54 m (28 ft 0 in); wing area 16,5 m² (177·6 ft²).

ENGINE (1) one 950 hp M-87 (later M-87A), (2) 1100 hp M-87B, (series) 1100 hp M-88.

WEIGHTS Empty (1) 2257 kg (4976 lb), (2) similar; fuel 275 kg; loaded (1) 2670 (5886), (2) 2720 (5996).

PERFORMANCE Max speed at SL (1) 412 km/h (256 mph), (2) 421 (262); max speed at 6 km (1) 545 (339), (2) 576 (358); time to 5 km (1) 6·3 min, (2) 6·1; service ceiling (1) 10,5 km, (2) 10,8 (35,430 ft); range 800 km (497 miles), 2 h; time 360° circle at height 25/26 s; landing speed 140 km/h.

Yermolayev

Vladimir Grigor'yevich Yermolayev was born 1908 and graduated 1930 from physics faculty of Moscow state university. Joined Bartini's design group following year as estimator, working on Stal-6 and Stal-7. A political activist, he saw his chance when Bartini was arrested January

I-28 (first aircraft)

1938, and became prominent member of small KB formed under Zakhar Borisovich Tsentsiper to continue Stal-7 programme and design a bomber version. All Stal-7 record flights organized by this group, funded by Aeroflot deputy head M.F. Kartushyev, but VVS (and Stalin) interest in bomber meant priority for bomber version from January 1939, before 5068 km flight. Large OKB immediately established within Aeroflot based on existing factory group of D.S. Maksimov, and Kartushyev appointed Yermolayev head and M.V. Orlov his deputy. According to Shavrov Bartini was consultant; he does not add Italian was still in prison. Large and effective organization swiftly created outstanding long-range bomber, flown June 1940 and ordered into production October. OKB at this time transferred to NKAP and aircraft redesignated Yer-2 for Yermolayev (number 2 because bomber, ie, even number). Potentially great programme hampered by circumstances, and Yermolayev died at height of effort 31 December 1944 (Simakov states 1943), according to Western report, of typhoid. OKB taken over March 1945 by Sukhoi and programme slowly ran down to full stop in 1947.

Yer-2, DB-240 Originally allotted VVS designation DB-240 (*Dalnyi Bombardirovshchik*, long-range bomber), little remained but general shape of Stal-7. Wing redesigned as modern stressed-skin structure in D16, extensive rubber-presswork in simple ribs and details but heavy plate spars and extruded/machined spar booms and simple open top-hat or angle stringers, all suited to rapid mass-production. Centre section little changed, still electro-welded steel-tube space-frame, but because of increased aircraft weight KhMA replaced by 30KhNZA and changed in detail. Two main spars 2,5 m (98·4 in) apart at root left room for capacious bomb bay in redesigned semi-monocoque fuselage, which retained slightly triangular oval section of Stal-7 but longer and much stronger with heavy pressed frames, multiple stringers and skin 0,8/1,0 mm. Flush riveting extensively used, a bold step forward. Accommodation for nav/bomb in fully glazed streamlined nose with hand-aimed UB, pilot in fully glazed blister cockpit on left of centreline, radio alongside on right with side windows (in combat to go aft and man lower rear ShKAS firing through sliding floor panel) and gunner in dorsal turret with single ShKAS. New stressed-skin twin-finned tail, 5,8 m span, inset hinges and tabs on all surfaces and rudders with forward-projecting mass balances. Selected 960 hp M-103 replaced by M-105 during prototype build, in neat cowlings with coolant radiator in outer wing with LE slit inlet and flush cascade outlet in upper surface, carb and oil-cooler inlet on underside, oil-cooler outlet in top of nacelle over wing. AV-5L series three-blade props. Twin-oleo main gears stronger than Stal-7 and larger tyres (size on DB-240 not recorded). Retractable tailwheel. Slotted two-section tabbed ailerons, slotted Schrenk flaps in four large sections, max 45°. Operation of gear, flaps, bomb doors and turret all believed electric. Fuel in four large protected tanks in centre section, provision for outer-wing tanks used later. Normal bombload 1 t internal.

DB-240 flown (Něměcek/Green state by N.P. Shyebanov, lead pilot in Stal-7 programme) June 1940, with excellent results. OKB testing completed September and NII testing October 1940, with immediate instruction for series production as Yer-2 at Voronezh (probably GAZ-64) under A.B. Shyenkman. Tooling swift and aircraft available from spring 1941, with around 50 delivered by 22 June 1941. Second *dubler* prototype complete September 1940 handled VVS TTT evaluation. Believed it was this aircraft (not commonly reported first) which at start of 1941 flew round-trip Moscow/Omsk/Moscow loaded to represent dropping of 1 t bomb at Omsk (common Western story is bomb actually dropped; Russian wording 'dropping there a symbolic bomb').

Operational service began immediately, with virtually no training, by two regiments hastily formed at Smolyensk from GVF (civil) personnel collected from local Aeroflot line crews. Same two regiments, by July named *Novodranov* and *Gusyev* (numbers not known), increasingly flew long-range missions as far as Königsberg and Berlin with 100 or 250 kg bombloads, total strength averaging 40/60 during late summer despite severe casualties in low close-support missions totally unlike those for which Yer-2 designed. Production continued at Voronezh until 128th aircraft at evacuation July 1941. Western histories commonly suggest concentration on short-range aircraft almost halted further work, but in fact developement never quite came to a stop, Yer-2 was flown with several more powerful engines and at much greater weights. Despite severe difficulties, production of diesel-engined variant was restarted late 1943 and added almost 300 to total.

Deep penetration of Nazi forces accentuated need for greater range and bombload, and as

Yer-2 (series, AM-35)

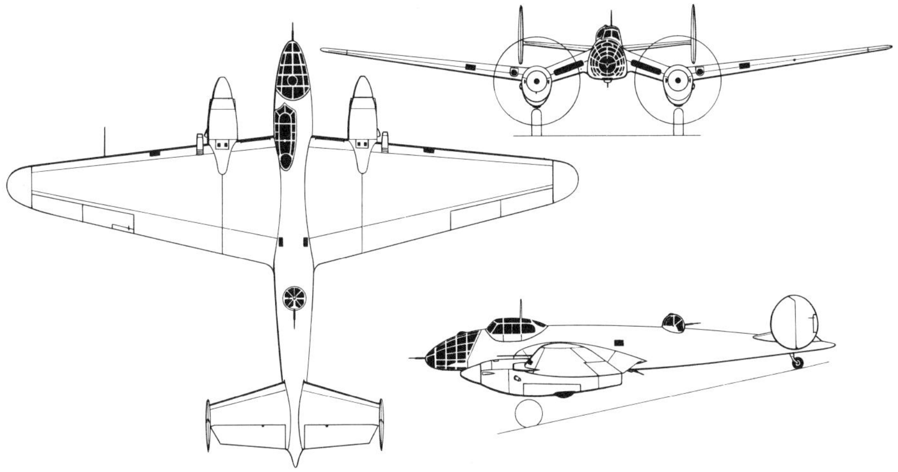

Yer-2 (AM-35)

early as December 1940 studies began of more powerful engines and mods to increase weight. Western report engine change demanded by M-105 being earmarked for fighters incorrect; no problem in supply of this engine in modest numbers required. Engines studied included AM-35, AM-37, AM-40, ASh-71, ASh-82, M-30, M-40, M-120, MB-100 and, most importantly, ACh-30 series. First re-engined aircraft flown April 1942 by A.D. Alekseyev with M-35 (AM-35) engines. Large VISh-24 prop necessitated angling engines outwards (Shavrov says loosely 3° to 5°) and increased engine mass was countered by bringing c.p. of wing forward. Western (Green) account states LE taper increased and TE taper reduced by 5°; this would have opposite of desired effect. Shavrov merely states area and angle of wing altered, and clearly objective would be to bring tip forward. OKB data show that, while area was slightly increased, span was slightly reduced. Later span was restored, whilst maintaining new area. Plan view by Simakov certainly shows wing tapered mainly on TE, with tip further forward, but it is poor drawing and unreliable in detail. At least one Yer-2 also flown with AM-37 engines. OKB received order spring 1941 to fit M-120 engine(s) to DB-240, but work never completed. In late 1942 two aircraft earmarked for powerful MB-100, which might have made tremendous bomber (far better than He 177) but cooling this engine posed severe difficulties and believed never flown. Only successful engine installation concerned Charomskii diesels. About July 1942 section under chief designer Tulupov converted Yer-2 No 4, an aircraft retained at OKB for testing, to M-30 and later M-40 engines. As before, larger propeller required 5° outward cant of engines. Installation successful and aircraft flew usual Moscow/Omsk/Moscow mission with simulated 1 t bomb drop. Low fuel consumption but engines unreliable. Spring 1943 during search for permanent OKB home one aircraft, believed No 4, fitted with ACh-30B. This proved to be excellent, despite imperfect running of engine, with slim cowl, AV-5LV-116 prop and completely redesigned cooling system with main radiators transferred to centre section (usual LE slit inlet and flush cascade discharge in upper surface) and oil coolers in prominent circular ducts projecting ahead of LE outboard of cowl. Nacelle reprofiled to extend to TE providing enlarged bay for 1200 × 600 mm tyres to support new overload weight 18,58 t. Prolonged trials showed excellent characteristics marred only by engine faults. Later VISh-24 props fitted, and NII tests completed December 1943.

By this time OKB had settled at GAZ-153 in Siberia where series manufacture quickly organized and new **Yer-2ACh-30B** came off line with remarkable speed. As noted, almost 300 delivered by termination late 1944, forming core of newly created ADD force and winning major competitive evaluation against Il-6. Production aircraft had added AMTs protected tanks in outer wings, modified bomb bay able to take three FAB-1000 or three 980 kg torpedoes (or wide variety other stores), improved radiator discharge giving positive thrust in cruise, GS-1000 generators, TN-12 fuel pumps, new 15° flap setting for take-off, and usual defensive armament one UBT in nose, one UBT in lower rear and one ShVAK in TUM-5 turret. Modifications introduced during production included addition of co-pilot (both tandem and side-by-side cockpits flown, latter giving aircraft symmetry and being accepted despite increased drag) and various tinkering with wing area, sweep (ie, LE-TE angles in plan) and dihedral, in all cases confining changes to outer wings. None adopted except fifth crew-member. One of first Soviet aircraft with properly assembled Pilot's Notes.

Numerous test programmes. In man-hours most important was **Yer-2ON** (*Osobogo Naznachyeniya*, personal assignment or special allocation) modified from series Yer-2/ACh-30B. Bomb bay, turret and ventral gun position removed and fuselage modified to accommodate two large passenger cabins each seating nine. Sukhoi OKB had major role in design (shared same location) and assisted in manufacture of cabins. Four-hour missions in comfort on test at end 1944, and three built of which two used for liaison between GAZ and Moscow. As always engine unreliability was major drawback. **Yer-2N** (*Nocitel*, carrier or bearer of load) used late 1945 to fly As 014 resonant-duct engines from V-1 missiles; five flights showing 'poor power, high drag'. Final variant **Yer-4** was series aircraft No 11 (originally M-105s) rebuilt 1945 with ACh-30BF engines and redesigned coolant system with wing ducts on each side of nacelle (not just on one side) further developed to give better positive thrust in cruise. Tail also improved and enlarged (one Western report states tailplane span increased).

DIMENSIONS Span (most) 23,0 m (75 ft 5½ in), (AM-35, AM-37) 21,7 m (71 ft 2¼ in); length (DB) 16,3 m, (series) 16,34 m (53 ft 7⅓ in), (ACh-30B series) 16,42 m (53 ft 10½ in); wing area (DB, M-105 series) 72,0 m² (775 ft²), (AM, ACh) 73,1 (787).

ENGINES (DB, initial series) two 1050 hp M-105, (second series) 1500 hp ACh-30B, (experimental) see text.

WEIGHTS Empty (DB) 5991 kg (13,208 lb), M-105 series) not known, about 6200 kg (13,670), (ACh) not known, about 8 t (17,640 lb); fuel (series) in all cases over 5 t; loaded (DB) 11,3 (24,912), (first series) 11.92 (26,279), (second) 14,85 normal, 18,58 max (32,738/40,961), (ON) 19 (41,887).

PERFORMANCE Max speed at SL (DB) 395 km/h (245 mph), (first) 372 (231), (AM-37) 418 (260), (second) 360 (224); max speed at height (DB) 500 (311) at 6 km, (first) 491 (305) at 6, (AM-37) 520 (323) at 5, (second) 446 (277) at 5; time to 5 km (DB) 18·4 min, (first) about 20, (AM) not known, (second) 30·4; service ceiling (DB) 7,7 km, (first) not known, (AM-37) 9,2, (second) 7,7; range (DB) 4100 km (2548 miles), (first) not known, about 4000, (AM) not known, (second) 5000 (3110 miles); cruise consumption (second) 95 l/h per eng; take-off (second) 1860 m/175 km/h (safety speed 230); landing (second) 1450 m/210 km/h.

Zlokazov

Aleksandr Ivanovich Zlokazov was senior airframe engineer at GVF repair plant at Irkutsk in 1930s. About end 1933 he formed small KB to create new transport for Arctic regions.

ARK-Z-1 Cast in Junkers mould, this low-wing monoplane was of substantial size for single engine, and embodied such advanced features as air/oil oleo legs and powered landing flaps. Much of airframe based on PS-4, and wing used corrugated skin of identical rolled profile. Enclosed and heated cockpit, main cabin for ten passengers or 880 kg cargo with double door on left, fuel tanks in inner wings, fixed-pitch wooden prop, large low-pressure tyres replaceable by skis. Completed spring 1935, satisfactory test programme and then flown in stages to Moscow for NII GVF testing. Completed programme, including long-range flight, during October/November 1935 but decision not to produce in series because of obsolescent structure and claimed inadequate reserve factor of strength.

DIMENSIONS Span 21,8 m (71 ft 6¼ in); length 15,0 m (49 ft 2½ in); wing area 70,2 m² (755·6 ft²).

ENGINE One 750 hp M-34R.

WEIGHTS Empty 3,2 t (7055 lb); fuel/oil 900 kg total; loaded 5150 kg (11,354 lb).

PERFORMANCE Max speed 240 km/h (149 mph) at SL, 180 (112) at 2,5 km; time to 1/2/3 km, 4·3/10·5/20 min; service ceiling 3,8 km (12,500 ft); range, not recorded; take-off 280 m/15 s; landing 450 m/25 s/95 km/h.

Avietka

In this section are grouped light aircraft produced by designers not part of a recognised OKB. They are listed in chronological order rather than by alphabetical order of designer's name, aircraft name or designation. Some entries are classed as *motor planer* (powered gliders), but gliders and sailplanes are not included. A few entries were the result of nationwide competitions, organised for example by Dosaaf, but the majority were the result of individuals and small groups, and organised student bodies in aviation institutes, managing to obtain official authority or scrounging materials and building to their own design, usually without state backing or test facilities. Before the Second World War, M-11 engines were available on loan or at a reduced price to individual constructors, on the understanding that the state had free use of any successful design.

Shyukov Little is known of this triplane, begun in 1919 but not completed. Clearly a single-seater.
DIMENSIONS Span 7,8 m (25 ft 7 in); length 5,8 m (19 ft 0 in); wing area 16 m² (172 ft²).
ENGINE One 120 hp Le Rhône 9-cylinder rotary.
WEIGHTS Empty 360 kg (794 lb); fuel 70 kg (154 lb); loaded 557 kg (1228 lb).
PERFORMANCE Speed at sea level 190 km/h (118 mph).

Vigulya Pyetra Antonovich Vigulya was behind a new design built at the Aviarabotnik (aviation-worker) repair factory in Moscow in 1920. Based on the Farman 30 pusher, it had the original wings but tandem 80 hp Le Rhône engines, one at each end of the two-seat nacelle. It suffered rudder failure and crashed. No data.

ShM No details are available of this biplane built in 1921, beyond the following data.
DIMENSIONS Span 11,5 m (37 ft 9 in); length 8,9 m (29 ft $2\frac{1}{2}$ in); wing area 35 m² (376·7 ft²).
ENGINE One 100 hp Gnome Monosoupape 9-cylinder rotary.
WEIGHTS Empty 500 kg (1100 lb); fuel/oil 98/31 kg (216/68 lb); loaded 800 kg (1764 lb).
PERFORMANCE Max speed 120 km/h (75 mph) at sea level.

Kasyanenko No 6 Known as the Cavalry Aeroplane, described as a diminutive but neat design. Intended for army reconnaissance. Construction begun 1921 at No 6 Aircraft Repair Factory in Kiev. Never completed; no data.

SP The *Sinyaya Ptitsa* (Bluebird) was almost too large to be included here, for it carried three passengers in a cabin behind the open cockpit. Designed 1922 and built 1923 at the Aviarabotnik factory; the work of Ignatii Aleksandrovich Valentei and Nikolai Efimovich Shvaryev, the latter being the designer, the basis being a captured Schneider reconnaissance aircraft. Fuselage completely rebuilt, aircraft doped blue overall, and flown in summer of 1923 by I.G. Savin. Rear fuselage too large (heavy?) and aircraft inherently unstable.
DIMENSIONS Span 13,0 m (42 ft $7\frac{3}{4}$ in); length 8,0 m (26 ft 3 in).
ENGINE One 220 hp Benz Bz III 6-cylinder inline.
WEIGHTS Empty 980 kg (2160 lb); loaded 1490 kg (3285 lb).
PERFORMANCE Max speed 180 km/h (112 mph).

VOP-1 First of two attractive sporting machines created by one of the most famed aviators, Victor Osipovich Pissarenko. Single-seat low-wing cantilever monoplane, with open cockpit and discontinuity in fuselage underside where deep cockpit joined slim tail boom. Structure wood, with birch veneer glued and pinned to form skin. Pissarenko flew it on 27 November 1923; ferried to Moscow and flown by over 100 pilots. Described as the first successful Soviet light aircraft.
DIMENSIONS Span 7,5 m (24 ft $7\frac{1}{4}$ in); length 5,0 m (16 ft $4\frac{3}{4}$ in); wing area 10 m² (107·6 ft²).
ENGINE One 35 hp Anzani.
WEIGHTS Empty 222 kg (489 lb); fuel/oil 20 kg (44 lb); loaded 322 kg (710 lb).
PERFORMANCE Max speed 120 km/h (75 mph); practical ceiling 1,2 km (3940 ft).

Savelyeva Though it looked neat, this tandem-seat quadruplane — a configuration adopted to minimize overall dimensions — was a failure. Handling poor, and attempts to improve manoeuvrability made things worse, landing being especially difficult. Photographs show it on skis. Designer V.F. Savelyeva; flown 1923, by which time generally considered obsolete.
DIMENSIONS Span 5,6 m (18 ft $4\frac{1}{2}$ in); length 6,4 m (21 ft 0 in); wing area 20,7 m² (222·8 ft²).
ENGINE One 120 hp Le Rhône 9-cylinder rotary.
WEIGHTS Empty 506 kg (1116 lb); fuel/oil 106/40 kg (234/88 lb); loaded 802 kg (1768 lb).
PERFORMANCE Max speed 164 km/h (102 mph); time to 1 km alt 4 min; service ceiling 3500 m (11,480 ft).

LM Despite its trivial power this ultralight monoplane was a complete success. Designed and built by V.A. Likoshin and N.G. Mikhelson (whose later work is described under his own OKB). Built at Red Airman plant in Leningrad and flown about February 1924.
DIMENSIONS Span 8,4 m (27 ft $6\frac{3}{4}$ in); length 5,2 m (17 ft 0 in); wing area 12,7 m² (136·7 ft²).
ENGINE One $7\frac{1}{2}$ hp Indian (motorcycle).
WEIGHTS Empty 89 kg (196 lb); fuel/oil 5 kg (11 lb); loaded 174 kg (386 lb).
PERFORMANCE Not published.

Buryevestnik This name (Stormy Petrel) identified ultralight monoplanes created in the 1920s by Vyacheslav Pavlovich Nyevdachin. He had been a glider pioneer at the meetings at Koktebel. His **P-5** (*Planer* No 5) was flown by Jungmeister to a national record of 532 m in November 1923, 18 months after it appeared. In 1924 Nyevdachin fitted a P-5 with a Harley-Davidson engine, the first of numerous motorcycle engines that offered power at minimal cost. Tested on 3 August 1924 the resulting Buryevestnik **S-2** managed to take-off but the power was too low. Construction mainly pine, with glued and pinned veneer on the fuselage and leading part of the wing. Main gear, an arc of ash laminates carrying two wheels. Several made, with different engines and reduced dimensions.
DIMENSIONS (No 1) Span 10,0 (32 ft $9\frac{1}{2}$ in); length 6,0 m (19 ft $8\frac{1}{4}$ in); wing area 15 m² (161·5 ft²).
ENGINE One motorcycle type, originally 5/7 hp Harley-Davidson V-twin.
WEIGHTS (No 1) Empty 120 kg (264·5 lb); fuel/oil 5 kg (11 lb); loaded 220 kg (485 lb).
PERFORMANCE (No 1) Max speed 70 km/h (43·5 mph).

Buryevestnik S-3 Despite its more powerful engine, this 1926 machine never managed to fly further than 300 m. Tested with wheels and skis.

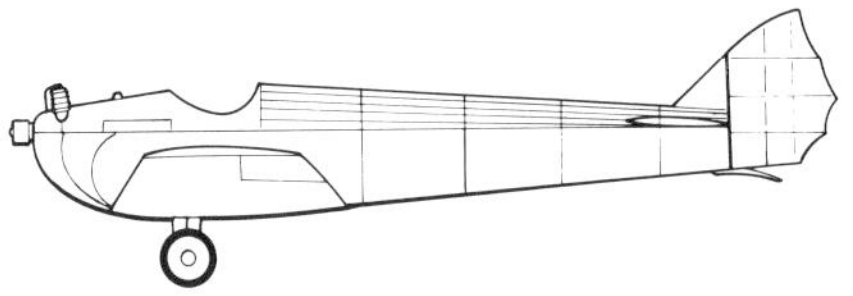

Buryevestnik S-3

DIMENSIONS Span 9,8 m (32 ft $1\frac{3}{4}$ in); length 5,8 m (19 ft 0 in); wing area 12,5 m² (134·5 ft²).
ENGINE One 12 hp Harley-Davidson V-twin.
WEIGHTS Empty 135 kg (298 lb); fuel/oil 7 kg (15·4 lb); loaded 220 kg (485 lb).
PERFORMANCE Poor.

Buryevestnik S-4 This at last performed like a real aeroplane, the key lying in the engine. On 29 July 1927 A.I. Zhyukov set ultralight height record. Take-off and landing run 30 m, and 360° turn made in 14 seconds. Fame followed a flight in five stages from Moscow to Odessa. Numerous pilots flew S-4, most performing aerobatics.
DIMENSIONS Span 9,0 m (29 ft $6\frac{1}{4}$ in); length 5,8 m (19 ft 0 in); wing area 9,6 m² (103 ft²).
ENGINE One 18 hp Blackburn Tomtit.
WEIGHTS Empty 130 kg (287 lb); fuel/oil 20 kg (44 lb); loaded 230 kg (507 lb).
PERFORMANCE Max speed 140 km/h (87 mph); landing speed 60 km/h (37 mph).

Buryevestnik S-5 Last of Nyevdachin's ultralights, this was the most powerful, the State Aviatrust having imported a few Bristol Cherubs along with its licence for the Jupiter. This made the S-5 a first-class performer and it was exhibited at the 1929 International Aviation show in Berlin, after eight months of successful flying. The same aircraft was later given to the Osoaviakhim club of Irkutsk.
DIMENSIONS As S-4.
ENGINE One 32 hp Bristol Cherub flat-twin.
WEIGHTS Empty 145 kg (320 lb); fuel/oil 25 kg (55 lb); loaded 250 kg (551 lb).
PERFORMANCE Max speed 160 km/h (100 mph).

Pissarenko T A small monoplane like its predecessor, the T (for Trainer) was a different machine, for it outperformed most aircraft of its day. Data are lacking, but it flew in 1925, the engine being a 150 hp Hispano. Single-seat parasol monoplane, of wooden construction, with ply covering on the wing leading edge and fuselage back to the cockpit, which was behind the trailing edge. Wide spacing of wing bracing struts suggested spars at about 5 and 80% chord. Maximum speed approached 300 km/h (186 mph); studied as a *Strelbom* (fighter/bomber), considered a novel idea.

Alekseyev It is not known if Igor G. Alekseyev was related to the OKB chief of the 1950s, but he was son of the painter Georgiya Alekseyev. He produced two of the real ultralights of the early Soviet period when civil war had not completely stopped. His **IgA-1** *Blokhi* (Flea) was one of the simplest machines imaginable,

being a parasol monoplane of backyard appearance. In 1924 K.K. Artseulov offered to test it, but it is doubtful that it flew.
DIMENSIONS Span 4,5 m (14 ft 9 in); length 3,0 m (9 ft 10 in); wing area 5 m^2 (53·8 ft^2).
ENGINE One 8 hp JAP V-twin.
WEIGHTS Empty 65 kg (143 lb); fuel/oil 5 kg (11 lb); loaded 130 kg (287 lb).

IgA-2 This 1926 machine used the same engine but was larger. It broke after making several attempts to fly.
DIMENSIONS Span 6,0 m (19 ft 8 in); length 4,5 (14 ft 9 in).
No other data.

OSO-1 This ultralight was a diploma project by Sergeya Sergei Ivanovich Kamenyev, supervised by the head of OSO TsAGI, A.A. Baikov. Designed 1925, flown in 1926 by AGOS engineer N.I. Petrov. Considered to be underpowered.
DIMENSIONS Span 10,9 m (35 ft 9 in); length 5,8 m (19 ft ⅓ in); wing area 15 m^2 (161·5 ft^2).
ENGINE One 18 hp Blackburn Tomtit.
WEIGHTS Empty 180 kg (397 lb); fuel/oil 20 kg (44 lb); loaded 267 kg (589 lb).
PERFORMANCE Max speed 120 km/h (74·5 mph); landing speed 55 km/h (34 mph).

SK Designation derived from A.N. Sedyelnikov and V.L. Korvin (who collaborated with Mikhelson on the MK-1 described later). Well-braced biplane, unusual in having interplane struts just outboard of the fuselage; further struts linked upper and lower ailerons on each side. Fuselage skinned with glued ply.
DIMENSIONS Span 9,0 m (29 ft 6¼ in); length 5,3 m (17 ft 4½ in); wing area 19,8 m^2 (213 ft^2).
ENGINE One 12 hp Harley-Davidson tuned to 16 hp.
WEIGHTS No data.
PERFORMANCE Max speed 100 km/h (62 mph); landing speed 50 km/h (32 mph).

VEK Named *Strekoza* (Dragonfly), neat monoplane built at Kharkov OAVUK by student A.A. Bromberg, supervised by professor G.F. Proskur. Made several flights, powered by 27/35 hp ABC Dragonfly engine. No other data.

IT-2 One of three powered machines designed by Igor Pavlovich Tolstikh, his other designs being gliders. Fuselage ply-skinned, the seat being ingeniously incorporated into the structure. Bad workmanship in the engine prevented take-off. Date, late 1925.
DIMENSIONS Span 6,5 m (21 ft 4 in); length 3,2 m (10 ft 6 in); wing area 10,5 m^2 (113 ft^2).
ENGINE One IEL motorcycle, nominal 9/12 hp.
WEIGHTS Empty 85 kg (187 lb); fuel/oil 10 kg (22 lb); loaded 170 kg (375 lb).

Ivanov Ultralight created by Viktor Appollonovich Ivanov and pilot N.D. Anoshchenko. Made numerous flights in 1925–1926.
DIMENSIONS Span 7,5 m (24 ft 7¼ in); length 4,5 m (14 ft 9 in); wing area 11 m^2 (118 ft^2).
ENGINE One 8/12 hp JAP.
WEIGHTS Empty 150 kg (331 lb); fuel/oil 20 kg (44 lb); loaded 250 kg (551 lb).
PERFORMANCE Max speed 100 km/h (62 mph); landing speed 63 km/h (39 mph).

MB This small biplane flew in 1926; designer not reported.
DIMENSIONS Span 6,2 m (20 ft 4 in); length 5,2 m (17 ft 0¾ in); wing area 9,8 m^2 (105·5 ft^2).
ENGINE One 45 hp Anzani.
WEIGHTS Empty 160 kg (353 lb); fuel/oil 20 kg (44 lb); loaded 260 kg (573 lb).
PERFORMANCE Max speed 145 km/h (90 mph).

Dzerzhinski Biplane also known as **SCh**, from builder Sergei Dmitryevich Chernikhovsky. Fuselage and tail welded steel tube, wings being wood. Work began 1925; from 1927 numerous flights in Moscow and Odessa.
DIMENSIONS Span 8,8 m (28 ft 10½ in); length 5,3 m (17 ft 4¾ in); wing area 12,8 m^2 (138 ft^2).
ENGINE 27/35 hp ABC Scorpion.
WEIGHTS Empty 170 kg (375 lb); fuel/oil 20 kg (44 lb); loaded 270 kg (595 lb).
PERFORMANCE No data.

Pishchalnikov N.N. Pishchalnikov, an engineer at OMOS, made his lightplane alone at home; then took it by rail to a Finnish beach where he made the first flight in late 1926.
DIMENSIONS Span 8,0 m (26 ft 3 in); length 5,1 m (16 ft 9 in); wing area 12,5 m^2 (135 ft^2).
ENGINE 15 hp Reading-Standard.
No other data.

Mars A rebuild of a glider of the same name, both by Kharkov constructor S.N. Ruiltsyev. Parasol monoplane, flown 1927 wheels and skis.
DIMENSIONS Span 12,0 m (39 ft 4½ in); length 5,5 m (18 ft 0½ in); wing area 13 m^2 (140 ft^2).
ENGINE One 27/35 hp ABC Scorpion.
WEIGHTS Empty 190 kg (419 lb); fuel/oil 20 kg (44 lb); loaded 290 kg (639 lb).
PERFORMANCE Max speed 110 km/h (68 mph); landing speed 55 km/h (34 mph).

STI Two-seater designed and built by students at Siberian Technical Institute, Tomsk, under professors G.V. Trapeznikov (airframe) and A.V. Kvasnikov (engine), 1925-1927. Engine, designated for five students who built it, used parts from a Le Rhône rotary; airframe had braced low wing and incorporated tail of Nieuport and landing gear from Morane. First flight 1927; later flew as far as Kansk.
DIMENSIONS Span 10,0 m (32 ft 9½ in); length 7,0 m (22 ft 11½ in); wing area 15 m^2 (161·4 ft^2).
ENGINE One Tuzhkut flat twin, 24 hp.
WEIGHTS Empty 300 kg (661 lb); fuel/oil 20 kg (44 lb); loaded 400 kg (882 lb).
PERFORMANCE Max speed 100 km/h (62 mph).

Tri Druga Name of this attractive parasol monoplane (Three Friends) reflected those who built it: S.A. Semyenov, L.I. Sutugin and S.N. Goryelov – and motto of 1923 Aviakhim contest 'strength, simplicity, cheapness, three friends of aviation'. In fact less simple than most, because it was a refined design with monocoque fuselage of glued veneer, with cantilever main gear of original design. Pilot ahead of front spar; two-seater carried passenger behind under the wing. Flew 1928 and exhibited in Berlin.
DIMENSIONS Span 12,0 m (39 ft 4½ in); length 6,9 m (22 ft 8 in); wing area 18,7 m^2 (201 ft^2).
ENGINE Bristol Cherub 30 hp.
WEIGHTS Empty 245 kg (540 lb); fuel/oil 22 kg (48·5 lb); loaded 417 kg (919 lb).
PERFORMANCE Max speed 127 km/h (79 mph); landing speed 45 km/h (28 mph); ceiling 3,2 km (10,500 ft) (single-seat, 4,3 km, 14,100 ft).

Budilnik No data on this ultralight built by group of railwaymen at Krasnoyarsk and flown 1927. Had motorcycle engine, described as 'weak'. Name, however, means 'alarm-clock'.

LAKM Designation from Leningrad Aero Club-Museum. Possibly only machine to fly with neat flat-twin engine designed by L.Ya. Palmen. Low-wing single-seater, designed with Osoaviakhim support by M.V. Smirnov (famed *Ilya Mouromets* pilot) and Ya.L. Zarkhi. First flight 27 November 1928; still flying 1931.
DIMENSIONS Span 10,4 m (34 ft 1½ in); length 5,6 m (18 ft 4½ in); wing area 12 m^2 (129 ft^2).
ENGINE One 20 hp Palmen flat-twin.
WEIGHTS Empty 175 kg (386 lb); fuel/oil 27/13 kg (59·5/28·7 lb); loaded 285 kg (628 lb).
PERFORMANCE Max speed 115 km/h (71·5 mph); landing speed 50 km/h (31 mph); ceiling 1620 m (5300 ft).

S-1 Little known about this parasol single-seater designed by test-pilot Vasili Andreevich Stepanchenok. Despite poor engine performance (bad workmanship) the S-1 managed to fly moderately well. First flight 1928, demonstrations in Moscow 1929.
DIMENSIONS Span 7,7 m (25 ft 3 in); length 5,0 m (16 ft 4¾ in); wing area 9,2 m^2 (99 ft^2).
ENGINE One 40 hp Anzani.
WEIGHTS Empty 207 kg (456 lb); fuel/oil 27 kg (59·5 lb); loaded 314 kg (692 lb).
PERFORMANCE Max speed 150 km/h (93 mph); landing speed 75 km/h (46·6 mph).

Pavlov Built by Aleksei Nikolayevich Pavlov, famous instructor at Orenburg flying school, this was another parasol single-seater. Flown spring 1929; made several flights, including one from Orenburg to Moscow, but crashed fatally in late 1929.
DIMENSIONS Span 7,5 m (24 ft 7¼ in); length 5,5 m (18 ft 0½ in); wing area 10 m^2 (107·6 ft^2).
ENGINE 100 hp Bristol Lucifer.
WEIGHTS Empty 480 kg (1058 lb); fuel/oil 90 kg (198 lb); loaded 650 kg (1433 lb).
PERFORMANCE Max speed 190 km/h (118 mph); landing speed 85 km/h (53 mph).

Ivensen Pavel Albertovich Ivensen (Yevyensyen) was famous for his gliders, but his single-seat aeroplane, flown 1929, was a new design. Parasol wing, a single wooden structure, held by four short struts. Flew with wheels and skis. In 1930s Ivensen was deputy to Isacco.
DIMENSIONS Span 9,0 m (29 ft 6¼ in); wing area 13,5 m^2 (145 ft^2).
ENGINE One 30 hp Bristol Cherub.
No other data.

IT-6 Next in IT family of I.P. Tolstikh to be powered. Parasol two-seat tandem, named *Komakademiya* or *Krupskoi*. Again a refined veneer-skinned aircraft which made many flights 1929–1930.
DIMENSIONS Span 10,6 m (34 ft 9¼ in); length 6,7 m (22 ft 0 in); wing area 16 m^2 (172 ft^2).
ENGINE One 60 hp Cirrus Hermes.
WEIGHTS Empty 430 kg (948 lb); fuel/oil 60 kg (132 lb); loaded 650 kg (1433 lb).
PERFORMANCE Max speed 105 km/h (65 mph).

RG-1 Designed by Sergei Nikolayevich Goryelov, unusual in being STOL sesquiplane with slatted main wing. First Soviet lightplane powered by Czech Walter radial, which though expensive was reliable. This machine had the more powerful seven-cylinder model. Wooden, with monocoque fuselage, and engine fully cowled. Tandem-seater, said to be 'easily understood'.
DIMENSIONS Span 10,0 m (32 ft 9½ in); length not recorded; wing area 20 m^2 (215 ft^2).

ENGINE One 85 hp Walter.
WEIGHTS Empty not recorded; loaded 900 kg (1984 lb).
PERFORMANCE Max speed 135 km/h (84 mph); landing speed 45 km/h (28 mph).

Prokopenko A bus-driver in Krivoi Rog, Ukraine, G.I. Prokopenko built a parasol monoplane that flew on 24 February 1930 with complete success. Data lacking, but wing was upper plane from Hanriot 14 and engine incorporated parts from 80 hp Le Rhône. Wing collapsed during later flight, constructor being killed.

Omega Attractive low-wing cabin monoplane built at Kharkov 1931 by Aleksei Nikolayevich Gratsianski, later Hero of the Soviet Union; tested by none other than B.N. Kudrin. Efficient wooden single-spar wing with aspect ratio of 9; welded steel-tube fuselage. Description states seating side-by-side, but photograph shows tandem; dual control. Original 60 hp Walter ran with severe vibration, and was replaced. This type (a number were built) served as trainer at Poltava Osoaviakhim school.
DIMENSIONS Span 11,0 m (36 ft 1 in); length 7,5 m (24 ft 7¼ in); wing area 13,4 m² (144 ft²).
ENGINE One 65 hp M-23 (NAMI-65).
WEIGHTS Empty 500 kg (1,100 lb); fuel/oil 110 kg (243 lb); loaded 760 kg (1,675 lb).
PERFORMANCE Max speed 170 km/h (106 mph); to 1 km, 6 min; to 2 km, 13 min; service ceiling 4,5 km (14,750 ft); landing speed 60 km/h (37 mph).

Vinogradov 3B/M Named *Igrado* (plaything), neat biplane designed by Ivan Nikolayevich Vinogradov and constructed at FZU plant at Frunze 1929-1930. Construction mixed, forward fuselage being corrugated duralumin and rear wood, with veneer skin. Wings wood, with fabric covering, with streamlined I interplane struts. Test flying 1931. In final form ailerons were full-span, but on lower wings only.
DIMENSIONS Span 10,2 m (33 ft 5½ in); length 5,4 m (17 ft 9 in); wing area 22,4 m² (241 ft²).
ENGINE 60 hp Walter 5-cylinder.
WEIGHTS Empty 500 kg (1100 lb); loaded 675 kg (1488 lb).
PERFORMANCE Max speed 120 km/h (74·5 mph); cruising speed 92 km/h (57 mph).

Gup-1 Designation of this two-seat tourer intended to be surname of German designer, Friedrich Guep, rendered in Russian with sound Gyoop. He was invited to build by ZOK-NII-GVF; first flight October 1933. Tandem open cockpits in steel-tube truss fuselage; wooden wings of constant section braced by four compression struts to top of fuselage. Control surfaces skinned with glued ply; stability and handling 'put it in a class of its own'.
DIMENSIONS Span, reported as 10,5 m, Shavrov declines to quote.
ENGINE One 100 hp M-11, with ring cowl.
WEIGHTS Empty 615 kg (1356 lb); fuel/oil 190 kg (419 lb); loaded 880 kg (1940 lb).
PERFORMANCE Max speed 160 km/h (100 mph); climb to 1 km, 8 min; service ceiling 3,5 km (11,500 ft); landing speed 70 km/h (43·5 mph).

IT-9 Last and best aeroplane of I.P. Tolstikh. Tandem two-seat parasol, demonstrated outstanding performance and handling. Fuselage welded steel-tube truss; folding wings were wooden, of constant (TsAGI R-IIS) section, with slats ahead of ailerons and manually lowered flaps inboard. Metal tail, with tight fabric covering. Bungee shock-absorbers on long-stroke landing gears, fitted with either wheels or skis. Test-flying early 1934; IT-9 was so good it was considered for mass-production, but familiarity and experience of U-2 (Po-2) rendered the biplane unassailable.
DIMENSIONS Span 12,9 m (42 ft 4 in); length 7,7 m (25 ft 3 in); wing area 28 m² (301 ft²).
ENGINE One 100 hp M-11 with ring cowl.
WEIGHTS Empty 625 kg (1378 lb); fuel/oil 65/5 kg (143/11 lb); loaded 1000 kg (2205 lb).
PERFORMANCE Max speed 140 km/h (87 mph); take-off 80 m (262 ft) in 7 s; range 400 km (248 miles); landing speed 55 km/h (34 mph).

EMAI A bold effort to determine to what extent aircraft could safely be constructed from magnesium. First flown 1934, EMAI (Elektron-MAI), also designated **EMAI-1-34** or **E-1**, and named *Sergei Ordzhonikidze*, was major project at MAI (Moscow Aviation Institute) whose other aircraft are mainly listed under designer's names. Lead designers were Professors S.O. Zonshain, supervising A.L. Gimmelfarb, with full authority of GUAP. Low-wing monoplane with tandem seats in enclosed cockpit, spatted main wheels and tailplane high on fin. Entire airframe Elektron magnesium alloy, mainly welded but some bolted or riveted joints. Fuselage basically hexagonal-section monocoque; cantilever wing based on Stieger's (Monospar) principles. Structure painted, and covered with doped fabric. Judged a complete success; MAI report claimed weight-saving of 42% overall compared with aluminium, wood or steel tube. Widespread opinion this was superior method of construction, despite fire-risk, but shortage of electricity for producing the metal, as much as other factors, prohibited adoption. EMAI flew about 600 times by 1940.
DIMENSIONS Span 12,0 m (39 ft 4½ in); length 7,0 m (22 ft 11½ in); wing area 20 m² (215 ft²).
ENGINE One 175 hp Salmson radial.
WEIGHTS Empty 700 kg (1543 lb); fuel/oil 165 kg (364 lb); loaded 1200 kg (2646 lb).
PERFORMANCE Max speed 170 km/h (106 mph); range 800 km (500 miles); landing speed 75 km/h (47 mph).

E-2 Named for *Klim Voroshilov*, this second magnesium (Elektron) research aircraft was smaller, and had no major backing, though builder M.L. Babad enjoyed active participation of Gimmelfarb and Petrov-Gubish who had worked on EMAI. Tandem-seat mid-wing monoplane, riveted and screwed from heavy (10 mm) sheet, with thinner secondary sections and thin skin over single-spar wing. Flown on 27 hp Anzani by A.I. Zhukov in late 1934, 18 hp Blackburn Tomtit then being substituted to improve reliability. Thought that corrosion made structure suspect, and flights ceased early 1935. No data.

VVA-1 In 1934 Osoaviakhim and the Aviavnito (aviation technical society) sponsored a competition for a superior touring aircraft. It was hoped to create 'a flying Ford'. Many entries submitted and several of designs built, including the winner, VVA-1. Though one of the 'official' entries, it was rejected as being structurally difficult. Designer one of chief VVA professors, Vladimir Sergeyevich Puishnov, who played a part in many aircraft prior to 1941. Tandem-seat cabin sesquiplane, with N-Warren interplane bracing of rear-folding wings, and neat landing gears using copies of Dowty internally sprung wheels. What the committee found too much was the beautiful monocoque wooden fuselage, of streamlined profile and circular section. Tailplane was ahead of fin, on top of rear fuselage.

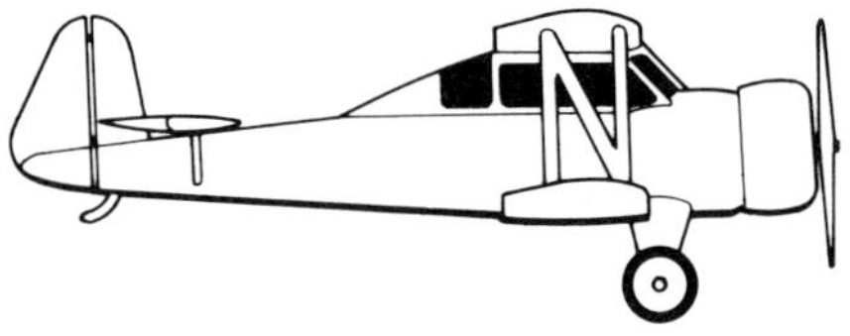

VVA-1

DIMENSIONS Span 10,9 m (35 ft 9 in); length 7,8 m (25 ft 7 in); wing area 24 m² (258 ft²).
ENGINE One 100 hp M-11 in long-chord NACA cowling.
WEIGHTS Empty 800 kg (1764 lb); loaded 1120 kg (2470 lb).
PERFORMANCE (Est) Max speed 170 km/h (106 mph); range 550 km (342 miles); landing speed 60 km/h (37 mph).

Anito-1 Another attractive contest entry, name being abbreviation of sponsoring society. Low-drag low-wing monoplane, seating pilot and two passengers one behind the other in enclosed (seemingly rather cramped) cabin. Wooden, elliptical-section monocoque fuselage, two-spar wing with split flaps, veneer-covered balanced control surfaces, and helmeted engine cowl. Designer/builders Nikolai Georgievich Nurov and Suren Alekseyevich Elibekyan. Flight testing 2–9 September 1935.
DIMENSIONS Span 12,6 m (41 ft 4 in); length 8,4 m (27 ft 6¾ in); wing area 24 m² (258 ft²).
ENGINE One 100 hp M-11.
WEIGHTS Empty 815 kg (1797 lb); fuel/oil 86/14 kg (186/31 lb); loaded 1160 kg (2557 lb).
PERFORMANCE Max speed 204 km/h (127 mph); take-off 190 m in 15 s; service ceiling 5040 m (16,535 ft); range 666 km (414 miles); landing speed 60 km/h (37 mph).

Komarov No details of Aviavnito contest entry by A.A. Komarov built at Novocherkassk and flown 1935, beyond the fact it had an M-11. It crashed, killing the designer.

Chyerednichenko Ultralight built from parts of a glider and another powered aircraft by engineer/pilot Vladimir Grigoryevich Chyerednichenko in 1935. Wooden low-wing monoplane, with main wheels protruding from underside of wing. Powered by locally created engine, made several ground runs and one flight.
DIMENSIONS Span 11,0 m (36 ft 1 in); length not recorded; wing area 24 m² (258 ft²).
ENGINE One 18 hp Stulov flat-twin.
WEIGHTS Empty 270 kg (595 lb); fuel/oil 20 kg (44 lb); loaded 370 kg (816 lb).
PERFORMANCE Not recorded.

Pleskov Another of bumper 1935 crop was simple parasol monoplane seating two in tandem built by famed glider pilot A.I. Pleskov, assisted by colleagues Kovalyenko and Mazalov, and also Sevastyanov, mechanic at Saratov aero club. Of wood/fabric construction, it managed to fly despite its car engine (56 hp GAZ-M-1 as described in KSM-1 entry), adopted to save expense. No data.

Vasilyev A *Motoplaner* (powered glider) constructed 1935–1936 by G.S. Vasilyev who mounted a 12 hp outboard motor from a boat on parasol wing, driving tractor propeller above cockpit canopy. Wing said to have 'freely floating ailerons', which may explain why it slid one wingtip along ground and crashed. No data.

Blokhi family News of Henri Mignet's *Flying Flea* triggered a rash of Fleas in the Soviet Union, and as elsewhere most never flew. Of those that were completed, many were greatly (and probably advantageously) modified by their builders. One of the first, flown in 1935, was the *Blokha* (Flea) built at GAZ-1. Main constructor A.A. Shteiner. Became a prototype for further construction, examples of which went to newspapers *Pravda* and *Izvestya* and adopted their names. Another placed in Polytechnic Museum in Moscow. Data typical.
DIMENSIONS Span 5,6 m (18 ft 4½ in); length 3,5 m (11 ft 5¾ in); wing area 10 m² (108 ft²).
ENGINE One 18 hp Aubier-Dunne.
WEIGHTS Empty 100 kg (220 lb); fuel/oil 20 kg (44 lb); loaded 200 kg (441 lb).
PERFORMANCE Max speed 105 km/h (65 mph); ceiling 1800 m (5900 ft).

Grushin His *Oktyabrnok* is described under his own OKB.

Sheremetyev One of the more attractive Fleas was flown 1935 by glider factory engineer Boris Nikolayevich Sheremetyev. Also known as **ShBM** and **ZAOR**. Rear wing pivoted at 25% chord and left/right halves could function as ailerons and as elevators. This was an important improvement; described as having flown quite well.
DIMENSIONS Span 5,8/6,1 m (19 ft 0 in/20 ft 0 in); length 3,9 m (12 ft 9½ in); wing area (total) 12,5 m² (135 ft²).
ENGINE One 18 hp Aubier-Dunne.
WEIGHTS Empty 150 kg (331 lb); fuel/oil 18 kg (40 lb); loaded 253 kg (558 lb).
PERFORMANCE Max speed 115 km/h (71·5 mph); ceiling 2 km (6500 ft); range 290 km (180 miles); landing speed 48 km/h (30 mph).

Moskit Built by S.V. Konstantinov, assistant professor at Novocherkassk, assisted by V.V. Belyaninuim, this was not quite a Mignet type but almost a Flea-sized regular aeroplane with full-span ailerons and large slab tailplanes pivoted at 25% chord. All these surfaces were operated by the stick with rudder interlinked, there being no pedals. Test-flown by head of experimental KB, G.M. Zhuravlyev.
DIMENSIONS Span 6,0/4,0 m (19 ft 7 in/13 ft 1½ in); length 4,0 m (13 ft 1½ in); wing area 7,5/4,8 m² (81/51·6 ft²).
ENGINE One 27/35 hp ABC Scorpion.
WEIGHTS Empty 120 kg (265 lb); fuel/oil 30 kg (66 lb); loaded 230 kg (507 lb).
PERFORMANCE Max speed 100 km/h (62 mph); landing speed 45 km/h (28 mph).

Katsur VO-4 Katsur was an engineer in Kharkov, whose *Avietka-Blokha* had a rear wing pivoted to function as an elevator and also carrying ailerons; front wing fixed and without movable surfaces. First flight early 1936.
DIMENSIONS Span 6,0 m (19 ft 7 in); length 3,9 m (12 ft 9½ in); wing area 13,8 m² (148·5 ft²).
ENGINE One 27 hp, believed ABC Scorpion.
WEIGHTS Empty 120 kg (265 lb); fuel/oil 21 kg (46 lb); loaded 238 kg (524·5 lb).
PERFORMANCE Max speed 115 km/h (71·5 mph); ceiling 3 km (9850 ft); landing speed 47 km/h (29 mph).

Ruibchinsko In 1935–1936 three Flea-type machines were built at GAZ-1 in Moscow by Ruibchinsko, assistant professor (reader) at Dniepropetrovsk metallurgical institute and associates from Chardzhou and Gomel. No data.

Mikoyan A.I. Mikoyan's first creation is best covered here because it was designed and built with K. Samarin and N.A. Pavlov in 1936 as their diploma project at the VVA. Neat pusher, with shoulder wing and open cockpit offering almost perfect view ahead of long-stroke main gears.
DIMENSIONS Span 8,0 m (26 ft 3 in); length 6,2 m (20 ft 4 in); wing area 11,4 m² (123 ft²).
ENGINE One 25 hp flat-twin by P. Labur.
WEIGHTS Empty 150 kg (331 lb); fuel/oil 20 kg (44 lb); loaded 264 kg (582 lb).
PERFORMANCE Max speed 126 km/h (78 mph); take-off/landing 85/50 m; ceiling 3 km (9850 ft); landing speed 45 km/h (28 mph).

Sidoryenko Another tandem-wing ultralight, built in Tashkent by this constructor, flying 1936.
DIMENSIONS Span 9,5 m (31 ft 2 in); length 5,4 m (17 ft 8½ in); wing area 12 m² (129 ft²).
ENGINE One 17 hp Aubier-Dunne.
WEIGHTS Empty 154 kg (340 lb); fuel/oil 6 kg (13 lb); loaded 240 kg (529 lb).
PERFORMANCE Max speed 110 km/h (68 mph); ceiling 1,5 km (4900 ft); landing speed 42 km/h (26 mph).

KSM-1 Shortage of good yet cheap light aircraft engines led in the early 1930s to attempts to use car engines or engines using car components. Most important Soviet attempt, under direction of E.V. Agitov, was GAZ-M-1 four-in-line, with water cooling and electric starter. KSM-1 *Komsomolyets*-1 was first aircraft designed for this engine, though beaten into the air by simpler Pleskov. Low-wing tandem two-seater of wooden construction, monocoque fuselage and leading edge having skin of *shpon* (birch ply) and wing fabric behind front spar. Split flaps fitted, and engine cowled in circular casing with radial nose apertures for radiator air. Designer Aleksei Andreyevich Smolin. Built under expert supervision at GVF; experimental shop at Gorki car works made one-piece propeller. Construction complete 1935; first flight 1936. Performance unimpressive because of heavy engine installation. At least two built. Attempts continued to 1939 to improve matters. Gribovskii assisted, and used same type of engine in G-23.
DIMENSIONS Span 12,0 m (39 ft 4½ in); length 7,0 m (22 ft 11½ in); wing area 18 m² (194 ft²).
ENGINE One 56 hp GAZ-M-1 (possibly 80 hp development fitted later).
WEIGHTS Empty 605 kg (1334 lb); loaded 860 kg (1896 lb).
PERFORMANCE Max speed 121 km/h (75 mph); take-off 400 m/20 s; ceiling 1620 m (5315 ft); landing speed 57 km/h (35 mph).

MIIT Student at MIIT, Sergei Vasilyevich Popov, built neat single-seater in 1936 as diploma project. Named *Miitovyets*, said to grow more beautiful in flight, and to have passed factory tests with commendation.
DIMENSIONS Span 10,6 m (34 ft 9 in); length 6,0 m (19 ft 9 in); wing area, not recorded.
ENGINE One 25 hp (possibly ABC).
WEIGHTS Empty 175 kg (386 lb); fuel/oil 30 kg (66 lb); loaded 285 kg (628 lb).
PERFORMANCE Max speed 120 km/h (75 mph); landing speed 50 km/h (31 mph).

E-3 Another experimental machine with airframe of Elektron magnesium alloy; monoplane amphibian designed by P.M. Danilov in 1936. During construction wing and tail were modified to be covered in tight fabric, hull remaining magnesium. M-11 engine mounted on centreline pylon driving tractor propeller. Work halted 1937, apparently because of corrosion.

MB-1 In 1936 M.P. Beschastnov, skilled aviation worker in far east of Siberia, built single-seat trainer looking very much like an I-16.
ENGINE One M-11; trials successful, speed being 230 km/h (143 mph). No other information.

Vlasov Another *motor planer*, built and flown at Kuibyshev 1937 by A. Vlasov. Based on Antonov PS-2, plus 12 hp LM-4 flat-twin (outboard boat engine).

Caudron/Dubrovin In 1936–1939 a major effort was made to develop the Caudron-Renault racers and their engines. Main types involved were the C.690 and C.713, the former a main competitor in Coupe Deutsch de la Meurthe races in 1934–1935, and the latter related to light fighters of 1937–1940. The Renault inverted in-line engines were adopted in 4, 6 and 12-cylinder (inverted-V) forms, Soviet designations being MV-4, MV-6 and MV-12. MV-6 was used in Soviet aircraft during 1938–1941 period. Airframe bureau chief was A.A. Dubrovin, with A.G. Brunov as chief deputy; others were Z.I. Itskovich (of KAI) and Ye.G. Adler (of Yak). Work discontinued 1939.

Sh-13 Another design of Boris Nikolayevich Sheremetyev actually built, this was intended to be a super-efficient sporting single-seater to take the world absolute long-range record in its class. Construction described as 'one-piece wooden' and its outstanding feature was the wing whose aspect ratio had not been approached before (in the Soviet Union, at least) except for two sailplanes. Well streamlined, with single-seat cockpit having moulded plastics panels in hinged canopy. Test flown by P.G. Golovin 1939; pleasant at light weights, but had no chance of lifting design fuel load which would have given endurance calculated to be 17 hours.
DIMENSIONS Span 13,0 m (42 ft 8 in); length 5,92 m (19 ft 5 in); wing area 10,56 m² (113·7 ft²).
ENGINE One 40 hp Salmson radial.
WEIGHTS Empty 397 kg (875 lb); fuel/oil 176 kg (388 lb); loaded 663 kg (1462 lb).
PERFORMANCE Max speed 180 km/h (112 mph); range 2500 km (1553 miles) with normal tankage; landing speed 90 km/h (56 mph).

G-5 From 1937 the purges and terrifying environment almost halted light aircraft construction, until in 1940 a refined *motor planer* was built at Kharkov with this designation. Constructor was Stepan Vasilyevich Grizodubov. Wooden, built for low-drag penetration, with single open cockpit and pylon-mounted wing. Engine on steel-tube framework above wing, driving pusher propeller (cannot be seen in heavily re-

touched photo that survives). Flights successful, but performance measurement, and attempts to improve engine output, thwarted by urgent evacuation in 1941.
DIMENSIONS Span 12,15 m (39 ft 10 in); length 6,0 m (19 ft 8¾ in); wing area 17,65 m² (190 ft²).
ENGINE One 35 hp ADG-4 flat-twin.
WEIGHTS Empty 178 kg (392 lb); fuel/oil 32 kg (70·5 lb); loaded 300 kg (661 lb).

UPO-22 Having achieved indifferent results with KSM-1, A.A. Smolin persisted with low-wing two-seaters with car engines and by 1941 completed this refined and more powerful machine. Assumed similar to KSM in construction, and engine was 80 hp GAZ-M-4 (surprisingly Shavrov identifies engine as MV-4; this was not a car-type but much more powerful Renault). All documents lost in Second World War.

Boldrev Following natural hiatus in 1941–1945, next recorded amateur aeroplane is ultralight by Aleksandr Ivanovich Boldrev, senior engineer holding chair of aerodynamics at MAI. Financially assisted by TsAGI, and skilfully made at MAI in 1946–1947. Intended as STOL research machine to explore flight control systems. Main feature was a fore-wing looking like a slat but of 286 mm (11¼ in) chord, symmetrical section and mounted on tubular pivots ahead of and above the NACA 23020-section main surface to investigate how its angle and spacing affected lift coefficient. Structure mainly of wood, gondola occupied by pilot being a truss and tail boom a monocoque. Concept does not seem to have been successful, and work ceased at end of 1947.
DIMENSIONS Span 6,07 m (19 ft 11 in); length 5,0 m (16 ft 4¾ in); wing area 7,2 m² (77·5 ft²).
ENGINE One 22/25 hp M-72.
WEIGHTS, performance not recorded.

Dosav During its two-year life, in 1950, this organization sponsored the first (and almost only) nationwide design competition since the Second World War. Objective: a training and utility machine worthy of succeeding Po-2. Numerous entries received, from which five designs listed below were selected for prototype construction. Contest then abandoned.
Elibekyan S.A. Elibekyan, one of the designers of *Anito* of 1935, produced entrant with simple (mixed steel tube, wood and fabric) construction and adequate performance. Side-by-side dual trainer, high-wing cabin machine with slats, slotted flaps and high tailplane.
DIMENSIONS Span 11,6 m (38 ft 0¾ in); length 7,6 m (24 ft 11½ in); wing area, not recorded.
ENGINE One 90 hp radial by Mikulin.
WEIGHTS Empty 560 kg (1235 lb); loaded 830 kg (1830 lb).
PERFORMANCE Max speed 190 km/h (118 mph); landing speed 60 km/h (37 mph).
Golayev Pure sporting machine, entry by A. Golayev was small wooden racer with wings of 'laminar' section and high aspect ratio for long range.
DIMENSIONS Span 7,0 m (22 ft 11¾ in); length 5,7 m (18 ft 8¾ in); wing area 7 m² (75 ft²).
ENGINE One 90 hp radial.
WEIGHTS Empty not recorded, loaded 500 kg (1100 lb).
PERFORMANCE (Est) Max speed 306 km/h (190 mph); landing speed 110 km/h (68 mph).
Gribovskii This experienced designer proposed stressed-skin low-wing two-seater, with side-by-side seating in enclosed cockpit with dual control. Wings high aspect-ratio, elevator one piece behind rudder, fixed tricycle landing gear.
DIMENSIONS Span 11,4 m (37 ft 5 in); length 7,05 m (23 ft 2 in); wing area 12,2 m² (131 ft²).
ENGINE One 90 hp radial.
WEIGHTS Empty 502 kg (1107 lb); loaded 750 kg (1653 lb).
PERFORMANCE Max speed 195 km/h (121 mph); landing speed 65 km/h (40 mph).
Nikitin Another experienced builder, V.V. Nikitin adopted stressed-skin for small ultralight single-seater. Braced high wing, tricycle gear and liberal slats and flaps.
DIMENSIONS Span 9,3 m (30 ft 6½ in); length 6,4 m (21 ft 0 in); wing area 13 m² (140 ft²).
ENGINE One 50 hp flat-twin.
WEIGHTS Empty 272 kg (600 lb); loaded 400 kg (882 lb).
PERFORMANCE Max speed 145 km/h (90 mph); landing speed 55 km/h (34 mph).
Ollo/Shprangel Only successful entry by a new team, low-wing single-seater with light-alloy framework and fabric covering. Wing resembled Blanik in being swept slightly forward, with flaps.
DIMENSIONS Span 8,5 m (27 ft 11 in); length 7,1 m (23 ft 3¾ in); wing area 12 m² (129 ft²).
ENGINE One 225 hp radial.
WEIGHTS Empty 430 kg (948 lb); loaded 830 kg (1830 lb).
PERFORMANCE Max speed 318 km/h (198 mph); landing speed 88 km/h (55 mph).

Zherebtsov One of several post-war ultralight tip-drive helicopters. Designed from 1947 by B.Ya. Zherebtsov, Yu.S. Braginski and Yu.L. Starinin, mainly to test proposed pulsejet drive; the three engineers led group formed for this project. Rotor had two blades, of 7,0 m (23 ft 0 in) diameter, intention being to substitute 9 m unit later. Pulsejets of 250 mm (10 in) length gave up to 17 kg (37·5 lb) thrust. In 1950 prototype flown (pilot Smirnov) with Zis-150 truck engine on ground driving rotor up to speed.

Ilyin Soviet Union has persistently produced ideas for flapping-wing aircraft (ornithopters). In 1957 reported that small machine built by Dmitri V. Ilyin had flown, using engine of 5 hp. Said to be based on widely published principles of I.N. Vinogradov (lead designer of 3B/M described earlier in this section); official Soviet view is that it flew 3 km non-stop.

Leningradets Built and flown 1962, one of world's smallest two-seaters. Designers Lyev Sekinin, Valentin Tatsiturnov and Lyev Kostin, in Leningrad. Tandem cabin parasol monoplane of traditional form.
DIMENSIONS Span 7,0 m (23 ft 0 in); length 4,8 m (15 ft 9 in).
ENGINE One 51 hp Zündapp Z9 inverted 4-inline.
PERFORMANCE Max speed 150 km/h (93 mph). No other data.

Malysh Meaning *Little One*, only designation of primitive but creditable ultralight by aeromodelling section of Young Pioneers of Zlatoust, Urals. Wood/fabric single-seat parasol monoplane designed and built under direction of Lyev Aleksandrovich Komarov. Flown on skis, 12 April 1964.
DIMENSIONS Span 6,9 m (22 ft 7¾ in); length 4,74 m (15 ft 6¾ in); wing area 7,8 m² (84 ft²).
ENGINE One 30 hp flat-twin motorcycle.
WEIGHTS Empty 110 kg (242·5 lb); loaded 200 kg (441 lb).
PERFORMANCE Max speed 130 km/h (81 mph); landing speed (min) 50 km/h (31 mph).

Riga-1 Formed 1962, Riga RIIGA (institute of civil aero engineers) immediately launched this ultralight, diploma project of students G. Ivanov and F. Mukhamedov, assisted by others. Strongly reminiscent of Tipsy Nipper, though high aspect-ratio wings were from BRO glider. Steel-tube/wood/fabric fuselage carried balanced rudder but no fin. Not certain Riga-1 flew, but complete 1965.
DIMENSIONS Span 9,0 m (29 ft 6¼ in); length 5,2 m (17 ft 1 in); wing area 9,0 m² (97 ft²).
ENGINE Various 26/30 hp (eg, M-61/M-62/K-750).
WEIGHTS Empty about 190 kg (419 lb); loaded about 300 kg (661 lb).
PERFORMANCE (Est) max speed 140 km/h (87 mph); landing speed 65 km/h (40 mph).

Riga-50 Following at least two other sailplane-derived ultralights RIIGA built this autogyro mid-1960s, completed 1967. Designed by diploma student V. Ustinov, assisted by D. Osokin and V. Prishlyuk. Difficult parts – rotor blades, hub and dynamics – based on Bensen philosophy, though Ka-18 served as pattern for blade design. Duralumin keel provided foundation for nacelle, with glassfibre casings. Original 28 hp M-61 (one of engines tested in Riga-1) replaced (one report says developed into) that listed. No spin-up auxiliary drive provided. Later autogyro, possibly this machine rebuilt, is Riga-50M with nacelle of welded steel tube and plywood.
DIMENSIONS Rotor diameter 6,1 m (20 ft 0 in); length (discounting rotor) 3,4 m (11 ft 2 in); disc area 29,2 m² (314 ft²).
ENGINE One 45 hp M-77 flat-twin.
WEIGHTS Empty 140 kg (309 lb); loaded 225 kg (496 lb).
PERFORMANCE Max speed 85 km/h (53 mph); take-off run about 100 m (330 ft).

Chaika Using same design of main rotor and control rods as on Riga-50, this rotor-kite, also designated **Ch-1**, was designed for towing behind car or boat. First flown by V. Tseitlin in August 1970 (listed here to be near its predecessor). Structure built from standard thin sheet-steel U-sections resembling Dexion, empty weight under 50 kg (110 lb). Normal towing speed 30 to 45 km/h (19–28 mph).

VIGR-1 Another ultralight rotorcraft, early student project at KuAI (Kuibyshev Aviation Institute). Two-blade rotor driven by tip pulsejets similar to Zherebtsov's. First hovering flight October 1965. No spin-up engine fitted.
DIMENSIONS Rotor diameter 8,5 m (27 ft 11 in); disc area 56,75 m² (611 ft²).
WEIGHTS Empty 95 kg (209 lb); loaded 190 kg (419 lb).
PERFORMANCE Not recorded.

Sverchok-1 Meaning *Cricket*, KuAI's second light rotorcraft. Autogyro, diploma project by student group led by S. Pyatinitskii and tested 1971. Simple structure of light alloy and glassfibre, with veneer-skinned rotor blades on steel spar.
DIMENSIONS Rotor diameter 6,4 m (21 ft 0 in);

length (discounting rotor) 3,75 m (12 ft 3½ in); disc area 32,2 m² (346 ft²).
ENGINE One 38 hp M-61.
WEIGHTS Empty 110/125 kg (242/278 lb); loaded 180/196 kg (397/432 lb).
PERFORMANCE Max speed 100 km/h (62 mph); take-off speed 30/40 km/h (19/25 mph); landing speed 20/25 km/h (12/16 mph).

MAI-62 Designed 1962, but not flown until later (possibly not at all), this single-seater resembled baby jet fighter. Tailless and virtually all-wing, surface having leading-edge sweep of 45° and centre section of delta shape, joined to swept outer panels with almost square tip ailerons. Cockpit immediately ahead of broad stumpy fin containing engine, driving pusher propeller. Fixed tricycle landing gear. Structure probably wooden, but little known about this possibly unsuccessful beast.
DIMENSIONS Span 4,9 m (16 ft 1 in); length 5,25 m (17 ft 2¾ in).
ENGINE One 80 hp M-71.
WEIGHTS Loaded 440 kg (881 lb).
PERFORMANCE Max speed 220 km/h (137 mph); range 800 km (497 miles).

MAI Kvant Displayed in Moscow October 1967, this single-seater had name meaning Quantum and designation **MAI-OSKB-1-EPM**, for experimental production workshop at MAI. Most ambitious student project yet seen; clearly a 'hot ship' having no chance of replacing Yak-18/50 in world aerobatic championships (as was suggested) but no mean performer. Steel-tube truss fuselage, three-spar wing, pneumatic gear and flaps. Stressed to +9/−7 g; made ten flights in all.
DIMENSIONS Span 7,5 m (24 ft 7¼ in); length 5,7 m (18 ft 8½ in); height (tail up) 2,8 m (9 ft 2¼ in).
ENGINE One 300 hp M-14P, fan-cooled and driving c/s prop.
WEIGHTS Not disclosed.
PERFORMANCE Design speed 420 km/h (261 mph).

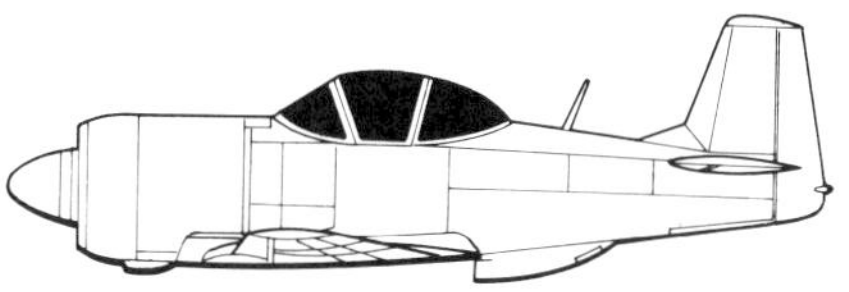
Kvant

Semburg Meaning bird of happiness, name applied to small passenger jet exhibited as model 1980 and stated to have flown 1981. Design group under Professor A. Badyagin, with assistance from Tashkent Poly and local aviation plants. Pilot plus 5/7 passengers or two stretchers or 800 kg (1323 lb) cargo. Clean high wing, T-tail, engine located in rear fuselage and fed by dorsal inlet. Small APU turbine provides thrust for emergencies.
ENGINE One 1500 kg AI-25 turbofan
WEIGHTS Max 3200 kg (7055 lb).
PERFORMANCE Cruise 360 km/h (223 mph); take-off 150 m (492 ft).
No other data.

Chkalov Ch-1 Also designated **C-12** and **VAT** (Voronezh Aero-Technical college); qualified for inclusion in 'Flea' section for same layout. Metal construction, fabric covering. Fixed tricycle gear with twin nosewheels; mainwheels, Yak-12 tailwheels. Full-span ailerons on front wing, enormous horn-balanced elevators at rear. Motorcycle saddle and handlebars, though conventional flight controls with pedals for rudder. First flight 1970.
DIMENSIONS Span (wing) 5,4 m (17 ft 8½ in), (tail) 4,4 m (14 ft 5 in); length 3,7 m (12 ft 1½ in); height 1,64 m (5 ft 4½ in); areas (wing) 6,72 m² (72·3 ft²), (tail) 5,58 m² (60·1 ft²).
ENGINE One 28 hp K-750.
WEIGHTS Empty 230 kg (507 lb); loaded 330 kg (726 lb).
PERFORMANCE Max speed 105 km/h (65 mph); take-off 15 m (49 ft); landing speed 31 km/h (20 mph); range up to 620 km (358 miles).

Tourist In February 1970 Kiev engineers, Demchyenko, Khitry and Gusyev, said to have completed nine years' development of personal helicopter foldable into 1 m (39 in) suitcase. Coaxial rotors 'inflated hydraulically' and driven by 'kerosene turbine of kind used to start turboprops of large aircraft' (NK-12MV). Unfolding said to take 3 min. Empty weight 25,5 kg (56 lb) with two-way radio; max speed 160 km/h (99 mph).

ESKA-1 Experimental ground-effect 'surface skimmer' developed at Central Laboratory of Lifesaving Technology under Y.V. Makarov, with assistance by V.B. Shavrov. Light-alloy hull seating two in side-by-side cabin, sharply tapered high wings sloping down to stabilizing floats, with upturned tip winglets. Braced T-tail, and retractable land wheels. Engine on braced pylon. Capable of operation above ground effect but normally intended to skim at about 1 m (39 in) above land or water. Probably scale model of larger rescue vehicle. First operated 1973.

ESKA-1

DIMENSIONS Span 6,0 m (19 ft 8½ in); length 7,75 m (25 ft 5¼ in); wing area 13 m^2 (140 ft^2).
ENGINE One 30 hp MT-8 flat twin driving tractor propeller.
WEIGHTS Empty 230 kg (507 lb); loaded, max 450 kg (992 lb).
PERFORMANCE Operating speed 110 km/h (68 mph).

AT-1 Named *Mriy* (meaning is obscure) this lightplane was joint work of Mikhail Artyumov and Viktor Timofeyev in early 1970s. No further details.

Omega Artyumov and Timofeyev then designed their own aircraft; Artyumov's was an attempt to use channel-wing idea unsuccessfully worked on by Baumann in USA in 1948–1960. Small metal/fabric amphibian with gull wings forming channel ahead of propeller. Tricycle landing gear with main wheels non-retractable but raised clear of water; nose wheel replaced by ski for first flight from ice on 8 January 1975.
DIMENSIONS Span 8,22 m (26 ft 11¼ in); length 5,4 m (17 ft 8½ in).
ENGINE One 32 hp IZ-56 flat-twin driving glassfibre-skinned pusher propeller.
WEIGHT Max loaded 270 kg (595 lb).
PERFORMANCE Max speed 100 km/h (62 mph); landing 65 km/h (40 mph).

T-1 Mustang Timofeyev built a conventional and attractive high-wing pusher with configuration almost indistinguishable from Polish Janowski J-1 of same period. Mixed construction, cantilever main legs in line with front wing-struts, tailskid, streamlined nose cockpit open at sides. Flew early 1975.
DIMENSIONS Span 8,0 m (26 ft 3 in); length 5,6 m (18 ft 4½ in).
ENGINE One 32 hp IZ-56 flat-twin driving pusher propeller.
WEIGHTS Empty 150 kg (331 lb); max 270 kg (595 lb).
PERFORMANCE Max speed 105 km/h (65 mph); take-off 65 km/h (40 mph) in 100 m (328 ft).

RKIIGA-74 Also called Riga-74, and named *Experiment*, this novel amphibian used hull of a Progress speedboat, wings and tail of a Primoryets glider and powerful Czech aero engine. Windshield moved 0,15 m (6 in) back to avoid propeller; hull strengthened at attachments of the wings, landing gear and tail. Side-by-side seats with 90 lit (19·8 gal) fuel tank behind. First flight by V. Abramov and Riga professor V. Cezhtlin on 17 September 1974, as flying boat. Water rudders and retracting landing gear then added.

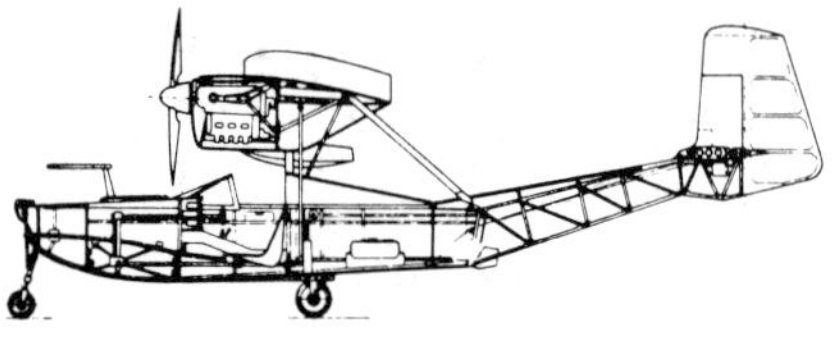

RKIIGA-74

DIMENSIONS Span 13,2 m (43 ft 4 in); length 8,1 m (26 ft 7 in); height 2,4 m (7 ft 10½ in) on wheels; wing area 20,2 m^2 (217 ft^2).
ENGINE One 140 hp Avia M 332 4-inline driving tractor propeller.
WEIGHTS Empty 600 kg (1323 lb); max 900 kg (1984 lb).
PERFORMANCE Max speed 160 km/h (99 mph); climb at 90 km/h, 6 m/s (1180 ft/min); range 500 km (311 miles).

Mikrosamolyet Low-wing cabin single-seater (named Micro-aeroplane) designed and built in Frunze by team led by V. Dmitriyev. Mainly wood and fabric, disclosed 1975, no details except 40 hp engine, empty weight 250 kg (551 lb) and (optimistic?) design speed 270 km/h (168 mph).

Enthusiast Streamlined low-wing single-seater with spatted landing gear built by RIIGA (Riga) to attack national long-distance class record. Completed 1975 and exhibited in Moscow in 1976, possibly without having flown.
DIMENSIONS Span 8,0 m (26 ft 3 in); length 7,6 m (24 ft 11¼ in).
ENGINE One 140 hp Avia M 332 inverted 4-inline.
WEIGHT Max 750 kg (1653 lb).
PERFORMANCE Max speed 265 km/h (165 mph); service ceiling 6 km (19,700 ft); range 3000 km (1864 miles).

MVTU Curious reverse-delta (straight leading edge, trailing edges meeting at extreme tail) with 25 hp pylon-mounted engine described as 'trainer and for testing future lunar vehicles' when displayed at 6th Scientific and Technical Youth Exhibition in 1976.

Strekoza Second avietka with this name (Dragonfly), built 1977 by SKB at Kuibyshev Aviation Institute, marking their return to fixed wings. Materials steel tube, light alloy, fabric and glassfibre. Junkers-type double-wing of R-P-14 profile with flaps inboard and ailerons outboard. Engine mounted far ahead of leading edge on centreline, with pilot gondola underneath hung from spars and carrying tail on lattice boom of inverted-triangle section. Two bracing struts to wing, and two linking main gears to rear of engine mount.
DIMENSIONS Span 7,2 m (23 ft 7½ in); length 6,07 m (19 ft 11 in); height 2,0 m (6 ft 7 in); wing area 9,8 m^2 (105·5 ft^2).
ENGINE One 25 hp VIKhR-25 flat twin.
WEIGHTS Empty 150 kg (331 lb); max 230 kg (507 lb).
PERFORMANCE Max speed 100 km/h (62 mph); cruise 90 km/h (56 mph); landing 45 km/h (28 mph).

KuAI Szmiel Built in parallel with *Strekoza*, this has more conventional layout, with engine on nose and wings attached each side above single-seat cabin. Triangular truss fuselage has apex along underside instead of top, and is fabric-covered throughout; tailplane part-way up fin. Name means bumblebee.
DIMENSIONS Span 7,6 m (24 ft 11¼ in); length 5,42 m (17 ft 9½ in); wing area 10,24 m^2 (110·2 ft^2).
ENGINE One 38 hp M-73 flat-twin aircooled.
WEIGHTS Empty 220 kg (485 lb); loaded 310 kg (683 lb).
PERFORMANCE Maximum speed 120 km/h (74 mph); take-off 400 m/55 km/h; landing 300 m/50 km/h.

X-12C Second homebuilt by Viktor Dmitriyev, driver at Kirghiz University, Frunze, flew early 1981. Ultralight built by KB formed with various friends.
DIMENSIONS Span 5,54 m (18 ft 2 in); length 3,35 m (11 ft 0 in; height 1,26 m (4 ft 1⅔ in).
ENGINE One 20 hp by Nikolai Kitz.
WEIGHT Empty 51 kg (112 lb).
PERFORMANCE Speed 105 km/h (65 mph); take-off 30 m (98 ft).

Viktor Dmitriyev waving to his helpers from X-12C

Index

No index is provided because the content is, in the English language, totally alphabetical. Within each design bureau (OKB), entries are in numerical (or chronological) order. Difficult pre-1940 designations can be resolved with the help of the list beginning on page 17.